ECONOMICS

Economics

JOSEPH E. STIGLITZ

Stanford University

W • W • NORTON & COMPANY • NEW YORK • LONDON

Cover painting: Laszlo Moholy-Nagy, *LIS*, 1922
Oil on canvas, 131 × 100 centimeters
Courtesy of the Kunsthaus, Zurich
Special thanks to Hattula Moholy-Nagy
Cover design: Antonina Krass

The text of this book is set in Electra with display set in Kabel and Binner Gothic.
Composition and Manufacturing by Arcata Graphics.
Book design and Interior Graphics by Antonina Krass.
The Interior Graphics were inspired by the cover painting, *LIS* by Moholy-Nagy.

Library of Congress cataloging-in-publication data
Stiglitz, Joseph E.
Economics / Joseph Stiglitz.
    p. cm.
1. Economics. I. Title.
HB171.5.S884 19936
330—dc20 92–37303

ISBN 0-393-96110-9

W.W. Norton & Company, Inc., 500 Fifth Avenue, New York, N.Y. 10110
W.W. Norton & Company Ltd., 10 Coptic Street, London WC1A 1PU

1 2 3 4 5 6 7 8 9 0

To Jane,
my harshest critic and best friend,
from whom I have learned the strengths and limits of economics;

and to
Julia, Jed, Michael, and Siobhan
in the hope, and belief, that a better understanding of economics
will lead to a better world for them to inherit.

ABOUT THE AUTHOR:

Internationally recognized as one of the leading economists of his generation, Joseph Stiglitz has made important contributions to virtually all of the major subdisciplines of economics: macroeconomics, monetary economics, public and corporate finance, trade, development, and industrial organization. He is professor of economics at Stanford University, where he currently teaches Economics 1, one of the most popular courses on campus. He is the author and editor of hundreds of scholarly articles and books, including the best-selling undergraduate text *Economics of the Public Sector* (Norton) and, with Anthony Atkinson, *Lectures in Public Economics.* Professor Stiglitz is the founding editor of the *Journal of Economic Perspectives,* established in 1987 to lower the barriers of specialization erected by other major economic journals, and a former vice president of the American Economic Association. Among his many prizes and awards, Professor Stiglitz has received the American Economic Association's John Bates Clark Award, given to the economist under forty who has made the most significant contributions to economics. Joe Stiglitz lives in Palo Alto with his wife and four children.

CONTENTS IN BRIEF

CONTENTS

CHAPTER 2 THINKING LIKE AN ECONOMIST • 27

CHAPTER 3 EXCHANGE AND PRODUCTION • 53

PART TWO

PERFECT MARKETS

CHAPTER **8** THE CONSUMPTION
DECISION • 197

CHAPTER **9** THE SAVINGS DECISION • 229

CHAPTER **10** A STUDENT'S GUIDE TO
INVESTING • **252**

CHAPTER **11** THE LABOR SUPPLY
DECISION • **279**

CHAPTER **12**   **THE FIRM'S COSTS • 308**

CHAPTER **13**   **THE FIRM'S PRODUCTION**
DECISION • 341

CHAPTER **14** **COMPETITIVE
EQUILIBRIUM • 368**

PART THREE

IMPERFECT MARKETS

CHAPTER **22** MANAGING THE FIRM • 565

CHAPTER **23** EXTERNALITIES, MERIT GOODS,
PUBLIC DECISION MAKING • 586

PART FOUR

AGGREGATE MARKETS

CHAPTER **25** MACROECONOMIC GOALS
AND MEASURES • 643

CHAPTER **26** AN OVERVIEW OF MACROECONOMICS • 679

CHAPTER **27** THE AGGREGATE LABOR
MARKET • **709**

CHAPTER **28** AGGREGATE DEMAND • **737**

CHAPTER **29** CONSUMPTION AND
INVESTMENT • **766**

CHAPTER **30** GOVERNMENT EXPENDITURES AND TRADE • 798

CHAPTER **31** AGGREGATE DEMAND AND SUPPLY • 828

CHAPTER **32** STICKY PRICES • 860

PART FIVE

MONEY'S ROLE

CHAPTER **35** MONETARY POLICY: THE INTERNATIONAL SIDE • 941

CHAPTER **36** PRICE STABILITY • 964

PART SIX

POLICIES FOR GROWTH AND STABILITY

CHAPTER **37** GROWTH AND PRODUCTIVITY • 993

CHAPTER 40   ALTERNATIVE ECONOMIC SYSTEMS • 1081

CHAPTER 41   DEVELOPMENT • 1110

PREFACE

The last fifty years have been an exciting time for economics. The world has changed in so many fundamental ways. And the discipline of economics has changed in fundamental ways too, partly to reflect these changes.

In the years immediately following World War II, the United States dominated the world economy. International trade was relatively unimportant, in part because of the prevalence of trade barriers. American firms were investing widely abroad, helping to rebuild a Europe that had been devastated by the war. The Cold War put the market economies of the United States and Western Europe in military and economic competition with the Soviet Union, with its very different form of economy. These postwar years saw the U.S. economy growing vigorously and living standards rising rapidly. Countries in Asia and Africa, freed from their colonial status, looked forward as well to rising living standards that they believed would accompany their newly acquired freedom.

All of this has changed. The economies of the former Soviet Union nations have collapsed, along with their political systems. International trade has grown in importance, and Japan and other countries of east Asia and Europe now provide formidable competition for American firms. The United States has lost its lead in the growth sweepstakes: while the rates of growth in east Asia were phenomenal, virtually unprecedented in the history of mankind, the rate of increase of productivity in the United States and Western Europe has slowed down markedly. Indeed, wages of less skilled workers in these Western countries have actually been falling during the past two decades. The dream that each generation would be better off than its parents has been lost. The

United States has gone from being the largest creditor nation in the world—foreigners owed it billions of dollars—to being the largest debtor nation; the country now owes foreigners hundreds of billions of dollars. A major part of the U.S. banking system, the savings and loan associations (S & L's), required a government bailout costing huge sums of money, and the banking systems of several other countries also appear to be on shaky ground.

International capital markets have played an important role in the globalization of the world economy, with hundreds of billions of dollars moving daily from one country to another. Multinational companies have grown beyond belief, to the point where the largest are now larger than many small countries. In the battles for the control of some of these large companies, the capital markets have provided the large sums of money required by the different contestants.

It is not only that the world has changed; expectations have changed as well. While there has been enormous improvement in the quality of air in cities like Pittsburgh and Gary, Indiana, and while Lake Erie has been rescued from becoming polluted to the point where life could not survive, our expectations about the environment have grown even faster; we have become increasingly aware of environmental costs. Longevity has increased, but our knowledge of how to prolong life has grown more rapidly, and rising medical costs have become a major political issue. The economic role of women has changed: not only have they taken a more active part in the labor force, there has been a revolution in expectations concerning the kinds of jobs women can hold.

And in virtually every one of the major issues facing the economy, there is a debate about the role of government. Government in the United States has grown enormously. Before World War II, government took less than one out of every five dollars; today it takes one out of three. There are differing views of government responsibility. For instance, people expect, even demand, that government do something about unemployment. But at the same time, there is a wider understanding of the limitations of government. The deficits over the past decade, the largest in America's peacetime history, have meant that the richest country in the world seems short of money to initiate needed public programs. Issues concerning the responsibility, capabilities, and strategies of government in economics have come to the center of the political debate.

These are exciting issues and events, and they fill the front pages of our newspapers and the evening television news shows. Yet in the past, as a teacher of the introductory course in economics, I felt frustrated: none of the textbooks really conveyed this sense of excitement. Try as they might, none seemed to prepare the student adequately for interpreting and understanding these important economic events.

As I thought about it more, one of the reasons for this became clear: the principles expounded in the classic textbook of Alfred Marshall of a hundred years ago, or that of Paul Samuelson, now almost fifty years old, were not the principles for today. The way we economists understand our discipline had changed to reflect the changing world, but the textbooks had not kept pace. Our professional discourse was built on a *modern* economics, but these new developments simply were not adequately reflected in any of the vast array of textbooks that were available to me as a teacher.

Indeed, changes in the economics discipline over the past half century have been as significant as the changes in world events. The basic competitive model of the economy was perfected in the 1950s. Since then, economists have gone beyond that model in several directions as they have come to better understand its limitations. Earlier researchers had paid lip service to the importance of incentives and to problems posed by limited information. However, it was only in the last two decades that real progress was made in understanding these issues, and the advances found immediate application. Both the collapse of the former Soviet bloc economies and the failure of the American S & L's can be viewed as consequences of the failure to provide appropriate incentives. A central question in the debate over growth and productivity has been, how can an economy provide stronger incentives for innovation? The debate over pollution and the environment centers around the relative merits of regulation and providing incentives not to pollute and to conserve resources.

The past fifty years have also seen a reexamination of the boundary between economics and business. Subjects like finance and management used to be relegated to business schools, where they were taught without reference to economic principles. Today we know that to understand how market economies actually work, we have to understand how firms finance and manage themselves. Tremendous insights can be gleaned through the application of basic economic principles, particularly those grounded in an understanding of incentives. Stories of corporate takeovers have been replaced on the front page by stories of bankruptcies as acquiring corporations have found themselves overextended. The 1990 Nobel Prize was awarded to three economists who had contributed most to the endeavor to integrate finance and economics. Yet the introductory textbooks had not yet built in the basic economics of finance and management.

We have also come to better appreciate the virtues of competition. We now understand, for instance, how the benefits of competition extend beyond price to competition for technological innovation. At the same time, we have come to see better why, in so many circumstances, competition appears limited. Again, as I looked over the available textbooks, none seemed to provide my students with a sense of this new understanding.

Samuelson's path-breaking textbook is credited with being the first to integrate successfully the (then) new insights of Keynesian economics with traditional microeconomics. Samuelson employed the concept of the neoclassical synthesis—the view that once the economy was restored to full employment, the old classical principles applied. In effect, there were two distinct regimes to the economy. In one, when the economy's resources were underemployed, macroeconomic principles applied; in the other, when the economy's resources were fully employed, microeconomic principles were relevant. That these were distinct and hardly related regimes was reflected in how texts were written and courses were taught; it made no difference whether micro was taught before macro, or vice versa. In the last few decades, economists came to question the split that had developed between microeconomics and macroeconomics. The profession as a whole came to believe that macroeconomic behavior had to be related to underlying microeconomic principles; there was one set of economic principles, not two. But this view simply was not reflected in any of the available texts.

Thus, as a teacher of introductory economics, I felt that none of the books provided an understanding of the *principles* of *modern* economics—both the principles that are necessary to understand how modern economists think about the world and the principles that are required to understand current economic issues. As we approach a new century, we need principles that go beyond those of Marshall and Samuelson. To be sure, *some*, even much, of what was contained in these older texts remains in this book. Demand curves and supply curves are tools that have continued to be useful. A thorough understanding of concepts such as comparative advantage, opportunity costs, and marginal analysis is necessary if students are to adequately understand the problems facing market economies. One of the challenges I faced was how to integrate the new principles with the old.

Economics is often characterized as the science of choice. Writing a textbook involves many choices; there is limited space, and the subject matter is vast. As I wrote the book, I continually asked, "What are the basic principles every student of economics should know? What are the most relevant, current applications with which to illustrate each of these principles?" Let me illustrate some of my answers by mentioning several ways in which this text is different.

- The macroeconomic analysis is based on sound microeconomic principles, and the microeconomics is presented in a way that builds a foundation for macroeconomics. While it is fashionable today for most texts to be coauthored by two economists, one specializing in microeconomics and the other in macroeconomics, I have deliberately undertaken the more ambitious task of writing both, believing that doing so will result in a more integrated view of the entire subject. (This reflects my teaching over the past quarter century; I have regularly taught both parts, and have always attempted to show how each throws light on the other.)

- Finance is recognized as an important part of economics, in both the microeconomic and macroeconomic discussions. Chapter 6 introduces the basic ideas of time and risk, Chapter 10 presents "A Student's Guide to Investing," and Chapter 21 discusses how firms raise the funds they need for investment and relates finance to the struggles for corporate control. This new understanding of the microeconomics of finance is then reflected in the macroeconomic discussions, in the analysis of investment in Chapter 29 and in the analysis of monetary economics in Chapters 33–36.

- Problems of growth and international competitiveness are discussed at length. Chapter 18, for instance, provides an analysis of technological change, and Chapter 37 discusses explanations for the slowdown of growth in the United States.

- The importance of international trade and finance is recognized, and not just by adding more chapters or pages. For instance, the role of trade and exchange, including the gains from trade, is developed in Chapter 3. In the macroeconomics discussion, exports and imports and capital flows are an integral part of the analysis. And a separate chapter (38) is devoted to the relationship between the trade deficit and the fiscal deficit.

- Throughout, issues of incentives and the problems posed by incomplete information are given prominence. To take two of many examples, Chapter 22 discusses how firms try to motivate their managers and how managers try to motivate their workers— and the problems they encounter in doing so. Similarly, Chapter 10 takes up the problems investors face when they do not know which investments are likely to be successful.

- As our understanding of the limitations of markets has increased, so has our understanding of the limitations of government, and the age-old questions of the appropriate balance between government and the private sector have to be reexamined. This book looks at a wide range of policy issues, including what the government should do to preserve the environment (Chapter 23) and to promote greater equality (Chapter 24).

I emphasize in this book that most economic tasks are beyond the scope of any one individual. This lesson certainly applies to the writing of this text. In the years during which the book was being written, I benefited greatly from the reactions of my students in the introductory economics courses at Princeton and Stanford who class-tested earlier versions. Their enthusiastic response to drafts of the manuscript provided much-needed boosts to motivate me at several critical stages.

I have also benefited from a large number of reviewers. Their enthusiasm too carried me on, and confirmed my judgment about the need for a new principles book of the kind I was attempting to write. Beyond that, they provided thoughtful criticism and suggestions about both substance and exposition. The book has been improved immeasurably from their advice—some of which, quite naturally, was conflicting. In particular, I would like to thank Robert T. Averitt, Smith College; Mohsen Bahmani-Oskooee, University of Wisconsin, Milwaukee; H. Scott Bierman, Carleton College; John Payne Bigelow, University of Missouri; Bruce R. Bolnick, Northeastern University; Michael D. Curley, Kennesaw State College; John Devereux, University of Miami; K. K. Fung, Memphis State; Christophre Georges, Hamilton College; Ronald D. Gilbert, Texas Tech University; Robert E. Graf, Jr., United States Military Academy; Glenn W. Harrison, University of South Carolina; Marc Hayford, Loyola University; Sheng Cheng Hu, Purdue University; Glenn Hubbard, Columbia University; Allen C. Kelley, Duke University; Michael M. Knetter, Dartmouth College; Stefan Lutz, Purdue University; Mark J. Machina, University of California, San Diego; Burton G. Malkiel, Princeton University; Lawrence Martin, Michigan State University; Thomas Mayer, University of California, Davis; Craig J. McCann, University of South Carolina; Henry N. McCarl, University of Alabama, Birmingham; Marshall H. Medoff, University of California, Irvine; Peter Mieszkowski, Rice University; W. Douglas Morgan, University of California, Santa Barbara; John S. Murphy, Canisius College; David H. Papell, University of Houston; James E. Price, Syracuse University; Daniel M. G. Raff, Harvard Business School; Christina D. Romer, University of California, Berkeley; Richard Rosenberg, Pennsylvania State University; Christopher J. Ruhm, Boston University; Suzanne A. Scotchmer, University of California, Berkeley; Andrei Shleifer, Harvard University; John L. Solow, University of Iowa; George Spiva, University of Tennessee; Raghu Sundaram, University of Rochester; Hal R. Varian, University of Michigan; Franklin V. Walker, State University of New York at Albany; James M. Walker, Indiana University; Andrew Weiss, Boston University; Gilbert R. Yochum, Old Dominion University.

It is a pleasure also to acknowledge the help of a number of research assistants. Many of them went well beyond the assigned tasks of looking up, assembling, and graphing data to providing helpful criticism of the manuscript. These include Edwin Lai, now at Vanderbilt University, Chulsoo Kim, now at Rutgers University, Alexander Dyck, Patricia Nabti, Andrés Rodríguez, Marcie Smith, and Kevin Woodruff. I am particularly indebted to John Williams, who supervised and coordinated the final stages of preparation of the manuscript.

I have also been fortunate in having secretarial support from Linda Handelman and Jean Koentop. Not only did they make preparation of the manuscript easier, they improved it in the process by bringing an unusual degree of intelligence and concern to their work.

This is the second book I have written with Norton, a company that reflects many of the aspects of organizational design that I discuss in the text. This book would not be nearly the one it is without the care, attention, and, most important, deep thought devoted to my work by so many there. A few deserve special mention. Donald Lamm, Norton's president, not only manages to keep the incentives straight within his firm, but also found time to read drafts of this manuscript at several critical stages and offer his usual insightful suggestions. I cannot sufficiently acknowledge my indebtedness to Drake McFeely, my editor on both books: he was concerned about the ideas *and* their presentation. He was a tough critic, but a constructive one, and was as convinced as I was about the importance of the project. The work of Susan Gaustad, the manuscript editor, was as energetic as it was cheerful. All three made my work harder, so that readers of this book would have an easier time. Three others at Norton also deserve mention: Kelly Nusser for her work on the photographs, Antonina Krass for the splendid design of the book, and Roy Tedoff for coordinating its production.

On the editorial front, there was one other person whose contribution was invaluable: Timothy Taylor. Tim's remarkable editorial skills are known to most members of the economics profession through his role as managing editor of the *Journal of Economic Perspectives*. He has long been committed to the notion that it is important that modern economic ideas be communicated widely, and that they *can* be in a way that is both enlightening and enjoyable. At Stanford, he has earned a reputation as one of the finest teachers of the introductory course. Within the wider San Francisco Bay area, he is known as a prolific writer of provocative and informed editorials on economic themes.

In this project, Tim has performed many roles. We have worked together on each draft. We have discussed extensively both the content and the exposition. His editorial skills have not only made the prose more lively, they have, I believe, enabled me to make accessible ideas that might otherwise appear to be difficult and complex. Finally, Tim applied his journalistic talents to the drafting of many of the boxed "Close-ups" that appear here. He did his job so well that many of the boxes he wrote for earlier drafts were incorporated into the main text in later drafts.

I owe special thanks to those who prepared the ancillary materials that accompany the text. Given the fact that this book represents a departure from the standard mold of the past, the tasks they faced were both more important and more difficult. They too shared with me a vision of what this new introductory textbook was about, and their enthusiasm, insight, and hard work has produced a set of truly superb ancillaries: Lawrence Martin of Michigan State prepared the Study Guide, Glenn Harrison and Elisabet Rutström of the University of South Carolina wrote the Instructor's Manual, Dale Bails of Iowa Wesleyan College prepared the test bank, and Stephen R. King and Rick M. McConnell are responsible for the unusual and effective computer tutorials.

It is common practice at this point in the preface to thank one's spouse and children, who have had to sacrifice so much (presumably time that the author would otherwise have spent with them). My debt goes beyond these commonplaces. My wife and children have motivated me, partly by the thirst for economic understanding they have evidenced by their questions about the rapidly changing economic scene, and partly by their challenging spirit—easy explanations, making heavy use of standard economics jargon, would not satisfy them. Moreover, in their perspective, the only justification for diverting my attention away from them and from my principal job as a teacher and researcher was the production of a textbook that would succeed in communicating the basic ideas of modern economics more effectively than those already available. I hope that what I—together with all of those who have helped me so much—have produced will please them.

Suggested Outline for a Short Course

The following is my suggestion for an abbreviated course. I would cover all of the chapters in Part One. In Part Two, Chapter 8 provides the basic tools for analyzing the behavior of the household. Chapters 9 and 11 apply the basic analysis to decisions concerning savings and labor supply; the first parts of those chapters will serve to introduce students to the basic ideas as well as reinforce the ideas taught in Chapter 8. Chapters 11 and 12 are the core chapters for analyzing the theory of the firm. Chapter 14 introduces, in an elementary way, one of the most important concepts in economics, that of general equilibrium, and it explains why economists have such faith in the market economy. These topics have traditionally been viewed as too advanced for the introductory course, but they really do form part of the principles of modern economics, and I believe I have succeeded in presenting them in an elementary way.

There is considerable room for choice in Part Three. Many teachers looking to shorten the course will drop Chapter 22, on managing the firm. While one of the achievements of the text is the integration of financial economics into introductory economics, some teachers of a shortened course may need to drop Chapter 10 and 21; Chapter 10 presents issues of finance from the perspective of the household (the investor), while Chapter 21 discusses issues of corporate finance and takeovers. Again, while one of the contributions of the text is the recognition of the importance of technological change, Chapter 18 can be dropped without impairing the understanding of subsequent chapters. Other teachers may decide to drop Chapter 20, on labor markets.[1] Chapter 19, on imperfect information in the product market, can be skipped as well, though it should be noted that some sections in Chapters 20–22 draw upon the material presented there. Finally, some teachers may find it desirable to provide a more abbreviated discussion of imperfect competition than I provide in Chapters 15–17. I suggest focusing on Chapter 15 and supplementing this with some of the earlier sections of Chapter 17. Similarly, some teachers may find it desirable to provide a more abbreviated discussion of government. In that case, I would recommend dropping Chapter 24.

In Part Four, Chapters 29, 30, and 32 may be dropped without loss of continuity. In Part Five, Chapter 35, which presents monetary theory in an open economy, may be dropped, though I recommend against it, since I do not believe that monetary policy can be adequately understood today from the more traditional closed economy perspective. Finally, Part Six provides, again, wide scope for choice: although each of the chapters draws upon ideas presented in earlier chapters, any may be dropped without impeding the understanding of subsequent chapters.

---

[1] This chapter builds on Chapter 11, so if there is time for only a single chapter on labor markets, it should probably be 11. Chapter 22, on management, builds on some of the ideas concerning incentives presented in the latter part of Chapter 20.

PART ONE

INTRODUCTION

These days economics is big news. If we pick up a newspaper or turn on the television for the prime-time news report, we are likely to be bombarded with statistics on unemployment rates, inflation rates, exports, and imports. How well are we doing in competition with other countries, such as Japan? Everyone seems to want to know. Political fortunes as well as the fortunes of countries, firms, and individuals depend on how well the economy does.

What is economics all about? That is the subject of Part One. Chapter 1 uses the story of the automobile industry to illustrate many of the fundamental issues with which economics is concerned. The chapter describes the four basic questions at the heart of economics, and how economists attempt to answer those questions.

Chapter 2 introduces the economists' basic model and explains why notions of property, profits, prices, and cost play such a central role in economists' thinking.

A fact of life in the modern world is that individuals and countries are interdependent. Even a wealthy country like the United States is dependent on foreign countries for vital imports. Chapter 3 discusses the gains that result from trade; why trade, for instance, allows greater specialization, and why greater specialization results in increased productivity. It also explains the patterns of trade—why each country imports and exports the particular goods it does.

Prices play a central role in enabling economies to function. Chapters 4 and 5 take up the question of what determines prices. Also, what causes prices to change over time? Why is water, without which we cannot live, normally so inexpensive, while diamonds, which we surely can do without, are very expensive? What happens to the prices of beer and cigarettes if the government imposes a tax on these goods? Sometimes the government passes laws requiring firms to pay wages of at least so much, or forbidding landlords to charge rents that exceed a certain level. What are the consequences of these government interventions?

Chapter 6 introduces two important realities: economic life takes place not in a single moment of time but over long periods, and life is fraught with risk. Decisions today have effects on the future, and there is usually much uncertainty about what those effects will be. How do economists deal with problems posed by time and risk?

Finally, Chapter 7 turns to the pervasive role of the government in modern economies. Its focus is on why the government undertakes the economic roles it does and on the economic rationale for government actions. It also describes the various forms that government actions might take and the changing roles of the government over time.

THE AUTOMOBILE AND ECONOMICS

For a teenager, an automobile can symbolize status, freedom of movement, and adventure. For a mechanic, a car can seem like a sick creature to be healed. For a commuter stuck in traffic, a car can feel like a padded prison. For an assembly-line worker, an automobile may be only a partially completed collection of loose pieces, and a job. For a bank robber or a race car driver, a car is a modernized mechanical horse. In the lives of each of these different people—and their example could be multiplied indefinitely—the combination of metal and rubber and plastic that we call an automobile plays an important role, whose nature varies from the grease and grit of utmost practicality to the romanticism of an open convertible on a moonlit highway.

For an economist, the automobile can serve as a starting place for illustrating almost any part of economics. By looking at this familiar subject from the perspective of economics, we can learn a great deal about the economic way of thinking.

"Shame on you, Jamie! Mr. Huntington will be here in a few minutes and he'll say, 'Henry, is my car ready?' And what am I going to say?...Am I going to say, 'Mr. Huntington...Jamie made a boo-boo'?"

KEY QUESTIONS

1. What *is* economics? What are the basic questions it addresses?

2. In economies such as that of the United States, what are the respective roles of government and the private, or "market," sector?

3. What are markets, and what are the principal markets that make up the economy?

4. Why is economics called a science?

5. Why, if economics is a science, do economists so often seem to disagree?

THE AUTOMOBILE: A BRIEF HISTORY

After nearly one hundred years of automobile production, it is hard to imagine a time when cars did not exist. But just like any other new product, the automobile had to start with an idea. Of course, ideas by themselves are not enough. Ideas must be translated into marketable products and produced at affordable prices, and the production process must be financed. Before investors will provide financial support, they have to be convinced that the proposed idea is not only feasible, but likely to be profitable enough to compensate them for the risks of the investment.

No single discovery led to the development of the automobile, and the idea of a motorized carriage occurred to many individuals in the United States, Germany, France, and Great Britain in the late nineteenth century. The technical problems that had to be solved were easy to state, if difficult to tackle. For instance, unlike a steam locomotive, a horseless carriage could not carry its fuel in a separate car, so the development of a powerful but relatively light internal combustion engine was critical.

If you visit a museum of early cars, you will see that the technical problems were resolved independently in a variety of ways. At the end of the nineteenth and beginning of the twentieth centuries, the area around Detroit was full of innovators developing their various cars—Ransom E. Olds, the Dodge brothers, and Henry Ford, ultimately the most successful of them all. The spirit must have been much like that of "Silicon Valley" (the area in California between San Francisco and San Jose) in the past quarter century, which has been at the center of the development of new computer technologies: a spirit of excitement and of important breakthroughs being made and new milestones being reached. The various automobile innovators could draw upon a stock of ideas that were "floating in the air." Then too they had the help of specialized firms that had developed a variety of new technologies and skills unusual for that time: for example, new alloys that enabled lighter motors to be constructed and new techniques for machining that allowed for greater power, precision, and durability. Innovators could draw upon these new technologies to supplement their own ideas.

Henry Ford is generally given credit for having recognized the potential value of a vehicle that could be made available at a reasonable price. Before Ford came along, automobiles were luxuries, affordable only by the very rich. He saw the potential benefit from providing inexpensive transportation. Even after he introduced the Model T in 1909 at a seeming "bargain" price of $900, he subsequently cut the price in half, to $440, in 1914 and then reduced the price by almost a fifth again, to $360, by 1916. The public responded: sales skyrocketed from 58,000 in 1909 to 730,000 in 1916. Ford's prediction of a mass market for inexpensive cars had proved correct.

There was more to Ford's success than simply putting a lower price tag on his cars. He also devised a way to produce cars less expensively. His major innovation was the assembly line, which allowed mass production; this was the key to his lower car prices. Furthermore, Ford managed to obtain the needed financial resources to hire and train a labor force that could produce the automobiles. Underlying all his other successes was the creation of the organization—the Ford Motor Company—within which the production, financing, and marketing took place.

The riskiness of the venture was great. Would Ford be successful in developing his automobile? Would someone else beat him to it? Would the price of a car be low enough for many people to buy it? If he was successful, would imitators copy his invention and produce so many cars that he could not make any money?

Investors in Ford's venture contemplated these risks as they thought about whether to provide him the funds he needed. As it turned out, the investors should have anticipated—but probably did not—a further problem. Ford formed a partnership to develop his first car. He was primarily to supply the ideas and work, while his partners supplied the funds. But the partnership went broke before production began, and Ford's critics claimed that the reason was that he spent all his time and energy thinking about his next set of ideas, rather than actually making any cars.

On the basis of his more developed ideas, Ford then persuaded a new set of investors to finance him. The previous experience should, perhaps, have made them suspicious, but they went ahead. Again the partnership failed, and again Ford seemed to be spending his time developing new ideas.

In his third partnership, Ford finally succeeded in producing cars. Were Ford's first two sets of partners treated unfairly? Ford might well have argued that he entered each of the partnerships in good faith, but he simply was not able to pull off the feat of producing cars until the third time around. Besides, Ford might say, the success of that venture was more attributable to his ideas and efforts than to the money supplied by his partners. Whatever the truth of Ford's particular case, this general sort of problem—one or more partners feels he has contributed proportionately more than his share of profits indicates, or one or more partners tries to "cheat" the others of what they consider their due—occurs over and over again.

Ford's success was due as much to his ability to come up with innovative ways of providing incentives and organizing production as to his skill in solving technical problems. He demonstrated this ability with his original labor policies. Instead of trying to hold down worker pay, he offered more than double the going wage and paid his workers the then princely sum of $5 a day. In exchange, though, Ford worked his employees hard; the moving assembly line he invented enabled him to set his workers a fast pace and push them to keep up. The amount produced per worker increased enormously. Still, it was clear that the high wages were ample compensation for the extra effort. In fact, riots almost broke out as workers clamored for the jobs being offered. Ford had rediscovered an old truth: by paying workers more than they could earn elsewhere, it is possible to obtain a labor force that is harder working and more loyal, with less quitting and absenteeism. In some cases, higher wages for employees can repay the employer in higher productivity.

Ford's success in using incentives to compensate his workers for increasing productivity meant that he could sell his cars far more cheaply than his rivals could. The lower prices and the high level of sales that accompanied them made it possible for him to take full advantage of the mass production techniques he had developed. At one point, however, Ford's plans were almost thwarted when a lawyer-inventor named George Baldwin Selden claimed that Ford had infringed on his patent.

The U.S. government grants patents to enable inventors to reap the rewards of their innovative activity. These are generally for specific inventions, like a new type of braking system or transmission mechanism. A patent gives the inventor the exclusive right to produce his invention for a limited time, thus helping to assure that inventors will be able to make some money from their successful inventions. Patents may lead to higher prices for these new products, since there is no competition from others making the same product, but the presumption is that the gains to society from the stimulation to innovative activity more than compensate for the losses to consumers from the temporarily higher prices.

To obtain a patent, one has to meet certain criteria. Ford's idea of an assembly line, for example, was not an invention that could be patented, and it was imitated by other car manufacturers. One of the criteria for granting a patent (and judging whether someone else is infringing on that patent) is a standard of "novelty." Ideas cannot, in general, be patented; only specific innovations can. Selden had applied for, and been granted, a patent for a horseless, self-propelled carriage. He demanded that other car manufacturers pay him a royalty, which is a payment for the right to use a patented innovation. Simultaneously, he established an association that would ensure that prices of automobiles remained high.

Ford challenged Selden's patent in court on the grounds that the concept of a "horseless, self-propelled carriage," which Selden claimed he had patented, was too vague to be patentable. Ford won and became a national hero. Providing cars to the masses at reasonably low prices made Ford millions of dollars and made many millions of Americans better off, by enabling them to go where they wanted to go more easily, cheaply, and speedily.

THE REBIRTH OF THE AMERICAN AUTOMOBILE INDUSTRY

Today people think of computers and gene-splicing, not automobiles, as the new technologies. The story of the automobile is no longer emblematic of the latest technological breakthroughs. The changing fortunes of the American automobile industry during the past two decades reflect a redefinition of American industry.

There were more than a hundred automobile manufacturers in the fall of 1903, twenty-seven of which accounted for more than 70 percent of the total sales of the industry. By the early 1960s, however, only three companies were responsible for 88 percent of U.S. auto sales. Of the car manufacturers that existed at the beginning of the century, many had gone bankrupt or left for more profitable businesses, and the remainder had been agglomerated into or taken over by the dominant firms. In the 1960s, with only one or two exceptions, foreign car manufacturers simply could not make cars of a quality and price that many Americans wanted to buy. Without the spur of competition pitting many companies against one another, the prices of American-made automobiles were relatively high, and the industry's rate of innovation was relatively low.

The most serious problems faced by the auto industry in the 1960s involved the quality of the environment and automobile safety. It became recognized that the automobile was contributing significantly to air pollution. The government, through the Environmental Protection Agency, regulated the kind of exhaust fumes a car could produce, and design changes followed. On the safety front, automobile companies quickly responded to demands for increased safety by providing seat belts. They balked, however, at supplying air bags that would inflate automatically if a car crashed.

This relatively rosy picture changed dramatically in 1973. That year, the Organization of Petroleum Exporting Countries (OPEC)—mainly countries in the Middle East—combined forces to hold down the supply of oil, create a scarcity, and thus push up its price. In fact, OPEC actually cut off all oil exports for a few tense weeks late in 1973. The power of OPEC was a surprise to many, including the American automobile industry. American cars then tended to be bigger and heavier than those in Japan and Europe. This was easily explained: incomes in the United States were higher, which meant that Americans could afford larger cars and the gasoline they guzzled. Also, Japan and Europe imposed heavy taxes on gasoline, thus encouraging consumers in those countries to buy smaller and more fuel-efficient cars.

The U.S. auto industry had expected that the American taste for large, gas-guzzling cars would continue, which left them ill-prepared for the shock of the higher gas prices caused by OPEC's move. But other countries, especially Japan, stood ready to gain, with smaller, cheaper, and more fuel-efficient cars. Auto imports as a whole nearly doubled in the 1970s, from 15 percent of the total cars sold in the United States in 1970 to 27 percent by 1980, and they remained at that high level throughout the 1980s and into the 1990s. Figure 1.1 shows the imports of new passenger cars from Canada, Japan, and Germany from 1965 to 1990. The figure immediately tells a story: car imports from Japan increased quickly, both absolutely and in comparison with those from other countries. To an economist, such a sudden change from a past trend can be the trigger for a deeper investigation of causes.

It was clear that the Japanese firms were supplying what was wanted by American

Figure 1.1 U.S. AUTO-MOBILE IMPORTS FROM CANADA, JAPAN, AND GERMANY

Imports from Canada and Germany increased in the late 1960s. In the 1970s, however, imports from Japan rose sharply, and the Japanese manufacturers attained a powerful market position that they still enjoy today. *Source: Ward's Automotive Reports* (1991).

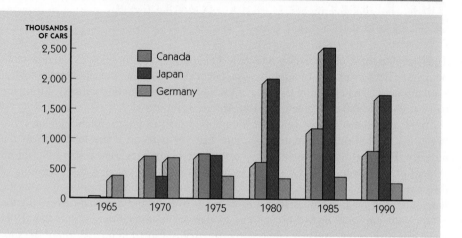

consumers, but the explosion of imports had a devastating effect on the American automobile industry. Profits fell and workers were laid off. Whereas Henry Ford had believed that by paying workers higher wages one could obtain a more productive labor force, the high price of American-made cars in the 1970s was blamed, in large part, on the high wages that the auto industry was paying. The wages could not be justified by the level of productivity of the workers.

CHRYSLER: GOVERNMENT TO THE RESCUE

In the late 1970s, one firm, Chrysler, was on the verge of bankruptcy. Banks refused to lend it money, fearing that it would not be able to repay. The company did not have the cash to pay off loans that were due, so it asked for help from the government. In the ensuing debate about whether the government should do something to save Chrysler, advocates of a bailout (a rescue from financial ruin) painted a picture of unemployed workers—the government has long seen as one of its responsibilities maintaining full employment—and empty, wasted factories.

Critics of the bailout pointed out that workers and other resources could be redeployed. After all, the workers, machines, and buildings of a bankrupt company do not disappear; instead, they are hired by or sold to new companies under new management. Redeployment was appropriate, critics argued, because the bankruptcy demonstrated that Chrysler management had failed to manage its resources well.

Traditional political roles were sometimes reversed in the debate. Some conservatives who had long favored a limited role for the government, who had criticized government "handouts" for the poor and destitute on the grounds that such welfare payments discourage the poor from self-reliance, became advocates of this handout to Chrysler. Some liberals who believed in government spending to help solve many other social problems suddenly became champions of the free market, arguing that a federal subsidy to Chrysler would reduce the incentive for other companies to manage their assets well.

In the end, the government provided a bailout by guaranteeing some new loans for Chrysler. The guarantees meant that if Chrysler failed to pay back its loans, the government would do so with tax money. Because of this guarantee, Chrysler was able to obtain loans from private investors and banks, and at a relatively low rate of interest. The money Chrysler received thus came at least partly at the expense of other firms that were trying to borrow money at the same time, so resources were effectively diverted to Chrysler. Chrysler was able to pay back the loans without going bankrupt, and the company got back on its feet. The subsequent success is by now an often-told tale, with the president of Chrysler, Lee Iacocca, claiming a large share of the credit for himself.

It turns out that the government had strong incentives to step in and help Chrysler. Not only was there concern about losing one of the three major firms in the automobile industry, but the government stood to lose quite a bit of money through an insurance program it had set up several years before for workers' pensions. The insurance program guaranteed that even if a company went bankrupt, workers would still receive their pensions. Had Chrysler gone bankrupt, the government might have had to pay Chrysler workers hundreds of millions of dollars in pensions.

The government also ended up making a lot of money in bailing out Chrysler. In return for guaranteeing the loans, the government insisted that, in effect, it be granted some share of ownership in the firm. With the company's subsequent success, these shares turned out to be quite valuable. Not surprisingly, Chrysler asked the government to forgo what (in retrospect) looked like unconscionable payments for nothing more than a promise, a guarantee on which the government had never had to pay anything. The government refused, and took the money.

PROTECTION FROM FOREIGN COMPETITION

The problems at Chrysler also existed, although in somewhat reduced form, at General Motors and Ford. But in the early 1980s, all three auto companies began to make a recovery from the hard times of the 1970s, for several reasons. The unions dramatically reduced their wage demands. Smaller and more fuel-efficient cars were developed. And while these changes were occurring, the government again stepped in, this time to help protect the industry from foreign competition. Again there was concern about layoffs in the domestic automobile industry: in 1980, unemployment in Michigan, a major auto-producing state, had reached 12.6 percent (as contrasted with the total U.S. unemployment rate of 7.1 percent). But rather than imposing a tariff (a tax) on car imports, the American government negotiated with the Japanese government to restrain Japan's automobile exports. Although the export limits were called voluntary, they were actually negotiated under pressure. If the Japanese had not taken the "voluntary" step of limiting exports, Congress probably would have passed a law forcing them to do so involuntarily.

In any event, the reduced supply of Japanese cars led not only to increased sales of American cars, but to higher prices, both for Japanese cars and for American cars. The American industry was subsidized not by the taxpayers in general but by those who bought cars, through these higher prices. Even the Japanese car manufacturers had little to complain about, since they too benefited from the higher prices. Indeed, had a group of American manufacturers gotten together and agreed to reduce their production and raise prices, it would have been viewed as a violation of U.S. antitrust laws, which were designed to enforce competition. But here the American government itself was encouraging less competition!

The Japanese responded in still another way to these restrictions. They decided to circumvent the limitations on their exports by manufacturing cars here in the United States. This was an ironic reversal of pattern. In the decades immediately after World War II, American firms had set up plants all over the world, showing how American technical knowledge and managerial skills could produce better goods more cheaply. Now the Japanese were coming to America with technological and managerial lessons of their own to teach. Table 1.1, which shows who produced the cars purchased by American consumers in both 1960 and 1990, is powerful testimony to the rising importance of imports and domestically produced foreign cars over that period.

Economists often like to translate numbers into graphs and figures. Figure 1.2 summarizes some of the information in Table 1.1. Panel A shows the fraction of total U.S. production accounted for by General Motors, Ford, Chrysler, and "other" firms in 1960 and 1990. While in 1960 the other firms were all American owned, in 1990 the other firms were all foreign owned. The figure shows that production is highly concentrated. Thus, GM, with slightly less than 50 percent of the total production, is shown as having slightly less than half the pie. Panel B depicts graphically the substantial increase in the share of imports during the period.

By the end of the 1980s, while the American automobile industry had not regained the dominant position it had held some twenty-five years earlier, it showed increasing signs of vitality, reflected not only in high levels of profits, but also in new designs and

Table 1.1 WHO MAKES AMERICA'S CARS

	1960	1990
Domestic production (United States and Canada)		
General Motors	2,869,799	3,141,157
Ford	1,749,308	1,880,389
Chrysler	921,337	795,096
Small producers[a]	528,517	0
Total produced by U.S.-owned companies in America	6,068,955	5,816,642
Total produced by foreign-owned companies in America[b]	0	1,080,246
Total U.S. car production	6,068,955	6,896,888
Plus imports	498,785	2,404,416
Total purchases of cars in the United States	6,567,740	9,301,304

Source: Ward's Automotive Yearbook (1961, 1991).
[a] In 1960, small producers included American Motors, Studebaker, and Packard; by 1990, none of these firms had survived as independent companies.
[b] Includes Honda, Nissan, Toyota, Mazda, Mitsubishi, and Subaru-Isuzu.

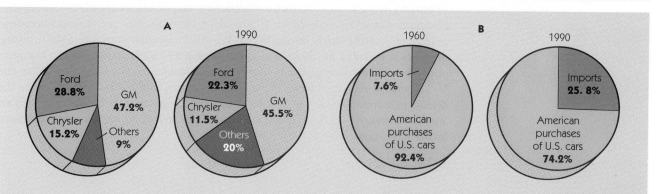

Figure 1.2 SHARES OF THE U.S. AUTOMOBILE MARKET

These pie charts show some of the changes in the U.S. auto market in recent decades. The charts in panel A show that production has remained concentrated. In 1960, the "other" firms were small American firms such as Studebaker and American Motors; in 1990, they were foreign-owned firms like Honda. The charts in panel B show the dramatic increase in imports. *Source: Ward's Automotive Reports* (1961, 1991).

innovations. But the recession of 1991 brought with it record levels of losses. GM alone lost nearly $4.5 billion that year, a new record for any corporation.

Figure 1.3 illustrates the history of U.S. car production. The ups and downs of the curve reflect the story told above of the rise, fall, and recovery of the industry. Car production has been set against a backdrop of the major events affecting the economy as a whole. Different years are listed on the horizontal axis, while the number of cars sold is provided on the vertical axis. The figure shows at a glance that annual auto

Figure 1.3 ANNUAL U.S. AUTOMOBILE PRODUCTION, 1900 TO THE PRESENT

Changes in U.S. automobile production have both reflected and influenced events in the U.S. economy and the world during the twentieth century. *Source: Ward's Automotive Reports* (various years).

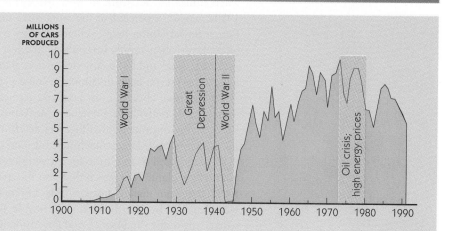

production has declined markedly from its peak in the 1960s. The improvements in techniques of mass production led to the boom in automobile sales early in this century. During the Great Depression of the 1930s, sales declined sharply, and civilian automobile production halted entirely during World War II. Production then rose quickly during the postwar boom of the 1950s and 1960s. In the 1970s, sharp increases in the price of gasoline helped to trigger two worldwide recessions, reducing car sales, before the U.S. economy recovered to a pattern of steady growth in the mid-1980s, allowing the decline in automobile sales at least to be halted. Competition from abroad brought on another downturn in U.S. car production in the late 1980s; the downturn was exacerbated by the 1991 recession.

WHAT IS ECONOMICS?

This short narrative illustrates many facets of economics, but now a definition of our subject is in order. **Economics** studies how individuals, firms, governments, and other organizations within our society make **choices,** and how those choices determine how the resources of society are used. **Scarcity** figures prominently in economics: choices matter because resources are scarce. Imagine an enormously wealthy individual who can have everything he wants. We might think that scarcity is not in his vocabulary—until we consider that time is a resource, and he must decide what expensive toy to devote his time to each day. Taking time into account, then, scarcity is a fact in everyone's life.

To produce a single product, like an automobile, thousands of decisions and choices have to be made. Since any economy is made up not only of automobiles but of millions of products, it is a marvel that the economy functions at all, let alone functions as well as it does most of the time. This marvel is particularly clear if you consider instances when things do not work so well: the Great Depression in the United States in the 1930s, when 25 percent of the work force could not find a job; the countries of the former Soviet Union today, where ordinary consumer goods like carrots or toilet paper or boots are often simply unavailable; the less developed economies of many countries in Africa, Asia, and Latin America, where standards of living have remained stubbornly low, or have even been declining in some places.

The fact that choices must be made applies as well to the economy as a whole as it does to each individual. Somehow, decisions are made—by individuals, households, firms, and government—that together determine how the economy's limited resources, including its land, labor, machines, oil, and other natural resources, are used. Why is it that land used at one time for growing crops may, at another time, be used for an automobile plant? How was it that over the space of a couple of decades, resources were transferred from making horse carriages to making automobile bodies? that blacksmiths were replaced by auto mechanics? How do the decisions of thousands of consumers, workers, investors, managers, and government officials all interact to determine the use of the scarce resources available to society? Economists reduce such matters to four basic questions concerning how economies function:

1. What is produced, and in what quantities?   There have been important changes in consumption over the past fifty years. Spending for medical care, for example, was only 3.5 percent of total personal consumption in 1950. By 1990, more than one out of every eight dollars was spent on medical care. In 1950, more than one out of every four dollars was spent on food. By the late 1980s, the figure was only one out of six dollars. In the past twenty years, consumers have switched from gas guzzlers to more fuel-efficient cars. What can account for changes like these? The economy seems to spew out new products like videocassette recorders and new services like automated bank tellers. What causes this process of innovation? The overall level of production has also shifted from year to year, often accompanied by large changes in the levels of employment and unemployment. How can economists explain these changes?

In the United States, the question of what is produced, and in what quantities, is answered largely by the private interaction of firms and consumers, but government also plays a role. Prices are critical in determining what goods are produced. When the price of some good rises, firms are induced to produce more of that good, to increase their profits. A central question with which economists have thus been concerned is, why are some goods more expensive than others? And why is it that the price of some good has increased or decreased?

2. How are these goods produced?   There are often many ways of making something. Textiles can be made with hand looms. Modern machines enable fewer workers to produce more cloth. Very modern machines may be highly computerized, allowing one worker to monitor many more machines than was possible earlier. The better machines generally cost more, but they require less labor. Which technique will be used, the advanced technology or the labor-intensive one? Henry Ford introduced a new way of making cars, the assembly line. More recently, car manufacturers have begun using robots. What determines how rapidly technology changes?

In the U.S. economy, firms answer the question of how goods are produced, again with help from the government, which sets regulations and enacts laws that affect everything from the overall organization of firms to the ways they interact with their employees and customers.

3. For whom are these goods produced?   With goods produced, the issue of distribution arises. Who gets to consume the goods that are produced in any society? In the United States, individuals who have higher incomes can consume more goods. But that answer only pushes the question back one step: What determines the differences in income and wages? What is the role of luck? of education? of inheritance? of savings? of experience and hard work? These questions are difficult to answer. For now, suffice it to say that while, again, incomes are primarily determined by the private interaction of firms and households, government also plays a strong role, with taxes as well as programs that redistribute income.

Figure 1.4 shows the relative pay in a variety of different occupations. To judge by income, each physician receives five times as much of the economy's output as a firefighter, and seven times as much as a butcher.

4. Who makes economic decisions, and by what process?   In a **centrally planned economy,** as the Soviet Union used to be, the government takes responsibility for virtually every aspect of economic activity. The first three questions, as well as the fourth, are

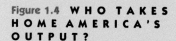

Figure 1.4 WHO TAKES HOME AMERICA'S OUTPUT?

This chart measures the earnings of a variety of professions relative to the wages of an average worker. Firefighters make 25 percent more than an average worker, while physicians make over six times as much.

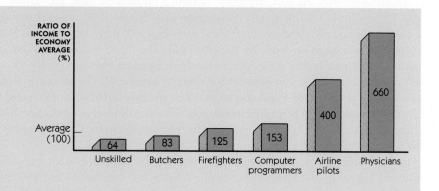

thus answered by the government. A central economic planning agency works through a bureaucracy to say what will be produced and by what method, and who shall consume it.

At the other end of the spectrum are economies that rely primarily on the free interchange of producers and their customers to determine what, how, and for whom. The United States, which lies near this latter end, is said to have a **mixed economy;** that is, there is a mix between public (governmental) and private decision making. Within limits, producers make what they want to make; they use whatever method of production seems appropriate to them; and the collective output is distributed to consumers according to their income. When economists examine an economy, they want to know to what extent economic decisions are made by the government, and to what extent they are made by private individuals. In the United States, while individuals are allowed for the most part to make their own decisions about what kind of car to purchase, the government has intruded in a number of ways: it has taken actions that affect the imports of Japanese cars, that restrict the amount of pollutants a car can produce, and that promote fuel efficiency and automobile safety.

A related question is whether economic decisions are made by individuals for their own interests or for the interest of an employer such as a business firm or government agency. This is an important distinction. We can expect people acting on their own behalf to make decisions that benefit themselves. When they act on behalf of organizations, however, a conflict of interest may arise. Observers often refer to corporations and governments as if they were a single individual. Economists point out that organizations consist, by definition, of a multitude of individuals and that the interests of these individuals do not necessarily coincide with one another or, for that matter, with the interests of the organization itself. This is but one example of the fact that organizations bring a number of distinctive problems to the analysis of choice.

As you can see by their concern with decision making, economists are concerned not only with *how* the economy answers the four basic questions, but also *how well*. They ask, is the economy efficient? Could it produce more of some goods without producing fewer of others? Could it make some individuals better off without making some other individuals worse off?

MARKETS AND GOVERNMENT IN THE MIXED ECONOMY

The primary reliance on private decision making in the United States reflects economists' beliefs that this reliance is appropriate and necessary for economic efficiency; however, economists also believe that certain kinds of interventions by the government are desirable. Finding the appropriate balance between the public and the private sectors of the economy is one of the central issues of economic analysis.

MARKETS

When economists argue for a basic reliance on private decision making, they often say that economic decisions should be left "to the market." The modern concept of the **market** is an extension of the traditional village market, where buyers and sellers came together to exchange goods. This kind of market still exists in many less developed countries, and in most cities some farmers still bring their produce to sell in a farmers' market. In modern economies, some markets exist in well-defined locations: stocks, for instance, are mostly traded on the "stock market" at locations like the New York Stock Exchange, the American Stock Exchange, and the Pacific Stock Exchange.

Today the concept of markets is used to include any situation where exchange takes place, though this exchange may not necessarily resemble the village market. In department stores and shopping malls, customers rarely haggle over the price. When manufacturers purchase the materials they need for production, they exchange money for them, not other goods. Most goods, from cameras to clothes, are not sold directly from producers to consumers. They are sold from producers to distributors, from distributors to retailers, from retailers to consumers. All of these transactions are embraced by the concept of the **market economy.**

In market economies with competition, individuals make choices that reflect their own desires. And firms make choices that maximize their profits; to do so, they must produce the goods that consumers want, and they must produce them at lower cost than other firms. As firms compete against one another in the quest for profits, consumers are benefited, both in the kinds of goods produced and the prices at which they are supplied. The market economy thus provides answers to three of the four basic economic questions—what is produced, how it is produced, and how these decisions are made—and on the whole, the answers ensure the efficiency of the economy.

The market economy also provides an answer to the remaining question—**for** whom goods are produced—but it is an answer that not everyone finds acceptable. Markets allocate goods to those who are willing and able to pay the most for them. Like bidders at an auction, the market participants willing and able to pay the highest price take home the goods. But what people are willing and able to pay depends on their income. It is possible that some groups of individuals—including those without skills that are valued by the market—may receive such a low income that they could not survive or feed and educate their children without outside assistance. Government provides the assistance by taking steps to increase income equality. These steps, however, often blunt economic incentives. While welfare payments provide an important safety net for the poor, the high taxation required to finance them may discourage work and savings. After all, if the government takes one out of three or even two dollars that a high-income individual earns, she may not be inclined to work so hard. She may decide not to work every Saturday and to take a longer vacation. And if the government takes one out of two or three dollars a person earns from interest on savings, she may decide to spend more now and save less. Like the question of the appropriate balance between the public and private sectors, the question of the appropriate balance between concerns about equality, often referred to as **equity concerns,** and efficiency is one of the central issues of modern economics.

THE ROLE OF GOVERNMENT

While the market provides, *on the whole*, answers to the basic economic questions that ensure efficiency, there are certain areas in which the solutions are inadequate, or appear to be so to many people. When the market is not working well, or is not perceived to be working well, people often turn to government. This, however, is only part of government's function.

The government plays a major role in modern economies, and we need to understand both what that role is and why government undertakes the activities that it does. In the narrative of the automobile industry, we encountered several instances of government action. Early in the history of the automobile, George Baldwin Selden was almost able to use the government-created patent laws to change the course of the industry. In the late 1970s, government loan guarantees enabled Chrysler to survive. The automobile industry was greatly helped by government restrictions on Japanese imports, but probably hurt by other government regulations, like those concerning safety and pollution. The strength of the auto unions, when they succeeded in raising wages to high levels, was partly a result of the rights that federal legislation had granted to them. Later in this book, we will see more ways in which government policy has affected the automobile and other industries.

In general, the U.S. government sets the legal structure under which private firms and individuals operate. It regulates businesses to ensure that they do not discriminate by race or sex, that they do not mislead customers, that they are careful about the safety of their employees, that they do not pollute the air and water. In some industries, the government operates like a private business: the government-owned Tennessee Valley Authority (TVA) is one of the nation's largest producers of electricity; most children attend government-owned public schools; and most mail is still delivered by the government-owned post office. In other cases, such as providing for the national defense, building roads, and printing money, the government supplies goods and services that the private sector does not. Government programs provide for the elderly through Social Security (which pays income to retired individuals) and Medicare (which funds medical needs of the aged). The government helps those who have suffered some sort of economic dislocation, through unemployment insurance for those temporarily unemployed and disability insurance for those who are no longer able to work. The government also attempts to provide a "safety net" of support for the poor, particularly poor children, through various welfare programs.

One can, however, easily imagine a government controlling the economy more directly. In countries where decision-making authority is centralized and concentrated in the government, government bureaucrats might decide what and how much a factory should produce and pass laws on the level of wages that should be paid. Various European governments run steel companies, coal mines, and the telephone system. At least until recently, governments in countries like the former Soviet Union and China attempted to control practically all major decisions regarding resource allocation.

THE THREE MAJOR MARKETS

In simple form, the market economy revolves around exchange between individuals (or households), who buy goods and services from firms, and firms, which take **inputs,** the various materials of production, and produce **outputs,** the goods and services that they sell. In thinking about a market economy, economists focus their attention on three broad categories of markets in which individuals and firms interact. The markets in which firms sell their outputs to households are referred to collectively as the **product market,** or the market for goods. Many firms also sell their goods to other firms; the outputs of the first firm become the inputs of the second. These transactions too are said to occur in the product market.

On the input side, firms need (besides the materials that they buy in the product market) some combination of labor and machinery with which their goods can be produced. They purchase the services of workers in the **labor market.** They raise funds, with which to buy inputs, in the **capital market.** Traditionally, economists have also highlighted the importance of a third input, land, but in modern industrial economies, land is of secondary importance. Hence, for most purposes, it suffices to focus attention on the three major markets listed here, and this text will follow this pattern.

As Figure 1.5 shows, individuals participate in all three markets. When individuals buy goods or services, they act as **consumers** in the product market. When people act as **workers,** economists say that they "sell their labor services" in the labor market.

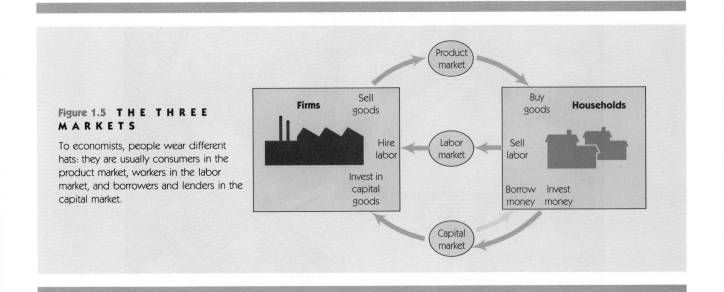

Figure 1.5 THE THREE MARKETS

To economists, people wear different hats: they are usually consumers in the product market, workers in the labor market, and borrowers and lenders in the capital market.

Close-up: Russia and Eastern Europe Try New Answers to Old Questions

For most of the twentieth century, the centrally planned economic system of the former Soviet Union gave straightforward answers to the four basic economic questions.

What was produced in such an economy, and in what quantities? Government planners set the targets, which workers and firms then struggled to fulfill.

How were these goods produced? Again, since government planners decided what supplies would be delivered to each factory, they effectively chose how production occurred.

For whom were these goods produced? The government made decisions about what each job was paid, which affected how much people could consume. In principle, individuals could choose what to buy at government-operated stores, at prices set by the government. But in practice, many goods

were unavailable at these stores. Those who held positions of power and influence could find alternate sources of goods, but average consumers could not. The government also directly controlled many goods like apartments, deciding who could live where.

Who made economic decisions, and by what process? The government planners decided, basing the decisions on their view of national economic goals.

At one time, all this planning sounded very sensible, but as former Soviet premier Nikita Khrushchev once said, "Economics is a subject that does not greatly respect one's wishes." By the time that Mikhail Gorbachev rose to power in the mid-1980s, it was clear to Soviet citizens and outsiders alike that some change was needed. Many examples of Soviet economic woes could be cited, but two will

suffice. In the shoe market, the Soviet Union was the largest national producer in the world. However, the average shoe was of such low quality that it fell apart in a few weeks, and inventories of unwanted shoes rotted in warehouses. In agriculture, the Soviet government had traditionally allowed small private agricultural plots. Although the government limited the amount of time that farmers could spend on these plots, publicly run farming was so unproductive that the 3 percent of Soviet land that was privately run usually produced about 25 percent of the total farm output.

Today the standard of living in the former Soviet Union is not only below that in industrialized nations like the United States and those of Western Europe, but it is barely ahead of developing nations like Brazil and Mexico. Workers in the Soviet Union shared a grim one-liner: "We pretend to work and they pretend to pay us."

Gorbachev came to power promoting the ideas of *perestroika* (restructuring) and *glasnost* (openness). In political terms, these ideas had very rapid and powerful consequences. In the countries of Eastern Europe, the Communist leaders were overthrown in 1989 and 1990. The Soviet Union itself disintegrated at the end of 1991, breaking up into Russia, Ukraine, and a number of other independent states. Many of these countries held elections to determine, at least in part, who would hold the power of government.

Deciding to hold an election, however, is relatively easy compared with the job of restructuring an entire economy. The political desires of people striving for freedom often seemed to overshadow economic considerations. Yet by early in the 1990s, some general pathways toward economic reform of these economies were becoming clear. Workers need increased incentives to work hard, even if that means greater inequality of wages. Firms need greater incentives to become more efficient and produce what people want, even if that occasionally means unemployment and bankruptcy. It seems evident that the role of government planners must be reduced. Programs along these lines were instituted in many Eastern European nations in 1989 and 1990, and in Russia under Boris Yeltsin at the start of 1992.

But after seven decades of central economic planning, making the transition to an economy in which market forces have greater power promises to be excruciatingly difficult. Things may very well become worse before they get better. The eventual payoff may be years or even decades in the future.

When individuals buy shares of stock in a firm or lend money to a business, economists note that they are participating in the capital market, and refer to them as **investors.** The automobile industry provides some vivid examples of the complexity of all three markets.

The Product Market Economists use the term "product market" to refer to the sale of goods by firms to households and to other firms. Among the most important characteristics of the product market is the degree of competition. In the early 1900s, the automobile industry was made up of a large number of auto companies competing against one another; more recently, in the 1960s, three firms dominated the industry; and today foreign firms provide strong competition for U.S. companies.

Economic competition, however, is only one of several important economic concerns. Patent rights provide one case where society is willing to risk a lack of competition for a limited amount of time in exchange for an incentive to inventors to produce new products. The near-collapse of Chrysler is an example of where the results of market competition—a major company driven bankrupt—were judged to be unacceptable by the American political system.

The Labor Market   Economists use the term "labor market" to refer to the transactions in which workers are hired or labor services are purchased. Firms not only must hire and train workers, they must provide them with incentives to work hard and not to quit. Henry Ford discovered that it might be profitable to pay higher wages than competitors, and auto companies in the early 1980s found that excessively high wages may prevent them from competing against imported cars.

The Capital Market   The term "capital" is used in two different but closely related ways in economics. The first refers to machines and buildings, what are sometimes called **capital goods.** The second refers to the money used to buy and sell capital goods, or to buy and sell firms (which may, in turn, own capital goods). When economists refer to the "capital market," they generally mean the markets in which funds are raised and transferred, including all the institutions involved in borrowing and lending money. Care is taken in this book to use the term "capital goods" whenever it is just the machines and buildings themselves that are of concern.

The capital market includes the whole array of institutions by which firms (and individuals) raise money from other firms and individuals. From the economist's perspective, people have two choices about what to do with their money: they can spend it or they can save it. What they save goes into bank accounts, stock brokerage accounts, and a variety of other forms by which funds enter the market for capital. The capital market plays an important role not only in financing new ventures and new investment—as when Henry Ford sought out investors, with whom he was supposed to share the proceeds from his innovative activity—but also in sustaining established firms when they face hard times. Chrysler's inability to raise funds without a government guarantee took the company to the verge of bankruptcy.

Capital markets play a critical role in determining how America's savings are allocated. Individual investors and companies like banks or pension funds that collect and hold the savings of individuals must decide not only which industries look most promising, but which firms within those industries look most likely to be profitable. To fund his automobile companies, Henry Ford had to compete with a large number of innovators and established companies, many of whom had as much faith in their own ideas as Ford did in his.

THE BRANCHES OF ECONOMICS

Economics is a broad subject. Understanding even the development of a single industry, such as the automobile industry, requires studying economics from several different perspectives.

MICROECONOMICS AND MACROECONOMICS

The detailed study of product, labor, and capital markets is called **microeconomics.** Microeconomics ("micro" is derived from the Greek word meaning "small") focuses on the behavior of the units—the firms, households, and individuals—that make up the economy. It is concerned with how the individual units make decisions and what affects those decisions. By contrast, **macroeconomics** ("macro" comes from the Greek word meaning "large") looks at the behavior of the economy as a whole, in particular the behavior of such aggregate measures as overall rates of unemployment, inflation, economic growth, and the balance of trade. The aggregate numbers do not tell us what any firm or household is doing. They tell us what is happening in total, or on average.

It is important to remember that these economic perspectives are just two ways of looking at the same thing. Microeconomics is the bottom-up view of the economy; macroeconomics is the top-down view. The behavior of the economy as a whole is dependent on the behavior of the units that make it up; for example, the overall unemployment rate is, in part, the result of the employment decisions of the thousands of firms that make up the economy; the inflation rate is the result of thousands of decisions about what prices should be charged; the rate of economic growth is determined by thousands of decisions about investment, research and development, and new products.

The automobile industry is a story of both micro- and macroeconomics. In part, it is a story of microeconomic interactions of individual companies, investors, and labor unions. In part, it is a story of global macroeconomic forces like oil shortages and a surge in foreign competition. When auto companies laid off workers in the late 1970s, their problems boosted the overall unemployment rate. The recession of the early 1990s brought heavy reductions in car sales.

THE SCIENCE OF ECONOMICS

Economics is a **social science.** It studies the social problem of choice from a scientific viewpoint, which means that it is built on a systematic exploration of the problem of choice. This systematic exploration involves both the formulation of theories and the examination of data.

A **theory** consists of a set of assumptions (or hypotheses), and conclusions derived from those assumptions. Theories are logical exercises: *if* the assumptions are correct, *then* the results follow. If all college graduates have a better chance of getting jobs and Ellen is a college graduate, then Ellen has a better chance of getting a job than a nongraduate. Economists make predictions with their theories. They might use a theory to predict what will happen if a tax is increased, or if some regulation is removed, or if imports of foreign cars are limited. The predictions of a theory are of the form "If a tax is increased and if the market is competitive, then output will decrease and prices will increase."

In economics, another word for theory is **model.** To understand how economists use models, consider a modern car manufacturer trying to design a new automobile. It is extremely expensive to construct a new car. Rather than creating a separate, fully developed car for every engineer's or designer's conception of what she would like to see the new car be, the company uses models. The designers might use a plastic model to study the general shape of the vehicle and to assess reactions to the car's aesthetics. The engineers might use a computer model to study the air resistance, from which they can calculate fuel consumption. Another major question concerns the comfort of the passengers; engineers might construct a separate model for the interior of the car. And the interior designers may have little interest in details of the exterior shape, and use an interior model of their own.

Just as the engineers construct different models to study a particular feature of a car, so too an economist constructs a model of the economy—in words or equations—to depict the particular features of the economy with which he is concerned. An economic model might describe a general relationship ("When incomes rise, the number of cars purchased increases"), describe a quantitative relationship ("When incomes rise by 10 percent, the number of cars purchased rises, on average, by 12 percent"), or make a general prediction ("An increase in the tax on gasoline will decrease the demand for cars").

AN ECONOMIC EXAMPLE: CHOOSING HOW TO GET TO WORK

Traffic congestion is a major problem in almost all of America's major cities. Urban planners would like to encourage more commuters to use public transport. In thinking about how best to do this, they have found simple models of how commuters decide on how to get to work extremely useful. While recognizing that there are a wide variety of considerations in deciding whether to take a bus or subway versus driving, planners might focus on two: cost and time. But as the expression goes, time is money. The planners thus add up the actual transportation cost plus the value of the time. Again, while recognizing that different people value their time differently, the planners might simplify by saying that time is valued at the wage a person receives.

To see how such a model can be used, consider the city of Urbania, contemplating replacing its current slow rail service to Idyllic Park with a high-speed train line, which would reduce travel time by 30 minutes. The train ride currently takes 1 hour, and the car commute takes 45 minutes. The current cost of a train ride is $1; for driving, the estimated cost of gasoline plus wear and tear on the car is $1.25. The average commuter in Idyllic Park makes $20 an hour, so the value of the extra quarter of an hour is $5. The total cost of going by car is $15 (value of time) + $1.25 = $16.25, and by train is $20 (value of time) + $1 (fare) = $21. The model predicts that few commuters will take the current, slow train.

The high-speed train will necessitate raising the fare to $2. The total cost of a train ride will then be $2 (fare) + $10 (value of time) = $12, considerably cheaper than the $16.25 cost of going by car. The model predicts that many commuters will switch, and argues that considerable attention should be placed on speed.

While this example is hypothetical, similar considerations arose in discussions concerning the construction of BART, the Bay Area Rapid Transit system in the San Francisco area. And they arise repeatedly as cities consider whether to extend or improve their subway systems.

DISCOVERING AND INTERPRETING RELATIONSHIPS

A **variable** is any item that can be measured and that changes. Prices, wages, interest rates, quantities bought and sold, are all variables. The price of bread changes over time, as does the quantity sold. So does the price of wheat, the number of people who have jobs, the interest rate your bank pays. What interests economists is the connection between variables. When economists see what appears to be a systematic relationship among variables, they ask, could it have arisen by chance, or is there indeed a relationship? This is the question of **correlation.**

Economists use statistical tests to measure and test correlations. For instance, consider the problem of deciding whether a coin is biased. If you flip a coin 10 times and get 6 heads and 4 tails, is the coin a fair one? Or is it weighted to heads? Statistical tests will say that the result of 6 heads and 4 tails could easily happen by chance, so the evidence does not prove that the coin is weighted. Of course, it does not prove that it is *not* slightly weighted either. The evidence is just not strong enough for either conclusion. On the other hand, if you flip a coin 100 times and get 80 heads, then statistical tests will tell you that the possibility of this happening by blind chance with a fair coin is extremely small. Thus, the evidence would support the assertion that the coin is weighted.

A similar logic can be used on questions about correlations in economic data. People with more education tend to earn higher wages. Is the connection merely one of chance? Statistical tests show whether the evidence is too weak for a conclusion, or whether it supports a particular answer.

CAUSATION VERSUS CORRELATION

Economists would like to accomplish more than just asserting that different variables are indeed correlated. They would like to conclude that changes in one variable *cause* the changes in the other variable. This distinction between correlation and **causation** is an important one. If one variable "causes" the other, then changing one variable necessarily will change the second. If the relationship is just a correlation, this may not be true.

For instance, Figure 1.6 shows the relationship between years of schooling completed and annual income. There is no doubt that those with more years of schooling receive a higher income. But there are at least two possible explanations. One is that firms are willing to pay more for workers who are more productive and that education increases individuals' productivity. In this explanation, there is causation. More education "causes" greater productivity, which "causes" higher wages. The other explanation is that firms

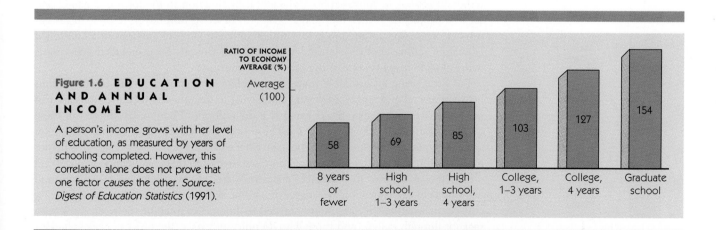

Figure 1.6 EDUCATION AND ANNUAL INCOME

A person's income grows with her level of education, as measured by years of schooling completed. However, this correlation alone does not prove that one factor *causes* the other. *Source: Digest of Education Statistics* (1991).

RATIO OF INCOME TO ECONOMY AVERAGE (%)

Average (100)

8 years or fewer	High school, 1–3 years	High school, 4 years	College, 1–3 years	College, 4 years	Graduate school
58	69	85	103	127	154

are willing to pay higher wages to those who are smarter even though they may not yet have many productive skills (and what skills they have may have little to do with what they have learned at school), and those who are smarter survive longer in school. In this view, more able individuals stay in school longer and receive higher wages, but the schools do not cause increased productivity. There is a correlation, but no causation.

Sometimes there are systematic relationships between variables in which it is difficult to tell which variable is the cause, which the effect. For example, there is a systematic relationship between the number of children a woman has and the wages she earns. But the explanation for this relationship is not clear. Low wages mean that the income the woman must give up when she takes off work to have a child is less; in a sense, children are "less expensive." Do low wages, then, induce women to have more children? Or does having many children distract a woman from pursuing her career as avidly, and thus lead to low wages? Or is there a third factor, accounting for both the level of wages and the number of children?

EXPERIMENTS IN ECONOMICS

Many sciences use experiments to test alternative explanations, since experiments allow the scientist to change one factor at a time and see what happens. But the economy is not a chemistry lab. Instead, economics is like astronomy, in that both sciences must use the experiments that nature provides. Economists look for situations in which only one factor changes, and study the consequences of changing that factor. A change in the income tax system is an example of a natural experiment. But nature is usually not kind to economists; the world does not hold still. As the tax system changes, so do other features of the economy, and economists often have a difficult time deciding whether changes that they perceive are the result of the new tax system or of some other economic change. Sometimes they can use what is called **econometrics,** the branch of statistics that has developed to analyze the particular sorts of measurement problems that arise in economics.

In a few cases, economists have engaged in social experiments. For example, they have given a selected group of individuals a different income tax schedule or a different welfare program. They have tried experiments with alternative ways of providing housing or education to the poor. Also, in recent years, economists have studied certain aspects of economic behavior in "laboratory" situations. One way of seeing how individuals respond to risk is to construct an artificially risky situation in the form of a game, and see how people react when they play it. One way of seeing how buyers respond to various ways of organizing an auction is to simulate different kinds of auctions in a controlled laboratory setting. Both social and laboratory experiments have provided economists with valuable insights concerning economic behavior.

But even using all available tools, the problem of finding a variety of correlations between several different types of data and having to discern which connections are real and which are only apparent is obviously a difficult one. Economists' interest in these questions is motivated by more than just curiosity—though this plays an important role. Often important policy questions depend on what one believes is really going on. Whether a country thinks it worthwhile to pour more resources into higher education may depend on whether it believes that the differences in wages observed between those with and without a college education are largely due to the skills and knowledge acquired during college, or whether they are mainly related to differences in ability between those who make it through college and those who do not.

The important lessons to remember here are (1) the fact of a correlation does not prove a causation; (2) the way to test different explanations of causation is to hold all of the factors constant except for one, and then allow that one to vary; (3) data do not always speak clearly, and sometimes they just do not allow any conclusions to be drawn.

WHY ECONOMISTS DISAGREE

Economists are frequently called upon to make judgments on matters of public policy. Should the government reduce the deficit? Should inflation be reduced? If so, how? In these public policy discussions, the disagreements among economists often get considerable attention. But disagreement can be a productive way of learning more, if approached properly. Economists try carefully to define the sources and reasons for their differences.

Two major sources of disagreement exist within the scientific realm of economics. First, economists may differ over what is the appropriate model of the economy. They may disagree about how well people and firms are able to perceive and calculate their self-interest, and whether their interactions take place in a competitive or a noncompetitive market. Different models will often produce different results. Often the data that we currently have available do not allow us to say which of two competing models provides a better description of some market.

Second, even when they agree about the appropriate theoretical model, economists may disagree about quantitative magnitudes, and accordingly their predictions will differ. They may agree, for instance, that reducing the tax on interest income will encourage individuals to save more. But some economists may claim, on the basis of their studies, that individuals will increase their savings only a little; others, that people will increase their savings a lot. Again, many of these disagreements arise because of the lack of relevant data. We may have considerable data concerning savings in the United States over the past century. But institutions and economic conditions today are markedly different from those of fifty or even ten years ago.

There is another source of disagreement, but this one lies outside the scientific realm. It is common for economists to be asked questions like "Should the government cut the capital gains tax to encourage savings?" "Should the government cut taxes to stimulate the economy and reduce unemployment?" To answer such questions, economists must determine the consequences of the policy in question, which makes it necessary first to formulate a model of the economy or the market. Even if the goals of the policy are clear, disagreements may occur for either of the reasons given above. But if the goals are unclear, then the economist's own values may intrude, and this is where the third source of disagreement comes in.

There are generally many consequences of any policy, some beneficial, some harmful. In comparing two policies, one may benefit some people more, another may benefit others. One policy is not unambiguously better than another. It depends on what you care more about. A cut in the tax on the profits from the sale of stocks might encourage savings, but at the same time, most of the benefits accrue to the very wealthy; hence, it increases inequality. A reduction in taxes to stimulate the economy may reduce unemployment, but it may also increase inflation. Even though two economists agree about the model, they may make different recommendations. In assessing the effect of a tax cut on unemployment and inflation, for instance, an economist who is worried more about unemployment may recommend in favor of the tax cut, while the other, concerned about inflation, may recommend against it. In this case, the source of the disagreement is a difference in values.

POSITIVE AND NORMATIVE ECONOMICS

Economists try to identify carefully the points in their analysis where values are brought in. When they describe the economy, and construct models that predict either how the economy will change or the effects of different policies, they are engaged in what is called **positive economics.** When they attempt to evaluate alternative policies, weighing up the various benefits and costs, they are engaged in what is called **normative economics.** Positive economics is concerned with what "is," with describing how the economy functions; normative economics deals with what "should be," with making judgments about the desirability of various courses of action. Normative economics makes use of positive economics. We cannot make judgments about whether a policy is desirable unless we have a clear picture of its consequences. Good normative economics also tries to be explicit about precisely what values or objectives it is incorporating. It tries to couch its statements in the form "If these are your objectives . . . , then this is the best possible policy."

Consider the positive and normative aspects of a proposal to levy a $1-per-case tax on beer. Positive economics would describe what effect the tax would have on the price of beer—would the price rise by the full $1, or would producers absorb some of the price rise? On the basis of that analysis, economists would go on to predict how much beer consumption would be reduced, and who would be affected by the tax. They might find, for instance, that since lower-income individuals spend a larger fraction of their income on beer, these people would be affected proportionately more. Studies may have indicated that there is a systematic relationship between the quantity of beer consumed and road accidents. Using this information, economists might attempt to estimate how the beer tax would affect the number of accidents. These steps are all part of describing the full consequences of the tax, without making judgments. In the end, however, the question is, *should* the tax be adopted? This is a normative question, and in responding to it, economists will weigh the benefits of the tax revenue, the distortions it induces in consumption, the inequities caused by the fact that proportionately more of the tax is borne by lower-income individuals, and the lives saved in road accidents. Furthermore, in evaluating the tax, economists will also want to compare it with other ways of raising similar amounts of revenue.

REVIEW AND PRACTICE

SUMMARY

1. Economics is the study of how individuals, firms, and governments within our society make choices. Choices are unavoidable because desired goods, services, and resources are inevitably scarce.

2. There are four basic questions that economists ask about any economy. (1) What is produced, and in what quantities? (2) How are these goods produced? (3) For whom are these goods produced? (4) Who makes economic decisions, and by what process?

3. The United States has a mixed economy; there is a mix between public and private decision making. The economy relies primarily on the private interaction of individuals and firms to answer the four basic questions, but government plays a large role as well. A central question for any mixed economy is the balance between the public and private sectors.

4. The term "market" is used to describe any situation where exchange takes place. In America's market economy, individuals, firms, and government interact in product markets, labor markets, and capital markets.

5. Economists use models to study how the economy works and to make predictions about what will happen if something is changed. A model can be expressed in words or equations, and is designed to mirror the essential characteristics of the particular phenomena under study.

6. A correlation exists when a change in one variable leads to a predictable change in another variable. However, the simple existence of a correlation does not prove that one factor causes the other to change. Additional outside factors may be influencing both.

7. Economists may disagree for three main reasons: they differ on the appropriate model of the economy or market; they differ about the value of some important empirical estimate, and thus about the quantitative magnitudes of the consequences of a change; and they differ in values, in how they weigh the various costs and benefits resulting from a change.

KEY TERMS

mixed economy
centrally planned
  economy
market economy
product market
labor market

capital market
capital goods
microeconomics
macroeconomics
theory

model
correlation
causation
positive economics
normative economics

REVIEW QUESTIONS

1. Why are choices unavoidable?

2. How are the four basic economic questions answered in the U.S. economy?

3. What is a mixed economy? Describe some of the roles government might play, or not play, in a mixed economy.

4. Name the three main economic markets, and describe how an individual might participate in each one as a buyer and seller.

5. Give two examples of economic issues that are primarily microeconomic, and two examples that are primarily macroeconomic. What is the general difference between microeconomics and macroeconomics?

6. What is a model? Why do economists use models?

7. When causation exists, would you also expect a correlation to exist? When a correlation exists, would you also expect causation to exist? Explain.

8. "All disagreements between economists are purely subjective." Comment.

PROBLEMS

1. Characterize the following events as microeconomic, macroeconomic, or both.
    (a) Unemployment increases this month.
    (b) A drug company invents and begins to market a new medicine.
    (c) A bank loans money to a large company but turns down a small business.
    (d) Interest rates decline for all borrowers.
    (e) A union negotiates for higher pay and better health insurance.
    (f) The price of oil increases.

2. Characterize the following events as part of the labor market, the capital market, or the product market.
    (a) An investor tries to decide which company to invest in.
    (b) With practice, the workers on an assembly line become more efficient.
    (c) The opening up of the economies in Eastern Europe offers new markets for American products.
    (d) A big company that is losing money decides to offer its workers a special set of incentives to retire early, hoping to reduce its costs.
    (e) A consumer roams around a shopping mall, looking for birthday gifts.
    (f) The federal government needs to borrow more money to finance its level of spending.

3. Discuss the incentive issues that might arise in each of the following situations. (Hint: Remember the history of the automobile industry at the start of this chapter.)
    (a) You have some money to invest, and your financial adviser introduces you to a couple of software executives who want to start their own company. What should you worry about as you decide whether to invest?
    (b) You are running a small company, and your workers promise that if you increase their pay, they will work harder.
    (c) A large industry is going bankrupt and appeals for government assistance.

4. Name ways in which government intervention has helped the automobile industry in the last two decades, and ways in which it has injured the industry.

5. The back of a bag of cat litter claims, "Cats that use cat litter live three years longer than cats that don't." Do you think that cat litter actually causes an increased life expectancy of cats, or can you think of some other factors to explain this correlation? What evidence might you try to collect to test your explanation?

6. Life expectancy in Sweden is 78 years; life expectancy in India is 57 years. Does this prove that if an Indian moved to Sweden he would live longer? That is, does this prove that living in Sweden causes an increase in life expectancy, or can you think of some other factors to explain these facts? What evidence might you try to collect to test your explanation?

THINKING LIKE AN ECONOMIST

I n Chapter 1, economics was defined as the science that studies how individuals, firms, governments, and other organizations make choices, and how those choices determine how the resources of society are used. We also learned how economists formulate models to study these questions. This chapter begins with a basic model of the economy. We follow this with a closer look at how the basic units that comprise the economy—individuals, firms, and governments—make choices in situations where they are faced with scarcity. In Chapters 3 through 5, we study ways in which these units interact with one another, and how those interactions "add up" to determine how society's resources are allocated.

"Mrs. Ritterhouse charges her violin students six dollars an hour. That's two bunches of asparagus and a black-and-white cookie."

KEY QUESTIONS

1. What is the basic competitive model of the economy?

2. What are incentives, property rights, prices, and the profit motive, and what roles do these essential ingredients of a market economy play?

3. What alternatives for allocating resources are there to the market system, and why do economists tend not to favor these alternatives?

4. What are some of the basic techniques economists use in their study of how people make choices? What are the various concepts of costs that economists use?

THE BASIC COMPETITIVE MODEL

Though different economists employ different models of the economy—and as a result sometimes reach markedly different conclusions—they all commonly use a basic set of assumptions as a point of departure. This is the economist's basic model, and it has three components: assumptions about how consumers behave, assumptions about how firms behave, and assumptions about the markets in which these consumers and firms interact. The model ignores government, not because government is not important, but because before we can understand the role of government we need to see how an economy without a government might function.

RATIONAL CONSUMERS AND PROFIT-MAXIMIZING FIRMS

The fact of scarcity, which we encountered in Chapter 1, implies that individuals and firms must make choices. Underlying much of economic analysis is the basic assumption of **rational choice,** that people weigh the costs and benefits of each possibility. This assumption is based on the expectation that individuals and firms will act in a consistent manner, with a reasonably well-defined notion of what they like and what their objectives are, and with a reasonable understanding of how to attain those objectives.

In the case of an individual, the rationality assumption is taken to mean that he makes choices and decisions in pursuit of his own self-interest. Different people will, of course, have different goals and desires. Sally may want to drive a Porsche, own a yacht, and have a large house; to attain those objectives, she knows she needs to work long hours and sacrifice time with her family. Andrew prefers a less harried life-style; he is willing to accept a lower income for longer vacations and more leisure throughout the year.

Economists make no judgments about whether Sally's preferences are "better" or "worse" in some sense than Andrew's. They do not even spend much time asking why it is that different individuals have different views on these matters, or why tastes change over time. These are important questions, but they are more the province of psychology, sociology, and other social sciences. What economists are concerned about are the consequences of these different preferences. What decisions can they expect Sally and Andrew, rationally pursuing their respective interests, to make?

In the case of firms, the rationality assumption is taken to mean that firms operate to maximize either their profits or stock market value. If a company pays adequate attention to profits in the long run as well as the short, it turns out that profit maximization and maximization of stock market value are essentially the same. We will therefore stick to profit maximization as the firm's goal.

Individuals and firms often have to make choices without being sure about the consequences. Fred has to decide on Monday whether to buy a ticket for Saturday's football game. He knows it may rain. He also knows that if he waits until Saturday to decide he wants to go to the game and it is a beautiful day, it will be too late to get a ticket. The assumption of rationality implies that individuals think through the consequences, forming judgments about the likelihood of various possibilities. Thus, Fred decides to buy the ticket on Monday. When it rains on Saturday, he has no regrets about his decision; he wishes it hadn't rained, but he knows his decision was made rationally. He felt it was fairly likely not going to rain, and he knew he would be much unhappier not being able to go to the game if the sun shone on Saturday than he would if he lost the $10 on an unused ticket. Given the information he had about the likelihood of rain, he made the best possible decision.

The principle of rationality applies to decisions about gathering information as well. Rational individuals and firms decide whether to spend money and time to become more informed—say, about whether it will rain on Saturday—by weighing the costs and benefits. Fred looked up the week's weather forecast in Monday's newspaper, but he did not bother to go to the library to look up the forecast in the *Farmers Almanac*. The *Almanac*'s track record in predicting weather accurately, he felt, was sufficiently weak that the cost, in terms of time, was not worth the possible benefit, in terms of improved accuracy of forecast.

While rational choices involve the careful balancing of costs and benefits, economists spend more time discussing costs than benefits. This is largely because individuals and firms often see clearly the benefits of each alternative; where they make mistakes is in evaluating the costs. In later sections of this chapter, we will see how economists think systematically about costs.

COMPETITIVE MARKETS

To complete the model, economists make some assumptions about the places where self-interested consumers and profit-maximizing firms meet: markets. Economists often begin by focusing on the case where there are many buyers and sellers, all buying and selling the same thing. You might picture a crowded farmers' market to get a sense of the number of buyers and sellers—except that you have to picture everyone buying and selling just one good. Let's say we are in Florida, and the booths are all full of oranges.

Each of the farmers—our profit-maximizing firm—would like to raise his prices. That way, if he can still sell his oranges, his profits go up. Yet with a large number of sellers, each is forced to charge close to the same price, since if any farmer charged much more, he would lose business to the farmer next door. Firms are in the same position. In an extreme case, it may even be expected that if a firm charged any more than the going price, it would lose *all* of its sales. Economists label this case **perfect competition.** In perfect competition, each firm is a **price taker,** which simply means that because it cannot influence the market price, it must accept that price. The firm takes the market price as given because it cannot raise its price without losing all sales, and at the market price it can sell as much as it wishes. Even if it multiplied sales by a factor of ten, this would have a negligible effect on the total quantity marketed. Perhaps the best example of real markets that, in the absence of government intervention, would probably be perfectly competitive is the various markets for agricultural goods. There are so many wheat farmers, for instance, that each farmer believes that he can grow and sell as much wheat as he wishes and have essentially no effect on the price of wheat. (Later in the book, we will encounter markets with limited or no competition, like monopolies, where firms can raise prices without losing all their sales. Firms with such market power are called **price makers.**)

On the other side of our farmers' market are rational individuals, each of whom would like to pay as little as possible for her oranges. Why can't she pay less than the going price? Because the seller sees another buyer in the crowd who will pay the going price. Thus, the consumers take the market price as given, and focus their attention on other factors—their taste for oranges, primarily—in deciding how many to buy.

This description of the farmers' market is an economic model. It pulls together the assumptions of self-interested consumers, profit-maximizing firms, and perfectly competitive markets in a combination that has predictive power. These predictions can be tested against empirical observation. As we just saw, for instance, the model predicts that when there are many firms, they will not be able to charge more than their competitors, and if we went to a farmers' market, we could check to see if this is true.

This model of consumers, firms, and markets is the **basic competitive model.** Economists generally believe that, to the extent that it can be duplicated by market systems in the real world, the competitive model will provide answers to the basic economic questions of what is produced and in what quantities, how it is produced, and for whom it is produced that result in the greatest economic efficiency. Resources are not wasted: it is not possible to produce more of one good without producing less of another, and indeed it is not even possible to make anyone better off without making someone else worse off. In the basic competitive model, these results are obtained without any help from the government. Unfortunately, the model is not duplicated in the real world, and governments frequently intervene. Nevertheless, it is a convenient benchmark. Some economists believe that the competitive model describes many markets well, even if it does not describe them exactly. Even those who do not think real markets can be described by the competitive model nonetheless often find that the model is a useful jumping-off point. By observing the difference between its predictions and the observed outcomes, they know what other models to employ.

INGREDIENTS IN THE BASIC COMPETITIVE MODEL

1. Rational, self-interested consumers
2. Rational, profit-maximizing firms
3. Competitive markets with price-taking behavior

PROPERTY RIGHTS AND INCENTIVES

A healthy economy depends on people who work and firms that are as efficient as possible. What, then, makes self-interested individuals get out of bed in the morning? How can we expect that profit-maximizing firms will invest their hard-earned profits trying to find more efficient ways to produce goods? The government could pass a law, perhaps, requiring that individuals and firms behave properly. However, market economies, like that of the United States, accomplish this with a carrot rather than a stick.

The carrot that provides incentives to firms in a market economy is profits. The carrot for households is income. Economists assume that individuals would prefer not to work hard, at least beyond a certain point. But they also assume that people would prefer more goods to fewer goods. If you want more goods, you have to work harder or longer. For business firms, the goal of more profits gives them an incentive to produce efficiently, develop new products, discover unmet needs, and find better production techniques.

For the profit motive to be effective, firms need to be able to keep at least some of their profits. Households, in turn, need to be able to keep at least some of what they earn or receive as a return on their investments. (The return on their investments is simply what they receive back in excess of what they invested. If they receive back less than they invested, the return is negative.) There must, in short, be **private property,** with its attendant **rights.** Property rights include both the right of the owner to use the property as she sees fit and the right to sell it.

These two attributes of property rights give individuals the incentive to use property that is under their control efficiently. The owner of a piece of land tries to figure out

CLOSE-UP: ECONOMISTS AGREE!

Try the following seven statements out on your classmates or your family to see whether they, like the economists surveyed, disagree, agree with provisos, or agree:

	Percentage of economists who		
	Disagree	Agree with provisos	Agree
1. Tariffs and import quotas usually reduce general economic welfare.	6.5%	21.3%	71.3%
2. A minimum wage increases unemployment among young and unskilled workers.	20.5%	22.4%	56.5%
3. A ceiling on rents reduces the quantity and quality of housing available.	6.5%	16.6%	76.3%
4. If the federal budget is to be balanced, it should be done over the business cycle rather than yearly.	13.4%	24.8%	60.1%
5. The cause of the rise in gasoline prices that occurred in the wake of the Iraqi invasion of Kuwait is the monopoly power of large oil companies.	67.5%	20.3%	11.4%
6. The trade deficit is primarily a consequence of the inability of U.S. firms to compete.	51.5%	29.7%	18.1%
7. Cash payments increase the welfare of recipients to a greater degree than do transfers-in-kind of equal cash value.	15.1%	25.9%	58.0%

Among the general population, these are controversial questions. You will find many people who believe that restricting foreign imports is a good thing; that government regulation of wages and rents has few ill effects; that the federal budget should be balanced every year; that the trade deficit is mainly caused by the inability of U.S. companies to compete; that government should avoid giving cash to poor people (because they are likely to waste it); and that oil companies are the cause of higher oil prices.

But when professional economists are surveyed, there is broad agreement that many of those popular answers are misguided. The percentages listed above are from a survey carried out by economists at Weber State University and Brigham Young University in 1990. Notice that healthy percentages of economists apparently believe that most import quotas are economically harmful; that government control of wages and rents does lead to adverse consequences; that thinking about an annually balanced budget is improper; that oil companies are not to blame for higher oil prices; that the trade deficit is not caused by the competitive problems of individual companies; that cash payments benefit the poor more than direct (in-kind) transfers of food, shelter, and medical care.

Sources: Richard M. Alston, J. R. Kearl, and Michael B. Vaughan, "Is There a Consensus Among Economists in the 1990s?" *American Economic Review* (May 1992); J. R. Kearl, Clayne L. Pope, Gordon C. Whiting, and Larry T. Wimmer, "A Confusion of Economists?" *American Economic Review* (May 1979), pp. 28–37.

the most profitable use of the land; for example, whether to build a store or a restaurant. If he makes a mistake and opens a restaurant when he should have opened a store, he bears the consequences: the loss in income. The profits he earns if he makes the right decisions—and the losses he bears if he makes the wrong ones—give him an incentive to think carefully about the decision and do the requisite research. The owner of a store tries to make sure that her customers get the kind of merchandise and the quality of service they want. She has an incentive to establish a good reputation, because if she does so, she will do more business and earn more profits.

The store owner will also want to maintain her property—which is not just the land anymore, but includes the store as well—because she will get more for it when the time comes to sell her business to someone else. Similarly, the owner of a house has an incentive to maintain *his* property, so that he can sell it for more when he wishes to move. Again, the profit motive combines with private property to provide incentives.

How the Profit Motive Drives the Market System

In market economies, incentives are supplied to individuals and firms by the chance to own property and to retain some of the profits of working and producing.

When Property Rights Fail

Property rights and the profit motive are so pervasive in our society that most of us take them for granted. To see why economists put such emphasis on property rights, it is worth examining a few cases where property rights are interfered with.

Ill-Defined Property Rights: The Grand Banks   Fish are a valuable resource. Not long ago, the area between Newfoundland and Maine, called the Grand Banks, was teeming with fish. Not surprisingly, it was also teeming with fishermen, who saw an easy livelihood scooping out the fish from the sea. Since there were no property rights, everyone tried to catch as many fish as he could. They failed not only to consider that as they fished more, others would find it harder to catch fish, but even to consider that if they caught too many fish, the number of fish in future years would decline. A self-interested fisherman would rationally reason that if he did not catch the fish, someone else would. The result was a tragedy: the Grand Banks was overfished, to the point where not only was it not teeming with fish, but commercial fishing became unprofitable. Today Canada and the United States have a treaty limiting the amount of fish that fishermen from each country can take from the Grand Banks, and gradually, over the years, the fish population has been restored.

Similar problems arise even today in the American West. The U.S. government owns enormous amounts of land, which it leases out for grazing. Since the leases are often short-term and there always seem to be other tracts of land available for lease, the ranchers who lease the land have no incentive to take care of the land and avoid overgrazing. (When land is overgrazed, the grasses are killed so the land can support fewer animals in future years.) It is easier to lease a new tract than to maintain the one they have.

The problem of ill-defined property rights is more general than the situation of fishermen and ranchers. *Any* time society fails to define the owners of its resources and does not allow the highest bidder to use them, we can expect inefficiencies to result. Resources will be wasted or will not be used in the most productive way.

Restricted Property Rights   In California, the government has given water rights to certain groups. Farmers, ranchers, city residents, are each entitled to a certain amount of water. Currently, for instance, cattle grazers have the right to about 10 percent of the state's water, just slightly less than the fraction that is consumed in residences. This property right comes with a restriction, however: it is not transferable; that is, the cattle grazers cannot sell the water to urban water users. Water is scarce, and hence these rights to water are extremely valuable.

The total value of the grass grown for the cattle to graze on is only about $100 million, a mere $\frac{1}{60}$ of 1 percent of California's $600 billion economy. Using water to irrigate land for grazing is not the most valuable use of water. Those in the cities would be willing to pay more for the water than it is worth to the ranchers. Today some cattle owners pay as little as $50 per acre-foot for water, while residents of San Francisco pay $256 per acre-foot, five times as much. In one California county, some city residents paid fifty times as much for a gallon of water as some farmers. If the water rights could be sold, those in the cattle industry would have a strong incentive to sell their rights to the towns. The value of water to thirsty urban consumers—what they would be willing to pay for the additional water—exceeds the profits from raising cattle. If cattle owners could get out of the cattle business and sell their water rights to urban residents instead, everyone would be better off.[1] In this case, restrictions on property rights have led to inefficiencies.

Entitlements as Property Rights   Property rights do not always mean that you have full ownership or control. A **legal entitlement,** such as the right to occupy an apartment for life at a rent that is controlled, common in some large cities, is viewed by economists as a property right. Individuals do not own the apartment and thus cannot sell it, but they cannot be thrown out, either.

A similar situation exists with gate slots at airports. These slots are allocated to different airlines. As a result, small airlines that were lucky enough to get the slots have property rights that, because the slots are not owned, cannot be sold. Yet the slots are far more valuable to major carriers, with their many passengers, than to the small airlines. For instance, Princeton Airways was a small commuter airline that had a gate slot at Washington National Airport, one of the nation's busiest airports. When, during a brief period, airlines were able to sell their slots, Princeton Airways sold its slot for a large amount of money to a major carrier.

Economists found legal entitlements even in countries like the former Soviet Union, which claimed to have abolished private property. Economists argue that such countries changed, but did not eliminate, property rights. The manager of a Soviet firm had

---

[1] The calculation of benefits and losses does not take into account the feelings of the cattle.

considerable discretion over who got his products, which were often in very short supply. This right was much like a property right. He exchanged "favors" with other managers who had the right to decide on who got their own products. Thus, a market emerged even in an economic system where free markets were outlawed.

In market economies, these partial and restricted property rights result in many inefficiencies. Because the individual in a rent-controlled apartment cannot (legally) sell the right to live in her apartment, as she gets older she may have limited incentives to maintain its condition, let alone improve it. (In the Soviet example, the effects of these restricted property rights may have had the opposite effect, improving the economy's efficiency from what it would have been in the absence of *any* market.)

INCENTIVES VERSUS EQUALITY

One way to provide incentives, whether for an individual or a company, is to relate compensation to performance. There are some problems, however, with tying compensation closely to performance. Commission plans for sales representatives, for instance, link compensation to sales. However, a salesperson's sales may be up not because he did a better job of selling, but because more customers wanted to buy the product. The salesperson will claim it was superior skill and effort, while his colleague may argue that it was dumb luck.

Providing incentives by tying compensation to performance also means that those who are successful will earn a higher income. Thus, if there are incentives, there must be some inequality. This is called the **incentive-equality trade-off.** The inequality may arise not just because one individual has worked harder than another, but also because she has been luckier than another, as the sales commission story makes clear.

If society provides greater incentives, total output is likely to be higher, but there will also probably be greater inequality. The relationship is depicted in Figure 2.1, whose vertical axis shows a measure of equality and whose horizontal axis shows some measure of output. At a point such as A, incentives are strong because taxes are low and government welfare programs are limited, so how hard a person works determines how well off he is. Thus, output is high, but equality is low (inequality is high). At point B, by contrast, there are weak incentives; taxes are high and government welfare programs are generous, so that the differences in the levels of consumption someone can enjoy,

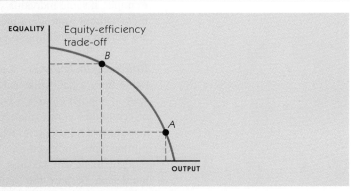

Figure 2.1 THE EQUITY AND EFFICIENCY TRADE-OFF

Point A shows a situation where incentives, and thus efficiency and output, are high, but equality is low; point B shows the reverse.

whether he works hard or not, are small. So there is not much incentive to work hard. Output is low, but equality is high.

One of the basic questions facing members of society in their choice of tax rates and welfare systems is, how much would incentives be diminished by an increase in tax rates to finance a better welfare system and thus reduce inequality? What would be the results of those reduced incentives?

RATIONING

In a market economy, goods go to those individuals who are most willing and able to pay for them. Thus, the market economy is called a **price system.** But the price system is only one of several ways of allocating resources, and a comparison with other systems will help to clarify the advantages of markets. When individuals get less of a good than they would like at the terms being offered, the good is said to be **rationed.** Different rationing schemes are different ways of deciding who gets society's scarce resources.

Rationing by Queues   Rather than supplying goods to those most willing and able to pay the most for them, a society could give them instead to those most willing to wait in line. This system is called **rationing by queues,** after the British term for lines. Tickets are often allocated by queues, whether they are for movies, sporting events, or rock concerts. A price is set, and it will not change no matter how many people line up to buy at that price. (The high price that scalpers can get for "hot" tickets is a good indication of how much more than the ticket price people would have been willing to pay.)

Rationing by queues is thought by many to be a more desirable way of supplying medical services than the price system. Why, it is argued, should the rich—who are most able to pay for medical services—be the ones to get better or more medical care? Using this reasoning, Britain, in the 1940s, decided to provide free medical care to everyone on its soil. To see a doctor there, all you have to do is wait in line. Rationing medicine by queues turns the allocation problem around: since the value of time for low-wage workers is lower, they are more willing to wait, and therefore they get a disproportionate share of (government-supplied) medical services.

In general, rationing by queues is an inefficient way of distributing resources. The time spent in line is a wasted resource. There are usually ways of achieving the same goal within a price system that can make everyone better off. Again using the medical example, if some individuals were allowed to pay for doctors' services and could obtain them without waiting in line, more doctors could be hired, and the lines for those who are unable or unwilling to pay could actually be reduced.

Rationing by Lotteries   **Lotteries** allocate goods by a random process, like picking a name from a hat. University dormitory rooms are usually assigned by lottery. So are seats in popular courses; when more students want to enroll in a section of a principles of economics course than the size of the section allows, there may be a lottery to determine the lucky ones who get to enroll. The United States used to allocate certain mining rights and licenses to radio airwaves by lottery. Like queue systems, lotteries are thought to be fair because everyone has an equal chance. However, they are also inefficient, because the scarce resources do not go to the individual or firm who is willing and able to pay the most.

Rationing by Coupons   Most governments in wartime use systems of **coupon rationing.** People are allowed so many gallons of gasoline, so many pounds of sugar, so much meat, and so much flour each month. To get the good, you have to pay the market price *and* produce a coupon. The reason this system of rationing is used is that it is thought that without coupons prices would soar, and these extremely high prices would inflict a hardship on poorer individuals.

Coupon systems take two forms depending on whether coupons are tradable or not. Systems in which coupons are not tradable give rise to the same inefficiency that occurs with most of the other nonprice systems—goods do not in general go to the individuals who are willing and able to pay the most. There is generally room for a deal, a trade that will make all parties better off. For instance, I might be willing to trade some of my flour ration for some of your sugar ration. But in a nontradable coupon system, the law prohibits such transactions. Usually when coupons cannot be legally traded, there are strong incentives for the establishment of a **black market,** an illegal market in which the goods or the coupons for goods are traded.

OPPORTUNITY SETS

We have covered a lot of ground so far in this chapter. We have seen the economist's basic model, which relies on competitive markets. We have seen how the profit motive and private property supply the incentives that drive a market economy. And we have gotten our first glimpse at why economists believe that market systems, which supply goods to those who are willing and able to pay the most, provide the most efficient means of allocating what the economy produces. They are far better than the variety of nonprice rationing schemes that have been employed. It is time now to return to the question of choice. Market systems leave to individuals and firms the question of what to consume. How are these decisions made?

For a rational individual or firm, the first step in the economic analysis of any choice is to identify what is possible, what economists call the **opportunity set,** which is simply the group of available options. If you want a sandwich and you have only roast beef and tuna fish in the refrigerator, then your opportunity set consists of a roast beef sandwich, a tuna fish sandwich, a strange sandwich combining roast beef and tuna fish, or no sandwich. A ham sandwich is out of the question. Defining the limitations facing an individual or firm is a critical step in economic analysis. One can spend time yearning after the ham sandwich, or anything else outside the opportunity set, but when it comes to making choices and facing decisions, only what is within the opportunity set is relevant.

BUDGET AND TIME CONSTRAINTS

What limits choices are **constraints.** Constraints define the opportunity set. In most economic situations, the constraints that limit a person's choices—that is, those constraints that actually are relevant—are not sandwich fixings, but time and money. Opportunity sets whose constraints are imposed by money are referred to as **budget constraints;** opportunity sets whose constraints are prescribed by time are called **time constraints.** A billionaire may feel that his choices are limited not by money but by time; while for an unemployed worker, time hangs heavy—it is the lack of money rather than time that limits his choices.

The budget constraint defines a typical opportunity set. Consider the budget constraint of Alfred, who has decided to spend $100 on either cassette recordings or compact discs. A CD costs $10, a cassette $5. So Alfred can buy either 10 CDs or 20 cassettes. Or he can buy 9 CDs and 2 cassettes; or 8 CDs and 4 cassettes. The various possibilities are set forth in Table 2.1. And they are depicted graphically in Figure 2.2:[2] along the vertical axis, we measure the number of cassettes purchased, and along the horizontal axis, we measure the number of CDs. The line marked $B_1 B_2$ is Alfred's budget constraint. The extreme cases, where Alfred buys only CDs or cassettes, are represented by the points B_1 and B_2 in the figure. The dots between these two points, along the budget constraint, represent the other possible combinations. The cost of each combination of CDs and cassettes must add up to $100. The point actually chosen by Alfred is labeled E, where he purchases 4 CDs (for $40) and 12 cassettes (for $60).

While Alfred's budget constraint is the line that defines the outer limits of his opportunity set, the whole opportunity set is larger. It also includes all points below the budget constraint. This is the shaded area in the figure. The budget constraint shows the maximum number of cassettes Alfred can buy for each number of CDs purchased, and vice versa. Alfred is always happiest when he is on (chooses a point on) his budget constraint. To see why, compare the points E and D. At point E, he has more of both goods than at point D. He would be even happier at point F, where he has still more cassettes and CDs, but that point, by definition, is unattainable.

Figure 2.3 depicts a time constraint. The most common time constraint simply says that the sum of what an individual spends her time on each day—including sleeping—must add up to 24 hours. The figure plots the hours spent watching television on the horizontal axis and the hours spent on all other activities on the vertical axis. People—no matter how rich or how poor—have only 24 hours a day to spend on different

---

[2] See the Chapter Appendix for help in reading graphs.

Table 2.1 ALFRED'S OPPORTUNITY SET

Cassettes	CDs
0	10
2	9
4	8
6	7
8	6
10	5
12	4
14	3
16	2
18	1
20	0

Figure 2.2 ALFRED'S BUDGET CONSTRAINT

The budget constraint identifies the limits of an individual's opportunity set between CDs and cassettes. Points B_1 and B_2 are the extreme options, where he chooses all of one and none of the other. His actual choice is point E. Choices from the shaded area are possible, but less attractive than choices actually on the budget constraint.

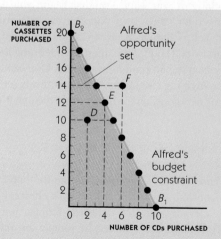

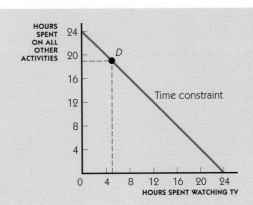

Figure 2.3 AN OPPORTUNITY SET FOR WATCHING TV AND OTHER ACTIVITIES

This opportunity set is limited by a time constraint, which shows the trade-off a person faces between spending time watching television and spending it on other activities. At 5 hours of TV time per day, point D represents a typical choice for an American.

activities. The time constraint is quite like the budget constraint. A person cannot spend more than 24 hours or fewer than zero hours a day watching TV. The more time she spends watching television the less time she has available for all other activities. Point D (for dazed) has been added to the diagram at 5 hours a day—this is the amount of time the typical American chooses to spend watching TV.

THE PRODUCTION POSSIBILITIES CURVE

Business firms and whole societies face constraints. They too must make choices limited to opportunity sets. The amounts of goods a firm or society could produce, given a fixed amount of land, labor, and other inputs, are referred to as its **production possibilities.**

As one commonly discussed example, consider a simple description of a society in which all economic production is divided into two categories, military spending and civilian spending. Of course, each of these two kinds of spending has many different elements, but for the moment, let's discuss the choice between the two broad categories. For simplicity, Figure 2.4 refers to military spending as "guns" and civilian spending as "butter." The production of guns is given along the vertical axis, the production of butter along the horizontal. The possible combinations of military and civilian spending—of guns and butter—is the opportunity set. Table 2.2 sets out some of the possible combinations: 90 million guns and 40 million tons of butter, or 40 million guns and 90 million tons of butter. These various possibilities are depicted in the figure. In the case of a choice involving production decisions, the boundary of the opportunity set—giving the maximum amount of guns that can be produced for each amount of butter and vice versa—is called the **production possibilities curve.**

When we compare the individual's opportunity set and that of society, reflected in its production possibilities curve, we notice one major difference. The individual's budget constraint is a straight line, while the production possibilities curve bows outward. There is a good reason for this. An individual typically faces fixed **trade-offs:** if Alfred spends $10 more on CDs (that is, he buys one more CD), he has $10 less to spend on cassettes (he can buy two fewer cassettes).

Table 2.2 PRODUCTION POSSIBILITIES FOR THE ECONOMY

Guns (millions)	Butter (millions of tons)
100	0
90	40
70	70
40	90
0	100

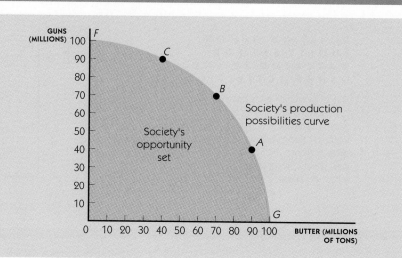

Figure 2.4 THE GUNS AND BUTTER TRADE-OFF

A production possibilities curve can show society's opportunity set. This one describes the trade-off between military spending ("guns") and civilian spending ("butter"). Points *F* and *G* show the extreme choices, where the economy produces all guns or all butter. Notice that unlike the budget and time constraint, the production possibilities line curves, reflecting diminishing returns.

On the other hand, the trade-offs faced by society are not fixed. If a society produces only a few guns, it will use those resources—the men and machines—that are best equipped for gun making. But as society tries to produce more and more guns, it finds that doing so becomes more difficult; it will increasingly have to rely on those who are less and less good at producing guns. It will be drawing these resources out of the production of other goods, in this case, butter. This means that for each successive increment in gun production, society will have to reduce the production of butter more. Thus, when the economy increases its production of guns from 40 million a year (point *A*) to 70 million (*B*), butter production falls by 20 million tons, from 90 million tons to 70 million tons. But if production of guns is increased further, to 90 million (*C*), an increase of 20 million, butter production has to decrease by 30 million tons, to only 40 million tons. The change in the number of tons of butter produced, for each increase in the number of guns, does not stay constant. That is why the production possibilities curve is curved.

The importance of the guns-butter trade-off can be seen dramatically by looking back at Figure 1.3, which shows that during World War II, car production plummeted almost to zero as the automobile factories were diverted to the production of tanks and other military vehicles.

In another example, assume that a firm owns land that can be used for growing wheat but not corn, and land that can grow corn but not wheat. In this case, the only way to increase wheat production is to move workers from the cornfields to the wheat fields. As more and more workers are put into the wheat fields, production of wheat goes up, but each successive worker increases production less. The first workers might pick the largest and most destructive weeds. Additional workers lead to better weeding, and better weeding leads to higher output. But the additional weeds rooted up are smaller and less destructive, so output is increased by a correspondingly smaller amount. This is an example of the general principle of **diminishing returns.** Adding successive units of any input such as fertilizer, labor, or machines to a fixed amount of other inputs— seeds or land—increases the output, or amount produced, but by less and less.

Table 2.3 DIMINISHING RETURNS

Labor in cornfield (no. of workers)	Corn output (bushels)	Labor in wheat field (no. of workers)	Wheat output (bushels)
1,000	60,000	5,000	200,000
2,000	110,000	4,000	180,000
3,000	150,000	3,000	150,000
4,000	180,000	2,000	110,000
5,000	200,000	1,000	60,000

Table 2.3 shows the output of the corn and wheat fields as labor is increased in each field. Assume the firm has 6,000 workers to divide between wheat production and corn production. Thus, the second and fourth columns together give the firm's production possibilities, which are depicted in Figure 2.5.

INEFFICIENCIES: BEING OFF THE PRODUCTION POSSIBILITIES CURVE

There is no reason to assume that a firm or an economy will always be on its production possibilities curve. Any inefficiency in the economy will result in a point such as A in Figure 2.5, below the production possibilities curve, where society could obtain more of everything, both more wheat and corn. One of the major quests of economists is to look for instances in which the economy is inefficient in this way.

Whenever the economy is operating below the production possibilities curve, it is

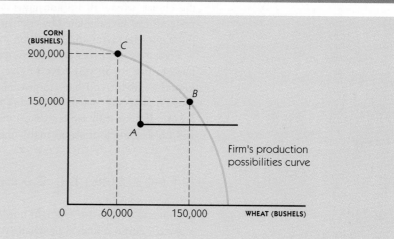

Figure 2.5 THE WHEAT AND CORN TRADE-OFF

This production possibilities curve shows that as wheat production increases, it becomes necessary to give up larger and larger amounts of corn. Or to put the same point a different way, as corn production falls, the resulting increase in wheat production gets smaller and smaller. Point A illustrates an inefficient outcome in this opportunity set.

possible for us to have more of every good—more wheat and more corn, more guns and more butter. No matter what goods we like, we can have more of them. That is why we can unambiguously say that points below the production possibilities curve are undesirable. But this does not mean that every point on the production possibilities curve is better than any point below it. Compare points A and C in Figure 2.5. Corn production is higher at C, but wheat production is lower. If people do not like corn very much, the increased corn production may not adequately compensate them for the decreased wheat production.

There are many reasons why the economy may be below the production possibilities curve. If land that is better suited for the production of corn is mistakenly devoted to the production of wheat, the economy will operate below its production possibilities curve. If some of society's resources—its land, labor, and capital goods—are simply left idle, as happens when there is a depression, the economy operates below the production possibilities curve. The kinds of problems discussed earlier in the chapter with inadequately or improperly defined property rights also give rise to inefficiencies.

COST

The beauty of a well-defined opportunity set like the budget constraint, the time constraint, or the production possibilities curve is that it specifies the cost of one option in terms of another. If the individual, the firm, or the society is operating on the constraint or curve, then it is possible to get more of one thing only by sacrificing some of another. The "cost" of one more unit of one good is how much you have to give up of the other.

Economists thus think about cost in terms of trade-offs within opportunity sets. Let's go back to Alfred choosing between CDs and cassettes in Figure 2.2. The trade-off is given by the **relative price,** the ratio of the prices of CDs and cassettes. In our example, a CD cost $10, a cassette $5. The relative price is $10 ÷ $5 = 2; for every CD Alfred gives up, he can get two cassettes. Likewise, societies and firms face trade-offs along the production possibilities curve, like the one shown in Figure 2.4. There, point A is the choice where 40 million guns and 90 million tons of butter are produced. The trade-off can be calculated by comparing points A and B. Society can have 30 million more guns by giving up 20 million tons of butter.

Trade-offs are necessary because resources are scarce. If you want something, you have to pay for it; you have to give up something. If you want to go to the library tomorrow night, you have to give up going to the movies. If you want to have more income to spend, you have to work more; that is, you have to give up some of your leisure. If a sawmill wants to make more two-by-four beams from its stock of wood, it will not be able to make as many one-by-four boards.

OPPORTUNITY COSTS

If someone were to ask you right now what it costs to go to a movie, you would probably answer, "Seven dollars," or whatever you paid the last time you went to the movies. But with the concept of trade-offs, you can see that a *full* answer is not that simple. To begin with, the cost is not so much the $7 as it is what that $7 could otherwise buy.

CLOSE-UP: OPPORTUNITY COSTS OF MEETINGS

Businesses often neglect one of the most important opportunity costs of all: the time of their top employees. The personnel agency Accountemps tried to measure some of that wasted time by surveying 200 executives from the 1,000 largest U.S. companies. The executives estimated that they spent an average of 15 minutes a day on hold on the telephone; an average of 32 minutes a day reading or writing unnecessary memos; and an average of 72 minutes a day at unnecessary meetings. Now multiply those numbers by 48 weeks (assuming that the executives take four weeks of vacation each year). The average executive would be spending 60 hours per year on telephone hold; 128 hours per year on unnecessary memos; and 288 hours a year in unnecessary meetings!

Of course, estimates like these are more for illustration than precision. Moreover, it may be impossible to tell in advance whether a meeting will be useful; the only way to have a productive meeting, after all, may be to risk having an unproductive one. But even taking the particular numbers with a grain of salt, it seems likely that many businesses schedule meetings believing that since they do not have to pay extra for people to attend, the cost of the meetings is zero. They ignore the opportunity cost, the fact that their highly paid managers could be doing something else with their time.

One semi-serious proposal is that businesses should measure and display the opportunity cost of their meetings with a scoreboard placed discreetly in the corner of their meeting rooms. As everyone entered the meeting room, she would enter her hourly salary, and the scoreboard would then start adding up the cost of everyone's time. For example, if there were twenty executives in a meeting who earned an average of $45 per hour, then the scoreboard would ring up $900 for every hour of meeting time. We could also include an opportunity cost of using the meeting room, of needing to call back people from other companies who called during the meeting, and so on. Surely, as the scoreboard showed the opportunity cost of the regular afternoon meeting climbing into four figures, there would be powerful incentive to finish quickly and let everyone return to her other tasks.

Source: "Executives on Hold 60 Hours a Year," *San Jose Mercury News,* July 10, 1990, p. 7A.

Furthermore, your time is a scarce resource that must be figured into the calculation. Both the money and the time represent opportunities forgone in favor of going to the movie, or what economists refer to as the **opportunity cost** of the movie. To apply a resource to one use means that it cannot be put to any other use. Thus, we should consider the next-best, alternative use of any resource when we think about putting it to use. This next-best use is the formal measurement of opportunity cost.

Some examples will help to clarify the idea of opportunity cost. Consider a student, Sarah, who enrolls in college. She thinks that the check for tuition and room and board represents the costs of her education. But the economist's mind immediately turns to the job she might have had if she had not enrolled in college. If Sarah could have earned $15,000 from September to June, her next-best choice of what to do this year, then this is the opportunity cost of her time, and this forgone income must be added to the college bills in calculating the total economic cost of the school year.

Now consider a business firm that has bought a building for its headquarters that is bigger than necessary. If the firm, by renting out the space that is not needed, could receive $3 per month for each square foot, then this is the opportunity cost of leaving the space idle. The firm would be wise to pretend it has to pay itself rent for all the space it owns, and to balance the benefits of using space against this cost.

The analysis can be applied to the government level as well. The federal government owns a vast amount of wilderness. In deciding whether it is worthwhile to convert some of that land into a national park, the government needs to take into account the opportunity cost of the land. The land might be used for growing timber or for grazing sheep. Whatever the value of the land in its next-best use, this is the economic cost of the national park. The fact that the government does not have to buy the land does not mean that the land should be treated as a free good.

Thus, in the economist's view, when rational firms and individuals make decisions—whether to undertake one investment project rather than another, whether to buy one product rather than another—they take into account *all* of the costs, the full opportunity costs, not just the direct expenditures.

SUNK COSTS

Economic cost includes costs, as we have just seen, that noneconomists often exclude, but it also ignores costs that noneconomists tend to include. If an expenditure has already been made and cannot be recovered no matter what choice is made, a rational person would ignore it. Such expenditures are called **sunk costs.**

To understand sunk costs, let's go back to the movies, assuming now that you have spent $7 to buy a movie ticket. You were skeptical about whether the movie was worth $7. Half an hour into the movie, your worst suspicions are realized: the movie is a disaster. Should you leave the movie theater? In making that decision, the $7 should be ignored. It is a sunk cost; your money is gone whether you stay or leave. The only relevant choice now is how to spend the next 90 minutes of your time: watch a terrible movie or go do something else.

We can also return to Fred, who at the beginning of the chapter was deciding whether to buy a nonrefundable ticket to a football game for Saturday. He decides to buy it, knowing that if he waits until Saturday, there is a good chance that all the tickets will be sold. When Saturday arrives, it is raining. Fred hates sitting out in the rainy weather. But he feels that since he has already spent the money on the ticket, it would be a waste not to go to the game. Is this rational?

An economist would ask Fred, "What if someone had offered you a free ticket to the game on Saturday?" Fred hates sitting in the rain so much that he would have said, "Thanks, but no thanks." The economist would then say that if he feels this way, it would be irrational for him to go to the game even if he had already paid for the ticket. The money he paid for it is gone, and the decision to buy it is a bygone; Monday's expenditures on the ticket are sunk costs, and should be ignored in Saturday's decision about whether to go to the game.

Or assume you have just purchased a fancy laptop computer for $2,000. You are feeling very pleased with your purchase. But then the next week, the manufacturer announces a new computer with twice the power for $1,000; you can trade in your old computer for the new one by paying an additional $400. You are angry. You feel you have just paid $2,000 for a computer that is now almost worthless, and you have gotten hardly any use out of it. You decide not to buy the new computer for another year, until you have gotten at least some return for your investment. Again, an economist would say that you are not approaching the question rationally. The past decision is a sunk cost. The only question you should ask yourself is whether the extra power of the fancier computer is worth the additional $400. If it is, buy it. If not, do not.

MARGINAL COSTS

The third aspect of cost that economists emphasize is the extra costs and extra benefits, or what economists call the **marginal costs** and **marginal benefits.** The most difficult decisions we make are not whether to do something or not. They are whether to do a little more or a little less of something. Few of us waste much time deciding whether or not to work. We have to work; the decision is whether to work a few more or a few less hours. When we need an apartment or a house, the tough question is whether to buy (or rent) a bigger or a smaller place. A country does not consider whether or not to have an army; it decides whether to have a larger or smaller army.

Jim has just obtained a job for which he needs a car. He must decide how much to spend on the car. By spending more, he can get a newer, bigger, and more luxurious car. But he has to decide whether it is worth a few hundred (or thousand) marginal dollars for extra items like cute hubcaps, power windows, a stereo system, a model that is a year newer, and so on.

Similarly, Polly is thinking about flying to Colorado for a ski weekend. She has three days off from work. The air fare is $200, the hotel room costs $100 a night, and the ski ticket costs $35 a day. Food costs the same as at home. She is trying to decide whether to go for two or three days. The *marginal* cost of the third day is $135, the hotel cost plus the cost of the ski ticket. There are no additional transportation costs involved in staying the third day. She needs to compare the marginal cost with the additional enjoyment she will have from the third day.

Marginal analysis can be addictive. You are at a refreshment stand, trying to decide what size drink to order. A small 6-ounce cup costs $.75, a 12-ounce cup costs $1.00, and a big 20-ounce cup costs $1.25. In going from the small to the medium size, the marginal cost for the extra 6 ounces is $.25. In deciding whether to buy a small or medium Coke, you have to decide whether the benefit of an additional (marginal) 6 ounces is worth the $.25 cost. In deciding whether to buy a medium or large Coke, you have to decide whether the benefit of an additional (marginal) 8 ounces is worth an extra quarter.

People, consciously or not, think about the trade-offs at the margin in most of their

CLOSE-UP: OREGON MAKES TOUGH CHOICES ABOUT HEALTH CARE

The miracles of modern medicine do not come cheaply. While consumer prices rose by about 50 percent during the 1980s, prices for medical care doubled. By the start of the 1990s, American spending on medical care was exceeding $700 billion per year. At the same time, an estimated 30 million or more Americans had no health insurance at all.

In 1990, the state of Oregon decided to tackle head-on the problem of expensive care for many and little health care for others. The state decided to try to rank 1,600 medical procedures with a computer program that would balance the costs and benefits of the procedures. The idea was that by eliminating coverage for those medical problems that were disproportionately expensive, the state could double the number of poor people who were eligible for Medicaid, the government program of basic health insurance for the poor.

Of course, the list is controversial. For example, detection of the AIDS (H.I.V.) virus and protection against it ranks high on the list of procedures to provide for everyone, but treatment for AIDS when a patient is already near death might be greatly reduced under the plan. Other procedures that

might be dropped include organ transplants and treatments for chronic ulcers, sleep disorders, and varicose veins. Implementing such a list inevitably means that the state will have to refuse to help some people who would benefit from certain medical procedures, and that some of those people will die sooner than they otherwise would.

But having Oregon tax its citizens to provide everyone with all the medical care they could ever want is not a realistic choice, either. Scarcity cannot be avoided. The issue is how to make the hard decisions.

Today those with private health insurance or the support of a program like Medicaid can receive a great deal of expensive medical care, while those without private health insurance but not poor enough to qualify for Medicaid fall through the cracks. The Oregon plan proposes to shift extra spending on medical care toward procedures that will provide greater public health benefits. This is marginal analysis in a truly life-or-death situation.

Source: Timothy Egan, "Oregon Lists Illnesses by Priority to See Who Gets Medicaid Care," *New York Times,* May 3, 1990.

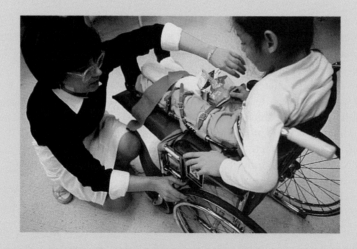

decisions. Economists, however, bring them into the foreground. Like opportunity costs and sunk costs, marginal analysis is one of the critical concepts that enable economists to think systematically about the costs of alternative choices.

BASIC STEPS OF RATIONAL CHOICE

Identify the opportunity sets.

Define the trade-offs.

Calculate the costs correctly, taking into account opportunity costs, sunk costs, and
marginal costs.

REVIEW AND PRACTICE

SUMMARY

1. The economists' basic model consists of rational, self-interested individuals and profit-maximizing firms, interacting in competitive markets.

2. The profit motive and private property provide incentives for rational individuals and firms to work hard and efficiently. Ill-defined or restricted property rights can lead to inefficient or counterproductive behavior.

3. Society often faces choices between equality, which means allowing people more or less equal amounts of consumption, and efficiency, which requires incentives that enable people or firms to receive different benefits depending on their behavior.

4. The price system in a market economy is one way of allocating goods and services. Other methods include rationing by queue, by lottery, and by coupon.

5. An opportunity set illustrates what choices are possible. Budget constraints and time constraints define individuals' opportunity sets. Both show the trade-offs of how much of one thing a person must give up to get more of another.

6. A production possibilities curve defines a firm or society's opportunity set, representing the possible combinations of goods that the firm or society can produce. If a firm or society is producing below its production possibilities curve, it is said to be inefficient, since it could produce more of either good (or both goods) without producing less of the other.

7. The opportunity cost is the cost of using any resource. It is measured by looking at the next-best, alternative use to which that resource could be put.

8. A sunk cost is a past expenditure that cannot be recovered, no matter what choice is made in the present. Thus, rational decision makers ignore them.

9. Most economic decisions concentrate on choices at the margin, where the marginal (or extra) cost of a course of action is compared with its extra benefits.

KEY TERMS

perfect competition	opportunity sets	sunk cost
basic competitive model	diminishing returns	marginal costs and benefits
rationing systems	opportunity cost	

REVIEW QUESTIONS

1. What are the goals of individuals and of firms in economists' basic competitive model?

2. Consider a lake in a state park where everyone is allowed to fish as much as he wants. What outcome do you predict? Might this problem be averted if the lake were privately owned and fishing licenses were sold?

3. Why might government policy to make the distribution of income more equitable lead to less efficiency?

4. List advantages and disadvantages of rationing by queue, by lottery, and by coupon. If the government permitted a black market to develop, might some of the disadvantages of these systems be reduced?

5. What are some of the opportunity costs of going to college? What are some of the opportunity costs a state should consider when deciding whether to widen a highway?

6. Give two examples of a sunk cost, and explain why they should be irrelevant to current decisions.

7. How is the decision to purchase a good such as a car or a house different from the marginal decisions involved in that purchase?

PROBLEMS

1. Imagine that many businesses are located beside a river, into which they discharge industrial waste. There is a city downstream, which uses the river as a water supply and for recreation. If property rights to the river are ill-defined, what problems may occur?

2. Suppose an underground reservoir of oil may reside under properties owned by several different individuals. As each well is drilled, it reduces the amount of oil that others can take out. Compare how quickly the oil is likely to be extracted in this situation with how quickly it would be extracted if one person owned the property rights to drill for the entire pool of oil.

3. In some states, hunting licenses are allocated by lottery; if you want a license, you send in your name to enter the lottery. If the purpose of the system is to ensure that those who want to hunt the most get a chance to do so, what are the flaws of this system? How would the situation improve if people who won licenses were allowed to sell them to others?

4. Imagine that during time of war, the government imposes coupon rationing. What are the advantages of allowing people to buy and sell their coupons? What are the disadvantages?

5. Kathy, a college student, has $20 a week to spend; she spends it either on junk food at $2.50 a snack, or on gasoline at $1 per gallon. Draw Kathy's opportunity set. What is the trade-off between junk food and gasoline? Now draw each new budget constraint she would face if
   (a) a kind relative started sending her an additional $10 per week;
   (b) the price of a junk food snack fell to $2;
   (c) the price of gasoline rose to $1.20 per gallon.
In each case, how does the trade-off between junk food and gasoline change?

6. Why is the opportunity cost of going to medical school likely to be greater than the opportunity cost of going to college? Why is the opportunity cost of a woman with a college education having a child greater than the opportunity cost of a woman with just a high school education having a child?

APPENDIX: READING GRAPHS

Whether the old saying that a picture is worth a thousand words under- or overestimates the value of a picture, economists find graphs extremely useful.

For instance, look at Figure 2.6; it is a redrawn version of Figure 2.2, showing the budget constraint—the various combinations of CDs and cassettes he can purchase—of an individual, Alfred. More generally, a graph shows the relationship between two variables, here, the number of CDs and the number of cassettes that can be purchased. The budget constraint gives the maximum number of cassettes that can be purchased, given the number of CDs that have been bought.

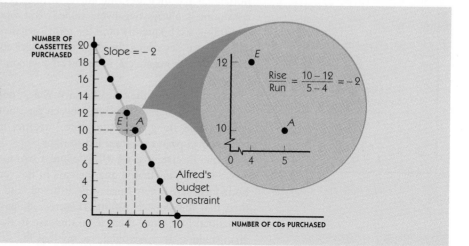

Figure 2.6 READING A GRAPH: THE BUDGET CONSTRAINT

Graphs can be used to show the relationship between two variables. This one shows the relationship between the variable on the vertical axis (the number of cassettes Alfred can buy) and the variable on the horizontal axis (the number of CDs).

The slope of a curve like the budget constraint gives the change in the number of cassettes that can be purchased as Alfred buys one more CD. The slope of the budget constraint is negative.

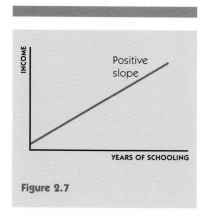

Figure 2.7

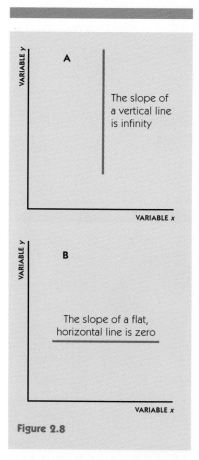

Figure 2.8

In a graph, one variable (here, CDs) is put on the horizontal axis and the other variable on the vertical axis. We read a point such as E by looking down to the horizontal axis and seeing that it corresponds to 4 CDs, and by looking across to the vertical axis and seeing that it corresponds to 12 cassettes. Similarly, we read point A by looking down to the horizontal axis and seeing that it corresponds to 5 CDs, and by looking across to the vertical axis and seeing that it corresponds to 10 cassettes.

In the figure, each of the points from the table has been plotted, and then a curve has been drawn through those points. The "curve" turns out to be a straight line in this case, but we still use the more general term. The advantage of the curve over the individual points is that with it, we can read off from the graph points on the budget constraint that are not in the table.

Sometimes, of course, not every point on the graph is economically meaningful. You cannot buy half a cassette or half a CD. For the most part, we ignore these considerations when drawing our graphs; we simply pretend that any point on the budget constraint is actually possible.

SLOPE

In any diagram, the amount by which the value along the vertical axis increases from a change in a unit along the horizontal axis is called the **slope,** just like the slope of a mountain. Slope is sometimes described as "rise over run," meaning that the slope of a line can be calculated by dividing the change on the vertical axis (the "rise") by the change on the horizontal axis (the "run").

Look at Figure 2.6. As we move from E to A, increasing the number of CDs by 1, the number of cassettes purchased falls from 12 to 10. For each additional CD bought, the feasible number of cassettes that can be purchased falls by 2. So the slope of the line is

$$\frac{\text{rise}}{\text{run}} = \frac{10 - 12}{5 - 4} = \frac{-2}{1} = -2.$$

When, as in Figure 2.6, the variable on the vertical axis falls when the variable on the horizontal axis increases, the curve, or line, is said to be **negatively sloped.** A budget constraint is always negatively sloped. But when we describe the slope of a budget constraint, we frequently omit the term "negative." We say the slope is 2, knowing that since we are describing the slope of a budget constraint, we should more formally say that the slope is negative 2. Alternatively, we sometimes say that the slope has an absolute value of 2.

Figure 2.7 shows the case of a curve that is **positively sloped.** (Figure 1.6 in Chapter 1 suggested such a relationship between the number of years of schooling and income.) The variable along the vertical axis, income, increases as schooling increases, giving the line its upward tilt from left to right.

In later discussions, we will encounter two special cases. A line that is very steep has a very large slope; that is, the increase in the vertical axis for every unit increase in the horizontal axis is very large. The extreme case is a perfectly vertical line, and we say then that the slope is infinite (Figure 2.8, panel A). At the other extreme is a flat, horizontal line; since there is no increase in the vertical axis no matter how large the change along the horizontal, we say that the slope of such a curve is zero (panel B).

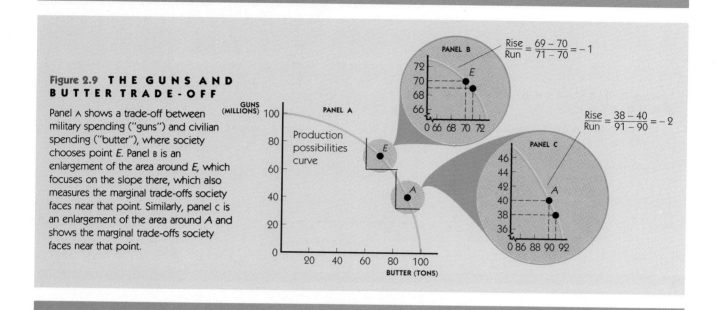

Figure 2.9 THE GUNS AND BUTTER TRADE-OFF

Panel A shows a trade-off between military spending ("guns") and civilian spending ("butter"), where society chooses point E. Panel B is an enlargement of the area around E, which focuses on the slope there, which also measures the marginal trade-offs society faces near that point. Similarly, panel C is an enlargement of the area around A and shows the marginal trade-offs society faces near that point.

Figures 2.6 and 2.7 both show straight lines. Everywhere along the straight line, the slope is the same. This is not true in Figure 2.9, which repeats the production possibilities curve shown originally in Figure 2.4. Look first at point E. Panel B of the figure blows up the area around E, so that we can see what happens to the output of guns when we increase the output of butter by 1. From the figure, you can see that the output of guns decreases by 1. Thus, the slope is

$$\frac{\text{rise}}{\text{run}} = \frac{69 - 70}{71 - 70} = -1.$$

Now look at point A, where the economy is producing more butter. The area around A has been blown up in panel C. Here, we see that when we increase butter by 1 more unit, the reduction in guns is greater than before. The slope at A is

$$\frac{\text{rise}}{\text{run}} = \frac{38 - 40}{91 - 90} = -2.$$

With curves such as the production possibilities curve, the slope differs as we move along the curve.

INTERPRETING CURVES

Look at Figure 2.10. Which of the two curves has a larger slope? The one on the left appears to have a slope that has a larger absolute value. But look carefully at the axes. Notice that in panel A, the vertical axis is stretched relative to panel B. The same distance that represents 20 cassettes in panel B represents only 10 cassettes in panel A. In fact,

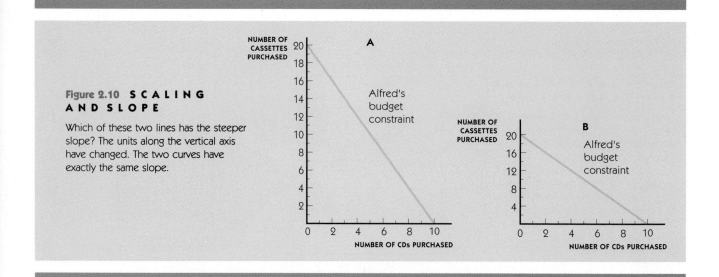

Figure 2.10 SCALING AND SLOPE

Which of these two lines has the steeper slope? The units along the vertical axis have changed. The two curves have exactly the same slope.

both panels represent the same budget constraint. They have exactly the same slope.

This kind of cautionary tale is as important in looking at the graphs of data that were common in Chapter 1 as it is in looking at the relationships presented in this chapter that produce smooth curves. Compare, for instance, panels A and B of Figure 2.11. Which of the two curves exhibits more variability? Which looks more stable? Panel B appears to show that car production does not change much over time. But again, a closer look reveals that the axes have been stretched in panel A. The two curves are based on exactly the same data, and there is really no difference between them.

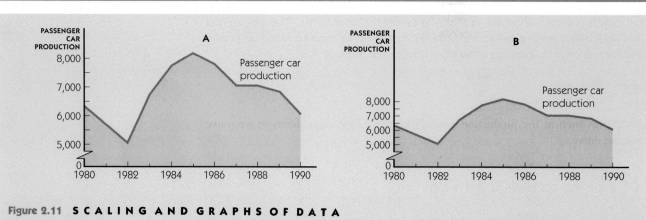

Figure 2.11 SCALING AND GRAPHS OF DATA

Which of these two curves shows greater variability in the output of cars over time? The two curves plot the same data. The vertical scale has again been changed. *Source: Ward's Automotive Reports* (1991).

CHAPTER 3

EXCHANGE AND PRODUCTION

A creature on another planet looking down at a developed modern economy on earth might compare human activity to an enormous ant colony. Each ant seemingly has an assigned task. Some stand guard. Some feed the young. Some harvest food and others distribute it. Some of these peculiar human ants also spend a lot of time shuffling paper, scribbling notes in books, and keyboarding at computer consoles. Others work in factories, tightening screws, running machines, and so on. Still others move goods from one place to another. How is all of this activity coordinated? Who decides who does what? No dictator or superintelligent computer is giving instructions. Yet somehow an immense amount is accomplished in a reasonably coordinated way. Understanding how a complex economy operates—how it is that certain individuals do one task, others do another, how information is communicated and decisions are made—is a central objective of economics.

This chapter discusses the problem of economic interdependence at two levels: of individuals and firms within a country, and of countries within the world economic community. Many of the same principles apply at both levels. Economic interdependence has its benefits—and its costs.

"You got into the college of my choice, and I got into the college of your choice. Now, if we could just work something out . . ."

KEY QUESTIONS

1. Why is trade (exchange) mutually beneficial?

2. What are the similarities and differences between trade (exchange) between individuals within a country and trade between countries?

3. What determines what any particular country produces and sells on the international market? What is meant by comparative advantage, and why does it play such an important role?

4. What are the gains from specialization?

5. How valid is the argument, so often heard in political circles, that trade should be restricted?

THE BENEFITS OF ECONOMIC INTERDEPENDENCE

We begin by considering the benefits of trade, specifically the exchange of those goods that are already available in the economy.

THE GAINS FROM TRADE

When individuals own different goods, have different desires, or both, there is an opportunity for mutually beneficial trades: trades that benefit all parties to the trade. Kids trading baseball cards learn the basic principles of exchange. One has two Kirby Puckett cards, the other has two Jose Canseco cards. A trade will probably benefit both of them. The same lesson applies to countries. Nigeria has more oil than it can possibly use, but it does not produce enough food to feed its populace. The United States has more wheat than Americans can possibly consume, but needs oil. Trade can benefit both countries.

Voluntary trade between two individuals involves not a winner and loser, but only two winners. After all, if the trade would make a loser of either party, that party would choose not to trade. Thus, a fundamental consequence of voluntary exchange is that it benefits everyone involved.

"FEELING JILTED" IN TRADE

In spite of the seemingly persuasive argument that individuals only voluntarily engage in a trade if they think they will be better off as a result, people often walk away from a deal believing they have been hurt. It is important to understand that when economists say that a voluntary trade makes the two traders better off, they do not mean that it makes them both happy.

Imagine, for example, that Frank brings an antique rocking chair to a flea market to sell. He is willing to sell it for $100—at any lower price, he would rather keep it himself—but he hopes to sell it for $200. Helen comes to the flea market planning to buy such a chair, hoping to spend only $100, but willing to pay as much as $200. They argue and negotiate, eventually settle on a price of $150, and make the deal. But when they go home, they both complain. Frank complains the price was too low, and Helen that it was too high. It is common to hear people complain that a product cost "too much," but that they went ahead and bought it anyway.

From an economist's point of view, such complaints are self-contradictory. If Frank *really* thought $150 was too low, he should not have sold at that price. If Helen *really* thought $150 was too high, she should not have paid the price. Of course, sellers always wish they could have received more money, and buyers always wish they could have paid less. But economists argue that people reveal their preferences not by what they say, but by what they do. If one voluntarily agrees to make a deal, one also agrees that the deal is, if not perfect, at least better than the alternative of not making the deal.

There are two common objections to this line of reasoning. Both of them involve the idea of Frank or Helen "taking advantage" of the other. The implication, of course, is that if a buyer or a seller can take advantage, then the other party may be a loser rather than a winner.

The first objection is that either Frank or Helen may not really know what is being agreed to. Perhaps Helen recognizes that the chair is actually a rare antique, worth $5,000, but by neglecting to tell Frank this fact, manages to buy it for only $150. Perhaps Frank knows that the rockers fall off the chair if one rocks in it for ten minutes, but sells the chair anyway without telling Helen, thus keeping the price high. In either case, by keeping hidden information a secret, the party without this information becomes a loser after the trade, rather than a winner.

The second objection concerns the division of the **gains from trade.** Since Helen would have been willing to pay as much as $200, anything she pays less than that is **surplus,** the term economists use for a gain from trade. Similarly, since Frank would have been willing to sell the chair for as little as $100, anything he receives more than that is also surplus. The total dollar value of the gain from trade is $100—the difference between the maximum price Helen would have been willing to pay and the minimum price at which Frank would have been willing to sell. At a price of $150, they split the gain in half; each gets a surplus of $50. But if the price had been $125, $25 of the gain would have gone to Frank, $75 to Helen. The split would thus not have been an equitable one.

Economists do not have much patience with these objections. Like most people, they favor making as much information public as possible, and they think vendors and customers should be made to stand behind their promises. Thus, many economists support laws against selling defective products or misrepresenting products. But economists also point out that second thoughts and the "If only I had known" argument are just not relevant. If Frank sells his antique at a flea market instead of taking it around to several different reputable antique dealers and asking them what it might be worth, he has made a voluntary decision to save his time and energy. If Helen buys an antique at a flea market instead of going to a reputable dealer who will guarantee that the product is in good condition, she knows she is taking a risk. Maybe both Frank and Helen would like to go back and do things differently. Maybe they acted prematurely or foolishly. As for the negotiations, it is only natural that both would like to get more of the gains from trade.

The logic of free exchange, however, does not say that everyone must express great happiness with the result either at the time of the sale or forever after. It simply says that when people choose to make a deal, they prefer making the deal to not making the deal. And if they prefer making the deal, they are by definition better off *in their own minds* making the deal, at the time the transaction takes place.

The objections to trade nonetheless carry an important message: exchanges that happen in the real world tend to be considerably more complicated than swapping baseball cards. They involve problems of information, problems of estimating risks, and problems of forming expectations about what will happen in the future. These complications will be discussed throughout the book. So without going into too much detail at the moment, let's just say that if you are worried that you do not have the proper information to make a trade, then shop around, or get a guarantee or an expert opinion, or buy insurance; such precautions are a legitimate part of voluntary exchange. If you feel there is too much risk even taking these steps, don't go through with the trade. But if you choose to plunge ahead without any of these precautions, you can't pretend you didn't have other choices. Like those who buy a ticket in a lottery, you know you are taking chances.

ECONOMIC RELATIONS AS EXCHANGES

Individuals in our economy can be thought of as involved in a multiplicity of voluntary trades. They "trade" their labor services (their time and skills) to their employer in exchange for dollars. They then trade some of those dollars with a multitude of merchants for goods, like gasoline and groceries; other dollars they trade for services, like those of plumbers and hair stylists. The firm for which an individual works trades the goods it produces for dollars, and then it turns around and trades dollars for labor services. Even your savings account at a bank can be viewed as a trade: you give the bank $100 today, and in exchange, the bank promises to give you $105, for example, at the end of the year (your original deposit plus 5 percent interest).

TRADE BETWEEN COUNTRIES

Why is it that people engage in this complex set of economic relations with others? Wouldn't life be easier and simpler if all people were self-sufficient and relied on their own resources? The answer is that people are better off as a result of trading. And this applies not just to trade and economic relations between individuals but to trade and economic relations between countries as well. Just as individuals *within* a country find it advantageous to trade with one another, so too do countries find trade advantageous. Just as it is virtually impossible for any individual to be self-sufficient, it is almost impossible for any country to be completely self-reliant without sacrificing a great deal of its standard of living. The United States has long been part of an international economic community, and this participation has grown in recent decades. Let's look at how interdependence has affected the three main markets in the U.S. economy.

Interdependence in the Product Market Foreign-produced goods are commonplace in U.S. markets. In the late 1980s, for instance, more than a quarter of the cars sold in the United States were **imported** (imports are goods produced abroad but bought domestically), along with a third of apparel items, a third of the oil, and virtually all of the diamonds. Many of the minerals essential for the U.S. economy must also be imported from abroad. At the same time, U.S. farmers **export** almost two-fifths of the agricultural goods they produce (exports are goods produced domestically but sold abroad), including almost three-fourths of the wheat and one-third of the cotton.

Imports have grown in recent decades, not only when measured in dollars, but also as a percentage of overall production. Exports, while they have not quite kept pace, have grown almost commensurately. Figure 3.1 shows how exports and imports have grown relative to the nation's total output: as a percentage of national output, both have more than doubled. Smaller countries are typically even more dependent on international trade than the United States. Britain and Canada import a quarter of their goods, France 20 percent.

Earnings from abroad constitute a major source of income for some of our largest corporations; exports account for 45 percent of sales for Boeing, 20 percent for Hewlett-Packard, and 12 percent for Ford. Table 3.1 gives some other examples of large companies that rely heavily on exports.

Interdependence in the Labor Market International interdependence extends beyond simply the shipping of goods between countries. More than 99 percent of U.S. citizens either immigrated here from abroad or are descended from people who did so. Though the flow of immigrants, relative to the size of the population, has slowed since its peak at the turn of the century, it is still substantial. Today many rural American areas are

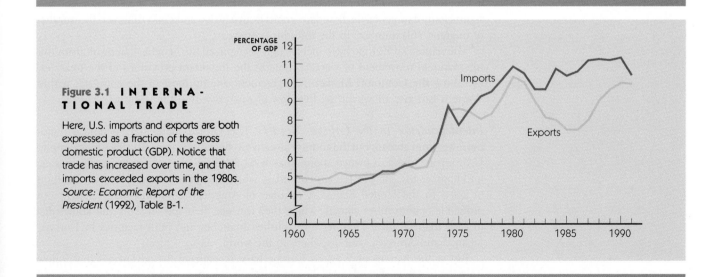

Figure 3.1 INTERNA-TIONAL TRADE

Here, U.S. imports and exports are both expressed as a fraction of the gross domestic product (GDP). Notice that trade has increased over time, and that imports exceeded exports in the 1980s. *Source: Economic Report of the President* (1992), Table B-1.

Table 3.1 **E X P O R T - D E P E N D E N T   B I G   C O M P A N I E S**

Company and product	Rank in the Fortune 500	Exports as share of sales
Prime Computer (computers)	338	47%
Boeing (aircraft)	16	45%
Intel (semiconductors)	256	29%
Caterpillar (heavy machinery)	47	28%
McDonnell Douglas (aerospace)	23	22%
FMC (defense equipment)	131	20%
Hewlett-Packard (computers)	51	20%
Archer Daniels Midland (food products)	67	19%
Celanese (chemicals)	134	19%
Motorola (radio equipment)	60	18%
Digital Equipment (computers)	44	18%
Dresser Industries (pumps)	105	18%
Eastman Kodak (photographic equipment)	26	18%
Weyerhauser (wood products)	62	16%
Textron (aerospace)	69	15%
Ford (automobiles)	3	12%

Source: Fortune, July 20, 1987, p. 73.

dependent upon foreign-born doctors and nurses. Half of the engineers currently receiving doctorates at American universities are foreign-born. The harvests of many crops are highly dependent on migrant laborers from Mexico. Though recent legislation has significantly dampened the flow of migrants from Mexico and Latin America, the number of migrants still numbers in the millions every year.

The nations of Europe have increasingly recognized the benefits that result from this international movement of workers. One of the important provisions of the treaty establishing the Common Market, an agreement among most of the countries within Western Europe, allows for the free flow of workers within the Common Market.

Interdependence in the Capital Market   The United States has become a major borrower from abroad, but the country also invests heavily overseas. In 1990, for example, U.S. private investors owned approximately $1.9 trillion of assets (factories, businesses, buildings, loans, etc.) in foreign countries, while foreign investors owned $2.2 trillion of assets in the United States. A number of American companies have sought out profitable opportunities abroad, where they can use their special skills and knowledge to earn high returns. They have established branches and built factories in Europe, Japan, Latin America, and elsewhere in the world.

Just as the nations of Western Europe have recognized the advantages that follow from the free flow of goods and labor among their countries, so too they have recognized the gains from the free flow of capital. Funds can be invested where they yield the highest returns. Knowledge and skills from one country can be combined with capital from another to produce goods that will be enjoyed by citizens of all countries. Though the process of liberalizing the flow of goods, labor, and capital among the countries of the European Common Market has been going on for more than twenty years, 1992 marks the crucial date at which all remaining barriers are supposed to be removed.

MULTILATERAL TRADE

Many of the examples to this point have emphasized two-way trade between individuals or nations. Trade between two individuals or countries is called **bilateral trade.** But in most cases, exchanges between two parties may be less advantageous than **multilateral trade,** which is trade between several parties. Sometimes such trades are observed between sports teams. The New York Mets send a catcher to the St. Louis Cardinals, the Cardinals send a pitcher to the Los Angeles Dodgers, and the Dodgers send an outfielder to the Mets (see Figure 3.2A). No two of the teams might have been willing to make a two-way trade, but all can benefit from the three-way swap.

Countries may function in a similar way. Japan has no domestic sources of oil; it imports oil from Arabian countries. The Arabian countries want to sell their oil, but they want wheat and food, not the cars and television sets that Japan can provide. The United States can provide the missing link by buying cars and televisions from Japan and selling food to the Arab nations. Again, this three-way trade, shown in Figure 3.2B, offers gains that two-way trade cannot. The scores of nations active in the world economy create patterns far more complex than these simplified examples.

Figure 3.3 illustrates the construction of a Ford Escort in Europe, and dramatizes the importance of multilateral and interconnected trade relations. The parts that go into an Escort come from all over the world. Similar diagrams could be constructed for many of the components in the diagram; the aluminum alloys may contain bauxite

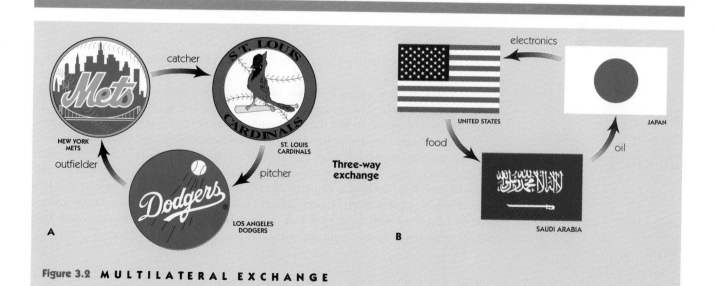

Figure 3.2 MULTILATERAL EXCHANGE

Panel A shows a multilateral, three-way trade between baseball teams. Notice that no two of the teams have the ingredients for a mutually beneficial exchange. Panel B illustrates a multilateral exchange in international trade.

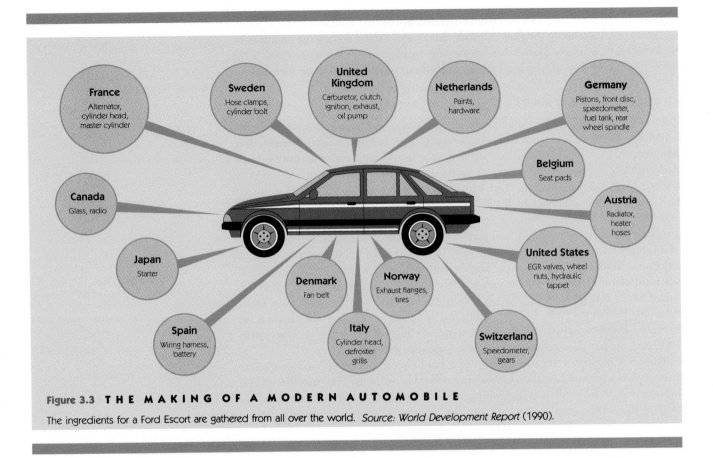

Figure 3.3 THE MAKING OF A MODERN AUTOMOBILE

The ingredients for a Ford Escort are gathered from all over the world. *Source: World Development Report* (1990).

from Jamaica, the chrome plate may use chromium from Africa, the copper for wiring may come from Chile.

Multilateral trade means that trade between any two participants may not balance. In Figure 3.2B, the Arab countries send oil to Japan but get no goods (only yen) in return. No one would say that the Arab countries have an unfair trade policy with Japan. Yet some congressional representatives, newspaper columnists, and business executives complain that since the United States imports more from a particular country (often Japan) than it exports to that country, the trade balance is "unfair." A misguided popular cliché says that "trade is a two-way street." But trade in the world market involves hundreds of possible streets between different nations. While there are legitimate reasons to be concerned with the overall U.S. trade deficit, there is no particular reason that U.S. exports and imports with any particular country should be balanced.

COMPARATIVE ADVANTAGE

Up to this point, it has been assumed that exchange occurs with existing goods, and no new goods are produced. But clearly, most of what is exchanged must first be produced. Another advantage of trade is that it allows individuals and countries to concentrate on what they produce best. As a result, the gains from trade are even larger when production is allowed for.

Some countries are more efficient at producing almost all goods than are other countries. The possession of superior production skills is called having an **absolute advantage,** and these advanced countries are said to have an absolute advantage over the others. How can the countries with disadvantages successfully engage in trade? The answer lies in the principle of **comparative advantage,** which states that individuals and countries specialize in producing those goods in which they are *relatively*, not absolutely, more efficient.

To see what comparative advantage means, let's say that both the United States and Japan produce two goods, computers and wheat. The amount of labor needed to produce these goods is shown in Table 3.2. In the United States, say that it takes 100 worker hours to make a computer (that is, if we add up all the time spent by all the people working to make a computer, the sum is 100 hours); in Japan, it takes 120 worker hours. In the United States, it takes 5 man hours to make a ton of wheat; in Japan, it takes 8 man hours. The United States is more efficient at making both products. America can rightfully claim to have the most efficient computer industry in the world, and yet it imports computers from Japan. Why? The answer is comparative advantage. The *relative* cost of making a computer (in terms of labor used) in Japan, relative to the cost of producing a ton of wheat, is low, compared with the United States. That is, in Japan, it takes 15 times as many hours (120/8) to produce a computer as it does to produce a ton of wheat; in the United States, it takes 20 times as many hours (100/5) to produce a computer as it does to produce a ton of wheat. While Japan has an absolute *dis*advantage in producing computers, it has a *comparative* advantage.

The principle of comparative advantage applies to individuals as well as countries. The president of a company might type faster than her secretary, but it still pays to have the secretary type her letters, because the president may have a comparative advantage at bringing in new clients, while the secretary has a comparative (but not absolute) advantage at typing.

A CLOSER LOOK AT THE GAINS FROM COMPARATIVE ADVANTAGE

When two countries exploit their comparative advantage, the gains from trade that result can benefit both countries. Assume that in both the United States and Japan, 120,000 worker hours are spent altogether making computers, and 120,000 worker hours are spent growing wheat. So, according to the information given in Table 3.2, Japan produces

Table 3.2 LABOR COST OF PRODUCING COMPUTERS AND WHEAT (worker hours)

	United States	Japan
Labor required to make a computer	100	120
Labor required to make a ton of wheat	5	8

CLOSE-UP: EUROPE IN 1992

The nations of Western Europe have long been one another's most frequent trading partners, but the trade was not without its obstacles. Each nation had its own currency, its own health and safety rules, its own economic interest groups to protect from foreign competition with import quotas and other restrictions. Starting in the late 1980s, however, the twelve nations that make up the European Community (EC) decided to aim at becoming a single economic market at the end of 1992. As the diagram here shows, the nations of the EC collectively outstrip the United States in both population and output.

The process of creating free trade has been time-consuming, and it is not over yet. New disputes and issues continually arise and require resolution. But although the eventual impact is difficult to predict, economists have formed some rough estimates of what it would be. One report commissioned by the EC forecast that economic unification would lead to additional growth of 4.3 to 6.4 percent in the medium term. In other words, the combined EC economy could be more than $300 billion better off in a decade because of the single-market initiative. A more specific report estimated that if the EC nations were willing to purchase their weapons from one another instead of each country making its own, the EC nations as a group could save one-fifth of their total weapons budget.

Europe's trading partners are concerned that European companies, many of which are already large and tough, will become even stronger international competitors in the future. They also worry that the single European market may become a mechanism for promoting trade within Europe while at the same time reducing international trade between Europe and the rest of the world. These trading ties will be especially important for the

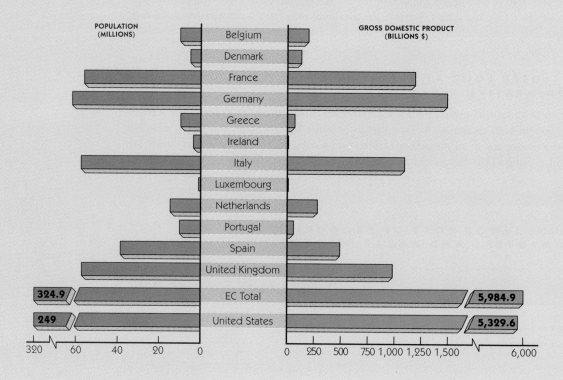

1,000 computers and 15,000 tons of wheat; the United States produces (with the same amount of labor) 1,200 computers and 24,000 tons of wheat. There is no reason that all 240,000 worker hours have to be divided equally between the two products, however. Table 3.3 shows what happens when each country changes its level of production to benefit from its comparative advantage.

Suppose the United States devotes 200,000 worker hours to producing wheat, and the remaining 40,000 worker hours to producing computers. Japan concentrates on producing computers and shifts 100,000 worker hours from producing wheat to producing computers. Japan then produces 1,833 (220,000 ÷ 120) computers, and output of computers goes up by 833; but wheat production has fallen, to 2,500 tons. Meanwhile, the shift of 80,000 man hours from computers to wheat in the United States has reduced computer output by 800 and increased wheat output by 16,000 tons; the United States now produces 400 computers and 40,000 tons of wheat. The total combined production of the two countries of both wheat and computers has gone up: computers from 2,200 to 2,233, and wheat from 39,000 tons to 42,500 tons. There are clearly gains from trade and specialization—an extra 33 computers and an extra 3,500 tons of wheat. By focusing on their comparative advantages and then trading, Japan and the United States can both be better off.

Table 3.3 HOW TRADE INCREASES OUTPUT FROM THE SAME LABOR FORCE

United States		Japan		Combined output	
Labor devoted to wheat (worker hours)	Labor devoted to computers (worker hours)	Labor devoted to wheat (worker hours)	Labor devoted to computers (worker hours)	Wheat (tons)	Computers
120,000	120,000	120,000	120,000	39,000	2,200
200,000	40,000	20,000	220,000	42,500	2,233

HOW COMPARATIVE ADVANTAGE IMPROVES PRODUCTION POSSIBILITIES

The wheat-computer example can also be illustrated with production possibility curves, developed in Chapter 2. Consider Figure 3.4, which shows the trade-off between computers and wheat for the United States and Japan. The trade-offs are pictured as straight lines in this case because we are assuming that the two goods are produced by labor alone, and in each country a given amount of labor is required to produce each unit of each good. Thus, every time 100 worker hours in the United States are switched from producing computers to producing wheat, 1 less computer and 20 more tons of wheat are produced. The trade-off between computers and wheat is determined by their *relative* costs—in terms of the labor required. In the figure, both countries start at A and then move to B.

Notice that the production possibilities curve for the United States is sloped less sharply downward than the line for Japan. If Japan wants to produce 1 more computer, it must reduce its wheat production by 15 tons. If the United States wants to produce 1 less computer, it can produce 20 tons more of wheat.

The differences in trade-offs facing the two countries reflect their differences in comparative advantage. Because the United States has a comparative advantage in wheat, the increase in the wheat it produces (20 tons) when it reduces its computer production by 1 is much greater than the increase in wheat Japan produces (15 tons) when it reduces its computer production by 1. When both countries focus on their comparative advantage, with U.S. computer production decreasing by 1 and Japan's increasing by 1, net world production of wheat is increased by 5 tons.

The figure also shows what happens when production moves all the way from A to B: the output of both products goes up. Both countries—including the United States, with its absolute advantage in both products—gain from the increased production.

The principle of comparative advantage implies that trade can always provide mutual benefits to both countries, even trade between countries where one is more efficient in

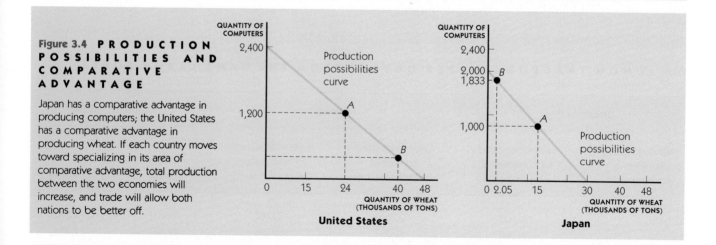

Figure 3.4 PRODUCTION POSSIBILITIES AND COMPARATIVE ADVANTAGE

Japan has a comparative advantage in producing computers; the United States has a comparative advantage in producing wheat. If each country moves toward specializing in its area of comparative advantage, total production between the two economies will increase, and trade will allow both nations to be better off.

producing every single individual product than its trading partner. While smaller countries will often specialize, larger countries, like the United States, continue to produce a larger variety of products. Still, there are some products that, because of comparative advantage, it simply does not pay for the United States to produce: TVs, VCRs, and a host of other electronic gadgets, for example. The United States is still, however, a major producer of textiles, in spite of heavy imports from the Far East.

The same general principles of comparative advantage that apply to countries apply as well to individuals: from an economic standpoint, individuals as well as nations should play to their comparative strengths.

COMPARATIVE ADVANTAGE AND SPECIALIZATION

Both nations and individuals frequently wind up specializing in the goods in which they have a comparative advantage, producing little or none of the goods in which they have a comparative disadvantage. Comparative advantage thus leads to specialization, and specialization leads to increased competence in those specialized activities, reinforcing the original comparative advantage.

To see the benefits of specialization, consider the lowly pencil. It is a simple tool, but there may be no single person in the world who knows how to make all that goes into a pencil. Some tree, containing the right kind of wood, must be felled somewhere; it must be transported somehow to a sawmill, and there cut into pieces that can be further processed in the shape of the casings. The graphite that runs through the pencil's center, the eraser at its tip, the metal that holds the two together, are all relatively simple materials, yet it takes specially trained people to produce each one of them.

Why Specialization Increases Productivity   Specialization increases productivity, thus enhancing the benefits of trade, for three reasons. First, specializing avoids the time it takes a worker to switch from one production task to another. Second, by repeating the same task, the worker becomes more skilled at it. And third, specialization creates a fertile environment for invention.

Workers may possess roughly equal skills before they begin specializing in their jobs. The choice of who specializes in what particular job could be made at random. But after workers have begun specializing, switching them back and forth between jobs will tend to make production less efficient.

Note the immense productive power that can result from the division of labor. Dividing jobs so that each worker can practice a particular skill may increase productivity hundreds or thousands of times. Almost anyone who practices simple activities like sewing on a button, shooting a basketball, or adding a column of numbers for a week or two will be quite a lot better than someone who has not practiced. Similarly, a country that specializes in producing sports cars may develop a comparative advantage, because with its relatively large scale of production, it can divide tasks into separate assignments for different people; as each becomes better at his own tasks, productivity is increased.

At the same time, the division of labor often leads to invention. As someone learns a particular job extremely well, she might figure out ways of doing the job better. Also, a simple job may be a job that a machine can be invented to do. One can argue over whether necessity or laziness is the mother of this sort of invention, but whatever its cause, such an invention is more likely to occur with specialization. Specialization and invention reinforce each other. A slight initial advantage in some good leads to greater production of that good, thence to more invention, and thence to even greater production and further specialization.

Limits of Specialization The extent of division of labor, or specialization, that is possible is limited by the size of the market. There is greater scope for specialization in mass-produced manufactured goods like picture frames than in custom-made items like the artwork that goes into picture frames. That is one of the reasons why the costs of production of mass-produced goods have declined so much. Similarly, there is greater scope for specialization in a big city than a small town. That is why in any big city, one will find small stores that specialize in a particular food or sport or type of clothing. The size of a market in a city provides an opportunity for dividing the labor of retail sales, and owners of specialty shops take advantage of that opportunity.

The gains from specialization also may be limited. The repetition of specialized jobs sometimes leads to bored, sloppy, and unproductive workers. Also, new insights and ideas can often arise from the cross-fertilization of disciplines, rather than from single-tracked specialization. Still, even in these cases, a certain degree of specialization adds greatly to productivity.

WHAT DETERMINES COMPARATIVE ADVANTAGE?

A close look at what each country in the world exports and imports presents a complex picture of trade. For example, the United States imports bananas from Central America, cars, TVs, and personal computers from Japan, cloth from Taiwan and Hong Kong; it exports jet airplanes, wheat, and large computers. Earlier we learned that comparative advantage determines the pattern of trade. But what determines comparative advantage? In the modern world, this turns out to be a fairly complex matter.

Natural Endowments In first laying down the principle of comparative advantage in the early 1800s, the great British economist David Ricardo used the example of Portugal's trade with Britain. In Ricardo's example, Portugal had an absolute advantage in producing both wool and wine. But it had a comparative advantage in producing wine, because it could produce wine better than it could produce wool, compared with Britain. Thus, Britain had a comparative advantage in producing wool.

In this and other early examples, economists tended to assume that a nation's comparative advantage was determined largely by its **natural endowments.** Countries with soil and climate that are *relatively* better for grapes than for pasture will produce wine; countries with soil and climate that are relatively better for pasture than for grapes will produce sheep (and hence wool). In the modern economy, America's abundance of arable farmland gives the country a comparative advantage in agriculture. Countries that have an abundance of low-skilled labor relative to other resources, such as South Korea and Hong Kong, have a comparative advantage in producing goods like textiles, which require a lot of handwork.

While this theory, called **geographical determinism,** can still be applied in some places, it has clearly been outdated by developments in the modern world economy. Rather than searching for whatever comparative advantage nature has bestowed, nations in today's technological age can act to acquire a comparative advantage.

Acquired Endowments A nation's endowments need not be limited by accidents of geography. The Japanese have little in the way of natural resources, yet they are a major player in international trade, in part because they have **acquired endowments.** Their case underscores the principle that by saving and accumulating capital and building large factories, a nation can acquire a comparative advantage in goods, like steel, that require large amounts of capital in their production. And by devoting resources to education, a nation can develop a comparative advantage in those goods that require a skilled labor force. Thus, the resources—human and physical—that a country has managed to acquire for itself can also give rise to comparative advantage.

Superior Knowledge   In the modern economy, what is important is not only possessing resources, but having the knowledge to use those resources productively. Switzerland's comparative advantage in watches is not based on a larger store of capital goods or better-educated laborers, nor does it have a better natural endowment of the materials that go into making watches. It is simply that over the years, the country has accumulated superior knowledge and expertise in watch making. In some cases, such as with Swiss watches, the knowledge that one country accumulates is largely a matter of historical accident. Belgium has a comparative advantage in fine lace; its workers have developed the requisite skills. A quirk of fate might have led Belgium to acquire a comparative advantage in watches and Switzerland in lace.

While sometimes patterns of specialization occur almost as an accident of history, in modern economies they are more likely to be a consequence of deliberate decisions. One of the principal ways that countries acquire a comparative advantage is by establishing or increasing their technological knowledge in a particular area. The United States' semiconductor industry is a case in point. This industry manufactures the tiny silicon brains that control computers. Semiconductors were invented by an American, Robert Noyce, and in the 1970s, the United States had a powerful comparative advantage in manufacturing semiconductors; but Japan managed to become a close competitor (some would say the dominant producer) in the 1980s. The rise of the U.S. semiconductor industry was built in part on decisions by the federal government to fund the necessary research (usually so the semiconductors could be used in guided missiles and other weapons), and the rise of the Japanese industry was similarly based on decisions by that government to subsidize and support its semiconductor industry.

Thus, the semiconductor industry provides an example where a comparative advantage was first gained, then equaled by another competitor, and now may be lost, through the cumulative effect of many business and government decisions taken in Japan and the United States. If U.S. producers today concede the comparative advantage of Japanese producers and leave the market, the United States will be in an even worse position for competing in the future, as still more sophisticated computer chips are developed.

Stories like that of the semiconductor industry have led some economists to argue that government should encourage certain industries, in order for them to gain a technological advantage. This would happen either through trade protection or through the support of research. A school of economists led by Paul Krugman of MIT has argued for a **strategic trade policy**; just as dynamic companies have a strategy for growth, these economists maintain, so too should nations.

Specialization   Earlier we saw how comparative advantage leads to specialization. At the same time, specialization may lead to comparative advantage. The Swiss make fine watches, and have a comparative advantage in that market based on years of unique experience. Such superior knowledge, however, does not explain why Britain, Germany, and the United States, which are at roughly the same level of technological expertise in building cars, all trade cars with one another. How can each country have a comparative advantage in making cars? The answer lies in specialization.

Both Britain and Germany may be better off if Britain specializes in producing sports cars and Germany in producing luxury cars, or conversely, because specialization increases productivity. Countries enhance, or simply develop, a comparative advantage by specializing just as individuals do. As a result, similar countries enjoy the advantages of specialization even when they specialize in different but similar products.

THE FOUR BASES OF COMPARATIVE ADVANTAGE

Natural endowments, which consist of geographical determinants such as land, natural resources, and climate

Acquired endowments, which are the physical capital and human skills a nation has developed

Superior knowledge, including technological advantages, which may be acquired either by the accident of history or through deliberate policies

Specialization, which may create comparative advantages between countries that are similar in all other respects

THE PERCEIVED COSTS OF INTERNATIONAL INTERDEPENDENCE

The argument that voluntary trade must be mutually beneficial seems so compelling that one wonders why there has been, from time to time, such strong antitrade sentiment in the United States and many other countries. This antitrade feeling is often labeled **protectionism,** because it calls for "protecting" the economy from the effects of trade. Those who favor protectionism raise a number of concerns: (1) trade leads to a loss of jobs; (2) dependence on trade makes a country vulnerable, particularly in times of war; (3) *fair* trade may be good, but foreign countries subsidize their producers, and thus trade unfairly; (4) trade imbalances make a country indebted to foreigners; and (5) weak countries can be hurt by trade. Most of these objections make little sense to economists, as we will see in the following paragraphs.

LOSS OF DOMESTIC JOBS

With the onslaught of Japanese imported cars in the mid-1970s, sales of American cars plummeted, and unemployment in Michigan (where the auto industry dominates the state's economy) soared. Protection from foreign imports was an easy and obvious answer. From an economic viewpoint, however, this protectionism meant forgoing the gains from trade. Economists argue that government always has better means at its disposal for accomplishing the goals that trade restriction is designed to achieve. There are, for instance, other ways of stimulating employment.

One of the dangers in drawing analogies between individuals and countries is that countries as a whole do not actually trade or make decisions. Instead, some person or company within one country makes a beneficial trade with some person or company from another country. Perhaps a U.S. consumer buys an automobile from a Japanese company, or a U.S. computer manufacturer makes a sale to a German company. Those making the trade are, by definition, better off, but others in the country may feel disadvantaged. An American autoworker may say, "If only those American consumers were buying cars from us, this company would not be losing money." Similarly, a German computer maker might say, "If only those American computer companies were forbidden to sell in Germany, then German computer companies would benefit."

CLOSE-UP: REELING AND WRITHING TO ESCAPE SUGAR QUOTAS

To assist American sugar farmers, the U.S. government has long had a policy of restricting sugar imports from the rest of the world. This policy has paid sweet dividends for those who produce sugar. Protected from competition from poor sugar-growing nations around the world, such as the Philippines and many countries in Latin America, U.S. sugar prices have averaged about twice as high as prices on the world market. Consumers foot the bill for the higher price. Various economic studies have estimated that the sugar import quotas cost consumers $2 to $3 billion annually.

But the adaptations of the economy to restrictions on imported sugar have been complex. In the early 1980s, one common dodge around the sugar import quotas was to import a blend of sugar and something else, because the quotas applied only to pure sugar, not to mixtures. Different kinds of sugar were blended together, and sugar was also mixed with honey, chocolate, corn syrup, and maple syrup. Some of these loopholes were later closed off, but there continued to be doubts about whether sugar imported in the form of cake mixes or breakfast cereal should count under the import quotas.

If the United States keeps sugar prices high by restricting imported sugar, then imported products that *contain* sugar have an advantage. If foreign candy manufacturers, for example, can buy cheap sugar outside the United States and then sell their candy bars in the United States, they will be able to sell more cheaply than domestic candy manufacturers. For exactly these reasons, E. J. Brach, America's third-largest candy maker, has threatened to close up shop and move to Canada or Mexico, rather than trying to match prices with for-

eign competitors who have access to cheaper sugar.

Trying to help farmers become more productive is one thing, but many economists would argue that the sugar quotas are an example of good intentions run amok. Sugar import quotas cause American firms using sugar to shut down or move elsewhere, help keep farmers poor in impoverished countries close to the United States, and cost consumers billions of dollars each year.

Sources: Stephen Chapman, "Sugar Boondoggle Is a Sour Deal for Almost Everyone," *Chicago Tribune,* July 12, 1990; Clyde H. Farnsworth, "Beating the Quota on Sugar Imports," *New York Times,* April 20, 1983, p. D1.

For this reason, trade between people from different countries will often create a situation in which the country as a whole is better off, but particular groups within the country may be worse off. American consumers benefit greatly from being able to buy quality imported products at a good price. Many U.S. workers benefit because their companies export products abroad. But certain industries within the country that are facing stiffer competition may be hurt. And when companies are struggling and people are losing their jobs, those who are suffering will get a lot of attention. Nevertheless, while trade costs some workers their jobs, it creates jobs for others. Beyond that, consumers benefit because trade enables them to buy those goods that foreigners can make less expensively and better than Americans can.

When economic circumstances change, it may be desirable for the government to help those in industries that have been hurt by imports to get jobs in other sectors of the economy, and to provide them support during the transition process. Government assistance may be particularly valuable when jobs are lost in import-competing industries faster than jobs are created in export industries. Several countries (including the United States) have programs to provide such assistance.

The argument that trade leads to a loss of jobs is also used by those who would restrict immigration. Once proud of being a "melting pot" of immigrants, the United States in the twentieth century has restricted the flow of immigrants. Most of the immigrants today from Mexico and Latin America are unskilled. Because they are willing to take low-wage jobs, wages in those jobs can stay low. The lower wages mean that consumers can buy goods such as lettuce and grapes at lower prices. The country as a whole thus benefits. The immigrants also benefit; after all, though the wages are low by American standards, they are very high in comparison with the opportunities these workers faced in their own countries. However, low-skilled U.S. workers who are in direct competition with the immigrants lose.

As with free trade, there are both winners and losers with free immigration. Again the gains to the winners exceed the losses to the losers. That is, the gainers could pay the losers enough to make them as well off as they were before, and the gainers would still be better off than before the immigration. Thus, from the perspective of economic efficiency, both free trade and free immigration make sense. But political opposition to the two remains strong. The gains (other than to the immigrants themselves, who do not vote) are dispersed widely throughout the population, and the costs, in loss of jobs, are concentrated and visible. Congress responded to the visible suffering by enacting the Immigration Reform and Control Act of 1986, which continued the restrictions on immigration and made it more difficult for illegal immigrants to get jobs.

VULNERABILITY

Another objection to free trade has to do with the vulnerability of a nation that depends on other nations for critical resources. Countries should treasure their independence, critics argue, and this requires a degree of self-sufficiency. There is some merit to this line of reasoning, although not as much as the special interests who seek trade protection would have us believe. Back in the 1950s, the oil industry was successful in lobbying for quotas—that is, strict numerical limits—on the amount of oil that could be imported. The argument was that the United States should not depend on other nations for its oil. "Drill America First" was the industry's motto. As a result, the United States used up much of its own oil reserves during the 1950s and 1960s, making the country *more* dependent on foreign oil in later years. This was hardly the best strategy for long-run energy independence. The appropriate response to the risk of a cut-off of oil is to have alternative sources of energy developed and ready, to establish (as has now been done to some extent) a strategic stockpile of resources like oil, and to formulate contingency plans, that is, plans of what to do should oil supplies be interrupted.

There is, however, a more fundamental concern with vulnerability as America's comparative advantage may be shifting away from manufacturing and certain high-technology fields to agriculture and service sectors such as banking and higher education. Were the United States to become involved in a war, unless it maintains a technological capability in these areas, it could be at a marked disadvantage in producing steel, tanks, and ships. However, as in the case of oil imports, antitrade proposals couched in terms of vulnerability should be eyed with caution. The costs of maintaining complete self-sufficiency are enormous, partly because they require forgoing the mutual benefits of trade. Maintaining the country's technological capabilities for defense purposes usually does not require the abandonment of trade.

UNFAIR TRADE

Another objection to trade holds that foreign governments subsidize their producers, and thus compete unfairly. If foreign governments subsidized their products continually, then there would be no problem. After all, if the Japanese government wants to provide an endless parade of subsidized products for American consumers, enabling them to buy those goods more cheaply than they otherwise could, why should the U.S. government complain? More difficult issues arise if one believes that the subsidies are temporary, and will only persist long enough to drive American producers from desirable markets. After forcing out the U.S. competition, foreign firms will be in a position to exploit American consumers by charging higher prices. This argument makes theoretical sense, but in most industries, competition among the several foreign and U.S. firms is sufficiently keen that it does not appear to be a serious threat in practice.

INDEBTEDNESS

Since the early 1980s, the United States has been importing far more than it exports, as we can see in Figure 3.5. The excess of imports over exports is called the **trade deficit,** and the trade deficit has exceeded 3 percent of the country's output in recent

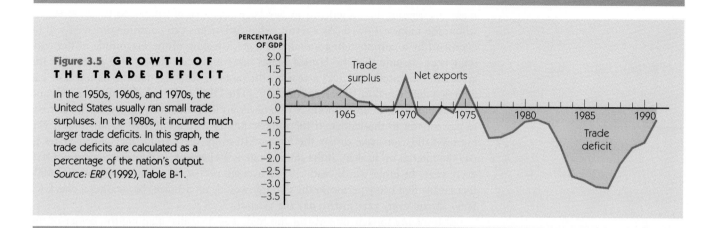

Figure 3.5 GROWTH OF THE TRADE DEFICIT

In the 1950s, 1960s, and 1970s, the United States usually ran small trade surpluses. In the 1980s, it incurred much larger trade deficits. In this graph, the trade deficits are calculated as a percentage of the nation's output. *Source: ERP* (1992), Table B-1.

years. As the figure shows, such a trade deficit represents a dramatic reversal from the situation that prevailed when U.S. exports exceeded imports in the 1950s and 1960s.

The only way the United States can afford to consume more products from foreign countries than it sells to foreign countries is to borrow from those same countries to pay for the excess. In effect, the U.S. economy is borrowing from Germany, Japan, Canada, and other countries and using the proceeds to buy German, Japanese, Canadian, and other nations' products. As a result of this pattern of borrowing and trade deficits, the United States has become a net debtor country; that is, the total amount Americans owe to foreign countries exceeds the total amount that foreign countries owe to American companies and individuals. Indeed, as shown in Figure 3.6, the United States has moved in just a few years from being the largest creditor nation in the world to being the largest debtor nation, though the size of its debt relative to its national income remains much smaller than in the poorer countries.

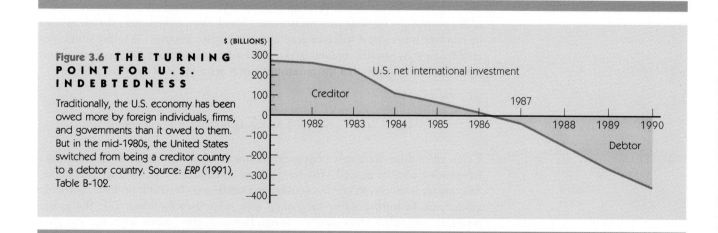

Figure 3.6 THE TURNING POINT FOR U.S. INDEBTEDNESS

Traditionally, the U.S. economy has been owed more by foreign individuals, firms, and governments than it owed to them. But in the mid-1980s, the United States switched from being a creditor country to a debtor country. Source: *ERP* (1991), Table B-102.

These numbers are of concern because the increasing indebtedness to foreigners will make it necessary for Americans to pay large amounts of interest to those abroad to whom the money is owed. As a result, what Americans can consume or invest will be decreased by a corresponding amount. To get a feeling of the magnitude of the consequences, assume that the United States has run a trade deficit of 3 percent of the gross domestic product (GDP) a year for the past ten years, so that the nation now has a foreign debt equal to 30 percent of GDP. (The GDP is the value of all the goods and services produced in an economy.) Whenever an individual or country borrows, it has to pay interest to the lender. If the interest rate is 10 percent, that means that if you borrow $100, you have to pay the lender $10 every year. So for the United States to pay the interest on its debt, if the interest rate is 10 percent, will take 3 percent of GDP every year. In other words, with 1990's average per capita GDP of around $22,000, this means that every person in the country would, on average, be sending a check for $660 abroad every year *just to pay the interest.*

But to blame foreign imports for the trade deficit is like blaming the owner of the candy store for the stomachache that results from eating too much candy. The problem, as will be explained in future chapters, is that the U.S. economy as a whole has been consuming more than it produces, not that nasty foreigners are snookering virtuous Americans.

WEAK COUNTRIES HURT BY TRADE

The final objection to trade is that poorer countries are exploited by richer countries, and therefore they should protect themselves. Again, this political rhetoric misses the basic point of trade: both sides gain from exchanges that are entered into voluntarily. The relative strength of the trading partners may determine how the mutual gains from trade are shared. The weaker trading partner may wind up just a little bit better than it was without trade, with most of the advantages of trade reaped by the stronger partner. This may seem unfair, but it does not contradict the result that both sides gain.

This conclusion, however, is predicated on the assumption that countries rationally pursue their self-interest in making their decisions to trade, and that they take into account the long-term consequences. Weaker nations may not be so farsighted, particularly if those who are making the trading decisions do not adequately reflect the interests of the country. In the long run, for instance, Brazil may not be better off cutting down its rain forests because it will take generations to replace the trees. Wealthy landowners might view it as privately profitable to sell their trees, knowing there is a good chance within a decade or two that the government may seize the land away from them.

WHY PROTECTIONISM SURVIVES

Given all of these seemingly persuasive arguments against protectionism, why does it have such a popular appeal? Why have almost all countries enacted trade restrictions? The answer is simple. While the country as a whole may benefit from trade, particular groups may be hurt. Because the gainers gain more than the losers lose, the gainers could, in principle, compensate the losers. However, this seldom happens. The gains to society come in the form of a slight reduction in the prices consumers pay. But the losses—the lower wages and lost jobs that result in industries facing competition—are often more visible than the gains. Unless people who suffer such losses receive some compensation, they will fight free trade.

REVIEW AND PRACTICE

SUMMARY

1. The benefits and costs of economic interdependence apply to individuals and firms within a country as well as to countries within the world. No individual and no country is self-sufficient.

2. Both individuals and countries gain from voluntary trade. There may be cases when there are only limited possibilities for bilateral trade (exchange between two parties), but the gains from multilateral trade (exchange between several parties) may be great.

3. The principle of comparative advantage asserts that countries should export the goods in which their production costs are *relatively* low.

4. Specialization tends to increase productivity for three reasons: specializing avoids the time it takes a worker to switch from one production task to another; workers who repeat a task become more skilled at it; specialization creates a fertile environment for invention.

5. A country's comparative advantage can arise from natural endowments, or as a result of acquired endowments, superior knowledge, or specialization.

6. Those who favor protectionism say that trade leads to a loss of domestic jobs, makes a country vulnerable, gives foreign nations the chance to trade unfairly, creates foreign debt, and hurts weak countries. Most of these objections are of doubtful validity, and even when there is some truth to the problem, protectionist policies are usually a costly and inappropriate response.

KEY TERMS

gains from trade	multilateral trade	natural endowments
imports	absolute advantage	acquired endowments
exports	comparative	protectionism
bilateral trade	advantage	trade deficit

REVIEW QUESTIONS

1. Why are all voluntary trades mutually beneficial?

2. Describe a situation (hypothetical, if need be) where bilateral trade does not work, but multilateral trade is possible.

3. What are some of the similarities of trade between individuals and trade between countries? What is a key way in which they differ?

4. Does a country with an absolute advantage in a product necessarily have a comparative advantage in that product? Does a country with an absolute disadvantage in a product necessarily not have a comparative advantage in that product? Explain.

5. Does specialization tend to increase or decrease productivity? Explain.

6. "A country's comparative advantage is dictated by its natural endowments." Discuss.

7. "If trade with a foreign country injures anyone in this country, the government should react by passing protectionist laws to limit or stop that particular trade." Comment.

PROBLEMS

1. Four players on a Little League baseball team discover that they have each been collecting baseball cards, and they agree to get together and trade. Is it possible for everyone to benefit from this agreement? Does the fact that one player starts off with many more cards than any of the others affect your answer?

2. Leaders in many less developed countries of Latin America and Africa have often argued that because they are so much poorer than the wealthy nations of the world, trade with the more developed economies of North America and Europe will injure them. They maintain that they must first become self-sufficient before they can benefit from trade. How might an economist respond to these claims?

3. If the United States changes its immigration quotas to allow many more unskilled workers into the country, who is likely to gain? Who is likely to lose? Consider the impact on consumers, on businesses that hire low-skilled labor, and on low-skilled labor in both the United States and the workers' countries of origin.

4. David Ricardo illustrated the principle of comparative advantage in terms of the trade between England and Portugal in wine (port) and wool. Suppose that in England it takes 120 laborers to produce a certain quantity of wine, while in Portugal it takes only 80 laborers to produce that same quantity. Similarly, in England it takes 100 laborers to produce a certain quantity of wool, while in Portugal it takes only 90. Draw the opportunity set for each country, assuming that each has 72,000 laborers. Assume that each country commits half its labor to each product in the absence of trade, and designate that point on your graph. Now describe a new production plan, with trade, that can benefit both countries.

5. In 1981, the U.S. government prodded Japanese automakers to limit the number of cars they would export to the United States. Who benefited from this protectionism in the United States and in Japan? Who was injured in the United States and in Japan? Consider companies that produce cars (and their workers) and consumers who buy cars.

6. For many years, an international agreement called the Multifiber Agreement has limited the amount of textiles that the developed economies of North America and Europe can buy from poor countries in Latin America and Asia. Textiles can be produced by relatively unskilled labor with a reasonably small amount of capital. Who benefits from the protectionism of the Multifiber Agreement, and who suffers?

APPENDIX: ORGANIZATIONS AND THE REAL COSTS OF INTERDEPENDENCE

Almost everyone has reflected at one time or another that life would be simpler if we did not have to depend on others. Emerging from their reveries, however, most individuals decide that the gains from interdependence exceed the costs; so too in the realm of economics.

Many of the problems of economic interdependence are similar to those that arise in daily life. You rely on someone to pick you up at a particular time to go to a concert. He is late, and you find that the tickets are sold out. Two friends are trying to decide how to spend the day. One wants to go biking, the other hiking. There are conflicts that have to be resolved. Two couples want to go on summer vacation together, but they find it difficult coordinating their schedules. Think of the time it takes for a group of more than five people to decide on what restaurant to go to or what movie to see!

Individuals who specialize in doing what they have a comparative advantage in have to rely on others for everything else. The frustrations of interdependence often make one recall the old adage "If you want something done right, do it yourself." Someone you hire to do a task for you seldom has the incentive to do it with the care that you would exercise.

Beyond misplaced incentives, economic interdependence also introduces problems of communication and coordination, of selecting individuals to perform different tasks, and of collective decision making. In our economy, these problems are addressed in a variety of ways. Each has its costs. Much of this book will discuss how the price system provides appropriate incentives, how it communicates information about scarcity, how it guides individuals and countries in their choices of specializations, and how it serves to coordinate economic activity.

Even the price system has its costs, however. When a firm wants to buy some input, it has two alternatives. For example, when Ford needed steel, it could have bought the steel from another firm or it could have produced the steel itself. In the first case, we say that the firm is using the market. But there are costs involved. The steel producers have to hire salespeople and set prices. Ford would have to hire buyers to search among alternative suppliers and to negotiate the best price. The costs of engaging in transactions are called, quite naturally, **transactions costs.** In some markets, transactions costs may be quite high, motivating firms to produce the goods they need themselves. Thus, Ford decided to produce its own steel. Or to take another example, a large builder may employ plumbers, electricians, and carpenters directly rather than buying these services from other firms. These workers' activities are then controlled not by prices, primarily, but by the orders of the firm's managers. Within organizations, managers, not markets, take on the role of coordinating the workers and supervising them to make sure that they work hard.

There are real costs associated with addressing such problems, whether within organizations or markets; and while the benefits of economic interdependence far outweigh the costs, it is important to bear these costs in mind. When we think about technological progress, we often have a picture of lasers and transistors, computers and VCRs. No less important for the economy, however, have been those advances that have reduced the costs of economic interdependence and allowed markets and organizations to function more efficiently.

FOUR ECONOMIC PROBLEMS WITHIN ORGANIZATIONS

Most production takes place inside organizations; in fact about one-fourth of U.S. manufacturing takes place inside the fifty largest manufacturing corporations. Most consumption takes place in households, which can be viewed as small organizations. Local, state, and federal governments are nothing more than large organizations. In fact, the whole economy can be thought of as an organization—an organization made up of smaller organizations. The following sections explore four common economic problems that these different kinds of organizations face.

INCENTIVES

When you do something for yourself, you know the costs (both in materials and effort) and the benefits. If you own a car and you get a thrill out of screeching the tires, both the benefit (the feeling of going fast) and the cost (the wear and tear on the tires) are yours to consider. Because you reap the benefits and pay the costs yourself, you have the right economic incentives: you only burn rubber if the benefits exceed the costs. However, the teenager driving the family car may be able to enjoy the benefits while letting her parents pay the costs. As this simple example illustrates, *whenever costs and benefits do not accrue to the same person, there is an incentive problem.*

Incentive problems arise in every economic organization, from families to households to government, because the interests of the individual and those of the organization are rarely identical. People must be motivated to exert effort and do high-quality work. But many workers are paid an agreed-upon salary. Even when a company makes an attempt to link pay to overall levels of performance, there is no close connection between any particular action and the worker's pay. A sales representative may know that if he drives a company car too hard, it will shorten the life of the car; but he may enjoy driving it hard, and doing so will enable him to get his job done more quickly and get home to watch his favorite TV show. The sales representative has no incentive to take care of the car. He knows that his supervisor has no way to tell whether he drove the car too hard; even if the car actually breaks down while he is hot-rodding, it will be almost impossible to tell whether it was his fault or a mechanical defect in the car.

There is an obvious solution to this incentive problem—make the salesperson provide his own car. But many incentive problems do not have such an easy answer. A store's employee may know that if all the windows of the store are not double-locked, the probability of a break-in increases. But it takes effort to go around to check whether they are locked, and the employee may feel he has no incentive to exert that effort. Even the owner herself may not exert much effort, if she has purchased insurance against burglary for the store.

Those in decision-making positions must also be motivated to make good decisions, decisions that benefit not just themselves but the organization. The retiring manager of a firm may know that one of two candidates for the job as his successor is better than the other; but it may require some effort to convince the others who are involved in the decision. Since the manager is retiring, there may not be a sufficient incentive to induce him to exert that effort.

In Chapter 2, we learned that prices play a central role in providing incentives in market economies. Within organizations, prices rarely play this role. The Production Department does not pay the Personnel Department for its services. One manager does not charge another for the value of her time used in a consultation on whether to go ahead on a project. When the manager of a division calls a meeting, she often does not weigh carefully the opportunity cost of those attending the meeting—what their time is worth on other tasks. Finding substitutes for prices as the basis of incentives is a key problem within many organizations.

COMMUNICATION AND COORDINATION

When you are on your own, you do not have to communicate with anyone; you do not have to coordinate what you do with anyone else. But as soon as there is economic interdependence, communication and coordination become extremely important—and there are considerable costs involved, both in communicating and coordinating and in failing to communicate and coordinate.

Communication and coordination are essential in any team play, if each individual is to do his part. Any organization can be viewed as a team. Information is divided and dispersed throughout the divisions of the firm, and throughout the people in those divisions. If the organization is to get its job done, there has to be communication and coordination. Individuals within the organization must have incentives to communicate essential information.

A dramatic example where information was not collected and communicated properly was the explosion of the space shuttle *Challenger* in 1987, which killed the seven astronauts aboard. The source of the problem turned out to be a defective "O-ring," which performed badly in the low temperatures that Florida was experiencing at the time of the launch. Some of the engineers had had concerns about the O-ring, but the managers to whom they communicated their concerns did not pay attention. The managers' concern was to get the project done on schedule.

After the tragedy, the concerns of the engineers finally reached the ears of the late physicist Richard Feynman, who was part of a committee appointed to investigate the disaster. In a simple but dramatic experiment, Feynman dropped the O-ring in a glass of ice water and pointed out that it became less flexible. The failure to incorporate such simple but vital information was an obvious organizational failure. Those building the space shuttle had had insufficient incentives to obtain the requisite information, and indeed were motivated to press ahead without the vital information.

SELECTION

When an individual is on her own, not only does she avoid the costs of communication and coordination, she also avoids the costs of deciding who should do what tasks. She does everything herself!

We saw earlier that there are gains from specialization, and that it pays to have individuals do the tasks for which they have a comparative advantage. But knowing what is each individual's comparative advantage is no easy matter. A central problem facing any organization is deciding whom to hire, whom to assign to what job, whom to promote to the company presidency, and whom to fire.

STRUCTURING DECISION MAKING

All organizations must make decisions, just as individuals do. Organizations have to decide what to produce and how to produce it, and what investment projects to undertake. It used to be thought that decision making could be reduced to a simple formula: decide on your objectives; find out what the alternative possible actions are; ascertain the consequences of each action; evaluate the extent to which each action meets your goals; and choose the action that most clearly meets your objective. Life, unfortunately, is not so simple.

This formula may actually do more to reveal the problems of decision making than to solve them. In most organizations, different individuals may have different objectives. Even when they agree on the firm's objectives, such as maximizing its profits, they may disagree about the best way of accomplishing these objectives. They may disagree because of different information or different beliefs about the consequences of certain policies.

In the final analysis, individual interests and those of the organization may not precisely coincide. The manager of one division may truly believe that the best way for the firm to make money is to expand his division, but it surely does not escape his attention that if his division is expanded, his status within the firm and probably his salary will also increase.

Even after the event, it is often difficult to judge whether a decision made was the correct one, and whether it was made for the right reason. With the perspective of twenty-twenty hindsight, we can say that a wrong (or a right) decision was made. The investors in Henry Ford's first two enterprises undertook great risks, for which they never received a return. In the 1960s, the managers of U.S. automobile firms had to forecast what kind of cars American consumers would want in the 1970s. They predicted that consumers would continue to want big cars. In both of these cases, wrong decisions were made. But relying on the benefits of hindsight is not fair. The real question is whether those making the decisions gathered the necessary amount of information, and whether their decisions were appropriate given the information that was available to them at the time.

Thus, a central problem facing all organizations is how to structure decision making. All organizations face a general choice between **centralized systems,** where a lot of control is vested in those at the top, and **decentralized systems,** where considerable discretion remains with subordinates. In the former Soviet Union, a single government ministry decided on how much steel each steel mill should produce. Economic decisions in that country were highly centralized. By contrast, in the United States, these decisions are made by many different firms.

Centralized systems are sometimes better than decentralized ones for making substantial changes, but such changes can turn out to be big mistakes as well as successes. When Communist China, under the direction of Mao Tse-tung, decided that more land should be converted from growing rice to growing wheat, the economy responded quickly, with disastrous consequences. Land that was ill-suited for wheat was converted, erosion set in, and by the time the decision was reversed, some of the land had been largely ruined—not even rice could be grown on it.

Centralized systems also have greater problems of collecting information and providing incentives to all the members of the organization. The economic ills that plagued the centralized economy of the former USSR were largely attributed to the country's failure to provide incentives, to its inability to elicit information about what was going on in the economy, and to its consequent inability to coordinate economic activity. For instance, hospitals wanting to give an impression of their effectiveness had an incentive *not* to report the number of babies that died. And schools had an incentive to overreport the number of children in attendance, so they would get bigger budgets. As a result, phantom children passed through the school system. It was not until these children were drafted into the military—and failed to report for duty—that the mistakes became evident. Thus, the inaccuracy of Soviet statistics on population (as in other areas) was not just a matter of distortions by the leaders at the top. The information on which those statistics were compiled, supplied by those beneath, was simply inaccurate. Worse still, the system provided incentives for inaccurate reporting.

The issue of centralization versus decentralization also arises within firms. Many companies have several divisions, each of which operates almost autonomously, with only general oversight provided by the central headquarters. Some firms, such as Hewlett-Packard (a major computer and high-tech electronics firm), decentralize even further, allowing a large number of project managers to decide for themselves what research projects to pursue.

There are several advantages to decentralization: firms can respond quickly to current conditions, avoid the bureaucracies almost always associated with centralized control, and provide greater incentives and motivation by allowing more employees to participate in decision making. Advocates of centralization, on the other hand, cite the advantages of the stronger sense of control, which at times (such as war) may allow the organization to respond more quickly, and the greater ability to coordinate. Whether or not this greater sense of control, ability to respond quickly, and ability to coordinate are illusory remains controversial. While those at the top might be able to control matters better *if* they had all the information that those under them have, they never do have all such information, and this puts them at a disadvantage.

Of course, when, say, a manager delegates responsibility to a subordinate, the subordinate may not do exactly what the manager would have done in that situation; she may make a mistake (though the manager too may have made a mistake). The possibility of mistaken judgments drives many organizations to try to retain more central control. But again, there are trade-offs. Mistakes will occur under any system. And the subordinate may have more of the detailed information required to make a good decision; she may see more of what goes on in the workplace than the manager, who cannot be everywhere at once. The manager may indeed make better decisions when he has the requisite information and time. But as we saw earlier, there are advantages to specialization; it pays him to spend his time making the bigger decisions. The manager needs to stick to his comparative advantage too.

Direct versus Indirect Control   Issues of centralization and decentralization are closely related to issues of *how* control is exercised. When one individual attempts to affect or control the behavior of another individual by "ordering" her to do something, with an implicit or explicit threat of dire consequences if the order is not followed, he is using a direct control mechanism. Many politicians have argued that the government should control automobile pollution by issuing regulations. Some old-style management textbooks suggested that the managers of a firm should decide what they want, and then order their employees to carry out those decisions.

But economists argue that better results are often obtained by using incentive systems as indirect control mechanisms, where individuals are *motivated* to act in the desired manner by the rewards they receive from doing so, rather than as a result of being told or ordered to do something. Noneconomists frequently fail to recognize the limitations of direct control and the power of indirect control mechanisms and incentives.

Imperfect and Costly Information   If information were perfect—complete and accurate—problems of how to allocate resources would be relatively easy to solve. If consumers had perfect information, they would know the prices of each seller's products, all the characteristics of each product, and thus whether a price was lower because the product was shoddier or simply because it was a better deal. Firms would know precisely what the skills of every employee were, so that each could be assigned to an appropriate job. But information is imperfect—less than complete and accurate—and costly to acquire. It is, for instance, costly even to administer tests that give only an imperfect assessment of each worker's skills.

All four of the organizational problems named above can be viewed as largely resulting from the fact that information is imperfect and costly. Even the problem of incentives is essentially an information problem. If an employer could costlessly observe everything the worker does, and if he could easily ascertain what it is that the worker should do, then he would simply tell the worker what to do and pay her if and only if she complied. The questions of communication and coordination are quite clearly information problems; how to convey, for instance, information about the scarcity, measured by their opportunity costs, of the various raw materials used in production. If an employer had perfect (complete and accurate) information about the skills of a worker as well as the characteristics making for success on the job, the selection problem would be trivial.

Finally, if all decision makers had perfect information concerning the consequences of their decisions, decision making would be a relatively easy matter. But they have imperfect and often contradicting information, and different decision makers come to different conclusions about the desirability of a project. These information problems are at the core of understanding how economics and economic organizations function. As a result, the "economics of information" has become one of the most active areas of research in economics during the past two decades.

ECONOMIC ORGANIZATION AND POLITICAL FREEDOM

There is a widespread feeling that there is a relationship between the economic and the political organization of a society. Totalitarian regimes, such as the former Soviet Union under Stalin, centralized economic as well as political power at the top. They restricted the rights of individuals to engage in economic activities just as they restricted people's political rights.

The notion that concentrations of economic power might lead to concentrations of political power found expression in the early days of the American Republic. Thomas Jefferson, in particular, thought that the vitality of the Republic depended on small landholders. Though the structure of the economy changed dramatically in the next two hundred years as it moved from a rural, agrarian base to an urban, industrial society, similar concerns have repeatedly arisen; in the late nineteenth century, for instance, as a few large firms such as Standard Oil and the larger railroads assumed enormous economic power.

These concerns have often played an important role in discussions about economic policy. They probably were a more important factor, for instance, in the legislation aimed at limiting the power of large corporations than arguments that focused on economic efficiency. And fear that the government was assuming too much power formed an important basis of the criticisms leveled against some of President Franklin D. Roosevelt's proposals designed to bring the economy out of the Great Depression.

Among the former Soviet bloc economies during the 1980s, there was growing recognition of the importance of increased economic decentralization if these economies were to improve their dismal records. Finally, at the end of the decade, these countries openly embraced the idea of a market economy. The notion that any central authority could run an economy efficiently was abandoned. With these economic changes has come a further benefit: the rights to make economic decisions, to enter a business, to make a new product, to hire workers, have been accompanied by greater political rights.

Today in the United States and the other industrialized democracies, there is a widespread consensus in favor of the mixed economy, where government's economic power is limited. But even given this consensus, there is considerable debate over precisely what role the government should take. Frequently concerns have been raised that a particular government program would represent an unreasonable aggrandizement of power on the part of the government. The debate over the role of the government in providing medical services is one example, though there is little evidence that countries in which the government dominates the medical sector, such as the United Kingdom, are any less democratic on that account. In the discussions of economic policy in this book, we will focus our attention more narrowly on economic costs and benefits, but many of the policy controversies touch on broader issues—such as the consequences for the U.S. political system.

DEMAND, SUPPLY, AND PRICES

conomics, as we have seen, is concerned with choice in the face of scarcity. This chapter is about prices. **Price** is defined as what is given in exchange for a good or a service. When the forces of supply and demand are permitted to operate freely, price measures scarcity. As such, prices are a thing of beauty to economists, for they convey critical economic information. When the price of a resource used by a firm is high, the company has a greater incentive to economize on its use. When the price of a good that the firm produces is high, the company has a greater incentive to produce more of that good, and its customers have an incentive to economize on its use. In these ways and others, prices provide our economy with incentives to use scarce resources efficiently.

"Push the Scotch salmon with dill sauce."

KEY QUESTIONS

1. What is meant by demand? Why do demand curves normally slope downward? On what variables, other than price, does the quantity demanded depend?

2. What is meant by supply? Why do supply curves normally slope upward? On what variables, other than price, does the quantity supplied depend?

3. Why do economists say that the equilibrium price occurs at the intersection of the demand and supply curves?

4. How do shifts in the demand and supply curves affect the equilibrium price?

THE ROLE OF PRICES

Prices are the way that the participants in the economy communicate with one another. Assume a drought hits the country, reducing drastically the supply of corn. Households will consequently need to reduce their consumption of corn. But how will they know this? Suppose newspapers across the country ran an article informing people that they would have to eat less corn. Would it be read? If so, would people pay attention to it? Why should they? What incentive do they have? How would each family know how much it ought to reduce its consumption? As an alternative to the newspaper, consider the effect of an increase in the price of corn. The higher price quickly and effectively conveys all of the relevant information. Households do not need to know why the price is high. They do not need to know the details of the drought. All they need to know is that there is a greater scarcity of corn, and that they would be wise to reduce their consumption. The higher price tells them that corn is scarce at the same time that it encourages families to consume less of it.

Prices present interesting problems and puzzles. In the early 1980s, while the price of an average house in Los Angeles went up by 41 percent, the price of a house in Milwaukee, Wisconsin, increased by only 4 percent. Why? During the same period, the price of computers fell dramatically, while the price of bread rose, but at a much slower rate than the price of housing in Los Angeles. Why? The "price" of labor is just the wage or salary that is paid. Why does a physician earn three times as much as a college professor, though the college professor may have performed better in the college courses they took together? Why do women, on average, earn two-thirds the amount that men do? Why did average wage rates fall in the United States between 1973 and

1983? Why is the price of water, without which we cannot live, very low in most cases, but the price of diamonds, which we can surely live without, very high? The simple answer to all of these questions is that in market economies like the United States, price is determined by supply and demand. Changes in prices are determined by changes in supply and demand.

Noneconomists see much more in prices than the impersonal forces of supply and demand. One of the events that precipitated the French Revolution was the rise in the price of bread, for which the people blamed the government. More recently, large price changes have given rise to political turmoil in several countries, including Morocco, the Dominican Republic, Russia, and Poland.

On a personal level, individuals tend to blame the owner of an enterprise for the higher prices he charges. It was the landlord who raised the rent on the apartment; it was the oil company or the owner of the gas station who raised the price of gasoline; it was the owner of the movie theater or movie studio who raised the price of movie tickets. These people and companies *chose* to raise their prices, says the noneconomist, in moral indignation. True, replies the economist, but there must be a reason why they decided to raise their prices at this particular time. After all, it is not plausible to say that the landlord or the oil company or the movie theater just had a brainstorm one day and decided to charge more. There must be some factor that made these people and companies believe that a higher price was not a good idea yesterday, but is today.

When all the gas stations in a state or all the landlords in a town start charging roughly the same amount more at the same time, economists argue that there must be a reason. And economists point out that at a different time, these same impersonal forces often oblige these same landlords and oil companies and movie theaters to cut their prices. Economists see prices, then, as symptoms of underlying causes, and they encourage those who are outraged by higher prices to focus on the forces of supply and demand behind the price changes.

DEMAND

Economists use the concept of **demand** to describe the quantity of a good or service that a household or firm chooses to buy at a given price. It is important to understand that economists are concerned not just with what people desire, but with what they choose to buy given the spending limits imposed by their budget constraint and given the prices of various goods. Of course, the total demand for a good in the economy depends on more than price. Demand for a product at any price may change with the population (more babies result in a higher demand for diapers) or with the style (demand for miniskirts changes over the years) or with broad social trends (Americans drink more wine and less whiskey now than they did several decades ago).

If analyzing demand meant analyzing all the possible influences on the demand for all possible products, the job of economists would be hopelessly complex. Economists deal with this problem of complexity and multiple factors by focusing on one variable at a time, while keeping all of the other factors fixed. They focus their attention particularly on factors that are most important in causing *changes* in demand. Of these, the factor that receives the most attention is price. When other changes are important, such as changes in people's income or the structure of the population, then economists take these changes, as well as the effect of these changes on prices, into account.

THE INDIVIDUAL DEMAND CURVE

Think about what happens as the price of candy bars changes. At a price of $5.00, you might never buy one. At $3.00, you might buy one as a special treat. At $1.25, you might buy a few, and if somehow the price declined to $.50, you might buy a lot. Table 4.1 summarizes the weekly demand of one individual, Roger, for candy bars at these different prices. We can see that the lower the price, the larger the quantity demanded.

We can also summarize the information in this table in a graph that shows the quantity Roger demands at each price. By convention, the quantity demanded is measured along the horizontal axis, and the price is measured along the vertical axis. Figure 4.1 plots the points in Table 4.1.

A smooth curve can be drawn to connect the points. This curve is called the **demand curve.** The demand curve gives the quantity demanded at each price. Thus, if we want to know how many candy bars a week Roger will demand at a price of $1.00, we simply look along the vertical axis at the price $1.00, find the corresponding point A along the demand curve, and then read down to the horizontal axis. At a price of $1.00, Roger buys 6 candy bars each week. Alternatively, if we want to know at what price he will buy just 3 candy bars, we look along the horizontal axis at the quantity 3, find the corresponding point B along the demand curve, and then read across to the vertical axis. Roger will buy 3 candy bars at a price of $1.50.

The fact that as the price of candy bars increases the quantity demanded decreases can be seen in Table 4.1, or from the fact that the demand curve in Figure 4.1 slopes

Table 4.1 ROGER'S DEMAND FOR CANDY BARS AT VARIOUS PRICES

Price	Quantity demanded
$5.00	0
$3.00	1
$2.00	2
$1.50	3
$1.25	4
$1.00	6
$ .75	9
$ .50	15

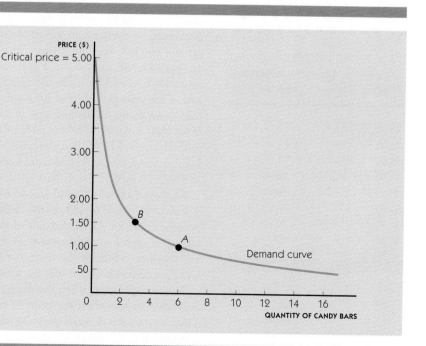

Figure 4.1 AN INDIVIDUAL'S DEMAND CURVE

This demand curve shows the quantity of candy bars that Roger consumes at each price. Notice that quantity demanded falls as the price increases, and the demand curve slopes down.

downward from left to right. This relationship is typical of most demand curves, and it makes common sense: the cheaper a good is (the lower down we look on the vertical axis), the more of it a person will buy (the farther right on the horizontal axis); the more expensive, the less a person will buy.

DEMAND CURVE

The demand curve gives the quantity of the good demanded at each price.

THE MARKET DEMAND CURVE

Table 4.1 gave the quantity of candy bars Roger demanded each week at various prices, while Figure 4.1 presented his demand curve. Table 4.2 gives the total quantity of candy bars demanded by everybody in the economy at various prices. If we had a table like Table 4.1 for each person in the economy, we would construct Table 4.2 simply by adding up, at each price, the total quantity of candy bars purchased. Table 4.2 tells us, for instance, that at a price of $3.00 per candy bar, the total market demand for candy bars is 1 million candy bars, and that lowering the price to $2.00 increases market demand to 3 million candy bars.

Figure 4.2 depicts in a graph the information from Table 4.2. As with Figure 4.1, price lies along the vertical axis, but now the horizontal axis measures the quantity demanded by everyone in the economy. Joining the points in the figure together, we get the **market demand curve.** The market demand curve gives the total quantity demanded by all individuals. For instance, if we want to know what the total demand for candy bars will be when the price is $1.50 per candy bar, we look on the vertical axis at the price $1.50, find the corresponding point A along the demand curve, and read down to the horizontal axis; at that price, total demand is 4 million candy bars. If we want to know what the price of candy bars will be when the demand equals 20 million, we find 20 million along the horizontal axis, look up to find the corresponding point *B* along the market demand curve, and read across to the vertical axis; the price at which 20 million candy bars are demanded is $.75.

Suppose there was a simple economy made up of two people, Roger and Jane. Figure 4.3 illustrates how to add up the demand curves of these two individuals to obtain a demand curve for the market as a whole. We "add" the demand curves horizontally by taking, at each price, the quantities demanded by Roger and by Jane and adding the two together. Thus, in the figure, at the price of $.75, Roger demands 9 candy bars and Jane demands 11, so that the total market demand is 20 candy bars.

Notice that just as when the price of candy bars increases, the individual's demand decreases, so too when the price of candy bars increases, market demand decreases. Thus, the market demand curve also slopes downward from left to right. This general rule holds both because each individual's demand curve is downward sloping and because as prices change, some individuals will decide to enter or exit the market. We have

Table 4.2 TOTAL MARKET DEMAND FOR CANDY BARS AT VARIOUS PRICES

Price	Quantity demanded (millions)
$5.00	0
$3.00	1
$2.00	3
$1.50	4
$1.25	8
$1.00	13
$ .75	20
$ .50	30

Figure 4.2 THE MARKET DEMAND CURVE

The market demand curve shows the quantity of the good demanded by all consumers in the market at each price. The market demand curve is downward sloping, for two reasons: at a higher price, each consumer buys less, and at high enough prices, some consumers decide not to buy at all—they exit the market.

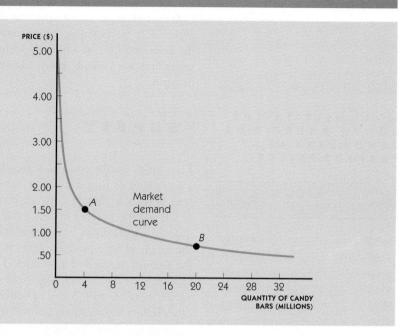

Figure 4.3 DERIVING THE MARKET DEMAND CURVE

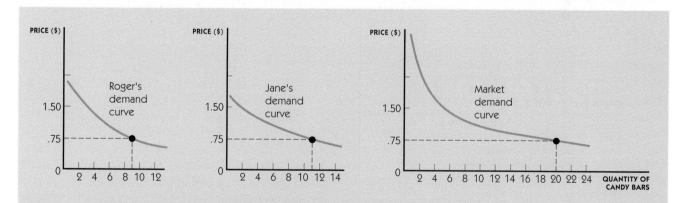

The market demand curve is constructed by adding up, at each price, the total of the quantities consumed by each individual. It shows what market demand would be if there were only two consumers. Actual market demand, as depicted in Figure 4.2, is much larger because there are many consumers.

already examined the first of these reasons, but the second deserves a closer look. At a high enough price, consumers may drop out of the market for a particular product. In Figure 4.1, for example, Roger **exits the market**—consumes a quantity of zero—at the price of $5.00, at which the demand curve hits the vertical axis. Similarly, when prices drop low enough, more consumers will **enter the market** and thus increase the demand.

SUPPLY

Economists use the concept of **supply** to describe the quantity of a good or service that a household or firm would like to sell at a particular price. They use the concept to refer to such seemingly disparate choices as the number of candy bars that firms want to sell and the number of hours that a worker is willing to work. As with demand, the quantity supplied can change according to a variety of factors. A drought can reduce the supply of farm products dramatically. A better production technique may increase the amount supplied of a product. The birth of a child may lead one parent to supply less labor, as that parent takes time off to raise the child, while the other parent may supply more. As in the case of demand, economists focus on price first, while keeping other factors like weather, technology, and so on constant for the moment.

Table 4.3 shows the number of candy bars that the Melt-in-the-Mouth Chocolate Company would like to sell, or supply to the market, at each price. Below $1.00, the firm finds it unprofitable to produce. At $2.00, it would like to sell 85,000 candy bars. As the price rises, so does the quantity supplied—at $5.00, the firm would like to sell 100,000.

Table 4.3 MELT-IN-THE-MOUTH'S SUPPLY OF CANDY BARS AT VARIOUS PRICES

Price	Supply
$5.00	100,000
$3.00	95,000
$2.00	85,000
$1.50	70,000
$1.25	50,000
$1.00	25,000
$ .75	0
$ .50	0

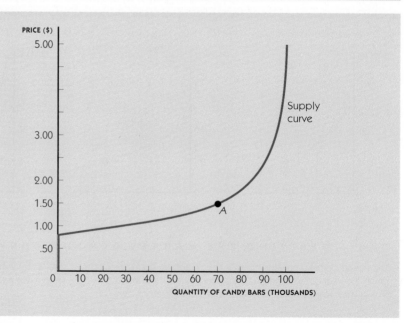

Figure 4.4 ONE FIRM'S SUPPLY CURVE

The supply curve shows the quantity of a good a firm is willing to produce at each price. Normally a firm is willing to produce more as the price increases, which is why the supply curve slopes upward.

Figure 4.4 depicts these points in a graph. The curve drawn by connecting the points is called the **supply curve.** It shows the quantity that Melt-in-the-Mouth will supply at each price, holding all other factors constant. As with the demand curve, we put the price on the vertical axis. The quantity supplied is on the horizontal axis. Thus, we can read point A on the curve as indicating that at a price of $1.50 the firm would like to supply 70,000 candy bars.

Unlike the demand curve, the typical supply curve slopes upward from left to right; at higher prices, firms will supply more.[1] This is because suppliers find it more profitable to produce the goods with higher prices; the higher prices provide them with an incentive to do so.

SUPPLY CURVE

The supply curve gives the quantity of the good supplied at each price.

MARKET SUPPLY

The **market supply** of a good is simply the total quantity that all the firms in the economy are willing to supply at a given price. Similarly, the market supply of labor is simply the total quantity of labor that all the households in the economy are willing to supply at a given wage. As with market demand, market supply is calculated by adding up the quantities of the good that each of the firms or households is willing to supply at each price. Table 4.4 tells us, for instance, that at a price of $2.00, firms will supply 70 million candy bars, while at a price of $.50, they will supply only 5 million.

Figure 4.5 shows the same information graphically. The curve joining the points in the figure is the **market supply curve.** The market supply curve gives the total quantity of a good that firms are willing to produce at each price. Thus, we read point A on the market supply curve as showing that at a price of $.75, the firms in the economy would like to sell 20 million candy bars.

As the price of candy bars increases, the quantity supplied increases. The market supply curve generally slopes upward from left to right for two reasons: at higher prices, each firm in the market is willing to produce more; and at higher prices, more firms are willing to enter the market to produce the good.

The market supply curve is calculated from the supply curves of the different firms in the same way that the market demand curve is calculated from the demand curves of the different households: at each price, we add horizontally the quantities that each of the firms is willing to produce.

Figure 4.6 shows how this is done in a market with only two producers. At a price of $1.25, Melt-in-the-Mouth Chocolate produces 50,000 candy bars, while the Chocolates of Choice Company produces 40,000. So the market supply is 90,000 bars.

Table 4.4 TOTAL MARKET SUPPLY FOR CANDY BARS AT VARIOUS PRICES

Price	Total market supply (millions)
$5.00	82
$3.00	80
$2.00	70
$1.50	59
$1.25	47
$1.00	34
$ .75	20
$ .50	5

[1] Chapter 11 will describe some unusual situations where supply curves may not be upward sloping.

Figure 4.5 THE MARKET SUPPLY CURVE

The market supply curve shows the quantity of a good all firms in the market are willing to supply at each price. The market supply curve is normally upward sloping, both because each firm is willing to supply more of the good at a higher price and because higher prices entice new firms to produce.

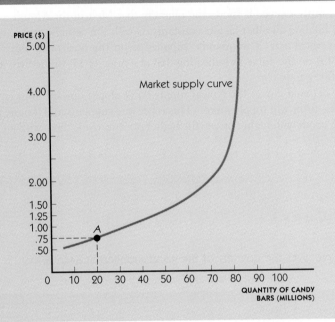

Figure 4.6 DERIVING THE MARKET SUPPLY CURVE

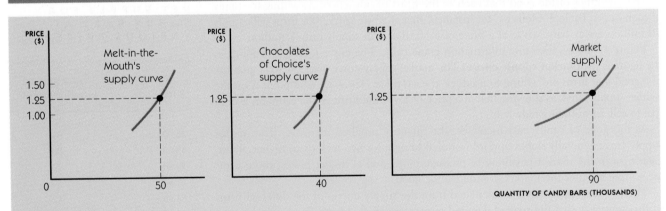

The market supply curve is constructed by adding up the quantity that each of the firms in the economy is willing to supply at each price. It shows what market supply would be if there were only two producers. Actual market supply, as depicted in Figure 4.5, is much larger because there are many producers.

LAW OF SUPPLY AND DEMAND

This chapter began with the assertion that supply and demand work together to determine the market price in competitive markets. Figure 4.7 puts a market supply curve and a market demand curve on the same graph to show how this happens. The price actually paid and received in the market will be determined by the intersection of the two curves. This point is labeled E_0, for equilibrium, and the corresponding price ($.75) and quantity (20 million) are called, respectively, the **equilibrium price** and the **equilibrium quantity.**

Since the term **equilibrium** will recur throughout the book, it is important to understand the concept clearly. Equilibrium describes a situation where there are no forces (reasons) for change. No one has an incentive to change the result—the price or quantity in the case of supply and demand.

In describing a weight hanging from the end of a spring, physicists also speak of equilibrium. There are two forces working on the weight. Gravity is pulling it down; the spring is pulling it up. When the weight is at rest, it is in equilibrium, with the two forces just offsetting each other. If the weight is pulled down a little bit, the force of the spring will be greater than the force of gravity, and the weight will spring up. In the absence of any further intrusions, the weight will eventually bob back and forth to its equilibrium position.

An economic equilibrium is established in roughly the same way. At the equilibrium price, consumers get precisely the quantity of the good they are willing to buy at that price, and producers sell precisely the quantity they are willing to sell at that price.

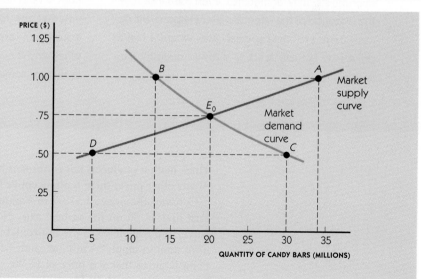

Figure 4.7 SUPPLY AND DEMAND EQUILIBRIUM

Equilibrium occurs at the intersection of the demand and supply curves, at point E_0. At any price above E_0, the quantity supplied will exceed the quantity demanded, the market will be out of equilibrium, and there will be excess supply. At any price below E_0, the quantity demanded will exceed the quantity supplied, the market will be out of equilibrium, and there will be excess demand.

CLOSE-UP: THE STRUCTURE OF ECONOMIC MODELS

Every economic model, including the model of how supply and demand determine the equilibrium price and quantity in a market, is constructed of three kinds of relationships: identities, behavioral relationships, and equilibrium relationships. Recognizing these component parts will help in understanding how economists think and understanding the source of many of their disagreements.

As described in the text, the demand curve represents a relationship between the price and the quantity demanded. The statement that normally, as prices rise, the quantity of a good demanded decreases is a description of how individuals behave. It is called a behavioral relationship. The supply curve for each firm is also a behavioral relationship.

Economists disagree over behavioral relationships, in at least two ways. First, they may differ over the strength of the connection. For any given product, does a change in price lead to a large change in the quantity demanded or a small one? Second, economists may sometimes even disagree over the direction of the effect. As later chapters will discuss, there are some special cases where a higher price may actually lead to a *lower* quantity supplied.

The statement that the market demand is equal to the sum of the individual demands is an identity. An identity is a statement that is true according to the definition of the terms; in other words, market demand is *defined* to be the sum of the demands of all individuals. Similarly, it is an identity that market supply is equal to the sum of the supplies of all firms; the terms are defined in that way. Economists rarely disagree over identities, since disagreements over definitions are pointless.

Finally, an equilibrium relationship exists when there are no forces for change. In the supply and demand model, the equilibrium occurs when the quantity demanded is equal to the quantity supplied. An equilibrium relationship is not the same as an identity. It is possible for the economy to be out of equilibrium, at least for a time. Of course, being out of equilibrium implies that there are forces for change pushing toward equilibrium. But an identity must always hold true at all times, as a matter of definition.

Economists usually agree about what an equilibrium would look like, but they often differ on whether the forces pushing the markets toward equilibrium are strong or weak, and thus on whether the economy is usually fairly close to equilibrium or sometimes rather far from it.

Thus, neither producers nor consumers have an incentive to alter the price or quantity. At any other price, there is an incentive for either buyers or sellers to change the price.

Consider the price of $1.00 in Figure 4.7. There is no equilibrium quantity here. First find $1.00 on the vertical axis. Now look across to find point A on the supply curve, and read down to the horizontal axis; point A tells you that at a price of $1.00, firms want to supply 34 million candy bars. Now look at point B on the demand curve. Point B shows that at a price of $1.00, consumers only want to buy 13 million candy bars. Like the weight bobbing on a spring however, this market will work its way back to equilibrium. At a price of $1.00, there is **excess supply.** As producers discover that they cannot sell as much as they would like at this price, some of them will lower their prices slightly, hoping to take business from other producers. When one producer lowers prices, his competitors will have to respond, for fear that they will end up unable to sell their goods. As prices come down, consumers will also buy more, and so on until the market reaches the equilibrium price and quantity.

Similarly, assume that the price is lower than $.75, say $.50. At the lower price, there is **excess demand:** individuals want to buy 30 million candy bars (point C), while firms only want to produce 5 million (point D). Consumers unable to purchase all they want will offer to pay a little bit more; other consumers, afraid of having to do without, will match these higher bids or raise them. As prices start to increase, suppliers will also have a greater incentive to produce more. Again the market will tend toward the equilibrium point.

At equilibrium, no purchaser and no supplier has an incentive to change the price or quantity. The observation that in competitive market economies actual prices tend to be the equilibrium prices, at which demand equals supply, is called the **law of supply and demand.** It is important to note that this law does not mean that at every moment of time the price is precisely at the intersection of the demand and supply curves. As with the example of the weight and the spring, the market may bounce around a little bit when it is in the process of adjusting. The law of supply and demand does say that when a market is out of equilibrium, there are predictable forces for change.

PRICE, VALUE, AND COST

As noted above, price is easily defined in the economist's impersonal language as what is given in exchange for a good or service. Price is determined by the forces of supply and demand. Adam Smith called our notion of price "value in exchange," and contrasted it to the notion of "value in use":

> The word VALUE, it is to be observed, has two different meanings, and sometimes expresses the utility of some particular object, and sometimes the power of purchasing other goods which the possession of that object conveys. The one may be called "value in use"; the other, "value in exchange." The things which have the greatest value in use have frequently little or no value in exchange; and, on the contrary, those which have the greatest value in exchange have frequently little or no value in use. Nothing is more useful than water, but it will purchase scarce any thing; scarce any thing can be had in exchange for it. A diamond, on the contrary, has scarce any value in use; but a very great quantity of other goods may frequently be had in exchange for it.[2]

Why is it that water, which is a basic necessity for life, has a lower price than diamonds or other luxuries that most people could easily live without? The law of supply and demand can help to explain the diamond-water paradox, and many similar examples

---

[2] *The Wealth of Nations* (1776), Book I, Chapter IV.

CLOSE-UP: GASOLINE PRICES AND DEMAND FOR SMALL CARS

When demands for several products are intertwined, then conditions affecting the price for one product will also affect the demand for the other. When gasoline prices in the United States increased in the 1970s, for example, the change affected the demand for small cars.

Actually, the price of gasoline soared twice in the 1970s: once when the Organization of Petroleum Exporting Countries (OPEC) got together and shut off the flow of oil to the United States late in 1973, and again when the Shah of Iran was driven from power in 1979, leading to a disruption in oil supplies. The price of gasoline at the pump rose from $.27 a gallon in 1973 to $.50 a gallon in 1977, before shooting up to $1.40 a gallon by 1981.

When the price of gasoline soared, many public figures and commentators turned green. How, they asked, could Americans ever conserve on gasoline? After all, the distance from home to office was not going to shrink, and people had to commute to their jobs. What were workers to do? One solution found by American drivers was that when the time came to replace their old cars, they purchased smaller cars that offered more miles to the gallon.

Analysts classify car sales according to the size of the car—subcompact, compact, midsize, large, and so on. In both 1976 and 1977, just after the first rise in gas prices, about 2.5 million large cars, 2.8 million compacts, and 2.3 million subcompacts were bought per year. Roughly speaking, the same number of cars were being sold in all three categories. By 1985, however, the proportions had shifted drastically. About 1.5 million large cars were sold that year, a significant decline from the mid-1970s. However, 2.2 million subcompacts were sold, and the number of compact cars sold had climbed to 3.7 million.

The demand curve for any good (like cars) as-

sumes that the price of complementary goods (like gasoline) is fixed. The rise in gasoline prices caused the demand curve for small cars to shift out to the right and the demand curve for large cars to shift back to the left.

The reason is easy to see. Imagine that you drive 15,000 miles per year. A large car gets 15 miles to the gallon, meaning that you would need to buy 1,000 gallons of gasoline per year, while a small car gets 30 miles to the gallon, meaning that you would only have to buy 500 gallons of gas per year. When the price of gasoline was at its 1981 peak of $1.40 per gallon, this higher mileage translated into a savings of $700 per year, for the life of the car.

Sources: Gasoline prices taken from various issues of *Survey of Current Business;* auto sales figures from Linda Williams and Patricia Hu of Oak Ridge National Laboratory; *Light Duty Vehicle Summary: Model Year 1976 to the First Half of Model Year 1989.*

where "value in use" seems very different from "value in exchange." Figure 4.8 presents a demand and a supply curve for water. Individuals are willing to pay a high price for the water they need to live, as illustrated by point A on the demand curve. But above some quantity, B, people will pay almost nothing more for additional water. In most of the inhabited parts of the world, water is readily available, so it gets supplied in plentiful quantities at low prices. Normally, the supply curve of water intersects the demand curve to the right of B, as in the figure; hence the low equilibrium price. Of course, in the desert, the water supply may be very limited, and then the price may rise to very high levels.

To an economist, the statements that the price of diamonds is high and the price of water is low are statements about supply and demand conditions, not a deep philosophical assertion that diamonds are "more important" than water or "better" than water. They are not statements about value in use. Similarly, the fact that many writers or artists

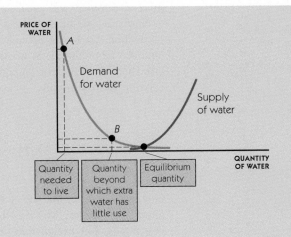

Figure 4.8 SUPPLY AND DEMAND FOR WATER

Point A shows that people are willing to pay a relatively high price for the first few units of water. But to the right of B, people have plenty of water already and are not willing to pay much for an additional amount. The price of water will be determined at the point where the supply curve crosses the demand curve. In most cases, the resulting price is extremely low.

make no money, while a few make fortunes, does not necessarily mean that those who make more money are "better," just that the conditions of supply and demand allow them to receive more money.

Price is related to the *marginal* value of an object, that is, the value of an additional unit of the object. Water has a low price not because the *total* value of water is low—it is obviously high, since we could not live without it—but because the marginal value, what we would be willing to pay to be able to drink one more glass of water a year, is not very high.

Supply and demand analysis provides an organized and logical framework for searching for an explanation of both the level of prices and their changes. When confronted by a question about prices, economists think about what the shape of the demand and supply curves look like, and where they might intersect. For example, why are doctors paid so much, and why have their salaries been declining relative to salaries in other professions?

In the short run, the supply of doctors is relatively fixed; it can only be augmented gradually, as more doctors are trained. If the supply is low, relative to the demand, the price paid for medical services will be high, and doctors' incomes will be high. For many years, the American Medical Association was able to keep the supply of doctors artificially low by controlling the number of places in approved medical schools. When those constraints were eliminated, medical schools expanded, and the high incomes attracted large numbers of students. In recent years, the supply of doctors has increased markedly, and as the law of supply and demand predicts, the relative income of doctors has declined. As in any other real-life example, there are numerous other factors that may partially account for the changing income of doctors too. But almost all of them can be analyzed, compared, and accommodated within the framework of supply and demand.

Just as economists take care to distinguish the words "price" and "value," they also distinguish the *price* of an object (what it sells for) from its *cost* (the expense of making the object). The two are distinct concepts. The costs of producing a good affect the price at which firms are willing to supply that good. An increase in the costs of production will normally cause prices to rise. While under some conditions, *in equilibrium*, the price of an object will equal its cost of production, this need not be the case.

Normally, we think of land as something that cannot be produced, so its cost of production can be considered infinite (though, admittedly, there are situations where land can be produced, as when Chicago filled in part of Lake Michigan to expand its lake shore). Yet there is an equilibrium price of land—where the demand for land is equal to its fixed supply.

SHIFTS IN DEMAND CURVES

One of the uses of the law of supply and demand is to be able to explain changes in prices; for instance, why it is that in one year the price of wheat rises and in another year it falls. The explanation lies in changes in the market demand curve, changes in the market supply curve, or both. We will take up changes in demand first.

The analysis so far has focused on one major determinant of how much will be demanded of a good: its price. Changes in the price of a good move us up and down

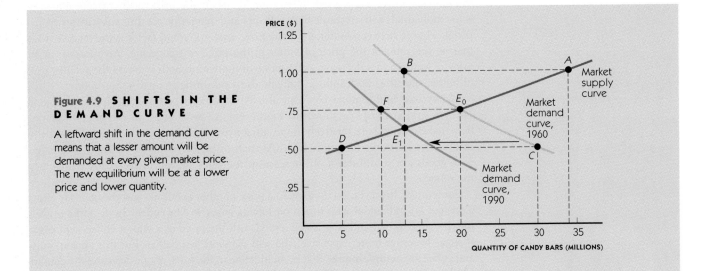

Figure 4.9 SHIFTS IN THE DEMAND CURVE

A leftward shift in the demand curve means that a lesser amount will be demanded at every given market price. The new equilibrium will be at a lower price and lower quantity.

the existing demand curve; they do not *shift* it. But what about the other factors that affect the quantity demanded, like income, the price of other goods, style, and season? Changes in any of these will lead to shifts in the demand curve.

Figure 4.9 shows hypothetical demand curves for candy bars in 1960 and in 1990. The 1960 curve replicates the demand curve in Figure 4.7. As Americans have become more health conscious, the demand curve for candy bars has shifted to the left, which means that the demand for candy bars at each price is less in 1990. We can see from the figure, for instance, that the demand for candy bars at a price of $.75 has decreased from 20 million candy bars (point E_0, the original equilibrium) to 10 million (point F).

Figure 4.9 also shows the supply curve for candy bars, which by assumption is unchanged from 1960 to 1990. For simplicity, we assume that the overall price level has remained unchanged over that period. The equilibrium is at the intersection of the demand and supply curves. The leftward shift in the demand curve thus has had two effects: the equilibrium price is lower and the equilibrium quantity is lower. Price is lowered from $.75 to $.62, and quantity is lowered from 20 million candy bars to 12.5 million. The new equilibrium is E_1. Notice that the reduction in quantity sold (from 20 million to 12.5 million) is less than would have occurred if the price had not fallen from $.75 to $.62 (in which case only 10 million candy bars would have been bought).

SOURCES OF SHIFTS IN DEMAND CURVES

Of the various factors that shift the demand curve, two—changes in income and in the price of other goods—are specifically economic factors. As an individual's income increases, she normally purchases more of any good. As we see in Figure 4.10, rising incomes shift the demand curve to the right. At each price, she consumes more of the good.

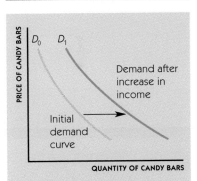

Figure 4.10 HOW IN-COME SHIFTS THE DEMAND CURVE

Normally, an increase in income leads to a higher quantity demanded of a good at each price. This is shown as a rightward shift of the demand curve.

Changes in the price of other goods, particularly closely related goods, will also shift the demand curve for a good. For example, when the price of margarine increases, some individuals will substitute butter. Butter and margarine are thus **substitutes.** When people choose between butter and margarine, one important factor is the relative price, that is, the ratio of the price of butter to the price of margarine. An increase in the price of butter and a decrease in the price of margarine both increase the relative price of butter, and thus both induce individuals to substitute margarine for butter.

Candy bars and granola bars can also be considered substitutes, as the two goods satisfy a similar need. As shown in Figure 4.11A, an increase in the price of granola bars makes candy bars relatively more attractive, and hence leads to a rightward shift in the demand curve for candy bars. (At each price, the demand for candy is greater.) Two goods are substitutes if an increase in the price of one *increases* the demand for the other.

Sometimes, however, an increase in a price of other goods has just the opposite effect. Consider an individual who insists on having sugar in her coffee. In deciding on how much coffee to demand, she is concerned with the price of a cup of coffee *with* sugar. If sugar becomes more expensive, she will demand less coffee. For this person, sugar and coffee are **complements;** that is, an increase in the price of one *decreases* the demand for the other. As shown in Figure 4.11B, the price increase of sugar shifts the demand curve of coffee to the left. (At each price, the demand for coffee is less.)

Noneconomic factors can also shift market demand curves. The major ones are changes in population and in taste. The demand for many goods differs markedly among different age groups. Young families with babies purchase disposable diapers. The demand for new houses and apartments is closely related to the number of newly formed households, which in turn depends on the number of individuals of marriageable age. The U.S. population has been growing older, on average, both because life expectancies are increasing and because birthrates fell somewhat after the baby boom that followed World War II; so there has been a shift in demand away from diapers and new houses. Economists working for particular firms and industries spend a considerable amount of energy ascertaining the population effects, called **demographic effects,** on the demand for the goods their firms sell.

Sometimes demand curves shift simply because of a shift in tastes. Since the 1970s,

Figure 4.11 SUBSTITUTES AND COMPLEMENTS

As shown in panel A, the demand curve for a particular good shifts to the right when the price of a substitute increases. As shown in panel B, the demand curve for a particular good shifts to the left when the price of a complement increases.

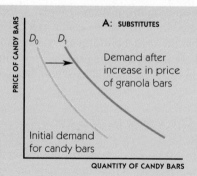

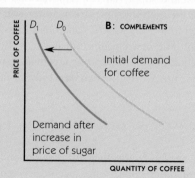

Americans have changed their drinking habits; they now consume more wine and less hard liquor than they did previously. There has been a shift in taste toward yogurt and away from buttermilk, toward low-cholesterol foods and away from fatty meats. Each of these changes has shifted the demand curve for the good in question.

Sometimes demand curves shift as the result of a change in information. Part of the change in the demand for alcohol may be due to improved consumer information about the dangers of alcohol. Certainly the shift in the demand for cigarettes is largely the result of heightened awareness of the effects of smoking.

People typically borrow to buy goods like cars and houses. At times, they may simply not be able to borrow from their usual sources, such as the bank. This reduced availability of credit may also give rise to a shift in the demand curve.

What households demand today depends not only on current income and prices but also on their expectations about the future. If people think they may become unemployed, they will reduce their spending in general, and the demand curve for certain goods like cars will shift. In this case, economists say that their demand curve depends on expectations.

SOURCES OF SHIFTS IN MARKET DEMAND CURVES

A change in income

A change in the price of a substitute

A change in the price of a complement

A change in the composition of the population

A change in tastes

A change in information

A change in the availability of credit

A change in expectations

SHIFTS IN A DEMAND CURVE VERSUS MOVEMENTS ALONG A DEMAND CURVE

It is important to distinguish between changes that result from a shift in the demand curve and changes that result from a *movement* along the demand curve. A movement along a demand curve is simply the change in the quantity demanded as the price changes. Figure 4.12A illustrates a movement along the demand curve from point A to point B; *given a demand curve*, at lower prices, more is consumed. Figure 4.12B illustrates a shift; the demand curve has shifted to the right, so that at a *given price*, more is consumed. Quantity again increases from Q_0 to Q_1, but the price stays the same.

Figure 4.12

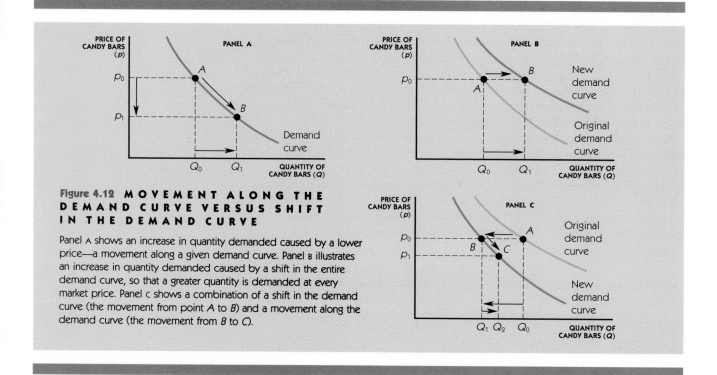

Figure 4.12 MOVEMENT ALONG THE DEMAND CURVE VERSUS SHIFT IN THE DEMAND CURVE

Panel A shows an increase in quantity demanded caused by a lower price—a movement along a given demand curve. Panel B illustrates an increase in quantity demanded caused by a shift in the entire demand curve, so that a greater quantity is demanded at every market price. Panel C shows a combination of a shift in the demand curve (the movement from point A to B) and a movement along the demand curve (the movement from B to C).

In practice, both effects are often present. Thus, in panel C, the movement from point A to point C—where the quantity demanded has been reduced from Q_0 to Q_2—can be thought of as consisting of two parts: a change in quantity demanded resulting from a shift in the demand curve (the reduction in quantity from Q_0 to Q_1) and a movement along the demand curve (the change from Q_1 to Q_2).

SHIFTS IN SUPPLY CURVES

Supply curves too can shift. Suppose a drought hits the breadbasket states of mid-America. Figure 4.13 illustrates the predictions of the law of supply and demand in this situation. The supply curve for wheat shifts to the left, which means that at each price of wheat, the quantity firms are willing to supply is smaller. The shift in the supply curve results in a lower equilibrium quantity (Q_3) and a higher equilibrium price (p_3). Notice that if the price had remained unchanged, the quantity produced would have fallen from Q_1 to Q_2. The increase in the price induces farmers to produce more. Thus, the equilibrium reduction in quantity from Q_1 to Q_3 is somewhat smaller than it would have been had price remained unchanged.

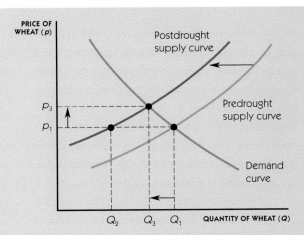

Figure 4.13 SHIFTING THE SUPPLY CURVE TO THE LEFT

A drought or other disaster (among other possible factors) will cause the supply curve to shift to the left, so that at each price, a smaller quantity is supplied. The new equilibrium will be at a higher market price but a lower quantity.

SOURCES OF SHIFTS IN SUPPLY CURVES

There are several sources of shifts in market supply curves. One is lower prices of the inputs used to produce a good. Figure 4.14 shows that as corn becomes less expensive, the supply curve for cornflakes shifts to the right. Producing cornflakes costs less, so at every price, firms are willing to supply a greater quantity. That is why the quantity supplied along the curve S_1 is greater than the quantity supplied, at the same price, along the curve S_0.

Improvements in technology, such as have occurred in the computer industry over the past two decades, will also lead to a rightward shift in the market supply curve. Another source of shifts is nature. The supply curve for agricultural goods may shift to the right or left depending on whether nature is kind or unkind, in the form of weather conditions, insect infestations, or animal diseases. Some economists would even categorize these changes in the natural environment as technology shifts, but this blurs an important distinction between changes in the known technology of farming and the vagaries to which these technologies are subjected.

Just as changed expectations concerning future income and prices can lead to a shift in the demand curve, changed expectations concerning new technologies or prices of inputs can lead to a shift in the supply curve. If firms believe that a new technology for making cars will become available in two years' time, this belief will discourage investment today and will lead to a temporary leftward shift in the supply curve. By the same token, a reduction in the availability of credit may curtail firms' ability to borrow to obtain inputs needed for production, and this too will induce a leftward shift in the supply curve.

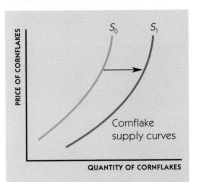

Figure 4.14 SHIFTING THE SUPPLY CURVE TO THE RIGHT

An improvement in technology or a reduction in input prices (among other possible factors) will cause the supply curve to shift to the right, so that at each price, a larger quantity is supplied.

CLOSE-UP: THE DROUGHT OF 1988 AS A SUPPLY SHOCK

For the midwestern United States, 1988 brought one of the worst droughts ever recorded. Corn production was 35 percent lower than had been expected before the drought; soybean production was down more than 20 percent, wheat was down more than 10 percent, and oats and barley were down more than 40 percent. The examples could go on and on. From an economist's perspective, an unpredictable event like a severe drought is a good example of a shift in the supply curve. The drought reduced the amount of any crop that could be supplied at any given price, which means that the supply curve itself shifted to the left.

As an economist would predict, this shift in the supply curve led to higher prices for these farm products. To cite some of the extreme examples, corn prices rose by 80 percent by the end of the summer, soybeans by almost 70 percent, and wheat by 50 percent.

The drought also had a number of predictable side effects on substitute and complement goods. For example, higher prices in the United States stimulated foreign agricultural production. Since much grain is fed to cattle, the higher price of grain led many farmers to slaughter their cattle sooner than they had originally planned. As a result, meat production rose slightly in 1988, and meat prices (adjusted for inflation) dropped slightly. Supermarket prices increased sharply for consumers in the middle of the summer; fruit and vegetable prices were up 5 percent in July 1988, and egg prices were up nearly 10 percent in that month alone.

Despite these many side effects, the drought of 1988 had only a temporary effect on prices and quantities. Because of stockpiles of goods and the possibility of buying farm products from other nations, the agricultural system has enough flexibility to get through a bad year.

SOURCES OF SHIFTS IN MARKET SUPPLY CURVES

A change in the prices of inputs
A change in technology
A change in the natural environment
A change in expectations
A change in the availability of credit

SHIFTS IN A SUPPLY CURVE VERSUS MOVEMENTS ALONG A SUPPLY CURVE

The same care that is taken in distinguishing between a movement along a demand curve and a shift in the demand curve must be taken with market supply curves. In Figure 4.15A, the price of candy bars has gone up, with a corresponding increase in quantity supplied. There has been a movement along the supply curve. The increase in price may itself have arisen from a rightward shift in the market demand curve.

By contrast, in Figure 4.15B, the supply curve has shifted to the right, perhaps because a new production technique has made it cheaper to produce candy bars. Now, even though the price does not change, the quantity supplied increases. The quantity supplied in the market can increase either because the price of the good has increased—and at a higher price, for a *given supply curve*, the quantity produced is higher; or because the supply curve has shifted, so that at a *given price*, the quantity supplied has increased.

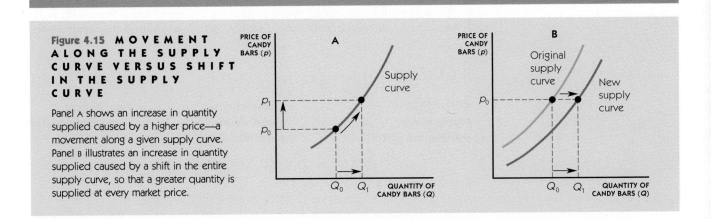

Figure 4.15 MOVEMENT ALONG THE SUPPLY CURVE VERSUS SHIFT IN THE SUPPLY CURVE

Panel A shows an increase in quantity supplied caused by a higher price—a movement along a given supply curve. Panel B illustrates an increase in quantity supplied caused by a shift in the entire supply curve, so that a greater quantity is supplied at every market price.

REVIEW AND PRACTICE

SUMMARY

1. An individual's demand curve gives the quantity demanded of a good at each possible price. It normally slopes down, which means that the person demands a greater quantity of the good at lower prices and a lesser quantity at higher prices.

2. The market demand curve gives the total quantity of a good demanded by all individuals in an economy at each price. As the price rises, demand falls, both because each person demands less of the good and because some people exit the market.

3. A firm's supply curve gives the amount of a good the firm is willing to supply at each price. It is normally upward sloping, which means that firms supply a greater quantity of the good at higher prices and a lesser quantity at lower prices.

4. The market supply curve gives the total quantity of a good that all firms in the economy are willing to produce at each price. As the price rises, supply rises, both because each firm supplies more of the good and because some additional firms enter the market.

5. The law of supply and demand says that in competitive markets, the equilibrium price is that price at which quantity demanded equals quantity supplied. It is represented on a graph by the intersection of the demand and supply curves.

6. A demand curve *only* shows the relationship between quantity demanded and price. Changes in tastes, in demographic factors, in income, in the prices of other goods, in information, in the availability of credit, or in expectations are reflected in a shift of the entire demand curve.

7. A supply curve *only* shows the relationship between quantity supplied and price. Changes in factors such as technology, the prices of inputs, the natural environment, expectations, or the availability of credit are reflected in a shift of the entire supply curve.

8. It is important to distinguish movements along a demand curve from shifts in the demand curve, and movements along a supply curve from shifts in the supply curve.

KEY TERMS

demand curve	excess supply	complement
supply curve	excess demand	demographic effects
equilibrium price	substitute	

REVIEW QUESTIONS

1. Why does an individual's demand curve normally slope down? Why does a market demand curve normally slope down?

2. Why does a firm's supply curve normally slope up? Why does a market supply curve normally slope up?

3. What is the significance of the point where supply and demand curves intersect?

4. Explain why, if the price of a good is above the equilibrium price, the forces of supply and demand will tend to push the price toward equilibrium. Explain why, if the price of the good is below the equilibrium price, the market will tend to adjust toward equilibrium.

5. Name some factors that could shift the demand curve out to the right.

6. Name some factors that could shift the supply curve in to the left.

PROBLEMS

1. Imagine a company lunchroom that sells pizza by the slice. Using the following data, plot the points and graph the demand and supply curves. What is the equilibrium price and quantity? Find a price at which excess demand would exist and a price at which excess supply would exist, and plot them on your diagram.

Price per slice	Demand (number of slices)	Supply (number of slices)
$1	420	0
$2	210	100
$3	140	140
$4	105	160
$5	84	170

2. Suppose a severe drought hit the sugarcane crop. Predict how this would affect the equilibrium price and quantity in the market for sugar and the market for honey. Draw supply and demand diagrams to illustrate your answers.

3. Imagine that a new invention allows each mine worker to mine twice as much coal. Predict how this will affect the equilibrium price and quantity in the market for coal and the market for heating oil. Draw supply and demand diagrams to illustrate your answer.

4. Americans' tastes have shifted away from beef and toward chicken. Predict how this change affects the equilibrium price and quantity in the market for beef, the market for chicken, and the market for roadside hamburger stands. Draw supply and demand diagrams to illustrate your answer.

5. During the 1970s, the postwar baby boomers reached working age, and it became more acceptable for married women with children to work. Predict how this increase in the number of workers is likely to affect the equilibrium wage and quantity of employment. Draw supply and demand curves to illustrate your answer.

CHAPTER 5

USING DEMAND AND SUPPLY

The concepts of demand and supply are among the most useful in economics. The demand and supply framework explains why doctors are paid more than lawyers, or why the income of unskilled workers has increased less than that of skilled workers. It can also be used to predict what the demand for condominiums or disposable diapers will be fifteen years from now, or what will happen if the government increases the tax on cigarettes. Not only can we predict that prices will change, we can predict by how much they will change.

This chapter has two purposes. The first is to develop some of the concepts required to make these kinds of predictions, and to illustrate how the demand and supply framework can be used in a variety of contexts.

The second is to look at what happens when people interfere with the workings of competitive markets. Rents may seem too high for poor people to afford adequate housing. The wages of unskilled workers may seem too low for people to live on. Prices of corn may seem unfairly low, not adequate to compensate farmers for their work. With such hardship, it is only natural that political pressures develop to intervene on behalf of the disadvantaged. (Political pressures do not come only from the disadvantaged. Voters in California, for instance, elected to force insurance companies to reduce their premiums.) In the second part of this chapter, we explore the consequences of these interventions.

It was a dark and stormy night. From the heavy, brooding clouds poured great torrents of rain, a cold rain, whipped to a frenzy by a biting, metallic wind.

"If this keeps up," he thought, "I should be able to sell at least two dozen umbrellas an hour . . ."

KEY QUESTIONS

1. What is meant by the concept of elasticity? Why does it play such an important role in predicting market outcomes?

2. What happens when market outcomes are interfered with, as when the government imposes price floors and ceilings? Why do such interferences give rise to shortages and surpluses?

SENSITIVITY TO PRICE CHANGES

If tomorrow supermarkets across the country were to cut the price of bread or milk by 50 percent, the quantity demanded of these items would not change much. If stores offered the same reduction on ice cream, however, demand would increase substantially. Why do price changes sometimes have small effects and at other times large ones? The answer lies in the shape of the demand and supply curves.

The demand for ice cream is more sensitive to price changes than is the demand for milk, and this is reflected in the shape of the demand curves as illustrated in Figure 5.1. The demand curve for ice cream (panel A) is flatter than the one for milk (panel B). When the demand curve is very flat, it means that a change in price, say by 5 percent, from $2.00 a gallon to $2.10, has a large effect on the quantity consumed. In panel A, the demand for ice cream decreases from 100 million pints at a price of $2.00 a pint to 90 million pints at a price of $2.10 per pint.

By contrast, when the demand curve is very steep, it means that a change in price has little effect on quantity. In panel B, the demand for milk decreases from 100 million gallons at $2.00 per gallon to 99 million gallons at $2.10 per gallon. But saying that the demand curve is steep or flat just pushes the question back a step: why are some demand curves steeper than others?

The answer is that though substitutes exist for almost every good or service, substitution will be more difficult for some goods and services than for others. When substitution is difficult, then even when the price increases, the quantity demanded will not decrease by very much. Similarly, when the price falls, demand does not increase very much.

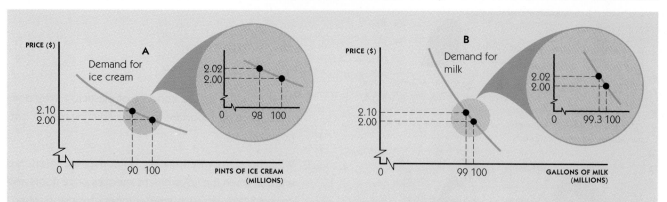

Figure 5.1 ELASTIC VERSUS INELASTIC DEMAND CURVES

Panel A shows a hypothetical demand curve for ice cream. Note that quantity demanded changes rapidly with fairly small price changes, indicating that demand for ice cream is elastic. The telescoped portion of the demand curve shows that a 1 percent rise in price leads to a 2 percent fall in quantity demanded. Panel B shows a hypothetical demand curve for milk. Note that quantity demanded changes very little, regardless of changes in price, meaning that demand for milk is inelastic. The telescoped portion of the demand curve shows that a 1 percent rise in price leads to a .7 percent fall in quantity demanded.

The typical consumer does not substitute milk for beer—or for anything else—even if milk becomes a good deal cheaper.

When substitution is easy, on the other hand, a fall in price may lead to a very large increase in quantity demanded. For instance, there are many very good substitutes for ice cream, including sherbets and frozen yogurts. The price decrease for ice cream means that these close substitutes have become relatively more expensive, and the demand for ice cream would thus increase significantly.

THE PRICE ELASTICITY OF DEMAND

For many purposes, economists need to be more precise about how steep or how flat the demand curve is. They use the concept of the **price elasticity of demand** (for short, the price elasticity or the elasticity of demand). The price elasticity of demand is defined as the percentage change in the quantity demanded divided by the percentage change in price. In mathematical terms,

$$\text{elasticity of demand} = \frac{\text{percent change in quantity demanded}}{\text{percent change in price}}.$$

If the quantity demanded changes 8 percent in response to a 2 percent change in price, then the elasticity of demand is 4.

(Price elasticities of demand are really *negative* numbers; that is, when the price increases, quantities demanded are reduced. Usually, however, we simply write the price elasticity of, say, tobacco as .6, understanding that this means that when the price increases by 1 percent, the quantity demanded decreases by .6 percent.)

It is easiest to calculate the elasticity of demand when there is just a 1 percent change in price. Then the elasticity of demand is just the percent change in the quantity demanded. In the telescoped portion of Figure 5.1A, we see that increasing the price of ice cream from $2.00 a pint to $2.02—a 1 percent increase in price—reduces the demand from 100 million pints to 98 million, a 2 percent decline. So we say the price elasticity of demand for ice cream is 2.

By contrast, assume that the price of milk increases from $2.00 a gallon to $2.02 (again a 1 percent increase in price), as shown in the telescoped portion of Figure 5.1B. This reduces demand from 100 million gallons per year to 99.3 million. Demand has gone down by .7 percent, so the price elasticity of demand is therefore .7. Larger numerical values for price elasticity indicate that demand is more sensitive to changes in price, while smaller values indicate that demand is less sensitive to price changes.

It behooves business firms to pay attention to the price elasticity of demand for their products. Suppose that a cement producer, the only one in town, is considering a 1 percent price increase and wants to know what that will do to revenues. The firm hires an economist to estimate the elasticity of demand, so that it will know what will happen to sales when it raises its price. The economist tells the firm that its demand elasticity is 2. This means that if the price of cement rises by 1 percent, the quantity sold will decline by 2 percent.[1]

The firm's executives will not be pleased by the findings. To see why, assume that initially the price of cement was $1,000 per ton, and 100,000 tons were sold. To calculate revenues, you multiply the price times the quantity sold. So initially revenues were $1,000 × 100,000 = $100 million. With a 1 percent increase, the price will be $1,010. If the elasticity of demand is 2, then a 1 percent price increase results in a 2 percent decrease in the quantity sold. With a 2 percent quantity decrease, sales are now 98,000 tons. Revenues are down to $98.98 million ($1,010 × 98,000), just slightly over 1 percent. Because of the high elasticity figure, this cement firm's price *increase* leads to a *decrease* in revenues.

The price elasticity of demand works the same way for price decreases. Suppose the cement producer decided to decrease the price of cement 1 percent, to $990. With an elasticity of demand of 2, sales would then increase 2 percent, to 102,000 tons. Thus, revenues would *increase* to $100,980,000 ($990 × 102,000), that is, by almost 1 percent.

In the case where the price elasticity is **unity,** or 1, the decrease in the quantity demanded just offsets the increase in the price, so price increases have no effect on revenues. If the price elasticity is less than unity, then when the price of a good increases by 1 percent, the quantity demanded is reduced by less than 1 percent. Since there is not much reduction in demand, elasticities in this range, between 0 and 1, mean that price increases will also increase revenues. And price decreases will decrease revenues. We say that the demand for that good is **relatively inelastic,** or *insensitive* to price changes.

On the other hand, if the price elasticity for a good is greater than unity, then when the price increases by 1 percent, the quantity demanded is reduced by more than 1 percent. Thus, price increases mean that total revenues for that good will be reduced. Price decreases will increase revenues. The increase in sales more than offsets the

---

[1] There is a simple relationship between price elasticity and revenue. Revenue is just price times quantity. If prices go up by 1 percent and quantity remains unchanged, then revenue rises by 1 percent. But normally the quantity sold decreases. The amount it decreases depends on the elasticity of demand. The percentage change in revenues from a 1 percent change in price = 1 − elasticity of demand.

Table 5.1 SOME PRICE ELASTICITIES IN THE U.S. ECONOMY

Industry	Elasticity
Elastic demands	
Purchased meals	2.27
Metals	1.52
Furniture, timber	1.25
Motor vehicles	1.14
Transportation	1.03
Inelastic demands	
Gas, electricity, water	.92
Oil	.91
Chemicals	.89
Beverages	.78
Tobacco	.61
Food	.58
Housing services	.55
Clothing	.49
Books, magazines, newspapers	.34
Meat	.2

Sources: Ahson Mansur and John Whalley, "Numerical Specification of Applied General Equilibrium Models: Estimation, Calibration, and Data," in Scarf and Shoven, eds., *Applied General Equilibrium Analysis* (New York: Cambridge University Press, 1984), p. 109; Hendrik S. Houthakker and Lester D. Taylor, *Consumer Demand in the United States: Analysis and Projections* (Cambridge: Harvard University Press, 1970).

decreased price. We say that the demand for that good is **relatively elastic,** or *sensitive* to price changes.

There are two extreme cases that deserve attention. One is that of a flat demand curve, a curve that is perfectly horizontal. We say that such a demand curve is perfectly elastic, or has infinite elasticity, since even a slight increase in the price results in demand dropping to zero. The other case is that of a steep demand curve, a curve that is perfectly vertical. We say that such a demand curve is perfectly inelastic, or has zero elasticity, since no matter what the change in price, demand remains the same.

The elasticity of demand for most foods is low (an increase in price will not affect demand much), while the elasticity of demand for most luxuries, such as perfume, ski trips, and Mercedes cars, is relatively high (an increase in price will lead to much less demand). Table 5.1 gives the elasticities of demand for some important goods. For example, the price elasticity of food and of tobacco is about .6, in contrast to the price elasticity for motor vehicles, which is 1.14. The table also shows the price elasticities for broad groups of goods. While it may be easy to substitute purchased meals for home-cooked food, it is difficult to do without food. Thus, the price elasticity of purchased meals is 2.27, while the price elasticity of all food is much lower, at .58. More generally, goods for which it is easy to find substitutes will have high price elasticities; goods for which substitutes cannot easily be found will have low price elasticities.

SMALL VERSUS LARGE PRICE CHANGES

So far, we have focused our attention on small price changes. If the elasticity of demand for apples is 2 (a 1 percent increase in price will lead to a 2 percent decrease in quantity demanded), then an increase in the price of apples by 1 percent will decrease the quantity demanded by 2 percent (2×1). A decrease in the price of apples by 3 percent will increase the quantity demanded by 6 percent (2×3).

But what about large price changes? With a price elasticity of 2, will a 25 percent price increase reduce demand by 50 percent? The answer is, in general, no, and the reason is illustrated in Figure 5.2. For high prices, such as at point A, the demand curve is very inelastic, while for low prices, demand is very elastic. Many demand curves have this shape. At low prices, such as at point B, there are many substitutes for the product. For example, when the price of aluminum is low, it is used as a food wrap (aluminum foil), for cans, and for airplanes. As the price increases, customers constantly seek out more and more substitutes. At first, substitutes are easy to find, and the demand for the product is greatly reduced. For example, plastic wrap can be used instead of aluminum foil. As the price rises still further, tin is used instead of aluminum for cans. At very high prices, say near point A, aluminum is used only where its lightweight properties are essential, such as in airplane frames. At this point, a price increase will not affect the demand for aluminum very much; it may take a *huge* price increase before steel or some other material becomes an economical substitute. [2]

USING THE PRICE ELASTICITY OF DEMAND

Using the elasticity of demand to predict the consequences of price changes is a fairly straightforward process. Assume prices of oil are expected to rise by 10 percent over the

___

[2] It is important to note that even along a straight-line demand curve, the elasticity changes, as explained in the appendix to this chapter.

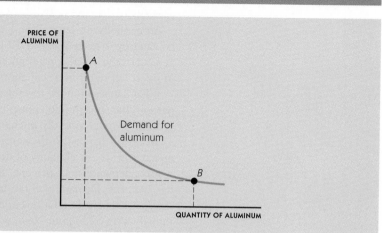

Figure 5.2 CHANGING ELASTICITY ALONG A DEMAND CURVE

Near point A, where the price is high, the demand curve is quite steep and inelastic. In the area of the demand curve near B, the demand curve is very flat and elastic.

PRICE OF ALUMINUM

Demand for aluminum

QUANTITY OF ALUMINUM

PRICE ELASTICITY OF DEMAND

ELASTICITY	DESCRIPTION	EFFECT ON QUANTITY DEMANDED OF 1% INCREASE IN PRICE	EFFECT ON REVENUES OF 1% INCREASE IN PRICE
Zero	Perfectly inelastic (vertical demand curve)	Zero	Increased by 1%
Between 0 and 1	Inelastic	Reduced by less than 1%	Increased by less than 1%
1	Unitary elasticity	Reduced by 1%	Unchanged
Greater than 1	Elastic	Reduced by more than 1%	Reduced; the greater the elasticity, the more revenue is reduced
Infinite	Perfectly elastic (horizontal demand curve)	Reduced to zero	Reduced to zero

next two years. What will this do to the consumption of oil in the United States, if the elasticity of demand is 1?

An elasticity of demand of 1 means that a 1 percent increase in price will reduce demand by 1 percent. So a 10 percent increase in price will reduce demand by 10 percent. If the initial consumption was 100 million barrels, then the 10 percent increase in price will result in a reduction in demand by 10 million barrels, to 90 million.

What happens to total revenues from oil consumption? The price has gone up by 10 percent, the consumption down by 10 percent. The two effects are just offsetting. Total revenues remain virtually unchanged.

What will happen to the consumption of oil in the United States if the elasticity of demand is .7? An elasticity of demand of .7 means that a 1 percent increase in price reduces demand by .7 percent. So a 10 percent increase in price will reduce demand by 7 percent. Demand will fall from 100 million barrels to 93 million.

What happens to total revenues? If the initial price was $20 a barrel, total revenues initially were $2 billion. Now, with a price of $22 a barrel (a 10 percent increase from $20), they have gone up to $22 × 93 million = $2.04 billion.

SHORT RUN VERSUS LONG RUN

It is always easier to make adjustments when you have a longer time to make them. Economists distinguish between the long run, the period in which all adjustments can be made, and the short run, in which at least some adjustments cannot be made. As a result, demand is likely to be less elastic (less sensitive to price changes) in the short run than in the long run, when consumers have time to adapt. Figure 5.3 illustrates the difference in shape between short-run and long-run demand curves.

The sharp increase in oil prices in the 1970s provides an outstanding example. The short-run price elasticity of gasoline was .2 (a 1 percent increase in price led to only a .2 percent decrease in quantity demanded), while the long-run elasticity was .7 or more; the short-run elasticity of fuel oil was .2, and the long-run elasticity was 1.2. In the short run, consumers were stuck with their old gas-guzzling cars, their drafty houses, and their old fuel-wasting habits. In the long run, however, consumers bought smaller

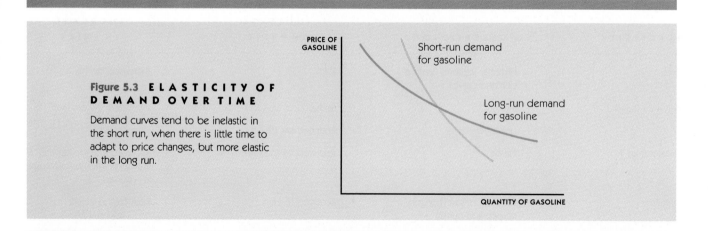

Figure 5.3 ELASTICITY OF DEMAND OVER TIME

Demand curves tend to be inelastic in the short run, when there is little time to adapt to price changes, but more elastic in the long run.

PRICE OF GASOLINE

Short-run demand for gasoline

Long-run demand for gasoline

QUANTITY OF GASOLINE

cars, became used to houses with slightly lower temperatures, installed better insulation in their homes, and turned to wood-burning stoves, coal, natural gas, and other alternative energy sources. The long-run demand curve was therefore much more elastic (flat) than the short-run curve; and indeed, the long-run elasticity turned out to be much larger than anticipated.

How long is the long run, and how short is the short run? The example of the response to the oil price increases shows that there is no simple answer to that question. It will vary from product to product. In some cases, adjustments can occur rapidly; in other cases, they are very gradual. As old gas guzzlers wore out, they were replaced with fuel-efficient compact cars. As furnaces wore out, they were replaced with more efficient ones. New homes are now constructed with more insulation, so that gradually, over time, the fraction of houses that are well insulated is increasing. Thus, two decades after the initial increase in the price of oil, the adjustments are not yet completed.

THE PRICE ELASTICITY OF SUPPLY

Supply curves normally slope upward, but they are very steep in some cases and very flat in others. As with demand curves, the degree of steepness reflects sensitivity to price changes. A steep supply curve, like the one for oil in Figure 5.4A, means that a very large change in price generates only a small change in the quantity firms would like to produce. By contrast, a flatter curve, like the one for chicken in Figure 5.4B, means that a small change in price generates a large change in supply. Just as with demand, economists have developed a more precise way of representing the sensitivity of supply to prices. They use a concept that parallels the one already introduced: the **price elasticity of supply** is defined as the percentage change in quantity supplied divided by the percentage change in price (or the percentage change in quantity supplied corresponding to a price change of 1 percent).

The elasticity of supply of oil is low—an increase in the price of oil will not have a significant effect on the total supply. The elasticity of supply of chicken is very high, as President Nixon found out when he imposed price controls in August 1971. When the price of chicken was forced to slightly lower than the market equilibrium price, less than 10 percent lower, farmers found it was simply unprofitable to produce chickens and sell them at that price; there was a large decrease in the quantity supplied, and the result was huge shortages.

As is the case with demand, if a 1 percent increase in price results in more than a 1 percent increase in supply, we say that the supply curve is elastic, and if a 1 percent increase in price results in less than a 1 percent increase in supply, we say that the supply curve is inelastic. In the extreme case of a vertical supply curve—where the amount supplied does not depend at all on price—the curve is said to be perfectly inelastic, or to have zero elasticity; and in the extreme case of a horizontal supply curve, the curve is said to be perfectly elastic, or to have infinite elasticity.

Just as the demand elasticity differs at different points of the demand curve, so too for the supply curve. Figure 5.5 shows a typical supply curve in manufacturing. An example might be ball bearings. At very low prices, plants are just covering their operating costs. Some plants shut down. In this situation, a small increase in price elicits a large increase in supply. The supply curve is relatively flat (elastic). But eventually, not only

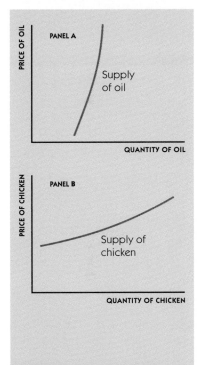

Figure 5.4 DIFFERING ELASTICITIES OF SUPPLY

Panel A shows a supply curve for oil. It is inelastic: quantity supplied increases only a small amount with a rise in price. Panel B shows a supply curve for chicken. It is elastic: quantity supplied increases substantially with a rise in price.

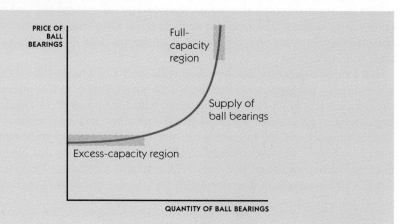

Figure 5.5 CHANGING ELASTICITY ALONG A SUPPLY CURVE

When output is low and many machines are idle, a small change in price can lead to a large increase in quantity produced, so the supply curve is flat and elastic. When output is high and all machines are working close to their limit, it takes a very large price change to induce even a small change in output; the supply curve is steep and inelastic.

are all machines being worked, factories are working all three shifts. In this situation, it may be hard to increase supply further, so that beyond some point, the supply curve becomes close to vertical (inelastic); that is, however much the price increases, the supply will not change very much.

USING THE PRICE ELASTICITY OF SUPPLY

Again, it is easy to use the concept of price elasticity of supply to predict what will happen to the quantity produced when prices increase. Assume that prices of oil are expected to rise by 10 percent over the next two years. What will this do to the supply of oil in the United States, if the elasticity of supply is .5?

An elasticity of supply of .5 means that a 1 percent increase in price results in a .5 percent increase in quantity produced. Thus, a 10 percent increase in price will result in a 5 percent (10 × .5) increase in quantity produced. (Note that with elasticity of demand, a price increase leads to a decrease in quantity demanded, but with elasticity of supply, a price increase leads to an *increase* in supply.)

SHORT RUN VERSUS LONG RUN

Just as economists distinguish between the responsiveness of demand to price in the short run and in the long run, so too with supply. The fact that firms can respond to an increase in prices in the long run in ways that they cannot in the short run means that the long-run supply elasticity is greater than the short-run. We define the short-run supply curve as the supply response *given the current stock of machines and buildings;* by contrast, in the long run, we assume that the stock of machines and buildings can adjust.

Farm crops are a typical example of a good whose supply in the short run is not very sensitive to changes in price; that is, the supply curve is steep (inelastic). After farmers have done their spring planting, they are committed to a certain level of production. If the price of their crop goes up, they cannot go back and plant more. If the price falls, theoretically farmers could decide to cut the supply by not harvesting their crops, but

CLOSE-UP: THE SURPRISING ELASTICITY OF DEMAND FOR LUXURIES

Late in 1990, as part of an overall package to reduce the U.S. budget deficit, the Congress adopted a 10 percent "luxury tax" on such big-ticket items as pleasure boats, private airplanes, high-priced cars, jewelry, and furs. Such luxury taxes are often popular because most people do not have to pay them. All taxes are painful to someone, but surely a tax that weighs only on rich people who are buying frivolous luxuries is one of the more socially painless ways to raise money.

However, the discussion of elasticity and inelasticity in this chapter should make you suspicious of a key assumption underlying this tax. The assumption was that the demand for these luxury goods was quite inelastic. We can think of the luxury tax as increasing the total cost the producers face in bringing a good to market, so the supply curve effectively shifts up. Thus, when the industry supply curve shifted up in response to the new luxury tax, the equilibrium quantity would change little while the equilibrium price would rise, as the rich simply paid the extra cost.

If the demand for these luxury goods was reasonably elastic, however, then the upward shift in the supply curve would lead to a much smaller rise in equilibrium price and a large fall in equilibrium quantity. As it happened, sales of pleasure boats fell by nearly 90 percent in south Florida in early 1991, as prospective buyers bought boats in the Bahamas to avoid paying the tax. Sales of high-priced cars like Mercedes and Lexus also fell substantially in early 1991. The situation of sellers of luxury goods was made even worse by the recession in 1991, which reduced the income of many prospective buyers, thus shifting the demand curve for luxuries back to the left as well.

This unexpected elasticity of demand carried two bits of bad news for the economy. First, rather than falling on the wealthy as had been hoped, the burden of the new luxury tax actually ended up falling on the workers and retailers who manufacture and sell these luxury items, many of whom are middle class at best. Second, the luxury tax raised far less money than had been expected. The Congressional Budget Office had forecast that the tax would raise about $1.5 billion over five years. But in 1991, it raised only about $30 million. Once the costs of setting up and enforcing the new tax were considered, it probably lost money for the government in its first year.

Sources: Bernard Baumohl, "Tempest in a Yacht Basin," *Time,* July 1, 1991, p. 52; Nick Ravo, "Big Boats Take It on the Chin," *New York Times,* April 14, 1991, sec. III, p. 9.

PRICE ELASTICITY OF SUPPLY

ELASTICITY	DESCRIPTION	EFFECT ON QUANTITY SUPPLIED OF 1% INCREASE IN PRICE
Zero	Perfectly inelastic (vertical supply curve)	Zero
Between 0 and 1	Inelastic	Increased by less than 1%
1	Unitary elasticity	Increased by 1%
Greater than 1	Elastic	Increased by more than 1%
Infinite	Perfectly elastic (horizontal supply curve)	Infinite increase

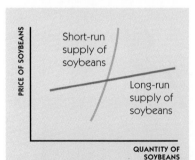

Figure 5.6 ELASTICITY OF SUPPLY OVER TIME

Supply curves may be inelastic in the short run and very elastic in the long run, as in the case of agricultural crops like soybeans.

the price would have to fall very, very low to justify that sort of waste. Thus, in this case, the supply curve is relatively close to vertical, as illustrated by the steeper curve in Figure 5.6.

On the other hand, the long-run supply curve for many crops is very flat (elastic). A relatively small change in price can lead to a large change in the quantity supplied. A small increase in the price of soybeans relative to the price of corn may induce many farmers to shift their planting from corn and other crops to soybeans, generating a large increase in the quantity of soybeans. This is also illustrated in Figure 5.6.

Earlier, we noted the response of consumers to the marked increase in the price of oil in the 1970s. The long-run demand elasticity was much higher than the short-run. So too for supply. The higher prices drove firms, both in the United States and abroad in places like Canada, Mexico, and the North Sea off the coast of Great Britain, to explore for more oil. Though the alternative supplies could only be increased to a limited extent in the short run (the short-run supply curve was inelastic, or steep), the long run had greater potential for increasing supply. Because new supplies were found, the long-run supply elasticity was much higher (the supply curve was flatter) than the short-run supply elasticity.

To know when long-run effects set in, we need to know the industry. Consider truck transportation. In the short run, we can increase the "supply" (miles driven) simply by having existing drivers drive all night and on weekends. In the long run, we can increase the number of trucks and drivers on the road. This will only take a few months, at most; it does not take long to increase the supply of trucks. The long run for other industries, on the other hand, can be a longer time. It takes years to build a new electric power–generating station.

IDENTIFYING PRICE AND QUANTITY ADJUSTMENTS

When the demand curve for a good such as wine shifts to the right—when, for instance, wine becomes more popular, so that at each price the demand is greater—there is an increase in both the equilibrium price of wine and the quantity demanded, or consumed. Similarly, when the supply curve for a good such as corn shifts to the left—because, for instance, of a drought that hurt the year's crop, so that at each price farmers supply less—there is an increase in the equilibrium price of corn and a decrease in quantity. Knowing that the shifts in the demand or supply curve will lead to an adjustment in both price *and* quantity is helpful, but it is even more useful to know whether most of the impact of a change will be on price or on quantity. For this, we have to consider the price elasticity of both the demand and supply curves.

SOME EXTREME CASES

At the extreme, all of the effect of a change in supply or demand will be translated fully into either price changes or quantity changes. These extreme cases are somewhat hypothetical, but they should help in understanding what happens in the more usual cases.

Figure 5.7 depicts the two extreme cases for a shift in the demand curve. In panel A, the supply curve is perfectly flat. A situation where this might be the case is in the yo-yo industry. Each yo-yo manufacturer could easily increase its output just by buying more machines and hiring proportionately more workers. If the firm doubled the number of machines and doubled its work force, its output would double. Because the industry is so small, if the producers of yo-yos doubled or even quadrupled their output, it would have little effect on what they have to pay either for machines or workers. In short, a small change in the price would elicit an enormous increase in quantity supplied. If yo-yos sold for a price just above what it costs to produce them, producers would rush in to supply more; at a lower price, firms would rather shut down than incur losses.

Figure 5.7 INFINITE AND ZERO ELASTICITY OF SUPPLY

Panel A shows a flat, infinitely elastic supply curve. Since, in this case, industry is willing to supply any amount at a certain price, shifts in demand will only affect the equilibrium quantity. Panel B shows a vertical, zero-elasticity supply curve. Here, since the quantity supplied does not change regardless of price, shifts in the demand curve will now affect only price, not quantity.

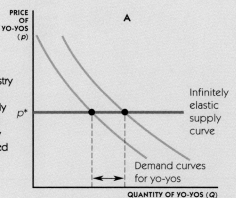

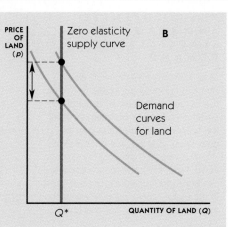

In the extreme case depicted in Figure 5.7A, below p^*, firms are not willing to supply any of the good, but at or above p^*, they are willing to supply an unlimited quantity. Since a small change in the price around p^* leads to an **infinite** rise or fall in the quantity supplied, this is a case where the price elasticity of supply is infinite. *A shift in demand is reflected only in a change in quantity purchased*; since the firms are willing to produce any amount at the price p^*, the market equilibrium price remains unchanged.

In Figure 5.7B, the supply curve is vertical. The supply curve of natural resources, such as land, is generally vertical. Nature, not prices, determines the quantity available. Likewise, the supply of paintings by van Gogh—or for that matter, any painter who has passed on—is also vertical, or inelastic. Firms simply cannot increase the quantity produced beyond Q^*; but they are willing to produce Q^* regardless of the price. Here, the supply curve has **zero elasticity,** because no change in price, no matter how large, will change the quantity produced. In that case, as eager consumers bid more for the fixed supply, *the shifts in the demand are reflected only in price changes.*

Similarly, different demand elasticities lead to very different consequences of a shift in the supply curve. Figure 5.8 depicts two special cases. When the demand curve for a good is horizontal (perfectly elastic)—that is, consumers are willing to consume an indefinite amount at the price p^*, but nothing at a price beyond p^*—the market equilibrium price remains unchanged, and *the shift in the supply curve simply increases the quantity purchased.* The demand curve will be horizontal if there exists a *perfect* substitute for the good. If two goods are perfect substitutes, consumers will choose the cheapest. If Coca-Cola and Pepsi were perfect substitutes, then if the price of Coke were a penny higher than the price of Pepsi, everyone would switch to Pepsi; everyone would drink Coke if its price were a penny lower. Thus, a small change in the price causes a very large change in quantity demanded. Figure 5.8A depicts the extreme case where the demand curve is horizontal.

The other extreme is where the demand curve is vertical, as shown in Figure 5.8B. Here the elasticity of demand is zero. Consumers demand the quantity Q^*; they are

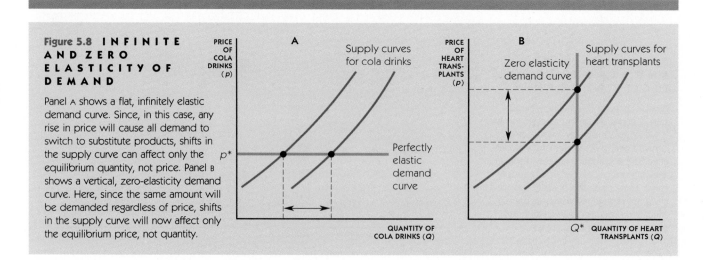

Figure 5.8 INFINITE AND ZERO ELASTICITY OF DEMAND

Panel A shows a flat, infinitely elastic demand curve. Since, in this case, any rise in price will cause all demand to switch to substitute products, shifts in the supply curve can affect only the equilibrium quantity, not price. Panel B shows a vertical, zero-elasticity demand curve. Here, since the same amount will be demanded regardless of price, shifts in the supply curve will now affect only the equilibrium price, not quantity.

unwilling, even at a zero price, to consume any more, and even at very high prices they refuse to consume any less. The demand for heart transplants provides an example of an almost perfectly inelastic demand curve. People who need them will buy them at any price they are able to pay. In that case, *the shift in the supply curve is completely reflected in price.*

THE MORE USUAL IN-BETWEEN CASES

Panels A and B of Figures 5.7 and 5.8 depict the extreme cases, but it should be clear how the results generalize to in-between examples, as illustrated in Figure 5.9. If the supply curve is highly elastic (horizontal), then shifts in the demand curve will be mostly reflected in changes in quantities; if the supply curve is *relatively* inelastic (vertical), then shifts in the demand curve will be *mostly* reflected in changes in price. If the demand curve is highly elastic, then shifts in the supply curve will be mostly reflected in changes in quantities; if the demand curve is relatively inelastic, then shifts in the supply curve will be mostly reflected in changes in price.

Figure 5.9 ELASTICITY OF DEMAND AND SUPPLY CURVES: THE NORMAL CASES

Normally, shifts in the demand curve will be reflected in changes in both price and quantity, as seen in panels A and B. When the supply curve is highly elastic, shifts in the demand curve will result mainly in changes in quantities; if it is relatively inelastic, shifts in the demand curve will result mainly in price changes. Likewise, shifts in the supply curve will be reflected in changes in both price and quantity, as seen in panels C and D. If the demand curve is highly elastic, shifts in the supply curve will result mainly in changes in quantities; if it is relatively inelastic, shifts in the supply curve will result mainly in price changes.

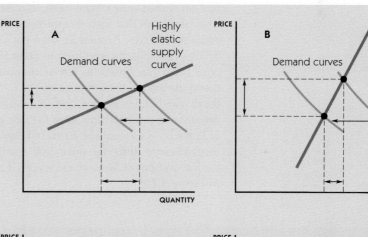

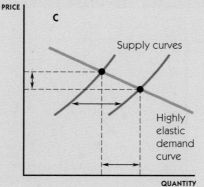

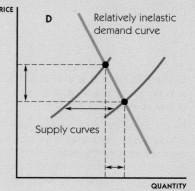

LONG-RUN VERSUS SHORT-RUN ADJUSTMENTS

Because demand and supply curves are likely to be less elastic (more vertical) in the short run than in the long run, shifts in the demand and supply curves are more likely to be reflected in price changes in the short run, but in quantity changes in the long run. In fact, the increases in prices that take place in the short run provide the signals to firms to increase their production. Short-run price increases can be thought of as being responsible for the output increases that occur in the long run.

USING MARKET DATA TO DERIVE DEMAND AND SUPPLY CURVES

In the real world, it is sometimes not as easy to draw demand and supply curves as it is in textbooks. Because the shape of the demand and supply curves is so important for understanding how the market behaves, economists have put an enormous effort into calculating their position and shape precisely. In some cases, this can be relatively easy. For instance, consider the case where economists *know* that the demand for some crop has not shifted over several years, but that supply has varied (as a result of rainfall). They also know that each year the price is determined at the intersection of the demand and supply curves. Economists draw the supply curve for each year, as shown in Figure 5.10A. They plot the equilibrium point for each year. This point, which represents a price and a quantity, is the intersection where demand and supply meet. Therefore, by taking the intersections of price and quantity for several years, economists can trace out the demand curve, as illustrated in the figure. The market data thus provide a basis for determining precisely how steep the demand curve is. Conversely, if the supply curve of Popsicles is *known* to be fixed, but demand varies, say with the weather, then as the demand curve shifts, the prices and quantities observed indicate equilibrium points—the intersections of demand and supply. Thus, they trace out the supply curve, as shown in Figure 5.10B.

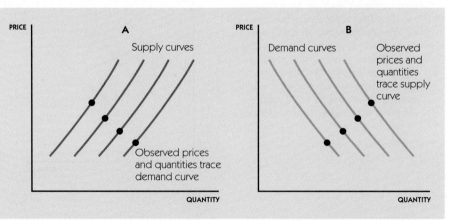

Figure 5.10 MARKET DATA AND SUPPLY AND DEMAND CURVES

Panel A shows that if the demand curve is known to be fixed, shifts in the supply curve will trace out the points on the demand curve. Panel B shows that if the supply curve is known to be fixed, shifts in the demand curve will trace out the points on the supply curve.

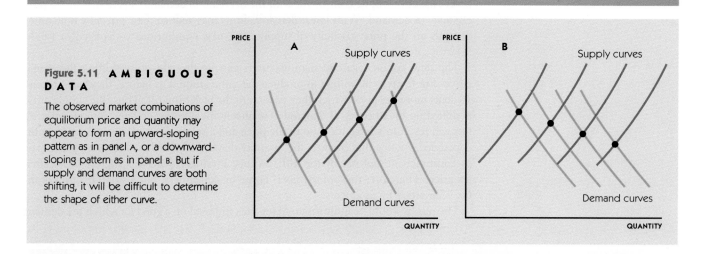

Figure 5.11 AMBIGUOUS DATA

The observed market combinations of equilibrium price and quantity may appear to form an upward-sloping pattern as in panel A, or a downward-sloping pattern as in panel B. But if supply and demand curves are both shifting, it will be difficult to determine the shape of either curve.

The more common case, however, is where every year there are some disturbances to both the demand and supply curves, as illustrated in Figure 5.11. For instance, the demand curve for yogurt may shift as America's health consciousness changes, and the supply curve may shift as the cost of milk changes with different farm programs. Note that the observed prices and quantities now are tracing out neither a demand curve nor a supply curve. They might produce a shape as in panel A, where the points traced out are upward sloping. Alternatively, the points traced out might be downward sloping, as in panel B.

Because of their shapes, many a noneconomist has been fooled into thinking that the points in panel A trace out a supply curve, and those in panel B trace out a demand curve. This is not the case. Because both demand and supply are shifting, identifying either the demand curve or the supply curve from the set of observed equilibrium points is, to say the least, difficult if not impossible. Devising mathematical methods for doing this has been one of the central goals of research over the past fifty years in econometrics, the branch of statistics that focuses on the special problems arising in economics. The Norwegian economist Trygve Haavelmo was awarded the Nobel Prize in 1989 for his pioneering work in developing methods for separating out the effects of demand and supply shifts.

TAX POLICY AND THE LAW OF SUPPLY AND DEMAND

For many questions of public policy, understanding the law of supply and demand is vital. One of the important ways economists use this law is to help them understand what will happen if the government imposes a tax, say on cigarettes. Assume that the tax on a pack of cigarettes is increased by 10 cents, and that the tax is imposed on cigarette manufacturers. Let's assume that all the companies try to pass on the cost increase to consumers, by raising the price of a pack by 10 cents. At the higher price, fewer cigarettes will be consumed, with the decrease in demand depending on the price elasticity of demand. With lower demand, firms may reduce their price; by how much depends on the price elasticity of supply. The new equilibrium is depicted in Figure 5.12A.

The new tax on cigarette manufacturers can be thought of as shifting the supply curve. For firms to be willing to produce the same amount as before, they must receive 10 cents more per pack (which they pass on to the government). Thus, the supply curve is shifted up by 10 cents. If demand is relatively inelastic (as demand for cigarettes is), this will result in a large increase in the price and a relatively small decrease in quantity demanded. Notice that because the quantity demanded is reduced slightly, prices paid by consumers do not rise by the full 10 cents. Producers receive a slightly lower after-tax price. Therefore, most of the tax is borne by consumers, but a small fraction of the tax is absorbed by producers.

The results would be quite different for a tax imposed on a good for which the demand

Figure 5.12 PASSING ALONG A TAX TO CONSUMERS

A tax on the output of an industry shifts the supply curve up by the amount of the tax. Panel A shows that if the demand curve is relatively inelastic, as it is for cigarettes, then most of the tax will be passed on to consumers in higher prices. Panel B shows that if the demand curve is relatively elastic, as it is for cheddar cheese, then the tax cannot be passed along to consumers in higher prices, and must instead be absorbed by producers.

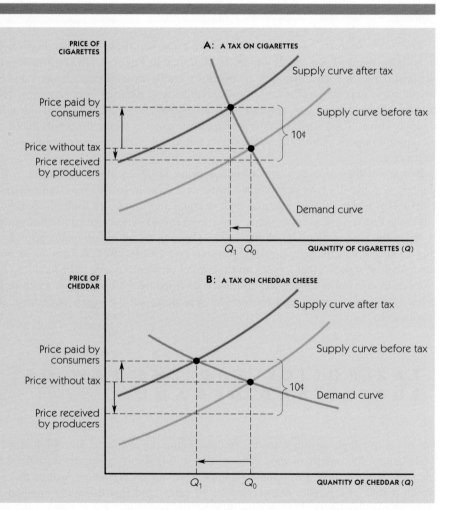

is very elastic. Assume, for instance, that the government decided to tax cheddar cheese (but no other cheeses). There are many cheeses that are almost like cheddar, and fewer people are addicted to cheese than are addicted to cigarettes, so the demand curve for cheddar cheese is very elastic. Now, as Figure 5.12B makes clear, most of the tax is absorbed by the producer, who receives (net of tax) a lower price. Production of cheddar cheese is reduced drastically.

When, as in the case of a tax on cigarettes, a tax on producers results in consumers paying a higher price, economists say the tax is "passed on" or "shifted" to consumers. The fact that the consumer bears the tax (even though it is collected from the producers) does not mean that the producers are "powerful" or have conspired together. It is simply the reflection of the workings of supply and demand.

SHORTAGES AND SURPLUSES

Most of the time, the law of supply and demand works so well in a developed modern economy that everyone can take it for granted. Americans rarely stop to marvel that they can walk into a shopping mall or grocery store and select what they want from a dizzying array of products. If you are willing to pay the "market price"—the prevailing price of the good, determined by the intersection of demand and supply—you can obtain almost any good or service, without needing access to some powerful politician or friend. Similarly, if a seller of a good or service is willing to charge no more than the market price, he can always sell what he wants to.

When the price is set so that demand equals supply—so that any individual can get as much as she wants at that price, and any supplier can sell the amount he wants at that price—economists say that the market **clears.** But there are also times when the market does not clear, when there are dramatic shortages or surpluses. To an economist, a **shortage** means that people would like to buy something, but they simply cannot find it for sale at the going price. A **surplus** means that sellers would like to sell their product, but they cannot sell as much of it as they would like at the going price. These cases where the market does not seem to be working are often the most forceful reminders of the importance of the law of supply and demand. The problem is that the "going price" is not the market equilibrium price.

Shortages and surpluses can be seen in the standard supply and demand diagram shown in Figure 5.13. In both panels A and B, the market equilibrium price is p^*. In panel A, the going price, p_1, is below p^*. At this low price, demand exceeds supply; you can see this by reading down to the horizontal axis. Demand is Q_d; supply is Q_s. The gap between the two points is the "shortage." With the shortage, consumers scramble to get the limited supply available at the going price.

In panel B, the going price, p_1, is above p^*. At this high price, demand is less than supply. Again we denote the demand by Q_d and the supply by Q_s. There is a surplus in the market of $Q_s - Q_d$. Now sellers are scrambling to find buyers.

At various times and for various goods, markets have not cleared. There have been shortages of apartments in New York; farm surpluses have plagued both Western Europe and the United States; in 1973, there was a shortage of gasoline, with cars lined up in long lines outside of gasoline stations. Perhaps the most important example of a surplus is unemployment: at some times, significant fractions of the labor force find that they cannot sell their labor services at the going wage.

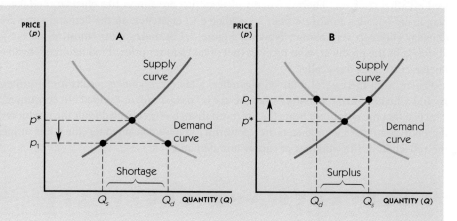

Figure 5.13 SHORTAGES AND SURPLUSES

In panel A, the actual price p_1 is below the market-clearing price p^*. At a price of p_1, quantity demanded exceeds quantity supplied, and a shortage exists. In panel B, the actual price p_1 is above the equilibrium price p^*. In this case, quantity supplied exceeds quantity demanded, and there is a surplus, or glut, in the market.

In some markets, like the stock market, the adjustment of prices to shifts in the demand and supply curves tends to be very rapid. In other cases, such as in the housing market, the adjustments tend to be very sluggish. Decreased demand for housing translates slowly into lower housing prices. When price adjustments are sluggish, shortages or surpluses may appear as prices adjust. Houses tend not to sell quickly, for instance, during periods of decreased demand.

When the market does not seem to be adjusting quickly toward equilibrium, economists say that prices are **sticky.** Even in these cases, the analysis of market equilibrium is useful. It indicates the direction of the changes—if the equilibrium price exceeds the current price, prices will tend to rise. Moreover, the rate at which prices fall or rise is often related to the gap, at the current market price, between the quantity demanded and supplied.

INTERFERING WITH THE LAW OF SUPPLY AND DEMAND

Many of the complaints about market economies and the law of supply and demand, which governs how prices are set, are not that they do not work, but that they produce results that some individuals or groups do not like. For example, a reduced supply of oil may lead to a higher equilibrium price for oil. The higher price is not a malfunction of the law of supply and demand, but this is little comfort to those who use gasoline to power their cars and oil to heat their homes. Increased farm productivity during this century has led to a rightward shift in the supply curve; at any price, farmers are willing to produce more. While the demand for agricultural products has also increased with the increase in population and income, the shifts in the supply curve have outpaced those in the demand curve. This shift in the supply curve results in lower farm prices—an unhappy prospect for farmers.

Low demand for unskilled labor may similarly lead to very low wages for unskilled workers. By the same token, an increase in the demand for apartments in New York City leads, in the short run (with an inelastic supply), to an increase in rents—to the delight of landlords, but an unfortunate development for renters.

In each of these cases, dissatisfaction with the outcome of market processes has led to government actions. The price of oil and natural gas was, at one time, regulated; minimum wage laws set a minimum limit on what employers can pay their workers, even if the workers would be willing to work for less; and rent control laws limit rents that can be charged. The concerns behind these interferences with the market are understandable, but the agitation for government action is based on two errors.

First, someone (or some group) was assigned blame for the change in the price (wages, rents): the oil price rises were blamed on the oil companies, low wages on the employer, and rent increases on the landlord. As already explained, economists emphasize the role of anonymous market forces in determining these prices. After all, if landlords or oil companies are basically the same people today as they were last week, there must be some reason that they started charging different prices this week. To be sure, sometimes the price increase is the result of producers colluding to raise prices. This was the case in 1973, when the oil-exporting countries got together to raise the price of oil. The more common situation, however, is illustrated by the increase in the price of oil in August 1990, after Iraq's invasion of Kuwait. The higher price simply reflected the anticipated reduction in the supply of oil.

The second error was to forget that as powerful as governments may be, they can no more repeal the law of supply and demand than they can repeal the law of gravity. When they attempt to interfere with its working, the forces of supply and demand will not be balanced. There will either be excess supply or excess demand. Shortages and surpluses create problems of their own, often far worse than the original problem the government policy was supposed to resolve.

This is precisely what happened in the former Soviet Union and other former socialist economies. In those countries, governments did not allow the law of supply and demand to work. The government set prices by decree. In some cases, the government tried to figure out what the prices would have been had the law of supply and demand been allowed to function naturally. This may seem a little pointless—after all, why not just let the market work? Even if the government was successful in deciding on an appropriate price, it could do so only after a lengthy bureaucratic process. But economic conditions were changing while the bureaucrats were deliberating, which means that the government-announced price was rarely the same as the market price. Moreover, the government-announced price was usually inflexible.

In some cases, the government set prices to assure that important products were "affordable." The result of government price setting was that in those socialist countries, shortages became the rule rather than the exception. Consumers in Russia and Poland spent hours each day waiting in line to buy the foods they needed. They waited months or years to get a car or an apartment.

Two of the more straightforward examples of government overruling the law of supply and demand are **price ceilings,** which are attempts to impose a maximum price that can be charged for a product, and **price floors,** which are attempts to impose a minimum price. Rent control laws are price ceilings, and minimum wage laws are price floors. A closer look at each will help to highlight the perils of interfering with the law of supply and demand.

New York City adopted rent control on a "temporary" basis during World War II. Half a century later, it is still in effect. As a result, people who have lived in the city a long time (or whose families have) may have spectacularly cheap apartments, while a newcomer to New York might pay $1,500 a month for a one-bedroom apartment in midtown Manhattan, if one can be found at all.

Over the last few years, journalist William Tucker has been collecting stories of well-to-do New Yorkers who benefit from this situation. The minority leader in the state senate, for example, pays $1,800 a month for a *ten-room* apartment overlooking Central Park. A housing court judge who hears rent-control cases pays $93 a month for a two-bedroom apartment in a building where studio apartments (with no separate bedroom) now rent for $1,200. Former mayor Ed Koch was paying $351 a month for a Greenwich Village apartment that, according

to Tucker, would easily go for $1,500 a month in the absence of the price controls.

Of course, people who have been able to pay far below market value for decades tend to favor rent control. The problems it causes are less obvious. Rent control is effectively a price ceiling, so economists, looking to the law of supply and demand, would expect it to lead to a shortage of housing. Indeed, this has been the case.

For example, despite a serious shortage of housing in New York City, over 300,000 rental units have simply been abandoned. Almost no new rental housing is being built. Only about 2 percent of the apartments in New York are vacant at any time, as opposed to vacancy rates that are commonly at 6 percent in other East Coast cities, like Baltimore, that do not have rent control. When many people are struggling to obtain one of the few available apartments, poor people will tend to lose out, and

may end up living in the subways or on the streets.

Even with rent control, the *average* rent in New York City seems little different from some other large cities, like Chicago. The difference is that in Chicago, a newcomer can find an apartment at something close to the average rent. In New York, newcomers often have to make special payments to secure an apartment, and then pay extraordinarily high rents that help to subsidize those who have been living there for a long time. Tucker refers to this process as a "tenant aristocracy," emphasizing the irony that while rent control is often promoted as an aid to the poor, it tends to end up benefiting the well-established upper middle class and wealthy.

Attempting to provide moderate and low-cost housing is a worthy public goal. But the example of New York and other rent-controlled cities shows that even when the goal is worthy, the law of supply and demand does not simply fade away.

Sources: William Tucker, "We All Pay for Others' Great Apartment Deals," *Newsday,* May 24, 1986; Tucker, "Moscow on the Hudson," *The American Spectator* (July 1986), pp. 19–21; Tucker, "Where Do the Homeless Come From?" *National Review,* September 25, 1987, pp. 32–43.

PRICE CEILINGS: THE CASE OF RENT CONTROL

Price ceilings are always tempting to governments because they seem an easy way to assure that everyone will be able to afford a particular product. Thus, in the last couple of decades in the United States, price ceilings have been set for a wide range of goods, from chickens to oil to interest rates. In each case where the government has attempted to set a price ceiling, the result has been to create shortages at the controlled price; more people want to buy the product than there are products, because producers have no incentive to produce more of the good. Those who can buy at the cheaper price benefit; producers and those unable to buy suffer.

Rent control is one example of a price ceiling. The effect of rent control laws—setting the maximum rent that a landlord can charge for a one-bedroom apartment, for example—is illustrated by Figure 5.14. In panel A, R^* is the market equilibrium rental rate, at which the demand for housing equals the supply. However, the local government is concerned that at R^*, many poor people cannot afford housing in the city, so it imposes a law that says that rents may be no higher than R_1. At R_1, there is an excess demand for apartments. While the motives behind the government action may well have been praiseworthy—after all, making sure that everyone can afford housing is a laudable goal—the government has created an artificial scarcity.

The problems caused by rent control are likely to be worse in the long run than in the short run. In the short run, the quantity of apartments does not change much; in other words, the supply of apartments is inelastic in the short run. But in the long run, the quantity of apartments can decline for several reasons. They may be abandoned as they deteriorate; they can be converted to condominiums and sold instead of rented; and apartment owners may not wish to construct new ones if they cannot charge enough in rent to cover their costs. As argued earlier, long-run supply curves are likely to be more elastic than short-run supply curves.

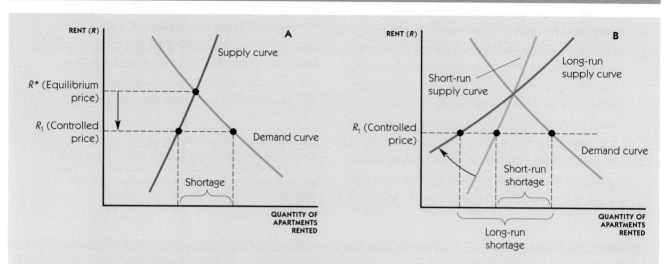

Figure 5.14 A PRICE CEILING: RENT CONTROL

Rent control laws limit the rents apartment owners may charge. If rents are held down to R_1, below the market-clearing level R^*, as in panel A, there will be excess demand for apartments. Panel B shows the long-run response. The supply of rental housing is more elastic in the long run, since landlords can refuse to build new apartment buildings, or they can sell existing apartments as condominiums. The price ceiling eventually leads to the quantity supplied being even farther below the quantity demanded.

Panel B illustrates the probable result. Rent control leads to a housing shortage that is likely to increase over time. Rent control results in all *existing* renters being better off, whether they are poor or rich, at least as long as the landlord stays in the business. But the quantity of available rental housing will decrease, so that many would-be residents will be unable to find rental housing in the market. Since renters tend to be poorer than those who can buy a home, a shortage of rental housing will tend to hurt the poor most.

PRICE FLOORS: THE CASE OF THE MINIMUM WAGE

To many Americans, it has long seemed that if you work full time fifty-two weeks a year at some job, you ought to earn enough to support yourself and a family. During the Great Depression of the 1930s, Congress gave force to that feeling by enacting the Fair Labor Standards Act of 1938. Among the provisions of the act was a requirement that most businesses pay at least a **minimum wage** to all workers. Since then, Congress has raised the minimum wage as the cost of living in the economy has increased; because of these increases, the minimum wage has generally been about half the average wage for all workers.

The minimum wage is an example of a price floor. While price ceilings are meant to help consumers (buyers), price floors are meant to help producers (sellers). With a price floor such as the minimum wage, buyers (employers) cannot pay less than the government-set minimum price.

Price floors have predictable effects too. The reasoning is simply the reverse of the reasoning for price ceilings. If the government attempts to raise the minimum wage higher than the equilibrium wage, the demand for workers will be reduced and the supply increased. There will be an excess supply of labor. Of course, those who are lucky enough to get a job will be better off at the higher wage than at the market equilibrium wage; but there are others, who might have been employed at the lower market equilibrium wage, who cannot find employment and are worse off.

How much unemployment does the minimum wage create? That depends on the level at which the minimum wage is set and on the elasticity of demand and supply for labor. If the minimum wage is set low enough, then it has little effect, either on wages or on unemployment. Panel A of Figure 5.15 shows a market in which an equilibrium wage is above the minimum wage. A small increase in the minimum wage thus has no effect on either the wage rate or the employment level. With the current level of minimum wages, only the very unskilled individuals—those whose wages would have been below the minimum wage—are affected. In the United States, perhaps the major unemployment effect of minimum wages is on teenagers. Most other workers, even the unskilled, get paid more than the minimum wage.

Panel B of Figure 5.15 shows a case where the demand and supply for unskilled labor are very inelastic, so that wages can be increased significantly, with little increase in unemployment. In panel C, the demand and supply for unskilled labor are both very elastic, and the minimum wage has been set substantially above the market equilibrium price. As a result, substantial unemployment is generated with any increase in the minimum wage.

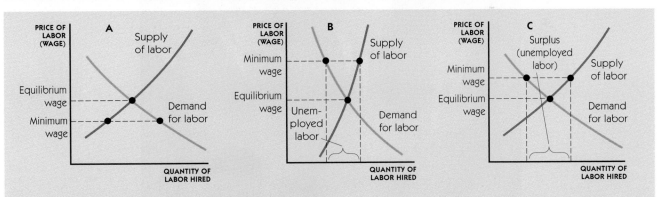

Figure 5.15 EFFECTS OF MINIMUM WAGES

In panel A, the minimum wage is below the equilibrium wage. However, since the minimum wage is a price floor, there is nothing to stop the market from paying the higher equilibrium wage, and any increase in the minimum wage will have no effect so long as the minimum wage remains below the equilibrium wage. In panel B, an increase in the minimum wage will result in very little increase in unemployment, as the demand and supply curves for labor are inelastic. In panel C, the demand and supply curves are more elastic; the minimum wage is above the equilibrium wage, creating a large surplus of workers who would like to work but cannot find jobs. Increases in the minimum wage in this case will increase unemployment significantly.

CLOSE-UP: PRICE FLOORS ON THE FARM

Farmers are exposed to risks from both the environment and the market. After all the investment of hard work and money in plowing and planting, bad weather or bugs can decimate a crop. But unexpectedly wonderful weather causes an outward shift of the supply curve, driving down equilibrium prices and hurting farmers as well.

Starting in the 1930s, the federal government tried to stabilize the prices of grain, cotton, rice, dairy foods, sugar, wool, honey, peanuts, and other products. The programs to achieve this stability are complex. But over time, under pressure from congressmen from agricultural states and their lobbyists, the details of the programs have been manipulated to assure that the average prices received by farmers are actually somewhat above what would have been the average market price. In other words, the government programs have acted as a price floor, and as economists would

expect, they have led to excess supply and government-owned stockpiles. In 1987, for example (a year chosen because it is just before the drought of 1988), the federal government held 4.1 billion bushels of corn (57 percent of that year's production), 1.33 billion bushels of wheat (63 percent), and 4.8 million bales of cotton (33 percent).

A grand revision of the farm programs occurs every five years or so, and in November 1990, President Bush signed a new five-year farm bill. One of the goals of the bill was to hold down the price floors, and thus gradually to reduce the stockpiles and move closer to the market equilibrium.

In mid-1991, the Congressional Budget Office estimated that because of the new farm bill, stocks of corn would be only 1.6 billion bushels by 1996 (18 percent of expected 1996 production) and stocks of wheat would be 872 million bushels (35 percent). Stocks of cotton, on the other hand,

President Bush signs the 1990 farm bill.

would still be at 4.8 million bales in 1996 (30 percent). These predictions are based on estimates of how many farm products the United States will export to other countries, on expected weather and technology, and on other variables.

The holding of some stocks of agricultural products by the government does protect consumers against a rapid price rise brought on by a drought or other agricultural disaster. But the stockpiles should be as small as possible to achieve that end. By gradually reducing the price floors in agriculture and thereby reducing stockpiles, the government hopes that farmers will respond more to market incentives than to government-set price levels.

Sources: Congressional Budget Office, *The Outlook for Farm Commodity Program Spending, Fiscal Years 1991–1996* (June 1991) and *Fiscal Years 1988–1993* (June 1988); Keith Schneider, "Plan Would Revise Farm Subsidies," *New York Times,* October 17, 1990.

Recent policy discussions on minimum wages have focused on whether the original intent of minimum wage legislation—to ensure that those who work earn enough to support a family—makes any sense. While it may have been reasonable back in the 1930s to assume that one man needed to earn a certain minimum wage to support a wife and family, today's labor market often has both spouses and even a teenage child or two working. Surely they do not *all* need to earn enough to support their own family. In addition, a higher minimum wage does not seem a particularly useful way to help the poor. Most poor people earn more than the minimum wage *when they are working*; their problem is not low wages. The problem comes when they are not working. And this may be either because they cannot find a job, in which case the problem is the level of unemployment, not the level of wages, and increasing wages may make it even more difficult to find a job; or because they are not well enough to work. Only about 10 percent of people in poverty work at jobs that pay at or near the minimum wage. Thus, the minimum wage is not a good way of trying to deal with problems of poverty. Other government programs need to be designed to address those problems.

ALTERNATIVE SOLUTIONS

Widespread unhappiness with the workings of the law of supply and demand is understandable because large changes in prices cause distress. It is natural to try to find scapegoats and to look to the government for a solution. Such situations call for compassion, and the economists' caution against the use of scapegoats and government action can seem coldhearted. But the fact remains that in competitive markets, the price changes are simply the impersonal workings of the law of supply and demand; without the price changes, there will be shortages and surpluses. The examples of government attempts to interfere with the workings of supply and demand provide an important cautionary tale: one ignores the workings of the law of supply and demand only at one's peril. It is a lesson that politicians seem to need to learn over and over again. This does not mean, however, that the government should simply ignore the distress caused by large price and wage changes. It only means that government must take care in addressing the problems; price controls, including price ceilings and floors, are unlikely to be effective instruments.

Later chapters will discuss some of the ways in which the government can try to address the problems that arise from dissatisfaction with the consequences of the law of supply and demand, by making use of the power of the market rather than trying to fight against it. For example, if the government is concerned with low wages paid to unskilled workers, it can try to increase the demand for these workers. A shift to the right in the demand curve will increase the wages these workers receive. The government can do this either by subsidizing firms that hire unskilled workers or by providing more training to these workers and thus increasing their productivity.

If the government wants to increase the supply of housing to the poor, it can provide housing subsidies for the poor, which will elicit a greater supply. If government wants to conserve on the use of gasoline, it can impose a tax on gasoline. Noneconomists often object that these sorts of economic incentives have other distasteful consequences, and sometimes they do. But government policies that take account of the law of supply and demand will tend to be more effective, with fewer unfortunate side effects, than policies that try to ignore the predictable economic consequences that follow from disregarding the law of supply and demand.

REVIEW AND PRACTICE

SUMMARY

1. The price elasticity of demand describes how sensitive the quantity demanded of a good is to changes in the price of the good. When demand is inelastic, an increase in the price has little effect on quantity demanded; when demand is elastic, an increase in the price has a large effect on quantity demanded.

2. If price changes do not induce much change in demand, the demand curve is very steep and is said to be inelastic, or insensitive to price changes. If the demand curve is very flat, indicating that price changes induce large changes in demand, demand is said to be elastic, or sensitive to price changes. Demand for necessities is usually quite inelastic; demand for luxuries is elastic.

3. The price elasticity of supply describes how sensitive the quantity supplied of a good is to changes in the price of the good.

4. If price changes do not induce much change in supply, the supply curve is very steep and is said to be inelastic. If the supply curve is very flat, indicating that price changes cause large changes in supply, supply is said to be elastic.

5. The extent to which a shift in the supply curve is reflected in price or quantity depends on the shape of the demand curve. The more elastic the demand, the more a given shift in the supply curve will be reflected in changes in equilibrium quantities and the less it will be reflected in changes in equilibrium prices. The more inelastic the demand, the more a given shift in the supply curve will be reflected in changes in equilibrium prices and the less it will be reflected in changes in equilibrium quantities.

6. Likewise, the extent to which a shift in the demand curve is reflected in price or quantity depends on the shape of the supply curve.

7. Demand and supply curves are likely to be more elastic in the long run than in the short run. Therefore a shift in the demand or supply curve is likely to have a larger price effect in the short run and a larger quantity effect in the long run.

8. Elasticities can be used to predict to what extent consumer prices rise when a tax is imposed on a good. If the demand curve for a good is very inelastic, consumers in effect have to pay the tax. If the demand curve is very elastic, the quantities produced and the price received by producers are likely to decline considerably.

9. Government regulations may prevent a market from moving toward its equilibrium price, leading to shortages or surpluses. Price ceilings lead to excess demand. Price floors lead to excess supply.

KEY TERMS

price elasticity of
   demand
price elasticity of
   supply
infinite elasticity of
   demand

infinite elasticity of
   supply
zero elasticity of
   demand
zero elasticity of
   supply

market clearing
sticky prices
price ceiling
price floor

REVIEW QUESTIONS

1. What is meant by the elasticity of demand and the elasticity of supply? Why do economists find these concepts useful?

2. Is the slope of a perfectly elastic demand or supply curve horizontal or vertical? Is the slope of a perfectly inelastic demand or supply curve horizontal or vertical? Explain.

3. If the elasticity of demand is unity, what happens to total revenue as the price increases? What if the demand for a product is very inelastic? What if it is very elastic?

4. Under what condition will a shift in the demand curve result mainly in a change in quantity? in price?

5. Under what condition will a shift in the supply curve result mainly in a change in price? in quantity?

6. Why do the elasticities of demand and supply tend to change from the short run to the long run?

7. Under what circumstances will a tax on a product be passed along to consumers?

8. Why do price ceilings tend to lead to shortages? Why do price floors tend to lead to surpluses?

PROBLEMS

1. Suppose the price elasticity of demand for gasoline is .2 in the short run and .7 in the long run. If the price of gasoline rises 28 percent, what effect on quantity demanded will this have in the short run? in the long run?

2. Imagine that the short-run price elasticity of supply for a farmer's corn is .3, while the long-run price elasticity is 2. If prices for corn fall 30 percent, what are the short-run and long-run changes in quantity supplied? What are the short- and long-run changes in quantity supplied if prices rise by 15 percent? What happens to the farmer's revenues in each of these situations?

3. Assume that the demand curve for hard liquor is highly inelastic and the supply curve for hard liquor is highly elastic. If the tastes of the drinking public shift away from hard liquor, will the effect be larger on price or on quantity? If the federal government decides to impose a tax on manufacturers of hard liquor, will the effects be larger on price or on quantity? What is the effect of an advertising program that succeeds in discouraging people from drinking? Draw diagrams to illustrate each of your answers.

4. Imagine that wages (the price of labor) are sticky in the labor market, and that a supply of new workers enters that market. Will the market be in equilibrium in the short run? Why or why not? If not, explain the relationship you would expect to see between the quantity demanded and supplied, and draw a diagram to illustrate. Explain how sticky wages in the labor market affect unemployment.

5. For each of the following markets, explain whether you would expect prices in that market to be relatively sticky or not:
    (a) the stock market;
    (b) the market for autoworkers;
    (c) the housing market;
    (d) the market for cut flowers;
    (e) the market for pizza-delivery people.

6. Suppose a government wishes to assure that its citizens can afford adequate housing. Consider three ways of pursuing that goal. One method is to pass a law requiring that all rents be cut by one-quarter. A second method offers a subsidy to all builders of homes. A third provides a subsidy directly to renters equal to one-quarter of the rent they pay. Predict what effect each of these proposals would have on the price and quantity of rental housing in the short run and the long run.

APPENDIX: ALGEBRAIC DERIVATION OF ELASTICITIES

The association of the steepness of demand curves with their elasticities implies some relationship between the elasticity and the slope of a demand curve. But while the two concepts are related, there are also important differences.

In the appendix to Chapter 2, the slope of a line was defined as the change in the vertical axis resulting from a change of one unit along the horizontal axis—the rise over the run. Figure 5.16 shows a demand curve for CDs; it is called a **linear demand curve** because it is a straight line. We write the slope as

$$\text{slope} = \frac{\Delta p}{\Delta Q},$$

where the symbol **Δ**, the Greek letter delta, is used to represent change. Thus, the above expression reads, "Slope equals delta p divided by delta Q" or, "Slope equals the change in price divided by the change in quantity." At point A, the slope is $-\$.50$ per CD, because an increase in the quantity by 1 reduces the price from $10.00 to $9.50. In fact, the slope is $-\$.50$ all along this demand curve, a result of the general rule that the slope of a straight line is the same at all points along the line.

The elasticity of demand, as stated in this chapter, is the percentage change in quantity demanded corresponding to a 1 percent change in price or, more generally in mathematical terms,

$$\text{elasticity of demand} = \frac{\text{percentage change in quantity demanded}}{\text{percentage change in price}}.$$

When there is a 1 percent change in price, then the elasticity is equal to the percentage change in quantity demanded.

The percentage change in price is taken as the change in the price divided by the price,[3] and likewise for quantity:

$$\text{percentage change in price} = \frac{\Delta p}{p},$$

$$\text{percentage change in quantity demanded} = \frac{\Delta Q_d}{Q_d},$$

where Q_d is the quantity demanded. Thus, the elasticity of demand is defined as

$$\text{elasticity of demand} = \frac{\Delta Q_d / Q_d}{\Delta p / p} = \frac{\Delta Q_d}{\Delta p} \times \frac{p}{Q_d},$$

the percentage change in the quantity demanded divided by the percentage change in price.[4]

If the price of a CD decreases by $.50 and the price initially is $10.00, that represents a decrease in price of 5 percent ($.50/$10.00). The quantity increase of 1, from 25 CDs to 26 CDs, represents an increase in quantity demanded of 4 percent (1/25). So in our example, the elasticity of demand for CDs would be .8 (.04/.05) at point A.

The equation for elasticity is closely related to the one above for slope, with two important differences. First, the elasticity equation puts quantity on top and price on the bottom, while slope does the opposite. This reflects, in the case of slope, a mathematical convention (price is usually on the vertical axis) and, in the case of elasticity, the economist's focus on quantity changes induced by price changes.

Second, elasticity is stated in percentage terms, which means that it is free of the units (in this case, number of CDs) that carry over in the calculation of slope. The

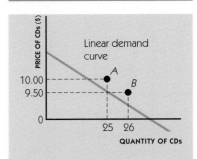

Figure 5.16 **LINEAR DEMAND CURVE**

The slope of this linear demand curve, the change in price divided by the change in quantity (rise over run), is the same at all points on the curve. But the elasticity of demand, the percentage change in quantity divided by the percentage change in price, changes as we move along the curve. At point A, elasticity of demand is higher than it is at B.

---

[3] This raises a slight technical problem: do we express the change as a percentage of the initial price, the final price, or a price somewhere in between? If the change is small enough, the percentages we calculate each of these ways will be approximately the same; it makes little difference. In our example, if we had calculated the change as a percentage of final price, we would have obtained $.50/$9.50 = .052 rather than .050.

[4] Students familiar with calculus will note that the elasticity can be written in a simple form. We simply substitute the expression dQ/dp for the expression $\Delta Q_d/\Delta p$.

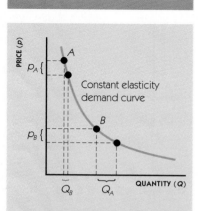

Figure 5.17 C O N S T A N T E L A S T I C I T Y D E M A N D   C U R V E

The elasticity of demand is the same for every price along this demand curve; the slope, however, is not constant.

reason percentages are used is that they mean elasticities will be the same no matter what units are used. If the good in questions is eggs, it will not matter if we measure them singly or by the dozen. But the calculation of the slope of a linear demand curve for eggs will change if we change our unit of measurement from eggs to dozens of eggs.

Note that even though the slope of a linear demand curve is constant, the elasticity changes as we move along the curve. In Figure 5.16, the slopes at A and B are the same, but at A the ratio of price to quantity, p/Q, is much higher than at B: price is higher and quantity is lower. Hence the elasticity of demand at A is higher than at B. Figure 5.17 shows a demand curve for which the elasticity is the same at every price. This demand curve is called the **constant elasticity demand curve.** (Note that the slope in this case is not constant.)

The fact that the elasticity of demand is constant means that we can take any two points along the curve, such as A and B, and calculate the elasticity, and it would be the same. At A, the elasticity is

$$\frac{\Delta Q_A}{\Delta p_A} \times \frac{p_A}{Q_A},$$

and at B, it is

$$\frac{\Delta Q_B}{\Delta p_B} \times \frac{p_B}{Q_B}.$$

Because the curve has constant elasticity, the two numbers are the same.

The analysis for elasticity of supply proceeds in an analogous fashion. The elasticity of supply is the percentage change in quantity supplied corresponding to a 1 percent increase in price or, more generally,

$$\text{elasticity of supply} = \frac{\text{percentage change in quantity supplied}}{\text{percentage change in price}}.$$

Again, when there is a 1 percent change in price, the elasticity of supply is equal to the percentage change in quantity supplied. As before, we can write the percentage change in price as $\Delta p/p$ and the percentage change in quantity supplied as $\Delta Q_s/Q_s$, where Q_s denotes the quantity supplied. Thus, the elasticity of supply is defined as

$$\text{elasticity of supply} = \frac{\Delta Q_s/Q_s}{\Delta p/p}.$$

T he discussion of markets in Chapters 4 and 5 might lead an astute observer to ask two questions. First, how do markets take account of the future? The pint of ice cream you buy today is for consumption in the present and has no value five years down the road, but real estate, gold coins, and other goods may retain their value or even increase in value over time. The first part of this chapter shows how prices in the present are linked to expectations of prices in the future.

Since we never know for sure what the future will bring, we can never be sure what future prices will be. This raises the second question, that of risk. How does uncertainty affect markets? Firms build new plants; they also fund projects designed to produce new products or new techniques of production. In both cases, they cannot know with certainty what the future value of the plant or product will be. When individuals face risk, sometimes they can buy insurance, as when a home owner buys fire insurance. But sometimes they cannot. Nor can a firm buy insurance against the risk that its newest product will be a failure. How well market economies handle the problems posed by risk has much to do with their successes. Conversely, shortcomings in their ability to handle risk will have much to do with their failures. In the latter part of this chapter, we investigate insurance and other markets for risk.

KEY QUESTIONS

1. How do we compare a dollar received next year or in five years' time with a dollar received today?

2. What determines the demand for an asset like gold, which is purchased mainly with the intent of selling it at some later date? What determines shifts in the demand curve for assets?

3. Why do people buy insurance?

4. Why are there many risks for which insurance is not available?

5. How do the different ways that firms raise funds in the capital market affect the risks borne by the investors who provide those funds? Why do some firms have to pay a higher interest rate on what they borrow than do others?

"Have you and your bear ever had a loan with us before?"

INTEREST

The simplest future-oriented transaction occurs when you put money into a bank account. In effect, you have loaned your money to the bank, and the bank has promised to pay you back whenever you say. But banks offer more than security; they offer you a *return* on your savings. This return, like the return on any loan, is called **interest.** If you put $1,000 in the bank at the beginning of the year, and the interest rate is 10 percent per year, you will receive $1,100 at the end of the year. The $100 is the payment of interest, while the $1,000 is the repayment of the **principal,** the original amount lent to the bank.

To an economist, the interest rate is like a price. Normally, we express prices in terms of dollars. If the price of an orange is $1.00, that means we must give up $1.00 to get one orange. Economists talk about the relative price of two goods as the amount of one good you have to give up to get one more unit of the other. The relative price is just the ratio of the "dollar" prices.

For example, if the price of an apple is $.50 and the price of an orange is $1.00, then the relative price (that is, the ratio of the prices) is 2. If we wish to consume one more orange, we have to give up two apples. The relative price is thus just a way of describing a trade-off. Similarly, if the interest rate is 10 percent, by giving up $1.00 worth of consumption today, a saver can have $1.10 worth of consumption next year.

Thus, the rate of interest tells us how much future consumption we can get by giving up $1.00 worth of current consumption. It tells us the relative price between the present and the future.

THE TIME VALUE OF MONEY

Interest rates are normally positive. This means that *$1.00 today is worth more than $1.00 in the future*. If you have $1.00 today, you can put it into the bank and, if the interest rate is 5 percent, receive $1.05 at the end of next year. Similarly, if you wanted $1.00 today, you could borrow it and promise to pay $1.05 in a year. In short, $1.00 today is worth, in this example, $1.05 next year.

Economists use the concept of **present discounted value** to calculate and express how much less $1.00 in the future is worth than $1.00 today. The present discounted value of $100 a year from now is what you would pay today for $100 a year from now. Suppose the interest rate is 10 percent. If you put $90.91 in the bank today, at the end of the year you will receive $9.09 interest, which together with the original amount will total $100. Thus, $90.91 is the present discounted value of $100 a year from now, if the interest rate is 10 percent.

There is a simple formula for calculating the present discounted value of any amount to be received a year from now: just divide the amount by 1 plus the annual rate of interest. The annual rate of interest is often denoted by r.

To check this formula, consider the present discounted value of $100. According to the formula, it is $100 / (1 + r). That means that if you put $100 in the bank today, at the end of the year you will have the principal ($100) *times* $(1 + r)$. Thus, if you take the present discounted value, $100 / (1 + r), and put it in the bank, at the end of the year you will have

$$\frac{\$100}{1 + r} \times (1 + r) = \$100,$$

confirming our conclusion that $100 / (1 + r) today is the same as $100 one year from now.

A similar calculation can be performed to figure the present discounted value of $100 to be received two years from now. The problem now is to take **compound interest**

PRESENT DISCOUNTED VALUE

Present discounted value of $1.00 next year $= \dfrac{\$1.00}{1 + \text{interest rate}}$.

Often the annual interest rate is denoted by r, so the right-hand side of the equation becomes $\dfrac{\$1.00}{1 + r}$.

into account. In the second year, you earn interest on the interest you earned the first year. (By contrast, **simple interest** does not take into account the interest you earn on interest you have previously earned.) If the rate of interest is 10 percent and is compounded annually, $100 today is worth $110 a year from now and $121 (*not* $120) in two years' time. Thus, the present discounted value today of $121 two years from now is $100. Table 6.1 shows how to calculate the present discounted value of $100 received next year, two years from now, and three years from now.

Table 6.1 PRESENT DISCOUNTED VALUE OF $100

Year received	Present discounted value
Next year	$\dfrac{1}{1 + r} \times 100 = \dfrac{100}{1 + r}$
Two years from now	$\dfrac{1}{1 + r} \times \dfrac{100}{1 + r} = \dfrac{100}{(1 + r)^2}$
Three years from now	$\dfrac{1}{1 + r} \times \dfrac{100}{(1 + r)^2} = \dfrac{100}{(1 + r)^3}$

We can now see how to calculate the value of an investment project that will yield a return over several years. We look at what the returns will be each year, adjust them to their present discounted values, and then add these values up. Table 6.2 shows how this is done for a project that yields $10,000 next year and $15,000 the year after, and

Table 6.2 CALCULATING PRESENT DISCOUNTED VALUE OF A THREE-YEAR PROJECT

Year	Return	Discount factor ($r = 0.10$)	Present discounted value ($r = 0.10$)
1	$10,000	$\dfrac{1}{1.10}$	$ 9,091
2	$15,000	$\dfrac{1}{(1.10)^2} = \dfrac{1}{1.21}$	$12,397
3	$50,000	$\dfrac{1}{(1.10)^3} = \dfrac{1}{1.331}$	$37,566
Total	$75,000	—	$59,054

that you plan to sell in the third year for $50,000. The second column of the table shows the return in each year. The third column shows the discount factor—what we multiply the return by to obtain the present discounted value of that year's return. The calculations assume an interest rate of 10 percent. The fourth column multiplies the return by the discount factor to obtain the present discounted value of that year's return. In the bottom row of the table, the present discounted values of each year's return have been added up to obtain the total present discounted value of the project. Notice that it is much smaller than the number we obtain simply by adding up the returns, the "undiscounted" yield of the project.

EFFECTS OF CHANGES IN THE INTEREST RATE

If the interest rate increases, the present discounted value of $100 a year from now will decrease. If the interest rate should rise to 20 percent, for example, the present discounted value of $100 a year from now becomes $83.33 (100/1.2).

Thus, if the interest rate rises, the present discounted value of the returns from any investment project will be diminished. This can be seen in Table 6.3, where the value of the project shown in Table 6.2 has been calculated at a 20 percent as well as a 10 percent interest rate. The present value, $47,685, is now even lower.

Table 6.3 CHANGING THE INTEREST RATE

Year	Return	Present discounted value ($r = 0.10$)	Present discounted value ($r = 0.20$)
1	$10,000	$ 9,091	$ 8,333
2	$15,000	$12,397	$10,417
3	$50,000	$37,566	$28,935
Total	$75,000	$59,054	$47,685

The concept of present discounted value is an important one because so many decisions in economics are oriented to the future. Whether the decision is made by a person buying a house or saving money for retirement or a company building a factory or making an investment, it is necessary to be able to calculate how to value money that will be received one, two, five, or ten years in the future. Economists say that it is necessary to remember the **time value of money.** The concept of present discounted value tells us precisely how to do that.

THE MARKET FOR LOANABLE FUNDS

The previous section explained how the interest rate is a price, similar to the price of any other good, like apples and oranges. The price of borrowing a dollar is the dollar plus the annual rate of interest. How is the interest rate determined? Like other prices, the interest rate is determined by the law of supply and demand.

At any given time, there are some people and companies who would like to borrow, so they can spend more than they currently have. Rachel has her first job and knows she needs a car for transportation; George needs kitchen equipment, tables, and chairs to open his sandwich shop. Others would like to save, or spend less than they currently have. John is putting aside money for his children's college education and for his retirement; Sandy's Sauces has become a huge success, and Sandy cannot spend the money as fast as it is coming in.

The gains from trade, discussed in Chapter 3, apply equally well to what economists call **intertemporal** trades, which are exchanges that occur over time. When one individual lends money to another, both gain. John and Sandy can lend money to Rachel and George. John and Sandy will get paid interest in the future, to compensate them for letting Rachel and George use their funds now. Rachel and George are willing to pay the interest because to them, having the funds today is particularly valuable. The borrower may be a business firm like the one owned by George, who believes that with these funds he will be able to make an investment that will yield a return far higher than the interest rate charged. Or the borrower may be an individual facing some emergency, such as a medical crisis, that requires funds today. The borrower may even simply be a free spirit, wishing to consume as much as he can (as much as lenders are willing to give him), and letting the future take care of itself.

How is the supply of funds to be equated with the demand? Those who wish to borrow will have to pay interest, while those who save will receive interest. As the interest rate rises, some borrowers will be discouraged from borrowing. Rachel may decide to ride her bicycle to work and postpone buying a new car until she can save up the money herself (or until interest rates come down). At the same time, as the interest rate rises, some savers may be induced to save more. Their incentives for savings have increased. John realizes that every extra dollar he saves today will produce more money in the future, so he may put more aside.[1] Figure 6.1 shows the supply and demand curves for loanable funds. Here the interest rate is the "price," and the amount of money loaned and borrowed is the quantity. At r^*, the demand for funds equals the supply of funds.

Below r^*, the demand for funds exceeds the supply. The would-be borrowers who cannot get loans bid up the interest rate; those least desirous of borrowing drop out of the competition for the scarce funds. At the higher interest rates, savers save more, so there are more funds to go around. The process goes on until the interest rate is bid

---

[1] In Chapter 9, we will see that there is some controversy about whether higher interest rates really induce people to save more. Under some circumstances, increasing the interest rates can have even the perverse effect of reducing the supply of savings.

Figure 6.1 SUPPLY AND DEMAND FOR LOAN-ABLE FUNDS

The amount of money loaned and borrowed is the quantity, and the interest rate is the price. At the equilibrium interest rate *r**, the supply of loanable funds equals the demand.

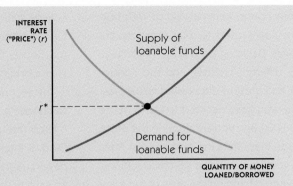

up to the level where supply equals demand. Exactly the converse process goes on if initially the interest rate is above *r**, where the supply of funds exceeds the demand.

We can now explain why the equilibrium interest rate is normally positive. If it were zero percent or negative, prospective borrowers would demand more funds than prospective savers would be willing to supply. Indeed, negative interest rates would mean that people could borrow to consume today and pay back less in the future, and that savers would receive less in the future than the amount they saved. Only at a positive interest rate can the demand for loans be equated to the supply.

In our economy, borrowers and lenders do not usually meet face to face. Instead, banks and other financial institutions serve as intermediaries, collecting savings from those who want to save and disbursing money to those who want to borrow. These intermediaries help make the market for loans work smoothly. For their services, the intermediaries charge fees, which can be measured as the difference between the interest rate they pay savers and the interest rate they charge borrowers.

TWO PROBLEMS IN INTERPRETING INTEREST RATES

When borrowers look at loan options and when savers look at investment options, they are confounded with an array of possibilities. Borrowers can pay back the money they borrow in two years or three years. One bank offers 9.5 percent interest compounded monthly; another offers 10 percent, compounded annually. These are exchanges, and as in any other exchanges, individuals should take care that what they are trading for matches their needs and expectations. Economists encourage people to consider two, often hidden, issues: the effect of compounding, and the effect of inflation on the true cost of borrowing or on the true return from investing.

THE EFFECT OF COMPOUNDING

The rate of compounding affects the total interest received or paid. We have already seen the benefits to the saver of interest compounded annually. Interest compounded

People who buy houses generally do so with borrowed money. Loans used to buy property are called mortgages. Deciding on the right mortgage involves many different choices, and the consideration of risk and present discounted value is essential. Let's say you have decided to buy a house that costs $100,000, and you are sitting in the office of the institution that offers the best interest rates around. Now you have to make several decisions.

First you have to decide on the term of the loan: the time period over which the loan will be repaid. Two common terms for mortgage loans are 15 years and 30 years. A 15-year mortgage commonly involves higher payments—for example, $200 a month or so higher at current rates of interest—but the loan is totally repaid in half the time as a 30-year loan. What are the reasons for choosing one loan over the other?

Sometimes it is suggested that the 15-year loan will save the borrower a lot of money. The reasoning goes that if you add up the extra $200 a month you would be paying over the 15 years, you would find that it is much less than the amount you would pay over the second half of a 30-year mortgage. The flaw in this argument relates to the ideas of present value and the time value of money.

By definition, the present value of a 15-year loan and a 30-year loan must be the same; after all, each loan is enough to buy the same $100,000 house. The basic lesson is that *choosing the shorter loan period means that you will have less money to spend on other goods during the next 15 years and more money to spend in the subsequent 15 years.*

The main consideration in choosing between 15- and 30-year mortgages is how fast you want to pay off a debt of a given size. For example, a young family starting off may reason that by paying off the loan in 15 years, they will be better able to afford college tuition when their children turn eighteen. On the other hand, if they feel they can barely afford the house, the lower monthly payments of a 30-year mortgage may make more sense.

The second major mortgage decision is whether to choose a fixed-rate or a variable-rate loan. With a fixed-rate mortgage your interest payments are fixed. If interest rates go up, you do not have to pay any more than your fixed rate. If rates go down, you still have to pay the amount agreed upon.

With a variable-rate mortgage, interest payments are variable; the rate you have to pay is usually related to some recognized market rate of interest. But interest rates tend to rise when the rate of inflation increases. So *real* interest rates (the nominal interest rate minus the rate of inflation) may actually be *less* variable than with a fixed-rate mortgage.

Thus, if you had taken out a fixed-rate mortgage at 15 percent in 1980 when the rate of inflation was around 11 percent, so that the real interest rate was 4 percent, in 1981 you would have suddenly found yourself paying twice that real interest rate as the inflation rate came down to 7 percent. Since one of the things borrowers really care about is how many extra *goods* they have to give up in the future for consuming more today—that is, the real interest rate—they find variable-rate mortgages, where real rates are in fact less variable, attractive. Still, the difficulty of making increased payments should the interest rate rise substantially makes variable-rate mortgages unattractive to many borrowers; wages may not move in tandem with interest rates.

Of course, if you think you are smarter than the market, and you *know* what is going to happen to interest rates, your decision may be easier. If you see interest rates rising rapidly, take advantage of a fixed-rate mortgage. But before betting your bucks, just remember: even experts find it difficult to predict what is going to happen to interest rates, especially over a span of 15 to 30 years.

A final question home buyers have to face is how much to borrow. The bank will require a down payment of perhaps 20 percent of the purchase value. With a $100,000 house, the minimum down payment would then be $20,000. Imagine that you could make a down payment of $25,000, more than enough. But then you realize that you would like to furnish your house, which will cost $5,000. You could buy furniture on credit, but you would have to pay a much higher interest rate of 18 or 20 percent. (Sometimes firms think it sounds better to call interest "finance charges.") It obviously makes sense to borrow $80,000 for the house rather than the $75,000 you need, and use the extra $5,000 to pay cash for the furniture, thus avoiding finance charges. Economists say, "Funds are fungible," that is, it is easy to distribute funds nominally designed for one purpose (here, to buy a house) to another (to buy furniture). There is another reason you should consider taking out a larger mortgage than you might absolutely need: the government allows you to deduct interest on mortgage payments for income tax purposes, but not interest on other loans.

monthly is even better because you start earning interest on interest more quickly, and most banks now have accounts that compound interest on a daily basis.

To see the advantage of more frequent compounding, consider the choice between an account that pays 10 percent compounded annually and one that pays 9.6 percent compounded daily. If you put $1,000 in the first account, at the end of the year you will get $1,100, and $1,210 at the end of two years. At 9.6 percent compounded daily, you will have $1,100.75 at the end of the year and $1,211.64 at the end of two. The faster rate of compounding makes the 9.6 percent rate better than the 10 percent rate.

The same story holds in reverse for borrowers. If you borrow $1,000 for two years at 10 percent annual interest, then with simple interest, you will pay the bank $1,200 at the end of two years. With annual compounding, at the end of the first year, you will owe the bank $1,100. At the end of two years, you will owe interest on the $100 interest you already owe, for a total of $1,210. With *daily* compounding, matters are worse—you will owe $1,221.37.

Banks used to offer loans with the rate of compounding in the fine print, until the confusion this caused led Congress to enact a Truth in Lending Act. This law requires lenders to convert all interest rates to an annual percentage rate (APR). This provision has been helpful to borrowers; savers too are wise to make the same conversion. For simplicity, in this book we will normally assume that interest is compounded annually.

THE EFFECT OF INFLATION

Borrowers and savers are also wise to consider the effect of **inflation** on loans and investments. Goods and services generally have higher prices this year than they did last year. This general upward creep of all prices is what economists call inflation.

Consider the case of an individual who decides to deposit $1,000 in a savings account. At the end of the year, at a 10 percent interest rate, she will have $1,100. But prices meanwhile have risen by 6 percent. That means that a good that cost $1,000 in the beginning of the year now costs $1,060. In terms of "purchasing power," she has only $40 extra to spend ($1,100 − $1,060)—4 percent more than she had at the beginning of the year. This is her real return. On the other hand, a borrower knows that if he borrows money, the dollars he gives back to repay the loan will be worth less than the dollars he receives today. Thus, what is relevant for individuals to know when deciding either how much to borrow or how much to lend (save) is the *real* interest rate, which takes account of inflation. It is the real interest rate that should appear on the vertical axis of Figure 6.1.

Economists separate interest rate measures into **nominal interest rates,** which name the amount you are paid in dollars, and **real interest rates,** which give the nominal interest rate minus the rate of inflation. The real interest rate tells how much extra *consumption*, or goods, you can get next year if you give up some consumption today. If the nominal interest rate is 10 percent and the rate of inflation is 6 percent, then the real interest rate is 4 percent. By lending out (or saving) a dollar today, you can increase the amount of goods that you can get in one year's time by 4 percent.

REAL INTEREST RATE

Real interest rate = nominal interest rate − rate of inflation

THE MARKET FOR ASSETS

Gardeners today would have been shocked at the price of tulip bulbs in seventeenth-century Holland, which rose to the point where one bulb sold for the equivalent of $16,000 in today's dollars. The golden age of tulips did not last long, however, and in

1637, prices of bulbs fell by over 90 percent. Such a dramatic price swing is by no means a quirk of history. Between 1973 and 1980, the price of gold rose from $98 to $613, or by 525 percent; then from 1980 to 1985, it fell to $318. Between 1977 and 1980, the price of farmland in Iowa increased by 40 percent, only to fall by over 60 percent from 1980 to 1987. In yet another example, on October 19, 1987, prices plummeted in the U.S. stock market. In that single day, the total value of stock in U.S. companies decreased by $.5 trillion, almost 25 percent. Even a major war would be unlikely to destroy a quarter of the U.S. capital stock in a day. But there was no war or any other external event sufficient to explain the 1987 drop.

Just how large these price swings have been can be seen graphically in Figure 6.2, which shows how the prices of four assets have risen and fallen. If you bought at the low points and sold at the high, you could have made a fortune, but if you bought at the high points and sold at the low, you could have easily lost a fortune.

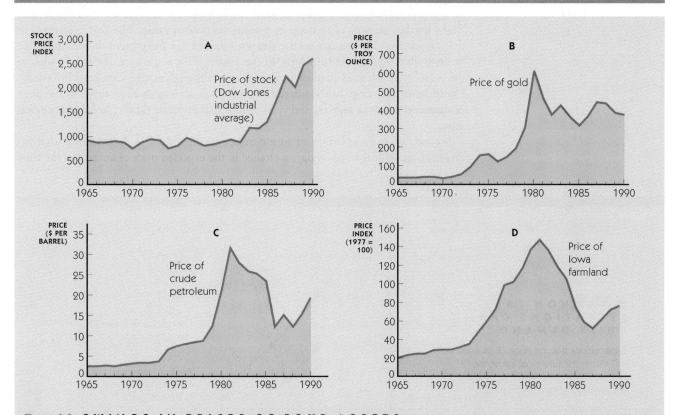

Figure 6.2 **SWINGS IN PRICES OF FOUR ASSETS**

Prices for some assets—such as stocks, gold, oil, and farmland— changed dramatically between 1965 and 1990. *Sources: Economic Report of the President* (1991), Table B-93; *Mineral Commodity* *Summaries* (1991); *Monthly Energy Review* (1991); *Farm Real Estate Market* (1987–88); Economic Research Service (1989–90).

How can the demand and supply model of Chapters 4 and 5 explain these huge price swings? Surely the supply curves for these goods did not shift dramatically in such short intervals. Nor is it plausible that the uses to which the goods could be put suddenly expanded and then contracted, causing some fantastic shifts in demand. The solution to this puzzle lies in shifts of the demand curve, but not directly for the reasons we saw in Chapter 4.

The first step in the solution is to recognize that the goods in the examples above are unlike ice cream cones, newspapers, or any other goods that are valued by the consumer mainly for their present use. Gold, land, stock, and even tulips in seventeenth-century Holland are all examples of **assets.** Assets are long-lived and thus can be bought at one date and sold at another. For this reason, the price individuals are willing to pay for them today depends not only on today's conditions, the immediate return or benefits, but also on some expectation as to what tomorrow's conditions will be; in particular, on what the assets will be worth in the future, what they can be sold for.

The concept of present discounted value tells us how to measure and compare returns anticipated in the future. Changes in present discounted value shift demand curves, as shown in Figure 6.3, because the amount that someone is willing to pay today depends on the present discounted value of what she believes she can get for it in the future. There are two sources of changes in present discounted value. The first is changes in the interest rate: an increase in the interest rate reduces the present discounted value of the dollars you expect to receive in the future. This is the explanation of much of the volatility of the stock markets in recent years (although not the October 1987 crash). For instance, increases in the interest rate are often accompanied by drops in the price of shares on the stock market, and vice versa. Smart investors thus try to forecast interest rates.

Second, since expectations of future prices are important in determining what individuals are willing to pay today, a change in the expected price of an asset at the time

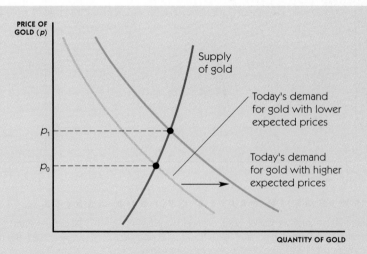

Figure 6.3 HOW EX-PECTATIONS CAN SHIFT DEMAND

Expectations that the price of an asset will rise in the future can cause the demand curve to shift out to the right, thus raising the current price.

one expects to sell it will change the present discounted value. Again, this will lead to a shift in the demand curve. Expectations can be quite volatile, and this volatility in expectations explains a great deal of the volatility in asset prices.

To see how expectations concerning future events affect *current* prices, consider a hypothetical example. People suddenly realize that new smog-control devices will, ten years from now, make certain parts of Los Angeles much more inhabitable than they are today. As a result, future-oriented individuals will think that ten years from now, the price of land in those areas will be much higher, say $1 million an acre. But, they think, nine years from now surely it will be recognized that in one short year an acre will be worth $1 million. Hence, nine years from now investors will be willing to pay almost $1 million for the land; even if, at that date (nine years from now), the smog has not yet been eliminated. But then, these same individuals think, eight years from now investors will realize that in one short year the price will rise to almost $1 million and will pay close to that amount. So working backward, it becomes apparent that if people are confident that land is going to be much more valuable in ten years, its price rises today.

Thus, while changes in tastes or technology or incomes or the prices of other goods *today* could not account for some of the sharp changes in asset values described at the start of this section, changes in expectations concerning any of these variables in the future will have an effect *today* on the demand. Markets for assets are linked together over time. An event that will happen—or is expected to happen—ten or fifteen or even fifty years hence can have a direct bearing on today's market.

FORMING EXPECTATIONS

Changes in expectations of the future, about either returns or interest rates, thus can be reflected today in large changes in asset prices. How do individuals and firms form expectations? Partly by looking at past experience. If a company has steadily grown more valuable, investors may come to expect that pattern to continue. If every time inflation rates increase rapidly the banking authorities act to slow down the economy by raising interest rates, people come to expect inflation to be followed by higher interest rates.

Psychologists and economists have extensively studied how individuals form their expectations. Sometimes people are **myopic,** or short-sighted. They simply expect what is true today to be true tomorrow. The price of gold today is what it will be tomorrow. Sometimes they are **adaptive,** extrapolating events of the recent past into the future. For instance, if the price of gold today is 5 percent higher than it was last year, they expect its price next year to be 5 percent higher than it is today.

When people make full use of all the relevant available past data to form their expectations, economists say that their expectations are **rational.** While the price of gold rises during an inflationary period, the individual also knows that the price of gold goes down when inflation subsides. Thus, if a person knows that economic analysts are predicting lower inflation, he will not expect the gold price increases to continue. When individuals form their expectations rationally, they will not be right all the time. Sometimes they will be overly optimistic, sometimes overly pessimistic (although in making their decisions, they are aware of these possibilities), but the assumption of rational expectations is that on average they will be right.

The 1970s were a period when adaptive expectations reigned, as many investors came to expect prices to continue to rise at a rapid rate. The more you invested, the more money you made. The idea that the price of a house or of land might actually fall seemed beyond belief—in spite of the fact that historically there had been a number of episodes (most recently during the 1930s) when prices fell dramatically. The weak real estate markets of the 1980s in many regions became a reminder of the importance of incorporating more historical data in forming expectations.

The problem in all types of fortune-telling, however, is that history never repeats itself exactly. Since the situation today is never precisely like any past experience, it is never completely clear which facts will turn out to be the relevant ones. The last fifty years have seen a variety of gradual changes as corporations have expanded and diversified, governments have taken on new responsibilities, tax rates have bounced up and down, and tax loopholes have opened and closed. Indeed, all of society's institutions are in a state of flux that can be gradual or violent in turn. Even the best-informed experts are likely to disagree on which changes are likely to be most relevant. When it comes to predicting the future, everyone has a cloudy crystal ball.

FORECASTING: A FIRST LOOK

Despite the difficulty of making good forecasts, they are in great demand. Many economists have grown rich on the basis of a good forecasting record, and a whole industry has developed trying to provide better forecasts of everything—from the number of babies in ten years' time to the size of the economy to the demand for steel to the price of IBM shares on the stock market. There is money to be made if you can tell which stocks are going to do better in the market. If you know when the demand for your product is going to drop, you can make a better investment decision.

Forecasters often construct statistical models of an industry or of the economy to predict what will happen. Thus, a model of the industry will include an estimate of the demand curve and the supply curve (including an estimate of the price elasticity of demand and supply), and an analysis of the major factors that are likely to shift either the demand curve or the supply curve. These models can incorporate more of the relevant information than a "seat of the pants" guess about the future.

Some forecasters seem to predict a new Great Depression every other year, while others seem to perpetually believe that the United States is about to enter a golden age of unparalleled prosperity. Many of the forecasters are reminiscent of newspaper advertisements of long ago that promised to predict the sex of a child, with a money-back guarantee. Even if these seers had always predicted a boy, they would have been right half the time. So too—thanks to blind chance—practically all economic forecasters, no matter how incompetent, eventually have a day when they can crow, "I told you so!"

The real test of forecasters, of course, is not whether they are ever correct, but whether they are correct more consistently than mere chance can explain, and correct when it really counts. Despite the many jokes made about economic forecasters—for example, the claim that economists have predicted twelve out of the last five recessions—they have actually done a fairly credible job. The main failure has been in attempting to forecast turning points, when the economy switches from growth to stagnation, or stagnation to growth. But because one of the predicaments of business is to plan for turning points and one of the main objectives of government policy is to forestall downturns, this inability to predict turning points has been a major limitation.

THE MARKET FOR RISK

Risk accompanies most future-oriented economic activity, and most of us do not like this uncertainty about outcomes. We might spend a few dollars on some lottery tickets or playing the slot machines at Las Vegas or Atlantic City, but for the most part, we try to avoid or minimize serious risks. Psychologists have extensively studied this "risk-avoidance behavior," focusing, for instance, on the anxiety to which uncertainty gives rise. Economists refer to risk-avoidance behavior by saying that individuals are **risk averse.**

Individuals are risk averse, and yet our economy needs to encourage risk taking. New ventures are risky, but they are the engine of economic growth. Our economy has developed a number of ways by which risks are transferred, transformed, and shared. The collection of institutions and arrangements by which this is done is known as the **market for risk.**

INSURANCE

Among the most important parts of the market for risk is the insurance market, in which people buy security from the financial risk of specified events—illness, accidents, and other misfortunes. A look at the insurance market will supply us with some of the general issues and concerns in the market for risk.

When an individual takes out an insurance policy, she pays a fixed amount to the insurance company, the **premium,** in return for which she receives a promise that some payment will be made if the insured-against event occurs. Thus, the individual transfers the risk (at least the financial part of it) to the insurance firm. The insurance firm is able to absorb this risk for two reasons. First, it spreads the risk among a large number of people. If the insurance firm has many owners, as most do, the risks it takes are effectively carried by all of them.

Second, the insurance firm can predict risk quite accurately because it insures a large pool of individuals who face similar risks. The company may be looking at a population of a million people, all of whom want fire insurance. It can estimate with a fair degree of accuracy the number of individuals who will have a fire in a given year. If there is a 1 in 100 chance of a fire, with 1 million people insured, the firm can be fairly sure that approximately 10,000 will have fires. In a lucky year, 9,000 may have fires; in an unlucky year, 11,000. If the firm sets the premium at just slightly greater than the amount it expects to pay out on each policy, it can be quite confident that the premiums it collects will cover its disbursements.

Unfortunately, while individuals and firms can divest themselves of many risks through insurance, there are many important risks for which they cannot buy insurance. A business cannot buy insurance that protects it against the risk that the demand for its product will fall, or the risk that a competitor will develop a better product that will drive the company into bankruptcy. Economists have identified two inherent problems that limit the use of insurance as a mechanism for handling risk: adverse selection and moral hazard.

ADVERSE SELECTION

Some individuals are more likely to have an accident than others. Consider, for example, the issues posed by automobile insurance. Some people may drink more frequently before they drive. They may drive when they are tired. They may drive carelessly. An insurance company can ask what sort of car you drive and how far a typical commute is, but many accident-related attributes are hard or impossible for an insurance firm to detect. A firm certainly does not expect an individual to admit that he is an accident-prone driver, which would practically beg the company to charge him a higher rate.

Insurance companies do make some effort to divide people into better and worse risk categories. This general problem—knowing that there are differences among individuals, differences in their likelihood of collecting on insurance, but not knowing which people are high risk and which are low—is an example of what is called a selection problem. The insurance company would like to select the best risks to insure, just as the employer would like to select the most productive employees to hire. Before selling life insurance, insurance firms often ask an individual to submit to a medical exam. Before selling fire or theft insurance, they may send around a building inspector to inspect the premises and make suggestions for greater security and safety. But although these examinations will gather some information, they will not reveal everything.

If an insurance company knows an individual is a bad risk, it may still be willing to provide insurance but only at a higher premium, such as automobile insurance for drivers under the age of twenty-five. Not surprisingly, then, people who are bad risks and are attempting to purchase insurance do not readily tell the insurance company that they are bad risks. For example, the prospective buyer of life insurance may try to hide any malady from the doctor examining him; he is certainly unlikely to draw any problems to the attention of the doctor. Someone thinking of buying fire or theft insurance is not likely to point out faulty electrical wiring or unlocked back windows to the insurance company's building inspector.

Worse still for the insurance company is the general rule that those who are most likely to collect from insurance—for example, those who are most accident-prone—are often among the most eager to purchase it. Those who are least likely to collect—for example, those who are most safety conscious—may still want to buy some insurance; but since they know they are relatively safe, they will not be willing to pay too much for the insurance.

To understand the insurance firm's problem, we need to see how insurance markets work. In simple terms, firms collect premiums from a pool of customers to cover those customers against a specified risk. As long as the average losses and the costs of doing business match up with the premiums, an insurance market is viable. To keep the story simple, we can ignore wages and the other costs of doing business, and say the premiums must be at least as high as average losses for the market to be viable. The 45-degree line in Figure 6.4A shows the points where premiums equal average losses: on the line and below it, the market is viable, while above the line, the market is not viable because the firm is paying out more than it is taking in.

As premiums rise, the "best" risks decide not to buy insurance, so the *average* loss per policy increases. Panel B shows a curve relating average losses per policy to the level of the premium. At very low premiums, the market is not viable because the firm is simply not charging enough to cover losses. At some level of premiums, the market passes into the viable side of the 45-degree line. The question is, why does it not remain

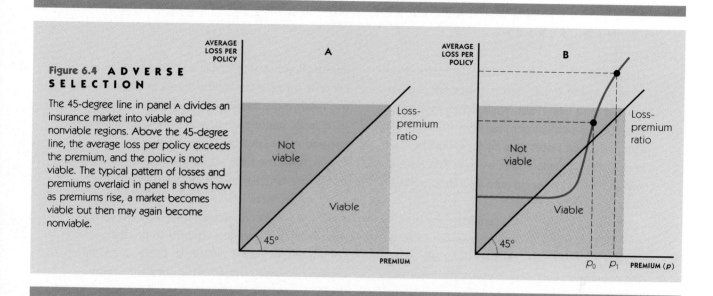

Figure 6.4 ADVERSE SELECTION

The 45-degree line in panel A divides an insurance market into viable and nonviable regions. Above the 45-degree line, the average loss per policy exceeds the premium, and the policy is not viable. The typical pattern of losses and premiums overlaid in panel B shows how as premiums rise, a market becomes viable but then may again become nonviable.

viable forever as premiums get higher and higher? The answer is that higher premiums drive low-risk customers from the market, leaving a smaller pool with a higher fraction of customers who will have an accident.

The fact that the insurance company cannot completely discern between good risks and bad risks presents it with a serious dilemma. Consider an insurance firm that finds that the current premiums on its policies, p_0 in panel B, do not pay for the losses covered by these policies. The natural response if premiums are failing to pay for losses is to raise the premiums to p_1. But if the insurance firm raises its premiums, those who are not very accident-prone will decide that the price is too high, and they will demand less insurance. As they drop out of the market, however, the change in the proportion of "bad" customers may swamp the direct effect of the increase in premiums. Rather than reducing the insurance firm's gap between losses and premiums, the price increase will widen the gap. The company could raise the price of its insurance further in another attempt to make up the difference, but it will lose still more of the remaining safety-conscious people.

The effect is called **adverse selection:** those who tend to buy insurance tend to be those most at risk, and charging higher prices for insurance will discourage those at less risk from buying insurance at all. This adverse selection effect is a consequence of the limited information available to the insurance firm. The firm knows that among its customers, some people are better risks than others, but it does not know who are the better risks. The insurance firm knows less about the individual than the individual knows about herself, and the person has no incentive to supply possibly damaging information to the insurance firm.

For many kinds of insurance, such as fire insurance, adverse selection problems may not be too bad. The critical information (determining the likelihood of a fire) can easily enough be observed—for instance, by building inspectors. But for many of the kinds of risks against which individuals would like to buy insurance, adverse selection effects

CLOSE-UP: AUTO INSURANCE AND ADVERSE SELECTION IN NEW JERSEY

The charge for private passenger automobile insurance in the United States skyrocketed during the mid- and late 1980s. While prices rose on average by 3.5 percent per year from 1984 to 1989, auto insurance prices rose by 9 percent per year during that time, more than twice as fast. But perhaps no state had worse auto insurance problems than New Jersey.

New Jersey was a likely candidate for auto insurance problems, for several reasons. It has the highest population per square mile of any state in the country, making drivers somewhat more likely to bump into one another. Nine of the nation's top twenty-five cities for car theft are in New Jersey, a statistic that does not do much to hold down auto insurance rates. Finally, New Jersey was one of only two states without any upper limit on the amount of medical costs that could be claimed from any accident. When we combine these factors with the national surge in auto insurance premiums, it should

be little surprise that it cost $1,000 a year on average to insure a car in New Jersey at the start of the 1990s, more than double the national average.

To make matters even worse, New Jersey was trapped in the jaws of an adverse selection problem. In 1983, the state set up a Joint Underwriting Authority (JUA), which was intended to offer auto insurance to those who were too risky for private companies to insure. Rates in the JUA were supposed to be comparable to those in private companies, which is a bit difficult to figure, since the private insurance companies did not want to insure these risky drivers at all. In practice, anyone could be insured by the JUA, at rates not much different from the average for low-risk drivers.

This well-intended but poorly thought-out law set up what should have been anticipated patterns of adverse selection. Private insurance companies directed their worst risks to the JUA and insured only the lowest risks. By the end of the 1980s, half

of New Jersey's drivers were enrolled in the JUA, which had accumulated a deficit of $3 billion that was growing by $1 billion a year; extra taxes were needed to cover the lost money, creating a political furor in the Garden State.

In 1990, newly elected governor Jim Florio pushed through an insurance reform plan. The plan abolished the JUA and called upon auto insurance companies to pay for half its deficit and absorb all the drivers it had insured. The insurance companies argued that this was unfair, unprofitable, and illegal, and lengthy court battles seem to be looming ahead. Companies like the Hartford, Cigna, Colonial Penn, and the Travelers have all announced that they want to stop doing auto insurance business in New Jersey altogether, and Allstate has actually withdrawn from the state.

It is a hard reality, in New Jersey and elsewhere, that even with the rapid increases in auto insurance premiums during the 1980s, companies in the business have lost money. The amount going out in claims has increased even faster than the amount coming in. Insurance spreads and shares risk, but it cannot provide something for nothing. What goes in (the premiums) can only be reduced if what goes out (the claims) is also reduced. Either safe drivers must be willing to subsidize risky ones—not very likely—or drivers who run a higher risk of being in an accident will need to be charged higher rates.

While voters are eager to have their premiums reduced, they are less enthusiastic about fundamental reforms that would limit how much they could recover in an accident, or limit their right to sue. But in the long run, these sorts of reforms are probably the only way out of the auto insurance crisis.

Sources: Insurance Information Institute, *1990 Property/ Casualty Insurance Facts;* "Insurers Under Siege: Lawmakers, Consumers, and Corporate Customers Are Fighting Mad," *Business Week,* August 21, 1989, pp. 72–79; Joseph J. Sullivan, "Compromise on Insurance Isn't Working in New Jersey," *New York Times,* January 15, 1989, p. D6; Jay Romano, "Why Auto Insurance Costs So Much," *New York Times,* October 22, 1989, sec. XII, p. 1; Romano, "New Law on Auto Insurance Draws Fire," *New York Times,* March 18, 1990, sec. XII, p. 1.

are important. With health or automobile insurance, for instance, an insurance firm is likely to find it difficult to determine any particular individual's risk. Even worse, consider the problem of measuring the risk that a firm's new product will fail to meet expectations. It would be nearly impossible for an insurance company to decide precisely what the prospects for the product are. The business firm itself is certainly more likely to be better informed about the markets in which it is trying to sell the product. Not surprisingly, then, because of their disadvantage in obtaining crucial information, insurance firms do not supply insurance against such business risks.

MORAL HAZARD

A second problem faced by insurance companies is an incentive problem: insurance affects people's incentives to avoid whatever contingencies they are insured against. A person who has no fire insurance on a house, for example, may choose to limit the risk of fire by buying smoke alarms and home fire extinguishers and being especially cautious. But if that same person had fire insurance, he might not be so careful. Indeed, if the insurance would pay more than the house's market value, he might even be tempted to burn his own house down. This would be rational but, most people would say, immoral.

This general feature of insurance, that it reduces the individual's incentives to avoid the insured-against accident, is called **moral hazard.** Of course, from an economist's point of view, what is at issue is not a question of morality, but only a question of incentives. If a person bears only a portion, or none, of the consequences of his actions—as he does when he has purchased insurance—then his incentives are altered.

In the late 1960s, after urban riots plagued many major cities in the United States, inner-city property values plunged. Insurance coverage adjusted slowly, so that for a while many buildings were insured at amounts that considerably exceeded their reduced market value. Was it purely coincidental that the value of fire losses nationwide increased 55 percent between 1966 and 1970?

Moral hazard concerns may not be too important for many kinds of insurance; an individual who buys a large life insurance policy and thus knows that her children will be well cared for in the event of her demise is hardly likely to take much bigger risks with her life. (There was, however, a grisly case in California some years ago in which a person cut off one foot with an axe to try to collect on disability insurance.) But for many kinds of risks against which a firm's managers would *like* to buy insurance, moral hazard concerns are important. For example, if a company could buy insurance to guarantee a minimum level of profit, managers would have less incentive to exert effort. When moral hazard problems are strong, insurance firms will offer limited—or even no—insurance.

THE CAPITAL MARKET: SHARING RISKS AND RAISING CAPITAL

The insurance market is concerned with risks: risks are transferred from an individual to an insurance firm, which is better able to bear those risks. Other markets are concerned with time: an individual gives up consumption today in return for more consumption in the future. Bank accounts illustrate in simple form the time aspect of markets. When we look more generally at the broad class of markets called the capital market—the general set of institutions involved in lending and borrowing and in raising funds—we can see that generally both the risk and time aspects arise at the same time.

Trades in the capital market are intertemporal: they occur over time. For this reason, there is also risk: individuals and households who give up funds today to other individuals and firms face uncertainty about how much will be repaid in the future and in what circumstances. Because most of the important risks cannot be insured through an insurance company, in the capital market issues of time and risk are intricately interconnected. How the capital is raised determines how the risks are apportioned, who bears what risks.

In modern capital markets, there are two principal ways in which capital is raised: through debt (also referred to as credit or loans) and through equity (also referred to as shares). In loan markets, the borrower promises to pay back certain fixed amounts of money at certain times in the future. Firms can obtain loans not only from banks, but also by issuing **bonds,** which are purchased by households and other firms. A bond is a promise the firm makes to pay a certain amount, say thirty years from now, and to make regular interest payments on the amount borrowed, say twice a year. Just as it does with a bank, the firm thus receives money today in return for a promise to repay a certain amount in the future (to whoever owns the bond at the time). Economists often lump bonds and bank credit (outstanding loans) together, and refer to funds raised in this way as **debt.** Alternatively, firms raise **equity capital,** which is the money the firm's owners supply directly to the firm. The most popular form of ownership in the United States is the corporation, on which we will focus for now. Ownership of the corporation is established through the sale of **shares,** also called **stock.** The initial owner of a company gives up a fraction of her company to people who supply her with capital. Those who provide the capital are then said to have a "share" in the company; they are the firm's **shareholders.** If a company issues 2,000,000 shares, for example, an individual who owns 100,000 shares then is entitled to 100,000 / 2,000,000 = 5 percent of the firm's profits, and to cast 5 percent of the votes in deciding who should run the company. Thus, Henry Ford may have had the ideas that led to the success of Ford Motor Company, but he needed capital, and he received much of the capital by giving a fraction of his company to those who provided it. If a company's new shareholders own 50 percent of the shares, that means they get 50 percent of the profits. If the value of the firm goes up, they receive 50 percent of the gains.

RISKS OF STOCKS

With shares, investors (shareholders) do not receive back a fixed amount. What they get depends on how well the firm does. If it fails, they may receive nothing. If it is a roaring success, they may make a fortune. For example, there is the case of Microsoft, a computer software company. If you had bought $1,000 worth of stock in 1986, by 1991 the stock would have been worth $7,000, a return of over 600 percent, or a rate of return of nearly 50 percent per year. But there are many other computer firms whose shareholders have received no returns at all.

There are thus considerable risks associated with investing in stocks. But the risks are limited, a feature that sets the corporate form of ownership apart from other, less popular forms. The investor in a corporation can lose all the money he invests in shares, but no more. He is said to have **limited liability.** By contrast, owners who do not protect themselves with the corporate form may be personally liable for the firm's debts and thus may lose *more* than the amount they have invested in their firm.

RISKS OF LOANS

There are risks associated with any investment, loans as well as stocks. In the case of a loan, as we have seen, the borrower promises to pay back a certain amount of money. But promises are sometimes broken. Sometimes a borrower may **default;** that is, fail to make a promised payment. Indeed, about 2 to 3 percent of all bank loans to consumers go into default every year, and every year thousands of firms—including several major firms—go bankrupt. They find themselves in a situation in which they cannot fulfill their obligations to creditors, including the banks that have lent them money and the

CLOSE-UP: THE S&L CRISIS

The savings and loan crisis was waiting for George Bush when he assumed the presidency in 1989. Savings and loan associations (S & L's, for short) are banks whose traditional function is to accept deposits from savers, and to use this money to make mortgage loans to home buyers. In this, S & L's have been successful. America is a nation of home owners, with almost two-thirds of families owning their own home. In contrast, less than half of French families own their own home. But as President Bush entered office, hundreds of S & L's were going bankrupt.

To the public, this debacle was the result of greed and fraud; stories of high-living bank presidents and big campaign contributions attracted national attention. But bank officers seem no more prone to corruption than those in other sectors of the economy; indeed, they have more of a reputation for dull respectability than for high living. Economists argued that the S & L crisis resulted from a combination of bad economic luck and bad government incentives.

The government has long been involved with savings and loans, both as a regulator and as a provider of insurance. In the past, if an S & L went bankrupt, a government agency, the Federal Savings and Loan Insurance Corporation (FSLIC), stepped in and paid off the depositors. The savings and loan crisis occurred because so many of them had gone bankrupt that the FSLIC did not have the money to pay off the depositors. Either people would lose their savings, or taxpayers had to step in.

These bankruptcies were rooted in the economic problems of the late 1970s and early 1980s. Until the 1970s, S & L's mainly loaned money for home mortgages at an interest rate of about 6 percent and were allowed by law to pay only 5 percent interest to depositors.

But interest rates skyrocketed in the late 1970s and early 1980s. The value of home mortgages—the principal asset of the S & L's—fell. The value of a mortgage is the present discounted value of the money that borrowers promise to pay back (interest and principal). Those promises were based on mortgage interest rates often fixed at around 6 percent or even lower. When interest rates jumped to 14 percent or higher, the present discounted value of these mortgages was cut by half or more. This is just another example of the principle that when interest rates rise, the present discounted value of future income is reduced.

In the early 1980s, the federal government was forced to react, or else the entire savings and loan

industry might have gone bankrupt. The government allowed S & L's to invest in many things besides mortgages. Many S & L's worked themselves back to financial stability.

But for a smaller group of S & L's, matters went from bad to worse. Some S & L managers tried a strategy of making high-risk loans, for which they could charge high interest rates. If the loans worked out, these S & L's could make a lot of money.

Incentives were all awry. Depositors had no reason to worry about this high-risk strategy; if the loans failed, as high-risk loans have a nasty tendency to do, government insurance would pay them off. Thus, money poured into these high-risk S & L's, which offered higher interest rates to depositors.

The situation was a classic example of a moral hazard problem. Because of depositor insurance, the S & L's not only lacked incentives to invest in safe investments, they actually had incentives to undertake quite risky investments. Since if they did not take these risks they would have almost surely gone bankrupt anyway, they were in a no-lose situation.

If the government had simply shut down all the bankrupt savings and loans in 1984 or 1985, it might have cost $20 billion or so to pay off the depositors. But by the end of the 1980s, the total bill was estimated at well over $100 billion in present discounted value. Together with accumulated interest payments, the undiscounted value of the payments over forty years could run as high as $500 billion.

In August 1989, Congress passed and President Bush signed legislation that was billed as the solution to the S & L troubles. The bill called for tighter monitoring of the S & L's, and it made some bureaucratic changes. But critics of the bill claim that there is still need for more fundamental reforms.

suppliers who have delivered goods with the stipulation that payment be made in thirty to sixty days. Eastern Airlines and International Harvester are among the large companies that have recently gone "belly-up."

The fact that there is some risk of default explains why some borrowers must pay higher rates of interest than others. The U.S. government, which borrows money just as individuals and firms do, can usually borrow what it wants by promising to pay a relatively low interest rate. That is because the government is generally thought of as having an extremely low risk of defaulting, practically zero. Well-established, healthy companies like General Electric and Exxon pay a slightly higher rate than the government, because even big companies like these, although their risk of defaulting is low, are slightly more likely to default than the federal government. The rate of interest these firms and others judged to have a low risk of default are charged is called the **prime rate.** Other borrowers pay even higher rates.

The law of supply and demand explains how these differences in interest rates are determined. The discussion of interest rates early in this chapter ignored default. It implicitly assumed that the amount borrowed was so low that the default risk was negligible. A more realistic scenario is one where lenders are aware that there are differences between the default rates on, say, loans made to people for the purpose of buying a car and on loans to major corporations. Figure 6.5 shows the demand and supply curves for car loans and loans to major corporations. The equilibrium interest

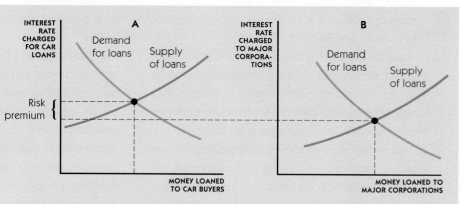

Figure 6.5 RISK AND EQUILIBRIUM INTEREST RATES

Panel A shows the supply and demand for loans to buy automobiles. Panel B shows the supply and demand for loans to major corporations. The equilibrium interest rate is higher in the automobile loan market, which reflects the higher riskiness of these loans.

rate in panel A (car loans) is higher than in panel B (loans to major corporations). The difference in interest rates reflects the difference in default risks. It is not that lenders discriminate against car buyers or in favor of large corporations. It is just that they must receive a higher return from the car loan to compensate them for bearing the greater risk. This higher return is sometimes referred to as a **risk premium.**

Even though there is some chance of loans not being repaid, lending money to a firm is much less risky than giving money to a firm by buying shares of stock. The only risk lenders bear is that of default. Otherwise, the lender gets back the promised amount regardless of how well the firm does. By contrast, not only do shareholders bear the risk of getting back nothing if the firm goes bankrupt, but how much they get back depends completely on the vagaries of how well the firm does. Stock must therefore yield a higher return to shareholders in order to compensate them for the extra risk.

But what may be an advantage from the perspective of a lender may be a disadvantage from the perspective of a borrower. The higher return on stocks, while an advantage to shareholders, who provide capital, is a disadvantage for firms trying to raise capital; these firms, on average, have to pay more to get equity capital. On the other hand,

THE TWO PRINCIPAL WAYS FIRMS RAISE FUNDS

Debt: issuing bonds, taking out loans, and otherwise obtaining funds with a commitment to repay

Equity: selling ownership shares (stock)

investors share the risk; this is an advantage for firms trying to raise capital, but generally viewed as a disadvantage by shareholders. How these advantages and disadvantages are weighed out in determining the mix of debt (outstanding loans and bonds) and stocks we see in the market is a question we will turn to in later chapters.

THE RISK-INCENTIVE TRADE-OFF

Those who supply capital share with insurance companies the problem that risk sharing distorts incentives. Indeed, it is a general rule that as we reduce risk, we also reduce incentives. A store manager whose salary is guaranteed faces little risk but also has little incentive. If his pay depends on the store's sales, he has stronger incentives but faces greater risk. In spite of his best efforts, sales may be low—perhaps because of an economic downturn, perhaps because buyers have simply turned away from his products; in either case, his income will be low.

In many cases, the market reaches a compromise: partial insurance, providing the purchaser of insurance with some incentives, but making her also bear some risk. With medical insurance, for example, it is common for an insurance company to pay only some percentage (like 80 percent) of expenses (this is called coinsurance). In this case, an individual will have a financial motivation to be cautious in the use of medical care, but still be largely protected.

Similarly, a firm that borrows money for a project is generally required to invest some of its own funds in the project, or to supply the lender with collateral; that is, provide the lender with an asset that the firm forfeits if it fails to repay the loan. Lenders know that with more of their own money at stake, borrowers will have better incentives to use the funds wisely.

Figure 6.6 shows the trade-off between risks and incentives. Along the horizontal axis, we have some measure of risk; along the vertical, some measure of incentives. It is a general rule that as we reduce the proportion of the medical costs the insurance

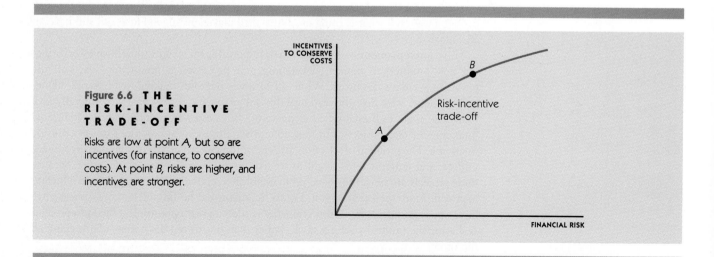

Figure 6.6 THE RISK-INCENTIVE TRADE-OFF

Risks are low at point A, but so are incentives (for instance, to conserve costs). At point B, risks are higher, and incentives are stronger.

INCENTIVES TO CONSERVE COSTS

Risk-incentive trade-off

FINANCIAL RISK

policy pays, we move along the risk-incentive trade-off from point *A*, where the individual faces little risk and has little incentive to economize on medical costs, to point *B*, where she faces considerable risk but has strong incentives for keeping costs down.

ENTREPRENEURSHIP

Innovation gives life to a capitalist economy. It also demonstrates the vital roles played by time and risk. Consider for a moment the many new products and new processes of production that have so enriched (or at least altered) everyone's life in the last century: fast food, transistors, computers, airplanes, cars, televisions—the list is endless. Each of these innovations required more than just an idea. It needed people willing to follow the advice of David Lloyd George, once prime minister of Great Britain, who said: "Don't be afraid to take a big step if one is indicated. You can't cross a chasm in two small jumps."

Innovations require people and businesses to take risks. Innovators need capital too, since those who have innovative ideas, like Henry Ford, often do not have the capital to carry them out. They must turn to others to supply them with resources, generally in exchange for a fraction of the return. After all, someone who lends to an innovator bears a risk, and he must receive compensation to be willing to undertake these risks.

In forming judgments about whether to pursue a possible innovation, innovators and investors must form expectations about the future. But because they are dealing with new ideas, products, and processes, the expectations of reasonable men and women may well differ. When the returns are in and the project has proved to be a success or a failure, it is often difficult to ascertain the reasons why, even with the wisdom of hindsight. Thus, those whose jobs require them to make decisions—the lending officers of banks, the managers of pension funds and other financial institutions, the leaders of corporations—face a difficult task. But the lack of any simple formula does not mean that there are not better and worse ways of going about making these decisions. Forming expectations and evaluating risks are like trying to play football in a heavy fog; you cannot always tell what is going on, but skilled players with good foresight still have an advantage.

Thus, **entrepreneurs**—the individuals responsible for creating new businesses, bringing new products to market, developing new processes of production—face all the problems we have discussed. While all business decision making involves risk taking, entrepreneurs who take the responsibility for managing a new business generally face more risk than well-established companies. Businesses frequently require additional financing for new projects, but new enterprises almost always require extensive outside financing. The problem of selection, of determining which of a set of potential investment projects and entrepreneurs ought to receive funds, is particularly acute, since because these projects are new, they have yet to establish a reputation. Lenders may be reluctant to provide funds for fear of default. Equity financing may be difficult too, since prospective buyers may wonder why, if this company is such a great opportunity, the entrepreneur is sharing the profits by selling stock, rather than borrowing the money and keeping all the profit.

The entrepreneur cannot buy insurance to cover most of the risks he faces. Thus, entrepreneurs must be willing to bear the risks themselves. Entrepreneurs need a return to compensate them for their efforts and the risks they undertake. Similarly, those who provide these new enterprises with capital must receive a return greater than they might receive elsewhere, to compensate them for the additional risks they have to bear. There has been ongoing concern about the effect of a variety of public policies, especially tax policy, on these returns. Does the current tax system discourage entrepreneurship? Are there policies that can be designed to encourage it? These questions will be addressed later in the book.

REVIEW AND PRACTICE

SUMMARY

1. Much of economics is future-oriented, which means that households and firms must form expectations about the future and cope with problems of risk and uncertainty.

2. The interest rate is a price. It equates the supply of funds by savers and the demand by borrowers. Savers receive interest for deferring consumption, and borrowers pay interest so that they can consume or invest now and pay later.

3. The fact that the market interest rate is positive means that a dollar received today is worth more than a dollar received in the future; this is the time value of money. The present discounted value of a dollar in the future is the amount that, if received today, is equal to what a dollar will be worth in the future, given the prevailing rate of interest.

4. The real interest rate, which measures a person's actual increase in buying power when she saves money, is equal to the nominal interest rate (the amount paid in dollars) minus the inflation rate.

5. What investors are willing to pay today for an asset depends largely on what they believe they can sell it for in the future. Changes in expectations can thus shift the demand curve for an asset and change current prices.

6. Most people are risk averse. Insurance is one way they attempt to reduce the risks they face. Insurance companies face two problems. One is that people who buy insurance tend to be those most at risk, and charging higher prices for insurance will discourage those less at risk from buying insurance at all. This effect is called adverse selection. The second problem is that insurance reduces the incentives individuals have to avoid whatever they are insured against. This is called the moral hazard problem.

7. Firms can raise money through either debt (issuing bonds or taking out loans) or equity (selling stock, or shares). Purchasers of equities share the firm's risks, its losses as well as gains.

8. With every loan, there is a risk the borrower will default. This risk explains why some borrowers must pay higher rates of interest than others.

9. Entrepreneurial innovation plays a central role in modern economies.

KEY TERMS

interest	real interest rate	debt
principal	asset	equity capital
present discounted value	risk averse	equity, shares, stock
	moral hazard	risk premium

REVIEW QUESTIONS

1. Who is on the demand side and who is on the supply side in the market for loanable funds? What is the price in that market?

2. Would you prefer to receive $100 one year from now, or five years from now? Why? Does your answer change if the rate of inflation is zero?

3. How does compound interest differ from simple interest?

4. What is the relationship between the nominal interest rate and the real interest rate?

5. True or false: "Demand curves depend on what people want now, not on their expectations about the future." Explain your answer.

6. What is meant by risk aversion? What are some consequences of the fact that most people are risk averse?

7. Why do people pay insurance premiums if they hope and expect that nothing bad is going to happen to them?

8. Would you expect a borrower's rate of interest to be higher if the borrower was a large automobile company or a small restaurant owner? Why?

9. Why is there a trade-off between risk and incentives? Give an example of this trade-off.

PROBLEMS

1. Imagine that $1,000 is deposited in an account for five years; the account pays 10 percent interest per year, compounded annually. How much money will be in the account after five years? What if the rate of interest is 12 percent? What if the annual rate of interest is 12 percent, but the interest is compounded monthly?

2. Suppose you want to buy a car three years from now, and you know that the price of a car at that time will be $10,000. If the interest rate is 7 percent per year, how much would you have to set aside today to have the money ready when you need it? If the interest rate is 5 percent, how much would you have to set aside today?

3. Many states have passed laws that put a ceiling on the rate of interest that can be charged; these laws are called usury laws. Using a supply and demand diagram, show

the effect of interest rate ceilings on the quantity (supply) of lending. Who is better off as a result of usury laws? Who is worse off?

4. Imagine that you win the lottery, but find that your $10 million prize is paid out in five chunks: a $2 million payment right away, and then $2 million every five years until you have received the total. Calculate the present discounted value of your winnings if the interest rate is 10 percent. What would it be if the interest rate were 15 percent? How does a higher interest rate affect the present discounted value?

5. Suppose the workers at a particular company have been complaining that their medical insurance does not cover enough items. To help build loyalty among the staff, the company agrees to cover more items. However, it finds that the number of sick days taken and its expenses for health care both rise sharply. Why might this happen? What is the name for it?

6. You hire someone to paint your house. Since it is a large job, you agree to pay him by the hour. What moral hazard problem must you consider? Explain the trade-off between risk and incentives in this situation.

CHAPTER 7

THE PUBLIC SECTOR

Most Americans have a great deal of faith in our economic system, with its primary reliance on private markets. In earlier chapters, we have seen how the profit system provides firms with the incentive to produce the goods that consumers want. Prices give firms the incentive to economize on scarce resources, and serve to coordinate economic activity and to signal changes in economic conditions. Private property provides incentives for individuals to invest in and to maintain buildings, machines, land, cars, and other possessions. Chapter 3 demonstrated the incentives individuals and countries have to engage in mutually advantageous trades and to specialize in areas of comparative advantage. Chapters 4 and 5 showed how, in free markets, prices are determined by the interaction of demand and supply.

We have thus seen how the private market provides answers to the four basic questions set out in Chapter 1: what is produced and in what quantities, how it is produced, for whom it is produced, and who makes the decisions. What is produced is determined by the interaction of demand and supply, reflecting both the goods consumers want and what it costs firms to produce those goods. Firms, competing against one another, produce the goods in the least expensive way possible. The answer to the "for whom" question is given by the incomes of individuals in the economy. Those with high incomes get more of the economy's goods and services, and those with low incomes receive less. These incomes, in turn, are established by the demand and supply for labor, which determines what workers are paid, and the demand and supply for capital, which determines the return people get on their savings. The answer to the "who decides" question is "everyone." Decisions about which goods are produced are the result of millions of decisions made in households and firms throughout the economy. Moreover, firms, competing against one another, have incentives to choose as managers those most able to make the hard decisions—whether to enter some new market or develop some new product—that every firm must face if it is to survive.

Yet in spite of this basic faith in the market economy, the United States has an enormous public, or governmental, sector, reaching out into all spheres of economic activity. Why is this? What role do economists see for the government? Economists tend to look hard at any function government serves, not because they are antigovernment, but because they are promarket. They recognize that the government must set and enforce the basic laws of society, and provide a framework within which firms can compete fairly against one another. Beyond this, however, economists' understanding of the market's ability to answer the basic economic questions leads them to wonder at any additional function the government serves: why is it that private markets do not serve this function? This chapter will explore the roles the government has undertaken, and how and why it carries out those roles.

"Approximately one-third of our income goes for defense."

Key Questions

1. What distinguishes the private from the public sector?

2. What explains the economic roles the government has undertaken?

3. What are externalities and public goods, and why do they imply that markets may not work well?

4. What are the various ways the government can affect the economy and attempt to achieve its economic objectives?

5. How has the role of government changed in recent decades? And how does the role of government in the United States compare with its role in other industrial countries?

6. What are some of the current controversies concerning the roles of government? Why do failures of the market system not necessarily imply that government action is desirable?

WHAT OR WHO IS GOVERNMENT?

Most countries of the world have an ongoing debate over what the appropriate balance between the public and private sectors should be, and different countries have supplied different answers to this question. In some nations, like Switzerland, the public sector is small and government economic activities are severely limited. In the former Soviet Union and China, the government tried to control virtually all aspects of economic activity, though the difficulty of doing this created increasing pressures for change.

There is a wide spectrum between these extremes: free market economies like Hong Kong, where businesses are free from most of the regulations that they encounter in the United States and Western Europe; welfare state economies like Sweden, where the government takes major responsibilities for health care, child care, and a host of other social services, but where there is also a large private sector; and a number of European economies, like Great Britain, where the government has dominated major industries like steel, coal, railroads, airlines, and public utilities. The United States falls within this spectrum, placing heavier reliance on the private sector than do most other countries with industrialized, developed economies.

The balance between government and the private sector seems to swing over time. From 1930 to 1970, for example, government took on an increasing role in most countries. Many private industries were **nationalized** in this period, or taken over and run by the government. Since 1970, there has been a time of retrenchment for the public sector and a reevaluation of its role. This is true no less for communist countries like China and the former Soviet Union, which have recently begun to allow a greater degree of private enterprise, than it is of the European countries. Some of these countries have been selling off their government enterprises to the private sector; this is known as **privatization.** Similarly, government regulations that were in force in many industries, such as airlines, railroads, and trucking, have been reduced or eliminated, a process called **deregulation.**

In the United States, decisions concerning taxes, expenditures, and regulations are made by thousands of different governmental bodies. The United States has a **federal** governmental structure, which means that government activities take place at several levels: national, state, and local. This federal structure is the reason that the national government is generally referred to as the federal government; it is responsible for defense, the post office, the printing of money, and the regulation of interstate and international commerce. On the other hand, the states and localities have traditionally been responsible for education, welfare, police and fire protection, and the provision of the other local services, such as libraries, sewage disposal, and garbage collection. Although the U.S. Constitution asserts that all rights not explicitly delegated to the federal government reside with the states and the people, the Constitution has proved to be a flexible enough document that the exact boundaries are ambiguous. For example, while education is primarily a local responsibility, the federal government has become increasingly involved.

Moreover, neither at the national level nor at the local level is there any single entity we can call "the government." The Constitution explicitly provides for the separation of powers among the executive, legislative, and judicial branches, so that there is no single decision maker. At the federal level, there are a myriad of agencies, each responsible for certain functions. For instance, the Securities and Exchange Commission (SEC) regulates the securities industry, in which stocks and bonds are traded; the Federal Aviation Agency (FAA) is responsible for air safety; the Environmental Protection Agency (EPA) is in charge of regulations protecting the environment; and the Federal Trade Commission (FTC) is charged with stopping unfair trade practices.

At the local level, there are a large number of separate governmental bodies. Even a small town might have an elected school board, an elected town council, an elected library board, and an elected sewage board, each with the right to set policies and levy taxes. In fact, today the United States contains over eighty thousand separate governmental entities. This number may seem surprisingly large, but it is only about half the number that existed in 1942.

WHAT DISTINGUISHES THE PRIVATE AND PUBLIC SECTORS?

Private institutions include not only profit-maximizing firms but a large number of not-for-profit organizations like churches, hospitals, and private universities. What distinguishes those institutions that are labeled as "government" from private institutions?

In a democracy, there are two important differences between private and public institutions. First, the people responsible for running public institutions are elected or appointed by someone who is elected (or appointed by someone who is appointed by someone who is elected . . .). The legitimacy of the person holding the position is derived directly or indirectly from the electoral process.

Second, the government is endowed with certain rights of compulsion that private institutions do not have. For instance, the U.S. government has the right to force its citizens to pay taxes; if they fail to do so, it can confiscate their property and even imprison them. The government has the right to force its young people to serve in the armed forces at wages below those that would induce them to volunteer. The government also has the right of **eminent domain,** which is the right to seize private property for public use, provided it compensates the owner fairly.

Private institutions and individuals do not have these rights. Moreover, the government restricts such coercion by private institutions, even if the individuals involved agree to it; for instance, the government does not allow you to sell yourself into slavery. Private exchanges are voluntary. One person may want another to work for him, but he cannot coerce that person into doing so. One person may need another's property to construct an office building, but she cannot force the owner to sell. You may think that some deal is advantageous to the person you are proposing the deal to, but you cannot legally force him to engage in the deal.

Its ability to use compulsion means that the government may be able to do some things that private institutions cannot do. Once a decision has been made to build a public road, for instance, a local government can make sure that everyone in town helps to pay for it. On the other hand, governments sometimes create rules to bind their own hands, so that they cannot do *anything* they wish. For instance, the government has established elaborate hiring procedures for government organizations that private firms generally do not find worthwhile. The owner of a private firm can decide whom she wants to hire; if she hires someone incompetent, she and her firm suffer. If the manager of a public enterprise hires someone incompetent, however, the public pays. The government's strict hiring procedures help avoid bad hiring, but they may also result in rigidities that often make it difficult for government enterprises to compete against private firms for the most talented individuals.

Economists, concerned with the most efficient solutions to economic problems, focus on government's powers of compulsion, including its power to tax, when they try to find a role for government. They focus on its limitations, such as its limited flexibility and the special problems posed by the political processes that govern its behavior, when they try to delineate the extent of that role. Before looking more closely at the economic role of government, it is instructive to observe how governmental and private solutions are combined in the United States.

THE PERVASIVENESS OF GOVERNMENT

The United States, as we saw in Chapter 1, is a mixed economy; this means that like most countries, it combines private and public solutions to its economic problems. The emphasis is on private market solutions, but to think that the United States has a simple market economy is to ignore the pervasiveness of government.

From the moment Americans are born to the moment they die, government touches their lives. Births are recorded by a government bureau to aid in establishing citizenship, and a variety of rights (and obligations) of citizenship follow. Most children attend publicly run schools as they grow up, where they may eat publicly subsidized school lunches. Many then go on to attend public universities; others attend private universities that receive large government grants, or obtain government-subsidized loans to pay their tuition. The currency in their pockets is printed by the government. Americans travel on a transportation system that is publicly built and maintained, with publicly provided roads and publicly run airports. Air safety is supervised by a federal agency, and interstate rail passenger service is run by AMTRAK, a government enterprise.

The elderly have been increasingly supported by government. Much of what they live upon is provided by the government, through Social Security; many of their medical expenses are covered through a government program called Medicare; and even the pensions they receive from private companies are affected by government regulations, with the government ensuring that the private firms actually pay what they promise. Government issues death certificates for Americans when they die, and government rules oversee inheritances by and property settlements for the next generation.

In all of these activities, the government plays a variety of roles. First, it sets the legal framework within which all private actions take place. Second, it acts as a producer: most of elementary and secondary education and a large fraction of higher education is produced publicly, as are police and fire services; and in many communities, water and garbage collection lie within the public sector. Government is also a "consumer," buying goods and services that it then provides freely to the public. Expenditures on national defense and the highway system are examples. Much of government production goes directly to consumption—education, for example—but the two roles of producer and consumer are distinct. The government buys, but does not produce, airplanes and tanks; it also pays for, but does not itself produce, medical services for the aged.

Equally as important as these direct roles of the government are its indirect roles, in affecting how households and firms behave. The government regulates and it subsidizes. There are regulations designed, for instance, to restrict anticompetitive practices, to protect consumers, and to promote general social objectives, such as the elimination of discrimination. Subsidies too are directed at a multitude of objectives, from the drilling of oil to the construction of low-income housing to the provision by employers of medical insurance for their employees. In the United States, most subsidies are indirect, through the tax system.

The functions of government have been changing during the past century. Consider railroads, for example. During the nineteenth century, the U.S. government subsidized the establishment of many railroads, primarily by donating the land on which they were built. Later, with the Interstate Commerce Act of 1887, the government regulated how much the railroads could charge. Still later, in the 1960s, as passenger service became unprofitable, the government, through AMTRAK, began to run the passenger railroad system; and in 1975, when the railroads in the Northeast faced bankruptcy, it took over freight service there as well, establishing a government enterprise called Conrail. Still later, in 1986, the government privatized Conrail; that is, sold it back to the private sector.

Just because government today customarily provides certain goods and services does not mean that it must do so; and the fact that government customarily does not provide some good or service does not mean that it should not. There are other dramatic examples of the changing role of the government besides railroads. Take currency, for instance. Today, it is hard to imagine private firms producing bills and coins. However, until 1913, when a central banking law was passed, many private banks in the United States printed their own "bank notes," and these notes circulated as currency. Even today, in Scotland, private banks provide currency.

Or consider the U.S. mail. The U.S. Constitution consigns first-class postal service to the government, but private firms have happily jumped at the chance to provide other mail services. Today United Parcel Service delivers over half of all parcels, and private services dominate the market in providing overnight mail delivery.

Finally, consider highway construction. Few of us could imagine starting a business whose function it was to build and sell the use of a highway. Yet many of the early turnpikes in the United States were built by private firms that then charged tolls for use of the roads. Even today, the Autostrada in Italy, the Italian superhighway system, is a private enterprise.

AN ECONOMIC ROLE FOR GOVERNMENT

The previous section teaches us that we cannot simply look at the services and goods provided by government and assume that only government can provide them. The economist does not say that grade school education or currency or postal service has to be provided by the government. Economists ask how societies can supply these and any other needs most efficiently. The tax, expenditure, and regulatory policies of government have a profound effect on how the basic economic questions are answered. If economic models of the private market are accurate, and the general faith in market solutions is justified, then a good question to ask would be, why is there *any* economic role for government? Another visit with Adam Smith is a good place to start in answering this question.

ADAM SMITH'S ''INVISIBLE HAND'' AND THE CENTRAL ROLE OF MARKETS

Most of the time, private markets provide the best way of maintaining economic efficiency, of ensuring that goods are produced at least cost and that the goods produced are in fact those consumers want. The modern economic faith in private markets can be traced back to Adam Smith's 1776 masterpiece *The Wealth of Nations*. Smith argued that workers and producers, interested only in helping themselves and their families, were the root of economic production. The public interest would best be promoted by individuals pursuing their own self-interest. As Smith put it:

> Man has almost constant occasion for the help of his brethren, and it is in vain for him to expect it from their benevolence only. He will be more likely to prevail if he can interest their self-love in his favor, and show them that it is for their own advantage to do for him what he requires of them. . . . It is not from the benevolence of the butcher, the brewer, or the baker, that we expect our dinner, but from their regard to their own interest. We address ourselves, not to their humanity but to their self-love, and never talk to them of our own necessities but of their advantages.[1]

Smith's insight was that individuals work hardest to help the overall economic production of society when their efforts help themselves. He argued that an "obvious and simple system of liberty" provided the greatest opportunities for people to help themselves and thus, by extension, to create the greatest wealth for a society.

In another famous passage, Smith used the metaphor of the **"invisible hand"** to describe how self-interest led to social good: "He intends only his own gain, and he is in this as in many other cases, led by an invisible hand to promote an end which was no part of his intention. Nor is it always the worse for the society that it was no part of it. By pursuing his own interest he frequently promotes that of the society more effectually than when he really intends to promote it."

Economics has progressed a long way since Adam Smith, but his fundamental argument has had great appeal over the past two centuries. In practice, although there are certainly exceptions, greater liberty for individuals in country after country has indeed led to huge increases in production that have benefited if not everyone, almost everyone. The general belief in the productivity of a market system can largely be considered a legacy from Adam Smith.

While today's economists stress the central place of private firms in modern economies, most also believe that government must play a role as well, because there are certain problems with which the market does not deal well.

[1] Book 1, Chapter 2.

CLOSE-UP: THE DIVISION OF FEDERAL AND STATE RESPONSIBILITIES

You often hear federal politicians talking about how they will fight crime and improve education. When George Bush first ran for president, for example, he said that he wanted to be known as "the education president" and ran televised advertisements arguing that Michael Dukakis had been too soft on criminals. To those who have a bit of familiarity with the difference between state and federal budgets, these were odd issues for a presidential campaign.

Most of the U.S. spending on education and on criminal justice, along with most of the responsibility for proposing and carrying out reforms, has traditionally occurred at the state and local levels, not at the federal level. In fact, education is the single largest expenditure at the state and local levels, accounting for more than a third of all spending. As shown in the chart, other important categories are highways and welfare payments. The remaining 45 percent of state and local government spending is a hodgepodge of different categories, including police and fire protection, prisons, libraries, hospitals, health care, air transportation, parking facilities, transit subsidies, sewerage, natural resources, parks and recreation, housing and community development, solid waste management, public buildings, interest on government debt, and more.

Federal spending is also concentrated in a few areas. Although you often hear about federal initiatives in areas like international affairs, science, space, energy, natural resources and the environment, agriculture, commerce and housing, transportation, community and regional development, manpower and training, employment, income security, veterans' benefits, and administration of justice, all of those categories taken together are less than one-third of all federal spending.

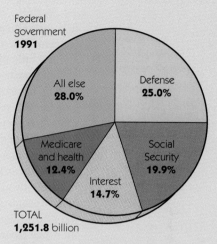

Federal government
1991

Defense 25.0%

All else 28.0%

Social Security 19.9%

Medicare and health 12.4%

Interest 14.7%

TOTAL
1,251.8 billion

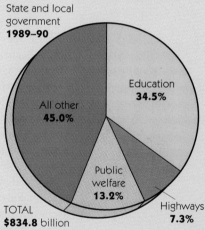

State and local government
1989–90

Education 34.5%

All other 45.0%

Public welfare 13.2%

Highways 7.3%

TOTAL
$834.8 billion

The big-ticket items for the federal government are four: defense, Social Security for the elderly, interest payments on the money it has borrowed, and Medicare and other health payments. Any attempt to reduce the growth in federal spending must come to grips with reducing spending in these categories.

Source: Economic Report of the President (1991), Tables B-77, B-83.

GOVERNMENT AS A RESPONSE TO DISAPPOINTMENTS WITH THE MARKET

It is not difficult to find complaints about and discontent with the market. There is concern that markets produce too much of some things, like air and water pollution, and too little of other things, such as support for the arts or child care facilities. Much of the growth in government this century has stemmed from a concern that private markets fail to achieve the social goals of high levels of employment, economic stability, growth, and security for workers. Indeed, in the United States, the past two hundred years have been marked by periodic episodes of high unemployment. In the Great Depression of the 1930s, the unemployment rate reached 25 percent and national output fell by 30 percent from its pre-Depression peak in 1929. The Depression brought to the fore problems that, in less severe form, had existed for a long time. Many individuals lost virtually all of their money when banks failed and the stock market crashed. Many elderly people did not have the resources on which to survive. Many farmers found that the prices they received for their products were so low that they could not make their mortgage payments, and defaults became commonplace.

In response to the Depression, the federal government not only took a more active role in attempting to stabilize the level of economic activity, it also passed legislation aimed at alleviating many of the specific problems, including unemployment insurance, Social Security, federal insurance of bank deposits, and federal programs aimed at supporting agricultural prices. These programs were proposed by President Franklin D. Roosevelt, who referred to the collection of policies as the New Deal.

After World War II, the economy recovered, and the country experienced an unprecedented level of prosperity. But it became clear that the fruits of that prosperity were not being enjoyed by all. Many people seemed to be born into a life of squalor and poverty; they received inadequate education, and their prospects for obtaining good jobs were bleak. These inequities provided the impetus for many of the government programs that were enacted in the 1960s, as part of what President Johnson called the War on Poverty. Some poverty programs attempted to provide a "safety net" for the needy; for instance, by supplying food and medical care to the poor. Other programs, such as job-retraining programs, were directed at improving the economic opportunities of the disadvantaged.

In the late 1980s, a new set of concerns emerged having to do with the competitiveness of the American economy. Americans were saving less than were citizens of other industrialized powers. The high rates of increases in productivity that marked the 1950s and early 1960s seemed to have come to an end. There were new calls for government activity to spur the economy.

Anyone who follows the news can come up with many other examples of discontent with the outcome of private markets. The concerns listed here, as well as many others, can be placed into three broad categories: those that are based on an ignorance of the laws of economics, those having to do with redistribution of income, and those having to do with genuine failures of private markets.

GOVERNMENT AND THE LAWS OF ECONOMICS

Some of the complaints about markets are of the "Wouldn't the world be a better place if we still lived in the Garden of Eden?" variety. Things have a price because they are scarce. The price of oil may be high not because oil companies are trying to take advantage of consumers, but simply because oil is scarce, and the high prices reflect that scarcity. In Chapter 4, we saw that economists regard these situations not as market failures but as the hard facts of economic life. Much as everyone would like to live in a world where all individuals could have almost everything they wanted at a price they could afford, this is simply unrealistic. Some pretend that the government can "solve" the problem of scarcity by passing laws about prices; but this simply shifts the problem around, leading to reduced prices for some and shortages for everyone else.

GOVERNMENT AND REDISTRIBUTION

A second category of complaints against the market represents a dissatisfaction with the distribution of income. Market economies may be productive and efficient at producing wealth, but they may also yield a distribution of income where some people become very rich and others starve. Someone who has a rare and valuable skill will, by the laws of supply and demand, receive a high income. Someone else who has few skills, and common ones at that, will find his wage to be low—perhaps even too low for survival.

Most economists see an important role for the government in income redistribution, taking income from those who have more and giving it to those who have less. In their view, society does not need to sit passively by the side and accept whatever distribution of income results from the workings of private markets. Federal income and estate taxes on the rich and welfare programs for the poor can be seen as part of the government's role in redistribution.

While concern for greater economic equality is a generally accepted role for government, there is still room for much disagreement about the benefits and costs of programs aimed at reducing inequality. Also, if the government does want to reduce inequality, economists will disagree as to what is the best method. Redistributive tax systems and welfare programs often interfere with economic incentives. Questions of redistribution are often posed as, How should the economy's pie be divided? What size slice should each person get?

By looking at the pie in panel A of Figure 7.1, you can see that the poorest 20 percent of the population get a relatively small slice—that is, 20 percent only receive 5 percent of the economy's income—while the richest 20 percent of the population get a relatively large slice, 46 percent of the economy's income. Often redistribution is viewed as simply cutting the pie differently, giving the poor somewhat larger slices and the rich somewhat smaller, as in panel B. But if the process of redistributing income makes the economy less productive, the size of the whole pie will shrink, as illustrated in panel C. There the poor get a larger share of a smaller pie. The rich are much worse off now—they get a smaller share of a smaller pie. If the size of the pie has shrunk enough, even the poor may be worse off. By designing government redistribution programs appropriately, it may be possible to limit the size of these effects on productivity.

GOVERNMENT AND MARKET FAILURES

The final category of discontent with private markets represents cases where the market does indeed fail in its role of producing economic efficiency. Economists refer to these problems as **market failures,** and have studied them closely. When there is a market failure, there may be a role for government if it can correct the market failure and enhance the economy's efficiency. The correction of market failures leads to two main

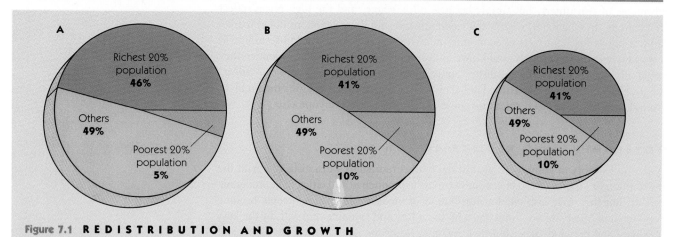

Figure 7.1 **REDISTRIBUTION AND GROWTH**

Panel A shows that the poor receive only a small share of the economy's output. Plans for redistribution often assume that they will create the situation in panel B, where the poor simply receive a larger share. But if the redistribution is poorly managed or too great, it may substantially reduce the size of the overall pie, as in panel C, making all groups worse off. *Source: Current Population Report* (1990), p. 5.

functions for government: stabilization of the aggregate economy and reallocation of its resources.

Stabilization of the Economy   The most dramatic example of market failures is the periodic episodes of high unemployment that have plagued capitalist economies. It is hard to tout the virtues of an efficient market when a third of the industrial labor force and capital stock sits idle, as it did in the Great Depression of the 1930s. While many economists believe there are forces that might eventually restore the economy to full employment, the costs of waiting for the economy to correct itself—in terms of both forgone output and human misery—are enormous, and today virtually all governments take it as their responsibility to stabilize the economy. They *try* to avoid the extreme fluctuations in economic activity—both the downturns, when much of the economy's resources, its workers and machines, remain idle, and the booms, which may result in high inflation. The causes of these fluctuations, and how and whether the government can succeed in significantly reducing them, are one of the main topics discussed in macroeconomics, to which Parts Four to Six of this book are devoted.

When the economy's scarce resources are idle, the economy is operating below its production possibilities curve, as shown in Figure 7.2. As usual, the curve has been simplified to two goods, guns and butter, which represent the general output levels in the public and private sectors. The government attempts to move the economy from point E to a point closer to the production possibilities curve, *E'*.

Reallocation of Resources   Even when an economy's resources are fully utilized, they may not be utilized well. Socialist countries such as the former Soviet Union used to

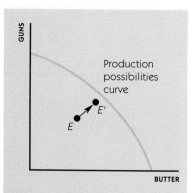

Figure 7.2 **AN ECONOMY OPERATING BELOW FULL POTENTIAL**

The economy is at point E, below the edge of its production possibilities curve. The government seeks to have it operate closer to the curve, at point E', for instance.

brag that they had developed an economic system in which there was no unemployment, but the economies were extremely inefficient. They even had trouble getting food from the rural sector where it was produced to the cities where it was needed. During the past quarter century, economists have come to understand much better the circumstances under which market economies are efficient. There must be competition, and government has taken it as a responsibility to ensure that there is at least some level of competition in most markets. But even when there is competition, the market may supply too much of some goods and too little of others.

One of the most important instances of this kind of market failure occurs when there are **externalities.** These are present whenever an individual or a firm can take an action that directly affects others and for which it neither pays nor is paid compensation. It therefore does not bear all the consequences of its action. (The effect of the action is "external" to the individual or firm.) Externalities are pervasive. Someone who litters, a driver whose car emits pollution, a child who leaves a mess behind after he finishes playing, a person who smokes a cigarette in a crowded room, all create externalities. In each case, the actor is not the only one who must suffer the consequences of his action; others suffer them too. Externalities can be thought of as instances when the price system works imperfectly. The individual is not "charged" for the litter she creates, nor does the car owner pay for the pollution it makes.

Externalities can be negative or positive. A common example of a negative externality is a factory that emits air pollution. The factory benefits from emitting the pollution, since by doing so, the company can make its product more cheaply than it could if it put in pollution-control devices. However, society as a whole bears the negative external costs. If the factory had to pay for its pollution, it would find ways to produce less of it. And indeed, government environmental regulations are often aimed at just that goal.

A common example of a positive externality is a new invention. Almost always, when someone makes a new discovery that leads to greater economic productivity, other people (or companies) benefit. The inventor receives, through the prices he charges, only a fraction of the total gains to society from the invention. Other firms, for instance, will copy it and learn from it. Inventions like the laser and the transistor have benefited consumers, both by providing new products and allowing other products to be made less expensively. While the individual researcher bears the costs of making a discovery, society receives positive external benefits. If everyone who benefited from an invention had to pay money to the inventor, there would be far higher incentives for research and development. And indeed, patents and other government laws enable the investors to get a larger return than they otherwise would.

With externalities present, the market's allocation of goods is inefficient. When the production of a good such as steel entails a negative externality—like smoke and its effect on the air—the level of production is too high. This is because the producer fails to take into account the "social costs" in deciding how much to produce. To put it another way, the price of steel determined in competitive markets by the law of supply and demand only reflects *private* costs, the costs actually faced by firms. If firms do not have to pay *all* of the costs (including the costs of pollution), equilibrium prices will be lower and output higher than they would be if firms took social costs into account.

The government can try to offset this effect in several ways. For instance, it might impose a tax. Panel A of Figure 7.3 shows the demand and supply curves for steel, and depicts the market equilibrium at the intersection of the two curves, Q_0. If the government imposes a tax on the production of steel, the supply curve will shift to the left—the

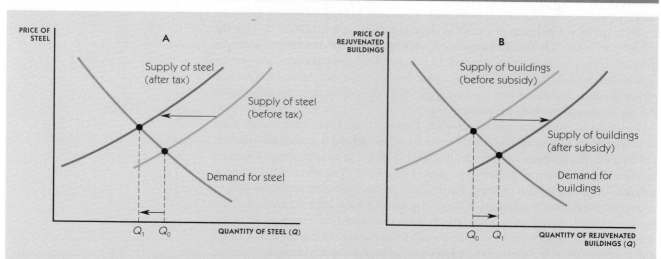

Figure 7.3 SUPPLY, DEMAND, AND EXTERNALITIES

The steel industry produces a negative externality of pollution. In panel A, a tax on steel production shifts the supply curve to the left, reducing both steel production and pollution. In panel B, a subsidy for rejuvenated buildings, which create the positive externality of neighborhood beautification, shifts the supply curve to the right, causing more buildings and neighborhoods to be renovated.

quantity produced at each price will be lower—and the equilibrium level of production will be less, Q_1.

Similarly, there is an undersupply of goods that produce positive externalities, and the government can try to enlarge the supply. The rejuvenation of an apartment building in a decaying part of a city is an example of a positive externality; it will probably enhance the value of buildings around it. Panel B of Figure 7.3 shows the demand and supply curve for rejuvenated buildings. A government subsidy to rejuvenation shifts the supply curve to the right, increasing the number of rejuvenated buildings from Q_0 to Q_1.

Public Goods   There is a category of goods, called **public goods,** that can be viewed as an extreme case of positive externalities. Public goods are goods that it costs nothing extra for an additional individual to enjoy (their consumption is **nonrivalrous**), and that it costs a great deal to exclude any individual from enjoying (they are **nonexcludable**). The standard example of a public good is defense. Once the United States is protected from attack, it costs nothing extra to protect each new baby from foreign invasion. Furthermore, it would be virtually impossible to exclude a newborn baby from the benefits of this protection.

Public parks along the sides of a highway are another example. Anyone driving along the highway enjoys the view; the fact that one person is enjoying the view does not exclude others from enjoying it; and it would in fact be expensive to stop anyone who is driving along the highway from benefiting from the view. A lighthouse to guide ships around dangerous shoals or rocks is still another example of a public good. There are no additional costs incurred as an additional ship navigates near the lighthouse, and it would be difficult to shut off the light in the lighthouse at just the right time to prevent a ship passing by from taking advantage of the lighthouse.

A **pure public good** is one where the marginal costs of providing it to an additional person are strictly zero and where it is impossible to exclude people from receiving the good. Many public goods that government provides are not *pure* public goods in this sense. It is possible, but relatively expensive, to exclude people from (or charge people for) using an uncrowded interstate highway; the cost of an additional person using an uncrowded interstate highway is very, very small, but not zero.

Figure 7.4 compares some examples of publicly provided goods against the strict definition of a pure public good. It shows the ease of exclusion along the horizontal axis and the (marginal) cost of an additional individual using the good along the vertical axis. The lower left-hand corner represents a pure public good. Of the major public expenditures, only national defense is close to a pure public good. Uncongested highways, to the extent that they exist, are also an example. The upper right-hand corner represents a pure private good (health services or education), where the cost of exclusion is low and the marginal cost of an additional individual using the good is high.

There are many goods that are not pure public goods but that have one or the other property to some degree. Fire protection is a good for which exclusion is relatively easy—individuals who refuse to contribute to the fire department could simply not be helped in the event of a fire. But fire protection is like a public good in that the marginal cost of covering an additional person is low. Most of the time, firefighters are not engaged in fighting fires but are waiting for calls. Protecting an additional individual has little extra cost. Only in that rare event when two fires break out simultaneously will there be a significant cost to extending the protection to an additional person.

Figure 7.4 PUBLICLY PROVIDED GOODS

Pure public goods are characterized by nonrivalrous consumption (the marginal cost of an additional individual enjoying the good is zero) and nonexcludability (the cost of excluding an individual from enjoying the good is prohibitively high). Goods provided by the public sector differ in the extent to which they have these two properties.

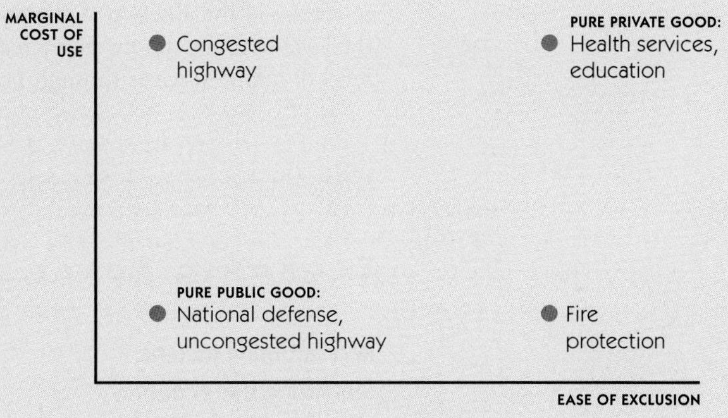

MARGINAL COST OF USE

● Congested highway

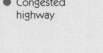
PURE PRIVATE GOOD:
● Health services, education

PURE PUBLIC GOOD:
● National defense, uncongested highway

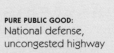
● Fire protection

EASE OF EXCLUSION

Sometimes the marginal cost of using a good to which access is easy (a good that possesses the property of nonexcludability) will be high. When an uncongested highway turns congested, the costs of using it rise dramatically, not in terms of wear and tear on the road but in terms of the time lost by drivers using the road then. It is costly to exclude by charging for road use—as a practical matter, this can only be done on toll roads, and, ironically, the toll booths often contribute to the congestion.

Many of the goods that are publicly provided, such as education and health services, have high costs associated with providing the service to additional individuals. For most of these goods, exclusion is also relatively easy. In fact, many of these goods and services are provided privately in some countries, or provided both publicly and privately. Though they are publicly provided, they are not *pure* public goods, in the technical sense in which the term is defined.

Private markets undersupply public goods. If there were a single shipowner using the port near which a lighthouse is constructed, he could weigh the costs and benefits of the lighthouse. But if there were one large shipowner and many smaller owners, it would not pay any one of the small owners to build the lighthouse; and the large shipowner, in deciding whether to construct the lighthouse, would only take into account the benefits he would receive, not the benefits to the small shipowners. If the costs of construction exceeded the benefits that he alone would receive, he would not build the lighthouse. But at the same time, if the benefits accruing to *all* the shipowners, large and small, were taken into account, those benefits would exceed the costs; it would then be desirable to build the lighthouse.

One can imagine a voluntary association of shipowners getting together to construct a lighthouse in this situation. But what happens if some small shipowner refuses to contribute, thinking that even if he does not contribute, the lighthouse will be built anyway? This is the **free-rider** aspect of public goods; because it is difficult to preclude anyone from using them, those who benefit from the goods have an incentive to avoid paying for them. Every shipowner has an incentive to "free ride" on the efforts of others. When too many decide to do this, the lighthouse will not get built.

Governments bring an important advantage to bear on the problem of public goods. They have the power to coerce citizens to pay for them. It is true that there might be *some* level of purchase of public goods—lighthouses, highway parks, even police or fire services—in the absence of government intervention. But society would be better off if the level of production were increased, and citizens were forced to pay for the increased level of public services through taxes.

ECONOMIC ROLES FOR THE GOVERNMENT

Redistributing income
Stabilizing the economy
Reallocating resources

CLOSE-UP: A GREAT BUY ON A TANK OF GAS

How long would you be willing to wait in line for a bargain? That is the question that radio station KJLH posed to gasoline purchasers in Los Angeles on August 23, 1990. On that day, the station agreed to subsidize the gasoline purchased at a downtown Union 76 station between 6:15 and 8:30 in the morning. Although gasoline prices were shooting up to over $1.20 a gallon at most stations, since Iraq had just invaded Kuwait, KJLH offered gas at $.76 a gallon, which was the price back in 1978.

On that morning, the line of eager bargain hunters extended for three blocks; it took more than an hour to reach the pumps. Since saving $.50 a gallon on 15 gallons of gas is worth $7.50, it appeared that at least 400 drivers were willing to value the opportunity cost of their time at less than $7.50 an hour. Or perhaps they simply did not review their introductory economics courses and both forgot to take into account opportunity costs and allowed the sunk costs—the time they had already spent in getting to the gas station—to influence their decision.

In fact, the lines were long enough that they added to the morning traffic jams that plague the Los Angeles area. While those who stayed in line revealed by their actions that they preferred to wait, those who were delayed in traffic without buying any cheap gasoline suffered a negative externality from the station's publicity stunt. If station KJLH had had to face the actual social costs of its stunt and subsidize those drivers who suffered the negative externality of greater delay, the whole idea might well have never been launched.

Source: "L.A. Radio Station Stunt Revives '70s Gas Prices and '70s Gas Lines," *San Jose Mercury News,* August 24, 1990, p. F1.

GOVERNMENT'S OPTIONS

Once it has been decided that government should do something, there is a second question: how can government accomplish society's ends most efficiently? The government will have to choose among several courses of action. It could do something directly, it could provide incentives for the private sector to do something, it could mandate that the private sector do something, or it could take some combination of these three courses of action.

TAKING DIRECT ACTION

Faced with a market failure, the government could simply take charge itself. If it believes there is a market failure in the provision of medical care, for instance, it can nationalize the medical sector, as Britain did after World War II. If the government believes there is a market failure in the airline or railroad industry, it can nationalize the industry, or the part of the industry with which it is discontent, and run the industry itself. If it believes there is a market failure in the provision of housing for the poor, it can build government housing projects.

Sometimes the direct action the government takes is not to produce the good itself, but to purchase the good from the private sector. While the government itself runs a large system of hospitals for veterans, it pays for most of the costs of medical care for the aged and the poor but allows them to obtain these medical services from private doctors and hospitals.

PROVIDING INCENTIVES TO THE PRIVATE SECTOR

Another alternative is for the government to operate at a distance, providing incentives that attempt to alter the workings of private markets in desirable ways. It can provide incentives directly through subsidies, as it does for agriculture, or, as is more commonly done in the United States, indirectly through the tax system. The government has used energy tax credits to encourage energy conservation. It has also used an investment tax credit, which gives firms a tax break for investing in new machines, to encourage investment. Special provisions of the tax code encourage employers to provide health insurance and pensions for their employees.

Both of these strategies, subsidies and taxes, put the government in the position of manipulating the price system to achieve its ends. If the government is worried about the supply of adequate housing for the poor, for example, it can provide incentives for builders to construct low-income housing in inner cities—it can provide the builders with direct payments, or it can grant tax reductions for those who make investments in slum areas. If the government wants to encourage oil conservation, it can impose a tax on oil or gasoline, which will encourage conservation by raising the price. Similarly, the government can impose a tax on cars that are not energy efficient.

MANDATING ACTION IN THE PRIVATE SECTOR

Sometimes, however, there is concern about whether the private sector will respond to incentives, or uncertainty about what effect particular incentives will have. Or there is concern that providing subsidies is too costly. In these circumstances, the government often mandates the desired action, which means that it forces the private sector to do something, under threat of some legal punishment. The government may mandate, for instance, that private firms provide health insurance to their employees. The government may mandate that automobile manufacturers produce fuel-efficient cars, specifying particular standards for miles per gallon of gas. In some localities, real estate developers who want to get a permit for a large housing project may be required to provide a certain number of units for low-income individuals, or to help improve a local road or build a local school. In all these cases, the fact that the government requirement does not show up on the government's budget does not mean that there is not a cost to such a requirement. The costs—borne indirectly by workers, firms, and consumers—can be very high.

COMBINING OPTIONS

The government often combines two or more courses of action in its attempts to achieve some objective. Consider, for instance, the concern over medical care. The U.S. government pays for medical care for the aged and the poor; it provides actual medical care for veterans in hospitals it operates; it provides incentives for employers to offer health insurance, by giving these expenditures favorable tax treatment; and there are proposals to mandate firms to provide a minimum level of health insurance for employees. Different countries have chosen different mixes of these policies. In several countries, such as the United Kingdom, the government actually runs the entire health service; in other countries, government supplies health insurance to everyone and charges the taxpayers.

GOVERNMENT'S OPTIONS

Taking direct action
   Production of a good or service
   Purchase of a good or service
Providing incentives to the private sector
   Subsidies
   Taxes
Mandating private sector action

THE SIZE OF GOVERNMENT

A central question of debate in the United States and in other mixed economies is what the appropriate size of the public sector should be. Those like Nobel laureate Milton Friedman, formerly at the University of Chicago and now at Stanford University's Hoover Institution, who believe that the public sector is too large, generally have two reasons: they are skeptical of government's ability to solve social and economic problems, and they fear that bigger government undermines economic and political freedom. Others believe that the public sector is too small. In their view, greater government spending could ameliorate some problems, like blighted inner cities and inadequate schools. Harvard economist John Kenneth Galbraith, for example, has argued that public spending for these activities has been inadequate given the affluence of the U.S. economy.

Regardless of one's views on this question, there is no doubt that the impact of government today is far larger than it was a half century ago. The government produces more, it regulates more, it taxes more, and it spends more. The growth in expenditures is the easiest of these to quantify. A standard measure of the size of the economy is the gross domestic product (GDP), which measures the value of all the goods and services produced in an economy. In the United States today, government expenditures are approximately one-third of GDP. In 1913, before World War I, government accounted for less than a tenth of the nation's output.

SOURCES OF GROWTH IN GOVERNMENT EXPENDITURES

The United States, as was noted earlier, has a federal government structure. The states and localities are primarily responsible for education and basic local services like police and fire protection. The federal government is responsible for defense, and has assumed increasing responsibility for the aged, through Social Security and Medicare. There are many areas of joint responsibility, like roads and welfare, though in each of these areas the federal government has in recent decades assumed an increasingly important role.

Expenditures at the federal, state, and local levels have increased over the past four decades. And as shown in Figure 7.5, they have increased faster than the nation's output, so that the *fraction* of the nation's output that is spent by the federal, state, and local governments has grown larger.

Figure 7.6, which shows the relative importance of different categories of federal expenditures in 1950, 1970, and 1990, helps us see what accounts for this increase. One of the major contributors to growth in federal public expenditures during the past quarter century has been expenditures on programs for the aged—on Social Security and Medicare.

A second factor contributing to the growth in public expenditures in the last decade has been the interest the government must pay on the huge debt it has been accumulating. During the 1980s, the government spent more than it took in in taxes and had to borrow to finance the difference; it consequently had to pay interest on that debt. These interest payments grew significantly during the 1980s, and they now account for about one-seventh of the federal budget.

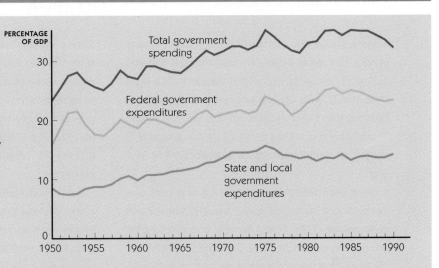

Figure 7.5 FEDERAL, STATE, AND LOCAL EXPENDITURES

Expenditures at all levels of government, as a proportion of the size of the total economy, have increased substantially from 1950 to 1990. *Source: Economic Report of the President* (1992), Tables B-1, B-77.

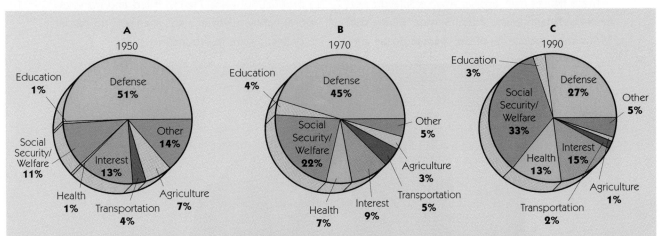

Figure 7.6 THE CHANGING PATTERN OF FEDERAL EXPENDITURES

The period 1950–1990 has seen a marked decrease in the share of defense expenditures, and marked increases in expenditures on Social Security and welfare. Interest expenses declined from 1950 to 1970, but then rose. *Sources: Historical Statistics of the United States* (1975), p. 1116; *ERP* (1991), Table B-77.

CLOSE-UP: PRODUCTIVITY IN THE U.S. POSTAL SERVICE

Griping about the shortcomings of the U.S. Postal Service is a great American tradition. But the anguished complaints every time the price of a first-class stamp goes up are not really about money. After all, even if you sent a letter every day, which is probably more than most of us do, an extra 5 cents per stamp adds up to only about $18 in a year.

More likely, knocking the post office is part of a deep-rooted suspicion about the inefficiencies of government. If the Postal Service is controlled by the government, it must be inefficient, right? Well, the prejudice used to have some truth in it, but no longer.

About four-fifths of total Postal Service expenditures go to paying postal employees, so measuring the productivity of these employees is the real test of the Postal Service. In 1950, the Postal Service delivered 90,000 pieces of mail per employee. By 1960, it was 113,000 per employee; in 1970, 115,000; and in 1975, 127,000.

These figures help explain why people do not have much faith in the Postal Service. During the 1960s, the productivity of the average postal employee barely budged. Over the quarter century from 1950 to 1975, the productivity of the typical employee increased by 41 percent. By way of comparison, business sector productivity for the economy as a whole increased by 85 percent from 1950 to 1975. The Postal Service spent twenty-five years building its reputation for backwardness and inefficiency.

But unfortunately for all the complainers who enjoy bashing the Postal Service, the productivity figures have now reversed themselves. By 1980, the post office was delivering 159,000 pieces of mail per employee. By the end of the 1980s, the average had risen to 198,000 per employee. From 1975 to the end of the 1980s, the letters delivered per postal employee increased by 56 percent, which is a substantially larger increase in fifteen years than had been managed in the preceding quarter century. Over that same time, business sector productivity increased by only 18.4 percent.

The post office has become an American leader in productivity gains. Clearly, if led and managed appropriately, a government agency is no barrier to dramatic gains in productivity.

Defense expenditures have fluctuated. After declining in the years after the Vietnam War, they increased in the early 1980s as President Reagan made improved defense capabilities a central part of his platform. But subsequently, defense expenditures as a percentage of GDP declined. With the end of the Cold War, there are prospects for a substantial reduction in defense expenditures. The money available has been called the peace dividend. How to spend the peace dividend—and how large it should be—is a question of major importance.

While public assistance is often made a scapegoat for increased expenditures, a look at the numbers shows that it has remained relatively constant over the past fifteen years, at approximately a tenth of the government budget. Similarly, other areas of government expenditures, like the cost of running government itself, have played only a small role in the increased level of public expenditures.

COMPARISON WITH OTHER COUNTRIES

The increase in government expenditures during the twentieth century has been dramatic, but still, expenditures in the United States are among the smallest of any of the major industrial countries in proportion to the size of the economy. In France and Germany, government expenditures are approximately half of the GDP, as Figure 7.7 illustrates. Of the countries listed, only Japan and Australia spend a smaller share on the public sector than the United States.

A large portion of U.S. federal expenditures goes to defense, and so the relative size of nondefense expenditures is particularly low viewed from this international perspective.

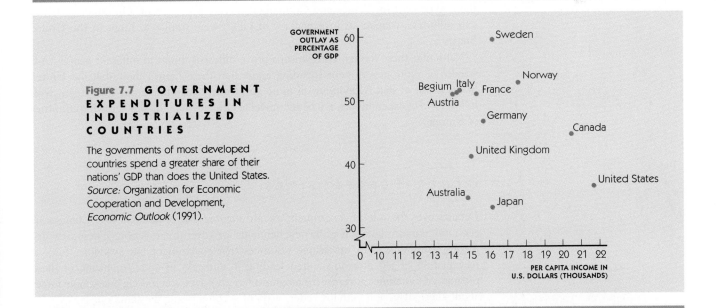

Figure 7.7 GOVERNMENT EXPENDITURES IN INDUSTRIALIZED COUNTRIES

The governments of most developed countries spend a greater share of their nations' GDP than does the United States. *Source:* Organization for Economic Cooperation and Development, *Economic Outlook* (1991).

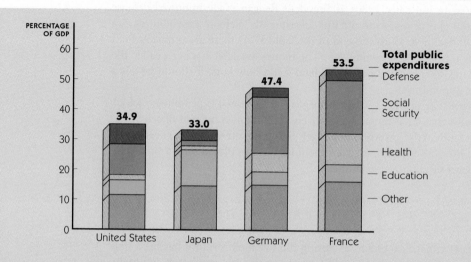

Figure 7.8 EXPENDITURE PATTERNS OF INDUSTRIALIZED COUNTRIES

U.S. government expenditures (as a percentage of GDP) are smaller than those of European countries. Moreover, since defense expenditures in the United States are relatively larger, its nondefense government spending is especially relatively smaller. *Sources: Government Finance Statistics Yearbook* (1990); *National Accounts Statistics* (1990).

The red portion at the top of the bars of Figure 7.8 represents defense expenditures. So the height of the bar up to the red area represents the percentage of GDP spent on nondefense public sector programs. While in the United States this was slightly less than 30 percent, in France and Germany it exceeded 45 percent. On the other hand, expenditures in Japan (as a percentage of GDP) were similar to those in the United States.

Naturally, these foreign comparisons prove different things to different people. Advocates of more government spending argue that these figures show that the United States is out of step. Opponents of more government spending argue that Japan, with its low level of expenditures, is a better model to emulate than the slow-growing countries of Europe.

OTHER PERSPECTIVES

Debates over the role of government are an ongoing part of political life. Changes in economic circumstances lead to new demands for government action. These new demands, combined with the scarce resources that government has available, force a reevaluation of old programs, often leading to cutbacks in or restructuring of these programs. Sometimes government programs have been around so long that people forget about alternative, and perhaps better, ways of accomplishing the same objectives.

Each of these debates has many facets. In areas such as health, banking, and housing for the poor, where there already is extensive government involvement, people disagree about whether there should be more or less government involvement, and whether the form of government involvement should be changed. While some claim that the presently perceived problems are the result of, or are at least exacerbated by, government programs, others believe that the main problem is too little government, or misdirected government programs.

A central issue in all of these debates is how resources are to be allocated. These are economic issues. But behind the economic issues are value judgments. Is it more important to spend an extra dollar trying to prolong the life of an octogenarian, or trying to improve the life opportunities of an underprivileged child from one of the nation's urban ghettos? These are hard choices, and it would be nice to say, let's do both. The fact of scarcity means that we cannot have everything we want.

Another set of noneconomic issues relates to how much government *should* intervene in the lives of its citizens, and the rights of individuals to make decisions for themselves, for better or worse. The principle that individuals are the best judges of what is in their own interests, and that their preferences should be respected, is called the **principle of consumer sovereignty.** For example, even though our society as a whole might be greatly benefited if everyone stopped eating fatty foods, which cause debilitating heart disease and death, should the government make laws to prevent the sale and consumption of ice cream?

Some claim that a major responsibility of government is establishing a just and humane society. John Rawls, professor of philosophy at Harvard and widely regarded as one of the world's leading moral philosophers, has argued in his book A *Theory of Justice* that a society is to be judged on how well it treats its worst-off members. Others, such as Harvard philosopher Robert Nozick, question the moral right of government to take away the fruits of any individual's labor. The conflicting views of the role of government in our society lead, quite naturally, to conflicting views about the role of government in the economy.

GOVERNMENT ACTION AND PUBLIC FAILURES

The call for government action is a natural one. Individuals feel powerless to correct broad social problems. If such problems are to be addressed, collective action will be required, and the government is the one collective institution to which all of us, in some sense, belong. But the fact that a market failure exists does not necessarily mean that the government should do something. It has to be shown that government action could improve matters.

When demanding that the government take action, individuals often forget the budget constraints facing society as a whole; sometimes observed deficiencies are merely the reflection of scarcity. If members of society wish to guarantee first-rate nursing home care to all of the elderly, it will be expensive. It is no less expensive—and, indeed, it may be more expensive—when it is paid for collectively than when the families of the elderly have to pay for it as individuals. The funds for increased expenditures must

Like any people, Americans have opinions about what their government should and should not do. The following are some of the rallying cries, pro and con, in the current debates.

MORE GOVERNMENT!

Health The U.S. government now finances a fifth of the nation's expenditures on medical care, a dramatic increase from past decades. But deficiencies in America's medical care system are still easy to find. Nursing home care is a growing need, but few public or private programs cover it. Some tens of millions of individuals have no health insurance. They are too young to be covered by Medicare, the government's program for the aged; they have too high an income to be eligible for Medicaid, the government's program for the poor; and their employers do not provide insurance. Finally, the cost of medical care has been rising rapidly. In the 1990s, health care has become a major political issue.

The American Banking System In the 1970s and 1980s, America's banks, including savings and loan associations (S & L's), which make loans for mortgages, made a number of investment decisions that turned out badly. The S & L's in particular made billions of dollars of real estate loans that went sour. Since the federal government provides insurance for deposits in banks and savings and loans, it was responsible for paying back the billions of dollars lost by the S & L's. Many economists believe that other parts of the banking system face similar problems. They believe that strong government action is required, not only to save the taxpayer from having to foot the bill for another multibillion-dollar bailout, but also to ensure the stability of America's financial system.

Children While the government was spending billions on banks, poverty was growing among America's children. Infant mortality rates in Washington, D.C., compare unfavorably with much poorer countries, such as Cuba. As more and more women have entered the labor force, the demand for government-supported day care (particularly for preschool children) has been rising.

The Homeless A walk through any major American city reveals a sight that is common in poor countries, such as India, but has not been seen on such a scale in the United States since the Great Depression: homeless individuals sleeping in doorways or makeshift shelters along the street. While there is widespread acknowledgment of the problem, budgetary pressures force discussions to focus only on modest government proposals.

LESS GOVERNMENT!

Agriculture During the 1980s, programs to help the farmers grew out of hand, to the point where they were costing the government in excess of $20 billion a year, or about $10,000 for each farm family. While by 1990 the expenditures were down to $12 billion, they were still large enough to remain a source of concern. Some of these programs actually paid farmers not to produce. In a world of scarcity, where people starve to death every day, programs that paid farmers *not* to produce seemed tragically misdirected. More generally, there was a belief that the farm programs as a whole had grown out of bounds.

Competition Policies The government has a responsibility to make sure there is effective competition among firms. For example, it restricts mergers that result in any one firm dominating an industry. There are some who claim that in focusing on competition in the United States, the government has lost sight of foreign competition. They believe American firms should be allowed greater freedom to combine, so that they can compete more effectively against foreign firms. Critics of this view believe this is just another smokescreen for the desire of companies to merge and attain more economic power and higher profits.

CHANGE GOVERNMENT POLICIES SOMEHOW!

Education Elementary and secondary education has long been primarily a responsibility of government. There is growing concern that our education system is not as effective as it could be, or needs to be. There is also a general consensus that money alone will not solve the problem; the United States already spends more on a per pupil basis than other countries such as Japan and Germany, whose students considerably outperform American students, at least on standardized tests.

One group of reformers would like more federal direction and assistance for the schools. Those holding the opposite view would give greater power to local officials like school principals, encourage students to choose between schools, and perhaps even encourage more competition between the public schools and private schools.

Welfare Government welfare policies have two main goals: to provide the poor with a basic level of subsistence and to help the poor become economically independent members of society. In 1965, President Johnson declared a War on Poverty. By the mid-1980s, however, it was clear that the war had not been won. Not only did statistics indicate that poverty was still an important problem, homelessness became a major issue in many cities. In 1988, Congress passed a welfare reform bill aimed at encouraging poor people to move from welfare to "workfare"; that is, in return for receiving welfare benefits, poor people were required to look for jobs, participate in job training, or take government-provided jobs.

come from somewhere, either from reallocating current expenditures or by increasing taxes (that is, increasing the size of the public sector at the expense of the private). Clearly, if it were costless, everyone would favor providing first-rate nursing home care for all of the elderly who want or need it. Given the costs, people may choose not to do so.

Some calls for government programs may simply be slightly veiled attempts to redistribute income. Those who want the government to pay for nursing care for the aged or child care for the young know that it takes resources to provide these services. They want someone else—the anonymous taxpayer—to pick up the bill. These groups may feel that they are particularly deserving, or that they cannot "afford" to pay for the services themselves. Evaluating whether these claims are justified is a question to which we will turn in later chapters.

In recent years, there has been increasing awareness of government failures, that it is not sufficient simply for government programs to have lofty objectives to redress the inadequacies of the market. While inner-city slums represent a serious social problem, many government housing projects have proved to be little if any better. While private nuclear power plants now comply (partly at the government's prodding) with high standards that make serious nuclear contamination unlikely, some of the government-run nuclear power plants are thought to represent a real potential hazard.

Thus, an analysis of the role of the government requires an understanding of the strengths and weaknesses of governments as well as those of markets. Governments can fail just as markets can. Careful analysis is required to determine whether the government should actually take action, and what form that action should take. What is the cause of the problem? Is there reason to believe the government can do a more effective job? What will it cost in the short and long run? Where will the funds come from?

An understanding of the basic tools and techniques economists use in making evaluations about the benefits or costs of particular government interventions can help greatly to put contemporary economic issues in perspective. Subsequent chapters will develop these tools and techniques.

REVIEW AND PRACTICE

SUMMARY

1. The government plays a pervasive role in the economy of almost every industrialized country. U.S. government expenditures are approximately one-third of national output—a much larger proportion than forty years ago, but a smaller proportion than in most countries of Western Europe.

2. In a democracy, the public sector differs from the private in two main ways. Its legitimacy and authority are derived from the electoral process; it has certain powers of compulsion, such as requiring households and firms to pay taxes and obey laws.

3. By and large, economists believe that private markets allocate resources efficiently. But there are a number of areas in which they do not, as is the case with externalities and public goods. Moreover, at times, when the economy fails to use the available resources fully, there may be idle industrial capacity and unemployed workers. And even when the economy is efficient, there may be dissatisfaction with the distribution of income.

4. Individuals and firms tend to produce too much of a good with a negative externality, such as air or water pollution, since they do not bear all the costs. On the other hand, they tend to produce too little of a good with a positive externality, such as a new invention, since they cannot receive all the benefits.

5. Public goods are goods that it costs little or nothing for an additional individual to enjoy, and that it costs a great deal to exclude any individual from enjoying. National defense and lighthouses are two examples. Free markets tend to underproduce public goods, since it is (by definition) difficult to prevent anyone from using them without paying for them.

6. Government has a variety of instruments it can use to attain its objectives. It can take direct action, provide incentives to the private sector, or mandate action by the private sector.

7. The proper balance between the public and private sectors is a major concern of economics. Recent years have seen an increased reliance on the private sector, with movements toward deregulation and privatization.

8. Government expenditures have grown in the past four decades, as a result of increased spending on programs for the aged and the growing interest government must pay on the national debt, among other reasons.

KEY TERMS

nationalization
privatization
deregulation
federal governmental
   structure

Smith's "invisible
   hand"
market failure
externality

public good
free-rider problem
principle of consumer
   sovereignty

REVIEW QUESTIONS

1. Name some of the ways government touches the lives of all citizens, both in and out of the economic sphere.

2. "Since democratic governments are elected by the consent of a majority of the people, they have no need for compulsion." Comment.

3. How can individual selfishness end up promoting social welfare?

4. Name areas in which market failure can occur.

5. Why do goods with negative externalities tend to be overproduced? Why do goods with positive externalities tend to be underproduced? Give an example for each.

6. What two characteristics define a public good? Give an example.

7. What three broad types of instruments does government have to try to achieve its goals?

8. Does the presence of a market failure necessarily mean that government action is desirable? If not, why not?

9. Describe some of the major economic roles of government.

10. How has the size of government changed over time? How does the size of the U.S. government compare with that of other industrialized countries?

PROBLEMS

1. In each of the following areas, specify how the government is involved, either as a direct producer, a regulator, a purchaser of final goods and services distributed directly to individuals or used within government, or in some other role:
   (a) education
   (b) mail delivery
   (c) housing

    (d) air travel

    (e) national defense.

In each of these cases, can you think of ways that part of the public role could be provided by the private sector?

2. Can you explain why even a benevolent and well-meaning government may sometimes have to use the power of eminent domain? (Hint: Consider the incentives of one person who knows that her property is the last obstacle to building a highway.)

3. Explain why government redistribution programs involve a trade-off between risk and incentives for *both* rich and poor.

4. Each of the situations below involves an externality. Tell whether it is a positive or negative externality, or both, and explain why free markets will overproduce or underproduce the good in question:

    (a) a business performing research and development projects;

    (b) a business that discharges waste into a nearby river;

    (c) a concert given in the middle of a large city park;

    (d) an individual who smokes cigarettes in a meeting held in a small, unventilated room.

5. When some activity causes a negative externality like pollution, would it be a good idea to ban the activity altogether? Why or why not? (Hint: Consider marginal costs and benefits.)

6. Highways are often referred to as public goods. That designation is basically fair, but not perfect. What are the costs of "exclusion"? Can you describe a case where the marginal cost of an additional driver on a highway might be relatively high? How might society deal with this problem?

PART TWO

PERFECT MARKETS

Microeconomics and macroeconomics provide two perspectives from which we can view the economy. One focuses on the behavior of the parts, the other on the behavior of the whole; one focuses on the choices of households and the production decisions of firms, the other on the aggregate consequences of those individual decisions and actions for the nation's output, employment levels, productivity growth, balance of payments, and inflation rates.

Parts Two and Three of this book focus on microeconomics. Part Two explores in depth the basic microeconomic assumptions of rational, well-informed consumers interacting with profit-maximizing firms in competitive markets. This set of assumptions, as we learned in Chapter 2, constitutes economists' basic model. Here, we study the implications of this model and examine the powerful insights it affords. It turns out that while this basic model is a good starting point, consumers are often not as well-informed, and markets are often not as competitive, as the model assumes them to be. Part Three expands on and enriches the basic model in ways that make it more realistic.

The economy consists of three groups of participants—individuals or households, firms, and government—interacting in three markets, the labor, capital, and product markets. Part Two follows those divisions, with one important exception: the discussion of government is postponed to Part Three. The objective in Part Two is to understand how a purely private market economy might operate. Chapters 8–11 discuss how individuals and households make their choices of what goods to consume, how much to save, how to invest their savings, and how much labor to supply. Chapters 12 and 13 analyze how firms make their decisions concerning how much to produce and how to produce it.

Finally, Chapter 14 brings households and firms together in the three markets. Households supply labor, and firms demand labor. The interaction of this supply and demand for labor determines the wage rate and the level of employment. Households supply savings or capital, and firms demand capital so that they can build factories and buy new machines. Their interaction in the capital market determines the interest rate and the equilibrium level of savings and investment in the economy. Households take their income, both what they earn as workers and the return on their savings, and use it to buy goods. They demand goods. With the workers they have hired, machines they have purchased, and factories they have built, firms produce goods. Firms' supply of goods and households' demand for goods interact in the product market, and this interaction determines the prices of the myriad of goods we consume.

8

THE CONSUMPTION DECISION

T here are more than 95 million households in the United States. The choices made by each one contribute to the overall demand for cars and bicycles, beer and wine, clothes and housing, and many other products available in U.S. markets. The members of each household also make decisions that affect how much income they will have to spend, like whether to work overtime or whether both partners in a marriage should work. They decide how much of their income to save and, if they do save, where to put their nest eggs. Their choices about whether to have children, and if so how many, affect the demand for schools, diapers, and strollers.

Naturally, these microeconomic decisions have macroeconomic consequences as well. Household decisions about whether to buy a car that's imported from Japan or one that's American-made will affect the U.S. trade deficit. Choices about how much to work will affect the level of unemployment and the overall level of production in the economy. Household decisions about savings and investment will affect the future growth of the economy.

We now take a closer look at the decisions of individual consumers and households concerning how to spend their income, and how these decisions can be affected by taxes and other government policies. Chapters 9, 10, and 11 focus, respectively, on the ways households make decisions concerning how much to save, how to invest their savings, and how much to work. Together, these four decisions represent the basic economic choices facing the household. The tools and concepts developed here will find repeated application throughout this book.

"What would you do if you had a million dollars—tax free, I mean?"

KEY QUESTIONS

1. Where does the demand curve come from? Why is it normally downward sloping?

2. How does an increase in income shift the demand curve? How do changes in the prices of other goods shift the curve?

3. How can the concepts of budget constraint and trade-off, introduced in Chapter 2, be applied to these questions?

4. How do changes in income and prices change the budget constraint?

5. How do the choices individuals make—their consumption, or demands—relate to these changes in the budget constraint?

THE BUDGET CONSTRAINT

Each consumer has a certain amount of income that he can spend. A consumer must allocate (that is, divide) his available income among alternative goods. His opportunity set—the choices he has available—is defined by a budget constraint, as we saw in Chapter 2. If, after taxes, a person's weekly paycheck comes to $300, then this is his budget constraint (assuming that he has no other source of income); total expenditures on food, clothing, rent, entertainment, travel, and all other categories cannot exceed $300 per week. For the present purposes, we will ignore the possibilities that individuals may borrow money, or save money, or change their budget constraints by working longer or shorter hours.

The line *BC* in Figure 8.1A is a simple example of an individual's budget constraint. In this case, a student, Fran, has a total of $300 each semester to spend on "fun" items.

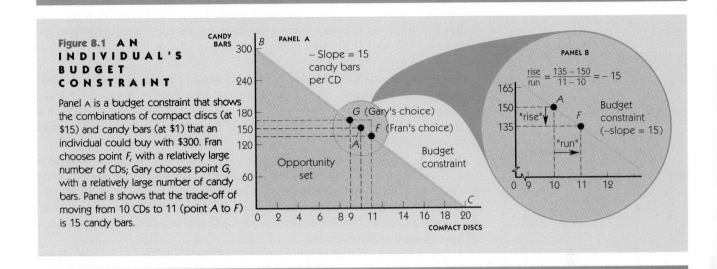

Figure 8.1 AN INDIVIDUAL'S BUDGET CONSTRAINT

Panel A is a budget constraint that shows the combinations of compact discs (at $15) and candy bars (at $1) that an individual could buy with $300. Fran chooses point F, with a relatively large number of CDs; Gary chooses point G, with a relatively large number of candy bars. Panel B shows that the trade-off of moving from 10 CDs to 11 (point A to F) is 15 candy bars.

Figure 8.1 assumes that there are two goods, candy bars and compact discs. The assumption of only two goods is obviously an abstraction from the real world of millions of goods, but it is an abstraction that should help to highlight the main points of the analysis.

For the purposes of the example, let's say that a candy bar costs $1, while a compact disc costs $15. Thus, if Fran spent all of her income on candy bars, she could purchase 300 candy bars (point B on the budget constraint). If she spent all of her income on CDs, she could buy 20 CDs (point C on the budget constraint). Fran can also choose any of the intermediate choices on line BC. For example, she could buy 10 CDs (for $150) and 150 candy bars (for $150), or 15 CDs ($225) and 75 candy bars ($75). Each combination of purchases along the budget constraint totals $300.

We learned in Chapter 2 that there are two important features of a budget constraint diagram. First, although any point in the shaded area of Figure 8.1A is feasible, only the points on the line BC, where Fran is actually operating on her budget constraint and consuming her entire budget, are really relevant. Second, by looking along the budget constraint, we can see the trade-offs she faces—how many candy bars she has to give up to get 1 more CD, and vice versa. For example, look at points F and A. This part of the budget constraint is blown up in panel B. At point A, Fran has 10 CDs; at F, she has 11. At F, she has 135 candy bars; at A, 150. To get 1 more CD, she has to give up 15 candy bars. That is the trade-off.

The trade-off is determined by the relative prices of the two goods. If one good costs twice as much as another, to get 1 more unit of the costly good, we have to give up 2 units of the cheaper good. If, as here, one good costs fifteen times as much as another, to get 1 more unit of the costly good, we have to give up 15 units of the less costly good.

The **slope** of the budget constraint also tells us what the trade-off is. The slope of a line simply measures how steep it is; that is, as we move 1 unit along the horizontal axis (from 10 to 11 CDs), the slope measures the size of the change along the vertical axis. The slope is the rise (the movement up or down on the vertical axis) divided by the run (the corresponding horizontal movement). The slope of this budget constraint is thus 15.[1] It tells us how much of one good, at a given price, we need to give up if we want 1 more unit of the other good; it tells us, in other words, what the trade-off is.

Notice that the relative price of CDs to candy bars is 15; that is, a CD costs fifteen times as much as a candy bar. But we have just seen that the slope of the budget constraint is 15, and that the trade-off, the number of candy bars Fran has to give up to get 1 more CD, is 15. It is no accident that these three numbers—relative price, slope, and trade-off—are the same.

This two-product example was chosen for simplicity, and because it is easy to illustrate with a two-dimensional graph. But this sort of logic can easily cover any number of products. A certain amount of income can be spent on any one item, or on a combination of items. The budget constraint defines what that amount of income can buy, which depends on the prices of the items. Giving up some of one item would allow the purchase of more of another item or items.

To avoid drawing figures in three or more dimensions to represent these choices, economists use a trick. On the horizontal axis, they put the purchases of the good upon which they are focusing attention, say CDs. On the vertical axis, they put "all other goods." Obviously, by definition, what is not spent on CDs is available to be spent on all other goods. Fran has $300 to spend altogether. We can draw a more realistic budget constraint for her like the one in Figure 8.2. The intersection of the budget constraint with the vertical axis, point *B*—where purchases of CDs are zero—is $300. If Fran spends nothing on CDs, she has $300 to spend on other goods. The budget constraint intersects the horizontal axis at 20 CDs (point *C*); if she spends all of her income on CDs and CDs cost $15 each, she can buy 20 of them. If Fran chooses a point such as *F*, she will buy 11 CDs, costing $165, and she will have $135 to spend on other goods ($300 − $165). The distance *OD* on the vertical axis measures what she spends on other goods; the distance *BD* measures what she spends on CDs.

CHOOSING A POINT ON THE BUDGET CONSTRAINT: INDIVIDUAL PREFERENCES

The study of consumer behavior always begins with the budget constraint and a recognition of possible trade-offs. The process of identifying the budget constraints and the trade-offs is the same for *any* two people. If a person walks into a store (that only accepts cash) with $300, any economist can tell you his budget constraint and the trade-offs he faces by looking at the money in his pocket and the prices on the shelves. What choice will he actually make? Economists narrow their predictions to points on his budget constraint; individuals will choose *some* point along the budget constraint. But the point actually chosen depends on the individual's preferences: Fran, who likes to listen to music a great deal, might choose point *F* in Figure 8.1, while Gary, who loves candy, might choose *G*.

Few people will choose either of the extreme points on the budget constraint, *B* or

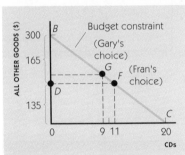

Figure 8.2 ALLOCATING A BUDGET BETWEEN A SINGLE GOOD AND ALL OTHERS

Some budget constraints show the choice between a particular good, in this case CDs, and all other goods. The other goods that might be purchased are collectively measured in money terms, as shown on the vertical axis.

---

[1] We ignore the negative sign. See the appendix to Chapter 2 for a more detailed explanation of the slope of a line.

C in Figure 8.1, where only one of the goods is consumed. The reason for this is that the more you have of a good—say, the more CDs you have relative to another good such as candy—the less valuable is an additional unit of that good relative to additional units of another good. At points near C, it seems safe to assume that to most individuals, an extra CD does not look as attractive as some candy bars. Certainly, at B, most people would be so full of candy bars that an extra CD would look preferable.

Where the individual's choice lies depends on how she values the two goods. Chapter 2 emphasized the idea that in making decisions, people look at the *margin*; they look at the extra costs and benefits. In this case, the choice at each point along the budget constraint is between 1 more CD and 15 more candy bars. If Gary and Fran choose different points along the budget constraint, it is because they value the marginal benefits (how much better off they feel with an *extra* CD) and the marginal costs (how much giving up 15 candy bars hurts) differently. Gary chooses point G in Figure 8.1 because that is the point where, for him, the marginal benefit of an extra CD is just offset by what he has to give up to get the extra CD, which is 15 candy bars. When Fran, who loves listening to music, considers point G, she realizes that for her, at that point, CDs are more important and candy bars less important than they are for Gary. So she trades along the line until she has enough CDs and few enough candy bars that, for her, the marginal benefits of an extra CD and the marginal costs of 15 fewer candy bars are equal. This point, as we have supposed, is F.

The same reasoning holds for a budget constraint like the one shown in Figure 8.2. Here, Gary and Fran are choosing between CDs and all other goods, measured in dollar terms. Now in deciding to buy an extra CD, each one compares the marginal benefit of an extra CD with the marginal cost, what has to be given up in other goods. With CDs priced at $15, choosing to buy a CD means giving up $15 of other goods. For Gary, the marginal benefit of an extra CD equals the cost, $15, when he has only 9 CDs and can therefore spend $165 on other goods. For Fran, who has more of a taste for CDs, the marginal benefit of an extra CD does not equal this marginal cost until she reaches 11 CDs, with $135 to spend elsewhere. Thus, the price can be thought of as giving a quantitative measure of the marginal benefit.

CHANGES IN THE BUDGET CONSTRAINT

Broadly speaking, there are two reasons that budget constraints can change: relative prices change, or incomes change. Figure 8.3 shows what happens to Fran's budget constraint when relative prices change. Again, the horizontal axis represents CDs and the vertical axis all other goods. As the price of CDs changes, the budget constraint rotates around point B. It tilts down to the left, from BC to BC_i, when the price of CDs increases, and rotates up to the right, from BC to BC_d, when the price of CDs decreases. The direction of rotation is due to the change in the amount of other goods Fran has to give up to get 1 more CD. The steeper the line, the more other goods must be given up to get a CD, and the flatter the line, the fewer other goods must be given up for a CD. With CDs priced at $15, Fran chooses point F, or 11 CDs. At the increased price of $30, she chooses F_i (6 CDs), and at the decreased price of $10, she chooses F_d (15 CDs). Notice that when CDs are more expensive Fran buys fewer of them, and when CDs are less expensive she buys more of them. Later in the chapter, we will take a closer look at why this is so.

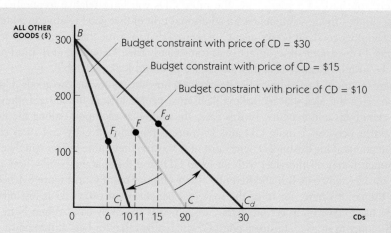

Figure 8.3 HOW A CHANGE IN PRICE AFFECTS THE BUDGET CONSTRAINT

Starting from BC, where the price of CDs is $15, the budget constraint rotates down to BC_i when the price of CDs increases to $30. It rotates up to BC_d when the price of CDs decreases to $10.

Now suppose Fran's *income* changes, but relative prices do not. The budget constraint shifts outward or inward in parallel lines, as shown in Figure 8.4. The budget constraint does not rotate here because if income alone changes, the relative prices of the goods remain unchanged, and therefore the trade-off remains unchanged. As Fran's income increases from $300 to $450, her budget constraint shifts out to the right from BC to B_iC_i, and as her income decreases to $150, her budget constraint shifts down to the left, to B_dC_d.

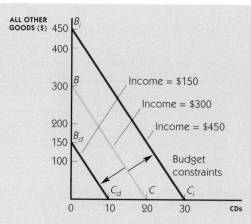

Figure 8.4 HOW A CHANGE IN INCOME AFFECTS THE BUDGET CONSTRAINT

Starting from BC, where income is $300, the budget constraint shifts out to the right in a parallel line, to B_iC_i, when income increases. It shifts down to the left, to B_dC_d, when income decreases.

WHAT HAPPENS TO CONSUMPTION WHEN INCOME CHANGES

When an individual's income changes, we have seen that his budget constraint shifts in a parallel line—outward if his income rises, inward if his income declines. The point the person chooses on this new budget constraint is again a matter of individual taste. To study how changes in income affect consumption, we continue to assume that prices do not also change.

Normally, consumption of a good will increase when a person's income rises. Indeed, goods that exhibit this property are called **normal goods.** Figure 8.5A shows the choice between CDs and all other goods. When Fran's income goes up, the budget constraint shifts out from BC to B_iC_i. Fran, predictably, chooses to move to point F_i from point F, increasing her consumption both of CDs and of all other goods.

It is possible that consumption of a particular good will go *down* when income goes up. This is an exceptional case, however, and goods that exhibit this trait are called **inferior goods.** If Fran, who has been riding the bus to work, gets a large raise, she may find that she can afford a car. After buying the car, she will spend less on bus tokens. A trip by car is, in Fran's opinion, preferable to a bus ride. Or, to put it another way, the bus ride is an inferior good in this situation. Panel B shows Fran's income rising, the budget constraint shifting out from BC to B_iC_i, and the consumption of bus tokens declining as a result.

Economists often attempt to measure how much the consumption of a good changes in response to a change in income, what they call the **income elasticity of demand** (this parallels the price elasticity of demand, which we encountered in Chapter 5). The income elasticity of demand gives the percentage change in demand divided by the percentage change in income (the percentage change in demand as the result of a 1 percent change in income). If the income elasticity of demand of a certain good is greater than one, a 1 percent increase in an individual's income results in a more than 1 percent increase in expenditures on that good. That is, the amount he spends on that good increases more than proportionately with income. By definition, if the income elasticity of demand is less than one, then a 1 percent increase in income results in a less than 1 percent increase in expenditures. The share of income a consumer spends on that good decreases with a rise in income. So long as the income elasticity is greater than zero, the good is, by definition, normal.

As people's incomes increase, they have more money to spend on goods other than those required just to survive. For instance, while they may spend some of the extra income to buy better-quality food and other necessities, more money goes toward movies, more expensive automobiles, vacations, and other luxuries. Accordingly, poor individuals spend a larger percentage of their income on food and housing and a smaller percentage of their income on perfume.

Figure 8.6 illustrates this point by showing how typical families at different income levels spend their income. In the figure, we see that *on average*, the poorest 20 percent of the population spend more than 100 percent of their before-tax income on housing—such a high percentage is only possible because of government subsidies. This should be contrasted with the richest 20 percent, who spend only a fifth of their income on housing. Similarly, the poorest 20 percent spend nearly half of their before-tax income

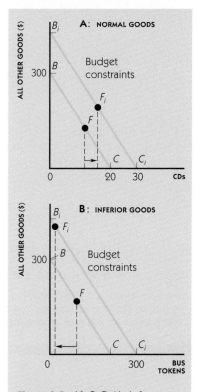

Figure 8.5 **NORMAL VERSUS INFERIOR GOODS**

The effect on consumption of a change in income depends on the nature of the good. For normal goods, higher income leads to higher consumption, as shown for CDs in panel A. For inferior goods, higher income leads to lower consumption, as shown for bus tokens in panel B.

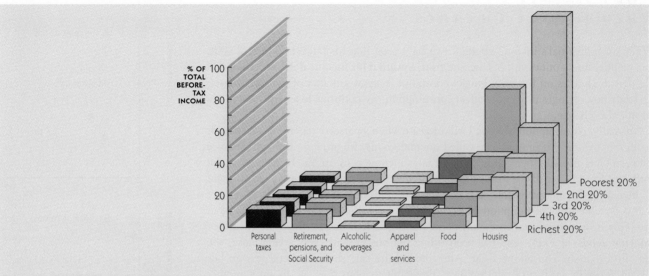

Figure 8.6 **HOW HOUSEHOLDS OF DIFFERENT INCOMES SPEND THEIR MONEY**

The poor spend far higher proportions of their income on basic necessities like food and housing than do the rich. *Note:* Before-tax income does not include borrowing or benefits received from government programs, which explains expenditures greater than 100 percent. *Source: Consumer Expenditure Survey Data, 1984–87,* Bulletin 2333.

on food, while the richest 20 percent spend less than a tenth.

Table 8.1 provides the income elasticities of some consumer goods. Chapters 4 and 5 pointed out that consumers and firms could make greater adjustments the longer the time they had to make changes. Thus, long-run price elasticities are normally larger—and often much larger—than short-run price elasticities. The same is true for responses to changes in income. Long-run income elasticities are larger—often much larger—than short-run income elasticities. The data provided in the table are long-run elasticities. An example of the difference between long-run and short-run elasticity is provided by gasoline and oil; the long-run elasticity is 1.36, but the short-run has been measured to be only .55.

Note that the income elasticity of water is .59. It may seem surprising that water has any elasticity at all—don't poor people have to drink water just as much as rich people do to survive? The fact that there is a systematic relationship between income and water consumption simply emphasizes the point that, with effort, you can economize on almost any resource, and that this process of economizing often proceeds almost unconsciously. At lower income levels, you may wash your car less often, water your lawn less often, and so on.

Information like that contained in Figure 8.6 is often of great practical importance. For example, it helps to determine how a tax will affect different groups. Clearly,

Table 8.1 SOME INCOME ELASTICITIES OF DEMAND

Elastic (long-run)		Inelastic (long-run)	
Motion pictures	3.41	Car repairs	.90
Drugs and medicines	3.04	Tobacco products	.86
Owner-occupied housing	2.45	China, glassware, and utensils	.77
Nondurable toys	2.01	Shoe repairs	.72
Electricity	1.94	Alcoholic beverages	.62
Restaurant meals	1.61	Water	.59
Local buses and trains	1.38	Furniture	.53
Gasoline and oil	1.36	Clothing	.51
Car insurance	1.26		
Physicians' services	1.15		
Car purchases	1.07		

Source: H. S. Houthakker and Lester D. Taylor, *Consumer Demand in the United States* (Cambridge, Mass.: Harvard University Press, 1970).

anybody who consumes alcohol will be hurt by a tax on alcohol, but if the poor spend a larger fraction of their income on alcohol, as the figure suggests, they will bear a disproportionately large share of the tax.

WHAT HAPPENS TO CONSUMPTION WHEN PRICES CHANGE: DERIVING THE DEMAND CURVE

When prices change, an individual's budget constraint rotates, as we saw in Figure 8.3, which is repeated as panel A of Figure 8.7. By analyzing the choices Fran is likely to make in response to these price changes, we can derive her demand curve, which, as we learned in Chapter 4, traces out the quantity demanded of a good at different prices. Thus, at the original price of $15 a CD, Fran buys 11 CDs (point F), while at the higher price of $30, she buys only 6 (point F_i). By the same token, consider what happens to the demand for CDs as the price falls. Now the budget constraint is flatter and Fran buys 15 (point F_d).

Panel B in the figure plots, for each price of CDs, the quantity consumed. This is the demand curve. Note that the vertical axis now represents the price of CDs. The points F_i, F, and F_d correspond to the prices and quantities given in panel A, and the smooth line connecting the points is based on the assumption that the analysis of the previous paragraph could be applied to smaller price changes, and that it would produce all the points shown as the demand curve.

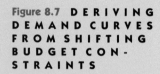

Figure 8.7 DERIVING DEMAND CURVES FROM SHIFTING BUDGET CON-STRAINTS

In panel A, the budget constraint rotates down to the left as the price of CDs increases, leading Fran to change consumption from F to F_i. The budget constraint rotates to the right when the price of CDs decreases, and Fran moves from F to F_d. Panel B shows the corresponding demand curve for CDs, illustrating how the rising prices lead to a declining quantity consumed.

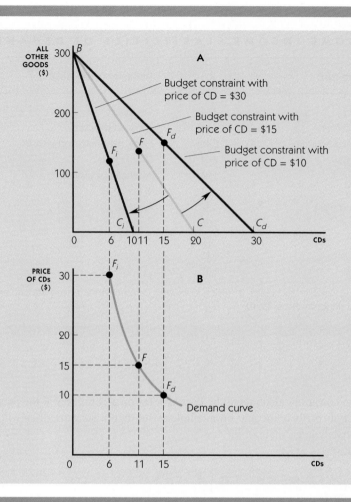

WHY DEMAND CURVES NORMALLY SLOPE DOWNWARD: SUBSTITUTION AND INCOME EFFECTS

An individual's demand curve normally slopes downward. There are two separate reasons for this, and both are also related to the change of the budget line caused by price changes.

When the price of CDs increases, Fran's budget constraint rotates downward, as was shown in Figure 8.3. The new line is steeper, reflecting the fact that CDs are now more expensive relative to other goods. Fran will thus be encouraged to substitute other goods for CDs, perhaps buying tapes to satisfy her interest in music. This is called the **substitution effect,** and it reduces the demand for CDs as the price goes up.

The downward rotation of the budget constraint also diminishes the opportunity set; Fran is made worse off by the price increase. Even though her income remains the same, she is able to buy less with it. Economists would say that her **real income** has gone down. What Fran cares about is not just what her income is in dollars, but what those dollars will buy. If prices go up and her dollar income stays the same, her real income has declined. This is the **income effect** of a rise in price. Like the change in income shown in Figure 8.5A, it encourages Fran to consume fewer of all goods.[2] The magnitude of the income effect will depend on how largely the higher-priced good figured in a person's preferred bundle of goods. An increase in the price of CDs will have a relatively small effect on a typical individual's real income; higher overall food prices would produce a more serious blow.

The substitution effect reflects the changes in the trade-offs facing an individual, while the income effect reflects changes in her well-being. With normal goods, both the substitution and income effects work in the same direction. As the price of a normal good drops, people substitute it for other goods; they consume more of it. The income effect normally reinforces this increase in consumption; as the price of a good drops, individuals are made better off, so they consume more of all goods, including the good whose price has been lowered. Similarly, when the price of a normal good rises, the substitution and income effects lead people to consume less of the good.

Figure 8.8 GIFFEN GOODS

In exceptional cases of inferior goods, the income effect may be strong enough to outweigh the substitution effect. The result is that the demand curve loses its characteristic downward slope.

The Exception to the Rule: Inferior Goods   In the case of inferior goods, the substitution effect continues to encourage more consumption of a good whose price has decreased, but the income effect acts in the opposite direction. Bus tokens were the example of an inferior good in Figure 8.5. There, we were holding prices constant while Fran's income changed. Now let's say the price of a token changes from $1.10 to $1.00 while Fran's income remains constant. The income effect of the cheaper bus tokens simply makes her feel slightly better off, but probably not better enough off to buy a car. The more significant effect, the substitution effect, is that she is probably tempted to substitute bus rides for worn shoe leather. This scenario, in which the substitution effect outweighs the countervailing income effect, and the demand curve therefore slopes downward, is typical of most inferior goods. The demand curve for bus tokens is still downward sloping.

With extreme cases of inferior goods, the income effect will be strong enough to overcome the substitution effect. Such goods are known as Giffen goods after the nineteenth-century British economist Robert Giffen, who first studied them. The demand curve now will have a shape like the one shown in Figure 8.8. The traditional example of a Giffen good was potatoes in nineteenth-century Ireland. Potatoes constituted a very large fraction of expenditures, and an increase in the price of potatoes made people so much worse off that in order to survive, they had to economize strongly on all other purchases. The only way they could meet their nutritional requirements was to cut back on meat, cheeses, and other high-cost foods and to increase their consumption of potatoes. Today within the industrial economies, there are probably no inferior goods that loom so large in anyone's budget that an increase in the price would produce an income effect large enough actually to lead to an increase in consumption.

THE SUBSTITUTION AND INCOME EFFECTS: SOME EXAMPLES

To see the importance of distinguishing between the substitution and income effects, let's contrast three cases. In the first, the supply of oil declines, as occurred with the

---

[2] For a precise breakdown of how the substitution and income effects lead to a change in consumption when there is a price change, see the Chapter Appendix.

Agencies of the federal government often use information about demand curves and price elasticities to estimate the effects of different taxes. For example, the Congressional Budget Office, which provides nonpartisan analysis of issues before Congress, published a report in August 1990 on "Federal Taxation of Tobacco, Alcoholic Beverages, and Motor Fuels."

One chapter of the report is devoted to analyzing the various consequences of three proposed changes:

1. doubling the cigarette tax from 16 cents to 32 cents per pack;

2. raising the gasoline tax from 9 cents to 21 cents per gallon and the diesel fuel tax from 15 cents to 27 cents per gallon; and

3. raising the tax on all alcoholic beverages to 25 cents per ounce of pure alcohol, which would raise the tax on a typical bottle of 80-proof liquor from $1.98 to $2.54, on a typical bottle of wine from 3 cents to 76 cents, and on a six-pack of beer from 16 cents to 81 cents.

The CBO estimated that the cigarette tax increase would raise an additional $2.8 billion, the combined alcoholic beverage tax increases would raise an additional $7.2 billion, and the motor fuels tax increase would raise an additional $12.1 billion.

Estimates of revenues to be collected by the government must include an analysis of the elasticities of demand for these products. If demand for a product is extremely elastic, then an attempt by the producer to raise prices (to pass the tax along to the consumer) will lead to a large decline in quantity demanded, and the government may not collect much from such a tax. However, demands for cigarettes, alcohol, and gasoline are relatively inelastic.

The CBO analysis showed that these taxes would have the effects on price and quantity demanded in the short run given in the second and third columns of the table below. The implied estimates of price elasticity of demand could then be derived from this data; they are presented in the fourth column.

	Percentage change in price	Predicted percentage change in quantity demanded	Elasticity of demand
Cigarettes	11	4–8	.36–.72
Beer	18	5–13	.28–.72
Wine	25	17–25	.68–1.0
Distilled spirits	7	4–7	.57–1.0
Gasoline	11	2	.18

The CBO went on to argue that there is little evidence that changes in the price of one alcoholic beverage affect the quantity consumed of other alcoholic beverages. Thus, the fact that the suggested tax increase would cause a greater change in the price of wine and beer than in the price of distilled spirits does not complicate the analysis. Also, the CBO reported that although the short-term elasticity of demand for gasoline is only about .2, the long-run elasticity may be between .7 and 1.0, implying that a gasoline tax will not lead to much conservation in the short run, but it will change driving habits in the long run.

Source: Congressional Budget Office, *Federal Taxation of Tobacco, Alcoholic Beverages, and Motor Fuels* (August 1990).

oil embargo in 1973. This leads to higher prices of gasoline and other oil products. This in turn rotates downward the individual's budget constraint between gasoline and "all other goods." The consumer responds by substituting against gasoline (substitution effect). He is also worse off. It is as if he has suffered a pay cut equal to the extra amount of his budget he would have to spend to get the same amount of gasoline as before (income effect).

In the second case, gasoline prices also rise, but this time it is because the government imposes a tax specifically on gasoline. The impact on the individual is the same as that of the embargo-based price increase (both the substitution and income effects cause him to use less gasoline). But there is one important difference. In the case of the oil embargo, when the consumer substitutes against gasoline, this is the economically efficient response, given the decreased supply of oil. But in the case of the tax, there is no decrease in the supply of oil; when the consumer substitutes against gasoline, this does not reflect a greater scarcity of gasoline. Prices should reflect the scarcity value of resources. The gasoline tax distorts this principle. The substitution effect of the tax is associated with economic inefficiency.

The purpose of most taxes, of course, is to collect revenue for the government, and the consequence is lower income for taxpayers. Therefore, there will necessarily be an income effect from any tax. As the third case, consider a tax that every citizen, regardless of income or consumption, has to pay—let's say each taxpayer must pay $50. There is *only* an income effect from such a tax. This kind of tax is economically more efficient than a tax that has both income and substitution effects, like the gasoline tax, because it does not disturb the pattern of consumption. Relative prices still reflect scarcities. The only change is what arises naturally from the lower income. Such taxes, however, are not considered to share the burden of taxation equitably, which is why most countries do not use them (Britain under Prime Minister Thatcher in the late 1980s and early 1990s was an exception). Still, some taxes have more distortions than others. These distortions are related to the substitution effect produced by the taxes as they change relative prices (the slope of the budget constraint); one thing a *good* tax policy does is look for taxes that have small substitution effects.

THE SUBSTITUTION AND INCOME EFFECTS AND THE DEMAND CURVE

1. The substitution effect: When the price of a good changes, the budget constraint rotates. A higher price means that an individual has to give up more of other goods for each extra unit of the good whose price has risen. The new trade-off discourages consumption of that good, and the consumer will substitute other products for the good. In similar fashion, a lower price of a good encourages consumption of that good.

2. The income effect: When the price of a good changes, any individual who consumes the good has, in effect, had a change in his purchasing power. A lower price makes a person better off, while a higher one makes him worse off. Normally, a higher real income leads the individual to consume more of all goods, including the good whose price has changed.

3. The demand curve: The demand curve normally slopes downward. This is because except in the case of inferior goods, both the substitution and income effects operate in the same direction; when the price of a normal good rises, consumers buy less of the good. With inferior goods, the income effect works in the opposite direction from the substitution effect. Still, the substitution effect almost always dominates the income effect.

HOW A PRICE CHANGE AFFECTS THE DEMAND FOR ALL OTHER GOODS: SUBSTITUTES AND COMPLEMENTS

We have seen how, as the price of a good increases, the demand for that good normally decreases. When the price of one good, say gasoline, increases, demand for other goods is likely to be affected as well. The increase in price reduces the buying power of individuals' income. As a result, people tend to consume *less* of every good. This is the income effect. But an increase in the price of a good (like gasoline) makes all other goods *relatively* less expensive. The substitution effect thus tends to make people consume *more* of these other goods. We have learned that when the price of a good increases, the substitution and income effects usually work in the same direction; in both cases, demand for that good is reduced. (The exception is the case of inferior goods.) When considering the effect of a price increase for one good on the quantity demanded for all other goods, however, we find that the income and substitution effects work in opposite directions. Thus, it is quite possible that an increase in the price of one good leads to either an increase or decrease in the consumption of another good.

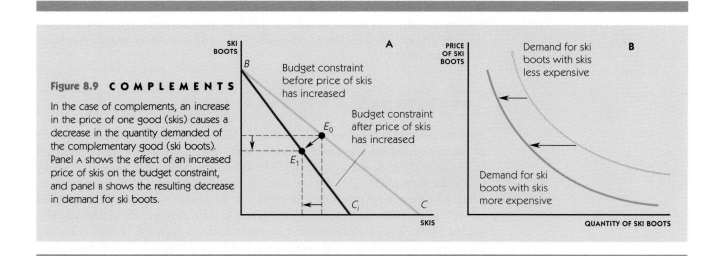

Figure 8.9 COMPLEMENTS

In the case of complements, an increase in the price of one good (skis) causes a decrease in the quantity demanded of the complementary good (ski boots). Panel A shows the effect of an increased price of skis on the budget constraint, and panel B shows the resulting decrease in demand for ski boots.

Figure 8.9A shows the case of *complements*, where an increase in the price of one good *decreases* the demand for the other good. When the price of skis goes up, the budget constraint tilts down, and with it the demand for ski boots. The demand for ski boots is not only reduced at their original price, it is reduced at *every* price of ski boots. In short, the demand *curve* for ski boots has shifted as a result of the increased price of skis. Skis and ski boots are complements; tennis rackets and tennis balls are complements. If two goods are complements, an increase in the price of one good leads to a leftward shift in the demand curve for the other good (panel B); that is, at each price, individuals will consume less of the other good.

Figure 8.10, on the other hand, illustrates the case of *substitutes*, where an increase

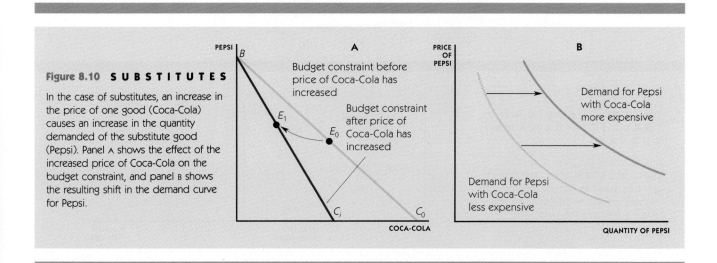

Figure 8.10 SUBSTITUTES

In the case of substitutes, an increase in the price of one good (Coca-Cola) causes an increase in the quantity demanded of the substitute good (Pepsi). Panel A shows the effect of the increased price of Coca-Cola on the budget constraint, and panel B shows the resulting shift in the demand curve for Pepsi.

in the price of one good *increases* the demand for the other. Coca-Cola and Pepsi are substitutes; coffee and tea are substitutes. Thus, an increase in the price of Coca-Cola shifts the demand curve for Pepsi to the right. The substitution effect strongly dominates the income effect.

SUBSTITUTES AND ELASTICITY

Demand curves generally slope downward, as we have seen, as a result of the combination of substitution and income effects. However, some of them are steeper than others, and one individual curve can vary in steepness from nearly vertical at the upper left to nearly horizontal at the lower right. We measure "steepness" by the price elasticity of demand, which gives the percent reduction in demand from a 1 percent increase in price. Demand curves that are flatter are more elastic (sensitive to price changes); those that are steep are less elastic. Why is demand curve D_1 more elastic in Figure 8.11 than curve D_2? Also, why is it that each of these two demand curves is relatively inelastic at the upper left and relatively elastic at the lower right?

The reason some demand curves are more elastic than others usually has to do with the availability of substitutes. Consider a product for which substitutes are fairly limited, like skis. When the price of skis increases, most individuals do not substitute snowshoes. Some continue to buy skis at the higher price; others may decide to go skiing less often, or to save money on some complementary purchase like ski clothing and use it for skis. The price increase leads to a relatively small decline in quantity demanded; the demand curve is thus inelastic, or steep.

On the other hand, consider a product for which substitution is easy, like Coca-Cola. If the price of Coca-Cola increases sharply, people can easily switch to Pepsi. As a result, a relatively small change in price will have a large substitution effect. A small increase in price will lead to a large decline in quantity demanded, which is to say that the demand curve is quite elastic, or flat.

Understanding why the shape of individual demand curves changes, from inelastic at the upper left to elastic at the lower right, can be explained with similar logic. Assume

Figure 8.11 ELASTIC AND INELASTIC DEMAND CURVES

Demand curve D_1 (panel A) is more elastic, with a flatter slope, than demand curve D_2 (panel B). Both curves are relatively inelastic at the upper left and relatively elastic at the lower right.

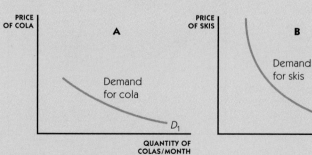
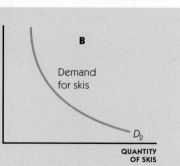

Bob is purchasing steaks 25 times a month, because the price is so low—a point such as *B* in Figure 8.12. As the price rises, Bob purchases fewer steaks. It is easy to cut back on eating steaks. He simply substitutes hamburger, ham, lamb chops, or chicken. But at a very high price, point *A*, Bob is consuming only 3 steaks a month. Now he really relishes each of his steaks. He is less willing to substitute. A further increase in price will still lead to a decline in quantity demanded, but not a large one. Generally, when an individual is consuming lots of some good, substitutes for the good are easy to find, and a small increase in price leads to a large reduction in the quantity demanded; but as consumption gets lower, it becomes increasingly difficult to find good substitutes.

THE SUBSTITUTION AND INCOME EFFECTS IN ACTION

To better understand the substitution and income effects, consider an idea proposed during the 1979 presidential campaign. To encourage conservation of oil, this plan proposed raising the price of gasoline by imposing a tax, but then refunding the tax to consumers by reducing their income taxes. Some commentators ridiculed this idea. What's the point of collecting a tax and then refunding it? But Figure 8.13 shows how an economist might look at such a proposal. This figure sets gasoline on the horizontal axis and "all other goods" on the vertical.

The original budget constraint of this particular consumer, Lucy, is the line BC_1. Now, an increase in the price of gasoline involves a clockwise rotation of the budget constraint around point *B* on the vertical axis. The new budget constraint is BC_2.

Imagine that before this plan, Lucy has an income of $20,000. She spends $500 a year on gasoline; at a price of $1.00 a gallon, that buys 500 gallons of gas. This choice is represented by point E_1 on the line BC_1. Now imagine the gasoline plan in two separate steps. First, the tax on a gallon of gasoline is raised by $.20, increasing the price Lucy pays to $1.20 a gallon. This shift in prices tilts the budget constraint down to BC_2. The higher price leads Lucy to choose the new point E_2, with a lower level of gasoline consumption. If the price elasticity of demand for gasoline is .5, then this price increase will lead to a fall in quantity demanded of 10 percent (20 percent × .5 = 10 percent). Now Lucy is buying 450 gallons (90 percent of 500) at a price of $1.20 a gallon; she spends a total of $540 ($1.20 × 450 gallons) on gasoline, with $90 ($.20 × 450 gallons) of that going to the gasoline tax.

Now, in the second step of the plan, the government refunds the $90 it has collected from Lucy through the gasoline tax by reducing the income tax rate. (The refund depends not on the actual amount of the gasoline tax paid by Lucy but on the average amount paid by all taxpayers. In this example, Lucy is an average person, so her refund is just equal to the gasoline tax she paid.) We could say the government is undoing the income effect of the higher gasoline prices by giving consumers income. This increase in income creates a new budget constraint *parallel* to BC_2, line B_3C_3. Let's say that Lucy chooses point E_3 on the new budget constraint. If she spends about 2½ percent of her additional income on gasoline, expenditures on gasoline go up by just over $2 (2½ percent × $90 refund). Notice that her consumption of gasoline is still lower than

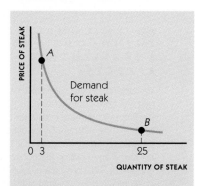

Figure 8.12 THE CHANGING ELASTICITY OF A SINGLE DEMAND CURVE

At point *B*, a lot of steak is being consumed, and the benefit derived from an extra steak is relatively low. As the price of steak rises from point *B*, many substitutes are available, and the demand curve is elastic. But by the time point *A* is reached and little steak is being consumed, the benefit of an extra steak is relatively high, most of the readily available substitutes have been tried, and the demand curve is relatively inelastic.

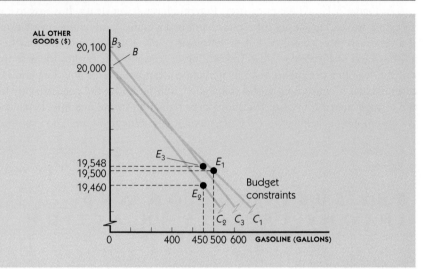

Figure 8.13 COMBINING THE INCOME AND SUBSTITUTION EFFECTS

The original budget constraint between gasoline and all other goods is given by the line BC_1, with the consumer choosing point E_1. The new tax on gasoline shifts the budget constraint in to BC_2, changing the slope and leading the consumer to choose E_2. Refunding the amount of tax collected to the consumer shifts the budget constraint out in a parallel line, B_3C_3, and the consumer chooses E_3.

it originally was before the plan started, but not as low as it was before the refund was distributed. (It is now about 452 gallons.)

If the tax rate is very low, individuals' welfare will not be much affected by the tax combined with the refund; what they lose in gas consumption they gain in consumption of other goods. Thus, the tax proposal, though it would have generated no revenue, would have succeeded in reducing consumption of gasoline, reflected in the diagram by the movement from E_1 (where consumption is 500 gallons per year) to E_3 (where consumption is 452 gallons per year). The plan, having stripped away the income effect of higher gasoline prices, has left a pure substitution effect. This was, of course, the intent of the proposal: to encourage conservation of energy.

UTILITY AND THE DESCRIPTION OF PREFERENCES

We have seen that people choose a point along their budget constraint by weighing the benefits of consuming more of one good against the costs, what they have to forgo of other goods. Economists sometimes describe the benefits of consumption by referring to the **utility** that individuals get from the combination of goods they consume. Presumably a person can tell you whether or not he prefers a certain combination of goods to another. Economists say that the preferred bundle of goods gives that individual a higher level of utility. Similarly, economists sometimes say that the individual will choose the bundle of goods—within the budget constraint—that maximizes his utility.

In the nineteenth century, social scientists, including the British philosopher Jeremy Bentham, hoped that science would someday develop a machine that could actually

CLOSE-UP: OWNERSHIP OF CARS BY LOCATION

In focusing on how price and income affect demand, it is important not to lose sight of other factors that matter, like geography and taste. In 1990, the average number of cars nationwide was .57 per person, but that number varied considerably between states, as the map here shows.

States with higher levels of auto ownership formed two bands. One stretched from Washington and Oregon in the West through to Minnesota and Iowa in the upper Midwest; the other ran up the East Coast, from Florida up to Tennessee, then to Virginia and north along the coast to Maine. What can these states have in common?

One possible connection is that with one exception, none of the states with car ownership above .60 per person contains any of the nation's ten largest urban areas (New York, Los Angeles, Chicago, San Jose/San Francisco/Oakland, Philadelphia, Detroit, Boston, Washington, D.C., Dallas,

and Houston). The single exception is Michigan, home of Detroit, the automobile city itself. It is plausible that urban dwellers have less reliance on cars. In Washington, D.C., which is almost entirely urban *and* has a well-developed mass transit, there are only .40 cars per person.

At the other extreme, some of the most rural states, like Arkansas and West Virginia, have the fewest cars. It is tempting to explain this by citing the relatively low income levels in these states, but that explanation will not do. Georgia, Mississippi, Alabama, and Kentucky are similarly poor, but have much higher levels of auto ownership. Perhaps the underlying cause is different tastes, different living patterns, or something in the state tax code. Part of the economist's job is to consider and test such explanations, not just those related to price and income.

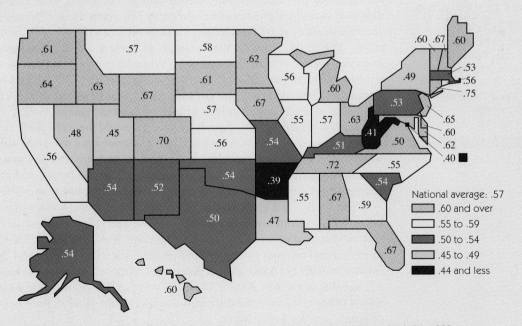

Source: U.S. Department of Transportation, Federal Highway Administration, *Highway Statistics 1990.*

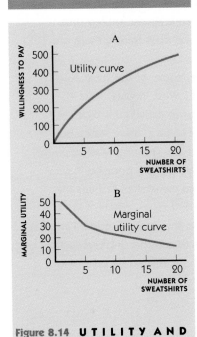

Figure 8.14 UTILITY AND MARGINAL UTILITY

Panel A shows that utility increases continually with consumption, but tends to level off as consumption climbs higher. Panel B explicitly shows marginal utility; notice that it declines as consumption increases.

measure utility. A scientist could simply hook up some electrodes to an individual's head and read off how "happy" she was. Modern economists have become more sophisticated about this issue. Most of them believe that there is no *unique* way to measure utility, but that there are useful ways of measuring changes in how well-off a person is.

For our purposes, a relatively simple way to measure utility will suffice: we ask how much an individual would be willing to pay to be in one situation rather than another. For example, if Joe likes chocolate ice cream more than vanilla, it stands to reason that he would be willing to pay more for a scoop of chocolate ice cream than for a scoop of vanilla. Or if Diane would rather live in California than in New Jersey, it stands to reason that she would be willing to pay more for the West Coast location.

Notice that how much a person is willing to pay is different from how much he *has* to pay. Just because Joe is willing to pay more for chocolate ice cream than for vanilla does not mean he will have to pay more. What he has to pay depends on market prices; what he is willing to pay reflects his preferences. Willingness to pay is an acceptable measure of utility, which is useful for purposes such as thinking about how an individual allocates his income along his budget constraint. But the early hopes of nineteenth-century economists, that we could find some way of measuring utility that would allow us to compare how much utility Fran got from a bundle of goods with how much utility Gary obtained, are now viewed as pipe dreams.

Using willingness to pay as our measure of utility, we can construct a diagram like Figure 8.14A, which shows the level of utility Mary receives from sweatshirts as the number of sweatshirts she buys increases. This information is also given in Table 8.2. Here we assume that Mary is willing to pay $200 for 5 sweatshirts, $228 for 6 sweatshirts, $254 for 7 sweatshirts, and so on; that is, 5 sweatshirts give her a utility of 200, 6 sweatshirts give her a utility of 228, and 7 sweatshirts give her a utility of 254. Mary's willingness to pay increases with the number of sweatshirts, reflecting the fact that additional sweatshirts give her additional utility. The extra utility of an additional sweatshirt, measured here by the additional amount she is willing to pay, is the **marginal utility.** The numbers in the third column of Table 8.2 give the marginal (or extra) utility she received from her last sweatshirt. When Mary owns 5 sweatshirts, an additional sweatshirt yields her an additional or marginal utility of 28 (228 − 200); when she owns 6 sweatshirts, an additional one gives her a marginal utility of only 26 (254 − 228). Panel B traces the marginal utilities of each of these increments.[3]

As an individual's bundle of goods includes more and more of a good, each successive increment increases her utility by less. There is **diminishing marginal utility.** The first sweatshirt will seem very desirable, and additional ones are attractive as well. But each sweatshirt does not increase utility by as much as the one before, and at some point, Mary may get almost no additional pleasure from adding to her sweatshirt wardrobe.

When Mary has a given budget and must choose between two goods that cost the same, say sweatshirts and pizza, each of which costs $15, she will make her choice so that the marginal utility of each good is the same. Table 8.2 shows Mary's willingness to pay (utility) for both sweatshirts and pizza. Look at what happens if Mary buys 20 sweatshirts with her $300 and no pizza. The marginal utility of the last sweatshirt is 12, and that of the first pizza is 18. If she switches $15 from sweatshirts to pizza, she loses a utility of 12 from the decreased sweatshirts, but gains 18 from her first pizza. It obviously pays for her to switch.

[3] Since marginal utility is the extra utility from an extra unit of consumption, it is simply measured by the slope of the utility curve in panel B.

Now look at the situation when she has decreased her purchases of sweatshirts to 17 and increased purchases of pizza to 3. The marginal utility of the last sweatshirt is 15, and that of the last pizza is also 15. At this point, she will not want to switch anymore. If she buys another sweatshirt, she gains 14, but the *last* pizza, her 3rd, which she will have to give up, has a marginal utility of 15; she loses more than she gains. If she buys another pizza, she gains 14, but the last sweatshirt (her 17th) gave her 15; again, she loses in net. We can thus see that with her budget, she is best off when the marginal utility of the two goods is the same.

The same general principle applies when the prices of two goods differ. Assume that a sweatshirt costs twice as much as a pizza. Now, so long as the marginal utility of sweatshirts is more than twice that of pizzas, it pays for Mary to switch to sweatshirts. To get one more sweatshirt, she has to give up two pizzas, and we reason as before that she will adjust her consumption until she gets to the point where the marginal utilities of the two goods, *per dollar spent*, are equal. This is a general rule: in choosing between two goods, a consumer will adjust her choices to the point where the marginal utilities are proportional to the prices. Thus, the last unit purchased of a good that costs twice

Table 8.2 **UTILITY AND MARGINAL UTILITY**

Number of sweatshirts	Mary's willingness to pay (utility)	Marginal utility	Number of pizzas	Mary's willingness to pay (utility)	Marginal utility
0	0		0	0	
1	50	50	1	18	18
2	95	45	2	34	16
3	135	40	3	49	15
4	170	35	4	63	14
5	200	30	5	76	13
6	228	28	6	88	12
7	254	26	7	99	11
8	278	24	8	109	10
9	301	23	9	118	9
10	323	22	10	126	8
11	344	21	11	133	7
12	364	20	12	139	6
13	383	19	13	144	5
14	401	18	14	148	4
15	418	17			
16	434	16			
17	449	15			
18	463	14			
19	476	13			
20	488	12			

as much as another must generate twice the marginal utility as the last unit purchased of the other good; the last unit purchased of a good that costs three times as much must generate three times the marginal utility as the last unit purchased of the other good; and so on.

This general rule becomes even more powerful if we think about it in relation to a budget constraint diagram. We saw earlier that Fran chose the point along the budget constraint where the marginal *benefit* of an extra CD was equal to its price. The price measured what she had to give up in other goods to get one more CD. It was the marginal or opportunity cost of the extra CD. The reason Fran chose point *F* rather than *G* in Figure 8.1 is that *F* was the point where the marginal utilities of CDs and candy bars were proportional to their prices, or 15 to 1. For Fran, at *G* the marginal utility of an extra CD exceeded its price, while that of a candy bar was less than its price. As she moved down the budget constraint to *F*, the marginal utility of CDs decreased and that of candy bars increased until the marginal utility of each equaled its price. We can express this in an equation,

$$MU_x = P_x,$$

which says that the marginal utility (MU) of any good (x) must equal its price (p).[4]

In the example we have just analyzed, we assumed Mary's willingness to pay for sweatshirts, her measure of utility, does not depend on how many pizzas, or other goods, she has. This is seldom the case. The utility, and hence marginal utility, of sweatshirts will depend on the number of pizzas, books, and other goods she has. Thus, even when the price of sweatshirts remains the same, if the price of other goods changes, she will change her consumption of those other goods *and* sweatshirts. The same thing will happen if Mary's income changes. The number of sweatshirts at which her marginal utility of an extra sweatshirt equals 15 will change. What matters for choices is *relative* price, so Mary will also change her choices if the price of sweatshirts changes and other prices remain unchanged.

CONSUMER SURPLUS

We have now seen how, in order to determine the quantity of a good they wish to purchase, people set marginal utility equal to price. Since utility is measured by willingness to pay, the marginal utility is just equal to the marginal willingness to pay—the extra amount a person is willing to pay for a good. If we draw a curve with marginal utility (or marginal willingness to pay) on one axis and the quantity of the good on the other (panel B of Figure 8.14), we see that marginal utility (or marginal willingness to pay) decreases with the quantity consumed.

We can bring the discussion of utility together with the discussion of budget constraints by recognizing that the demand curve corresponds to the marginal utility (or marginal willingness to pay) curve. At 11 pizzas, Mary is willing to pay $6 for one more; at 12, she is willing to pay $5.

Mary buys pizza up to the point where the price is equal to the marginal utility of the last pizza she chooses to buy. Of course, she pays the same price for each of the

---

[4] The result holds because of the way we are measuring utility, as willingness to pay. More generally, the result cited earlier, that the marginal utility per dollar spent must be the same for all goods, can be written $MU_x/p_x = MU_y/p_y$ for any two goods, x and y; or $MU_x/MU_y = p_x/p_y$, the ratio of marginal utilities must equal the price ratio.

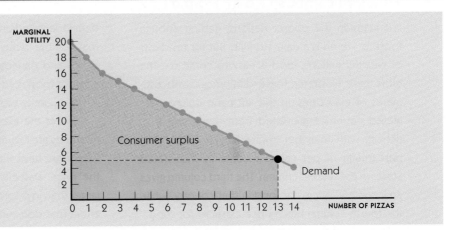

Figure 8.15 CONSUMER SURPLUS

The demand curve plots the amount Mary would be willing to pay for her 1st, 2nd, 3rd, and so on, pizza. The total amount she is willing to pay for 13 pizzas is the area under the demand curve up to the 13th pizza. The amount she actually has to pay is the heavily shaded area. The consumer surplus is the difference between the two, the lightly shaded area above the line and below the demand curve, over the range of the quantity purchased.

pizzas she purchases. Suppose pizzas cost $5 and Mary buys 13. The 13th pizza gives her a marginal utility of 5 and costs $5. Mary is getting a bargain: she would have been willing to pay more for the earlier pizzas. For her first pizza, she would have been willing to pay $18, for the second $16, and so forth. She would have been willing to pay a total of $144 ($18 + $16 + $15 + $14 + $13 + $12 + $11 + $10 + $9 + $8 + $7 + $6 + $5) for the 13 pizzas. The difference between what she *has* to pay for 13 pizzas—$5 × 13, or $65—and what she would have been willing to pay, $144, is called her **consumer surplus.** In this case, her consumer surplus is $79.

More generally, there is always some consumer surplus, so long as a consumer has to pay only a fixed price for all the items she purchases. The fact that demand curves are downward sloping means that the first units that the consumer purchases are more valuable than the marginal unit; she would have been willing to pay more for these earlier units than for the last unit, but she does not have to.

In Figure 8.15, the total amount Mary would have been willing to pay for 13 pizzas is the total area under the demand curve between the vertical axis and 13, the combination of the lightly and heavily shaded areas. This area is nothing but the sum of the willingness to pay for the 1st, 2nd, 3rd, and so on, up to 13 pizzas. The amount Mary actually has to pay is the heavily shaded area—the price, $5, times the quantity, 13 pizzas. Thus, the consumer surplus is the *difference*, the lightly shaded area above the price line and below the demand curve, over the range of the quantity of purchases.

LOOKING BEYOND THE BASIC MODEL: HOW WELL DO THE UNDERLYING ASSUMPTIONS MATCH REALITY?

In the market economy, the answer to the question "For whom are goods produced?" is that goods are produced for consumers, and thus a theory of consumer choice is

CLOSE-UP: INTERNATIONAL PRICE AND INCOME ELASTICITIES FOR FOOD

For many in the poorer nations, getting enough food to live on is a daily struggle. But for residents of wealthy nations, food is easy to come by. The table here illustrates these differences with estimates of elasticities. In the left-hand column, selected countries are listed from the poorest to richest, with their per capita income given as a percentage of per capita income in the United States in the second column. The third column gives an income elasticity for food in that country, while the fourth column lists a price elasticity for food.

Notice that the income elasticity of demand for food declines as income rises. This makes intuitive sense: as poor people receive more income, they will tend to spend a larger proportion of their additional money on food than wealthier people will. In India, a 10 percent increase in income will lead to a 7.6 percent increase in the quantity of food demanded. Looking at the fourth column, we see that for the richer countries such as the United States and Canada, a 10 percent increase in the price of food leads only to a 1 percent reduction in the quantity of food purchased.

More of the expenditures on food in the richer countries are luxuries—restaurants, lobsters, steaks. One might have thought that this would imply that the price elasticity in richer countries would be larger than in poorer countries. But there is another effect that dominates. In poorer countries, people spend a much larger fraction of their income on food. When the price of food goes up, they almost have to reduce food consumption. This is not the case in the wealthier countries. Because expenditures on food represent a larger fraction of total expenditures in poor countries, the income effect of a rise in the price of food there is larger.

Country	Per capita income (as % of U.S.)	Income elasticity of food	Price elasticity of food
India	5.2%	.76	− .32
Nigeria	6.7%	.74	− .33
Indonesia	7.2%	.72	− .34
Bolivia	14.4%	.68	− .35
Philippines	16.8%	.67	− .35
Korea	20.4%	.64	− .35
Poland	34.6%	.55	− .33
Brazil	36.8%	.54	− .33
Israel	45.6%	.49	− .31
Spain	55.9%	.43	− .36
Japan	61.6%	.39	− .35
Italy	69.7%	.34	− .30
United Kingdom	71.7%	.33	− .22
France	81.1%	.27	− .19
Germany	85.0%	.25	− .17
Canada	99.2%	.15	− .10
United States	100.0%	.14	− .10

Source: Ching-Fun Cling and James Peale, Jr., "Income and Price Elasticities," in Henri Theil, ed., *Advances in Econometrics Supplement* (Greenwich, CT: JAI Press, 1989). Data are from 1980.

critical to understanding market economies. The model of budget constraints and in-dividual preferences sketched in this chapter is the economist's basic model of consumer choice. It is a powerful one whose insights carry well beyond this chapter; indeed they carry well beyond this course. Still, there is room to criticize the model.

A first criticism might be that the model does not reflect the thought processes that consumers really go through. Who pauses while shopping for CDs to sketch a budget constraint or weigh marginal benefits? But this line of criticism is unfair. It is like criticizing the physicist's model of motion, which predicts with great precision how billiard balls will interact, because most pool players do not go through the equations before taking a shot. The question is whether the economic model of consumer choice can reliably be used to make predictions, and by and large it can. Many businesses, for example, have found the model useful for predicting the demand for their products.

Another criticism has to do with the model's assumption that individuals know what they like, which is to say that they have well-defined preferences. Having well-defined preferences means that if you gave someone a choice between two bundles of goods, one consisting of two apples, three oranges, and one pear and the other consisting of three apples, two oranges, and four pears, she could tell you quickly which she preferred. Furthermore, well-defined preferences imply that if you asked her tomorrow and the day after, she would give you the same answer. But in many cases, if you asked someone which of two things he preferred, he would say, "I don't know. Let me try them out." And what he likes may change from day to day. His preferences may, moreover, be affected by what others like. How else can we account for the frequent fads in foods and fashions as well as other aspects of our lives?

A third criticism has to do with the model's assumption that individuals know the prices of each of the goods in the market, which is to say that they know with precision their budget constraint. Outside the economics textbooks, people often do not know well their budget constraints. They know that there are bargains to be found, but they know it is costly to search for them. While we can talk meaningfully about the price of a bushel of wheat, what do we mean by the "price" of a couch, or a house? If we are lucky and stumble onto a deal, we might find a leather couch for $1,000. If unlucky, even after searching all day, we may not find one for under $1,500. When we get the bargain leather couch home, if we are lucky, we will find it is even better than we thought; if we are unlucky, the couch will fall apart just after the guarantee expires.

Suppose Inez likes the idea of going sailing, but has never done so. She does not know how much it will cost, but she knows it is costly to find out. When she is quoted a price over the phone, she may not even know the right questions to ask. For instance, what size sailboat? How long does it take to rig up the boat? Is this included in the time for which she is charged? Inez has to guess what the costs are, and then, with that best guess, if she thinks it is a real possibility, she checks it out further.

Finally, a fourth criticism points out that sometimes prices and preferences interact in a more complicated way than this chapter has depicted. Sometimes people's attitudes toward a good depend on its price. More expensive goods may have snob appeal. Or when the quality of certain goods cannot easily and quickly be checked, individuals may judge quality by price. Because, on average, better (more durable) things are more costly, when people see something that is very cheap, they infer that it could not be very good; or when they see something that is very expensive, they think it must be of high quality. In either case, demand curves may look quite different from those described in this chapter. Lowering the price for a good may actually *lower* the demand.

The fact that there are some goods and some instances for which the basic economic model needs to be extended or modified does not mean that the model is not useful. There are many situations where it provides just the information that businesses and governments need for making important decisions. And in those instances where the model does not work so well, it provides a basic framework that allows us to enhance our understanding of the behavior of households. We ask, which of the assumptions underlying the model seems inappropriate in that particular situation? The answer to that question guides our search for a better or more general model of consumption.

REVIEW AND PRACTICE

SUMMARY

1. The amount of one good a person must give up to purchase another good is determined by the relative prices of the two goods, and is illustrated by the slope of the budget constraint.

2. The demand curve for an individual is derived by tracing out the different quantities demanded of a good along a budget constraint as the price of the good changes and the budget constraint rotates.

3. Consumption of a normal good rises as income rises. Consumption of an inferior good falls as income rises.

4. As a good becomes more expensive relative to other goods, an individual will substitute other goods for the higher-priced good. This is the substitution effect. In addition, as the price of a good rises, a person's buying power is reduced. This is the income effect. Normally, both the substitution effect and the income effect reduce the quantity demanded of a good as its price rises.

5. If two goods are complements, the demand for one falls when the price of the other increases. If two goods are substitutes, the demand for one increases when the price of the other rises.

6. When substitution is easy, demand curves tend to be elastic, or flat. If substitution is difficult, demand curves tend to be inelastic, or steep.

7. Economists sometimes describe the benefits of consumption by referring to the utility that people get from a combination of goods. The extra utility of consuming one more unit of a good is referred to as the marginal utility of that good.

KEY TERMS

slope	real income	marginal utility
normal good	substitution effect	diminishing marginal
inferior good	income effect	utility
income elasticity of	utility	consumer surplus
demand		

REVIEW QUESTIONS

1. How is the slope of the budget constraint related to the relative prices of the goods on the horizontal and vertical axes?

2. How can the budget constraint appear the same even for individuals whose tastes and preferences differ dramatically?

3. Describe how a demand curve is derived.

4. Is the income elasticity of demand positive or negative for a normal good? for an inferior good? Explain.

5. If the price of a normal good increases, how will the income effect cause the quantity demanded of that good to change?

6. If the price of a good increases, how will the substitution effect cause the quantity demanded of that good to change?

7. Does a greater availability of substitutes make a demand curve more or less elastic? Explain.

8. Why does marginal utility tend to diminish?

PROBLEMS

1. Consider a student who has an entertainment budget of $120 per term, and spends it on either concert tickets at $10 apiece or movie tickets at $6 apiece. Imagine that movie tickets start decreasing in price, first falling to $4, then $3, then $2. Graph the four budget constraints, with movies on the horizontal axis. If the student's demand curve for movies is represented by the function $D = 60 - 10P$, graph both her demand curve for movies and the point she will choose at each price on the budget line.

2. Choose two normal goods and draw a budget constraint illustrating the trade-off between them. Show how the budget line shifts if income increases. Arbitrarily choose a point on the first budget line as the point a particular consumer will select. Now find two points on the new budget line such that the new preferred choice of the consumer must fall between these points.

3. DINKs are households with "double income, no kids," and such households are invading your neighborhood. You decide to take advantage of this influx by starting a gourmet take-out food store. You know that the price elasticity of demand for your food from DINKs is .5 and the income elasticity of demand is 1.5. From the standpoint of the quantity that you sell, which of the following changes would concern you the most?
    (a) The number of DINKs in your neighborhood falls by 10 percent.
    (b) The average income of DINKs falls by 5 percent.

4. Compare one relatively poor person, with an income of $10,000 per year, with a relatively wealthy person who has an income of $60,000 per year. Imagine that the poor person drinks 15 bottles of wine per year at an average price of $10 per bottle, while the wealthy person drinks 50 bottles of wine per year at an average price of $20 per bottle. If a tax of $1 per bottle is imposed on wine, who pays the greater amount?

Who pays the greater amount as a percentage of income? If a tax equal to 10 percent of the value of the wine is imposed, who pays the greater amount? Who pays the greater amount as a percentage of income?

The data in Table 8.1 show an income elasticity of .62 for alcoholic beverages. Consider two people with incomes of $20,000 and $40,000. If all alcohol is taxed at the same rate, by what percentage more will the tax paid by the $40,000 earner be greater than that paid by the $20,000 earner? Why might some people think this unfair?

5. Consider two ways of encouraging local governments to build or expand public parks. One proposal is for the federal government to provide grants for public parks. A second proposal is for the government to agree to pay 25 percent of any expenditures for building or expansion. If the same amount of money would be spent on each program, which do you predict would be most effective in encouraging local parks? Explain your answer, using the ideas of income and substitution effects.

6. The text showed the effect of an increase in the price of CDs on the budget constraint between CDs and candy bars. Show the effect of an increase in the price of candy bars on the same budget constraint.

APPENDIX: INDIFFERENCE CURVES AND THE CONSUMPTION DECISION

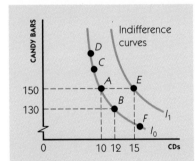

Figure 8.16 AN INDIFFERENCE CURVE

An indifference curve traces combinations of goods among which an individual is indifferent. This one reflects Fran's taste for CDs and for candy bars. She is just as well off (has an identical amount of utility) at all points on the indifference curve: A, B, C, D, or F.

The point on a budget constraint that an individual chooses depends on her preferences. To help us see which point will be chosen, economists use the concept of **indifference curves.** The indifference curve shows the various combinations of goods that make a person equally happy. For example, in Figure 8.16, the indifference curve I_0 gives all those combinations of candy bars and compact discs that Fran finds just as attractive as 150 candy bars and 10 CDs (point A on the curve). At B, for instance, she has 12 CDs but only 130 candy bars—not so much candy, but in her mind the extra CDs make up for the loss. The fact that B and A are on the same indifference curve means that Fran is indifferent. That is, if you asked her whether she preferred A to B or B to A, she would answer that she couldn't care less.

Indifference curves simply reflect preferences between pairs of goods. Unlike demand curves, they have nothing to do with budget constraints or prices. The different combinations of goods along the indifference curve cost different amounts of money. The indifference curves are drawn by asking an individual, which do you prefer, 10 candy bars and 2 CDs or 15 candy bars and 1 CD? or 11 candy bars and 2 CDs or 15 candy bars and 1 CD? or 12 candy bars and 2 CDs or 15 candy bars and 1 CD? When he answers, "I am indifferent between the two," the two points that represent those choices are on the same indifference curve.

Moving along the curve in one direction, Fran is willing to accept more CDs in exchange for fewer candy bars; moving in the other direction, she is willing to accept more candy bars in exchange for fewer CDs. Any point on the indifference curve, by definition, makes her just as happy as any other—whether it is point A or C or an extreme point like D, where she has many candy bars and very few CDs, or F, where she has relatively few candy bars but more CDs.

However, if Fran were to receive the same number of candy bars but more CDs than at A—say 150 candy bars and 15 CDs (point E)—she would be better off on the principle that "more is better." The new indifference curve I_1 illustrates all those combinations of candy bars and CDs that make her just as well off as the combination of 150 candy bars and 15 CDs.

The logic of indifference curves is such that we could find one for *any* point in an indifference curve diagram. Figure 8.17 shows a variety of indifference curves for Fran. Because more is better, Fran (or any individual) will prefer a choice on an indifference curve that is higher than another. On the higher indifference curve, she can have more of both items. Also by definition, indifference curves cannot cross, as Figure 8.18 makes clear. Assume that the indifference curves I_0 and I_1 cross at point A. That would mean that Fran is indifferent between A and all points on I_0, and between A and all points on I_1. In particular, she would be indifferent between A and B, between A and C, and accordingly between B and C. But B is clearly preferred to C; therefore, indifference curves cannot cross.

INDIFFERENCE CURVES AND MARGINAL RATES OF SUBSTITUTION

The slope of the indifference curve measures the number of compact discs that the individual is willing to give up to get another candy bar. The technical term for the slope of an indifference curve is the **marginal rate of substitution.** The marginal rate of substitution tells us how much of one good an individual is *willing* to give up in return for one more unit of another. This concept is quite distinct from the amount a consumer *must* give up, which is determined by the budget constraint and relative prices.

If Fran's marginal rate of substitution of candy bars for CDs is 15 to 1, this means that if she is given 1 more CD, she is willing to give up 15 candy bars. If she only had to give up 12 candy bars, she would be happier. If she had to give up 20, she would say, "That's too much—having one more CD isn't worth giving up twenty candy bars." Of course, Gary could have quite different attitudes toward CDs and candy bars. His marginal rate of substitution might be 25 to 1. He would be willing to give up 25 candy bars to get 1 more CD.

The marginal rate of substitution rises and falls according to how much of an item an individual already has. For example, consider point F in Figure 8.16, where Fran has a lot of CDs and few candy bars. In this case, Fran already has bought all her favorite CDs; the marginal CD she buys now will be something she likes, but not something she is wild over. In other words, because she already has a large number of CDs, having an additional one is less important. She would rather have some candy bars instead. Her marginal rate of substitution of candy bars for CDs at F is very low; for the sake of illustration, let's say that she would be willing to give up the marginal CD for only 10 candy bars. Her marginal rate of substitution is 10 to 1 (candy bars per CD).

The opposite situation prevails when Fran has lots of candy bars and few CDs. Since she is eating several candy bars almost every day, the chance to have more is just not worth much to her. But since she has few CDs, she does not yet own all of her favorites. The marginal value of another candy bar is relatively low, while the marginal value of another CD is relatively high. Accordingly, in this situation, Fran might insist on getting

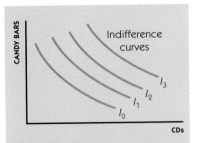

Figure 8.17 **MULTIPLE INDIFFERENCE CURVES**

By definition, an indifference curve describing Fran's tastes can be drawn through any point in the diagram. Four of the infinite number of possibilities are shown here. Because more is better, Fran will prefer indifference curves that are higher, like I_3, to those that are lower, like I_0.

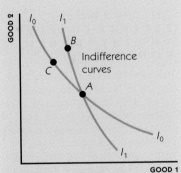

Figure 8.18 **WHY INDIFFERENCE CURVES CANNOT CROSS**

If two indifference curves crossed, a logical contradiction would occur. If curves crossed at point A, then Fran would be indifferent between A and B, between A and C, and therefore between B and C. But since B involves higher consumption of both goods than C, B is clearly preferred to C.

30 extra candy bars before she gives up 1 CD. Her marginal rate of substitution is 30 to 1 (candy bars per CD).

As we move along an indifference curve, we increase the amount of one good (like CDs) that an individual has. She thus requires less and less of the other good (candy bars) to compensate her for each one-unit decrease in the quantity of the first good (CDs). This principle is known as the **diminishing marginal rate of substitution.** As a result of the principle of diminishing marginal rate of substitution, the slope of the indifference curve becomes flatter as we move from left to right along the curve.

USING INDIFFERENCE CURVES TO ILLUSTRATE CHOICES

By definition, an individual does not care where he sits on any given indifference curve. But he would prefer to be on the highest indifference curve possible. What pins him down is his budget constraint. As Figure 8.19 illustrates, the highest indifference curve that a person can attain is the one that just touches the budget constraint—that is, the indifference curve that is *tangent* to the budget constraint. The point of tangency (labeled *E*) is the point the individual will choose. Consider any other point on the budget constraint, say *A*. The indifference curve through *A* is below the curve through *E*; the individual is better off at *E* than at *A*. On the other hand, consider an indifference curve above I_0, for instance I_1. Since every point on I_1 lies above the budget constraint, there is no point on I_1 that is feasible, that the individual can purchase with his given income.

When a curve is tangent to a line, the curve and line have the same slope at the point of tangency. Thus, the slope of the indifference curve equals the slope of the budget constraint at the point of tangency. The slope of the indifference curve is the marginal rate of substitution; the slope of the budget constraint is the relative price. This two-dimensional diagram is therefore a way of illustrating a basic principle of consumer choice: *individuals choose the point where the marginal rate of substitution equals the relative price.*

This principle makes sense. If the relative price of CDs and candy bars is 15 (CDs cost $15 and candy bars cost $1) and Fran's marginal rate of substitution is 20, that means that Fran is willing to give up 20 candy bars to get 1 more CD, but only *has* to give up 15; it clearly pays her to buy more CDs and fewer candy bars. If her marginal rate of substitution is 10, she is willing to give up 1 CD for just 10 candy bars; but if she gives up 1 CD, she can get 15 candy bars. She will be better off buying more candy bars and fewer CDs. Thus, if the marginal rate of substitution exceeds the relative price, Fran is better off if she buys more CDs; if it is less, she is better off if she buys fewer CDs. When the marginal rate of substitution *equals* the relative price, it does not pay for her to either increase or decrease her purchases.

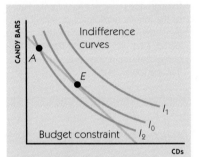

Figure 8.19 INDIF- FERENCE CURVES AND THE BUDGET CONSTRAINT

The highest feasible indifference curve that can be reached is the one just tangent to the budget constraint, or indifference curve I_0 here. This individual's budget constraint does not permit her to reach I_1, nor would she want to choose point A, which would put her on I_2, since along I_2 she is worse off.

INCOME ELASTICITY

Budget constraints and indifference curves show why, while goods normally have a positive income elasticity, some goods may have a negative income elasticity. As incomes increase, the budget constraint shifts out to the right in a parallel line, say from *BC* in

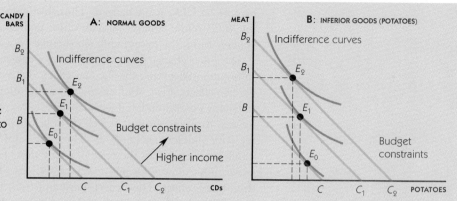

Figure 8.20 NORMAL AND INFERIOR GOODS WITH INDIFFERENCE CURVES

Panel A shows the case of two normal goods. An increase in income shifts the budget constraint out from BC to B_1C_1 to B_2C_2, and the consumption of both goods rises from E_0 to E_1 to E_2. Panel B shows the case of an inferior good. As the budget constraint shifts out, consumption of potatoes falls.

Figure 8.20 to B_1C_1 to B_2C_2. The choices—the points of tangency with the indifference curves—are represented by the points E_0, E_1, and E_2. In panel A, we see the normal case, where as the budget constraint shifts out, more of both candy bars and CDs are consumed. But panel B illustrates the case of inferior goods. Potatoes are on the horizontal axis, and meat is on the vertical. As incomes rise, the points of tangency E_1 and E_2 move to the left; potato consumption actually falls.

SUBSTITUTION AND INCOME EFFECTS

Indifference curves also permit a precise definition of the substitution and income effects. Figure 8.21 plots Jeremy's indifference curve between CDs and candy. Jeremy's original budget constraint is line BC and his indifference curve is I_0; the point of tangency, the

Figure 8.21 SUBSTITUTION AND INCOME EFFECTS WITH INDIFFERENCE CURVES

As the price of a good increases, the budget constraint rotates down. The change of Jeremy's choice from E_0 to E_1 can be broken down into an income and a substitution effect. The line B_1C_1 shows the substitution effect, the change that would occur if relative prices shifted but the level of utility remained the same. (Notice that Jeremy stays on the same indifference curve in this scenario.) The substitution effect alone causes a shift from E_0 to E_2. The movement between B_1C_1 and the new budget constraint B_2C shows the income effect, the change that results from changing the amount of income but leaving relative prices unchanged. The income effect alone causes a shift from E_2 to E_1.

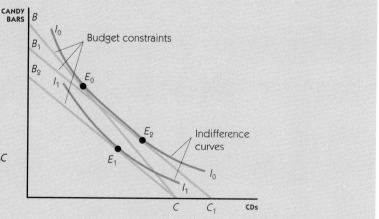

point he chooses, is point E_0. Suppose the price of candy increases. Now he can buy fewer candy bars, but the number of CDs he can buy, were he to spend all of his income on CDs, is unchanged. Thus, his budget constraint becomes flatter; it is now line B_2C. While Jeremy originally chose point E_0 on the indifference curve I_0, now he chooses E_1 on the *lower* indifference curve I_1.

The price change has moved Jeremy's choice from E_0 to E_1 for two reasons: the substitution effect and the income effect. To see how this has happened, let's isolate the two effects. First, we focus on the substitution effect by asking what would happen to Jeremy's consumption if we changed relative prices, but did not change how well off he was. To keep him just as well off as before the price change, we must keep him on the same indifference curve, I_0. Thus, the substitution effect is a movement along an indifference curve. As the price of candy rises, Jeremy, moving down the indifference curve, buys more CDs and fewer candy bars. The movement from E_0 to E_2 is the substitution effect. The budget constraint B_1C_1 represents the *new* prices, but it does not account for the income effect, by definition, since Jeremy is on the same indifference curve that he was on before.

To keep Jeremy on the same indifference curve when we increase the price of candy requires giving Jeremy more income. The line B_1C_1 is the budget constraint with the *new* prices that would leave Jeremy on the same indifference curve. Because prices are the same, the budget constraint B_1C_1 is parallel to B_2C. We now need to take away the income that left Jeremy on the same indifference curve. We keep prices the same (at the new levels), and we take away income until we arrive at the new budget constraint B_2C, and the corresponding new equilibrium E_1. The movement from E_2 to E_1 is called the income effect, since only income is changed. We have thus broken down the movement from the old equilibrium, E_0, to the new one, E_1, into the movement from E_0 to E_2, the substitution effect, and the movement from E_2 to E_1, the income effect.

9

THE SAVINGS
DECISION

C hapter 8 described how individuals choose how to spend their money, one of the three basic decisions of the household. This and the next chapter show how the tools and concepts developed there can also be used to analyze people's decisions about how much to save and how to invest their savings. Chapter 11 will take up the third household-level decision: work and the choice of a job.

Traditional folklore has emphasized the virtues of saving. As Benjamin Franklin put it, "A penny saved is a penny earned." Policymakers have also recognized the importance of savings for the long-run prosperity of the country. Yet in spite of the lip service paid to their importance, savings in the United States have declined significantly in recent years, and devising policies to reverse this trend has proved difficult. Household savings, to take one example, fell from 9.2 percent of disposable income (income available to households after taxes) in 1975 to only 2.9 percent in 1987; they then rose to 4.5 percent in 1990. In recent years, savings rates in the United States have been less than half the rate in Japan, Germany, France, Canada, and many other industrialized countries.

The level of national savings is a consequence of separate savings decisions made in each of the 95 million households in the United States. To understand the relatively low level of U.S. savings, it is necessary to examine the motivations that influence the level of individual savings. For example, people save for retirement and for emergencies such as an illness or an injury. They save for their children's education, for a down payment on major purchases like a house or car, or because they want to leave an inheritance. To some extent, they save because they will receive interest payments. These reasons for saving are discussed in more detail below.

"Papa doesn't want Tsi Tsu in the bedroom while he's hiding his little nest egg."

KEY QUESTIONS

1. How can the tools and insights of Chapter 8 be applied to the analysis of savings?

2. How do changes in the real interest rate affect savers and borrowers?

3. Normally, income and substitution effects are reinforcing, so that demand curves for goods are downward sloping; why are the effects of a change in the real interest rate ambiguous?

4. What might account for the decrease in savings in the United States, and what will be the effect of some of the current proposed policies aimed at stimulating savings?

BUDGET CONSTRAINTS AND SAVINGS

In Chapter 8, it was assumed that individuals spend their money in a rational manner, thinking through the alternatives clearly. The same assumption holds for the savings decision. Indeed, the two decisions are closely related: in making their savings decisions, individuals are essentially making a decision about *when* to spend, or consume. If they consume less today—if, that is, they save more today—they can consume more tomorrow.

We can use the budget constraint to analyze this choice. Instead of showing the choice between two goods, the budget constraint can show, as in Figure 9.1, the choice between spending in two time periods. For example, consider the case of Joan, who leads a simple life consisting of two time periods: in the first time period, she works; in the second, she is retired. Joan faces the lifetime budget constraint depicted in the figure. The first period is represented on the horizontal axis, the second on the vertical.

Figure 9.1 THE TWO-PERIOD BUDGET CONSTRAINT

The two-period budget constraint *BC* describes the possible combinations of current and future consumption available. Wages not spent in period 1 become savings, which earn interest. As a result, forgoing a dollar of consumption today increases future consumption by more than a dollar.

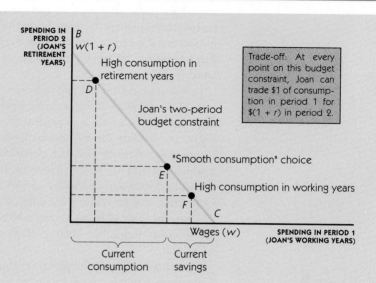

Her wages during her working life (the first period) are *w*. Thus, at one extreme, she could consume all of *w* the first period (point C) and have nothing for her retirement in the second period. At the other extreme, she could consume nothing in the first period, save all of her income, and consume her savings, with accumulated interest, in the second (point B). If we use *r* to denote the rate of interest, her consumption in the second period is $w(1 + r)$. In between these extremes lies a straight line that defines the rest of her choices. She can choose any combination of first- and second-period consumption on this line. This is Joan's two-period budget constraint.

By postponing consumption—that is, by saving—Joan can increase the total amount of goods that she can obtain because she is paid interest on her savings. The cost, however, is that she must wait to enjoy the goods. But what is the relative price, the amount of future consumption she has to trade off for one more unit of current consumption? Or to put it another way, how much extra future consumption can she get if she gives up one unit of current consumption?

If Joan decides not to consume one more dollar today, she can take that dollar, put it in the bank, and get back at the end of the year that dollar plus interest. If the interest rate is 10 percent, then for every dollar of consumption that Joan gives up today, she can get $1.10 of consumption next year. The relative price (of consumption today relative to consumption tomorrow) is thus 1 plus the interest rate. Because Joan must give up more than $1.00 of consumption in the second period to get an additional $1.00 worth of consumption today, current consumption can be thought of as being more expensive than future consumption. As was emphasized in Chapter 6, what Joan cares about in evaluating the trade-offs between consumption during her working years versus consumption in retirement is the *real* rate of interest, taking into account inflation.

In this example, where Joan's life is divided into a working period and a retirement period, what is relevant is the average length of time between the time that money is earned and saved, and the time that the savings are used in retirement. For an average person, this is perhaps 35 years. In making her calculations, Joan will take into account the fact that if she leaves her money in the bank, it will earn compound interest, meaning that interest will be paid on interest already earned, not just on the amount of principal saved.

In recent years, the real rate of interest has been around 4 percent a year. If interest were not compounded, then earning 4 percent a year for 35 years would simply provide an overall return of 35×4 percent $= 140$ percent. If Joan puts \$1.00 in the bank today, in 35 years she will get back—in real terms—\$2.40. However, if interest is compounded annually, for each dollar deposited the calculation is $(1 + .04)^{35}$, so the total interest paid will be 294.6 percent. If she puts \$1.00 in the bank today, in 35 years she will get back—in real terms—\$3.94 (that is, her original dollar *plus* the interest). Compound interest makes a big difference.

Thus, the slope of Joan's budget constraint is 3.94—for every dollar of consumption she gives up during her working years, she gets \$3.94 of additional consumption in retirement.

Joan chooses among the points on this budget constraint according to her personal preferences. Consider, for example, point *D*, where Joan is consuming very little during her working life. Since she is spending very little in the present, any additional consumption now will have a high marginal value. She will be relatively eager to substitute present consumption for future consumption. At the other extreme, if she is consuming a great deal in the present, say at point *F*, additional consumption today will have a relatively low marginal value, while future consumption will have a high marginal value. Hence, she will be relatively eager to save more for the future. She chooses a point in between, *E*, where consumption in the two periods is not too different. She has **smoothed** her consumption; that is, consumption in each of the two different periods is about the same.

SAVINGS AND THE INTEREST RATE

What happens to Joan's savings if the interest rate increases? Her new budget constraint is shown in Figure 9.2 as *B'C*. If she does no saving, the interest rate has no effect on her consumption. She simply consumes her income during her working years, with nothing left over for retirement. But for all other choices, she now gets more consumption during her retirement years. Thus, her budget constraint has rotated upward. As we saw in Chapter 8, the rotation of the budget constraint produces both income and substitution effects. There we studied these effects in connection with the choice between the goods, and found that normally they reinforce each other, working in the same direction.

With savings, the substitution and income effects work in different directions. The higher (after-tax) interest rates mean that Joan is better off, because she will receive more for her savings. Since she feels better off—the budget constraint has rotated out—there is an income effect: she wishes to consume more in *both* periods. Higher interest rates thus tend to increase consumption in period 1 (and period 2).

On the other hand, the increased return to savings changes the relative price between consumption in the future and in the present, making it more attractive to postpone

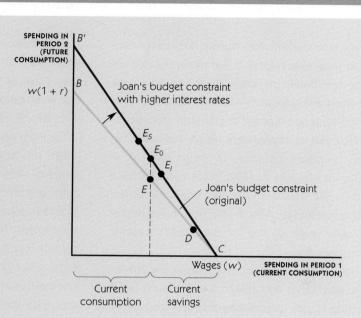

Figure 9.2 SAVINGS AND THE INTEREST RATE

An increase in interest rates rotates the budget constraint out from *BC* to *B'C*. The fact that the individual is better off means that there is an income effect, leading to greater consumption in the present (and the future). However, the higher interest rate makes future consumption cheaper; the substitution effect, associated with the changed slope, leads to greater savings now.

consumption. This shift in relative prices is the substitution effect. As prices change, individuals switch (substitute) their consumption and choose less of the relatively expensive good, in this case consumption in period 1. The higher interest rate makes current consumption relatively more expensive. That is, to obtain one more unit of current consumption, Joan has to give up more future consumption; similarly, by giving up one more unit of current consumption, she obtains relatively more future consumption.

In Figure 9.2, Joan chooses point E_0 on the new budget constraint: she consumes exactly as much in period 1 after the increase in real interest rates as before. The change in real interest rates thus has no effect on Joan's savings. Other people might have chosen a point like E_s, slightly to the left of E_0—their savings would have gone up, with the substitution effect dominating the income effect. Still others might have chosen a point like E_I, slightly to the right of E_0—their savings would have decreased, with the income effect dominating the substitution effect. Either is possible.

What happens on *average* is a difficult empirical question. Most estimates indicate that the substitution effect outweighs the income effect, so that an increase in real interest rates has a slightly positive effect on the rate of savings.

The question of the magnitude of the response of savings to interest rates is quite an important one, as we will see. Government policies aimed at increasing the interest rate individuals receive, perhaps by exempting certain forms of savings from taxation, are predicated on the belief that there is a significant positive effect of an increase in the interest rate on savings. Since wealthy people save more, reducing taxes on interest—which increases the rate of return to the saver—obviously benefits them more. If it were established that these tax benefits had only limited effects in stimulating savings, political support for them would probably diminish. In fact, it has proved very difficult to devise plans that substantially stimulate savings.

LIFE-CYCLE SAVINGS

Because of the importance of savings to the nation's economy, economists have worked hard to provide a systematic explanation of why people save. As the budget constraints above suggested, one of the most important motives for saving is retirement. This motivation is often called **life-cycle savings**. People put away money during their working years so that they can enjoy consumption during retirement, an aspect of savings emphasized by MIT's Nobel laureate Franco Modigliani. People generally prefer to smooth out their income over time, rather than to consume a lot in the years while they work and very little in their retirement years.

Figure 9.3 shows a simple version of the life-cycle savings model. The total wealth of an individual at any given time is simply the sum of the savings from past years. Thus, the figure shows the accumulated wealth and savings of a fellow named Paul, who gets his first job at age 25, works until he is 60, and expects to live to the age of 95. It assumes that Paul earns and saves the same amount each year from age 25 to age 59 and then retires, planning to live off the savings each year until age 95. At age 20, he has saved nothing. Savings reach a peak at age 60, when he starts to spend savings until they are gone at 95. The shape of the curve reflects compound interest; as Paul's wealth grows, his interest earnings grow, as these are added each year to new savings.

Naturally, the life cycle for most people is considerably more complex than is indicated by this simple diagram. Because of increased skills and experience, most people earn considerably more when they are 40 or 50 than when they are 20 or 30. Thus, many people save relatively little in their 20s and relatively more in their 40s and 50s.

However, the simplified example shown in the figure still gives a good feeling for the general pattern of savings behavior. The example also makes it easier to think about what interest rate is appropriate for this problem. Notice that Paul plans to work for 35 years and be retired for 35 years. As a result, it is possible to imagine that the savings from when he is 25, with accumulated interest, will be what he lives on when he reaches age 60. Savings from age 26, plus interest, will be spent at age 61, and so on. That is why when Paul thinks about the return on savings, he must consider a 35-year horizon. Money that he puts aside has a chance to earn interest for 35 years.

Of course, by the time Paul comes to retire, he will have put aside a considerable nest egg—his accumulated savings, with interest, will be substantial. If the real interest rate is 4 percent, and if he saves $4,000 a year, he will have, at retirement at the age of 59, a total of $310,400 (in real terms). If his annual income is $20,000, he will be able to smooth his consumption over his life. The $4,000 he saved at 25 will amount to $15,760 (3.94 × $4,000) when he is 60. Thus, what he consumes at 60 is only slightly less than the $16,000 he had to consume when he was 25.

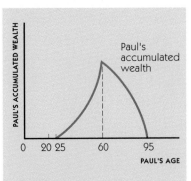

Figure 9.3 LIFE-CYCLE SAVINGS

Savings gradually build up during Paul's working life, and then are gradually drawn upon after retirement.

THE SAVINGS DECISION

The savings decision is essentially a decision of *when* to consume: today or tomorrow.

The slope of the budget constraint between consumption today and consumption tomorrow is determined by the rate of interest.

A principal motive of savings is to smooth consumption, so that consumption during working years and consumption during retirement years is about the same.

LOOKING BEYOND THE BASIC MODEL: OTHER MOTIVES FOR SAVINGS

Life-cycle motives are only one possible reason for saving. Some of the other important reasons take us beyond the basic model of rational, self-interested individuals and profit-maximizing firms interacting in perfectly functioning competitive markets. Four are discussed briefly below.

Some people save so that they can leave a bequest or inheritance to their children. This is called the **bequest motive.** A person with such a motive is, in some sense, not acting in a self-interested way. He is sacrificing some of what he could have consumed to enhance the consumption of his children and grandchildren. The less the parent consumes, the more is left for the child. (There is a sense, however, in which the parent can be thought of as acting in a self-interested manner: he gets pleasure from giving to his children, and it may be increasing this pleasure, not any sense of altruism, that motivates these gifts. It is also true that some people use the promise of bequests to get better treatment from children and grandchildren.)

There is some debate among economists about the actual importance of bequest savings. Beyond funding their children's college education, to which they often contribute significantly, most parents do not leave a substantial amount to their children. Nevertheless, a few wealthy individuals leave their children huge amounts of money. Wealth in the United States is concentrated; only one-fifth of U.S. households have more than $100,000 in net wealth. By contrast, at least one-third have a net wealth of less than $10,000. Rich individuals save a considerable amount, often more than they need for their own retirement. Lawrence Summers of Harvard and Laurence Kotlikoff of Boston University have argued that the bequest savings of the few relatively wealthy people are larger, in total, than the life-cycle savings of poorer people, who are much more numerous. If confirmed, these economists' findings would be important for government policymakers, who have thus far directed their efforts primarily at encouraging savings for retirement. If the bequest motive is more important than was previously thought, then to be effective, government policies attempting to stimulate savings may have to focus there as well; for instance, lower inheritance taxes may have substantial effects.

The possible unexpected need for funds, for expenses related to illness or an accident, provides another motive for savings. This "saving for a rainy day" is called **precautionary savings.** It arises out of another problem with the basic competitive model. There are no markets for some of the important things individuals would like; in particular, as we saw in Chapter 6, a person cannot buy insurance against many of the risks she faces. If she is to have funds in these times of emergency, she must save. Today there is less need for precautionary savings than there used to be. People are protected against many risks by insurance, both private (health, automobile, accident) and social (unemployment, Social Security, disability). And in emergencies, it is easier for individuals today to borrow.

A related motivation for savings is the uncertainty that many people face in their year-to-year income. This is particularly true for small businessmen and farmers, whose income may vary greatly from year to year. Again, individuals cannot buy insurance against the risks of varying income. For these people, savings are necessary not just for the retirement years (the life-cycle motive), but also to tide them over bad years during their working lives. They want to smooth out the year-to-year fluctuations in their income. Milton Friedman, a Nobel laureate currently at Stanford University, observed that such individuals do save more than those with more stable incomes. More generally, Friedman emphasized that consumption was related to people's **permanent income,** averaging out the good years with the bad. Thus, if people have an unusually good year, most of the "extra" income will be saved for use in unusually bad years.

Friedman's permanent-income theory and Modigliani's life-cycle theory are in fact very similar. They both argue that people use savings to smooth out consumption. Friedman emphasized the role savings play in smoothing between bad and good working years, Modigliani between working and retirement years.

A final motive for savings is referred to as **target savings.** Individuals save for specific goals, such as for the down payment for a house or to pay for their children's education. Part of this savings too is a result of competitive markets' not working the way envisaged by the basic model. Until the federal government came forward to guarantee student loans, banks seldom made such loans. Students could not borrow to finance their education; if they could not get a scholarship, they or their parents had to save up for it.

CAUSES OF LOW SAVINGS

A variety of changes, from increased Social Security benefits to improved private capital markets, have led to a lower level of savings in the United States in recent years. It is not clear how much of the reduced savings can be attributed to these factors and how much to a change in preferences—a stronger preference for consumption today rather than consumption tomorrow. But regardless of the cause, the U.S. government has become concerned about the low level of savings, and has considered incentives to stimulate savings. We can use our two-period diagram to help us see how various changes in the economy have affected savings, and how different policies might be able to stimulate them. These questions are of sufficient importance that we will return to them in the discussion of economic growth in Chapter 35.

CHANGES IN TASTES: LIVING FOR THE PRESENT

Some economists believe that the major explanation for the low level of savings is an increase in the number of people who advocate living for the present, letting the future take care of itself, sometimes referred to as the "Now" generation. In this view, people today, when faced with the same opportunity set as previous generations, would choose a higher level of current consumption and a lower level of savings. While inquiring into whether or why there have been fundamental changes in attitudes would take us

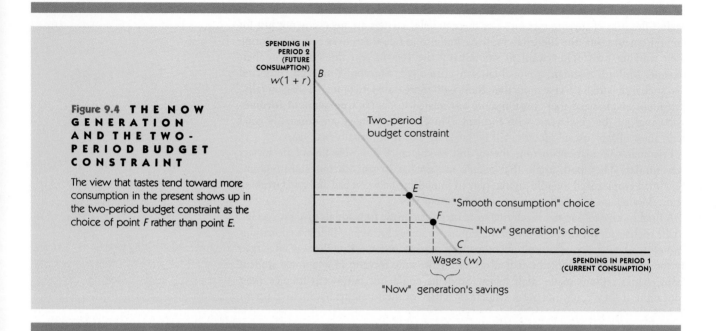

Figure 9.4 THE NOW GENERATION AND THE TWO-PERIOD BUDGET CONSTRAINT

The view that tastes tend toward more consumption in the present shows up in the two-period budget constraint as the choice of point *F* rather than point *E*.

beyond the bounds of economics, we can see what such changes do in terms of a two-period budget constraint. In Figure 9.4, which is similar to Figure 9.1, the contention is that the Now generation might choose point *F* on the budget line *BC*, rather than point *E*.

SOCIAL SECURITY

Some economists, such as Martin Feldstein, a chairman of the Council of Economic Advisers in the Reagan administration, allege that the recent growth in Social Security benefits has contributed strongly to the decrease in savings rates. To understand their argument, we need to know how the Social Security system is structured.

The common belief is that Social Security operates like a pension: people pay money into Social Security while they work and get it back, with interest, when they retire. In fact, Social Security is not this kind of bank-account-style pension. It is built on the premise that if there are sufficiently more workers than there are retired individuals, a relatively low tax on today's workers can go directly to pay substantial benefits to today's retirees. This is called a **pay-as-you-go** system, to distinguish it from standard pensions where accounts build up over time to be paid out after individuals retire.

Thus, the Social Security program is a tax program, not a savings account. It is financed by levying a tax, *T*, on today's workers, out of which the government has to turn around and pay benefits to today's retirees. To see the argument that pay-as-you-go may affect the savings rate, look at Figure 9.5, which shows Joan's budget constraint

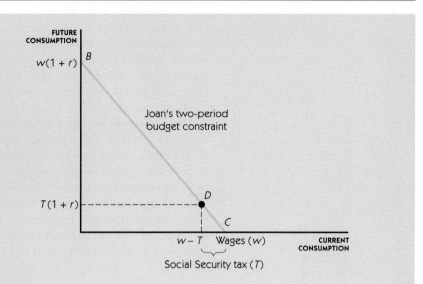

Figure 9.5 THE EFFECT OF SOCIAL SECURITY ON SAVINGS

A Social Security system that taxes workers an amount T and provides a retirement benefit of $T(1 + r)$, comparable to what Joan would have obtained had she saved and invested the money, leaves the budget constraint unchanged. Accordingly, individuals will choose the same consumption as before. Because Social Security is operated as a pay-as-you-go system rather than bank-account-style, savings are now reduced by the full magnitude of the tax.

BC from Figure 9.1. Assume that the population is growing at a rate of growth g, so that a tax of T per worker can finance a Social Security benefit of $T(1 + g)$ for each retiree. For simplicity, assume $g = r$: the rate of growth equals the rate of interest. Then the Social Security benefit is $T(1 + r)$; that is, individuals get back what they contributed with interest. (In fact, in recent years, they have gotten back far more than this.) Assume for the moment that Joan did no other saving. She would now consume $w - T$ (her wage minus her Social Security tax payments) the first period, and $T(1 + r)$ the second period. Her consumption in the two periods is represented by the point D. The first period's consumption is reduced by T as a result of the Social Security program; the second period's consumption is increased by $T(1 + r)$. But this is a point on the original budget constraint—it is precisely what Joan would have had, had she saved T dollars herself.

If Joan decides to save still more, of course, her consumption during her retirement will increase; and again, for each dollar of reduced current consumption, her retirement consumption increases by $1 + r$. If she would like to save less than T, she could theoretically borrow money in the present and pay it back in the future. It is apparent that this hypothetical Social Security program has left Joan's budget constraint completely unaffected. Since the budget constraint is unaffected, her consumption is unaffected; that is, she will choose to consume the same amount the first period (while she is working) and the same amount the second period (in retirement).

But the Social Security program nonetheless has some consequences. Individuals no longer need to save as much for retirement. The government is, in effect, doing the saving for them. Before this program went into effect, the amount of current Social Security tax payments, T, was part of the nation's savings. Now national savings go down by T. (Of course, this would not be the case with a savings-account type of social security. The Social Security program would still have effects: "public" savings through

Social Security would supplant private savings, but total savings would be unaffected.)

The importance of the effect of Social Security on savings has remained a subject of controversy. Martin Feldstein has claimed that as a result of Social Security, savings are a third lower than they otherwise would be, and that the growth in Social Security benefits in the 1970s played an important role in the declining savings rates in the United States. Indeed, Japan and Taiwan, two countries with very high savings rates, have more limited social security programs.

Other economists, such as Henry Aaron of the Brookings Institution, are not convinced that Social Security has had a substantial negative effect on savings. They cite the many European countries that have even more generous social security programs than the United States and yet have higher savings rates as well. They further suggest that Social Security has enabled individuals to retire earlier, and as they have retired earlier, their need for savings has increased. As always, interpreting the evidence is difficult. The period since 1935, when Social Security was established, has been marked by many other important changes. For instance, people can now borrow more easily, and more Americans are insured against a variety of risks. The low level of savings in the United States may be attributed to one of these other changes as well.

CAPITAL MARKETS

Blame for low savings rates has also been attributed to the improved functioning of capital markets in today's economy. To understand this argument, the two-period budget constraint can again be put to use. This diagram applies to borrowing as well as to saving because borrowing is simply the negative of saving. Instead of storing up money with the idea of spending it in the future, borrowers spend today with the idea of repaying it in the future.

Consider, for example, the case of a fortunate 30-year-old named Alan who today has $50,000 and knows that he will receive an inheritance worth $500,000 when he reaches the age of 40. His alternatives are shown in Figure 9.6. Instead of waiting 10 years to spend his inheritance, he might choose to borrow money now, knowing that in 10 years he will be able to repay his debts. Again, the budget constraint BC describes the trade-offs he faces. If he consumes more than $50,000 now, he will have to borrow. If he consumes less than $50,000, he will be saving. At point H, his consumption is $50,000; he is neither borrowing nor saving. Choices like D on the budget constraint that are up and to the left involve saving; choices like F that are down and to the right involve borrowing. The simple budget diagram assumes that the interest rate is the same whether Alan borrows or saves. If he gives up $1 of consumption today, he gets $1 + r$ more consumption tomorrow. This is true whether he is a borrower or a saver.

The situation just envisioned, in which the rate of interest paid as a borrower is the same as that received as a saver (or lender), is not the typical case. Individuals usually must pay a higher interest rate when they borrow than the interest rate they receive from saving. The difference, often 3 or 4 percent more, is due to the administrative costs and profits for the lending institution and to the chance of default by the borrower.

Figure 9.7A illustrates the choices available to Alan when he faces these different interest rates. In this case, the budget constraint is not a straight line but has a kink, at point H, where again Alan is neither a borrower nor a lender. By giving up further current consumption (moving leftward from H), Alan obtains $1 + r_s$ next period for

Figure 9.6 **BORROWING (NEGATIVE SAVINGS)**

At point *H*, Alan is neither borrowing nor saving. At points below *H* on the budget constraint, he is borrowing, knowing that he will repay the loan with the money to be received in 10 years. At points above *H*, he is saving his current income to increase the amount he can consume in

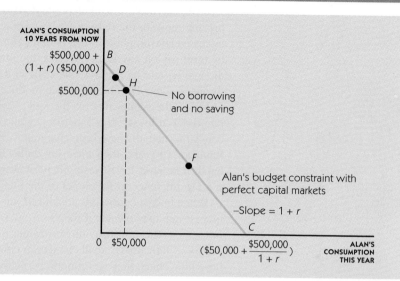

Figure 9.7 **EFFECTS OF LOWER INTEREST RATES FOR BORROWERS**

In panel A, the interest rate at which a person can borrow and the rate at which he can save are different. As a result, the budget line has a kink. Panel B shows what happens if the interest rate at which people can borrow is reduced. The kink there is less severe because the rate at which people can borrow is closer to the rate they receive on savings. For borrowers, both the income and substitution effects of lowered interest rates lead to more current consumption.

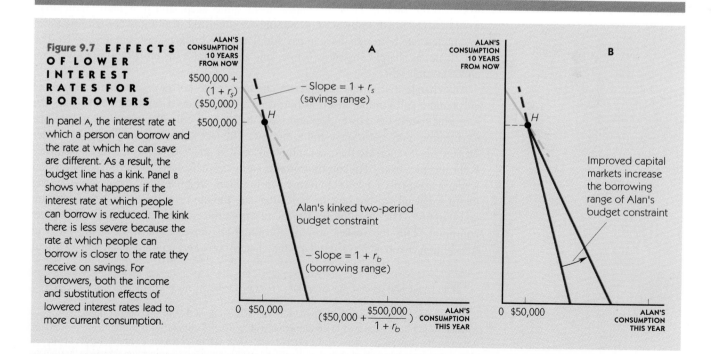

each dollar given up this period. The interest rate that applies here, r_s, is the rate he receives, say, from a bank deposit. If Alan wants to consume more than he currently has and move to the right of H, he must give up $1 + r_b$ next period for each dollar of increased consumption in this period. The interest rate that applies here, r_b, is the rate he must pay on any loans. Because the interest rate he must pay is much greater than the interest rate he receives, the slope of the budget constraint below H is greater than the slope above H. The difference produces the kink at H.

To see the significance of the kink, assume, for instance, that the annual interest rate received by savers is 7 percent, while borrowers must pay 12 percent (credit card companies actually have been charging 15 to 20 percent in recent years). If Alan borrows funds for 10 years, then for every dollar borrowed, he has to pay $3.[1] On the other hand, if he saves for 10 years, then for every dollar saved, he gets back only $2.[2] There is a big difference in the slopes of the budget constraint both left and right of H.

When budget constraints are kinked, many people will neither borrow nor save. The interest rate they receive if they save, r_s, is too low to convince them to save; and the interest rate they must pay on borrowing, r_b, is so high that they do not want to borrow. For these individuals, small changes in either the saving or borrowing interest rates may have little effect; they continue to be neither savers nor borrowers.

MAKING IT LESS EXPENSIVE TO BORROW

The effect of any innovation that lowers administrative costs, and thus reduces the difference between the rate at which people can borrow and the rate at which they can lend, can easily be seen by the slight modification of panel A shown in panel B. Assume initially that the interest rate charged to borrowers is extremely high. The budget constraint to the right of H would appear to be quite steep, and thus many individuals would choose to consume at H. Now suppose improved institutions for lending lower the interest rate borrowers have to pay and flatten the budget constraint beyond H. The kink is not as sharply angled as before, and interest rates for borrowers and savers are closer to each other.

Any change that lowers the interest rate charged to borrowers has both an income effect and a substitution effect on borrowers. The improved capital market makes the individual better off. His budget constraint has moved out—this means he would like to consume more both today and tomorrow. The fact that when individuals are better off they like to increase their consumption of most goods is, as we learned in Chapter 8, the income effect.[3] The substitution effect arises from the fact that current consumption is now less expensive relative to future consumption, which is just another way of saying that it is cheaper to borrow; the individual substitutes current consumption for future consumption. The substitution effect results from the change in the *slope* of the budget constraint. This too makes current consumption more desirable. The income and substitution effects of lowered interest rates facing borrowers reinforce each other; current

---

[1] With compound interest, for every dollar borrowed today he must repay $(1.12)^{10}$ in 10 years.

[2] For every dollar saved, he receives $(1.07)^{10}$ in 10 years.

[3] The appendix to Chapter 8 explained how the *magnitude* of the income effect is found by looking at what would have happened to consumption with a parallel outward shift in the budget constraint, i.e, with *no* changes in prices (real interest rates). Here we are concerned only with identifying the *presence* of an income effect. There is a positive income effect on consumption whenever the budget constraint rotates outward.

CLOSE-UP: SOCIAL SECURITY AND SAVINGS

Social Security payments to the elderly have expanded dramatically, rising from $30 billion in 1970 to about $250 billion at the start of the 1990s. At the same time, personal savings declined from slightly over 8 percent of disposable personal income in 1970 to about 4.5 percent at the start of the 1990s. Is there a connection?

Martin Feldstein, a professor at Harvard University and chairman of the Council of Economic Advisers under Ronald Reagan from 1982 to 1984, has argued that as Social Security payments rise, people feel less need to save for their retirement. He estimated late in the 1970s that every dollar people expect to receive in Social Security leads them to save at least 50 cents less. With $250 billion being paid out in Social Security, the potential effect on private savings is at least $125 billion.

The nature of the Social Security program, however, is changing in two ways that should raise future savings. Traditionally, Social Security taxes were not saved in any government account, but instead were paid out immediately to the elderly. But in the early 1980s, a process began of building up a surplus in the Social Security fund. By law, these surpluses are loaned to the rest of the federal government, thus reducing the need of the government to borrow from the public to cover its budget deficits, and increasing overall national savings.

In addition, the level of benefits each retiree receives from Social Security, relative to tax contributions that she pays in as a worker, is declining. In 1991, the present value of the Social Security benefits an average male earner who was just retiring expected to receive was 1.6 times the present value of the taxes he had paid to the system. But today's earners are paying in more money to help build the Social Security surpluses, and will be receiving back amounts much closer to the value of their contributions. With less of a Social Security bonus waiting, workers today have an incentive to increase savings now.

Source: Martin S. Feldstein, "The Effect of Social Security on Saving," in D. Currie, R. Nobay, and D. Peel, eds., *Macroeconomic Analysis: Essays in Macroeconomics and Econometrics* (London: Croom Helm, 1981), pp. 1–23; Committee on Ways and Means, *Overview of Entitlement Programs: 1991 Green Book,* May 7, 1991, pp. 1128–29.

consumption is increased, and savings are reduced. Changes that make it easier for people to borrow will always tend to reduce savings.

In recent decades, it has become easier and easier for Americans to borrow, and the average middle-class American can borrow much more easily than the average person in Europe or Japan. In the United States, individuals can obtain mortgages to finance the purchase of a house that cover 80 or 90 percent of the cost of the house, meaning that the buyers only need to put up 10 or 20 percent of their own money as a down payment. (Some government-backed mortgages even allow people to borrow 95 percent of the cost of a house.) By contrast, in some European countries, mortgages in excess of 50 percent of the cost of the house are rare. Thus, home buyers in these countries must save much more before they can borrow the rest and buy their houses.

Other developments in the United States have also encouraged consumers to borrow. The development of "home equity loans" in the 1980s allowed individuals who already owned houses to borrow up to 80 percent of the value of a house. Credit cards like Visa and MasterCard became much more popular in the 1980s, enabling U.S. consumers to obtain credit more easily than before, and more easily than consumers in other countries. Federally guaranteed loans to finance education mean that one main reason for people to save—to finance college education for their children—may have become less significant. In short, these kinds of improvements in the capital market make it easier for people to borrow and allow them to make choices that they would otherwise have been unable to make. However, by encouraging borrowing, these steps also reduce savings.

SOME EXPLANATIONS OF LOW SAVINGS RATE

Changed preferences: There are more people who believe in living for the present; sometimes referred to as the "Now" generation, they choose a higher level of current consumption and a lower level of savings.

High Social Security benefits: The recent growth in Social Security benefits people receive when they retire has discouraged them from saving.

Improved capital markets: The market for borrowers is more perfect—the rate of interest paid by a borrower is closer to the rate paid to a saver—so, since it is cheaper to borrow, current consumption is increased and savings are reduced.

STIMULATING SAVINGS

Even if it were known that changed preferences, Social Security, and improved capital markets have contributed to the reduction in the savings rate, the government would be hard-pressed to reverse these changes. Appeals to national patriotism were successful in inducing people to buy government bonds during World War II, but outside the crisis of war, there is little hope of turning the Now generation into frugal savers—at least just as a result of an appeal from the government. Cutting back substantially on Social Security would be politically unpopular. As for capital markets, there is a general consensus that improving them is all for the good. For these reasons, the government has focused on tax incentives as a device for stimulating savings, and has enacted or proposed a number of programs to reduce the tax burden on some forms of savings. The following sections discuss some of these programs.

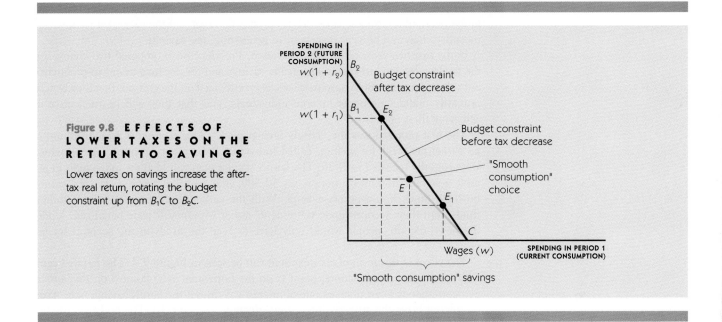

Figure 9.8 EFFECTS OF LOWER TAXES ON THE RETURN TO SAVINGS

Lower taxes on savings increase the after-tax real return, rotating the budget constraint up from B_1C to B_2C.

INTEREST RATE INCENTIVES

The two-period diagram of consumption and savings can also be used to analyze the effect of changes in the real, after-tax interest rate paid on savings, as in Figure 9.8. The slope of both budget constraints is 1 plus the *after-tax* interest rate. It represents the extra consumption an individual can get next period by giving up a unit of consumption today. Higher after-tax interest rates represent a change in the relative prices of present and future consumption. This change in relative prices makes the budget constraint steeper. The line B_1C is the original budget constraint, and B_2C represents the budget constraint after the return to savings has been given special tax treatment. The reduction in the tax on the return to savings has precisely the same effect as an increase from r_1 to r_2 in the real rate of interest received by savers. What savers care about is the after-tax return.

What effect will the increase in after-tax interest rates have? The original point chosen is depicted as point E on the original budget constraint. Will the choice on the new budget constraint increase current consumption (E_1) or current savings (E_2)?

That is the question addressed earlier in the chapter: what is the effect of an increase in the real rate of interest? There we saw that the substitution and income effects work in opposite directions, and that the net effect on savings is probably positive, but small.

THE FAMILY SAVINGS PLAN

How best to stimulate savings through tax policy has been a hotly contested issue in recent years. There are two central issues. One is the concern that since a disproportionate amount of saving is done by the rich—the cumulative savings of the poorest 40 percent of the population is negligible—giving tax breaks for savings amounts to giving tax breaks to the rich and the middle class. The second is that many of the suggested forms of tax incentives may not be very successful in generating new savings.

In the first two years of his administration, President Bush proposed two changes in the tax law designed to encourage greater savings and greater investment in productive but risky enterprises. Both proposals have been criticized on the grounds that they benefit primarily middle- or upper-income individuals, and that they will be ineffective in achieving their objectives.

The first proposal was the "family savings plan." This represents a modification of an earlier tax break for savings, called Individual Retirement Accounts (IRAs), which were partially repealed in 1986. The family savings plan would allow individuals to put aside a certain amount of money, say $2,500, into a special account. Interest earned on these funds would be tax-exempt. With the earlier IRAs, people could withdraw funds from their account upon retirement; earlier withdrawals were penalized. Under the new program, people would only have to keep the funds in the account for ten years.

The effect of this form of tax treatment can be seen in Figure 9.9. The family begins with its after-tax wage income, point C on the horizontal axis. Point B on the vertical axis corresponds to an untaxed rate of interest r. Without the family savings plan, taxes on interest bring the after-tax interest rate down to r_1 (point B_1). The budget constraint with total tax exemption of interest income is thus BC, while that with a standard tax on interest is B_1C. The family savings plan combines these two budget constraints. For savings of up to $2,500, there is no tax on the return to savings, and the corresponding budget constraint thus matches tax-exempt budget constraint BC. For savings beyond $2,500, the trade-off is the same as when interest is taxed, but the family has some

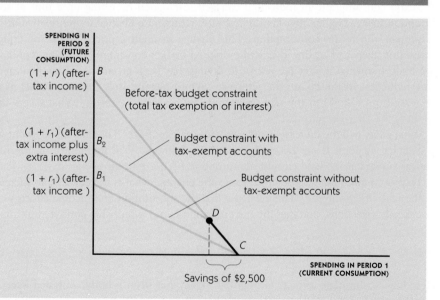

Figure 9.9 THE EFFECT OF THE FAMILY SAVINGS PLAN ON SAVINGS

The line BC shows the budget constraint before taxes and before the implementation of the savings plan. The line B_1C shows the after-tax budget constraint, without the savings plan. Finally, the kinked line B_2DC shows the budget constraint with the savings plan.

SPENDING IN PERIOD 2 (FUTURE CONSUMPTION)

$(1 + r)$ (after-tax income) B

$(1 + r_1)$ (after-tax income plus extra interest) B_2

$(1 + r_1)$ (after-tax income) B_1

Before-tax budget constraint (total tax exemption of interest)

Budget constraint with tax-exempt accounts

Budget constraint without tax-exempt accounts

D

C

Savings of $2,500

SPENDING IN PERIOD 1 (CURRENT CONSUMPTION)

more money in the bank thanks to what it saved tax-free. Thus, to the left of point D, the family's budget constraint is parallel to B_1C but higher, as shown by the line B_2D. The budget constraint with the family savings plan is the kinked line B_2DC.

The effect of the family savings plan depends on how much saving the family has been doing. High savers are better off, since they do not have to pay tax on the interest on their first $2,500 of savings. There is an income effect, but no substitution effect, since in the relevant portion of the budget constraint, the trade-off (the slope of the budget constraint) is unchanged. Hence, in *theory*, for high savers, the tax-exempt account should increase consumption during working years, actually reducing savings.

For low savers, there is an income effect and a substitution effect. The income effect leads individuals to save less, since they feel better off and want to consume more in both periods; the substitution effect causes them to save more, since by giving up one unit of current consumption, they can get relatively more future consumption. The net effect is ambiguous. Therefore, in theory, with a tax-exempt account, high savers save less, while low savers may save either more or less. But since what the high savers do is so much more important for what happens to total national savings, there is some presumption that net savings for the country will be lowered. There is a further reason for concern that tax-exempt accounts may not stimulate savings, at least in the initial years after they are introduced. Individuals with previously accumulated savings may simply transfer funds from ordinary savings accounts (or holdings of bonds and stocks) into tax-exempt accounts. They do not have to do any new saving to get the tax breaks.

In spite of these concerns, there is some evidence that, at least in the past, tax-exempt accounts, particularly IRAs, have actually stimulated savings, though to a limited extent. One explanation suggests that the competition among banks to attract the accounts has led to extensive advertising, that the advertising and publicity surrounding IRA accounts has helped focus attention on retirement, and that this has stimulated savings.

DECREASING THE CAPITAL GAINS TAX

President Bush's second proposal was to lower the tax rates on **capital gains,** the increase in the value of an asset between the time it is purchased and the time it is sold. Until 1986, capital gains received very favorable tax treatment. Not only was the tax due only when the asset was sold, the tax rate on long-term capital gains was 40 percent that on ordinary income. And if an individual managed to die before he sold the asset, no income tax was ever paid on the capital gain accumulated over his life. Beginning in 1986, capital gains were taxed at the same rate as ordinary income. Some special treatment of capital gains was justified on the grounds that much of the capital gain was due to inflation; the gains were not *real*. Economists argued that the appropriate way of handling this problem was to tax only the real capital gain. Another argument for special treatment of capital gains was that risky investments—such as those in the new high-tech companies—normally yield a large fraction of their returns in the form of capital gains, and so giving tax preference to capital gains encourages these investments.

But critics of special treatment of capital gains claim that the benefits are even more concentrated among the wealthy than would be the benefits of a family savings plan. Moreover, the proposed reduction in capital gains is a very crude way of encouraging risky high-tech investments; other forms of investment, like real estate speculation, which also typically receive most of their returns in capital gains, benefit just as much.

REVIEW AND PRACTICE

SUMMARY

1. In making a decision to save, people face a trade-off between current and future consumption. The amount of extra consumption an individual can obtain in the future by reducing present consumption is determined by the real rate of interest.

2. Life-cycle savings are what individuals save now so that they will be able to consume more after retirement. People also save to leave a bequest to children; as a precaution against unexpected illnesses or accidents; to smooth out year-to-year fluctuations in their income; and to meet a particular target, like a down payment on a house or college tuition.

3. An increase in the real rate of interest makes individuals better off and rotates the budget constraint. The resulting income effect leads to an increase in current consumption (*and* future consumption) and a decrease in savings. An increase in the real rate of interest also makes it more attractive to save; this is the substitution effect, and it leads to a decrease in current consumption. The net effect is thus ambiguous, though in practice it appears that an increase in the real interest rate has a slightly positive effect on savings.

4. Normally the interest rate for borrowing exceeds the interest rate for saving. As a result, budget constraints are kinked and many people will choose neither to save nor to borrow, regardless of small changes in interest rates. The cost of borrowing (at least for some purposes) is reduced. Because borrowing is now cheaper, the substitution effect tends to increase borrowing. Borrowers are better off. There is thus an income effect, which also leads to more current consumption and more borrowing (less savings).

KEY TERMS

smoothing consumption	precautionary savings	target savings motive
life-cycle savings	motive	capital gains
motive	permanent-income	
bequest savings motive	savings motive	

REVIEW QUESTIONS

1. How can a choice of consumption in the present determine the amount of consumption in the future?

2. How is the price of future consumption, in terms of present consumption, determined?

3. Name some of the motivations for saving.

4. For savers, how will the income effect of a higher interest rate affect current savings? How will the substitution effect of a higher interest rate affect current savings? What

will be the income and substitution effects of a lower interest rate on current savings? Explain your answers.

5. How will the income effect of lowered interest rates for borrowers affect current consumption? How will the substitution effect influence current consumption?

6. How does a government system of old-age pensions, run on a pay-as-you-go basis, affect the level of savings?

PROBLEMS

1. In the context of the life-cycle model of savings, explain whether you would expect each of the following situations to increase or decrease household savings.
    (a) More people retire before age 65.
    (b) There is an increase in life expectancy.
    (c) The government passes a law requiring private businesses to provide more lucrative pensions.

2. Explain how each of the following changes might affect people's motivation for saving.
    (a) Inheritance taxes are increased.
    (b) A government program allows college students to obtain student loans more easily.
    (c) The government promises to assist anyone injured by natural disasters like hurricanes, tornadoes, and earthquakes.
    (d) More couples decide against having children.
    (e) The economy does far worse than anyone was expecting in a given year.

3. Economists are fairly certain that a rise in the price of most goods will cause people to consume less of those goods, but they are not sure whether a rise in interest rates will cause people to save more. Use the ideas of substitution and income effects to explain why economists are confident of the conclusion in the first case, but not in the second.

APPENDIX: INDIFFERENCE CURVES AND THE SAVINGS DECISION

The appendix to Chapter 8 explained how to use indifference curves to analyze how households decide what amounts to spend on different goods. The same analysis can be applied to the savings decision.

The decision of how much to save is viewed as a decision about how much of lifetime income to consume now and how much to consume in the future. This trade-off is summarized in the two-period budget constraint introduced in the chapter, with present consumption measured along the horizontal axis and future consumption along the vertical axis. The slope of the budget constraint is $1 + r$, where r is the rate of interest, the extra consumption we get in the future from forgoing a unit of consumption today.

Figure 9.10 shows three indifference curves. The indifference curve through point

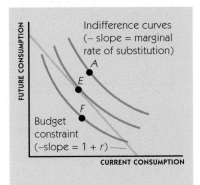

Figure 9.10 INDIF-FERENCE CURVES AND SAVINGS BEHAVIOR

An individual will choose the combination of present and future consumption at E. Point A would be more desirable, but it is not feasible. Point F is feasible, but it lies on a lower indifference curve and is therefore less desirable.

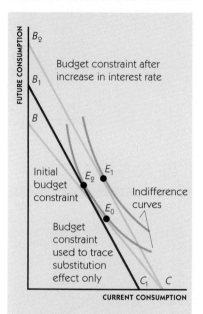

Figure 9.11 INCOME AND SUBSTITUTION EFFECTS OF A HIGHER INTEREST RATE

An increase in the interest rate rotates the budget constraint, moving it from BC to B_2C. The substitution effect describes what happens when relative prices are changed but Maggie remains on the same indifference curve; there is a shift in the budget line from BC to B_1C_1, and an increase in savings from E_0 to E_2. The income effect is the result of an outward shift of the budget line, keeping relative prices the same; the income effect is described by the shift from B_1C_1 to B_2C, and the increase in present consumption from E_2 to E_1.

A gives all the combinations of consumption today and consumption in the future among which the individual is indifferent (she would be just as well off, no better and no worse, at any point along the curve as at A). Since people generally prefer more consumption to less consumption, they would rather be on a higher than a lower indifference curve. The highest indifference curve a person can attain is one that just touches—that is, is tangent to—the budget constraint. The point of tangency we denote by E. The individual would clearly prefer the indifference curve through A, but no point on that curve is attainable; the indifference curve is everywhere above the budget constraint. She could consume at F, but the indifference curve through F lies below that through E.

As we learned in the appendix to Chapter 8, the slope of the indifference curve at a certain point is equal to the marginal rate of substitution at that point. In this case, it tells us how much future consumption a person requires to compensate him for a decrease in current consumption by 1 unit, to leave him just as well off. At the point of tangency, the slope of the indifference curve is equal to the slope of the budget constraint. The marginal rate of substitution at that point, E, equals $1 + r$. If the individual forgoes a unit of consumption, he gets $1 + r$ more units of consumption in the future, and this is exactly the amount he requires to compensate him for giving up current consumption. On the other hand, if the marginal rate of substitution is less than $1 + r$, it pays the individual to save more. To see why, assume $1 + r = 1.5$, while the person's marginal rate of substitution is 1.2. By reducing his consumption by a unit, he gets 1.5 more units in the future, but he would have been content getting only 1.2 units. He is better off saving more.

EFFECT OF CHANGES IN THE INTEREST RATE

With indifference curves and budget constraints, we can see the effect of an increase in the interest rate. Figure 9.11 shows the case of an individual, Maggie, who works while she is young and saves for her retirement. The vertical axis gives consumption during retirement years, the horizontal axis consumption during working years. An increase in the rate of interest rotates the budget constraint, moving it from BC to B_2C. It is useful to break the change down into two steps. In the first, we ask what would have happened if the interest rate had changed but Maggie remained on the same indifference curve. This is represented by the movement of the budget constraint from BC to B_1C_1. As a result of the increased interest rate, Maggie consumes less today—she saves more. This is the substitution effect, and it is seen in the movement from E_0 to E_2 in the figure.

Since Maggie is a saver, the increased interest rate makes her better off. To leave Maggie on the same indifference curve after the increase in the interest rate, we need to reduce her income. Her true budget constraint, after the interest rate increase, is B_2C, parallel to B_1C_1. The two budget constraints have the same slope because the after-tax interest rates are the same. The movement from B_1C_1 to B_2C is the second step. It induces Maggie to increase her consumption from E_2 to E_1. At higher incomes and the same relative prices (interest rates), people consume more every period, which implies that they save less. The movement from E_2 to E_1 is the income effect.

Thus, the substitution effect leads her to save more, the income effect to save less, and the net effect is ambiguous. In this case, there is a slight increase in savings.

Figure 9.12 SHIFTING INCOME FROM FUTURE TO PRESENT

In this case, all income will be received in the future, unless borrowing takes place. A higher interest rate for borrowing shifts the budget line in from BC to BC_2. The substitution effect is the decrease in current consumption along an indifference curve from E_0 to E_2, while the income effect is the decrease in current consumption between the two indifference curves, from E_2 to E_1.

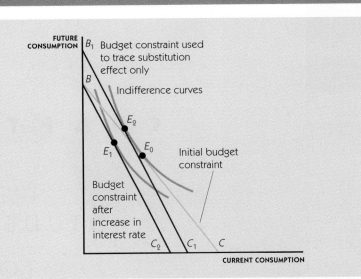

But consider now rich Nelly, prospective heir to the fortune her grandfather made when he invented chocolate-covered pretzels. She has never worked, and never intends to work. Her problem is that she will not get her small fortune until she is fifty. Her bankers, however, are willing to lend her money now. Figure 9.12 shows her budget constraint, with consumption before coming into her fortune along the horizontal axis, and consumption after coming into her fortune along the vertical. Assume that the interest rate increases. Again, the budget constraint rotates, from BC to BC_2, but note that it now rotates around the vertical axis. If Nelly chooses to consume nothing now, and accordingly borrow nothing, she will be unaffected by interest rate changes. But if she decides to consume before she gets her fortune, she must borrow; and if she has to pay a higher interest rate, she will clearly be worse off. Originally, she chose point E_0; now she chooses point E_1. We can again break the movement down into two steps: a substitution effect—the movement from E_0 to E_2 (what would have happened if the real interest had changed, but Nelly was given enough additional income to remain on the same indifference curve, so she faces the budget constraint B_1C_1); and an income effect—the movement from E_2 to E_1 (what happens as income is taken away, at unchanged real interest rates). At the higher interest rate, she consumes less, both because of the income effect (she is worse off) and because of the substitution effect (it costs more in terms of forgone future consumption to consume now).

CHAPTER 10

A STUDENT'S GUIDE TO INVESTING

E very decision to save is accompanied by a decision about what to do with the savings. They might go under a mattress, but usually savings are invested—in bank accounts, the stock or bond market, the real estate market, and other financial opportunities. Individually and collectively, these opportunities can be thought of as enticements to defer consumption—to save.

Broadly speaking, an **investment** is the purchase of an asset in the expectation of receiving a return. From the point of view of the economy as a whole, it is worth distinguishing between real investment and financial investment. The former includes the purchase of new factories and new machines, while the latter includes bank accounts, stocks, bonds, and so on. The two markets are linked: the financial investments people make provide firms with the funds they need to undertake real investments.

This chapter is about financial investment. It first takes up the major alternatives available to savers and discusses the characteristics of these alternatives that are important to investors. From these characteristics, a simple theory is established of how asset prices are determined. The chapter closes with some strategies for intelligent investing.

"Oh, Joe, not your portfolio again!"

KEY QUESTIONS

1. What are the principal alternatives available in which to invest savings?

2. What are the important characteristics of each?

3. Why are the prices of some assets sufficiently low that these assets yield a higher return than others?

4. What is meant by an efficient market? Is it possible to "beat the market"?

5. What are some of the basic ingredients in an intelligent investment strategy?

INVESTMENT ALTERNATIVES

Every saver faces a myriad of possibilities when it comes to investing her savings. The choices she makes depend on the amount of money she has to invest, what originally motivated her to save, her willingness to bear risk, and where she is in life.

BANK DEPOSITS

As a student, your major savings are likely to be earnings from a summer job that will be spent during the next school year. If so, the decision of where to invest is generally uncomplicated. A **bank savings account** (or a similar account) offers three advantages: it pays you interest, it allows easy access to your money, and it offers security, because the federal government, through the Federal Deposit Insurance Corporation, insures bank deposits of up to $100,000 even if the bank itself goes broke.

After leaving school, investment decisions become more difficult. You may want to put away some savings to make a down payment on a house (with the average house price today approximately $120,000, a 20 percent down payment would be $24,000). As savings increase, a few extra percentage points of interest become worth more. A **certificate of deposit (CD),** in which you deposit money in a bank for a preset length of time, is just as safe as an ordinary bank account and yields a slightly higher return. The drawback of a CD is that if you withdraw the money before the preset time has expired, you must pay a penalty. The ease with which an investment can be turned into cash is called its **liquidity.** Perfectly liquid investments can be converted into cash speedily and without any loss in value. CDs are less liquid than standard savings accounts.

Money Market Mutual Funds

Instead of putting your funds in a banking account or a certificate of deposit, you may decide to put them into a **money market mutual fund.** These funds became popular in the 1970s when many banks were limited by law in how much interest they could pay. A **mutual fund** gathers funds from a large number of investors, creating a single large pool of funds. With these funds, it can then purchase a large number of assets. A *money market* mutual fund invests its funds in CDs and comparably safe assets.

The advantage of a money market mutual fund is that you get higher rates of interest than bank accounts and still enjoy liquidity. The managers of the fund know that on average, most individuals will leave their money in the account, and some will be adding money to the account as others pull money out. They are thus able to put a large proportion of the fund in certificates of deposit and still not have to pay the penalties for early withdrawal. In this way, money market mutual funds give investors easy access to their funds, while providing them the higher returns associated with CDs.

Money market mutual funds may also invest their customers' money in short-term government bonds, usually called **Treasury bills,** or **T-bills.** Treasury bills are available only in large denominations ($10,000 or more). They promise to repay a certain amount (say, $10,000) in a relatively short period, less than 90 or 180 days, and investors buy them at less than their face value. The difference between the amount paid and the face value becomes the return to the purchaser.

With most money market mutual funds, you can even write a limited number of checks a month. Their major disadvantage is that they are not guaranteed by the federal government, as bank accounts are. However, some money market funds invest only in government securities or government-insured securities and so are virtually as safe as bank accounts.

Housing

About two-thirds of American households invest by owning their own homes. This investment is far riskier than putting money into a bank or a certificate of deposit. While home prices usually increase over time, there are exceptions. In 1986, the price of housing in Houston declined by 11 percent, and in 1990, the price of housing in the Northeast and in the West declined by 6.8 percent and 3.5 percent, respectively. In addition, when prices do rise, the rate of increase is uncertain. Prices may be almost level for a number of years, and then shoot up by 20 percent in a single year. Note that while the bank may provide most of the funds for the purchase of a house, the owner bears the risk, since she is responsible for paying back the loan regardless of the market price of the house.

There is one sense in which the return to investing in housing is relatively safe. An individual who rents a home faces uncertainty about what the rent will be. But when he purchases a house, there is a considerable reduction in the uncertainty over housing costs, though uncertainty about maintenance costs and taxes remains.

Housing has one other attractive attribute—and one unattractive attribute. On the positive side, real estate taxes, property taxes, and the interest on the mortgage are tax deductible, and the capital gains usually escape taxation altogether. On the other hand, housing is usually fairly illiquid. Houses differ one from another, and it often takes a considerable length of time to find someone who really likes your house; if you try to sell your house quickly, on average you will receive considerably less than you would if you had two or three months in which to sell it. Moreover, the costs of selling a house are substantial, often more than 5 percent of the value of the house, and in any case more than the costs of selling other assets such as stocks and bonds.

BONDS

Bonds are simply a way for corporations and government to borrow. The borrower—whether it is a company, a state, a school district, or the U.S. government—promises to pay the lender (the purchaser of the bond, or investor) a fixed amount in a specified time: say 5, 10, 20, or 40 years. In addition, the borrower agrees to pay the lender each year a fixed return on the amount borrowed. Thus, if the interest rate is 10 percent, a $10,000 bond will pay the lender $1,000 every year, and $10,000 in the prearranged number of years. The period remaining until a loan or bond is to be paid in full is called its **maturity.** Bonds that mature within a few years are called **short-term bonds;** those that mature in more than 10 years are called **long-term bonds.** A long-term government bond may have a maturity of 20 or even 30 years.

Bonds may seem relatively safe, because the investor knows what amounts will be paid. But consider a corporate bond that promises to pay $10,000 in 10 years and pays $1,000 every year until then. Imagine that an investor buys the bond, collects interest for a couple of years, and then realizes that he needs cash and wants to sell the bond. There is no guarantee that he will get $10,000 for it. He may get more and he may get less. If the market interest rate has fallen to 5 percent since the original bond was issued, a new $10,000 bond now would pay only $500 a year. Clearly, the original bond, which pays $1,000 a year, is worth considerably more. Thus, a decline in the interest rate (which is expected to be permanent) leads to a rise in the value of bonds; and by reverse logic, a rise in the interest rate leads to a decline in the value of bonds. This uncertainty about market value is what makes long-term bonds risky.[1]

Even if the investor holds the bond to maturity, that is, until the date at which it

---

[1] The market price of the bond will equal the present discounted value of what it pays. For instance, a 3-year bond that pays $10 per year each of 2 years and $110 at the end of the 3rd year has a value of

$$\frac{10}{1 + r} + \frac{10}{(1 + r)^2} + \frac{110}{(1 + r)^3},$$

where r is the market rate of interest. We can see that as r goes up, the value of the bond goes down, and vice versa.

pays the promised $10,000, there is still a risk, since he cannot know for sure what $10,000 will purchase 10 years from now. If the general level of prices increases at a rate of 7 percent over these 10 years, the value of the $10,000 will be just one-half what it would have been had prices remained stable during that decade.[2]

Because of the higher risk caused by these uncertainties, long-term bonds must compensate investors by paying slightly higher returns, on average, than comparable short-term bonds. And because every corporation has at least a slight chance of going bankrupt, corporate bonds must compensate investors for the higher risk by paying slightly higher returns than government bonds. However, economic studies suggest that the higher returns more than compensate for the additional bankruptcy risk. That is, if an investor purchases a very large number of good-quality corporate bonds, the likelihood that more than one or two will default is very small, and the overall return will be considerably higher than the return from purchasing government bonds of the same maturity (the same number of years until they come due).

Some corporate bonds are riskier than others—that is, there is a higher probability of default—and these bonds must pay extremely high returns to induce investors to take a chance on them. Back in 1980, when Chrysler looked as if it might be on the verge of bankruptcy, Chrysler bonds were yielding very high returns of 23 percent. Obviously, the more a firm borrows, the more likely it is that it will not be able to meet its commitments, and accordingly the riskier are its bonds. In recent years, several firms have issued what are sometimes called **junk bonds,** bonds considered highly risky, usually because the firms issuing them have taken on huge amounts of debt. While over long periods of time the average return on junk bonds has been higher than the return on good-quality corporate bonds, in 1990, as the economy went into a recession, there were many defaults. Junk bonds declined dramatically in value, causing some insurance companies that had invested heavily in them, like Executive Life, to go bankrupt.

SHARES OF STOCK

A household might also choose to invest in shares of corporate stock. When a person buys shares in a firm, she literally owns a fraction (a share) of the total firm. Thus, if the firm issues 1 million shares, an individual who owns 100 shares owns .01 percent of the firm. If the firm paid out all its earnings—all its receipts after paying workers, other suppliers of materials, and all interest due on bank and other loans—the shareholder would receive .01 percent of the total amount. However, firms usually retain a fraction, on average around two-thirds, of their total earnings. The money that they pay to shareholders directly is called **dividends,** and the expectation of receiving dividends is one reason investors buy stocks. So the amount of a dividend, unlike the return on a bond, depends on a firm's earnings, as well as on how much of those earnings it chooses to distribute to shareholders.

In addition to dividends, those who invest in stocks receive a return in the form of the change in the stock's value between the time they buy it and the time they sell it. This is the other reason investors choose stocks as investments. They hope to make money by selling the stocks at a higher price, which, as we learned in Chapter 9, is called a capital gain.

---

[2] If prices rise at 7 percent a year, with compounding, the price level in 10 years is $(1.07)^{10}$ times the level it is today; $(1.07)^{10}$ is approximately equal to 2; prices have doubled.

The money that the firm does not distribute as dividends but retains, called **retained earnings,** is invested in the company. If it is invested well, the value of the company increases and thus the price of the shares increases too.

Shares of stock are risky for a number of reasons. First, the earnings of firms vary greatly. Even if firms do not vary their dividends, differences in profits will lead to differences in retained earnings, and these will be reflected in the variability of the value of the shares. In addition, the stock price of a company depends on the beliefs of investors as to, for instance, the prospects of the economy, the industry, and that particular firm. A loss of faith in any one could lead to a drop in stock price. Thus, an individual who suddenly had to sell all of his shares because of some medical emergency might find that they had declined significantly in value. Even if the investor believes that the shares will eventually return to a higher value, he may be unable to wait.

Shares of stock are riskier than bonds. According to law, when a firm goes bankrupt and must pay off its investors, bondholders must be paid off as fully as possible before shareholders receive any money at all. As a result, a bondholder in a bankrupt company is likely to be paid some share of her original investment, while a shareholder may receive nothing. Over the long run, shares of stock have yielded very high returns. While corporate bonds yielded on average an annual real rate of return of 2 percent in the period from 1926 to 1991, shares of stock yielded a real return of about 6.7 percent in the same period.

COMMON AND PREFERRED SHARES

The financial markets have created an enormous and bewildering variety of assets, many of which can be thought of as various mixtures of bonds and stocks. Thus, a **common share** is distinguished from a **preferred share.** A common share refers to the usual stock ownership discussed above. A preferred share promises to pay a given amount, just as a bond does. However, if the firm fails to meet its commitment to preferred shareholders, the firm is not bankrupt. It simply cannot pay anything to its common shareholders until it pays the amount promised to preferred shareholders. And if the company does go bankrupt, bondholders must be fully paid before preferred shareholders get anything. The preferred share has an advantage over common shares: before a firm pays anything to its other shareholders, it must meet all of its obligations to preferred shareholders. But it can choose to pay nothing to either. Most preferred shares have a cumulative provision: if a company suspends payments to preferred shareholders, before it can start paying other shareholders anything, it must make up for all the amounts it had previously failed to pay preferred shareholders. Preferred shares are thus riskier than bonds, but somewhat safer than common shares.

THE DESIRABLE ATTRIBUTES OF INVESTMENTS

As investors survey the broad range of opportunities available to them, they balance their personal needs against the characteristics of investment options. The ideal investment would combine a high and sure rate of return with liquidity, and it would not be taxed. But the search for such an asset has as much chance of success as the search for the fountain of eternal youth. Usually you get only more of one desirable property—

say, greater returns—at the expense of another desirable property, such as safety. To understand what is entailed in these trade-offs, we have to take a closer look at each of the principal attributes.

EXPECTED RETURNS

First on the list of desirable properties are high returns. Returns have two components: the interest payments or dividend payments and the capital gain. The capital gain is the difference between what you spent on an asset and what you receive when you sell it. Thus, if you buy some stock for $1,000, receive $150 in dividends during the year, and at the end of the year sell the stock for $1,200, your total return is $150 + $200 = $350. If you sell the stock for $900, your total return is $150 − $100 = $50. If you sell it for $800, your total return is a *negative* $50.

Returns can take on a number of different forms. In the case of a bond, the amount you get back in excess of the amount you invest, or principal, is referred to as interest. Stocks may pay dividends. Real estate returns may come in the form of rent, or payment for the use of the real estate.[3] Bonds, stocks, and real estate all produce returns in the form of capital gains (or losses) when they are sold. If you buy an apartment building for $150,000 and sell it for $160,000, you have made a capital gain of $10,000 (note that this is in addition to any rent you may have collected while you owned the house).

In estimating the total return to an asset, the wise investor combines the asset's ongoing return (interest payments on a bank account or bond, dividends, rent, and so on) with its potential capital gain. There remain, however, two problems in comparing the returns to different assets. First, the returns may occur in different years. An asset that costs $1,000 and yields a $300 return next year is far preferable to one that costs the same amount and yields $300 in ten years' time. Dollars received at later dates are worth less than dollars today, as was demonstrated in Chapter 6. To make adjustments for the difference in timing, we need to compare the present discounted value of the returns.

But even if we have two assets, each of which will yield all of its returns next year, we have a problem. Like most assets, neither will have a guaranteed return. The return may be high or low. To evaluate such variable returns, we apply the concept of **expected returns.** The expected return to an asset is a statistical summing up—a single number that combines the various possible returns per dollar invested with the chances that each of these returns will actually be paid. What are relevant are not the average returns that have been experienced in the past but the average returns that are *expected* in the future. Of course, past performance may give a clue about future expected performance.

For simplicity, suppose that one of the two assets is a stock costing $100 that has a long tradition of paying $4 each year in dividends. The dividend thus supplies a 4 percent return; but some estimate is needed of its potential capital gain. Figure 10.1 plots the probabilities of different expected returns for this stock, and gives three possible outcomes for when the stock is sold a year from now. One possibility is that the stock will fetch only $97. The stock will nevertheless produce a 1 percent return ($97 + $4 = $101). Experts give this outcome a 1 in 4 chance of occurring (a 25 percent probability).

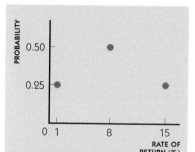

Figure 10.1 A PROBABILITY DISTRIBUTION OF POSSIBLE RATES OF RETURN

There are three possible levels of return for this asset: a 1 in 4 chance of a 1 percent return, a 2 in 4 chance of an 8 percent return, and a 1 in 4 chance of a 15 percent return. The expected return is calculated by multiplying the possible returns times their probability of happening, and adding the results.

---

[3] In Chapter 13, we will encounter a more technical economic definition of rent that differs slightly from the usage here.

A second possibility is that the stock's price will be $104 and thus produce an 8 percent return ($104 + $4 = $108). This possibility is given a 2 in 4 chance of occurring (a 50 percent probability). The third possibility is that the stock will sell for $111, producing a return of 15 percent ($111 + $4 = $115). Like the first possibility, this is given a 1 in 4 chance of occurring (a 25 percent probability). (The sum of the probabilities, by definition, must add up to 1.)

The next step in calculating the expected return is to multiply each of the possible outcomes by the chance, or probability, that it will occur, as illustrated in Table 10.1. The sum of these products, 8 percent, is the expected return. We would then go through the same series of calculations with the other investment opportunity. If all other important characteristics of the two opportunities were the same, we would presumably choose the one with the higher expected return.

Different individuals may differ in their judgments concerning the likelihood of various returns. To some extent, people's views are based on historical experience. When economists say that the average return to stocks is higher than the return to bonds, what they mean is that historically, on average, over the past century, the returns to stocks have been higher. This does not necessarily mean that the return to stocks next year will be higher than the return to bonds, or that the return to particular stocks will be higher than the return to particular bonds. An individual who believes that a major economic downturn is likely may believe that the expected return to stocks next year will be lower than the return to bonds, and will weight his expected return calculation accordingly.

An important first lesson in investment theory is that *if there were no differences between assets other than the ways in which they produce returns (interest, dividends, etc.), then the expected returns to all assets would be the same.* Why? Because investors seeing the return to an asset that yielded more than this average would bid more for the asset. If the 8 percent return given in the stock example above looked high relative to other options, then investors desirous of that return would bid the stock price up above $100. As the price rose, the expected return would decline. The upward pressure would continue until the expected return declined to match the level of all other investments. The process by which expected returns to all assets that are identical in every essential respect are equated is referred to as **arbitrage.**

In fact, the expected returns per dollar invested for different assets differ markedly from one another. The reason is that there are a number of other important attributes

Table 10.1 CALCULATING EXPECTED RETURNS

Outcome (return)	Probability	Outcome × probability
1 percent	25 percent	0.25 percent
8 percent	50 percent	4 percent
15 percent	25 percent	3.75 percent
		Sum = 8 percent

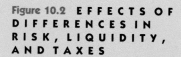

Figure 10.2 EFFECTS OF DIFFERENCES IN RISK, LIQUIDITY, AND TAXES

Lowering risk, increasing liquidity, or granting more favorable tax treatment shifts the demand curve for the asset to the right, increasing the equilibrium price and lowering the average return.

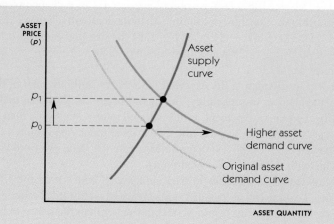

that affect an asset's return: the risk that it will not pay the expected return; its treatment under tax law; and the liquidity, or ease with which it can be sold. An asset that is less risky or more liquid or receives favorable tax treatment will have a higher demand. The higher demand will lead to higher prices and thus to lower returns. Therefore, the before-tax expected return will be lower on assets that are safer, more liquid, or tax-favored. Economists sometimes say that such desirable assets sell at a **premium,** while assets that are riskier or more illiquid sell at a **discount.** Even in these circumstances, a process of arbitrage is at work; assets of comparable risk and liquidity must yield the same expected returns.

We can see this in Figure 10.2. A reduction in the riskiness of an asset, a reduction in the taxes that are imposed on it, or an increase in its liquidity shifts the demand curve for the asset to the right. In the short run, the supply of an asset is inelastic. Even in the longer run, supply is likely not to be perfectly elastic. Accordingly, as illustrated in the figure, the price of the assets goes up, from p_0 to p_1. Accompanying the increase in price is a reduction in the return per dollar invested.

The next three sections explore the additional attributes of investments—risk, tax considerations, and liquidity—and how they create premiums and discounts.

RISK

There are important risks associated with most assets. The investor may receive a high return, a low return, or even a loss—that is, the investor may get back less than what she put in. Often this uncertainty is concerned with what the asset will be worth next week, next month, or next year. The price of a stock may go up or down. Long-term bonds are risky; even though the interest they pay is known, their market value may fluctuate. Moreover, because there is uncertainty about the rate of inflation, there is uncertainty about the *real* return paid by a bond, even though the nominal return is fixed.

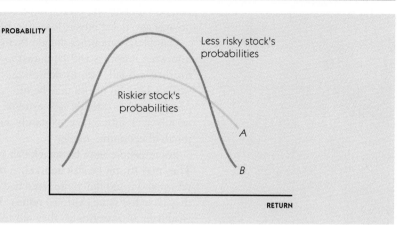

Figure 10.3
ILLUSTRATING RISK WITH PROBABILITY DISTRIBUTIONS

These two probability distributions are both symmetrical, around the same midpoint; thus, they both have the same expected return. However, the stock shown by curve A has a higher chance of very high or very low returns, and thus is riskier than the stock shown by curve B.

Some have said that financial markets are the places where risk is bought and sold. A full appreciation of this insight is beyond the scope of this book, but certainly a prime consideration for any investor is the riskiness of any investment alternative. Bank accounts, in this regard, are safe. Since government deposit insurance came into play in the 1930s, no one in the United States has lost her money in an insured bank account. But investments in housing, stocks, bonds, and most other investments all involve risk. You may lose some or all of your money, or the return may be substantially lower than what you expected.

Some assets are riskier than others; that is, they may have a greater chance of very low returns and a greater chance of very high returns. Figure 10.3 provides a slightly more complex version of Figure 10.1. This time, instead of describing only three possible payoffs, the diagram depicts all the possible payoffs. The two stocks represented here have the same average return, but the stock whose return is described by curve A is riskier than the stock whose return is described by curve B. There is a greater chance of very low and of very high returns.

ATTITUDES TOWARD RISK

Chapter 6 introduced the idea that individuals are risk averse, which means that if they can get the same average return with less risk, they will generally choose to do so. The fact that most people are risk averse means that risky assets must offer a higher average return to induce investors to buy them. Stocks are considered riskier than corporate bonds, and corporate bonds in turn are riskier than government bonds. That is why, on average, stocks yield a higher return than bonds, why corporate bonds must pay a slightly higher interest than government bonds, and so on.

The fact that individuals are, by and large, risk averse is not inconsistent with the observation that in certain situations they enjoy risks—they are **risk loving.** The popularity of Atlantic City and Las Vegas, not to mention numerous state lotteries and church bingo games, is testimony to the pleasure that many people get from gambling. Overall, the bets individuals make in these situations are losers; the losses are what allow casinos and fund-raisers to make money. Lotteries are an extreme example. In a state lottery, the state often takes 50 percent of the money spent on tickets, which means that on average, ticket buyers lose 50 cents of every dollar—before any numbers are drawn.

Gamblers sometimes delude themselves into thinking that they have special insights into what numbers will be drawn in a lottery or which horse will win a race or where the dice will fall, but, by definition, luck chooses the winners in games of chance. And while a little bit of risk may be fun, economists and society as a whole tend to think of people who persistently take extreme risks with a significant portion of their income or wealth as a little crazy, certainly not goal-oriented and rational in the spirit of the standard economic model.

Some people may be smack-dab in between risk-aversion and risk-loving behavior. They may simply be **risk neutral.** A risk-neutral individual cares only about the expected return and is indifferent between two assets that pose different amounts of risk, provided they have the same expected return. When people have a very small proportion of their wealth in an investment, they are likely to act in a risk-neutral manner.

Consider a wealthy individual who thinks an investment project has a 50–50 chance of being successful. If the project succeeds, it will yield a return of $2.12 for each dollar invested. If it fails, it pays nothing. The expected return per dollar invested is therefore .5 × $2.12 = $1.06, or 6 percent. This person might be willing to invest $1,000; the 6 percent return is just slightly greater than the 5 percent return from a bank savings account. If he has little at stake, he might go for the higher expected return—but he would probably not be willing to invest all his life savings in this gamble. When it comes to large risks, people tend to act in a risk-averse manner.

CORRELATION WITH THE ECONOMY

The risk associated with any asset, however, is not just related to the magnitude of the possible gains and losses. It also depends on the circumstances under which unusually large gains and losses occur. If some asset yields its high return when the economy is in a recession and its low return when the economy is in a boom, it will be more desirable than if it yields its high return when the economy is in a boom and its low return when there is a recession. An asset that yields a high return in a recession does so when money is particularly valuable, and investors take that into account. An example of such an asset might be stock in a food-processing firm, since people need to eat even in bad times. Stocks like these are similar to a type of insurance. They can offset some of the losses on other assets when the economy goes into a tailspin. Thus, investors are willing to pay more for these stocks than they otherwise would.

Most stocks, in contrast, tend to go up when the economy is strong, with employment, output, and growth at high levels, and down when it is weak; economists say that stocks that go up when the economy is up are **procyclical.** Construction varies a great deal with the business cycle, so that construction-related industries, like lumber, are highly cyclical. Similarly, when times are bad, people cut down on their purchases of luxuries like power motorboats, so those stocks are also cyclical. Stocks that rise with other stocks contribute to the total riskiness on an individual's income or wealth, and investors are willing to pay less for these.

Figure 10.4, which shows the relationship between risk and return, demonstrates that investors can only obtain higher returns by absorbing more risk. The measure of risk used along the horizontal axis is called systematic risk, because it reflects the extent to

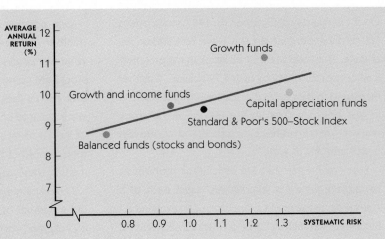

Figure 10.4 RISK-RETURN TRADE-OFF

In general, investors receive a higher return for bearing greater risk. Contrast the high returns of growth funds, which also have high risks, with "balanced funds" that consist largely of more conservative stocks and bonds.
Source: Burton Malkiel, *A Random Walk Down Wall Street* (New York: Norton, 1991, 5th ed.).

which the asset goes up when the rest of the market goes up. The figure shows how various mutual funds, funds that invest their money in bonds and stocks of different firms, have performed. Standard & Poor's 500-Stock Index is a mixture of 500 stocks designed to reflect the stock market as a whole. Growth funds are funds that try to buy stocks that are going to increase in value rapidly. They take greater risk, and during the twenty years in question, they obtained marginally high returns. Funds that bought both stocks and bonds undertook much less risk and received much lower returns.

TAX CONSIDERATIONS

A third general way in which assets differ is in their tax considerations. The government is a silent partner in almost all investments. He is not the kind of partner you would ordinarily choose—he takes a fraction of the profits, but leaves you with almost all the losses. Still, investors must take into account the fact that a substantial fraction of the returns to a successful investment will go to the government as taxes. Since different assets are treated differently in the tax code, tax considerations obviously can play an important role in choosing a portfolio. After all, individuals care about after-tax returns, not before-tax returns. Investments that face relatively low tax rates are sometimes said to be **tax-favored.**

The example of state and municipal bonds illustrates this point. These bonds yield a lower return than do corporate bonds of comparable risk and liquidity. So why do people buy them? The answer is that the interest on bonds issued by states and municipalities is generally exempt from federal tax. The higher your income, the more valuable this tax exemption is, because your tax savings are greater. The higher demand for these tax-exempt bonds from high-income investors drives up their price, thus driving down the interest rate received on the bonds. We can expect the interest rate to decline

On the single day of October 19, 1987, stock prices fell by 22.6 percent on the New York Stock Exchange. The total value of all stock in major American corporations fell by over $500 billion. Whether measured in percentage or dollar terms, it was the largest one-day crash in the history of the stock market. The market has experienced other one-day crash landings as well.

Stock market crashes are difficult for economists to explain; who can explain the exact path of a stampede or the precise direction of an avalanche? But a Presidential Task Force on Market Mechanisms, appointed almost immediately after the crash of October 1987 and headed by Nicholas Brady, who was later appointed secretary of the Treasury, offered some insights about the causes of the crash.

In an efficient stock market, one in which most information was widely distributed and new information was what caused prices to move, a stock market crash would make sense *if* it was preceded by some extremely bad news. However, while the weeks before October 19 held their share of good and bad news, there does not appear in retrospect to have been any news severe enough—like an earthquake or a plague—to cause this sort of collapse. In fact, the economy continued to grow after the crash until the recession that began in mid-1990.

If the cause of the crash was not fundamental economic factors, the task force reasoned, it must have been related to the mechanisms through which stocks are traded. In theory, at least, it is conceivable that the existing mechanisms for trading stocks somehow pushed stock prices too high, higher than the underlying value of the company could justify, and then pushed them too low during the crash. Economists have been working for some time on the issue of how price movements might become exaggerated in this way.

One possible explanation, for example, is that a number of stock traders have a tendency to buy whatever stocks are going up and to sell whatever stocks are going down, perhaps on the philosophy that even if they do not know what is causing the stock price to change, they can still take advantage of it. In a rising stock market, these traders would tend to bid stock prices still higher; in a falling market, they would push prices still lower.

This explanation may sound plausible enough, but a number of economists are not happy with it. It presumes, for example, that a high stock price leads to more purchasers for that stock, which violates the basic notion that demand curves slope down. And wouldn't these investors learn from the stock market crash that the market cannot be

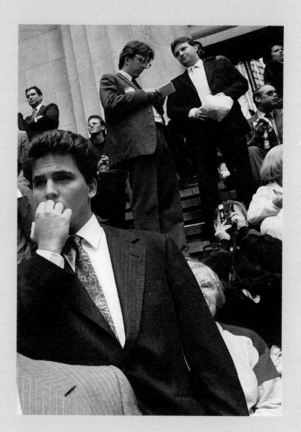

to the point where the after-tax return for high-income individuals is at most only slightly higher than for an ordinary taxable bond of comparable risk.

Consider two bonds, identical in all respects except their tax treatment. Both promise to pay $110 next year, $10 of which is interest. The price of the taxable bond is $100. The equilibrium price for a municipal bond is greater than $100. This means that its average return, before tax, is less than 10 percent—less than the return on the taxable bond. If most investors have to pay 30 percent of any interest income in taxes, then the after-tax return is $7, not $10. They will be willing to buy the tax-exempt bond so long as its yield is at least 7 percent. Below that level, they will buy the taxable bond instead. Thus, the equilibrium price of the tax-exempt bond is $110 ÷ $107 = $102.80; that is, at a price of approximately $103, the tax-exempt bond yields the same return as the taxable bond does at $100.

Investing in housing, particularly a house to live in, is another tax-favored form of investment enjoyed by most Americans. You can deduct the interest payments on your mortgage and real estate taxes when you calculate your income for tax purposes. In addition, the capital gain from owning the house is not taxed until the house is sold. Even then, if you use the money to buy another house or if you are above age fifty-five, the capital gain (up to $155,000) from selling your house is not taxed at all. If the tax advantages of home ownership were ever withdrawn, we could expect housing prices to decline precipitously, as illustrated in Figure 10.5. It is not likely that tax preferences for housing will be suddenly removed, however, because so many voters own houses, and politicians are unlikely to take any action against home owners.

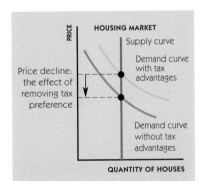

Figure 10.5 EFFECT OF REMOVING TAX PREFERENCES FOR HOUSING

Removing tax preferences for housing will shift the demand curve for housing down, and this will, in the short run (with an inelastic housing supply), cause marked decreases in the price of housing.

LOOKING BEYOND THE BASIC MODEL: LIQUIDITY

The fourth important attribute is liquidity. Liquid assets are assets for which the costs of selling are very low or for which it takes a short time to find a "suitable" buyer. Corporate stock in a major company is considered fairly liquid, because anyone who reads a newspaper can find the current price, and the costs of selling at that price are relatively small. A bank account is completely liquid (except when the bank goes bankrupt), because you can turn it into cash at virtually no charge by writing a check.

In the basic competitive model, all assets are assumed to be perfectly liquid. There is a well-defined price at which anything can be bought and sold; any household or firm can buy or sell as much as it wants at that price. And the model typically ignores the costs of engaging in these transactions. But there are often significant costs of selling or buying an asset. For houses, the costs run as high as 7 percent to 10 percent of the value of the house. It often takes a long time to find a suitable buyer; different potential buyers of a house are willing to pay different amounts. The longer you wait, the more likely it is you will find someone who really likes your house, and who is therefore willing to pay considerably more for it than others are. At times, municipal bonds have also been fairly illiquid: the prices at which a bond could be bought and sold have differed by more than 20 percent.

EFFICIENT MARKET THEORY

The demand for any asset depends on all of its attributes—average return, risk, tax treatment, and liquidity. In a well-functioning market, there are no bargains to be had; you get what you pay for. If some asset yields a higher average return than most other investments, it is because that asset has a higher risk, has a lower liquidity, or receives unfavorable tax treatment.

The fact that there are no bargains does not mean the investor's life is easy. He still must decide what he wants, just as he does when he goes into a grocery store. Figure 10.6A shows the kind of choices an individual faces. For simplicity, we ignore liquidity and tax considerations and focus only on average returns and risk. The figure shows the opportunity set, in the way that is usual for this case. Because "risk" is bad, to get less risk we have to give up some average returns. That is why the trade-off has its unusual positive slope. To show the more familiar version of an opportunity set, we could have drawn it by putting a measure of "safety" on the horizontal axis. Panel B

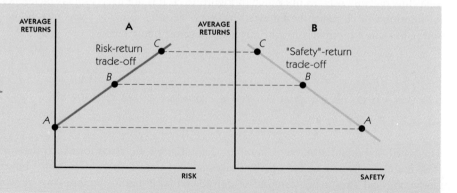

Figure 10.6 THE RISK-RETURN TRADE-OFF

To get more return, an investor must accept more risk, as is shown in panel A. Safety can be thought of as the inverse of risk. In panel B, the corresponding trade-off between safety and return is shown; to get more safety, an investor gives up some return.

does this. Greater safety can only be obtained at the expense of a lower average return. Reading from either panel, we can see that assets with greater risk have a higher average return. Point A represents a government T-bill—no risk, but low return. Point B might represent a stock or mix of stocks of average riskiness, point C one of high risk. A very risk-averse person might choose A, a less risk-averse person B, a still less risk-averse person C.

The theory that prices perfectly reflect the characteristics of assets—there are no bargains—is called the **efficient market theory.** Much of the work on efficient market theory has been done on publicly traded stocks, and so our discussion centers on them. The lessons, however, can be applied to all asset prices.

EFFICIENCY AND THE STOCK MARKET

While most people are skeptical about their ability to wander over to the racetrack and make a fortune, they are not so skeptical about the stock market. They believe that even if they themselves cannot sit down with the *Wall Street Journal* and pick out all the best stocks, someone who studies the stock market for a living could do so. But economists startled the investment community in the early 1960s by pointing out that choosing successful stocks is no easier—and no harder—than choosing the fastest horses.

The efficient market theory explains this discrepancy in views. When economists refer to an efficient market, they are referring to one in which relevant information is widely known and quickly distributed to all participants. To oversimplify a bit, they envision a stock market where all investors have access to the *Wall Street Journal* and *Barron's* and *Fortune* magazines and many other sources of good information about business, and where government requires businesses to disclose certain information to the public. Thus, each stock's average return, its risk, its tax treatment, and so on will be fully known by all investors. Because participants have all the information, asset prices will reflect it.

It turns out, however, that this broad dissemination of information is not only unrealistic but unnecessary. Economists have shown that efficient markets do not require that *all* participants have information. If enough participants have information, then prices will move as if the whole market had the information. All it takes is a few people knowledgeable enough to recognize a bargain, and prices will quickly be bid up or down to levels that reflect complete information. And if prices reflect complete information, even uninformed buyers, purchasing at current prices, will reap the benefit.

You cannot "beat" an efficient market any more than you can beat the track; you can only get lucky in it. All the research done by the many big brokerage houses and individual investors adds up to a market that is in some respects like a casino. This is the irony of the view, held by most economists, that the stock market is an efficient one. If you are trying to make money in an efficient stock market, it is not enough to choose companies that you expect to be successful in the future. If you expect a company to be successful and everyone else also expects it to be successful, based on the available information, then the price of shares in that company will already be quite high. The only way to make abnormally high profits on stock purchases is to pick companies that will surprise the market by doing better than is generally expected, which will thus force everyone to change their expectations, and then to invest in those companies before the expectations of the rest of the market change.

Because prices in an efficient market already reflect all of the available information, any price changes are a response to unanticipated news. After all, if the event was anticipated, it would have already been reflected in the price. If it was already known that something good was going to occur, for instance some new computer that was going to be better than all previous computers was going to be unveiled, the price of its stock would reflect this (it would be high) before the computer actually hit the market. You might not know precisely how much better than its competitors the new computer was, and hence you could not predict precisely by how much future earnings were likely to rise. The market will reflect an average value of these estimates. When the new computer is presented, there is some chance that it will be better than this average, in which case the price will rise further; but there is an equal chance that it will not be quite as good as this average estimate, in which case the price will fall, even though the computer is better than anything else on the market. In this case, the "surprise" is that the computer is not as good as the market anticipated.

Since tomorrow's news is, by definition, unanticipated, no one can predict whether it will cause the stock price to rise or fall. In an efficient stock market, prices will move unpredictably, depending on unexpected news. When a stock has an equal chance of going up in value more or less than the market as a whole, economists say that its price moves like a **random walk,** a term that conjures up the image of a drunk who rambles down the street with generally unstable—and unpredictable—movements. Figure 10.7 shows a computer-generated random walk and gives the idea of how unpredictable such a path is.

The image of a random walk combines the drunk's step-by-step unpredictability with the likelihood that he will probably get to the end of the block. So too with the stock market: there is an upward drift in the level of all stock prices, but whether any particular stock will do better or worse than that average is unpredictable. If the stock market is indeed a random walk, then it is virtually impossible for investors to beat the market. You can do just as well by throwing darts at the newspaper financial page as you can by carefully studying the prospects of each firm. The only way to do better than the

Figure 10.7 A COMPUTER-GENERATED RANDOM WALK

The series plotted here can be thought of as the closing price for a stock over 60 consecutive trading sessions. There is no predicting at the end of each day where the stock will close the next day.

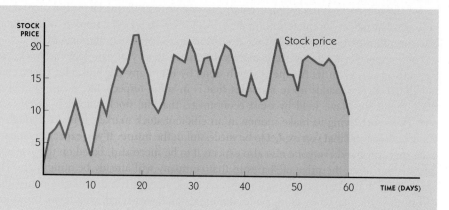

market, on average, is to take greater risks; but taking greater risks means that there is a larger chance of doing much worse than the market too.

The randomness of the market has one important consequence: *some* individuals are going to be successful. However, people have a desire to believe that their insights, rather than luck, enable them to beat the market.

INSIDER TRADING: AN EXCEPTION TO THE EFFICIENT MARKET THEORY

Insider trading provides an exception to the rule that you cannot beat the market. Insiders are the people who manage firms, and they often have information that is not publicly available. However, insiders are required by law to disclose when they buy and sell shares in their own company. There is some evidence that insiders can obtain returns that are above average, and that those who imitate insiders can also obtain a slightly higher than average return. The advantages that insiders enjoy has been the subject of considerable controversy; there is a widespread feeling that everyone trading in the stock market should have an equal chance of winning, and this is not true if there are some who, by the nature of their job, have an advantage. Federal rules restrict the ability of insiders to profit from their knowledge, or to pass that information on to others; the question is, should these rules be tightened? In a famous case in the late 1980s, Ivan Boesky and a number of other wealthy investors paid large fines and went to jail for violating the insider trading laws.

EFFICIENT MARKETS OR RANDOM NOISE?

While most economists agree that there is little evidence that individuals can, even by spending considerable money on information, consistently beat the market, there is controversy about how to interpret this finding. Some see it as evidence of the efficiency of the market, as we have seen; but others view it as evidence of nothing more than the market's randomness. Those who hold this latter view point out that stock market prices seem to vary far more than the efficient market theory would suggest. There often seem to be large changes in stock market prices without any "news" of sufficient magnitude to account for these changes. For example, there are usually ten or fifteen days in the year when the stock market changes by more than 2 percent—a very large change for a single day—for which there does not seem to be any obvious news-related explanation.

The most telling examples where the market seems to move more than the efficient market theory would predict are during so-called crashes. For example, on October 19, 1987, stock prices fell by 22.6 percent on the New York Stock Exchange. However, there was no news on the day of the crash—or in the days or the week before—that would justify such a huge decline.

The famous economist John Maynard Keynes compared the predictions of the stock market to predictions of the winner of a beauty contest, where what one had to decide was not who was the greatest beauty, but who the other judges would think was the most beautiful. If investors suddenly "lose confidence" in a particular stock or in the

Charles Albers, manager of the $259 million Guardian Park Avenue Fund, is on the honor roll. So are George Vanderheiden, who manages the $2,024 million Fidelity Destiny Portfolio I fund; G. Kenneth Heebner, who manages the $734 million New England Growth Fund; and Albert O. Nicholas, who runs the $1,715 million Nicholas Growth Fund.

An honor role of top investors in mutual funds is compiled by *Forbes* magazine each year. Between 1980 and 1991, these fund managers and sixteen others racked up average annual gains of between 15 and 20 percent on the money they managed.

Mutual funds provide one test of the efficient market hypothesis. Are there some professionals who *systematically* do better than the market? Any manager may do better in one month or in one year simply by catching a lucky wave in the economy. In choosing its honor roll, *Forbes* tries to minimize that possibility by looking at how fund managers perform during an entire decade, including periods of economic growth and recession.

Fund managers tend to advertise their successes and not their failures, so that one may get the mistaken impression that they are almost all successful. But economic research has shown that of those who handle stock investments for colleges and universities, state and local governments, insurance companies, and pension funds, more than two-thirds do *worse* by trying to pick stocks than they would have done by just buying a little bit of everything in the market. So one interpretation of the *Forbes* honor roll is that some people are especially gifted, by their analysis or their intuition, in picking stocks that are likely to rise in value.

But economists who believe in the random walk theory of stock movements would respond that *Forbes* monitors over 1,400 mutual funds. By blind chance, at least a few of those funds will do very well over any ten-year period, while others will not do as well. The question is, are those who are successful in one ten-year period any more likely to be successful in the next decade than pure chance would predict? The answer seems to be no! Attributing special skills to those who make large gains in the stock market is like attributing special skills to people who win the lottery; either attribution will confuse a process that essentially depends on luck.

Source: Steve Kichen, "The Honor Roll," *Forbes,* September 2, 1991, pp. 160–61; Burton G. Malkiel, *A Random Walk Down Wall Street* (New York: Norton, 1991, 5th ed.), pp. 169–77.

TNE Growth Fund

For long-term growth

whole stock market, or if they believe that others are losing confidence, then the price of shares may fall dramatically. Since confidence is a psychological phenomenon, not necessarily closely related to real economic events, it can shift in quite unpredictable ways. This sort of loss of confidence, combined with investors all trying to sell their stocks before the market fell further, seems to be what happened in October 1987. To be sure, there may have been events that triggered the loss of confidence, such as increases in interest rates, but the magnitude of the decline seemed out of proportion with such news. And at other times, similar news did not trigger a similar decline in prices.

The aftermath of the stock market crash illustrated how the approach of economists differs from more popular approaches. After the crash, the media tried to explain it by talking about the country's budget deficits, trade deficits, and the possibility of new taxes. But economists pointed out that these factors had existed for a while, and still exist, without causing continual stock market crashes. Examining the historical record and the experience of other countries showed that most of the explanations provided by journalists and Wall Street analysts simply did not hold up. A thorough economic analysis is not a list of anecdotes, but a systematic examination of all the relevant data.

Journalists' explanations for the crash were typical of what can be read in the newspapers or heard on television most days. Sometimes reporters will say that good economic news made people fear that the government, worried about inflation, would do something to slow the economy down, and therefore the seemingly good news caused stocks to decline. Other times, they will say that good economic news bolstered the market. These explanations have little or no predictive value.

In short, the advice to the new investor is: be wary. Do not be misled by success. It may be—almost surely is—just luck. If you have inside information, which you can take advantage of without going to jail or going against your conscience, use it. But first, see a lawyer!

STRATEGIES FOR INTELLIGENT INVESTING

So far, we have investigated major investment alternatives available to those who save, some of the important attributes of each, and the ways in which their prices reflect these attributes. If you are lucky enough to be considering some of these alternatives, you should keep in mind the following four simple rules for intelligent investment. These rules will not tell you how to make a million by the time you are twenty-five, but at the very least, they will enable you to avoid some of the worst pitfalls of investing.

1. *Know the attributes of each asset, and relate them to your personal situation.* Each asset has characteristic returns, risk, tax treatment, and liquidity. In making choices among different assets, your attitude toward each of these attributes should be *compared with the average attitudes reflected in the marketplace.* Most individuals prefer safer, tax-favored, more liquid assets. That is why those assets sell at a premium (and produce a correspondingly lower average return). The question is, are you willing to pay the amount required by the market for the extra safety or extra liquidity? If you are less risk averse than average, then you will find riskier assets attractive. You will not be willing to pay the higher price—and accept the lower return—for a safer asset. And if you are

confident that you are not likely to need to sell an asset quickly, you will not be willing to pay the premium that more liquid assets require. If you are putting aside money for tuition next year, you probably will not want to buy common stocks. Table 10.2 lists some of the major assets discussed so far and compares their characteristics.

2. *Give your financial portfolio a broad base.* Particularly in choosing among financial assets, you need to look not only at each asset separately, but at all of your assets together. A person's entire collection of assets is called her **portfolio.** (The portfolio also includes liabilities, what she owes, but they take us beyond the scope of this chapter.) This rule is seen most clearly in the case of risk. One of the ways you reduce risk is by diversifying your investment portfolio. Investment advisers recognize that if all of an individual's

Table 10.2 ALTERNATIVE INVESTMENTS AND HOW THEY FARE

Investment	Return	Risk	Tax advantages	Liquidity
Bank savings accounts	Low	Low	None	High
CDs (certificates of deposit)	Slightly higher than savings accounts	Low	None	Slightly less than savings accounts
T-bills	About same as CDs	Low	Exempt from state income tax	Small charge for selling before maturity
Federal government long-term bonds	Normally slightly higher than T-bills	Uncertain market value next period; uncertain purchasing power in long run	Exempt from state income tax	Small charge for selling before maturity
Corporate bonds	Higher return than federal bonds	Risks of long-term federal bonds plus risk of default	None	Slightly less liquid than federal bonds (depends on corporation issuing bond)
Municipal bonds	Lower return than federal bonds of same maturity	Same risks as long-term federal bonds plus risk of default plus risk of changes in tax law	Exempt from federal income tax and, in state of issue, state income tax	Often quite illiquid (market for bonds is thin)
Stocks	High	High	Capital gains receive slight tax preference	Those listed on major stock exchange are highly liquid; others may be highly illiquid
Houses	High returns from mid-1970s to mid-1980s; in many areas, negative returns in late 1980s, early 1990s	Used to be thought safe; viewed to be somewhat riskier now	Many special tax advantages	Relatively illiquid; may take long time to find "good buyer"
Mutual funds	Reflect assets in which funds are invested	Reflect assets in which funds are invested; reduced risk from diversification	Reflect assets in which funds are invested	Highly liquid

wealth is in one asset, something might go wrong with the asset and wipe that person out. So they cite the old adage "Don't put all your eggs in one basket." By spreading investments among many assets, an investor's total wealth (and consumption) will not depend on the performance of any single asset, but on the average of all of them.

With a well-diversified portfolio, it is extremely unlikely that something will go wrong with all the assets simultaneously. An investor with a diversified portfolio must still worry about events like recessions or changes in the interest rate, which will tend to make all stocks go up or down; but events that affect primarily one firm alone—a strike against an airline, the death of the president of a firm, the shutting down of an electric power company's nuclear power plant—will have a relatively small impact on the overall portfolio. The investor with a diversified portfolio can, in effect, ignore these risks and focus on the expected return.

The trouble is that few of us are wealthy enough to own a large number of different assets. The average price of a share of stock sold on the New York Stock Exchange, for instance, is roughly $30. To own a single share of 500 firms would require $15,000—and few stockbrokers would be patient enough to handle 500 single-share transactions (not to mention the fact that the fees they would charge would make this an unattractive strategy). This is where broad-based mutual funds come in. These funds can pool the money of a large number of savers to create a super portfolio that can easily contain a large number of stocks, bonds, or other assets. It is not unusual for a mutual fund to pool well over $1 billion from investors who individually contribute as little as $2,000 or so.

The way mutual funds work is simple. Assume 10,000 investors got together, each contributing $3,000. The mutual fund would have $30 million to invest. The mutual fund can thus diversify much more broadly than any individual member could. At an average share price of $30, the fund could buy 1,000 shares each in 1,000 companies. An individual could (possibly) have bought 100 shares in only one of those firms. Nothing that happened to any single firm would have much effect on the value of the mutual fund's portfolio. The mutual fund will pass on the money it receives as dividends to the investors. If some investors decide they want their money back, the mutual fund might find other investors who want to join. If not, it will have to sell a corresponding amount of the shares it holds. If more investors want to join the mutual fund, it simply buys more stock in each of the companies, or further diversifies the number of companies in which it invests.

Diversification is the main advantage of mutual funds. A portfolio consisting of 1,000 corporate bonds from different firms will have a higher expected return with little more risk than a portfolio consisting of 1,000 government bonds. True, in any given year, none of the safe bonds will default, while one or two of the corporate bonds may default. But the higher return on the corporate bonds more than compensates. Generally, the return on corporate bonds is sufficiently higher than government bonds', so the corporate bond portfolio would yield a lower return only if, say, several of the bonds defaulted. Short of a major economic downturn, this sort of event seems quite unlikely.

A highly diversified portfolio reduces risk, but does not eliminate it. The return on a diversified portfolio will be very close to the average return for the market as a whole, since it is somewhat like a scaled-down slice of the entire market. Thus, an investor with a diversified portfolio can worry less about individual companies, but must still worry about the risks of the market as a whole.

Many mutual funds claim more than just diversification: they claim that their research and insight into markets enable them to pick winners. There is considerable doubt about these claims, however, as our discussion of efficient markets would suggest. Today there are a number of mutual funds that do no research, claim no insights, and do nothing more than provide portfolio diversification. These are called **indexed funds,** because they are linked to certain well-publicized indexes of how the stock market is performing. For instance, the Standard & Poor's (S & P's) 500 Index reflects the average price of 500 stocks chosen to be representative of the market as a whole. S & P's indexed funds buy exactly the same mix of stocks that constitute the S & P's 500 Index, so naturally these indexed funds do just as well as—no better and no worse than—the S & P's 500 Index.

Because the index funds have low expenses, particularly in comparison with funds that are trying to outguess the market, on average they yield higher returns to their investors than funds with comparable risk.

3. *Look at all of the risks you face, not just those in your financial portfolio.* Many people may be far less diversified than they believe. For example, consider someone who works for the one big company in town. She owns a house, has a good job, has stock in the company, some money in the bank, and a pension plan. This may sound like a fairly diversified portfolio. But if that single company goes broke, the person will lose her job, the value of her stock will fall, the price of her house is likely to decline as the local economy suffers, and even the pension plan may not pay as much as expected.

4. *Think twice before you think you can beat the market!* Efficient market theory delivers an important message to the personal investor: if an investment adviser tells you of an opportunity that beats the others on all counts, don't believe him. The bond that will produce a higher than average return usually carries with it more risk. The bank account that has a higher interest rate usually also has less liquidity. The dream house at an unbelievable price probably has a leaky roof. The tax-favored bond will

CLOSE-UP: THE INSOMNIA INDEX

Investing is never as easy as just choosing an asset with the highest interest rate. Considerations of risk, liquidity, and taxes all have a role to play. Individual investors will weigh and balance these issues according to their own circumstances. Some investors will be willing to accept a considerable amount of short-term risk, since they expect to be holding their investments for a long-term return. Others may rely on having their money within a few years, perhaps to make a down-payment on a house or to help a child with college expenses.

The key question, according to Burton G. Malkiel, professor of economics at Princeton University, is whether you can sleep at night, given the investment choices you have made. Malkiel has created an imaginative "Sleeping Scale of Major Investment Choices," given on the opposite page. Notice that the assets are ranked in order of increasing expected returns, from top to bottom, as shown in the third column. But they are also ranked in order of decreasing expected sleep, as shown in the first column, and increasing risk, as explained by the notes on the alternative choices in the last two columns.

THE SLEEPING SCALE OF MAJOR INVESTMENT CHOICES

Sleeping point	Type of asset	Expected rate of return, 1990 (before income taxes)	Length of time investment must be held to get expected rate of return	Risk level
Semicomatose state	Bank accounts	5–5½%	No specific investment period required. Many thrift institutions calculate interest from day of deposit to day of withdrawal.	No risk of losing what you put in. Deposits up to $100,000 guaranteed by an agency of the federal government. An almost sure loser with high inflation, however.
Sound night's sleep	Money market mutual funds	7½–8½%	No specific investment period required. Most funds provide check-writing privileges.	Very little, since most funds are invested in bank certificates. Not usually guaranteed, however, although some funds buy only government securities. Rates geared to expected inflation. Will vary.
	Special six-month certificates of deposit (CDs)	8–8½%	Money must be left on deposit for the entire six months to take advantage of higher rate.	Early withdrawals subject to penalty. Rates geared to expected inflation. Will vary.
An occasional dream or two—some possibly unpleasant	High-quality corporate bonds (prime-quality public utilities)	9–9½%	Investments must be made for the period until the maturity of the bond (20–30 years) to be assured of the stated rate. The bonds may be sold at any time, however, in which case the net return will depend on fluctuations in the market price of the bonds.	Very little if held to maturity. (Since the price level is uncertain, there is considerable risk concerning real returns.) Moderate to substantial fluctuations can be expected in realized return if bonds are sold prior to maturity. Rate geared to expected long-run inflation rate now. This may differ from *actual* rate over the term to maturity of the bond. "Junk bonds" promise much higher returns but with much higher risk.
Some tossing and turning before you doze and vivid dreams before awakening	Diversified portfolios of blue-chip common stocks (such as an index fund)[a]	9½–10%	No specific investment periods required, and stocks may be sold at any time. The average expected return assumes a fairly long investment period and can only be treated as a rough guide based on current conditions.	Moderate to substantial. In any one year, the actual return could in fact be negative. Diversified portfolios have at times lost 25% or more of their actual value. Contrary to some opinion—a good inflation hedge.
Nightmares not uncommon, but over the long run well rested	Diversified portfolios of relatively risky stocks (such as aggressive growth-oriented mutual funds)	11–12%	Same as above. The average expected return assumes a fairly long investment period and can only be treated as a rough guide based on current conditions.	Substantial. In any one year, the actual return could be negative. Diversified portfolios of very risky stocks have at times lost 50% or more of their value. Good inflation hedge.
Vivid dreams and occasional nightmares	Real estate	Similar to common stocks	Only makes sense as a very long-term investment. Heavy transactions costs in trading.	Can't sell in a hurry without substantial penalties. Hard to diversify. Very good inflation hedge if bought at reasonable price levels.
Bouts of insomnia	Gold	Impossible to predict	High returns could be earned in any new speculative craze as long as there are greater fools to be found.	Substantial. Believed to be a hedge against doomsday and hyperinflation. Can, however, play a useful role in balancing a diversified portfolio.

Source: Burton G. Malkiel, *A Random Walk Down Wall Street* (New York: Norton, 1991, 5th ed.).

[a] A blue-chip common stock is one in a successful, well-established firm.

have a lower return—and so on. Efficient market theory, as we have seen, says that information about these characteristics is built in to the price of assets, and hence built in to the returns. Basically, investors can adjust the return to their portfolio only by adjusting the risk they face. As Burton Malkiel, author of the best-selling book *A Random Walk Down Wall Street*, which applies this theory to personal investing, puts it: "Every investor must decide the trade-off he or she is willing to make between eating well and sleeping well. The decision is up to you. High investment rewards can be achieved only at the cost of substantial risk-taking."[4]

REVIEW AND PRACTICE

SUMMARY

1. Investment options for individuals include putting savings in a bank account of some kind or using them to buy real estate, bonds, or shares of stock.

2. Returns on investment can be received in four ways: interest, dividends, rent, and capital gains.

3. Assets can differ in four important ways: in their average returns, their riskiness, their treatment under tax law, and their liquidity.

4. The expected return of an asset is calculated by multiplying each of the possible outcomes times the probability of its occurring, and adding the results.

5. When choosing between two assets with an equal expected return but different levels of risk, a risk-averse individual will choose the less risky, a risk-loving person will choose the more risky, and a risk-neutral individual will be equally happy with either one.

6. By holding assets that are widely diversified, individuals can avoid many of the risks associated with specific assets, but not the risks associated with the market as a whole.

7. The efficient market theory holds that all available information is fully reflected in the price of an asset. Accordingly, changes in price reflect only unanticipated events and, therefore, must be random.

8. There are four rules for intelligent investors: (1) evaluate the characteristics of each asset and relate them to your personal situation; (2) give your financial portfolio a broad base; (3) look at all the risks you face, not just those in your financial portfolio; (4) think twice before believing you can beat the market.

KEY TERMS

investment	dividends	efficient market theory
certificate of deposit (CD)	expected return	random walk
	arbitrage	portfolio
liquidity	risk averse, risk	mutual fund
Treasury bills (T-bills)	loving, risk neutral	

[4] 5th ed. (New York: Norton, 1991).

REVIEW QUESTIONS

1. Suppose an investor is considering two assets with identical expected rates of return. What three characteristics of the assets might help differentiate the choice between them?

2. List the principal alternative forms of investment that are available. What are the returns on each called? Rate them in terms of the characteristics described in question #1.

3. True or false: "Two assets must have equal expected returns." If we modify the statement to read "Two assets that are equally risky must have equal expected returns," is the statement true? Explain your answer.

4. If you found out that several company presidents were buying or selling stock in their own companies, would you want to copy their behavior? Why or why not?

5. What is the efficient market theory? What implications does it have for whether you can beat the market? Does it imply that all stocks must yield the same expected return?

6. What are the theoretical reasons that economists expect the market to be efficient? What is some empirical evidence to support this belief?

7. Why are stock market crashes sometimes cited as evidence against the efficient market theory?

8. List and explain the four rules for intelligent investing.

9. True or false: "A single mutual fund may be a more diversified investment than a portfolio of a dozen stocks." Explain.

PROBLEMS

1. Imagine a lottery where 1 million tickets are sold at $1 apiece, and the winning ticket receives a prize of $700,000. What is the expected return to buying a ticket in this lottery? Will a risk-neutral person buy a ticket in this lottery? What about a risk-averse person?

2. Would you expect the rate of return on bonds to change with their length of maturity? Why or why not?

3. Why might a risk-averse investor put some money in junk bonds?

4. Would you predict that
   (a) the before-tax return on housing would be higher or lower than the before-tax return on other assets?
   (b) investors would be willing to pay more or less for a stock with a high return when the economy is booming and a low return when the economy is in a slump than they would pay for a stock with just the opposite pattern of returns?
   (c) an investment with low liquidity would sell at a premium or a discount compared with a similar investment with higher liquidity?

5. Each of two investments has a 1 in 10 chance of paying a return of −10 percent; a 1 in 5 chance of paying 2 percent; a 1 in 3 chance of paying 6 percent; a 1 in 5

chance of paying 10 percent; and a 1 in 6 chance of paying 12 percent. Draw this probability distribution, and calculate the expected return for these two investments. If investment A is a house and investment B is a share of corporate stock, how might liquidity or tax considerations help you decide which of these investments you prefer?

6. Imagine a short-term corporate $1,000 bond that promises to pay 8 percent interest over three years. This bond will pay $80 at the end of the first year and the second year, and $1,080 at the end of the third year. After one year, however, the market interest rate has increased to 12 percent. What will the bond be worth to a risk-neutral investor at that time? If the firm appears likely to go bankrupt, how will the expected return on this bond change?

7. Golfer Lee Trevino once said: "After losing two fortunes, I've learned. Now, when someone comes to me with a deal that's going to make me a million dollars, I say, 'Tell it to your mother.' Why would a stranger want to make me a million?" Explain how Trevino's perspective fits the efficient market theory.

11

THE LABOR SUPPLY DECISION

C hapter 8 focused on the household's spending decision, Chapter 9 examined its saving decision, and Chapter 10 looked at its investment decision.

This chapter rounds out our study of the household. We look at the choices people make that affect the amount of income they have to spend and save—choices such as how much to work, when to retire, and how much education and training to obtain. We also take a brief look at one other decision that fundamentally affects every other aspect of family decision making—how many children to have. People's decisions about these matters touch on basic philosophical and religious values. Many individuals choose a career because they want to be of service to others. They choose an education for enlightenment and self-improvement. They decide to have children and a family because they fall in love. To discuss these decisions in economic terms, as if they could be measured in dollars and cents, can seem demeaning and cynical.

Yet economic factors have a way of intruding even where they may be unwelcome. People's choices concerning a job affect what they earn, and thus what they can spend. Economics does not say that more income is morally superior or that people *should* take a higher-paying job, but it does say that individuals sense the trade-offs they face. They balance, for instance, the gains in extra goods they can obtain by working longer hours with the costs, usually measured in such terms as reduced leisure time or psychological toll. Similarly, a higher level of education will, on average, result in a higher income, but education involves an investment of money, time, and effort. Again, economists believe that people sense these trade-offs and respond to them.

Even decisions about marriage and whether to have children involve a series of economic costs and benefits. In the past, when women had limited employment options outside the home, many of them felt marriage was an economic necessity. As more women entered the labor market, broke into jobs that had been denied to them in the past, and gained independent incomes, divorce rates increased. There may have been many factors contributing to the increase in the divorce rate, yet the changed economic condition of women was surely an important one.

In many poor countries, it is customary to use young children as free labor to help work the farm and to expect adult children to support parents in their old age. Birthrates are high. But in wealthy countries, parents do not expect their children to work, and they know that the government provides social security for them in old age. Is it just coincidence that as countries grow wealthier, their birthrates tend to decline?

Such connections all rest on the same argument: economic factors enter into even the most personal decisions. These factors may not be the only, or even the major, consideration, but people do respond to them. It is therefore worth understanding how economic factors affect such decisions as how much to work, how much to study, and how many children to have. When these factors change substantially, people's behavior is also likely to change in important ways. Economists do not claim to be able to predict how any particular person would respond to a change in economic incentives. But they can do a remarkably good job at answering questions such as "Will the average American work more, study more, or have more children if her hourly wage increases?" In doing so, they apply the basic model of consumer behavior developed in Chapter 8.

"We have something with terrific fringe benefits. No salary—just fringe benefits."

KEY QUESTIONS

1. How can the basic tools introduced in Chapter 8 to analyze consumers' expenditure decisions be applied to such important aspects of life as work, education, and family size?

2. What determines the number of hours an individual works, or whether she chooses to work or not? How do income and substitution effects help us understand why labor supply may not be very responsive to changes in wages?

3. How do economists explain differences in the wages received by people of comparable skills working in different jobs?

4. Why do economists think of education as an investment, and refer to the result as human capital? What role does education play beyond the accumulation of human capital?

5. How do economic factors affect other aspects of family life, such as decisions concerning family size?

UNDERSTANDING THE LABOR SUPPLY DECISION

Patterns of labor supply have changed greatly in the past three decades. While the average work week for a production worker has declined from about 40 hours in 1950 to fewer than 35 hours today, the fraction of women in the labor force has increased enormously. As a result, the typical married household now devotes more hours to work outside the home than it did at the beginning of the century. The number of hours worked in different jobs and industries also varies; as Figure 11.1 shows, miners work an average of over 40 hours per week, for instance, while those in the retail sector work an average of fewer than 30 hours.

THE CHOICE BETWEEN LEISURE AND CONSUMPTION

Economists use the basic model of choice to help understand these patterns of labor supply. The decision about how much labor to supply is a choice between consumption, or income, and leisure: by giving up leisure, a person receives additional income, and therefore increases his consumption, and by working less and giving up some consumption, a person obtains more leisure. There are, of course, exceptions to the rule that when an individual's income increases his consumption increases—for instance, scrooges who simply enjoy accumulating money for its own sake, not for the goods it will buy. But we will ignore these exceptions. And as we saw in Chapter 9, an increase in income does not necessarily translate *immediately* into consumption; the individual

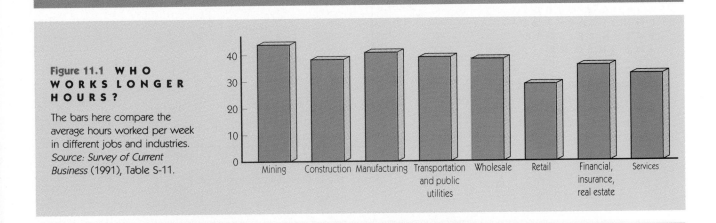

Figure 11.1 WHO WORKS LONGER HOURS?

The bars here compare the average hours worked per week in different jobs and industries. *Source: Survey of Current Business* (1991), Table S-11.

has to decide whether to spend his extra income now or in the future. But in this chapter, we do not make this distinction; we assume that the person spends all of his income, so that an increase in income translates directly into an increase in consumption.

In order to apply the model of choice to the decision between work and leisure, we have to establish that small trade-offs between the two are possible. At first glance, after all, the typical job seems to represent a fixed time requirement. Either you have a job—and you work the 35 or 40 hours a week that it requires—or you don't. Under these circumstances, how can a desire for more income trade itself into a small decrease in the amount of leisure time?

There are a variety of ways in which people can influence how much labor they will supply. Even though many workers may not have discretion as to whether they will work full time, they have some choice in whether or not they will work overtime. In addition, many individuals moonlight; they take up second jobs that provide them with additional income. Most of these jobs—like driving a taxi—provide considerable discretion in the number of hours worked. Hence, even when people do not face a choice at their primary job, they still have choices to make. Further, the fact that jobs differ in their normal work week means that a worker has some flexibility in choosing a job that allows her to work the amount of hours she wishes. Finally, economists believe that the social conventions concerning the "standard" work week—the 40-hour week that has become the 35-hour week—respond over time to the attitudes (preferences) of workers.

Returning to an individual's choice between work and leisure, we can easily apply the analysis of Chapter 8. Figure 11.2 shows the budget constraint of a person named Steve, who earns an hourly wage of $5. Accordingly, for each less hour of leisure that Steve enjoys—for each extra hour that he works—he earns $5 more; that is, his consumption increases by $5. Underlying this budget constraint is his time constraint. He

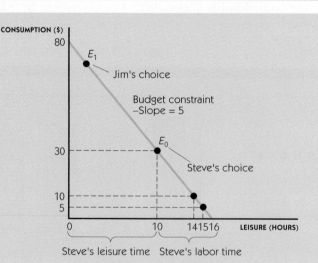

Figure 11.2 A BUDGET CONSTRAINT BE- TWEEN LEISURE AND INCOME

Individuals are willing to trade leisure for an increase in income, and thus in consumption. The budget constraint shows Steve choosing E_0 with 10 hours of daily leisure, 6 hours of work, and $30 in daily wages.

has only so many hours a day, say 16, to spend either working or at leisure. For each extra hour he works, he has 1 less hour of leisure. If he works 1 hour, his income is $5, if he works 2 hours, his income is $10, and so forth. If he works 16 hours—he has no leisure—his income is $5 × 16 = $80. The budget constraint trade-off is $5 per hour.

Steve will choose a point on the budget constraint according to his own preferences, just as he chose between two goods in Chapter 8. He must choose the appropriate trade-off between consumption and leisure. Let's suppose that he chooses point E_0. At E_0, he has 10 hours of leisure, which means that he works 6 hours out of a total available time of 16 hours, and makes $30.

In deciding which of the points along the budget constraint to choose, Steve balances out the marginal benefits of what he can buy with an additional hour's wages with the marginal costs—the value of the hour's worth of leisure that he will have to forgo. Steve and his workaholic brother Jim assess the marginal benefits and marginal costs differently, so Steve chooses point E_0, while his brother chooses point E_1. Jim values the material things in life more and leisure less.

For Steve, at E_0, the marginal benefit of the extra concert tickets or other goods he can buy with the money he earns from working an extra hour just offsets the marginal cost, the extra leisure he has to give up. At points to the left of E_0, Steve has less leisure, so the marginal value of leisure is greater, and he has more goods, so the marginal value of the extra goods he can get is lower. The marginal benefit of working more exceeds the marginal costs, and so he works more—he moves toward E_0. Converse arguments apply to Steve's thinking about points to the right of E_0.

We can use the same kind of reasoning to see why Jim chooses a point to the left of E_0. At E_0, Jim values goods more and leisure less; the marginal benefit of working more exceeds the marginal cost. At E_1, the marginal benefit of working an extra hour (the extra consumption) just offsets the marginal cost.

EFFECTS OF PARALLEL SHIFTS IN THE BUDGET CONSTRAINT

Diagrams like Figure 11.2 not only help to interpret the labor supply decision, they also help in understanding how other sources of income will affect labor supply. Figure 11.3 shows the budget constraint of an individual whose nonwage income has increased, perhaps because he has received an inheritance of stocks and bonds from his parents. These investments produce $20 per day. For any given amount of work he chooses to do, this person can now have a higher level of consumption. His budget constraint shifts out, parallel to the original budget constraint. The level of consumption when the individual does no work—when he enjoys 16 hours of leisure—is his income from nonwage sources. With the initial budget constraint, BC, the level of this income is zero. But with the new budget constraint, B_1C_1, the level of this income is $20.

Normally, as individuals become better off—a situation represented by an outward shift in the budget constraint—they wish to enjoy more of all goods. Leisure, in this context, is very much like any other good, and a shift in the budget constraint will therefore be reflected in an increased demand for leisure; that is, a decrease in labor supply.

Figure 11.3 A PURE INCOME EFFECT ON LABOR SUPPLY

When people become wealthier, the budget constraint shifts up, parallel to the previous constraint, and they will wish to enjoy more of all normal goods. Thus, an increase in wealth will normally lead to a rise in leisure and a decrease in labor supply.

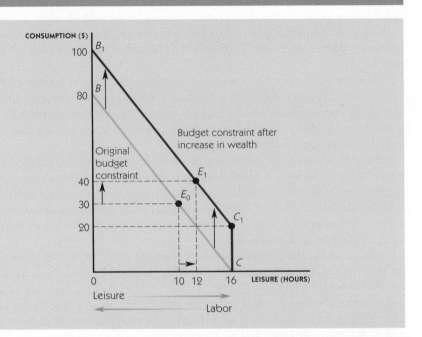

EFFECT OF CHANGES IN WEALTH ON LABOR SUPPLY

Normally, as individuals become better off, their labor supply is decreased. Conversely, as they become worse off, their labor supply is increased.

EFFECTS OF CHANGES IN WAGES: ROTATION OF THE BUDGET CONSTRAINT

An increase in wages is essentially a change in price. It rotates the budget constraint, as illustrated in Figure 11.4. Martha has no income other than from wages. When her wages rise, the slope of the budget constraint is changed; the trade-off between leisure and consumption is altered. Now, for each hour of leisure that Martha gives up, she gets more consumption. The new budget constraint lies outside the old one (except when Martha does no work at all, at point C, in which case the change in the wage rate is irrelevant). Martha is clearly better off after the wage increase.

In Chapter 8, we saw how to separate the effect of a price increase into two parts—an income effect, reflecting the fact that at the higher price the individual's real income is lower; and a substitution effect, reflecting the changed trade-offs. The same concepts

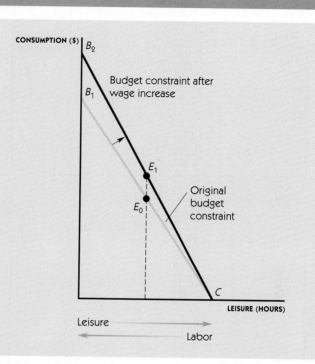

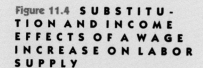

Figure 11.4 SUBSTITUTION AND INCOME EFFECTS OF A WAGE INCREASE ON LABOR SUPPLY

A rising wage rate shifts the budget constraint from B_1C to B_2C. The original leisure-income choice is at point E_0. The income effect of higher wages will lead to more leisure and less work, while the substitution effect will lead to more work and less leisure.

apply to the effect of a wage increase. At the higher wage, at each level of work, Martha is better off than she was with the lower wage; she wishes to enjoy more leisure and work less. This is the income effect, which induces a reduction in the labor supply. The better off an individual is, the more leisure she would like to enjoy. Leisure is a normal good. At the same time, because the wage is higher, Martha obtains a larger increase in consumption for each extra hour worked, and so she is motivated to work more. This is the substitution effect, which stimulates an increase in labor supply.

Before the wage increase, Martha balanced her individual preferences in the trade-off between income (consumption) and leisure, and chose point E_0. After the change in wages, she will choose some point on the new budget constraint. Will she supply more, or less, labor? While the income effect of a wage increase induces Martha to work less, the substitution effect motivates her to work more. Depending on the relative size of the income and substitution effects, the net effect of an increase in the wage rate may be positive, negative, or zero. For some individuals, the income effect will be larger than the substitution effect; these people will respond to a wage increase by working less. For others, the income effect will be smaller; these people will work more when their wages rise.

THE LABOR SUPPLY CURVE

The labor supply curve can be developed from this model of choice in the same way that the demand curve for CDs was developed in Chapter 8. As the wage level changes, an individual chooses the amount of labor that will be supplied, that is, the number

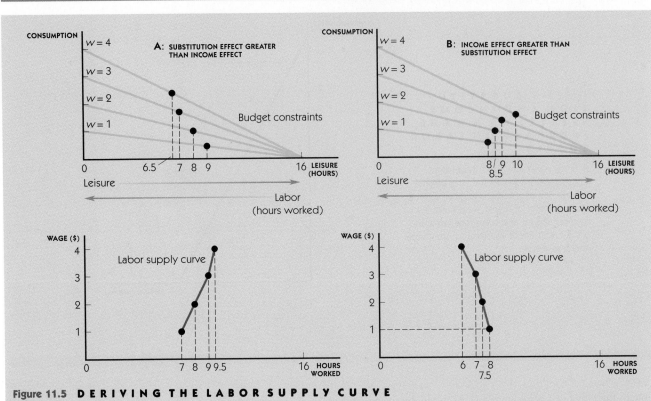

Figure 11.5 DERIVING THE LABOR SUPPLY CURVE

Panel A shows the case where the substitution effect exceeds the income effect by just a bit, so increases in wages lead to only a small change in labor supply, and the labor supply curve is almost vertical.

Panel B illustrates the case where the income effect exceeds the substitution effect, so increases in wages lead to a decline in labor supply, and the labor supply curve is downward sloping.

of hours that he would like to work. Figure 11.5 plots two versions of the labor supply curve, or hours worked, for each wage level. (As the vertical axis represented price in the demand curve for CDs, so here the vertical axis represents wage.) Panel A shows the case where the substitution effect exceeds the income effect by just a bit, so that the labor supply curve is almost vertical. This is typical of the labor supply decision for adult men in the short run. There is only a slight increase in labor supply (hours worked) when men's wages are increased. We measure the magnitude of the response of labor supply to wages by the **elasticity of labor supply,** or the percentage change in labor supplied resulting from a 1 percent change in the wage. Thus, in panel A, the labor supply elasticity is very low; when there is a 1 percent increase in wages, men increase their working hours only slightly.

It is also possible that the income effect could dominate the substitution effect, so that as the wage increases, the amount of labor supplied actually decreases. The long-run labor supply for men seems to accord best with panel B, where the labor supply elasticity is *negative*. As wages have increased during this century, hours worked have decreased.

Figure 11.6 illustrates an interesting combination case. At a low wage rate, the substitution effect dominates the income effect, so that as the wage increases, labor supply increases; while at high wages, the income effect dominates, so that labor supply decreases. Because of the shape of this curve, it is called a **backward-bending labor supply curve.** Doctors, dentists, and other high-income professionals who work only a four-day week may be evidence of a labor supply curve that is backward bending at high-income levels.

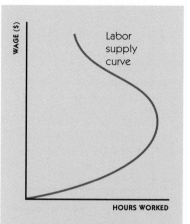

Figure 11.6 BACKWARD-BENDING LABOR SUPPLY CURVE

In this figure, the substitution effect dominates the income effect at low wages, so that the labor supply curve is upward sloping; the substitution effect roughly equals the income effect at an intermediate wage level, so the labor supply curve is close to vertical; and the income effect dominates the substitution effect at high wages, so that the labor supply is downward sloping over that range. Thus, the labor supply curve bends backward.

WAGE CHANGES AND LABOR SUPPLY

As wages rise, individuals become better off. This income effect induces them to work less. Offsetting this is the substitution effect—the greater return to working provides an incentive to work longer hours. Either effect may dominate—the quantity of labor supplied may increase or decrease with wage increases.

TAX POLICY AND LABOR SUPPLY

The question of what effect a change in wages has on labor supply has important policy implications. For example, one often hears it said that an increase in taxes discourages people from working. An increase in tax rates is equivalent to a decrease in wages, since it decreases the after-tax wage received by the worker. But if the labor supply curve is backward bending, then an increase in the income tax and its accompanying reduction in the after-tax wage can actually increase the labor supply.

Differences in views about the relative magnitudes of the income and substitution effects on labor supply have played an important role in recent debates over tax policy. How would workers respond to a tax increase? We could survey them, asking, for instance, doctors or taxi drivers how the lower wages resulting from an increase in income tax has affected their decisions about how much to work. They will not say, "I work more because the income effect outweighs the substitution effect" or "I work less because the substitution effect outweighs the income effect." They say things like "I have to work longer hours to maintain the living standard to which I have become accustomed" or "I work less, because it doesn't pay to work so hard." But economists can interpret these different responses in the analytical framework of income and substitution effects. Economists are interested not in how any particular individual responds, but what happens *on average*, and what happens to particular groups of people within the economy. Women may react differently from men, and the elderly differently from the young.

To study how the market as a whole is affected by a tax increase, we need to look at the **market labor supply curve,** illustrated in Figure 11.7. Panel A shows an individual's labor supply curve; the market labor supply curve in panel B is found by adding up the labor supply curves of all the individuals in the economy (just as we saw, in Chapter 4, that the market demand for any good is found by adding up the demand curves of

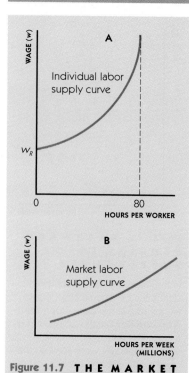

Figure 11.7 THE MARKET LABOR SUPPLY CURVE

Panel A shows an individual's labor supply curve. By summing labor supply curves for all individuals, we obtain the market labor supply curve, shown in panel B.

each person). In the curve illustrated in panel A, one point stands out—the wage at which the supply curve hits the vertical axis, w_R. At wages lower than this, people decide simply not to work; they do not *participate* in the market. As we move along the market labor supply curve, the total supply (say, total number of hours all individuals together would like to work) changes for two reasons: each person changes how much he would like to work, and the number of people who would like to work changes. Since for many jobs discretion over the number of hours worked may be limited, the effects of taxes on the level of labor force participation may be more important than the effects on the number of hours each person wishes to work.

In 1987, marginal tax rates were substantially reduced. A few economists and politicians argued that the substitution effect would be enormous. Their view was that labor supply would respond so strongly to lower tax rates that tax revenues would actually increase. For the most part, however, economists argued that most of the available evidence suggested that the substitution effect would not be so strong and that the labor supply would not increase by very much. Their predictions were borne out.

LABOR FORCE PARTICIPATION

As we have seen, the decision about how much labor to supply can be divided into two parts: whether to work and, if so, how much to work. For men, the first question has traditionally had a quick and obvious answer. Unless they were very wealthy, they have had to work to support themselves. There are, admittedly, other situations; a man who is laid off and is receiving unemployment compensation must decide whether to look for another job immediately, or wait until either he gets recalled to his former job or his unemployment compensation expires. But such cases are more the exception than the rule. Thus, for most men, a change in the wage does not affect their decision of whether to work. It affects only their decision about how many hours to work, and even this effect is small.

Most women work for pay now too. Women, however, have faced different social expectations from those facing men. Only a few decades ago, not only was there some question as to whether women should work, the social presumption was that women with small children would drop out of the labor market. And many mothers did not reenter the market even after their children had grown. Whether by social convention or by choice, most women seemed almost indifferent about whether they worked. Small changes in the wage rate thus had the potential of causing large changes in the fraction of women who worked. The labor supply curve for women appeared to be very flat, or elastic. Some economists have estimated a female labor supply elasticity as large as .9; that is, a 1 percent increase in wages leads to a .9 percent increase in labor supply.

Today the traditional presumptions about the role of women have changed. Most women without small children are in the labor market, and many with children leave only for relatively short periods of time. The labor force is defined to include those who either have jobs or are looking for one—it is broader than just those with jobs, but not as broad as the entire population. In 1890, only 17 percent of all women were in the labor force; the figure now stands at 57 percent. Figure 11.8 shows the dramatic increase in female labor force participation during the past quarter century.

This change can be viewed partly as a *shift* in the labor supply curve and partly as a *movement* along it. Figure 11.9 shows how the number of women participating in the labor force increases with the wage rate. Such a curve is called the labor force participation curve. If all women supplied a fixed number of hours (say, 35 hours per week), then

Figure 11.8 FEMALE LABOR FORCE PARTICIPA- TION

While only one-third of all women were in the labor force in 1950, more than half are in the labor force today. *Source: Economic Report of the President* (1991), Table B-36.

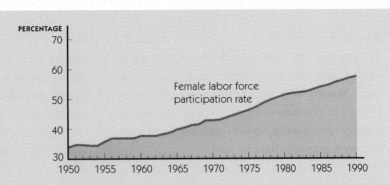

the labor force participation curve and the female labor supply curve would look the same.

Job opportunities for women have increased enormously in the past thirty years, and relative wages have risen. Thus, the return to working has increased; the opportunity cost of being out of the labor force has gone up. Even in the absence of any other social changes, economists would predict that these factors would have led to an increased labor force participation by women. The increased participation of women as a result of the higher wages they are receiving today is a movement along the labor force participation curve. This change is seen in Figure 11.9 as the increase in labor force participation from L_0 to L_1.

But two other changes have contributed to the trend as well. The first is that beginning around 1973, (real) wages stopped growing at the rate they had been during the period following World War II. Individuals and families had come to expect regular increases in their income. When these increases stopped, they felt the loss. It was not that their income had actually declined, only that it had not grown as much as they had come to expect. This development encouraged many married women to take part-time or full-time jobs as a way of keeping the family income increasing.

The second change is a change in attitudes, both on the part of women, concerning their desires for work, and on the part of employers. Outright discrimination against women was barred by federal law in 1963. Large employers adopted affirmative action programs, in which they made a commitment to increase the number of women, particularly in managerial and more highly skilled jobs. Enrollments of women in professional schools increased dramatically, reflecting changed attitudes. These changes represent a shift of the labor force participation curve for women. Figure 11.9 shows the effect of the shift in the curve in the increased labor force participation from L_1 to L_2.

The fact that relatively small changes in the wages received by women can have large effects on the fraction of women who work means that the tax system can have significant effects on the decision of women to work. A look at the U.S. income tax makes it easy to see both why the labor supply curve for women is relatively flat and why taxes can have such a large effect on female labor force participation. For a family of four, no tax is imposed on approximately the first $15,000 of earned income. But if the household's

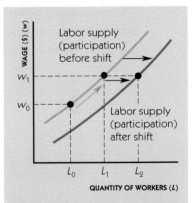

Figure 11.9 EXPLAINING CHANGES IN LABOR FORCE PARTICIPA- TION

The increased labor force participation of women results in part from a movement along the supply curve resulting from higher wages (the movement from L_0 to L_1), and in part from a shift of the supply curve itself (the movement from L_1 to L_2.).

CLOSE-UP: THE MIXED LEGACY OF COMPARABLE WORTH

The pay of an average female worker is about 30 percent less than the pay of an average male worker. Moreover, many women feel that they have been guided and pushed into a "pink-collar ghetto" of predominantly female jobs, like secretaries or receptionists, where wages are lower than in comparable jobs held by men.

One way to address this complaint would be to raise wage levels in the jobs traditionally held by women. In 1986, the state of Washington decided to do just this. It assigned to every state job a certain number of points in each of four categories: knowledge and skills required, mental demands, accountability, and work conditions. These points would be used to find the "comparable worth" of each job, and wages would then be adjusted accordingly.

When the rankings were completed, there were many cases of male-dominated jobs with fewer points but higher wages. For example, the predominantly male job of delivery truck driver received 97 total points, while the predominantly female job of a "grade III" secretary received 197 total points. However, truck drivers were then being paid about one-fourth more than secretaries.

To adjust wages toward comparable worth, as defined by total points, no one's salary was cut. Instead, cost-of-living adjustments and raises were concentrated on "underpaid" jobs. By the end of the 1980s, the gap between the average wages of men and women in Washington state government had been cut to almost nothing. Many women working for the state also reported that their work was being treated with greater respect.

So far, so good. But although the forces of supply and demand had led to a situation that Washington state wanted to change, those market forces cannot be simply ignored. Wages for Washington state workers in some male-dominated jobs have fallen nearly one-third below what private sector com-

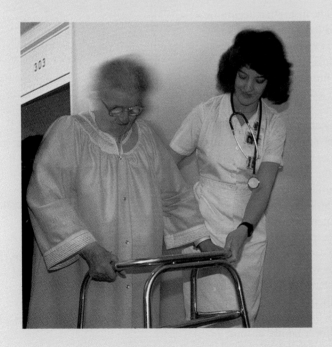

panies are offering, so men are quitting. The state has had to break the comparable worth guidelines and offer special raises to keep and attract workers in certain areas. Many men do not see why their "worth" should be determined by a survey or a personnel consultant, rather than by the forces of supply and demand. Moreover, since comparable worth has tended to make wages higher in jobs dominated by women, women have less economic incentive to leave those jobs, and their separation into a pink-collar ghetto has continued.

Washington will periodically review its comparable worth plan. The 62,000 state employees and labor economists everywhere will be watching.

Sources: Barbara R. Bergmann, "Does the Market for Women's Labor Need Fixing?" *Journal of Economic Perspectives* (Winter 1989) 3:43–60; Peter T. Kilborn, "Wage Gap Between Sexes Is Cut in Test, but at a Price," *New York Times,* May 31, 1990, p. A1.

primary breadwinner earns more than this, then every dollar the spouse earns is taxed. In fact, if the primary breadwinner earns more than about $50,000, the household faces a federal income tax rate of 28 percent (not to speak of the Social Security and state income taxes).

Not only does a household face high taxes on the additional income when both adults work, but these families have some additional costs, like child care or the higher food bills from eating out or buying frozen dinners. Between the higher tax rate and the fact that much of the extra income may go to cover the extra expenses, the financial incentive for secondary earners to work may be low, and thus changes in the after-tax wage rate can have large effects on the number of secondary earners who decide to work. Again, a sobering fact of American life is that the spouse looking for the household's second job is usually the wife.

Before 1986, the tax laws recognized this problem, and did not tax the wages of the second worker in a family as heavily. But this tax provision created inequities as well. Consider a single-earner family where the father is working two jobs, one full-time and one part-time, for a total of 60 hours a week. Compare that with a two-earner family where the two wage earners' combined hours equal 60 hours a week. Why should the two-earner family deserve a lower tax rate than the man working overtime? Arguments like this one led to the repeal in 1986 of the tax provision that benefited the second wage earner in a family.

THE RETIREMENT DECISION

Retirement is another important aspect of the labor force participation decision. In 1900, a 40-year-old American man could expect to live until age 68. At the same time, however, 68 percent of the men over age 65 were in the labor force. These statistics meant that the typical worker stayed on the job until he died, or until he was too sick to work.

By 1950, the situation had changed. Life expectancy for a 40-year-old man had risen to 71 years, but only 41 percent of the men over 65 were in the labor force. Retirement was becoming a popular option, if you lived long enough. Today the average 40-year-old man can expect to live to be 74, but only 16 percent of the men over 65 are working or looking for work. In addition, only 68 percent of the men between the ages of 55 and 64 are in the labor force. Retirement after 65 has become the expectation, and retirement before 65 is becoming ever more common. The number of middle-aged retirees is expected to continue to grow.

These retirement decisions too can be understood in terms of a basic economic model. Increased lifetime wealth has led individuals to choose more leisure over their lifetime. The fact that when people are better off they wish to enjoy more leisure is, as we saw earlier, the income effect. The decision to retire earlier can be thought of as a decision to enjoy more leisure; indeed, it makes sense for people to choose more leisure in the later years of life, when their productivity is relatively low and their wages are not going to increase much further.

At the same time, the fact that wages today are much higher than they were fifty years ago means that it is more costly for people to retire early—the amount of consumption (income) they have to give up is larger. This is the substitution effect. In fact, improved health has meant that workers' productivity probably declines less rapidly with age than it did a half century ago. Evidently, for many men, the income effect dominates the substitution effect.

HUMAN CAPITAL AND EDUCATION

The nation's output depends not only on the number of hours people work but also on how productive those hours are. One of the important determinants of workers' productivity—and therefore wages—is education.

By staying in school longer, which usually means delaying entry into the labor force, people can increase their expected annual income. In addition, working *harder* in school and giving up leisure may result in better grades and skills, which in turn will tend to result in higher wages in the future. Thus, students face a trade-off between leisure today and consumption, or income, in the future.

Spending a year in college has its obvious costs, like fees for tuition, room, and board. But there are also opportunity costs, such as the income that would have been received from taking a job. These opportunity costs are as much a part of the costs of going to school as are any direct tuition payments. Economists say that the investment in education produces **human capital,** making an analogy to the **physical capital** investments that businesses make in plant and equipment. Human capital is developed by formal schooling, on-the-job learning, and many investments of time and money that parents make in their children.

The United States invests an enormous amount in human capital. The investment is financed both publicly and privately. The local, state, and federal governments alone spend about $.25 trillion a year on education. Government expenditures on primary and secondary education are the largest category of expenditure at the local and state levels, accounting for more than 20 percent of total expenditures. In fact, human capital is actually more significant than physical capital. Some economists estimate that as much as two-thirds to three-fourths of all capital is human capital.

The enormous increase in education in the past fifty years is illustrated in Table 11.1. Among those 65 and older, less than a quarter have at least one year of college; almost half of those in the 35–44 age group do.

Table 11.1 YEARS OF SCHOOLING BY AGE

Age group (in 1989)	% with less than high school degree	% with only a high school degree	% with at least one college year
25–29	14.5	41.7	43.8
30–34	12.4	41.1	46.5
35–44	13.3	37.3	49.4
45–54	21.6	40.5	37.9
55–64	30.9	39.6	29.5
65 and older	45.1	33.2	21.7

EDUCATION AND ECONOMIC TRADE-OFFS

The production possibilities curve introduced in Chapter 2 can illustrate how decisions concerning investments in human capital are made. To accomplish this, we use the same trick that we employed in Chapter 9 of dividing an individual's life into two periods. There, the two periods were "working years" and "retirement years," but now our two periods are "youth" and "later working years." Figure 11.10 depicts the relationship between consumption in youth and in later life. As the individual gives up consumption in his youth, by staying in school longer, his expected future consumption increases because he can expect his income to go up. The curve has been drawn to show diminishing returns: spending more on education today (reducing consumption) raises future income, but each additional investment in education provides a smaller and smaller return.

Point A represents the case where Everett is a full-time student through four years of college, with little income until graduation (his youth) but with a high income in later life. Point B represents the consequences of dropping out of school after high school. When he does this, Everett has a higher income in his youth but a lower income in later life. Other possible points between A and B represent cases where Everett drops out of college after one or two years.

For individuals who can make the grade, college education pays off, at least on average. Today the average wage of workers with at least four years of college is about two-thirds greater than that of workers whose formal education ended with a high school diploma.

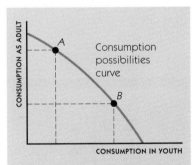

Figure 11.10 EDUCATION AND THE TRADE-OFF BETWEEN CURRENT AND FUTURE CONSUMPTION

Point A represents a choice of a reduced income and better education in the present, with a higher income in the future. Point B represents the choice of higher income and less education now, with a lower level of income in the future.

THE WIDENING WAGE GAP

Those who have a college education are paid more on average than those who fail to complete high school. Because unskilled workers generally cannot perform the same jobs as skilled workers, the wages of the two groups can be thought of as determined in separate labor markets, as illustrated in Figure 11.11. Panel A shows the demand and supply curves of unskilled workers, panel B those of skilled workers. The figure shows the equilibrium wage for skilled workers as being higher than that for unskilled workers.

What happens if a change in technology shifts the demand curve for skilled labor to the right, to DS_1, and the demand curve for unskilled labor to the left, to DU_1? The wages of unskilled workers will decrease from wu_0 to wu_1, and those of skilled workers will increase from ws_0 to ws_1. In the long run, this increased wage gap induces more people to acquire skills, so the supply of unskilled workers shifts to the left, and that of skilled workers shifts to the right. As a result, the wage of unskilled workers rises from wu_1 to wu_2, and that of skilled workers falls from ws_1 to ws_2. These long-run supply responses thus dampen the short-run movements in wages.

During the 1970s and 1980s, there were dramatic changes in technology, which resulted in real wages (wages adjusted for changes in the cost of living) of unskilled workers falling dramatically, by as much as 30 percent. Wage rates of skilled workers, while they remained stagnant for most of the 1970s, have increased substantially since then. Thus, there has been a dramatic increase in the skilled-unskilled worker wage gap. While the decline in unskilled wages seems to have been arrested, the gap remains large.

It is too early to tell whether the predicted shifts in supply, which result from unskilled workers' acquiring more skills and which should reduce the wage gap, will in fact occur, and if they do occur, how long it will take for the wage gap to be reduced to the levels that prevailed in the 1960s. Meanwhile, policymakers are concerned about the social consequences of this apparent large increase in inequality.

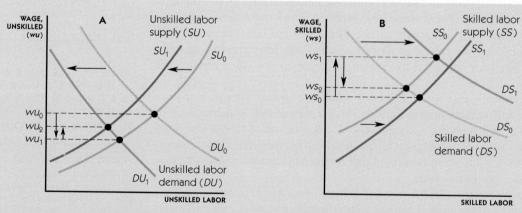

Figure 11.11 **THE MARKET FOR SKILLED AND UNSKILLED LABOR**

In panel A, the invention of a new machine shifts the demand curve for unskilled labor to the left, and reduces wages from wu_0 to wu_1. In panel B, the new machine shifts the demand curve for skilled labor out to the right, and thus raises wages from ws_0 to ws_1. Over time, this increased difference in wages may lead the supply curve for unskilled labor to shift back to the left, raising wages for unskilled labor somewhat from wu_1 to wu_2, and the supply curve for skilled labor to shift out to the right, reducing wages for skilled labor from ws_1 to ws_2.

Is the United States investing enough in education? American students at the elementary and secondary levels spend a third less time in the classroom than Japanese students of the same age. Recent tests suggest that American students are significantly behind not only Japanese students but also students in many European countries in mathematics. Average scores on the Scholastic Aptitude Test and many other standardized tests actually declined from the late 1960s to the early 1980s. There is concern that an undereducated America is ill-equipped for the challenge of outproducing foreign competitors.

There are bright spots in this picture, however. American universities attract the brightest students from every continent to their graduate schools. America can claim at least seven of the top ten universities in the world—there are few other industries in which its share of the top quality production is so high. At the same time, a larger share of American students go on to education past the high school level than in almost any other country. In the United States, more than a quarter of college-age Americans are enrolled in college; the corresponding figure for other countries is about a third to half of that of the United States.

There are two explanations frequently put forward for the plight of America's elementary and secondary education: Americans spend too little, and the school systems are not organized in a way to get as much out of each dollar spent as they should.

Level of Expenditures In some areas of the country, growth in the student population and concern about the size of government has led to a decline in real expenditures per student (that is, expenditures taking into account the effects of inflation).

However, during the 1960s and 1970s generally, real expenditures per student climbed dramatically in public and private schools, while average class sizes declined. The United States also spends more on a per-pupil basis than most of its competitors. Thus, spending more money might help, but it is inaccurate to say that a decline in spending on education has generally occurred, or that the plight would be cured by an increase in expenditure alone.

Organization James Coleman, a sociologist at the University of Chicago, has claimed that the problem with American schools is rooted in how they are organized. He showed that private schools (most of which are Catholic parochial schools) were able to achieve better student performance—and at the same time were more racially integrated—than public schools at roughly the same level of per-pupil expenditures. Private schools, he argued, were more successful in creating a favorable environment for learning.

One reason cited for this greater success is the greater autonomy in many private schools. Principal, teachers, and parents all feel they have more say in how the school is run, and their active involvement in the school leads to more learning by students. By contrast, control of most public school districts is vested in a school administration that often appears remote and more concerned with issues of budget and government regulations than with the children themselves.

Proposed Reforms A variety of reforms have been proposed to improve the quality of education in America. While more spending would undoubtedly help, critics of America's educational system see a need for more fundamental structural changes.

One proposed reform is a voucher system. In such a system, the government would give each student a certificate worth, say, $5,000, which could be used at any accredited school, public or private. Advocates claim that the competition among private schools and between public and private schools would improve the quality of all schools. Critics worry that the main benefits would accrue to children of the educated and highly motivated, who would be able to make better-informed judgments. In addition, critics raise the concern that some schools would skim off the intelligent and well-behaved students, while others would be stuck with the problem students. They contend that the observed superior performance of private schools is a mirage: it could not be duplicated on a national basis. In their view, it is a consequence of the fact that parents who have chosen to spend the extra money to send their children to private schools are more committed to education, and of the ability of private schools to expel students who misbehave. These critics further argue that there is a positive social value to having children forced to interact with a broad range of other students.

Many Americans adhere to the principle that everyone should play on as level a playing field as possible. Such people believe that while obviously some individuals are by virtue of their birth more fortunate than others—they may have greater athletic prowess, intellectual abilities, or wealthier parents—a major objective of the educational system is to equalize the life chances of all individuals. They worry that a voucher system might help reinforce the inequities and inequalities already present in American society.

Another scheme, somewhat less radical, focuses on how public schools are run. This plan encourages decentralization, which means giving the individual schools in a public system more autonomy. Principals, for instance, would be given considerable discretion in hiring and firing teachers in their schools, in allocating their budgets, and in deciding on curricular matters. Several states, such as Min-

nesota and New Mexico, are currently experimenting with different forms of decentralization.

Finally, to provide greater motivation for teachers, some states are looking for ways to reward excellence in teaching—for instance, by providing good teachers with public recognition or, more concretely, merit pay. Teachers' unions have often resisted proposals for merit pay. Usually the judgment about whether a teacher is particularly meritorious will be made by the principal, and there is concern about the capriciousness of these judgments, the discretionary power given to the principal, and the loss of seniority-based, union-controlled advancement and pay rules. On the other hand, if the judgment is based on the performance of students on standardized tests, teachers will be induced to teach so that students will perform well on the tests, diverting attention away from more fundamental objectives of schools, such as encouraging creativity, many of which cannot be easily measured by standardized tests.

Each of these approaches has potential risks and benefits. The success of each is uncertain. The experiments currently under way in various states and school districts should help provide some better answers to the question of how to improve America's system of education.

LOOKING BEYOND THE BASIC MODEL: CREDENTIALS COMPETITION

The basic competitive model, which is the focus of this part of the book, assumes that firms know how productive each worker is, and that competition ensures that wages paid correspond to each worker's productivity. The model also assumes that education results in higher wages because education results in increased productivity.

In fact, however, when employers hire workers, they cannot know all the pertinent characteristics of potential employees. As economists would put it, their information is not perfect. They know that some candidates will be far more productive than others, but they simply cannot tell who these candidates are. To make their hiring decisions, they have to use whatever information is available.

Education helps employers identify whom they should hire. In some jobs, what is important is brains, the ability to think quickly. Students who have done well in college taking difficult courses have demonstrated that they have the kinds of minds these employers want. From this perspective, what education does is not so much *increase* productivity but identify which people are more productive or have certain scarce abilities. Economists say that schools **screen** individuals, and that the level of education **signals** their abilities. Those who graduate from college get higher pay. The higher pay reflects their higher productivity; but the higher productivity is not acquired in college. Colleges simply identify talent.

Of course, what students learn at college does increase their productivity. College is not *just* a screening device. But there are some striking pieces of evidence suggesting just how important the screening and signaling role is. The discussion of investing in education and human capital so far has assumed (as the basic model would suggest)

Table 11.2 **RETURNS TO EDUCATION**

Level of education	Percent increase of average wage over preceding level of education
No high school diploma	—
High school diploma	14.2
1–3 years of college	14.8
College degree	37.6

Source: K. Murphy and F. Welch, "Wage Premiums for College Graduates," *Educational Researcher* (May 1989) 18:17–26.

that this form of investment has diminishing returns: as a student spends more and more years in school (forgoes more and more current consumption), the returns continue to add up, but the returns from additional years are less than the returns from earlier years.

However, closer examination of the year-by-year returns to education suggests that the final year of high school or college produces much higher returns than any other year. This seems a bit odd; one would expect that learning is a continuous and gradual process, implying a smoothly increasing relationship between years of education and earnings. Nevertheless, the evidence shown in Table 11.2 is well documented. What it seems to demonstrate is that there are definite increasing returns to *completing* college. A similar study of high school education shows that the return (percentage increase in wage) to the final year of school is three times that of the preceding (eleventh) year.[1]

There is another, related puzzle: if individuals who go to school receive higher wages because they have learned more, why does it seem to make so little difference what they study? Art history and music appreciation may enhance the quality of your life, but do they really contribute significantly to your productivity in the purchasing department or sales department of a company? Yet those who major in art history or other liberal arts subjects experience an increase in their wages just as do those who major in subjects more directly related to their future careers, such as engineering, nursing, or business.

One explanation for these facts is the one we have already learned, that education performs a screening and signaling role for employers. On average, those individuals who complete four years of college are better bets for, say, managerial jobs than those who drop out after three. Thus, employers look for a high school or a college degree not just because of the skills that job candidates acquire in their senior year, but because the completed degree is a signal that that person may be more productive. Completing four years of college shows a kind of perseverance that is highly valued in the business

[1] A. Weiss, "High School Graduation, Performance, and Wages," *Journal of Political Economy* (1988) 96:785–820.

community. Brighter students find it easier to do college work, and hence have less incentive to drop out. Students who know that they will not be able to make the grade may quit, figuring it is better not to waste another year; among those who drop out, there are likely to be some who would not have graduated even if they had tried.

Of course, employers know that not everyone who drops out after three years of college is a dud. Some of those who have not gone to college have made this decision not for lack of ability but from lack of resources. And not everyone who completes four years is a winner. But employers must make judgments on the basis of the limited information available. On average, completing four years of college is a good signal.

Such signals are important because it is costly to give a worker a try; the employer must advertise, search, interview, hire, and train each employee. Hiring a dud means wasted training expenses and having to go through the hiring procedure again. Hence, the employer is going to give a chance to the person she thinks has the greatest chance of succeeding; that is, the worker with the "best" signal or credential.

Naturally, students know that employers interpret the completion of a college education in this way. They are therefore induced to stay in school longer than they might otherwise; that is, individuals may stay in school not so much to acquire productive skills as to convince potential employers that they are among the more productive members of society, deserving of high wages. Get that diploma! Get that degree! This trend gives rise to what has been called the **credentials competition.** The more able individuals have an incentive to try to distinguish themselves, to persuade potential employers that they are truly among the gifted. To signal their higher ability, they stay in school still longer, acquiring still more advanced degrees. The increased qualifications required for many jobs over the past several decades may reflect this credentials competition as much as it reflects the increased knowledge required for performing these jobs.

JOB CHOICE

Choosing a job is not easy. Other things being equal, we would all prefer a higher salary to a lower salary. In general, however, other things are not equal. There are many characteristics of a job that are important. Some jobs have a longer work week, others a shorter work week. Some jobs require a higher intensity of work, while others are more relaxed. Teachers have long summer vacations. Surgeons work an average of thirty-five hours a week. Other kinds of doctors work eighty-hour weeks. Besides the salary, jobs offer different levels of fringe benefits such as health insurance and vacation time. Some jobs offer a chance to travel, while in others, you report to the same desk every day. People often care about how stimulating the job is, how pleasant the work surroundings are, and how much discretion they have over how they spend their time.

Why do jobs requiring roughly comparable skills often pay quite different wages? There are important **nonpecuniary,** or nonmoney, attributes of a job. In some cases, what is attractive to one individual may be unattractive to another. Some people like to be told what to do, others like to make their own decisions. Some individuals might like the radio on while they work, others might find it distracting. In other cases, there is a fair amount of agreement; most people would find garbage collecting unattractive, for example. Jobs that are generally less attractive must pay **compensating differentials,** which is the name economists give to the higher wages needed to offset unattractive nonpecuniary attributes.

Compensating differentials are like the premium returns paid on riskier or less liquid investments, which we encountered in Chapter 9. People who find these jobs less unattractive or who value income more may choose such jobs. Naturally, the fact that a compensating differential exists does not mean that workers in distasteful occupations will earn more than *anyone* else—sanitation workers will still be paid less than psychiatrists. A compensating differential in a job means only that workers are paid more in that job than they would be if they took another job available to someone with their skills.

RISK

One example of a nonpecuniary characteristic is the riskiness of a job. Some jobs, such as underground mining or construction work on tall buildings, have greater risks of injury or death than others do, like desk jobs. Workers who face these risks generally receive a compensating differential, to compensate them for the risks they bear.

The risk of injury on a job is not the only risk workers face. They also face the risk of being laid off. In some occupations, such as construction work, this risk is greater than in others, and the wages they pay should adjust accordingly. The fact that employers who provide less job security will have to pay higher wages is an incentive for employers to provide stable employment for their workers.

In fact, there is widespread public concern that the market mechanism does not work well in providing compensation for the risks of unemployment. Hence, the American government as well as the governments of most developed countries have unemployment compensation programs.

Increases in job security are not without their costs, however. Guaranteeing an individual a job, or making firing difficult, reduces the threat an employer can use to motivate workers. For some people—particularly those for whom promotion potential is limited—the threat of being fired may be an effective incentive device. It has long been argued, for example, that the job security the government provides its workers in the civil service accounts for the low level of effort that is often evidenced.

FAMILY DECISIONS AND THE LONG-RUN SUPPLY OF LABOR

The number of births today will have a powerful impact on the number of workers available in the next generation. It may seem implausible that economic factors have a powerful effect on the decision to have children, but there is strong evidence that they do.

Imagine the scene. A romantic, candlelit dinner. A newly married couple are discussing their future. These two know about family planning and want to make a rational

CLOSE-UP: ECONOMIC INCENTIVES FOR PARENTHOOD

Birthrates in Europe have fallen so low that the population of the European nations is likely to begin shrinking. It takes an average of 2.1 children per woman of childbearing age to keep the population at a steady level, and as the table here shows, only Ireland among European countries exceeds that rate. Meanwhile, birthrates in many African nations are three times as high. Of course, many cultural and historical factors go to make up these differences, but economists also argue that economic factors play a role.

In relatively poor countries, children are a source of labor for the family when they are young and a source of social security for aged parents. But as a society grows wealthier, moves away from a reliance on farming, and establishes systems of pensions and social security, the economic benefits of having children decrease while the opportunity costs rise. In nations around the world, birthrates tend to fall as people become wealthier.

Economists who study the labor market in Europe have pointed out that unless other factors intervene, the number of adult workers in Europe soon will not match the expected demand of business for labor at current wages. Employers in many European countries are already reporting that it is difficult to find workers for low-paid jobs like food servers and agricultural workers. If European wages rise sharply in all industries because of a lack of workers, it will push up costs for European companies and make it harder for them to compete in world markets.

One solution to the labor shortage problem would be immigration from African nations with higher birthrates. But while such immigration might be economically beneficial for all parties, it is often politically unpopular in Europe, usually from concerns over an influx of people from a different culture. France has attempted to implement a more direct solution, where mothers receive substantial welfare payments and tax breaks as an incentive to have more children. But so far, at least, the birthrate in France has remained low.

Source: Alan Riding, "Western Europe, Its Births Falling, Wonders Who'll Do All the Work," *New York Times,* July 22, 1990, p. A1.

European nations	Birthrate[a]	African nations	Birthrate[a]
Ireland	2.3	Ethiopia	7.5
United Kingdom	1.8	Niger	7.1
France	1.8	Mali	7.0
Spain	1.6	Somalia	6.8
Belgium	1.6	Tanzania	6.7
Netherlands	1.6	Nigeria	6.6
Greece	1.6	Burkina Faso	6.5
Portugal	1.6	Sudan	6.4
Germany	1.5	Mozambique	6.3
Denmark	1.5	Zaire	6.0
Italy	1.3	Chad	5.9

Source: World Development Report (1990), Table 27. Data are for 1988.
[a] Average number of children per woman.

decision about the size of their family. As their discussion of the shared anticipation of the joys of parenthood progresses, they push their plates away and bring out their yellow legal pads and calculators. Naturally, they have both taken economics.

They calculate that with each child, the wife will be out of the labor force for a total of nine months—three months before the birth of the baby, six months after. Fortunately, her job offers her the flexibility to take a nine-month unpaid leave and then to return. Since her monthly wage is $2,000, each baby costs $18,000—not including hospital and doctor bills. Then there are the costs of clothes and food over the ensuing eighteen years, and the bill for a college education looming at the end. Fortunately, they both remember about discounted present value (and feel gratified that they remembered to bring their calculators to the table).

The couple recall a study that showed that women with children earn lower wages than those without, perhaps because these women cannot devote as much attention to the job, perhaps because employers discriminate against such women. But since they feel confident that her employer is not the sort of person to discriminate, and she feels confident in her abilities to focus her attention, they decide not to make any adjustment for future reductions in wages. Eventually, they calculate that the present discounted value of the costs of a child is $60,000. They then discuss alternative ways in which $60,000 might be spent, and they recall the law of diminishing returns. After carefully balancing the costs and benefits of each additional child, they decide to have two children, but agree that if there are any major changes in economic circumstances, particularly those that affect the cost of having a child, they will have another romantic dinner to reassess their situation.

In case you have any doubt, this is *not* how the typical American family makes decisions about children. But economists argue that, though most families may only be vaguely aware of it, economic considerations do intrude even into these most personal decisions. Economics cannot explain why one family has one child while another family has three. Economists have observed, however, that women with higher real wages are,

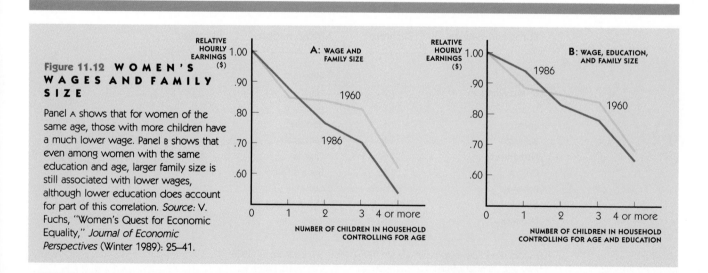

Figure 11.12 WOMEN'S WAGES AND FAMILY SIZE

Panel A shows that for women of the same age, those with more children have a much lower wage. Panel B shows that even among women with the same education and age, larger family size is still associated with lower wages, although lower education does account for part of this correlation. *Source:* V. Fuchs, "Women's Quest for Economic Equality," *Journal of Economic Perspectives* (Winter 1989): 25–41.

on average, associated with smaller families. This is illustrated in Figure 11.12, where, in panel A, we see that for women of the same age, those with more children have a much lower wage. The figure also shows that while this effect decreased from 1960 to 1986 for small families, it actually increased for women with many children over the same period.

There are a number of ways of interpreting such a relationship. One is that when the opportunity cost of having children is higher, families decide to have fewer children. In this view, high wages "cause" low family size. Another possibility is that women with large families spend more of their energies on the home, and thus have fewer energies to spend on the job. They may also be absent from the job more often, when children are sick; or they may choose lower-paying jobs that allow them greater flexibility in hours. In this view, then, large families "cause" (or explain) low wages.

A third possibility is that there is some other factor that explains both high wages and small family size. For example, it may be that more education enhances a variety of interests that make having children seem somewhat less attractive; and at the same time, more education leads to higher wages. Could this explain the observed relationship between wages and number of children? Panel B provides part of the answer. It shows that even among women with the same education and age, larger family size is associated with lower wages, though the relationship is not so strong as in panel A. Thus, some—but only some—of the negative correlation between wages and family size is explained by education.

Of course, decisions are not made by looking at this relationship and saying, "Since my wage is fifteen thousand a year, I should have four children." Instead, economists argue that decisions are made by individuals weighing the marginal costs and benefits of having additional children; when the opportunity costs of having children are higher—and wages are the dominant measure of the opportunity costs of children—there is a systematic tendency to have fewer children. The economists' model thus provides an explanation for this regularity. Economists speak of the decision to have children as the "demand" for children. Higher wages represent an increase in the "price" of a child; the lower demand is a movement along the demand curve for children in response to a higher price.

The economists' model also makes a prediction concerning the future growth of the population. If current trends continue and wage differentials between men and women of comparable education and experience continue to decline, birthrates will decline too.

In some circumstances, these predictions may be of only limited value, as changes in our society, in social attitudes toward family planning and large families, shift the demand curve for children; these shifts overwhelm the effects of movements along the demand curve. Standard theory might have predicted that the fall in wage rates during the late 1970s and early 1980s would have led to increased birthrates. (This is a movement along the demand curve; the lower the opportunity cost for having children, the greater the demand for children.) This did not, however, occur. Birth patterns were dominated by changing social attitudes.

Similarly, the postwar baby boom had little to do with wage or income changes. The birthrate soared after World War II as soldiers returned home to start the families they had postponed. Nevertheless, the economists' model has been able to provide a simple and powerful explanation of why birthrates tend to be lower in wealthy countries than in poor ones, and why birthrates tend to fall as a country's economy grows.

REVIEW AND PRACTICE

SUMMARY

1. The decision about how to allocate time between work and leisure can be analyzed using the basic ideas of budget constraints and preferences. Individuals face a trade-off along a budget constraint between leisure and income. The amount of income a person can obtain by giving up leisure is determined by the wage rate.

2. In labor markets, the substitution and income effects of a change in wages work in opposite directions. An increase in wages makes people feel better off, and they wish to enjoy more leisure now as well as more consumption; this is the income effect. But the substitution effect of an increase in wages raises the opportunity cost of leisure, and encourages more work. The overall effect of a rise in wages will depend on whether the substitution or income effect is actually larger.

3. An upward-sloping labor supply curve represents a case where the substitution effect of rising wages outweighs the income effect. A relatively vertical labor supply curve represents a case where the substitution and income effects of rising wages are nearly equal. A backward-bending labor supply curve represents a case where the substitution effect dominates at low wages (labor supply increases as the wage increases), but the income effect dominates at high wages (labor supply decreases as the wage increases).

4. The basic trade-off between leisure and income can also be used to analyze decisions such as when to enter the labor force (leave school) and when to retire (leave the labor force).

5. Human capital adds to economic productivity just as physical capital does. It is developed by education, on-the-job learning, and investments of time and money that parents make in their children.

6. Education may serve a screening and signaling function, identifying those workers who are, in some sense, likely to be more productive.

7. Jobs that have particularly unattractive features, like a high risk of physical injury or of fluctuating income, often pay compensating differentials, compared with other jobs that require similar skills and background.

8. Economic considerations have some impact on decisions about whether to have children and other seemingly noneconomic choices.

KEY TERMS

elasticity of labor supply	human capital	credentials
market labor supply curve	screening	competition
	signaling	compensating differentials

REVIEW QUESTIONS

1. How do people make choices about the amount of time to work, given their personal tastes and relative wages in the market?

2. How will the income effect of a fall in wages affect hours worked? How will the substitution effect of a fall in wages affect hours worked? What does the labor supply curve look like if the income effect dominates the substitution effect? if the substitution effect dominates the income effect?

3. Describe how students invest time and money to acquire human capital.

4. Wages often reflect the amount of human capital a person has. Explain why this will *not* be true in a situation where compensating differentials exist.

5. Describe the signaling role of education.

6. True or false: "If a person did not acquire any useful job skills when she got an educational degree, she would have no *economic* reason to get the education." Explain.

7. Would you expect an increase in women's wages to increase or decrease family size? What about an increase in men's wages?

PROBLEMS

1. Imagine that a wealthy relative dies and leaves you an inheritance in a trust fund that will provide you with $20,000 per year for the rest of your life. Draw a diagram to illustrate this shift in your budget constraint between leisure and consumption. After considering the ideas of income and substitution effects, decide whether this inheritance will cause you to work more or less.

2. Most individuals do not take a second job (moonlight), even if they could get one, for instance as a taxi driver. This is in spite of the fact that their "basic job" may require them to work only 37 hours a week. Most moonlighting jobs pay less per hour than the basic job. Draw a typical worker's budget constraint. Discuss the consequences of the kink in the budget constraint.

3. Under current economic conditions, let's say that an unskilled worker will be able to get a job at a wage of $5 per hour. Now assume the government decides to assure that all people with a weekly income of less than $150 will be given a check to bring them up to the $150 level. Draw one such worker's original budget constraint and the constraint with the welfare program. Will this welfare program be likely to cause a recipient who originally worked 30 hours to work less? How about a recipient who worked less than 30 hours? more than 30 hours? Explain how the government might reduce these negative effects by offering a wage subsidy that would increase the hourly wage to $6 per hour for each of the first 20 hours worked, and draw a revised budget constraint to illustrate.

4. "The fact that the average woman is paid less than the average man in the U.S. economy proves to most economists that discrimination against women is widespread." Discuss.

5. Name two jobs where you would expect positive compensating differentials to be paid, and two jobs where you might expect the compensating differential to reduce wages.

6. There is a negative correlation between a woman's real wage and her family size. This chapter discussed two possible interpretations: women with higher real wages *choose* to have smaller families; or larger family sizes might cause women to receive lower wages. What evidence might help you choose between these two explanations?

APPENDIX: INDIFFERENCE CURVES AND THE LABOR SUPPLY DECISION

This appendix investigates the labor supply decision using the concept of the indifference curve, first introduced in the appendix to Chapter 8. Indifference curve analysis is useful first because it helps to determine the point on the budget constraint that an individual will choose. It is further useful in analyzing what will happen as prices (wages, in this case) change.

Figure 11.13 shows Tom's budget constraint between leisure and consumption. As we saw in this chapter, the trade-off along this budget constraint is between leisure and consumption: the less leisure, the more consumption, and vice versa. The slope of the budget constraint is the wage. The figure also shows two indifference curves; each gives the combinations of leisure and consumption among which Tom is indifferent. As usual, since people prefer more of both consumption and leisure if that is possible, Tom will move to the highest indifference curve he can attain. This will be the one that is just tangent to the budget constraint.

The slope of the indifference curve is the marginal rate of substitution between leisure and consumption. It measures the amount of extra consumption Tom requires to compensate him for forgoing one additional hour of leisure. At the point of tangency between the indifference curve and the budget constraint, point E, both have the same slope. That is, the marginal rate of substitution equals the wage at this point.

As in the earlier appendices, we can easily see why Tom chooses this point. Assume his marginal rate of substitution is $15 (dollars per hour), while his wage is $20 (dollars per hour). If he works an hour more—gives up an hour's worth of leisure—his consumption goes up by $20. But to compensate him for the forgone leisure, he only requires $15. Since he gets more than he requires by working, he clearly prefers to work more.

DECIDING WHETHER TO WORK

We can also use indifference curve analysis to see how people make decisions about whether to work or not, as shown in Figure 11.14. Consider a low-wage individual facing a welfare system in which there is a fixed level of benefits if one's income is below a threshold level. Benefits are cut off once income exceeds a certain level. The indifference curve I_0 is tangent to the budget constraint without welfare, and the point

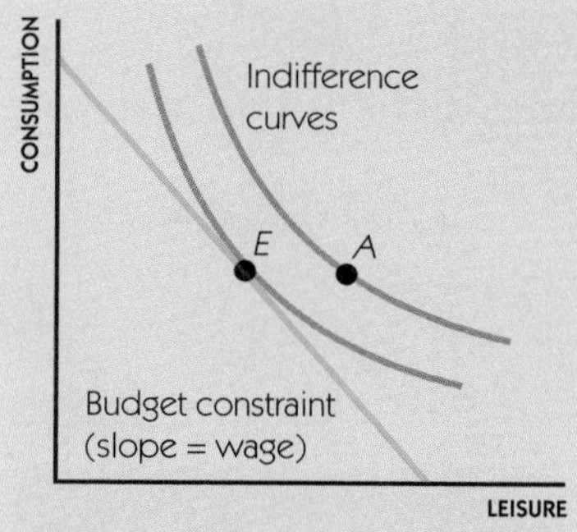

Figure 11.13 INDIFFERENCE CURVES AND LEISURE-INCOME CHOICES

An individual will choose the combination of leisure and income at E. Point A would be more desirable, but it is not feasible. Other points on the budget line or inside it are feasible, but they lie on lower indifference curves and are therefore not as desirable.

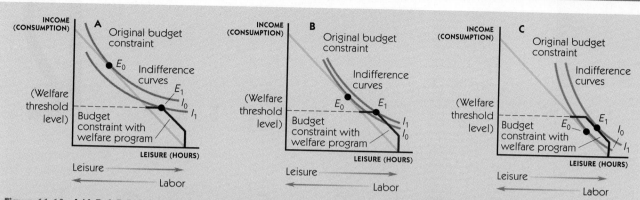

Figure 11.14 INDIFFERENCE CURVES AND WELFARE PROGRAMS

Panel A shows the case of an individual who chooses to work whether or not the welfare program exists. In panel B, the individual is earning more than the welfare threshold, but relies on welfare benefits to work less and move to a higher indifference curve. Panel C shows the case of someone who is earning less than the welfare threshold, but would choose to work still less if the welfare program existed.

of tangency is E_0. The curve I_1 is the highest indifference curve consistent with the person receiving welfare.

There are three possible cases, illustrated in panels A, B, and C. In panel A, the indifference curve through point E_0, I_0, is higher than the curve I_1. The individual chooses to work at E_0, and is unaffected by the welfare program. In panels B and C, the person works sufficiently little to be eligible for welfare; that is, I_1 is higher than I_0, and so he chooses point E_1. In panel B, the individual realizes that if he works more, he will lose his welfare benefits. He earns just (little) enough to be eligible for welfare. In panel C, his marginal rate of substitution is equal to the wage rate; that is, the indifference curve I_1 is tangent to the budget constraint. The welfare system has only an income effect.

CHAPTER 12

THE FIRM'S COSTS

T he previous four chapters focused on how households and individuals make choices about consumption, savings, investment, and labor supply. In this chapter, the focus shifts from households to firms. While households are assumed to make decisions in pursuit of satisfaction, firms have one primary consideration: they seek to maximize their profits for the present and, equally important, for the future. In their pursuit of profits, firms help to answer two of the four fundamental economic questions: "What goods should be produced, and in what quantities?" and "How should these goods be produced?" Firms also play a major role in answering the fourth question, "Who makes the decisions?" and this role will be explored in detail in Chapter 22.

Our attention continues to be centered on the basic competitive model, in which many firms all make the same product. The firms compete with one another to sell that product to well-informed customers, who instantaneously recognize and act upon any price differences. With competition among sellers, if a company does not lower its price when its competitors do, it will lose all of its customers. That is why it is said that firms in these competitive markets are, in effect, forced to be price takers; each must accept the price set by the forces of supply and demand in the rest of the market. The market for wheat or corn, which consists of thousands of farmers producing these crops, is a better example of a competitive market than cigarettes or automobiles, where a small number of firms dominate. (Even in the wheat market, however, we find extensive government intervention that does not match the pristine version of the competitive model.)

Chapter 13 will show where supply curves for goods and demand curves for labor, as well as other factors of production, come from and what determines their shape. But first we need a thorough understanding of the firm's costs. After taking a quick glimpse at what goods and services U.S. firms provide, this chapter focuses on these costs.

"Here is the way it works: We take from the rich and give to the poor—keeping only enough for salaries, travel, equipment, depreciation, and so on, and so on."

KEY QUESTIONS

1. What do cost curves—curves relating costs to the level of production—look like in an economy where output depends on a single input to production?

2. What additional issues are raised when there are several inputs?

3. In the long run, firms can vary some inputs that they cannot vary in the short run. As a result, in the long run, cost curves may look different than they do in the short run. What is the relationship between long-run and short-run cost curves?

WHAT U.S. FIRMS PRODUCE

Table 12.1 presents a snapshot of production in the U.S. economy, divided into broad categories. The precise dollar figures given in the second column do not matter all that much; even among professional economists, very few bother to memorize new statistics every year. However, most economists do carry around in their heads a rough sense of which categories are larger or smaller. Knowing the rough proportions of the economy will not answer every factual question, of course, but will provide a useful background for thinking about economic issues.

When we think about what American firms produce, images of General Motors, Ford, and Chrysler cars, Apple and IBM computers, and a host of other consumer products—shoes, shirts, tennis rackets, and so forth—come to mind. But this vision can lead to a false sense of what most companies actually produce. Of the millions of firms in the U.S. economy, most produce goods, called **intermediate goods,** that are used by companies in other industries as they in turn produce **final goods.** For example, iron ore is mined and sold to steel mills, and the steel is then sold as rods to a hardware factory that produces bolts. The bolts in turn are sold to a packager who also buys nuts and washers and sells packets of all three to hardware stores, where consumers buy them. In this chain, the packager produces the final good, and is therefore called the final goods producer. All the others are intermediate goods producers.

Table 12.1 shows that while the manufacture of intermediate and final goods is important (fourth and fifth categories), it is by no means the dominant productive activity

Table 12.1   1988 OUTPUT OF THE UNITED STATES, DIVIDED BY INDUSTRY (billions of current dollars)

Agriculture, forestry, fisheries	$ 99.8	2.0%
Mining	$ 80.4	1.6%
Construction	$ 232.6	4.8%
Durable goods manufacturing, including lumber and wood, furniture, stone, clay and glass products, metal, machinery, electrical equipment, automobiles and trucks, measuring instruments, computers	$ 530.5	10.9%
Nondurable goods manufacturing, including food, tobacco, textiles, clothing, paper, printing and publishing, chemicals, oil and coal, rubber and plastic, leather	$ 418.3	8.6%
Transportation Railroads, buses, trucking, water and air transportation, pipelines	$ 163.2	3.3%
Communications Telephone, radio, TV	$ 129.3	2.6%
Electric, gas, sanitary services	$ 148.8	3.0%
Wholesale and retail trade	$ 780.8	16.0%
Finance and insurance Banking, credit agencies, stock brokers, insurance and investment companies	$ 257.7	5.6%
Real estate	$ 554.6	11.4%
Services Hotels, business services, auto repair, motion pictures, recreation, health services, legal services, education	$ 872.5	17.9%
Government and government enterprises	$ 570.6	11.7%
Total	$4,880.6	100.0%

Source: Survey of Current Business (1991). This study used the GNP measure of output, defined in Chapter 25.

in the U.S. economy. The traditional industry categories—agriculture, mining, construction, and durable and nondurable manufacturing—add up to less than a third of total economic activity. Another sixth is accounted for by services such as recreational activities, education, and health care. The cost of marketing goods and services, wholesale and retail trade, amounts to another sixth of the economy. The transportation and communication categories—transporting goods and services to the market, moving people around the country, and providing the systems that allow them to communicate with one another—make up more than 6 percent of the nation's economy, while finance (running the nation's banks and brokerage houses) and insurance account for 5 percent.

Analysts have remarked on the extent to which ours is a **service economy,** meaning that we have shifted away from manufacturing industries to service-related ones. They point not only to the category called "services" in the table, but also to the finance and insurance and real estate categories, which, together with services, are considerably larger than manufacturing.

Thus, if you had to envision the modern economy, it would only be partly right to think of workers on assembly lines or on construction sites or in fields and mines. In addition, you should think of the many people who make their living sitting at desks, doing their work on paper or at a computer terminal.

PROFIT MAXIMIZATION

Firms are assumed to keep the profit motive constantly in mind as they approach the questions of what to produce and in what quantities, and how to produce it. The value of a company is ultimately determined by its long-run potential for profits. So we could also express the firm's profit-maximizing impulse by saying that the firm seeks to maximize its value. Naturally, there will be times when a company sacrifices returns over the next few years for long-run gains. In fact, every time the firm makes a decision to invest in a research and development program or a piece of equipment or a training program that will provide long-term returns, it is attempting to trade off dollars that it could distribute now as dividends to its shareholders for greater long-run profits. These profits will enable it to distribute even more money to its shareholders in the future.

Firms may not be driven only by profits and may not always succeed in making the decisions that maximize their profits, just as consumers are not driven only by self-interest and may not always behave rationally. Future chapters will explain both the difficulty of maximizing profits and the reasons why managers of large corporations may sometimes behave in ways that do not maximize the firm's market value. But one very real fact of life remains: a business that fails to make a profit over time will cease to exist. It will not have enough money to pay its bills. If businesses are to continue, they are under pressure to make money. The motivation of making as much money as possible provides a useful starting point for discussing the behavior of firms in competitive markets.

On the one hand, the business firm receives **revenues** from selling its products. Revenues can be calculated simply by multiplying the quantity of the product sold by the price received for the product. On the other hand, the firm incurs **costs,** or the total expense of bringing the good to the market. **Profits** are defined as the difference between revenues and costs. This relationship is expressed by the identity

profits = revenues − costs.

The firm's costs include labor, materials (raw materials and intermediate goods), and capital goods (machines and buildings). These are referred to as the firm's inputs, or **factors of production.** Labor costs are simply what the company has to pay for the workers it hires and the managers it employs to supervise the workers. The materials include whatever supplies it purchases from other firms—for a farm, these supplies would include such inputs as seeds, fertilizer, and gasoline; for a steel company, they would include the iron ore, coal, coke, limestone, electric power, and other fuels required to produce steel.

All firms work to keep their costs as low as possible without changing the quality of the good they produce. Within limits, they can vary the mix of labor, materials, capital goods, and production processes they use; and they will do so until they find the lowest cost method. To understand this process, let's look at the case of a firm with only one variable factor of production.

PRODUCTION WITH A SINGLE VARIABLE FACTOR

We begin with a simple example—a wheat farmer with a fixed amount of land. The more labor he applies to the farm (his own time, plus the time of workers that he hires), the greater the output. Of course, modern agriculture requires tractors and other expensive farm equipment as well as fertilizer and other inputs. For the moment, we focus on a short-run situation, where these other inputs do not change. Labor is the single variable factor (input).

The relationship between the inputs used in production and the level of output is called the **production function.** Figure 12.1 shows the farmer's production function; the data supporting the figure are set forth in Table 12.2. The figure shows that as the amount of labor increases, output is increased. The increase in the output corresponding to an increase in any factor of production, such as labor, is the **marginal product** for that factor. For example, when the number of hours worked per year rises from 7,000 to 8,000, output increases by 15,000 bushels, from 140,000 to 155,000. When the farmer is employing 8,000 hours, the marginal product of 1,000 more hours is 10,000

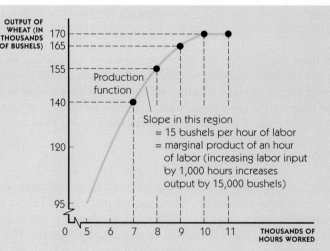

Figure 12.1 PRODUCTION FUNCTION WITH DIMINISHING RETURNS TO AN INPUT

As the amount of the input (labor) increases, so does the output (wheat). But there are diminishing returns to labor; increases in labor result in successively smaller increases in wheat output on the margin. Since the slope of the curve is the marginal product of labor, on the graph, this means the slope flattens out as the amount of labor increases.

Slope in this region
= 15 bushels per hour of labor
= marginal product of an hour of labor (increasing labor input by 1,000 hours increases output by 15,000 bushels)

Table 12.2   LEVEL OF OUTPUT WITH DIFFERENT AMOUNTS OF LABOR

Number of hours worked	Amount of wheat produced (bushels)	Marginal product (additional bushels produced by 1,000 additional hours of labor)
5,000	95,000	25,000
6,000	120,000	20,000
7,000	140,000	15,000
8,000	155,000	10,000
9,000	165,000	5,000
10,000	170,000	0
11,000	170,000	

bushels. The marginal product of an extra hour of labor will, accordingly, be 10 bushels. The marginal product is given in the last column of the table. Diagrammatically, it is given by the slope of the production function.

DIMINISHING RETURNS

As we can see from Figure 12.1 and Table 12.2, as more and more labor is added, while other inputs remain unchanged, the marginal product of labor diminishes. This is another application of the concept of **diminishing returns,** which we originally encountered in Chapter 2. Diminishing returns implies that output increases less than proportionately with input. If labor is doubled, output is less than doubled. It is an empirical regularity that has important consequences. Increasing the number of hours worked from 7,000 to 8,000 raises output by 15,000 bushels, but increasing the hours worked from 8,000 to 9,000 raises output by only 10,000 bushels. Diminishing returns sets in with a vengeance at higher levels of input; moving from 10,000 to 11,000 hours worked adds nothing.

DIMINISHING RETURNS

As more and more of one input is added, *while other inputs remain unchanged,* the marginal product of the added input diminishes.

One often-discussed application of the concept of diminishing returns comes from Thomas Malthus, an early nineteenth-century economist. Malthus was concerned with agriculture and the consequences of the kind of production function just described. According to Malthus, with a fixed supply of land and an increasing population, the extra output that each extra person produced would decline because the amount of land each farmer would have to work with would be less. Overall output would increase as the number of people working on each acre went up, but each extra farmer would produce less than the one before.

In Malthus' view, world population would increase more than proportionately to the available food supply. Therefore, unless people could be persuaded to have fewer children—and Malthus did not believe population control was very likely—starvation and famine would result. In some of today's poorest countries, the Malthusian prediction seems to have some force, as their high rates of population growth outstrip the growth of their economies. But in the developed countries and the world as a whole, technological changes like the use of fertilizer and machines have led food output to increase far faster than population. Technology, which raised the productivity of farm labor enormously, has thus far saved much of the world from a Malthusian fate.

OTHER SHAPES OF PRODUCTION FUNCTIONS

The critical property of the production function depicted in Figure 12.1 is that it exhibits diminishing returns. But not all production functions do so.

INCREASING RETURNS

Figure 12.2 shows a production function where increasing an input (here, labor) raises output more than proportionately. A firm with this kind of production function is said to have **increasing returns.** In the single-input case depicted, it is clear that the marginal product of the input increases with the amount produced; that is, when the firm is producing a lot, adding one more worker increases output by more than it does when the firm is producing little.

For example, imagine a business that picks up garbage. If this business counts only one out of every five houses as customers, it will have a certain cost of production. But if the company can expand to picking up the garbage from two out of every five houses, while it will need more workers, the workers will be able to drive a shorter distance and pick up more garbage faster. Thus, a doubling of output can result from a less than doubling of labor. Many examples of increasing returns involve providing service to more people in a given area, like the garbage collection example. Telephone companies and electric utilities are two familiar instances.

CONSTANT RETURNS

In the case of increasing returns, output grows faster than the input, while with diminishing returns, the input grows faster than output. The intermediate case is one where if the input doubles, output doubles too. In this case, economists say that there are **constant returns.** The relationship between input and output appears as the straight

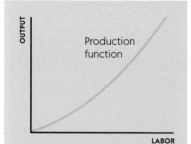

Figure 12.2 PRODUCTION FUNCTION WITH INCREASING RETURNS TO AN INPUT

As the amount of labor increases, so does output. But the returns to labor are increasing in this case; successive increases in labor result in successively larger increases in output. On the graph, this means the slope becomes steeper as the amount of labor increases.

line in Figure 12.3. In the single-input case depicted, it is clear that the marginal product of the input is constant.

FIXED INPUTS

Firms typically require a certain level of input just to start production. Before it can open its doors, for instance, a firm may need land (or space) and some machines. It will have to hire someone to run the personnel office and someone to supervise the workers. These are called **fixed,** or **overhead, inputs,** because they do not depend on the level of output. The quantities of **variable inputs,** on the other hand, rise and fall with the level of production. For instance, the firm can work its space and machines for one shift a day, or it can run them for all twenty-four hours. It simply hires more workers and uses more materials in the latter case. These workers and materials are variable inputs.

We often focus on buildings and capital goods as fixed inputs and labor as a variable input, but this is frequently not the case. If a firm rents more and more machines as it produces more goods, then those machines are variable inputs. On the other hand, wages paid to the firm's president, corporate treasurer, and some other workers required just to make the firm go are fixed. As long as the firm continues to operate, these payments will be required.

In Figure 12.4, L_0 is the fixed input. At first, when the firm increases inputs beyond L_0, output increases more than proportionately. As the firm expands production, initially it shows increasing returns. The output at L_2 is more than twice that at L_1, even though the input is just twice that of L_1. Beyond L_3, the effect of diminishing returns dominates. Each additional worker increases output by less and less; the output at L_5 is less than twice that at L_4, even though the input is twice as large. The ratio of output to input

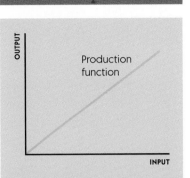

Figure 12.3 PRODUCTION FUNCTION WITH CONSTANT RETURNS TO AN INPUT

As the amount of the input (for example, labor) increases, so does output. But the returns to labor are constant in this case; a given increase in the input always results in the same increase in output. On the graph, this one-for-one match means that the slope does not change.

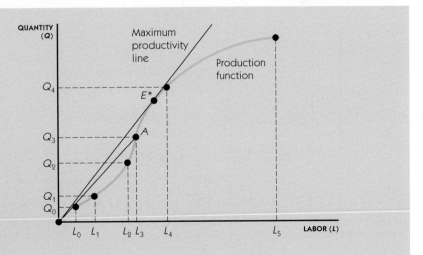

Figure 12.4 PRODUCTION FUNCTION WITH FIXED AND VARIABLE INPUTS

As the amount of labor increases, given the fixed inputs already in place, marginal returns to labor are increasing up to L_3, which is shown by the slope of the production function becoming steeper. They then decrease after L_3, which is shown by the slope of the production function becoming flatter. Average productivity is given by the slope of a line from any point on the production function to the origin, and will be highest at E^*.

is called the **average productivity.** The average productivity at any point on the production function—say, point A—is thus found by dividing the vertical distance (the output, Q_3) by the horizontal distance (the labor input, L_3). But this is just the slope of the line from the origin to A. Average productivity is highest at E^*; at this level of production, the output per unit input is maximized. This is the steepest line from the origin to the production function.

COST CURVES

The production function, no matter what shape it takes, is important to the firm and to the economist for one reason in particular: it determines the costs of production. The case of a production function with fixed inputs is the most common production function in the economy, and a look at the kinds of costs it generates will give us an overview of the major categories of cost upon which economists concentrate.

First, there is the cost of the fixed input. To begin production, a firm may need space, machines, and a core of workers. The costs associated with fixed inputs are called **fixed costs,** or **overhead costs.** Whether the firm produces nothing or produces at maximum capacity, it antes up the same fixed cost just to open for business. Figure 12.5 shows how costs depend on output. Panel A depicts fixed costs as a horizontal line—by definition, they do not depend on the level of output. As an example, consider

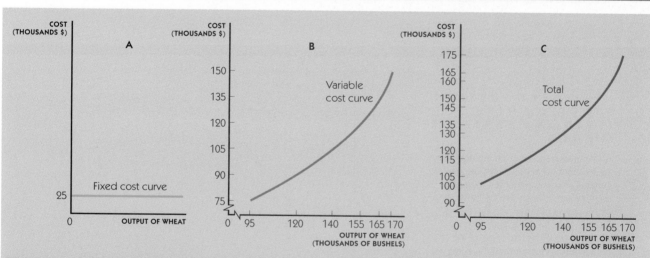

Figure 12.5 FIXED, VARIABLE, AND TOTAL COST CURVES

Panel A shows a fixed cost curve; by definition, fixed costs do not depend on the level of output. Panel B shows a variable cost curve, which rises with the level of production. The increasing slope of the curve indicates that it costs more and more to produce on the margin, which is a sign of diminishing returns. Panel C shows a total cost curve. It has the same slope as the variable cost curve, but is higher by the amount of the fixed costs.

Table 12.3   COST OF PRODUCING WHEAT

Output (bushels)	Labor required (hours)	Total variable cost (at a wage of $15 per hour)	Total cost ($)	Marginal cost ($ per bushel)	Average variable cost ($ per bushel)	Average cost ($ per bushel)
95,000	5,000	75,000	100,000	——	.79	1.05
120,000	6,000	90,000	115,000	.60	.75	.96
140,000	7,000	105,000	130,000	.75	.75	.93
155,000	8,000	120,000	145,000	1.00	.77	.94
165,000	9,000	135,000	160,000	1.50	.82	.97
170,000	10,000	150,000	175,000	3.00	.88	1.03

a would-be wheat farmer who has the opportunity to buy a farm together with its equipment for $25,000. His fixed costs are $25,000.

The counterpart to fixed costs is **variable costs,** which correspond to variable inputs. These costs rise or fall with the level of production. Any cost that the firm can change during the time period under study is a variable cost. To the extent that such items as labor costs or costs of materials can go up or down as output does, these are variable costs. If we give our farmer only one variable input, labor, then his variable costs would be, say, $15 per hour for each worker. The variable costs corresponding to levels of output listed in Table 12.2 are shown in Table 12.3 and plotted in Figure 12.5B. As output increases, so do variable costs, so the curve slopes upward.

Table 12.3 also includes a column labeled "Total cost." **Total costs** are defined as the sum of variable and fixed costs, so this column differs from the variable costs column by $25,000, the amount of the firm's fixed cost. The total cost curve, summarizing these points, is shown in Figure 12.5C.

MARGINAL PRODUCT AND MARGINAL COSTS

Knowing the total cost at every level of output, the firm's decision makers can determine the most important cost—the **marginal cost,** or extra cost corresponding to each additional unit produced[1] Let's return to our example of a wheat farmer. As we increase labor input from 7,000 hours to 8,000 hours, output increases by 15,000 bushels. Thus, to produce 1,000 extra bushels requires 1,000/15 = 66⅔ extra hours. The cost of producing an extra 1,000 bushels is 66⅔ hours × wage per hour. If the wage is $15 per hour, the marginal cost of 1,000 bushels is $1,000.

More generally, if *MPL* is the marginal product of labor (15 bushels per hour), and

[1] There is a simple relationship between the marginal cost curve and the total cost curve. The marginal cost is just the slope of the total cost—the change in total costs (movement along the vertical axis, in Figure 12.5C) resulting from a unit change in output (movement along the horizontal axis).

CLOSE-UP: THE SHRINKING IMPORTANCE OF THE FORTUNE 500

The model of small and very competitive companies may seem like an abstraction. When many people think of the American economy, they think of huge companies like Exxon, IBM, and General Motors. Each year, *Fortune* magazine lists the 500 largest companies in the United States; it is a sort of honor role of corporate America, where success is equated with size. But the existence of large companies does not disprove the importance of the competitive model.

Size by itself does not imply a lack of competition in markets for individual products. A true conglomerate may have corporate divisions in businesses that seem totally unrelated, such as food products, insurance, and mining. The enormous U.S. economy has room for many large firms of this kind without a loss of competition.

Moreover, large firms are not immune from competition, either from other large firms or from upstarts. For the last few decades, the importance of the Fortune 500 has been declining relative to growth in the rest of the economy. Competitive pressure is eating away at even the largest companies, while the importance of small- and middle-sized companies has been increasing. In 1970, for example, the Fortune 500 employed a total of 14.6 million workers. About 18.6 percent of the national employment (roughly one worker in five) was with a Fortune 500 company. By 1990, though, the Fortune 500 employed only 12.4 million, a decline of 15 percent from 1970. Since employment in the rest of the economy had been growing in that time, the share of total employment in the Fortune 500 fell to only 11.7 percent. Only about one person in ten worked for one of the biggest 500 companies.

Sales figures tell a similar story, although the trend is not quite as pronounced. In 1970, the Fortune 500 reported $463 billion in total sales. By 1990, total sales had climbed to $2,304 billion. Even after adjusting for price inflation during that time, that is an increase of 59 percent over those twenty years. However, the economy as a whole grew by 72 percent over that time, so the Fortune 500 was lagging well behind.

The biggest American corporations are certainly in no danger of an immediate demise, but their lessened role has given rise to considerable debate. Some argue that in a globally connected economy, bigness has its uses. Big companies can invest in larger projects, distribute and sell all over the globe, and compete with huge companies from other

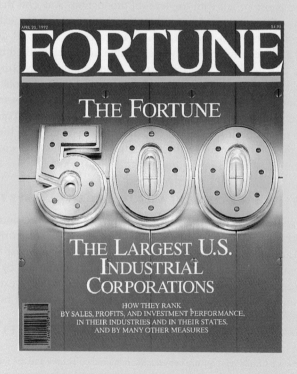

w is the (hourly) wage ($15 per hour), the marginal cost of producing an extra unit of output is just w/MPL ($1 per bushel).

The marginal cost curve depicted in Figure 12.6 is upward sloping. This is a reflection of the fact that as more is produced, it may become harder and harder to increase output further—an example of our familiar friend the principle of diminishing marginal returns. But while normally marginal cost curves are upward sloping, there are some important exceptions, which we will come to shortly.

AVERAGE COSTS AND AVERAGE VARIABLE COSTS

The final set of costs that concern the business firm are its **average costs.** These are simply total costs divided by output. The average cost curve gives average costs corresponding to different levels of output. Figure 12.6 also shows the average cost curve corresponding to the total cost curve depicted in Figure 12.5c. To find the average cost

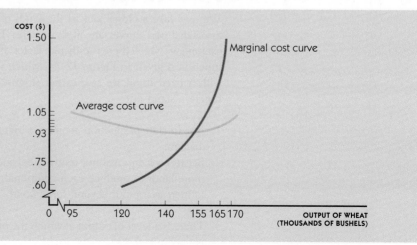

Figure 12.6 MARGINAL AND AVERAGE COST CURVES

The marginal cost is the extra cost of producing one more unit of output. With diminishing returns, marginal costs increase with the level of output. Average costs, also shown here, are total costs divided by output.

for any level of output, we draw a line from the origin to the point on the total cost curve for that level of output. The slope of that line is

$$\frac{\text{total costs}}{\text{output}} = \text{average costs.}$$

There is one more cost concept that will prove useful in the next chapter, **average variable costs;** these are just total variable costs divided by output.

Cost Concepts

Total costs:	Total costs of producing output = fixed costs + variable costs
Fixed, or overhead, costs:	Costs that do not depend on output
Variable costs:	Costs that do depend on output
Marginal costs:	Extra cost of producing an extra unit = total cost of ($Q + 1$) units minus total cost of Q units of output
Average costs:	Total costs divided by output
Average variable costs:	Total variable costs divided by output

U-SHAPED COST CURVES

We now take a closer look at the kinds of shapes that production functions and their associated cost curves are likely to take. For simplicity, we continue focusing on an example in which there is only one factor of production, labor. The "typical" production function is given in Figure 12.7A, which is a slight variant of the production function with a fixed input we saw earlier (Figure 12.4). Three properties of this production function stand out:

1. Just to start production requires a significant input of labor, marked by L_0 in the diagram.
2. Because of diminishing returns, beyond some level of output it requires more and more labor to produce each additional unit of output. It may be almost impossible to increase output beyond some point. That is why the production function flattens out.
3. There is a level of output at which the output per unit input—average productivity—is maximized, Q^*.

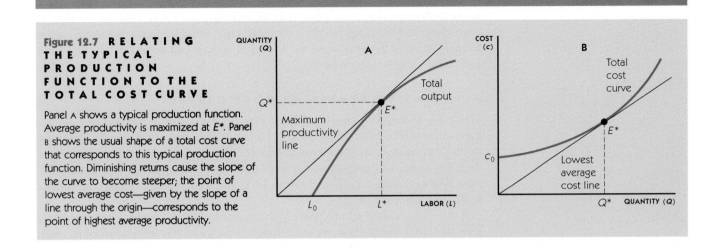

Figure 12.7 RELATING THE TYPICAL PRODUCTION FUNCTION TO THE TOTAL COST CURVE

Panel A shows a typical production function. Average productivity is maximized at E^*. Panel B shows the usual shape of a total cost curve that corresponds to this typical production function. Diminishing returns cause the slope of the curve to become steeper; the point of lowest average cost—given by the slope of a line through the origin—corresponds to the point of highest average productivity.

Panel B shows what these three properties imply for the total cost curve. First, there are fixed costs, c_0. Second, diminishing returns mean that not only do total costs rise as output increases, but the total cost curve becomes steeper and steeper.

Panel A shows that output per unit input is maximized at Q^*. This has one important implication: average costs, total costs divided by output, are minimized at the output level Q^*. This is shown in Figure 12.8. *The typical average cost curve is U-shaped.* With small outputs, average costs decline as output increases. If the *only* costs were fixed costs, then average costs (which would then equal the fixed costs divided by the output) would decrease in proportion to the increase in output. This same principle holds even if not all costs are fixed. Average costs still decline because there are more units of production by which to divide fixed costs. With large outputs, average costs increase, as the law of diminishing returns sets in with strength. Output increases less than proportionately with input; or equivalently, to get a 1 percent increase in output, one needs much more than a 1 percent increase in input.

Even if the average cost curve is U-shaped, the output at which average costs are minimized may be very great, so high that there is not enough demand to justify producing that much. Thus, when economists refer to declining average costs, they mean that those costs are declining over the level of output that is likely to prevail in the market.

Relationship Between Average and Marginal Cost Curves There is a simple relationship between average costs and marginal costs, reflected in Figure 12.8. The marginal cost curve intersects the average cost at the bottom of the U—the *minimum* average cost. That is no accident. To understand why the marginal cost curve will *always* intersect the average cost curve at its lowest point, consider the relationship between average and marginal costs. As long as the marginal cost is below the average cost, producing an additional unit will pull down the average. Thus, everywhere that the

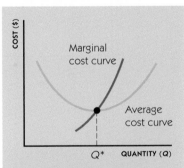

Figure 12.8 RELATING THE MARGINAL COST CURVE TO THE AVERAGE COST CURVE

The average cost curve is usually U-shaped. It initially declines as the fixed costs are spread over a larger amount of output, and then rises as diminishing returns to the variable input become important. With a U-shaped average cost curve, the marginal cost curve will cross the average cost curve at its minimum.

marginal cost is below average cost, the average cost curve is declining. If marginal cost is above average cost, then producing an additional unit will raise the average. So everywhere that the marginal cost is above average cost, the average cost curve must be rising. The point between where the U-shaped average cost curve is falling and where it is rising is the minimum point.

ALTERNATIVE SHAPES OF COST CURVES

While the U-shaped average cost curve may be thought of as the normal case, cost curves may exhibit other shapes as well. Earlier, we saw that production functions may exhibit increasing or constant returns. If there are increasing returns, then since output increases more than proportionately with the input, total costs increase more slowly than output, as seen in panel A of Figure 12.9, and average and marginal costs decline, as illustrated in panel B.

If there are constant returns, then doubling inputs doubles output. Correspondingly, if we wish to double output, we must double inputs, and this will cost twice as much.

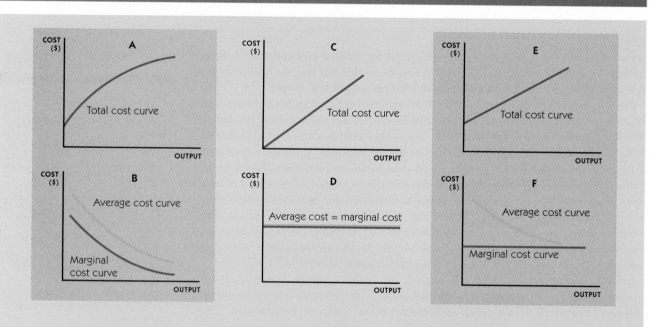

Figure 12.9 COST CURVES WITH INCREASING OR CONSTANT RETURNS

Panels A and B show total, marginal, and average cost curves with increasing returns. Since the cost of producing an additional unit of output is falling, average costs decline as production increases. Panel C shows a total cost curve with constant returns; since returns to the variable factor are constant and fixed costs are zero, the total cost curve begins at the origin and its slope does not change. Panel D shows marginal and average costs with constant returns; marginal cost does not change, and so the average cost does not change either. Panels E and F show total, average, and marginal costs for the case where there is a fixed cost, but the costs of producing each unit are constant.

Thus, total costs are simply proportional to output (panel C), and average and marginal costs are constant (panel D).

Finally, panels E and F show the case where there is a fixed cost, but beyond that, there are constant returns. In that case, marginal costs are constant, but average costs are declining.

CHANGING FACTOR PRICES AND COST CURVES

The cost curves shown thus far are based on the fixed prices of each of the inputs firms purchase. An increase in the price of any factor, such as the wage, the cost of machines, or the price of some raw material, shifts all of the cost curves—total, average, and marginal—upward, as illustrated in Figure 12.10.

PRODUCTION WITH MANY FACTORS

The basic principles we have learned in the previous section apply equally well to firms producing many products with many different inputs. Their application to such firms is somewhat more complicated; the appendix deals with some of these complications. There are, however, two additional important issues, to which we now turn.

COST MINIMIZATION

There are usually several ways a good can be produced, using different quantities of various inputs. For example, Table 12.4 illustrates two alternative ways of making car frames, one a highly automated process requiring little labor and the other a less automated process that uses more assembly-line workers. The table shows the daily wage and capital costs for each process. Each method produces the same number of cars (say, 10,000 car frames per day). In this simple example, we assume all workers are identical

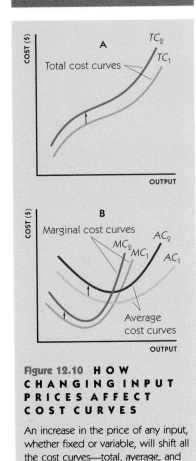

Figure 12.10 HOW CHANGING INPUT PRICES AFFECT COST CURVES

An increase in the price of any input, whether fixed or variable, will shift all the cost curves—total, average, and marginal—upward.

Table 12.4 COSTS OF PRODUCTION

Inputs	More automated process	Less automated process
Labor	50 man hours @ $20 = $1,000	500 man hours @ $20 = $10,000
Machines	5 machines @ $1,000 = $5,000	2 machines @ $1,000 = $ 2,000
Total	$6,000	$12,000

(of equal skill) and hence get paid the same wage, and that all machines cost the same. As we can see from the table, the less automated process clearly costs more at the given costs of labor ($20 per worker per hour) and machines (rental costs equal $1,000 per day).

Although this table provides only two stark alternatives, it should be clear that in some cases the alternative possibilities for production will form a continuum, where the cost of one input increases a bit, the cost of another falls a bit, and output remains the same. In other words, the firm can smoothly substitute one input for another. For instance, in producing cars, different machines vary slightly in the degree of automation. Machines requiring less and less labor to run them cost more. When firms make their decisions about investment, they thus have a wide range of intermediate choices between the two described in the table.

THE PRINCIPLE OF SUBSTITUTION

One of the most important consequences of the principle of cost minimization is that when the price of one input (say, oil) increases relative to that of other factors of production, the change in relative prices causes firms to substitute cheaper inputs for the more costly factor. This is an illustration of the general **principle of substitution** we encountered in Chapter 4.

THE PRINCIPLE OF SUBSTITUTION

An increase in the price of an input will lead the firm to substitute other inputs in its place.

In some cases, substitution is easy; in other cases, it may take time and be fairly difficult. When the price of oil increased fourfold in 1973 and doubled again in 1979, firms found many ways to economize on the use of oil. For instance, companies switched from oil to gas (and in the case of electric power companies, often to coal) as a source of energy. More energy-efficient cars and trucks were constructed, often using lighter materials like ceramics and plastics. These substitutions took time, but they did eventually occur.

The principle of substitution should serve as a warning to those who think they can simply raise prices without bearing any consequences. Argentina has almost a world monopoly on linseed oil. At one time, linseed oil was universally used for making high-quality paints. Since there was no competition, Argentina decided that it would raise the price of linseed oil and everyone would have to pay it. But as the price increased, paint manufacturers learned to substitute other natural oils that could do almost as well.

Another example has to do with raising the price of labor. Unions in the auto and steel industries successfully demanded higher wages for their members during the boom periods of the 1960s and 1970s, and firms paid the higher wages. At the same time, the firms redoubled their efforts to mechanize their production and to become less dependent on their labor force. Over time, this effect led to a decline in employment in those industries.

DIAGRAMMATIC ANALYSIS

We can see the principle of substitution at work using our average cost diagrams. The car manufacturer described earlier has two alternative ways of producing cars, each with its own average cost curve. Both are shown in Figure 12.11. The general principle of cost minimization requires that the firm use the method of production that has the lowest average costs at the level of production at which the firm plans to produce. In the figure, at high levels of production, the more mechanized process with average cost curve AC_2 dominates the less mechanized process with average cost curve AC_1. A smaller-scale producer, however, uses the less mechanized process. Assume now the cost of labor increases. This shifts up the cost curves for both ways of producing, but obviously, the less mechanized process—which is more dependent on labor—has its cost curve shifted up more. As a result, the critical output at which it pays to use the more mechanized production process is lowered, from Q_1 to Q_2. Thus, as the price of labor is increased, some firms switch to a more mechanized process—capital goods (machines) are substituted for labor.

An increase in the price of any input shifts the cost function up. The amount by which the cost function shifts up depends on several factors, including how much of the input was being used in the first place and how easy it is to substitute other inputs. If the production process uses a great deal of the input, then the cost will shift up a lot. If there is a large increase in the price of an input, and the firm cannot easily substitute other inputs, then the cost curve will shift up more than it would if substitution of other inputs were easy.

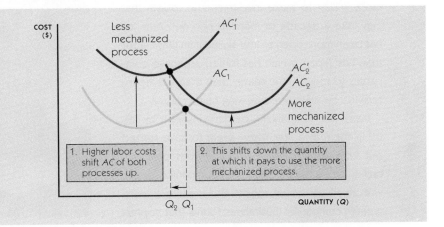

Figure 12.11 MINIMIZING COSTS AS INPUT PRICES CHANGE

With two production processes, as the price of an input increases—in this case, labor—both average cost curves shift up. However, AC_1 relies more heavily on labor, so it shifts up more. This means that firms will switch to the more mechanized technology of AC_2 at a lower level of output (Q_2 instead of Q_1), and there will tend to be a shift away from the more expensive input, labor, and toward the relatively cheaper capital.

1. Higher labor costs shift AC of both processes up.

2. This shifts down the quantity at which it pays to use the more mechanized process.

When many workers hear about robots, the principle of substitution is what leaps into their minds. Their concern is that the increased productivity of industrial robots will encourage industry to use more of them. They further believe that the declining price of computerized brainpower will hold down the price of robots, reinforcing the shift. As a result, workers will end up unemployed or facing lower wages. But this fear has not been realized in either the United States, where robots have not yet been used much, or in Japan, where robots have been widely used.

By the end of the 1980s, about two-thirds of the world's robots were employed in Japan. The total number of robots in the United States, about 37,000, was roughly equal to the *additional* number of new robots put into place in Japan in a single year. In the United States, 1987 was the best year of the 1980s for sales of industrial robots; purchases of new robots actually declined later in the decade.

A number of possibilities have been cited for why the United States might lag behind in number of robots. Interest rates have tended to be lower in Japan over time, which means that Japanese businesses can discount the future less heavily and are more willing to make investments in robots that may take a decade or more to pan out. America has been more open to low-skilled immigrant labor than has Japan, which has forced Japanese companies to focus more heavily than their U.S. counterparts on ways of conserving human labor.

Many U.S. companies—perhaps inspired by R2-D2 in the movie *Star Wars*—seem to have started out with very complex robots, which promptly broke down, while Japanese companies began with relatively simple robots and worked toward greater complexity. Businesses found that sophis-ticated robots were not easy to program and keep running. When some businesses redesigned their assembly lines to make it easy for the robots, they often found that the redesign had made it easier for human workers too, so the robots became unnecessary. Keith McKee, director of the Manufacturing Productivity Center at the Illinois Institute of Technology, described the overall reaction to robots this way: "A lot of companies will buy a robot or two and then find that its care and feeding is more difficult than the care and feeding of a man."

Instead of substituting for jobs that people can do, robots have proved to be best of all at jobs

that people *cannot* do, for reasons of size or safety. Such jobs include handling radioactive waste in nuclear reactors; mass spray-painting in a closed room where paint is thick in the air; welding with 200-pound machines; jobs of infinite repetition, like wrapping or screwing in bolts; or doing tasks that involve very small-scale work, perhaps even microscopic. But these are jobs that most people do not mind giving up.

In the United States, robots have yet to arrive in a way that could even threaten to displace human labor. In Japan, robots are demonstrating that they allow people to move on to more high-paid and flexible tasks. Evidently, robots (like many other new inventions) may add to the marginal product of labor, rather than subtracting from it.

Sources: Andrew Tanzer and Ruth Simon, "Why Japan Loves Robots and We Don't," *Forbes,* April 16, 1990, pp. 148–53; Peter T. Kilborn, "Brave New World Seen for Robots Appears Stalled by Quirks and Costs," *New York Times,* July 1, 1990, sec. I, p. 14.

SHORT-RUN AND LONG-RUN COST CURVES

When a firm uses several inputs, the time it takes to increase or decrease the supply of one input may be greater than that for another. Take the inputs of labor and machines, for example. In the short run, the supply of machines may be fixed. Output is then increased only by increasing labor. In the longer run, both machines and workers can be adjusted. The short-run cost curve is the cost of production with a *given* stock of machines. The long-run cost curve is the costs when all factors are adjusted.[2]

SHORT-RUN COST CURVES

If we think of the number of machines as being fixed in the short run, and labor as the principal input that can be varied, then our earlier analysis of production with a single variable factor provides a good description of short-run cost curves. Thus, short-run *average* cost curves are normally U-shaped.

The short-run *marginal* cost curve in Figure 12.12 presents a pattern often seen in manufacturing. Marginal costs are approximately constant over a wide range. As long as their newest machines are not being fully used, firms find that increasing production by 10 percent just requires increasing the number of production workers by 10 percent and the inputs of other materials (raw materials, intermediate goods) by 10 percent. Idle

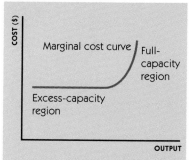

Figure 12.12 SHORT-RUN MARGINAL COSTS

When there is excess capacity, the marginal cost of producing an extra unit may not increase much, and so the marginal cost curve is flat. But when capacity is approached, marginal costs may rise rapidly.

[2] The distinction between short-run and long-run costs corresponds to the distinction between short-run and long-run supply curves introduced in Chapter 4. Chapter 13 will make clear the relationship. It is an exaggeration to think that only capital goods are fixed in the short run while all of labor is variable. In some cases, capital goods may easily be varied; a firm can, for instance, rent cars. And in some cases, as when a company has long-term contracts with its workers, it may be very difficult to vary labor in the short run.

machines are simply put to work. Eventually, however, the cost of producing extra units goes up. Workers have to work more hours (and often they get paid more—time and a half or double time—for these extra hours). Overworked machines break down more frequently. Older, poorer machines have to be put to use. At some level of output, it may be nearly impossible, without extraordinary costs, to push a factory to a higher level of production in the short run.

We have thus identified two key properties of the short-run marginal cost curve. When there is excess capacity, the marginal cost of producing each extra unit does not increase much; the marginal cost curve is relatively flat. Eventually, however, the marginal cost curve becomes steeply upward sloping. (Remember, we are focusing here on the short run, so we assume the number of machines is fixed; there is a particular capacity for which the plant was designed.)

Finally, recognizing that some factors can be adjusted in the short run and others cannot be forces us to think once again about our definition of fixed, or overhead, costs or inputs. These terms were defined earlier as costs or inputs that do not depend on the level of output. Sometimes they are also defined as costs or inputs that cannot be varied in the short run; that is, they do not depend on *current* output, though they may depend on output in the longer run. The two concepts are related, but distinct. Even if a firm could instantaneously adjust all inputs, some overhead inputs would still be required if the company is to exist at all. The firm may have long-term contracts with some of its laborers; their wages are, therefore, fixed. But these laborers are not considered overhead. They are production workers. To help us keep these concepts separate, the remainder of the chapter will refer to costs that are fixed in the short run (whether they represent overhead costs or not) as *fixed*, and costs that a firm must bear simply to operate (whether they can be varied in the short run or not) as *overhead costs*.

LONG-RUN COST CURVES

Even if the short-run average cost curves for a given manufacturing facility are U-shaped, the long-run average cost curve may not have the same shape. As production grows, it will pay at some point to build a second plant, and then a third, a fourth, and so on. Panel A of Figure 12.13 shows the total costs of producing different levels of output, assuming that the firm builds one plant. This curve is marked TC_1. It also shows the total costs of producing different levels of output assuming the firm builds two plants (TC_2) and three plants (TC_3). How many plants will the company build? Clearly, the firm wishes to minimize the (total) costs of producing at any level of output. Thus, the *relevant* total cost curve is the lower boundary of the three curves, which is heavily shaded. Between 0 and Q_1, the firm produces using one plant; between Q_1 and Q_2, it uses two plants; and for outputs larger than Q_2, it uses three plants.

We can see the same results in panel B, using average cost curves. Obviously, if the firm minimizes the total costs of producing any particular output, it minimizes the average cost of producing that output. The figure shows the average cost curves corresponding to the firm's producing with one, two, and three plants. The company chooses the number of plants that minimizes its average costs, given the level of output it plans to produce. Thus, if the firm plans to produce less than Q_1, it builds only one plant; AC_1 is less than AC_2 for all outputs less than Q_1. If the firm plans to produce between Q_1 and Q_2, it builds two plants, because AC_2 is, in this interval, less than either AC_1 or AC_3. Similarly, for outputs greater than Q_2, the firm builds three plants.

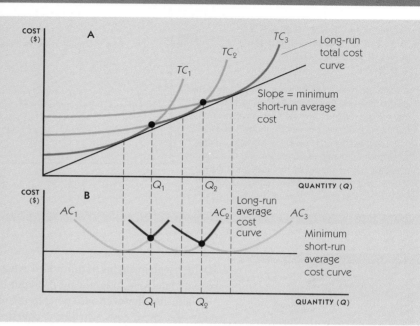

Figure 12.13 SHORT-RUN AND LONG-RUN COST CURVES

Panel A shows a series of short-run total cost curves, TC_1, TC_2, and TC_3, each representing a different level of fixed capital input. In the long run, a cost-minimizing firm can choose any of these, so the long-run total cost curve will be the lowest cost of producing any level of input, as shown by the heavily shaded lower boundary of the curves. Panel B shows a series of short-run average cost curves, AC_1, AC_2, and AC_3, each representing a different level of fixed capital input. In the long run, a cost-minimizing firm can choose any of these, so the long-run average cost curve will be the heavily shaded lower boundary of the curves.

In this case, the long-run average cost curve is the heavily shaded bumpy curve in Figure 12.13B. For large outputs, the bumps look very small. In drawing long-run average cost curves, we typically simply ignore the bumps, and draw smooth curves.

We now need to ask whether long-run average cost curves are normally flat or slope upward or downward. To answer this question, we need to remember how we analyzed the shape of the short-run average cost curve, or the average cost curve with a single variable input. We first described the production function, relating the level of input to the level of output. If output increases less than proportionately with the input, there are diminishing returns, and the average cost curve is rising. If output increases more than proportionately with the input, there are increasing returns, and the average cost curve is falling.

Exactly the same kind of analysis applies when there are many inputs. We ask, what happens when all of the inputs increase together? If, when all of the inputs increase together and in proportion, output increases just in proportion, there are **constant returns to scale**; if output increases less than proportionately, there are **diminishing returns to scale**; and if output increases more than proportionately, there are **increasing returns to scale**, or **economies of scale**.

Many economists argue that constant returns to scale are most prevalent in manufacturing; a firm can increase its production simply by replicating its plants. Then the long-run average and marginal costs equal minimum short-run average costs. The average and marginal cost curves for such a case are depicted in Figure 12.14, where there are many, many plants, and the long-run average cost curve is flat. (The small "bumps" are caused by the fact that output may not be a simple multiple of the output

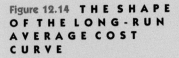

Figure 12.14 THE SHAPE OF THE LONG-RUN AVERAGE COST CURVE

If there are many possibilities for varying the scale of the firm, and thus many short-run average cost curves, the long-run average cost curve defined by their joint boundary can be thought of as very flat, or smooth. In this case, the long-run average cost curve is drawn as horizontal. The firm can increase output simply by replicating identical plants, and there are constant returns to scale.

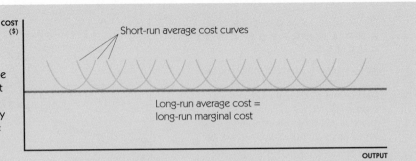

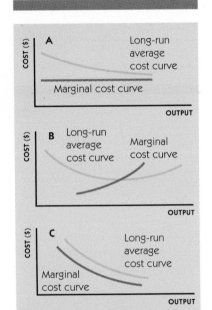

Figure 12.15 LONG-RUN AVERAGE COSTS

Panel A shows that with overhead costs, long-run average costs may be declining, but they flatten out as output increases. In panel B, with managerial costs increasing with the scale of the firm, eventually average and marginal costs may start to rise. Panel C shows that if there are increasing returns to scale, long-run costs may be continuously falling.

at which a plant attains its minimum average costs; but, as the figure shows, these bumps become relatively insignificant if output is very large.)

There are, however, also costs to establishing a firm—the overhead costs. The firm must bear these costs whether it operates 1, 2, or 100 plants. These overhead costs include not only the costs of the corporate headquarters, but also the basic costs of designing the original plant. Thus, we more commonly think of the long-run average cost curve as slightly downward sloping, as in Figure 12.15A.

Some economists believe, however, that "small is beautiful, and big is bad." As the firm tries to grow, adding additional plants, it faces increasing managerial problems; it may have to add layer upon layer of management, and each of these layers increases its cost. When the firm is very small, the owner can watch all of his workers. When the firm has grown to 10 employees, the owner may find that he can no longer supervise his workers effectively; a new supervisor may be needed every time his firm hires 10 more workers. Now the owner spends most of his time looking after the supervisors, not the workers directly. But by the time the firm has grown to 100 workers, he has 10 supervisors.

Now the owner finds it difficult to keep tabs on the supervisors, so it becomes necessary to hire a manager for them. Notice that in this pattern, the number of supervisors and managers is a growing proportion of the workers in the firm. An organization with 10 workers requires only 1 supervisor; with 100 workers, it requires 10 supervisors and a manager; with 1,000 workers, 100 supervisors, 10 managers, and 1 supermanager. Besides the raw numbers of administrative people, decisions now must pass through a number of layers of bureaucracy, and communication will often be slower.

Eventually, average costs may start to increase, as illustrated in Figure 12.15B. Whether any particular industry is best described by Figure 12.14, 12.15A, or 12.15B depends on the importance of overhead costs and the extent to which managerial problems grow with size.

As for the final possibility, in some industries, there may be increasing returns to scale even for very large outputs. As the firm produces a higher output, it can take advantage of larger and more efficient machines, which it would not pay a small firm to purchase. If there are increasing returns to scale, then the long-run average cost curve and the marginal cost curve will be downward sloping, as in Figure 12.15C.

LOOKING BEYOND THE BASIC MODEL: COST CURVES AND THE COMPETITIVENESS OF MARKETS

Industries with declining average costs tend not to have many firms, and thus are not very competitive, and this brings us to another insight that takes us beyond the basic model. Consider the case of one company that is producing all the market wants in an industry with declining average costs. If any new company wishes to enter this market and produce less than the incumbent firm, its average costs will be higher than that of the incumbent company, which will then be able to undersell it. So long as the original firm produces more than the entrant, its costs will be lower, so it can undercut the newcomer—and in fact charge a price so low that the new firm suffers a loss while the incumbent firm still makes a profit. Indeed, if the original merchant charges a price just equal to his average costs (or threatens to do so if an entrant tries to crash into his market), then there is no way that a rival can profitably enter.

On the other hand, if the incumbent firm is producing for the entire market but is on the upward-sloping portion of a U-shaped average cost curve, a new company might aim at producing less with a lower average cost. Now, at least one new company will be able to undersell the original firm, and competitive forces will have some power.

The magnitude of the output at which average costs are minimized depends largely on the size of fixed costs, relative to the costs that vary with the level of output. Fixed and variable costs take on different importance in different industries. In industries in which fixed costs are low, there will normally be many firms, since average costs will reach their minimum value at a relatively low level of output. Since the average cost curve may begin to rise quite rapidly beyond a relatively small output, small firms have the power to undersell larger firms, and there will tend to be many firms in the market. Businesses with low fixed costs include real estate and travel agencies. In these industries, the typical firm is small, and there are thousands of them.

On the other hand, in industries in which fixed costs are high, the minimum average costs will be attained at a very high output, so there will be relatively few firms. Low-cost producers in these industries tend to be large firms, and relatively few fill the market demand. Makers of automobiles and household appliances are examples. Fixed costs loom large in the chemical industry too, so it is not surprising that many major chemicals are produced by only a few firms. In some industries, fixed costs are so large that average costs are declining throughout the output levels demanded in the market. In these cases, at least within any locality, there will be only one firm. Examples include electricity and other utility companies and cement plants. A main cost for most utilities is the cost of the wires (for electricity and telephone) or pipes (for water and sewage).

Expenditures to develop a new product do not depend on the scale of production. Firms can, of course, choose to spend more or less on research or on developing new products, but these costs do not increase with the firm's level of output. It is not surprising, then, that in many of the sectors of the economy in which research and development

CLOSE-UP: ECONOMIES OF SCALE IN SAVINGS AND LOAN BRANCHES

Should a large savings and loan association put a branch office on every other corner to become a well-known presence in the community? Or should it centralize all its operations in one head office, hoping for greater efficiency? Part of the answer to this question must rely on estimating whether larger branches really do provide cost savings.

One way for analysts of the savings and loan industry to study this issue is to calculate an "operating ratio." They first add up all the costs of running a branch, including costs of salaries and benefits, the lease, utilities, maintenance, repairs, taxes and insurance, furniture, and other equipment from computers to light bulbs. They then divide these operating costs by the total deposits of the savings and loan; this provides the operating ratio.

One recent study found that the operating ratio for a branch of a savings and loan declined—that is, the operation became more efficient—as the branch increased in size up to about $50 million in deposits. It would be about 20 percent more expensive to have two branches with $25 million in deposits as it would be to have one branch with $50 million in deposits.

But for branch sizes in which the number of deposits exceeded $50 million, no additional efficiency gains occurred. Presumably, the reason is that the costs and problems of coordinating a larger office offset any lower costs from the expanded size.

Source: Linda Farrell, "Larger Branches Do Offer More Efficiency," *Savings Institutions* (April 1989), pp. S20–S24.

expenditures are important, there are relatively few firms, or that a few dominate the industry. For example, only a few companies control the chemical industry, and for years IBM dominated the computer industry.

ECONOMIES OF SCOPE

Most firms produce more than one good. Deciding which goods to produce and in what quantities, and how to produce them (the first and second basic economic questions), are central problems facing firm managers. The problems would be fairly straightforward, were it not for some important interrelations among the products. The production of one product may affect the costs of producing another.

In some cases, products are produced naturally together; we say they are **joint products.** Thus, a sheep farm naturally produces wool, lamb meat, and mutton. If more lambs are slaughtered for meat, there will be less wool and less mutton.

If it is less expensive to produce a set of goods together than separately, economists say that there are **economies of scope.** The concept of economies of scope helps us understand why certain activities are often undertaken by the same firms. Issues of economies of scope have also played an important role in discussions of regulation over the past two decades. At the time of the breakup of AT&T, which previously had dominated both local and long-distance telephone service as well as research in telecommunications, some economists argued against the breakup on the grounds that there were important economies of scope among these activities. As a result, the breakup, they feared, would reduce efficiency.

REVIEW AND PRACTICE

Summary

1. Only one-third of the U.S. economy consists of manufacturing, mining, construction, and agriculture industries. The rest of the economy consists largely of service industries like transportation, education, health care, wholesale and retail trade, and finance.

2. A firm's production function specifies the level of output resulting from any combination of inputs. The increase in output corresponding to an increase in any input is the marginal product of that input.

3. Short-run marginal cost curves are generally upward sloping, because diminishing returns to a factor of production imply that it will take ever increasing amounts of the input to produce a marginal unit of output.

4. The typical short-run average cost curve is U-shaped. With U-shaped average cost curves, the marginal and average cost curves will intersect at the minimum point of the average cost curve.

5. All profit-maximizing firms choose the method of production that will minimize costs for the level of output they wish to produce, because the lowest costs will allow the highest amount of profit.

6. When a number of different inputs can be varied, and the price of one input increases, the change in relative prices of inputs will encourage a firm to substitute relatively less expensive inputs; this is an application of the principle of substitution.

7. Economists often distinguish between short-run and long-run cost curves. In the short run, a firm is generally assumed not to be able to change its capital stock. In the long run, it can. Even if short-run average cost curves are U-shaped, long-run average cost curves can take on a variety of shapes. They can, for instance, be flat, continuously declining, or declining and then increasing.

8. Economies of scope exist when it is less expensive to produce two products together than it would be to produce each one separately.

KEY TERMS

revenues	average productivity	constant, diminishing,
profits	fixed or overhead costs	or increasing
production function	variable costs	returns to scale
marginal product	total costs	(economies of scale)
fixed or overhead	marginal cost	economies of scope
inputs	average costs	
variable inputs	average variable costs	

REVIEW QUESTIONS

1. What is a production function? When there is a single (variable) input, why does output normally increase less than in proportion to input? What are the alternative shapes that the relationship between input and output takes? What is the relationship between these shapes and the shape of the cost function?

2. What are decreasing, constant, and increasing returns to scale? When might you expect each to occur? What is the relationship between these properties of the production function and the shape of the long-run average and total cost curves?

3. What is meant by these various concepts of cost: total, average, average variable, marginal, and fixed? What are the relationships between these costs? What are short-run and long-run costs? What is the relationship between them?

4. Why are short-run average cost curves frequently U-shaped? With U-shaped average cost curves, what is the relationship between average and marginal costs? If the average cost curve is U-shaped, what does the total cost curve look like?

5. What happens to average, marginal, and total costs when the price of an input rises?

6. If a firm has a number of variable inputs and the price of one of them rises, will the firm use more or less of this input? Why?

7. What are economies of scope, and how do they affect what a firm choses to produce?

PROBLEMS

1. Tom and Dick, who own the Tom, Dick, and Hairy Barbershop, need to decide how many barbers to hire. The production function for their barbershop looks like this:

Number of barbers	Haircuts provided per day	Marginal product
0	0	
1	12	
2	36	
3	60	
4	72	
5	80	
6	84	

Calculate the marginal product of hiring additional barbers, and fill in the last column of the table. Over what range is the marginal product of labor increasing? constant? diminishing? Graph the production function. By looking at the graph, you should be able to tell at what point the average productivity of labor is highest. Calculate average productivity at each point to illustrate your answer.

2. The overhead costs of the Tom, Dick, and Hairy Barbershop are $160 per day, and the cost of paying a barber for a day is $80. With this information, and the information in problem #1, make up a table with column headings in this order: Output, Labor required, Total variable cost, Total cost, Marginal cost, Average variable cost, and Average cost. If the price of a haircut is $10 and the shop sells 80 per day, what is the daily profit?

3. Using the information in problems #1 and #2, draw the total cost curve for the Tom, Dick, and Hairy Barbershop on one graph. On a second graph, draw the marginal cost curve, the average cost curve, and the average variable cost curve. Do these curves have the shape you would expect? Do the minimum and average cost curves intersect at the point you expect?

4. Suppose a firm has the choice of two methods of producing: one method entails a fixed cost of $10 and a marginal cost of $2; the other entails a fixed cost of $20 and a marginal cost of $1. Draw the total and average cost curves for both methods. At what levels of output will the firm use the low fixed-cost technology? At what levels of output will it use the high fixed-cost technology?

5. A firm produces cars using labor and capital. Assume that average labor productivity—total output divided by the number of workers—has increased in the last few months. Does that mean that workers are working harder? Or that the firm has become more efficient? Explain.

APPENDIX: COST MINIMIZA-TION WITH MANY INPUTS

This appendix shows how the basic principles of cost minimization can be applied to a firm's choice of the mix of inputs to use in production. To do this, we make use of a set of concepts and tools similar to those presented in the appendix to Chapter 8, in the analysis of how households make decisions about what mix of goods to purchase.

ISOQUANTS

The alternative ways of producing a particular quantity of output can be graphically represented by **isoquants.** The first part of the term comes from the Greek word *iso,* meaning "same," while "quant" is just shorthand for quantity. Thus, isoquants illustrate the different combinations of inputs that produce the same quantity.

Consider this simple extension of the example of Table 12.4 on page 323. A firm can buy three different kinds of machines, each of which produces car frames. One is a highly mechanized machine that requires very little labor. Another is much less automated and requires considerably more labor. In between is another technique. These represent three different ways of producing the same quantity.

Assume the firm wishes to produce 10,000 car frames a day. It could do this by using 5 highly mechanized machines or 2 of the moderately mechanized machines or 1 of the nonmechanized machines. The total capital and labor requirements for each of these possibilities are represented in Figure 12.16. The horizontal axis shows the capital requirements, while the vertical axis shows the labor requirements. The labor and capital associated with the highly mechanized production process is shown by point A, the moderately mechanized by point B, and the unmechanized by point C.

If the firm wishes, it can produce half of its output on the highly mechanized machines and half on the moderately mechanized machines. If it chooses this option, its capital requirements will be halfway between the capital that would be required if it used only A or only B, and its labor requirements will also be halfway between. This halfway-between choice is illustrated by point X. By similar logic, the firm can achieve any combination of capital and labor requirements on the straight line joining A and B by changing the proportion of highly mechanized and moderately mechanized machines. And by changing the proportion of moderately mechanized and low-mechanized machines, it can achieve any combination of capital and labor requirements on the straight line joining B and C. The curve ABC is the isoquant. It gives all those combinations of capital and labor requirements that can produce 10,000 automobile frames per day. All of these input combinations give the same output.

Consider now what happens if many techniques are available instead of only three. The isoquant consists of points designating each of the techniques, and the short line segments connecting these points that represent combinations of two techniques, as shown in Figure 12.17A. When many, many production techniques are available, the isoquant looks much like a smooth curve, and economists often draw it that way, as in panel B.

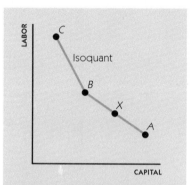

Figure 12.16 THREE ALTERNATIVE METHODS OF PRODUCING A CERTAIN AMOUNT

Point A represents the inputs for a highly mechanized way of producing a certain number of car frames; point C represents a technique of production that uses a much less expensive machine, but more labor; point B represents a technique that is in between. By using different techniques in different proportions, the firm can use a combination of labor and capital on the line joining A and B, such as point X. The curve ABC is an isoquant.

Many different isoquants can be drawn, each representing one particular level of output, as in panel B. Higher isoquants represent higher levels of production; lower isoquants represent lower levels.[3] There is also a simple relationship between the production functions discussed above and isoquants. The production function gives the output corresponding to each level of inputs. The isoquant tells what are the levels of inputs that can yield a given level of output.

MARGINAL RATE OF TECHNICAL SUBSTITUTION

The idea of marginal rate of substitution was introduced in the appendix to Chapter 8 to describe how individuals are willing to trade off less of one good for more of another. The concept is also useful in analyzing what technology firms will choose. In the case of firms, the marginal rate of substitution is defined not by individual preferences but by actual physical facts. If a firm reduces one input by a unit and then raises another input enough so that the final output remains the same, the amount of extra input required is called the **marginal rate of technical substitution.**

An example should help to clarify this idea. If a firm can reduce the amount of capital it uses by 1 machine, hire 2 more workers, and produce the same quantity, then it is possible for 2 workers to replace 1 machine. In this case, the marginal rate of technical substitution between workers and machines is 2/1. The marginal rate of technical substitution is just the slope of the isoquant, as Figure 12.17B shows diagrammatically: the slope simply tells how much of an increase in labor is needed to offset a one-unit decrease in capital to produce the same amount of output.[4]

Notice that the marginal rate of technical substitution and the slope of the isoquant change with the quantities of labor and capital involved. With fewer and fewer machines, it becomes increasingly difficult to substitute workers for machines. The marginal rate of technical substitution rises, and the slope of the isoquant becomes steeper and steeper. At the other end of the isoquant, with more and more machines, it becomes easier and easier to replace one of them. The marginal rate of technical substitution diminishes as the number of workers increases, and the slope of the isoquant becomes flatter. There is a **diminishing marginal rate of technical substitution** in production, just as there was a diminishing marginal rate of substitution in consumption.

The marginal rate of technical substitution can be calculated from the marginal products of labor and capital. If adding 1 more worker increases the output of automobile frames by 1, the marginal product of an extra worker in this industrial process is 1. Let us also imagine that adding 1 machine leads to an increase in car output of, say, 2 a

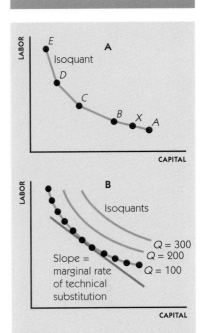

Figure 12.17 ISOQUANTS AND THE MRS

Panel A shows an isoquant defined with many alternative techniques of production. Panel B shows that as the number of production techniques increases, isoquants appear as a smooth curve. The slope of the isoquant tells how much of one input must be added to make up for the loss of a marginal amount of the other input; this is the marginal rate of technical substitution.

---

[3] Readers who have read the Chapter 8 Appendix on indifference curves should recognize the similarities between isoquants and indifference curves: while indifference curves give those combinations of goods that yield the individual the same level of utility, the isoquant gives those combinations of goods (inputs) that yield the firm the same level of output.

[4] Again, readers who earlier studied indifference curves will recall that the slope of the indifference curve is also called the marginal rate of substitution; it tells us how much extra of one good is required when consumption of another good is reduced by one unit, if we wish to leave the individual at the same level of welfare—on his indifference curve.

day. So in this industrial process, the marginal product of a machine is 2. In this example, adding 2 workers and reducing machine input by 1 leaves output unchanged. Thus, the marginal rate of technical substitution is 2/1. In general, the marginal rate of technical substitution is equal to the ratio of the marginal products.

The principle of diminishing returns explains why the marginal rate of technical substitution diminishes as a firm adds more and more workers. As it adds more workers, the marginal product of an additional worker diminishes. As the number of machines is reduced, the marginal product of an additional machine is increased. When a firm considers the choices along an isoquant where machines are becoming more productive at the margin and workers are becoming less productive at the margin, it becomes increasingly costly to replace machines with additional workers.

Notice that calculating the marginal rate of substitution does not tell the firm whether it *should* substitute workers for machines, or machines for workers. The number itself only provides factual information about what the trade-off would be, based on the technology available to the firm. To decide which combination of inputs should be chosen, the firm must also know the market prices of the various inputs.

COST MINIMIZATION

Minimizing costs will require marginal decision making. Firms know the technology they are currently using and can consider changing it by trading off some inputs against others. To decide whether such a trade-off will reduce costs, they can simply compare the market price of the input they are reducing with the price of the input they are increasing. If a firm can replace 1 machine with 2 workers and maintain the same output, and if a worker costs $12,000 a year and a machine costs $25,000 a year to rent, then by reducing machines by 1 and hiring 2 workers, the firm can reduce total costs. On the other hand, if a worker costs $13,000, it would pay to use 2 fewer workers (for a saving of $26,000) and rent 1 machine (for a cost of $25,000).

The only time that it would not pay the firm either to increase labor and reduce the number of machines or to decrease labor and increase the number of machines is when the marginal rate of technical substitution is equal to the relative price of the two factors. The reason for this is similar to the reason why individuals set their personal marginal rates of substitution equal to the ratio of market prices. The difference is that the individual's marginal rate of substitution is determined by individual preferences, while the firm's marginal rate of technical substitution is determined by technology.

ISOCOST CURVES

The **isocost** curve gives those combinations of inputs that cost the same amount. The isocost curve is analogous to an individual's budget constraint, which gives those combinations of goods that cost the same amount. If a firm faces fixed prices for its inputs, the isocost curve is a straight line, whose slope indicates the relative prices; that is, if each worker costs, say, $50 per day, then if the firm reduces the labor used by one, it could spend $50 per day on renting more machines. If renting a machine for a day costs $100, then the firm can rent one more machine with the amount it would save by reducing the input of labor by two. There are, of course, many isocost lines, one for each level of expenditure. Lower isocost lines represent lower expenditures on inputs. Costs along line C_1C_1 in Figure 12.18 are lower than costs along CC. The different

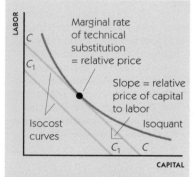

Figure 12.18 COST MINIMIZATION

Cost-minimizing firms will wish to produce as much output as they can given a particular level of expenditure, so they will choose the highest isoquant they can reach with a given isocost curve, which will be the isoquant tangent to the isocost curve.

isocost lines are parallel to one another, just as different household budget constraints representing different income levels are parallel.

Notice that all firms facing the same prices for inputs will have the same isocost lines. Similarly, different individuals with the same income face the same budget constraint, even when their preferences differ. However, the isoquant curves that describe each firm are based on the product the firm is making and the technology and knowledge available to the firm. Thus, isoquant curves will differ from firm to firm.

Isoquant curves and isocost lines can illuminate the behavior of a cost-minimizing firm. For example, any efficient profit-maximizing firm will wish to maximize the output it obtains from any given expenditure. Or to rephrase the same point, the firm must reach the highest possible isoquant, given a particular level of expenditure on inputs, represented by a particular isocost line. The highest possible isoquant will touch the isocost line at a single point; the two curves will be tangent.

The problem of cost minimization can be described in a different way. Consider a firm that has a desired level of output and wishes to minimize its costs. The firm chooses an isoquant, and then tries to find the point on the isoquant that is on the lowest possible isocost line. Again, the cost-minimizing firm will choose the point of tangency between the isocost line and the isoquant.

At the point of tangency, the slopes of the two curves are the same. The slope of the isoquant is the marginal rate of substitution. The slope of the isocost line is the relative price. Thus, *the marginal rate of technical substitution must equal the relative price*.

APPLYING THE DIAGRAMMATIC ANALYSIS

The isoquant/isocost diagram can be used to show how a change in relative prices affects the optimal mix of inputs. A change in relative prices changes the isocost line. In Figure 12.19, an increase in the wage makes the isocost curves flatter. CC is the original isocost curve that minimizes the costs of producing output Q_0 (that is, CC is tangent to the

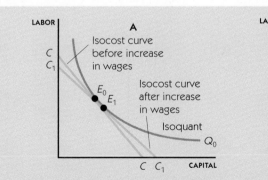
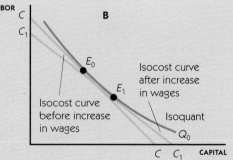

Figure 12.19 CHANGING FACTOR PRICES

This firm has chosen the level of production associated with the isoquant shown, and the cost-minimizing combination of labor and capital for producing that amount is originally at E_0. But as wages rise, relative prices shift, and the cost-minimizing method of producing the given amount becomes E_1. In panel A, an increase in wages leads to little substitution. But in panel B, an increase in wages leads to a much larger amount of substitution.

isoquant Q_0). C_1C_1 is the isocost line with the new higher wages that is tangent to the original isoquant. Obviously, to produce the same level of output will cost more, if wages are increased. The figure also shows what this change in relative prices in the form of higher wages does to the cost-minimizing combination of inputs: as one would expect, the firm substitutes away from labor toward capital (from point E_0 to E_1).

Of course, the magnitude of the substitution will differ from industry to industry, depending on an industry's isoquant. In addition, substitution is likely to be much greater in the long run than in the short run, as machines wear out, firms engage in research to find out how to conserve on the more expensive inputs, and so on. The figure represents these different possibilities for substitution. In panel A, the possibilities for substitution are very limited. The isoquant is very "curved." This figure might illustrate a case where it is very difficult to substitute (at least in the short run) machines for labor—illustrated, perhaps, by the use of blast furnaces in producing steel. In panel B, substitution is very easy; the isoquant is very flat. This would illustrate an opposite case; for example, given the increased possibilities for automation afforded by modern technology, it is often relatively easy for a firm to substitute machines for labor.

DERIVING COST CURVES

The cost curves in this chapter represent the minimum cost of producing each level of output, at a particular level of input prices. Figure 12.20A shows the cost-minimizing way of producing three different levels of output, Q_1, Q_2, and Q_3. Panel B then plots the actual level of costs associated with each of these levels of output. That is, the isocost curves tangent to the isoquants in panel A show the minimum level of costs associated with each output. Tracing out the costs associated with each level of output provides the total cost curve. And once we have the total cost curve, we know how to derive the marginal cost curve (the slope of the total cost curve) and the average cost curve (the slope of a line from the origin to the total cost curve).

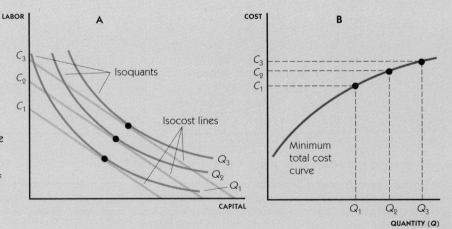

Figure 12.20 DERIVING THE TOTAL COST CURVE

The total cost curve describes how total cost changes at different levels of output. Panel A shows three isoquants representing different levels of output, and three isocost curves tangent to those isoquants, representing the least-cost way of producing each of these amounts. Panel B plots the actual level of costs for each of these levels of output, producing the familiar total cost curve.

THE FIRM'S PRODUCTION DECISION

Chapter 12 defined profits as the difference between revenues and costs. Firms maximize their profits by balancing the extra benefit from producing one more unit, hiring one more worker, or buying one more machine with the extra costs. We also learned the basic tools for assessing the extra costs. In this chapter, we learn how to calculate the extra benefits, and examine more closely how firms weigh extra costs against these extra benefits. This balancing process dictates the (rational) firm's production decision.

In making their production decisions, firms also provide the final ingredients for a complete model of the economy. Households consume goods; firms supply them. Households and firms both operate on the two sides of the capital market: households supply money by saving and demand it by borrowing, and firms do roughly the same thing; on balance, however, households supply capital and firms demand it. Finally, households supply labor, while firms demand it. Thus, this chapter rounds out the discussion of markets. With all the ingredients in hand, we will be able to construct a complete model of the economy in Chapter 14.

"As for me and Bertie here, we will endeavor, in the face of constantly rising costs, to maintain our criteria of excellence. Ain't that right, Bertie?"

KEY QUESTIONS

1. What determines the level of output a firm will supply at any given price? How do we derive, in other words, the firm's supply curve?

2. What determines whether or when a firm will enter or exit a market?

3. How do the answers to these questions enable us to analyze the market supply curve, why it is upward sloping and why it may be more elastic than the supply curve of any single firm?

4. How do we reconcile economists' view that competition drives profits to zero with accountants' reports showing that most of the time most firms earn positive profits?

5. What determines firms' demand for inputs, such as labor or capital? Why is firms' demand curve for labor downward sloping?

REVENUE

Consider the hypothetical example of the High Strung Violin Company, manufacturers of world-class violins. The company hires labor; it buys wood, utilities, and other materials; and it rents a building and machines. Its violins sell for $40,000 each. Last year the company sold 7 of them, for a gross revenue of $280,000. Table 13.1 gives a snapshot of the firm's financial health, its **profit-and-loss statement** for last year.

We see that High Strung's revenues were $280,000, and its costs were $180,000, so its profits were $100,000. If its costs had been $400,000 instead of $180,000, its profits would have been −$120,000. The firm would have made a negative profit, or as it is normally described, a **loss.**

The relationship between revenue and output is shown by the **revenue curve** in Figure 13.1. The horizontal axis measures the firm's output, while the vertical axis measures the revenues. When the price of a violin is $40,000 and the firm sells 9 violins, its revenue is $360,000; when it sells 10, revenue rises to $400,000.

Table 13.1 PROFIT-AND-LOSS STATEMENT FOR THE HIGH STRUNG VIOLIN COMPANY

Gross revenues		$280,000
Costs		$180,000
Wages (including fringe benefits)	$150,000	
Purchases of wood and other materials	$ 20,000	
Utilities	$ 1,000	
Rent of building	$ 5,000	
Rent of machinery	$ 2,000	
Miscellaneous expenses	$ 2,000	
Profits		$100,000

The extra revenue that a firm receives from selling an extra unit is called its **marginal revenue.** Figure 13.1 shows that increasing output from 9 violins to 10 increases revenue by $40,000. Thus, $40,000 is the extra (or marginal) revenue from selling the tenth violin. It is no accident that the marginal revenue equals the price of the violin. A fundamental feature of competitive markets is that firms receive the same, market price for each unit they sell. Thus, the extra revenue that firms in competitive markets receive from selling one more unit—the marginal revenue—is the same as the price of the unit.

Figure 13.1 THE REVENUE CURVE

The revenue curve shows a firm's revenues at each level of output. For the firm in a competitive industry, price does not change as more is produced, so the revenue curve is a straight line with a constant slope. In this example, the revenue of each additional violin is always $40,000.

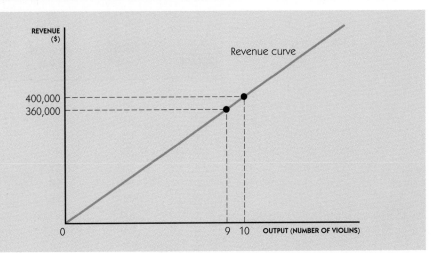

COSTS

High Strung incurs costs corresponding to each level of output. Total costs are given in column 1 of Table 13.2 and depicted diagrammatically in Figure 13.2A. Panel B shows the corresponding average and marginal costs. High Strung's average cost curve exhibits the typical U-shape that we associate with manufacturing firms.

Even before it builds its first violin, the company must spend $90,000. Space must be rented. Some employees will have to be hired. Equipment must be purchased. No matter how many or how few violins High Strung produces, its overhead or fixed costs will remain $90,000.

The *extra* cost of producing an additional violin, the marginal cost, is shown in column 3. The marginal cost of increasing production from 1 to 2 violins, for example, is $10,000. Each additional violin costs $10,000 more until production reaches 6 violins. To increase production from 6 to 7, the extra (or marginal) cost is $30,000; to increase production from 7 to 8, it costs $40,000. (In the table and figure, the marginal cost associated with any output is the additional cost of producing *that* unit: the marginal

Table 13.2 HIGH STRUNG VIOLIN COMPANY'S COSTS OF PRODUCTION (thousands of dollars)

Output	(1) Total cost	(2) Average cost	(3) Marginal cost	(4) Total variable cost	(5) Average variable cost
0	90				
1	100	100	10	10	10
2	110	55	10	20	10
3	120	40	10	30	10
4	130	32.5	10	40	10
5	140	28	10	50	10
6	150	25	10	60	10
7	180	25.72	30	90	12.72
8	220	27.5	40	130	16.25
9	270	30	50	180	20
10	400	40	130	310	31

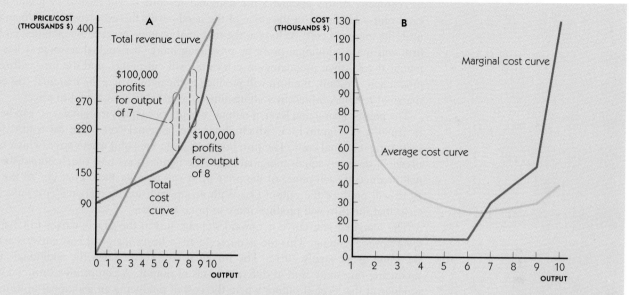

Figure 13.2 RELATING REVENUES AND COSTS

The firm's revenue and total cost curves can be diagrammed on the same graph, as in panel A. When total revenue exceeds total costs, the firm is making profits at that level of output. Profits, the difference between revenues and costs, are measured by the distance between the two curves; in this case, the highest level of profit is being made at a production level of 7 or 8. When total costs exceed total revenue, the firm is making losses at that level of output. When the two lines cross, the firm is making zero profits. The marginal and average cost curves for this company have their expected shape in panel B. Marginal costs are constant until a production level of 6, and then they begin to increase. The average cost curve is U-shaped.

cost associated with 7 violins is $30,000, which is the marginal cost of producing the *7th* violin.)

The High Strung Violin Company's average costs initially decline as its production increases, since the fixed costs can be divided among more units of production. But between 6 and 7 violins, average costs begin to increase, as the effect of the increasing average variable costs dominates the effect of the fixed costs.

BASIC CONDITIONS OF COMPETITIVE SUPPLY

In choosing how much to produce, a profit-maximizing firm, such as the High Strung Violin Company, can be expected to focus its decision at the margin. Having incurred the fixed cost of getting into this market, the decision is generally not the stark one of whether or not to produce, but whether to produce one more unit of a good or one less. For a firm in a competitive market, the answer to this problem is relatively simple: the company simply compares the marginal revenue it will receive by producing an extra unit—which is just the price of the good—with the extra cost of producing that unit, the marginal cost. As long as the marginal revenue exceeds the marginal cost, the firm will make additional profit by producing more. If marginal revenue is less than marginal cost, then producing an extra unit will cut profits, and the firm will reduce production. In short, the firm will produce to the point where the marginal cost equals marginal revenue, which in a competitive market is, in turn, equal to price.

The profit-maximizing level of output, where price equals marginal cost, can be seen in panel A of Figure 13.3, which shows the marginal cost curve for a firm facing increasing marginal costs. The firm produces up to the point where price (which equals marginal revenue) equals marginal cost. The figure shows how much output the firm will produce at each price. At the price p_1, it will produce the output Q_1. At the price p_2, it will produce the output Q_2. With an upward-sloping marginal cost curve, it is clear that the firm will produce more as price increases.

The marginal cost curve is upward sloping, just as the supply curves in Chapter 4 were upward sloping. This too is no accident: a firm's marginal cost curve is actually the same as its supply curve. The marginal cost curve shows the additional cost of producing one more unit at different levels of output. A competitive firm chooses to produce at the level of output where the cost of producing an additional unit (that is, the marginal cost) is equal to the market price. We can thus read from the marginal cost curve what the firm's supply will be at any price: it will be that output at which marginal cost equals that price. Therefore, the marginal cost curve *is* the firm's supply curve.

For the High Strung Violin Company, the marginal revenue (price) is $40,000. Looking down column 3 of Table 13.2, we find that marginal costs reach $40,000 at 8 violins. Total revenues at 8 violins are $320,000, and total costs are $220,000, so profits are $100,000. The same calculation for 9 violins gives us profits of $90,000. This is because at 9 violins, extra (marginal) costs are $50,000; but the extra violin fetches only $40,000, so the firm does not recover its *extra* costs. At 7 violins, profits

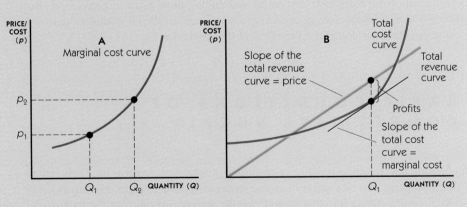

Figure 13.3 THE PROFIT-MAXIMIZING LEVEL OF OUTPUT

A competitive firm maximizes profits by setting output at the point where price equals marginal cost. In panel A, at the price of p_1, this quantity is Q_1. Panel B shows total revenue and total costs. Profits are maximized when the distance between the two curves is maximized, which is the point where the two lines are parallel (and thus have the same slope).

are also \$100,000, but at 6 they are down to \$90,000 again. Figure 13.2A shows total revenues as well as total costs. We can see that profits—the gap between revenues and costs—are maximized at an output of either 7 or 8. If the price were just slightly lower than \$40,000, profits would be maximized at 7, and if the price were just slightly higher than \$40,000, profits would be maximized at 8.

More generally, the profit-maximizing level of output can be seen in panel B of Figure 13.3, which shows the total revenue and total cost curves. Profits are the difference between revenues and costs. In this diagram as in Figure 13.2A, profits are the distance between the revenue curve and the cost curve. The profit-maximizing firm will choose the output where that distance is greatest. This occurs at Q_1. Below Q_1, price (the slope of the revenue curve) exceeds marginal costs (the slope of the total cost curve), so profits increase as output increases; above Q_1, price is less than marginal cost, so profits decrease as output increases.

EQUILIBRIUM OUTPUT FOR COMPETITIVE FIRMS

In competitive markets, firms produce at the level where price equals marginal costs.

ENTRY, EXIT, AND SUPPLY

We are now in a position to tackle the market supply curve. To do so, we need to know a little more about each firm's decision to produce. First let's consider a firm that is currently not producing. Under what circumstances should it incur the fixed costs of entering the industry? This is a relatively easy problem: the company simply looks at the average cost curve and the price. *If price exceeds minimum average costs, it pays the firm to enter.* This is because if it enters, the firm will make a profit, since it can sell the goods for more than the cost of producing them.

Figure 13.4A shows the U-shaped average cost curve. Minimum average cost is c_{min}. If the price is less than c_{min}, then there is no level of output at which the firm could produce and make a profit. If the price is above c_{min}, then the firm will produce at the level of output at which price (p) equals marginal cost, Q^*. At Q^*, marginal cost exceeds average costs. (This is always true at output levels greater than that at which average costs are minimum.) Profit per unit is the difference between price and average costs. Total profits are the product of profit per unit and the level of output, the shaded area in the figure.

Figure 13.4B shows the U-shaped average cost curves for three different firms. Firm 1's minimum average cost is AC_1, firm 2's minimum average cost is AC_2, and firm 3's minimum average cost is AC_3. Different companies may have different average cost curves. Some will have better management. Some will have a better location. Accord-

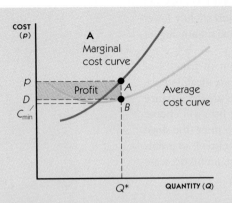

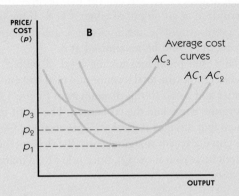

Figure 13.4 COST CURVES, PROFITS, AND ENTRY

Panel A shows that if price is above the minimum of the average cost curve, profits will exist. Profits are measured by the area formed by the shaded rectangle, the profit per unit (price minus average cost, corresponding to the distance *AB*) times the output, *Q**. Panel B shows average cost curves for three different firms. At price p_1, only one firm will enter the market. As price rises to p_2 and then to p_3, first the firm whose cost curve is AC_2 and then the firm whose cost curve is AC_3 will enter the market.

ingly, firms will differ in their minimum average cost. As prices rise, some firms—those with the lowest minimum average costs—will find it attractive to enter the market. Thus, firm 1 enters at the price p_1, firm 2 at the price p_2, and firm 3 at the price p_3.

SUNK COSTS AND EXIT

The converse of the decision of a firm to enter the market is the decision of a firm already producing to exit the market. If there were no sunk costs (sunk costs are costs that are not recoverable), firms would exit the market when their average costs rose above the price. The decision to enter and the decision to exit would be mirror images of each other. The reason why they are not is that some of the costs a firm has incurred when it entered will not be recovered if it leaves. The simple question facing a firm already producing is whether it will be better off producing or shutting down. The company that is losing money—taking into account the money it has already spent—may find that it will lose less money if it continues to produce rather than shutting down. In that case, it obviously pays to produce.

Assume, for instance, that if a firm shuts down, its costs become zero, and it recovers all of its fixed costs; that is, there are no sunk costs. If there is no cost to shutting down, firms will shut down and produce nothing whenever price falls below their minimum average cost, the cost at the bottom of the U-shaped cost curve. Shutting down avoids losses.

The more realistic case is one where some, perhaps all, of the fixed costs are sunk. Figure 13.5A depicts a case where all of the fixed costs are sunk. (Fixed costs, as has been noted, are costs that do not depend on output.) Both the average variable cost

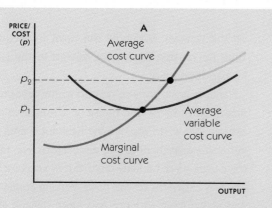

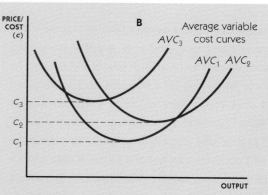

Figure 13.5 AVERAGE VARIABLE COSTS AND THE DECISION TO PRODUCE

Panel A illustrates that in the short run, firms will produce as long as price exceeds average variable costs. Panel B shows that firms with different average variable cost curves will decide to shut down at different price levels. As price falls below c_3, the minimum average

variable cost for firm 3, firm 3 shuts down; as price falls still lower, below c_2, firm 2 shuts down. Finally, when price falls below c_1, firm 1 shuts down.

curve and the average cost curve are shown. The firm shuts down when price is below minimum average *variable* costs (costs that vary with the level of output), p_1. But if the price is between average variable costs and average costs, the firm will continue to produce, even though it will show a loss. It continues to produce because it would show an even bigger loss if it ceased operating. Since price exceeds average variable costs, the revenues it obtains exceed the additional costs it incurs from producing.

If its fixed costs are sunk, High Strung Violins will produce so long as the price exceeds $10,000 (the minimum average variable cost, given in column 5 of Table 13.2). On the other hand, if its fixed costs are not sunk, it will shut down as soon as price falls below $25,000, the minimum average costs.

Different firms in an industry will have different average variable costs, and so will find it desirable to exit the market at different prices. Figure 13.5B shows the average variable cost curves for three different firms. Their cost curves differ; some may, for instance, have newer equipment than others. As the price falls, the firm with the highest minimum average variable costs finds it is no longer able to make money at the going price, and decides not to operate. Thus, firm 3 (represented by the curve AVC_3) shuts down as soon as the price falls below c_3, firm 2 shuts down as soon as the price falls below c_2, and firm 1 shuts down as soon as the price falls below c_1.

FIXED COSTS VERSUS SUNK COSTS

It is important to note that sunk costs and fixed costs are not necessarily the same. Fixed costs are costs that are incurred regardless of the scale of production of the firm. Some of these costs might be recoverable if it went out of production. For instance, a firm

House painting is a summer business, for days that are hot and long, and with available low-skilled labor on vacation from high school and college. As a way of picking up some cash, Michael decided to start Presto Painters during the summer after taking introductory economics.

Just getting started involves some substantial fixed costs. Michael needed to buy a used van for transportation; supplies like brushes and paint; a phone line and answering machine for making appointments; flyers and signs for advertising the business and people to distribute them around town; and business cards and estimate sheets. However, he ran the business out of his parents' home so he had no costs for office space. The fixed costs for Presto Painters ended up looking like this:

Fixed costs

Used van	$5,000
Paint and supplies	$2,000
Flyers and signs	$1,200
Business cards and estimate sheets	$ 500
Phone line and answering machine	$ 300
Total	$9,000

Michael went to work drumming up business. He took calls from potential customers and knocked on doors, made estimates of what he thought it would cost to paint someone's home, and then offered them a price. Of course, he was in direct competition with many other painters and had to meet the competition's price to get a job.

Michael was also a price taker in the market for inputs, and he found that the going rate for labor was $10 per hour. In the real world, there are also costs from buying additional paint and brushes, but for the sake of simplicity, let's assume that he started off the summer buying all the paint he needed. Thus, his variable costs were related to the labor he needed to hire.

Variable costs are also related to the amount of time it takes to paint a house. It is reasonable to assume that when you hire the best applicants you get and assign them to the easiest jobs you have, the painting will be fairly rapid. But as you hire less and less experienced and hard-working applicants and assign them to more and more difficult jobs, the painting will be considerably slower. The variable costs for Presto Painters were as follows:

Houses painted	Hours of labor hired	Payroll cost
5	100	$ 1,000
10	300	$ 3,000
15	600	$ 6,000
20	1,000	$10,000
25	1,500	$15,000
30	2,100	$21,000

Given this information, Michael could calculate cost curves for Presto Painters (see next page).

The hardest thing to figure out was how much time it would actually take to paint the typical house. How can anyone know in advance, for example, how efficient workers will actually be or how long painting a particular house will actually take? Michael learned with experience, of course, but he knew that if he made a serious mistake, he could end up losing money for the summer.

Based on his marginal and average cost curves, Michael figured that if market conditions allowed him to charge $1,000 or more for a typical house, then he could make a profit by painting at least 25 houses. Roughly speaking, that is how his summer worked out; painting 25 houses for $1,000 apiece. Thus, he earned $1,000 in profits.

Or so he thought. Nowhere in this list of costs did Michael consider the opportunity cost of his time. He was not getting paid $10 an hour for painting houses; he was out there stirring up business, hiring and organizing workers, taking calls from customers, dealing with complaints.

Imagine that Michael had an alternate job possibility waiting on tables. He could earn $6 per hour (including tips) and work 40-hour weeks during a 12-week summer vacation. Thus, he could have earned $2,880 during the summer with little stress or risk. If this opportunity cost is added to the fixed costs of running the business, then his apparent profit turns into a loss. If Presto Painters did not cover Michael's opportunity cost *and* compensate him for the risk and aggravation of running his own business, he would have been financially better off sticking to the business of filling people's stomachs rather than painting their houses.

Number of homes	Variable cost	Total cost	Average cost	Marginal cost (per house)
0	0	$ 9,000		
				$2,000
5	$ 1,000	$10,000	$2,000	
				$ 400
10	$ 3,000	$12,000	$1,200	
				$ 600
15	$ 6,000	$15,000	$1,000	
				$ 800
20	$10,000	$19,000	$ 950	
				$1,000
25	$15,000	$24,000	$ 960	
				$1,200
30	$21,000	$30,000	$1,000	

might buy a building in which to locate itself. It may spend a considerable amount of money decorating the building with the company's logo. If the firm should go out of business, it can resell the building and recover its cost. No one will pay much (or anything) for the logo, so the expenditures on the logo are not recoverable. Both the building and the logo are fixed costs, but only the logo is a sunk cost. Advertising expenditures are typically sunk. Expenditures on assets that can readily be put to other uses—such as buildings and cars—are, for the most part, not sunk.

THE FIRM'S SUPPLY CURVE

We can now draw the firm's supply curve. As Figure 13.6A shows, for a firm contemplating entering the market, supply is zero up to a critical price, equal to the minimum average cost. Thus, for price below $p = c_{min}$, the firm produces zero output. For prices greater than c_{min}, the firm produces up to the point where price equals marginal cost, so the firm's supply curve coincides with the marginal cost curve. For a firm that has incurred sunk costs of entering the market (panel B), the supply curve coincides with the marginal cost curve so long as price exceeds the minimum value of average *variable*

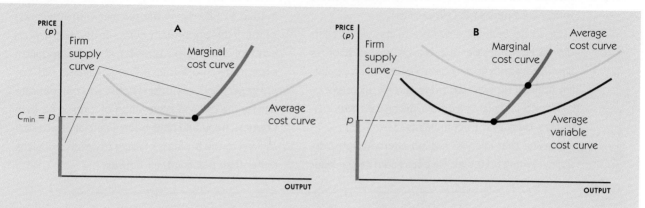

Figure 13.6 THE SUPPLY CURVE FOR A FIRM

Panel A shows that for a firm contemplating entering the market, supply is zero up to a critical price, equal to the firm's minimum average cost, after which the firm's supply curve coincides with the marginal cost curve. Panel B shows a firm that has already entered the market, incurring positive sunk, fixed costs; this firm will produce as long as price exceeds the minimum of the average variable cost curve.

costs; when price is below the minimum value of average variable costs, the firm exits, so supply is again zero.

THE MARKET SUPPLY CURVE

With this information about the cost curves of individual firms, we can derive the overall market supply curve. Back in Chapter 4, the market supply curve was defined as the sum of the amounts that each firm was willing to supply at any given price. Figure 13.7 provides a graphical description.

Figure 13.7 THE MARKET SUPPLY CURVE

The market supply curve is derived by horizontally adding up the supply curves for each of the firms. As price rises, each firm produces more and new firms enter the market.

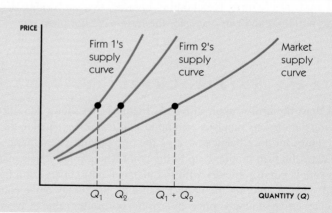

At very high prices, all firms in the industry will produce and some new firms may enter the industry. Because price increases induce more firms to enter a competitive market, the response of output to any change in price is greater than it would be if the number of firms were fixed. But at lower prices, some firms will decide not to produce. In Figure 13.5B, we saw that firm 3 shuts down when the price falls below c_3, firm 2 when the price falls below c_2, and firm 1 when the price falls below c_1. Thus, as prices decline, supply decreases for two reasons: each firm is willing to supply less, and some firms decide not to produce at all. As price falls, the high-cost producers drop out first. That is one way a competitive market assures that whatever is produced is produced at the lowest possible cost, by the firms that can produce the goods most efficiently.

LONG-RUN VERSUS SHORT-RUN SUPPLY

Adjustments to market conditions take time. It may take a while for firms to decide whether or not to discontinue production in the face of lower prices, or to expand in a market when prices rise. In the short run, for example, the plant and equipment of firms represent fixed costs. Variations in output are accomplished by adding more workers, having employees work additional shifts, running the machines harder, and so on. In the longer run, the firm can acquire more buildings and more machines, or sell off those it already has. Thus, the response of output to price changes is likely to be larger in the long run than in the short; that is, the long-run supply curve is likely to be more elastic (flatter) than the short-run supply curve, as illustrated in Figure 13.8A. In some cases, the long-run supply curve may be close to horizontal; that is, the long-run supply elasticity is close to infinite (panel B).

We saw in Chapter 12 that even if the firm has a U-shaped average cost curve in the short run, its long-run average and marginal costs may be close to horizontal. If the firm doubles its output by doubling the number of plants, its average cost remains the same, and the marginal cost of doubling output—the extra cost of producing this extra output—equals the average cost. Since in the long run, firms produce up to the point where price equals long-run marginal costs, and since long-run marginal costs are approximately constant (and equal to long-run average costs), the firm's long-run supply curve is horizontal.

The same argument holds even if each firm can operate only one plant, but a number of new firms can enter the market. The industry's output can be increased by 5 percent simply by increasing the number of firms by 5 percent. The extra costs of increasing output by 5 percent are approximately the same as the average costs. Accordingly, the long-run market supply curve is approximately horizontal. Under these conditions, even if the demand curve for the product shifts drastically, the market will supply much more of the product at pretty much the same price, as additional plants are constructed and additional firms enter the market.

Thus, the market supply curve is much more elastic in the long run than in the short run. Indeed, in the very short run, a firm may find it impossible to hire more skilled labor or to increase its capacity. Its supply curve, and the market supply curve, would be nearly vertical. In what was called the short run in Chapter 12, machines and the number of firms are fixed, but labor and other inputs can be varied. Figure 13.9 shows the short-run supply curve. It is upward sloping. In the short run, a shift in the demand curve has a larger effect on price and a smaller effect on quantity than it does in the long run, as illustrated in panel A. In the long run, if the supply curve is horizontal, shifts in the demand curve have an effect only on quantity, as in panel B. Price remains

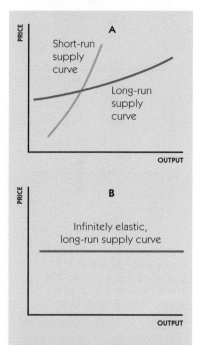

Figure 13.8 ELASTICITY OF SHORT-RUN AND LONG-RUN SUPPLY CURVES

Panel A shows that because there is a greater chance for firms to adjust to changes in price in the long run, the price elasticity of the supply curve is greater in the long run than in the short run. Panel B illustrates the special case where the elasticity of supply is infinite in the long run.

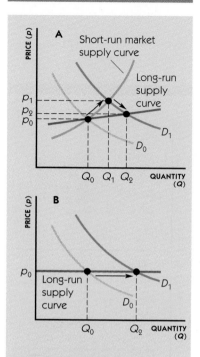

Figure 13.9 MARKET EQUILIBRIUM IN THE SHORT RUN AND LONG RUN

In panel A, the market equilibrium is originally at a price p_0 and an output Q_0. In the short run, a shift in the demand curve from D_0 to D_1 raises the price to p_1 and quantity to Q_1. In the long run, the supply elasticity is greater, so the increase in price is smaller—price is only p_2—and quantity is greater, Q_2. If supply is perfectly elastic in the long run, as shown in panel B, shifts in demand will only change the quantity produced in the long run, not the market price.

at the level of minimum average costs; competition leads to entry to the point where there are zero profits.

Again, it is worth asking, "How long is the long run?" That depends on the industry. For an electric power company to change its capacity takes years. For most other firms, buildings and equipment can be added, if not within months, certainly within a year or two. Recent improvements in technology, like computer-aided design and manufacturing, have made it possible for many companies to change what they are producing more rapidly, and thus have reduced the length of the long run and made supply curves more elastic than in the past.

ADJUSTMENTS IN THE SHORT RUN AND THE LONG RUN

In the very short run, firms may be unable to adjust production at all; only the price changes.

In the short run, firms may be able to hire more labor and adjust other variable inputs.

In the long run, firms may be able to buy more machines, and firms may decide to enter or to exit.

The times required for these adjustments may vary from industry to industry.

LOOKING BEYOND THE BASIC MODEL: SUNK COSTS, ENTRY, AND COMPETITION

The degree of competition envisioned in the basic competitive model requires a large number of firms. Vying with one another to sell a product, these firms drive the market price down to a level where there are no profits (as economists define them) in the market.

Even without a large number of firms in the market, the predictions of the basic competitive model may still hold. The theory of **contestable markets** predicts that even in a market with only one firm, that firm will make zero profits, just as in a market with many firms, *if* sunk costs are low. The threat that other firms will enter is sufficient to deter the single firm from raising its price beyond average cost. This result holds even in the presence of high fixed costs, so long as those fixed costs consist of buildings, cars, airplanes, and other assets that can easily be sold. A firm entering the industry has little to lose, since it can always reverse its decision and recover its investment.

When the assets include major ones with no alternative use, such as a nuclear power plant, then the fixed costs become sunk costs, and the threat of competition diminishes. The firm that would otherwise have entered the market might now worry that if it enters, competition will get fierce. This will indeed be the case, as high sunk costs will make

CLOSE-UP: PAM AM'S EXIT

Pan American World Airways passed away on December 4, 1991. The company had been flying since 1927, and for many decades had been the dominant global airline. In fact, some said that the Pan Am logo may have been the most widely recognized corporate logo in the world at one time.

The death came as no surprise. Pan Am had lost money in every year except one between 1980 and 1991—losses that totaled nearly $2 billion. It had officially declared bankruptcy in January 1991. But what life support system delayed the exit of Pan Am from commercial aviation? How can our economic model account for a company that makes losses for a decade and even continues to operate after it has officially declared bankruptcy?

The model of entry and exit based on cost curves gives a useful explanation of why Pan Am would not exit after a single year of losses. As long as a firm can charge a price above average variable costs, it makes economic sense to stay in business, even if the price is below average costs and the firm is making losses.

To stay in business while making losses, though, a company must have assets to sell. In its many profitable years, Pan Am had built up many such assets, and in the 1980s it proceeded to sell them off. The company sold the Pan Am Building to Metropolitan Life Insurance for $400 million; its Intercontinental Hotels subsidiary for $500 million; its Pacific operations and later its London routes to United Airlines; and a considerable amount of Tokyo real estate. By the end of 1991, Pan Am was proposing to sell off most of its other routes to Delta and become a small airline based in Miami, serving mainly Latin American destinations. In other words, although Pan Am continued to fly during the 1980s while losing money, it was slowly exiting during most of that time. In the real world, an "exit" often means a reduction in size.

In fact, economists sometimes disagree over whether a market economy forces exit to happen quickly enough. As the case of Pan Am demonstrates, exit can be a drawn-out process. This surely benefits some workers who could avoid switching jobs for a longer time. But shareholders in Pan Am would have been better off if the company had been sold off in the early 1980s before it had a chance to lose more money.

Sources: Brett Pulley, "Pan Am Ceases Operations, Race Opens to Get Its Valuable Latin American Routes," *Wall Street Journal,* December 5, 1991, p. A7; Agis Salpukas, "Its Cash Depleted, Pan Am Shuts," *New York Times,* December 5, 1991, p. D1; Severin Borenstein, "The Evolution of U.S. Airline Competition," *Journal of Economic Perspectives* (Spring 1992).

all firms reluctant to exit. If competition is fierce enough, the price might even drop below average costs, and still the firm's rivals may not leave. With prices below average costs, the firm will not be able to get a return on its investment. Until it enters the market, the firm has an advantage: it has not taken on the sunk costs. Given the scenario just described, it may very well avert its gaze from the lure of the higher market prices, knowing they are like a mirage; they will disappear if the firm tries to grab them by entering. But this tells us that markets with high sunk costs may be able to sustain high profits without much fear of entry—a clear departure from the basic competitive model.

ACCOUNTING PROFITS AND ECONOMIC PROFITS

We have learned in previous chapters that firms maximize profits, but now it appears that with competition, profits are driven to zero. To most individuals, this seems like a contradiction: if profits were truly zero, why would firms ever produce? If firms stopped producing, wouldn't prices rise? And wouldn't profits then become positive? How do we reconcile the conclusion that with competition, profits are driven to zero with the fact that throughout the economy, firms regularly report that they are making profits?

The concept of profits is more complicated than it may seem at first glance. The way accountants report profits—the difference between the firm's revenues and its costs—coincides only imperfectly with how economists think about profits. There are two important differences between how economists and accountants look at profits. The first is that economists take opportunity costs into account, and the second has to do with the economic concept of rent. Both deserve a closer look.

OPPORTUNITY COSTS

To begin to see how opportunity costs affect the economist's view of profits, consider a small firm in which the owner has invested $100,000. Assume the owner receives a small salary, and devotes sixty hours a week to running the enterprise. An economist would argue that the owner ought to calculate the best wage available from working sixty hours a week at an alternate job and the return the $100,000 invested in this enterprise would produce in another investment, and use this sum as the true cost of the owner's time and capital investment. To calculate profits of the firm as the economist sees them, these opportunity costs have to be subtracted out.

One can easily imagine a business whose accountant reports a low level of profit—say, 3 percent—while an economist notes that if the investment capital had been put in a bank account, it would have earned at least 5 percent. Thus, the economist would say that the business is making losses, rather than profits. Failure to take into account opportunity costs means that reported profits often overstate true economic profits.

Taking opportunity costs into account is not always a simple matter. Firms often make use of resources they do not buy on an ongoing basis from the market. A company may operate in buildings that it bought ten or twenty years ago. Managerial time spent in expanding the firm in one direction might have been spent in controlling costs or expanding the firm in another direction. Land that is used for a golf course for the firm's employees might have been used for some other purpose, perhaps saving enough money to buy golf club memberships for all who want them. In making decisions about resources like these, firms ought to try to take into account the opportunity costs of these resources; in other words, they must constantly ask what price the resources might fetch in other uses.

Sometimes the market data can provide appropriate prices for calculating opportunity costs. For example, the opportunity cost of giving huge offices to top executives can be gauged by the money those offices would bring in if they were rented to some other company. But other times such calculations are difficult: how can a company measure the opportunity cost of the vice-president who cannot be fired and will not retire for five years?

Sometimes the principle that sunk costs should be ignored is misunderstood to mean that if the firm has bought a building or signed a long-term lease, it should ignore any costs associated with the use of that building. However, even if a firm has signed a lease for a building, and it cannot extricate itself from the deal except at prohibitively high costs, there is an opportunity cost to the building space. The space can be used in alternative ways within the firm, and it may even be possible to rent out some space to other companies. There are real economic costs associated with using the building, but those costs may have little or nothing to do with the actual expenditures on the building.

The flip side of the mistake of ignoring opportunity costs associated with a previously made expenditure, such as the purchase of a building, is the mistake of overestimating opportunity costs by basing calculations on past expenditures. Consider an automaker that has purchased a parcel of land for $1 million an acre. It turns out, however, that the company made a mistake and the land is worth only $100,000 an acre. The firm now must choose between two different plants for producing new cars, one of which uses much more land than the other. In figuring opportunity costs, should the land be valued at the purchase price of $1 million an acre, or at the current opportunity cost— what the land could be sold for—of $100,000 an acre? The answer can make a difference between whether or not the firm chooses to conserve on land. From an economics viewpoint, the answer to this valuation problem should be obvious: the firm should evaluate costs according to the current opportunity costs. The fact that the company made a mistake in purchasing the land should be irrelevant for the current decision.

Individuals and firms frequently do compound their economic errors, however. Business executives who were originally responsible for making a bad decision may be particularly reluctant to let bygones be bygones. They know if it is widely recognized that a mistake has been made, this knowledge may jeopardize their future with the firm, and certainly their future promotion prospects. Publicly announcing that the correct market price of land is $100,000 an acre would be equivalent to announcing that a mistake had been made. Using the $1-million-an-acre price says, in effect, that the market is wrong in its evaluation, that the firm believes it made the right original assessment, and that eventually it expects to be proved correct.

RENTS

There is a second reason that an accountant may say a firm in a competitive market is making money while an economist says it is making zero profits. Some of the returns that accountants call profit, economists call **rent.** The economic concept of rent has its historic origins in the payments made by farmers to landlords for the use of land, but today its application is much broader.

The critical characteristic of land in this regard is that it is inelastically supplied, so that higher payments for land (higher rents) will not elicit a greater supply. Even if landlords received virtually nothing for their land, the same land would be available. Many other factors of production have the same inelastic character. Even if you doubled his $5 million salary, Roger Clemens would not "produce" more pitches for the Boston Red Sox. Luciano Pavarotti, who makes plenty of money as a tenor, might not be able to schedule any more performances even if concertgoers were willing to pay twice what he now receives. The extra payments for this kind of rare talent also fall into the economist's definition of rent. Anyone who is in a position to receive economic rents is fortunate indeed, because those "rents" are a sort of gravy, payments determined entirely by demand that lie above and beyond what is required to put forth effort.

In the case of firms, we saw earlier that a firm would be willing to produce at a price equal to its minimum average cost. Some firms might be more efficient than others (as was the case in Figure 13.4B), so that their average cost curves are lower. Consider a case where all firms except one, which is more efficient, have the same average cost curve, and the market price corresponds to the minimum average cost of these firms. The one superefficient company would enjoy what an accountant might call profits as a result of the fact that its average costs are far below those of the other firms. But an economist would refer to these returns as rents on the firm's superior technological capabilities. The company would have been willing to produce at a lower price, at its minimum average cost. What it receives in excess of what is required to induce it to enter the market are rents.

Thus, when economists say that competition drives profits to zero, they are focusing on the fact that in competitive equilibrium, price equals marginal cost for every firm producing. A company will not increase profits by expanding production, and it will not pay for firms outside the industry to enter. We say that competition drives profits to zero at the margin.

In some cases, supplies of inputs are inelastic in the short run but elastic in the long run. Payments made for such an input may be viewed as rents in the short run, but not in the long run. An example is a payment for the use of a building. In the short run, the supply of buildings does not depend on the return, and hence payments for the use of a building are rents, in the economists' sense. But in the long run, the supply of buildings does depend on the return—investors will not construct new buildings unless they receive a return equal to what they could obtain elsewhere—and so the "rent" received by the building's owner is not really a rent, in the sense in which economists use that term.[1]

It should now be clear how to reconcile the fact that firms in competitive industries show profits, according to accountants, with economists' claim that competition drives profits to zero. Economists include as costs opportunity costs, both the value of the capital and the value of the owner's time, and they note that more efficient firms may obtain a return, a rent, on their better technological capabilities.

---

[1] Economists sometimes use the term "quasi-rents" to describe payments for the use of buildings or other factors that are inelastically supplied in the short run, but elastically supplied in the long run.

ACCOUNTANTS' VERSUS ECONOMISTS' PROFITS

Accounting profits: revenues minus expenditures

Economic profits: revenues minus rents minus economic costs (including opportunity costs of labor and capital)

FACTOR DEMAND

In the process of deciding how much of each good to supply and the cost-minimizing method of producing those goods, firms also decide how much of various inputs they will use. This is called **factor demand.** It is sometimes called a derived demand, because it flows from other decisions the profit-maximizing firm makes. In Chapter 12, the analysis of cost was broken up into two cases, one in which there was a single input, or factor of production, and one in which there were several factors. We proceed along similar lines here, in both cases using labor as the main example of an input. The same principles apply to any factor of production.

When there is only a single factor of production, say labor, then the decision about how much to produce is the same as the decision about how much labor to hire. As soon as we know the price of the good, we can calculate the supply (output) from the marginal cost curve; and as soon as we know the output the firm plans to produce, we know the labor required, simply by looking at the production function, which gives the output for any level of input of labor, or, equivalently, the labor required for any level of output. Thus, in Figure 13.10 at the price p_1, the output is Q_1 (panel A), and the labor required to produce that output (factor demand) is L_1 (panel B).

There is another way of deriving the demand for a factor. In the case of labor, if a firm hires one more worker, the extra cost is the wage, w. The extra benefit of the worker is the price of the good times the extra output. The extra output corresponding to the extra worker is the marginal product of labor. (Marginal products can be calculated for any other factor of production as well.) The price of the good times the marginal product of labor is referred to as the **value of the marginal product of labor.** The firm hires labor, or purchases any other factor of production, up to the point where the value of its marginal product (the marginal benefit) equals its price, in this case, the wage.

Using p for the price of the good, MPL for the marginal product of labor, and w for the wage of the worker, we can write this equilibrium condition as

$$\text{value of marginal product of labor} = p \times MPL = w = \text{wage}.$$

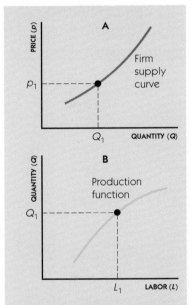

Figure 13.10 THE DEMAND FOR LABOR

The demand for labor can be calculated from the firm's supply curve and the production function. Panel A shows how the firm, given a market price p_1, chooses a level of output Q_1 from its supply curve. Panel B shows how the firm, given the level of output Q_1 it has chosen, then chooses a level of labor L_1 to demand from its production function.

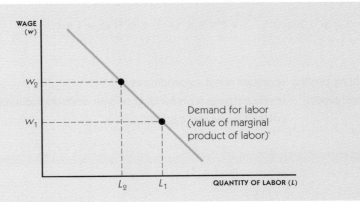

Figure 13.11 THE DEMAND CURVE FOR LABOR

The value of the marginal product of labor declines with the level of employment. Since labor is hired up to the point where the wage equals the value of the marginal product, at wage w_1, employment is L_1, and at wage w_2, employment is L_2. The demand curve for labor thus traces out the values of the marginal product of labor at different levels of employment.

We can then derive from this equilibrium condition the demand curve for labor. Figure 13.11 plots the value of the marginal product of labor for each level of labor. Since the marginal product of labor decreases as labor increases, the value of the marginal product of labor decreases. When the wage is w_1, the value of the marginal product of labor equals the wage with a level of labor at L_1. This is the demand for labor at a wage w_1. When the wage is w_2, the value of the marginal product of labor equals the wage with a level of labor at L_2. This is the demand for labor at a wage w_2. Thus, the curve giving the value of the marginal product of labor at each wage *is* the demand curve for labor.

It is easy to use this diagram to see the effect of an increase in the price of the good the firm produces. In Figure 13.12, the higher price increases the value of the marginal

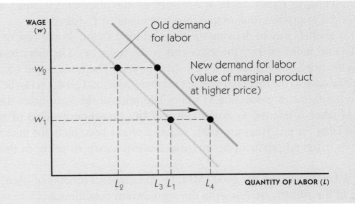

Figure 13.12 EFFECT OF PRICE CHANGE ON THE DEMAND CURVE FOR LABOR

An increase in the price received by a firm shifts the value of the marginal product of labor curve up, so that at each wage, the demand for labor is increased. At wage w_1, employment rises from L_1 to L_4; at wage w_2, employment rises from L_2 to L_3.

product of labor at each level of employment, and it immediately follows that at each wage, the demand for labor increases; the demand curve shifts to the right.

It is thus apparent that the demand for labor depends on both the wage and the price the firm receives for the goods it sells. In fact, the demand for labor depends only on the ratio of the two, as we will now see.

If we divide both sides of the equation above by the price, we obtain the condition

$$MPL = w/p.$$

The wage divided by the price of the good being produced is defined as the **real product wage.** It measures what firms pay workers in terms of the goods the worker produces rather than in dollar terms. Thus, the firm hires workers up to the point where the real product wage equals the marginal product of labor.

This principle is illustrated in Figure 13.13, which shows the marginal product of labor. Because of diminishing returns, the marginal product diminishes as labor (and output) increases. The demand for labor at the real product wage w_1/p is L_1, while the demand for labor at the real product wage w_2/p is L_2. As the real product wage increases, the demand for labor decreases.

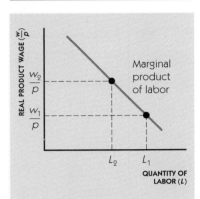

Figure 13.13 **THE FIRM'S DEMAND CURVE FOR LABOR AND THE REAL PRODUCT WAGE**

Firms hire labor up to the point where the real product wage equals the marginal product of labor. The demand for labor at the real product wage w_1/p is L_1, while the demand for labor at the real product wage w_2/p is L_2. As the real product wage increases, the demand for labor decreases.

FACTOR DEMAND

A factor of production will be demanded up to the point where the value of the marginal product of that factor equals the price. In the case of labor, this is the same as saying that the marginal product of labor equals the real product wage.

FROM THE FIRM'S FACTOR DEMAND TO THE MARKET'S FACTOR DEMAND

Once we have derived the firm's demand curve for labor, it is an easy matter to derive the total market demand for labor. At a given set of prices, we simply add up the demand for labor by each firm at any particular wage rate. The total is the market demand at that wage rate. Since as the wage increases, each firm reduces the amount of labor that it demands, the market demand curve is downward sloping. Figure 13.14 shows how we add up diagrammatically the demand curves for labor for two firms, the High Strung Violin Company and Max's Fine Tunes Violin Company. At a wage of w_1, High Strung demands 30 workers and Max's Fine Tunes demands 30 workers, for a total demand of 60 workers. At a wage of w_2, High Strung demands 20 workers and Max's demands 10 workers, for a total demand of 30 workers.

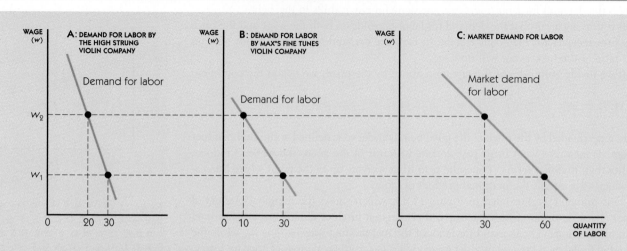

Figure 13.14 THE MARKET DEMAND CURVE FOR LABOR

The market demand curve for labor at each wage is obtained by horizontally adding up the demand curves for labor of each individual firm. As the wage rises, at a fixed price of output, less labor is demanded.

FACTOR DEMANDS WITH TWO OR MORE FACTORS

It is now time to relax our assumption that firms require only one factor of production. With more than one factor, when the price of any input falls, the demand for that input will increase for two reasons. First, the firm (and the industry as a whole) substitutes the cheaper input for other inputs, so that for each unit of output produced, more of the cheaper input is employed. Second, the lower price of the input lowers the marginal cost of production at each level of output, and this leads to an increase in the level of production. Since

total demand for an input = demand for input per unit output × output,

and since both factor demand per unit of output and output have been increased, total demand for the input has increased.

When we draw the demand curve for labor, which shows the quantity of labor demanded at each wage, in the background we are keeping the price of output and the price of other inputs fixed. When any of these prices changes, the demand curve for labor shifts. For instance, as we have seen, if the price of output increases, the value of the marginal product of labor increases and the demand curve shifts to the right.

On the farm, basic inputs like durable equipment, real estate, hired labor, and energy can be used to produce a variety of different outputs. However, as the price of an input rises, it may be harder to conserve on its use for some products than for others. A higher price of land, for example, is likely to have a larger effect on the production of grain than on the production of dairy products.

The elasticity relationships between four farm inputs and four outputs are shown in the table here. The first four rows of the table show how much the output of livestock, milk, grains, and oilseeds will change as the price of the four inputs changes. For example, a 10 percent rise in the price of energy will lead to a decline of 4.09 percent in the amount of fluid milk produced. These figures allow an analyst to predict which products' supply would be affected most severely by changes in the price of various inputs. For example, a 10 percent change in the price of durable equipment would have by far the smallest impact on the supply of grain, while a 10 percent change in the price of hired labor would have the largest effect on the supply of milk.

Another result of a change in input prices will be that less of the input itself is demanded, because less of it will be used for every unit of output, and output will be lower; this is where the second four rows come in. For example, the first column in the row for durable equipment shows that demand for durable equipment will fall 12.71 percent if the price of that equipment rises by 10 percent. Similarly, the second column of the row for real estate shows how demand for real estate inputs will change with the price of real estate.

The third effect of a change in input prices will be on how much other inputs are demanded. In this example, raising the price of any particular input will lead to less of other inputs being used as well. This may seem surprising at first; as the price of one input increases, shouldn't a sensible farmer substitute other inputs so that the demand for those inputs will increase? Such substitution is surely likely to occur. But the overall decrease in the amount produced will mean that fewer of all inputs are needed, even if the proportion of the inputs that are used shifts. If the price of energy increases by

| | Elasticity with respect to the price of | | | |
	Durable equipment	Real estate	Hired labor	Energy
Livestock	−.534	−.275	−.419	−.286
Fluid milk	−.556	−.319	−.554	−.409
Grains	−.192	−.425	−.307	−.166
Oilseeds	−.519	−.342	−.358	−.321
Durable equipment	−1.271	−.192	−.443	−.321
Real estate	−.237	−.584	−.252	−.206
Hired labor	−.674	−.310	−1.50	−.379
Energy	−.647	−.336	−.503	−.941

10 percent, for example, the quantity of energy demanded will fall by 9.41 percent, the quantity of durable equipment demanded will fall by 3.21 percent, the quantity of real estate by 2.06 percent, and the quantity of hired labor by 3.79 percent. Since the amount of energy demanded will decline by the greatest amount, the production process will now be using a smaller proportion of energy than before. But since overall supply of all products will fall, as shown by the supply elasticities in the first four rows of the fourth column, fewer of all inputs will be needed.

Source: U. F. Ball, *American Journal of Agricultural Economics* (November 1988), p. 823. Data are from 1978 and 1979, and all elasticities are short-run.

THE THEORY OF THE COMPETITIVE FIRM

We have now completed our description of the theory of the competitive firm. The firm takes the prices it receives for the goods it sells as given, and it takes the prices it pays for the inputs it uses, including the wages it pays workers and the costs of capital goods, as given. The firm chooses its outputs and inputs in order to maximize its profits.

We have seen where the supply curves for output and the demand curves for labor and capital that were used in Part One came from, and why they have the shape they do. As prices increase, output increases; firms produce more, and more firms produce. Thus, supply curves are upward sloping.

As wages increase, with the price of other inputs fixed, firms' marginal cost curve shifts up. This causes them to produce less at each price of their output. The higher *relative* price of labor induces firms to substitute other inputs for labor; they use less labor to produce each unit of output. Therefore, the demand curve for labor (and other inputs) is downward sloping.

In the next chapter, we will use these results, together with the analysis of the household's behavior in Chapters 8–11, to form a model of the entire economy.

REVIEW AND PRACTICE

SUMMARY

1. A revenue curve shows the relationship between a firm's total output and its revenue. For a competitive firm, the marginal revenue it receives from selling an additional unit of output is the price of that unit.

2. A firm in a competitive market will choose the output where the market price—the marginal revenue it receives from producing an extra unit—equals the marginal cost.

3. If the market price for a good exceeds minimum average costs, firms will enter the market, since they can make a profit by selling the good for more than it costs to produce the good.

4. If the market price is below minimum average costs and a firm has no sunk costs, the firm will exit the market immediately. If the market price is below minimum average costs and a firm has sunk costs, it will continue to produce in the short run as long as it can at least cover its variable costs.

5. For a firm contemplating entering a market, its supply is zero up to the point where price equals minimum average costs. Above that price, the supply curve is the same as the marginal cost curve.

6. The market supply curve is constructed by adding up the supply curves of all firms in an industry. As prices rise, more firms are willing to produce, and each firm is willing to produce more, so that the market supply curve is normally upward sloping.

7. The economist's and the accountant's concepts of profits differ in how they treat opportunity costs and rents.

8. A firm's demand for factors of production is derived from its decision about how much to produce. Inputs will be demanded up to the point where the value of the marginal product of the input equals its price.

9. The demand curve for factors of production is downward sloping, because output is reduced as the price of the factor increases, and because at each level of output, the firm substitutes away from the factor whose price has increased.

KEY TERMS

revenue curve	economic rents	real product wage
marginal revenue	factor demand	

REVIEW QUESTIONS

1. In a competitive market, what rule determines the profit-maximizing level of output? What is the relationship between a firm's supply curve and its marginal cost curve?

2. What determines firms' decisions to enter a market? to exit a market?

3. What is the relationship between the way accountants use the concept of profits and the way economists use that term?

4. How do firms decide how much of an input to demand? Why is the demand curve for inputs (like labor) downward sloping?

5. Explain when and how the average variable cost curve determines whether firms will enter or exit the market.

PROBLEMS

1. The market price for painting a house in Centerville is $10,000. The Total Cover-up House-Painting Company has fixed costs of $4,000 for ladders, brushes, and so on, and the company's variable costs for house painting follow this pattern:

Output (houses painted)	2	3	4	5	6	7	8	9	10
Variable cost (in thousands of dollars)	26	32	36	42	50	60	72	86	102

Calculate the company's total costs, and graph the revenue curve and the total cost curve. Do the curves have the shape you expect? Over what range of production is the company making profits?

2. Calculate and graph the marginal cost, the average costs, and the average variable costs for the Total Cover-up House-Painting Company. Given the market price, at what level of output will this firm maximize profits? What profit (or loss) is it making at that level? At what price will the firm no longer make a profit? Assume its fixed costs are sunk; there is no market for used ladders, brushes, etc. At what price will the company shut down?

3. Draw a U-shaped average cost curve. On your diagram, designate at what price levels you would expect entry and at what price levels you would expect exit if half the fixed costs are sunk. Explain your reasoning.

4. Jose is a skilled electrician at a local company, a job that pays $50,000 per year, but he is considering quitting to start his own business. He talks it over with an accountant, who helps him to draw up this chart with their best predictions about costs and revenues.

Predicted annual costs		Predicted annual revenues
Basic wage	$20,000	$75,000
Rent of space	$12,000	
Rent of equipment	$18,000	
Utilities	$ 2,000	
Miscellaneous	$ 5,000	

The basic wage does seem a bit low, the accountant admits, but she tells Jose to remember that as owner of the business, Jose will get to keep any profits as well. From an economist's point of view, is the accountant's list of costs complete? From an economist's point of view, what are Jose's expected profits?

APPENDIX: ALTERNATIVE WAYS OF CALCULATING THE DEMAND FOR LABOR

We have now seen three different ways for determining the demand for labor. One uses the condition for equilibrium output, that price equals marginal cost—to determine the equilibrium level of output and then determine the required labor. The second is derived directly from the profit-maximizing condition for the demand for labor: the value of the marginal product of labor is set equal to the wage. The third is to set the real product wage equal to the marginal product of labor. This appendix shows how these conditions are, in fact, alternative ways of writing the same condition.

With a single factor of production, labor, the extra cost of producing an extra unit of output is just the extra labor required times the wage. The extra labor required is $1/MPL$, 1 divided by the marginal product of labor. If 1 extra worker produces 2 violins a year, it takes $\frac{1}{2}$ of a worker to produce an extra violin. Hence, the competitive equilibrium condition, price equals marginal cost, can be rewritten as

$$p = w/MPL.$$

If we multiply both sides of this equation by MPL, we obtain

$$p \times MPL = w,$$

the familiar condition that the value of the marginal product ($p \times MPL$) equals the wage. And if we now divide both sides of the equation by p, we obtain

$$MPL = w/p,$$

the condition that the marginal product of labor equals the real wage. All of these conditions are in fact three ways of writing the same equation.

Two important consequences follow from these conditions. First, note that the demand for labor depends only on the real product wage, that is, the wage divided by the price of the good produced. If wages and prices both double, then the demand for labor and the supply of output are unaffected. Second, an increase in the wage, keeping prices fixed, reduces the demand for labor. This effect can be seen in several different ways. The real product wage has increased. Therefore, for the condition "the marginal product of labor equals the real wage" to be satisfied, the marginal product of labor must increase. But the principle of diminishing returns says that to increase the marginal product of labor, the input of labor must be reduced.

Alternatively, an increase in the wage can be seen as increasing the marginal cost of hiring an additional unit of labor, while with a fixed price, the marginal benefit remains the same. Thus, at the old level of employment, the marginal benefit of the last worker hired is less than the marginal cost, and it pays firms to lower their level of production. At a high enough wage, the average variable costs of production may exceed the price, and the firm will shut down.

COMPETITIVE EQUILIBRIUM

E ach of the last six chapters has taken up an aspect of the basic competitive model: consumer demand, household savings and investment, labor supply, the firm's costs, and the firm's production decision. Now it is time to put the pieces together. In doing so, we will come to understand how markets answer the basic economic questions posed in Chapter 1: what is to be produced and in what quantities, how these goods are to be produced, for whom they are to be produced, and, most fundamental, how these resource allocation decisions are to be made.

At the same time, this chapter provides a first glance at the interconnectedness of a modern economy. The U.S. economy is a web of transactions involving many workers and companies. A pressure or tension on any one part will affect all the rest. For instance, when the price of oil fell sharply in 1982, there was a decline in oil-drilling activity in the United States. This led to a lower level of economic activity in oil-drilling states, most notably Texas; this in turn resulted in lower real estate prices. Many real estate developers were unable to pay off the money they had borrowed to build new homes, and some of them defaulted on their loans. Most of these loans had been made through savings and loan associations (S & L's), and because so many borrowers defaulted, many S & L's went bankrupt. The cost of rescuing the Texas S & L's was so great that it threatened the nation's entire system of S & L's, requiring a federal bailout. Thus, a shiver in one part of the economic web sent a chill through many other sectors.

Finally, this chapter explains why economists believe that, by and large, the market answers the fundamental economic questions efficiently, although there are certain circumstances in which markets may not work well.

"The Connecticut Turnpike's connected to the New York Thruway,
The Thruway's connected to the Garden State Parkway,
The Garden State's connected to the New Jersey Turnpike,
The Jersey Turnpike's connected to the Pennsylvania Turnpike . . ."

KEY QUESTIONS

1. What is meant by the competitive equilibrium of the economy? Why is it that in competitive equilibrium, a disturbance to one part of the economy may have reverberations in others?

2. What implications does the interconnectedness of the economy have for such important policy issues as the corporation income tax?

3. What is the circular flow diagram, and how does it show the many links between the different parts of the economy?

4. Why do so many economists believe that, by and large, reliance on private markets is desirable? How do competitive markets result in economic efficiency?

5. If markets result in distributions of income that society views as unacceptable, should the market be abandoned, or can the government intervene in a more limited way to combine efficient outcomes with acceptable distributions?

THE BASIC COMPETITIVE EQUILIBRIUM MODEL

Chapter 4 introduced the idea of a market equilibrium, in which demand equals supply. In that chapter, we focused on one market at a time. The wage rate was determined when the demand for labor equaled its supply; the interest rate was determined when the demand for savings equaled the supply; and the price of a good was determined when the demand for the good equaled its supply. This kind of analysis is called **partial**

equilibrium analysis, because in analyzing what is going on in one market, we ignore what is going on in other markets.

Interdependencies in the economy often make partial equilibrium analysis overly simple. Demands and supplies in one market depend on prices determined in other markets. For instance, the demand for skis depends on the price of ski tickets, ski boots, and possibly even airline tickets. Thus, the equilibrium price of skis will depend on the price of ski tickets, ski boots, and airline tickets. But by the same token, the demand for ski tickets and ski boots will depend on the price of skis; and accordingly, the equilibrium price of ski tickets and ski boots will depend on the price of skis. **General equilibrium analysis** broadens the perspective, taking into account all of the interactions and interdependencies between the various parts of the economy. General equilibrium analysis seeks an understanding of the wages, interest rates, and prices at which the markets for labor, capital, and goods and services clear simultaneously. It also provides a framework within which to trace out how a disturbance in one market—say, an increase in the supply of labor—leads to a new equilibrium in all markets.

By its nature, taking all of these interdependencies into account is complicated. However, we can see the basic principles at work by focusing on a simplified model of the economy. In this simplified model, we assume all workers are identical in their ability. We ignore, in other words, differences in skill level, and accordingly we can talk about the labor market as if all workers received the same wage. Similarly, we ignore all aspects of risk in our analysis of the capital market; there is only a single interest rate. Finally, we assume that all firms produce the same good; in other words, the product market consists of only one good. In this simplified three-market economy, we will be able to see how all three markets are interdependent.

In Chapter 11, we saw how households determine the amount of labor they wish to supply. Households supply labor because they want to buy goods. Hence, their labor supply depends on both wages and prices. It also depends on other sources of income. If we assume, for simplicity, that households' only other source of income is the return to their investments (their return to capital, or the interest on their investments), then we can see that the labor supply is connected to all three markets. It depends on the wage, the price of the single good, and the return to capital. Similarly, in Chapter 12, we saw that the demand for labor depends on the wage, on the interest rate, and on the price at which the firm sells its product.

Equilibrium in the labor market requires that the demand for labor equal the supply.[1] Normally, when we draw the demand curve for labor, we simply assume that p, the price of the good(s) being produced, and the interest rate (here, r) are kept fixed. We focus our attention solely on the wage rate, the price of labor. *Given p and r,* we look for the wage at which the demand and supply for labor are equal, as illustrated in panel

---

[1] Labor-market equilibrium can be expressed in mathematical terms. If we represent the wage as w, the price of a single good as p, and the return to capital, or interest rate, as r, then

$$L^s = L^s(w, p, r),$$

where L^s represents the supply of labor. This equation says that labor supply is a function of these three prices. Likewise,

$$L^d = L^d(w, p, r),$$

where L^d is the demand for labor. The equilibrium condition is then

$$L^d = L^s.$$

A of Figure 14.1. This is a partial equilibrium analysis of the labor market.

The labor market is only one of the three markets, even in our highly simplified economy. There is also the market for capital to consider. In Chapter 9, we saw how households determine their savings, which in turn determine the available supply of capital. The supply of capital is affected, in general, by the return it yields (the interest rate, r) plus the income individuals have from other sources, in particular from wages. Since the amount individuals are willing to save may depend on how well off they feel, and how well off they feel depends on the wage rate relative to prices, we can think of the supply of capital too as depending on wages, interest rates, and prices. In Chapter 12, we learned how to derive firms' demand for capital. This too will depend on the interest rate they must pay, the price at which goods can be sold, and the cost of other inputs.

Equilibrium in the capital market occurs at the point where the demand and supply for capital are equal, illustrated in panel B of Figure 14.1.[2] Again, partial equilibrium analysis of the capital market focuses on the return to capital, r, at which the demand and supply of capital are equal, but both the demand and the supply depend on the wage and the price of goods as well.

Finally, there is the market for goods. Chapters 8 and 9 showed how to derive households' demand for goods. We can think of the household as first deciding on how much to spend (Chapter 9), and then deciding how to allocate what it spends over different goods (Chapter 8). Of course, with a single consumption good, the latter problem no longer exists. In our simplified model, then, we can think of the demand for goods as being determined by household income, which in turn depends on the wage, the interest rate, and the price of goods.

Similarly, in Chapter 13, we analyzed how firms determine how much to produce: they set price equal to marginal cost, where marginal cost depends on wages and the interest rate. Equilibrium in the goods market requires that the demand for goods equal the supply of goods. Again, while in the simple partial equilibrium analysis we focus on how the demand and supply of goods depend on price, p, we know that the demand and supply of goods also depend on both the wage rate and the return to capital. The equilibrium is illustrated in panel C of Figure 14.1.[3]

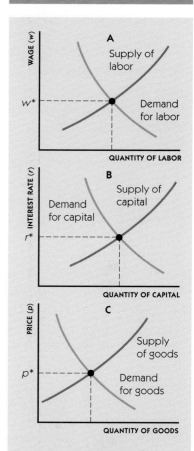

Figure 14.1 GENERAL EQUILIBRIUM

Panel A shows that supply equals demand in the labor market at the wage w^*, given the price level p^* and the interest rate r^*. Panel B shows that supply equals demand in the capital market at the interest rate r^*, given the price level p^* and the wage w^*. Panel C shows that supply equals demand in the product market at price p^*, given wages w^* and interest rate r^*. For a general equilibrium to exist, all markets must clear.

---

[2] Using mathematical terms,

$$K^s = K^s(w, p, r),$$

where K^s is the supply of capital;

$$K^d = K^d(w, p, r),$$

where K^d is the demand for capital. The equilibrium condition is then

$$K^d = K^s.$$

[3] In mathematical terms,

$$Q^s = Q^s(w, p, r),$$

where Q^s is the supply of goods;

$$Q^d = Q^d(w, p, r),$$

where Q^d is the demand for goods. The equilibrium condition is then

$$Q^d = Q^s.$$

EQUILIBRIUM IN THE BASIC COMPETITIVE MODEL

The labor market clearing condition: The demand for labor must equal the supply.
The capital market clearing condition: The demand for capital must equal the supply.
The goods market clearing condition: The demand for goods must equal the supply.

While the labor market is said to be in equilibrium when the demand for labor equals the supply, the product market is in equilibrium when the demand for goods equals the supply, and the capital market is in equilibrium when the demand for capital equals the supply, the economy as a whole is in equilibrium only when all markets clear simultaneously (demand equals supply in all markets). The general equilibrium for our simple economy occurs at a common wage rate, w, price, p, and interest rate, r, at which all three markets are also in equilibrium.[4]

In the basic equilibrium model, there is only a single good, but it is easy to extend the analysis to the more realistic case where there are many goods. The same web of interconnections exists between different goods and between different goods and different inputs. Recall from Chapter 4 that the demand curve depicts the quantity of a good—for instance, beer—demanded at each price; the supply curve shows the quantity of a good that firms supply at each price. But the demand curve for beer depends on the prices of other goods and the income levels of different consumers; similarly, the supply curve for beer depends on the prices of inputs, including the wage rate, the interest rate, and the price of hops and other ingredients. Those prices, in turn, depend on supply and demand in their respective markets. The general equilibrium of the economy requires finding the prices for each good and for each input such that the demand for each good equals the supply, and the demand for each input equals the supply.

GENERAL EQUILIBRIUM ANALYSIS

The basic competitive equilibrium model, or slight variants of it, has proved useful in examining a variety of economic problems, from the effect of a change in tax policy to the effect of restrictions on imports to the effect of decreased defense expenditures.

The procedure for using general equilibrium analysis to describe the effect of some change is straightforward. There is an initial equilibrium, in which all markets clear. Then, with the change, there is a disturbance to some market. This results in a new equilibrium price where that market clears. But the disturbance is now translated to other markets. When the prices in those markets adjust, to equate demand with supply,

---

[4] Thus, the market equilibrium is described as the simultaneous solution to the three equations

$$L^d = L^s, \ K^d = K^s, \ Q^d = Q^s.$$

reverberations are felt in the first market. Eventually, a new equilibrium is attained, in which all markets simultaneously clear. We compare the new equilibrium with the old. The *general* equilibrium effect of the shift consists of the differences—in prices, wages, returns to capital, output, employment, etc.—between the two equilibriums.

EXAMPLE: THE CORPORATION INCOME TAX

Ascertaining the effect of the corporate income tax—the tax the federal government imposes on the net income of corporations—provides an example of why general equilibrium analysis is essential. Over 80 percent of nonfarm business takes place in the corporate sector. Since much of the income of a corporation can be viewed as a return on the capital that has been invested in it, the corporation income tax is often seen as a tax on capital in the corporate sector. Such a tax will make it less attractive for corporations to use capital; savings will flow into the unincorporated sector, reducing the return to capital there.

A partial equilibrium analysis might conclude that the effect of a tax on capital in the corporate sector is to reduce the return to capital in the corporate sector—and stop there. A general equilibrium analysis will note that in equilibrium, investors bid up or down the price of different investments available, so that all the investments, whether in the corporate or noncorporate sector, provide roughly the same rate of return, that is, the same return per dollar invested. If one investment paid a higher return per dollar invested than other investments, all investors would want to put their money there. As a result of this high demand, its price would increase; in fact, its price would increase until its rate of return (the total return divided by the price) was reduced to the point that it yielded the same return, per dollar invested, as any other investment. If an investment paid a lower return, demand for it would fall; its price would decrease until its rate of return increased.

Thus, the after-tax rate of return on all investments, whether in the corporate or the noncorporate sector, will be lowered to the same extent, even though the tax is only imposed on the corporate sector. The effect on other sectors is no less important than the effect on the sector in which the tax is imposed. An analysis of the corporate income tax that failed to take into account these general equilibrium responses would be, at best, incomplete; at worst, seriously misleading.

One of the important lessons to emerge from a general equilibrium analysis of any tax is that those who bear the burden of the tax may be quite different from those who actually pay it. There is a widespread belief that corporations are rich and thus should pay the corporation income tax. But it is not corporations, in the end, who bear the burden of a tax on corporations. Individuals do, either as consumers, through higher prices; as workers, through lower wages; or as shareholders, through lower returns on their investments. Which group or groups are affected depends on the general equilibrium responses of the economy to the tax. The most commonly accepted view among economists is that in the long run, most of the burden of the tax rests on workers and consumers, and relatively little is shouldered by the firms' shareholders or those who have lent the firm money. This is quite contrary to popular impressions.

WHEN PARTIAL EQUILIBRIUM ANALYSIS WILL DO

In the example just given, the importance of general equilibrium analysis is apparent. Can we ever simply focus on what goes on in a single market, without worrying about the reverberations in the rest of the economy? Are there circumstances in which partial equilibrium analysis will provide a fairly accurate answer to the effect of, say, a change in a tax? Fortunately, the answer to these questions is yes.

For some tax changes, for instance, partial equilibrium analysis is adequate and appropriate because the reverberations from the initial imposition of the tax can be ignored. That is, as individuals shift their demand away from the taxed good, they shift their demand a little bit toward many, many other goods. Each of the prices of those goods changes only a very little, and the total demand for factors of production like capital and labor changes only negligibly, so that the prices of different factors are virtually unchanged. Moreover, the slight changes in the prices of different goods and inputs have only a slight feedback effect on the demand and supply curve of the industry upon which the analysis is focusing. In these circumstances, partial equilibrium analysis may provide a good approximation to what will actually happen.

EXAMPLE: A TAX ON CIGARETTES

The effect of a tax on cigarettes is an example where partial equilibrium analysis works well. Back in 1951, the federal tax on a pack of cigarettes was worth 42 percent of the total price paid by a consumer. Since then, the tax has not been adjusted for inflation, so as the price of cigarettes (and everything else) has increased over the past few decades, the tax has not. By the late 1980s, the tax was only about 15 percent of the total market price of a pack. A case could be made for increasing the tax, particularly since even doubling the tax—still well within the 42 percent figure—on each pack of cigarettes would raise nearly $3 billion a year. What predictions can be made about the consequences of adding an additional 15 percent tax?

The tax can be thought of as shifting the supply curve of cigarettes up by the amount of the tax. As Figure 14.2 illustrates, demand is reduced from Q_0 to Q_1. Since expenditures on cigarettes are a small proportion of anyone's income, a 15 percent increase in their price will have only a small effect on overall consumption patterns. While the reduced quantity demanded of cigarettes (and the indirect changed demand for other goods) will have a slight effect on the total demand for labor, this effect is really so small

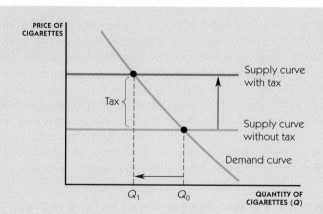

Figure 14.2 PARTIAL EQUILIBRIUM ANALYSIS OF THE EFFECT OF A TAX ON CIGARETTES

A tax on cigarettes raises the price of cigarettes and reduces consumption slightly. The second-round reverberations of this tax are sufficiently slight that they can be ignored.

as to be negligible, and so one would not expect any noticeable change in the wage rate. Similarly, the tax will not have a real effect on the return to capital.

So under these circumstances, where more distant general equilibrium effects are likely to be so faint as to be indiscernible, a partial equilibrium analysis of a tax on cigarettes may well be appropriate.

THE CIRCULAR FLOW OF FUNDS

General equilibrium analysis is one way to think about the interrelations of the various parts of the economy. Another is to consider the flow of funds through the economy. Households buy goods and services from firms. Households supply labor and capital to firms. The income individuals receive, whether in the form of wages or the return on their savings, is spent to buy the goods that firms produce.

Figure 14.3 depicts this **circular flow** for a simplified economy in which there are no savings (and therefore no capital), no government, and no foreign trade. Firms hire labor from households and sell goods to households. The income they receive from selling their products goes to pay their workers, and anything left over is paid out to households as profits.

A circular flow can be analyzed from any starting point, but let's start on the upper arrow (at point A), moving from left to right. Consumers pay money to firms to buy their goods and services, and this money then flows back through the firms to households at *B* in the form of wages, rents on land, and profits. Not only is the circular flow diagram useful in keeping track of how funds flow through the economy, it also enables us to focus on certain balance conditions, which must always be satisfied. Thus, in the figure, the income of households (the flow of funds from firms) must equal the expenditures of households (the flow of funds to firms).

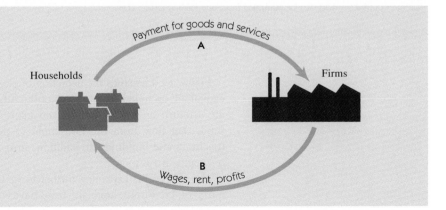

Figure 14.3 A SIMPLE CIRCULAR FLOW DIAGRAM

In this simple circular flow diagram, only labor and product markets and only the household and firm sectors are represented. It can be analyzed from any starting point. For example, funds flow from households to firms in the form of purchases of goods and services. Funds flow from firms to households in the form of payments for the labor of workers and profits paid to owners.

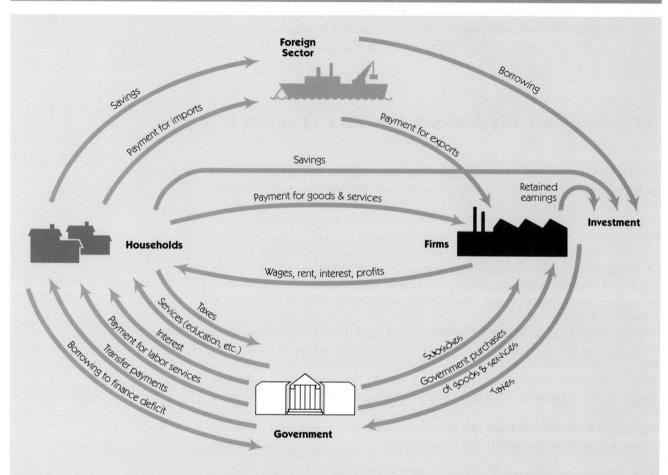

Figure 14.4 CIRCULAR FLOW WITH GOVERNMENT AND FOREIGN SECTOR ADDED

This expanded circular flow diagram shows the labor, capital, and product markets along with households, firms, government, and foreign countries; it too can be analyzed from any starting point. The flow of funds into each sector must balance the flow of funds out of each sector.

Figure 14.4 expands the depiction of circular flow in several ways. First, savings and capital are included. Here, some of the funds that flow from the firm to the household are a return on capital (interest on loans, dividends on equities), while some of the funds that flow from the household to the firm are savings, which go to purchase machines and buildings. In addition, firms retain some of their earnings and use them to finance investment.

The diagram is expanded further to include funds flowing into and out of the government. Now households and firms have both additional sources of funds and additional places where funds go. Some households receive money from the government (like

Social Security and welfare payments); some sell their labor services to the government rather than private firms; and some receive interest on loans to the government (U.S. government bonds). And there is now an important additional outflow: part of household income goes to the government, in the form of taxes. Similarly, firms have additional sources of inflow in the sales of goods and services they make to the government and in government subsidies to firms, and an additional outflow in the taxes they must pay to the government.

Just as the flow of funds into and out of households and firms must balance, the flow of funds into the government must balance the flow of funds out.[5] Funds go out as purchases of goods and services from firms, purchases of labor services from households, and payments of interest to households on the government debt. Funds also go out as direct flows to households, for Social Security, welfare payments, and so forth (called "transfer payments" in the diagram), and to firms as subsidies. Funds flow into the government from taxes on both households and firms. When there is a deficit—that is, when the government spends more than it collects in taxes—as there has been in recent years, funds go into the government as borrowings from households. The government finances the difference between what it spends and what it raises in taxes by borrowing (in our diagram, from households).

Figure 14.4 also includes the flow to and from foreign countries. Firms sell goods to foreigners (exports) and borrow funds from foreigners. Households buy goods from foreigners (imports) and invest funds in foreign firms. Again, there must be a balance in the flow of funds: U.S. exports plus what the country borrows from abroad (the flow of funds from abroad) must equal its imports plus what it lends abroad (the flow of funds to other countries).[6]

The flow of funds diagram is useful as a way of keeping track of the various relationships in the economy. The various balance conditions that make up the diagram are basically identities. Identities, as we know, are statements that are always true; they follow from the basic definitions of the concepts involved. Household income, for example, must equal expenditures on goods plus savings (the flow of funds to firms).

The interconnections and balance conditions making up circular flow analysis are the same as those that arise in the competitive equilibrium model discussed earlier in the chapter. Even if the economy were not competitive, however, the interrelationships and balance conditions of the circular flow diagram would still be true. The circular flow diagram is useful, for it reminds us that whether the economy is competitive or not, if one element of a balance changes, some other element *must* change.

Let's put the circular flow diagram to work. Consider a reduction in the personal income tax, such as occurred in 1981 under President Reagan. The flow of funds into the government was reduced. The circular flow diagram reminds us that if flows in and out are to remain balanced, then either some other flow into the government must be increased or some flow out of the government must be decreased. That is, either some other tax must be increased, government borrowing must increase, or government expenditures must decrease.

[5] We ignore here the possibility that the government can simply pay for what it obtains by printing money. In the United States, the government always finances any shortfall in revenue by borrowing.

[6] This condition will play an important role in the discussion of Chapter 38. It can be put another way: the difference between U.S. imports and exports must equal the net flow of funds from abroad (the difference between what the country borrows from abroad and what it lends).

CLOSE-UP: THE MINIMUM WAGE AND GENERAL EQUILIBRIUM

Today the issue of a minimum wage seems of interest mostly to those who work in the fast food business. But when the first minimum wage law was adopted by the passage of the Fair Labor Standard Act of 1938, it had general equilibrium effects that altered the economic character of northern and southern states.

From the end of the Civil War until the 1930s, the South was poorer than the North, and the Southern economy was centered on industries and technologies that made use of the lower wages commonly paid in the South. When enacted, the minimum wage law required that wages be no lower than 32.5 cents per hour. But because wages were so much lower in the South, many more workers were affected there. For example, 44 percent of Southern textile workers were paid below the minimum wage, but only 6 percent of Northern

textile workers were. African-Americans in the South, who often tended to hold the lowest-paying jobs, were particularly affected. Many of them lost their jobs and migrated North. However, the economy of the South, no longer able to pay low wages, adapted by seeking out investment, which over the last few decades has helped to make some southern states like Texas and Florida among the fastest-growing in the country.

Gavin Wright, professor of economics at Stanford University, described the situation this way: "The overall effect of this history on black Americans is complex, mixed, and ironic. Displacement and suffering were severe. Yet in abolishing the low-wage South, the federal government also destroyed the nation's most powerful bastion of racism and white supremacy. The civil rights movement of the 1960s was able to use the South's hunger for capital in-

flows as an effective weapon in forcing desegregation. Similarly, migration to the North allowed dramatic increases in incomes and educational opportunities for many blacks; yet the same migration channeled other blacks into the high-unemployment ghettos which if anything have worsened with the passage of time."

A partial equilibrium analysis of the effects of enacting a minimum wage would only look at how the law affected labor markets. But for society as a whole, the effects of enacting such a law were far more momentous, touching on issues like racial desegregation and the growth of urban ghettos, which continue to plague many northern cities to this day.

Source: Gavin Wright, "The Economic Revolution in the American South," *Journal of Economic Perspectives* (Summer 1987) 1:161–78.

COMPETITIVE EQUILIBRIUM AND ECONOMIC EFFICIENCY

The first part of this chapter introduced the basic model of competitive equilibrium. The equilibrium entails prices, wages, and returns to capital such that all markets—for goods, labor, capital (and other factors of production)—clear. The model of competitive equilibrium provides basic answers to the fundamental economic questions posed in Chapter 1. The input prices (wages and returns to capital) determine the income of different individuals. To calculate a person's income, we simply have to know how much labor he supplies and how much capital he has. In a market economy, goods go to individuals in proportion to their income. Thus, markets, by determining the receipts to different factors of production, provide an answer to the question "For whom are the goods produced?"

The input prices also determine *how* goods are produced; for instance, whether firms use techniques of production that require a great deal of labor or methods that require a great deal of capital. Finally, the input prices, together with the goods prices, determine how much of each good is produced. Firms produce up to the point where price equals marginal cost. Input prices and goods prices are all determined simultaneously, by the balancing required for demand to equal supply in all markets.

A change in economic conditions, such as the imposition of a tax, the migration of labor, or a sudden decline in supply of some good, results in a new equilibrium to the economy. We have seen how the effects of such changes can be traced out. In the new equilibrium, each of the economic questions will be answered slightly differently. Input prices will change; some individuals may be better off, while others are worse off. There is a new answer to the question "For whom are the goods produced?" The change in input prices will also change how firms produce their goods. Moreover, the demand for different goods may change with the change in the distribution of income. Thus, the questions "What is produced, and in what quantities?" and "How is it produced?" will have new answers.

Economists are interested, however, not only in describing the market equilibrium, but in evaluating it. Do competitive markets do a "good" job in allocating resources? Chapter 7 introduced the idea of Adam Smith's "invisible hand," which said that market economies are efficient. One of the most important achievements of modern economic theory has been to establish in what sense and under what conditions the market is efficient.

PARETO EFFICIENCY

To economists, the concept of efficiency is related to a concern with the well-being of those in the economy. Resource allocations that have the property that no one can be made better off without making someone else worse off are called **Pareto-efficient allocations,** after the great Italian economist and sociologist Vilfredo Pareto (1848–1923). When economists refer to efficiency, Pareto efficiency is what they normally mean. Saying that a market is efficient is a compliment; in the same way that an efficient machine uses its inputs as productively as it can, an efficient market leaves no unexploited gains to trade, no unexploited way of increasing output with the same level of inputs—the only way one person can be made better off is by taking resources away from another, and making the second person worse off.

It is easy to see how a resource allocation might not be Pareto efficient. Assume the government is given the job of distributing chocolate and vanilla ice cream and that it pays no attention to people's preferences. Assume, moreover, that some individuals love chocolate and hate vanilla, while others love vanilla and hate chocolate. Some chocolate lovers will get vanilla ice cream, and some vanilla lovers will get chocolate ice cream. Clearly, this is Pareto inefficient. Allowing people to trade makes both groups better off.

To illustrate further the idea of Pareto efficiency, consider a simple island economy with only two individuals, Robinson Crusoe and Friday. Crusoe and Friday will have individual desires to supply labor and demand products, and they will be willing to specialize according to their comparative advantages and trade according to their preferences. By trading, each has the capability to become enriched beyond what he could accomplish on his own.

We can represent the Pareto efficiency of this island economy diagrammatically, using the concept of utility introduced in Chapter 8. For now, we can think of utility as simply any way of measuring how well off someone is. Given the level of utility of Crusoe, how well off can we make Friday? How high a utility level can Friday obtain? The curve giving the maximum level of utility that one individual can attain, given the level of utility attained by the other, is called the **utility possibilities curve.** It is shown in Figure 14.5. For our purposes, the only important property of the utility possibilities curve is that it is downward sloping. This simply reflects the fact that we cannot make one person, Crusoe, better off without making the other person, Friday, worse off. Thus, all the points on the utility possibilities curve are Pareto efficient.

Movements along the utility possibilities curve, say from E_0 to E_1, represent redistributions. One individual is better off, the other worse off. Movements from a point below the utility curve to a point on the curve, say from F to E_0, represent an increase in efficiency. Both individuals are better off. An economy is Pareto efficient if and only if it operates along its utility possibilities curve.

There is a mistaken view that *all* economic changes represent nothing more than

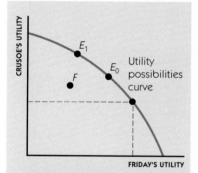

Figure 14.5 THE UTILITY POSSIBILITIES CURVE

The utility possibilities curve shows the maximum level of utility of one individual given the level of utility of other individuals. Pareto efficiency requires that the economy be on its utility possibilities curve. Along the curve, one individual can only gain at the expense of other individuals.

redistributions, that gains to one group are nothing more than subtractions from others. In this view, the only effect of rent control is redistribution—landlords receive less, and are worse off, by the same amount that their tenants' rents are reduced (and the tenants are better off). In some countries, unions have expressed similar views, and see wage increases as having no further consequences than redistributing income to workers from those who own or who manage firms. This view is mistaken, because in each of these instances, there are consequences beyond the redistribution. Rent control and minimum wages above those that clear the labor market both result in the economy being below the utility possibilities curve. They result, in other words, in inefficiencies.

CONDITIONS FOR THE PARETO EFFICIENCY OF THE MARKET ECONOMY

For the economy to be Pareto efficient, it must meet the conditions of exchange efficiency, production efficiency, and product-mix efficiency. Let's consider each of these conditions separately; in so doing, we will see why the basic competitive model attains Pareto efficiency. (Recall the basic ingredients of that model: rational, perfectly informed households interacting with rational, profit-maximizing firms in competitive markets, and in an environment in which the market failures discussed in Chapter 7, such as externalities, do not occur.)

EXCHANGE EFFICIENCY

Exchange efficiency requires that whatever the economy produces must be distributed among individuals in an efficient way. If I like chocolate ice cream and you like vanilla ice cream, exchange efficiency requires that I get the chocolate and you get the vanilla.

When there is exchange efficiency, there is no scope for further trade among individuals. Chapter 3 discussed the advantages of free exchange among individuals and nations. Any prohibition or restriction on trade results in exchange inefficiency. For instance, in war times, governments often ration scarce goods, like sugar. People are given coupons that allow them to buy, say, a pound of sugar a month. If sugar carries a price of $1 a pound, having $1 is not enough; you must also have the coupon. There is often considerable controversy about whether people should be allowed to sell their coupons, or trade their sugar coupons for, say, a butter coupon. If the government prohibits the sale or trading of coupons, then the economy will not be exchange efficient—and so it will not be Pareto efficient.

The price system ensures that exchange efficiency is attained. In deciding how much of a good to buy, people balance the marginal benefit they receive by buying an extra unit with the cost of that extra unit, its price. Hence, price can be thought of as a rough measure of the *marginal* benefit that an individual receives from a good; that is, the benefit a person receives from one more unit of the good. If all individuals face the same prices, their *marginal* benefits will be the same at the quantities they actually consume. For those who like chocolate ice cream a great deal and vanilla ice cream very little, this will entail consuming many more chocolate ice cream cones than vanilla; and conversely for the vanilla ice cream lover. Notice that to make sure that goods get delivered to the right person, no single individual or agency needs to know who is a chocolate ice cream lover and who is a vanilla ice cream lover; indeed, not even the

Airlines want their planes to fly as full as possible. However, they also know that a certain small percentage of people who purchased a ticket for any given flight are not going to show up. This gives the airlines an incentive to "overbook" flights; that is, to sell more tickets than there are seats in the reasonable expectation that there will still be room to take everyone who actually shows up. But sometimes everyone does show up, and a decision must then be made about who will be bumped from the flight. Several methods of making this choice are possible.

In the 1960s, the airlines simply bumped whoever showed up last, and gave those people tickets for a later flight. Bumped passengers had no recourse. This is the sort of policy that causes high blood pressure.

To avoid imposing these costs on frustrated passengers, a second policy might be for the government to forbid airlines to overbook flights. But in this case, some planes will be forced to fly with empty seats that some people would have been willing to buy. Both the airlines and travelers who could not get a ticket would be losers.

A third possibility was proposed by economist Julian Simon in a paper published in 1968. Simon wrote: "The solution is simple. All that need happen when there is overbooking is that an airline agent distributes among the ticket-holders an envelope and a bid form, instructing each person to write down the lowest sum of money he is willing to accept in return for waiting for the next flight. The lowest bidder is paid in cash and given a ticket for the next flight. All other passengers board the plane and complete the flight to their destination. All parties benefit, and no party loses."

As you may know if you have recently traveled on an overbooked flight, the airlines eventually adopted a policy very similar to this one. Today airlines often offer a free ticket on a separate future flight as compensation to anyone willing to wait. (Sometimes they offer a coupon good for a certain amount of money off on a future flight instead.) People willing to accept such a deal are clearly

owners of stores have to know the preferences of each person. Each consumer, by her own action, helps to ensure that exchange efficiency is attained.

Notice too that if different individuals face *different* prices, then the economy will not, in general, be exchange efficient, because the marginal benefit of the good to the person who has to pay the high price will be far greater than to the person who pays a low price. If manufacturers charge some customers (say, those who buy in bulk) a lower price than others, then the economy will not be exchange efficient. If airlines charge different customers different prices, then the economy will also not be exchange efficient.

Currently, in California, the government charges higher prices for water to those who live in cities than it charges farmers, as much as ten times more. However, it does not allow the farmers to trade. If the farmers were allowed to sell their water, they might willingly sell a substantial amount, because the value of the water is so much higher to urban dwellers than it is to farmers. The trade could make both better off. The prohibition on trade results in a Pareto inefficiency.

PRODUCTION EFFICIENCY

For an economy to be Pareto efficient, it must also be **productively efficient;** that is, it must not be possible to produce more of some goods without producing less of other goods. In Chapter 2, the production possibilities curve was introduced to illustrate the maximum amount of one good that the economy could produce, given the level of production of other goods. Pareto efficiency requires that the economy operate along the production possibilities curve, such as the one shown in Figure 14.6.

This figure shows the production possibilities curve for a simple economy that produces only two goods, apples and oranges. Clearly, if the economy is at point *I*, inside the production possibilities curve, it cannot be Pareto efficient. Society could produce more of both apples and oranges, and by distributing them to different individuals, it could make people better off. Thus, if the economy is below its production possibilities curve, it must also be below its utility possibilities curve; but being on the production possibilities curve does not guarantee that the economy is on its utility possibilities curve. For that to be true, the two other conditions for Pareto efficiency have to be satisfied, the exchange efficiency condition discussed above and the product-mix efficiency condition to be discussed below.

Prices signal to firms the scarcity of each of the inputs they use. When all firms face the same prices of labor, capital goods, and other inputs, they will take the appropriate actions to economize on each of these inputs, ensuring that the economy operates along its production possibilities curve.

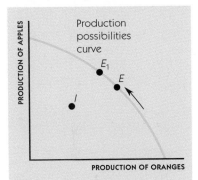

Figure 14.6 THE PRODUCTION POSSIBILITIES CURVE

The production possibilities curve shows the maximum level of output of one good given the level of output of other goods. Production efficiency requires that the economy be on its production possibilities curve. Along the curve, the only way to increase production of one good (here, apples) is to decrease the production of other goods (oranges).

Taxes may interfere with the production efficiency of the economy. Suppose the government imposes a tax on corporations, the effect of which is generally thought to increase how much corporations have to pay to obtain funds. Because corporations thus face a higher cost of obtaining funds, with which they can then purchase capital goods, they will economize more on their use of capital goods (substituting labor) than will unincorporated firms that do not have to pay the corporate income tax. The effect of the corporation income tax is thus to move the economy below its production possibilities curve.

PRODUCT-MIX EFFICIENCY

The third condition for Pareto efficiency is that there be **product-mix efficiency;** that is, that the mix of goods produced by the economy reflect the preferences of those in the economy, or that the economy produce along the production possibilities curve at a point that reflects the preferences of consumers. The price system again ensures that this condition will be satisfied. Assume that the economy is initially producing at a point along the production possibilities curve, E in Figure 14.6. Consumers decide that they like apples more and oranges less. The increased demand for apples will result in the price of apples increasing, and this will lead to an increased output of apples; at the same time, the decreased demand for oranges will result in the price of oranges falling, and this in turn will lead to a decreased output of oranges. The economy will move from E to a point such as E_1, where there are more apples and fewer oranges produced; the mix of goods produced in the economy will have changed to reflect the changed preferences of consumers.

THREE CONDITIONS FOR PARETO EFFICIENCY

1. Exchange efficiency: Goods must be distributed among individuals in a way that means there are no gains from further trade.

2. Production efficiency: The economy must be on its production possibilities curve.

3. Product-mix efficiency: The economy must produce a mix of goods reflecting the preferences of consumers.

COMPETITIVE MARKETS AND PARETO EFFICIENCY

We now know what economists mean when they say that market economies are efficient, or that the price system results in economic efficiency. What they mean is that the economy is Pareto efficient; no one can be made better off without making someone else worse off. We have also learned why competitive markets ensure that all three of the basic conditions for Pareto efficiency are attained: exchange efficiency, production efficiency, and product-mix efficiency.

The argument that competitive markets ensure Pareto efficiency can be put somewhat loosely in another way: a rearrangement of resources can only benefit people who voluntarily agree to it. But in competitive equilibrium, people have already agreed to all the exchanges they are willing to make; no one wishes to produce more or less or to demand more or less, given the prices he faces. If no one desires to change, then no one can benefit except at the expense of someone else.

Pareto efficiency does *not* say that there are no ways to make one or many individuals better off. Obviously, resources could be taken from some and given to others, and the recipients would be better off. We have seen how, for instance, government interventions with the market, such as rent control, do benefit some individuals—those who are lucky enough to get the rent-controlled apartments. But in the process, someone is made worse off. Indeed, in each of the cases where government interferes with competitive markets, some people are worse off.

COMPETITIVE MARKETS AND INCOME DISTRIBUTION

Efficiency is better than inefficiency, but it is not everything. In the competitive equilibrium, some individuals might be very rich, while others live in dire poverty. One person might have skills that are highly valued, while another does not. Competition may result in an efficient economy with a very unequal distribution of resources. In terms of the utility possibilities curve, the competitive equilibrium might be at a point such as E in Figure 14.7, where Crusoe is very well off and Friday can hardly survive.

On a broader scale, the circular flow diagrams presented earlier showed that funds flow between different sectors of the economy in a variety of forms. Funds flow from firms to households, for example, as wages, rents on land, interest, and profits. However, different households would prefer that funds flow in different ways. Households that have no capital would prefer to receive more money from the corporate sector as wages. Retired households that depend on payments of interest and dividends may prefer to receive more money from the corporate sector as a return on the use of capital. The form in which funds actually flow from firms to households will affect the distribution of income in the economy.

The law of supply and demand in a competitive economy determines how the available income will be divided up. The result will be economically efficient, but it may also produce distributions of income that seem, at least to some, morally repugnant. An economy where some individuals live in mansions while others barely eke out a living may be efficient, but that still hardly makes the situation desirable. Left to themselves, competitive markets may provide an answer to the question "For whom are goods produced?" that seems unacceptable.

This unacceptable response does not mean that the competitive market mechanism should be abandoned, at least not under the conditions assumed in our basic model, with perfectly informed, rational consumers and firms interacting in perfectly competitive markets. Even if society as a whole wishes to redistribute income, it should not dispense with competitive markets. Instead, all that is needed is to redistribute the wealth that people possess, and then leave the rest to the workings of a competitive market. Under some conditions, every point on the utility possibilities curve can be attained by such a redistribution of wealth.

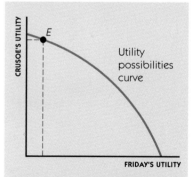

Figure 14.7 PARETO EFFICIENCY AND INCOME INEQUALITY

The Pareto-efficient competitive equilibrium might occur at a point like E, where one individual is extremely well off and the other can barely subsist.

EFFICIENCY

An economy in competitive equilibrium is Pareto efficient.
Any Pareto-efficient resource allocation that society desires can be obtained through
    the market mechanism.

Frequently government interferences with the market are justified on the grounds
that they increase equality. These government policies are often based on the widely
held but mistaken (as we have already seen) view that all redistributions are just that;
some individuals get more, others get less, but there are no further repercussions. We
now know that changing relative prices to achieve redistribution—such as imposing
minimum wage laws or subsidizing some good—will have effects in addition to redistributing income. Such changes interfere with the economy's efficiency. Or to put it
another way, the economy will be operating below its utility possibilities curve. One
consequence of lower rents for apartments, for example, is that the return on capital
invested in rental housing will fall, and the economy will as a result invest too little in
rental housing. Because of this underinvestment, the economy is not efficient.

Thus, interventions in the economy justified on the grounds that they increase equality
need to be treated with caution. To attain an efficient allocation of resources with the
desired distribution of income, *if* the assumptions of the competitive model are satisfied
by the economy, the *sole* role of the government is to redistribute initial wealth. Not
only can one rely on the market mechanism thereafter, but interfering with the market
will actually put the economy below its utility possibilities curve.

Both of the results just presented—that competitive markets are Pareto efficient, and
that every Pareto-efficient allocation, regardless of the desired distribution of income,
can be obtained through the market mechanism—are **theorems.** That is, they are logical
propositions that follow from basic definitions and assumptions, such as what is meant
by a competitive economy and what is meant by Pareto efficiency. These theorems are
based on other assumptions as well, such as the absence of externalities. When these
assumptions are not satisfied, market economies may not be Pareto efficient, and more
extensive government interventions may be required to obtain Pareto-efficient allocations. Later chapters will explore these circumstances in greater detail.

LOOKING BEYOND THE BASIC MODEL: MARKET FAILURES AND THE ROLE OF GOVERNMENT

This chapter has brought together the pieces of the basic competitive model. It has
shown how the competitive equilibrium in an ideal economy is achieved. To the extent
that conditions in the real world match the approximations of the basic competitive

CLOSE-UP: THE COST OF AIR SAFETY FOR CHILDREN

Many states require that small children in cars ride in specially designed safety seats. So why shouldn't small children traveling by plane be required to ride in safety seats as well? Congressional hearings were held on this subject in the summer of 1990. Everyone agreed that in at least a few cases, such seats would save a child's life in an airplane crash. Nevertheless, after considering the potential consequences and side effects of such a rule, the Federal Aviation Administration argued against it.

On the benefit side, the FAA estimated that mandatory safety seats would save the life of one child in an airline crash each decade. But with a rule requiring safety seats, parents would have to pay perhaps $185 to buy the safety seats themselves, in addition to paying for a seat for the child; now, when children sit in their parents' laps, parents do not have to buy them tickets. With those extra costs, the FAA estimated that 20 percent of the families who now fly with small children would either stay home or drive. The additional driving would lead to 9 additional highway deaths, 52 serious injuries, and about 2,300 minor injuries over the same ten-year period, according to FAA estimates.

Saving an additional child's life is tremendously valuable. But in this case, the attempt to save a life appears likely to cause an even greater loss of life.

Source: Jim Mitchell, "Valley Execs Remain Upbeat," *San Jose Mercury News,* July 17, 1990, p. D1.

model, there will be economic efficiency. Government will have little role in the economy beyond establishing a legal framework within which to enforce market transactions.

A group of economists, referred to as **free-market economists** for their strong faith in unfettered markets as the path to economic efficiency, believe that the competitive model provides a good description of most markets most of the time. These economists, who have included Nobel laureates Milton Friedman of Stanford University's Hoover Institution and the late George Stigler of the University of Chicago, believe that there is a very limited role for government in economic affairs. In their view, government intervention should be restricted mainly to changing unacceptable distributions of income, and even in this area government should operate with restraint.

Most economists agree that the model itself is tremendously powerful, but many are not quite so sure that it provides an accurate description of the real-world economy. These economists, who can collectively be called **imperfect-market economists,** see significant discrepancies between the basic competitive model and the conditions they observe when they study actual consumers, firms, and markets. Such discrepancies lead them to question whether private markets, left to operate on their own, will produce economically efficient outcomes.

Imperfect-market economists would not, however, discard the model: for them, it is still an important baseline for investigation. For example, many economists who specialize in the study of the economy's industrial structure, such as Joseph Bain of the University of California at Berkeley or F. M. Scherer of Harvard, argue that competition is limited, and try to explain why this is so. If the cigarette market is not competitive, the competitive model will yield incorrect predictions concerning, for instance, the consequences of an increase in the tax on cigarettes.

Other economists, such as Nobel laureate Kenneth J. Arrow of Stanford University, contend that the assumptions that firms have perfect information about the quality of their workers or that investors have perfect information about the returns to different investment opportunities are not good assumptions, and that imperfect information results in capital and labor markets functioning in ways quite different from that described by the basic competitive model.

Still other economists, such as MIT's Nobel laureate Robert Solow, argue that even if the model is generally appropriate, there are important instances where markets cannot be relied upon without government intervention. They are concerned about the pollution of the environment and about unemployment. They believe that these instances of market failures, where one or more of the assumptions of the basic competitive model are violated, imply that there may be some scope for government intervention to increase economic efficiency.

Thus, whether or not economists believe that the real-world economy matches the basic competitive model, they find the model to be a useful way of organizing their thinking about the economy. What are the consequences when the underlying assumptions are not valid? Which of the assumptions are most suspect? What evidence do we have with which we can assess either the validity of the model's underlying assumptions or its implications? The next part of this book is devoted to these questions, and to the role of government that emerges from the answers.

One final word of warning is in order before we embark on our study of market imperfections. That is, while the fact that markets do not work perfectly suggests a possible role for government, it does not necessarily mean that government intervention will improve matters. Those who argue against government intervention might concede that there are important market failures, but also argue that there are inherent problems in the attempts by government to improve matters.

TWO VIEWS OF THE BASIC COMPETITIVE MODEL

Free-market view: The competitive model provides a good description of the economy, and government intervention is not required.

Imperfect-market view: In many markets, the competitive model does not provide a good description—for instance, because competition is limited and information is imperfect. There are important market failures, evidenced by unemployment and environmental pollution, requiring at least selective government intervention.

REVIEW AND PRACTICE

SUMMARY

1. When an economic change affects many markets at once, general equilibrium analysis is used to study the interactions among various parts of the economy. But when the secondary repercussions of a change are small, partial equilibrium analysis, focusing on only one or a few markets, is sufficient.

2. General equilibrium in the basic competitive model occurs when wages, interest rates, and prices are such that demand is equal to supply in all labor markets, in all capital markets, and in all product markets. All markets clear.

3. Circular flow of funds diagrams show capital, labor, and product market interrelationships between households, firms, government, and the foreign sector. The flow of funds in and out of each sector must balance.

4. Under the conditions of the basic competitive model, the economy's resource allocation is Pareto efficient; that is, no one can be made better off without making someone else worse off.

5. The distribution of income that emerges from competitive markets may possibly be very unequal. However, under the conditions of the basic competitive model, a redistribution of wealth can move the economy to a more equal allocation that is also Pareto efficient. No further government intervention is required.

6. Some economists hold that the basic competitive model provides an essentially accurate view of most of the economy; markets ensure economic efficiency, and there

is only a limited role for government. Others maintain that many markets are quite imperfect, the basic competitive model provides no more than a starting point for analysis, and government intervention is required to deal with some of society's problems.

KEY TERMS

partial equilibrium analysis

general equilibrium analysis

circular flow

Pareto-efficient allocations

utility possibilities curve

exchange efficiency

production efficiency

product-mix efficiency

REVIEW QUESTIONS

1. What is the difference between partial and general equilibrium analysis? When is each one especially appropriate?

2. List the principal flows into and out of firms, households, government, and the foreign sector.

3. How does the economy in general equilibrium answer the four basic economic questions: What is produced, and in what quantities? How are these goods produced? For whom are they produced? Who decides how resources are allocated?

4. What is meant by Pareto efficiency? What is required for the economy to be Pareto efficient? If the conditions of the basic competitive model are satisfied, is the economy Pareto efficient?

5. If the distribution of income in the economy is quite unequal, is it necessary to impose price controls or otherwise change prices in the competitive marketplace to make it more equal?

PROBLEMS

1. Decide whether partial equilibrium analysis would suffice in each of these cases, or whether it would be wise to undertake a general equilibrium analysis:
   (a) a tax on alcohol;
   (b) an increase in the Social Security tax;
   (c) a drought that affects farm production in the Midwestern states;
   (d) a rise in the price of crude oil;
   (e) a major airline going out of business.
Explain your answers.

2. Use the extended circular flow diagram, with the foreign sector included, to trace out the possible consequences of the following:
   (a) a law requiring that businesses raise the wages of their employees;
   (b) a decision by consumers to import more and save less;
   (c) an increase in government expenditure financed by a corporate income tax;
   (d) an increase in government expenditure without an accompanying increase in taxes.

3. Explain how each of the following might interfere with exchange efficiency:
   (a) airlines that limit the number of seats they sell at a discount price;
   (b) doctors who charge poor patients less than rich patients;
   (c) firms that give volume discounts.
In each case, what additional trades might be possible?

4. Assume that in the steel industry, given current production levels and technology, 1 machine costing $10,000 can replace 1 worker. Given current production levels and technology in the automobile industry, 1 machine costing $10,000 can replace 2 workers. Is this economy Pareto efficient; that is, is it on its production possibilities curve? If not, explain how total output of both goods can be increased by shifting machines and labor between industries.

5. Consider three ways of helping poor people to buy food, clothing, and shelter. The first way is to pass laws setting price ceilings to keep these basic goods affordable. The second is to have the government distribute coupons that give poor people a discount when they buy these necessities. The third is for the government to distribute income to poor people. Which program is more likely to have a Pareto-efficient outcome? Describe why the other programs are not likely to be Pareto efficient.

APPENDIX: PARETO EFFICIENCY AND COMPETITIVE MARKETS

The concept of the marginal rate of substitution, introduced in the appendices to Chapters 8 and 10, can be used to see more clearly why competitive markets are Pareto efficient.

EXCHANGE EFFICIENCY

Exchange efficiency can be achieved only when all individuals have the same marginal rate of substitution, the amount of one good a person is willing to give up to get one unit of another. In competitive markets, individuals choose a mix of goods for which the marginal rate of substitution is equal to relative prices. Since all individuals face the same relative prices, they all have identical marginal rates of substitution, ensuring the exchange efficiency of the economy.

To see why exchange efficiency requires that all people have the same marginal rate of substitution, let's return to our simple example of Crusoe and Friday and their island economy. Assume that Crusoe's marginal rate of substitution between apples and oranges is 2; that is, he is willing to give up 2 apples for 1 extra orange. Friday's marginal rate of substitution between apples and oranges is 1; he is willing to give up 1 apple for 1 orange. Since their marginal rates of substitution are not equal, we can make one of them better off without making the other worse off (or we can make both of them better off). The allocation is not Pareto efficient.

To see how this is done, suppose we take 1 orange away from Friday and give it to Crusoe. Crusoe would then be willing to give up 2 apples, and be just as well off as before. If he gave up only $1\frac{1}{2}$ apples to Friday, Friday would also be better off. Friday would have given up 1 orange in return for $1\frac{1}{2}$ apples; he would have been willing to make the trade if he had received just 1 apple in return.

It is easy to see that Crusoe and Friday will continue to trade until their marginal rates of substitution are equal. As Friday gives up oranges for apples, his marginal rate of substitution increases; he insists on getting more and more apples for each orange he gives up. Similarly, as Crusoe gives up apples and gets more oranges, his marginal rate of substitution decreases; he is willing to give up fewer apples for each extra orange he gets. Eventually, the two will have identical marginal rates of substitution, at which point trade will stop. Thus, the basic condition for exchange efficiency is that the marginal rates of substitution of all individuals must be the same.

PRODUCTION EFFICIENCY

The condition of production efficiency—when the economy is on its production possibilities curve—is very similar to the condition of exchange efficiency. An economy can only be productively efficient if the marginal rate of technical substitution between any two inputs in any two firms is the same. The marginal rate of technical substitution is the amount that one input can be reduced if another input is increased by one unit, while total output remains constant (see appendix to Chapter 12).

Profit-maximizing firms in a competitive economy choose a mix of inputs such that the marginal rate of technical substitution of different inputs is equal to the relative prices of those inputs. If all firms face the same relative prices of inputs, their marginal rates of technical substitution will all be the same, and production efficiency will result.

For example, consider a case involving the steel and auto industries. Assume that in steel, the marginal rate of substitution between capital expenditures and labor is $2,000; that is, if a company uses one more worker, it can save $2,000 on equipment (or equivalently, two $1,000 machines substitute for one worker). In the auto industry, the marginal rate of substitution is $1,000; one $1,000 machine substitutes for one worker. The marginal rates of substitution between inputs are not equal, which means that the economy is not productively efficient.

Consider a worker moving from the auto to the steel industry. If the steel industry keeps its output at the same level, the additional worker in that industry frees up two machines. One of those machines can be transferred to the auto industry, and production in that industry would stay at the same level. (We are assuming that in the auto industry one $1,000 machine substitutes for one worker.) But one machine is left over. It can be used in the steel industry, the auto industry, or both to increase production.

As we increase the number of workers in steel, the marginal productivity of labor in that industry will diminish, while as we reduce workers in the automobile industry, the marginal productivity of labor in that industry will increase; conversely for machines. As a result, the marginal rates of technical substitution will shift in the two industries, so that they are closer. Spurred on by the profit motive of the individual companies in competitive markets, labor and capital will tend to move between companies until marginal rates of technical substitution are equated, and production efficiency is reached. Thus, production efficiency, which means that the economy is on its production possibilities curve, requires that the marginal rate of technical substitution between any two inputs be the same in all uses.

PRODUCT-MIX EFFICIENCY

This third condition of Pareto efficiency requires that the economy operate at the point along the production possibilities curve that reflects consumers' preferences. Look at a particular point on the production possibilities curve in Figure 14.6, say point E. The **marginal rate of transformation** tells us how many extra units of one good the economy can get if it gives up one unit of another good—how many extra cases of beer the economy can produce if it reduces production of potato chips by a ton, or how many extra cars the economy can get if it gives up one tank. The slope of the production possibilities curve is equal to the marginal rate of transformation. The slope tells us how much of one good, measured along the vertical axis, can be increased if the economy gives up one unit of the good along the horizontal axis.

Product-mix efficiency requires that consumers' marginal rate of substitution equal the marginal rate of transformation. To see why this is so, and how competitive economies ensure product-mix efficiency, consider an economy producing two fruits, apples and oranges. Assume that the marginal rate of substitution between apples and oranges is 2—that is, individuals are willing to give up 2 apples for an additional orange; while the marginal rate of transformation is 1—they only have to give up 1 apple to get an additional orange. Clearly, it pays firms to increase orange production and reduce apple production.

The competitive price system ensures that the economy satisfies the condition for product-mix efficiency. We know that consumers set the marginal rate of substitution equal to the relative price. In a similar way, profit-maximizing firms have an incentive to produce more of some goods and less of others according to the prices they can sell them for, until their marginal rate of transformation is equal to the relative price. If consumers and producers both face the same relative prices, the marginal rate of substitution will equal the marginal rate of transformation. Thus, product-mix efficiency comes about when both consumers and firms face the same prices.

To see more clearly why competitive firms will set the marginal rate of transformation equal to relative prices, consider a firm that produces both apples and oranges. If the company reallocates labor from apples to oranges, apple production is reduced and orange production is increased. Assume apple production goes down by 2 cases and orange production goes up by 1 case. The marginal rate of transformation is 2. If a case of apples sells for $4 and a case of oranges sells for $10, the firm loses $8 on apple sales but gains $10 on orange sales. It is clearly profitable for the firm to make the switch. The firm will continue to switch resources from apples to oranges until the marginal rate of transformation equals the relative price. The same result will occur even if oranges and apples are produced by different firms.[7]

Thus, the basic condition for product-mix efficiency, that the marginal rate of substitution must equal the marginal rate of transformation, will be satisfied in competitive economies because firms set the marginal rate of transformation equal to relative prices, and consumers set their marginal rate of substitution equal to relative prices.

[7] The concept of product-mix efficiency can be illustrated by superimposing a family of indifference curves (Chapter 8, appendix) in the same diagram with the production possibilities curve. Assume, for simplicity, that all individuals are the same. The highest level of welfare that one representative individual can attain is represented by the tangency of her indifference curve with the production possibilities curve. The slopes of two curves that are tangent to each other are equal at the point of tangency. The slope of the indifference curve is the consumer's marginal rate of substitution; the slope of the production possibilities curve is the marginal rate of transformation. Thus, the tangency—and Pareto efficiency—requires that the marginal rate of substitution equal the marginal rate of transformation.

PART THREE

IMPERFECT MARKETS

I n Part Two, the basic model of perfectly competitive markets was developed. If the real world matched up to its assumptions, then markets could be given free rein. They would supply efficient outcomes. If an outcome seemed inequitable, society would simply redistribute initial wealth and let markets take care of the rest.

In the two centuries since Adam Smith first enunciated the view that markets ensure economic efficiency, economists have investigated the model with great care. Nothing they have discovered has shaken their belief that markets are, by and large, the most efficient way to coordinate an economy. However, they have found significant departures between modern economies and the competitive model. Few would go so far as to condemn the model totally for its flaws; its insights are simply too powerful. Rather, most economists use the basic competitive model as the starting point for building a richer, more complete model that recognizes the following qualifications.

1. Most markets are not as competitive as those envisioned by the basic model. For evidence, one need look only as far as the nearest brand name. When we think of beer, we think of Budweiser, Miller, and Coors (among domestic beers). Automobiles bring to mind Chevrolets, Fords, Chryslers, and Toyotas. The examples go on forever; in fact, it is hard to think of a consumer product without attaching a brand name to it. *Brand names should not exist,* according to the basic model, because they mean that every twelve-ounce bottle of beer, every four-cylinder, five-passenger car, and so on is not a perfect substitute for another. A Budweiser enthusiast would probably pay 10 cents more for a six-pack of Bud than for one of Coors. As soon as this becomes possible, Budweiser is no longer strictly the price taker we assumed firms to be in the basic model of Chapter 8. In Chapters 15–17, we will take up failures of competition in product markets and government responses to them. In Chapter 20, we will also encounter restricted competition in the labor market.

2. The basic model simply ignores technological change. It tells us about the striving for efficiency that occurs as consumers and firms meet in competitive markets, but it assumes that all firms operate with a given technology. Competition in the basic model is over price, yet in the real world, the primary focus of competition is the development of new and better products and the improvements in production, transportation, and marketing that allow products to be brought to customers at lower costs and thus at a lower price. This competition takes place not between the multitude of small producers envisaged in the basic competitive model, but often between industrial giants like Du Pont and Dow Chemical, and between the industrial giants and upstarts, like IBM and the slew of small computer firms that eventually took away a major share of the computer market. Chapter 18 will enrich the model to help us understand better this more general view of competition, and to enable us to see how technological change can be encouraged.

3. The individuals and firms envisioned in the basic model have easy and inexpensive access to the information they need in order to operate in any market they enter. Buyers know what they are

buying, whether it is stocks or bonds, a house, a car, or a refrigerator. Firms know perfectly the productivity of each worker they hire, and when a worker goes to work for a firm, he knows precisely what is expected of him in return for his promised pay.

We have already encountered, in Chapter 6, instances in which information problems are important and may fundamentally affect how markets work. One example is the problem of adverse selection in the insurance market. Insurance firms cannot always tell who the best risks are among applicants. As the price of insurance rises, the mix of applicants changes adversely; the best risks drop out of the market. If initially the insurance firm was making a loss, as it raised the price of its premiums its losses might increase rather than decrease. Eventually, it might be "forced" to raise its premium to such a high level that essentially no one would want insurance. Adverse selection may thus effectively destroy a market.

We will see in the following chapters that information problems arise not only in insurance markets, but in other product markets (Chapter 19), labor markets (Chapter 20), and capital markets (Chapter 21). As we will see, many of the ways in which these markets differ from the markets analyzed in Part Two are a consequence of information problems.

4. The basic model assumes that the costs of bringing a good to the market accrue fully and completely to the seller, and that the benefits of consuming a good go fully and completely to the buyer. In Chapter 7, however, we encountered the possibility of externalities, which are extra costs or benefits that do not figure in the market calculation. There we focused on the extreme case of positive externalities known as public goods. These are goods that benefit everyone, like national defense. More precisely, the enjoyment of the good by one person does not detract from what is available to others. Not only is consumption in this sense nonrival, but it is difficult to exclude anyone from benefiting. If an individual were to purchase such a good for herself, she would ignore the benefits that accrue to others in deciding how much to purchase. As a result, private markets do not result in efficient levels of consumption of public goods.

Conversely, private markets oversupply goods characterized by negative externalities, or extra costs not captured in the market transaction. Unchecked pollution is a case in point, as when a firm's output costs society some dirty air or water but the firm does not have to figure this cost of production into the price it charges. In Chapter 23, we will look more closely at both public goods and negative externalities.

5. The basic model answers the question "What goods will be produced, and in what quantities?" by assuming that all desired goods that *can* be brought to market *will* be brought to market. Trees that bloom in gold coins and tablets that guarantee an eternal youth are out of the question. But if customers want to buy green hair coloring, cancer-causing tobacco products, or life insurance policies overladen with extras, then producers can be expected to supply such goods. There are, however, some products consumers would like to buy but cannot that are so similar to

existing products that we can expect they *could* be supplied.

The most obvious examples are in insurance and capital markets. Governments today provide flood insurance, crop insurance, crime insurance in inner cities, medical insurance for the aged, unemployment insurance, disability insurance, and retirement insurance, partly because at the time these programs were instituted the market did not provide them or provided them at a cost that was popularly viewed as prohibitive. Similarly, the government today provides loans and guarantees for loans to students, farmers, small businesses, and home buyers, partly because people felt that the market was not providing these loans by itself. Whether these were real failures of the basic model or whether the individuals demanding these government services simply did not take into account the full costs is one of the questions we will address in Chapter 23, where we will encounter further examples of incomplete markets.

6. In the basic model, all markets hover at or near equilibrium. That is, they clear: supply meets demand at the market price. Decades of evidence, however, suggest that labor markets often do not clear. Workers sometimes want to supply their labor services at the market wage, but cannot do so. The Great Depression of the 1930s is the most dramatic example of large-scale unemployment. During that period, unemployment rates rose as high as 25 percent of those willing and able to work. Theories of unemployment, and of related macroeconomic phenomena, are complex enough that they are postponed until Parts Four and Five, where they can be given the attention they deserve.

7. Even if markets are efficient, the way they allocate resources may appear to be socially unacceptable; there may be massive pockets of poverty, or other social needs may remain unmet. Income distribution is a major concern of modern societies and their governments. Chapter 24 deals with this issue, and includes a description and analysis of the major government programs and policies aimed at changing income distribution.

THE BASIC MODEL VERSUS THE REAL WORLD

The Basic Model	The Real World
1. All markets are competitive.	1. Most markets are *not* characterized by the degree of competition envisioned in the basic model.

2. Technological know-how is fixed and cannot change.

3. Firms, consumers, and any other market participants have easy access to information that is relevant to the markets in which they participate.

4. Sellers bear the full and complete costs of bringing goods to market, and buyers reap the full benefit.

5. All desired markets exist.

6. There is no involuntary unemployment.

7. Competitive markets provide an efficient allocation of resources.

2. Technological change is a central part of competition in modern industrial economies.

3. Good information may be impossible to come by, and in most cases is costly to obtain. In many markets, buyers of products know less than the sellers.

4. Externalities mean that market transactions may not accurately account for costs and benefits and the private market provides an inadequate supply of public goods.

5. Some markets may not exist, even though goods or services in that market might be provided at a cost consumers would be willing to pay.

6. There is involuntary unemployment.

7. Efficiency is not enough. The income distribution generated by the market may be socially unacceptable.

CHAPTER 15

MONOPOLIES AND IMPERFECT COMPETITION

I n the competitive model discussed in Part Two, markets are assumed to have so many buyers and sellers that none of them believe their actions will have any effect on the market equilibrium price. The buyer or seller takes the price as given, and then decides how much to buy or sell. At the "market" price, the seller can sell as much as she wants. But any effort to outfox the market has particularly dramatic consequences: if, for instance, she raises her price above that of her competitors, her sales will be zero.

That there are instances in which markets are not very competitive seems transparent. For years, almost all of the aluminum in the United States was produced by a single firm, Alcoa, and Kodak controlled the market for film. Some firms so dominated a product that their brand name became synonymous with the product, as with Kleenex "brand" tissues or Jell-O brand gelatin.

In some industries, such as the automobile (before the onslaught of Japanese cars in the early 1970s) or soft drink (Coca-Cola, Pepsi, Canada Dry), a handful of firms dominate a market, producing similar but different products. When one such firm raises its price a little—say, by 2 or 3 percent—it loses some customers but far from all; if it lowers its price by 2 or 3 percent, it gains additional customers, but it does not succeed in getting the entire market for itself. As a result, these companies do not simply "take" the price they charge as dictated to them by the market. They "make" the price. Markets like these, in which competition is limited, are the subject of this chapter and the next.

1. If there is only one firm in a market—a monopoly—how does it set its price and output? In what sense is the monopoly price too high?

2. Why do firms with no competition or imperfect competition face downward-sloping demand curves?

3. What are the barriers to entry that limit the number of firms in a market?

4. What does equilibrium look like in a market with imperfect competition, where barriers to entry are small enough that profits are driven to zero, yet in which there are sufficiently few firms that each faces a downward-sloping demand curve?

MARKET STRUCTURES

One way to simplify an economy is to break it up into its constituent markets and look at the **industries,** or groups of firms that supply those markets. An example of one market in the United States is the automobile market. Ford, General Motors, Chrysler, and various foreign firms, among others, supply passenger cars; these firms make up the automobile industry.

When economists look at markets, they look first at the **market structure,** that is, at how the industry in that market is organized. The market structure that forms the basis of the competitive model of Part Two, in which there are a very large number of firms, each a price taker, is called perfect competition. In the wheat industry, for example, there are so many farmers (producers) that no individual wheat farmer can realistically hope to single-handedly move the price of wheat from that produced by the law of supply and demand.

Frequently, however, competition is not "perfect." Rather, it is limited. Economists group markets in which competition is limited into three broad structures. In the first, the most extreme, there is no competition; there is a single firm that supplies the entire market. This is the case of **monopoly.** Your local telephone company and electric company probably have a monopoly on their respective markets. One would normally expect the profits of a monopolist to attract entry into that market. For a firm to maintain its monopoly position, there must be some barrier to entry. Below, we learn what these barriers are.

In the second structure, **oligopoly,** several firms supply the market, so there is *some* competition. The automobile industry is an example, with three main producers in the United States. The interesting thing about oligopolies—indeed, their defining characteristic—is that there are so few firms that each one has to be concerned with how its rivals will react to any action it undertakes. If General Motors offers low-interest-rate financing, for instance, the other companies may feel compelled to match the offer; and before making any such offer, GM will have to take this into account. By contrast, a monopolist has no rivals and thus considers only whether special offers help or hurt itself. And a firm facing perfect competition can sell as much as it wants at the market price without having recourse to any special offers.

In the final market structure, there are more firms involved than there are in an oligopoly, but not enough for perfect competition. This is called **monopolistic competition.** An example is the market for moderately priced clothing as represented by J.C. Penney, Sears, K-Mart, and other such chains of stores. Each chain has a monopoly on its own make of clothing; no other chain can sell it. However, the clothing in each chain is similar enough to that supplied by other chains that there is considerable competition, but not enough to make the chain a price taker. The degree of competition under monopolistic competition is generally greater than that of an oligopoly; monopolistic competition involves a sufficiently large number of firms that each firm ignores the reactions of any of its rivals. If one company lowers its price, for instance, it may garner for itself a large number of customers, but the number of customers it takes away from any single rival is so small that none of the rivals is motivated to retaliate.

With monopoly, there is no entry; there are no rival firms. With oligopoly, there are some barriers to entry that limit the number of firms. With monopolistic competition, entry is sufficiently easy that profits are driven to zero. With both oligopolies and monopolistic competition, there is some competition, but it is more limited than under perfect competition; for this reason, these market structures are referred to as **imperfect competition.**

ALTERNATIVE MARKET STRUCTURES

Perfect competition: Many, many firms; each believes that nothing it does will have any effect on the market price.

Monopoly: One firm.

Imperfect competition: Several firms, each aware that its sales depend on the price it charges and possibly other actions it takes, such as advertising. There are two special cases:

> Oligopoly: Sufficiently few firms that each worries about how rivals will respond to any action it undertakes.

> Monopolistic competition: Each firm faces a downward-sloping demand curve; there are sufficiently many firms that each believes that its rivals will not change the price they charge should it lower its own price; and entry drives profits to zero.

This chapter focuses primarily on the monopoly and monopolistic competition market structures. Oligopolies are left for Chapter 16 because of the interesting features that arise as small numbers of firms develop strategies to deal with one another. We begin here with an analysis of how a monopolist sets its price and quantity, and how monopoly outcomes compare with competitive outcomes. We then switch to imperfect competition, a more common structure, and analyze the principal determinants of the extent of competition within any market. You might normally expect that imperfect competition gives rise to profits, and the profits attract entry, thus increasing the level of competition. The next section analyzes the barriers to entry that enable imperfectly competitive firms to sustain higher than normal profits for long periods of time. The final section looks at the case where the barriers to entry are weak enough that profits are driven to zero, but nonetheless competition is sufficiently limited that each firm can change its prices without losing all of its customers.

MONOPOLY OUTPUT

Most of economists' concerns about monopolies and other forms of restricted competition stem from the observation that the output, or supply, of firms within these market structures is less than that of firms faced with perfect competition. In what follows, we will see how monopoly output is determined, as we consider a monopolist that charges the same price to all its customers.

The manager of a monopoly and the manager of a firm in a competitive industry both share the desire to maximize their firm's profits. But the profit-maximizing decision for a monopolist is more complicated than that of the manager of a firm in a competitive industry. In a competitive industry, the firm that increases production increases revenues in a simple way: if the company doubles its output, it doubles its revenues. The firm is assumed to be a price taker. Since there are many, many firms producing, an increase in the production level of any one firm can be absorbed by the market with a negligible effect on price.

Figure 15.1A shows the demand curve facing one such firm. This is not the same thing as the demand curve facing the industry. The demand curve facing the firm describes what happens to the quantity the firm can sell as it changes its price; or equivalently, the curve describes the price a firm can charge if it wishes to sell various quantities. With perfect competition, the firm faces a *horizontal* demand curve. The price, p^*, is the market price. The firm can sell as much as it wants at that price, and nothing at any higher price. Panel B shows the firm's total revenue, which increases proportionately as the quantity sold increases.

In an industry such as wheat, if there are one million wheat farmers, each farmer on average accounts for one-millionth of the market. If a single average farmer even *doubled* his production, the total production would increase by one-millionth—a truly negligible amount that could be absorbed by the market with barely a change in price.

On the other hand, the monopolist by definition controls the entire industry. The demand curve it faces *is* the industry demand curve. If Alcoa, in the days when it had a monopoly on aluminum, had increased its production by 1 percent, the total supply of aluminum would have increased by 1 percent. Market prices would have had to respond to a change in supply of that magnitude. Because as the monopoly increases

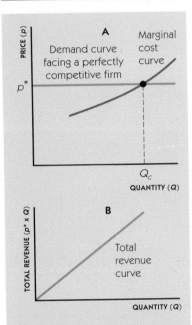

Figure 15.1 THE DEMAND AND TOTAL REVENUE CURVES FACING A PERFECTLY COMPETITIVE FIRM

A price-taking, perfectly competitive firm can sell any quantity it wishes at the market price, but cannot raise the price at all without losing all its business. It faces the horizontal demand curve shown in panel A. Since the marginal revenue from increasing or decreasing sales is always the same market price, the total revenue curve has a constant upward slope, as shown in panel B.

production market supply increases proportionately and the equilibrium price falls, the monopolist performs a balancing act. If the monopolist firm sets its price too low, it might produce and sell a huge quantity, but not make any money doing so. If the firm sets its price too high, it might make a large profit on each item sold, but sell so few that it still does not make much money. The trick for the monopolist is to find the combination of price and quantity that will result in the highest profit; and figuring that out requires knowing by how much the quantity it can sell will change as the company changes the price it charges. This is precisely the information conveyed by the price elasticity of demand (see Chapter 5), which tells the percentage change in quantity as a result of a percentage change in price.

Figure 15.2A shows the demand curve facing a monopolist; it slopes downward, in contrast to the horizontal demand curve faced by perfectly competitive firms. Because the monopolist is the only firm producing the given good, the demand curve facing such a firm is the same as the demand curve for the product. Hence, to sell more, it must lower its price. And since the price falls as the quantity sold increases, revenue increases less than proportionately with output, as illustrated in panel B.

Chapter 12 described the firm as maximizing its profits, which were defined as the difference between revenues (what it receives from selling its goods) and costs. Like the firm in the competitive industry, the monopolist compares the revenue it receives from producing an extra unit of output with the extra cost—that is, the marginal revenue with the marginal cost—and produces at the point where the marginal revenue equals the marginal cost. If the marginal revenue exceeds the marginal cost, it pays for the monopolist to increase production. If the marginal revenue is less, it pays for the company to reduce production.

Thus, both competitive firms and monopolies set marginal revenue equal to marginal cost, as illustrated in Figure 15.3. The essential difference between them is that a competitive firm is a price taker, accepting the price set by market forces as given. When such a firm increases production by one unit, its marginal revenue is just the price; for instance, the marginal revenue a wheat farmer receives from producing one more bushel of wheat is the price of a bushel of wheat. But the only way a monopolist can sell more is to lower the price it charges, so marginal revenue is *not* equal to the present market price.

The marginal revenue a monopolist receives from producing one more unit can be broken into two components. First, the firm receives revenue from selling the additional output. This additional revenue is just the market price. But to sell more, the firm must reduce its price. Unless it does so, it simply cannot sell the extra output. Marginal revenue is the *net* effect, the price it receives from the sale of the one additional unit *minus* the loss in revenues from the price reduction on all other units. For a monopolist, marginal revenue for producing one extra unit is always less than the price received for that extra unit. (Only at the "first" unit produced are marginal revenue and price the same.)

Thus, in Figure 15.3A, which shows the output decision of a competitive firm, marginal revenue is just equal to the market price, p^*, while in panel B, which shows the output decision of a monopolist, marginal revenue always is less than price. Note that with a monopoly, since marginal revenue is less than price and marginal revenue equals marginal cost, marginal cost is less than the price. The price is what individuals are willing to pay for an extra unit of the product; it measures the marginal benefit to the consumer of an extra unit. Thus, the marginal benefit of an extra unit exceeds the

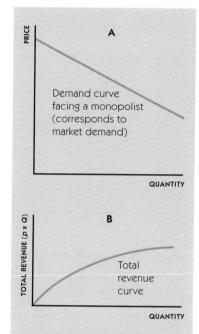

Figure 15.2 THE DEMAND AND TOTAL REVENUE CURVES FACING A MONOPOLIST

A monopolist provides all the output in a market, so an increased amount in the market can only be sold at a reduced price. Panel A shows the downward-sloping demand curve—the market demand curve—faced by a monopolist. Since the price falls as output rises, total revenue for a monopolist increases less than proportionately with output, as shown in panel B.

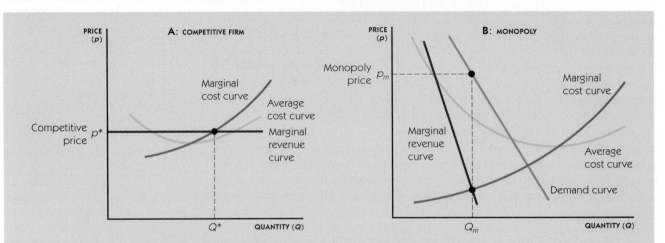

Figure 15.3 MARGINAL REVENUE EQUALS MARGINAL COST

A perfectly competitive firm gains or loses exactly the market price (p^*) when it changes the quantity produced. To maximize profits, the firm produces the quantity where marginal cost equals marginal revenue, which in the competitive case also equals price. Panel B shows the downward-sloping marginal revenue curve for a monopolist. A monopolist also chooses the level of quantity where marginal cost equals marginal revenue. In the monopolistic case, however, marginal revenue is lower than price.

marginal cost. This is the fundamental reason that monopolies interfere with economic efficiency.[1]

The extent to which output is curtailed depends on the magnitude of the difference between marginal revenue and price. This in turn depends on the shape of the demand curve. When demand curves are very elastic (flat), prices do not fall much when output increases. Hence, as shown in Figure 15.4A, marginal revenue is not much less than

[1] Chapter 17 will describe more precisely how the magnitudes of the losses associated with monopoly can be quantified.

Figure 15.4 MONOPOLY AND THE ELASTICITY OF DEMAND

In panel A, a monopoly faces a very elastic market demand, so prices do not fall much as output increases, and marginal cost is not much less than price. In panel B, a monopoly faces a less elastic market demand, so prices fall quite a lot as output increases, and price is substantially above marginal cost.

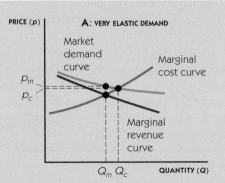

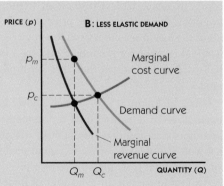

price. The firm produces at Q_m, where marginal revenue equals marginal cost. Q_m is slightly less than the competitive output, Q_c, where price equals marginal cost. When demand curves are less elastic, as in panel B, prices may fall a considerable amount when output increases, and then the extra revenue the firm receives from producing an extra unit of output will be much less than the price received from selling that unit.

THE FIRM'S SUPPLY DECISION

All firms maximize profits at the point where marginal revenue (the revenue from selling an extra unit of the product) equals marginal cost.

For a competitive firm, marginal revenue equals price.

For a monopoly, marginal revenue is less than price.

AN EXAMPLE: THE ABC-MENT COMPANY

Table 15.1 gives the demand curve facing the ABC-ment Company, which has a monopoly on the production of cement in its area. There is a particular price at which it can sell each level of output. As it lowers its price, it can sell more cement. Local builders will, for instance, use more cement and less wood and other materials in constructing a house.

For simplicity, we assume cement is sold in units of 1,000 cubic yards. At a price of $10,000 per unit (of 1,000 cubic yards), the firm sells 1 unit, at a price of $9,000, it sells 2 units, and at a price of $8,000, 3 units. The third column of the table shows the total revenues at each of these levels of production. The total revenues are just price

Table 15.1 DEMAND CURVE FACING ABC-MENT COMPANY

Cubic yards (thousands)	Price	Total revenues	Marginal revenues	Total costs	Marginal costs
1	$10,000	$10,000		$15,000	
			$8,000		$2,000
2	$ 9,000	$18,000		$17,000	
			$6,000		$3,000
3	$ 8,000	$24,000		$20,000	
			$4,000		$4,000
4	$ 7,000	$28,000		$24,000	
			$2,000		$5,000
5	$ 6,000	$30,000		$29,000	
			0		$6,000
6	$ 5,000	$30,000		$35,000	

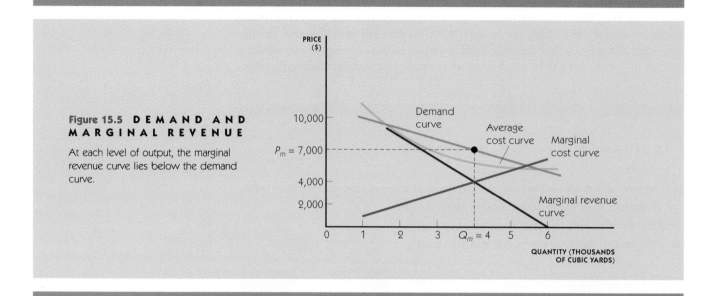

Figure 15.5 DEMAND AND MARGINAL REVENUE

At each level of output, the marginal revenue curve lies below the demand curve.

times quantity. The marginal revenue from producing an extra unit (of 1,000 cubic yards) is just the difference between, say, the revenues received at 3 units and 2 units or 2 units and 1 unit. Notice that in each case, the marginal revenue is less than the price.

Figure 15.5 shows the demand and marginal revenues curves, using data from Table 15.1. At each level of output, the marginal revenue curve lies below the demand curve. As can be seen from the table, not only does price decrease as output increases, but so does marginal revenue.

The output at which marginal revenues equal marginal costs—the output chosen by the profit-maximizing monopolist—is denoted by Q_m. In our example, $Q_m = 4,000$ cubic yards. When the number of cubic yards increases from 3,000 to 4,000, the marginal revenue is \$4,000, and so is the marginal cost. At this level of output, the price is p_m, \$7,000 (per 1,000 cubic yards), which is considerably in excess of marginal costs, \$4,000. Total revenues, \$28,000, are also in excess of total costs, \$24,000.[2]

MONOPOLY PROFITS

We have seen that monopolists maximize their profits by setting marginal revenue equal to marginal cost. There are two ways of seeing the total level of monopoly profits. Figure 15.6A shows the total revenues and total costs (from Table 15.1) for each level of output of the ABC-ment Company. The difference between revenues and costs is profits—the distance between the two curves. This distance is maximized at the output $Q_m = 4,000$

[2] In this example, the firm is indifferent between producing 3,000 or 4,000 cubic yards. If the marginal cost of producing the extra output exceeds \$4,000 by a little, then it will produce 3,000 cubic yards; if the marginal cost is a little less than \$4,000, then it will produce 4,000 cubic yards.

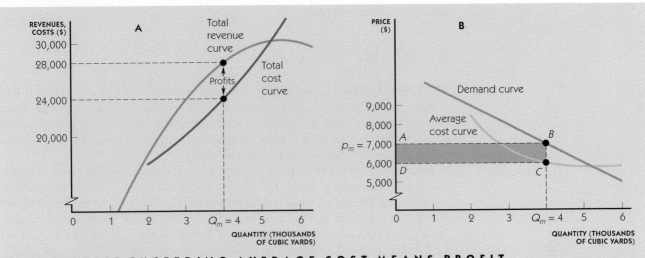

Figure 15.6 **PRICE EXCEEDING AVERAGE COST MEANS PROFIT**

Panel A shows profits to be the distance between the total revenue and total cost curves, maximized at the output Q_m = 4,000 cubic yards. Profits occur when the market price is above average cost, as in panel B, so that the company is (on average) making a profit on each unit it sells. Monopoly profits are the area $ABCD$, which is average profit per unit times the number of units sold.

cubic yards. We can see that at this level of output, profits are $4,000 ($28,000 − $24,000). We can also calculate profits using the average cost diagram (panel B). Total profits are equal to the profit per unit multiplied by the number of units produced; the profit per unit is the difference between the unit price and the average cost. The figure depicts monopoly profits as the shaded area $ABCD$. Again, the sum is $4,000: ($7,000 − $6,000) × 4.

In Chapter 12, we saw that competition drives profits to zero. What that means is that price is equal to the minimum average cost of the least efficient firm in the industry. There may, of course, be firms who, by dint of superior knowledge, managerial ability, or other advantages, have lower costs. Even in a competitive industry, these more efficient firms will enjoy a situation where price exceeds average costs. The return on such differential knowledge or managerial ability, which accountants would consider a profit, is called by economists a rent. In addition, as we saw in Chapter 12, accountants commonly ignore opportunity costs—the return that the owner of the firm could have received on his capital if he had invested it elsewhere, or the return on his time (his wage) if he worked elsewhere.

For monopolists, there is a return that cannot be traced to opportunity cost or rents on technological capabilities. Even after taking these factors into account, monopolies enjoy what is called a **pure profit,** the extra return that results from the fact that the monopolist has reduced its output and increased its price from the level that would have prevailed had there been competition. Because these payments are not required to elicit greater effort or production on the part of the monopolist (in fact, they derive from the monopolist's reducing the output from what it would be under competition), they are also called **monopoly rents.**

PRICE DISCRIMINATION

The basic objective of monopolists is to maximize profits, and they accomplish this by setting marginal revenue equal to marginal cost, so price exceeds marginal cost. Some monopolists also engage in a variety of other practices to increase their profits. Among the most important of these is **price discrimination,** which means charging different prices to different customers or in different markets.

Figure 15.7 shows a monopolist setting marginal revenue equal to marginal cost in the United States and in Japan. The demand curves the firm faces in the two countries are different. Though marginal costs are the same, the firm will charge different prices for the same good in the two countries. (By contrast, in competitive markets, price equals marginal cost, so that regardless of the shape of the demand curves, price will be the same in the two markets, apart from the different costs of delivering the good to each market.) With prices in the two countries differing, middlemen firms will enter the market, buying the product in the country with the low price and selling it in the other country. A company may attempt to thwart the middlemen, as many Japanese companies do, by, for instance, having distinct labels on the two products and refusing to provide service or honor any guarantees outside the country in which the good is originally delivered.

Within a country, a monopolist can sometimes price discriminate if resale is difficult and if it can distinguish between buyers with high and low elasticities of demand. An electricity company can make its charge for each kilowatt hour depend on how much electricity the customer uses, because of restrictions on the retransmission of electricity. If the company worries that large customers faced with the same high prices that it charges small customers might install their own electric generators, or switch to some other energy source, it may charge them a lower price. An airline that has a monopoly on a particular route might charge business customers a higher fare than vacationers. They do so knowing that business customers often have no choice but to make the trip,

Figure 15.7 **PRICE DISCRIMINATION**

A monopolist who sells products in two different countries may recognize that the demand curve it faces in the two countries is different. Though it sets marginal revenue equal to the same marginal cost in both countries, it will charge different prices.

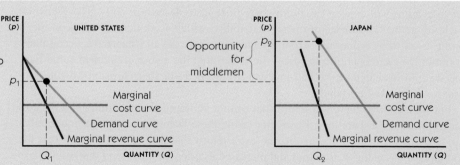

CLOSE-UP: THE SOVIET LEGACY OF MONOPOLY POWER

In the planned economy of the former Soviet Union, it was common for one government ministry to oversee production of a particular product for the entire economy. In fact, the chart below shows that a large proportion of total Soviet output was produced in a single factory.

Product	Share of total Soviet production from the single largest plant (%)
Automatic washing machines	90
Coking equipment	100
Concrete mixers	93
Deep-oil-well sucker rods	87
Diesel locomotives	95
Electric locomotives and trains	70
Forklift trucks	87
Hoists for coal mines	100
Locomotive cranes	100
Polypropylene	73
Reinforced steel	55
Road-building cranes	75
Sewing machines	100
Sucker-rod pumps	100
Tram rails	100
Trolley buses	97

Source: "The Best of All Monopoly Profits . . . ," *The Economist,* August 11, 1990, p. 67.

Those huge factories have created several significant problems for economic reform of the economies of Russia, Ukraine, and the other states that used to form the Soviet Union. First, if the large producers are simply freed from government control and allowed to charge what the market will bear, they are likely to act as monopolies. The Russian economy may thus attempt to eliminate the inefficiencies of central planning and end up instead with the inefficiencies of monopoly. Yet it is not clear how to break up the single factory that makes sewing machines or tram rails or hoists for coal mines to form anything that resembles a competitive industry.

A second problem, and the seeds of a potential solution, may be found in international trade. The problem is that if the one plant for producing, say, sewing machines is in Ukraine, then none of the other former Soviet republics can produce sewing machines immediately. Even if the various republics seek political independence, they will still be economically interdependent. However, trade with the countries of Western Europe and the rest of the world offers an alternative source for those republics that do not produce a certain product. If a republic has inherited a monopoly producer, international trade can supply an instant dose of competition.

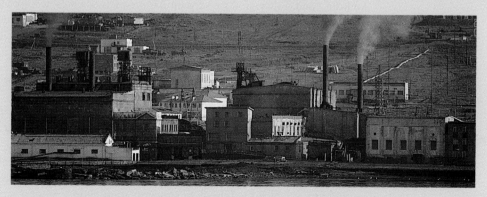

while the vacationers have many alternatives; they could travel elsewhere, on another day or by car or train. These sharp business practices enable the monopolist to increase its profits relative to what they would be if it charged a single price in the market. Firms facing imperfect competition also engage in these practices as we will see; the airlines again provide the most telling example. Though the Robinson-Patman Act, which Congress passed in 1936, was designed to restrict price discrimination, it does so only imperfectly.

IMPERFECT COMPETITION

In most markets, there is more than a single firm. Firms compete, often vigorously, against one another. Still, each firm believes it faces a downward-sloping demand curve. That is, if it lowers its price, it captures some sales from other firms, but it does not capture the whole market; if it raises its price, it loses some customers, but not all. Recall that the perfectly competitive model of Part Two assumed that all firms face a horizontal demand curve. But outside of agriculture, the more general case is that of imperfect competition, where firms face a downward-sloping demand curve. The imperfectly competitive market may be an oligopoly or have monopolistic competition, but for now we will ignore the distinction and discuss in broad terms the factors that determine the competitiveness of any market.

One way of thinking about the competitiveness of a market is to consider what will happen if a firm in that market raises its price. What percentage of its sales will it lose—in other words, what is its elasticity of demand? Firms in a perfectly competitive market face horizontal demand curves. The elasticity of demand for their output is infinite. By the same token, they are price takers; if they raise their price at all, they lose all of their customers. They have no **market power,** a term meant to suggest the ability of a firm to throw its weight around, the way a monopoly can. As imperfect competition sets in, the demand curve facing a firm in the industry begins to slope downward. The more downward sloping the demand curve, the more market power the firm has.

There are two factors that affect the elasticity of the demand curve facing a firm, that is, that determine a firm's market power: the number of firms in an industry or, more generally, how concentrated production is within a few firms; and how similar the goods produced by the different firms in the industry are. If there are many firms in the industry, and if they produce very similar products, then each firm will face a very flat demand curve. If there are many firms in the industry, but they produce quite different products, a typical firm may face a demand curve with limited price elasticity.

NUMBER OF FIRMS IN THE INDUSTRY

Competition is likely to be greater when there are many firms in an industry (textiles, shoes) and less when a few companies dominate an industry (home refrigerators and freezers, greeting cards, soft drinks). Table 15.2 gives the percentage of output that is produced by the top four firms in a variety of industries ranging from breakfast cereals to wood household furniture. The fraction of output produced by the top four firms in an industry is called the **four-firm concentration ratio,** one of several measures used by those who study industry concentration. When the four-firm percentage is high, as

Table 15.2 DEGREE OF COMPETITION IN VARIOUS INDUSTRIES

	Market share of top 4 firms (percent)
Breakfast cereals	81
Burial caskets	53
Motor vehicles and car bodies	92
Primary copper	92
Semiconductors and related devices	36
Women's suits and coats	14
Wood household furniture	15

Source: Census of Manufacturing (1982), vol. 7, Table 6.

it is in the automobile or copper industry, we can expect to find companies with considerable market power. This is true even when they produce similar or identical products, as in the case of copper. When it is low, as in the case of furniture or women's clothes, we can expect market power to be low; each firm in that industry faces a close to horizontal demand curve.[3]

PRODUCT DIFFERENTIATION

The extent to which competition is limited depends not only on the number of firms in a market—and how concentrated production is—but on how similar the goods are that are produced by the different firms. In some industries, the goods produced are essentially identical—the wheat produced by one farm is no diferent from that produced by its neighbor; copper produced by Kennecott Copper is essentially identical to that produced by Anaconda Copper. More typically, the firms in an industry with imperfect competition produce goods that are **imperfect substitutes,** goods sufficiently similar that they can be used for many of the same purposes, but still different enough that one may be somewhat better than another, at least for some purposes or in some people's minds. The producers of soft drinks do not produce drinks that are identical; there is a difference between Pepsi and Coca-Cola. Kellogg's Corn Flakes and the store brand may look alike, but more people purchase the Kellogg's version, even though it is more expensive.

The fact that similar products nonetheless differ from one another is referred to as **product differentiation.** Firms often spend considerable effort in trying to produce goods that are slightly different from those of their competitors.

SOURCES OF PRODUCT DIFFERENTIATION

Many of the differences between products can be seen, heard, or tasted by consumers. But geography also often provides the basis for product differentiation. People are willing to pay slightly more for service at a neighborhood garage, rather than driving fifty miles to a discount garage. They are willing to pay slightly more for milk at the neighborhood grocery store than at the supermarket out on the main road.

In cases where consumers find it difficult to assess the quality of a product before they purchase it, they come to rely heavily on firm reputations. They may buy Bayer aspirin even though it is more expensive than the store brand, because they believe it is of a higher quality (though in fact, aspirin is just a white crystalline substance, acetylsalicylic acid, nothing more or less; still, the binding agents that hold the pill together may differ, so the effects may differ). Consumers are often willing to pay more for goods with a trademark than for generic brands.

Ignorance and the costs of obtaining information often serve to make the products of one firm an imperfect substitute for another. A consumer sees a dress for $45. She might know or suspect that some other store is selling the same dress for $35, but she does not know where, she is not sure it is in stock there, it will cost her money to drive around looking for it, and so she goes ahead and buys the dress anyway. If the store had raised its price to $55, she probably would have made the effort to search. If a store raises its prices, more customers decide to search out the bargains, and sales go down.

---

[3] In both theory and practice, a critical issue in evaluating the extent of competition is defining the relevant market, an issue taken up in Chapter 17.

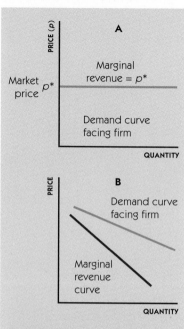

Figure 15.8 DEMAND CURVES WITH PERFECT AND IMPERFECT COMPETITION

Panel A shows the demand curve for a perfectly competitive firm: if it raises its price, all its customers will find substitutes. The marginal revenue curve for the firm is the same as its demand curve. Panel B shows the demand curve and marginal revenue curve facing a firm with only imperfect substitutes for its products.

HOW PRODUCT DIFFERENTIATION IMPLIES IMPERFECT COMPETITION

When goods are perfect substitutes, individuals will choose whichever good is cheapest. It may be hard to imagine a world in which all the different brands of cornflakes really are perfect substitutes for all consumers, but if they were, they would all sell at the same price. If one brand lowered its price slightly, all consumers (assuming they knew this) would switch to it; if it raised its price slightly, all consumers would switch to the rival brand. That is why the demand curve facing the manufacturer of a perfectly substitutable good is horizontal, as illustrated in Figure 15.8A.

By contrast, if most consumers viewed the different brands as imperfect substitutes, the demand curve facing each firm would be downward sloping as in panel B, which, as we have already learned, implies a departure from perfect competition. Some individuals may prefer sogginess and be willing to pay more for cornflakes that rapidly become soggy. Others may prefer crispness and be willing to pay more for cereal that does not become soggy. Assume that Kellogg's Corn Flakes become soggy more slowly than the store brand. As the price of Kellogg's increases above that of the store brand, some individuals—those who care less about crispness—switch to the store brand. They are not willing to pay the price differential. But there are some who are willing to pay a lot more for crisp flakes. Hence, Kellogg's does not lose all of its customers, even if it charges considerably more than the store brand. By the same token, when Kellogg's lowers its price below that of the store brand, it does not steal all of the customers. Those who love sogginess are willing to pay more for the store brand.

It makes little difference whether the differences between the brands are true differences or simply perceived differences. The store brand and Kellogg's Corn Flakes could be identical, but if Kellogg's advertisements have convinced some consumers that there is a difference, they will not switch even if the price of Kellogg's is higher. Numerous studies have attested to the fact that consumers often see differences where none exist. One study put the same soap into two kinds of packages, one marked Brand A, the other marked Brand B. Homemakers were asked to judge which brand cleaned their clothes more effectively. Half saw no difference, but the other half claimed to see significant differences. Another study put the same beer into three kinds of bottles, one labeled premium, the second labeled standard, the third labeled discount. After drinking the differently bottled beers over an extended period of time, consumers were asked which they preferred. The "premium" beer was consistently chosen.

BASES OF PRODUCT DIFFERENTIATION

1. Differences in characteristics of products produced by different firms

2. Differences in location of different firms

3. Perceived differences, often induced by advertising

Close-up: Is Xerox the Same as Photocopy?

You may have heard someone say, "I'm going to Xerox that document." What that person usually means is, "I'm going to photocopy that document on a machine that may or may not have been made by Xerox." Up until the early 1970s, though, the Xerox company was almost synonymous with photocopying. The company had invented the photocopier; it held a group of more than 1,700 closely interrelated patents on the photocopying process; and it received about 95 percent of all copying machine sales in the United States.

In 1972, the Federal Trade Commission charged that Xerox was using its many patents as a way of monopolizing the photocopy market. Instead of using the patents to protect a new invention for a limited amount of time, the FTC argued, Xerox was making them part of a strategy to monopolize the market indefinitely.

After several years of investigation and argument, a "consent order" was announced. Essentially, that meant that Xerox did not admit it had done anything wrong, but it agreed to change anyway. In July 1975, Xerox agreed to allow other competitors to use its patents and even to give its competitors access to some future patents. In addition, Xerox was required to drop all outstanding lawsuits against other companies for infringing on its patents. A spokesman for the FTC maintained that these steps (and some others) would "eliminate the principal sources of Xerox's dominance of the office copier industry."

No longer fearing a lawsuit for infringing on a Xerox patent, entrants started pouring into the photocopy market, led by the Japanese firm Ricoh. Prices for photocopiers fell sharply. By 1980, Xerox was receiving only 46 percent of U.S. copier sales. Among the cheaper machines, the company held only 31 percent of the market. And the downward trend was continuing.

Through the 1980s, Xerox made several efforts to regain its growth path. It tried to move into the fields of computers and computer systems. It bought an insurance company and two investment banking firms. The move into computers was apparently more successful than the one into finance. As the 1990s began, the company was trying to sell off its financial subsidiaries and refocus its attention on laser printers and "smart" copying machines that could be linked with computers and fax machines. No longer collecting the profits of limited competition, Xerox had been transformed into another scrambling firm, worried about being surpassed by other firms and looking for an edge in the highly competitive market for office systems products.

Sources: Business Week, December 16, 1972, p. 24, October 12, 1981, p. 126, February 13, 1989, p. 90; Wall Street Journal, April 17, 1975, p. 8, July 31, 1975, p. 7; Fortune, June 17, 1991, p. 38.

The Ricoh DT1200 entered the market in 1975, and by 1976 Ricoh was the domestic market leader.

BARRIERS TO ENTRY: WHY IS COMPETITION LIMITED?

Normally, the profits that arise where there is a monopoly or imperfect competition should encourage other firms to enter the market. For a monopoly to persist, some factors must prevent competition from springing up. Similarly, when there are profits with imperfect competition, some factors must prevent other firms' entering and eroding those profits. Such factors are called **barriers to entry.** They can take a variety of forms, ranging from government rules that prohibit or limit competition (for reasons that may be good or bad), to technological reasons that naturally limit the number of firms in a market, to market strategies that keep potential competitors at bay.

When there are few barriers to entry, the government need not worry much about a monopoly. It can only be temporary—the profits of the monopolist will attract entry, and the firm's monopoly position will be lost. When there are many barriers, even if they only serve to delay entry, there *is* cause for concern, particularly when firms themselves take actions to create the barriers.

GOVERNMENT POLICIES

Many early monopolies were established by governments. In the seventeenth century, the British government gave the East India Company a monopoly on trade with India. The salt monopoly in eighteenth-century France had the exclusive right to sell salt. Even today, governments grant certain monopoly franchises; for example, government grants monopolies for electric and telephone service within a locality.

The most important monopolies granted by government today, however, are patents. As we learned in Chapter 1, a patent gives inventors the exclusive right to produce or to license others to produce their discoveries for a limited period of time, currently seventeen years. The argument for patents is that without them, copycat firms would spring up with every new invention, and an inventor would make little money from a discovery. Without some assurance that inventors could benefit from their inventions, they would have no economic incentive to invent. Patents are so important that the framers of the U.S. Constitution included a provision enabling the newly created federal government to grant patents.

Occasionally governments set policies that restrict entry, allowing some, but only limited, competition. Licensing requirements in many of the professions (law, accounting, medicine), whose ostensible purpose is to protect consumers against incompetent practitioners, may at the same time limit the number of qualified practitioners, and thus limit competition.

SINGLE OWNERSHIP OF AN ESSENTIAL INPUT

Another easily understood barrier to entry and source of monopoly power is a firm's exclusive ownership of something that is not producible. For example, an aluminum company might attempt to become a monopolist in aluminum by buying all the sources of bauxite, the essential ingredient. A single South African company, De Beers, has come close to monopolizing the world's supply of diamonds. But there are in fact relatively few instances of such monopolies.

INFORMATION

Information does not pass through the economy in the full and complete way envisioned in the basic competitive model of Part Two. In considering barriers to entry, we encounter two of many ways that information—and the lack thereof—affects market outcomes. First, firms engage in research to give them a technological advantage over competitors. Even if they do not get a patent, it will take time before what they learn disseminates through the economy to rivals. The fact that firms outside the industry do not know the trade secrets of the industry provides an important barrier to entry.

Second, consumers have imperfect information concerning the products being sold by different firms. As a new firm, you must not only let potential buyers know about your product, you must convince them that the product is a better value than that of your rivals. When goods differ markedly in qualities that cannot easily be detected, it may not suffice simply to offer to sell at a lower price; customers may infer that the reason your mousetrap is cheaper than the rival brand is that it is an inferior mousetrap. Thus, to get customers to try your product, you may have to advertise heavily and give away free samples. These costs of entering a market constitute another significant barrier to entry.

ECONOMIES OF SCALE AND NATURAL MONOPOLIES

In some cases, the technology used to produce a good can result in a market with only one firm or with very few firms. For example, it would be inefficient to have two firms construct power lines on each street in a city, with one company delivering electricity to one house and another company to the house next door. Likewise, single firms are generally the most efficient way of delivering telephone, water, and gas service. In most locales, there is only one gravel pit or concrete plant. These situations are called **natural monopolies** because the lack of competition arises naturally; one cannot envision a way that competition would be viable, or that the entry of additional firms would improve on the efficiency of the industry.

A natural monopoly occurs whenever the average costs of production for a single firm are declining up to levels of output that are beyond those likely to emerge in the market. When the average costs of production fall as the scale of production increases, we say there are economies of scale, a concept first introduced in Chapter 12. In Figure 15.9, the demand curve facing a monopoly intersects the average cost curve at an output that is so low that average costs are still declining. At large enough outputs, average costs might start to increase, but that level of output would be so high as to be irrelevant to the actual market equilibrium. For instance, firms in the cement industry have U-shaped average cost curves, and the level of output at which costs are minimized is quite high. Accordingly, in smaller, isolated communities, there is a natural monopoly in cement. (If the monopolist raised its price *too* high, customers would find that it paid

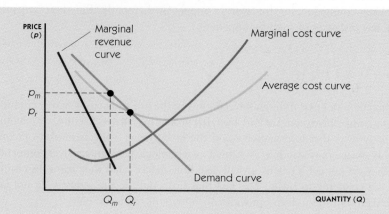

Figure 15.9 NATURAL MONOPOLY

In a natural monopoly, market demand intersects average cost in the downward-sloping portion of the average cost curve, at quantity Q_r and price p_r. Any firm that attempts to enter the market and produce less than Q_r will have higher average costs than the natural monopoly. Any firm that tries to enter the market and produce more than Q_r will find that it cannot sell all its output at a price that will cover its average costs.

to ship cement in; there are still some limits to monopoly power.) The fact that eventually average costs start to increase may become relevant as the size of the market grows. Thus, in medium-sized cities, there may be several producers of cement, so that instead of a monopoly, there is an oligopoly.

A natural monopolist is protected by the knowledge that it can undercut its rivals should they enter. Since entrants typically are smaller and average costs decline with size, their average costs are higher. Therefore the monopolist feels relatively immune from the threat of entry. So long as it does not have to worry about entry, it acts like any other monopolist, setting marginal revenue equal to marginal cost, as in Figure 15.9, where it produces at the output Q_m and charges p_m.

Whether a particular industry is a natural monopoly depends on the size of the output at which average costs are minimized relative to the size of the market. With high enough demand, the monopolist will be operating along the rising part of the average cost curve. At this point, the monopolist can be undercut by an entrant, since a new firm that enters at the output at which average costs are minimized has costs that are lower. Thus, with high enough demand, the industry is no longer a natural monopoly.

Among the most important determinants of the size of the market are transportation costs. Among the most important determinants of the quantity of output at which average costs are minimized is the size of the fixed costs: the larger the expenditures of the firm just to begin production, the larger the scale of production at which average costs are minimized.

ECONOMIES OF SCALE AND IMPERFECT COMPETITION

Similar arguments explain why only a limited number of firms produce each variety of a good, and why the variety of goods is limited. There are fixed costs associated with producing each variety of a product. Setting up the dyes to make a slight variant of an existing car, for example, may be very expensive. Because of the fixed costs associated with painting a car a slightly different color, firms tend to produce only a limited range of colors. Some individuals might prefer that the color of their car be different from the colors currently provided, but car manufacturers do not offer this option, presumably because they realize that the marginal costs would be greater than the marginal revenue they would receive from providing it.

Because over time both technology and transportation costs may change, the number of firms in a market may change. Long-distance telephone service used to be a natural monopoly. Telephone messages were transmitted over wires, and it would have been inefficient to duplicate wires. As the demand for telephone services increased, and as alternative technologies like satellites developed, long-distance service ceased to be a natural monopoly. Several major firms now provide the service.

MARKET STRATEGIES

There are some monopolies and oligopolies that cannot be explained by any of the factors discussed so far. They are not the result of government policies and are not natural monopolies; nor can information problems explain the lack of entry. Many firms, whose original monopoly position may have been based on some technological innovation or patent, manage to maintain their dominant positions even after their patents expire, at least for a time. IBM, Kodak, and Polaroid are three examples. These firms maintained their dominant positions by the pursuit of market strategies that deterred other firms from entering the market.

When a company thinks about entering an industry dominated by a single firm, it must assess not only the current level of profits being earned by that firm but also what profits will be like after it has entered. If a potential entrant believes that the incumbent firm is likely to respond to entry by lowering its price and fighting a fierce competitive battle, then the potential newcomer may come to believe that while prices and profits look high now, they are likely to drop precipitously if it actually does enter the market.

Established firms would thus like to pursue a strategy to convince potential entrants that even though they are currently making high levels of profit, these profits will disappear should the new firm enter the market. There are three major ways to create this belief, collectively called **entry-deterring practices:** predatory pricing, excess capacity, and limit pricing.

Predatory Pricing   If prices have fallen drastically in a certain market every time there has been entry in the past, then new firms may be reluctant to enter. This situation has often occurred in the airline industry. For instance, in the mid-1970s, Laker Airways, headed by a brash British businessman named Freddy Laker, began flying the London–New York route at prices far below those of the established carriers. Other airlines responded by drastically cutting their prices to the point where Laker was eventually driven into bankruptcy. Upon his withdrawal from the market, prices returned to their previously high level.

In this case, the competing carriers were declared to have engaged in an unfair trade practice. But the experience was sufficiently unpleasant that other low-cost carriers have not tried to break into the market, at least not on the scale attempted by Laker. At times, even on some large and active airline routes such as those between Los Angeles and San Francisco, the threat of entry appears low, although prices and profits are high. The explanation may lie in the fact that the last few times an upstart airline has attempted to enter, it has been knocked out of the market by extremely aggressive price cutting by incumbent airlines.

In some cases, an incumbent firm may go so far as to deliberately lower its price below the new entrant's cost of production, in order to drive the new arrival out and discourage future entry. This practice is called **predatory pricing** and is generally viewed as an illegal trade practice. However, with shifting technologies and shifting demand, it is often difficult to ascertain whether a firm has actually engaged in predatory pricing or simply lowered its price to meet the competition. Firms that lower their prices always claim that they were "forced" to do so by their competitors. When they subsequently raise their prices, they talk about how costs have increased or how demand has increased (and, of course, the exit of the rival will result in the firm facing increased demand). These problems make it very difficult for the government to prosecute successfully a case in which a firm has engaged in predatory pricing.

Excess Capacity   Another action that firms can take to convince potential rivals that prices are likely to fall if they enter the market is to build up **excess capacity,** or production facilities in excess of those currently needed. By building extra plants and equipment, even if they are rarely used, a firm poses an extra threat to potential entrants. A newcomer will look at those plants and equipment and realize that the incumbent firm can increase production a great deal with minimal effort. The excess capacity serves as a signal that the incumbent is willing and able to engage in fierce price competition.

Limit Pricing   Other strategies for deterring entry can involve clever patterns of pricing. A potential entrant may know what price is charged on the market and may have a good idea of its own costs of production, but it is not likely to know precisely the cost curve of the incumbent firm. The established firm can try to persuade potential entrants that its marginal costs are low. It wants the new firm to believe that it could easily reduce its price, making entry unprofitable.

Suppose a potential entrant knew that a monopolist firm's marginal revenue was 70 percent of price. If the monopolist charges a price of $10, then the marginal revenue (the extra revenue from selling one more unit) is $7. Reasoning that the monopolist was setting marginal revenue equal to marginal cost, the potential entrant might use a $7 marginal cost figure in deciding whether it pays to enter. If its costs are lower, it might decide to enter.

The monopolist, on the other hand, knows that the price it charges conveys information. Therefore, it might pay the firm to charge a slightly lower price, and thereby trick a potential rival into believing that the firm's marginal costs are lower and hence that entry is less attractive. This is an example of a broader practice known as **limit pricing,** in which firms limit the prices they charge (they charge less than the ordinary monopoly price and produce at a level beyond that at which marginal revenue equals marginal cost) because they are afraid that at higher prices, entry will be encouraged. This may happen simply because a firm realizes that high profits attract attention; the greater attention focused on a market, the more likely it is that some entrepreneur will believe that entry is profitable. Even if that entrant proves to be wrong, no firm wants to fight a money-losing competitive battle unless it is strictly necessary.

Some entry-deterring devices, such as maintaining excess capacity, may be socially wasteful. Others, such as limit pricing, will benefit consumers, at least in the short run, though the long-run deleterious effects of monopoly or limited competition remain.

BARRIERS TO ENTRY

Government policies: These include grants of monopoly (patents) and restrictions on entry (licensing).

Single ownership of an essential input: When a single firm owns the entire supply of a nonproducible input, entry is by definition precluded.

Information: Lack of technical information by potential competitors inhibits their entry; lack of information by consumers concerning the quality of a new entrant's product discourages consumers from switching to the new product, and thus inhibits entry.

Economies of scale: With a natural monopoly, economies of scale are so strong that it is efficient to have only one firm in an industry.

Market strategies: These include policies (such as predatory pricing, excess capacity, and limit pricing) aimed at convincing potential entrants that entry would be met with resistance, and thus would be unprofitable.

EQUILIBRIUM WITH MONOPOLISTIC COMPETITION

Sometimes barriers to entry are sufficiently weak that firms enter to the point where profits are driven to zero. But even then, if products are differentiated, competition is imperfect. With each firm producing a slightly different product, each faces a downward-sloping demand curve. In this section, we briefly analyze the case where fixed costs are sufficiently large to ensure that each firm faces a downward-sloping demand curve, but sufficiently small that there are *enough* firms so that each firm ignores the consequences of its actions on others. This is the case of monopolistic competition.

The behavior of firms in markets with monopolistic competition was first analyzed by Edward Chamberlin of Harvard University in 1933 in an influential book, *Theory of Monopolistic Competition*. Chamberlin considered a market in which there were initially a fixed number of similar firms with identical cost curves, producing goods that were imperfect substitutes. If they all charged the same price, they divided the market equally.

Figure 15.10 illustrates a market in which there is monopolistic competition. Assume initially that all firms are charging the same price, say p_1. If one firm were to charge a slightly lower price, it would steal some customers away from other stores. If there were twenty firms in the market, this price-cutting firm would attract more than one-twentieth

CLOSE-UP: IBM: FROM THE EDGE OF MONOPOLY TO THE EDGE OF COMPETITION

IBM committed itself to computers in the 1950s, and rapidly asserted its dominance in the business of large "mainframe" computers. IBM machines were often the most technologically advanced, and in the few cases where they might not have been the best, they still had an extraordinary reputation for great service and support. Back in the days when computers were more than a little mysterious to most of their users, that reputation mattered a lot.

IBM was never a literal monopoly; throughout the 1960s and 1970s, competition came from firms like Control Data, Honeywell, Sperry Univac, Burroughs, and NCR. But by 1980, IBM still had over 80 percent of the world market for mainframe computers. It was common for the company's sales to grow every year by double-digit percentages.

In the mid-1980s, IBM executives predicted publicly that the company would earn $100 billion in sales in 1990. The actual figure turned out to be $69 billion. The company was still the fourth largest in the United States, but it had missed its target for corporate growth by an embarrassingly large amount. What happened?

The computer industry shifted dramatically in the 1980s. In 1980, it was still quite unusual for a college student, say, to have her own computer. Now, personal computers are on their way to replacing the typewriter. On the business side, the different departments in a company may all have their own computer systems, and top management has a new saying: "We used to have a goal of putting a computer on every desk. Now we have a goal of putting *only* one computer on every desk."

While IBM has remained the world's dominant producer of large mainframe computers, it has faced more of a struggle to compete effectively in this new world of personal, laptop, and notebook computers, networks of smaller machines, and computers controlled by a pen or a mouse. In the tough competition with Apple, Compaq, Toshiba, Dell, and a legion of others, no company can be said to dominate. The 1980s were a time of monopolistic competition in the computer business, when a company had a technological edge for a few months or a year and then was overtaken by competitors. The hottest computer businesses of

 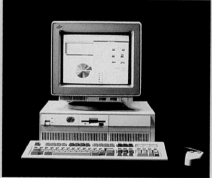 

Three offerings from IBM: the ES/9000 mainframe, the PS/2 personal computer, and the PS/2 laptop.

the early 1990s have focused on specialized applications of computers and on putting together networks.

Computer technology has moved toward "open systems," in which it is possible, for example, to plug together a computer from one company, a screen from a second company, a printer from a third, and software from a fourth, and have the whole system work. Instead of running over its smaller rivals, IBM has been nibbled from all directions in markets that have become highly, even viciously, competitive.

From 1969 to 1982, IBM was the target of a government antitrust suit, which argued that the company was too close to a monopoly in the computer business and should be broken up. After an incredible blizzard of paperwork, the government prosecution stalled and was finally called off in 1982. But when the government regulators called off their chase, the competitive struggles of IBM were just beginning. The upheaval of computer markets in the 1980s has shown the power of markets and competition to affect even a company with tens of billions of dollars in annual sales.

Sources: "The New IBM," *Business Week,* December 16, 1991, p. 112; Joel Dreyfuss, "Reinventing IBM," August 14, 1989, pp. 30–39.

of the total market demand. By the same token, if it should raise its price above that of its rivals, it would lose customers to them. Each firm assumes that the prices charged by other firms will remain unchanged as it changes its price or the quantity it produces. The demand curve facing each firm is thus the one shown in the figure.

In deciding how much to produce, the firm sets marginal revenue equal to marginal cost. The market equilibrium is (p_1, Q_1), with marginal revenue equaling marginal cost. In the equilibrium depicted in the figure, price exceeds average costs. There are profits. In a way, one can almost think of this situation as a sort of minimonopoly, where each firm has a monopoly on its own brand name or its own store location.

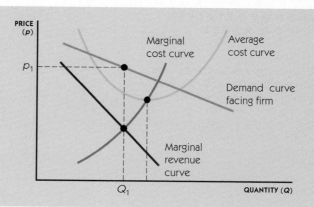

Figure 15.10 PROFIT-MAXIMIZING FOR A MONOPOLISTIC COMPETITOR

A monopolistic competitor chooses the quantity it will produce by setting marginal revenue equal to marginal cost (Q_1), and then selling that quantity for the price given on its demand curve (p_1). In this diagram, the price charged is above average cost, and the monopolistic competitor is making a profit.

But if existing firms are earning monopoly profits, there is an incentive for new competitors to enter the market. In fact, firms will enter until profits are driven to zero, as in the perfectly competitive model. This is the vital distinction between monopolies and monopolistic competition. In both cases, firms face downward-sloping demand curves. In both cases, they set marginal revenue equal to marginal cost. But in monopolistic competition, there is entry. Entry continues so long as profits are positive. As firms enter, the share of the industry demand of each firm is reduced. The demand curve facing each firm thus shifts to the left, as depicted in Figure 15.11. The demand curve may also get flatter (more elastic), as more substitutes become available. This process continues until the demand curve just touches the average cost curve, at point (p_e, Q_e). At that point, profits are zero.

The figure also shows the firm's marginal revenue and marginal cost curves. The firm acts like any other in an imperfectly competitive industry, by setting its marginal revenue equal to its marginal cost. This occurs at exactly the level of output at which the demand curve is tangent to the average cost curve. This is because at any other point, average costs exceed price, so profits are negative. Only at this point are profits zero. Accordingly, this is the profit-maximizing output.

The equilibrium of monopolistic competition has some interesting characteristics. Notice that in equilibrium, price and average costs exceed the minimum average costs at which the goods could be produced. *Less is produced at a higher price.* But there is a trade-off here: whereas in the perfectly competitive market every product was a perfect substitute for every other one, in the world of monopolistic competition there is variety among the products available. In general, people value variety, and are willing to pay a higher price to obtain it. Thus, the fact that in this market goods are sold at a price above the minimum average cost does not necessarily mean that the economy is inefficient.

Whether the market results in too little or too much product variety remains a hotly contested subject. Either can occur. For our purposes, the important point to realize is that there is a trade-off. Greater variety can only be obtained at greater costs.

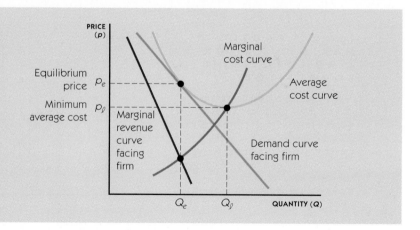

Figure 15.11 MONOPOLISTIC COMPETITION AFTER ENTRY

If a monopolistic competitor is earning profits, other firms will enter the market. As firms enter, the share of the market demand of each firm is reduced, and the demand curve facing each firm shifts to the left, until it just touches the average cost curve. Now, setting marginal revenue equal to marginal cost leads the firm to choose quantity Q_e, which it can sell for price p_e. But since this point is on the average cost curve, the monopolistic competitor is no longer earning a profit.

SCHUMPETERIAN COMPETITION

The famous Harvard economist Joseph Schumpeter envisaged a rather different form of monopolistic competition. He saw different markets being dominated at different times by one or two firms, as a result of their technological superiority. But these firms were constantly subjected to competition for supremacy as new innovations supplanted old. For example, Apple and Compaq and a host of other companies have challenged IBM's domination over the computer industry, and have won the battle for at least one important segment, the personal computer market.

Even when the lead firm is not supplanted by another, the threat of entry keeps it on its toes. While each company dominates the market, it acts like a monopolist: it sets marginal revenue equal to marginal cost, producing less than would be produced under perfect competition. But the firm has limited discretion over how to use its profits: if it wishes to maintain its position, it must reinvest those profits in further expenditures to make new products and to develop new, cheaper ways of producing. In Schumpeter's view, the disadvantage of monopoly—the reduction in output—was more than offset by the advantages of the greater research the monopoly profits funded. Chapter 18 will take a closer look at these questions.

REVIEW AND PRACTICE

SUMMARY

1. Economists isolate four broad categories of market structure: perfect competition, monopoly, oligopoly, and monopolistic competition (the last two are collectively referred to as imperfect competition).

2. A perfectly competitive firm faces a horizontal demand curve; it is a price taker. In markets in which there is imperfect or no competition, each firm faces a downward-sloping demand curve.

3. Both monopolists and firms facing perfect competition maximize profit by producing at the quantity where marginal revenue is equal to marginal cost. However, marginal revenue for a perfect competitor is the same as the market price of an extra unit, while marginal revenue for a monopolist is less than the market price.

4. Since with a monopoly price exceeds marginal revenue, buyers pay more for the product than the marginal cost to produce it; there is thus less production in a monopoly than there would be if price were set equal to marginal cost.

5. Imperfect competition occurs because a relatively small number of firms dominate the market and/or because firms produce goods that are differentiated by their characteristics, by the location of the firms, or in the perception of consumers.

6. Monopolies and imperfect competition involve both natural and manmade barriers to entry.

7. With monopolistic competition, barriers to entry are sufficiently weak that entry occurs until profits are driven to zero; there are few enough firms that each faces a downward-sloping demand curve, but a sufficiently large number of firms that each ignores rivals' reactions to what it does.

KEY TERMS

monopoly	pure profit or	barriers to entry
oligopoly	monopoly rents	natural monopoly
monopolistic	price discrimination	predatory pricing
competition	product differentiation	limit pricing
imperfect competition		

REVIEW QUESTIONS

1. What is the difference between perfect and imperfect competition? between oligopoly and monopolistic competition?

2. Why is price equal to marginal revenue for a perfectly competitive firm, but not for a monopolist or with imperfect competition?

3. How should a monopoly choose its quantity of production to maximize profits? Explain why producing either less or more than the level of output at which marginal revenue equals marginal cost will reduce profits. Since a monopolist need not fear competition, what prevents it from raising its price as high as it wishes to make higher profits?

4. What are the primary sources of product differentiation?

5. What are barriers to entry? Describe the principal ones.

6. What is a natural monopoly?

7. Describe market equilibrium under monopolistic competition. Why does the price charged by the typical firm exceed the minimum average cost, even though there is entry?

PROBLEMS

1. Explain how it is possible that at a high enough level of output, if a monopoly produced and sold more, its revenue would actually decline.

2. Assume there is a single firm producing cigarettes, and the marginal cost of producing cigarettes is a constant. Suppose the government imposes a 10-cent tax on each pack of cigarettes. If the demand curve for cigarettes is linear, will the price rise by more or less than the tax?

3. Describe possible strategies a furniture firm might use to differentiate its products.

4. Suppose a gas station at a busy intersection is surrounded by many competitors, all of whom sell identical gas. Draw the demand curve the gas station faces, and draw its

marginal and average cost curves. Explain the rule for maximizing profit in this situation. Now imagine that the gas station offers a new gasoline additive called zoomine, and begins an advertising campaign that says: "Get zoomine in your gasoline." No other station offers zoomine. Draw the demand curve faced by the station after this advertising campaign. Explain the rule for maximizing profit in this situation, and illustrate it with an appropriate diagram.

5. Explain how consumers may benefit from predatory pricing and limit pricing in the short run, but not in the long run.

6. Why might it make sense for a monopolist to choose a point on the demand curve where the price is somewhat lower than the price at which marginal revenue equals marginal costs?

APPENDIX A: MONOPSONY

In any market, imperfections of competition can arise on either the buyer or seller side. In this chapter, we have focused on imperfect competition among the sellers of goods. When there is a single buyer in a market, the buyer is called a **monopsonist**. Though monopsonies are relatively rare, they do exist. The government is a monopsonist in the market for a variety of high-technology defense systems.

In some labor markets, a single firm may be close to a monopsonist, or there may be "monopsonistic competition," analogous to monopolistic competition. That is, in that labor market, an employer may face an upward-sloping supply curve for labor, or at least labor with particular skills. Firms in one-company towns—like Gary, Indiana, which was founded and is dominated by U.S. Steel—particularly when they are geographically isolated, are most likely to face upward-sloping supply curves for labor. In one town, for example, most of the plumbers may work for one company. The firm is not a price taker in plumbing services. It cannot hire all the plumbing services it would like at the going wage. If the company wants more plumbing services, it has to pay a higher wage (just as the monopolist must charge a lower price when it wants to sell more goods). At higher wages, the plumbers in the town are willing to work longer hours. And at a high enough wage, plumbers from the neighboring town are willing to incur the costs of commuting, or, if they could be sure that the high wages would continue, they might even be willing to move.

The consequences of monopsony are similar to those for monopoly. The basic rule remains: produce at the point where marginal revenue equals marginal cost. The buyer firm is aware, however, that if it buys more units, it will have to pay a higher price. Then if the firm cannot price discriminate, the marginal cost of buying one more unit is not only what the company has to pay for the last unit, but also the higher price it must pay for all previously purchased units.

In the case of a labor market, Figure 15.12 illustrates the consequence. Chapter 13 showed that in competitive markets, firms hire labor up to the point where the value of the marginal product of labor (MPL) equals the wage, the marginal cost of hiring an additional worker. The figure shows the curve that represents the value of the marginal product of labor; it declines as the number of workers hired increases. The figure also shows the labor supply curve, which is upward sloping. From this, the firm can calculate

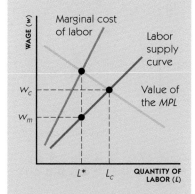

Figure 15.12 MONOPSONY

A monopsony wants to choose the most profitable point on the market supply curve. It knows the value of the marginal product of additional units of an input. As a monopsonist buys more of an input, it must pay not only a higher price for the marginal unit but a higher price for all the units it buys; thus, the marginal cost of buying an input will exceed the price. The monopsonist will set the marginal cost of the input equal to the value of its marginal product at employment level L^*, and set the wage at w_m. The firm hiring in a competitive labor market would hire up to the point where the value of its marginal product equals the wage; that is, up to point L_c, at wage w_c. Thus, a monopsonist hires less labor at a lower wage than competitive firms would.

the marginal cost of hiring an additional worker, the wage *plus* the increase in the wage paid to all previously hired workers. Clearly, the marginal cost curve lies above the labor supply curve. The firm hires workers up to the point L^*, where the value of the marginal product of labor is equal to the marginal cost. Employment is lower than it would have been had the firm ignored the fact that as it hires more labor, the wage it pays increases.

APPENDIX B: DEMAND FOR INPUTS UNDER MONOPOLY AND IMPERFECT COMPETITION

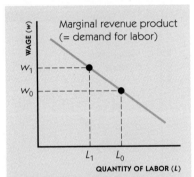

Figure 15.13 MARGINAL REVENUE PRODUCT CURVE

Firms hire labor up to the point where the marginal revenue product of an extra worker equals the marginal cost. In a competitive labor market, the marginal cost of labor is just the wage.

In Chapter 13, we saw that competitive firms hire labor up to the point where the value of the marginal product (the value of what an extra hour of labor would produce) is equal to the wage. Similarly, any other factor of production is hired up to the point where the value of its marginal product is equal to its price. From this, we could derive the demand curve for labor (or any other input).

A quite similar analysis applies with imperfect competition. A monopolist hires labor up to the point where the extra revenue it produces—what economists call the marginal revenue product—is equal to the wage. In competitive markets, the value of the marginal product is just equal to the price of the output times the marginal physical product, the extra quantity that is produced. In a monopoly, the marginal revenue product (MRP) is equal to the marginal revenue yielded by producing one more unit (MR) times the marginal physical product (MPP): $MRP = MR \times MPP$.

The quantity of labor that will be hired is illustrated in Figure 15.13, which shows the marginal revenue product curve. It is downward sloping, for two reasons: the more that is produced, the smaller the marginal physical product (this is just the law of diminishing returns), and the more that is produced, the smaller the marginal revenue. The firm hires labor up to the point where the marginal revenue product equals the wage, point L_o. If the wage increases from w_0 to w_1, the amount of labor hired will fall, from L_0 to L_1. Thus, the demand curve for labor is downward sloping with imperfect competition, just as it is with perfect competition.

OLIGOPOLIES

In industries characterized by monopolistic competition, we assume there are enough firms that each operates under the belief that its actions have no effect on the actions of its competitors. But in many industries, called oligopolies, there are sufficiently few firms that each worries about how its rivals will react to anything it does. This is true of the airline, cigarette, aluminum, automobile, and a host of other industries. Airlines that offer frequent flier bonuses, for instance, can expect their competitors to respond with similar offers.

Some industries may include many firms, but only a few that produce goods that are close substitutes. For example, while there are many manufacturers of dishes, there are relatively few that produce fine china (such as Wedgewood and Royal Doulton). Although every town of any size has many gas stations, any particular gas station may view itself as being in competition with the two or three others at the same intersection. In these cases as well, each of the firms may worry about the reactions of its immediate rivals. If any such firm lowers its price, it worries that rivals will do the same and it will gain no competitive advantage. Worse still, a competitor may react to a price cut by engaging in a price war and cutting the price still further.

Different oligopolies seem to behave in quite different ways. The oligopolist is always torn between its desire to outwit competitors and the knowledge that by cooperating with other oligopolists to reduce output, it might manage to earn a portion of the pure profits of a true monopolist. This is a key question facing an oligopolistic firm—whether it will earn higher profits by colluding with rivals to act as a joint monopolist or by competing with rivals by charging lower prices. There is no obvious answer; the answer depends in part on what rival companies do, and firms in an oligopoly can only guess what their rivals will do in response to any action they take.

In this chapter, the analysis of oligopoly behavior is divided into three sections. The first discusses collusion, or cooperation, and the problems firms confront in colluding; the second shows how firms may restrict competition, even when they do not formally collude; and the third describes what happens if firms in an oligopoly compete.

"Given the downward slope of our demand curve and the ease with which other firms can enter the industry, we can strengthen our profit position only by equating marginal cost and marginal revenue. Order more jelly beans."

KEY QUESTIONS

1. Under what conditions will the firms in an industry collude in order to charge high prices? What are the incentives to collude?

2. What practices do firms in an oligopoly engage in to restrict the force of competition and hence increase their profits?

3. What are the main forms that competition among oligopolists takes? How do they compare in terms of the level of prices and output, and how the market responds to changes in economic conditions?

COLLUSION

In some cases, oligopolists try to **collude** to maximize their profits. In effect, they act jointly as if they were a monopoly, and split up the resulting profits. The prevalence of collusion was long ago noted by Adam Smith, the founder of modern economics, who was not at all naive about where the self-interestedness of businessmen would lead. He remarked, "People of the same trade seldom meet together, even for merriment and diversion, but the conversation ends in a conspiracy against the public, or in some contrivance to raise prices."[1] A group of companies that formally operate in collusion is called a **cartel.** The Organization of Petroleum Exporting Countries (OPEC), for instance, acts collusively to restrict the output of oil, to raise oil prices and hence the profits of member countries.

In the late nineteenth century, there were often two or more railroads between major cities. When they competed vigorously, profits were low. It did not take them long, however, to discover that if they acted collusively, they could raise prices and profits.

[1] *Wealth of Nations*, Book 1, Chapter 10, Part II.

New York Central and the other major carriers connecting the Midwest with the East Coast got together and set the price of shipping grain from the Midwest to the East. To stop the railroads from gouging their customers, the Interstate Commerce Commission was formed in 1887 and given the right to set railroad rates. The intent was to bring prices down closer to precollusion levels. However, while the Interstate Commerce Commission did limit the prices the railroads could charge, it also ensured that the railroads did not compete too vigorously. Before the onset of government regulations, there were periodic price wars, in which rates fell dramatically; the Interstate Commerce Commission stopped these. The outcome is often cited as a classic example of **regulatory capture,** a term meaning that the regulators end up serving the interests of the regulated industry rather than the interests of consumers.

In the steel industry at the turn of the century, Judge Elbert H. Gary, who headed the U.S. Steel Company, the largest of the steel firms, regularly presided over Sunday dinners for prominent members of his industry at which steel prices were set. And over the years, there have been cartels in a variety of industries, such as tin and coffee. Today cartels and explicit agreements to fix prices are illegal in the United States, so that collusive price setting cannot be done openly. Most states also have laws prohibiting collusion. But aside from their illegality, cartels by their very nature face inherent problems. We now look at three of these problems.

THE PROBLEM OF SELF-ENFORCEMENT

Cartels seek to restrict output and thus to raise prices above marginal costs. The central difficulty facing cartels is that it pays any single member of the cartel to cheat; that is, if all other members of the cartel restrict output, so that price exceeds marginal cost, it pays the last member of the cartel to increase its output and take advantage of the higher price. This firm is said to be free riding on the cartel—the other firms pay the price of collusion by restricting their output, while the free rider gets the advantage, the higher price, without giving up any sales. But if too many members of a cartel cheat by increasing their output beyond the agreed-upon levels, the cartel breaks down. This is what happened to the OPEC oil cartel during the 1980s: producers (other than Saudi Arabia) systematically increased production beyond their allotted quotas.

Similarly, if all other members of the cartel have set their prices at a high level, it pays any single member to undercut that price slightly, thereby stealing customers away from the other members and increasing its own profits. This happened to the nineteenth-century railroad cartels. At the high prices to which they had agreed—the prices that maximized their *joint* profits—each railroad had excess capacity. It paid each railroad to try to recruit business from its competitors, and the best way to recruit business was to offer a discount.

The incentives for any member of a cartel to cheat are illustrated in Figure 16.1, in which all members of a cartel face the same constant marginal costs. The figure shows the market demand curve and the output, Q_c, and price, p_c, at which the cartel's joint profits are maximized—that is, where marginal revenue for the cartel as a whole equals marginal costs. But the marginal revenue for the cartel as a whole is not the marginal revenue for any one firm. Any firm thinks it can cheat on the cartel and get away with it. If it shaves its price just lower than p_c and increases its production, it makes a profit of approximately p_c minus the marginal cost on that additional unit. With a large gap between price and marginal costs, there are strong incentives to cheat.

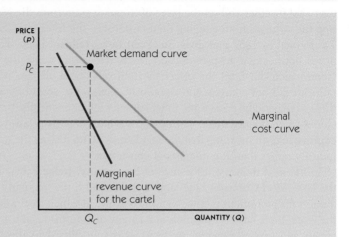

Figure 16.1 INCENTIVES TO CHEAT ON A CARTEL

The existence of a large gap between price and marginal costs provides a strong incentive for each member of a cartel to cheat; p_c is the cartel price.

A factor that further encourages some members of a cartel to cheat on the collusive agreement is that frequently one or more members believe they are not getting their fair share. This problem has plagued the oil cartel. Each country within the cartel faces different economic circumstances. Oil-rich sheikdoms have per capita incomes among the highest in the world, while for poor countries like Indonesia, oil revenues are necessary if there is to be any hope of development. There are no simple principles these countries can call upon to decide how much each should produce, or who should bear the burden of cutting back production, to sustain the market price at a high level. Those who feel they are being unfairly treated are more likely to try to cheat on the collusive agreement.

Thus, the first major problem facing cartels is how to enforce their collusive arrangement on their members. This self-enforcement is a particular problem because both state and federal governments have passed **antitrust laws** prohibiting collusive behavior. This makes it impossible, of course, for firms to get together and sign legally binding contracts that would require each firm to keep output low and prices high.

Sometimes the profits from collusion have been so great that firms have taken the risks involved in violating the law. The most famous recent case involved manufacturers of electrical machinery, including Westinghouse and General Electric, who were caught conspiring in their bids for major projects, like the electric turbines for a dam. The companies arranged to take turns winning, using an elaborate scheme that involved the phases of the moon and the lunar calendar; their precautions were sufficiently good that the conspiracy went on for years before they were caught.

GAME THEORY: THE PRISONER'S DILEMMA

In recent years, economists have used a branch of mathematics called game theory to study collusion among oligopolists. The participants in a game are allowed to make certain moves, defined by the rules of the game. The outcomes of the game—what each participant receives—are referred to as its payoffs, and depend on what each player does. Each participant in the game chooses a strategy; he decides what moves to make. In games in which each player has the chance to make more than one move (there is more than one round, or period), moves can depend on what has happened in previous periods. Game theory begins with the assumption that each player in the game is rational and knows that his rival is rational. Each is trying to maximize his own payoff. The theory then tries to predict what each player will do. The answer depends on the rules of the game and the payoffs.

One example of such a game is called the **Prisoner's Dilemma.** Two prisoners, A and B, alleged to be conspirators in a crime, are put into separate rooms. A police officer goes into each room and makes a little speech: "Now here's the situation. If your partner confesses and you remain silent, you'll get five years in prison. But if your partner confesses and you confess also, you'll only get three years. On the other hand, perhaps your partner remains silent. If you're quiet also, we can only send you to prison for one year. But if your partner remains silent and you confess, we'll let you out in three months. So if your partner confesses, you are better off confessing, and if your partner doesn't confess, you are better off confessing. Why not confess?" This deal is offered to both prisoners.

The diagram below shows the results of this deal. The upper left-hand box, for example, shows the result if both A and B confess. The upper right-hand box shows the result if prisoner A confesses but prisoner B remains silent. And so on.

		Prisoner B	
		Confesses	Remains silent
Prisoner A	Confesses	A gets 3 years B gets 3 years	A gets 3 months B gets 5 years
	Remains silent	A gets 5 years B gets 3 months	A gets 1 year B gets 1 year

From the combined standpoint of the two prisoners, the best option is clearly that they both remain silent and each serve their one year. But the self-interest of each individual prisoner says that confession is best, whether his partner confesses or not. However, if they both follow their self-interest and confess, they both end up worse off, each serving three years. The Prisoner's Dilemma is a simple game in which both parties are made worse off by independently following their own self-interest. Both would be better off if they could get together to agree on a story, and to threaten the other if he deviated from the story.

The Prisoner's Dilemma comes up in a variety of contexts. For example, during the years of the Cold War, the arms race between the United States and the former USSR was described in these terms. Each party reasoned that if the other side built weapons, it needed to match the buildup. And if the other side did not build, it could acquire an advantage by building. Even though both sides might have been better off by agreeing not to build, their incentives pushed them toward a situation where both continued to do so.

The game can also be directly applied to collusion between two oligopolists. Assume that both firms agree to cut back their production, so they obtain higher prices and higher profits. But each oligopolist reasons in the following way. Whether my rival cheats or not, it pays for me to expand production. If my rival cheats, then he gets all the advantages of my restricting output but pays none of the price. And if he does not cheat and keeps production low, it pays for me to cheat. As both firms reason that way, production expands and prices fall to a level below that at which their joint profits are maximized.

In the examples of the Prisoner's Dilemma presented so far, each party makes only one decision. But if firms (or countries) interact over time, then they have additional ways to try to enforce their agreement. For example, suppose each oligopolist announces that it will refrain from cutting prices as long as its rival does. But if the rival cheats on the collusive agreement, then the first oligopolist will respond by increasing production and lowering prices. Won't this threat ensure that the two firms cooperate?

Consider what happens if the two firms expect to compete in the same market over the next ten years, after which time a new product is expected to come along and shift the entire configuration of the industry. It will pay each firm to cheat in the tenth year, when there is no possibility of retaliation, because the industry will be completely altered in the next year. Now consider what happens in the ninth year. Both firms can figure out that it will not pay either one of them to cooperate in the tenth year. But if they are not going to cooperate in the tenth year anyway, then the *threat* of not cooperating in the future is completely ineffective. Hence in the ninth year, each firm will reason that it pays to cheat on the collusive agreement by producing more than the agreed-upon amount. Collusion breaks down in the ninth year. Reasoning backward through time, this logic will lead collusion to break down almost immediately.

Economists have tried to set up laboratory experiments, much like those used by other sciences, to test how individuals actually behave in these different games. The advantage of this sort of **experimental economics** is that the researcher can change one aspect of what is going on at a time, to try to determine what are the crucial determinants of behavior. One set of experiments has looked at how individuals cooperate with one another in situations like the Prisoner's Dilemma. These experiments have a tendency to show that participants often evolve simple strategies that, although they may appear irrational in the short run, can be effective in inducing cooperation (collusion) as the game is repeated a number of times. One common strategy is "tit for tat": if you increase your output, I will do the same, even if doing so does not maximize my profits. If the rival firm believes this threat, especially after it has been carried out a few times, the rival may decide that it is more profitable to cooperate and keep production low rather than to cheat. In the real world, such simple strategies may play an important role in ensuring in those markets where there are only three or four dominant firms that the firms do not compete too vigorously.

THE PROBLEM OF COORDINATION

Because explicit collusion is illegal in the United States, members of an oligopoly who wish to take advantage of their market power must rely on **tacit collusion.** Tacit collusion is an implicit understanding that the oligopoly's interests are best served if its members do not compete too vigorously and particularly if they avoid price cutting. However, the interests of particular firms may not coincide exactly, and it is difficult to specify what each firm should do in every situation in an implicit agreement. When cost or demand curves shift, perhaps because of changes in technology or changes in tastes, the members of a cartel need to get together to agree upon the appropriate changes in output and prices. A new technology or development may benefit one firm more than another, and that firm will wish to increase output more than the others. Naturally, if the oligopolists could bargain together openly, they might be able to cut a deal. But since these sorts of deals are illegal, the agreements the oligopolists make cannot be upheld in courts. Inventive oligopolists have developed a number of ways to circumvent this coordination problem.

One solution is for one firm to become the **price leader;** that firm, often the second- or third-largest member of the industry, sets the price, and others follow. According to some economists, American Airlines used to be the price leader in its industry. As costs (say, of fuel) or demand conditions changed in the airline industry, American would announce new fare structures, and the other airlines would simply match them. It is usually hard to prove that collusion has occurred—the firms simply claim that they are responding to similar market forces.

Some oligopolies have also developed **facilitating practices** that serve to make collusion easier. One example is the "meeting-the-competition clause," in which at least some members of the oligopoly commit themselves, often in advertisements, to charging no more than any competitor. Electronics shops often make such claims. To the consumer, this looks like a great deal. But to see why this practice may actually lead to higher prices, think about it from the perspective of rival firms. Assume that the electronics store is selling for $100 an item that costs the store $90; its selling costs are $5, so it is making a $5 dollar profit on the sale. Consider another store that would like to steal some customers away. It would be willing to sell the item for $95, undercutting the first store. But then it reasons that if it cuts its price, it will not gain any customers, since the first store has already guaranteed to match the lower price. Further, the second store knows that it will make less money on each sale to its current customers. Price cutting simply does not pay. It thus appears that a practice that seemingly is highly competitive in fact may facilitate collusion.

In many cases, oligopolists create a variety of cooperative arrangements that involve sharing inventories, research findings, or other information. In electronics and other high-technology industries, exchanging research information is particularly important. In retail and wholesale markets, helping one another out in the case of inventory shortages is important; for example, one distributor of beer may provide beer to another, when the latter's inventory is insufficient to meet his retailers' demand. Any firm that cheated on the collusive price arrangement would find itself cut out from these cooperative arrangements.

THE PROBLEM OF ENTRY

The third major problem that cartels face is similar to the problem faced by a monopolist: the high profits enjoyed by the members of the cartel attract entry from other firms or cause nonmembers of the cartel to expand production. Often simply referred to as the problem of **entry,** this was one of the fates that befell OPEC; when its members raised the price of oil, noncartel countries like Britain, Canada, and Mexico increased their production of oil.

Some economists, such as William Baumol of New York and Princeton universities, have argued that in some markets just the threat of entry is so strong that even if a firm controlled 90 or 95 percent of the market, the threat of entry would keep prices low.

CLOSE-UP: PRICE FIXING IN ACTION

Price-fixing cases are often hard to prosecute, since the parties go to great lengths to hide their activities. Occasionally, however, a private conversation becomes public, as happened in a 1983 antitrust suit against American and Braniff Airlines. The following is part of a recorded telephone call between Robert Crandall, president of American Airlines, and Howard Putnam, president of Braniff Airlines, that was introduced at the trial. (The two companies had been acting as oligopolistic competitors and cutting prices as they competed in the Dallas market.)

CRANDALL: I think it's dumb as hell . . . to sit here and pound the (deleted) out of each other and neither one of us making a (deleted) dime. . . . We can both live here and there ain't no room for Delta. But there's, ah, no reason that I can see, all right, to put both companies out of business.

PUTNAM: Do you have a suggestion for me?

CRANDALL: Yes, I have a suggestion for you. Raise your goddamn fares twenty percent. I'll raise mine the next morning. . . . You'll make more money, and I will too.

PUTNAM: We can't talk about pricing.

CRANDALL: Oh (deleted), Howard. We can talk about any goddamn thing we want to talk about.

The Justice Department released a transcript of the conversation as it charged American Airlines and Crandall with an attempt to monopolize airline routes and fix prices with Braniff. However, after some months of litigation, a federal judge dismissed the charge. The decision held that while the conversation was clearly an offer to raise prices, it was not an attempt to monopolize according to the meaning of the law. The judge also wrote that "Crandall's conduct was at best unprofessional and his choice of words distasteful," but concluded that since Putnam turned down the offer, no conspiracy to monopolize existed.

Crandall was lucky. If his phrasing had been a bit different, or if Putnam had taken him up on his offer, he could easily have been found guilty. But how many other, similar conversations are occurring among other executives today, without any government recording devices on the line?

Sources: Robert E. Taylor and Dean Rotbart, "American Air Accused of Bid to Fix Prices," *Wall Street Journal,* February 24, 1983, p. 2; Dean Rotbart, "American Air, Its President Get Trust Suit Voided," *Wall Street Journal,* September 14, 1983, p. 2.

If prices were ever so slightly above costs of production, there would be rapid entry, forcing prices down. In these cases, **potential competition,** the possibility of entry, is all that is required to keep prices low, not actual competition. The costs of entry and exit have to be relatively small, however, for potential competition to be effective. Otherwise, firms will not enter, even when they see high prices, unless they have reason to believe that prices will remain high after entry.

Markets such as these, in which potential competition suffices to ensure competitive prices, are called **contestable.** At one time, advocates of the theory of contestable markets used airlines as the basic example of a contestable entry. An airline could easily enter a market in which price exceeded costs (for example, the San Francisco–Los Angeles market or the New York–Chicago market), and thus potential competition would ensure low prices, even when there were only one or two airlines flying a particular route. But by the end of the 1980s, as airline prices skyrocketed on many routes on which competition was limited, potential competition did not seem strong enough to keep prices down. Potential entrants recognized that there were significant costs to entering a market—customers had to be informed, they had to be persuaded to switch from the usual carrier, airline offices had to be opened, and so forth—and experience had taught them that once they entered, prices would fall, making it impossible for them to recover these costs.

Indeed, it is perhaps remarkable how many oligopolies seem to persist with limited entry. There has been some entry into the film industry (Fuji), but it remains dominated by a few firms. Other oligopolies, such as the automobile, cigarette, and aluminum industries, have remained relatively intact over long periods of time. Even the number of attempts at entry has been limited; Tucker and Kaiser represent the two most famous cases of failure in automobiles. This suggests that if the barriers to entry discussed in Chapter 15 are strong enough, as appears to be the case in many situations, entry may not pose an important limit to collusion.

LIMITS TO COLLUSION

Self-enforcement; incentives for each firm to cheat

Coordination problems in responding to changed economic circumstances

Entry

RESTRICTIVE PRACTICES

If the members of an oligopoly could easily get together and collude, they frequently would; their joint profits would thereby be increased. They would have a problem of how to divide the profits, but each of the members of the oligopoly could be better off than it would be if they competed. We have seen, however, that there are significant impediments to collusion. If the members of an industry cannot collude to stop competition and cannot prevent entry, at least they can act to reduce competition and deter entry.

Chapter 15 described some of the ways firms act to deter entry. Here, we look at practices firms engage in that *may* serve to restrict competition, called **restrictive practices.** While these practices may not be quite as successful in increasing profits for the firms as the collusive arrangements discussed above, they do succeed in raising prices. In some cases, consumers may be even worse off than with outright collusive behavior. Some of these practices were made illegal by the Federal Trade Commission Act of 1914; this act also established the Federal Trade Commission itself, an agency whose responsibility is to ascertain what are unfair trade practices and to design regulations prohibiting them. Many of the restrictive practices are aimed at the wholesalers and retailers who sell a producer's goods. When one firm buys or sells another firm's products, the two companies are said to have a "vertical" relationship. Accordingly, such restrictive practices are called **vertical restrictions,** as opposed to the price-fixing arrangements among producers or among wholesalers in a local market, which are referred to as **horizontal restrictions.**

One example of a vertical restriction is that of **exclusive territories,** in which a producer gives a wholesaler or retailer the exclusive right to sell a good within a certain region. Beer and soft drink producers, for instance, typically give their distributors exclusive territories. Coca-Cola manufactures its own syrup, which it then sells to bottlers who add the soda water. Coca-Cola gives these bottlers exclusive territories, so the supermarkets in a particular area can buy Coke in only one place. A store in Michigan cannot buy the soft drink from Coca-Cola bottlers in New Jersey, even if the price there is lower.

Similarly, in most locales, there are only one, two, or three beer distributors. One distributor might carry Budweiser, Michelob, and some imports, while another carries Miller, Löwenbräu, and other imports. Exclusive territorial arrangements ensure that only one distributor can sell Budweiser in any locale. There is no "intrabrand" competition, only interbrand competition. The arrangements limit competition, enabling the two or three local distributors to raise prices above competitive levels. Indiana passed a law prohibiting exclusive territories for beer within the state, and as a result, beer prices there appear substantially lower (adjusting for other differences) than in other states.

Slight changes in competition can have big effects on prices. In the 1930s, the state of New York passed a law prohibiting dairies outside New York from selling milk in the state. The law benefited New York milk producers at the expense of the broad spectrum of New York consumers, not to mention milk producers in other states. In 1979, the New Jersey–based Farmland Dairies challenged the New York law. After an eight-year legal battle, a court decision gave Farmland Dairies the chance to sell milk in New York City. Before the legal decision, five local milk producers controlled over 90 percent of the milk market in New York City. After the decision, when Farmland Dairy and others entered the market, milk prices in New York City dropped by as much as 70 cents a gallon. In total, the new competition saved New York consumers as much as $100 million every year in lower milk prices.

Another example of a restrictive practice is **exclusive dealing,** in which a producer insists that any firm selling its products not sell those of its rivals. When you go into an Exxon gas station, for instance, you can be sure you are buying gas refined by the

Exxon Corporation, not by Texaco or Mobil. Like most refiners, Exxon insists that stations that want to sell Exxon sell only its brand of gasoline.

A third example of a restrictive practice is **tie-ins,** in which a customer who buys one product must buy another. Mortgage companies, for example, used to insist that those who obtained mortgages from them purchase fire insurance as well. Nintendo, the dominating firm in electronic games, designs its console so that it can only be used with Nintendo games. In effect, they force a tie-in sale between the console and the computer games. Some manufacturers of copying machines produced paper that was designed specially for their machines, again effectively forcing a tie-in sale. In the early days of computers, IBM designed its computers so that they could only be used with IBM "peripherals" such as printers.

A final example of a restrictive practice is **resale price maintenance.** Under resale price maintenance, a producer insists that any retailer selling his product must sell it at the "list" price. Like exclusive territories, this practice is designed to reduce competitive pressures at the retail level.

FORMS OF RESTRICTIVE PRACTICES

Exclusive territories
Exclusive dealing
Tie-ins
Resale price maintenance

CONSEQUENCES OF RESTRICTIVE PRACTICES

In each of these cases, firms engaging in the restrictive practice *claim* they are doing so not because they wish to restrict competition, but because they want to enhance economic efficiency. Exclusive territories, they argue, provide companies with a better incentive to "cultivate" their territory. They know they will get any enhanced business for the product that is generated within their territory. Exclusive dealing contracts provide incentives for firms to focus their attention on one producer's goods.

However, in many cases, restrictive practices actually reduce economic efficiency in their attempt to limit competition. Exclusive territories for beer have sometimes limited the ability of very large firms, with stores in many different territories, to set up a central warehouse and distribute beer to their stores in a more efficient manner.

Regardless of whether they enhance or hurt efficiency, restrictive practices may lead to higher prices by limiting competitive pressures. Practices like exclusive territories limit the number of firms competing directly against one another; and as we saw in Chapter 15, the number of firms in a market is one of the key determinants of the level of competition.

The beer-brewing industry is divided into three parts: producers, wholesalers, and retailers. Retailers are the ones who sell to the public, in stores, taverns, and restaurants.

Producers brew the beer. They create the brand names—Budweiser, Coors, and so on—and they are the ones who buy most of the television advertising. Wholesalers operate in between the producers and the retailers.

For years now, beer wholesalers have been arguing that to serve the public properly, each wholesaler needs an exclusive right to sell a certain brand of beer within a given territory. The laws of forty-five states either encourage such exclusive arrangements or at least do not prohibit them. However, Arizona, Connecticut, Idaho, and Texas explicitly authorize brewers to contract with more than one wholesaler for a given territory, and Indiana prohibits exclusive territories altogether.

The argument for exclusive territories runs like this. A wholesaler often has to invest money and energy in encouraging stores and bars to carry a certain brand of beer. If the wholesaler does not have an exclusive territory, then another distributor could come along after these costs of establishing the market have been incurred and try to take over the market. The threat of this happening would discourage wholesalers from investing in new markets, just as the threat of having an invention copied would discourage an innovator from investing in a new product. In 1982, Anheuser-Busch, the nation's largest brewer, announced that because of this threat, it was adopting a policy that was tantamount to requiring all wholesalers who carried its brands to sell beer only within assigned territories.

But to owners of groceries and bars, as well as to many government regulators, the argument for exclusive territories sounds like a justification for shutting off competition. Reduced competition, they reason, is likely to lead to higher prices. Retailers find that they can buy a given brand of beer from only one wholesaler—take it or leave it. Sometimes they find that one wholesaler is the exclusive dealer for several different brands of beer, so they cannot even play one exclusive wholesaler off against another.

Moreover, government regulators have argued that when a small number of wholesalers supply beer to an entire market, new breweries are discouraged from entering the market, since they cannot be sure that an existing wholesaler will be eager to offend the producers with which it has established relations and distribute the newcomer's beer. AT the end of World War II, there were about six hundred breweries in the United States; by the mid-1980s, there were less than one hundred, and the top four brewers controlled 80 percent of the market. A few "boutique" breweries and "brewpubs" have opened up in recent years, but they have made almost no dent in the overall market.

Supporters of exclusive territories counter that even if competition between wholesalers is limited, the competition between different beers for the consumer's drinking dollar persists. Whether exclusive territories are a violation of antitrust laws has remained unclear. To eliminate this ambiguity, during the 1980s, beer producers pushed for an official act of Congress that would prohibit any antitrust suits against exclusive territories. The law has failed to pass, but the exclusive territories continue.

Source: Peter C. Carstensen and Richard F. Dahlson, "Vertical Restraints in Beer Distribution: A Study of the Business Justifications for and Legal Analysis of Restricting Competition," *Wisconsin Law Review* (1986) 1:1–81.

Some restrictive practices work by increasing the costs of, or otherwise impeding, one's rivals. In the 1980s, several major airlines developed computer reservation systems that they sold at very attractive prices to travel agents. If the primary goal of these systems had been to serve consumers, they would have been designed to display all the departures near the approximate time the passenger desired. Instead, each airline's system displayed only its own flights—United's, for instance, focused on United flights—although with additional work, the travel agent could find out the flights of other airlines. Airlines benefited from these computer systems, not because they best met the needs of the consumer, but because they put competitors at a disadvantage and thereby reduced the effectiveness of competition.

An exclusive dealing contract between a producer and a distributor is another example of how one firm may benefit from hurting its rivals. The contract may force a rival producer to set up its own distribution system, at great cost. The already-existing distributor might have been able to undertake the distribution of the second product at relatively low incremental cost. Thus, the exclusive dealing contract increases total resources spent on distribution.

Because these practices may both serve valid business objectives (such as providing enhanced incentives to distributors) and reduce competition, in many cases it is not clear whether they should be judged illegal. Courts have taken varying attitudes, in some circumstances ruling that they are illegal, while in others, having been persuaded by the argument that they represent reasonable business practices, allowing them.

CONSEQUENCES OF RESTRICTIVE PRACTICES: ALTERNATIVE VIEWS

Lower prices from
    Enhanced economic efficiency

Higher prices from
    Reduced competition
    Increased costs for rivals

COMPETITION AMONG OLIGOPOLISTS

At one level of analysis, the oligopolist is just like a firm facing monopolistic competition. The oligopolist firm faces a demand curve, specifying how much output it believes it can sell at each price it charges, or what the firm believes it will receive if it tries to sell a particular quantity. The oligopolist chooses the point along that demand curve at which its profits are maximized. It sets, in other words, marginal revenue equal to marginal cost. But while true, this statement hides all the real difficulties in an analysis of oligopoly. What an oligopolist will sell at any particular price, or what the market price will be if it produces a particular level of output, depends on what its rivals do. And what its rivals do may depend on what the oligopolist does. There are no simple answers; oligopolies in different industries seem to behave in quite different ways.

Earlier we saw how game theory is useful in describing the problems of firms in an oligopoly trying to collude. When oligopolists compete, game theory is again useful. But in real life, competition among oligopolists is a game in which not all the rules are clear, let alone written down. If you can think of a new move, unlike that taken by any of your rivals, it may give you an advantage. On the other hand, they may respond in a way that you did not fully anticipate. You may be worse off in the end. For example, American Airlines might have thought it was getting a leg up on its rivals when it introduced its frequent flier program, and Delta Airlines might have thought it was doing likewise when it offered triple mileage. But some of the rival airlines had more empty seats, so giving away free tickets may have been less costly for them, and they could respond by offering even more attractive programs. Were American and Delta, then, really better off?

We now take a look at three possible patterns of behavior for an oligopoly. In each, the oligopolists take different actions and make different assumptions about how rivals will respond. We also look at the circumstances under which each of these possibilities is more likely to be relevant. But it should be remembered that these are only three of many possible patterns.

COURNOT COMPETITION

An oligopolist firm may believe that its rivals are committed to producing a given quantity and selling it on the market, and that they will keep this quantity fixed no matter what level of output the firm chooses to produce. If the firm considers producing more, it expects that its rivals will cut their prices until they sell the production level to which they are committed. This is the kind of competition that might result in an industry such as aluminum or steel, where the major part of the cost of production is the cost of machinery, and once capital goods are in place, variable costs are relatively unimportant. Adding new machinery would be expensive, and not using machinery to its capacity would save the firm relatively little money. Output is then determined, at least in the short run, by the production capacity of the firm's capital goods. Competition of this sort is called **Cournot competition,** after Augustin Cournot, a French economist and engineer who first studied it in 1838.

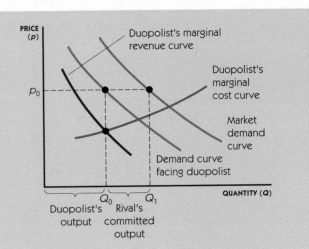

Figure 16.2 COURNOT COMPETITION IN A DUOPOLY

For a duopolist in a situation of Cournot competition, the firm's demand curve and the market demand curve are parallel, separated by the amount that the rival firm is committed to producing. Given the demand curve, the duopolist maximizes profit in the usual way, by setting its marginal revenue equal to marginal cost.

Figure 16.2 illustrates the case where there are two firms in an industry—a **duopoly,** like Alcoa and Reynolds, which at one time dominated the aluminum industry.[2] The analysis of the equilibrium behavior of a duopolist begins much the same as the analysis of the behavior of a monopolist or a firm in monopolistic competition. We first ask, what is the demand curve facing the firm—that is, what is the price it would receive if it attempted to sell so many units of a good? Once we know the firm's demand curve, we know what it will do: maximize its profit, by setting marginal revenue equal to marginal cost.

The demand curve facing a duopolist depends on the behavior of its rival. In the case we are considering here, the rival has a fixed level of output. The duopolist's demand curve is then simply the market demand curve shifted over to the left by the amount of output the rival is committed to producing.[3] Given this demand curve, we can draw the marginal revenue curve, and the firm produces at the point where marginal revenue equals marginal cost.

Normally, the equilibrium output with Cournot competition is less than with perfect competition but greater than with monopoly. The reason for this is easy to see. With a monopoly, firms can be thought of as setting marginal revenue equal to marginal cost. With perfect competition, marginal revenue is just price. With a monopoly, marginal revenue is lower than price. It is price minus what the firm loses on its earlier sales; that is, the reduction in price from producing one more unit. This is also the case with Cournot competition. Thus, output is lower than it is with perfect competition. But if there are two identical firms, each is producing only half the total output. Hence, what it loses in profits on earlier sales is smaller than under monopoly. Part of the lost revenue from lower prices is borne by the rival firm, which, under the Cournot as-

---

[2] Actually, the aluminum industry in the early post–World War II period was dominated by three firms: Alcoa, Reynolds, and Kaiser. Since then, the market shares of all three have declined as other producers have gained ground. Focusing on only two firms simplifies the discussion.

[3] This demand curve is sometimes referred to as the residual demand curve.

sumption, is expected to maintain its output. Marginal revenue is closer to price. So because at any level of output the marginal revenue is higher with Cournot competition than with monopoly, equilibrium output is also higher.

BERTRAND COMPETITION

In Cournot competition, each firm decides what quantity to produce; it chooses the quantity that will maximize its profits. In making its calculations, each firm assumes that the level of output of its rivals is fixed. This assumption, we saw, is plausible for industries in which it takes time to change production capacity, and in which capital goods represent the bulk of all production costs.

But this assumption does not hold in many industries. In some, it is easy to expand capacity. A taxicab company in a large city can easily buy a new car and hire new drivers. While increasing the total number of planes in service may take some time, an airline that wishes to increase the number of planes flying the Chicago–New York route can do so quickly.

Firms in these industries can be thought of as choosing a price to charge, and adjusting their output to meet whatever demand arises at that price. They choose the price so as to maximize their profits, given their beliefs about the behavior of their rivals. One commonly made assumption is that rivals' prices are fixed. Oligopolies in which each firm chooses its price to maximize its profits on the assumption that rivals' prices are fixed are said to have **Bertrand competition,** after the French economist Joseph Bertrand, who first studied this form of competition in 1883.

If rivals keep their prices unchanged, then the oligopolist may steal many of its rivals' customers when it lowers its price. If the goods produced by the two rivals are imperfect substitutes (for any of the reasons discussed in Chapter 15), when one firm lowers its price below that of its rivals, it does not capture *all* of the customers. That is the case depicted in Figure 16.3, which shows the demand curve facing one of the firms in a

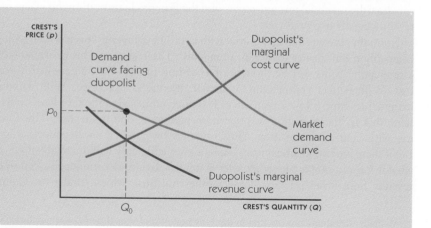

Figure 16.3 BERTRAND COMPETITION IN A DUOPOLY

The demand curve facing a duopolist in a situation of Bertrand competition is drawn under the assumption that its rival's price is fixed. Thus, the demand curve facing the firm is more elastic than the market demand curve. Given the demand curve, the duopolist maximizes profit in the usual way, by setting marginal revenue equal to marginal cost.

duopoly. It is very elastic. As the firm charges slightly more than its rival, it loses many customers; if it charges slightly less, it gains many customers. The firm chooses the profit-maximizing price; given the demand curve it believes it is facing, this is just the output Q_0, where marginal revenue equals marginal cost. (The figure also shows the market demand curve. This curve represents the total demand for, say, toothpaste, given that both Colgate and Crest charge the same price. The demand curve facing Crest is drawn with the assumption that Colgate's price is fixed, and vice versa.)

With price-setting (Bertrand) competition, firms believe that they face more elastic demand curves than they do with quantity-setting (Cournot) competition. This can easily be seen when we consider the extreme case where the two goods produced by two different firms are perfect substitutes. Then if one firm charges slightly less than its rival, it garners for itself the entire market; if it charges slightly more, it loses all of its sales. Each firm faces a horizontal demand curve. Thus, even when there are only two firms, if each believes the other has fixed its price and will not change the price in response to changes in prices it charges, and if the two firms produce *perfect* substitutes, the market outcome is competitive.

We can see this process of competition as follows. Assume both firms have constant marginal and average costs of production. Since each company believes its rival will not budge its price so long as price exceeds marginal costs, each one will find that it pays it to shave its price by a small amount. By doing so, it steals the whole market. But the rival firm, thinking the same way, then undercuts still further. The process continues until the price is bid down to the point where there are zero profits. It does not pay to cut prices any further.

In general, the products produced by two duopolists are not perfect substitutes but differ somewhat, so that each firm faces a downward-sloping demand curve. In equilibrium, price exceeds marginal costs. Output is less than it would be with perfect competition, but more than it would be with Cournot competition.

KINKED DEMAND CURVES

A third simple hypothesis about how oligopolistic rivals may respond says that rivals match price cuts but do not respond to price increases. In this situation, an oligopolist believes that it will not gain much in sales if it lowers its price, because rivals will match the price cut, but it will lose considerably if it raises its price, since it will be undersold by rivals who do not change their prices. The demand curve facing such an oligopolist appears kinked, as in Figure 16.4. The curve is very steep below the current price, p_1, reflecting the fact that few sales are gained as price is lowered; but it is relatively flat above p_1, indicating that the firm loses many customers to its rivals, who refuse to match the price increases.

The figure also presents the marginal revenue curve, which has a sharp drop at the output level corresponding to the kink. Why does the marginal revenue curve have this

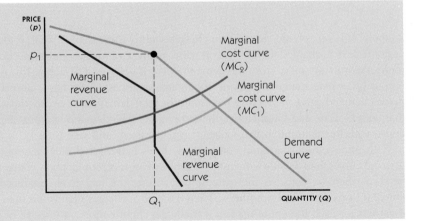

Figure 16.4 A KINKED DEMAND CURVE

The demand curve facing a firm is relatively flat at price levels above the current level (p_1), showing that an oligopolist will lose a large amount of sales if it increases its price and rivals do not. However, the demand curve is relatively steep at prices below the current level, showing that the oligopolist will not gain much in sales if it lowers its price, since rivals will follow. The sharp drop in marginal revenue means that a firm may not change its level of price or output, even if marginal costs shift.

shape, and what are the consequences? The drop in the marginal revenue curve follows from the fact that the increase in the price from a reduction in sales by a unit is much smaller than the fall in the price if the firm wants to increase sales by a unit. Increases in output beyond Q_1 raise relatively little additional revenue, since to sell the increased output, price must fall by a considerable amount; any price cut by a firm is matched by its rivals, so relatively few customers are gained. On the other hand, at levels of output less than those at the kink, marginal revenue is quite high, because as we have seen, the demand curve is relatively flat to the left of Q_1. With a flat demand curve, price and marginal revenue are close together.

The drop in the marginal revenue curve means that at the output at which the drop occurs, Q_1, the extra revenue lost from cutting back production is much greater than the extra revenue gained from increasing production. This in turn has one important implication: small changes in marginal cost, from MC_1 to MC_2, have no effect on output or price. Thus, firms that believe they face a kinked demand curve have good reason to hesitate before changing their prices.

COMPETITION AMONG OLIGOPOLISTS

Cournot competition: Each firm believes its rivals will leave their output unchanged in response to changes in the firm's output.

Bertrand competition: Each firm sets its price believing its rivals will leave their own price unchanged in response to changes in the firm's price.

Kinked demand curves: Each firm believes its rivals will match price cuts but not price increases.

REVIEW AND PRACTICE

SUMMARY

1. Oligopolists must choose whether to seek higher profits by colluding with rival firms or by competing. They must decide what their rivals will do in response to any action they take.

2. Firms that have an explicit and open agreement to collude are known as a cartel. Although cartels are illegal under U.S. law, firms have tried to find tacit ways of facilitating collusion; for example, by using price leaders and "meeting the competition" pricing policies.

3. If the threat of potential entry is sufficient to cause firms to set price and output at

competitive levels, the industry is said to be contestable.

4. Even when they do not collude, firms attempt to restrict competition, with practices like exclusive territories, exclusive dealing, tie-ins, and resale price maintenance. In some cases, a firm's profits may be increased by raising its rival's costs and making the rival a less effective competitor.

5. Cournot competition leads to a combination of price and output that is between monopoly and perfect competition; price exceeds marginal cost, but by an amount that is less than under monopoly.

6. In Bertrand competition, when the goods produced by each firm are perfect substitutes, the firms will keep trying to undercut one another on price until they reach the perfectly competitive outcome, with price equal to marginal cost.

7. If the rivals to an oligopolist match all price cuts but do not match any price increases, then the oligopolist faces a kinked demand curve. A kinked demand curve will lead to a marginal revenue curve with a vertical segment, which implies that the firm will often not change its level of output or its price in response to small changes in costs.

KEY TERMS

cartel	Prisoner's Dilemma	Bertrand competition
regulatory capture	Cournot competition	kinked demand curve
antitrust laws	duopoly	

REVIEW QUESTIONS

1. Why is the analysis of oligopoly more complicated than that of monopoly, perfect competition, or monopolistic competition?

2. Name some ways that firms might use tacit collusion, if explicit collusion is ruled out by law.

3. What is a contestable market?

4. Name and define three restrictive practices.

5. How does a Cournot competitor in a duopoly choose its profit-maximizing level of output?

6. Explain why Cournot competitors will produce more and charge a lower price than monopolists, but produce less and charge a higher price than perfect competitors.

7. How does a Bertrand competitor in a duopoly choose its profit-maximizing level of output?

8. Explain why oligopolists producing perfect substitutes in Bertrand competition will end up at the perfectly competitive level of price and output.

9. What expectations must an oligopolist have about the behavior of its rivals if it believes that it faces a kinked demand curve?

10. Why might a firm that faces a kinked demand curve not change its price even when its costs change?

PROBLEMS

1. Explain why every member of a cartel has an incentive to cheat on its agreement. How does this fact strengthen the ability of antitrust laws that outlaw explicit collusion to do their job?

2. How might cooperative agreements between firms—to share research information, share the costs of cleaning up pollution, or help avoid shortfalls of supplies—end up helping firms to collude in reducing quantity and raising price?

3. Consider two oligopolists, with each choosing between a "high" and a "low" level of production. Given their choices of how much to produce, their profits will be:

		Firm A	
		High production	Low production
	High production	A gets $2 million profit	A gets $1 million profit
		B gets $2 million profit	B gets $5 million profit
Firm B			
	Low production	A gets $5 million profit	A gets $4 million profit
		B gets $1 million profit	B gets $4 million profit.

Explain how firm B will reason that it makes sense to produce the high amount, regardless of what firm A chooses. Then explain how firm A will reason that it makes sense to produce the high amount, regardless of what firm B chooses. How might collusion assist the two firms in this case?

4. Explain how exclusive territories, exclusive dealing, tie-ins, and resale price maintenance might help an oligopolist to make higher profits. How might a firm make the case that these practices add to efficiency?

APPENDIX: DESCRIBING THE MARKET EQUILIBRIUM FOR OLIGOPOLY

In this appendix, we learn how the firms in a duopoly interact to determine the market equilibrium. We first consider the Cournot and Bertrand equilibrium, and then see what happens if the firms in an industry engage in certain restrictive practices.

COURNOT COMPETITION

The central tool in this analysis is the **reaction function**, which specifies the level of output of each firm given the level of output of the other firm. It shows, in other words, the reaction of one firm to the actions of the other. Consider the aluminum industry in the period after World War II; the two largest firms were Alcoa and Reynolds. The reaction function for Alcoa is plotted in Figure 16.5A. It is downward sloping.

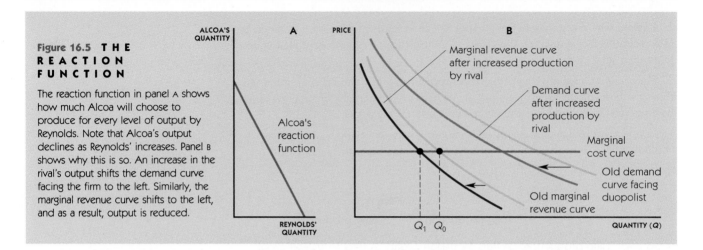

Figure 16.5 THE REACTION FUNCTION

The reaction function in panel A shows how much Alcoa will choose to produce for every level of output by Reynolds. Note that Alcoa's output declines as Reynolds' increases. Panel B shows why this is so. An increase in the rival's output shifts the demand curve facing the firm to the left. Similarly, the marginal revenue curve shifts to the left, and as a result, output is reduced.

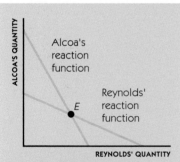

Figure 16.6 MARKET EQUILIBRIUM WITH COURNOT COMPETITION

Equilibrium will be at the intersection of the two reaction functions, where each firm is maximizing its profits given its belief that the output of the other firm is fixed. At that point, there is no pressure for either firm to change output.

To see why this is so, we need to recall how each Cournot oligopolist decides how much to produce. It sets marginal revenue equal to marginal cost, as in panel B. If Reynolds increases production, the demand facing Alcoa at any given price is reduced. Equivalently, if Alcoa wants to sell the same amount as before, it must lower its price. The figure shows the new demand and marginal revenue curves; they are to the left of the corresponding curves when Reynolds produced less. Accordingly, the optimal level of output is lower: as Reynolds increases production, Alcoa decreases production.

We can apply the same analysis to Reynolds, in Figure 16.6. The reaction curve shows Reynolds' level of output along the horizontal axis, given Alcoa's output along the vertical axis. The market equilibrium is the intersection of the reaction functions, point E. This point depicts the equilibrium output of Alcoa given the output of Reynolds, and it depicts the output of Reynolds given the output of Alcoa. The intersection of the reaction functions is an equilibrium because, given each firm's beliefs about the behavior of its rival, neither firm wishes to change what it does. There are, in short, no pressures to change. Each firm is maximizing its profits, given its belief that the rival is committed to producing its current level of output.

BERTRAND COMPETITION

Figure 16.7 uses reaction functions to describe the market equilibrium of a Bertrand duopoly consisting of two mattress companies, Supersleepers and Heavenlyrest, which produce imperfect substitutes. The reaction function in this case gives the price charged by one firm, given the price charged by its rival. As Supersleepers increases its price, Heavenlyrest finds it optimal to increase its own price. That is why the reaction function is positively sloped. The equilibrium is at E.

The figure also shows how Supersleepers can increase its profits by insisting that wholesalers deal only with it. Once Supersleepers has accomplished this, Heavenlyrest finds its costs of distribution have increased. As a result, the optimal price Heavenlyrest

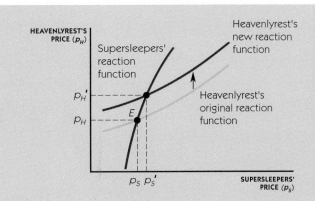

Figure 16.7 EXCLUSIVE DEALING TO RAISE RIVALS' COSTS

If Supersleepers is able to set up an exclusive dealing agreement with most of the experienced distributors in a market, it will force its rival, Heavenlyrest, to bear higher costs by using less skilled distributors. Thus, Heavenlyrest will charge a higher price for any level of price chosen by Supersleepers, which leads to a higher equilibrium price for Supersleepers.

charges, given any price charged by Supersleepers, is higher. Its reaction function shifts up. The new equilibrium price for Supersleepers is higher: it has increased from p_S to p_S'. Because Heavenlyrest's price is also higher, Supersleepers may have lost few if any sales to the rival firm; its profits are higher. Thus, even if Supersleepers had to pay its distributors to sign exclusive dealing contracts, it may be better off.

RESTRICTIVE PRACTICES

Figure 16.8 shows what happens if both firms adopt restrictive practices. The restrictive practices serve to shift out both reaction functions; because of the limitations on competition at any price of one firm, the optimal price of the other firm is higher. Given that both reaction functions shift out, the equilibrium prices will be higher.

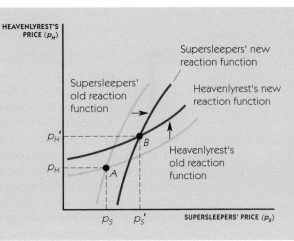

Figure 16.8 RESTRICTIVE PRACTICES WITH BERTRAND COMPETITION

Restrictive practices allow both firms to charge more than they otherwise would, since they have less to fear from competition. If both firms adopt restrictive practices, the equilibrium of the reaction functions shifts from A to B.

CHAPTER 17

GOVERNMENT POLICIES TOWARD COMPETITION

T here is a general consensus in the United States that monopolies are not a good thing. Popular disapproval is probably based more on concerns of politics and equity than on concern for how they affect economic efficiency. Leaders of near-monopolies in the early part of this century, like John D. Rockefeller of Standard Oil and Andrew Carnegie in the steel industry, were the subject of populist envy as well as concern that such concentrations of wealth could give rise to undemocratic concentrations of political power. Economists' disapproval, however, is based on the ways in which the concentration of economic power affects the workings of the market economy. Motivated by both political and economic concerns, government has taken an active role in promoting competition and in limiting the abuses of excessive market power. In this chapter, we review the economic effects of limited competition and then look at government policies designed to surmount its negative effects.

"But if we do merge with Amalgamated, we'll have enough resources to fight the antitrust violation caused by the merger."

1. Why is government concerned with monopolies and imperfect competition? In what sense do markets with monopolies and imperfect competition result in inefficiency?

2. How have different governments attempted to address the problem posed by a natural monopoly?

3. How have governments used antitrust policies to break up monopolies; to impede the ability of any single firm to attain a dominant position in a market; and to outlaw practices designed to restrict competition?

THE DRAWBACKS OF MONOPOLIES

Economists have identified four major problems resulting from monopolies and other imperfectly competitive industries. These include a restricted output, managerial slack, insufficient attention to research and development, and the dissipation of profits through rent-seeking behavior. The problems can be seen most simply in the context of monopolies, and therefore the discussion focuses on this market structure. However, it is worth noting that many of these problems also arise in the imperfectly competitive markets discussed in Chapters 15 and 16.

RESTRICTED OUTPUT

Monopolists, like competitive firms, are in business to make profits. Like competitive firms, they try to make profits by producing the kinds of goods and services customers want. But monopolists can make profits in ways not available to competitive firms. Monopolists can drive up the price of a good by restricting their output. They can, to use the popular term, gouge their customers. Consumers, by *choosing* to buy the monopolist's good, are revealing that they are better off than they would be without the

Figure 17.1 WHY MONOPOLY OUTPUT IS INEFFICIENT

A perfect competitor will set price equal to marginal cost, and produce at quantity Q_c and price p_c. A monopolist will set marginal revenue equal to marginal cost, and produce at quantity Q_m and price p_m, where the market price exceeds marginal cost.

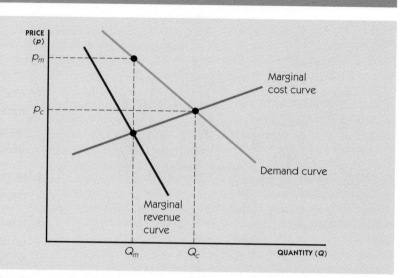

product. But they are paying more than they would if the industry were competitive.

A monopolist who sets marginal revenue equal to marginal cost produces at a lower level of output than a corresponding competitive industry—an industry with the same demand curve and costs but in which there are many producers rather than one—where price equals marginal cost. Figure 17.1 shows that the monopoly output, Q_m, is much smaller than the competitive output, Q_c, where price (p_c) equals marginal cost; the price under monopoly, p_m, is thus much higher.

But in what sense is the monopoly output "too little"? Remember that the price of a good, by definition, measures how much an individual is willing to pay for an extra unit of a good; it measures, in other words, the marginal benefit of the good to the purchaser. With perfect competition, price equals marginal cost, so that in equilibrium the marginal benefit of an extra unit of a good to the individual (the price) is just equal to the marginal cost to the firm of producing it. On the other hand, because for a monopolist the market price exceeds marginal revenue, when the monopolist chooses its output so that marginal revenue equals marginal cost, the marginal benefit of producing an extra unit—the price individuals are willing to pay for an extra unit—exceeds marginal cost. Output is too low: the marginal benefit of producing an extra unit exceeds the marginal cost. This reduction in output is one of the reasons why economists object so strongly to monopolies.

The effects of limited competition for some consumer goods can be seen in Figure 17.2, which shows the production possibilities curve between automobiles and wheat. The wheat sector is assumed to be competitive, the automobile sector imperfectly competitive. However, a monopoly in an industry that produces goods that consumers purchase does not interfere with the *productive* efficiency of the economy. Any profit-maximizing firm has an incentive to minimize the costs of whatever it produces and thus to produce efficiently. The problem is that imperfect competition will lead to a smaller output (in this case, of automobiles) being produced in that sector. Chapter 14 showed that one of the conditions for economic efficiency is product-mix efficiency, that the goods produced by the economy accord with the preferences of consumers.[1] In Figure 17.2, the competitive equilibrium is at point E. This is the efficient level of production. As a result of imperfect competition, too few automobiles are produced. The economy operates at point E', where consumers are worse off.[2]

It is difficult to quantify precisely how much worse off society as a whole is as a result of monopolists' restrictions on output. The reduction in output, and the consequent higher prices, makes the owners of the monopoly better off (than they would otherwise be) and makes consumers worse off. There may be a large *transfer* of resources, of "purchasing power," from consumers to the monopolist. But setting aside this issue of distribution, how significant is the fact that the production of some good is somewhat lower than it otherwise would have been? Lower production levels mean less use of society's resources within an industry. Thus, resources that the monopoly might have used are deployed elsewhere, and production of other goods increases. From society's point of view, the cost of the monopoly's reduced output is only the *net* difference in the value of how these resources are used. In Figure 17.2, more wheat is produced and fewer cars. The gain to consumers from the increased wheat production is less than the loss to consumers of the reduced car production; the net loss to society is just the difference between the two.

By comparing the monopolist's production decision to the collective output decisions of firms in a competitive market, we can estimate the value of the loss to society when there is a monopoly. To simplify the analysis, in Figure 17.3 marginal cost is assumed to be constant, the horizontal line at the competitive price p_c. The monopolist produces an output of Q_m, at the point where marginal revenue equals marginal cost, and finds that it can charge p_m, the price on the demand curve corresponding to the output Q_m.

There are two kinds of loss to be measured. Both are related to the concept of consumer surplus introduced in Chapter 8. There we learned that the downward-sloping demand curve implies a sort of bounty to most consumers: at points to the left of the intersection of the price line and the demand curve, people are willing to pay more for the good than they have to. With competition, the consumer surplus in Figure 17.3 would be the entire shaded area between the demand curve and the line at p_c. The monopolist cuts into this surplus first because it charges a higher price, p_m, than would be obtained in the competitive situation. This loss is measured by the rectangle $ABCD$, the extra price times the quantity actually produced and consumed. The loss to consumers is not a loss to society as a whole; it is a transfer of income as the higher price winds up as revenues for the monopoly.

The second kind of loss is a complete loss to society, and is thus called the **deadweight loss** of a monopoly. While production in a competitive market would be Q_c, with a monopoly it is the lower amount Q_m. Consumers lose the surplus to the right of Q_m, denoted by ABG, with no resulting gain to the monopolist.

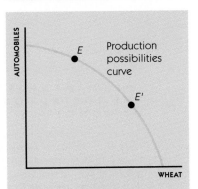

Figure 17.2 IMPERFECT COMPETITION AND THE PRODUCTION POSSIBILITIES CURVE

The efficient product mix for the economy, given the preferences of consumers, would lead the economy to choose point E. However, imperfect competition in the automobile sector would lead to fewer cars being produced, which causes a shift to the less efficient product mix at E'. Notice that the products are being produced efficiently; the problem is that the wrong combination is being produced.

---

[1] Using the concept of marginal rate of substitution introduced in the appendices to Chapters 8 and 12, we say that product-mix efficiency requires that the marginal rate of substitution for consumers equal the marginal rate of transformation for producers.

[2] For those who studied the appendix to Chapter 8, this can be described using indifference curves. Assume for simplicity that all individuals are identical. Then the indifference curve will be tangent to the production possibilities curve at E. The indifference curve through E' will correspond to a lower level of welfare.

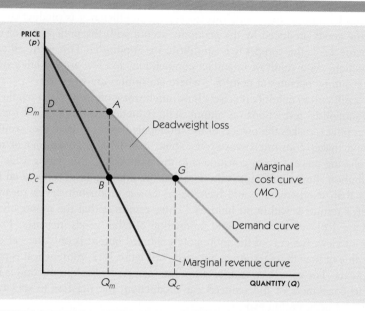

Figure 17.3 MEASURING THE SOCIAL COST OF MONOPOLY

The higher, monopoly price removes some of the consumer surplus. Part of this loss (the rectangle *ABCD*) is simply a transfer of income from consumers to the monopolist; the remainder (the triangle *ABG*) is known as the deadweight loss of monopoly.

Some economists, such as Arnold Harberger of UCLA, have argued that these costs of monopoly are relatively small; even in sectors in which competition is extremely limited, they may amount to only 3 percent of the value of the output of that sector. Even if these estimates are correct, however, monopolies introduce further inefficiencies in the economy.

MANAGERIAL SLACK

Chapter 12 argued that any company wants to minimize its cost of production, and any profit-maximizing firm (competitive or monopoly) will make the highest possible level of profits when it keeps its costs as low as possible. (The discussion above showed that even with imperfect competition in consumer goods, the economy operates along its production possibilities curve. In this view, imperfect competition only affects the mix of goods produced.) But in practice, companies that are already making a lot of money without much competition usually lack the incentive to hold costs as low as possible. The lack of efficiency when firms are insulated from the pressures of competition is referred to as **managerial slack**.

In the absence of competition, it can be very difficult to tell whether managers are being efficient. How much, for instance, should it cost for AT&T to put a call through from New York to Chicago? In the days when AT&T had a monopoly on long-distance telephone service, it might have claimed that its costs were as low as possible. However, not even trained engineers could really tell whether this was true. When competition developed for intercity telephone calls, shareholders in AT&T could compare its costs with those of Sprint, MCI, and other competitors, and the competition provided each company with an incentive to be as efficient as possible. In the absence of the discipline provided by competition, resources are often not utilized efficiently. The discipline provided by competition limits the extent of managerial slack.

RESEARCH AND DEVELOPMENT

Competition motivates firms to develop new products and less expensive ways of producing goods. A monopoly, by contrast, may be willing to stand pat and let the profits roll in, without aggressively encouraging technological progress.

There are surely exceptions to this general observation, cases where monopolists have pushed hard for technological progress. Bell Labs, the research division of AT&T, was a fountain of important innovations throughout the period during which AT&T was a virtual monopolist in telephone service. The development of the laser and the transistor are but two of the innovations for which it is often given credit. On the other hand, AT&T was in a unique position. The prices it charged were set by government regulators, and those prices were set to encourage the expenditure of money on research. From this perspective, AT&T's research contribution was as much a consequence of government regulatory policy as of anything else.

Critics of the American automobile and steel industries argue that limited competition resulted in their falling behind foreign competitors. By the end of World War II, these industries had attained a dominant position in the world. After enjoying high profits for a number of years, they received quite a surprise when in the 1970s, upstarts such as Japan not only caught up but surpassed them technologically. Today Japan is able to sell these goods at lower prices not just because their labor is less well paid; they are actually more efficient in producing steel and automobiles. While the U.S. automobile industry made a strong comeback in the 1980s, the steel industry has simply continued its pattern of decline.

RENT SEEKING

Finally, monopolists may spend the extra profits they enjoy in economically unproductive ways. In particular, society loses when monopolies devote resources to obtaining or maintaining their monopoly position or deterring entry. Since the profits a monopolist receives are called monopoly rents, the attempt to acquire or maintain already existing rents by acquiring or maintaining a monopoly position in some industry is referred to as **rent seeking**.

Ordinarily, the profits earned by monopolies would serve to encourage competitors to enter the business. However, we saw in Chapter 15 how firms use entry-deterring devices to discourage such entry. These practices often harm consumers to some extent, since the benefits to the firm (high profits) are not necessarily beneficial to consumers.

Sometimes a firm's monopoly position is at least partly the result of government protection. Many less developed countries grant a company within their country a monopoly to produce a good, and they bar imports of that good from abroad. In these circumstances, firms will give money to lobbyists and politicians to maintain regulations that restrict competition so that they can keep their profits high. These lobbying and political activities are, for the most part, socially wasteful. Real resources (including labor time) are used to win favorable rules, not to produce goods and services. There is thus legitimate concern that the willingness of governments to restrict competition will encourage firms to spend money on rent-seeking activities rather than on making a better product.

How much would a firm be willing to spend to gain a monopoly position? The firm would be willing to spend up to the amount it would obtain as monopoly profits. The waste from this rent-seeking activity can be much larger than the loss from the reduced output.

POLICIES TOWARD NATURAL MONOPOLIES

If imperfect competition is as disadvantageous as the previous analysis has suggested, why does society not simply get rid of it? Why not simply require that competition be perfect? To answer these questions, we need to recall some of the reasons, discussed in Chapter 15, that competition is imperfect.

One of the reasons is government-granted patents: monopoly profits provide the return to inventors and innovators, a return that is necessary to stimulate activities vital to a capitalist economy. We will discuss these issues more extensively in Chapter 18.

A second reason is that the cost of production may be lower if there is a single firm in the industry; this is the case with natural monopoly. Natural monopolies offer a vexing problem for legislators and policymakers. Like any other monopolist, a natural monopolist will produce at the level where marginal revenue equals marginal cost, at Q_m in Figure 17.4. It will charge a price of p_m. It will produce less and charge more

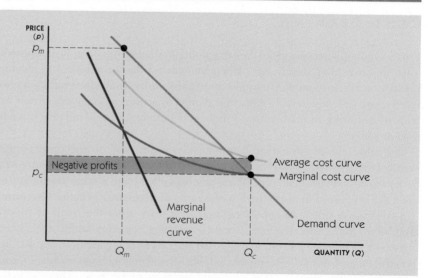

Figure 17.4 A PROBLEM WITH REGULATING NATURAL MONOPOLY

A natural monopoly will set marginal revenue equal to marginal cost, and produce at quantity Q_c and price p_m. In perfect competition, price would be equal to marginal cost, at Q_c and p_c. However, the perfectly competitive outcome is not possible in this case, since it would force the natural monopoly to produce at below its average cost, and thus to be making losses.

than it would if price were equal to marginal cost, as would be the case with perfect competition (the output level Q_c and the price p_c in the figure).

But in the case of natural monopoly, the very nature of the decreasing cost of technology precludes perfect competition. Indeed, consider what would happen if price were set equal to marginal cost. With a natural monopoly, average costs are declining, and marginal costs are below average costs. Hence, if price were equal to marginal cost, it would be less than average costs, and the firm would be losing money. Profits would be negative, as shown by the shaded area in the figure. If the government wanted a natural monopoly to produce at the point where marginal cost equaled price, it would have to subsidize the company to offset these losses. Taxes would have to be raised to generate the money for the subsidies, and raising taxes obviously imposes other economic costs. Moreover, the government would likely have a difficult time ascertaining the magnitude of the required subsidy, with the managers and workers in the firm claiming that they needed a greater subsidy to pay them the high wages they think they really deserve.

Following are three different solutions government has found to the problem of natural monopolies.

NATIONALIZATION

In many foreign countries, government has taken over ownership of an industry, or nationalized it. Britain and France nationalized their electric power companies, telephone companies, and other public utilities like gas and water companies. There are problems with this approach, however. Governments often are not particularly efficient as producers. The managers of nationalized industries often lack adequate incentives to cut costs and modernize vigorously, particularly given the fact that government is frequently willing to subsidize the industry when it loses money.

In addition, the nationalization of natural monopolies subjects them to a number of political pressures. For example, political pressure may affect where firms locate their plants—politicians like to see jobs created in their home districts—and whether they prune their labor force in attempts to increase efficiency. Firms may also be under pressure to provide some services at prices much below marginal cost, and make up the deficit from the revenues from other services, a practice referred to as **cross subsidization**. Thus, business customers of utilities are sometimes charged more, relative to the costs of serving them, than are households. There is in effect a hidden tax and a hidden subsidy; businesses are taxed to subsidize households. Though the United States has no major nationalized industries, the same phenomena can be seen in our most important public monopoly, the U.S. postal service. It charges the same price for delivering mail to small rural communities as it does to major cities, in spite of the large differences in costs; the small rural communities have their mail service subsidized by the large ones.

It is difficult to determine exactly how much less efficient the government is as a producer than the private sector. Comparisons of the efficiency of the nationalized telephone companies in Europe and America's private firms provided a large part of the motivation for the movement of privatization—of converting these government enterprises into private firms. Britain sold its telephone services and some other utilities, Japan its telephones and railroads, France its banks and many other enterprises. Not

CLOSE-UP: CONCENTRATION OVER TIME

About every five years, the U.S. government takes a voluminous Census of Manufacturing. Among the mounds of data collected by this census is information on how concentrated different industries have been over time. Information on the overall concentration in a handful of industries appears in the table, expressed in the form of the four-firm concentration ratio, which in this case was measured as the share of total shipments by the four largest firms in each industry.

The table shows widely varying levels of concentration between different industries. The producers of fluid milk and canned fruits and vegetables, for example, appear quite unconcentrated, while the manufacture of cereals has stayed concentrated. Overall, there does not seem to be a general pattern of increasing concentration in American industry, although some industries, like chewing gum, have become more concentrated in the past few decades.

Sometimes such numbers, taken at a national level, can be a bit misleading. Consider the three publishing industries listed in the table: newspapers, periodicals, and books. At first glance, it appears that all are unconcentrated. However, it is possible to subscribe to a given periodical or buy a particular book just about anywhere you live in the country. It is not possible to buy any newspaper

FOUR-FIRM CONCENTRATION RATIOS

Industry	1967	1977	1987
Canned fruits and vegetables	22	22	29
Cereal breakfast foods	88	89	87
Chewing gum	86	93	96
Fluid milk	22	18	21
Books	20	17	24
Newspapers	16	19	25
Periodicals	24	22	18
Environmental controls	56	59	50
Calculating and accounting equipment	83	59	50
Semiconductors and related devices	47	42	40
Surgical and medical instruments	38	32	30
Aircraft	69	59	72
Motor vehicles	92	93	90
Truck and bus bodies	21	33	29

Source: U.S. Department of Commerce, Bureau of the Census, *1987 Census of Manufactures: Concentration Ratios in Manufacturing* (February 1992).

you want. If the concentration ratios were measured on a city-by-city basis, the newspaper industry would certainly appear far more concentrated than the other two. Another interesting trend appears in the four high-technology industries listed. All have become less concentrated in the last couple of decades, which reflects the fact that many new companies and competitors have been springing up in industries like electronics and scientific instruments.

The fact that industrial concentration has not increased in many industries should not, of course, be taken to imply that antitrust laws have served no purpose or are no longer needed. It may be that without such laws holding firms back, concentration would have increased dramatically.

all nationalized enterprises are inefficient, however. For example, Canada has two major rail lines, one operated by the government and one private, with little difference in the efficiency with which they are run. This may be because the competition between the two forces the government railroad to be as efficient as the private. Many of the nationalized enterprises in France seem to run as efficiently as private firms. This may be because of the high prestige afforded to those who work in the French civil service, and their ability to recruit many of the most talented people in their country. There may be less difference between government enterprises and large corporations, particularly when both are subjected to some degree of market pressure and competition, than the popular conceptions of inefficient government would suggest.

REGULATION

Some countries, rather than nationalizing an industry, leave the industry in the private sector but regulate it; this has generally been the U.S. practice. Local utilities, for instance, remain private, but their rates are regulated by the states. At the national level, federal agencies regulate interstate telephone services and the prices that can be charged for the interstate transport of natural gas and oil.

In principle, regulators try to ensure that price is kept at the lowest possible level, commensurate with the monopolist's obtaining an adequate return on its investment. In other words, they try to keep price equal to average costs—where average costs include a "normal return" on the firm's capital, on what the firm's owners have invested in the firm. If the regulators are successful, the natural monopoly will earn no monopoly profits. Such a regulated output and price are shown in Figure 17.5 as Q_r and p_r.

Two criticisms have been leveled against the regulatory system. The first is that regulations often take an inefficient form. Prices are set so that firms obtain a "fair" return on their capital. To make the highest possible level of profit, firms respond by increasing their amount of capital as much as possible, which can lead to too much or too costly investment. In many cases, the structure of prices is set so that some groups, often businesses, may be charged extra-high prices to make it possible to subsidize other groups. The problem of cross subsidies is no less a problem for natural monopolies if they are privately owned and regulated than it is if they are owned and operated by the government.

Figure 17.5

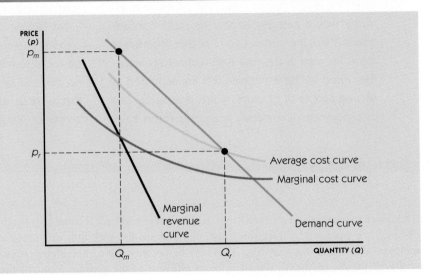

Figure 17.5 REGULATING NATURAL MONOPOLY

Government regulators will often seek to choose the point on the market demand curve where the firm provides the greatest quantity at the lowest price consistent with the firm's covering its costs. The point is the quantity Q_r and price p_r, where the demand curve intersects the average cost curve.

Firms' incentives to innovate are greatly attenuated if every time they succeed in lowering costs, the regulators quickly force them to lower their prices as well, giving all or even most of the benefits to consumers. This problem is exacerbated when regulators require the shareholders to absorb all the costs of unsuccessful attempts at cost reduction. For example, many regulators have forced utilities to absorb the costs of aborted nuclear power plants. When construction on the plants started, it was widely believed that they were the most efficient way of providing electricity. Increasing concerns about safety and strong local opposition led to skyrocketing costs and the abandonment of several of these plants. The question was, who should pay for what in retrospect appeared to be a major mistake? Some regulators, such as those in New Hampshire, took a hard line and insisted that the costs could not be passed on to consumers. As a result, the Public Service Company of New Hampshire went into bankruptcy.

More recently, regulators have recognized that unless they provide some reward for innovation, it will not be forthcoming. They have agreed to allow the utilities to retain much of the increased profits they obtain from improved efficiency, at least for a period of a few years.

The second criticism of regulation is that the regulators sometimes lose track of the public interest. The theory of regulatory capture, first mentioned in Chapter 16, argues that regulators frequently are pulled into the camps of those they regulate. This could happen through bribery and corruption, of course, but the much likelier way is just that over time, employees of a regulated industry, who have more of the information necessary to regulate the industry, develop personal friendships with the regulators, who in turn come to rely on their expertise and judgment. Even worse, regulatory agencies (of necessity) tend to do their hiring from among those in the regulated industry; by the same token, regulators who demonstrate an "understanding" of the industry may be rewarded with good jobs in that industry after they leave government service.

COMPETITION

The final way in which government deals with the hard choices posed by natural monopolies is to encourage competition, recognizing that while perfect competition will not arise in this situation, limited competition may bring some of the same benefits. Let us first review why it is that when average costs are declining over the relevant range of outputs, competition may not be viable.

If two firms divide the market between them, each faces higher average costs than it would if any one firm grabbed the whole market, as illustrated in Figure 17.6, where Q_d denotes the output of each firm in the initial duopoly and AC_d its average costs. By undercutting its rival, a firm would be able to capture the entire market *and* have its average costs reduced. The firm (which has now become a monopoly) gains on both counts. By the same token, a natural monopolist knows that it can charge a price slightly above its average cost, AC_m, without worrying about entry. Rivals that might enter, trying to capture some of the profits, know that the monopolist, because of its larger scale of production, has lower costs and so can always undercut them.

Some economists, such as William Baumol of New York and Princeton universities, have argued that even when there is a natural monopoly, potential competition—the threat of entry—will keep prices from rising above average costs. Potential competition will force the price to the same level that a regulator would. The figure shows this zero profit equilibrium: the intersection of the demand curve with the average cost curve, with output Q_1 and price $p_1 = AC_1$.

If the monopolist was charging the price p_m (or any price higher than AC_1), a *large*

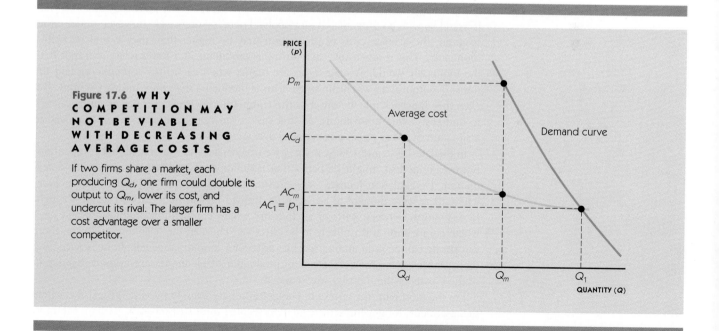

Figure 17.6 WHY COMPETITION MAY NOT BE VIABLE WITH DECREASING AVERAGE COSTS

If two firms share a market, each producing Q_d, one firm could double its output to Q_m, lower its cost, and undercut its rival. The larger firm has a cost advantage over a smaller competitor.

firm could enter, charge a slightly lower price, and grab the whole market; and as it did so, its average costs would be lower than the monopolist's. But this firm, in turn, would be subjected to competitive pressures; another large firm could enter, charging still less, and grab the entire market. The process would continue until price was driven down to AC_1. Thus, potential competition is all that is required, not actual competition. Competition to be the monopolist drives the monopolist's profits to zero. In this view, no government action is required.

Most economists are not so sanguine about the effectiveness of potential, as opposed to actual, competition. When there is a natural monopoly, an entrant would have to enter on a large scale to incur costs comparable with the existing firm's, and this is unlikely. Moreover, as we saw in Chapter 16, the entrant worries that should it enter, the existing firm will compete sufficiently keenly that what promised to be high profits will disappear. Entry is even less enticing when there are large sunk costs: if the existing firm does compete and the entrant decides to exit, the entrant will be unable to recoup much of its investment. Thus, potential competition may not serve as a very effective check on the exercise of monopoly power.

There are some situations where actual competition is not feasible. Because average costs may sharply increase when the market is divided between two firms, a firm with half the market may not be able to break even no matter what it does.

Where actual competition *is* feasible, it can provide a check on high monopoly prices. This is true where average costs are not declining too rapidly (at the relevant levels of output). When the average cost curve is relatively flat, the difference in average costs between one firm operating and two firms operating is relatively small. Average costs would be lower if only one firm operated, but not much.

This might be the case, for instance, for airline travel between two medium-sized cities. With only one airline, the price will be the monopoly price. Competition between two airlines will serve to reduce prices. If competition is fierce enough, prices might fall to the average cost. Even if competition is not that severe, price may be lower than it would be with an unregulated monopoly. There is a drawback, however: under either scenario, the average costs of production may be higher than they would be with a monopoly. This is a because each airline is producing at a lower level of output than the monopoly would. Average costs are higher when each firm is producing half the industry output than when the single firm is producing the entire industry output. But even this drawback may be offset as the competition between airlines encourages each to find cost-saving innovations. In that case, even imperfect competition may lead to a situation of lower prices and reduced average costs.

In the late 1970s and 1980s, many governments became convinced that competition, however imperfect, might be better than regulation. There began a process of deregulation. Deregulation focused on industries such as airlines, railroads, and trucking, where there were thought to be, at most, limited increasing returns to scale. It sought to distinguish between parts of an industry where competition might work and parts where competition was unlikely to be effective. Thus, in the telephone industry, there was strong competition among several carriers for long-distance telephone service, and there were few economies of scale in the production of telephones; accordingly, regulation of these parts of the industry was reduced.

For the most part, the virtues of competition have been borne out. Trucking—where the arguments for government regulation seemed most suspect—was perhaps the most unambiguous success story, with prices falling significantly. Today railroads appear more

CLOSE-UP: THE BREAK-UP OF AT&T

When the phone system was deregulated in January 1984, the general tone of discussion was a resigned and long-suffering cynicism: the federal government had in its unerring manner sought out one of the few things in life that worked—phone service—and decided to muck it up. Before deregulation, AT&T provided local and long-distance service to essentially everyone. After deregulation, a regional phone company (sometimes called a "Baby Bell") provided local phone service as a regulated monopoly, while the long-distance market was opened up to competition between AT&T, MCI, Sprint, and others. From the public reaction, you would have thought it was the end of modern communication. People complained about dialing a separate long-distance code before dialing a long-distance number. They complained about how confusing it was to receive two phone bills, one for local service and one for long-distance. They complained about how phone service declined.

Well, fair is fair. The results are now starting to come in on how phone deregulation has worked, and they are reasonably positive. It is time to give the deregulation decision a little credit.

In the five years following deregulation, the cost of leasing a phone fell by half. New phone services like call waiting, phone mail, three-way calling, automatic redialing, and call forwarding have become popular. Phone cards are nearly as common as credit cards. Fax machines are now in almost every office. Of course, many of these technological changes would have happened over time, with or without phone deregulation. But the increased competitive pressure helped speed them up.

The price story, however, is a little more ambiguous. The price of long-distance service fell as much as 40 percent in these five years. However, local phone bills increased substantially; not enough to absorb all of the 40 percent fall, but enough to absorb most of it. Much of this change had been predicted by economists. Before deregulation, AT&T used to charge long-distance callers more heavily in order to subsidize local phone service. With deregulation, both local and long-distance service are now closer to paying their own way. Overall phone service (combining local and long-distance) was slowly getting cheaper before deregulation; it has continued to gradually fall in price.

Clearly, phone deregulation has had its benefits. Just as clearly, the main benefits have gone to those who make the most use of the new phone services and who use long-distance heavily. The ordinary household has not been hurt, but has not benefited greatly, either.

financially sound than they did under regulation, but coal producers, who rely on railroads to ship their coal, complain that railroads have used their monopoly power to charge them much higher tariffs.

After its initial success—with new firms, lower fares, and more extensive routings—airline deregulation has become more controversial in recent years. A rash of bankruptcies has reduced the number of airlines. Many airports, including those at St. Louis, Atlanta, and Denver, are dominated by one or two carriers, and these communities often find themselves facing extremely high fares. Potential competition—the possibility of new entrants—has not sufficed to keep fares low. The fares between Los Angeles and San Francisco gyrate from $50 round trip to $300 round trip with the entry and exit of airlines and as price wars break out and are won and lost. A pattern of discriminatory pricing has developed, with businessmen who cannot make reservations weeks in advance paying four or more times the fare for the same seat as a vacationer. While airline deregulation is not the unmitigated success that it appeared to be a decade ago, the problems of reregulating appear so severe that, at this juncture, there are few serious proposals to do so.

Deregulation has not yet extended to natural monopolies like electricity and water, but there are suggestions for extending its reach further. The electricity industry could be divided into electric power generation and the transmission of electricity. Some competition may be viable in electric power generation, necessitating less government regulation.

APPROACHES TO NATURAL MONOPOLY

Nationalization
Regulation
Competition

ANTITRUST POLICIES

While some of the failures of competition in our economy arise from natural monopolies, other imperfections are the result of sharp business practices. Firms that are not natural monopolies may develop market power by strategies designed to deter the entry of competitors and to promote collusive behavior among the firms in the industry. Just as with natural monopolies, this restricted competition results in higher prices and lower output than would prevail under competition. It is for this reason that most economists have argued for government policies to promote competition. As we will see, these policies have been controversial. Consumer groups and injured businesses tend to support them, arguing that otherwise firms would focus more on competition-reducing strategies than on producing products that customers like in a less expensive way. It is easier to garner profits by reducing competition than by producing a better product.

Many businesses, however, claim that government policies designed to promote competition interfere with economic efficiency. For instance, even if a firm believed that the most efficient way to distribute its products was to guarantee exclusive territories for its distributors, the firm might worry that such a contract might be illegal. Antitrust policy, as government efforts to enhance competition are known, has ebbed and flowed between the view that focuses on the benefits from increased competition and the view that emphasizes the potential costs of antitrust policies.

OUTLAWING MARKET DOMINATION

The U.S. government has been officially concerned about the negative consequences of imperfect competition since the late nineteenth century. It has tried to encourage competition in two ways. First, it has tried to ensure that no firm, or combination of firms, has too much economic power. Second, it has tried to curb restrictive practices. In this section, we look at how government uses the first method.

In the decades following the Civil War, entrepreneurs in several industries attempted to form **trusts**, which were organizations that controlled a market: one individual had a controlling interest in a firm, which in turn had a controlling interest in all of the other firms in the industry. By adding more layers—firms that controlled firms that controlled firms, and so on—a relatively small ownership stake could be leveraged into very large economic power.

A controlling interest need not be a majority interest when the shares of a company are widely held; an individual or group of individuals owning only 10 or 20 percent of the shares can frequently exercise control, since the rest of the shareholders will either split their votes or be apathetic about the outcome. Among the most famous of the nineteenth-century trusts was the oil industry trust, with Rockefeller and his partners eventually controlling 90 percent of oil sold in America between 1870 and 1899. In the early 1900s, Andrew Carnegie and J. P. Morgan put together many smaller steel companies to form U.S. Steel, which in its heyday sold 65 percent of American steel.

Concern about these robber barons led to the passage of the Sherman Antitrust Act of 1890, which outlaws "every contract, combination in the form of a trust or otherwise, or conspiracy in restraint of trade or commerce." Further, "every person who shall monopolize, or attempt to monopolize, or combine or conspire with any other person or persons, to monopolize any part of the trade or commerce among the several States, or with foreign nations, shall be deemed guilty of a misdemeanor." (As a result of a 1974 amendment, violations are now treated as felonies.)

The Sherman Act was supplemented by the Clayton Act in 1914, which forbade any firm to acquire shares of a competing firm when that purchase would substantially reduce competition. The act also outlawed interlocking directorates (in which the same individuals serve as directors of several firms) among competing firms, on the presumption that they would naturally lead to reduced competition. These antimerger provisions were further strengthened in 1950 by the Celler-Kefauver Antimerger Act. Collectively, the laws designed to restrict anticompetitive practices are called antitrust laws, though today their reach is far broader than in the nineteenth century, when trust fighting was their original objective. The Sherman Antitrust Act was successful in breaking up two of the most famous trusts, Standard Oil and American Tobacco.

The government does not care about absolute size itself. In the 1960s, huge firms called conglomerates were formed, which brought together such disparate enterprises as a steel company, an oil company, and a company making films. For example, United Airlines bought Hertz rental cars and Westin Hotels. But while large, these conglomerates might not have had a dominant position in any one market, and thus the antitrust laws were not concerned with them. The early antitrust laws were particularly concerned with **horizontal mergers**, with competition within a market. These are distinguished from **vertical mergers**, in which a firm buys a supplier or a distributor, amalgamating the various stages in the production process within a firm. Thus, Ford made its own steel, and General Motors bought out Fisher Body (the maker of GM's car bodies), as well as many of the specialized firms that produced batteries, spark plugs, and other components.

DEFINING MARKETS

In practice, the question of whether a firm is too big is usually phrased, "What is its size relative to the market?" and thus the debate centers on the question of what is the relevant market. The concept of a market is one of the most fundamental in economics. We talk about the market for steel or the market for aluminum. But when the government sets out to enforce a policy of competition within a certain market, it must have a concrete way of defining that market. We have learned that the extent to which a firm's demand curve is downward sloping, so it can raise prices without losing all of its customers—that is, a firm's market power—is related to the number of firms in the industry and the extent of product differentiation. The problem of defining markets is related to both of these factors.

Geographical Bounds   During the last quarter century, international trade has become ever more important to the United States and the world economy. This change has affected all aspects of economic analysis, including the extent of competition in many markets. Today, imports exceed 9 percent of national output—three times the level in the 1950s and 1960s.

Thus, while the degree of concentration among domestic producers of automobiles has increased—three firms are responsible for more than 90 percent of all U.S. auto production—the industry has become more competitive in the 1980s and 1990s, as foreign competition has become much more effective and as foreign companies such as Toyota and Honda have established plants in the United States. It used to be that American firms could increase their price without worrying about their consumers switching to Japanese or European imports, but no longer. Today, the degree of competition in a market must be assessed from a global viewpoint, rather than looking simply at how many firms produce a good in the United States.

Product Differentiation   While all firms that produce the same good and sell in the same location are clearly in the same market, when the goods produced by different firms are close but imperfect substitutes, there may be problems of defining the boundaries of the market. Though we naturally speak of the "market for beer," those in the industry might claim that premium beers and discount beers are really two different markets, with relatively few customers crossing over from one to the other. In the early 1950s, Du Pont's cellophane had a virtual monopoly on the market for clear wrapping paper. In 1956, the company managed to fight off charges of monopoly by claiming that this market was part of a larger one for "wrapping materials"; it claimed that brown paper was a good, though not perfect, substitute for cellophane, and in this broader market, Du Pont did not have a particularly large share (roughly 18 percent).

Legal Criteria   Today the courts tend to look at two criteria for defining a market and market power. First, they consider the extent to which the change in prices for one product affects the demand for another. If an increase in the price of aluminum has a large positive effect on the demand for steel, then steel and aluminum may be considered to be in the same market, the market for metals. Second, if a firm can raise its price, say by 10 percent, and lose only a relatively small fraction of its sales, then it is "large"— that is, it has market power. (In a perfectly competitive market, a firm that raised its price by 10 percent would lose all of its customers, so this is a natural approach to measuring the degree of competitiveness in the market.)

Before one large company can acquire a competitor or merge with another, it must convince the government that the acquisition would not seriously interfere with competition. Thus, although Dr. Pepper made up only a small part of the soft drink market, the government was concerned that the acquisition of Dr. Pepper by Coca-Cola would have a significantly adverse affect on competition in a market that was already highly concentrated.

What happens if a firm comes to dominate a market, not by acquiring other firms, but simply by being more efficient and undercutting rivals? Usually matters are not clear-cut; firms grow both by being efficient and by engaging in sharp business practices. In the 1970s, the government attempted to break up IBM on the grounds that simply by virtue of its size, it dominated the market. While the government claimed that IBM achieved its success partly by practices that deterred the entry of rivals, it could not deny the pioneering role the company had played in introducing new technologies and the fact that much of its position came from being a more efficient and innovative firm. The suit lasted more than a decade, during which time IBM's dominant position was succesfully challenged by a number of new entrants. The government finally gave up, after millions of dollars were spent on the litigation.

Today the focus of antitrust policy is not so much on breaking up dominant firms as it is on preventing firms from acquiring market power, either through mergers or through anticompetitive practices. For example, it is illegal to engage in predatory pricing. When TWA, British Air, and other international carriers responded to Laker Airways' low transatlantic fares by deeply cutting their own prices, they were successfully sued for violating the antitrust laws.

CURBING RESTRICTIVE PRACTICES

We have seen that one method the government uses to promote competition is to try to limit the extent of concentration within an industry—for instance, restricting mergers when they would result in increased concentration in already concentrated industries.

Coca-Cola Company and PepsiCo, Inc., dominate the market for carbonated soft drinks. Early in 1986, they each proposed to grow larger through acquisition. In January, PepsiCo proposed buying 7-Up, the fourth largest soft drink manufacturer, for $380 million. In February, Coca-Cola proposed buying Dr. Pepper, the third largest, for $470 million.

The mergers would have made the big even bigger. Coca-Cola and PepsiCo already held 39 percent and 28 percent of the market, respectively, while Dr. Pepper had 7 percent and 7-Up had 6 percent. The next largest firm in the market after 7-Up was R.J. Reynolds, which made Canada Dry and Sunkist and held 5 percent of the market.

After a few months of skirmishing, the Federal Trade Commission announced that it would oppose the mergers. The rule the government often uses in such cases is called the Herfindahl-Hirschman Index (HHI). The index is calculated by summing the squares of the market shares. If the industry consists of a single firm, then the HHI is $(100)^2 = 10,000$. If the industry consists of 1,000 firms, each with .1 percent of the market, then the HHI is $(.1)^2 \times 1,000 = 10$. Thus, higher values of the HHI indicate less competitive industries.

Merger guidelines adopted by the federal government in 1982 divided markets into three categories, with the following policies.

Level of HHI	Type of industry	Policy recommendation
Less than 1,000	Unconcentrated	Mergers allowed without government challenge
Between 1,000 and 1,800	Moderately concentrated	Mergers challenged if they raise the industry HHI by more than 100 points
Above 1,800	Concentrated	Mergers challenged if they raise the industry HHI by more than 50 points

Before the mergers, the HHI for the soft drink industry would appear as follows. For ease of calculation, we assume that the 15 percent of the market not covered by the top five firms consists of fifteen small companies, each with 1 percent of the market:

$$HHI = 39^2 + 28^2 + 7^2 + 6^2 + 5^2 + 15\,(1)^2$$
$$= 2,410.$$

If we plug in the 34 percent share PepsiCo would have after acquiring 7-Up, the PepsiCo–7-Up merger alone would raise the HHI to 2,766. The two proposed mergers together would raise the HHI to 3,312.

With numbers like these, the announced FTC opposition to the merger should have come as no surprise. In fact, PepsiCo immediately gave up on purchasing 7-Up. Coca-Cola pushed ahead with its plan to buy Dr. Pepper, though, until a federal judge ruled in August 1986 that it was a "stark, unvarnished" attempt to eliminate competition that "totally [lacked] any apparent redeeming feature."

The court case did bring a secret to the surface, however. The trial disclosed certain Coca-Cola company memos written in February, after PepsiCo's offer for 7-Up had been made. In the memos, Coca-Cola executives expressed fear that the FTC might allow the PepsiCo merger, despite the merger guidelines. By announcing plans to buy Dr. Pepper, Coca-Cola hoped that the FTC would step in and block *both* mergers, thus preventing PepsiCo from using a merger to catch up in size to Coke.

Sources: Timothy K. Smith and Scott Kilman, "Coke to Acquire Dr. Pepper Co. for $470 Million," *Wall Street Journal,* February 21, 1986, p. 2; Andy Pasztor and Timothy K. Smith, "FTC Opposes Purchase Plans by Coke, Pepsi," *Wall Street Journal,* June 23, 1986, p. 2; Pasztor and Smith,

"Coke Launched Dr. Pepper Bid to Scuttle Plans by PepsiCo, Documents Indicate," *ibid.,* July 29, 1986, p. 3; Pasztor and Smith, "Coke's Plan to Buy Dr. Pepper Is Blocked by U.S. Judge, Pending Decision by FTC," *ibid.,* August 1, 1986, p. 3.

The second method the government uses to promote competition is to limit restrictive practices. The history here begins with the 1914 Federal Trade Commission Act. The first ten words of the act read: "Unfair methods of competition in commerce are hereby declared unlawful." President Wilson defined the purpose of the new commission a little more poetically, by saying it existed to "plead the voiceless consumer's case." Since then, a number of laws have been passed by Congress to make these general statements more specific.

Many of the restrictive practices targeted by the government involve the relations between a firm and its distributors and suppliers. Such practices include tying, exclusive dealing, and price discrimination. We have already encountered all three. Tying requires a buyer to purchase additional items when she buys a product. A producer engaged in exclusive dealing says to a firm that wants to sell its product, "If you want to sell my product, you cannot sell that of my rival." Price discrimination entails charging different customers different prices, when those price differences are not related to the costs of serving those customers. The Robinson-Patman Act of 1936 strengthened the provisions outlawing price discrimination, making it easier to convict firms engaged in the practice. Other practices discussed in Chapters 15 and 16, designed to deter entry or promote collusion, are illegal as well.

The precise definition of what is an illegal restrictive practice has changed over time with varying court interpretations of the antitrust laws. Some practices are *per se* illegal (from the Latin, meaning "by itself")—firms getting together to conspire to fix prices, for example. In 1961, General Electric, Westinghouse, and other producers of electrical equipment were found guilty of this practice. They paid millions of dollars in fines, and some of their officials went to prison. Today, however, for most practices a "rule of reason" prevails. Under a rule of reason, the practice is acceptable if it can be shown to be reasonable business practice, designed to promote economic efficiency. The efficiency gains are balanced against the higher prices resulting from the reduced competition.

Thus, Budweiser beer delivers its product through distributors; in any area, there is only one distributor, and the distributors are not allowed to compete against one another. The New York attorney general has argued that this system, by restricting competition, raises prices. Anheuser Busch has replied that the system of exclusive territories enhances the efficiency with which beer is delivered and is necessary to ensure that customers receive fresh beer. They have maintained that their distribution system satisfies the rule of reason, and thus far their view has been upheld by the courts.

ENFORCING THE ANTITRUST LAWS

Today there are antitrust laws at both the state and federal levels, enforced by both criminal and civil courts. The government takes action not only to break up existing monopolies but also to prevent firms from obtaining excessive market power.

The Federal Trade Commission and the Antitrust Division of the Department of Justice are at the center of the government's efforts to promote competition. The FTC works like a law enforcement agency, investigating complaints it receives. It can provide advisory opinions on how an individual business should interpret the law, provide guidelines for entire industries, or even issue specific rules and regulations that businesses must follow. When necessary, the FTC enforces these decisions in court.

Both Presidents Reagan and Bush have been generally viewed to be pro–big business, but antitrust matters are sufficiently complex that they cannot always be easily categorized. Reagan, for instance, appointed Stanford Law School professor William Baxter to be in charge of the antitrust division of the Department of Justice. Baxter took seriously the provisions of the antitrust laws making conspiracies in restraint of trade a crime, and a large number of businessmen were charged, convicted, and sent to jail for violation of the antitrust laws. While Baxter dropped the antitrust case against IBM, he successfully prosecuted the case against AT&T.

One interesting and controversial aspect of the antitrust laws is the use they make of *private* law enforcement. Any firm that believes it has been injured by the anticompetitive practices of another firm can sue, and if successful, it can receive three times the dollar value of the damages and attorney fees. The treble damage provision helps to encourage private firms to call violations to the attention of the government. For example, MCI sued AT&T, claiming that the latter had used unfair trade practices to hurt MCI in its attempt to enter the long-distance telephone business. The jury estimated that MCI had, as a result of AT&T's activities, lost $600 million in profits, and accordingly ordered AT&T to pay triple that amount—$1.8 billion—in damages to MCI, although the award was subsequently reduced on appeal to higher courts.

There are two arguments in favor of the private enforcement of antitrust laws. First, those who are injured by anticompetitive practices are in the best position to detect a violation of the law. Second, there is a concern that government may be lax in the enforcement of these laws, because of the potential political influence of cartels and dominant firms.

At the same time, however, there is concern about the rising costs of antitrust litigation—the number of private suits doubled between the 1960s and the 1970s. There is also concern that some businesses use the threat of an antitrust suit as a weapon, as a way of raising a rival's costs. Thus, Chrysler charged General Motors with an antitrust violation when GM proposed a joint venture with a Japanese firm, only to drop the action when it subsequently found a Japanese partner for its own joint venture. Also, there is the possibility that whenever a firm is successful in winning customers from a rival, the rival will accuse the firm of unfair practices and bring suit. Firms that lower prices may worry that they will be accused of predatory pricing.

CURRENT ANTITRUST CONTROVERSIES

Exactly how and when antitrust laws should be enforced remains one of the most controversial subjects of economic policy. In recent years, the controversy has focused around two major issues. First, how stringent should the standards be for allowing mergers of competing firms? In 1982, the government adopted new guidelines for such mergers, which many critics thought to be too lax.

Those who favored the more lax rules argued that in today's international markets, competition is almost always sufficiently keen to ensure low prices and economic efficiency. Any firm that tried to exercise monopoly power by charging too high a price or that was slack in keeping costs down would be faced with an onslaught of competition. At most, the firm could enjoy a monopoly position for only a short time. Canon, followed by a host of other firms, unseated Xerox's monopoly position in copiers, and Fuji is now challenging Kodak's dominant position in film. Moreover, these advocates argue, attempts to restrict size penalize the more successful firms and inhibit their ability to take advantage of economies of scale and scope. Since foreign governments do not put similar restrictions on their own firms, American companies find themselves at a disadvantage. Size is particularly important for financing large-scale research endeavors, necessary if America is to keep its competitive edge.

Critics of this view contend that international competition is often not that keen and cannot be relied upon—though admittedly, markets are more competitive with than without international competition. Furthermore, they question the importance of the economies of scale and scope; many of America's leading exporters are relatively small companies, such as Compaq Computer. And the enhanced competition among firms in the United States not only makes consumers better off, through lower prices, but also sharpens the edge of businesses, making the more successful firms better able to compete not only at home but also abroad.

The second major controversial issue concerns disagreements about government policies toward restrictive practices, in particular the contractual arrangements between firms and their suppliers and customers, such as exclusive dealing, tying, and exclusive territories. Those who, like Richard Posner, formerly of the University of Chicago (now a federal judge), believe that by and large competition is effective think there should be a presumption that such practices are legal. Others, like Steven Salop of Georgetown Law School, believe that quite frequently, while there is competition, it is limited. A review of the alleged "efficiency" gains of such practices suggests to them that more often firms' objective is to restrict competition further. If a change is needed from the current rule of reason, they argue, it is to make the presumption that these practices are restrictive; the burden would be on any firm engaging in restrictive practices to show that the efficiency gains outweigh the losses from reduced competition.

REVIEW AND PRACTICE

SUMMARY

1. Economists have identified four major problems resulting from monopolies and imperfect competition: restricted output and excessive profits; managerial slack; a lack of incentives for technological progress; and a tendency toward wasteful rent-seeking expenditures.

2. Since for a natural monopoly average costs are declining over the range of market demand, a large firm can undercut its rivals; and since marginal cost for a natural monopoly lies below average cost, an attempt by regulators to require it to set price equal to marginal cost (as in the case of perfect competition) will force the firm to make losses.

3. Nationalizing a natural monopoly allows the government to set price and quantity directly, but it also subjects an industry to political pressures and the government may not be efficient.

4. In the United States, natural monopolies are regulated; government regulators seek to keep prices as low and quantity as high as is consistent with the natural monopolist covering its costs. However, regulators must also face problems of cross subsidies and the possibility of being "captured" by the industry they are regulating.

5. In some cases, competition may be as effective as nationalization or government regulation at keeping prices low.

6. Antitrust policy is concerned with promoting competition, both by prohibiting any firm from dominating a market and by restricting practices that interfere with competition.

7. Under the "rule of reason," companies may seek to defend themselves from accusations of anticompetitive behavior by claiming that the behavior also leads to greater efficiency. In such cases, courts must often decide whether the potential efficiency of restrictive practices outweighs their potential anticompetitive effects.

KEY TERMS

managerial slack	cross subsidization	vertical mergers
rent seeking	horizontal mergers	

REVIEW QUESTIONS

1. What does it mean when an economist says that monopoly output is "too little" or a monopoly price is "too high"? By what standard? Compared with what?

2. Why might a monopoly lack incentives to hold costs as low as possible?

3. Why might a monopoly lack incentives to pursue research and development opportunities aggressively?

4. What might an economist regard as a socially wasteful way of spending monopoly profits?

5. Explain why the marginal cost curve of a natural monopoly lies below its average cost curve. What are the consequences of this?

6. If government regulators of a natural monopoly set price equal to marginal cost, what problem will inevitably arise? How might nationalization or regulation address this problem?

7. What is the regulatory capture hypothesis?

8. Explain the difference between a horizontal and a vertical merger.

PROBLEMS

1. Before deregulation of the telephone industry in 1984, AT&T provided both local and long-distance telephone service. A number of firms argued that they could provide long-distance service between major cities more cheaply than AT&T, but AT&T argued against allowing firms to enter only the long-distance market. If those other firms could actually have offered long-distance service more cheaply, what does that imply about cross subsidies in AT&T's pricing of local and long-distance service? What would have happened if AT&T had been required to continue offering local service at the same price, but competition had been allowed in the long-distance market?

2. "The stories of $400 hammers and $1,000 toilet seats purchased by the Department of Defense prove that the private sector is more efficient than the public sector." Comment.

3. Explain the incentive problem involved if regulators assure that a natural monopoly will be able to cover its average costs.

4. Explain how some competition, even if not perfect, may be an improvement for consumers over an unregulated natural monopoly. Explain why such competition will not be as good for consumers as an extremely sophisticated regulator, and why it may be better than many real-world regulators.

5. Should greater efficiency be a defense against an accusation of an antitrust violation?

18

TECHNOLOGICAL CHANGE

T hroughout most of the twentieth century, the United States has led the way in the discovery and applications of new technologies. Alexander Graham Bell and the telephone, the Wright brothers and their airplane, and Thomas Edison and a host of electric devices are all familiar success stories. In some industries, Americans were not responsible for the original invention but did develop the mass production technology—this was the case in the automobile industry. This tradition of innovation and invention continued into the 1950s, as American inventors came up with products like the transistor and the laser. Well-known U.S. companies such as IBM, Eastman Kodak, and Xerox grew large mostly because of the new products they brought to the market.

In his 1942 book *Capitalism, Socialism, and Democracy*, Harvard economist Joseph Schumpeter described capitalism as a process of "creative destruction." The incentives built in to market-based economies, in Schumpeter's view, were the best solution available to the problem of creating new products and new technologies. However, these new technologies may destroy old jobs, old companies, even whole industries. The invention of the automobile, for example, destroyed the horse carriage industry and put blacksmiths out of business. Those who are injured by change will inevitably protest; after all, why should they suffer because someone else came up with a good idea? Often these arguments become the subject of bills before Congress or negotiation between a company and a union. The railroad unions succeeded in forcing the railroads to keep workers aboard trains to stoke the fires for years after steam engines had given way to diesel, and stokers were no longer needed.

Change is always painful and costly, but avoiding change and technological advance would be costly too. The average American citizen today lives longer, is better educated, travels more, and has an overall higher standard of living than did her parents or grandparents. These advances are mainly a result of technological progress. For society as a whole, the creativity of a market economy has a large positive impact that far outweighs the negative impact on those who are harmed.

That is why it has become a matter of concern that, despite the emergence of young technology-based companies such as Apple and Genentech, America's technological lead seems to be shrinking. Competitors like Japan and Germany seem to be catching up both in making discoveries and in applying them to new consumer products. Japanese firms make some of the most advanced computer chips, and one of the most important breakthroughs in superconductivity occurred in a Swiss laboratory. This chapter examines the choices made by individuals and firms that lead to new discoveries, and the government policies that affect those choices. It also examines the interrelationship between competition and technological change.

Studying these questions takes us beyond the basic competitive model that was the focus of Part Two. There are several reasons for this, beyond the obvious one that in Part Two we simply assumed the state of technology was given, and here our concern is with what makes it change. First, for reasons that will become clear, industries in which technological change is important are almost necessarily imperfectly competitive.

Second, in the basic competitive model of Part Two, we assumed that individuals and firms receive all the benefits and pay all the costs of their actions, but this assumption does not take externalities into account. There is little doubt that we have all benefited from the multitude of inventions that have occurred in the last century. Just imagine what life would be like without the radio, television, cars, airplanes, washing machines, dishwashers—the list is endless. Alexander Graham Bell, Henry Ford, the Wright brothers, were all rewarded for their inventions and innovations, some richly so. But innovations generate externalities—others besides the innovator and the innovating firm benefit. The creation of these new products confers benefits beyond what consumers have to pay for them.

Given the importance of the externalities yielded by technological innovation, it is no surprise that government, which played little role in the basic competitive model, is instrumental in promoting technological progress. At the same time, antitrust policies attempt to limit the harm done by any imperfections in competition resulting from technological innovation. But there is increasing concern that the more stringent antitrust laws faced by American firms, compared with those in Japan and Western Europe, may put American firms at a technological disadvantage.

"I didn't actually build *it, but it was based on my idea."*

KEY QUESTIONS

1. In what ways is the production of knowledge—including the knowledge of how to make new products and how to produce things more cheaply—different from the production of ordinary goods, like shoes and wheat?

2. Why is the patent system important in providing incentives to engage in research and development?

3. How may patents, as essential as they are for encouraging competition in research, at the same time reduce some aspects of competition?

4. How can government encourage technological progress?

LINKS BETWEEN TECHNOLOGICAL CHANGE AND IMPERFECT COMPETITION

In modern industrialized economies, much competition takes the form of trying to develop both new products and new ways of making old products. Firms devote a considerable amount of their resources to research (discovering new ideas, products, and processes) and development (perfecting, for instance, a new product to the point where it is brought to the market), or R & D for short. Industries in which technological change (and therefore R & D) is important, such as computers and drugs, are often very competitive in the sense that there is a great deal of rivalry, each firm trying to make new discoveries and bring new products to the market before its competitors do. But industries like these are not well described by the model of perfectly competitive markets, which is based on the assumption of many firms producing essentially identical products. Quite the contrary: high R & D expenditures are the result of an effort to gain the advantages of market power. The way for a company to earn a profit is to produce a good that is better than its rivals' goods, at least in the eyes of some consumers, so it can raise its price without losing all of its customers; or to develop a cheaper way of manufacturing, so the company can lower its price below the costs of competitors, thus driving them out of the market. By either method, a firm acquires market power.

Thus, the striving for at least temporary market power is one of the principal motivations for expenditures on research and development. And it is only because R & D is successful in giving the inventor or innovator some temporary market power that it can occur at all. The profits obtained are both the source of funds for future R & D and the reward for past R & D efforts.

Let us now take a closer look at the relationship between technological change and imperfect competition.

PATENTS

What drives firms to innovate is the desire to get ahead of their rivals. But if rival firms could quickly imitate the innovating firm, the latter would not be able to sustain its competitive advantage. Its incentives to take the risks of innovating would be greatly reduced. If the company were successful in developing a new product, for example, its profits would be quickly eliminated as others made their own version of the same product; if the firm were unsuccessful, it would simply bear the losses itself. That is a no-win situation.

The writers of the U.S. Constitution must have understood this. Section 8 of Article 1 grants Congress the power "to promote the progress of science and useful arts, by securing for limited times to authors and inventors the exclusive right to their respective writing and discoveries." The writers recognized that if inventors are to have an incentive to innovate, they must be able to reap or, as economists say, *appropriate* for themselves some of the fruits of their activities.

The holder of a patent has the exclusive right to produce and sell his invention or innovation for seventeen years. During this same time period, other producers are precluded from producing the same good, or even making use of the invention in a product of their own, without the permission of the patent holder. Patent holders will often sell to others the right to use the product in exchange for a payment called a royalty. As we will see later, not all inventions and innovations are patentable. New products and processes typically are, but many of the fruits of development expenditures, including small improvements in existing methods of production that cumulatively account for much of the technological progress in our society, are not.

In spite of the general advantages of competition in promoting economic efficiency, the government limits the extent of competition by providing patents, because without patents, firms would have insufficient incentives to carry on research. To understand this point, think of expenditures on research and development as an investment. The incentives of firms to make this kind of investment depend on their ability to realize a return from the investment. In a world with no patent protection, firms would have little incentive to fund R & D. They would simply copy any new inventions, thus enjoying the fruits of others' research while suffering none of the development costs. Inventors in this situation would not gain market power and thus would have little reason to work at making new discoveries.

The patent system grants the inventor a temporary monopoly, allowing her to appropriate some part of the returns on her inventive activity. Patents are limited to seventeen years, however, as a way of compromising between the objectives of providing an incentive for inventors to engage in research and allowing for an eventual transition to competitive markets. The longer the life of the patent, the greater the return to innovation, but the longer-lived the social costs of the temporary monopoly—reduced output and higher prices.

Chapter 14 explained why competitive markets, with price equal to marginal cost, ensure economic efficiency. But it also assumed that the technology was given. We refer to the kind of economic efficiency discussed in that chapter, which ignores concerns about invention and innovation, as short-run efficiency. Thus, when a patent expires, the patent-holding firm's monopoly power evaporates, and price falls to marginal cost, we say that there is an improvement in the short-run efficiency of the economy.

But the overall efficiency of the economy requires balancing these short-run concerns with the longer-run objectives of stimulating research and innovation. An economy in which this balancing is appropriately done is said to be dynamically efficient.

AN EXAMPLE: THE SWEET MELON COMPANY

Figure 18.1 illustrates the effect of a patent owned by the Sweet Melon Company for a new, cheaper process for producing frozen watermelon juice. For the sake of simplicity, the marginal cost of production is taken to be constant in this example. Before the

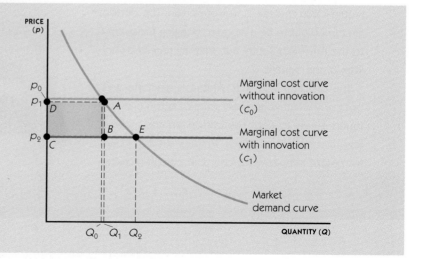

Figure 18.1 ECONOMIC EFFECT OF PATENTS

Here, an innovation has reduced the marginal cost of production from c_0 to c_1. Before the innovation, the equilibrium price is p_0, which equals c_0. However, an innovator with a patent will drop the price to p_1, just below p_0, and sell the quantity Q_1. Total profits are the shaded area $ABCD$. When the patent expires, competitors reenter the market, price falls to p_2, which equals c_1, and profits drop to zero.

CLOSE-UP: ELI WHITNEY AND THE COTTON GIN

Obtaining a patent does not necessarily guarantee that the inventor will receive a return on her discovery. Others may "infringe" on her patent—that is, use the idea without paying her for it—in which case the inventor will have to engage in costly litigation. Suits for patent infringement are common, even among supposedly respectable companies: in recent years, Apple Computer sued Microsoft and Polaroid sued Kodak, to name but two such cases. One of the most famous examples of an inventor who found it difficult to enforce his patents is that of Eli Whitney and the cotton gin.

Late in the eighteenth century, the textile mills of England and the northern American states were up and humming, but there seemed to be a perpetual shortage of cotton. The kind of cotton grown in the southern United States could have filled the need, but first someone had to find an inexpensive way to separate the seeds out of the cotton. Eli Whitney invented the cotton gin to perform that task. Whitney did what an inventor is supposed to do. He applied for a patent and received one in 1794. He found a partner to put up the money, and then started a business to make machines that would clean the seeds out of cotton. The cotton gin turned out to be a wonder, bringing prosperity to the American South. But Whitney received very little of the benefit.

The problem was that Whitney's machine was both very effective and very simple. Cotton planters found it easy to copy the cotton gin and make a few minor changes. When Whitney sued in court for patent infringement, courts in cotton-growing states tended to find that his patent had not actually been infringed. Eventually, the states of South Carolina, North Carolina, Tennessee, and Georgia agreed to pay a lump sum to Whitney to purchase the rights to his invention. The amount paid, though, was barely enough to allow Whitney and his partner to recoup their expenses.

Whitney continued his lifelong career as an inventor, but he never bothered to patent any of his other inventions. He once wrote that "an invention can be so valuable as to be worthless to the inventor." Whitney's experience was extreme. Today patent laws provide essential protection for scientific firms engaged in producing new and better products. For some firms, such as Texas Instruments, royalties represent a substantial fraction of their revenues.

Whitney's cotton gin, 1793.

innovation, all the producers face the same marginal cost of c_0. Sweet Melon's innovation reduces the marginal costs of production to c_1. Imagine that this industry is perfectly competitive before the innovation, so that price is equal to marginal cost, c_0. But now Sweet Melon is able to undercut its rivals. With patent protection, the firm sells the good for slightly less than p_0; its rivals drop out of the market because at the new, lower price, they cannot break even. Sweet Melon now has the whole market. The company sells the quantity Q_1 at the price p_1, making a profit of AB on each sale. Total profits are the shaded area $ABCD$ in the figure. The innovation pays off if the profits received exceed the cost of the research.

What happens when the patent expires? Other firms enter the industry, using the less expensive technology. Competition forces the price down to the now lower marginal costs, c_1, and output expands to Q_2. The new equilibrium is at E. Consumers are clearly better off. Short-run economic efficiency is enhanced, because price is now equal to marginal cost. But Sweet Melon reaps no further return from its expenditures on research and development.

If no patent were available, competitors would immediately copy the new juice-making process, and the price would drop to c_1 when the innovation became available. Sweet Melon would receive absolutely no returns. (In practice, of course, imitation takes time, during which the company would be able to obtain *some* returns from the innovation.) On the other hand, if the patent were made permanent, consumers would benefit only a small amount from the innovation, since other companies could not compete and therefore output would remain at Q_1, just slightly greater than the original output, and the price would remain high.

Figure 18.2 illustrates the trade-off involved in choosing how many years a patent should be in effect. With long-lived patents, incentives to innovate (measured along the horizontal axis) are high, but short-run efficiency (measured along the vertical axis) is low, because of the monopoly power derived from the patent. With short-lived patents, incentives to innovate are low, but short-run efficiency is high.

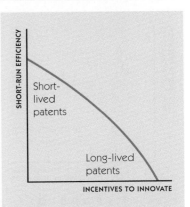

Figure 18.2 TRADE-OFF BETWEEN LONG AND SHORT PATENT LIFE

As the length of the patent increases, incentives to innovate are increased. However, the economy suffers from a longer period during which the firm exercises some degree of monopoly power; this interferes with the short-run efficiency of the economy.

THE BREADTH OF PATENT PROTECTION

The question of the breadth of a patent, how broadly it should be defined, is as important as the question of its duration. If an inventor comes up with a product quite similar to one that has already been patented yet slightly different, can this inventor also get a patent for his variant? Or does the original patent cover "minor" variants? Chapter 1 discussed the patent claim of George Baldwin Selden, who argued that his patent covered all self-propelled, gasoline-powered vehicles. He tried to force Henry Ford and the other pioneers of the automobile industry to pay royalties to him, but Ford successfully challenged the patent claim. Recently there have been controversies over patents in the fields of genetic engineering and superconductivity.

Generally, the original innovators try to claim a broad patent coverage, affecting their own product and those that are in any way related, while later entrants argue for narrow coverage so that they will be allowed to produce variants and applications without paying royalties. While a broad coverage ensures that the inventor reaps more of the returns of her innovation, an excessively broad coverage may inhibit innovation, as others see their returns to developing the idea further squeezed by the royalties they have to pay to the original inventor.

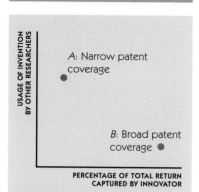

Figure 18.3 TRADE-OFF BETWEEN BROAD AND NARROW PATENTS

Broad patents help to assure that inventors receive a return on their innovations, but discourage other firms from pursuing ideas in the same area.

Figure 18.3 illustrates the trade-offs. The horizontal axis shows the fraction of total returns to the invention "captured," or enjoyed, by the innovator; the vertical axis depicts the availability of the invention to other researchers. Movements along either axis away from the origin serve to increase total innovative activity: the larger the fraction of returns captured, the greater the incentive to innovate; similarly, greater access to earlier inventions stimulates subsequent innovative activity. Increasing the breadth of patent coverage moves the economy from point A to point B, where a larger fraction of returns is captured, but access to new inventions by other researchers is restricted.

PATENT RACES

An important feature of the competition for patents is the fact that the winner takes all. An inventor who comes in second—a week, a day, or even an hour later than his rival—reaps no direct rewards. As a result, competition for patents may be very fierce, even when only a few firms are involved. This form of competition is called a **patent race**.

There are indirect rewards to coming in second, however. Generally, there is another lap in the race; superior products or processes remain to be discovered. So even if a firm loses one round, what it has learned in the process is likely to be helpful in the next. Thus, the monopoly power granted by a patent is limited by far more than the seventeen-year life of the patent: by the end of their lives, many patents are of little value, because the innovation has been superseded by something better.

The winner-take-all system may seem peculiar. Assume that a number of firms are on the verge of discovering a new product or process—say, a new way of freezing french fries. Why should the firm that completes the process a day ahead of the others get the entire returns? This company's contribution has been only to make the invention available a day ahead of when it otherwise would have occurred. Its reward seems all out of proportion with its contribution. Indeed, in some instances, the patent race may actually cause excessive and inefficient expenditures on R & D. Total costs of making the discovery might be lowered if a more balanced, more paced research program were followed. But the firm undertaking such a program will lose the race against a rival engaged in a crash research program.

Offsetting these incentives to engage in excessive research expenditures is the fact that the patent holder cannot appropriate *all* the social value of the invention; this reduces the incentive to overinvest in R & D. Besides, there is a simple answer why, in spite of the seeming disadvantages of patent races, all countries employ them: it is almost impossible to ascertain how close rivals were to having the same or similar ideas. We can tell who is the first person to apply for a patent. It is virtually impossible even to tell who would have been next in line.

PATENT LIMITATIONS

There are limits to the use of the patent system as a goad to innovation. The most important is the fact that not every idea is patentable. For instance, to obtain a patent, an applicant must convince the U.S. Patent Office that the invention is truly novel and not obvious.

Theoretical ideas—like the theory of gravity or Einstein's theory of relativity—are not patentable. In general, only inventions are patentable. You cannot patent the "idea" of a computer, though you can patent a specific design for the computer, or particular parts of the computer. At the same time, many of the design improvements made in the "development" stage of bringing a good to the market are not sufficiently novel to be patentable.

Marketing ideas are also generally not patentable. When the brokerage firm Merrill Lynch introduced Cash Management Accounts, which allowed its customers to combine their checking and securities accounts, this feature became popular, and other securities firms quickly followed suit. Merrill Lynch's only recourse was to register the Cash Management Account as a trademark, but this is not the same as a patent; it only ensured that no one could use the same name for the copycat accounts. Similarly, when Ray Kroc, the man behind the McDonald's restaurant chain, came up with his idea for selling hamburgers, he could not patent the idea, and his success was quickly imitated. (McDonald's was, however, able to patent its way of making french fries.)

Similarly, many of the most important developments in modern manufacturing were not, and probably could not have been, patented. These include the ideas of replaceable parts, conveyor belts, and assembly lines, ideas that revolutionized modern industry.

TRADE SECRETS

The patent system is imperfect. It does not allow inventors to reap all the benefits that result from their innovative activity. But it allows them to reap some, enough to stimulate considerable research. Yet, surprisingly, many firms do not even bother to seek patent protection for their new products and processes. To obtain a patent, a company has to disclose the details of the new product or process, and this information may be extremely helpful to its rivals in furthering their own R & D programs. Added to this is the fact that patents are granted on a case-by-case basis, and the questions of what is patentable and how broadly a patent should be defined are subject to considerable uncertainty and legal debate.

Because of these problems with patent protection, some companies prefer to try to keep their inventions a **trade secret**. A trade secret is simply an innovation or knowledge of a production process that a firm does not disclose to others. The formula for Coca-Cola, for example, is not protected by a patent; it is a closely guarded trade secret. Trade secrets play an important role in metallurgy, where new alloys are usually not patented. Trade secrets have one major disadvantage over patents: if a rival firm independently discovers the same new process, say for making an alloy, it can make use of the process without paying the innovative firm any royalties.

Whether an innovation is protected by patents or trade secrets, some of the returns come from being first in the market. Typically, the firm that first introduces a new product has a decided advantage over rivals, as it builds up customer loyalty and a reputation. Latecomers often have a hard time breaking in.

R & D AS A FIXED COST

Patents and trade secrets are not the only reason that industries in which technological change is important are generally not perfectly competitive, and why there are often relatively few firms in such industries. A second explanation has to do with the fact that R & D expenditures are fixed costs in the sense that they do not vary with the scale of

Intellectual property is the ownership of an idea, through a patent (which protects inventors) or a copyright (which protects authors, composers, and publishers). Intellectual property has become a fast-growing area of the law. Legal disputes arise concerning who actually was the first to invent a product, whether there really was an invention (as with Selden and the automobile), and what exactly the patent covers (as with Eli Whitney).

In one well-publicized case, Apple Computer sued Microsoft Software in 1988, claiming that Microsoft's windows program (a program making personal computers much more user-friendly) violated their copyright, not because it actually used the computer code, but because it imitated the "look and feel" of the Apple program. An interesting sidelight of that suit is the fact that the "look and feel" of the Apple programs were originally developed by computer scientists working for Xerox in California. But Xerox failed to convert their invention into a marketed computer, and did not obtain the appropriate legal protections; as a result, the computer scientists received little return from their research efforts.

The attractiveness of certain new technologies may depend on how they affect the ease with which intellectual property rights can be enforced. Recording studios like the compact disc and the old-fashioned record, because recordings cannot easily be copied at home; while this is precisely the reason many consumers prefer cassette tapes. Companies that produce CDs have been reluctant to share their patents with companies that might manufacture CD recorders, from a fear that the new invention might injure their current market.

As the high technology revolution continues, society will have to define and enforce new intellectual property rights and strike a balance between incentives for private innovation and the need for competition and a free flow of ideas.

The U.S. Patent Office library.

production; the cost of inventing something does not change according to how many times the idea is used in production.[1] And the size of fixed costs helps determine how competitive an industry is. The larger the fixed costs the more likely that there will be few firms and limited competition.

Because expenditures on research and development are fixed costs, industries with large R & D expenditures face declining average cost curves up to relatively high levels of output. We saw in Chapter 12 that firms typically have U-shaped average cost curves. The presence of fixed costs means that average costs initially decline as firms produce more, but for all the reasons discussed in Chapter 12, beyond some level of output, average costs increase. When there are large fixed costs, large firms (provided they are not *too* large) will have lower average costs than small firms and enjoy a competitive advantage. Industries with large fixed costs thus tend to have relatively few firms; competition is often limited. It is not surprising, therefore, that the chemical industry—where R & D is tremendously important—is highly concentrated.

Increased size also provides firms with greater incentives to undertake research. Suppose a small firm produces 1 million pens a year. If it discovers a better production technology that reduces its costs by $1 per pen, it saves $1 million a year. A large firm that makes the same discovery and produces 10 million pens a year will save $10 million a year. Thus, large firms have more incentive to engage in research and development, and as they do, they grow more than their smaller rivals do.

But while a large firm's research and development department may help the firm win a competitive advantage, it may also create managerial problems. Bright innovators can feel stifled in the bureaucratic environment of a large corporation, and they may also feel that they are inadequately compensated for their research efforts. In the computer industry, for example, many capable people have left the larger firms to start up new companies of their own.

Thus, size has both its advantages and disadvantages when it comes to innovation. Important inventions and innovations, such as nylon, transistors, and the laser have been produced by major corporations; on the other hand, small enterprises and individual inventors have produced Apple computers, Polaroid cameras, and Kodak film, all of which became major corporations as a result of their success. One objective of antitrust policies is to maintain an economic environment in which small, innovative firms can compete effectively against established giants.

LEARNING BY DOING

Some increases in productivity occur not as a result of explicit expenditures on research and development, but as a by-product of actual production. As firms gain experience from production, their costs fall. This kind of technological change is called **learning by doing**. Figure 18.4 depicts a **learning curve**, showing how the marginal cost of production declines as cumulative experience (output) increases. The horizontal axis represents not one year's output but the sum of all previous outputs. The more experience producing a good, as measured by cumulative output, the lower the marginal cost of producing one more unit. This systematic relationship between cumulative output and costs was first discovered in the airplane industry, where as more planes of a given type were produced, the costs of production fell dramatically.

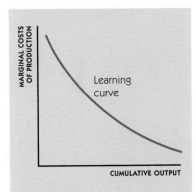

Figure 18.4 LEARNING CURVE

As firms produce more, the cost of producing each extra unit is reduced as they learn how to produce a good more efficiently. The result is that marginal costs decline with the cumulative output of a firm.

[1] The R & D expenditures can themselves be varied. Differences in the expenditure level will affect when new products will be brought to market and whether a firm will beat its rivals in the competition for new products.

In industries where learning by doing is important, the marginal cost falls as the scale of production increases. Accordingly, these markets have a built-in tendency to be imperfectly competitive, and this is a third reason why technological change and imperfect competition often go together. In particular, the first firm to enter an industry has a decided advantage over other firms. Even if some of what the first company has learned spills over into other firms, not all of it does. Because of the knowledge the first firm has gained, its costs will be below those of potential rivals, and thus it can always undercut them. Since potential entrants know this, they are reluctant to enter industries where learning by doing has a significant impact on costs. By the same token, companies realize that if they can find a product that provides significant benefits from learning by doing, the profits they earn will be relatively secure. Hence, just as firms race to be the first to obtain a patent, so too do they race to be the first to enter a product market in which there is a steep learning curve. This behavior is commonly displayed in the race to make the newest generation of computer chip.

When learning by doing is important, firms will produce beyond the point where marginal revenue equals *current* marginal costs, because producing more today has an extra benefit: it reduces future costs of production. How much extra a firm produces depends on the steepness of the learning curve.

ACCESS TO CAPITAL MARKETS

Because expenditures on research and development are often very risky and these risks cannot be insured, banks are generally unwilling to lend funds to finance them. When a bank makes a loan for a building, if the borrower defaults, at least the bank winds up with the building; it is protected. If the bank lends for R & D and the research project fails, or a rival beats the firm to the patent office, the borrower may not be able to repay the loan, and the bank winds up with nothing. Investors also often have a hard time judging the prospects of an R & D endeavor—inventors are always optimistic about their ideas. And an inventor may be reluctant to disclose fully all of the information about his idea, either to banks or potential investors, lest some among them steal his idea and beat him either to the market or the patent office.

For established firms in industries with limited competition and growing demand, financing their research expenditures may present no serious problem; they can pay for their R & D out of their profits. That is why, for the economy as a whole, most research and development occurs in such firms. But raising capital is a problem for new and small firms, and also for firms in industries where intense competition limits the profits that any one company can earn. Thus, a firm's dominant position in an industry may be self-perpetuating: its greater output means that it has more to gain from innovations that reduce the cost of production; its greater profits mean that it has more resources to expend on R & D.

Today, as we saw in Chapter 6, much of the research and development in new and small companies is financed by venture capital firms. These firms raise capital, mainly from pension funds, insurance companies, and wealthy individuals, which they then invest in the most promising R & D ventures. Venture capital firms often demand, as compensation for their risk taking, a significant share of the new enterprise, and they usually keep close tabs on how their money is spent. They also sometimes specialize in particular areas, such as computer technology or biotechnology. In less glamorous industries, it is often difficult to find financing for research and development.

COMPETITION AND TECHNOLOGICAL CHANGE

HOW COMPETITION AFFECTS TECHNOLOGICAL CHANGE

Competition spurs R & D:
>   A new innovation enables firms to enjoy profits (profits are driven to zero in standard markets).
>   Unless firms innovate, they will not survive.

Competition impedes R & D:
>   Competitors may imitate, thus eroding returns from innovation.
>   Competition erodes the profits required to finance R & D.

HOW TECHNOLOGICAL CHANGE AFFECTS COMPETITION

R & D spurs competition:
>   R & D provides an alternative to prices as a way for firms to compete; it is one of the most important arenas for competition in modern economies.

R & D impedes competition:
>   Patents give a single firm a protected position for a number of years.
>   The fixed costs of R & D give large firms an advantage, and mean that industries in which R & D is important may have few firms.
>   Learning by doing gives a decided advantage to the first entrant into a market.
>   Limited access to capital markets for financing R & D is a disadvantage to new and small firms.

BASIC RESEARCH AS A PUBLIC GOOD

As we learned in Chapter 7, externalities arise whenever there are costs or benefits of one individual's or firm's actions that accrue to others. There are almost always externalities associated with an invention or innovation. The sum of benefits produced by an invention is called the **social benefit** of the invention. Even with patents, inventors are able to appropriate only a fraction of these social benefits. For example, a firm that discovers a cheaper way of producing is likely to lower its price during the life of the patent in an attempt to steal customers away from its rivals, to the benefit of consumers; and after the patent expires, consumers benefit even more, as other companies compete and price falls further.

There are also social benefits for new products. Suppose the True Sound Company has invented a better compact disc player, and to maximize profits the firm sets the price at a level slightly higher than what its competitors charge. Some customers will see no advantage to the combination of new product and higher price—the improved quality will not be enough to offset the higher price. Others will be better off, because to them the new product seems like a really good deal.

The benefits of an invention in one area often spill over to other areas. The transistor, which revolutionized electronics, was invented at AT&T's Bell Laboratories. Yet when transistors spawned better radios, television sets, and other products, AT&T received little return from these huge benefits. The company's major return was the capacity to develop better and less expensive telephone equipment.

In deciding how much to spend on R & D, firms only focus on the returns they themselves receive, not on the benefits that accrue to others. We saw in Chapter 7 that when there are externalities, there is a role for government. Because of the positive externalities, government encourages R & D, particularly in the form of **basic research**. Basic research is the kind of fundamental inquiry that may produce a wide range of applications. It was, for instance, basic research in physics that led to the ideas behind so many of the things we take for granted today—the laser, the transistor, atomic energy. As we will see, basic research has both the characteristics of a public good.

A public good, it will be recalled from Chapter 7, can be viewed as an extreme form of externality. All individuals can benefit from the good. Public goods have two properties. First, it is difficult to exclude anyone from the benefits of a public good. Basic research involves the discovery of underlying scientific principles or facts of nature. Such facts—like superconductivity, or even the fact that there exist certain materials that exhibit superconductivity at temperatures considerably above absolute zero—cannot be patented, though a particular superconducting material may be. Nonetheless, discovering these facts of nature is of fundamental importance to technological progress. Because the fruits of basic research cannot be patented, private firms cannot be expected to undertake basic research.

The second characteristic of a public good is that the marginal cost of an additional individual enjoying the good is zero. We say that consumption is nonrivalrous. National defense is a public good, because when a new baby is born, hardly any additional costs for national defense are incurred. To put it another way, the additional person does not detract from the quality of the defense provided to others. Similarly, an additional person being informed of a basic discovery does not detract from the knowledge that the original discoverer has, though it may, of course, reduce the profits the original discoverer can make out of the discovery. Indeed, there are some marked advantages to having the fruits of basic research easily accessible; there may be large social gains when many researchers attempt to apply new basic ideas. Sealing up the basic ideas in a patent could slow the progress of others engaged in related lines of research.

Thus, basic research has both of the central properties of a public good: it is difficult to exclude others from the benefits of the research, and the marginal cost of an additional person making use of the new idea is zero. And as with all public goods, private markets are likely to provide an undersupply of basic research. Accordingly, the government supports basic research through the National Science Foundation, the National Institutes of Health, and a number of other organizations. Some of the expenditures of the Department of Defense on R & D also go into basic research. There is increasing concern that expenditures on basic research are inadequate.

Figure 18.5 shows that there has been a substantial decline in the support by the federal government of R & D, outside of defense, since 1967—a reduction of almost 50 percent after adjusting for inflation. Present expenditures on defense R & D consume

Figure 18.5 FEDERAL EXPENDITURES ON RESEARCH AND DEVELOPMENT

Real expenditures on R & D for nondefense purposes have declined markedly since 1967, while expenditures on defense research have increased over the late 1970s and 1980s. *Source: Budget of the U.S. Government* (1992), Table 10.1.

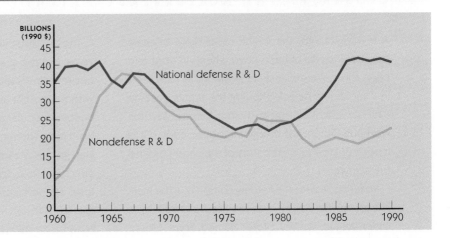

65 percent of overall U.S. government support for R & D. Thus, while the United States devotes about as large a proportion of its economy to R & D as do Japan and Germany, as shown in Figure 18.6, less of the total is spent in developing new products and processes to make American industry more competitive, and more is spent in developing better and more effective weapons. This may partly explain why today foreigners are getting almost one out of every two patents granted by the U.S. Patent Office. (Inventors have the right to obtain a patent from a foreign country as well as their own.)

Figure 18.6 COM-PARISON OF R & D EXPENDITURES ACROSS COUNTRIES

Total U.S. expenditures, as a percentage of the nation's output, are similar to that of other countries. The difference lies in how those expenditures are allocated, with U.S. expenditures concentrated more heavily in defense than those of Japan and Germany. *Source:* Organization for Economic Cooperation and Development, *Science and Technology Indicators* (1992).

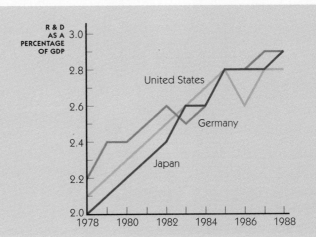

CLOSE-UP: THE ROLLERBLADE PATENT

A few years ago, the in-line roller skate became popular. Instead of having two wheels in front and back, the in-line roller skate positions all its wheels in a line. Some people thought the skates became a hit because it is faster and offers a better aerobic workout. Others just thought it looked cool. (Or is it hot?) But few knew the story of the patent behind the scenes.

Rollerblade, Inc., the leading company in the market for in-line skates, was founded in 1980 by a minor-league hockey player named Scott Olson. Olson originally planned to build a modern version of an in-line skate that had been designed back in the eighteenth century. However, he found that a patent on in-line skates was already owned by the Chicago Roller Skate Company, although they were not selling many of the skates. So Olson bought the patent and, with his brother Brennan, updated the design.

The two struggled to sell in-line skates for several years, but the skates only seemed popular among hockey players looking for a way to practice skating without ice. But around 1987, the skates started to become popular among a broad segment of buyers, both male and female, in the eighteen-to-thirty-five age group. Meanwhile, however, the patent expired in 1985. So when the in-line skate market took off, new competitors were free to enter the market without fear of infringing on any patent. Rollerblade still has an advantage, with about two-thirds of the market in 1990, but its share is eroding. Scott Olson, the original company founder, has left the company and at latest word was planning to start a new company to make skates that can glide on either blades or wheels.

Source: "Innovator Tries to Protect Its Lead," *New York Times,* August 7, 1990, p. C1.

ALTERNATE POLICIES TO PROMOTE TECHNOLOGICAL CHANGE

Patents and direct support of research and development are two of the most conspicuous ways that governments encourage technological progress, but other policies are helpful as well. Public expenditures on education determine the quantity and quality of the primary input into research and development: the scientists and engineers who do the work. Other policies involve encouraging R & D expenditures through the tax system, protecting American firms from unfair foreign competition until they can establish themselves technologically, and using antitrust policies to encourage, or at least not impede, innovation.

TAX SUBSIDIES

Since firms view research and development expenditures as a form of investment, R & D spending will be affected by some of the same factors that affect other forms of investment. In particular, tax changes that reduce a firm's profits may also be reflected in declined investments in research and development. Because of its concern that the level of R & D expenditures is too low, the government provides a tax credit for incremental expenditures on research and development. The credit works this way: firms that increase their R & D expenditures beyond the average of their expenditures during the preceding three years can subtract 25 percent of those increased expenditures from their tax bill. In effect, the government pays a quarter of the *increased* expenditures. However, both the amount of the credit and the formula for calculating the base seem to come under discussion almost every year, making firms uncertain of how much they can rely on the credit in the future.

PROTECTION

Government may also choose to subsidize R & D indirectly by protecting industries from foreign competition, thus allowing the domestic industry to charge a higher price. In effect, the consumers pay the subsidy directly to the firm in the form of these higher prices.

In recent years, several industries have asked for federal protection, arguing that without it America will lose its technological leadership in their area. Manufacturers of computer chips have been concerned about being undercut by Japanese firms. They have argued that Japan has tried to put them out of business by selling chips at prices below the cost of production. This practice is a form of predatory pricing, which was discussed in Chapter 15. The intent, claim the American producers, is to knock them out of the competition so that the Japanese companies can charge higher prices in the future. They argue that even if Japan can currently produce chips more cheaply than American firms, it pays to keep American producers in business, so that they can develop the next generation of chips—in the production of which they have at least a chance of competing effectively.

Similar arguments were raised by American automobile companies in the early 1980s, when they appealed to the government for protection from the competition of Japanese firms. The U.S. firms, it was argued, needed to get back on their feet after suffering the devastating effects of the oil price increases on the large-car market, in which they had been dominant. The U.S. government negotiated with Japan until Japan imposed "voluntary" export restraints on itself—voluntary only in the sense that Japan chose to impose them against the backdrop of a threat by the United States to impose more serious restraints if Japan did not do so.

These arguments are variants of what is called the **infant industry argument for protection**. Some industry may not be able to compete on the basis of current costs with competitors from abroad, but with the learning that will result from production, it believes that it will be able to do so later. But to obtain this learning, the industry must be temporarily protected from competition from abroad until it is ready to compete. This argument is made most often in less developed countries, but it arises in developed economies too.

The infant industry argument for protection has always been controversial, but the judgment among economists has tended to be critical. It is an argument for *temporary* protection, but once protection is granted, it is often not withdrawn. Thus, the restraints on Japan's exports to the United States remained years after the American automobile companies had recovered and were making record profits. Moreover, critics of the infant industry argument contend that protection is as likely to have a deleterious effect on innovation, by insulating domestic producers from the pressures of foreign competition.

Protection has a further disadvantage when the product in which import competition is limited is used in other industries: helping one industry to charge higher prices will affect not only consumers but other industries as well. One of the effects of restricting imports of computer chips is that it raises the price of chips that American computer manufacturers have to pay, making it more difficult for this industry to compete against foreign computer manufacturers who can buy cheaper chips.

If a temporary subsidy is desirable, trade protection is not the best way of providing it. By supplying the subsidy openly and directly, it is then possible to make informed judgments about whether the benefits are likely to be worth the costs. But, of course, industries and congressmen prefer trade protection precisely because the costs are so hidden. It is much easier for politicians to provide protection from imports rather than raising taxes, even though both policies adversely affect individuals—in one case as consumers, in the other as taxpayers.

RELAXING ANTITRUST POLICIES

The antitrust policies explored in Chapter 17 were founded on the belief that government's role in the economy was, as much as possible, to push markets toward the model of perfect competition. But the increasing awareness of the importance of R & D in modern industrial economies has changed views about the objectives of antitrust policy, and has led many to argue for less strenuous enforcement of antitrust laws.

One reason for these changed views is that a firm that makes a major innovation may not be able to exploit it fully, lest it be subjected to an antitrust prosecution. For example, assume that General Motors has made a discovery that would enable it to produce cars at half the cost. If it thoroughly exploited the invention, it would be in a position to expand sales dramatically. But worrying that it may then be subjected to antitrust prosecution, GM might not attempt to exploit the discovery fully. It would simply enjoy a much-increased profit on its present volume of sales. While the innovation has clear benefits for the firm, they are not as large as they would be if the firm felt it could enjoy a monopoly position with impunity from antitrust laws. Knowing that it cannot take full advantage of major discoveries, GM has less incentive to spend as much on research and development expenditures than it otherwise would.

The significance of this effect is hard to measure. After all, firms need not drive their rivals out of business to reap some rewards of their innovations. They might even sell to their rivals a license to use the new invention, and profit in that way. Under a **licensing agreement**, the other firms pay the patent holder a certain amount for each unit they produce. For example, RCA held the patent on color television, but licensed other firms to manufacture color TV sets. However, license fees in such circumstances are often set at sufficiently high levels that prices remain near what they would be in the absence of competition. It was not an accident that when RCA's patent expired, prices of color TVs fell dramatically.

The antitrust laws also inhibit firms from engaging in joint ventures, in which several firms undertake projects together—it might be to share research ideas and the risks and costs of their R & D expenditures or to produce a new product. The government has traditionally feared that cooperative R & D efforts might easily turn into collusion on pricing and production. For example, a group of firms that makes a discovery might decide to block new competitors from using the new discovery. It may also decide to charge all group members a high price for rights to use the innovation with the returns thereby generated being distributed back to the members. The high license fees lead each firm to charge high prices to consumers, since they increase the marginal cost of production. In this way, a joint research venture might end up as a mechanism for facilitating collusion, and there has been a presumption that joint ventures involving most of an industry would be a violation of the antitrust laws.

The arguments in *favor* of joint ventures have to do with the externalities of R & D. Any single firm knows that if it makes a new invention, other firms in the industry are likely to benefit either directly from imitation, or indirectly from some of the knowledge acquired in the process of making the discovery. Society as a whole would like those benefits, but no individual firm has a sufficient incentive to pursue them. As a result, spending on R & D is insufficient. On the other hand, much of research and development can be thought of as a public good for the industry; that is, all of the members of the industry benefit from it. They thus have an incentive to group together for research and development efforts.

In 1984, the National Cooperative Research Act was passed to allow some cooperative R & D ventures. Ventures registered under the act are shielded from the risk of paying triple damages in a private antitrust suit. The act also allows the government to scrutinize the ventures before they are formed. By the end of the 1980s, over a hundred joint R & D ventures had been registered. Among the best known are the Electric Power Research Institute, formed by electric power companies; Bell Communications Research, formed by local telephone companies; and Sematech, a cooperative research venture of the electronics industry centered in Austin, Texas.

Yet another concern that has led to arguments for less strenuous enforcement of antitrust laws is that larger size may give a distinct competitive advantage, particularly with regard to international competition. Here the logic is less clear-cut. The proponents cite the success of large firms like IBM as evidence of why bigness is important. However, the success of smaller firms, like Apple Computer and Compaq Computer against giant IBM in the computer industry, shows that size alone need not be the determining factor.

Arguments earlier in the chapter suggested that perfect competition is not an ideal to strive for, because markets that are highly competitive may undertake less research and development than their less competitive counterparts. On the other hand, if markets are not competitive enough, there will be both limited R & D (because of the lack of spur that competition provides) and losses in efficiency from the restrictions in output that are associated with imperfect competition. Thus, the economy must strive to strike a balance between enough competition to provide a spur to innovation and limited enough competition so that firms can appropriate sufficient returns to their innovative activity to give them both the incentive and resources to finance R & D expenditures.

TECHNOLOGICAL CHANGE AND THE BASIC COMPETITIVE MODEL

Basic competitive model	Industries in which technological change is important
Assumes fixed technology.	The central question is what determines the pace of technological change. Related issues include what determines expenditure on R & D and how learning by doing affects the level of production.
Assumes perfect competition, with many firms in industry.	Competition is not perfect; industries where technological change is important tend to have relatively few firms.
Perfect capital markets.	Firms find it difficult to borrow to finance R & D expenditures.
No externalities.	R & D confers benefits to those besides the inventor; even with patents, the inventor appropriates only a fraction of the social benefits of an invention.
No public goods.	Basic research is a public good: the marginal cost of an additional person making use of a new idea is zero (non-rivalrous consumption), and it is often difficult to exclude others from enjoying the benefits of basic research.

REVIEW AND PRACTICE

SUMMARY

1. Industries in which technological change is important are almost necessarily imperfectly competitive. Patents are one way the government makes it difficult and costly for firms to copy the technological innovations of others. A firm with a patent will have

a government-enforced monopoly. The expenditures on R & D are fixed costs; when they are large, there are likely to be few firms in the industry, and price competition is more likely to be limited.

2. Long-lived and broad patents discourage competition (at least in the short run), but provide greater incentives to innovate. Short-lived and narrow patents reduce the incentive to innovate, but encourage competition.

3. Learning by doing, in which companies (or countries) that begin making a product first enjoy an advantage over all later entrants, may be a source of technological advantage.

4. Research and development generally provides positive externalities to consumers and other firms. But since the innovating firm cannot capture all the social benefits from its invention, it will tend to invest less than a socially optimal amount.

5. Basic research has both the central properties of a public good: it is difficult to exclude others from the benefits of the research, and the marginal cost of an additional person making use of the new idea is zero.

6. There are a number of governmental policies to encourage technological advance: patents; direct spending on basic research; support for education; tax incentives to encourage corporate R & D; temporary protection from technologically advanced foreign competitors; and relaxing antitrust laws to allow potential competitors to work together on research projects.

KEY TERMS

| patent | learning by doing | infant industry |
| trade secret | learning curve | argument for protection |

REVIEW QUESTIONS

1. In what ways do industries in which technological change is important not satisfy the assumptions of the standard competitive model?

2. Why are industries in which technological change is important not likely to be competitive?

3. Why do governments grant patents, thereby conferring temporary monopoly rights? Explain the trade-off society faces in choosing whether to offer long-lived or short-lived patents, and whether to offer broad or narrow patents.

4. How does the existence of learning by doing provide an advantage to incumbent firms over prospective entrants?

5. Why might it be harder to raise capital for R & D than for other projects? How can established firms deal with this problem? What about start-up firms?

6. How do positive externalities arise from research and development? Why do externalities imply that there may be too little expenditure on research by private firms?

7. Explain how basic research can be thought of as a public good. Why is society likely to underinvest in basic research? What is the economist's reason for supporting gov-

ernment subsidies in areas that help produce new technology?

8. What is the infant industry argument for protection? What are criticisms of this argument?

9. What possible trade-off does society face when it considers loosening its antitrust laws to encourage joint research and development ventures?

PROBLEMS

1. Imagine that Congress was considering a bill to reduce the current seventeen-year life of patents to eight years. What negative effects might this change have on the rate of innovation? What positive effect might it have for the economy?

2. Suppose that many years ago, one inventor received a patent for orange juice, and then another inventor came forward and requested a patent for lemonade. The first inventor maintained that the orange juice patent should be interpreted to cover all fruit juices, while the second inventor argued that the original patent included only one particular method of making one kind of juice. What trade-offs does society face in setting rules for deciding cases like these?

3. Although a patent assures a monopoly on that particular invention for some time, it also requires that the inventor disclose the details of the invention. Given this requirement, under what conditions might a company (like Coca-Cola) prefer to use trade secret law rather than patents to protect its formulas?

4. Why might a company invest in research and development even if it does not believe it will be able to patent its discovery?

5. Learning by doing seems to be important in the semiconductor industry, where the United States and Japan are the main producers. Explain why U.S. and Japanese firms may race to try to bring out new generations of semiconductors. Draw a learning curve to illustrate your answers. If learning by doing is important in the semiconductor industry, why might other nations try to use an infant industry strategy to develop their own semiconductor industry?

IMPERFECT INFORMATION IN THE PRODUCT MARKET

I t was never any secret to economists that the real world did not match the one envisioned by the model of perfect competition. Theories of monopoly and imperfect competition such as those covered in Chapters 15–18 have been propounded from Adam Smith's time to the present.

Recently another flaw in the model of perfect competition has come to the fore: its assumption that market participants have full information about the goods being bought and sold. Economists describe such a situation by saying there is **perfect information**. Less-than-perfect information is called **imperfect information**. By incorporating imperfect information into their models of the economy, economists have come a long way in closing the gap between the real world and the world depicted by the perfect competition, perfect information model of Part Two.

This chapter is intended to provide a broad overview of the major information problems, the ways in which market economies deal with them, and how the basic model of Part Two has to be modified as a result. Here we focus on the product market. In the following chapters, we will see more clearly how information problems affect labor markets (Chapter 20), capital markets (Chapter 21), and the management of firms (Chapter 22). In Parts Four and Five, we will see how many of the most important macroeconomic problems—such as the failure of labor markets to clear—may, at least in part, be traced to information problems.

"It's not fair. You have classes and pep talks on selling, and I have to resist all on my own."

KEY QUESTIONS

1. Why is information different from other goods, such as hats and cameras? Why, in particular, do markets for information often not work well?

2. When does the market price affect the quality of what is being sold? How does the fact that consumers believe that price affects quality influence how firms behave?

3. When customers have trouble differentiating good from shoddy merchandise, what are the incentives that firms have to produce good merchandise? What role does reputation play?

4. Why is it that often in the same market one good, or similar goods, will sell at different prices? How does the fact that search is costly affect the nature of competition?

5. How does advertising affect firm demand curves and profits? Why may the firms in an industry be better off if they collectively agree not to advertise?

6. What has government done to address the problem of imperfect information? Why may these government attempts have only limited success?

THE INFORMATION PROBLEM

The basic competitive model assumes that households and firms are well informed, which means that they know their opportunity set, or what is available. Imagine knowing every good sold at every store and the price at which it is sold! More striking, they know every characteristic of every good, including how long it will last. Were these assumptions true, shopping would hardly be a chore.

Similarly, the model assumes that consumers know their preferences, what they like.

They know not only how many oranges they can trade for an apple, but also how many oranges they are willing to trade. While in the case of apples and oranges this may make sense, there are other situations in which such knowledge is less plausible. How do students know how much they are going to enjoy, or even benefit from, a college education before they have experienced it? How does an individual know whether she would like to be a doctor or a lawyer? She gets some idea about what different professions are like by observing those who practice them, but her information is at best very imperfect.

According to the basic model, firms too are perfectly well-informed. They all know the best available technology; they know the productivity of each applicant for a job; they know the prices at which inputs can be purchased from every possible supplier (and all of the inputs' characteristics). They know the prices at which they can sell the goods, not only today, but in every possible circumstance in the future.

How Big a Problem?

The fact that individuals and firms are not perfectly well-informed is, by itself, not necessarily a telling criticism of the competitive model, just as the criticism that markets are not perfectly competitive does not necessarily cause us to discard the model. The question is, are there important economic phenomena that can only be explained by taking into account these imperfections of information? Are there important predictions of the model that are incorrect, as a result of the assumptions concerning well-informed consumers and firms? Are there, in other words, important instances in which the model is either incomplete or misleading?

Increasingly, over the past two decades, economists have come to believe that the answer to these questions is yes. We have already seen evidence of this. Chapter 11, for instance, pointed out that college graduates may receive a higher income than high school graduates not only because they have learned things in college that make them more productive, but because their college degree helps them through a sorting process. Employers cannot glean from an interview which applicants for a job will be productive workers; they do not have perfect information. They therefore use a college degree to help them identify those who are better at learning. College graduates *are*, on average, more productive workers. But it is wrong to conclude from this that college has necessarily *increased* their productivity. It may simply have enabled firms to sort out more easily the more productive from the less productive.

Similarly, Chapter 10 discussed the problem of the investor choosing among alternative stocks. The basic maxim for success in investing is simple: buy when the price is low, and sell when the price is high. The problem is how to know when the price of a stock is low or high.

As the discussion of efficient market theory in Chapter 10 pointed out, the U.S. stock market may come close to realizing the ideal of a perfect, efficient market. This ideal includes the assumption of, if not perfect information, then the rapid and complete dissemination of what information is available to all market participants. Low prices signal low value, and high prices signal high value. With efficient stock markets, investors get rich only when they get lucky—or when information is imperfectly disseminated, as when investors trade illegally on inside information. But while the stock market may be relatively efficient, the quest for beating the market—for getting better information or getting information earlier than others—occupies the energies and talents of thousands of people on Wall Street.

HOW PRICES CONVEY INFORMATION

There are some information problems for which the price system provides brilliant solutions. We have seen how prices play an important role in coordinating production and communicating information about economic scarcity. Firms do not have to know the details about consumers' preferences; they do not have to know what John or Julia likes, what their trade-offs are. The price tells the producer the marginal benefit of producing an extra unit of the good, and that is all he needs to know. Similarly, a firm does not need to know how much iron ore there is left in Minnesota, the cost of refining iron ore, or a thousand other details; all it needs to know is the price of iron ore. This tells the company how scarce the resource is, how much effort it should expend in conserving. Prices and markets provide the basis of the economy's incentive system. But there are some information problems that markets do not handle, or do not handle well, and sometimes imperfect information inhibits the ability of markets to perform the tasks it performs so well when information is good.

MARKETS FOR INFORMATION

Information has value; people are willing to pay for it. We can thus consider information just as we do any other good. There is a market for information, with its price, just as there is a market for labor and a market for capital. Indeed, our economy is sometimes referred to as an information economy. Every year, investors spend millions of dollars on newsletters that give them information. Magazines sell specialized information about hundreds of goods.

However, the markets for information are far from perfect, and for good reasons. The most conspicuous one is that information is *not* just like any other good. When you buy a chair, the furniture dealer is happy to let you look at it, feel it, sit on it, and decide whether you like it. When you buy information, you cannot do the same. The seller can either say, "Trust me. I'll tell you what you need to know," or show you the information and say, "Here's what I know. If this is what you wanted to know, please pay me." You would rightfully be skeptical in the first scenario, and might be unwilling to pay in the second. After you were given the information, what incentive would you have to pay? You could claim you already knew it or that it was of little value to you.

In some cases, there is a basic credibility problem. You might think, if a stock tipster *really* knows that a stock is going to go up in price, why should he tell me, even if I pay him for the information? Why doesn't he go out and make his fortune with the information? Or is it that he really is not sure, and would just as soon have me risk my money rather than risk his?

For these and other reasons, markets for information are very limited and imperfect. Most important, even after the firm or consumer buys all the information he thinks is worth paying for, his information is still far from perfect. Let's look now at some of the consequences of imperfect information.

THE MARKET FOR LEMONS AND ADVERSE SELECTION

Have you ever wondered why a three-month-old used car sells for so much less—often 20 percent or more—than a new car? Surely cars do not deteriorate that fast. The pleasure of owning a new car may be worth something, but in three months, even the car you buy new will be "used." A couple of thousand dollars or more is a steep price to pay for this short-lived pleasure.

George Akerlof of the University of California at Berkeley has provided a simple explanation, based on imperfect information. Some cars are worse than others. They have hidden defects, which become apparent to the owner only after she has owned the car for a while. Such defective cars are called lemons; one thing after another seems to go wrong with them. While warranties may reduce the cost of having a lemon, they do not eliminate the bother—the time it takes to bring the car into the shop, the anxiety of knowing that with any long-term use, there is a good chance of a breakdown. The owners of lemons know, of course, that they were unlucky. They would like to pass the lemon along to someone else. At any price of a used car (of, say, a 1992 Chevrolet), those who have the *worst* lemons are most anxious to pass off their cars. As the price falls, those with the least bad cars decide it is worth keeping their car rather than selling it. That means that the average quality of those still being offered in the market is lowered. We say that there is an adverse selection effect as the price falls: the mix of those who elect to sell changes adversely as price falls.

Figure 19.1 shows the consequences of imperfect information for market equilibrium in the used car market. Panel A depicts, for each level of price (measured along the horizontal axis), the average quality of used cars being sold in the market. As price increases, quality increases. Panel B shows the supply curve of used cars. As price increases, the number of cars being sold in the market increases, for all of the usual

Figure 19.1 A MARKET WITH LEMONS

Panel A shows the average quality of a used car increasing as the price increases. Panel B shows a typical upward-sloping supply curve, but a backward-bending demand curve. Demand bends back because buyers know that quality is lower at lower prices, and they thus choose to buy less as the price falls. Panel B shows the market equilibrium.

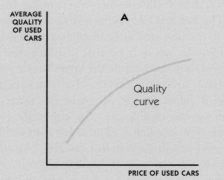

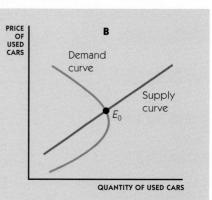

reasons. The demand curve is also shown. This curve, however, has a peculiar shape. It may be upward sloping as well as downward sloping. The reason for this is that as price increases, the average quality increases. And demand depends not just on price but on quality—on the "value" being offered on the market. If, as price falls, quality deteriorates rapidly, then the quantity demanded will actually *fall* as price falls—consumers are getting less for their dollars. The equilibrium is depicted in panel B.

This particular kind of example is often referred to as one with **asymmetric information**; that is, the seller of the used car has more information about the product than the buyer. Many markets are characterized by asymmetric information. One of the consequences of asymmetric information is that there may be relatively few buyers and sellers, far fewer than there would be with perfect information. Economists use the term **thin** to describe markets in which there are relatively few buyers and sellers. In some situations, a market may be so thin as to be essentially nonexistent; economists call such a market **incomplete**. The used car market, for example, is a thin one. Buyers may know that there are some legitimate sellers, those who for one reason or another always want to drive a new car (maybe because they just love having new cars all the time). But mixed in with these are people who are trying to dump their lemons. The buyers cannot tell the lemons apart from the good cars. Rather than risk it, they simply do not buy. (Of course, the fact that demand is low drives down the price, increasing the proportion of lemons; it is a vicious cycle.)

The problem with the used car market falls into the broader category of adverse selection. We encountered this phenomenon once before, in the insurance market (Chapter 6). As the price of insurance increases, those least likely to have an accident decide it is not worth paying the premium, and drop out. The mix of those applying for insurance changes adversely. In later chapters, we will encounter other instances of adverse selection effects in labor and capital markets.

SIGNALING

Of course, if you have a good car, you would like to persuade potential buyers that it is good. You could tell them that it is not a lemon, but why should they believe you? There is a simple principle: *actions speak louder than words*. What kind of actions can you take that will convince buyers of the quality of your car?

The fact that Chrysler is willing to provide a five-year, fifty-thousand mile warranty on its cars says something about the confidence Chrysler has in its product. The warranty is valuable, not only because it reduces the risks of having to spend a mint to repair the car, but also because the buyer believes that Chrysler would not have provided the warranty unless the chances of defects were fairly low. Actions such as this are said to "signal" higher quality. A signal is effective if it differentiates, here between high-quality cars and low-quality cars. The cost to the producer of a five-year guarantee is much higher for a car that is likely to fall apart within five years than for a car that is unlikely to break down. Customers know this, and thus can infer that if the firm is willing to provide this warranty, it is selling high-quality cars.

When you go to a car dealer, you want to know that it will be around if you have troubles in a year or two. Some firms try to signal that they are not fly-by-nights by spending a great deal of money on their showroom. This indicates that it would be costly for them to just pack up and leave. (There are, of course, other reasons why they may spend money on a fancy showroom.)

Thus, actions such as providing a better guarantee or a larger showroom are taken not just for the direct benefit that the consumer receives from them, but because those actions make consumers believe that the product is a better product or the firm is a better firm to deal with. In a sense, the information conveyed by the action "distorts" the decisions made relative to what they would have been in a perfect-information world.

JUDGING QUALITY BY PRICE

There is still another clue that buyers can use to judge the quality of what they are about to purchase: price. Consumers make inferences about the quality of goods being offered based on the price charged. For example, they know that on average, if the price of a used car is low, the chance of getting a lemon is higher. Firms know, of course, that consumers know this, and they try to take advantage of that information. Good firms seek to persuade consumers that their product is good.

In markets with imperfect information, firms do not simply act like the price takers envisaged in Part Two. They *set* their prices. And in setting their prices, they take into account what customers will think about the quality of the good being sold. Cutting the price may not be the best way for a firm to persuade its customers that its product is good. It knows that consumers may reason that the firm could not charge such a low price unless it cut corners, that is, unless it used shoddy materials. Concerns about consumers correctly or incorrectly making inferences like these impede the effectiveness of price competition.

In the used car example, we saw that as price rose, the average quality of cars increased. This relationship is redrawn in Figure 19.2. What consumers care most about is "value," which in this case can be thought of as quality divided by price. The quality divided by the price at any price is given by the slope of a line from the origin to the point on the curve corresponding to that price. Thus, the value at point A in panel A, corresponding to a price p_1, is given by q_1/p_1, the slope of a line from the origin to A. At p^*, the value (quality divided by price) is maximized. Panel B shows demand and supply curves. The demand curve does not have the usual downward-sloping shape because

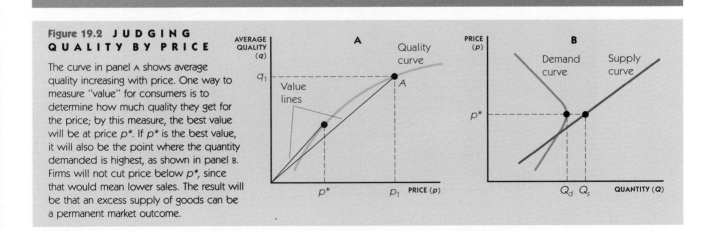

Figure 19.2 JUDGING QUALITY BY PRICE

The curve in panel A shows average quality increasing with price. One way to measure "value" for consumers is to determine how much quality they get for the price; by this measure, the best value will be at price p^*. If p^* is the best value, it will also be the point where the quantity demanded is highest, as shown in panel B. Firms will not cut price below p^*, since that would mean lower sales. The result will be that an excess supply of goods can be a permanent market outcome.

CLOSE-UP: AUTOMOBILE BROKERS AND IMPERFECT INFORMATION

A broker is someone who arranges contracts between two parties. In older times, marriage brokers brought together prospective couples. Stockbrokers bring together buyers and sellers of stocks. Car brokers bring together buyers and sellers of cars.

In every case, though, a broker is someone whose job exists only because of imperfect information. After all, why can't a person just go out and choose a spouse or a stock or a car? The obvious problem is that many different varieties are available, and it costs time and energy and money to collect the information to make an informed decision. A good broker is out there in the market all the time, keeping track of what is going on. Having a relatively small number of people keeping track of buyers and sellers is certainly more efficient than having all buyers and sellers duplicating one another's efforts.

Consider how car brokers work, for example. You call up a broker (usually they are listed in the Yellow Pages of the phone book) and describe what sort of car you want—make, model, year, accessories. The broker then finds you the best deal. He might just tell you where that deal is or actually buy the car and resell it to you. Sometimes the broker is paid directly by the buyer, sometimes by the seller.

Working as a broker may seem like a funny way to make a living. How can someone get paid for shopping for cars? Well, consider each side of the transaction. From the standpoint of the prospective car buyer, shopping for a car involves time and the energy of confronting dealers and haggling over price. Even if the buyer spends several days or weeks shopping, it is not clear that she will find the best deal. Paying a knowledgeable broker will certainly save time and energy, and might also result in a cheaper price too. A good broker will know about the amount of the sales representative's typical commission or the "preparation fee" that dealers receive for getting a car ready to sell. By taking factors like this into account, the broker can often negotiate a better price.

From the standpoint of the seller, matters are a bit more complicated. Why would the seller offer a good deal to the broker, rather than just waiting for a less savvy buyer to come in? The main reason

car dealers work with brokers is that they are under pressure to sell cars. Sure, they would rather hold out for a less knowledgeable consumer who will pay more for the car. But the car dealer has imperfect information about car buyers too—how can the dealer know who is out there ready to buy? When a broker offers a done deal at a purchase price that gives the dealer a small profit, the dealer is often better off taking the small profit and moving on.

Not everyone will need or want an automobile broker. But for those who feel that their information about the car market is extremely imperfect, a broker may be a wise choice.

Source: "A Better Way to Buy a Car?" *Consumer Reports,* September 1989, pp. 593–95.

at prices below p^*, the value (the quality-price ratio) is actually lower than at p^*. Because the value is lower, the quantity demanded is lower; that is why the demand curve bends backward.

Note that at p^*, the quantity demanded, Q_d, is less than the quantity supplied, Q_s. In a world with perfect information, we know what is supposed to happen: firms, unable to sell everything they would like to sell, cut their price. But now, firms know that customers might believe that the cars being sold not only have a lower price but are a worse value, that the quality deteriorates more than the price declines. Thus, lowering price does *not* garner more customers. In fact, it loses them customers. Since firms believe this, they have no incentive to cut prices. A situation can be sustained in which there is a seeming excess supply of goods. Imperfect information means that equilibrium will be achieved away from the intersection of supply and demand curves.

This is a profound result, one we will trace through many of the chapters that follow. Information problems fascinate economists because they turn the basic competitive model upside down. Prices convey critical information in a market economy. Participants in the market know that prices convey information, and that when they can, sellers will manipulate prices to control the information conveyed. Buyers, for their part, see through these manipulations. Their concern that the seller is trying to pass off a lemon discourages trade; when information problems like these are severe, markets are likely to be thin or nonexistent. Another possible outcome is that price competition may be limited; even when there is an excess supply of goods, firms may not cut their prices and the market may not clear.

SOLUTIONS TO ADVERSE SELECTION PROBLEMS IN MARKET ECONOMIES

Signaling
Judging quality by price

THE INCENTIVE PROBLEM

We have seen throughout this book that motivating individuals to do the right thing, to make the right choices, is one of the central economic problems. The central problem of incentives, in turn, is that individuals do not bear the full consequences of their actions. The multibillion-dollar collapse of the savings and loan associations—though fraud may have played a part—is largely attributable to incorrect incentives. Depositors had no incentives to check on what the S & L's were doing, because their deposits were guaranteed by the government; and the owners of many of the S & L's had an incentive to take high risks, since if they were successful, they kept the gains, while if they failed, the government picked up the loss.

In the basic competitive model of Part Two, private property and prices provide incentives; individuals are rewarded for performing particular tasks. The incentive problem arises when an individual is not rewarded for what he does, or when he does not have to pay the full costs of what he does. In our economy, incentive problems are pervasive. Chapter 6 discussed three such problems: the problem of moral hazard in the insurance industry, where, because a person is insured, she might take less care than she would if she had to bear all the losses herself; the incentive problem in equities, where the original owners and managers of a firm may have their incentives attenuated because they have to share the proceeds with the other shareholders; and the incentive problem in debt, that the managers of firms do not bear the losses that bondholders face in the event of bankruptcy.

In product markets, firms must be given the incentive to produce quality products. Again, the incentive problem is an information problem: if customers could always tell the quality of the product they were getting, firms that produced higher-quality products would always be able to charge a higher price, and no company could get away with producing shoddy goods. Most of us have had the experience of going to a newly established restaurant, having a good meal, and then returning some time later only to be disappointed with the deteriorated quality. Evidently something went wrong with incentives.

MARKET SOLUTIONS

In simple transactions, incentive problems can be solved with schemes of penalties and rewards. You would like a document typed. You sign a contract with someone to pay him $25 to deliver the typed document by tomorrow at 5:00 P.M. The contract stipulates that $.50 will be deducted from the total for each typographical error, and $1.00 will be deducted for every hour the paper is late. The contract has built-in incentives for the paper to be delivered on time and without errors.

But most transactions, even simple ones, are more complicated than this one, and the more complicated the transaction is, the more difficult it is to solve the incentive problem. You want your grass mowed, and your neighbor's twelve-year-old son wants to mow it. You want him to take care of your power mower. When he sees a rock in the mower's path, he should pick it up. But what incentive does he have to take care of the mower? If you plan to charge him for repairs if the mower does hit a rock, how can you tell whether the rock was hidden by the grass? Of course, if he owned his own mower, he would have the appropriate incentives. That is why private property combined with the price system provides such an effective solution to the incentive problem. But your neighbor's son probably does not have the money to buy his own power mower. Then an incentive problem is inevitable: either you let him use your lawn mower and bear the risk of his mistreating it, or you lend him money to buy his own, in which case you bear the risk of his not paying you back.

Many private companies must hire people to run machinery worth hundreds or thousands of times more than a lawn mower. Every company would like its workers to exert effort and care, to communicate clearly with one another and take responsibility. Beyond private property and prices, the market economy has several other partial solutions to these incentive problems, loosely categorized as contract solutions and reputation solutions.

CONTRACT SOLUTIONS

Most economic relations in our modern economy are not of the simple form "If you type my paper, I will pay you $25." As this example illustrates, you may be concerned both with the accuracy of the typing and with having the document delivered on time.

When one party (firm) agrees to do something for another, it typically signs a contract, which specifies the various conditions of the transaction. For example, a firm will agree to deliver a product of a particular quality at a certain time and place. There will normally be "escape" clauses: if there is a strike, if the weather is bad, and so on, the delivery can be postponed. These **contingency clauses** may also make the payment depend on the circumstances and manner in which the service is performed.

Contracts attempt to deal with incentive problems by specifying what each of the parties is to do in each situation. But no matter how thorough those who write the contract are, they cannot think of every possible contingency. And even if they could, it would take them a prohibitively long time to write down all of these possibilities.

Accordingly, there are times when it would be extremely expensive for the supplier to comply with all the terms of the contract. He could make the promised delivery on time, but only at a very great cost; if the buyer would only accept a one-day delay, there would be great savings. Of course, buyers know that sellers will always find excuses. Sometimes, however, there are real economic savings in violating the terms of the contract. To provide suppliers with the incentive to violate the terms only when it is really economically worthwhile, most contracts allow delivery delays, but with a penalty attached. The penalty is what gives the supplier the incentive to deliver in a timely way.

Sometimes the supplier may think it simply is not worth complying with the contract. If he violates the agreement, he is said to be in **breach** of the contract. One of the most famous examples of a breach of contract in recent years involved Westinghouse Electric, which agreed to supply uranium at a fixed price to the nuclear power plants it had built for a large number of electric utilities. When the price of energy skyrocketed in the early 1970s, Westinghouse found that the price it had to pay for uranium was many times the price at which it had agreed to sell the uranium. If the company had tried to fulfill the terms of the contract, it would eventually have been pushed near or over the bankruptcy threshold. It decided simply not to comply with the terms of the contract. Quite naturally, its customers were unhappy; they sued, but were only able to recover a fraction of what they lost as a result of Westinghouse's reneging on its promise.

Some contracts have explicit provisions allowing one or the other side to get out of the agreement upon payment of a penalty. If there is not such a clause, the parties usually wind up in court, and the legal system stipulates what damages the party breaking the contract must pay to the other side. We can see that no matter how complicated the contract, there will still be ambiguities and disputes. The contract typically specifies procedures for resolving these disputes, but again, many wind up in the courts.

Contracts, by stipulating what parties are supposed to do in a variety of circumstances, help resolve incentive problems. But contracts are incomplete and enforcement is costly, and thus they provide an imperfect resolution of the incentive problem.

REPUTATION SOLUTIONS

Reputations play an extremely important role in providing incentives in market economies. A reputation is a form of a guarantee. Even though you may know that you cannot collect from this guarantee yourself—it is not a "money-back" guarantee—you know that the reputation of the person or company will suffer if it does not perform well. The incentive to maintain a reputation is what provides firms with an incentive to produce high-quality goods. It provides the contractor with an incentive to complete a house on or near the promised date.

For reputation to be an effective incentive mechanism, firms must lose something if their reputation suffers. The "something" is, of course, profits; for reputations to provide incentives, there must be profits. Prices must remain above costs. These profits are known as **reputation rents**, returns that a firm earns on having a good reputation. In many industries, such as consumer durables and restaurants, where quality variation is large and hard to detect before purchasing a good, reputation rents are extremely important. These are goods for which brand names typically are also important.

Thus, we see another way that markets with imperfect information differ from markets with perfect information. In competitive markets with perfect information, competition drives price down to marginal cost. In markets in which quality is maintained as the result of a reputation mechanism, whether competitive or not, price must remain above marginal cost.

Why, in markets where reputation is important, doesn't competition lead to price cutting? Consumers know, perhaps from hard experience, that if price is "too low," firms do not have an incentive to maintain their reputation, and therefore they come to expect low-quality goods. This is another reason that cutting prices will not necessarily bring firms more customers. Most consumers, at one time or another, have encountered companies that tried to live off their reputation. For example, Head skis were the high-quality skis in the early 1970s. At high prices, of course, demand was limited. When the company lowered its price, sales increased, as consumers, knowing about the high quality, bought the skis thinking they were getting a bargain. But bargains are not so easy to come by. Consumers should have realized that at the lower prices, profits were lower; Head had little incentive to maintain its reputation, and may have let its quality deteriorate to achieve the lower prices.

Reputation as a Barrier to Entry   While for the reputation mechanism to work price must exceed costs, whether the market is competitive or not, in fact competition is frequently very imperfect in markets where reputation is important. The necessity of establishing a reputation acts as an important barrier to entry, and limits the degree of competition in these industries. Given a choice between purchasing the product of an established firm with a good reputation and the product of a newcomer with no reputation, at the same price, consumers will normally choose the established firm's good. Why try a new cola drink when you know what Pepsi and Coca-Cola taste like? The newcomer must offer a sufficiently low price, often accompanied with strong guarantees. In some cases, newcomers have almost to give away their product. Entering a market thus becomes extremely expensive. The firm has to spend a considerable amount of money to establish itself.

Commitment and Reputation   Economic relations often entail a commitment or promise by at least one of the participants to do something in the future. A contractor, for example, undertakes to complete a house by September 1. There is an understanding that a number of contingencies may arise that may prevent the house from being completed on the promised date, but there is also an understanding that if it is not possible to complete the house by September 1, the contractor will make every effort to complete it as soon thereafter as possible.

Reputations play an important role in providing incentives to live up to commitments. A contractor who repeatedly fails to complete the house on the dates promised may find it difficult to get new business.

SOLUTIONS TO INCENTIVE PROBLEMS IN MARKET ECONOMIES

Private property and prices
Contracts
Reputations

THE SEARCH PROBLEM

A basic information problem, as noted at the beginning of this chapter, is that consumers must find out what goods are available on the market, at what price, and where. Households must learn about job opportunities as well as opportunities for investing their funds. Firms, by the same token, have to figure out the demand curve they face, and where and at what price they can obtain inputs. Both sides of the market need, in other words, to find out about their opportunity sets.

CLOSE-UP: REFORMING THE U.S. MEDICAL CARE INDUSTRY

The United States spent almost $3,000 per person on medical care in 1991. This total was about 40 percent more per person than Canada spent; 70 percent more than Sweden; 90 percent more than Germany; 125 percent more than Japan; and a whopping 180 percent more than the United Kingdom. The U.S. total, in fact, was far higher than any nation in the world.

But this far higher spending does not seem to have purchased much better health. For example, the life expectancy for a woman in the United States in 78.5 years. This is slightly better than Germany (78.4 years) and the United Kingdom (78.1). However, it lags behind Canada (79.7), Sweden (80.6), and Japan (81.8). Another common health measure is the number of infants who die at less than a year of age. Out of every 10,000 infants born in the United States, 97 die in their first year of life. In Canada, the number is 72; in Sweden, 58; in Germany, 75; in Japan, 46; in the United Kingdom, 84. Moreover, approximately 30 million Americans do not have health insurance. They often postpone medical care until they are terribly ill, when earlier treatment might have saved money and promoted greater health. All other industrialized nations have some system that guarantees certain forms of care to all citizens.

Why does the United States spend so remarkably much on medical care, $738 billion in 1991, for health results that are so unremarkable? Economists have offered several explanations, many of which focus on the crucial role of imperfect information in the provision of medical care.

Sick people do not usually act as cautious self-interested consumers, carefully shopping around for different medical care providers and balancing the marginal benefits of various treatments. Most people have incomplete information about what is wrong with them, what treatment might help, and what medical actions are really needed. Moreover, most Americans have health insurance, so that they pay out-of-pocket only a small fraction of the bill (or sometimes nothing at all) for a doctor's visit or a hospital stay.

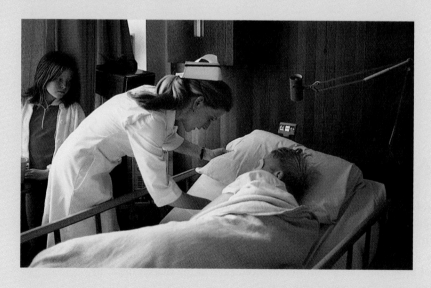

The resulting problem of moral hazard for patients is probably one reason why the United States pays so much for medical care. An insured patient, especially with incomplete information, has little reason to care about costs. Instead, her attitude is likely to be that if a trip to the doctor might help, it is worth a try. One economic study found that patients who pay nothing out-of-pocket for their medical care spend about 40 to 50 percent more than those who pay the first few hundred dollars for care (in the form of a "deductible"). However, the health status of those with full insurance is no better, despite the additional services they receive. The national health insurance systems in other countries usually deal with this moral hazard problem by rationing medical care. The government decrees that certain equipment will not be purchased, or that certain procedures will not be performed for the elderly or for anyone.

Uncertain information about what medical care is truly necessary presents another problem, this one to do with health care professionals. Under the traditional U.S. health insurance system, doctors are paid for the amount of care they provide, the number of tests they run, and the number of procedures they perform. When patients have both insurance and incomplete information, they are unlikely to question whether another test or procedure is really necessary. Moreover, health care professionals are trained to look after people's health. So they face strong economic and professional pressure to try everything, rather than weighing costs of treatment with potential benefits.

Today more and more doctors work in "managed care" organizations, where they are paid a flat fee up front and then provide whatever care is needed. They receive no extra income from doing extra procedures. Many managed care organizations display far lower rates of surgery and lower costs, again with no noticeable effect on the health of patients.

How to reform the U.S. medical care system to cut costs and assure universal access to some basic amount of care has been a hot political topic for years. Many have argued for offering health insurance to all, but few have been willing to advocate European-style rationing of health care, in which government puts direct limits on what care can be offered and how much can be spent. In fact, few reformers seem willing to come to grips with the uncomfortable reality of imperfect information and moral hazard in the provision of medical care.

Sources: Supplement to the *OECD Observer* (June/July 1991); Willard G. Manning, Joseph P. Newhouse, Naihua Duan, Emmett B. Keeler, Arleen Leibowitz, and M. Susan Marquis, "Health Insurance and the Demand for Medical Care: Evidence from a Randomized Experiment," *American Economic Review* (1987) 77: 251–77.

In the basic competitive model of Part Two, a particular good sells for the same price everywhere. If we see what look like identical shoes selling for two different prices at two neighboring stores—$25 at one and $35 at the other—it must mean (in that model) that the stores are really selling different products. If the shoes are in fact identical, then what the customer must really be getting is a combination package, the shoes plus the service of having the shoes fitted, and the more expensive store is providing a higher quality of service.

In fact, however, essentially the same good may be sold at different stores for different prices. And you may not be able to account for the observed differences in prices by differences in other attributes, like the location of the store or the quality of the service provided. In these cases, we say there is **price dispersion**. If search were costless (or information perfect, as in the standard competitive model), consumers would search until they found the cheapest price. No store charging more than the lowest price on the market would ever have any customers.

Price dispersion, combined with variations in quality, means that households and firms often must spend considerable energies in searching: workers search for a good job, firms look for good workers; consumers search for the lowest prices and best values. The process by which this kind of information is gathered is called **search**.

Search is an important, and costly, economic activity. Because it is costly, a search stops before you have *all* the relevant information. You know that there are some bargains out there to be found, but it is just too expensive to find them. You might worry that you will be disappointed the day or week after buying a new computer, if you find it for sale at 10 percent less—if only you had waited! But in truth, there should be no regrets. There was a chance that you would not find a better buy, or that next week you would not even be able to buy it at the price offered today. You looked at these risks, the costs of further search, the benefits of being able to get the computer today and use it now compared with the benefits of waiting and the chance of finding it at a still lower price; after a careful balancing of the benefits and costs of further waiting, you decided to purchase now.

In Figure 19.3, the horizontal axis plots the amount of search (for instance, time spent in searching), while the vertical axis measures the expected marginal benefit of searching. The expected marginal benefit of searching declines with the amount of search. In general, people search the best prospects first. As they search more and more, they look at less and less likely prospects. On the other hand, the marginal cost of additional search rises with increased search. This simply reflects the fact that the more time people spend in search, the less time they have to do other things. The opportunity cost of spending an extra hour searching thus increases. The amount of search chosen will be at the point where the expected marginal benefit just equals the marginal cost.

An increase in price (or quality) dispersion will normally increase the return to

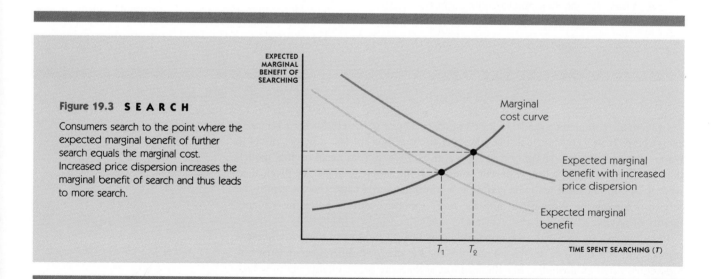

Figure 19.3 SEARCH

Consumers search to the point where the expected marginal benefit of further search equals the marginal cost. Increased price dispersion increases the marginal benefit of search and thus leads to more search.

searching—there is a chance of picking up a really good bargain, and the difference between a good buy and a bad buy is larger. Thus, the expected marginal benefit curve shifts up, as illustrated by the gray curve, and the amount of search will increase from T_1 to T_2.

Search is costly, and this has important implications for how *markets* work; the fact that in equilibrium there can exist price dispersion is only one example.

SEARCH AND IMPERFECT COMPETITION

Firms know that search is costly, and take advantage of that fact. They know they will not lose all their customers if they raise their prices. If a store lowers its price slightly, it will not immediately attract *all* the customers from the other stores. Customers have to learn about the competitive price advantage, and this takes time. Moreover, even when people do hear of the lower price, they may worry about the quality of the goods being sold, the nature of the service, whether the goods will be in stock, and so on.

Thus, the fact that search is costly means that the demand curve facing a firm will be downward sloping—in other words, the firm can change the price of its product without losing all of its customers. (Under perfect competition, the demand curve facing an individual firm is horizontal and the firm loses its entire market if it charges more than the going price.) Competition is necessarily imperfect.

Consider, for instance, the demand for a Walkman. When you walk into a store, you have some idea of what it should sell for. The store asks $70 for it. You may know that somewhere you might be able to purchase it for $5 less. But is it worth the additional time and trouble and gasoline to drive to the other stores that might have it, looking for a bargain? Some individuals are willing to pay the extra $5 simply not to bother with the additional search. As the store raises its price to, say, $75, $80, or $85, some people who would have bought the Walkman at $70 decide that it is worth continuing to shop around. The store, as it raises its price, loses some but not all of its customers. Thus, it faces demand that falls as its price increases: a downward-sloping demand curve. If search were costless, everyone would go to the store selling the Walkman at the lowest price. If a store charged any more than that lowest price, it would have no sales. Many markets are, accordingly, better described by the model of monopolistic competition or the other models of imperfect competition introduced in Chapters 15 and 16.

SEARCH AND INFORMATION INTERMEDIARIES

Some firms play an important role by gathering information and serving as intermediaries between producers and customers. These firms are part of the market for information discussed in the beginning of the chapter. One of the functions of good department stores, for example, is to economize on customers' search costs. The stores' buyers seek out literally hundreds of producers, looking for the best buys and the kinds of goods that the stores' customers will like. Good department stores earn a reputation for the quality of their buyers. Customers still have a search problem—they may have to visit several department stores—but the problem is far smaller than it would be if they had to search directly among producers.

ADVERTISING

While customers have an incentive to find out where the best buys are, firms have a corresponding incentive to tell customers about the good deals they are providing. Companies may spend a considerable amount of money on advertising to bring information about their products, prices, and locations to potential customers.

In the classic joke about advertising, an executive says, "We know that half the money we spend on advertising is entirely wasted, but we don't know which half." That joke summarizes some of the controversy over the economic function of advertising. In the United States, many firms spend 2 percent, 3 percent, or more of their total revenues on advertising. In 1990, total expenditures on advertising were $130 billion, with slightly more than half spent on national advertising. To put this number in perspective, these expenditures were only slightly less than those spent on all federal, state, and local public assistance programs in that year. Slightly more than a quarter of what was spent on advertising went to newspapers, slightly less than a quarter went to television, a sixth to direct mail, and the remainder to magazines (5 percent), radio (6 percent), and a miscellany of other methods, including outdoor advertising.

Advertising can serve the important economic function of providing information about what choices are available. When a new airline enters a market, it must convey that information to potential customers. When a new product is developed, that fact has to be made known. When a business is having a sale or a special deal, it must let people know somehow. A firm cannot just lower its price, sit on its haunches, and wait, if it wants to be successful. Companies need to recruit new customers and convey information in an active way.

But much advertising is not of this form. The famous Marlboro cigarette ad, of a man on horseback smoking Marlboros, does not seek to inform smokers of a new product—virtually everyone above the age of twelve, smokers as well as nonsmokers, has heard of Marlboro cigarettes. Nor does the fact that some rancher may smoke Marlboros convey much information about the product's quality. Horseback riders are no better and no worse than the average run of humanity. Instead, the advertising seeks to convey an image, one with which some smokers will identify.

The same is true of typical beer or car advertisements. The fact that these advertisements are successful—that they succeed in persuading individuals either to try a product or to stick with that product and not try another—is a reminder that consumer behavior is a much more complicated matter than the simple theories of competitive markets suggest. Of course, few people decide to go out and buy a car or a new suit solely because they saw a TV ad. But decisions about what kinds of clothes to wear, what beer to drink, what car to drive, may be affected by a variety of considerations; for instance, how peers will view them or how they will see themselves. These views, in turn, may be affected by advertising.

To emphasize the different roles played by advertising, economists sometimes distinguish between **informative advertising**, the intent of which is to provide consumers with information about the price of a good, where it may be acquired, or what its characteristics are, and **persuasive advertising**. In some cases, the intent of persuasive advertising is to provide "disinformation"—to confuse consumers into thinking that there is a difference among goods when there really is not. In other cases, the purpose is simply to make people have positive feelings about the good.

ADVERTISING AND COMPETITION

Advertising is both a cause and a consequence of imperfect competition. In a perfectly competitive industry, where many producers make identical goods, it would not pay any single producer to advertise the merits of a good. You do not see advertisements for wheat or corn. If such advertising were successful, it would simply shift the demand curve for the product out. The total demand for wheat might increase, but this would have a negligible effect on the wheat grower who paid for the advertisement. Of course, if all wheat farmers could get together, it might pay them to advertise as a group. In recent years, associations representing producers of milk, oranges, almonds, raisins, and beef have advertised.

ADVERTISING AND PROFITS

The objective of advertising is to shift the demand curve. The increase in advertising by one firm may divert customers away from rivals, or it may divert customers away from other products. Advertising a particular brand of cigarettes may be successful in inducing some smokers to switch brands and in inducing some nonsmokers to smoke (to spend money on cigarettes that they otherwise would have spent on something else).

The effect of advertising on profits can be illustrated in a diagram. When a firm is already in an imperfectly competitive situation, advertising shifts the demand curve for its product out, as in Figure 19.4. The increase in profits consists of two parts. First, the firm can sell the same quantity it sold before but at a higher price, p_3, rather than p_1. Profits then increase by the original quantity (Q_1) times the change in price ($p_3 - p_1$), the rectangle $ABCD$ in the figure. Second, by adjusting the quantity it sells, it can increase profits still further. This is because the advertising has shifted the firm's marginal revenue curve up. As usual, the imperfectly competitive firm sets marginal revenue equal to marginal cost, so it increases output from Q_1 to Q_2. The additional profits thus generated are measured by the area between the marginal revenue and marginal cost curves, between Q_1 and Q_2. Marginal cost remains the same, so the second source of extra profits is the shaded area EFG. The net increase in profits is the area $ABCD$ plus the area EFG minus the cost of advertising.

So far, in studying the effect of an increase in advertising on one firm's profits, we have assumed that other firms keep their level of advertising constant. The effect of advertising on both industry and firm profits is somewhat more problematical once the reactions of other firms in the industry are taken into account. To the extent that advertising diverts sales from one firm in an industry to another, advertising may, in equilibrium, have little effect on demand. For example, assume that Nike shoe ads divert customers from Reeboks to Nikes and vice versa for Reebok ads. Figure 19.5 shows the demand curve facing Reebok before advertising, then when only Reebok advertises, and finally when both companies advertise. The final demand curve is the same as the initial demand curve. Price and output are the same; profits are lower by the amount of the expenditures on advertising. We have here another example of a

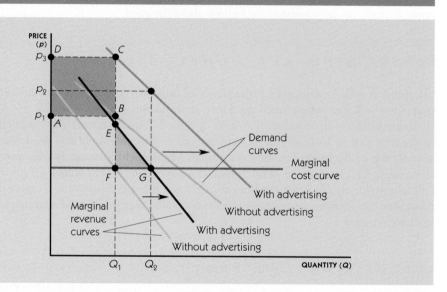

Figure 19.4 HOW ADVER-TISING CAN SHIFT THE DEMAND CURVE

Successful advertising shifts the demand curve facing a firm. When the imperfect competitor equates its new marginal revenue with its old marginal cost, it will be able to raise both its price and its output.

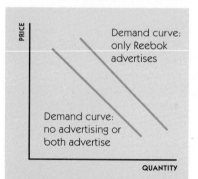

Figure 19.5 HOW ADVER-TISING CAN CANCEL OTHER ADVERTISING

If only one company advertises, the demand curve for its product may shift out. But if both companies advertise, the resulting demand curve may be the same as it would if neither advertised.

Prisoner's Dilemma. If the firms could cooperate and agree not to advertise, they would both be better off. But without such cooperation, it pays each to advertise, regardless of what the rival does. The government-mandated ban on cigarette advertising on radio and TV may have partially solved this Prisoner's Dilemma for the tobacco industry—in the name of health policy.

In practice, when all cigarette firms advertise, the ads do more than just cancel each other out; some people who might not otherwise have smoked are persuaded to do so, and some smokers are induced to smoke more than they otherwise would have. But the shift in the demand curve facing a particular firm when all companies advertise is still much smaller than it is when only the one firm advertises.

ADVERTISING AS A SIGNAL

A buyer often cannot tell the quality of a good before purchasing it. Most people cannot tell how long a television set will last or how good the food will be in a restaurant.

As we have seen, firms can deal with this uncertainty in several ways. One is to issue a guarantee promising that if the product proves to be unsatisfactory, it will be replaced or the price will be refunded. The fact that Chrysler is willing to guarantee its cars for five years or fifty thousand miles conveys considerable information; it suggests that the company has a high level of confidence in its cars. But even with a guarantee, buyers cannot know how much hassle they will have to go through to get a replacement or to get their money back, and there always seem to be exceptions in the fine print.

Another way that firms deal with the quality problem is to establish a reputation and then maintain it. For firms that are successful, price exceeds costs of production, and this provides them with an incentive to maintain their reputation.

In the simple model of perfect competition, a new orange juice company would announce that its product was ready, match or beat the price prevailing in the market, and sell its product. When Procter and Gamble entered the orange juice business in 1983, it competed by setting the price for its Citrus Hill juice a little lower than the price for established competitors like Tropicana and Minute Maid, and by blanketing the country with Citrus Hill coupons. But Procter and Gamble evidently felt that something more was needed to get its product started, so, according to *Business Week,* it set an advertising and promotion budget of $75 to $100 million. (By comparison, only $2.5 billion worth of orange juice was being sold in a year by all existing companies.) The venture paid off.

There are two lessons to be drawn from this and many similar episodes. First, by spending significant amounts of money on advertising, manufacturers demonstrate their belief that offering a lower price is not a sufficient way of competing. Second, manufacturers must believe that advertising helps to make people perceive their product as unique, even when, as in the case of orange juice, most consumers probably can barely distinguish the different brands. In a world of unique products and brand loyalty, companies are able to take advantage of such perceptions to earn higher profits.

Source: Business Week, October 31, 1983.

Advertising is another way for a firm to send a signal that it has a high-quality product. The fact that a firm is willing to spend a large amount on advertising may suggest to consumers that it has a great deal of confidence that once they try the good, they will like it. If the product is lousy—if a new brand of yogurt is indigestible—the firm will not gain any customers. Advertising will only pay if it actually attracts customers who, once they have tried the product, will become repeat purchasers. Of course, consumers do not have to go through this process of reasoning; they may simply have learned that there is a good chance that they will like a heavily advertised product.

SOME CONSEQUENCES OF IMPERFECT
INFORMATION

Adverse selection problems
    Thin or nonexistent markets
    Signaling
    Possibility that markets may not clear
Incentive problems
    Desirability of designing incentive schemes
    Increased importance of contracts and reputations
Search problems
    Price dispersion
    Imperfect competition

GOVERNMENT AND INFORMATION

When markets are not competitive, not only is the economy not likely to be efficient, information problems may result in market failures. The U.S. government has taken some interest in information problems, though the history of this interest is not as long and detailed as that of antitrust legislation. Governmental concern for ill-informed consumers has motivated a number of pieces of **consumer protection legislation**. For example, the Wheeler-Lea Act of 1938 made "deceptive" trade practices illegal and gave the Federal Trade Commission power to stop false and deceptive advertising. Truth-in-lending legislation requires lenders to disclose the true interest rate being charged; truth-in-packaging legislation makes it less likely that consumers will be misled by what is printed on the package; and the Securities and Exchange Commission, which regulates the sale of stocks and bonds, requires firms trying to sell these securities to disclose a considerable amount of information. Yet much of this legislation is of only limited effectiveness. One problem comes when consumers try to absorb and process the information. A cereal manufacturer may disclose not only what is required, but a host of other information, which may or may not be of importance. How is the consumer to know what to pay attention to? He simply cannot absorb everything.

Occasionally, as in the case of warnings about the dangers from smoking, government regulators, aware of these problems of information absorption, have required the disclosures to be of a specific form and size lettering to make them stand out. But that kind of intervention on a more massive scale would probably be, at the very least, extremely costly.

Another problem with outlawing deceptive advertising is that drawing a clear line between persuasion and deception is often difficult. Advertisers have developed a knack for walking along the edge of any line—a suggestive hint may do where an explicit claim might be called deceptive. Questions have been raised about the social usefulness of much of noninformative advertising, like the Marlboro cowboy. But as mentioned earlier, even noninformative advertising can convey a signal about quality, just because the firm is willing to spend money on it. And having congressmen or the courts draw a line between informative and noninformative advertising seems an impossible task.

REVIEW AND PRACTICE

SUMMARY

1. The model of perfect competition assumes that participants in the market have perfect information about the goods being bought and sold and their prices. But this is not the case in the real world, and economists have thus incorporated imperfect information into their models of the economy.

2. A problem of adverse selection may arise when consumers cannot judge the true quality of a product. As the price of the good falls, the quality mix changes adversely, and the quantity demanded at a lower price may actually be lower than at a higher price.

3. Producers of high-quality products may attempt to signal that their product is better than those of competitors, for instance by providing better guarantees.

4. When consumers judge quality by price, there may be some price that offers the best value. Firms will have no incentive to cut price below this "best value" price, even when, at this price, the amount they would be willing to supply exceeds demand. As a result, the market can settle in an equilibrium with an excess supply of goods.

5. When there is perfect information, private property and prices can provide correct incentives to all market participants. When information is imperfect, two methods of helping to provide correct incentives are contracts with contingency clauses, and reputations.

6. Advertising attempts to change consumers' buying behavior, either by providing relevant information about prices or characteristics, by persuasion, or both.

KEY TERMS

imperfect information
asymmetric
   information

thin or incomplete
   markets
contingency clauses

price dispersion
consumer protection
   legislation

REVIEW QUESTIONS

1. Why are markets for information not likely to work well?

2. Why would "lemons" not be a problem for consumers in a world of perfect information? Why do they lead to a backward-bending demand curve in a world of imperfect information?

3. Why is signaling unnecessary in a world of perfect information? What does it accomplish in a world of imperfect information?

4. Explain why, if consumers think that quality increases with price, there will be cases where firms will have no incentive to cut prices in an attempt to attract more business.

5. How do contingency clauses in contracts help provide appropriate incentives? What are some of the problems in writing contracts that provide for all the relevant contingencies?

6. What role does reputation have in maintaining incentives? What is required if firms are to have an incentive to maintain their reputations? How might the good reputation of existing firms serve as a barrier to the entry of new firms?

7. What are the benefits of searching for market information? What are the costs? How does the existence of price dispersion affect the benefits? Could price dispersion exist in a world of perfect information? How does the fact that search is costly affect the nature of competition in a market?

8. Describe how advertising might affect the demand curve facing a firm. How do these changes affect prices? profits?

9. "For most practical purposes, information problems can be solved by government requirements that information be disclosed to potential buyers and investors." Discuss.

PROBLEMS

1. The We Pick 'Em Company collects information about horse races, and sells a newsletter predicting the winners. Why might you possibly be predisposed to distrust the accuracy of the We Pick 'Em newsletter?

2. When you apply for a job, possible employers have imperfect information about your abilities. How might you try to signal that you would be a good employee?

3. Explain how the incentives of someone to look after a car she is renting may not suit the company that is renting the car. How might a contingent contract help to solve this problem? Is it likely to solve the problem completely?

4. L.L. Bean, a mail order company, has a long-standing policy that it will take back anything it has sold, at any time, for any reason. Why might it be worthwhile for a profit-maximizing firm to enact such a policy?

5. Would you expect to see greater price dispersion within a metropolitan area, or between several small towns that are fifty miles apart? Why?

6. How do costs of search help to explain the success of department stores?

CHAPTER 20

IMPERFECTIONS IN THE LABOR MARKET

P art Two emphasized the similarity between the labor market and markets for goods. Households demand goods and firms supply them, with the price system as intermediary. Likewise, firms demand labor and workers supply it, with the wage as intermediary. Firms hire labor up to the point where the value of the marginal product of labor is equal to the wage, just as they would buy coal up to the point where the value of the marginal product of coal is equal to the price of coal.

This chapter takes another look at the labor market. Just as we saw in the preceding five chapters some of the ways in which product markets differ from the way they are depicted in the basic competitive model, here we will also see some of the important ways in which the labor market differs. Like product markets, labor markets are characterized by imperfect competition. Unions are the most obvious manifestation of imperfect competition in the labor market, and we will take a look at their history as well as their impact on wages and employment—the prices and quantities of the labor market.

Information problems have an even more significant impact on the labor market than they do on product markets. This is partly because workers are not like lumps of coal. They have to be motivated to work hard; they are concerned with work conditions; they care about the steadiness of their employment and income; and they may be concerned with how their pay compares with others'. Firms are aware of the importance of these considerations, and design employment and compensation policies that take them into account.

SKILLED LABOR   UNSKILLED LABOR

KEY QUESTIONS

1. How do unions affect the wages of their workers? of workers in general? What limits the power of unions? Why have unions been declining in strength?

2. How do we explain the large differences in wages paid to different workers, even to workers that appear to have similar abilities? What role does discrimination play?

3. How do firms seek to motivate their workers, to ensure that they put out effort commensurate with their pay, and to select good workers? In what sense can the problem of providing workers incentives be viewed as a consequence of imperfect or limited information?

LABOR UNIONS

Labor unions are organizations of workers, formed to obtain better working conditions and higher wages for their members. The main weapon they have is the threat of a collective withdrawal of labor, commonly known as a **strike**.

A BRIEF HISTORY

Labor unions are important institutions in our economy, though they do not play quite the role in the United States that they do in many European countries. Unionization in the United States at first moved in fits and starts. In the late nineteenth and early twentieth centuries, a variety of craft unions were established, consisting of skilled workers such as carpenters, plumbers, and printers. In 1886, the American Federation of Labor (AFL) was formed. Led by Samuel Gompers, the AFL gathered together a number of craft unions to enhance the bargaining power of each.

The Rise of Unions Union power strengthened in the 1930s, with two events: the confederation of major industrial unions into the Congress of Industrial Organizations (CIO) and the passage of the Wagner Act in 1935, which provided legal status to unions. The Wagner Act set up a National Labor Relations Board, which established procedures for the certification of labor unions and for the prevention of unfair labor practices on the part of firms trying to prevent workers from unionizing. The CIO represented a major change in two respects. First, it embraced all workers, unskilled as well as skilled; and second, it represented all the workers in a company. A firm did not need to bargain separately with representatives of each of the different crafts. It did not have to put up with the squabbles among the craft unions about which jobs belonged to which craft, and what the relative pay of different crafts should be. (By contrast, in the United Kingdom, where craft unions have remained important, firms face the unpleasant situation of settling a dispute with one union, only to encounter a dispute and a threatened strike in another.)

At the same time, the industrial unions, by uniting all workers together, enhanced workers' bargaining strength. The leaders of these unions, such as Walter Reuther of the United Automobile Workers (UAW), attained national prominence, and the unions were able to obtain for their workers substantial wage increases and improvements in working conditions.

The Decline of Unions Prompted by concern that the balance had in fact swung too far in favor of unions, Congress passed the Taft-Hartley Act in 1947. This law addressed two issues. First, unions had claimed that when they negotiated a better contract or better working conditions, they were providing benefits to all workers at an establishment. Thus, they required all laborers at unionized companies to join the union, a requirement that established **union shops**. Critics of union shops thought that the right to work should not be limited to members of unions. The Taft-Hartley law left it to the individual states to decide whether to outlaw union shops, and many states subsequently passed **right-to-work laws**. The laws gave workers the right to hold a job without belonging to a union—or, to put it the way unions do, the right to receive union pay without paying union dues.

The second concern addressed by the Taft-Hartley Act was that strikes by national unions could have a devastating effect on the country. A shutdown of the railroads or the steel or coal industry could have ramifications far beyond the firms directly involved. The Taft-Hartley law gave the president the power to declare, when national welfare was at stake, an eighty-day cooling-off period, during which workers had to return to work.

Since the mid-1950s, union power has declined steadily in the United States. Figure 20.1 traces out the sharp increases of union membership in the 1930s, and again during World War II, when the government encouraged unionization in all military plants. But since then, unions have had only limited success in recruiting new members, so the union share of nonagricultural employment has been falling. It fell below 20 percent in 1984, where it remains today. In fact, not only has the union share been declining, the actual number of unionized workers has been falling. Today there are approximately 17 million union members, 1 million less than there were in 1960.

At the same time, there has been even more of a decline in unionization in the private sector. While in 1960 the percentage of union members working in the public sector was only 6 percent, today it is more than 35 percent. The decline in unionization is likely to continue, as suggested by the fact that workers of less than thirty-four years of age are much less likely to belong to unions than their older counterparts. What are the reasons for the recent and continuing decline?

One explanation is that, whether as a result of union pressure or technological progress, working conditions for workers have improved enormously. Workers see less need for unions.

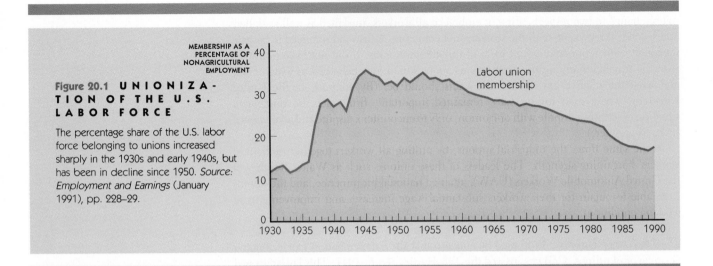

Figure 20.1 UNIONIZA-TION OF THE U.S. LABOR FORCE

The percentage share of the U.S. labor force belonging to unions increased sharply in the 1930s and early 1940s, but has been in decline since 1950. *Source: Employment and Earnings* (January 1991), pp. 228–29.

A second reason is related to the changing nature of the American economy. Unions have declined as the traditionally unionized sectors have weakened, and the service sector, in which unions have been weak, has grown. For instance, unions have been strong in the automobile and steel industries. These industries have declined, partially because the high union wages have made them less competitive with foreign firms.

Third, unions may be less effective in competitive markets. When competition is limited, there are monopoly (or imperfect competition) profits or rents. Unions may be successful in obtaining for their workers a share in those rents. But when markets are competitive, firms have no ability to charge more than the market price for their goods, and if they are to survive, they must try to keep their costs as low as possible. They simply cannot pay their workers more than the competitive wage.

For instance, in the late nineteenth and early twentieth centuries, high wages in shoe and textile mills in New England drove plants to the nonunionized South. High wages drive American firms to manufacture abroad. Unless unions somehow manage to ensure that their workers are more productive than average, it is only when these sources of competition are restricted that unions can succeed in keeping their wages above average for long, as they did in the steel and automobile industries. In this view, the increased competition to which American industry was subjected in the 1970s and 1980s, both from abroad and from the deregulation of trucking, oil, airlines, banking, telephone service, and so on, led to a decline in the potential effectiveness of unions in the private sector. The public sector still lacks competition, and so it is no surprise that it shows the major growth of unions over the past thirty years.

As a final explanation of the growth and decline of unions, it should be clear from this brief history that the ability of unions to organize and prosper depends heavily on the legal atmosphere. If encouraged by the laws, unions will prosper; if not, they will wither. Thus, the Wagner Act set the stage for the growth of unions in the 1930s, and the Taft-Hartley Act paved the way for their gradual decline in the post–World War II era.

ECONOMIC EFFECTS

The source of union power is collective action. When workers join together in a union, they no longer negotiate as isolated individuals. The threat of a strike (or a work slowdown) poses many more difficulties for an employer than does the threat of any single employee to quit and look for a better job.

In the perfectly competitive model of labor markets, workers are price takers, facing a given market wage. Unions, however, have some power to be price setters. It is possible to think of unions as a sort of monopoly. The autoworkers' union, in this view, is a monopoly that provides labor for automobile companies. Just as the corporate monopolists described in Chapter 15 generally make higher profits by charging more than the competitive price (and setting output lower than the competitive level), those who are inside a union are generally able to charge more than the competitive wage (with the result that there is less employment).

Figure 20.2 shows the demand curve for labor facing a union.[1] The union realizes that as it raises the price (the wage it is willing to accept), firms will employ fewer workers. Higher wages are obtained at the expense of lower levels of employment. When wages rise from the competitive level w_c to w_m, employment is reduced from L_c to L_m.

As a result of the union's monopolistic power, a worker at a given level of skill who works in a unionized establishment will be paid more than a comparable worker in a competitive industry. The firm would like to hire that lower-priced, nonunion worker, and the nonunionized worker could easily be induced to move, but the firm has a union contract that prevents it from doing so.

---

[1] Chapter 13 showed how the demand curve for labor is derived in competitive markets: firms hire labor up to the point where the wage equals the value of the marginal product of labor. The derivation of the demand curve for labor in monopolies and imperfectly competitive markets follows along similar lines. Firms hire labor up to the point where the marginal revenue, the extra revenue they obtain from selling the extra output they produce from hiring an extra unit of labor, is equal to the wage.

Figure 20.2 THE UNION AS A MONOPOLY SELLER OF LABOR

Unions can be viewed as sellers of labor, with market power. When they increase their wage demands, they reduce the demand for their members' labor services.

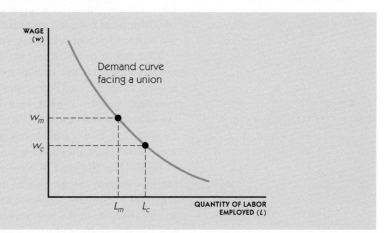

SHORT-RUN GAINS AT THE EXPENSE OF LONG-RUN LOSSES

Sometimes unions can even succeed in increasing both employment and wages. They present the employer with, in effect, two alternatives: either pay high wages *and* maintain the same employment level, or go out of business. If the employer already has sunk costs in machines and buildings, he may concede to the union demands. In effect, the union thus takes away some of the employer's monopoly profits and/or return to capital. In competitive markets, where there are no monopoly profits, the higher wages can only come out of employers' return to capital. But these employers will lose interest in investing in more capital. As capital wears out, the employer has less and less to lose from the union threat. As he refuses to invest more, jobs decrease. The union's short-run gains come at the expense of a long-run loss in jobs.

EFFECTS ON NONUNION WORKERS

Some of the gains of today's union members may be at the expense of future jobs, as we have seen. Some of the gains may also be at the expense of those in other sectors of the economy, for two reasons. First, the higher wages may well be passed on to consumers in the form of higher prices, particularly if product markets are not perfectly competitive. Second, the reduced employment of workers in the unionized sector increases the supply of labor in the nonunionized sector, driving down wages there.

This can be seen in Figure 20.3, where the economy is divided into two sectors, a union and a nonunion sector. The total demand for labor is shown in panel A, while panels B and C depict the demand curves for labor in the two sectors. Panel A also shows the labor supply curve. The competitive equilibrium in the labor market occurs at the intersection of the demand and supply curves, with employment L^* and wage w^*. Looking at panels B and C, we see that this entails an employment level of L_u in the unionized sector and L_n in the nonunion sector.

Now assume that the union succeeds in driving wages up in the unionized sector to w'_u. Employment in the union sector will decrease, to L'_u. But this means that there will be more workers seeking jobs in the nonunionized sector. The increased supply of labor in the nonunionized sector drives down the wage there to w'_n, until it absorbs the labor displaced from the unionized sector. Thus, some of the gains of union members are really at the expense of the nonunionized workers.

If we look at trends in average wages received by workers, there is little evidence that workers today, on the whole, receive more than they would have in the absence of unions. Over the past half century, wages have gone up and working conditions have improved, but this is what we would have expected from the normal workings of the law of supply and demand. Figure 20.4 shows demand and supply curves for labor. Because of technological change, the demand curve for labor shifts to the right; at each wage, firms are willing to hire more workers. There has also been a shift in the supply of labor. Over the last fifty to seventy-five years, the increase in the demand for labor has far exceeded the increase in the supply, so that employment has risen at the same time that wages have, depicted in the figure as the increase from L_0 to L_1 and w_0 to w_1. By contrast, in the past fifteen years, with the huge increase in the supply of labor and the slowdown in the increase in productivity, the shift in supply has been larger than the shift in demand, so real wages for unskilled workers have actually fallen. These changes in the real wages have primarily been determined by factors other than unions.

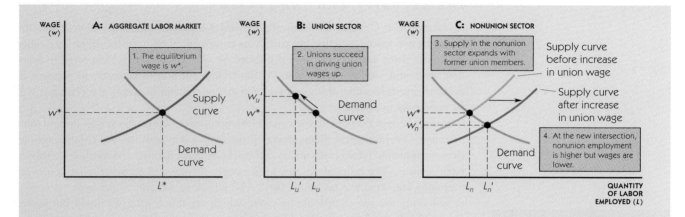

Figure 20.3 HOW HIGHER UNION WAGES DRIVE DOWN NONUNION WAGES

Panel A shows the aggregate labor market. Panel B depicts a demand curve for union labor. If a union acts to choose a point on the curve that will push up wages and hold down employment, it may move from employment L_u and wage w^* to employment L_u' and wage w_u'. Panel C shows demand and supply curves for nonunion labor. The reduction in union employment leads to an outward shift in the supply curve for nonunion labor. Employment in the nonunion sector rises from L_n to L_n', while wages fall from w^* to w_n'. Since the effects on employment and wages in the union and nonunion sectors are offsetting, the higher union wages may not greatly change the average wage or employment level in the economy; the gains to those still in unions come at the expense of those now in the nonunion sector.

Figure 20.4 WAGES RISE AS THE ECONOMY GROWS

A growing economy creates additional demand for labor, as well as additional supply. Equilibrium employment increases, shown here as the shift from L_0 to L_1. Whether wages increase or decrease depends on whether the supply or demand curve shifts more. Over the last fifty years, wages in the United States have risen along with employment.

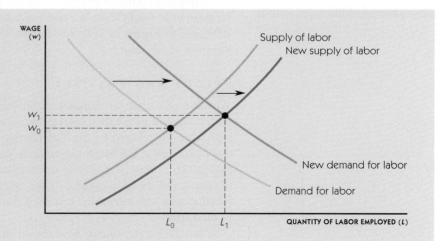

JOB SECURITY AND INNOVATION

As explained in Chapter 18, innovation involves a process of creative destruction; the economy as a whole benefits, but particular groups are likely to suffer. In an innovative economy, those workers who are dislocated by new inventions are expected to learn new skills and seek out new jobs. Without labor shifting in response to changes in demand (resulting either from new technologies or changes in tastes), the economy will be hopelessly inefficient.

Unions believe that one of their main functions is to increase the job security of their members. Technological changes may threaten that job security. As a result, unions have attempted to retard innovations that might decrease the demand for their members' labor services. The railroad unions, for instance, managed to require firemen on every train long after coal was no longer used. The plumbers' union has also been successful in restricting the use of new plastic pipes, which are much easier to install but would reduce the demand for plumbers' services.

Union opposition to innovation is understandable. Job transitions are desirable for economic efficiency, but they are costly and the costs are largely borne by the workers. Before the advent of unions and laws providing unemployment compensation, the human toll of these risks was considerable. Individuals could not buy insurance against these risks, but they could form unions, and union attempts to enhance job security were a response to this important problem. Today many countries are looking for ways of insulating workers against the risks of job transition without impeding the labor mobility that is so important for economic efficiency. For instance, the Swedish government has set up major programs to facilitate job transitions and job retraining.

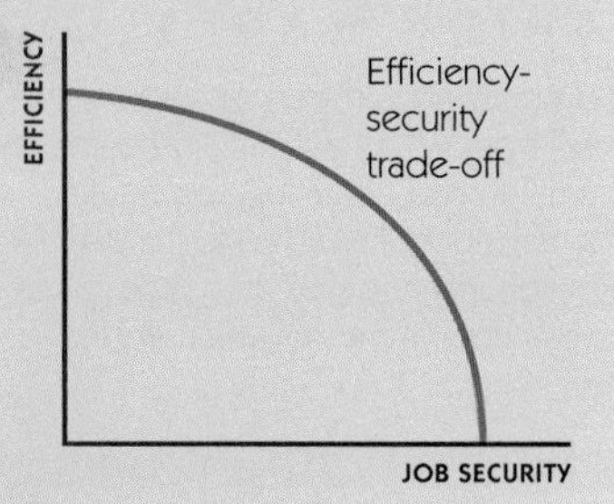

Innovations that lead to layoffs are only one source of insecurity facing workers. Employers have traditionally reserved the right to fire workers at will. Not surprisingly, workers have been concerned about unfair dismissal, and unions have bargained hard for procedures to ensure that workers are not fired capriciously. Of course, the fight for greater job security has not been without its economic cost. One of the important incentives that workers have for working hard is the threat of being fired. Reducing this threat reduces the motivation of workers. Some attribute a large part of the inefficiency of workers in the public sector to civil service procedures that make it particularly difficult for them to be fired. There is a trade-off between economic efficiency and job security, illustrated in Figure 20.5. In some areas, the economy may have gone too far in the direction of job security.

UNIONS AND POLITICS

We have seen that the fortunes of unions depend, to a large extent, on the legal environment in which they operate: they flourished under the Wagner Act, while they were adversely affected by the Taft-Hartley Act. Unions have also learned that what they cannot get at the bargaining table they may be able to obtain through the political process. Thus, they have actively campaigned for higher minimum wages. Unions are, of course, not always successful. Their attempt to preserve railroad cabooses (and the jobs that went with them) after modern technology made them unnecessary was rebuffed in most states.

At the same time, unions have shown in their political stances that they recognize the economic forces that determine both the strength of their bargaining positions and, more generally, the level of wages. Thus, they have been active supporters of policies

Figure 20.5 TRADE-OFF BETWEEN EFFICIENCY AND JOB SECURITY

Greater job security may lead people to work less hard, thus impairing economic efficiency.

of high employment, they have sought to restrict imports from abroad (believing that this will increase the demand for American products and therefore the demand for labor), and they have been proponents of restrictions on immigration (recognizing that increases in the supply of labor lead to reductions in wages).

Finally, unions have been strong advocates through the political process of safer working conditions. Today the Occupational Safety and Health Administration (OSHA) attempts to ensure that workers are not exposed to unnecessary hazards. The kinds of episodes such as occurred in the asbestos industry, where workers were exposed to life-threatening risks, probably could not occur today.

LIMITS ON UNION POWER

In the United States, no union has a monopoly on *all* workers. At most, a union has a monopoly on the workers currently working for a particular firm. Thus, the power of unions is partly attributable to the fact that a firm cannot easily replace its employees. When a union goes on strike, the firm may be able to hire some workers, but it is costly to bring in and train a whole new labor force. Indeed, most of the knowledge needed to train the new workers is in the hands of the union members. While one bushel of wheat may be very much like another, one worker is not very much like another. Workers outside the firm are not perfect substitutes for workers, particularly skilled ones, inside.

THE THREAT OF REPLACEMENT

In those industries in which skills are easily transferable across firms, or where a union has not been successful in enlisting the support of most of the skilled workers, a firm can replace striking workers, and union power will be limited. This happened in the airline industry in the early 1980s. Continental Airlines' pilots went on strike, and Continental found it easy to replace them because there were many pilots willing to work at wages far below the union wages. Similarly, TWA was faced with a strike of its flight attendants and found it easy to replace them.

In many cases, however, many of workers' skills are firm-specific. Workers would not be as productive at another firm. Just as, from the employers' perspective, workers outside the firm are not perfect substitutes for workers within, from the workers' perspective, one job is not a perfect substitute for another job. The fact that workers are not perfectly substitutable from the perspective of employers and likewise jobs are not perfectly substitutable from the perspective of employees means that there is often considerable value both to workers and firms in preserving ongoing employment relationships. The two parties are tied to each other in what is often referred to as a bargaining relationship. The bargaining strengths of the two sides are affected by the fact that a firm, at a cost, can obtain other employees, and employees, at a cost, can get other jobs. The total amount by which the two sides together are better off continuing their relationship than breaking it off is sometimes referred to as the "bargaining surplus." A large part of the negotiations between unions and management are about how to split this surplus.

THE THREAT OF UNEMPLOYMENT

Unions have gradually come to understand that in the long run, higher wages—other things being equal—mean lower levels of employment. When job opportunities in

Unions have been blamed for the declining low rates of productivity growth in the United States, even though union membership has been low and declining for decades. But unions in other countries offer a different perspective.

In the late 1980s, only 17 percent of U.S. workers belonged to unions. This number was comparable to the 16 percent of workers who belonged to unions in Spain, 12 percent in France, 19 percent in Turkey, and 25 percent in the Netherlands.

But in most developed countries, a somewhat higher percentage of workers belonged to unions. In Japan, the number was 27 percent; in Germany, 34 percent; in Canada, 35 percent. And in many other nations, the percentage was more than double the U.S. level: 40 percent in Italy, for example, and 42 percent in the United Kingdom and Australia. In Scandinavian countries, union membership was especially high: 55 percent in Norway, 71 percent in Finland, 73 percent in Denmark, and an astonishing 85 percent in Sweden.

Those who blame American unions for the decline of U.S. economic power must explain how nations like Japan and Germany have increased their rates of productivity with much higher rates of unionization. Moreover, although U.S. union membership has sunk steadily over the past two decades, unions around the world *gained* substantial numbers of members in the 1970s, before losing members in the 1980s. Those who blame the decline in unionization on the growth of the service sector or greater global competition must explain why those factors have led to lower union membership in the United States but much higher levels in other countries.

One key point to recognize is that unions are not the same everywhere. For example, in some nations, like Finland and Portugal, unions negotiate with employers and the government on overall national policy. in Germany, union negotiations tend to happen one industry at a time. By contrast, U.S. and Japanese unions tend to negotiate one *com-*

pany at a time. Some unions are organized along craft lines (as in the old American Federation of Labor), others are organized along industrial lines (automobile workers or coal workers); some unions are limited to one company (as in Japan); and some embrace many crafts and companies (as in Sweden). And a nation's legal environment can either encourage workers to form unions or make it easier for management to fight unions off. Margaret Thatcher, as prime minister of Britain in the 1970s, took as one of her main goals the redressing of what she saw as an imbalance of power in favor of unions.

This international perspective suggests that asking whether unions are generically "good" or "bad" is far too simplistic. Instead, the question should be whether unions, in some form, have a potentially useful role to play in the U.S. economy. Richard Freeman, of Harvard University, thinks so. He argues: "Although Scandinavian levels of unionization seem to me to be infeasible and undesirable in a large, diverse country like the United States . . . research supports the view that greater unionization is needed to give workers alternatives to the market or to governmental intervention in workplace arrangements." Freeman suggests that in the future, American unions will have to focus less attention on demanding higher wages and benefits and more attention on improving working conditions and helping to make investment decisions.

Just as American firms have been looking abroad to find alternative models for what makes success, unions in other countries may provide some alternative models for how American unions might help increase the country's productivity.

Sources: International Labour Office, *World Labour Report* (1992). Richard Freeman, "Is Declining Unionization of the U.S. Good, Bad, or Irrelevant?" in Lawrence Mishel and Paula Voos, eds., *Unions and Economic Competitiveness* (Armonk, N.Y.: Sharpe, 1992), pp. 143–72.

general are weak, concern about the employment consequences of union contracts increases. This was evident in the early 1980s, as a deep recession threatened a number of union jobs. It was especially evident in the automobile industry. Compounding the effects of the recession was the threat of Japanese imports; the steep rise in the price of oil in the 1970s had shifted demand away from large American automobiles to the smaller Japanese cars.

In the round of negotiations that began in 1981, Ford Motor Company was the first auto company to settle with the United Automobile Workers, in February 1982. In the new thirty-month contract, the UAW agreed to give up annual wage increases for two years, to defer what had been automatic increases in wages in response to increases in the cost of living, and to eliminate a number of paid personal holidays. The contract also provided for new employees to be paid at only 85 percent of the normal rate, thus creating a two-tier wage system. For its part, Ford offered a moratorium on closing any plants, a guarantee that extra profits arising during the term of the contract would be shared with workers, increased worker participation in decision making, and greater job security for workers. General Motors made a similar deal a few months later, and Chrysler was able to negotiate an even better deal because of its even worse financial condition. The dollar value of the total concessions from the union was estimated at about $3 billion for the contract period. Similar wage cuts occurred in the airline and steel industries, among others.

The deal between Ford and the UAW set the pattern for auto labor contracts in the 1980s: unions would make wage concessions in return for job security. In 1984, when the contracts came up for negotiation again, GM and the UAW agreed on a deal that gave the workers very little in the way of wage increases, but instituted some of the most comprehensive job protections ever negotiated. For example, GM agreed not to lay off for the next six years any worker with at least one year's seniority who was displaced by a new technology. Instead, such workers would stay on full salary while they were retrained and relocated.

In the long run, in the United States, the reduced employment in the unionized sector resulting from higher wages, when there is little overall unemployment, simply shifts labor into the nonunionized sector. Several European countries have national unions, which embrace a much larger fraction of the working force. If these unions are successful in attaining wages that are above the market-clearing level, it may be difficult, particularly for skilled workers, to obtain employment elsewhere. In these countries, unions are thought to contribute significantly to the overall unemployment level.

UNIONS AND IMPERFECT COMPETITION IN THE LABOR MARKET

Economic effects:

> Higher wages for union members, with fewer union jobs and lower wages for nonunion members

> Improved job security, sometimes at the expense of innovation and economic efficiency

> Minimum wages, restrictions on imports, improved working conditions, other gains achieved through the political process

Determinants of union power:

> Political and legal environment

> Economic environment: threat of replacement and unemployment

IMPERFECT INFORMATION AND THE LABOR MARKET

There are other ways besides the presence of unions in which the labor market differs from the basic competitive model. These can be loosely considered examples of imperfect information, and three of them are taken up in the next three sections: wage differentials, the motivation of workers, and the selection of workers.

WAGE DIFFERENTIALS

The basic competitive model suggests that if the goods being sold are the same, prices will also be the same. Wages are the price in the labor market; but differences in wages are conspicuous and widespread. Even in the absence of unions, similar types of workers performing similar types of jobs are sometimes paid quite different wages. For example, some secretaries are paid twice as much as others. How can economists explain differences like these? They begin by pointing to **compensating wage differentials**.

Understanding compensating wage differentials begins with the observation that although different jobs may have the same title, they can be quite different. Some jobs are less pleasant, require more overtime, and are in a less convenient location. Chapter 11 defined the nonpecuniary attributes of a job as all of its characteristics other than pay. They include the degree of autonomy provided the worker (that is, the closeness with which her actions are supervised) and the risk she must bear, whether in a physical sense or from the variability in income. Economists expect wages to adjust to reflect the attractiveness or unattractiveness of these nonpecuniary characteristics. Compensating wage differentials arise because firms have to compensate their workers for the negative aspects of a job.

Other differences are accounted for by differences in the productivity of workers; these are referred to as **productivity wage differentials**. Some workers are simply much more productive than others, even with the same experience and education. For example, some secretaries can type faster and make fewer mistakes than others.

The compensating and productivity wage differentials fall within the realm of basic competitive market analysis. But other wage differentials do not. Some are due to imperfect information. It takes time to search out different job opportunities. Just as one store may sell the same object for a higher price than another store, one firm may hire labor for a lower wage than another firm. The worker who accepts a lower-paying job simply because he did not know about the higher-paying one down the street faces an **information-based differential**.

IMPERFECT LABOR MOBILITY

If all workers were really identical or if employers could easily tell how productive each worker is, then it is unlikely that information-based wage differentials would persist for long. In a well-functioning market, firms would look for underpaid workers at other firms and try to recruit them. The process would continue until workers of a given productivity working in similar jobs were all paid the same amount.

But workers and jobs differ considerably. If an employer considers hiring a worker who currently receives low pay, that employer cannot know whether the worker is low-paid because she is unproductive and deserves to be low-paid, or because she is a highly productive worker who has not yet had a chance to prove herself.

Suppose an employer interviews a candidate who *appears* to be underpaid—that is, the worker is being paid less than his qualifications would seem to warrant. The employer might make him an offer above his current wage but below the wage of others with similar qualifications; the difference would enhance profits. But if an employer thought about this decision for a minute, she would also realize that the worker's current employer, who is in an advantageous position for judging true productivity, will respond to the higher wage offer. If this worker's productivity warrants it, the current employer will match the new offer; the new employer will be unsuccessful in her bid. If the worker's productivity does not warrant it, the current employer will not match the new job offer. Thus, the new employer will be successful in recruiting workers through competitive bidding only by paying too much. This scenario is an example of the adverse selection problem described in Chapter 19.

Recognizing the adverse selection problem makes it unattractive to attempt to recruit workers by bidding them away from others, except in one important instance: when the worker is better matched for working for the new employer. That is, if the worker's productivity will be higher working in the new job, it is worth paying more for that worker. Matching workers with the appropriate employers can clearly affect economic efficiency.

It is thus not surprising that with costly and imperfect information and with individuals of diverse abilities, large wage differentials for individuals of similar abilities can persist, and labor mobility can be impaired. In fact, in most hiring decisions, information is even more imperfect and incomplete than in the simple example given above. For instance, a prospective employer does not usually know the exact wage a potential employee is currently being paid.

DISCRIMINATION

Employers may try to exploit the fact that it is difficult for workers, particularly older workers, to switch jobs by offering lower wages. As a result, some workers may get paid lower wages than they would have received in perfectly competitive markets with perfect information. One objective of unions is to redress this seeming imbalance.

The attempt of employers to take advantage of the weaker market positions of the aged is referred to as age discrimination. It is only one of several forms of discrimination that occur in the labor market. Chapter 11 noted that women get paid less than men, and that blacks get paid less than whites. Some of the wage differences arise because of lower levels of job experience or education, but even among blacks and women of comparable education and job experience, wages are lower. In recent years, wage differentials for women, blacks, and Hispanics of comparable education, performing the same job, have been decreasing. Attention has shifted to **job discrimination**—the fact that these disadvantaged groups have less access to the better-paying jobs.

If qualified applicants are being systematically kept out of the labor market pool, then we have a departure from the basic competitive model, which assumes that all suppliers will be permitted to join the competition. Women, it is argued, are relegated to "pink collar" jobs—nursing, teaching, and other service sector jobs, which have traditionally been low paying. Figure 20.6 compares the fraction of jobs held by women, blacks, and Hispanics (as opposed to white males) in four occupations: managers, professionals, blue collar workers (operators, fabricators, and laborers), and service workers. Women, blacks, and Hispanics are underrepresented in managerial jobs and overrepresented in service jobs. By contrast, blacks and Hispanics are greatly overrepresented in blue collar jobs, while they are underrepresented in professions. There are huge earning differences among these occupations; on average, service workers receive only 45 percent of what managers receive. While professionals receive almost the same as managers, blue-collar workers receive only 61 percent of what managers get.

Prejudice, Statistical Discrimination, and the Old Boy Network Forty years ago, there was open and outright discrimination. Some employers simply refused to hire

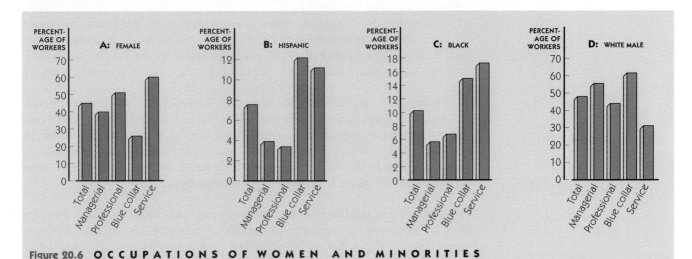

Figure 20.6 OCCUPATIONS OF WOMEN AND MINORITIES

Panel A shows women to be overrepresented in service occupations and underrepresented in blue collar jobs. Panels B and C show that Hispanics and blacks are overrepresented in blue collar jobs and service occupations, and underrepresented in managerial and professional positions. *Source: Employment and Earnings* (January 1991), pp. 185–87.

blacks. Today much of the discrimination that occurs is more subtle. Firms seek to hire the best workers they can for each job at the lowest cost possible, operating with imperfect information. We have seen how, in making predictions about future performance, employers use whatever information they have available. On average, employers may have found that those receiving a degree from a well-established school are more productive than those receiving a degree from a less-established college. Of those blacks and Hispanics who have managed to get a college education, more may have gone to the less-established schools. Screening the applicant pool to pick those with degrees from well-established colleges effectively screens out many blacks and Hispanics. This more subtle form of discrimination is called **statistical discrimination**.

Some discrimination is neither of the old-fashioned prejudice nor of the statistical variety. Employers may simply feel more comfortable dealing with people with whom they have dealt in the past. In a world in which there is so much uncertainty about who is a good worker, and in which a bad worker can do enormous damage, top management may rely on certain trusted employees for recommendations; and such judgments are inevitably affected by friendships and other ties. Many claim that if discrimination is to be eliminated, this form of discrimination, based on "old boy networks," has to be broken.

There are market forces that tend to limit the extent of discrimination. If a woman is paid less than a man of comparable productivity, it pays a firm to hire the woman. Not to hire her costs the firm profits. To put it another way, the firm pays a price for discriminating. If there are enough firms that put profits above prejudice, then the wages of women will be bid up close to the level of men of comparable productivity.

The only situation in which the firms' profits would not be lowered is if the firms' customers or workers were prejudiced, so that a firm would lose customers, for example, if it hired workers from a particular ethnic group at lower wages. But then the customers pay a price for the discrimination: the cost of producing the goods or services without those workers is higher than it otherwise would be. And again, if there are enough firms with customers who are not willing to pay that price, then wage differentials could not persist.

This argument, originally formulated by Gary Becker of the University of Chicago, does not say that statistical discrimination will not persist. It is rational for firms to pay different wages to workers whose expected productivity, based on whatever evidence the firm can collect, differs. Yet in many cases, wage differentials seem greater than can be accounted for by statistical discrimination. Evidently, in these cases, market forces are not sufficiently strong to eliminate the discrimination.

Public Policy Toward Discrimination   Beginning in the 1960s, the government has taken an increasingly active stance in combatting discrimination. In 1964, Congress passed the Civil Rights Act, which prohibited employment discrimination and set up the Equal Employment Opportunity Commission to prosecute cases of discrimination. The reach of these laws was extended in 1975 when the government banned age discrimination.

Beyond this, the government has required its contractors to undertake **affirmative action**. They must actively seek out minorities and women for jobs, and actively seek to promote them to better-paying positions. In order to be effective, affirmative action has often taken the form of quotas that specify that a certain number or fraction of positions be reserved for minorities or women. Quotas have been controversial. Critics claim that they are discriminatory—they imply that a minority individual would be chosen over a more qualified white male. One of the objectives of antidiscrimination laws was to discourage thinking in racial or gender terms. Accordingly, the Reagan and Bush administrations generally took a strong stance against quotas or policies that had quotalike effects. Proponents of quotas claim that without them discrimination will never be broken, because without them the concept of affirmative action has no teeth and cannot succeed in overcoming the subtler forms of discrimination pervasive in our economy.

EXPLANATIONS OF WAGE DIFFERENTIALS

Unions: Unions may succeed in obtaining higher wages for their workers.

Compensating differentials: Wage differences may correspond to differences in the nature of the job.

Productivity differentials: Wage differences may correspond to differences in the productivity between workers.

Information-based differentials: Wage differences may reflect the fact that workers do not have perfect information about the opportunities available in the market.

Imperfect labor mobility: Differentials will not be eliminated by individuals moving between jobs.

Discrimination: Wage differentials can sometimes be traced to nothing more than racial or gender differences. Discrimination once took the outright form of employers refusing to hire certain groups; today it is more subtle.

MOTIVATING WORKERS

The discussion to this point has treated workers as if they were machines. Workers have a price—the wage—analogous to the price of machines. But even to the most profit-hungry and coldhearted employer, people are different from machines; they bring adaptability and a multitude of skills and experiences to a job. Most machines can only do one task, and even robots can only do what they are programmed to do. However, machines have one advantage over humans: except when they break down, they do what they are told to do. To exercise their abilities to the fullest, workers have to be motivated to work hard and to exercise good judgment about when to show initiative and when to follow directions.

In a technical sense, this can be viewed as an information problem. In the basic competitive model of Part Two, workers were paid to perform particular tasks. The employer knew perfectly whether the worker performed the agreed-upon task in the agreed-upon manner. If the worker failed to do so, he did not get paid. The pay was the only form of motivation required. But in reality, workers frequently have considerable discretion. Employers have limited information about what a worker is doing at each moment. Firms see the problem of motivating workers as one of their central tasks.

Employers use two devices for motivating workers: the carrot and the stick. For instance, they may reward workers for performing well by making pay and promotion depend on performance, and they may punish workers for shirking by firing them. Sometimes a worker is given considerable discretion and autonomy—all the firm cares about is his output—and sometimes he is monitored quite closely. The mix of carrots and sticks, autonomy and direct supervision, varies from job to job and industry to industry. It depends partly on how easy it is to supervise workers directly and how easy it is to compensate workers on the basis of performance.

PIECE RATES AND INCENTIVES

When workers can be paid for exactly what they produce, with their pay increasing for higher productivity and falling for lower productivity, they will have appropriate incentives to work hard. The system of payment in which a worker is paid for each item produced or each task performed is called a **piece-rate system**. But relatively few Americans are paid largely, let alone exclusively, on a piece-rate system. Typically, even workers within a piece-rate system get a base pay *plus* additional pay, which increases the more they produce.

Why don't more employers enact a piece-rate system, if it would do so much to improve incentives? One major reason is that relying completely on piece rates would make workers bear a considerable amount of risk. Most conspicuously, if a worker is sick for a week, she will have no income that week. The worker may also have a bad week because of bad luck; for example, salesmen, who are often paid commissions on the basis of productivity—a form of piece rate—may simply find the demand for their wares lacking.

Workers, like firms, have bills to pay, but they are likely to find it much more difficult than firms to raise money to carry them over hard times. A firm, by providing a certain amount of guaranteed pay, gives the worker a steady income and reduces the risk she must bear. However, to provide this security, employers must reduce or eliminate piece-rate compensation. With lower piece-rate compensation, the worker has less incentive to work hard. There is thus a trade-off between risk and incentives. For a worker to be willing to work for a firm that pays entirely on a piece-rate system, she must expect to receive a higher total income as compensation for bearing all the risk.

Thus, compensation schemes must find some balance between offering some security and offering incentives linked to worker performance. A firm can offer a contract in which there is a very limited guarantee; the worker bears a lot of risk, but at the same time has strong incentives. Alternatively, the firm can offer a contract with a large guarantee and a low piece rate (a salesman, for example, could receive a very low commission on each sale). The worker then has a great deal of security and little risk, but also little incentive to work hard. In many jobs, employers or managers achieve a balance between risk and incentives by offering both a guaranteed minimum compensation (including fringe benefits) and a series of bonuses that depend on performance.

A second reason more employers do not use piece-rate systems is that they are unable to measure the quantity and quality of workers' output with any exactness. For workers on an assembly line, the quantity produced may be easily measured, but quality cannot. If the workers' pay just depends on the number of items produced, the worker has an incentive to emphasize quantity over quality. The result may not be particularly profitable for the firm.

In any case, most workers are engaged in a variety of tasks, only some of which can easily be defined and rewarded by means of a piece-rate system. For example, although employers would like experienced workers to train new workers, employees who are paid on a piece-rate system have little incentive to do this, or to help their co-workers in other ways. Similarly, when salesmen are paid on the basis of commissions, they have little incentive to provide information and service to potential customers whom they perceive as not likely to be immediate buyers. Even if providing information enhances the likelihood that a customer will return to the store to buy the good, there is a fair chance that some other salesperson will get the commission. Providing good service results in benefits that accrue to others; and since the salesman does not receive all the benefits, there is an undersupply of the activities that generate these positive externalities. To see this effect at work, visit a car dealer's showroom, make it clear that you are not going to buy a car immediately, and try to get information anyway.

MONITORING WORKERS

Many of the problems in setting up an appropriate system of incentives involve difficulties in monitoring worker performance. If day-to-day outputs can be monitored easily, then it is easier to set up a piece-rate system than it is in situations where monitoring is more costly.

When workers are not paid on a piece rate, one must monitor the more general activities of the workers, to attempt to ascertain how hard they are working. For some jobs, the cost of monitoring actions is very high. It is difficult to supervise workers in the field or salesmen calling on potential customers. The development of the factory system and the assembly line enabled firms to monitor more easily how hard their employees were working. To keep up with the assembly line, each worker had to perform a certain number of tasks per hour.

HIGH WAGES

In the simple model of perfect competition, wages are very closely linked to marginal productivity. Each worker gets paid on the basis of the tasks he actually performs. As in a piece-rate system, workers are rewarded for what they do. Wage differentials result from differences in productivity and in the attractiveness of the job. However, workers have no loyalty to the firm, because they can go to many other employers and receive the same pay for doing the same job.

One way for firms to provide incentives for loyalty and high-quality work and to reduce labor turnover is to pay workers more than they could get in alternative jobs. The theory that paying higher wages leads to a more productive labor force is called the **efficiency wage theory**. Note that not only does higher productivity result in higher wages, higher wages result in higher productivity. While wages increase with productivity, you cannot tell what is causing what.

If a worker receives a wage higher than he would be likely to receive elsewhere, then the cost of being fired is indeed great. One reason for employers to pay high wages is to raise the cost of being fired. The carrot of high compensation is thus the counterpart to the stick of being fired. The higher the wage, the greater the punishment from being fired.

Workers know, of course, that the managers cannot constantly monitor them. They balance the gain from shirking—the reduced effort on the job—with the cost, the chance of being caught and fired. If a worker thought there was little chance of being caught, he might more frequently slack off—unless the punishment for being caught was commensurately greater. Accordingly, in jobs where it is very costly to monitor workers on a day-to-day basis, or where the damage a worker can do is very great (where, for instance, the worker by punching the wrong button can destroy a machine), employers frequently pay high wages. The higher wages increase the incentive to do the job well.

These "wages of trust" may explain why wages in more capital-intensive industries (that require massive investments) appear higher for workers with otherwise comparable skills than do wages in industries using less capital, and why workers who are entrusted with the care of much cash (which they could abscond with) often are paid higher wages than are other workers of comparable skills. It is not so much that they receive high wages because they are trustworthy, but that they become more trustworthy because they receive high wages, and the threat of losing those high wages encourages moral behavior.

OTHER COMPENSATION INCENTIVES

Besides paying piece rates, bonuses, and higher-than-market wages, firms find other ways to induce workers to work hard. Among the most important incentives are enhanced promotion possibilities for those who perform well, with pay rising with promotions, and contests among workers. Contests are particularly useful when it is hard to determine the difficulty of the task a worker is performing. For example, consider the problem of

CLOSE-UP: FRINGE BENEFITS

The monetary pay a worker receives is often only a portion of the total compensation received. In 1990, for example, the average wage (or salary) received by a private industry worker in the United States was $10.84 per hour. However, the total compensation received was $14.96 per hour, a full 38 percent higher.

The reasons for the difference are sometimes referred to as "fringe benefits," although they are anything but unimportant. U.S. employers had to pay an average of $1.03 per hour to each employee for paid leave, including vacation time, paid holidays, and absence for illness. They set aside $.37 per hour for special bonuses and incentives. Employers also paid $.92 per hour for insurance, mainly health insurance, and $.45 an hour for company pensions. And employers set aside $1.35 per hour per employee for government-required programs like Social Security and unemployment insurance. All of these payments clearly have value to workers, but they do not show up in the typical week's take-home pay.

But fringe benefits have an impact that goes be-yond the bottom line; they complicate the straight-forward model of the labor market presented earlier in this book. In that model, workers try to seek out the firm that will give them the highest pay, while employers try to seek out those who will work for the lowest pay. But for employees, especially those with children, the health or dental insurance may be important enough that they are willing to accept less in salary in exchange for good insurance coverage. Other workers may value relatively lucrative retirement benefits, or incentive pay. The existence of fringe benefits complicates the problems workers face in deciding between jobs, since they must look beyond take-home pay and take all forms of compensation into account.

Why do employers offer fringe benefits, rather than simply paying a straight salary to workers? One main reason involves the tax code; if employees are paid income and then purchase health insurance on their own, they must pay income tax on the money, but if the company buys the insurance for them, the fringe benefit is not counted as income. In addition, many employers use fringe ben-

efits to offer an incentive for employees to stay with the company. For example, companies often increase the amount of vacation an employee receives the longer the worker is with the firm. Others require that the employee remain with the company for a period of several years before becoming eligible for the company pension plan. The fact that employers offer such benefits shows that they are not eager to lose their long-term employees, and would rather offer some added benefits than go through the cost and trouble of hiring and training new workers. But why—other than for tax reasons—they should rely so heavily on rewarding these workers through better fringe benefits rather than through cash bonuses remains unclear.

Source: U.S. Bureau of Labor Statistics, *News, Employer Costs for Employee Compensation* (June 1990).

a firm trying to figure out how much to pay its sales force when it is promoting a new product. If a salesperson is successful, does that represent good salesmanship, or is the new product able to "sell itself"? All sales representatives are in roughly the same position: the representative who sells the most gets a bonus—wins the contest.

At the top end of the corporate hierarchy, the very high pay received by the top executives of America's largest firms, often running into the millions of dollars, has been interpreted by some economists as the payoffs of contests. Whether contests can actually explain the high pay, whether the high pay really reflects the large contributions of these managers, whether it reflects wages of trust, or whether it stems from the fact that managers have considerable control over firms and can divert a considerable amount (though but a small fraction) of a firm's resources to their own betterment in the form of higher compensation are questions about which economists continue to argue.

In recent years, firms have explored the consequences of alternative ways of encouraging worker motivation and hence worker productivity. In some cases, employees may work more effectively as part of a team. When pay depends on team performance, members of a team have an incentive to monitor one another. They may rotate jobs, increasing the variety of tasks performed by any individual and making the work more interesting. The automaker Volvo believes that such team arrangements have increased the productivity of its own work force.

Some firms have encouraged worker participation in decision making, hoping thereby to increase employees' commitment to their jobs and reduce some of the antagonism that is sometimes felt between workers and management. Such participation may help both sides see that there is more to be gained by cooperation than by conflict. For instance, new ways of producing goods can make both the firm and workers better off; if the company sells more goods, all share in the benefits.

At least in the long run, wages and labor costs respond to reflect the attitudes of workers: if workers find that a certain firm provides an attractive workplace, the wages it must pay to recruit people may be lower than other firms' wages, and the people that it does recruit will work harder and stay longer. Firms thus have an incentive to pay attention to what workers like. If workers as a whole become concerned about having more autonomy, more say in decision making, or any other attribute of the workplace, it will pay firms to respond to these concerns.

WAYS OF MOTIVATING WORKERS

Piece rates, or pay based on measured output.

Efficiency wages, or higher wages to workers who work harder. These introduce an extra cost to those dismissed for unsatisfactory performance.

Relative performance: promotions, contests.

Team rewards, pay based on team performance.

SELECTING WORKERS

Besides motivating workers, a second major problem all firms face in real labor markets is selecting workers. In the idealized model of Part Two, we could divide up workers into various categories—workers without skills and workers with various specific skills. An employer knew precisely into which category each worker fit. Her only decision was how many workers of each skill category to hire.

In practice, firms spend a great deal of time and energy recruiting employees for a work force that is well matched to the needs of the firm. Firms try to predict how workers will perform under various situations. But no matter how much information they gather, they are still only making a guess. They look for clues that enable them to make better predictions. If some firm finds that those who have majored in English at a small liberal arts college do well, they will seek out similar graduates. Even if workers have a good idea about their own productivity, firms do not rely heavily on those statements. They cannot expect someone who is lazy or incompetent to say so on a job application.

In Chapters 11 and 19, we saw how graduating from college can be taken as a signal of higher ability. We learned about the credentials competition, in which individuals seek more and more credentials to prove they are "better" than others. The irony of the credentials competition is that often the competitors strive as hard as they do just to stay even. Jobs that three decades ago could have been taken by high school graduates are today reserved for college graduates. In some cases, the job has changed, so that more skills are required. But in other cases, it is the degree that is required. If you want to be a policeman and feel that a college education is unnecessary for the job and wish you did not have to complete your degree, you can blame the credentials competition. The police department wants the brightest individuals they can get, and in today's world, a college does a first pass at the sorting for them. The credentials competition has upped the ante.

There are many other instances of this kind of phenomena. In a world with perfect information, there might be no rational reason why young lawyers typically work sixty to ninety hours a week. It is not that they enjoy their work that much, nor that their hourly pay is so high that they set their leisure-consumption trade-off at this grinding level. Later in life, when their hourly rate increases, most of them will work much less. It is not even that they are learning that much during those extra hours—it is hard to imagine that their skills increase enough in the eighty-fifth to ninetieth hours each week to justify keeping them away from their other interests.

What are they trying to prove? They are trying to prove to their employers that they are extremely able individuals in love with and dedicated to their profession. In an interview, all workers would claim the same for themselves. But those who are really able and in love with their work find it *less* onerous to work that eighty-fifth or ninetieth hour a week. By working long enough hours, they can distinguish themselves from the others. Some argue that this "information" role of long hours and hard work is an important part of the explanation of the rat race in which many young professionals find themselves.

There are other characteristics besides willingness to work hard and long hours and intelligence that firms care about. Since training costs are high, a firm may want to know that workers are likely to stay with the firm a long time. Certain groups in the population, say teenage boys, may have a reputation for high turnover, and though any individual may think it unfair to be judged by these demographic characteristics, the employer simply must use whatever information she can get hold of. Again, while she cannot rely on the applicant's statement (of course the applicant is going to say that he plans to devote the remainder of his life to the firm, if he thinks that will get him the job), the employer can attempt to make the worker take an action that will reveal something about his true intentions. She might give the worker a choice between two contracts. In one, the salary is initially quite low, but if the worker sticks with the firm for five years, the salary becomes quite high; the other salary structure begins at a higher rate but does not increase as much. The worker who expects to stay will choose the first contract, the worker who expects to leave within five years will choose the second. This is sometimes called a **self-selection device**, a mechanism by which individuals, by the choices they make, reveal something about themselves. Having revealed this information, the firm can then assign the individual who plans to stay for a long time to a job where training costs are larger.

REVIEW AND PRACTICE

SUMMARY

1. The proportion of U.S. workers in unions has declined since the 1950s. Possible reasons include laws that have improved working conditions in general; the decline of manufacturing industries, where unions have traditionally been strong, relative to service industries; foreign competition; a more anti-union atmosphere in the U.S. legal structure.

2. Overall, there is little evidence that workers today receive higher pay than they would have in the absence of unions, though union workers may gain some at the expense of nonunion workers.

3. Union power is limited by the ability of companies to bring in new, nonunion workers and by the threat of unemployment to union workers.

4. Explanations for wage differentials include compensating differentials (differences in the nature of jobs), productivity differentials (differences in productivity between workers), imperfect information (workers do not know all the job opportunities that are available), and discrimination.

5. Employers try to motivate workers and induce high levels of effort through a combination of direct supervision, incentives for doing well, and penalties for doing badly. They pay wages higher than workers could get elsewhere (efficiency wages), give promotions and bonuses, base pay on relative performance (contests), and grant team rewards.

6. Firms face a problem of selecting workers, a problem of imperfect information. Workers attempt to signal that they have qualities valuable to the employer, and the employer tries to discern when those signals are accurate.

KEY TERMS

union shops
right-to-work laws

compensating wage
differentials

piece-rate system
efficiency wage theory

REVIEW QUESTIONS

1. Has the power of unions in the U.S. economy been shrinking or growing in the last few decades? Why? In what sector has union growth been largest? Why might this be so?

2. What effect will successful unions have on the level of wages paid by unionized companies? on the capital investment for those companies? What effect will they have on wages paid by nonunionized companies?

3. How might greater job security for union workers possibly lead them to become less efficient?

4. Does it make sense for a union to resist the introduction of an innovation in the short run? in the long run?

5. What are alternative explanations for wage differentials?

6. How do piece rates provide incentives to work hard? Why is there not a greater reliance on piece-rate systems?

7. What is efficiency wage theory?

8. Discuss some of the problems of selecting workers in a world of perfect information.

PROBLEMS

1. In what ways are labor markets similar to product markets? In what ways are they different?

2. Explain how both these points can be true simultaneously:
    (a) unions manage to raise the wage paid to their members;
    (b) unions do not affect the average level of wages paid in the economy.

3. How might each of the following factors affect the power of unions?
   (a) A state passes a right-to-work law.
   (b) Foreign imports increase.
   (c) The national unemployment rate falls.
   (d) Corporate profits increase.

4. Suppose a worker holding a job that pays $15 per hour applies for a job with another company that pays $18 per hour. Why might the second company be suspicious about whether the worker is really worth $18 per hour? How might the worker attempt to overcome those fears?

5. Imagine that a company knows that if it cuts wages 10 percent, then 10 percent of its employees will leave. How might adverse selection cause the amount of work done by the company to fall by more than 10 percent?

6. Advances in computer technology have allowed some firms to monitor their typists by a system that counts the number of keystrokes they make in a given workday. Telephone operators are sometimes monitored according to how many calls they take, and how long they spend on an average call. Would you expect these changes to increase productivity? Why or why not?

7. When someone is promoted from middle-management to top executive, his salary often doubles or more. Why does this seem puzzling, from the perspective of the theory of competitive markets? Why might a profit-maximizing firm do this?

CHAPTER 21

FINANCING AND CONTROLLING THE FIRM

Who controls a company? The simplest answer is that the executives do. Presidents, vice presidents, chief executive officers—no matter what the title, these are the people who make decisions, and they certainly deserve a major share of the responsibility for the actions of a company. But executives of most corporations are not entirely autonomous. There is an old saying: "He who pays the piper calls the tune." In the context of corporate behavior, investors who provide money to a firm certainly have some control over the executives who manage it.

This chapter explores the idea that the way a firm finances its investment and the way it is controlled are twin issues. While in Chapter 10 we looked at equity and debt from the perspective of the household investing its funds, here we look at these securities from the perspective of the corporation that issues them and receives the money. The branch of economics that is concerned with how firms raise capital—and the consequences of alternative methods—is called **corporate finance**. The importance of this topic to modern economics was recognized by the Nobel Foundation in 1990, when it awarded the Nobel Memorial Prize in economics to William Sharpe of Stanford University, Merton Miller of the University of Chicago, and Harry Markowitz of the City College of New York for their pioneering work in this field, some of which is described in this chapter.

Curiously enough, the issues with which we will be concerned here simply never arise in the basic competitive model of Part Two. There, firms all have a single objective, to maximize their profits or market value. That is also what all investors want. In the model, everyone, investors and managers alike, would agree about what that entails. And because there is unanimity about what the firm should do, the issue of "control" simply never arises. Indeed, even the issue of how the firm should raise its capital, whether by borrowing from the bank or issuing new shares or bonds, turns out to be unimportant in the model; it simply makes no difference. Nevertheless, issues of finance and control not only grab headlines but also absorb the attention of Wall Street and firm managers, and for good reason, as we will see.

"Don't ask me about stocks and bonds, or annual meetings. This is just a mom-and-pop steel mill."

KEY QUESTIONS

1. Are there circumstances in which whether a firm raises capital through debt or through equity makes no difference? How do concerns about taxes, bankruptcy, and managerial incentives affect firms' choice of financial structure?

2. What is the relationship between financial structure and control of the firm?

3. Why is credit frequently rationed? In the perfect markets model of Part Two, any firm can obtain as much of any input as it wants at the going price. Why, in the real world, can firms often not obtain as much capital at the going interest rate as they would like?

4. Why, in spite of the advantages in risk sharing, is so little new capital raised in the form of equity?

5. Why do most economists think that the large corporate takeovers of recent years play an important role in enhancing the efficiency of the economy? But why, at the same time, is there such criticism of these takeovers?

THE FIRM'S LEGAL FORM

Business firms in the United States take one of three legal forms: proprietorship, partnership, or corporation. A **proprietorship** is the simplest form: the firm has a single owner. If you went into business selling class notes to other students, your business would be listed as a proprietorship by the IRS. Because of the advantages of incorporation (which we will see below), only the smallest firms remain proprietorships.

When two or more individuals decide to go into business together, they may form a **partnership**. As with proprietorships, most partnerships are small—Sally and Sue's Delicatessen, or Bob and Andy's Laundromat. However, some partnerships are huge. Many of the major national accounting firms are organized as partnerships, with hundreds of partners; likewise, many law firms, from two-lawyer, small-town firms to big-city firms with one hundred or more lawyers, are organized as partnerships. Like proprietorships, partnerships have the alternative of organizing themselves into corporations. That major law and accounting firms choose not to do so tells us that the partnership is not entered into by accident. We will look at some of the reasons why these firms have remained partnerships after we consider the alternative.

The final form of organization is the **corporation**. Corporations divide ownership into shares, also known as the stock of a company. The purchase of a corporation's stock entitles the purchaser to a corresponding share of ownership in the firm.

The key feature of the corporation, and the one that has made possible the huge firms we know today, like IBM, General Motors, and Exxon, is limited liability. With proprietorships and partnerships, there is no limit to the liability of the owner(s). Consider Joe Smith, who decides to open up a restaurant and has not yet hired a lawyer to advise him of the advantages of the corporate form of business. He invests $50,000 of his savings and borrows $200,000 to buy furniture for the restaurant, to decorate it, and to pay for a five-year lease. Unfortunately, he has limited talents both as a chef and as a businessman, and the restaurant fails to attract customers. After trying to make a go of it for a year, he can no longer pay either the kitchen help or the waiters. He closes his business. But he is still responsible for the debts of the firm. Not only has he lost the $50,000 he took out of his savings, but he may be forced to sell his home to repay the $200,000 in loans because he is fully liable for them.

In partnerships, each partner is fully liable for all the debts of the firm. Now, when Joe Smith and his partner Alfred Jones go into business together, they each put up $25,000 and together borrow $200,000. If Alfred has no house or other form of wealth and thus cannot help to pay off the debt when the restaurant goes bankrupt, Joe will again find himself fully liable for the $200,000 debt.

By choosing the corporate form, owners avoid full liability. If Joe Smith sets his restaurant up as a corporation (and he can invite Alfred Jones and any others to purchase shares and join him as owners of the company), he can put his $50,000 into the corporation and have the corporation borrow the $200,000. The corporation is liable for all the debts it incurs, and in the case of bankruptcy, its assets will be sold. The money recouped in this way will go first to those who have lent the firm money (banks, bondholders), and then, if any is left over, to Joe and his fellow shareholders. In the event of bankruptcy, it is quite likely that the shareholders will lose all the money they invested in the corporation, but *they will not lose any more*. When Eastern Airlines declared bankruptcy in March 1989, none of the airline's shareholders had to worry about selling her house to help pay off the billions of dollars of Eastern's debts.

Limited liability provides larger corporations with another important advantage over other forms of organization: it facilitates public trading of the shares of the company. Buying a share of a corporation always involves the risk that the investor will lose all the money invested, as we have seen, yet this risk may be tiny compared with the risk faced by the investor in a partnership. In the latter, each partner is liable for all the

CORPORATE FINANCE • 545

partnerships' bills; if his fellow partners cannot pay their share, he will be left holding the bag. Therefore, an investor purchasing a partnership share needs to know something about the wealth of each of the other partners in order to know how much risk he faces. The fact that such information is unnecessary to the investor in a corporation means that the potential pool of investors in corporations is much, much larger. For firms that want to raise large amounts of money, this is an attractive feature.

The limited liability feature of corporations is attractive enough that today most businesses, small and large, are set up as corporations. Even the single proprietor, if he has a good lawyer, is likely to set his business up as a corporation to protect his family's assets. The corporate form is so attractive that a good question to ask is why law and accounting firms, which presumably know the advantages of incorporating, structure themselves as partnerships. The answer, in part, is that they feel their clients are more comfortable knowing that the firms are backed by the resources of all of the partners. Furthermore, joint liability provides each partner with strong incentives to monitor the actions of the others to ensure that they act appropriately.

Until very recently, the major Wall Street investment firms were also structured as partnerships. In the 1980s, however, both their liabilities and their slate of partners grew so large that each partner could not be sure what liabilities the other partners were undertaking. There was no way any one partner could be responsible for the actions of others. This growth occurred at a time when many of the investment firms also desired to enter riskier fields; they wanted not only to raise funds for other firms, but also to participate in the investments themselves. All in all, the disadvantages of unlimited liability outweighed the advantages, and most of the companies were accordingly re-organized as corporations. It may be no coincidence that some of these giant firms, E.F. Hutton, Drexel Burnham Lambert, McKinnon, and Shearson Lehman, subsequently got into trouble, winding up either in bankruptcy or being taken over by other firms.

There is another important distinction among the three legal forms. When there is a single proprietor, there is no question about who makes the final decisions. When there are many owners, whether they are partners or shareholders, there are potential disagreements. There must be a set of rules concerning how these disagreements are to be resolved. For instance, shareholders elect directors, who choose managers. If a majority of shareholders do not like what their board of directors is doing, they can elect new directors—though this seldom happens.

CORPORATE FINANCE

Corporations have a great deal of choice in how they finance their investments. We focus on three alternatives. First, a corporation can try to borrow funds, either from a bank or directly from investors by issuing bonds. Second, the corporation can issue new shares of stock. Those who purchase the new stock become partial owners of the corporation, entitled to a share of whatever profits the firm distributes to its owners in dividends. Finally, the profitable corporation can finance its investment by retaining earnings, rather than paying them out in dividends.

Figure 21.1 CORPORATE CASH FLOW

Money flows into a corporation from customers, bank loans, and investors who buy the company's bonds or new issues of stock. Money flows out to pay workers, purchase materials and equipment, repay lenders, and distribute dividends to shareholders.

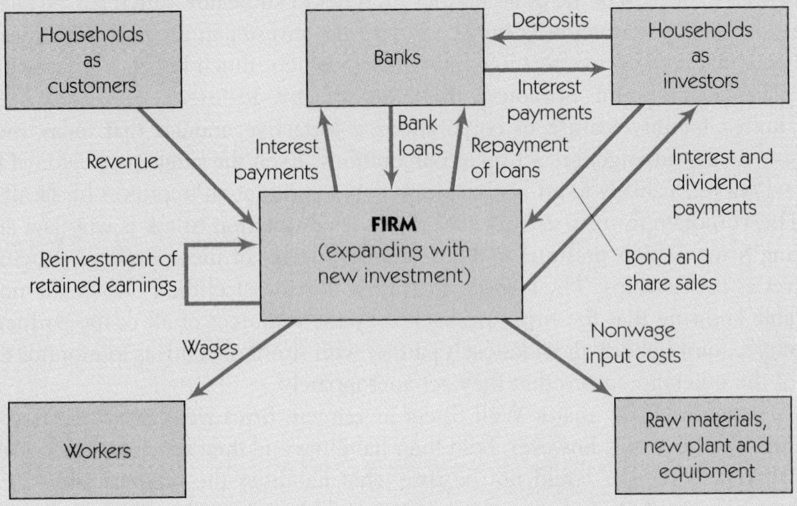

Figure 21.1 provides a schematic representation of a corporation's cash flow. The corporation receives cash in three forms: income from the sale of its products, borrowed funds from banks and bond sales, and funds from sales of new shares. The corporation uses its cash to pay its expenses—wages, raw materials, and other costs of production. It also pays back outstanding loans. If there is cash left over after expenses and debt payments, it may be distributed to the shareholders as dividends. The remaining cash, called retained earnings, is then available for the corporation to make further investments or simply to use as a cash reserve.

In Chapters 6 and 10, we learned the attributes of investments: average return, risk, tax treatment, and liquidity. There we took the perspective of the investor. Bonds yielded a lower average return and had lower risks than stocks; stocks yielded returns in the form of both dividends and capital gains; and capital gains had major tax advantages.

Here, we take the corporation's perspective. A corporation's management wants to raise capital in a way that is in the best interests of its shareholders. In particular, managers want to maximize the value of the firm's shares. Traditional theory reasoned that in deciding between debt and equity, a firm's treasurer focuses on two issues. First is the cost of capital, what the firm must pay to *new* investors in return for using their funds—the "average return" to investors. The average return paid to those who supply debt capital is lower than the average return paid to those who supply equity capital; debt is on this account less attractive from the viewpoint of new investors but more attractive from the viewpoint of the firm.

The second issue is risk, particularly the risk of bankruptcy. While firms do not have to pay their shareholders on any fixed schedule, they do have fixed obligations to pay certain amounts at certain times to bondholders and other lenders. Debt therefore imposes greater risks on the firm. If it does not have the cash to meet those obligations, and cannot get the cash by borrowing from someone else, then the company goes into bankruptcy. The more the firm borrows, the greater these fixed obligations, and the greater the chance that it will not be able to meet them. Thus, while to the investor debt appears to be safer, to the firm debt is riskier, and on this account equity is preferable.

The traditional analysis of corporate finance saw the firm as facing a risk-return trade-off: in general, the greater the debt, the lower the costs (lower payments, on average, to those who provided the capital), but the higher the risk, in terms of the likelihood of bankruptcy. The problem of the corporate treasurer was to choose the appropriate balance between risk and return.

THE MODIGLIANI-MILLER THEOREM

As economists thought about the problem more, they realized that matters were more complicated—and yet simpler. Under certain circumstances, *it appeared to be irrelevant whether the firm raised money by debt or equity financing*. This finding is known as the Modigliani-Miller theorem after its authors, both Nobel laureates: Franco Modigliani of MIT and Merton Miller of the University of Chicago. There are two steps to the theorem. The first step shows that firms wish to maximize their market value; the second, that the market value does not depend on the mix of debt or equity.

The **market value of the firm** is just the sum of the value of a firm's debt and equity; if an individual wanted to own a company free and clear, the market value is what it would cost her to buy all the shares and all the bonds and pay off all the firm's other debts. The concept of market value is an important one, because *if the firm makes its decisions with the objective of maximizing its market value, it maximizes the value of the shares of the original shareholders*. That means that the corporate treasurer has a simple task: maximize the market value of the firm.

Consider now the problem of a corporation that has identified a good project requiring $10 million of additional finance and is trying to decide whether to finance the project by issuing new debt or new equity. Modigliani and Miller showed that the market value of the firm was the same in either case, so the value of the shares of the original shareholders was the same in either case. How the company financed its new project simply made no difference.

What happened to the risk-return trade-off? How is it possible that the value of the firm could remain unchanged when, on average, the amount it must pay out to new investors is higher with new equity than with new debt? Here is how. If the firm borrows more—that is, if it becomes more **highly leveraged**—the equity becomes riskier. This will be reflected in the market value of the shares. And when this effect is taken into account, the total market value—the shares plus the bonds—is unchanged. After all, the risks associated with the firm and the extra payments that riskier firms have to make for capital do not just disappear when the firm decides to issue debt rather than equity. When it issues more debt, the risks are just concentrated on the smaller amount of equity.

We can liken the firm in the Modigliani-Miller perspective to a pie. Bondholders and shareholders get different pieces of the pie. But the size of the pie—the real value of the firm—is not affected at all by how it is sliced. The corporation's financial structure affects *who* gets the dollars earned by the corporation—how the profits pie is divided and who bears the risk of the firm—but that is all.

WHY CORPORATIONS CARE ABOUT FINANCIAL STRUCTURE

The conclusion that the financial structure of the firm makes no difference was a remarkable one, which contradicted the prevailing wisdom and provoked great consternation, particularly among corporate treasurers and old-fashioned corporate finance economists whose primary task had been to determine the appropriate balance between debt, equity, and retained earnings as sources of finance. They thought that a corporation's choice between debt and equity mattered a lot. And in the end, it became apparent that they were right.

In a way, the Modigliani-Miller result is like the simple model of profit-maximizing firms in perfectly competitive markets; even though it is not entirely true, it provides a useful starting point and organizing framework for thinking about the central issues. Describing when the corporate finance decision does not matter helped focus attention on what was truly important about corporate financial structure. The sections that follow examine the confounding factors of bankruptcy, taxation, management incentives, the market perception of a firm's value, and corporate control. These factors are not included in the simple model behind the Modigliani-Miller analysis, and each provides an explanation of why, in particular cases, a firm may care about its financial structure, its blend of debt and equity.

CONSEQUENCES FOR BANKRUPTCY

As we have already seen, increased debt imposes a greater risk of bankruptcy on a corporation. Modigliani and Miller's analysis ignored bankruptcy; what it essentially established was that if there was no risk of bankruptcy, the greater variability of shares as compared with bonds did not itself have any direct consequences. But bankruptcy is important. While 646,000 new businesses were incorporated in 1990, there were 642,000 filings of bankruptcy in that year. These statistics are typical; every year a substantial fraction of all businesses—including major firms like International Harvester, once one of the world's largest manufacturers of agricultural machinery, Western Union, Railroad Express, Pennsylvania Central Railroad, and Eastern Airlines—go bankrupt. And were it not for the fact that lenders limit the amounts they are willing to lend and monitor closely the firms to which they have lent money, bankruptcy rates might be substantially higher.

Bankruptcy has high costs, to shareholders, creditors, and managers. Concerns about bankruptcy thus provide an important limit on the use of debt. Banks are likely to limit the amount they are willing to lend, and even if they were willing to lend more, at high enough interest rates to compensate them for the risk of default, borrowers would limit the amount they borrow, recognizing that borrowing more exposes them to an excessively high risk of bankruptcy.

TAX CONSEQUENCES

Taxes affect a firm's choice of financial structure because while interest payments are tax deductible, payments to shareholders (dividends) are not. Thus, the firm would rather pay interest than dividends, if these are its options. Of course, the firm also should take into account the taxes that its shareholders have to pay on their individual incomes. Even if the corporate treasurer were inclined to say, "That's their problem, not ours," he must take into account the fact that the terms at which investors are willing to supply capital depend in part on the taxes they face; if the returns to equity are taxed more favorably than returns to debt, then the return shareholders require from the company will be correspondingly lower.

The tax law treats differently capital gains, dividends, and interest. Under the current tax law, capital gains receive slightly favored treatment. Since much of the return to stocks takes the form of capital gains, this aspect of the tax code gives shares a slight advantage over debt to individuals.

Overall, it appears that the tax code gives some advantage to corporate borrowing.

MANAGERIAL INCENTIVE CONSEQUENCES

Debt and equity provide managers with different incentives. There is a backs-to-the-wall theory of corporate finance that holds that firms should be encouraged to borrow so that managers are forced to work hard to avoid bankruptcy. If a firm is financed by equity and is making at least some money, then this theory holds that managers have little incentive to push hard for even greater efficiency.

In the 1970s, for example, the sharp increase in the price of oil led to enormous profits for oil firms. Though they distributed some of their profits to shareholders in the form of dividends, much of it they retained. Major oil companies such as Mobil and Exxon demonstrated enormous problems in investing these funds wisely; they made disastrous investments that lost hundreds of millions of dollars. Oil firms also expanded their oil exploration programs, with relatively low yields.

As the companies made unproductive investments, however, the price of their stock declined. There were a number of takeover bids that threatened to replace old management. Generally these takeover bids were financed with borrowed money. In some cases, the company that was threatened by a takeover borrowed a lot of money and used it to buy its own stock; sometimes by doing so, it was able to block the takeover bid. Gulf and Chevron merged, as did Getty and Texaco. The overall result of the mergers and threatened mergers was that the debt of those who owned the companies increased. The share price of these companies rose, and they seemed to make fewer foolish investments. One possible reason is that under the pressure of the increased debt, management became more effective.

Of course, the higher chance of bankruptcy that accompanies high debt loads can also cause a problem: all the managers' efforts may be directed at keeping the firm alive, not at making the sound long-run investments necessary for long-run prosperity. Firms near the threshold of bankruptcy may also undertake excessive risks—they gamble, knowing that if they fail, they are likely to have gone down anyway, but if the gamble pays off, they may be able to get themselves out of their hole. Thus, finding the right financial structure represents a real challenge: too little debt, and the firm's resources may be squandered; too much debt, and the threat of bankruptcy will disrupt the firm.

CONSEQUENCES FOR MARKET PERCEPTION OF VALUE

A firm's financial structure may also affect the market's beliefs about the firm's prospects. Most investors believe that a firm's managers are in a better position to judge the company's prospects than they are. If the managers believe that there is little risk, they will be willing to issue more debt, because they can do so without incurring a risk of bankruptcy. Their willingness to issue debt thus conveys in a forceful and concrete way management's confidence in the firm—a far more convincing display of confidence

Tens of thousands of businesses declare bankruptcy every year. In 1990, the assets of public corporations filing for bankruptcy totaled $83 billion, an increase of 5,000 percent from 1980. Once-healthy companies that have recently declared bankruptcy include Texaco, Continental Airlines, LTV (the nation's third-largest steel company), Manville (the country's largest asbestos company), Bank of New England, and others.

Is the penalty of bankruptcy too harsh? After all, totally disbanding a firm, pushing workers and managers into unemployment, and making the company's stock worthless can be hard on many people. But economists have pointed out that the penalties of bankruptcy may be less severe than they seem at first. After all, if product and labor markets are reasonably competitive, then suppliers can sell to others at much the same price; workers and managers can take new jobs at much the same wages; and customers can buy from surviving firms. Machines and buildings do not disappear when a company declares bankruptcy; they are sold to other firms. Bankruptcy does not eliminate human or physical resources. Instead, it reorganizes them, often putting them to a more efficient use.

But the costs of transition when a company goes out of business, especially for people who must shift to new jobs, are undeniably real. Thus, Congress reformed the bankruptcy laws in 1978 to make it *easier* to declare bankruptcy. Until then, a firm could only declare bankruptcy when it was completely broke, and after bankruptcy was declared, top management was almost always booted out. The argument for the new law was that these provisions discouraged managers from declaring bankruptcy until it was too late, when the company was damaged past saving. If managers could declare bankruptcy more easily and without losing their jobs, the argument went, then the company could start over with a clean slate and perhaps save the jobs of workers and the investment of shareholders.

This change in law helped cause the surge of bankruptcies during the 1980s. In fact, some are now arguing that the changes have gone too far and firms are using bankruptcy as a way to escape debts that they ought to pay. Manville, for example, declared bankruptcy in 1982 when it was found liable for the exposure of millions of people to Manville-produced asbestos. Texaco declared bankruptcy in an attempt to avoid paying a legal

judgment to Pennzoil. Continental Airlines declared bankruptcy in order to get out of a union contract.

This use of bankruptcy as a way of avoiding threatening events can have high, if not immediately obvious, costs for society. Reducing the threat to managers that bankruptcy will cost them their jobs encourages them to take on high debts and other risky behavior. The widespread use of bankruptcy diverts productive resources into legal fees; for example, Manville alone spent $100 million on bankruptcy fees over a six-year period. Moreover, the threat of an easy bankruptcy will make investors wary. A quick bankruptcy often means that bonds are not repaid in full. If investors cannot be sure that managers will suffer personally as a result of declaring bankruptcy, how can they be sure that managers have strong incentives to avoid bankruptcy?

Source: Stratford P. Sherman, "Bankruptcy's Spreading Blight," *Fortune,* June 3, 1991, p. 123; Matthew Scifrin, "Enough Already!" *Forbes,* May 28, 1990, p. 126; Mary Graham, "Bankrupt and Bullish," *The Atlantic,* March 1992, p. 24.

than simply a glossy and glowing report on the firm's future. Because debt both leads managers to work hard and convinces prospective shareholders about the value of the firm's prospects, issuing debt reduces the overall cost of capital to the firm and increases the company's market value.

We have seen that three of the factors discussed so far, tax considerations, managerial incentives, and market perceptions of value, tend to steer firms in the direction of debt financing, when they can obtain it; established firms tend to finance most of their investments, in excess of retained earnings, by borrowing from banks or issuing bonds.

FINANCE AND CONTROL

These financial factors differ in one more important respect: control of the corporation. At a simple level, the owners—the shareholders, through the board of directors, whom shareholders elect—control the firm. They hire managers who execute the day-to-day decisions, but these managers serve to carry out the interests of the owners. Bondholders and banks have no formal role in the management of the corporation, except when there is a bankruptcy.

Nonetheless, shareholders probably have less control of the firm, and bondholders and banks have more, than the formal arrangement suggests. Shareholders have less because of information problems—they have to rely on managers, who have more information than they do—and because of incentive problems. A small shareholder (who owns only a few shares) has little incentive to invest the effort and resources required to become well enough informed to make judgments about the quality of management. Yet if the quality of management is improved, leading to higher profits, all shareholders benefit. This is a classic public goods problem: all shareholders would benefit from better management, but none has the full incentive to learn how to judge the managers.

This incentive-information problem declines in corporations in which a majority of shares are owned by one or a few shareholders. Large shareholders have enough at stake that they are likely to take an active role in ensuring that "their" firm is well managed. They have an incentive to fire incompetent management and to detect incompetence early. In most large American firms, however, no shareholder has more than a few percent of the outstanding shares, and where the individual stockholder's interest declines, management's autonomy rises. Because of their expertise in information and because of the poor incentives for other stockholders to monitor their behavior, managers are often correctly able to answer the question "Who controls the firm?" with the response "We do." Of course, ultimate responsibility still rests with the board of directors. The important lesson that emerges from this is that "nominal" control and "effective" control often differ.

Once we recognize this difference, we also recognize that others may exercise considerable influence over the activities of the firm, and in some cases this influence is so strong as to amount to at least some degree of control. For instance, though banks have no formal role in the control of the corporation, most firms are dependent upon banks for funds, at least at certain critical times. Banks and other lenders are in a position to withdraw at any time the credit they have extended. Corporations know this, and accordingly their managers pay close attention to the views of their bankers. As a result, the corporation's bankers may exercise considerable control.

For firms that are large enough to issue bonds, these represent the least loss of control. Bonds often include "covenants," restrictions on what the firm can do, but they are typically far less onerous than the threat of day-to-day intervention associated with bank loans. Only when the firm is unable to meet its repayment commitments is there a significant loss of control. Perhaps for this reason, as firms grow in size to the point where they can easily raise capital by issuing bonds, they switch from bank financing to bonds.

Firms that worry about the risk of debt and the intrusion of bankers in their affairs may consider issuing new shares. But if enough new shares are issued, the new shareholders can seize control of the firm. There have been many such instances. Steve Jobs, one of the founders of Apple Computer, was eventually replaced by John Sculley, the former head of Pepsico and a man experienced at running a multibillion-dollar company. Sculley's experience was what was needed, not Jobs' genius for creativity.

Of course, the safest course for an entrepreneur who worries about the loss of control is to finance her investments with retained earnings. But if her retained earnings are small, as is typically the case with new firms, and if she believes that the return to additional investment is high enough, she will be tempted to turn to outside sources for funds. The expected return is worth the risk of loss of control.

WHY FINANCIAL POLICY MATTERS

The amount of debt affects the likelihood of bankruptcy.

Debt and equity receive different tax treatment.

The amount of debt affects managerial incentives.

The firm's choice of financial structure may affect the market's perception of the firm's value and risk.

Bonds, bank finance, and new equities have different implications for who controls the firm.

LIMITED FINANCIAL OPTIONS

The consequences of raising funds by different means help explain the choices that individual firms make in financing new investments. Also, some firms may not have the range of options we have seen. We have assumed that firms can finance the investments—beyond their retained earnings—by borrowing, as long as they are willing to pay the market rate of interest, or by issuing new shares, although the company cannot control the price the shares sell for. In many circumstances, however, firms may be able to neither borrow nor issue new equities, except at most disadvantageous terms, as we will see in the sections that follow. A company may then be forced to limit its investment to retained earnings.

CREDIT RATIONING

When individuals or firms are willing to pay the current interest rate but simply cannot obtain funds at that rate, they are said to be **credit rationed**. To understand credit rationing, picture a medium-sized corporation, Checkout Systems, that produces software that, when used in conjunction with retailers' checkout registers, handles inventory and all other accounting functions as well. The software has been popular, but Checkout Systems realizes that it would be much more successful if it sold the hardware—computer systems, terminals, and cash register drawers—that stores must have in order to use the software. Checkout can get the hardware from a computer manufacturer, but it needs $2 million for warehouse and inventory. The company is fully confident that the $2 million expansion will produce a steady return of at least 30 percent. However, it has no retained earnings with which to pay for the expansion.

This is only the beginning of Checkout's problems. The company has a line of credit, allowing it to borrow up to $400,000 from a local bank at 14 percent interest. It would happily borrow the $2 million at that rate (because the investment will throw off a 30 percent return). But the company's banker refuses to increase the credit limit, because the bank does not share Checkout's optimism. Checkout executives, who understand the law of supply and demand, offer to pay a higher price—16 percent interest for the $2 million. Surely the bankers would prefer 16 percent from their loan to 14 percent on someone else's. Indeed, given Checkout's confidence in its returns, it is willing to pay an even higher interest. The bank turns the company down. Is there any interest rate at which the bank would be willing to lend, the Checkout executives ask? The bank replies no.

The bank is aware that some borrowers are more likely to default than others, but it has no way of knowing which ones are most likely to do so. The bank faces an adverse selection problem: as it raises interest rates to accommodate firms like Checkout, its average returns may actually decrease. The reason for this is that at higher interest rates, the "best" borrowers—those with the lowest likelihood of default—decide not to borrow. People willing to take great risks may be willing to borrow even at very high interest rates.

Figure 21.2 shows the return to a lender being maximized at the interest rate r_0. The bank will not raise its interest rates beyond this level, even though at this rate the demand for funds may exceed the supply.

Let's look now at the market for funds for a particular category of loans, say small mortgages (under $100,000) for owner-occupied houses. The supply curve for funds for

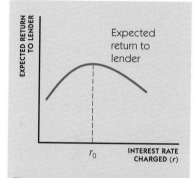

Figure 21.2 HIGHER INTEREST RATES, LOWER RETURN

As the interest rate increases, safe borrowers tend to drop out of the market, and only risky borrowers remain. Beyond some point, rises in the interest rate increase defaults on loans by enough to reduce the expected return to a lender. At higher interest rates, borrowers may also undertake greater risks, again lowering lenders' expected returns.

loans differs from the supply curve depicted in the basic model. Figure 21.3, which is based on the information in Figure 21.2, shows the supply curve for funds as backward bending. This shape reflects the reasonable assumption that as the average return to loans (which should not be confused with the interest rate charged for these loans) increases, the supply of funds increases. The supply curve thus bends backward beyond r_0. As the interest rate charged rises to this point, average returns increase and so does the supply of funds; but at interest rates beyond this point, average returns decline and so does the supply of funds.

Credit rationing takes three forms. Some borrowers get funds, but less than they would like. Some loan applicants are denied credit, even though similar applicants receive credit. And some whole categories of applicants are simply denied credit. A bank may, for instance, refuse to give loans for vacations or to finance a college education or to buy a house in a particular part of the town. In each of these cases, those who have their credit denied or limited will not be any more successful if they offer to pay a higher interest rate.

If lenders had perfect information, there would be no rationing. They would charge higher interest rates to reflect differences in the likelihood of default, but all applicants willing to pay the appropriate rate would get loans. Thus, underlying rationing is a lack of information. No matter how many forms are filled out, how many references are requested, or how many interviews are held, the lenders know there is a residual amount of missing information. They therefore develop rules of thumb for loans: yes to well-run, small businesses; no to vacation loans for college students or to new high-tech computer software firms, both of whom typically have high rates of default.

The lower the interest rate charged, of course, the greater the demand for funds. As the demand curve is drawn in Figure 21.3, average returns are maximized at interest rate r_0, but the supply of funds is less than the demand at this point. There is credit rationing; L_0 loans are actually made, while total demand is L_1. Many qualified borrowers would like to take out loans at the going interest rate but cannot. The magnitude of the credit rationing is measured by the gap between the demand, L_1, and the supply, L_0.

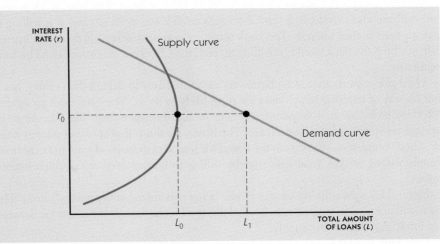

Figure 21.3 SUPPLY AND DEMAND FOR CAPITAL CREDIT WITH RATIONING

The supply of funds depends on the expected return. If that return begins to fall when the interest rate charged gets high, the supply of funds will be backward bending. Even if demand for funds exceeds supply at interest rate r_0, the lender will not raise his interest rate, since that would reduce expected returns. As a result, an excess demand for funds can exist in equilibrium.

There is a second reason that there may be credit rationing. Let's return to the example of Checkout Systems. The bank knows that Checkout's executives can engage in risky behavior, some of which the bank will find impossible to monitor. It may worry that the higher the interest rate charged, the more likely that such risk-taking behavior occurs. And if the firm is near bankruptcy, it will have no chance of survival unless it does take great risks. The bank knows that the higher the interest rate charged, the more likely that the firm will have trouble meeting its obligations and go bankrupt. As we saw in Figure 21.2, expected returns to the bank may actually decrease as the interest rate charged increases, because of this adverse incentive effect.

EQUITY RATIONING

We might suppose that firms that are unable to borrow would raise money by issuing more stock. However, established firms seldom raise capital in this way. In recent years, less than a tenth of new financing has occurred through the sale of equity. The reason is not hard to see—when firms issue new equity, the price of existing shares tends to decline, and by more than the amount that one would expect, given the dilution of the ownership of existing shareholders. For example, say that a firm worth $1 million issues $100,000 worth of new shares, and the price of the stock falls by 5 percent. The firm's existing shareholders have to give up $50,000 to raise $100,000 in funds from new investors. This is clearly an unattractive deal.

There are several reasons why issuing more equity frequently seems to have such an adverse effect on the price of shares. First, issuing equity adversely affects the market's perception of a firm's value. Investors reason that the firm's original owners and its managers will be most anxious to sell shares when these relatively informed individuals think that the market is overvaluing their shares, and they know that the owners and managers may refuse to issue shares if the shares are undervalued. These concerns are compounded by the fact that firms normally turn first to banks to raise funds. Investors wonder, "Is the reason the firm is trying to issue new shares that banks will not lend to it, or at least not on very favorable terms, or at least not as much as the firm wants? If banks, who have presumably looked closely into the firm and have a fair idea about what is going on, are reluctant to lend, why should I turn over my hard-earned money?" Reasoning this way, they will only invest in the firm if they believe they are getting a good enough deal, that is, if the price of the shares is low enough.

Also, we saw earlier that debt has a positive incentive effect on managers; by the same token, giving the firm more money to play with, without any fixed commitment to repay—which is exactly what equity does—may have an adverse effect on incentives.

For these, and possibly other, reasons, the issue of new shares on average depresses the value of firm shares. Accordingly, only infrequently do established firms raise new capital by issuing shares.

TAKEOVERS AND THE MARKET FOR MANAGERS

Firms buy other firms all the time, by mutual agreement. Whether a firm's stock is publicly traded or not, those with strong interests in the company do not mind friendly takeovers; at the right price, the company's founder is often willing to sell her firm,

Figure 21.4 NUMBER OF MERGERS AND ACQUISITIONS IN RECENT YEARS

The number of mergers and acquisitions rose sharply in the mid-1980s, tripling between 1981 and 1990. *Source: Mergerstat Review 1990* (1991), p. 5.

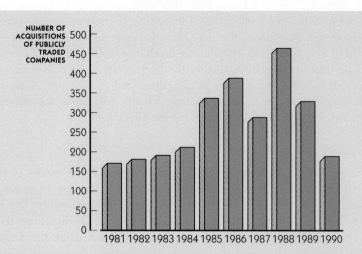

even if it means surrendering control. With publicly traded stocks, however, the takeover may not be friendly. Management may oppose the change of ownership, in which case the takeover turns hostile. Hostile takeovers, along with all other takeovers, increased sharply in the 1980s, as seen in Figures 21.4 and 21.5. So did the size of the companies taken over. It used to be thought that a company the size of TWA, Marathon Oil, or Nabisco would be immune from a takeover attempt; who, after all, had the capital required to buy the shares? But size has not turned out to be a barrier—in 1988, RJR Nabisco was bought for over $20 billion.

There has been much editorializing about the impact of hostile takeovers. The question that concerns us is, what impact do hostile takeovers and the threat of them have on the control and management of the firm?

Figure 21.5 VALUE OF MERGERS AND ACQUISITIONS IN RECENT YEARS

The value of the companies involved in mergers and acquisitions also rose sharply in the mid-1980s, quadrupling from 1983 to 1988. *Source: Mergerstat Review 1990* (1991), p. 9.

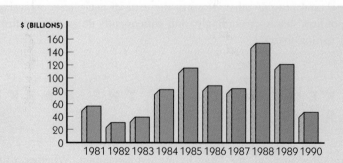

ARGUMENTS IN FAVOR OF TAKEOVERS

The central argument for takeovers is that they represent a successful way to replace ineffective managers. Under existing management, a firm may be worth $1 million, with 100,000 shares that trade at $10. An alternative management team may be able to use the firm's resources better, raising its value to $2 million ($20 per share). Even if the acquiring firm (the firm making the takeover) pays a 10 percent premium for the shares—that is, pays $1.1 million for the firm—it makes a profit of $900,000 on the deal. From this perspective, takeover battles are like auctions; the firm is sold to the bidder willing to pay the highest price, the one that thinks it can most effectively utilize the firm's resources.

Having won the auction, the highest bidder must get the company to earn enough money to justify its bid. If the post-takeover managers can indeed do a better job, the takeover firm realizes a profit. From this perspective, then, takeovers are nothing more than a reflection of the competition to be managers; they are evidence that the market for managers actually works. Much of the takeover activity of the 1980s in the oil industry can be interpreted as an attempt by various investors to redirect America's oil companies toward more profitable activities.

Takeovers provide an important discipline device even for managers whose companies have not been threatened with a takeover. Managers know that if they do not work hard, they may be threatened with a hostile takeover. They also know that a well-managed firm is unlikely to be taken over, because outsiders will recognize the quality of the management and know that they are unlikely to be able to raise the firm's profits. Even if the typical small shareholder has neither the ability nor the incentive to look over the shoulder of the existing management team to see that they are doing a good job, there is an army of corporate raiders always on the lookout for a mismanaged firm that could be renovated under new management.

Takeovers are particularly important, because the other methods of controlling managers of large corporations are relatively ineffective. We saw earlier, for instance, that most shareholders have neither the information, the incentives, nor the tools to exercise much control over management. The one way they have of exercising control is voting to elect members of the board of directors. Most investors, if they become dissatisfied with how the firm is being run, just sell their shares. In addition, supporters of takeovers (and of free markets) tend to believe that since shareholders are the real owners of a company, they should have a chance to sell what they own to the highest bidder when they desire to do so.

CRITICISMS OF HOSTILE TAKEOVERS

The primary criticism of hostile takeovers is that the corporate raiders who attempt to carry them out are more concerned with their own private interests than with the interests of the typical shareholder or bondholder, or of the workers, or of the communities in which the firms operate. Pursuing these private interests may be destructive for other groups or for the economy as a whole.

Sometimes the company taking over fires large numbers of workers and management. There is a general housecleaning. While in these circumstances one might say that some of the gains of the acquiring firm are at the expense of workers, most economists

CLOSE-UP: THE JARGON OF TAKEOVERS

Following the news about takeovers requires knowledge of the colorful jargon used in the corporate world. This glossary will help.

Takeover: Transaction that occurs when one company buys enough of the stock of another firm to take control of that firm. A takeover can be friendly, when the boards of directors of both companies agree willingly to the deal. Or it can be unfriendly, or hostile, when one company acquires the stock of the other company without the consent of its board of directors. Takeovers often go under the official names of mergers and acquisitions.

Raider: An investor or company who seeks to take over another company against the will of its board of directors.

White knight: An investor or company who "rides" to the rescue when a raider threatens a takeover. The white knight might offer a better deal to the company that is being taken over, or it might simply threaten to drive up the price of the takeover, thus persuading the raider to give up and try another target.

Poison pill: An action taken by a company to avoid being taken over. For example, the company may commit itself to paying out huge amounts of money to its stockholders in the event of a takeover. Because of these poison pills, a raider may decide that it is not worth trying to take over a company. Many poison pills have been challenged in court as protecting the board of directors to the detriment of shareholders.

Greenmail: Payment made to persuade a raider to leave a company alone. Boards of directors have sometimes agreed to buy back any stock the raider has purchased at higher than market value.

Golden parachute: Large payments given to top executives of companies that have been taken over, when those executives are fired. Golden parachutes have been attacked as a way of paying more money to incompetent managers, and have been defended as a way of encouraging managers to step aside quickly and willingly on behalf of new management.

would say that these "tough management" practices are precisely one of the benefits of takeovers. But the fact that the economy's overall economic efficiency may thereby be improved does not make the takeover any more loved by those who are put out of work.

The investors who organize takeover bids have found that they can borrow huge amounts to fund the takeover. After all, the funds are being used to buy valuable assets, and these assets provide collateral for the loan; that is, if the borrowers cannot pay back the amount promised, the lender at least can get back the value of the collateral. To finance their takeovers, some firms have issued so many dollars' worth of bonds that the market has insisted that these firms pay very high interest rates.

There is some concern that the high debt that firms typically undertake in the takeover process has adverse effects. Firms are put in a precarious position, as a number of them discovered in the late 1980s, when they found it impossible to meet their debt commitments and went into bankruptcy. There is concern not only that these bankruptcies represent a threat to the economic stability of the country, but also that high indebtedness will lead to less investment, particularly high-risk investments in research and development.

Critics of takeovers also claim that their alleged beneficial effects are overstated. They argue that takeovers do not necessarily replace one management with a more efficient management, and often represent the unbridled quest of one firm's management to aggrandize more power for itself. There is some evidence for this view. On average, the firms taking over do not see the value of their shares increase as a result of the takeover activity. This is particularly true in companies where management owns a relatively small share of the stock, in which case management may have little incentive to pay close attention to how their activities affect the market price. Further, Professor Andrei Shleifer of Harvard University has shown that managers with large egos—who, for instance, place their picture prominently within the company's annual report—are more likely to engage in takeovers.

Critics of takeovers also claim that even the threat of a takeover has bad consequences. It forces companies to try to make themselves look like unattractive candidates for a takeover. To accomplish this, a corporation may do several things. On the positive side, it can try to make itself more efficient. However, it may be tempted to sacrifice long-term projects for short-term profits, in the hope that short-term profits will trick investors into thinking that the company is better managed than it actually is. Additionally, since corporations with a lot of free cash are particularly attractive takeover targets, the corporation might be induced to spend its free cash so quickly that it makes bad investment decisions or takes on huge debts so that the return on the stock becomes riskier. Such actions rarely accord with the long-run interests of the corporation.

Finally, critics point out that a company that spends its scarce management time thwarting takeovers is less able to spend its time making better products at a better price. The threat of takeovers may thus weaken companies rather than strengthen them. To make matters worse, firms sometimes pay off takeover raiders to withdraw their bid. This is called "greenmail." By depleting its resources, the company is obviously hurt.

Supporters of takeovers see the payment of greenmail, however, as evidence of the importance of the takeover mechanism. Management may pay greenmail to preserve their jobs, even when the company would be better off if the deal were consummated. The fact that managers can undertake such actions to preserve their jobs and enhance their incomes is evidence of the need for the kind of discipline provided by the takeover threat, as imperfect as it may be in imposing constraints on management.

PUBLIC POLICY AND TAKEOVERS

The debate over takeovers is often a debate over how well markets work, in particular the markets for managers and for financial assets. Curiously, both those who believe strongly in the competitive model of Part Two and those who have great reservations

CLOSE-UP: WHY PENNSYLVANIA COMPANIES DO NOT WANT PROTECTION AGAINST TAKEOVERS

In early 1990, Pennsylvania passed a law aimed at allowing companies to block takeovers. The state's concern was that too many takeovers were not helping weed out inefficient management; instead, they were a way for financial arbitragers to make a quick buck by buying some stock, threatening a takeover and thus encouraging others to buy stock, and then selling out for a quick profit.

The new law had three main provisions. One made it very difficult for anyone who bought a large block of stock within twelve months of a takeover bid to vote either for or against the takeover. A second provision allowed corporate directors to put the interests of a firm's employees and customers above the interests of the company's shareholders. A third provision required that if a raider made any profits while attempting a takeover that turned out to be unsuccessful, those profits would have to be given to the target of the takeover.

One might think that companies would welcome this sort of protection. However, the law also al-lowed companies to choose to be exempt from any or all of the antitakeover provisions if they wished, and about two dozen of Pennsylvania's largest companies (including Westinghouse, H.J. Heinz, Mellon Bank, Allegheny Ludlum, and Quaker Chemical) chose not to be protected against take-overs in at least one of these ways.

Why would any company choose to remain vulnerable? Many shareholders, especially big institutional investors like state pension funds, tend to shy away from owning the stock of companies that are sheltered against takeovers, since eliminating the threat of a takeover may mean less pressure for efficiency. When a number of large buyers no longer demand a company's stock, the share price tends to fall. Indeed, one economic study showed that the stocks of Pennsylvania-based companies did 7 percent worse than the average performance of stocks from the time the antitakeover law was first proposed until it was passed.

Thus, with the passage of the antitakeover law,

Slab casting at U.S. Steel.

about that model often side together and oppose legislation curbing takeovers. Economists who believe strongly in the market system argue that hostile takeovers, like any change, produce gainers and losers, and that overall, the discipline that the market imposes makes the economy more efficient and most individuals better off.

Economists with less faith in the perfectly competitive markets envisioned in Part Two, including Andrei Shleifer of Harvard University and Rob Vishny of the University of Chicago Business School, argue that financial markets put only limited controls on management, and that without the threat—and reality—of hostile takeovers, management would be even more entrenched, more pursuant of its own interests, than it is today.

Proponents of takeovers also recognize potential abuses of a system that permits takeovers, such as greenmail. Still, they argue, in the imperfect world we live in, the gains from the discipline provided by takeovers exceed the costs of any of the abuses.

Despite the consensus (but by no means unanimous) view of economists that hostile takeovers should be left to the market, legislation has been enacted that would alter market outcomes. Some states have allowed corporations to create "poison pills," devices that provide for the partial destruction of the firm in the event of a successful takeover, and thus make the takeover less than attractive. And Congress, motivated partly by interest-group politics and partly by concern that the large debts accumulated to finance the takeovers might increase the chance of a wave of bankruptcies, has debated whether to remove some of the tax advantages of debt when used as part of a hostile takeover. But laws that restrict takeovers work to the detriment of shareholders, because shareholders do not benefit from the competition for shares that results from takeover battles, because the likelihood of incompetent management being replaced through takeover is reduced, and because current management, freed from the admittedly limited discipline provided by the takeover mechanism, is more likely to take actions that benefit the managers at the expense of shareholders.

IMPERFECT CAPITAL MARKETS AND GOVERNMENT POLICY

Throughout this chapter, we have seen that capital markets differ in important ways from the basic competitive model complete with perfectly informed borrowers and lenders envisioned in Part Two. There may, for instance, be credit rationing, limiting the amount that some borrowers can obtain, and some groups of borrowers may not be able to obtain loans at all. These examples of market failures are sometimes referred to as the market failure of "incomplete markets." The difficulties firms find in raising equity are related to another important instance of incomplete markets—the absence of risk markets. In effect, the original owners of a firm not only cannot buy insurance to cover some of the most important risks they face, they cannot even issue stock in order to share that risk with others.

Markets are called incomplete when they fail to bring buyers and sellers together at any price. When some group of borrowers cannot obtain loans at any interest rate or some group of entrepreneurs cannot issue stock at any price, capital markets are incomplete (or imperfect). Because capital markets are incomplete, and because access to capital is so important, government has intervened with a variety of programs. This should bring to mind another set of incomplete markets that were covered in Chapter 6, insurance markets. In effect, the two are related. Sharing the financial risk by spreading it out through the capital market is a way of sharing risk just as surely as buying insurance against the same financial risk would be. Typically, the risks with which capital markets are concerned are a kind with which the insurance industry does not deal.

Beginning with the New Deal in the 1930s, the government recognized that certain groups, such as small businesses and farmers, had difficulties obtaining loans. Students who wanted to borrow to finance their education found it almost impossible to do so. At one time, those of low and moderate income found it difficult to obtain a mortgage for more than 80 percent of the value of their house. In some cases, government lent money to these groups directly; in other cases, as in mortgages, it provided guarantees so that lenders were willing not only to lend their funds, but to lend them at a relatively low rate. These programs have grown to the point where more than a quarter of all loans made in the United States are made by the federal government or with government guarantees.

One of the reasons that some of these credit markets did not exist before is that default rates were so high that if interest rates had been set high enough to compensate for the high default rates, demand for the loans would have been extremely limited. It is not surprising, then, that the government has had to face extremely high default rates on the education loans it guarantees.

There is an important moral here: if the government goes where the private market has feared to tread, it needs to ask, "Why are private markets incomplete and imperfect?" Sometimes, as in the market's failure to provide good retirement insurance before 1930, there may be no good answer, at least no answer that provides a warning to the government. In other cases, the government may still want to go ahead—student loan programs may be desirable, even if the government has to subsidize them. But at the very least, the government should go into these programs with its eyes open.

REVIEW AND PRACTICE

SUMMARY

1. The three main forms of business ownership are proprietorships, partnerships, and corporations. Only corporate ownership has the advantage of limited liability, which means that investors will not be liable for debts incurred by the company.

2. The Modigliani-Miller theorem argues that under a simplified set of conditions, the manner in which a firm finances itself will not change its market value. The value of a firm is determined by its profits, not by how those profits are distributed. However, issues of bankruptcy, taxation, management incentives, and corporate control mean that firms care about their financial structure.

3. Shareholders have nominal control of corporations, but when share ownership is widely distributed, shareholders may not exercise effective control. While lenders (like banks) have nominal control over a corporation only if it declares bankruptcy, their ability to control the immediate flow of capital to the firm may give them a fair amount of say in what the firm does.

4. Credit rationing occurs when a borrower cannot find a source of funds even when he is willing to pay a higher-than-market interest rate. Lenders fear their average return may *decrease* (the chance of default is greater) as the nominal interest rate increases.

5. Firms will not be willing to issue new equity if doing so results in large decreases in the market value of outstanding shares.

6. The argument for takeovers is that they provide a means by which less efficient management teams can be replaced by more efficient teams. The argument against is that takeovers often are more matters of power or ego rather than efficiency, and that the threat of takeovers diverts companies from focusing on their actual business.

KEY TERMS

proprietorship	Modigliani-Miller
partnership	theorem
corporation	credit rationing

REVIEW QUESTIONS

1. Explain the difference between a proprietorship, a partnership, and a corporation.

2. According to the Modigliani-Miller theorem, how would financing a firm by borrowing rather than by equity change the value of the firm? Explain. If a firm wishes to raise additional capital to finance a new project, how should it do so, assuming the conditions of the Modigliani-Miller theorem are satisfied?

3. Explain how the risk of bankruptcy and the tax treatment of dividends and interest payments affect the attractiveness of equity to a business. How does debt provide incentives for management to work harder?

4. Why might the market interpret the issue of new equity as a negative signal concerning the value of a company?

5. Do banks or small shareholders have greater effective control over a corporation? Is your answer the same for large shareholders?

6. What is credit rationing? Why does it occur?

7. What are the arguments for and against takeovers?

Problems

1. Consider a firm that needs $350,000 in capital to get started. First, think about this firm organized as a proprietorship, where you put up $50,000 and borrow the rest from a bank. Second, think about this firm organized as a partnership, where you and nine friends each put up $5,000 and borrow the rest from a bank. Third, think about the firm organized as a corporation, where you and nine friends each buy $5,000 worth of stock and then borrow the rest from a bank. If the firm goes broke without earning any money, how large are your potential losses in each case?

2. The bankruptcy laws of the United States were changed in the mid-1980s to make it easier and less costly for a firm to declare bankruptcy. Would you expect these laws to lead to more partnerships or to more corporations? Why?

3. Speak Software, a small firm attempting to design new computer software, applies for a bank loan to purchase some new computer hardware. The bank turns the company down for the loan. When Speak Software offers to pay a higher interest rate, the bank still turns it down. Explain why the bank might practice this form of credit rationing, using a diagram that compares the interest rate charged with the bank's expected return.

4. A corporate raider is planning a hostile takeover, but the target company quickly finds a white knight and creates a poison pill. Describe each of these steps. How will they affect the raider's plans?

5. The Kitbits Company, which makes cat treats, has a stock price of $40 per share. A raider is trying to take over the company and is offering $50 per share. Shareholders must decide whether to sell their stock to the raider and take a $10 per share gain, or to hold on to the stock. Consider the effect of future management of the company. When might it make sense to hold on to the stock?

6. How might a firm harm itself in attempting to avoid a takeover? How might it strengthen itself in attempting to avoid a takeover?

CHAPTER 22

MANAGING THE FIRM

T he discussion of the firm in previous chapters treated "the firm" as if it were a monolithic entity. The firm decided when to invest, what and how much to produce, and how to produce it. It seemed to have a brain and perhaps even a personality of its own. That simple view of the firm serves well as an introduction, but we can do better. Firms are run by and made up of individuals, and as anyone who has ever worked inside a company of any size can tell you, they are full of disagreements.

Different employees have different priorities. Top managers, for example, may care more about keeping their own paychecks high than about whether the firm makes the highest possible profit. A middle-level manager may want her part of the firm to increase in size, whether or not that is good for the company as a whole. Most industrial production in the United States occurs in corporations that employ dozens or hundreds or thousands of individuals. Sometimes it seems miraculous that organizations of this complexity can function at all, let alone succeed in creating new products and innovations. The pages of the *Wall Street Journal, Forbes, Fortune,* and other business periodicals are full of stories of successes and failures. This chapter is concerned with certain key aspects of the internal design and management of these organizations.

We look at the major issues facing managers of firms—from the highest-level managers to those who manage a small department with a handful of employees—and learn why it is unlikely that any simple formula guaranteeing success will ever be found. However, even though there are no guarantees, understanding some of the basic principles and issues can improve the chances of success. Managers are at the center of the firm, and it is therefore important to understand more fully how they can be motivated to act in the interests of the firm, how they make decisions, and how the firm can be organized to ensure that better decisions are undertaken.

"Then it's moved and seconded that the compulsory retirement age be advanced to ninety-five."

KEY QUESTIONS

1. What are the central problems facing organizations in which the manager is not the sole owner? How do corporations select managers, motivate them, and induce them to make decisions that are in the interests of shareholders? How do the corporation's owners and managers ascertain the performance of different parts of the firm?

2. How are decisions within the corporation made in the presence of uncertainty? What difference does it make whether decision making is centralized or decentralized? What are the pros and cons to centralization and decentralization?

3. What determines what a firm produces *inside* the firm, as opposed to what it purchases from other companies? What determines, in other words, the boundaries of the firm?

DELEGATION

There is an old adage that says if you want something done right, do it yourself. Underlying this adage is the problem of incentives. For the individual who owns the firm and is its only employee, the economic incentives are clear: maximize the firm's profits, and you maximize your own income. The owner-worker can balance out the extra profits from working on weekends and late at night to fulfill a rush job with the lost leisure time that such effort involves.

But as soon as one employee is added, this equation changes. It may not be in the employee's best interest to maximize the firm's long-run profits. The lawn-care proprietor may find that his summer hires are not as careful as he would be in pushing the lawn mowers around the rose bushes or in picking up rocks in their path. By the same token, a corporation, having hired a new chief executive, may find that she has other matters on her mind than the corporation's long-run health.

Assigning to another the responsibility for a task is called **delegating**, and despite the apparent inefficiencies of delegation, it is a necessity in virtually all business firms. No executive has the time or even the knowledge necessary to do everything that the firm does; most executives could not even do the work of a moderately skilled blue-collar worker, and certainly could not replace a skilled engineer. Employees essentially are agents, carrying out the wishes of their superiors. The larger the company, the more likely it is that layers of delegation will build up. The owners (who may not even work at the firm) will have to delegate at least some of the management responsibility to others, who in turn will have to delegate to still others, resulting in a long chain of command and responsibility. In this delegation process, the manager or owner faces three central problems: choosing those to whom to delegate responsibility; motivating those to whom responsibility has been delegated to do the right thing; and monitoring the results (through an accounting process) to know whether the right thing has been done.

SELECTION

Just as managers face a selection problem when they hire an employee from outside the firm, they also have a problem when they delegate responsibility. If the task merits a full-time worker, then the manager must choose between hiring someone from outside the firm and transferring someone from another department inside the firm. For smaller tasks, new responsibilities may be assigned to a particular worker.

As workers spend time at one firm, supervisors gain more and more information about them by observing their performance. Still, there is always uncertainty about how an individual will perform at the next highest level, and this makes the promotion problem similar to that of hiring. Making judgments about whether someone in a management position is doing a good job is also difficult. If a project is delegated to someone who makes the right decision, was it good luck or foresight? If the project fails, was it bad luck or a bad decision? Managers have to make judgments concerning an individual's ability using whatever weak evidence they can get. Does the person seem well-informed? come to meetings well prepared? Those who want to be promoted know that managers are looking for evidence of this kind, and act accordingly. They may acquire more information than is really necessary to make a reasonable decision, because they wish to impress their superiors. They may go to meetings that they think are superfluous, mainly because it provides them an opportunity to put their competence on display.

These attempts to impress superiors can have positive or negative effects on a company. A company can benefit when promotion seekers try to impress their supervisors by doing their jobs especially well. On the other hand, individuals looking for a promotion can also waste the company's resources. For example, they may assign subordinates to help them prepare for meetings rather than assigning them to work on concerns that are more pressing from the company's perspective, or they may waste the time of others at meetings, vying with one another to convey a good impression of their qualities.

Job selections and promotions are generally made on the basis of **relative perfor-mance.** Because job promotions are inevitably made on the basis of relative performance, the selection process itself provides incentives. These contests may have a productive effect, by producing a strong motivating force. But they also sometimes take a destructive turn. The knowledge that promotions are based on relative performance may impede cooperative behavior; for instance, one individual may attempt to enhance his relative position by poor-mouthing rivals. To counteract these destructive effects, firms often base promotions partly on how good a team player the individual is.

MOTIVATION

Selecting a suitable manager is only the first step in the process of delegation. Many people are capable of doing a job, if properly motivated. Most people are also capable of not doing a good job, if not properly motivated. But there are problems in motivating workers. For example, firms could provide incentives to workers by basing pay on a piece-work measure of performance, but basing pay *exclusively* on performance imposes considerable risk on workers. As a result, relatively few firms pay their workers this way. When we shift our focus to the problem of managers, the problems differ from those of motivating other workers in one critical respect: it is even more difficult to ascertain what the output of managers is. A Volvo production team produces a certain number of cars every week. What exactly does a manager produce? And how can it be measured?

One of the main responsibilities of a manager is to make decisions. Owners of firms would like their managers to make the same decisions that the owners themselves would make, given the same information. However, typically the owner of the firm will not be there when the decision is made, and even if he is, he will probably not have the requisite information to make a good decision or to judge whether a good decision has been made.

Of course, the owner knows after the event whether some project was or was not successful; but even then he cannot tell whether the project was a reasonable gamble, given the information at the disposal of the subordinate. For example, the owner cannot tell whether it would have been cost effective for the subordinate to have gathered more information. Monday-morning quarterbacking may be enjoyable; hindsight is better than foresight. But it does not resolve the basic problem of the owner: how can he be sure that the manager will make the right decision in the future?

THE PRINCIPAL-AGENT PROBLEM

The problem of trying to motivate the manager to act in the same way that the owner would have acted is an example of a broad class of incentive problems. Chapter 6 noted that incentive problems arise whenever an individual does not bear, or receive, the full consequences of her action. If the manager makes a good decision, the firm prospers and the shareholders benefit. If she makes a bad decision, they suffer. Thus, shareholders would like to motivate the manager to act in a way that maximizes the value of their shares. In this form, the incentive problem is referred to as the **principal-agent problem**. The principal (here, the owner) would like to motivate the agent (here, the manager) to act in the principal's interests, with both parties knowing that the owner cannot judge whether the manager has taken the appropriate action simply by looking at the observable results.

The interests of managers and owners frequently differ. The manager going on a business trip may choose to buy a ticket on a more expensive airline because he is trying to accumulate frequent flier points for himself on that airline, rather than a cheaper alternative. An advertising agency may purchase spots for its client on a TV program more because of the gifts a TV station's sales representative brought than because of the audience reached by each station. The sales representative for a computer firm may give some account especially close attention not because of the prospects of increased sales, but because he is trying to land a new job; if he were acting in the interests of the firm, there are other accounts to which he would devote more time.

There are two important aspects of the principal-agent problem: how hard the agent works, and what risks the agent takes. On both counts, analysis of the problem involves ascertaining how the interests of the principal and agent differ, and attempting to devise ways to make the agent act more in accord with the interests of the principal. If a manager works especially hard, for example, the owners of the firm (often the shareholders) will receive some of the reward. But because the manager does not receive all the reward, she may have insufficient incentives for exerting maximum effort.

The manager's taste for risk will rarely match the owner's interests. On the one hand, managers may act in a more risk-averse (cautious) manner than the owners of the firm might like. After all, the managers know that should projects under their supervision fail, they may lose their jobs. So they will have something of a bias toward taking the most secure path. On the other hand, managers may be willing to take risks when the owners would not be willing to do so. After all, they are gambling with someone else's money. If the project is a flop, the firm loses money; if it is successful, the manager will receive credit. The consensus among economists is, however, that under most circumstances, managers act in a way that is more risk averse than the owners would like. To counteract this tendency, firms often seem deliberately to reward risk taking; for example, by providing large bonuses for large increases in profits.

Solving the Principal-Agent Problem: Ownership The most obvious solution to the principal-agent problem would be for the owner of the firm to sell each manager his own portion of the firm. As the owner, the manager would have all the right incentives. If he worked harder, he would reap the rewards. If he took more risks, he would receive the gains and bear the losses. In general, however, the manager does not have the requisite capital to buy the firm, and even if he did, he might not be willing to buy it. After all, an owner's income is a lot more variable than a paycheck. For one thing, the owner's income will depend not only on his own efforts but also on the vagaries of the market. A manager may not be willing to take that risk.

In any case, in most modern corporations, it would be difficult to "section" the company into different parts and make each manager an owner. Consider an assembly line: it is hard to imagine dividing the assembly line into two parts, making the manager of each part an owner. We can sometimes divide a large corporation into several parts, each run separately; but within each of these parts, there remain large principal-agent problems.

Solving the Principal-Agent Problem: Incentive Pay A second-best solution to the principal-agent problem is to include incentives in the agent's compensation package that reflect the principal's interest. Thus, sales representatives earn commissions, and many workers can qualify for performance bonuses if they or their department exceeds production quotas. One form that incentive programs for top managers has taken is the **stock option** bonus related to how well their firms perform. Suppose stock in a particular company is currently selling for $30. The stock option allows the manager to purchase

CLOSE-UP: THE BEST EXECUTIVES FOR THE MONEY?

As the table here shows, some top executives earn mind-bending sums of money, sometimes millions of dollars a year. Defenders of these high salaries point out that top executives make life-or-death decisions for their companies and that they deserve to be compensated for making those decisions wisely. Much of top executive pay comes in the form of stock options; their high pay is therefore due in part to the fact that the company's stock did well, which offers an incentive for top management to look out for the interests of shareholders.

However, in the past few years, critics of high executive salaries have become considerably more vocal. Here are some of their main arguments:

1. Pay for top executives has grown disproportionately. In 1974, for example, the typical chief executive officer (CEO) received pay that was 35 times that of the average manufacturing worker. In the early 1990s, the typical CEO earned about 120 times the pay of an average manufacturing worker.

2. Pay for U.S. top executives is out of line with what foreign companies pay. In Japan, the average CEO earns 20 times the pay of the average worker; in the United Kingdom, he earns 35 times the pay of the average worker. Yet Japanese managers often seem every bit as productive as U.S. managers.

3. Pay for top executives does not offer a true incentive, because it often rises even when the company does badly. During the recession in 1990, for example, corporate profits fell by an average of 7 percent, but compensation for top executives rose by an average of 7 percent.

Critics of high executive pay point out that compensation levels are often set by a board of directors chosen by the top executive, with the help of an outside consultant on the "appropriate" level of pay who is also chosen by the top executive. They argue that although a well-designed plan of linking the top executives' pay to the long-term price of the company's stock can provide useful incentives, too many stock plans have become a way to funnel money to the top executive, without limit or control.

Sources: "The Flap over Executive Pay," *Business Week,* May 6, 1991; Graef Crystal, *In Search of Excess* (New York: Norton, 1991).

THE 10 HIGHEST-PAID CHIEF EXECUTIVES FOR 1990

Name	Company	Total pay in 1990
1. Stephen M. Wolf	United Airlines	$18.3 million
2. John Sculley	Apple	$16.7 million
3. Paul B. Fireman	Reebok	$14.8 million
4. Dean L. Buntrock	Waste Management	$12.3 million
5. Leon C. Hirsch	U.S. Surgical	$11.7 million
6. Michael D. Eisner	Walt Disney	$11.2 million
7. Joseph D. Williams	Warner Lambert	$ 8.5 million
8. David O. Maxwell	Federal National Mortgage	$ 7.6 million
9. George V. Grune	Reader's Digest	$ 7.5 million
10. P. Roy Vagelos	Merck	$ 7.1 million

a specified number of shares at $30 for a specified period of time. For instance, the manager may be given the option to buy 100,000 shares at $30 any time during the next three years. If the firm's shares rise in value to $40, the manager can purchase the shares for $3 million and then immediately resell them for $4 million, receiving a bonus—presumably as a reward for her contribution in increasing the value of the firm—of $1 million. It is common for firms to provide their top managers with stock option bonuses valued in the millions of dollars.

Stock options make some economic sense as incentive devices. The better the firm does, the higher the manager's pay, so the manager has an incentive to try to maximize the firm's market value. If the manager succeeds in increasing the value of the firm by $100 million, it is likely that she will capture only a small fraction of that gain, on average perhaps less than 1 percent, or $1 million. But that reward is enough at least to head her in the right direction. And it is better than having no reward at all.

But there is some controversy over whether the popularity of stock option plans reflects their worth as an incentive mechanism, or whether the managers use these schemes to enrich themselves at the expense of current shareholders. When an employee exercises a stock option, he generally is purchasing shares of the firm that have not yet been issued. Since the total stock represents the total ownership of the firm, when a firm issues more shares of stock to fulfill a stock option plan, the holdings of current shareholders are diluted and will decline in value relative to what they would have otherwise been. In addition to paying the managers' salaries, then, shareholders are paying the managers indirectly through the decreased value of their shares. However, because share prices are constantly changing and the effect of dilution is less than 1 percent of the value of the shares, shareholders do not see clearly the true costs of the stock option.

If firms were really interested in providing managers with incentives, they would tie the compensation of their managers to how well their company did *relative to other firms*, particularly relative to other firms producing similar products. This cannot be done with stock options, which are just as likely to reward an executive for a boom in the stock market in general as they are to reward her for a better-managed firm. Firms can, however, easily base cash payments to their top managers on how well the company does—in terms of either profits or stock market value—relative to other firms.[1]

Other Solutions   Appropriately designed compensation schemes help align the interests of the agent with that of the principal. But they are only one of the ways that principal-agent problems are handled by the firm. Chapter 19 discussed some of the alternative ways incentive problems are dealt with in market economies, and we briefly review their application here.

The principal-agent problem arises because the principal does not know precisely the actions that the agent undertakes or should undertake. By spending more resources to obtain information, the problem is reduced. Thus, the owner of a firm could spend more time monitoring his managers, but there is a cost: he has less time to devote to other matters. He might hire someone to monitor his managers, but that only pushes the problem one step away—he must monitor the monitor. Sometimes the organization may be structured so that each individual is simultaneously monitoring others and being monitored by others. Still, monitoring is imperfect.

Long-term relationships between most principals and agents help them over this

---

[1] Such provisions increase the effective competition among firms. If there is collusion among firms—a possibility discussed in Chapter 16—then they will not want to design their executives' compensation in this way.

seeming impasse. Both sides see the gains from continuing the relationship. A manager will not take advantage of every opportunity to gain at the expense of the firm, knowing that even if the firm does not detect self-serving behavior every time, it is likely to observe it some of the time, and that even if the firm does not fire her, her behavior might affect prospects for promotion.

ACCOUNTING

Monitoring managers is only one aspect of the watchfulness necessary to the efficient operation of the business firm. For a firm to survive, it must have information about each of its parts.

This is a consideration in firms of almost any size beyond that of the owner who has no employees, but it is particularly important in large corporations. For them, detecting problems so that they can be corrected is an enormous task. The large corporation has to identify which of its units are more profitable, or potentially more profitable, so that it can allocate more resources to those units. This is the domain of **accounting**, the field that tracks the profits and losses of the firm and its various components. One of the major questions with which modern accounting is concerned is how to provide the information required to manage and control a firm to those responsible for making decisions.

The Valuation Problem   Since many of the outputs of units within a firm are not sold on the market but rather are supplied to other units within the firm, there are problems in valuing them. A secretary does not sell his services to a boss; the travel department does not sell its travel services to the sales representatives; and the research laboratory does not sell its services to the production department. But if a firm is losing money, it would like to know what departments are the main causes of the problem. Perhaps its secretarial department is too large or inefficient? To know whether the department has a problem, the manager has to know the value of the secretarial services. But since there are no prices within the firm, some other method is needed to establish value.

In the case of secretarial work, the problem may be solved relatively easily: the secretarial services can be valued at what the cost would have been had they been purchased from the outside. Firms often "charge" their units; that is, they pretend there is a market transaction. Thus, a company may give each department a typing budget, with which it can purchase typing services from the secretarial department. However, it would be far more difficult for the R & D department to determine in advance what the price would be for paying an outside laboratory to carry out a unique research project.

Allocating Fixed Costs   A second problem has to do with allocating the firm's fixed costs, sometimes referred to as overhead. How much of the salaries of top managers should be considered a cost for each of the departments they supervise? How much of the building's costs should be allocated to each department? the cafeteria's costs?

Accountants can provide numbers or estimates in many of these cases, but the numbers must be interpreted with care. Firms often use simple rules, like allocating the costs of the personnel department to the departments it serves in proportion to the number of workers hired in each department. Following such simple rules may distort firm behavior.

The fact that some unit within the firm—using these kinds of accounting conventions—is losing money does not mean that it should be shut down. The firm must compare carefully what will happen to profits assuming the division is or is not shut down. What will be the reduction in receipts? What will be the reduction in costs?

Assume, for instance, that the Computer Division of BC Research Laboratory accounts for 10 percent of the firm's employees, and that the company's cafeteria loses $1 million a year. As a result, the Computer Division is allocated a loss from cafeteria operations of $100,000, and appears to be losing money. Assume that apart from these "allocated" losses, the Computer Division makes a profit. But if the Computer Division is closed down, the cafeteria's losses might actually increase. Assume that the cafeteria charges slightly more than the *marginal* cost of each meal, but not enough to make up for the fixed costs of maintaining the cafeteria. Then shutting the Computer Division down makes the cafeteria's losses even bigger. Since apart from the cafeteria losses the Computer Division is making a profit, shutting down the Computer Division is clearly a mistake.

CONFLICTING OBJECTIVES OF ACCOUNTING SYSTEMS

In modern corporations, accounts serve at least three distinct, and sometimes conflicting, objectives. They provide information to the firm to help it operate efficiently; they provide information to the capital market, to be used to value the firm and to decide whether and on what terms it will be able to obtain additional funds; and they provide information to the Internal Revenue Service (IRS) to determine the firm's corporate income tax liability. While the firm would like to make its profits look high to the capital market, it would like to make them look low to the IRS. Firms have some discretion in how they keep their accounts. In several instances, companies have kept their books in such a way as to report higher profits—and pay higher taxes—than they needed to, presumably because they put greater emphasis on their position in the capital market than on their tax position.

Despite their limitations and the potential for misuse, accounting data make up one of the most important aspects of a large organization. Workers may sit up and pretend to be busy when the boss passes through; waste is not always obvious, even to a probing eye. But a good manager can use accounting data to track the flow of value throughout a firm without ever leaving the computer screen. When money is disappearing into one department as if it were a black hole, it is time to take a closer look.

CENTRAL PROBLEMS OF DELEGATING RESPONSIBILITY

1. Selecting the manager

2. Motivating and monitoring the manager

3. Tracking the performance of different parts of the organization

Close-up: What Is Good Management?

Despite conflicts of interests between managers and shareholders, American managers do see themselves as trying quite hard to the best job that they can for their firm. The bestseller list for books almost invariably includes one or two that promise a better way to manage a firm. The popularity of these books is testimony to the widespread concern about how to be a good manager; the fact that one book is followed by another with contradictory advice is testimony to the everlasting hope of American managers that the promised success formulas are just around the corner.

Back in the 1950s and 1960s, books often taught management skills as if following a few basic steps would always lead to a correct decision. Managers were urged to clarify their objectives, outline how best to attain those objectives, and constantly monitor the extent to which their objectives were being attained; good advice, but of only limited help. There may be little disagreement about the ultimate objectives of the firm—make profits and increase the market value of its shares. The difficulty is knowing how to attain those objectives. The simple prescriptions of forty years ago offered no assistance in dealing with the uncertainty and limited information that pervade decision making within firms; neither did they offer solutions for the difficulties of motivating individuals—the principal-agent problem.

More recent examples of this genre of books do not have a much better record of success. In 1983, Tom Peters and Robert Waterman wrote a book called *In Search of Excellence.* The book's main theme was that managers of businesses should learn from the example of the excellent companies identified in the book. The distinguishing feature of these companies was their commitment to excellence and the concern they showed for their employees. Business managers and students, dreaming of prosperity, bought millions of copies of the book, making it a bestseller.

However, the next couple of years were not kind

to many of the "excellent" companies identified by Peters and Waterman. For example, an airline called People Express, which had been growing like a weed for several years by offering no-frill flights, was cited as an excellent company with innovative personnel policies. But it went bankrupt and was bought by Continental Airlines two years after the book came out. Many of the other companies in the book suffered similar unglamorous fates. In fact, the firms selected as role models for excellence fared not much better over the five years following the book's publication than any randomly chosen group of firms.

But only five years later, both authors were back with new books that contained new guesses for success. In 1988, Tom Peters published a book called *Thriving on Chaos.* This book argued that "there are no excellent companies." Instead, it listed forty-five guidelines for dealing with a frenzied and chaotic business environment. Robert Waterman's 1988 book was called *The Renewal Factor,* and offered examples of companies that had achieved excellence by seeking out new products and strategies and renewing themselves. Of course, the list of companies was not the same as the list of five years earlier.

There are many other management books available, with a variety of themes. Some want U.S. firms to model themselves after Japanese firms. Others stress the need to build worker loyalty or customer loyalty. Some books argue for an "industrial policy," in which private firms coordinate their decisions with the federal government. Others suggest encouraging the decentralized growth of small businesses.

These books illustrate the difference between useful anecdotes and serious economic research. Citing a number of dramatic success stories or dramatic failures does not prove anything. The skeptical reader needs to remember that anyone can choose successful companies after they have become successful, but how many companies followed the same advice and were unsuccessful? Is the success rate of all firms with the attributes that the authors have identified higher than those who do not have these attributes? Showing that a few companies have the desired characteristics and made high profits does not establish a causal link between the two. It does not even show that on average, such firms have made higher profits than others. Systematic study of a subject requires looking at all the cases, failures as well as successes.

THE DECISION-MAKING PROCESS

The three central problems of delegating bear an intimate relation to two other big issues facing the firm: the decision-making process and the boundaries of the firm. We take up the decision-making process in this section, and the boundaries of the firm in the next.

Perhaps the most important problem facing a large enterprise is deciding how, and by whom, decisions are to be made. Most modern large corporations have given considerable thought to designing a decision-making structure that will make it more likely that good decisions are made.

THE ROLE OF UNCERTAINTY

Even if managers were able to resolve principal-agent problems, they would still face difficulties in making decisions. What makes decisions difficult—and interesting—is that most of the time managers do not know the full consequences of their decisions. For example, they face uncertainties about technology and costs of production. When electric utilities estimated in the early 1970s what it would cost to build nuclear power plants, the estimates often turned out to be wildly off the mark. Managers also face uncertainties about demand—the electric utilities misjudged the growth in demand for electricity, for example, because they failed to anticipate either the slowdown in the overall growth of the economy or the movement toward energy conservation in response to higher energy prices. As we saw in Chapter 16, in most imperfectly competitive markets, managers face uncertainties about what their rivals will do. Will Kodak's competitors introduce a disposable camera? At what price? Will Xerox's competitors introduce a color reproduction machine? At what price?

While most decision making still occurs by seat-of-the-pants judgments—managers' "hunches" and intuitions—large organizations have increasingly relied on more formal modes of analysis. The problems they face are too complex, and the costs of oversights and mistakes too large, to rely solely on hunches. These formal processes generally entail three steps. First, the firm attempts to identify the major sources of uncertainty, and the major alternative actions. Second, it tries to identify and evaluate the full range of consequences and, third, on the basis of that evaluation make a judgment about the best course of action to take.

Most decision making in large companies is made not by individuals but by committees. Even if a single individual is ultimately responsible, there is an attempt to arrive at a consensus. The formal processes of decision making provide a framework that is sometimes helpful in identifying the sources of disagreements.

The central element in most formal decision-making processes is the **decision tree**, which tries to show what decisions are linked together and to identify all the possible outcomes. It explicitly recognizes that some decisions can be postponed until further information has been acquired. Decision trees usually involve a diagram like the one in Figure 22.1 depicting the Dairy Deluxe Company's decision to bring out a new fat-free ice cream. Some individuals in the management committee think it is a good idea, some think it is a bad one. In a small company owned by one person, the owner would go with her personal hunch, and that would be the end of the matter. But in larger firms, the advocates must persuade the skeptics of the returns. The decision tree helps focus the discussion.

Perhaps there are two main alternative strategies. The first is depicted in the upper branch of the decision tree: to build a pilot plant. If the pilot plant is unsuccessful—the costs of production turn out to be prohibitively high—the project is terminated. Dairy Deluxe loses what it spent on the pilot plant, $1 million. If the project is successful—it demonstrates that the ice cream can be produced at a reasonable cost—the output of the pilot plant is marketed in selected areas. If the product is a marketing flop, the project is again terminated, but now the loss is $2 million. But if the ice cream is a marketing success, a large-scale plant is constructed and the product is marketed on a national scale, for a profit of $25 million.

The other possibility is depicted on the lower branch: to plunge ahead and build a

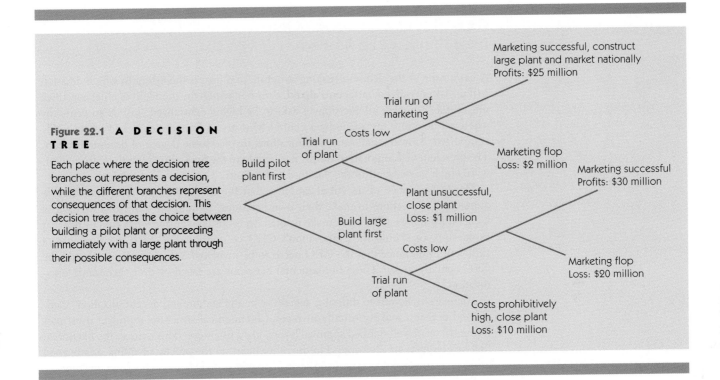

Figure 22.1 A DECISION TREE

Each place where the decision tree branches out represents a decision, while the different branches represent consequences of that decision. This decision tree traces the choice between building a pilot plant or proceeding immediately with a large plant through their possible consequences.

large-scale plant. There are again two possibilities. If the costs of production turn out to be prohibitive, the project is terminated. But now the loss is not $1 million but $10 million. If the costs of production are as low as originally estimated, the product is marketed on a national scale. If it is a flop, the project is again terminated, but now the losses have mounted to $20 million. But if it is successful, profits are higher, because Dairy Deluxe is able to bring its ice cream to the market more quickly than it could if it first constructed the pilot plant. The profits are, say, $30 million.

This decision tree is obviously oversimplified. There are far more decisions to be made, far more uncertainties to be faced, on the road to any successful project. But it is still useful. Comparing the two strategies, we see that if everything goes well, the decision to build the full-scale plant wins—a profit of $30 million compared with $25 million. But if everything does not go well, losses are far larger with the full-scale plant. Which decision is best depends on judgments about the likelihood of these various outcomes and on the firm's willingness to take risks.

When there is a great deal of uncertainty, firms prefer to keep their options open, in the hope that additional information will come along that will help them resolve the uncertainties. They are often willing to pay a considerable amount for these options. Thus, airlines typically pay millions of dollars to obtain an option to buy an aircraft two or three years later. They know that if they do not, and demand for air travel booms, they may miss the opportunity to compete effectively. The decision tree helps them to see clearly what options are foreclosed and what options remain open at each moment.

CENTRALIZATION AND DECENTRALIZATION

A basic issue of the decision-making structure in a firm is the extent to which decision making is **centralized** or **decentralized.** A firm in which the president or chief executive officer (CEO) makes all decisions is said to be highly centralized, just as an economy where all decisions are made by a central Ministry of Economics is said to be highly centralized. However, all large organizations involve some degree of decentralization. The president of a corporation simply does not have the time, much less the information, with which to make all of the day-to-day decisions.

The consequence of decentralization is that the firm's subunits have considerable autonomy, or freedom to make their own decisions. Should the Chevrolet division of General Motors be allowed to make its own decisions concerning what kind of new car to develop, or should the corporation's CEO be consulted? Which decisions are of sufficient importance that the CEO needs to be involved? Which decisions should the CEO actually make? These fundamental decisions are faced by every economic organization.

There are trade-offs to differing degrees of centralization and decentralization. Centralized decision making usually involves a hierarchical structure; a project must pass through a set of well-defined approval layers, like a fine sieve. This reduces the likelihood that bad projects are approved. On the other hand, in the process of sifting, many good projects get rejected. Decentralized decision making provides fewer checks on any project, so that it is more likely that some bad projects get adopted. By the same token, fewer good projects are rejected.

Figure 22.2 depicts the trade-offs between varying degrees of centralization and decentralization within an organization. For simplicity, the figure focuses on who has the authority to proceed with a project. With complete centralization, all decisions would have to pass through a set of layers until they reach the single chief decision maker. With high decentralization, there are many groups within the organization who can give the go-ahead. Point A corresponds to the highly decentralized organization, where there are many good projects being accepted but few bad projects being rejected, while B corresponds to the highly centralized organization, where there are many good projects being rejected but few bad projects being accepted.

ADVANTAGES OF CENTRALIZATION

Hierarchical decision making provides a structure for coordination across the divisions of a large corporation, which may be important in instances where there are externalities—where, for instance, the fruits of research in one part of the firm may be of benefit to another. Thus, in developing a new motor, it might pay the different divisions of General Motors to coordinate their research and development efforts. It is expensive to develop a new motor, and while Buick's ideal motor might be different from Chevrolet's ideal motor, the considerable economies that would result from a coordinated research program might far outweigh the fact that in the end, the motor that is developed is not exactly the one that any single division would have chosen. Even if, in the end, the different units decide to produce different motors, they will still find it profitable to coordinate their research programs and develop, for instance, new, lighter materials from which to make a motor.

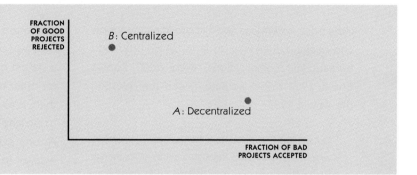

Figure 22.2 THE TRADE-OFF BETWEEN CENTRALIZATION AND DECENTRALIZATION

More centralized decision making reduces the likelihood of accepting bad projects, but increases the likelihood of rejecting good projects. Decentralized decision making reduces the likelihood of rejecting good projects, but increases the likelihood of accepting bad ones.

Another argument in favor of centralized decision making is that it avoids the duplication that results from operating autonomous corporate divisions, where personnel from several units are often engaged in quite similar activities. Thus, advocates of centralization claim that it is inefficient for each division of a firm to have its own legal staff or its own marketing department.

ADVANTAGES OF DECENTRALIZATION

Some of the arguments used by advocates of greater centralization are turned on their head and used as arguments for decentralization. For example, supporters of decentralization point out that having different units within an organization doing similar things may have decided advantages: the resulting competition not only provides a strong motivation for members of the different production units, but also provides a basis for judging whether one unit is doing better than another, and hence for making decisions about who is performing well and who should receive more funds.

Decentralized decision making also enables a production unit to adapt decisions to its own particular circumstances, so that they reflect the diversity of attitudes and skills among workers. As hard as they may try, centralized authorities have difficulty in obtaining the requisite information from those who are actually engaged in the production process. Decentralization also allows a range of experimentation greater than that found under more centralized regimes, and enables projects to be approved more quickly.

The advantages of decentralization are sufficiently great that many firms have considerable decentralization. Large corporations, like General Motors, are separated into divisions, each of which may have considerable autonomy, at least over some functions (such as marketing). While there may be centralization in certain issues—like the design of a new motor or body frame—there is a great deal of decentralization in others. Pontiac and Buick see their markets as slightly different, and even if they have the same basic engineering, each division believes it can adapt the car—with its own interior design, for example—and adopt a marketing strategy aimed at its part of the market far better than central headquarters could do. Some publishers have several different divisions producing books, sometimes competing directly against one another. The computer company Hewlett-Packard divides itself into a large number of units, each of which has the authority to undertake research projects.

CLOSE-UP: AN ECONOMIC JUSTIFICATION FOR THE FIRM

If the price system is so good at coordinating supply and demand, then why do firms, which often add bureaucratic complications, even exist? Ronald Coase, 1991 Nobel laureate, posed the question this way in 1937:

> Outside the firm, price movements direct production, which is coordinated through a series of exchange transactions on the market. Within a firm, these market transactions are eliminated and in place of the complicated market structure with exchange transactions is substituted the entrepreneur-coordinator, who directs production. It is clear that these are alternative methods of coordinating production. Yet, having regard to the fact that if production is regulated by price movements, production could be carried on without any organisation at all, well might we ask, why is there any organisation?

The answer Coase suggested is "transactions costs." There are costs associated with having a market, just as there are costs to running an or-ganization. The market system may offer the incentives best suited for some tasks at lower costs, while a system of bureaucratic coordination works best for other tasks. The trick for the manager of a firm, then, is to seek out the jobs that firms are suited to do and rely on the market for everything else. As one example, Coase offered the situation of a weaver in Lancashire, England, who could rent power and space and obtain supplies on credit. He was able to work for himself rather than going to work in a factory. Apparently, this system offered better incentives than having a large company hire many weavers. The reason is apparent: the incentives for the weaver to work hard were strongest when he was self-employed and able to keep all his own profits, rather than when he had to share the profits with an employer. And there were no (or insufficient) offsetting gains from organizing production inside a larger firm.

In the modern shopping malls of today, apparently it works better for the malls to sell space to

a variety of stores, large and small, rather than turning the mall into one huge super-store coordinated by a central bureaucracy. Often the more market-oriented approach (many small stores) and the more bureaucratic approach (some very large stores) coexist side by side, each offering its own advantages. Large stores may offer a wider selection and lower prices, while small stores concentrate on specialized styles and personalized service.

In the fast-food industry, a store might be either owned directly by a large chain or sold to an individual owner. An individual owner bears more of the risk, but reaps a greater reward for success (like the independent weaver in Lancashire). However, since an individual owner bears higher risks than the overall chain, it may have a harder time borrowing money and may have to pay higher interest rates. in the case of the McDonald's restaurant chain, about a third of the stores are owned directly by the company, while the rest are franchises owned by individuals.

Sometimes changes in a market or in the available technology will shift the balance between bureaucratic organization and the market. Late in 1991, for example, the enormous firm of IBM announced that it would try to decentralize its operations and allow each division to operate as a separate company, with responsibility for its own profits and losses. If this reorganization succeeds, IBM will become a sort of umbrella over many competing units, offering advice and sharing technology between its pieces, but providing far less intrusive central direction.

These examples and many others demonstrate that managers of firms must examine their operations on a case-by-case basis, looking for situations where market incentives might produce greater efficiency, or where a system of bureaucratic organization might work better than the market.

Source: Ronald H. Coase, "The Nature of the Firm," *Economica* (November 1937), pp. 386–405.

CENTRALIZATION AND DECENTRALIZATION WITHIN THE ECONOMY AS A WHOLE

The advantages and disadvantages of centralization within firms parallel those of the economy as a whole. The U.S. economy is characterized by a high degree of decentralization. Each firm in the economy has the right to undertake projects. With few exceptions, it does not have to get approval from any government agency. Projects and ideas that are rejected by one firm are taken up by others, and the same bad idea may be tried over and over by different companies. Yet there is a widespread consensus that the decentralization is desirable; the gains in increasing the likelihood that good projects get developed outweigh the disadvantages of having the same idea reexamined in what appears to be a duplicative manner. There are many stories of inventors and entrepreneurs who needed the many chances provided by a decentralized system in order to find one backer for their brilliant idea.

Despite the decentralization of the U.S. economy as a whole, many of its autonomous firms have only limited decentralization and retain a fairly strong hierarchy. Even multibillion-dollar companies like Exxon maintain a fairly high degree of centralization. Thus, our economy can be viewed as involving a mixture of decentralization and centralization. The question is one of balance; and the balance between centralization and decentralization is one that will continually be debated, both within firms and, more broadly, within society as a whole.

CENTRALIZED VERSUS DECENTRALIZED DECISION MAKING

CENTRALIZED	DECENTRALIZED
Fewer bad projects are accepted.	More good projects are accepted.
There is greater coordination; externalities are taken into account.	Comparison between competing units provides (a) incentives and (b) bases of selection.
Duplication is avoided.	There is greater diversity and experimentation.

THE BOUNDARIES OF THE FIRM

Many firms sell "clones" of IBM's personal computer. Most of them are "assemblers": they buy circuit boards, cases, monitors, and keyboards in bulk, assemble the parts into personal computers, and sell them. Why don't they expand, and make their own circuit boards, cases, monitors, and keyboards? To turn the question around, why don't those who make these parts assemble them? After all, firms always want more profits, and these expansions seem to be prime areas for growth.

Economists are interested in the conditions that cause a firm to limit itself in size or in the number of products it manufactures. What determines the boundaries of firms? Or to put the same question in a different way, when does a company find it easier to deal with another company through the market, rather than produce what it needs itself? What are the advantages and disadvantages of markets?

In modern economies, the degree of centralization and decentralization is closely related to the issue of what is produced within the firm, and what each firm purchases from other firms. In the case of the personal computer market, there is a great deal of decentralization; companies make extensive use of the market. The circuit board manufacturers have a much larger market than just personal computers, so they can achieve economies of scale that they would not enjoy if they restricted their output to the personal computer level. The same is true for those who make the other parts—they fear the loss of flexibility entailed in putting all their eggs in the personal computer market "basket." This pattern of specialization, however, leaves a profit opportunity for the assemblers, who can buy the parts from outside and still wind up with a computer they can sell at a good profit.

But the degree of decentralization within the personal computer market is unusual. Much economic activity occurs within firms, rather than between firms; that is, companies produce intermediate products that are used as inputs for the goods the company eventually sells, and firms may even produce the inputs that are used in these intermediate products. Such activity is known as **vertical integration**. (By contrast, **horizontal integration** involves bringing together firms producing the same goods.) At one time, U.S. Steel owned its own iron ore mines and its own fleet of vessels to transport the iron ore; it not only produced the pig iron, it also used the pig iron to make more finished steel products, such as the beams used in construction. Ford Motor Company at one time owned its own steel mill, for producing the steel used in making its cars.

Table 22.1 shows that the output of several large, vertically integrated firms is as large as the entire output of several medium-sized countries.[2] Within these firms, relationships are controlled by commands—direct decisions by the managers—though those commands themselves may be affected by accounting profits and prices (which can differ significantly from market prices and profits).

There are a number of factors that go into the decisions about whether to vertically integrate—that is, whether to produce the inputs used to produce the goods—or whether to use the market. One important factor is **transactions costs**—the extra costs (beyond the price of the purchase) of conducting a transaction, whether those costs are money, time, or inconvenience. Ronald Coase of the University of California at Los Angeles was awarded the Nobel Prize in 1991 partly for his work in identifying the role of transactions costs in determining the "boundaries" of the firm; that is, showing what activities occur within a firm and what activities occur between firms.

Consider, for instance, the problem of a large manufacturing company that offers health insurance to its employees. The company could continue to pay premiums to an outside insurance company that would then be liable for any claims. Because of its large number of employees, however, the option of paying its employees' medical bills directly has become economically viable. The company could set up a division to run its health insurance, but then it will face all the managerial problems discussed in this chapter. Although this company is good at manufacturing, it has no comparative advantage at running a health insurance company, and its managerial talent is scarce. Accordingly, the firm may find it cheaper, once these transactions costs are taken into account, to continue with the outside health insurance company. It is more efficient to make use of the market in obtaining health insurance services.

In other cases, transactions costs may be lower if the firm vertically integrates. Consider a chemical firm eager for new products to sell. It could hire an outside laboratory to try to develop a new drug, and use outside sales representatives to sell existing ones. But how can the company make sure that the outside laboratory really tries to make a breakthrough discovery? How can the company make sure that the outside sales firm makes a sincere effort to sell its products?

In some cases, where markets are stable, reputation mechanisms provide the answer. The chemical firm might hire a laboratory with which it has worked successfully in the past. But in new industries and in rapidly changing environments, reputation mechanisms may work most imperfectly.

In other cases, the parties will try to draw up a contract to specify clearly what each side is supposed to do. But once a contract has been signed, one side may attempt to take advantage of the other. The buyer may threaten to find an alternative supplier unless a large price concession is made, knowing that the supplier's equipment has been specially adapted to make products for him. Suppliers recognize this, and may be willing

---

[2] The comparison is not perfect. The appropriate comparison would be between the value added of U.S. corporations—the difference between their sales and the goods and services they purchase from other firms. Even in these terms, General Motors and Exxon are larger than Egypt and Greece.

Table 22.1 COMPARING LARGE CORPORATIONS AND SMALL COUNTRIES

1990 sales of large U.S. corporations	
General Motors	$125 billion
Exxon	$107 billion
Ford	$ 97 billion
IBM	$ 69 billion
Mobil	$ 64 billion

1989 national output of medium-sized economies	
Norway	$ 95 billion
Thailand	$ 70 billion
Argentina	$ 53 billion
Greece	$ 40 billion
Egypt	$ 32 billion

Sources: *Business Week*, March 18, 1991, p. 52; *World Development Report* (1991), pp. 208–9, Table 3.

to sign a contract only if the buyer puts down a lot of money to start with. But then the buyer may worry that the seller will try to take advantage of him. When the chemical company includes the problems of writing and enforcing contracts in the transactions costs of using markets, it may decide to try to develop its own drug.

Transactions costs are just as real and at least as important as the costs of production. Indeed, as innovations in manufacturing (such as the invention of the assembly line) have reduced production costs, transactions costs have taken on increasing importance. Many of the innovations of the past two decades, in turn, have reduced transactions costs. Computers have enhanced our ability to keep track of records and process other information required for engaging in transactions.

Finding a balance between centralization and decentralization and between what the firm produces and what it purchases from other firms are thus two of the central problems facing managers of all large enterprises.

REVIEW AND PRACTICE

SUMMARY

1. Large organizations face three central problems in delegating responsibility: selecting managers who will have responsibility delegated to them; motivating the managers; and monitoring the results.

2. The problem owners of firms have in motivating the managers to work hard and make decisions about risk in the general interests of the firm, rather than in their own personal interest, is known as the principal-agent problem.

3. Accountants provide information to a firm to help in management decisions; provide information to the capital market that helps to determine the firm's stock price and whether it can borrow funds; and supply the basis for calculating the firm's taxes.

4. Decision trees help structure decision making. They delineate the alternatives available at each point of decision making and the consequences of each action.

5. Centralized decision making reduces the likelihood that unproductive projects will be approved, improves coordination, and avoids duplication, but also tends to weed out good projects. Decentralized decision making reduces the likelihood that good projects will be rejected and provides a basis for experimentation and comparison, but also tends to allow a greater number of unproductive projects to go forward.

6. Every firm must decide whether to make a product or provide a service inside the firm or buy it in the marketplace. If transactions costs are low, firms will tend to buy goods or services in the market; if they are high, the firm will tend to supply the product or service itself.

KEY TERMS

relative performance	decision tree	centralization
principal-agent problem	transactions costs	decentralization

REVIEW QUESTIONS

1. Why must large companies delegate responsibility? What issues are raised by delegating authority?

2. What is a principal-agent problem? How might ownership and incentive pay address this problem?

3. What are three uses of accounting data? What problems do accountants face in determining the "profitability" of a unit within a firm?

4. What is a decision tree? Why might it be helpful?

5. What are the advantages and disadvantages of centralized and decentralized decision making within a firm?

6. When will a firm try to do a job itself, and when will it try to hire someone to do it in the market?

PROBLEMS

1. A middle manager for Hugific, Inc., supervises 20 employees, and must decide which one to promote. What signals might the manager attempt to use? Would he be wise to post a list of these signals for the information of all employees?

2. Try to think up an incentive scheme that would encourage managers to take more risks.

3. Explain why a profit-maximizing firm might find that a department was making losses when costs of overhead are included, but might still decide to keep that department open.

4. Make up a decision tree for the decision to open the Arctic Wildlife Refuge for oil exploration. When decisions are irreversible, economists stress the value of preserving options. Explain how the decision tree illustrates the advantages of preserving options in this case.

5. A company is considering setting up two new divisions. One division would be a corporate fleet of cars, as an alternative to renting cars from existing firms. The other division would be an R & D laboratory, as an alternative to contracting out projects to labs. Consider issues of transactions costs and comparative advantage, and analyze why these functions might be set up inside the company or bought from outside.

6. In several European countries, there have been strong movements for worker participation in management, entailing, for instance, unions sending representatives to sit on the board of directors. Discuss the problem of getting worker representatives to act in the interests of the workers in terms of the principal-agent problem.

CHAPTER 23

EXTERNALITIES, MERIT GOODS, PUBLIC DECISION MAKING

C hapters 21 and 22 provided a close-up look at the business firm. In this chapter and the next, we probe the economic role of government, a topic first treated in broad terms in Chapter 7. Beyond providing a legal framework within which economic relations take place, government may have an economic role to play when markets fail to produce efficient outcomes. This justification is known as the **market failures approach** to the role of government.

We now know of several ways in which markets can fail to produce efficient outcomes. For example, industries may be unsuccessful at producing the levels of competition envisaged by the basic model, and less-than-perfect competition produces inefficient economic outcomes. Competitive markets may, for all the reasons set forth in Chapter 18, fail to produce the technological innovation needed by a thriving economy. The government responds with patent laws and other legislative efforts to spur innovation.

Markets may also fail in the face of information problems (Chapter 19). For instance, producers tend to know more about their products than they reveal to customers; government has responded with truth-in-advertising laws. Information failures lead to incomplete markets (Chapter 21), and government has responded by providing certain kinds of insurance and student loans.

There is one market failure that has not yet been adequately discussed: the failure that arises when the extra costs and benefits of a transaction (externalities) are not fully summed up in the market price. We first encountered externalities in Chapter 7. There, our focus was more on positive externalities, such as those associated with goods that are publicly provided; the first section of this chapter shifts the focus to negative externalities and the issues of environmental protection and natural resource depletion.

Underlying the entire analysis of markets is the principle of consumer sovereignty, the notion that individuals know best what is in their own interests. Sometimes governments act as if they do not believe in consumer sovereignty. The second section of this chapter analyzes what happens when governments act in this way.

The existence of market failures suggests that government *may* have a role to play in correcting them, provided it can do better than the market. The final section of this chapter takes a closer look at government than we have had before, and asks whether there might be reasons why government has trouble acting in the public interest. Are there systematic "government failures," and if so, what accounts for them?

"*We create it, we clean it up—business couldn't be better.*"

Reproduced by special permission of *Playboy* Magazine.
Copyright © March 1971 by *Playboy*.

KEY QUESTIONS

1. Why do externalities such as pollution result in a market failure? What alternatives can government employ to remedy this market failure?

2. What are the market forces that lead to an efficient use of society's natural resources? What may impede markets from using scarce natural resources efficiently?

3. Why does government frequently not succeed in achieving its stated objectives? What are the sources of government failure?

4. Is there a determinate outcome of majority voting in democratic societies? If so, what can we say about it?

5. What is the role of bureaucrats and interest groups in democratic decision making?

EXTERNALITIES AND THE ENVIRONMENT

The description of perfect competition assumes that the costs of producing a good and the benefits of selling it all accrue fully to the seller, and that the benefits of receiving the good and the costs of buying it all accrue to the buyer. This is often not the case. As was explained in Chapter 7, the extra costs and benefits not captured by the market transaction are called externalities.

Externalities can be categorized as either positive or negative, depending on whether individuals enjoy extra benefits they did not pay for or suffer extra costs they did not incur. Goods for which there are positive externalities—such as research and development—will be undersupplied in the market. In deciding how much of the good to purchase, each individual or firm thinks only about the benefits it receives, not the benefits that are conferred upon others. By the same token, goods for which there are negative externalities, such as air and water pollution, will be oversupplied in the market. The fact that the market might not fully capture the costs and benefits of a trade provides a classic example of a market failure and a possible role for the public sector.

Figure 23.1A shows the demand and supply curves for a good, say steel. Market equilibrium is the intersection of the curves, the point labeled E, with output Q_p and price p_p. Chapter 14 explained why, in the absence of externalities, the equilibrium E is efficient: the price reflects the marginal benefit individuals receive from an extra unit of steel (it measures their marginal willingness to pay for an extra unit); and the price also reflects the marginal cost to the firm of producing an extra unit. At E, marginal benefits equal marginal costs.

But consider now what happens if, in the production of steel, there is an externality—producers are polluting the air and water without penalty. The **social marginal cost**—the marginal cost borne by all individuals in the economy—will now exceed the **private marginal cost**, the marginal cost borne by the producer alone. Note that in a competitive industry, the supply curve corresponds to the horizontal sum of all producers' *private* marginal cost curves. Panel B contrasts the two situations. It shows the social marginal

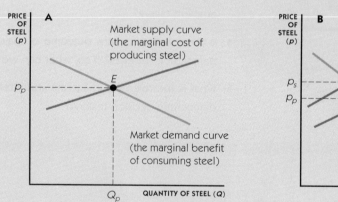
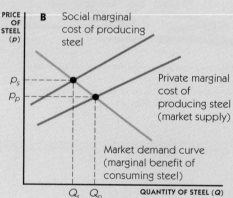

Figure 23.1 HOW NEGATIVE EXTERNALITIES CAUSE OVERSUPPLY

In a perfectly competitive market, the market supply curve is the (horizontal) sum of the marginal cost curves of all firms, while market demand reflects how much the marginal consumer is willing to pay. In panel A, the intersection or equilibrium, at quantity Q_p and price p_p, will be where marginal cost is equal to the marginal benefit for society as a whole.

The private marginal cost includes just the costs actually paid by the producing firm. If there are broader costs to society as a whole, like pollution, then the social costs will exceed the private costs. If the supplier is not required to take these additional costs into account (as in panel B), production will be at Q_p, greater than Q_s, where price equals social marginal cost, and the quantity will exceed the amount where marginal cost is equal to marginal benefit for society as a whole.

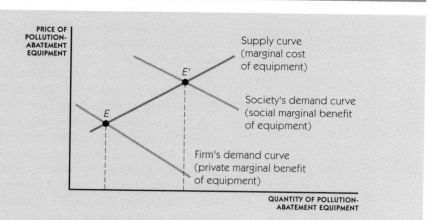

Figure 23.2 HOW POSITIVE EXTERNALITIES CAUSE UNDERSUPPLY

The private marginal benefit includes just the benefits received by the firm, but since pollution-abatement equipment provides a positive externality, it will have a social marginal benefit that is higher. If the firm takes only its private benefit into account, it will operate at point E, using less equipment than at the point where marginal benefits are equal to marginal costs for society as a whole (E').

cost curve for producing steel lying above the private marginal cost curve. Thus, with social marginal costs equated to social marginal benefits, the economically efficient level of production of steel will be lower, at Q_s, than it would be if private costs were the only ones, in which case output would be Q_p.

This analysis shows that the level of production of steel, which generates negative externalities, will be too high in a free market. We can also ask, what about the level of expenditure on pollution abatement? Such expenditures confer a positive externality on others—the benefits of the equipment, the cleaner air, mainly accrue to others. Figure 23.2 shows a firm's demand curve for pollution-abatement equipment. It is quite low, reflecting the fact that the firm itself derives little benefit (we are assuming the government does not regulate pollution). That is, the firm's marginal private benefit from expenditures on pollution-abatement equipment are small. The firm sets its marginal private benefit equal to the marginal cost of pollution abatement, which results in a level of expenditure on pollution abatement at E. The figure also depicts the marginal social benefit of pollution abatement, which is far greater than the marginal private benefit. Efficiency requires that the marginal social benefit equal the marginal cost, point E'. Thus, economic efficiency requires greater expenditures on pollution abatement than there would be in the free market.

One of government's major economic roles is to correct the inefficiencies resulting from externalities. There are plenty of categories of negative externalities, but perhaps the most conspicuous are those that harm the environment and lead to excessively rapid losses in our natural resources. These will be our focus in the section that follows.

ENVIRONMENTAL PROTECTION AND CONSERVATION: SOME EXAMPLES

Freon gas, used as the propellant in aerosol cans and as a coolant in air conditioners, appears to have destroyed some of the ozone layer of the atmosphere, thus risking major climatic changes and possibly exposing individuals to radiation that may result in cancer.

This is a worldwide externality; the cost of putting freon gas in the marketplace is borne by the entire world. A major treaty among the nations of the world was signed in early 1990 that would eventually ban the use of this and related gases. The nature of the externality in this case was clear: the use of the gas anywhere could have disastrous effects on everyone.

Similarly, there is concern that the cutting down of the Brazilian rain forests and the global warming caused by burning fossil fuels (coal, oil, and gas) will result in major climatic changes, with possibly catastrophic results.

In the late 1980s, two other major environmental disasters further underscored the problem of externalities. In 1989, in Alaska's Prince William Sound, millions of gallons of oil spilled out of an Exxon tanker, resulting in massive loss of wildlife, ruined fisheries, and damaged natural environment. Though Exxon claimed to spend more than $1 billion in the cleanup, much of the damage would take years to repair. Why didn't Exxon build a safer ship, or take more precautions? The answer lies in externalities: the cost of the spill to Exxon—even at $1 billion—is probably less than the full cost in terms of damage to the environment. Because Exxon, or any other oil company, bears only a part of the cost, it does not have adequate incentives to design and buy environmentally safe ships, or to enforce precautions among their crews.

The other major environmental disaster of recent years was the 1986 explosion at the nuclear power plant in Chernobyl, in the Ukraine (USSR), which spewed radioactive material over thousands of miles. Five years later, reindeer feeding on the grass in parts of Sweden were too radioactively contaminated to be eaten. Again, there was an externality—the USSR did not have to pay the costs of the damage done outside of the country.

THE PROPERTY RIGHTS RESPONSES

Large-scale environmental degradation is a conspicuous form of negative externalities. Having identified them as market failures, what can the government do to improve matters? Some economists, led by Nobel laureate Ronald Coase of the University of Chicago Law School, argue that government should simply rearrange property rights. With appropriately designed property rights, markets could take care of externalities without direct government intervention. Consider, for example, the case of a small lake in which anyone who wishes to can fish, without charge. Each fisherman ignores the fact that the more fish he takes out of the lake, the fewer fish there are for others to take out. In fact, they may take out so many fish that the fish cannot replenish themselves. If the government were to rearrange property rights and grant to a single individual the right to fish, then he would have every incentive to fish efficiently. There would be no externalities. He would take into account the long-run interests as well as the short-run. He would realize that if he fished too much this year, he would have fewer fish next year. If it were a large lake, he might let others do the fishing and charge them for each fish caught or regulate the amount of fish they could catch. But the prices he charged and the regulations he imposed would be designed to ensure that the lake was not overfished.

The point of this example is that the problem of overfishing is solved with only limited government intervention. All the government has to do is assign the property rights correctly.

This kind of problem arises repeatedly. The U.S. government leases public land to cattle ranchers. Since the ranchers only lease the land, they often impose a negative externality on future potential users by overgrazing the land, which leads to environmental damage like soil erosion. If the property rights were altered so that the land was sold to the ranchers, they would have reason to look after the land rather than abusing it. In deciding on how many cattle to graze this year, they would take into account the effect on the pasture, and thus on the number of cattle they could graze next year.

To take another example, consider a factory that discharges chemicals into a river. Suppose that the aggregate value of swimming in the river is $20,000 a year, and the property rights to the use of the river are assigned to the swimmers. The swimmers announce that the firm can pollute the river, provided it pays them $20,000 a year. If the cost of a filter to keep the chemicals out of the river is $15,000, then the firm chooses to install the filter; the result is efficient. If the cost of the filter is $25,000, then the firm pays the swimmers $20,000 and proceeds to pollute; the outcome is still efficient. Exactly the same outcomes obtain if the property rights are assigned to the factory. If the filter costs $15,000, the firm announces that it will stop polluting, providing the swimmers pay $15,000 for the cost of the filter. Since the value of swimming in the river is $20,000, the swimmers are willing to "bribe" the factory not to pollute. On the other hand, if the filter costs $25,000, they are not willing to bribe the factory, and the factory will pollute.

No matter how the property rights are assigned, the outcome is efficient. Pollution occurs when the cost of pollution abatement exceeds the value of clean water; pollution does not occur when the value of clean water exceeds the cost of abatement. What matters is that there are well-defined property rights. And who gets the property rights has implications for income distribution: in one case, the factory may make payments to swimmers; in the other, swimmers may have to make payments to the factory.

COASE'S THEOREM

That externality problems could be solved by reassigning property rights is a contention known as **Coase's theorem.** The appeal of Coase's theorem is that it assigns a minimal role to government. Government simply makes the property rights clear, and then leaves the efficient outcome to private markets. Opportunities to apply the theorem are limited because sometimes costs of reaching an agreement may be high, particularly when large numbers of individuals are involved.

Let's return to the problem of the factory negotiating with surrounding home owners who have been given the property right of clean air. In a world with perfect information, the factory owner could ascertain precisely what the clean air was worth to each home-owner—how much each would have to be compensated for the deterioration in the quality of the air. She would then compare that amount with the cost of buying equipment that would make the smoke emitted from the factory clean. If the costs of limiting pollution were greater than the amount required by the home owners to compensate them for polluted air, she would pay them. This would be the efficient solution. But the factory is unlikely to know precisely how much the neighbors need to be compensated. Each home owner might hold out for more money, knowing that without his agreement, the factory owner will be forced to buy the expensive equipment. Not only is bargaining in such situations expensive, in many cases it may even break down.

Today there is general agreement that while assigning property rights clearly may take

Close-up: The Market for Whales

The average American eats seventy-three pounds of beef, fifty-nine pounds of pork, and sixty-three pounds of chicken in a year, and one never hears concerns that this consumption will drive cows or pigs or chickens into extinction. Relatively few Americans eat whale meat, yet in certain countries like Japan, whale meat is considered a delicacy. In 1986, fearing that whales were being hunted into extinction, an international convention passed a moratorium on all commercial whaling. Why does the market system work to assure plenty of cows and pigs and chickens, but threaten to exterminate certain breeds of whales?

Economists approach this question by analyzing the property rights in each case. The farmers who raise cows and pigs and chickens own them, and thus have an incentive to build up the supply of animals. But no country or individual owns the ocean or the whales in it. Thus, although there is an economic incentive to hunt whales and sell their meat, there is no individual or company with a direct economic incentive to help nurture and increase the overall number of whales.

This pattern has been called "the tragedy of the commons." When an area is owned in common, like the ocean, everyone has an economic incentive to exploit it, but no one has an economic incentive to care for it. The result can be the disappearance of the whales in the ocean.

Of course, the problem of the commons is not limited to whales. The decimation of the bison on the commonly owned American prairie is another example, as is the pollution in the commonly owned air and water. In many cases, the answer to the problem of the commons is for society to band together and set up economic incentives or regulations that will prevent any resource from being exploited to destruction.

Sometimes even the passage of laws is not enough. Soon after the moratorium on whaling for commercial purposes was passed in 1986, several countries felt a sudden need to do a considerable amount of whaling for scientific purposes. Japan, for example, announced in 1987 an urgent need to kill for research purposes a number of whales equal to nearly half the number that they had been catching for commercial purposes. Iceland announced that it would be shipping much of the whale meat from its "research whales" to Japan, where the meat would sell at premium prices. More recently, international agreements have placed tight limits on the number of whales that can be caught, but the economic incentives to exploit the commons to the fullest remain.

Sources: Figures on meat consumption from *Statistical Abstract of the United States* (1990), Table 202; information about whaling in 1986 and 1987 comes from Timothy Appel, "Japan Finds Loophole in Whaling Ban," *Christian Science Monitor,* April 15, 1987, p. 1.

care of some externality problems, most externalities, particularly those concerning the environment, require more active government intervention. Some forms this intervention might take include regulatory measures, financial penalties, subsidization of corrective measures, and creating a market for the externality.

THE REGULATORY MEASURES RESPONSE

The strongest response government can make to a negative externality is to outlaw it. In the case of environmental externalities, many governments impose regulatory measures that define permissible levels of pollution and penalize firms that exceed them. Any level of pollution that falls within the regulated levels is permitted.

In most cases, economists see better alternatives than the strict, all-or-nothing standards called for in regulatory measures. This is because economists do not see pollution as an all-or-nothing matter. The air can be cleaner, or it can be dirtier. Water can be more or less polluted. There are, of course, certain limits beyond which air is unbreathable or water is undrinkable. But up to these points, one can ask, what is the extra cost of having slightly cleaner air? and compare that cost with the extra benefit. Economists believe in marginal analysis in the area of the environment as much as they do in any other area. Regulatory measures often do not allow for an exploration to find the efficient level of pollution.

Further, regulatory measures probably require more involvement of government than it can reasonably be expected to provide efficiently. The regulatory approach is sometimes called the **command and control** approach because it requires so much direction from the government. In the case of pollution, the government must ascertain the level at which emissions become dangerous, and then set appropriate standards for every smokestack and waste pipe. In practice, the government cannot have separate standards for each factory. Typically, it applies a uniform standard, regardless of the marginal costs firms face; it may, for instance, order the same cutback in pollution from everyone, without regard for differences in the costs of abatement. This may seem fair, but it is inefficient. In addition, although businesses clearly have an economic incentive to avoid the fines or legal penalties that the government can impose, once they have met the standard, they have no real incentive to find innovative ways of reducing pollution further or exceeding the standard.

Indeed, one of the criticisms of the regulatory system is that firms seem to spend more energy fighting the regulations and working to have them altered than they do trying to improve their performance with respect to the environment. If businesses have a chance of being exempted from the regulations, perhaps by arguing that such restrictions will produce a loss of jobs or other hardships, it may be more cost effective to pay lawyers to lobby the Environmental Protection Agency, the organization responsible for enforcing the regulations, than to pay engineers to develop a less polluting technology.

THE TAX AND SUBSIDY RESPONSE

Between property rights and regulatory measures lie other solutions to the problem of negative externalities. One is to use either taxes or subsidies to encourage the behavior society wants. Taxes are the stick, while subsidies are the carrot; both share the aim of adjusting private costs to account for social costs.

Fines for violating regulations and taxes for polluting are similar: they both increase the cost of and thereby discourage pollution. The central difference is that regulations tend to be black and white, while taxes or subsidies deal better with the gray area in between. Typically, regulations provide very high penalties for violating a specified level of pollution, but no reward for maintaining levels of pollution below the threshold. Systems of taxes offer more uniform, graduated rewards—the more pollution is reduced, the lower the tax paid. They thus provide firms with *marginal* incentives to reduce pollution. The extent of pollution abatement will depend on the costs of pollution abatement. Such systems lead to "efficient pollution," since firms with low abatement costs will reduce pollution more than firms with high abatement costs.

Rather than taxing firms in relation to the pollution they produce, the government might offer them subsidies, perhaps in the form of tax credits for pollution-abatement devices. Such a subsidy does not decrease a firm's output. If we take the extreme case where the government simply pays for the pollution-abatement equipment, output will remain the same. The marginal private costs of the production of steel, for example, are exactly the same as they were when there was no government intervention. The firm will fail to cut back its production to the socially efficient level.

The fact that some of the pollution has been abated means that the marginal social costs of production are lower. This is true even after we take into account the costs of the pollution-abatement equipment. The reason for this is that the value of the reduction in pollution exceeds the costs of the pollution-abatement equipment. Thus, the discrepancy between the socially efficient solution and the market solution is reduced; subsidies for pollution-abatement equipment are, in this sense, beneficial.

Firms prefer subsidies over taxes, for a reason that should be obvious: they are better off with subsidies. Economists, on the other hand, tend to favor using taxes to discourage pollution. If these taxes are set at the right level, they argue, pollution will be no higher than it would be under a command and control system. And taxes give companies an incentive to reduce their pollution as far as possible and to find new, low-cost ways of reducing pollution, rather than just keeping pollution under the legal standard.

The reason economists prefer taxes over subsidies is not that they are anti-industry. Rather, economic efficiency requires that the price of each good reflect its full (marginal) costs of production. Among those costs are the costs to the environment. If those costs are high, there should be less production of that good. With subsidies, firms are not paying the full costs; part of the costs are being picked up by the government. The true cost of steel includes the cost of pollution as well as the cost of pollution control. If pollution abatement is subsidized, then users of steel do not bear the true costs of steel. They do not pay the cost of the subsidy for pollution abatement, and they do not pay the cost that society must bear for the pollution that remains even after the pollution-abatement equipment is installed.

THE MARKETABLE PERMIT RESPONSE

Another approach to curbing pollution is the use of **marketable permits**. Companies purchase (or are granted) a permit from the government that allows them to emit a certain amount of pollution. Again, the government issues only enough permits so that the level of pollution would be the same as it would be under the command and control approach. However, companies are allowed to sell their permits. Thus, if a company cuts its pollution in half, it could sell some of its permits to another company that wants to expand production (and hence its emission of pollutants).

The incentive effects of marketable permits are very much like those of taxes. A market for pollution permits encourages the creation of the best possible antipollution devices, rather than just keeping the pollution under some government-set limit. If the government wishes to reduce pollution over time, the permits can be designed to reduce the amount of pollution they allow by a set amount each year. In the United States, this sort of shrinking marketable permit was used to reduce the amount of lead in gasoline during the early 1980s. Variants of this idea have recently been adopted to help control other forms of air pollution.

WEIGHING THE ALTERNATIVE APPROACHES

Incentive programs, such as taxes, subsidies, or marketable permits, have an important advantage over direct controls, like regulations. The issue of pollution is not whether it should be allowed—after all, it is virtually impossible to eliminate all pollution in an industrial economy. Nor would it be efficient; the costs of doing so would far exceed the benefits. The real issue is how sharply pollution should be limited; the *marginal* benefits have to be weighed against the marginal costs. If government ascertains the marginal social cost of pollution and sets charges and permits accordingly, private firms will engage in pollution control up to the point at which the marginal cost of pollution control equals the marginal social return of pollution abatement (which is, of course, just the marginal cost of pollution). Each firm will have the correct marginal incentives.

Governments often prefer direct regulations because they believe that they can control the outcomes better. But such control can be illusory. If an unreachable standard is set, it is likely to be repealed. For example, as automobile companies have found the costs of various regulations to be prohibitive, they have repeatedly appealed for a delay in the enforcement of the regulations, often with considerable success. Figuring out the right level of pollution fines or permits is no easy matter. There is uncertainty about the consequences of pollution and debate over how to value certain options: to what extent can environmental degradation be reversed? How much value should be placed on the extinction of a species like the spotted owl, or the preservation of the Arctic wilderness? No matter what approach is chosen to externalities and the environment, such questions will remain controversial.

SOLVING THE PROBLEM OF EXTERNALITIES

Externalities, which occur when the extra costs and benefits of a transaction are not fully summed up in the market price, give rise to market failure. Four main solutions have been proposed and used:

1. The reassignment of property rights
2. Regulations that outlaw the negative externality
3. Tax and subsidy measures to encourage the behavior society wants
4. Marketable permits

NATURAL RESOURCES

There is a recurrent theme among environmentalists that our society is squandering its natural resources too rapidly. We are using up oil and energy resources at an alarming rate, hardwood timber forests that took hundreds of years to grow are being cut down, and supplies of vital resources like phosphorus are dwindling. There are repeated calls for government intervention to enhance the conservation of our scarce natural resources. Those who believe in the infallibility of markets reply, nonsense! Prices give the same guidance to the use of natural resources that they give to any other resource, these people say. Prices measure scarcity, and send consumers and firms the right signals about how much effort to expend to conserve resources, so long as consumers and firms are well-informed, and so long as there is not some other source of market failure.

There is, in fact, some truth in both positions. Prices, in general, do provide signals concerning the scarcity of resources, and in the absence of market failures, those signals lead to economic efficiency. We have seen some cases where they do not: when there are externalities or when a resource (like the fish in the ocean) is not priced. In these cases, the rate at which fishing grounds are exploited or at which air is polluted in a private market economy without government intervention will not be efficient.

But what about a privately owned resource, like bauxite (from which aluminum is made) or copper? The owner of a bauxite mine has a clearly defined property right. Let's assume that he pays a tax appropriate to any pollution his mining operation causes. Thus, the price he charges will reflect both social and private costs. The question of resource depletion now boils down to the question of whether his bauxite is worth more to him in the market or in the ground. The answer depends on what bauxite will be worth in the future, say thirty years from now. If it is worth more thirty years from now, then even though he may not be alive, he will keep the bauxite in the ground. That way he maximizes the value of his property, and he can enjoy his wise decision by selling the mine when he retires, perhaps fifteen years from now. Its price should reflect the present discounted value of the bauxite.

If this miner and all other bauxite producers choose to bring the bauxite to market today, depleting the world's supply of bauxite, then we can assume either that this is the socially efficient outcome—society values bauxite more highly today than it will tomorrow—or that the miners have miscalculated the value of bauxite thirty years from now and underestimated future prices, though they have every incentive to get as accurate a forecast as they can. If they have indeed miscalculated, we might view the result as a market failure; but there would be no reason to expect a government bureaucracy to do any better than the firms at guessing future prices.

There are two plausible reasons why private owners may undervalue future benefits of a natural resource. First, in many countries where property rights are not secure, owners of a resource may feel that if they do not sell it soon, there is a reasonable chance that the resource will be taken away from them before they sell it. There may be a revolution in which the government will take over the resource and only partially compensate the owners. Even in countries like the United States, where owners are not worried about government confiscating their property, increased regulations might make it more expensive to extract the resource in the future, or higher taxes might make it less attractive to sell the resource in the future. Second, in many cases, individuals and firms face limited borrowing opportunities, and they must pay very high interest rates. In these circumstances, capital markets discount future returns at a high rate, far higher than society or the government would discount them.

Higher interest rates induce a more rapid depletion of resources. Suppose an oil company is deciding whether to extract some oil today or to wait until next year. For simplicity, assume there are no extraction costs, so the net return to selling the oil is just its price. If the price of a barrel of oil is the same today as a year from now, the firm's decision is simple: the value of a dollar today is greater than the value of a dollar a year from now, so the firm will clearly sell the oil today. But what if the price of oil is expected to go up by 10 percent? Now the firm must compare the present discounted value of the oil sold a year from now with what it could receive today. To calculate the present discounted value, we simply divide next year's price by 1 plus the interest rate. If the interest rate is 10 percent, then a dollar a year from now is worth 10 percent less than a dollar today. So if the interest rate is less than 10 percent, it pays the firm to wait; if the interest rate is more than 10 percent, it pays the firm to extract the oil today. At higher interest rates, firms have a greater incentive to extract oil earlier.

Rather than being the solution to the perceived waste of natural resources, government is sometimes the problem. In the United States, much of the timber lies on government lands, and the government, in making the land available, has paid less attention to concerns about economic efficiency than it has to the pleading of timber interest groups. Government policies aimed at restricting the import of foreign oil have encouraged the use of domestic resources, a seemingly perverse policy of "drain America first." Government policies in keeping the price of water for farmers low has led to excessive use of water, draining water from underground basins built up over centuries, lowering the water table, and in some cases, leaching out the soil. In each of these cases, private property rights and market outcomes would have supplied solutions that almost everyone in society would regard as better.

MERIT GOODS AND BADS

To some people, how we treat the environment and the earth's natural resources is not just a matter of economic efficiency; it is a moral issue. The question of whether we should allow whaling to the extent that some species become extinct cannot be approached narrowly from the perspective of economic costs and benefits. This is but one example of several in which government becomes involved not just because markets have failed to produce efficient outcomes, but because it believes there are values that supersede those reflected in individual preferences, and it has the right and duty to impose those values on its citizens.

The view that government can make better choices in some matters than individuals is called **paternalism**. When the government takes a paternalistic stance and either mandates or outlaws the consumption of a good, the good is called a **merit good** in the first case and a **merit bad** in the second. Education is an example of a merit good. All states have laws mandating that children attend school at least until the age of sixteen. There are many examples of merit bads. In 1919, a constitutional amendment was passed prohibiting the sale of alcoholic beverages. While the amendment was repealed in 1933, it remains illegal for customers under twenty-one to purchase alcoholic beverages in most states. Throughout the United States, it is illegal to buy, sell, or consume hard drugs. Laws against pornography vary from community to community, but are common throughout the United States.

In each of these cases, externalities are present. For instance, those who drink ex-

CLOSE-UP: VALUE OF A LIFE

Policy advocates who are not quite sure of their ground sometimes proclaim: "If this policy saves even one life, it is worth any cost." That rhetoric may be inspiring, but economists also argue that it is wrong. Life is extraordinarily precious, but a decision to save lives at any cost would mean, for example, that no one would be allowed to drive, because sooner or later driving would result in a death. Life cannot be lived in a cocoon.

In passing new regulations, government agencies must put some value on life, to determine when new regulations make economic sense. By how much should exposure to pesticides be reduced? Should air bags be required equipment in cars? What exposure to radiation is acceptable inside a nuclear power plant, and outside it? What chemicals must be controlled in the workplace, and to what extent? The table lists the value put on a life by different departments of the federal government. The larger figures indicate a more safety-conscious approach. The Nuclear Regulatory Commission's regulations, for instance will impose greater costs on nuclear power plants than the Department of Agriculture will impose on farms. Also, although the numbers are large, which is certainly appropriate, none claim that every step must be taken to save every life, no matter what the cost.

Source: Christopher Scanlan, "Federal Numbers Game: Putting a Price on Life," *San Jose Mercury News,* August 13, 1990, p. 2A.

Department of Agriculture	$1.1 million
Department of Transportation	$1 to $1.5 million
Office of Management and Budget	$1 to $2 million
Consumer Product Safety Commission	$1.5 to $2 million
Occupational Health and Safety Administration	$2 to $3.5 million
Nuclear Regulatory Commission	$5 million
Environmental Protection Agency	$1.6 to $8 million

cessively cause traffic accidents. But the argument for prohibition went beyond this externality to the contention that drinking was simply bad for the individual; likewise for hard drugs and pornography. Educating the citizenry produces extra, economy-wide benefits, but the legal requirement that parents send their children to school has a broader base than this: the government is responding to the view that any parent who would rather not send her child to school has made a fundamental mistake of judgment.

In most areas within economics, it is assumed that individuals know best what meets their needs, or what gives them satisfaction or pleasure (the principle of consumer sovereignty). If you like to wear loud red shirts, that is your privilege. No one from the government has the right to tell you that your tastes are wrong or misguided. If you enjoy listening to rock music on your Walkman, that is your right. The merit goods argument says that when such goods as alcohol, drugs, pornography, threatened species, and a child's education are involved, there are exceptions to this general principle. (In the case of education, since children do not make decisions for themselves, it is not so much a matter of consumer sovereignty as one of *who* should make decisions for them.) It is a noneconomic argument for government intervention, but no discussion of government's role would be complete without mentioning it.

PUBLIC FAILURES

Economists encourage those proposing government solutions to market failures and unequal income distribution to recall that governments are no more infallible than private markets. Government is not some sort of well-intentioned computer that only makes impersonal decisions about what is right for society as a whole. Instead, government is a group of people—some elected, some appointed, some hired—who are intertwined in a complex structure of decision making. Many of them have particular duties that conflict with the duties of others; for example, one official may be in charge of promoting U.S. exports, while another is in charge of making sure that no products are exported that will help enemy nations build better weapons. Some people are responsible to the district that elected them, some to the person who appointed them, and some (like judges) to an abstract rule of law.

Most people who work for government may care a lot about society as a whole, but they may disagree about how to make society better off. And their concern with society is tempered by other considerations; for elected officials, there is the question of getting reelected. So when government is proposed as a cure-all for what ails society, it is always appropriate to inquire into not only the extent of the problem, but also whether government can effectively address it.

Recent decades have provided numerous examples of government programs that have either failed or at least not succeeded to the extent that their sponsors had hoped. Urban renewal programs, meant to revive the inner cities and to provide housing for the poor, wound up destroying more low-income housing than they created. There is a concern that the welfare programs, intended to provide a safety net for the poor, have helped to perpetuate the cycle of poverty. Out of the failures and limited successes of government programs has emerged a better understanding of the causes of these failures.

IMPERFECT INFORMATION

Just as imperfect information poses a problem in the private sector, so too does it pose a problem in the public. The government would like to make sure, for instance, that public welfare assistance goes only to those who really need it. But it is costly to sort out the truly deserving from those who are not, and sometimes the undeserving receive funds. The existence of these errors should not be taken as a criticism, but simply as a statement of inevitable fact. By spending more on screening applicants, a better job can be done; but then resources that could have been spent on welfare recipients would be spent on administration. As always, there are trade-offs.

INCENTIVES AND THE EFFICIENCY OF GOVERNMENT

Problems of incentives in the public sector are probably even more important than similar problems in the private sector. For example, home owners have an incentive to maintain their property, not only because it is more enjoyable to live in an attractive house, but also because when they decide to sell, such a house will fetch a higher price. Those who live in public apartments have no such incentives. The quality of their apartment building from their perspective is like a public good; each individual has an insufficient incentive to exert the efforts required to maintain public amenities. And while the owner of a private apartment building has strong incentives both to maintain the building and to ensure that tenants do not abuse the property (he can refuse to renew leases for "bad" tenants), managers of public housing have no comparable incentives, and often have limited discretion in refusing to renew leases.

In general, public officials work under a set of civil service rules. The rules are often inflexible enough that it is difficult to pay good public officials a salary comparable to what similarly qualified and hardworking people receive in the private sector, or to offer them opportunities for rapid promotion; and it is even more difficult to fire or demote incompetent and lazy workers. Under these rules, providing incentives for efficiency and recruiting first-rate workers can be very difficult.

Some economists believe that incentives in the public sector actually lead to perverse decisions that are against broad social welfare. Legislators' concern about votes leads to "pork barrel" legislation, whose primary value is to create jobs or improve amenities in a legislator's home district. Presumably, most pork barrel projects would not be undertaken if those who lived in the district had to pay for it themselves, but the projects sound good if the rest of the country is footing the bill. It is widely believed, for instance, that a large number of unneeded military bases have been kept open because of congressional pressure.

Moreover, elected officials need funds to run their campaigns, and this makes them particularly attentive to those who can assist with campaign finances. The influence of the farm lobby in obtaining support, far out of proportion to the number of voters whose livelihood depends on agriculture, is frequently attributed to this sort of "special interest" lobbying. Unions and many other groups have formed Political Action Committees (PACs) to provide funds to congressional representatives who are sympathetic to their views. Naturally, lobbyists for these special interest groups claim that they are not buying politicians, simply providing them with information needed to make an informed judgment, and then supporting those who have seen the truth.

UNFORESEEN RESPONSES TO A PROGRAM

The success or failure of programs in the public sector depends not only on public officials, but also on how the private sector responds. Predicting those private responses is difficult, and many government programs have faced problems because of this difficulty. For example, providing almost free medical care to the aged, through Medicare, greatly increased the demand for medical services by the aged, leading to increases in costs well beyond those originally projected. Government education loan programs forgot to take into account the incentives of those with large debts to declare bankruptcy soon after completing their education, when they have almost no assets to lose.

As another example, in 1990, the government required that drug companies provide drugs to the government at the lowest price sold on the market. The government had observed that drug companies sold drugs to some customers at prices below those at which they were selling drugs to government under the Medicare program and calculated that it could save billions of dollars by taking advantage of these discounts. But the drug companies decided that it simply did not pay to discount at all if they had to give the government a discount every time they gave someone else a discount. As a result, instead of saving the government money, the legislation wound up costing other users of drugs more money!

Often a problem arises not from the overall design of a government program, but from a particular regulation. The Aid to Families with Dependent Children program (AFDC) used to have an eligibility requirement that there not be a man in the household (some states still have this requirement). The program may thus have contributed to the breakup of families. At other times, a problem occurs as an almost inevitable result of the program. Providing better Social Security has enabled many elderly to live on their own, rather than being dependent on their children. Whether it was the "push" of the children wanting to be freed of this burden, or the desire of the elderly for more independence, the consequence has been the same. These elderly, whose only or major source of income is Social Security, may (apart from the benefits of independence) be actually worse off than they were when they were living with their children. The true beneficiaries of increased Social Security may be not the elderly but their children, who have been relieved of a burden that they otherwise would have assumed.

SOURCES OF PUBLIC FAILURES

Imperfect information

Problems of incentives, particularly for those charged with administering government programs

Failure to assess the full consequences of government programs, including responses of the private sector

GOVERNMENT DECISION MAKING

Earlier chapters showed how the behavior of the household could be described as if it were maximizing its utility, subject to a budget constraint, and how the behavior of the firm could be described as if it were maximizing profits or market value. Is there any simple model that we can use to predict or explain the behavior of the government?

Understanding how and why the government makes the decisions it does has become an active field of research, referred to as **public choice theory.** James Buchanan of George Mason University received the Nobel Prize for his pioneering work in this area. Government is a collection of many individuals with differing interests and objectives. Therefore, it is not accurate to think of government as a single individual, or as if it has a well-defined set of objectives. In fact, the government often seems to behave in a somewhat inconsistent manner.

THE VOTING PARADOX

The seeming inconsistency of democratic governments is highlighted by what is called the **voting paradox.** This puzzle, first noted more than two hundred years ago by the Frenchman Marquis de Condorcet, involves three people choosing among three alternatives. As an illustration, consider three people who want to go to a movie together. They have narrowed their choices down to three movies, which they rank in this way.

	Jessica's preferences	Ralph's preferences	Brutus' preferences
First choice:	Young and Romantic	Third and Goal to Go	Automatic Avengers
Second choice:	Third and Goal to Go	Automatic Avengers	Young and Romantic
Third choice:	Automatic Avengers	Young and Romantic	Third and Goal to Go

Since the three people believe in democratic decision making, they decide to vote on a choice of movie. So they compare each of the movies. They find that *Young and Romantic* is preferred over *Third and Goal to Go* by a 2–1 margin. They find that *Third and Goal to Go* is preferred to *Automatic Avengers* by a 2–1 margin. It should stand to reason, since *Young and Romantic* is preferred over *Third and Goal to Go* and *Third and Goal to Go* is preferred over *Automatic Avengers*, that *Young and Romantic* is also preferred to *Automatic Avengers*. But when they put it to a vote, they find that *Automatic Avengers* is preferred to *Young and Romantic* by a 2–1 margin. There is no majority winner. This sets up a situation where majority vote can compare any two of these choices, but is incapable of ranking all three of them.

Nobel laureate Kenneth Arrow proved an even more remarkable result: there exists *no* voting system (two-thirds majority, weighted majority, or any other) that, under some circumstances, would not yield the same kind of indecision. Inconsistencies seem inherent in some of the decisions made by any democratic government. The only way around this problem, to ensure that consistent choices are made, is to entrust a single individual with all decisions. Such a system yields consistent choices, but is hardly democratic!

THE IMPORTANCE OF THE MEDIAN VOTER

Fortunately, inconsistencies in democratic decision making do not always arise. What happens if there is a vote over a simple issue like how much to spend on public schools? Some individuals want more to be spent, some less. Whose preferences dominate? The answer depends, of course, on the rules by which decisions are made. The **median voter theory** provides a remarkably simple prediction of the outcome in the case of majority voting. It is the median voter—half of the population want more to be spent than this voter, and half want less—whose preferences dominate. For instance, assume the median voter wants $5,000 to be spent per pupil and there are 40,001 voters. Consider a vote between $5,000 per pupil and $3,000, with 20,000 voters favoring $5,100 or more and 20,000 favoring $3,000 or less. Since all of those who want $5,100 or more spent will vote for $5,000, $5,000 will win. It gets 20,001 votes. This is the choice the median voter would have made by herself if the decision had been left to her. The same outcome would result if the vote was between $5,000 and a larger amount. The median voter would join those wanting even less than $5,000, ensuring that $5,000 wins.

Voters, of course, do not decide most issues directly, but elect politicians who vote on issues. Politicians, however, want to get elected. To increase the likelihood that they get elected, they take positions that will increase their vote. If both parties take positions to maximize their votes, both will take positions reflecting the views of the median voter.

To understand this point, imagine that the amounts different individuals would like the government to spend are arranged from the smallest to the largest. Suppose there are two parties, and one party takes the position reflecting the individual at the 40th percentile; that is, 40 percent would like the government to spend less, 60 percent would like it to spend more. The other party will win simply by taking a position close to that of the voter representing the 41st percentile. That party would get 59 percent of the vote, garnering the votes of all those who prefer higher spending; it would win by a landslide. Of course, the first party knows this and tries to find a position such that the opposition cannot undercut it and win a majority. There are thus strong incentives for both parties to take positions closely reflecting the views of the median voter.

This theory explains why voters often feel that they do not have a choice: the two parties are both trying to find the middle position, so that they will not be defeated. The theory also gives us a first theory for forecasting government behavior: government will approximate the interests of the median voter.[2]

There are many circumstances in which the median voter theory does not resolve the voting paradox. If there is a single variable being voted upon, say the level of expenditure on education, and different individuals have a "most preferred" level and will vote for outcomes closer to that level, then the median voter will determine the outcome. But in other cases, in which alternatives cannot be simply ranked in terms of "more" or "less" (as in the three-movie example given earlier), the voting paradox will arise and there is no clear theoretical prediction of the outcome of the electoral process.

INTEREST GROUPS AND RENT SEEKING

Frequently government action does not seem even to remotely approach behavior that would reflect the interests of the median voter. Rather, it more nearly represents interests of particular groups. Economists have sought economic explanations for this.

[2] The principle that both parties will gravitate toward the center (reflecting the views of the median voter) was first analyzed by the economist-statistician Harold Hotelling, who taught at Columbia University and North Carolina State.

It has become increasingly costly for candidates to run a campaign, to inform voters of their views, and to get out the vote. Special-interest groups find it worthwhile to support one party or person or another, provided that their interests are served. In American politics, these groups argue that it is in the general interest for their interests to be served. Thus, the dairy industry argues for huge subsidies; car manufacturers want protection from "unfair" foreign competition; and the gas and oil industries argue for huge subsidies through the tax system, stressing the importance of energy for the American economy.

Economists refer to these activities as **rent seeking**. Rents, as we learned in Chapter 13, are returns enjoyed by a factor of production that go beyond those required to elicit its supply. The term "rent *seeking*" is used generally when individuals or firms devote their energies to the procurement of rents or other special favors from the government. Government, through its power to tax, to set tariffs, to provide subsidies, and to intervene in other ways with private markets, can affect the profitability of various enterprises enormously. For example, the attempt by U.S. car producers to restrict foreign competition is referred to as rent seeking. As a result of protection from foreign competition, they find that they can get higher prices and make bigger profits.

As long as the government has the discretion to grant rents and other special favors, firms and individuals will find it pays to engage in rent-seeking behavior—that is, they will try to persuade government to grant them tariffs or other benefits—and the decisions of government accordingly get distorted. It may make little difference whether this behavior comes in the form of direct bribes, as is frequently the case in less developed countries, or campaign contributions that serve to influence how congressional representatives vote. Either way, a second aspect of government behavior has emerged: that governments respond to the rent-seeking behavior of special-interest groups.

BUREAUCRATS

The final aspect of government behavior that we will take up is the theory of bureaucracy. The government consists not only of elected officials, but also of those appointed by elected officials and the civil service, whose job it is to administer government programs. Just as in the private sector managers' interests may not perfectly coincide with those of shareholders, so too the government sector may suffer a principal-agent problem. Public managers may not do what the elected officials would ideally like, or what is, in some broader sense, in the public interest. The interests of the bureaucrats, responsible for administering the laws, do not always coincide exactly with the electorate, or their elected representatives.

Even if they are partly concerned with doing a good job, bureaucrats are also concerned with their own careers. For instance, concern about making mistakes may lead them to act in a risk-averse manner. Because it is so difficult to assess the "output" of administrators, judgments of performance may depend more on the extent to which an individual has conformed to certain "bureaucratic" procedures, which partially accounts for the proliferation of red tape. Bureaucrats may have an interest in expanding their spheres of influence, just as any businessperson has an interest in the growth of her business. But while a businessperson expands her business by providing a good at a cheaper price, bureaucrats expand their scale by persuading the legislature either that they need more funds or personnel to do what has to be done, or that there should be more of whatever it is they do.

Bureaucrats often compete against one another for funds, and this competition may have deleterious effects. The competition between the army, air force, and navy have led to some important problems in coordination among the U.S. armed services, with each service insisting on separate types of weapons systems, like separate airplanes, when costs might have been reduced if a common design had been agreed upon. These issues have been of sufficient concern that in 1986, Congress mandated a major reorganization of the military.

BINDING COMMITMENTS

Governments differ from individuals and firms in one other way. Individuals can sign a contract to agree to do something five or ten years from now. But each government is sovereign; the current government may not feel itself bound by the decision of a previous government. Thus, the current government may convince investors that it will pursue a noninflationary policy, but how can investors be sure that the next administration will not be more concerned with other objectives? Investors, worried about this long-term risk of inflation, may value long-term bonds less than they would if the current government could somehow commit future governments to a low-inflation policy. These difficulties in making binding commitments thus sometimes impose a serious impediment to the government in accomplishing its objectives.

Constitutions make it easier for governments to make commitments. Though a constitution can be amended, the process is difficult. Thus, in many societies without strong constitutional guarantees, incentives to invest are weakened by the concern that the government can at almost any time confiscate property without paying adequate compensation.

AGRICULTURE: A CASE STUDY IN MIXED MOTIVES

Government programs in agriculture provide an opportunity for studying the mixture of motives as well as public and market failures that so frequently characterize government activities. The United States has a major program of subsidies for agriculture; at their peak, in 1986, expenditures amounted to more than $25 billion per year, or $11,000 per farm. The total cost to the American consumer, however, is far higher, because the major objective of the program is to raise the prices farmers receive—and therefore the prices consumers pay.

There are two justifications the government gives for its agriculture programs. One relates to the fact that prices and output in agriculture are highly variable. These are risks against which a farmer cannot obtain adequate insurance. Thus, the programs are sometimes rationalized on the basis of "stabilizing" prices. But prices are not just stabilized around an average price, as they would be if the objective were truly risk reduction. Rather, prices are stabilized around a higher level, necessitating huge government purchases of some goods in order to sustain the prices. Moreover, the risk that farmers really care about is the risk to their income. Price stabilization programs do not eliminate income risk. Income depends on the price of outputs, the level of output, and costs; price stabilization programs only affect one of the three variables. If risk

CLOSE-UP: ECONOMICS, LIABILITY, AND THE LAW

At first glance, law and economics may seem like lines that do not cross. Law consists of the rules of conduct that a community formally recognizes as binding on its members. Economics is a study of the self-interested behavior of individuals who face choices imposed by the scarcity of resources.

However, in many contexts, it is possible to use economic reasoning to determine if the rules of law are the least costly way—or even an effective way at all—of reaching social goals. One of the most striking interactions between economics and law has been in the evolution of liability law.

Through the nineteenth century, one could only be held liable in a court case for behavior that deviated greatly from the norm; for example, if you kept a wild animal as a pet and it escaped, or if you kept explosives in your back garden and they blew up the neighbor's house. By definition, actions that were very different from normal do not happen all that often, so liability law was quite restricted.

By the early twentieth century, though, this sort of liability law was felt to be inadequate. After all, many people are injured in the normal course of events—in the workplace, while driving, while using various products, and so on. If liability only applied to the abnormal, these people would receive no compensation.

Economists pointed out in the 1930s and 1940s that if employers, drivers, or manufacturers could impose negative externalities on others without having to pay a price, they would cause far too many such injuries. Moreover, economists of that time argued that the liability system could be viewed as a sort of insurance system. In the case of injuries caused by products, for example, manufacturers would charge a little more to everyone (like an insurance premium) and use the money to pay off the lawsuits of those who were injured.

By the 1960s, the legal rule had evolved into "strict" liability. The economic arguments had per-

suaded the legal system that holding all parties responsible for *all* harm they did, whether they had behaved abnormally or not, was a useful way to encourage safer behavior and assure that victims of accidents received compensation. But this system of strict liability ran into problems. While it reduced the occurrence of negative externalities, it led to an explosion of lawsuits. Some of these seemed frivolous, like one brought by a person who was injured diving off a garage into a four-foot-deep pool of water; he sued the pool manufacturer for damages and won. As the number of lawsuits rose, so did the insurance premiums necessary to cover them. Moreover, when manufacturers knew that they would be liable for any harm resulting from a product, no matter how carefully they had tested it beforehand, they became more hesitant to introduce new, different products, even if they might be better than previous products.

Currently some students of the growing field of law and economics are working to redesign systems of liability law and insurance in the United States, so that they will provide compensation to victims and incentives to avoid harmful behavior but will also avoid the problems of frivolous lawsuits and discouragement of innovative new products. There are, however, no easy answers to be found.

Many other examples of the overlap between economics and law have already surfaced in this book: antitrust laws, patent law, laws prohibiting deceptive advertising, and the market-oriented environmental laws discussed in this chapter are just a few. The underlying lesson is that just as an economy relies on a physical infrastructure of roads, airports, telephone lines, electricity, and so on, it relies just as heavily on a legal infrastructure of stable rules.

Source: George Priest, "The Modern Expansion of Tort Liability: Its Sources, Its Effects, and Its Reform," *Journal of Economic Perspectives* (Summer 1991) 5:31–50.

reduction were really the objective, it would be possible to design a better program to meet that objective.

The second justification is to help disadvantaged farmers in the rural sector. But by their very nature, programs that provide support by raising the prices result in large farmers receiving more than small farmers. This is because the more farmers sell, the greater their subsidy. In assessing whether poverty alleviation is really the objective, one needs to ask two questions: Is there any reason why the United States should be more concerned about the poor in the rural sector than poor elsewhere in the economy? And even if a reason could be found for a program directed at poor farmers, couldn't a program be designed that got at this problem more directly, rather than providing larger subsidies to larger farmers?

A closer look at the farm programs suggests that at least some of them are principally motivated by special-interest groups trying to get subsidies for themselves, at the expense of taxpayers and consumers at large. Three of the subsidy programs are for milk, rice, and tobacco. Both milk and rice farmers are reasonably well off, and it is particularly hard to justify these programs in terms of distribution objectives. Many of the rice farms are in California, on irrigated land. Even with large government subsidies, rice farming is profitable only because the price of water is heavily subsidized. It is ironic that in a state that is facing major shortages of water, the government would be subsidizing rice. Similarly, there is a certain irony in the government spending large amounts of money trying to convince individuals that smoking is bad for your health at the same time it spends large amounts of money subsidizing tobacco farmers!

REVIEW AND PRACTICE

SUMMARY

1. Government may have a role in the economy when markets fail to produce an efficient outcome. When positive or negative externalities exist, markets will not provide an efficient outcome.

2. One way to deal with externalities is to assign clear-cut property rights.

3. Governments may deal with environmental externalities by imposing regulatory measures (the command and control approach), levying taxes and granting subsidies, or issuing marketable permits.

4. In a perfect market, natural resources are used up at an efficient rate. However, privately owned resources may be sold too soon, for two reasons. First, owners may fear that if they do not sell the resources soon, new government rules may prevent them from selling at all or, in any case, lower the return from selling it in the future. Second, interest rates facing owners may be higher, so they may value future income less than society in general. High interest rates lead to a faster exploitation of natural resources.

5. One argument for government intervention in the economy, called paternalism, is that some merit bads like alcohol, drugs, and pornography should simply not be available to some or all people, because it would not be good for those people.

6. Sources of public failure include imperfect information for designing and implementing programs; incentive problems facing public officials and bureaucrats, leading them to work in their own interest as well as a broader public interest; and the difficulties of foreseeing fully the consequences of government programs.

7. Different voters have, in general, different views about what the government should do. In some cases, the choice made in majority voting reflects the preferences of the median voter. In other cases, there is no determinate outcome to a process of majority voting.

KEY TERMS

market failures approach	Coase's theorem	voting paradox
social marginal cost	paternalism	median voter
private marginal cost	merit goods and bads	rent seeking

REVIEW QUESTIONS

1. Name several market failures. Why do economists see the existence of these market failures as a justification for government action?

2. Why will a free market produce too much of goods that have negative externalities, like pollution? Why will a free market produce too little of goods that have positive externalities, like pollution control?

3. What are the advantages and limitations of dealing with externalities by assigning property rights?

4. What are the advantages of marketable permits over command and control regulation? What are the advantages of using taxes for polluting rather than subsidies for pollution-abatement equipment?

5. How do markets work to allocate natural resources efficiently? In what cases will markets fail to give the correct signals for how quickly a resource like oil should be depleted?

6. How does the existence of merit goods provide a case for government intervention in markets?

7. What is meant by government failure? What are its sources?

8. What is the voting paradox?

9. What is the median voter? Why does the median voter matter so much in a system of majority rule?

PROBLEMS

1. Marple and Wolfe are two neighboring dormitories. Wolfe is considering giving a party with a very loud band, which will have a negative externality, a sort of sound pollution, for Marple. Imagine that the school administration decides that any dormitory has the right to prevent another dorm from hiring a band. If the band provides a negative externality, how might the residents of Wolfe apply the lessons of Coase's theorem to hire the band they want?

Now imagine that the school administration decides that no dormitory can prevent another dorm from hiring a band, no matter how loud. If the band provides a negative externality, how might the residents of Marple apply the lessons of Coase's theorem to reduce the amount of time they have to listen to the band? How would your answer change if the band provided a positive externality?

2. The manufacture of trucks produces pollution of various kinds; for the purposes of this example, let's call it all "glop." Producing a truck creates one unit of glop, and glop has a cost to society of $3,000. Imagine that the supply of trucks is competitive, and market supply and demand are given by the following data:

Price (thousands $)	19	20	21	22	23	24	25
Quantity supplied	480	540	600	660	720	780	840
Quantity demanded	660	630	600	570	540	510	480

Graph the supply curve for the industry and the demand curve. What are equilibrium price and output? Now graph the social marginal cost curve. If the social cost of glop were taken into account, what would be the new equilibrium price and output?

If the government is concerned about the pollution emitted by truck plants, explain how it might deal with the externality through fines or taxes and through subsidies. Illustrate the effects of taxes and subsidies by drawing the appropriate supply and demand graphs. (Don't bother worrying about the exact units.) Why are economists likely to prefer fines to subsidies?

3. Explain how the argument for government intervention in the case of merit goods is different from the argument for intervention in the case of externalities. Are merit goods a case of market failure? Explain.

4. Private markets have often failed to provide loans to college students. Because of imperfect information, lenders cannot be sure that students will be able to repay the loans, or even that they will be able to find the students after graduation. If the government attempts to deal with this market failure by offering student loans itself, what problems do you expect to arise?

5. Suppose you are considering building a food stand along a mile-long strip of beach, but you know that one other vendor is definitely planning to build a stand too. If visitors are evenly distributed along the beach, and people will buy from whichever food stand is closest to them, where should you decide to build your stand? If the goal is to have the shortest possible *average* distance for people to get to food, where should the two stands be located? (Hint: Think about the situation of two political parties competing for the median voter.)

6. Consider a small lake with a certain number of fish. The more fish that one fisherman takes out, the fewer fish are available for others to take out. Use graphs depicting private and social costs and benefits to fishing to describe the equilibrium and the socially efficient level of fishing. Explain how a tax on fishing could achieve the efficient outcome. Explain how giving a single individual the property right to the fish in the lake might also be used to obtain an efficient outcome.

The more fish taken out this year, the less fish will be available next year. Explain why if there is a single owner for the lake, the fish will be efficiently extracted from it. Assume that anyone who wants to fish can do so. Would you expect that too many fish would be taken out this year?

CHAPTER 24

TAXATION
AND REDISTRIBUTION

D uring this century, governments have become increasingly involved in altering the distribution of income. The distribution of income provided by the market sometimes seems to leave segments of the population with insufficient income upon which to survive. Children who have the bad fortune to be born into impoverished families face bleak prospects. Governments of most developed countries have therefore sought to provide a safety net for the poor, and some have taken an even more active stance in promoting equality of opportunity.

The subject of income redistribution is inextricably linked to that of taxation, because virtually every tax system in place in the world today changes or attempts to change the proportion of income enjoyed by different groups in society. After a look at the case for income redistribution, this chapter takes up taxes, redistribution programs, and the interplay between the two.

"Stop referring to my husband as 'he whose ox is gored'!"

KEY QUESTIONS

1. What are the characteristics of a good tax system, and how does America's current tax system fare under these criteria? What are the various ways that government raises revenues?

2. What do economists mean when they talk about a fair or equitable tax system? What arguments are used to decide how the burden of taxation should be shared among various groups in the population?

3. What are the basic programs designed to provide assistance for the poor? What are the trade-offs between equity and efficiency in the design of these programs?

4. What is the rationale for social insurance programs? What are some of the current public policy controversies concerning these programs?

THE CASE FOR INCOME REDISTRIBUTION

Policies of income redistribution are justified in ways different from other governmental economic policies. The roles of government developed in Chapters 15–23 are based on the premise that public sector intervention may be appropriate when private markets fail. When markets fail, the economy may not produce as much as it could, or may not produce the kinds of products consumers want. In short, markets may fail to provide completely satisfactory answers to two basic economic questions: "What goods are produced, and in what quantities?" and "How are the goods produced?" In the market economy, business firms make output decisions, but the answers they provide may be less than ideal if the markets in which they operate suffer failures of competition or of information. When markets fail to achieve efficient outcomes, government may get involved in making decisions.

When it comes to the question "For whom are the goods produced?," to which this chapter is devoted, the rationale for public sector intervention is different. Individuals' incomes determine who consumes the goods produced in a market economy. People with higher skills or more capital, for instance, earn higher incomes and therefore get to consume more of the goods produced. Labor and capital markets may be efficient, in the sense that wages and returns to capital get the incentive structure right for the economy. But it is entirely possible that the market distribution may result in some individuals having billions of dollars and others being homeless, with inadequate food and medical care. The case for income redistribution thus is not usually based on the pursuit of economic efficiency. It is based on overriding social values: there is a general consensus that when the market results in incomes so low that people cannot sustain a minimum standard of living, government should help these individuals out. When it does, however, care must be taken because redistribution programs often interfere with economic efficiency.

Income redistribution takes the overt form of welfare programs and unemployment benefits, but what is less clear is that the government's involvement with income distribution is an inevitable by-product of its day-to-day operations. The power to tax is basic to government, because without the coercive ability to raise funds, the government could not operate. People in different economic situations pay different amounts in taxes. In deciding how much they pay, the government reformulates the distribution of income set by private markets. If it decides that higher-income individuals should pay higher taxes and lower-income people lower taxes, that decision will alter how the goods available are consumed; the rich will be able to consume less, the poor more than they would if everyone paid the same proportion of their income to government.

We now take a closer look at the tax system.

TAXES

In the United States, government raises tax revenues from a variety of sources. There are taxes on the earnings of individuals and corporations, known as **individual income taxes** and **corporation income taxes**. Capital and income from capital are covered by special taxes and tax provisions. Real estate—buildings and land—is subject to taxation by most states; these taxes are known as **property taxes**. Large bequests and gifts are taxed, through **gift** and **estate taxes**. There are special provisions relating to the taxation of capital gains (the increase in value of an asset between the time an individual purchases it and the time she sells it). Furthermore, wage income is subject not only to the income tax, but also to the **payroll tax** (the tax levied on a company's payroll, half of which is deducted from employees' paychecks), the revenues of which are intended to finance the Social Security (retirement income) and Medicare (medical care for the aged) programs.

There are also taxes on the purchase of specific goods and services, known as **excise taxes**. The two heaviest excise taxes are on alcohol and tobacco; they are sometimes referred to as **sin taxes.** The excise taxes on air travel and gasoline are sometimes called **benefit taxes** because the proceeds are intended to be used to provide benefits, like airports and roads, to those who purchase the good. Excise taxes on perfume, large cars, yachts, and expensive fur coats, targeted to the rich, are referred to as luxury taxes. Other excise taxes, such as the one on telephone services, have no particular justification other than raising revenue. Most states impose a general tax on purchases of goods and services, known as a **sales tax**, though typically a wide variety of items (such as food) are exempted.

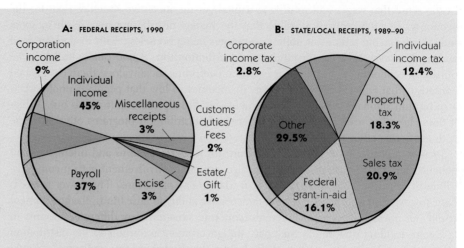

Figure 24.1 THE IMPORTANCE OF VARIOUS TAXES

At the federal level, the largest share of taxes comes from the individual income tax, followed by the payroll tax and the corporate income tax, as shown in panel A. Sources of revenue at the state and local level are more fragmented, as seen in panel B, but include sales and property taxes, as well as revenue received from other levels of government. *Source: Economic Report of the President* (1992), Tables B-76, B-81.

In short, there are few transactions in our economy that escape taxation. Figure 24.1 shows the relative importance of various taxes at the federal and the state and local levels. At the federal level (panel A), the single most important source of revenue is the tax on individuals' income (contributing almost half of total revenue), followed by the payroll tax. There have been marked variations in the importance of the corporation income tax, over time, partly because of changes in tax provisions and partly because corporate profits fluctuate a great deal with economic conditions. Currently the corporation income tax provides about a tenth of all tax revenue.

Historically, property taxes were the most important source of revenue at the state and local levels (panel B), but in the past few decades, sales taxes and income taxes have grown in importance. Those nickels, dimes, and dollars you pay in taxes every time you buy something add up to a fifth of all state and local tax revenue, over $3,000 for each family in the United States.

CHARACTERISTICS OF A GOOD TAX SYSTEM

Approximately one out of every three dollars produced by the U.S. economy goes to the government. Not surprisingly, there is a great deal of concern about how the government raises its revenue. At one time, the art of taxation was described as analogous to the problem of how to pluck a goose without making it squawk. The basic fact of life is that while everyone enjoys government services, few enjoy paying taxes; most people would rather someone else pick up the bill.

Following are five characteristics of a good tax system.

Fairness In most people's minds, the first criterion is fairness. Fairness, however, like beauty, is often in the eyes of the beholder. Economists have tried to define more precisely what should be meant by fairness, and they have focused on two principles:

horizontal equity, which says that individuals who are in identical or similar situations should pay identical or similar taxes, and **vertical equity**, which says that people who are better off should pay more taxes.

There are problems in applying both principles. For instance, what does it mean for different families to be in identical or similar situations? Consider three families with the same income. In one family, all of the income is earned by one individual; in another, both parents have to work full time; in the third, both parents work half time. Under current U.S. tax law, these three families are treated the same. But should they be? Clearly, the second family has much less leisure time than the other two. In most European countries, taxes do not depend on the total income of each household, but on the individual incomes of each worker. Thus, the second and third families (in which both parents work and each receives the same pay) would have the same taxes, but the first family would pay higher taxes, since there is only one breadwinner and his income is twice that of each of the parents in the other two families. Which system is more fair, America's or those in Europe?

Similarly, while the principle of vertical equity says that the rich should pay more in taxes than the poor, it does not say how much more. Tax systems in which the rich pay a larger fraction of their income than the poor are said to be **progressive**, while those in which the poor pay a larger fraction of their income than the rich are called **regressive**. If rich people pay more taxes than the poor but not proportionately more, the tax system is still considered regressive.

The U.S. income tax is, in principle, progressive, since the rates that apply to higher incomes are larger than for lower incomes. Taxes on tobacco and alcohol are examples of regressive taxes, since poor individuals spend a larger fraction of their income on these goods. State sales taxes, on the whole, are regressive, since in general not all goods—such as vacations in Europe—are taxed, and the fraction of income of the rich that thus escapes taxation is larger than that of the poor.

Views about how progressive the tax system *should* be reflect differences in both economic judgments about the costs of a progressive tax system and noneconomic judgments about the benefits. More progressive taxes have higher tax rates on the rich, and this may discourage work effort, entrepreneurial risk taking, and saving. How much is a matter of controversy. But even more controversial are the noneconomic judgments about the benefits. These judgments are based on views about what a "good" society should be like. Some, such as the philosopher Robert Nozick of Harvard University, argue that individuals have a basic right to enjoy the fruits of their labor; if someone works harder or is luckier in being more productive, then it is her basic *right* to have a higher income. Others, such as John Rawls, also a philosopher at Harvard, argue that a just society should do whatever it can to increase the welfare of the worst-off individual. Rawls asks, what would your conception of a just society be if you did not know beforehand whether your place in that society would be in a slum or in the house of a Rockefeller—if, in other words, you had to put aside self-interest and think about the problem of justice behind a "veil of ignorance"? He contends that behind that veil of ignorance people would agree that society should focus its attention on improving the plight of its poor.

In the nineteenth century, a group known as utilitarians argued that the benefit of an extra dollar to the rich was lower than the value of the same dollar to a poor individual. Therefore, they argued, transferring a dollar from the rich to the poor person made society better off: the gain of one person exceeded the loss of the other. Today most

In the 1992 presidential campaign, statistics on income inequality became a major issue. Many had sensed that the rich were getting richer and the poor poorer, but it took new statistics to confirm the fact of growing inequality. The political disagreement was about the possible causes of the growing disparity and about what, if anything, should be done about it.

Facts first: as the table here shows, the proportion of total income received by the highest fifth of all households (ranked by annual money income) rose from 44.1 percent in 1980 to 46.6 percent in 1990. Most of that increase was accounted for by the top 5 percent of households, whose share of total income increased from 16.5 percent to 18.6 percent. These changes by themselves may not look that dramatic, but cast in another way they suggest an alarming trend: other data show that while the average household in the lowest fifth saw its real income increased by 4.3 percent during the decade, an average household in the highest fifth saw its income rise by 18.1 percent. Of the total gain in income during the decade, between 60 and 70 percent went to the upper 1 percent. While the national income pie was getting bigger, almost all of the additional pie was going to very few people. The data suggest that the middle class was shrinking: this is disturbing to those who see America's strength as being a society in which almost everyone is in the middle class.

Looking at wealth (the amount accumulated over time) rather than income (the amount received in a year) makes the inequality look more extreme. One study showed that the top fifth of families (ranked by income) had an average wealth of $586,000 during the 1980s; wealth includes the value of homes, vehicles, businesses, and investments of all sorts. The lowest fifth, on the other hand, had an average of less than $30,000. The top

1 percent holds more total wealth than the bottom 90 percent.

There are inevitable problems that arise in any statistical measure. Did the data correctly account for the value of government subsidies to the poor (housing, medical care, food)? Should gains in the value of stocks and other assets be included in income? But almost any way the statistics are sliced, they still show that the rich became at least richer during the 1980s. In a sense, the statistics should have come as no surprise; economists had been well aware that real wages of the most unskilled workers had been falling since 1973, both absolutely and relatively to wages of skilled workers. Thus, the economic forces that led to the growing income inequality started well before the Bush and Reagan administrations.

Bush administration supporters tried to put as good a face on the statistics as they could. They pointed out that what was important was not income in any particular year, but income over an individual's lifetime. There were a myriad of circumstances that might make a person's income especially low one year and especially high another—a one-year snapshot gave a picture of more inequality than was truly there. They argued that what was important was mobility, the ability of those born into poor families to rise, as in Horatio Alger stories. There was some truth in these perspectives: while inequality was greater in America than in most other developed countries, upward mobility was also greater. But a cold look at the statistics showed that, if anything, it was getting more difficult for the poor to climb out of their poverty. The proportion of white high school graduates (who did not get further education) who would wind up earning less than the poverty level increased from 7 percent in the 1970s to 12 percent in the 1980s; while 16 percent of black males ended up in poverty in the

1970s, by the 1980s, 25 percent did.

Mobility statistics show that Horatio Alger stories are to a large extent myth. While someone whose father's income was in the top 5 percent has a 30 percent chance of being in the top 10 percent, someone whose father's income was in the bottom 5 percent has only a 1 percent chance of making it to the top 10 percent.

Wealth inequality exceeds income inequality partly because people save for their retirement. These life-cycle savings are a significant part of all savings. But the large inequality of wealth among members of any age cohort provides further evidence that the income inequality statistics represent more than just a statistical artifact.

The rising inequality, the shrinking middle class, and the limited income mobility all raised questions about some of America's basic beliefs about equality and opportunity. Yet it was not obvious what

government could or should do about the underlying factors. Those who saw the rise in inequality as a problem argued that whatever the cause, greater inequality called for government intervention. They have proposed policies of more progressive taxation, more redistribution through welfare programs, and, most important, more programs of education and job training to help otherwise low-skilled workers to participate in the opportunities available for the more highly skilled. Others argued that the best way to make the poor better off was to make the economy grow faster, and this required less, not more, government involvement.

Sources: U.S. Department of Commerce, Bureau of the Census, *Money Income of Households, Families, and Persons in the United States: 1990* (August 1991); Gary Burtless, ed., *A Future of Lousy Jobs?* (Washington, D.C.: Brookings Institution, 1990); "Charges in Family Finances from 1983 to 1989," *Federal Reserve Bulletin* (January 1992); *New York Times,* May 11, 1991, p. C1.

PERCENT DISTRIBUTION OF MONEY INCOME

	Lowest fifth	Second fifth	Third fifth	Fourth fifth	Highest fifth	Top 5 percent
1970	4.1	10.8	17.4	24.5	43.3	16.6
1975	4.3	10.4	17.0	24.7	43.6	16.6
1980	4.2	10.2	16.8	24.8	44.1	16.5
1985	3.9	9.8	16.2	24.4	45.6	17.6
1990	3.9	9.6	15.9	24.0	46.6	18.6

economists do not believe that there is any scientific basis for making these comparisons.[1] Nonetheless, such judgments are often at the heart of public policy discussions. There is an intuitive sense that it hurts a rich person less to take a dollar away from him than it hurts a poor person.

Finally, many people who do not subscribe to any of these general philosophies see

[1] Recall the discussion of utility in Chapter 8. The utilitarians believed that eventually, with scientific progress, people would be able to measure utility and compare the utility of one individual with that of another.

many of society's social ills, including high crime rates and drug usage, as deriving from the extremes of poverty. This perspective does not so much address the question of how progressive the tax system should be as it asks how much effort society should make to eradicate poverty, a question to which we will turn later in the chapter.

Efficiency   The second important criterion for a good tax system is efficiency. The tax system should interfere as little as possible with the way the economy allocates resources, and it should raise revenue with the least cost to taxpayers. Very high taxes may discourage work and savings, and therefore interfere with the efficiency of the economy. Taxes that select out particular goods to be taxed, such as excise taxes on alcohol, tobacco, and airline tickets, discourage individuals from purchasing those goods, and therefore also interfere with the efficiency of the economy.

The U.S. income tax system has many provisions that have the effect of encouraging some types of economic activity and discouraging others. For instance, the U.S. income tax allows certain child care payments to be taken as a credit against tax payments owed. The government thus subsidizes child care. Similarly, when firms spend money on R & D, their expenditures may reduce the amount they have to pay in taxes. Such arrangements are called **tax subsidies,** and they are an alternative to an outright grant; both change society's allocation of resources. These subsidies cost the government money just as if the government paid out money directly for child care or research. Accordingly, the revenue lost from a tax subsidy is called a **tax expenditure.**

Administrative Simplicity   The third important characteristic is administrative simplicity. It is costly—both to the government and to those who must pay taxes—to collect taxes and to administer a tax system. Billions of hours are spent each year in filling out tax forms, hours that might be spent producing valuable goods and services. Billions of dollars are spent on accountants and lawyers by taxpayers and by the IRS in the annual ritual of preparing and processing tax forms. In addition, with a good tax system, it should be difficult to evade the taxes imposed.

Flexibility   The fourth important criterion is flexibility. As economic circumstances change, it may be desirable to change tax rates. With a good tax system, it should be relatively easy to do this.

Transparency   The fifth important characteristic is transparency. A good tax system is one in which it can be ascertained what each person is paying in taxes. The principle of transparency is analogous to the principle of "truth in advertising." Taxpayers are consumers of public services. They should know what they (and others) are paying for the services they are getting.

GRADING THE U.S. TAX SYSTEM

How well does the U.S. tax system fare, based on these five criteria? Equally important, during the past decade there have been several major changes in the tax laws—have they resulted in a better tax system?

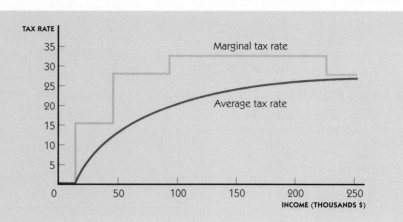

Figure 24.2 MARGINAL AND AVERAGE TAX RATES, 1990

Marginal tax rates change by jumps, as shown in the table, but average tax rates increase gradually. *Source:* Internal Revenue Service, Form 1040 (1991).

Fairness The U.S. federal income tax system is, over all, progressive. Low-income individuals are exempted from paying any income tax whatsoever. Beyond a certain level of income (depending on the size of the family—for a family of four, the critical level in 1990 was $13,650), the tax rate is 15 percent. This means that for each extra $100 an individual earns, he must pay an extra $15 of taxes; we thus speak of this tax rate as the **marginal tax rate**. At a still higher level of income, the marginal tax rate increases to 28 percent, then to 33 percent, before it declines again to 28 percent. The actual rates legislated, which you will see in the tax form, are the 15 and 28 percent rates. But the tax law is complicated; there are a variety of provisions that affect the additional taxes a person might pay as his income rises.

The **average tax rate** gives the ratio of taxes to taxable income. While there are big jumps in the marginal tax rate, the average tax rate increases smoothly. Figure 24.2 shows the 1990 marginal and average tax rates for a typical family of four that did not itemize its deductions.

The income tax is only one of several income-related taxes that U.S. citizens pay. The payroll (Social Security) tax is another one that increases with income up to some level. An **earned-income tax credit** is designed to supplement the income of low-income workers with families; as a person's income increases beyond some level, the payments he *receives* under this program decrease. Thus, while Figure 24.2 focuses only on income tax rates, Figure 24.3 collects together all income-related federal taxes: the income tax, the earned-income credit, and the payroll tax.

Again, the figure calculates the marginal and average taxes facing a family of four. For instance, it shows that at $18,000 of income, the marginal tax rate is slightly greater than 40 percent. This means that an increase in before-tax (and -subsidy) income of $100 results in an increase in after-tax (and -subsidy) income of approximately $60. The government takes away $40 in either increased taxes or reduced subsidies. Notice that there are high marginal tax rates even at low incomes—higher even than at upper incomes. This is because many upper-income individuals do not face payroll taxes on the last dollars they earn, and because the earned-income tax credit diminishes as a person's income increases.

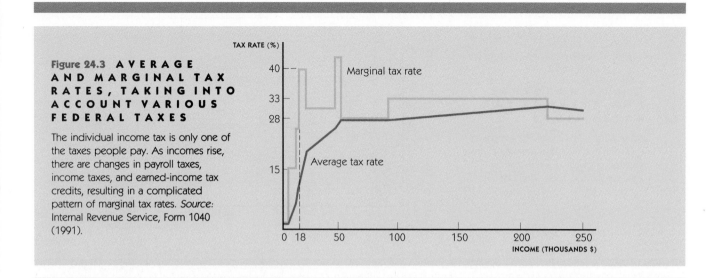

Figure 24.3 AVERAGE AND MARGINAL TAX RATES, TAKING INTO ACCOUNT VARIOUS FEDERAL TAXES

The individual income tax is only one of the taxes people pay. As incomes rise, there are changes in payroll taxes, income taxes, and earned-income tax credits, resulting in a complicated pattern of marginal tax rates. *Source:* Internal Revenue Service, Form 1040 (1991).

While the U.S. federal income tax system is intended to be progressive, it is less progressive than it seems, because of a variety of special provisions. One allows, for instance, the deduction from income of mortgage interest, another allows capital gains to escape taxation under certain special circumstances. These provisions—introduced for a variety of reasons, such as to stimulate investment and to help every American to be a home owner—are of more benefit to middle- and high-income taxpayers than to low-income taxpayers. Moreover, payroll taxes are proportional to income and subject to upper limits beyond which no such tax is imposed. In 1991, for instance, the U.S. payroll tax was 7.65 percent, levied on income up to $53,400. The Medicare portion, 2.9 percent, escaped this cap and was levied on wage income up to $125,000. And, as noted, the corporation tax may in fact really be borne largely by consumers.

To assess the progressiveness of the U.S. tax system, we have to look not only at the federal income tax but at all taxes—including the corporation income tax and state and local taxes. In the early 1980s, there were numerous articles about corporations that paid no taxes, even though they had a high income. It was charged that corporations were not paying their fair share of taxes. Economists stressed that corporations do not *ultimately* bear the costs of the taxes they pay. In the end, all taxes are paid by people. The question is, which people. In the case of the corporation income tax, the corporation's workers bear the tax in the form of lower wages, consumers bear the tax in the form of higher prices, or investors bear the tax in the form of lower returns on their investments.

The **incidence** of a tax describes who actually bears its economic burden as distinct from the individual or firm that sends the check for the tax in to the government. The incidence of a tax can be illustrated by means of a supply and demand diagram like Figure 24.4A, which shows the demand and supply curves for cigarettes before taxes. A 10-cent tax per pack on cigarettes is imposed on producers. For cigarette manufacturers to be willing to supply any given quantity of cigarettes, they have to receive 10 cents more per pack to compensate them for the 10-cent extra cost, the amount they have to pay the government. The supply curve shifts up. The new equilibrium entails a

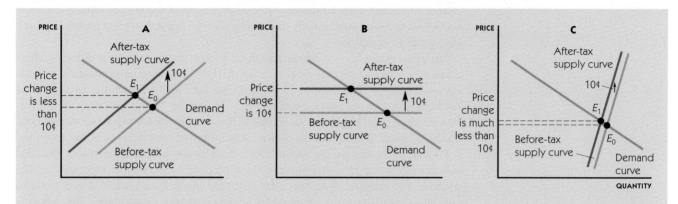

Figure 24.4 TAX INCIDENCE

The effect of a tax on a good depends on the elasticities of the demand and supply curves. In panel A, the tax increases the price paid by consumers, but by an amount less than the tax. Part of the tax is borne by consumers, part by producers. In panel B, the extreme case of a flat supply curve, the price rises by the full amount of the tax; the entire burden of the tax is borne by consumers. If the supply curve is relatively inelastic, as in panel C, the increase in the price paid by consumers is relatively small.

higher price and a lower quantity. The price paid by consumers goes up, but by *less* than 10 cents. That is, even though the tax is "paid" by the producer, consumers bear some of the costs. Panel B shows an extreme case where the producers' supply curve is horizontal. Then the price paid by consumers goes up by 10 cents; consumers bear the entire cost. Panel C shows the case of an inelastic supply curve. Then most of the tax is borne by producers. (In all three instances, output is lower than it would be in a competitive market without taxes.)

The correct question to ask is not whether corporations pay their fair share, but whether, taking into account the actual incidence of the corporation income tax, our tax system is fair. Unfortunately, it is difficult to tell precisely who does pay the cost of the corporation income tax. Those economists who believe that corporations typically pass on the tax in the form of higher prices think of the corporation tax as much like a sales tax, in which case increasing the corporation income tax makes the tax system *less*, not more, progressive. (They point out that since investors have the option of investments that are not subject to the corporation income tax—they can, for instance, invest abroad or in real estate—in the long run, the tax has relatively little effect on investors.)

Moreover, many state and local taxes are regressive. This is because lower- and middle-income individuals spend a larger fraction of their income on items that are subject to state sales taxes than do the very rich. In recent years, the general assessment of our *total* tax system—combining the slightly progressive federal tax system with the slightly regressive state and local tax system—has been that it is, at best, only slightly progressive.

Efficiency During the 1980s, the U.S. income tax system underwent two major reforms, one in 1981 and another in 1986. The announced intent of these reforms was to make the system more efficient, more fair, and administratively simpler. They did succeed in closing some loopholes—special provisions of the tax code that allow some individuals to reduce substantially their tax liabilities—but at the cost of greatly increased administrative complexity.

The other major accomplishment of these reforms was to reduce the distorting effect of taxes by lowering the marginal tax rate. In 1981, the maximum marginal tax rate was lowered from 70 percent to 50 percent, and then in 1986, with the passage of the Tax Reform Act, it was lowered still further to 33 percent. With a tax rate of 70 percent, the individual got to keep less than one out of three dollars she earned on her investments. On this account, the tax reforms of the 1980s improved the efficiency of the economy.

Prior to 1986, the tax law was riddled with a variety of special provisions designed to encourage what at least some members of Congress viewed as especially worthy activities. For example, there was a tax credit for energy conservation; if you insulated your house, you received a tax credit for a fraction of your expenditures, thus reducing your tax liability. (Tax credits work like this. An individual calculates how much he owes in taxes. Suppose he owes $4,000. Then he calculates his tax credits. With an energy tax credit at 20 percent, if he spent $1,000 on insulation, he would get a credit for $200. Thus, he would have to send the government a check for only $3,800.) In effect, the government was paying part of the cost of insulating your house; the government used the tax system to subsidize housing insulation.

But as worthy a cause as energy conservation may be, most economists believe that rational individuals know how to assess the costs and benefits of insulation without government assistance; if the savings in energy bills exceed the cost of the insulation, people will choose to install the insulation. The tax credit simply encouraged the inefficient use of insulation beyond the point where the savings in energy use were worth the cost of the insulation.

One of the major objectives of the 1986 act was to eliminate the energy conservation credit and a myriad of similar special provisions that had crept into the tax law over the years, costing the Treasury billions of dollars. In this it was not entirely successful. Employer expenditures on medical insurance is not taxed, and the oil and gas industry still receives some special treatment. Legislation in succeeding years has begun the process of reinserting special provisions for a variety of special causes, such as small businesses, research and development, and further aid to the oil and gas industry. Thus, in the area of efficiency, the U.S. tax system today, while considerably better than it was fifteen years ago, still shows much room for improvement.

Administrative Simplicity Americans live in a complex society, and their tax laws reflect and contribute to this complexity. As they have sought to make sure that the tax laws are fair and apply uniformly to all people in similar situations, the laws have become increasingly complex. Americans are clever people, and high tax rates make it worthwhile for them to think hard about how to avoid taxes (legally, without going to jail). With high tax rates, it may pay a businessperson to devote almost as much energy to how he can avoid taxes as to how he can produce a better product. The tax law has evolved out of this constant battle between the government and taxpayers; as each new way of reducing taxes is discovered, the law is modified to close the loophole. Inevitably another hole is discovered, and another repair job is attempted. Today the federal tax law amounts to a multitude of volumes.

The objective of administrative simplicity seems to have been an elusive one. Many economists are convinced that the United States could have a tax system that is truly administratively simple, but to do so, other objectives would have to be given up. Much of the complexity derives from the attempt to have a progressive income tax and to tax the income from capital.

Though overall the 1981 and 1986 tax reforms failed to simplify the U.S. tax code, two changes made life simpler for many individuals: first, the income below which no taxes were levied was increased substantially, so many lower-income individuals simply did not have to bother with paying taxes; and second, the lower marginal tax rates at the upper end made finding loopholes less attractive.

Flexibility   One of the weakest aspects of the U.S. tax system is its lack of flexibility. Any time a tax change is proposed, all of the issues discussed here are raised. There are debates about how different groups would be affected and about how efficiency is affected. Basic issues of values—how progressive should the tax system be?—are aired once again. Special-interest groups try to take the opportunity of any change in the tax law to get favorable treatment. It has turned out to be extremely difficult—and time-consuming—to change the tax law.

The lack of flexibility of the U.S. tax system has much to do with its political system. In Britain, the government simply announces the tax schedule. While there is debate, the government's proposal is substantially altered only if Parliament is so dissatisfied that it wants to force a change of prime minister. Still, with simpler tax structures, adjustments are easier: when the government wants to raise more revenue from taxes in which there is a single rate (such as sales taxes or property taxes), it simply raises the rate. If the income tax system were simpler—if it were agreed, for instance, that all income above some threshold level would be taxed at the same rate—then, when government needed to raise more revenue, the debate would narrow down to how much the threshold should change and how much the single rate should be increased.

Transparency   Of all the parts of the tax system, the corporation income tax is perhaps the least transparent. The 1986 Tax Reform Act increased the relative importance of the corporation income tax, and thus on average made the tax system less transparent. The sales tax ranks second: politicians love the sales tax, because they know that many, perhaps most, individuals never figure out the total amount they are spending on government services.

REDISTRIBUTION

Politicians frequently begin their appeal to voters by expressing their concern for the poor. Compassion for others not as fortunate is a fundamental human value. Government programs to aid the poor reflect the belief that there is a collective responsibility on the part of all citizens to take care of those among them who are in need. Though there is some disagreement about to what extent that responsibility should be borne by government and to what extent by voluntary charities, governments in all the developed countries have assumed a major role in at least providing a safety net to protect the most disadvantaged in society.

WHO ARE THE POOR?

Government programs have been mostly aimed at reducing the extremes of inequality—in particular, at preventing poverty and providing a safety net for the very poor. But before examining these programs, we need to take a closer look at who the poor actually are.

The poor include those who are not working and those with low wages. Those not working can be grouped into at least three categories: people who cannot work either because they are too old or too disabled; individuals who cannot find work, perhaps because the economy is in a recession and there is a shortage of jobs; and people who choose not to work, usually because the wages they would receive are so low relative to what they can get from government welfare and other assistance programs that it does not pay for them to work. Most of those who are not working fall into the first category and are thus assisted by the Social Security programs for the aged and disabled.

Most people who have been unemployed only for a short time (less than twenty-six weeks) receive unemployment compensation, which replaces a substantial fraction of their previous income. But for those who would like a job but have never held one, or who have been unemployed for a long time, there is no major federal program upon which they can fall back. The extent of this second category, often referred to as the **involuntarily unemployed**, varies with economic conditions. Also, the boundary between the second and third categories is often blurred. The laid-off automobile worker who had been receiving $20 an hour could get a job at McDonald's at $4 an hour, but cannot find a job that uses his skills or that pays anywhere near what he previously made. Should he be classified as involuntarily unemployed? Fortunately, to understand poverty and the effect of government programs on poverty, we do not need to answer this question.

We do need to understand how government programs will affect individuals' decisions. A reduction in unemployment compensation—what the government pays an individual while she is temporarily unemployed—might encourage people to search harder for a job; allowing a person to work part time without losing her unemployment benefits might induce her to accept a part-time job at McDonald's, while continuing to look for a better job.

There are also different reasons why individuals have low wages. First, many lack skills. These people have, to use the vocabulary introduced in Chapter 11, low levels of human capital.

Second, discrimination may play a role. As of the late 1980s, earnings of blacks were on average substantially less than those of whites of comparable age and education. While discrimination-based wage differentials have been reduced since the 1960s, there is still room for improvement.

The final group of workers with low wages are those who choose low-wage jobs because of certain advantages those jobs afford, or whose circumstances make it difficult for them to accept higher-wage jobs. For example, part-time work has usually been low paying. Women with children have often been attracted to part-time jobs, or to full-time jobs that provide a great deal of work flexibility. When such a woman's income is the second one in the household, the family is not likely to be poor. However, the low wages of part-time work are particularly tough on single women with children who may not be able to devote the time and energy required by a "fast-track" career.

In the United States, poverty is concentrated among certain groups in the population. There is a particular level of income (varying by family size) such that if a family's income falls below that level, they are considered to be in poverty. For instance, in 1990, the poverty threshold for a family of four was $13,359,[2] and 13.5 percent of the country was in poverty. But 32 percent of blacks were in poverty.

GOVERNMENT PROGRAMS FOR ALLEVIATING POVERTY

A quarter of a century ago, President Johnson declared a War on Poverty. He attempted to design a set of programs to provide support for those in poverty, and a ladder out of poverty. Yet today poverty remains. Concern about poverty is not just based on an altruistic, disinterested concern for others, or on the feeling that "there but for the grace of God go I." Problems of crime and drugs have been at the top of the political agenda for decades, and there is a strong feeling that these problems are closely related to the persistence of poverty. To use the vocabulary introduced in Chapter 23, poverty generates negative externalities for society as a whole.

The government has sought to reduce poverty by addressing each of its major causes; it has sought to reduce the number of unemployed, increase the income of those who are employed, provide support to those who for one reason or another cannot work, improve the skills of low-wage workers, and reduce discrimination.

Unemployment Governments attempt to reduce unemployment and its costs by three measures.

1. Unemployment insurance provides income for those *temporarily* unemployed.
2. The government's commitment to keeping the economy at close to full employment serves to reduce the total number of individuals who are involuntarily unemployed.
3. Job-retraining programs and employment placement bureaus help those who have lost one job to get another job.

There remain important gaps. The long-term unemployed and new entrants to the labor force do not receive unemployment compensation. In spite of the government's commitment to keeping the economy at close to full employment, there have been episodes, such as the 1981–82 recession, when one out of ten workers could not find a job; and in many European countries, for much of the decade of the 1980s, as many as one out of six workers was unable to find a job. The major recession that began in 1990 led to high unemployment rates for white-collar workers, something that had not occurred in previous recessions. The result was renewed concern for the plight of the unemployed.

Job-retraining programs, while helping a little, have had only limited success. The jobs that the economy is creating differ markedly in the skills they require from the jobs being destroyed. It is difficult to retrain the unemployed steel worker or autoworker in Pittsburgh or Detroit to qualify him for a computer job in California.

---

[2] Note that the poverty threshold was approximately the threshold below which families paid no taxes.

The official poverty line determines how many people the government counts as "poor." But what determines the poverty line itself?

In the late 1960s, an official at the Social Security Administration, Molly Orshansky, developed a method of measuring poverty. From a survey of household expenditures, she found that a typical family spent one-third of its income on food. She then gathered information on minimum food budgets for families of various sizes, and multiplied that number by three to get an estimate of the poverty line for the different family sizes. With minor changes, Orshansky's poverty line was officially adopted in 1969 and has been increased by the overall rate of inflation since then.

There are a number of questions one can ask about how poverty is measured: here are three.

First, the survey Orshansky relied on to find that households spent one-third of their income on food was taken in 1955. But since then, household expenditures have shifted. Households now spend a much lower percentage of income on food, perhaps one-fourth or one-fifth. If the minimum food budget were accordingly multiplied by four or five, the poverty line would be much higher. The smaller share of the typical family's expenditures spent on food is offset by larger fractions going elsewhere. Some expenses that were negligible in the 1950s, like child care, are now a large part of the family budget for single working parents.

Second, the poverty line does not take in-kind benefits into account. In-kind benefits include any benefits that are not received in cash form, like Medicaid, food stamps, and subsidized school lunches. If those benefits are measured as additional income, the number of people below the poverty line falls by about 20 percent.

Finally, some critics have proposed that poverty should be thought of as a relative concept rather than an absolute one. They argue that those at the bottom of society, say the bottom 5 or 10 or 20 percent, are poor relative to everyone else. They point out that poor people in the United States would qualify as middle class or even wealthy in some of the truly impoverished nations of the world, where malnutrition is common and running water and electricity are not. These critics argue that instead of trying to calculate a budget that allows a certain minimum life-style, we should view poverty more as an extreme case of inequality.

For many, this last criticism goes too far. After all, if poverty is just a statement that some people are relatively worse off, then poverty can never be re-

Income of the Employed The government further addresses income inequality by attempting to raise the incomes of those low-wage individuals who do work. There are two broad programs for this purpose.

1. Minimum wage legislation is intended to raise the wages of those without skills.
2. The earned-income tax credit is a subsidy that the government provides to low-income workers with families (through the tax system); in effect, the government augments their salaries.

The minimum wage legislation has been, at best, controversial. The higher wages may have made it more difficult for unskilled workers to obtain a job; thus, while wages of those working have risen slightly, the number of those who are poor because they cannot get a job may have increased.[3]

Support Programs The government sponsors several programs targeted at helping those who cannot participate, or participate fully, in the labor force.

1. Social Security and Supplementary Income (which supplements Social Security for the very poor aged) provide support for the aged and the disabled.
2. AFDC (Aid to Families with Dependent Children) originally provided support to families with only one adult, but in recent years the aid has been extended to other low-income families.

Ensuring Basic Necessities of Life: The Safety Net In addition, there are several programs to help ensure that the poor receive a minimal level of certain basic necessities: Medicaid provides medical care for the poor, and food stamps and housing subsidies help supply those goods. These programs, together with those designed to supplement the income of the very poor, provide a safety net that is intended to protect the most unfortunate members of society. What should be considered the minimal acceptable levels for each of these necessities remains controversial, however.

Getting at the Roots of the Problem To the extent that discrimination contributes to poverty, both by denying individuals access to jobs and human capital and by paying them lower wages, the government's commitment to the eradication of discrimination has played an important role in reducing poverty.

---

[3] Recall the discussion from Chapter 5, which showed that increasing the wage resulted in a reduction in the employment of unskilled workers, to a level below that where supply equaled demand.

To help improve the skills of the poor, the government initiated a major federal program of aid to schools where there were significant numbers of disadvantaged students. The program includes Project Head Start, which provides preschool education for the disadvantaged.

CURRENT PUBLIC POLICY ISSUES

In addressing the problems posed by poverty, the U.S. government has had to make some difficult choices. The country's compassion for the poor and its desire to provide a safety net for the unfortunate is balanced against its desire to provide incentives and its concern for efficiency. Programs that offer more extensive support are more costly and thus impose a larger tax burden on the rest of the population. They reduce the incentives of those who receive the benefits and those who have to contribute to support them. This is the equity-efficiency trade-off first discussed in Chapter 2.

Current policy discussions about the programs designed to alleviate poverty can be thought of as focusing on three questions. First, are these programs effective? Do they actually reduce poverty? For instance, while AFDC does increase the income of those families without a principal wage earner, there has been concern that when aid is restricted to families with only one adult, fathers are encouraged to desert their families, thus limiting the program's effectiveness in reducing poverty.

Second, are there changes in these programs that would make them more effective, that could provide a better safety net without adversely affecting incentives? That is, could the government make changes in the design of the programs that would enable the economy to move closer to the "equity-efficiency frontier," from a point such as A in Figure 24.5 to a point such as B?

Finally, has the government chosen the right point along the equity-efficiency frontier? In spite of the wide array of programs attempting to address the problem of poverty, there are several gaps in coverage. While those who value equity highly argue that closing these gaps is desirable, even if it entails some loss in efficiency, others argue that the programs we already have excessively attenuate incentives and should be cut back. The paragraphs below describe some of the specific contexts in which these debates are occurring.

Workfare   Welfare programs are criticized because for certain individuals, they reduce the incentive to work. The suggestion has been made that those who receive welfare ought to be required to work. Programs that provide support, but only on the condition that the person either join a job-training program, return to school, or seek employment, are called **workfare programs**.

Interest in these programs was motivated by concern about the perverse incentives of the AFDC program. Formerly, for a family to be eligible for the program, there could not be a man in the household. Payments increased as a woman had more children, and were reduced if she received an income. For every dollar she earned, the government reduced her payment by a dollar; it was as if she faced a marginal tax rate of 100 percent, a rate far in excess of that paid by even the very rich in our society. Since for many unskilled women, opportunities in the labor market were very limited, the AFDC program provided for them a viable though extremely limited means of financial independence.

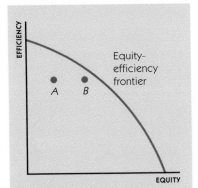

Figure 24.5 THE EQUITY-EFFICIENCY TRADE-OFF

Public assistance programs force society to face a trade-off between equity and efficiency. However, it may be possible that better-designed programs could create either more equity without reducing incentives to work, or greater incentives to work without reducing equity.

Although there is a debate about the extent to which the AFDC program contributed to the growth of female-headed families, the growth itself has been startling. A quarter of all babies born in the United States today are born out of wedlock; in 1970, the figure was just over 10 percent. The number of blacks born out of wedlock rose from 37.6 percent in 1970 to 62.4 percent today.

The AFDC program has been reformed to provide more work incentives—the woman can now keep a third of what she earns—and to remove incentives for the husband to leave. Half the states now allow families with both parents present to receive support. Some states, such as Massachusetts, have gone so far as to require those receiving AFDC to work or participate in job-retraining programs. Critics have argued that women with small children should not work. But changes in work norms for the population have made this argument less persuasive. As an ever-increasing fraction of women, including women with young children, have joined the labor force, there seems no compelling reason why poor women should not work. The real problem is that if young mothers are to work, assistance is often required for both child care and transportation, raising the cost and bureaucratic hassle.

Categorical Assistance versus General Assistance   Much of the assistance to the poor goes to particular groups—for instance, the aged and the disabled. This is known as **categorical assistance**, and examples include both the Social Security and AFDC programs. Some have argued that there should be a program of general assistance. Why should the *aged* poor be treated more favorably than the *young* poor? One way of treating all the impoverished the same, regardless of age, whether they work or not, whether they live in the city or the countryside, would be through the income tax system. A negative income tax, proposed by a number of analysts and politicians, would provide **general assistance** to the poor. Under the current tax law, those with low incomes pay no taxes, and those with higher incomes pay a tax. With a negative income tax, those with low incomes would actually receive money from the government. The amount they receive would depend only on their income and family size, and that alone (not on age or whether they live on a farm, or any other category).

General assistance proposals like the negative income tax have never been as popular as categorical assistance programs, and there is a good economic reason for this. General assistance attenuates incentives more than does categorical assistance. The decision of most eighty-five-year-olds not to work is not affected by the Social Security system, and would not be affected regardless of how generous it was. There are, of course, a few lucky eighty-five-year-olds who can work. However, they are a distinct minority. By targeting aid to those for whom incentive effects are limited, the government can provide more redistribution with a given loss of efficiency than it could with a broad-based program. Of course, this results in some inequities; the very poor who do not fall into one of the specially targeted groups are not treated as well as those who do.

Assistance in Kind   Besides aiming at specific groups in the population, assistance programs target particular categories of expenditures, such as food, medical care, or housing. Food stamps can be used only for food, Medicaid for medical care, and housing subsidies for housing. Such programs are called **assistance in kind**, to distinguish them from general and categorical assistance programs that supply income rather than goods.

Critics of food stamps, Medicaid, and housing subsidies claim that these programs distort people's choices. After all if an individual had been given cash, he might have chosen a different mix of medical care, food, and housing than the government chose

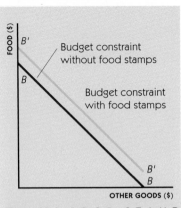

Figure 24.6 FOOD STAMP PROGRAM

A food stamp program that provides a fixed allotment of food stamps has only an income effect, not a substitution effect.

for him. Since an efficient economy allows people to choose what they want, letting the government choose instead is economically inefficient. Many supporters of in-kind programs agree with the charge that these programs are deliberately paternalistic. They are based on the belief that poor people should have roofs over their heads, medical care, and food, whether this is how the poor want to spend their money or not; these people should not be allowed to fritter away public assistance on other things.

In any case, it turns out that because of the way aid programs are designed in the United States, the in-kind programs may have limited effectiveness in increasing the consumption of the subsidized good. For example, food stamps may not lead to substantially increased consumption of food. They may simply result in individuals buying the same level of food and using the dollars they would have spent on food as cash for other goods. In this view, in-kind programs produce the same effects as general aid would.

To see whether this is so, consider the budget constraint shown in Figure 24.6. This individual has an income of $800 a month in the absence of the Food Stamp Program, which he can spend on food or other goods (the line *BB*). He then gets $100 in food stamps; this moves his budget constraint to *B'B'*. Notice that there is no substitution effect, only an income effect. Thus, the effect of the Food Stamp Program is exactly the same as the effect of a cash grant of $100. This is true so long as the food stamps are worth less than what he otherwise would have spent on food. In this case, the only difference between general and in-kind assistance is that the latter increases administrative costs.

Some welfare programs, such as Medicaid, involve thresholds. If your income is below the threshold, you are eligible for support; if your income is above it, you are not. There is no gradual phasing out of benefits. Thresholds produce a strange-looking budget constraint, as illustrated in Figure 24.7. At the threshold, extra work—resulting in extra income—actually reduces consumption, as government payments are reduced. For very low income individuals, these programs have an advantage: they have an income effect, but no substitution effect. But for individuals who might have chosen to work slightly more than the threshold level in the absence of the welfare program, the substitution effect is enormous; there are negative returns to working at the margin.

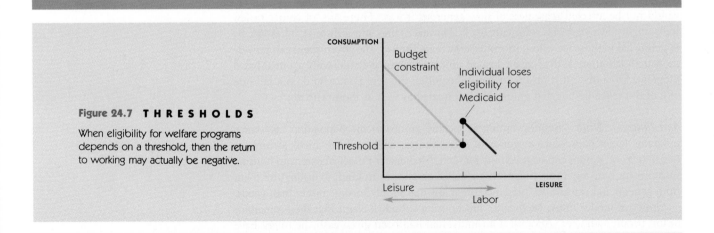

Figure 24.7 THRESHOLDS

When eligibility for welfare programs depends on a threshold, then the return to working may actually be negative.

Inevitably, welfare programs must be designed to give payments to very low income individuals, and not to higher-income individuals. Thus, payments must somehow decrease as income rises; there must, in effect, be a high tax rate as the poorest individuals work their way out of poverty. The design of welfare programs focuses on how these payments should decrease. If there are many people whose income is near the threshold, then the losses from the substitution effect will be large, and threshold systems are likely to be highly inefficient; similarly, if most of those who are poor and working are relatively insensitive to moderate rates of taxation, then the loss from forcing them to face an effective tax of 30 percent or 50 percent will be relatively low. Most economists believe that threshold systems create more distortions than systems with a more gradual phasing out of benefits.

Other Public Policy Debates   There are many other public policy initiatives to alleviate poverty that are currently under discussion.

During the mid-1980s, concern focused on the plight of the homeless. Not since the Great Depression were so many homeless people seen on the streets of the country's major cities. While some of the homeless were very poor families, others were individuals who had previously been institutionalized for mild mental disorders and seemed ill-equipped to care for themselves. In 1986, Congress passed legislation authorizing $.5 billion of aid for the homeless, but budget stringencies have kept expenditures down, and today the problem appears worse than it was then.

Medicare and Medicaid have made medical care much more available to the poor, though at a high public cost. The high costs have led some to advocate cutbacks, but the remaining gaps in coverage have caused others to argue for new government programs. In the 1992 presidential campaign, the gaps in medical coverage and what should be done about them became a major issue. The high costs of certain prolonged medical treatment, running into hundreds of thousands of dollars, not covered by regular insurance, led Congress to provide coverage for these catastrophic losses for the elderly under Medicare. But when it became known that the elderly would have to pay for the insurance, there was an outcry from the elderly, and the legislation was repealed.

Programs designed to alleviate the root causes of poverty also remain a subject of debate. While discrimination is illegal, there are ongoing debates about whether the government should compel employers to practice affirmative action—for instance, to require employers to actively recruit minority candidates—or even go further and establish job quotas for those from disadvantaged groups.

One of the reasons individuals are poor is that they lack skills; the problem is inadequate education and training. Education has traditionally been the responsibility of states and local communities. Differences in income and wealth across communities result in differences in expenditures on education and in the quality of education. Children who are born to parents who live in poor communities may, as a result, have a poorer chance of obtaining a good education. The way public education is provided in the United States thus contributes to an uneven playing field in the competition for jobs.

In several states, the courts have concluded that these inequalities are inconsistent with provisions within their state constitutions, such as those mandating equal treatment. The courts have capped the expenditures of rich communities, and they have required the state to provide additional financial resources to the poor communities. The caps on expenditures of rich communities have been particularly controversial. Why, critics claim, should parents not be allowed to spend more on their children if they want to? How can America win in international competition if it does not put forth the maximum effort possible in training its young? Moreover, the programs may be ineffective in their ultimate objective of promoting equality; they may result in more parents pulling their children out of public schools. This has the further side effect of eroding support for public education.

SOCIAL INSURANCE

Most Americans are neither rich nor poor. They belong to the "middle class." Members of this class have seen the poor get free medical care, while they struggle to pay their insurance and medical bills. They have heard about the rich hiring high-priced accountants to duck taxes by taking advantage of loopholes, while their own taxes are taken directly out of their pay checks. They have felt squeezed and unfairly treated. Some of this feeling is a matter of perception; the middle class actually receives the benefits of many "hidden" loopholes that reduce their taxes. For instance, fringe benefits, often representing between a quarter to a third of a person's salary (health insurance, retirement funds), generally escape taxation. Also, many people who are considerably above the U.S. median income think of themselves as middle class. When they are taxed according to their relatively high income, they feel cheated.

The middle class represents an enormous block of votes, and thus, whether or not middle-class frustrations are a result of accurate perceptions, it is not surprising that government has responded. In the United States today, there are a variety of what are referred to as **middle-class entitlement programs**, so named because individuals do not have to demonstrate poverty to receive benefits. The most important of these are the social insurance programs.

Earlier, we learned about a major set of programs—AFDC, the Food Stamp Program, and Medicaid—the *primary* objective of which is to improve the plight of the poor. These programs are directly concerned with redistribution; they are called **transfer programs**, because they move money from one group in society to another. The social insurance programs, while they help provide a safety net for the disadvantaged, also benefit the middle class. Individuals pay into a pool so that they themselves will be protected in times of need. Besides Social Security and Medicare, social insurance programs include disability insurance and unemployment insurance.

Social insurance programs are like private insurance, in that people nominally pay for their own protection. The programs are funded by a tax on wage income, the payroll tax. But in other, important ways, they are *not* like private insurance, as we will see in the paragraphs that follow.

THE BURDEN OF SOCIAL INSURANCE PROGRAMS

The first myth about social insurance concerns who pays for it. Social Security is supported by a tax on wages, 50 percent paid by the employer, 50 percent by the employee. This division of the tax is entirely superficial; the consequences of the tax are essentially the same as they would be if the worker paid the entire tax.

Figure 24.8 uses demand and supply curves for labor to show how this works. The payroll tax imposes a tax on the employer based on what she pays workers. The vertical axis measures the wage *received* by the employee. Since the cost of a worker is the wage received by the employee *plus* the tax, the tax shifts the demand curve down. In the new equilibrium, workers' wages have fallen. The wage received by a worker is precisely the same as it would have been had the same tax been imposed directly on the worker.

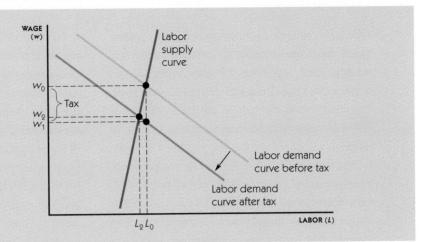

Figure 24.8 THE INCIDENCE OF PAYROLL TAXES

The payroll tax introduces a wedge between the cost to an employer of an individual working an hour more (wage plus tax) and what the worker receives. The magnitude of the wedge does not depend on whether the tax is levied on the employer or employee. The tax leads to fewer workers being hired at the equilibrium wage, reduced from w_0 to w_2.

While normally the wage falls by less than the amount of the tax, the extent to which it falls depends on the elasticity of the demand and supply curves. The figure shows the "normal" case where the supply of labor is relatively inelastic, in which case wages fall almost by the full amount of the tax.

HOW SOCIAL INSURANCE IS MORE THAN AN INSURANCE PROGRAM

The second myth about social insurance programs is that they are just like private insurance, and thus have no redistribution effect. In any insurance program, some individuals receive back more than they contribute, some less. That, in a sense, is the whole purpose of insurance. No one knows whether she will be sick enough next year to need hospitalization. So people buy hospital insurance. Those who are lucky enough not to need hospitalization in effect help pay for the hospitalization of those who need it. But with private insurance, on average, the premiums (what you pay for the insurance) cover the costs of what you receive (including the costs of administration, which are often substantial). With the social insurance programs, however, there is not a close connection between the amount actually contributed and the amount received back.

Here again, the Social Security program is a good example. On average, those receiving Social Security retirement benefits will receive much more than the value of what they and their employer contributed, even taking into account compound interest on those contributions. And the ratio of benefits to contributions is particularly large for those with low incomes; the Social Security program is thus a redistribution program as well as an insurance program.

To the extent that social insurance provides insurance that individuals want and the market has failed to provide, it performs an important economic function. To the extent that social insurance is popular because everyone believes someone else is picking up the tab, its role and function need to be reexamined. We learned earlier that part of the popularity of the social insurance programs is due to the fact that they seem to

CLOSE-UP: THE WEALTHIEST AMERICANS

America's capitalist economy provides the opportunity for some people to become extremely wealthy. Each year since the early 1980s, *Forbes* magazine has published a list of the 400 wealthiest. The chart shows the top 20 on the 1991 *Forbes* list—every one with personal wealth of at least $2 billion.

That amount of money is hard to comprehend. Imagine that you invested $2 billion at, say, 10 percent interest. That would mean an income of $200 million per year, forever, without ever diminishing the principal. People get awfully excited about the chance of winning a state lottery that pays $20 million. The billionaire is getting ten times this in interest—every year.

Can such amounts ever be justified or fair? That is a deep philosophical question, to which different people will give different answers. Defenders of extreme wealth note that most of the top 20 are not there because of inherited wealth, but because they started or managed very successful companies or made intelligent investments. If by a combination of clever ideas and hard work you build up a company that hires thousands of workers and offers a product that thousands or millions of consumers want to buy, why shouldn't you be extremely wealthy? In addition, the possibility of making a huge fortune motivates many talented people not on the list to exert their very best efforts, which is to the benefit of the entire economy.

Top 20 wealthiest Americans in 1991

John Kluge	$5.9 billion	Metromedia
William Gates III	$4.8 billion	Microsoft
Sam Walton	$4.4 billion	Wal-Mart, father and children
S. Robson Walton	$4.4 billion	
John Walton	$4.4 billion	
Jim Walton	$4.4 billion	
Alice Walton	$4.4 billion	
Warren Buffett	$4.2 billion	Berkshire Hathaway
Henry Hillman	$3.3 billion	Industrialist, venture capitalist, real estate
Richard DeVos	$3.0 billion	Amway
Jay Van Andel	$3.0 billion	Amway
Samuel Newhouse, Jr.	$2.8 billion	Newhouse newspapers,
Donald Newhouse	$2.8 billion	cable TV
Sumner Murray Redstone	$2.8 billion	Viacom, National Amusements
Leslie Wexner	$2.5 billion	The Limited
Paul Allen	$2.4 billion	Microsoft
Edgar Bronfman	$2.3 billion	Seagram's
Ted Arison	$2.3 billion	Carnival Cruise Lines
Jay Pritzker	$2.2 billion	Financier, manufacturing, Hyatt
Robert Pritzker	$2.2 billion	Marmon Group

The list does show some evidence of turnover from year to year. In 1990, for example, Donald Trump dropped from being one of the richest 400 people in the country to someone who appeared on the verge of bankruptcy. Recently declines in the value of stocks or real estate holdings have knocked others off the list. Moreover, most fortunes are eventually broken up into separate inheritances. Overall, 171 of those who were among the wealthiest 400 in 1982 were still on the list ten years later. Of course, most of the others did not exactly fall all the way to homelessness; nonetheless, even at the very top of the wealth pyramid, life is not altogether secure.

Source: "Billionaires," *Forbes,* October 22, 1990, pp. 122–30; "The Richest People in America," *Forbes,* October 21, 1991, p. 145.

benefit the majority of the population, the middle class. The problem facing the middle class, however, is that there are not enough "rich" people to pay for these programs, so the middle class must pay for them itself. These programs may have only a limited role in redistribution, and the taxes required to finance them may have serious disincentive effects.

THE COSTS AND BENEFITS OF REDISTRIBUTION

Tax, welfare, and social insurance programs in the United States all play an important role in answering one of the fundamental questions posed in Chapter 1: For whom are goods produced (who gets to enjoy the goods that are available)? Each group in society would like to pay as little in taxes as possible and receive as many benefits as possible. Of course, the claims of each are cloaked in fancier rhetoric. The rich may argue that "fairness" requires that since they have worked hard for what they earn, they should have the right to keep it. The poor claim that they have been dealt a bad hand, and they therefore deserve special benefits. Issues of what is fair may never be resolved, and economists worry that at least some attempts to redistribute the pieces of the economic pie, to make sure everyone has a fair slice, may so reduce the size of the pie that almost everyone is worse off.

EQUITY-EFFICIENCY TRADE-OFFS

Where economists enter the discussion of redistribution is to clarify the costs and consequences of various programs, including different tax systems. Systems that tax the rich more heavily or provide support for the poor regardless of their employability are likely to have adverse effects on incentives. Economists try to calculate precisely how important these effects are. How many people who are on welfare are really disabled, and thus could not work even if they wanted to? What do high taxes on estates and high-income tax rates do to the incentives of the rich to save?

As government redistributes more income to the poor, it has to raise taxes on the rich and middle-income individuals, which weakens their incentives to work. Once the government has designed an *efficient* tax system, one that is on the equity-efficiency frontier (depicted earlier in Figure 24.5), it faces a trade-off: it can only obtain more redistribution by sacrificing some efficiency.

Disagreements arise among economists both over the magnitudes of the trade-offs and over values. Some believe that the increased taxes necessary to achieve more redistribution in the United States would have a very large negative effect on incentives. These economists believe that individuals are very sensitive to changes in after-tax wages. Most economists agree that at high enough tax rates, incentives are greatly reduced; the high marginal tax rates that used to prevail in Europe (to the extent that they were enforced) of 60 percent or more probably had large negative effects on efficiency. But whether at current marginal tax rates in the United States an increase in taxation would have a *large* effect on incentives is more debatable.

Economists, like other citizens, disagree about how to compare gains in terms of redistribution with costs in terms of lost economic efficiency. Some are more concerned about the present inequality in incomes. Others argue that during the past century, the poor have been most helped by general increases in the prosperity of the country, not by programs of redistribution. In this view, the best way to help the poor in the long run is for the government to adopt policies that promote the growth of the economy.

We have seen how economists focus on the trade-offs—between equality (how the pie is divided) and efficiency (the size of the pie); and between reductions in the risks of life, through the provision of social insurance, and economic incentives. Beyond these trade-offs lie basic issues of social values, of what kind of society we want to have *recognizing the economic constraints on the choices that we can make*; values that touch not only upon issues of efficiency and equality, but also upon individual rights and social responsibilities.

How Well Does the United States Do?

Taking all of the government programs into account—the tax system, social insurance, the welfare programs—does the government succeed in changing the answer to the question "Who gets the goods produced in the economy?" To answer this question, we need to have some way of describing the distribution of income.

Economists often represent the degree of inequality in an economy by a diagram called the **Lorenz curve**, shown in Figure 24.9. The Lorenz curve shows the cumulative fraction of the country's total income earned by the poorest 5 percent, the poorest 10 percent, the poorest 15 percent, and so on. If there were complete equality, then 20 percent of the income would accrue to the lowest 20 percent of the population, 40 percent to the lowest 40 percent. The Lorenz curve would be a straight line, as depicted in panel A. On the other hand, if incomes were very concentrated, then the lowest 80 percent might receive almost nothing, and the top 5 percent might receive 80 percent of total income; in this case, the Lorenz curve would be bowed, as illustrated in panel B. When there is a great deal of inequality, the shaded area between the 45-degree line in panel B and the Lorenz curve is large. When there is complete equality, as in panel A, this area is zero. Twice the area between the 45-degree line and the Lorenz curve is a commonly employed measure of inequality, called the **Gini coefficient**.

Figure 24.10A shows Lorenz curves for the United States, both before and after the

Figure 24.9 THE LORENZ CURVE

Panel A shows a Lorenz curve for an economy in which income is evenly distributed. The bottom 20 percent of the economy has 20 percent of income, the bottom 40 percent has 40 percent of income, and so on. Panel B depicts a Lorenz curve for an economy where income is unequally distributed. The curvature of the line indicates that now the bottom 20 percent has less than 20 percent of income, the bottom 40 percent has less than 40 percent of income, and so on.

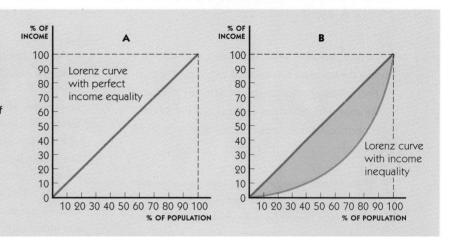

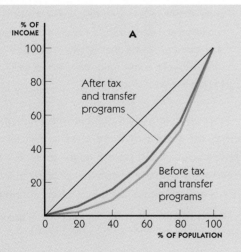

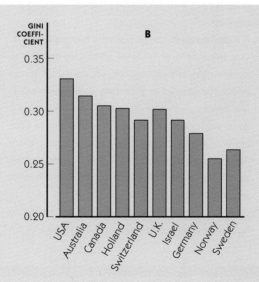

Figure 24.10 INEQUALITY MEASURES

Taxes and subsidies affect the distribution of income. Panel A shows two Lorenz curves for the United States in 1989, one for income before taxes have been levied and government transfers have been received, and the other after. Clearly, some redistribution does take place through these mechanisms, as they move the Lorenz curve toward greater equality. Panel B shows how other developed countries rank relative to the United States on one standard measure of inequality, the Gini coefficient. The United States ranks number one: it has the most unequal distribution of income among the ten.

Sources: Current Population Reports (1990), p. 5, Table B; *Luxembourg Income Study Database* (1989).

CLOSE-UP: BALANCING THE PUBLIC AND PRIVATE SECTORS

A central problem facing all mixed economies is finding the appropriate balance between the public and private sectors. Arthur Okun, an eloquent economist who served as chairman of the Council of Economic Advisers under President Johnson, put it this way:

> I have sounded a recurrent two-part theme: the market needs a place, and the market needs to be kept in its place. It must be given enough scope to accomplish the many things it does well. It limits the power of the bureaucracy and helps to protect our freedoms against transgression by the state. So long as a reasonable degree of competition is ensured, it responds reliably to the signals transmitted by consumers and producers. It permits decentralized management and encourages experiment and innovation.
>
> Most important, the prizes in the marketplace provide the incentives for work effort and productive contribution. In their absence, society would thrash about for alternative incentives—some unreliable, like altruism; some perilous, like collective loyalty; some intolerable, like coercion or oppression. Conceivably, the nation might instead stop caring about achievement itself and hence about incentives for effort; in that event, the living standards of the lowly would fall along with those of the mighty.
>
> For such reasons, I cheered the market; but I could not give it more than two cheers. The tyranny of the dollar yardstick restrained my enthusiasm. Given the chance, it would sweep away all other values, and establish a vending-machine society. The rights and powers that money should not buy must be protected with detailed regulations and sanctions, and with countervailing aids to those with low incomes. Once those rights are protected and economic deprivation is ended, I believe that our society would be more willing to let the competitive market have its place. Legislators might even enact effluent fees and repeal usury laws if they saw progress toward greater economic equality.
>
> A democratic capitalist society will keep searching for better ways of drawing the boundary lines between the domain of rights and the domain of dollars. And it can make progress. To be sure it will never solve the problem, for the conflict between equality and economic efficiency is inescapable. In that sense, capitalism and democracy are really a most improbable mixture. Maybe that is why they need each other—to put some rationality into equality and some humanity into efficiency.[1]

Other observers might quibble with Okun about where, on a scale of three cheers, the balance between public and private ought to lie. But few would argue with the notion that defining that balance is a fundamental issue in a mixed economy.

[1] "Equality and Efficiency: The Big Tradeoff" (Washington, D.C.: Brookings Institution, 1975), pp. 119–20.

government tax and transfer programs have had their effect. The after-tax curve is decidedly inside the pre-tax, indicating that the combined effect of government redistribution programs is to make incomes more equal than the market would have made them. Thus, while the efficiency costs are less clear-cut, the redistributive gains are undeniable.

Still, income inequality in the United States remains much larger than in other developed economies. Panel B gives the measure of inequality for ten developed countries. The United States ranks number one: it has the most *unequal* distribution of income among the ten.

THE ROLES OF GOVERNMENT: A REVIEW AND A LOOK AHEAD

Part Two, which set forth the basic competitive model, closed with a chapter that explained how the market system envisioned by that model will produce efficient economic outcomes. Beyond establishing a legal framework within which markets could operate, the only role seen for government in Part Two was possibly to correct the unacceptable distributions of income that have also been the subject of this chapter.

In this part, we have learned of many instances in which markets in the real world can be expected to depart from the basic competitive model. Failures of competition were discussed in Chapters 15 and 16, and government responses to them formed the subject of Chapter 17. Chapter 18 pointed out the absence of any analysis of technological advance in the basic model, and discussed the patent system and government support of research and development as responses to this shortcoming.

The basic model assumes that parties to transactions are armed with all the information they need about the goods being traded. Chapter 19 pointed out why this might not be the case in the product market, and Chapters 20 and 21 discussed problems of imperfect information in the labor and capital markets. Consumers may be ill-informed, for instance, because information is costly to obtain, so that it is seldom optimal to become perfectly informed; moreover, sellers tend to have better information than buyers and may try to take advantage of this. Government has responded with truth-in-advertising laws designed to protect consumers from this information imbalance. Similarly, the regulations surrounding securities trading were promulgated largely out of concern that buyers needed more information than they were given. In certain insurance and loan markets, where systematic information problems create a thin (incomplete) or nonexistent market, government has stepped in to supply the insurance or loans itself.

Chapter 23 discussed another market failure, externalities, which have so adversely affected our environment in recent decades, and the steps government has taken to remedy the situation. Moving beyond true market failures, Chapter 23 also took up merit goods and bads. Sometimes government takes a role simply because of a profound distrust in consumer sovereignty. In a free market for education, some parents might decide that their children should not go to school. When they do so out of ignorance about the benefits of education, there is an information problem. But they may also do so for religious beliefs or because they prefer that the children work. In either case, the government still insists that the children attend school; education is a merit good. Also in the realm beyond market failures is income redistribution, the subject of this chapter. As has been pointed out earlier, markets generally produce economically efficient outcomes, but there is nothing to say that the income shares they produce will be socially acceptable.

One final major category of market failure remains to be discussed. There are times when able workers eager to take jobs at the market wage nonetheless cannot find work.

The Great Depression, when 25 percent of the American labor force was out of work, is a dramatic example. In the basic competitive model, the price of labor (wages) adjusts so that the labor market always clears: the demand for labor equals the supply of labor. Unemployment should not exist. Understanding why unemployment arises and government's role in the face of unemployment are two of the central themes of the remainder of this book.

THE MARKET FAILURE ROLES OF GOVERNMENT

MARKET FAILURES	EXAMPLES OF GOVERNMENT RESPONSES

Market not competitive
    Product markets (Chapters
    15–18)
    Labor markets (Chapter 20)
	Antitrust policies

Public goods and externalities
    (Chapters 7, 23)
	Regulation of pollution; provision of
	    national defense

Basic research as a public good;
    externalities associated with
    R & D (Chapter 18)
	Public support of basic research;
	    patents

Imperfect information and thin
    (incomplete) markets (Chapters
    19, 21)
	Consumer protection legislation
	    (including securities
	    regulations); government loan
	    and insurance programs

Unemployment (to be discussed in
    Chapters 25–38)
	Macroeconomic policies to be
	    discussed

Merit goods and bads; distrust of
    consumer sovereignty (Chapter
    23)
	Compulsory education; prohibition
	    against drugs

Redistribution (Chapter 24)	Welfare and tax programs

REVIEW AND PRACTICE

SUMMARY

1. Even if markets are efficient, there may be dissatisfaction with the resulting distribution of income.

2. At the federal level, the largest share of taxes comes from the individual income tax, followed by the payroll tax. At the state level, main sources of revenue include sales and property taxes.

3. A tax system can be judged by five criteria: horizontal and vertical equity, efficiency, administrative simplicity, flexibility, and transparency.

4. The government has enacted a variety of programs to fight poverty, including unemployment insurance, job-retraining and placement programs, minimum wage laws, earned-income tax credits, and public assistance programs such as AFDC, Medicaid, and food stamps.

5. All public assistance programs force society to balance the concerns of equity, which involve helping those in need, with the concerns of efficiency, which involve making sure that both poor people and taxpayers have good incentives to work.

6. Social insurance programs, like Social Security and Medicare, are entitlement programs for everyone, regardless of income. But although everyone is entitled to benefits, some redistribution takes place, with some people getting back far more than they contribute.

KEY TERMS

individual income tax	horizontal equity	assistance in kind
corporate income tax	vertical equity	transfer programs
property tax	progressive tax	Lorenz curve
payroll tax	regressive tax	Gini coefficient
excise tax	categorical assistance	

REVIEW QUESTIONS

1. Will an efficient market necessarily produce a fairly equal distribution of income? Discuss.

2. What are the main sources of federal revenue? of state revenue?

3. What are the five characteristics of a good tax system? How well does the U.S. tax system fare in terms of their criteria? What is the difference between horizontal equity and vertical equity? What is the difference between a progressive and a regressive tax?

4. Make a list of government public assistance programs. How do the different programs affect the different causes and consequences of extreme poverty? What other government programs affect the overall number of poor people?

5. Define the difference between a social insurance program and a public assistance program, and give examples of each.

6. Why is in-kind assistance paternalistic? Do food stamps necessarily increase expenditure on food more than an equivalent cash subsidy?

7. How can redistribution take place through an entitlement program like Social Security, where all workers contribute and all retirees receive benefits?

8. Does it make any difference whether the payroll tax is officially paid by the employer or the employee? What determines who really bears the burden of the tax?

9. What is a Lorenz curve? What does it reveal?

PROBLEMS

1. Explain how a tax subsidy for a good with positive externalities (like research and development) can help economic efficiency. Then explain how a tax subsidy for other goods without such externalities could injure efficiency.

2. Explain how the following programs attempt to make sure that public assistance does not erode the incentive for poor people to work:
   (a) workfare;
   (b) categorical assistance;
   (c) negative income tax.

3. Assume that a country has a simple tax structure, in which all income over $10,000 was taxed at 20 percent. Evaluate a proposal to increase the progressivity of the tax structure by requiring all those with incomes over $100,000 to pay a tax of 80 percent on income in excess of $100,000. Draw a high-wage earner's budget constraint. How does the surtax affect his budget constraint? What happens to his incentives to work? Is it possible that imposing the tax actually will reduce the tax revenues the government receives from the rich?

4. Imagine that Congress decided to fund an increase in Social Security benefits by increasing the payroll tax on employers. Would this prevent employees from being affected by the higher tax? Draw a diagram to illustrate your answer.

5. Draw Lorenz curves for the following countries. Which country has the greatest and least inequality?

	Percentage of total income received by				
	Lowest fifth	Second fifth	Third fifth	Fourth fifth	Top fifth
United States	4.7	11.0	17.4	25.0	41.9
Japan	8.7	13.2	17.5	23.1	37.5
Germany	6.8	12.7	17.8	24.1	38.7

PART FOUR

Aggregate Markets

P eace and prosperity" is the slogan on which many political candidates have run for office, and the failure to maintain prosperity has led to many a government's defeat. There is widespread belief among the citizenry that government is responsible for maintaining the economy at full employment, with stable prices, and for creating an economic environment in which growth can occur. This belief is reflected in the Full Employment Act of 1946, which stated that "it is the continuing policy and responsibility of the Federal Government to use all practicable means . . . to promote maximum employment, production, and purchasing power."

Although most economists still agree with these sentiments, there are dissenting views. Some claim that the government has relatively little power to control most of the fluctuations in output and employment; some argue that, apart from isolated instances such as the Great Depression of the 1930s, neither inflation nor unemployment is a major *economic* problem (though they obviously remain political problems); and some believe that government has been as much a cause of the problems of unemployment, inflation, and slow growth as part of their solution. We will explore these various interpretations in greater depth in the chapters that follow.

The problems of unemployment, inflation, and growth relate to the performance of the entire economy. Earlier in the book, we learned how the law of supply and demand operates in the market for oranges, apples, or other goods. At any one time, one industry may be doing well, another poorly. Yet to understand the forces that determine how well the economy as a whole is doing, we want to see beyond the vagaries that affect any particular industry. This is the domain of macroeconomics. Macroeconomics focuses not on the output of single products like orange juice or peanut butter, nor on the demand for masons or bricklayers or computer programmers. Rather, it is concerned with the characteristics of an entire economy, such as the overall level of output, the total level of employment, and the stability of the overall level of prices. What accounts for the "diseases" that sometimes affect the economy—the episodes of massive unemployment, rising prices, or economic stagnation—and what can the government do, both to prevent the onset of these diseases and to cure them once they have occurred?

Macroeconomic *theory* is concerned with what determines the level of employment and output as well as the rate of inflation and the overall growth rate of the economy; while macroeconomic *policy* focuses on what government can do to stimulate employment, prevent inflation, and increase the economy's growth rate.

We begin our study of macroeconomics in Chapter 25 by learning the major statistics used to measure the economy—rates of unemployment, inflation, and growth. Chapter 26 then presents the main schools of macroeconomics and the principal analytical issues as they relate to the three aggregate markets—labor, product, and capital. It introduces the key concepts of *aggregate* demand

and *aggregate* supply curves, with which we can analyze price and output levels for the economy as a whole.

Chapter 27 looks in detail at the aggregate labor market and the reasons it might not clear. When the demand for labor decreases, real wages may not fall and unemployment is the result. But what causes the demand curve for labor to shift? The answer lies in the product market, to which Chapters 28–32 are devoted. Chapter 28 introduces the concept of aggregate expenditures, the total of what households, firms, and government, in the United States and abroad, would like to spend on goods produced in the United States. Chapters 29 and 30 examine each of the components of aggregate expenditures—consumption, investment, government spending, and net exports—to learn why aggregate expenditures fluctuate and how government policy can affect these fluctuations.

In Chapter 31, we learn how the aggregate demand and supply curves are derived, in order to understand what causes them to shift, how government policies can affect them, and why they have the shape they do. Finally, Chapter 32 explores why it is that prices may not adjust in the speedy way envisioned by the basic competitive model, as well as the consequences for the behavior of the economy and the role of government intervention. The third aggregate market, the capital market, is the subject of Part Five.

CHAPTER 25

MACROECONOMIC
GOALS AND
MEASURES

J ust as doctors find it useful to take a patient's temperature to help them determine just how sick the patient is, economists use statistics to get a quantitative measure of the economy's performance. This chapter introduces the major statistics that summarize the overall condition of the economy. In studying these measures, economists look for patterns. Are good years regularly followed by lean years? Does inflation usually accompany high employment levels? If they find patterns, they ask why.

This chapter also discusses problems of measurement that affect almost every economic variable. It often does not mean much when the rate of unemployment or inflation changes by a few tenths of a percent, just as there is rarely cause for alarm when a person's temperature changes by a tenth of a degree. But over time, the statistics describing the economy may change more dramatically. When unemployment statistics show an increase from 5 percent to 10 percent (that is, a change from one out of twenty workers without jobs to one out of ten), few would doubt that there has been a sizable increase in unemployment.

The sections below discuss the issues of unemployment, inflation, and growth and explain how each is measured.

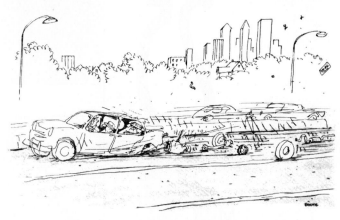

KEY QUESTIONS

1. What are the main objectives of government macro-economic policy?

2. How are unemployment, output, growth, the cost of living, and inflation measured?

3. What problems arise in measuring these variables?

4. What are some of the different forms of unemployment?

"The Administration sees a quick recovery, but Mrs. Fisher and I feel it's going to be deep and prolonged."

UNEMPLOYMENT

High on the list of economic goals the government sets for itself is maintaining full employment. Everyone who wants to get a job and is capable of working should be able to find gainful employment.

To an economist, unemployment represents an underutilization of resources: people who are willing and able to work are not being productively employed. To the unemployed individuals and their families, unemployment represents economic hardship and changes in their way of life: vacations will have to be given up, and children may have to forgo their dreams of going to college. If a person is unemployed for a long time, he will no longer be able to ignore the notices for missed rent or mortgage payments, and the family will have to find less expensive housing.

Unemployment not only costs individuals a paycheck, it can deal a powerful blow to their self-respect. Unemployed workers in today's urban America cannot fall back on farming or living off the land as they might have done in colonial times. Instead, they and their families may be forced to choose between poverty and the bitter taste of government or private charity. And many of these families may break up.

Unemployment presents different problems for each age group of workers. For the young, having a job is necessary for developing job skills, whether they are technical skills or such basic work prerequisites as punctuality and responsibility. Thus, persistent unemployment among the youth (and other workers too, to a lesser extent) not only wastes valuable human resources today but may also reduce the future productivity of the labor force. Furthermore, young people who remain unemployed for an extended period of time seem especially prone to becoming alienated from society and turning to antisocial activities such as crime and drugs.

For the middle-aged or elderly worker, losing a job poses particular problems as well. Despite various prohibitions on age discrimination enacted at the state and federal levels, employers are often hesitant to hire older workers. They wonder why such a worker lost her previous job and fear she is more likely to become sick or disabled than a younger person is. They may worry about being able to "teach old dogs new tricks." When the unemployed older worker succeeds in getting a job, it often entails a reduction in wages and status from her previous job and may make limited use of previously acquired skills. Even if the new job is challenging and interesting, these changes impose a heavy burden of stress on the newly reemployed worker and her family.

In addition to these personal losses, unemployment poses heavy costs for communities. If a number of people in a particular town are thrown out of work—say, because a big employer closes down or decides to move—then everyone else in town is likely to suffer as well, since there will be fewer dollars circulating around town to buy everything from cars and houses to gasoline and groceries. As more unemployment results in fewer people paying local taxes, it means downgrading the schools, libraries, parks, and police.

The existence of unemployment may also reinforce racial divisions that persist in society as a whole. The rate of unemployment for blacks is generally over twice that of whites; and during the 1980s, among blacks between the ages of sixteen and nineteen who were just beginning to look for work, the unemployment rate averaged almost 40 percent, nearly reaching 50 percent in the recession years of 1982–83.

Unemployment is thus often a tragedy for the individual, a source of dislocation and stress for a community, and a waste of productive resources for society as a whole.

THE MAGNITUDE OF THE PROBLEM

One shorthand description of the U.S. economy is that the economy is what happens when 120 million people get up and go to work. But living in the midst of those who have jobs is a fluctuating group of several million healthy people who do not. During the recession year of 1991, 8.5 million people were out of a job, and one-fourth of those people were out of work for fifteen weeks or more. As recently as the recession of 1983, 10.7 million potentially productive workers were looking for jobs. From the standpoint of the economy as a whole, these potentially productive workers who cannot find jobs are a major loss. Not only do the rest of the workers need to pay the costs of supporting the unemployed and their families, but even more important, the rest of society is deprived of the contributions the unemployed are capable of making.

During the 1980s, an average of 7.3 percent of those willing to work were unable to find jobs. Roughly speaking, that figure represents a loss of one worker in every thirteen, an unlucky number indeed for the American economy. One calculation puts the loss in output from the high unemployment of the early 1980s at between $122 billion and $320 billion a year, for a per capita loss of between $500 and more than $1,300.[1] That means that every man, woman, and child in the United States would have had (on average) as much as an additional $1,300 to spend if the unemployed workers had been gainfully employed. Clearly, society has many good reasons to be concerned with reducing the level of unemployment.

[1] A. Blinder, *Hard Heads, Soft Hearts* (Reading, Mass.: Addison-Wesley, 1987).

UNEMPLOYMENT STATISTICS

In the United States, unemployment data is collected by the Department of Labor, which surveys a representative mix of households and asks each whether a member of the household is currently seeking employment. The **unemployment rate** is the ratio of the number of those seeking employment to the total labor force. If there are 120 million Americans employed and 10 million say they are looking for a job but cannot find one, then the total labor force is 130 million, and the

$$\text{unemployment rate} = \frac{\text{number unemployed}}{\text{labor force}}$$

$$= \frac{\text{number unemployed}}{\text{number employed} + \text{number unemployed}}$$

$$= \frac{10 \text{ million}}{120 \text{ million} + 10 \text{ million}} = 7.7 \text{ percent.}$$

Figure 25.1 plots the unemployment rate for the United States since 1960. The figure illustrates two main facts. First, unemployment is clearly persistent; it never touches zero. Unemployment in foreign countries has often been even worse. As Figure 25.2 shows, unemployment in some European countries was more than 10 percent during much of the 1980s. Many cities in the less developed countries face unemployment rates in excess of 20 percent.

The second fact we can observe from Figure 25.1 is that the level of unemployment can fluctuate dramatically. In the worst days of the Great Depression, over 24 percent of the U.S. labor force was unemployed. The unemployment rate among those who worked in manufacturing was even worse—at one point, 33 percent of workers in manufacturing had lost their jobs. As recently as 1983, the unemployment rate in the

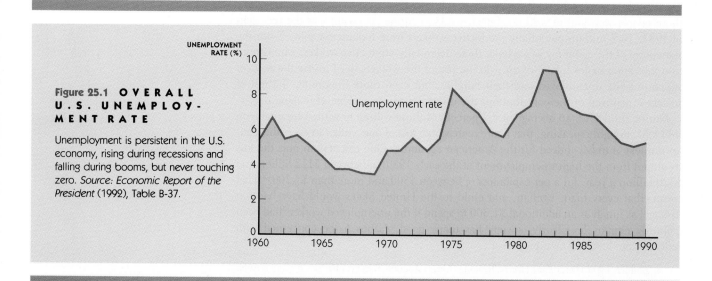

Figure 25.1 OVERALL U.S. UNEMPLOY-MENT RATE

Unemployment is persistent in the U.S. economy, rising during recessions and falling during booms, but never touching zero. *Source: Economic Report of the President* (1992), Table B-37.

Figure 25.2

INTERNATIONAL UNEMPLOYMENT COMPARISONS

In other developed countries, the unemployment rate is often much higher than has been observed in the United States in recent years. *Source: ERP* (1992), Tables B-37, B-106.

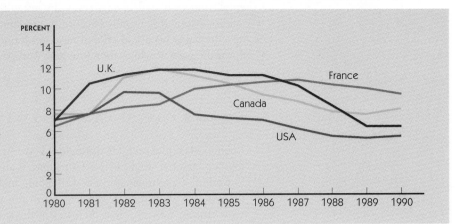

United States was 9.7 percent, before declining to about 5 percent at the end of the decade.

Underlying the overall unemployment rates plotted in Figure 25.1 is the important fact referred to earlier: there are marked differences in the unemployment rates of different groups. Unemployment among blacks and youths has been persistently larger—sometimes significantly so—than unemployment among adult white males. Economists seek to explain these differences in unemployment rates and how they change with varying economic circumstances.

PROBLEMS WITH UNEMPLOYMENT STATISTICS

Some economists believe that the answers to the Department of Labor survey provide too high an estimate of the true unemployment rate; some believe the estimate is too low. Some individuals who say they are actively seeking a job may not really be doing so in any meaningful way. Even if an unemployed person is actively looking for work, he may have turned down several reasonable job offers, hoping (unrealistically) for a job that is beyond his ability. Should an unskilled worker who turns down all job offers, insisting on waiting for a corporate vice-presidency or some other top executive job, be viewed as "actively seeking employment"?

Other people may have given up all hope of finding a job. They are referred to as **discouraged workers.** If some workers who want jobs have given up looking, the statistics will not count them as unemployed, and thus the reported rate may provide an underestimate of the number of people who would choose to work if a job were available.[2] The fraction of the working age population that is employed or seeking employment is called the **labor force participation rate.** Because of discouraged workers, the labor force participation rate tends to decline in recessions.

[2] There are other problems with the unemployment data. It has been suggested that the number of households reporting an unemployed worker depends on who is asked, which in turn depends in part on what time of day the household is surveyed. If the mother of a teenager is asked, she may report that her teenage son is seeking a job, while the teenager may not view himself as actively seeking employment.

Despite these ambiguities, there is little doubt that substantial changes in the unemployment rate reflect changes in the rest of the economy. When the unemployment rate increases, it is usually because the economy has slowed down. Some individuals have probably been laid off and have not found new jobs, and firms may have slowed down the pace at which they hire new workers.

FORMS OF UNEMPLOYMENT

Economists find it useful to distinguish between different kinds of unemployment. Some jobs are seasonal. Right before Christmas, there is a huge demand for retail salespeople to work in department stores and shopping malls across the country. In many parts of the country, construction slows down in the winter because of the climate. For the same reason, tourism often increases in the summer, and so does the number of jobs that cater to tourists. The supply of labor increases in the summer, as high school and college students enter the labor force on a temporary basis. Since the increase in the summertime supply of labor usually exceeds the increase in the summertime demand, the unemployment rate normally increases in the summer. Accordingly, it is important to make an adjustment for these seasonal changes.

Unemployment that varies with the seasons is called **seasonal unemployment,** and the adjustments that are made to the unemployment data to reflect normal seasonal patterns are called seasonal adjustments. Thus, if, on average, the unemployment rate is normally .4 percent higher in the summer than at other times, the seasonally adjusted unemployment rate for July will be the actually measured unemployment rate minus .4 percent. If between May and July the unemployment rate increases by much more than .4 percent, then there is something to worry about.

While workers in construction, agriculture, and tourism regularly face seasonal unemployment, still others are unemployed only as part of a normal transition from one job to another. This kind of unemployment is referred to as **frictional unemployment.** An individual who has grown sick of her job and has quit to look for a new one is among the frictionally unemployed. If people could move from job to job instantaneously, there would be no frictional unemployment. In a dynamic society such as America's, with some industries growing and others declining, there will always be movements from one job to another, and hence there will always be frictional unemployment.

Young people tend to switch jobs more often than older people, as they search for a job that matches their skills and interests. Thus, in periods in which there are an unusually large number of individuals entering the labor force, there is likely to be a higher level of frictional unemployment. In the late 1960s and early 1970s, when the post–World War II baby boomers reached working age, the level of frictional unemployment rose substantially.

Most bouts of unemployment are short-lived; the average person who loses a job is out of work for only three months. However, approximately 10 percent of the jobless have been unemployed for more than six months. This kind of long-term unemployment often results from structural factors in the economy, and so it is called **structural unemployment.** Quite often substantial structural unemployment is found side by side with job vacancies because the unemployed lack the skills required for the newly created jobs. For example, there may be vacancies for computer programmers, while construction workers are unemployed. By the same token, there may be job shortages in those parts of the economy that are expanding (as in the Sunbelt during much of the 1980s) and unemployment in areas that are suffering decline (as in Michigan during the period of decline in demand for U.S. cars). Older individuals, in particular, may find it difficult to adapt to structural change; and employers may be reluctant to spend the money required to retrain a fifty-five-year-old whose job has disappeared. Structural unemployment poses a particularly significant problem for society, since those who are unemployed for long periods of time become disaffected and can lose their work habits.

The kind of unemployment with which we will be most concerned in this part of the book is called **cyclical unemployment,** the unemployment that increases when the economy goes into a slowdown and decreases when the economy goes into a boom. Government policy is particularly concerned with reducing both the frequency and magnitude of this kind of unemployment, by reducing the frequency and magnitude of the recessions that give rise to it; and with reducing its impact, by providing unemployment compensation for those temporarily thrown out of work.

INFLATION

In the 1920s, the years of silent pictures, a movie ticket cost a nickel. By the late 1940s, in the heyday of Hollywood, the price was up to $.50. By the 1960s, the price of a movie was $2.00, and now it is well over $6.00. This steady price rise is no anomaly; most other goods have undergone similar increases over time. This increase in the general level of prices is called inflation, as we learned in Chapter 6. While unemployment tends to be concentrated in certain groups within the population, *everyone* is affected by inflation. Thus, it is not surprising that when inflation becomes high, it almost always rises to the top of the political agenda.

It is not inflation if the price of only one good goes up; it *is* inflation if the prices of *most* goods go up. The **inflation rate** is the rate at which the *general level* of prices increases.

MEASURING INFLATION

If the prices of all goods rose by the same proportion, say by 5 percent, over a period of a year, measuring inflation would be easy: the rate of inflation for that year would be 5 percent. The difficulties arise from the fact that the prices of different goods rise at different rates, and some goods may even decline in price. Over the past twenty years, while the price of fruits and vegetables has increased by 189 percent, the price of gasoline by 176 percent, and the price of medical care by 259 percent, the price of computers has declined. To determine the change in the overall price level, economists calculate the *average* percentage increase in prices. But in making this calculation, more importance must be placed on the change in the price of any goods that loom large in the budget (such as housing) than on the change in price of a relatively unimportant item, such as pencils. If the price of pencils goes down by 5 percent but the price of housing goes up by 5 percent, the overall measure of the price level should go up.

Economists have a straightforward way of measuring the price level. They ask, what would it cost consumers to purchase the same bundle of goods this year that they bought last year? If, for example, it cost $22,000 in 1991 to buy what it cost consumers only $20,000 to purchase in 1990, then we say that prices, *on average*, have risen by 10 percent. Such results are frequently expressed in the form of a **price index,** which, for ease of comparison, measures the price level in any given year relative to a common base year.

The price index for the base year is, by definition, 100. The price index for any other year is calculated by taking the ratio of the price level in that year to the price level in the base year and multiplying it by 100. For example, if 1990 is our base year and we want to know the price index for 1991, we first calculate the ratio of the cost of a certain bundle of goods in 1991 ($22,000) to the cost of the same bundle of goods in 1990 ($20,000), which is 1.1. The price index in 1991 is therefore $1.1 \times 100 = 110$. This does not mean that average prices are $1.10 or $110—whatever that would mean. The index of 110, using 1990 as a base, means that prices are 10 percent higher, on average, in 1991 than in 1990. In using price indices, one has to be careful to keep in mind both how they are calculated and the base year.

There are several different indices, each using a different bundle of goods. When the government, in calculating the price index, uses the bundle of goods that represents how the average American household spends its income, this index is called the **consumer price index,** or CPI. To determine this bundle, the government, through the Bureau of Labor Statistics of the Department of Labor, conducts a Consumer Expenditure Survey, which is updated once a decade or so.

The consumer price index tells us how much more the basket of goods that represents goods purchased by the average household costs today than it did at some earlier time. In Figure 25.3, 1983 is the base year and thus represents 100. Suppose in 1983 it took $857 to buy the basket of goods purchased by the average American family in a month.

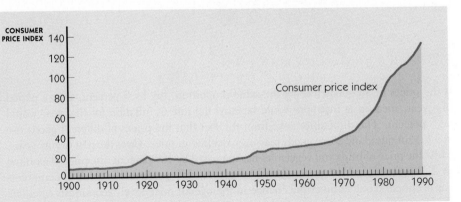

Figure 25.3 TWENTIETH-CENTURY U.S. INFLATION

The figure shows average prices in each year relative to what they were in 1983. For example, prices in 1920 were 20 percent of prices in 1983. *Source: ERP* (1992), Table B-56.

Assume in 1991 it cost $1,174 to buy the same basket. Then the price index for 1991 is just the ratio of the cost in 1991 to the cost in 1983, times 100; that is,

CPI for 1991 = (1,174/857) × 100 = 137.

The CPI rose 37 percent between 1983 and 1991.

Similarly, if the same basket cost $412 in 1973, then the consumer price index for 1973 (again, using 1983 as the base year) compares this figure with what the goods would have cost at 1983 prices:

CPI for 1973 = (412/857) × 100 = 48.

The CPI was 52 percent lower in 1973 than in 1983.

The advantage of an index is that once we have an index number for any year, we can compare it with any other year. The CPI for 1973 was 48, and for 1989 it was 111. Between those years, it rose by 63, so the increase was

63/48 = 131 percent.

On average, prices rose by 131 percent from 1973 to 1989.

THE AMERICAN EXPERIENCE
WITH INFLATION

As we have learned, the inflation rate is the percentage increase of the price level from one year to the next. Figure 25.4 shows the inflation rate for the United States during this century. Three interesting features about inflation emerge from the figure.

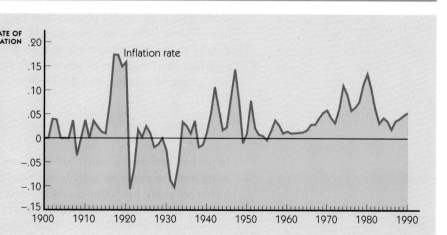

Figure 25.4 THE INFLATION RATE

The inflation rate is the percentage increase in the price level in a given year. Notice that inflation was low through most of the early part of this century (although high during World Wars I and II), rose sharply in the 1970s, and then fell somewhat in the 1980s. *Source: ERP (1992), Table B-56.*

First, prices were relatively stable for much of the century, with the inflation rate under 5 percent except in three periods: around World War I, around World War II, and during the period 1973–1981. Indeed, from the start of the twentieth century until the early 1960s, average inflation ran at only about 1 percent per year.

Second, the figure also shows that prices may actually come down. During the recession that followed World War I, prices fell by more than 15 percent, and in the Great Depression of the 1930s, prices fell by more than 30 percent. It may seem hard to believe, but just as today inflation seems an ever-present threat, at the end of the nineteenth century, there was great concern about **deflation,** which is a steady decline of the price level. Borrowers at that time who were in debt and had not anticipated the fall in prices found that the real value of the dollars they had to pay back were worth far more than the dollars that they had borrowed. They were as upset about this as investors today are about the fact that with inflation, the value of the dollars they get back from an investment or loan is worth less than the value of the dollars they originally spent.

Finally, while prices on average have been stable and there have even been periods of price decline, there have also been a few periods of high inflation, when prices increased rapidly. The most notable recent episode was in the late 1970s and early 1980s; in 1980, prices rose by more than 13 percent. Moreover, concern about inflation getting out of control led to government attempts to control prices in two instances: during World War II, when the rate rose to 10.7 percent in 1942, and in the early 1970s, when inflation went up to 4.5 percent. In the latter instance, President Nixon was concerned enough to implement a freeze on wages and prices; that is, a declaration that wages and prices could not increase under penalty of federal law. The Nixon price controls are now widely regarded as having been counterproductive; as the simple supply and demand model would predict, they resulted in shortages of some products. Furthermore, when Nixon lifted the controls, inflation shot up again, moving beyond 10 percent by the end of the decade.

Even the high level of inflation the United States experienced in the late 1970s and early 1980s—so-called "double-digit" inflation—is only the little brother of inflation that has occurred at other times and places. In Germany in the 1920s, for example, prices were increasing so rapidly that people rushed from the pay window to the market, fearful that prices would go up before they could get there. More recently, in Israel from 1980 to 1990, prices increased by over 100 percent each year. In Bolivia, prices rose by nearly 400 percent per year for the same period. On the other hand, some countries have managed to contain inflation quite well. In Japan, for example, the average rate of inflation over the 1980–90 period was only 1.3 percent.

THE IMPORTANCE OF INFLATION

In modern economies, much has been done to ease the pain of inflation. For workers, rising levels of prices are usually accompanied by higher wages, and if a worker faces higher prices but has commensurately more money in his pocket, he is just as well off. Many unions now often negotiate contracts with cost of living adjustments (COLAs); and nonunion firms often give bigger raises in inflationary times to keep up with the rising cost of living. Likewise, the U.S. government has taken steps to adjust the income of retirees to changes in the price level. Most significant, Social Security payments go up automatically as prices increase. We say that they are "indexed" to the cost of living.

Why, then, does fighting inflation rank so high as a priority in economic policy? There seem to be three answers.

The first is that there are still some groups who suffer. Anyone whose income does not adjust fully is made worse off by increases in the price level. Many retired people have fixed pension payments; they have saved all their lives with an expectation of the income they would need in retirement, but inflation may mean that their pensions will not enable them to live in the style they had expected to. As Social Security has become an increasingly important basis of support for the elderly, particularly for those of limited means, the importance of this problem has shrunk, but it still seems unfair that those on fixed incomes should suffer for reasons beyond their control.

Second, when the rate of inflation suddenly increases, those who have lent money find that the dollars they are being paid back with are worth less. Thus, creditors (those who lend money) are worse off, while debtors are better off. Just the reverse happens when the rate of inflation suddenly decreases. Those who owe money suddenly find that it is more expensive, in real terms, to pay back the loans than they had anticipated. When the inflation rate is variable, both borrowing and lending become riskier.

Third, many feel that something is fundamentally wrong with the economy when what cost $1 five years ago costs $2 today. Sometimes these observers are right: the inflation is often a reflection of gross errors in government economic policy, such as spending that is far in excess of revenues, or excessive provision of credit. Frequently inflation gets the blame when something else is the underlying problem. The steep increase in oil prices in 1973 set off a worldwide inflationary spiral. With Americans paying more to the oil-exporting countries, the United States was, in a sense, poorer. Someone had to take a cut. Furthermore, the worldwide economic downturn set off by the 1973 oil price rise made the cut that had to be taken that much larger. Thus, workers' real wages fell. They blamed inflation for their declining standard of living. But inflation was not really the culprit—higher oil prices were.

As the economy has adapted to inflation, economists have increasingly debated about how concerned we should be about moderate rates of inflation, the 3 to 6 percent inflation that has occurred regularly during the past few decades. They worry that in trying to stop the inflation, the cures may be worse than the disease. Still, most economists think that double-digit inflation levels, at the very least, are symptomatic of some kind of malfunction in the economy. Certainly there is a consensus that the kind of rapid rates of inflation experienced in Israel and some Latin American countries are extremely disruptive to the economy.

ALTERNATIVE PRICE INDICES

Other price indices besides the consumer price index can be calculated using different market baskets. One of them, the **producer price index,** measures the average level of prices of the goods sold by producers to wholesalers. The **wholesale price index** measures the average level of prices of the goods sold by wholesalers to retailers. These indices are useful because they give us an inkling of what will happen to consumer prices in the near future. Usually, if producers are receiving higher prices from their sales to wholesalers, in a short while wholesalers will have to charge higher prices to retailers; this will be reflected in a higher wholesale price index. A short while later, retailers will have to charge higher prices, and this will be reflected in an increase in the consumer price index.

CLOSE-UP: THE COST-OF-LIVING-EXTREMELY-WELL INDEX

Any calculation of an inflation rate involves choosing a basket of goods; the trick is to choose the correct basket for the question at hand. A basket of goods relevant for calculating the change in the cost of living for a student will differ considerably from a basket of goods appropriate for a retired person or for parents who are sending children to college.

Forbes magazine occasionally publishes an inflation index aimed at the very rich, called the "cost-of-living-extremely-well index" (CLEWI). In the category of clothes, the CLEWI basket contains an Adolfo Couture dress and Gucci loafers. In the cat-

egory of food at home, it includes a case of Dom Perignon champagne, seven pounds of filet mignon, and a kilogram of caviar. You get the idea. The transportation part of the basket contains a Rolls-Royce Silver Spirit, a Learjet, and an executive Sikorsky helicopter. Entertainment includes the price of a catered dinner for forty and two season tickets (box seats, Saturday night) to the New York Metropolitan Opera.

The retail prices of some items from the CLEWI are listed below, together with their rate of increase in 1990–91. Although most readers of this book will probably need to consider a somewhat dif-

Item	1991 price	Percentage rate of increase, 1990–91
Apparel		
Dress (Adolfo Couture)	$ 1,500	none
Loafers (Gucci)	$ 295	+14
Entertainment		
Catered dinner (for 40, by Ridgewells, Washington, D.C.)	$ 5,040	none
Opera (2 season tickets, Metropolitan Opera, Saturday night, box)	$ 2,250	+9
Food at home		
Caviar (Beluga Malossol, 1-kilo tin, average retail)	$ 1,478	none
Champagne (Dom Perignon, case)	$ 947	+7
Transportation		
Airplane (Learjet 35A, standard equipment, 10 passengers)	$4,625,000	+5
Helicopter (Sikorsky S-76, full executive options)	$6,300,000	+5
Automobile (Rolls-Royce Silver Spirit)	$ 151,700	+8

ferent basket of goods to reflect the changes in their personal cost of living, it should nonetheless be a great load off of everyone's mind to know that the cost of living extremely well increased by just 3.5 percent for the CLEWI set in 1991, the small-est increase in the five years *Forbes* has calculated the index. Over the same period, the consumer price index rose by 4.4 percent.

Source: Manjeet Kripalani, "Price Break for the Rich," *Forbes,* October 21, 1991, p. 49.

G R O W T H

For more than a century, Americans had become used to the idea that their children would have a higher standard of living than their own, and their grandchildren a still higher standard of living. Wages were increasing, so much so that each successive generation could enjoy both higher incomes and more leisure than the previous generation. Growth in the United States was more rapid than in other countries, so that by the mid-1950s, the United States accounted for more than 25 percent of the total output of the world, while it contained but 6 percent of the population. The high and rising standards of living formed the basis of American optimism. Even the poorest segments of society benefited from the economy's growth.

All of this has changed. In the 1970s and much of the 1980s, wages stagnated. Family incomes continued to increase, but only because of an increase in hours spent by family members in the workplace, as more and more women joined the labor force. And America's dominant economic position was challenged by Japan and several European countries. A major objective of macroeconomic policy today is to increase the economy's rate of growth. This, along with maintaining full employment and stable prices, constitutes the third major area of concern for macroeconomists.

If an economy is to compete effectively and grow rapidly, it must use its resources

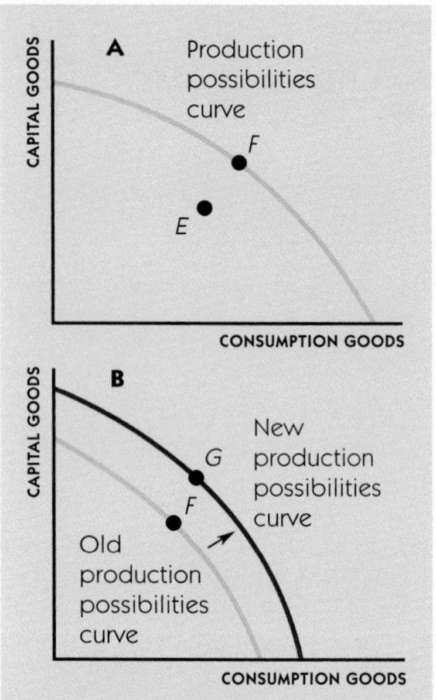

Figure 25.5 ECONOMIC EFFICIENCY AND GROWTH

In panel A, if the economy made efficient use of its resources, it could move from point E to F, on the production possibilities curve. Panel B shows that the economy can also expand if the production possibilities curve is shifted outward.

efficiently and it must invest in increasing its productive potential. To accomplish the first task—using resources efficiently—the economy must operate along its production possibilities curve. This concept was first introduced in Chapter 2, and it is fundamental to our thinking about macroeconomics. Figure 25.5A shows a production possibilities curve, which represents the *maximum* amount of one good that can be produced, given the amounts of other goods that are produced. In the figure, we focus on only two goods. The horizontal axis measures the amount of "consumption" goods that are produced, and the vertical axis measures the amount of capital goods (machines and buildings). If the economy is at point *E*, it is not using all of its resources, or at least not using them efficiently. Workers may be unemployed; machines may be idle. Production could be expanded to a point on the curve such as *F*, where the economy would be producing as efficiently as it possibly could. Here people would have more to consume, and there would be a higher level of investment.

The second task of an economy, increasing its productive potential, is illustrated in panel B of Figure 25.5: economic policy also seeks to move the production possibilities curve outward. The economy moves from point *F* to point *G*; there are both more consumption goods and more investment goods. (One has to be somewhat careful in interpreting what it means for the economy to be on its production possibilities curve. It does not mean that there is zero unemployment, or that all machines are fully used. There is, for instance, always some frictional unemployment, as workers move from one job to another. Normally, some machines may be idle, simply because they are being repaired or because they are being held in reserve for an emergency.)

MEASURING OUTPUT

The problem of measuring changes in output are similar to the problem of measuring changes in the price level. We could report how much of each good the economy produced: 1,362,478 hammers, 473,562,382 potatoes, 7,875,342 wristwatches, and so forth. Such data may be useful for some purposes, but they do not provide us with the information we want. If next year the output of hammers goes up by 5 percent, the output of potatoes goes down by 2 percent, and the output of wristwatches rises by 7 percent, has total output gone up or down? And by how much?

For many purposes, it is convenient to have a single number that summarizes the output of the economy. But how do we add up the hammers, potatoes, wristwatches, and billions of other products produced in the economy? We do this by adding the money value of all the final goods (goods that are not used to make other goods) produced and arriving at a single number that encapsulates the production of the economy. This number is called the **gross domestic product,** or **GDP.** It is the standard measure of the output of an economy, and sums up the total money value of the goods and services produced by the residents of a nation during a specified period. Thus, GDP includes everything from buttons to air travel, and from haircuts to barrels of oil. It makes no difference whether the production takes place in the public or private sector, or whether the goods and services are purchased by households or by the government.[3]

---

[3] We use prices not only because they are a convenient way of making comparisons, but also because prices reflect how consumers value different goods. If the price of an orange is twice that of an apple, it means an orange is worth twice as much (at the margin) as an apple.

There is one problem with using money as a measure of output. Inflation means that money changes in value over time. Candy bars, books, movie tickets, hammers, all cost more today than they did ten years ago. Another way of saying this is that a dollar does not buy as much now as it did ten years ago. We do not want to be misled into believing that the output is higher when in fact all that has happened is that the price level has risen.

To keep the comparisons of different years straight, economists adjust GDP for inflation. Unadjusted GDP is known as **nominal GDP.** The term **real GDP** is used for inflation-adjusted GDP figures, which are truer year-to-year measures of what the economy actually produces. To calculate real GDP, economists simply take the nominal value of GDP—the money value of all the goods and services produced in the economy—and divide it by a measure of the price level. Thus, real GDP is defined by the equation

$$\text{real GDP} = \frac{\text{nominal GDP}}{\text{price level}}.$$

If nominal GDP has risen 3 percent in the past year but inflation has also increased prices by 3 percent, then real GDP is unchanged. If nominal GDP has risen 3 percent in the past year but prices have increased by 6 percent, real GDP has actually decreased.

Earlier in the chapter, we learned how to measure the price level by analyzing how the cost of a particular bundle of goods changes over time. The measure of the price level that we use to adjust our GDP measure for inflation is the **GDP deflator,** which represents a comparison between what it would cost to buy the total mix of goods and services within the economy today and in a base year. In other words, the GDP deflator is a weighted average of the prices of different goods and services, where the weights represent the importance of each of the goods and services in GDP.

Between 1989 and 1990, nominal GDP rose by 5.1 percent, but the GDP deflator (using 1987 as a base year) went up from 108.4 to 112.9. Thus, the price level (measured this way) increased by 4.1 percent (112.9 ÷ 108.4 = 1.041). The percentage change in real GDP equals the percentage change in nominal GDP minus the inflation rate. Therefore, the percentage change in real GDP was 5.1 − 4.1 = 1.0.

INSIDE THE PRODUCTION POSSIBILITIES CURVE

While GDP provides a measure of how much the economy actually produces, it is also useful to know what the economy *could* produce if labor and machines were used fully to their capacity. Another measure, **potential GDP,** does just this. The gap between potential GDP and actual GDP is a measure of how far inside the production possibilities curve the economy is operating.

Figure 25.6 shows how potential (real) GDP and actual (real) GDP have increased over the past quarter century. Two features stand out.[4] First, output does not grow

[4] Figure 25.6 shows actual GDP exceeding potential GDP in a few years. How is this possible, if potential GDP really measures what the economy *could* produce? The answer is that the estimates of potential GDP are based on assumptions about "normal" levels of frictional unemployment and on the fact that even when the economy is quite strong, some capacity is not fully utilized. In fact, for short spurts of time, such as when a country goes to war, actual GDP can exceed estimates of potential GDP by a considerable amount.

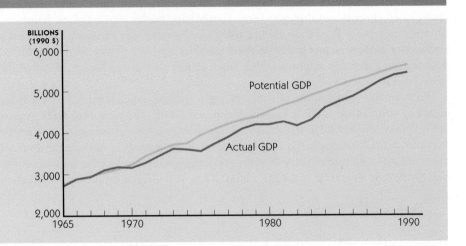

Figure 25.6 POTENTIAL AND REAL GDP

Potential GDP measures how much the economy would produce if it used all its resources efficiently. Actual GDP shows what the economy actually produces. Notice that both have been growing over time. *Source: ERP* (1992), Tables B-2, B-3, B-37.

smoothly, and there have been periods in which actual output has been far below potential output. The jagged progression in the figure shows the effect of short-term fluctuations around an upward trend. Sometimes these fluctuations represent only a slowdown in the rate of growth; sometimes output actually falls. The dips in real GDP from 1971 to 1973, from 1980 to 1981, and from 1990 to 1991 represent periods when U.S. economic output actually declined. Strong upward fluctuations are called **booms,** and downward ones are called **recessions.** Severe downturns are referred to as **depressions.** The last depression, called the Great Depression because of its length and depth, began in 1929. The economy did not fully recover from it until World War II. While there is no technical definition of a boom, a recession is said to have occurred when GDP falls for at least two consecutive quarters. (For statistical purposes, the year is divided into quarters. GDP data are reported at the end of each quarter.) An economic slowdown occurs when the rate of growth of the economy slows to the point where unemployment starts increasing. The economy suffers such a slowdown every few years. A notable exception to this rule is the period from 1983 to 1990, the longest upswing in peacetime in U.S. history.

Because the ups and downs seem to occur with such regularity, the economy's fluctuations are sometimes referred to as **business cycles.** Businessmen have a great interest in being able to predict when the cycle will **peak,** that is, when the economy will stop growing as rapidly and start turning down; by the same token, they want to know when the bottom or **trough** of a recession will occur. While economists have used sophisticated statistical models to try to predict output and employment over the next few months or next year or two, they have found it particularly difficult to predict these turning points in the business cycle.

There are some variables that usually (but not always) signal a downturn; a decline in producers' orders for new machines is an indicator of a lack of confidence in the future and the decline in orders may itself contribute to a slowdown in the economy, as fewer machines are built. Variables that anticipate a downturn or an upswing are called **leading indicators.**

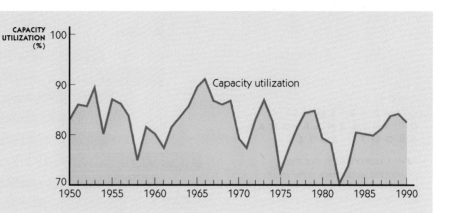

Figure 25.7 CAPACITY UTILIZATION

Capacity utilization measures the fraction of machines and buildings that are actually in use. Notice that the figure fluctuates between about 70 and 90 percent as the economy moves between booms and recessions. *Source: ERP* (1992), Table B-49.

Recessions are marked by the fact that the economy operates well below its potential; there are high levels of unemployment and a large fraction of its machines remain idle. Figure 25.7 shows the percentage of America's industrial capacity that was utilized for the past several decades. The figures vary from slightly more than 70 percent of industrial capacity being used when the economy is in a recession to over 90 percent of industrial capacity being used when the economy is in a boom. Again, notice the pattern. Capacity is never fully utilized—just as there is frictional and structural unemployment, which keeps unemployment rates from ever reaching zero, so too some machines, which are part of the nation's capacity statistics, are being repaired and maintained, while others are not suited for the economy's current structure. But there are fluctuations in how much goes unused. Low-capacity utilization can be thought of as unemployment of machines. Like unemployment of workers, it represents an economic waste, although it lacks the element of human loss. And, of course, the government does not have to make unemployment or welfare payments to an unused machine.

GROWTH IN THE UNITED STATES AND ELSEWHERE

The second important feature of output illustrated in Figure 25.6 is that it has risen over time; it has doubled since 1965 (and quadrupled since 1940). However, different countries grow at different rates, as Figure 25.8 shows. During the past quarter century, Japan's output has been growing much faster than that of the United States. During the fifteen years from 1965 to 1980, the United States was at the bottom of the league in the growth contest among industrialized economies—only the United Kingdom fared worse; but as panel B shows, in more recent years the country has fared better, especially in comparison with Europe. While the United States grew at slightly more than 3 percent per year during the 1980s, Japan grew at 3.7 percent and the Western European countries at rates of between 1.3 and 2.3 percent.

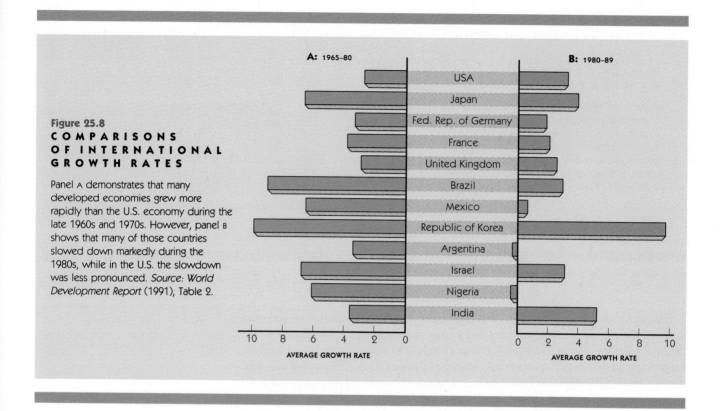

Figure 25.8

COMPARISONS OF INTERNATIONAL GROWTH RATES

Panel A demonstrates that many developed economies grew more rapidly than the U.S. economy during the late 1960s and 1970s. However, panel B shows that many of those countries slowed down markedly during the 1980s, while in the U.S. the slowdown was less pronounced. *Source: World Development Report* (1991), Table 2.

The difference between 3 percent and 3.7 percent may seem small, but these slight differences have large effects over time, just as compound interest rates do. If two countries had the same levels of output in 1900 but one country grew at .7 percent rate faster per year, at the end of the century its output would be twice that of the other. The persistent gap between the rates of growth in the United States and Japan has given rise to alarm and concern. Chapter 37 will discuss some of the causes of the differences in growth rates, some of the reasons for concern, and some of the proposed solutions.

MEASURING GDP: THE VALUE OF OUTPUT

There are three approaches to measuring GDP (whether real or nominal), each of which yields the same result. Two concentrate on output data. The third relies on the fact that the value of output all becomes income to someone, and uses income figures to obtain a measure of output.

THE FINAL GOODS APPROACH

On the face of it, measuring GDP is a straightforward task, albeit massive. One gathers together the dollar values of all goods and services sold in a country, and then adds them up. Unfortunately, matters are not this simple, because it is first necessary to distinguish between final goods and intermediate goods. Final goods, as we learned in Chapter 12, are those that are sold to consumers, like automobiles, books, bread, and shoes. Intermediate goods are those that are used to produce outputs, such as coal when it is used to make steel, or apples when they are used to make applesauce. A good such as an apple can be either a final or an intermediate good, depending on how it is used.

The reason it is so important to distinguish between final and intermediate goods is that the value of final goods includes the value of the intermediate goods that went into making them. When Ford sells a car for $12,000, that figure may include $100 worth of Uniroyal tires, and it would be double counting to list in GDP the revenues of both the car maker and the tire producer. Likewise for the steel, plastic, and other components that go into the car. In fact, cases where some intermediate goods are used to produce other intermediate goods could even lead to triple or quadruple counting.

The **final goods approach** to GDP adds up the total dollar value of goods and services produced, categorized by their ultimate users. One way of calculating the value of the final goods of the economy is to consider where those goods go. There are four possibilities. Some final goods are consumed by individuals—we call this aggregate **consumption** (and we include all consumption goods, regardless of where they are produced). Some are used by firms to build buildings and make machines—this is called aggregate **investment** (again, we include all investment goods, regardless of where they are produced). Some are purchased by government, and are called **government spending.** Finally, some of the goods go abroad; but at the same time, some outputs that we consume or invest or that the government uses are imported from abroad. Thus, the fourth category we refer to as **net exports,** the difference between exports and imports. We can also categorize goods by their "type"—whether they are consumption, investment, or government goods. There are some simple relationships between these two perspectives.

Let's say C = aggregate consumption, C_d = domestic production of consumption goods, M_C = imports of consumption goods, and X_C = exports of consumption goods. Consumption goods are either exported or purchased at home; and total purchases at home of domestically produced consumption goods consist of all purchases of consumption goods *minus* what is imported. Hence,

$$C_d = X_C + C - M_C.$$

Similarly, let I = aggregate investment, I_d = domestic production of investment goods, M_I = imports of investment goods, and X_I = exports of investment goods. Then, as for consumption goods,

$$I_d = X_I + I - M_I.$$

Finally, let G = total government expenditures, G_d = domestic production of "government goods," M_G = imports for government expenditures, and X_G = exports of "government goods." Then

$$G_d = X_G + G - M_G.$$

All of the goods produced in the economy, GDP, can be thought of as either (private) consumption goods, (private) investment goods, or government goods, so

$$GDP = C_d + I_d + G_d.$$

By the same token, aggregate imports, M, and aggregate exports, X, can be broken into the same three categories:

$$X = X_C + X_I + X_G;$$
$$M = M_C + M_I + M_G.$$

Using the expressions for C_d, I_d, and G_d that we have derived, we have the equation

$$GDP = X_C + X_I + X_G + C + I + G - (M_C + M_I + M_G)$$
$$= C + I + G + (X - M),$$

where $(X - M)$ is net exports.

Breaking down final goods this way is particularly useful for analyzing how the macroeconomy works, as we will see in Chapter 26.

THE VALUE-ADDED APPROACH

A second way to calculate the value of GDP is to study the intermediate goods directly. The production of most items occurs in several stages. Consider the automobile. At one stage in its production, iron ore, coal, and limestone are mined. At a second stage, these raw materials are shipped to a steel mill. A third stage finds a steel company combining these ingredients to make steel. Finally, the steel and other inputs, such as rubber and plastics, are combined by the automobile firm to make a car. The difference in value between what the automaker pays for intermediate goods and what it receives for the finished cars is called the firm's **value added.**

Value added = firm's revenues − cost of intermediate goods. GDP can be measured by calculating the value added at each stage of production.

GDP = sum of value added of all firms.

THE INCOME APPROACH

The third method used to calculate GDP involves measuring the income generated by selling products, rather than the value of the products themselves; this is known as the **income approach.** Firms do five things with their revenues: they pay for labor, they pay interest, they buy intermediate goods, they pay indirect taxes such as excise taxes, and what is left over they enjoy as profits.

Revenues = wages + interest payments + cost of intermediate inputs + taxes + profits.

But we already know that the firm's value added is its revenue minus the cost of intermediate goods. Therefore, value added = wages + interest payments + taxes + profits. And since the value of GDP is equal to the sum of the value added of all firms,

GDP must also equal the sum of the value of all wage payments, interest payments, taxes, and profits for all firms:

GDP = wages + interest payments + taxes + profits.

People receive income from wages, from capital, and from profits of the firms they own (or own shares in). Thus, the right-hand side of this identity is just the total income of all individuals plus government revenue from indirect taxes. This is an extremely important result, one economists use frequently, so it is worth highlighting: *aggregate output equals aggregate income*. A final way to measure output, then, is to add up the income of all the individuals in the society, whether received as wages, interest, or profits, and add to that indirect taxes.

Differences Between Individual Incomes and National Income   The notion of income used above to calculate GDP differs slightly from the way individuals commonly perceive income, and it is important to be aware of some of the distinctions.

First, people are likely to include in their view of income any capital gains they earn. Capital gains are the increase in value of assets, and accordingly do not represent production (output) in any way. The national income accounts used to calculate GDP, which are designed to focus on the production of goods and services, do not include capital gains.

Second, profits that are retained by a firm are included in national income, but individuals may not perceive these retained profits as part of their own income. Again, this is because the GDP accounts measure the value of production, and profits are part of the value of production, whether those profits are actually distributed to shareholders or retained by firms.

Third, and most conspicuous, people tend to concentrate on their **disposable income,** or what they have available to spend. To calculate disposable income, people subtract from their income the taxes they have to pay. Part of the value of production that GDP measures is the taxes collected at all stages. For instance, part of the value added of a firm is the total costs of its workers. But not all of what the firm spends for workers is actually received by the workers; the government takes part in the form of taxes. Thus, GDP exceeds the total disposable income of households by the value of taxes paid.

COMPARISON OF THE FINAL GOODS AND INCOME APPROACHES

Earlier we learned how to break down the output of the economy into four categories—consumption, investment, government expenditures, and net exports. Similarly, we typically break down the income of the economy into three categories—wages and other payments to workers; profits, interest, rents, and other payments to owners of capital; and taxes. As Table 25.1 shows, the value of GDP, calculated in both ways, is the same: in 1990, U.S. GDP was approximately $5,514 billion.

The fact that the value of output is equal to the value of income—that GDP measured either way is identical—is no accident. It is a consequence of what Chapter 14 described as the circular flow of the economy. What each firm receives from selling its goods must go back somewhere else into the economy—as wages, profits, interest, or taxes.

Table 25.1 **TWO APPROACHES TO U.S. GDP, 1990**

Final goods	Billions $	Income	Billions $
Consumption	3,742.7	Employee compensation	3,290.3
Investment	802.6	Profits, rents, interest, etc.	1,784.3
Government expenditures	1,042.9	Indirect taxes	439.2
Net exports	− 74.4	Total	5,513.8
Total	5,513.8		

The income to households flows back in turn to firms, either in the form of the consumption goods households purchase or in the form of savings, which eventually are used to purchase plant and equipment by firms; or it flows to the government, in the form of taxes or newly issued government bonds. Similarly, the money spent by the government must have come from somewhere—either from households or corporations in the form of taxes, or through borrowing.

THE THREE APPROACHES TO GDP: AN EXAMPLE

Each of the three approaches to measuring GDP has its uses. When studying how much income individuals and households receive from wages and profits, the income approach is natural. When studying the changing composition of national output, the final goods approach is used. Sometimes it is easier to obtain the numbers used in one approach than those used in another. For example, a large fraction of the value added is produced in large corporations, from whom reliable numbers can be obtained, while final goods are sold by a myriad of small retail establishments whose actual proceeds are much more difficult to track. One advantage of having three different approaches, in fact, is that they provide a check on one another. There will always be small statistical discrepancies, but if the work is done right, all three approaches should produce very close to the same number.

A numerical example will help to illustrate the basic principles. Consider an economy that produces only automobiles, and the automobiles are made entirely from steel. Automakers buy steel from steel companies and transform this steel into cars. They then sell the cars to retailers, who sell them to consumers. The steel industry has revenues of $100 billion, $80 billion of which it pays to its workers and $15 billion of which it pays in interest to creditors. The rest it pays out as dividends to its shareholders. The steel industry's accounts are given in Table 25.2.

The automobile industry pays the steel industry $100 billion for steel, pays its workers $60 billion, and sells its automobiles to the car dealers for $200 billion. It pays out $20 billion in interest. The difference—$200 billion minus the costs of $160 billion minus the $20 billion in interest—is the profits, which it pays out to shareholders. The automobile industry's accounts are also given in the table.

Table 25.2 INCOME AND EXPENDITURE ACCOUNTS (billions)

Steel industry			Automobile industry			Automobile retail industry		
Expenditures		Receipts	Expenditures		Receipts	Expenditures		Receipts
Wages	$80	$100	Wages	$ 60	$200	Purchases of cars	$200	$220
Dividends	$ 5		Purchases of steel	$100		Wages	$ 10	
Interest	$15		Dividends	$ 20		Dividends	$ 10	
			Interest	$ 20				

Finally, the car dealers sell the cars for $220 billion. For the sake of simplicity, we will assume that their only other costs are the wages they pay their workers, $10 billion.

Now let's use these accounts to calculate GDP. Using the final goods approach, we look only at the receipts of the automobile retailers and find that GDP is equal to $220 billion. (We do not also add the revenues of the steel or automobile industry because that would be double counting.) With the value-added approach, GDP is equal to the value of the sales of each industry, minus the value of inputs purchased from other industries. The value added of the three industries is given in Table 25.3.

Last, with the income approach, GDP is measured by the income received by households. Table 25.4 shows the different steps. First we add up all the wages received. Next we add the interest payments. Then we add the profits, which are paid out as dividends. GDP according to the income approach is $220 billion, the same total we reached using the first two approaches.

Table 25.3 APPLYING THE VALUE-ADDED APPROACH TO GDP

	Value of output		Less cost of intermediate goods		Value added
Steel	$100 billion	−	0	=	$100 billion
Automobile	$200 billion	−	$100 billion	=	$100 billion
Car retailers	$220 billion	−	$200 billion	=	$ 20 billion
			Total value added:		$220 billion

Table 25.4 APPLYING THE INCOME APPROACH TO GDP

Wages	
Steel	$ 80 billion
Automobile	$ 60 billion
Car retailers	$ 10 billion
Total wages:	$150 billion

Interest payments	
Steel	$ 15 billion
Automobile	$ 20 billion
Total interest paid:	$ 35 billion

Dividends	
Steel	$ 5 billion
Automobile	$ 20 billion
Car retailers	$ 10 billion
Total dividends:	$ 35 billion

GDP	
Total wages	$150 billion
Total interest	$ 35 billion
Total dividends	$ 35 billion
Total GDP:	$220 billion

ALTERNATIVE MEASURES OF OUTPUT

The U.S. government has used GDP as its main statistical measure of output since 1991; before then, **gross national product (GNP)** was used. Gross national product is a measure of the incomes of residents of a country, including income they receive from abroad (wages, returns on investment, interest payments), but subtracting similar payments made to those abroad. By contrast, GDP ignores income received from or paid overseas. It is thus a measure of the goods and services actually produced *within* the country. GDP was the standard measure of output used by most European countries, in which trade had traditionally been far more important than in the United States. As international trade became more important for the United States, it was natural for the country to switch. Besides, the switch made comparisons with the performance of other countries easier.

The treatment of machines and other capital goods (buildings) is a vexing problem in measuring national output. As machines are used to produce output, they wear out. Worn-out machines are a cost of production that should be balanced against total output.

As an example, consider a firm that has a machine worth $1,000 and that uses the machine, with $600 of labor, to produce $2,000 worth of output. Furthermore, assume that at the end of the year the machine is completely worn out. The firm then has a *net* output of $400: $2,000 minus the labor costs *and* minus the value of the machine, which has been worn out.

The reduction in the value of the machine is called the machine's **depreciation.** But machines wear out at all sorts of different rates, and accounting for how much the machines in the economy have depreciated is an extremely difficult problem. The GDP figures take the easy road, and make no allowance for depreciation. But in fact, the term "gross" in "gross domestic product" should serve as a reminder that the statistic covers all production. Economists sometimes use a separate measure that includes the effects of depreciation, called **net domestic product (NDP),** which subtracts an estimate of the value of depreciation from GDP:

$$NDP = GDP - \text{depreciation.}$$

But most economists have little confidence in the estimates of depreciation, and usually use the GDP or GNP figure as the measure of the economy's output.

GDP, GNP, and NDP go up and down together. For most purposes, it does not much matter which one you use.

MEASURING THE STANDARD OF LIVING

While the data on GDP or GNP tell something about the overall level of economic activity, ultimately economists are interested in how increases in the economy's output translate into increases in the standards of living of citizens of the nation.

One indicator of the standard of living is **GDP per capita,** which is found by dividing

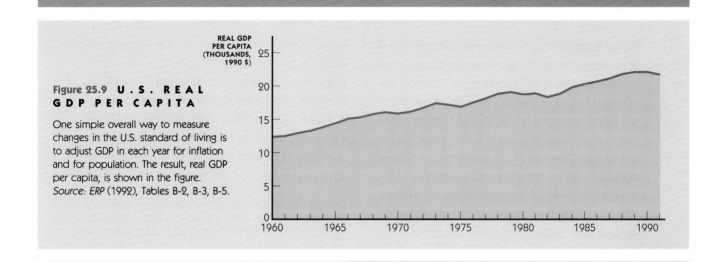

Figure 25.9 U.S. REAL GDP PER CAPITA

One simple overall way to measure changes in the U.S. standard of living is to adjust GDP in each year for inflation and for population. The result, real GDP per capita, is shown in the figure.
Source: ERP (1992), Tables B-2, B-3, B-5.

real GDP by population.[5] Figure 25.9 shows the growth in GDP per capita in the United States from 1960 to 1991. Over the past quarter century, the U.S. economy has gone from producing roughly $11,000 for every man, woman, and child to producing $22,000 (measured in 1990 dollars). Figure 25.10 shows that while per capita income

[5] Since we are concerned here with standards of living, GNP, which measures incomes of a country's residents, is a more appropriate measure than GDP. But for the United States the difference is small. Since we will be comparing per capita income across countries for which only comparable GDP per capita statistics are available, GDP per capita for the United States is given here.

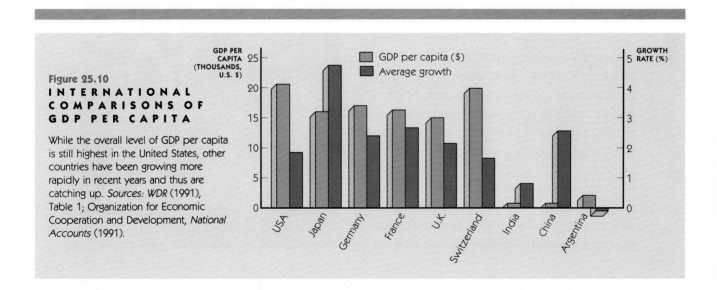

Figure 25.10 INTERNATIONAL COMPARISONS OF GDP PER CAPITA

While the overall level of GDP per capita is still highest in the United States, other countries have been growing more rapidly in recent years and thus are catching up. *Sources: WDR* (1991), Table 1; Organization for Economic Cooperation and Development, *National Accounts* (1991).

CLOSE-UP: HUMAN DEVELOPMENT AND GDP

Nobel laureate Robert Solow once wrote: "If you have to be obsessed by something, maximizing real national income is not a bad choice." Indeed, it is common among economists to rank the nations of the world according to the absolute or per capita size of their economies. But as Solow would be the first to admit, the size of the economy taken alone does not capture many important elements of the standard of living of the population. As a result, different groups have proposed alternatives to GDP or GDP per capita that make adjustments for changes to the environment, access to medical care, literacy, life expectancy, and so on.

The United Nations Development Program offers one example of an alternate index, called the Human Development Index (HDI), which includes in its measurement life expectancy, literacy, and the purchasing power of an average income. The United States is the richest country in the world measured by GDP per capita. But on the HDI, it falls behind seventeen other countries, including Germany, Japan, Australia, and Ireland, which tend to exceed the United States in life expectancy and literacy.

At the other end of the scale, Ethiopia and Kampuchea (Cambodia) are the two poorest countries in the world measured by GDP per capita. But measured by the HDI, Ethiopia is the nineteenth poorest and Kampuchea is the fortieth poorest. The two poorest countries in the world ranked by the HDI are Niger and Mali, where life expectancy is only forty-five years and the literacy rate is less than 20 percent.

But no alternate method of measuring national well-being seems likely to replace calculations based on GDP. The main difficulty of measurements like those of the U.N. Development Program is the difficulty of placing weights on the different elements. Is literacy just as important as life expectancy? only 90 percent as important? How should the value of an extra $1,000 of purchasing power compare with the value of life expectancy increasing by, say, two years? In the face of imponderable questions like these, calculations of GDP look relatively value-free and straightforward.

Sources: "Development Brief: The Human Condition," *The Economist,* May 26, 1990, pp. 80–81; Robert M. Solow, "James Meade at Eighty," *Economic Journal* (December 1986), pp. 986–88.

in the United States has not increased as rapidly as it has in Japan and other countries, still the U.S. *level* remains higher.

There are, to be sure, a number of difficulties in making international comparisons, partly resulting from the fact that people in different countries consume different goods. One should not make too much out of small differences, but large differences usually mean something.[6] GDP per capita in Sweden in 1990 was measured as roughly 3 percent lower than that of the United States. These figures are sufficiently close that it would be difficult to tell whether the standard of living in Sweden is really higher or lower than in the United States. But when GDP per capita is measured as $340 in India and $19,840 in the United States, it is fair to infer a big difference in the standard of living. The output of the state of California, for example, with a population of about 30 million, is $600 billion. It exceeds by more than twice the gross national product of India ($250 billion), which has over 800 million people. Output in California is also about 50 percent larger than the gross national product shared by over 1.1 billion citizens of China, which is $400 billion. These figures reflect large differences in standards of living.

There are marked differences not only in the levels of GDP per capita, but also in the rates of change. From 1965 to 1990, GDP per capita grew at 1.6 percent per year in the United States, 4.3 percent per year in Japan, but not at all in Argentina. Before World War II, Great Britain was one of the great powers of the world, while Japan's per capita income was below that of any of the major European countries. By 1990, Japan had a per capita income that was two-thirds higher than that of Great Britain. If per capita income continues to grow faster in Japan than in the United States, eventually Japan's living standards will become the highest in the world. In Niger, Zaire, and Ghana, GDP per capita actually fell from 1965 to 1990.

There are other measures of the standard of living, such as how long individuals live, or the number of infants who die. These different measures are correlated—that is, in general, in countries with higher GDP per capita, people live longer and infant mortality (the number of babies who die per 100,000 live births) is lower. But looking at Figure 25.11, we see that the United States does not fare as well on these other measures as might be expected, given the country's high per capita income. Life expectancy is not much different from that of several other countries, some of which, such as Ireland and Greece, have substantially lower per capita incomes; and infant mortality is significantly higher than in Japan, Sweden, and Ireland. In some ways, this is surprising, considering that Americans spend a much larger fraction of their GDP on health. It is perhaps explained by the fact, observed in Chapter 24, that inequality is greater in the United States than in many other developed countries.

---

[6] A particularly vexing problem is caused by changes in exchange rates, the rate at which the currencies used in different countries are exchanged for one another. In recent years, exchange rates have changed considerably. When the value of the dollar is low relative to that of the Swedish kronor—that is, $1 can be exchanged for, say, 5 kronor rather than 6—then if we translate per capita income in Sweden into dollars, Swedish per capita income looks very high. But the exchange rate may not accurately reflect purchasing power—what you can buy with the currency in each country. Even though the exchange rate between the dollar and the kronor is 5 kronor to the dollar, you can buy more in the United States with a dollar than you can buy in Sweden with 5 kronor. Making adjustments for differences in purchasing power makes the United States look better off.

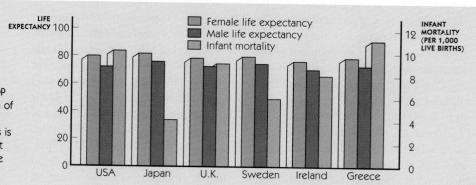

Figure 25.11 ALTER-NATE MEASURES OF STANDARD OF LIVING

A nation's standard of living can be measured in ways other than real GDP per capita. The health and education of its citizens, for example, are such measures. Although the United States is first in the world in GDP per capita, it does not do as well in many of these other measures. *Source: WDR* (1991), Tables 28, 32.

MEASURING PRODUCTIVITY

Increases in the average standard of living are brought about by increases in the average productivity of workers.[7] Economists calculate **productivity,** or **GDP per hour worked,** by dividing real GDP by an estimate of the number of hours worked in the economy. Increases in productivity will be reflected in either higher GDP per capita or more leisure, or both.

Figure 25.12 plots productivity growth in the United States for recent years. Two facts emerge. First, there are fluctuations. Output per hour climbs in boom times and grows more slowly, or sometimes even declines, in recessions. Second, there has been a slowdown in the growth of productivity during recent years. In the 1960s, for example,

[7] Since we are concerned here with output per worker, GDP per worker is a better measure than GNP. Again, the difference (for the United States) is small.

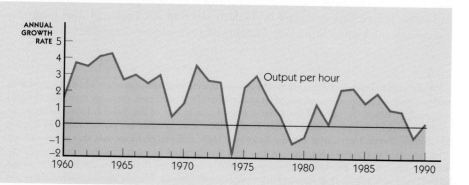

Figure 25.12 U.S. RATES OF PRODUCTIVITY GROWTH

Productivity growth fluctuates, rising in booms and declining in recessions. GDP per hour worked slowed down in the 1970s. *Source: ERP* (1992), Table B-44.

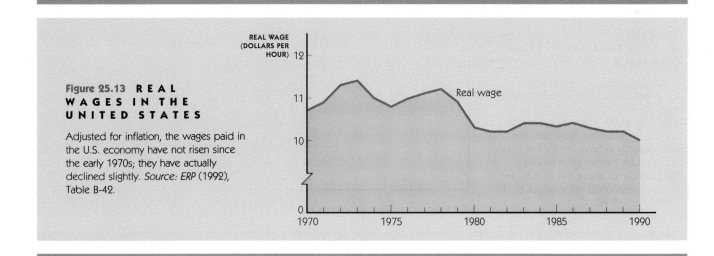

Figure 25.13 REAL WAGES IN THE UNITED STATES

Adjusted for inflation, the wages paid in the U.S. economy have not risen since the early 1970s; they have actually declined slightly. *Source: ERP (1992), Table B-42.*

productivity increased by 2.9 percent per year. In the 1970s and 1980s, it rose by only 1.4 percent per year.

One of the consequences of the slowdown of productivity increases is that wage rates have failed to grow. This is illustrated in Figure 25.13, which shows that real wages (wages taking into account inflation) were actually lower in 1990 than they were twenty years earlier.

These statistics on productivity and real wages, perhaps more than any others, have given rise to concern about the long-run prospects for the country; they have obvious implications for the future living standards of Americans.

RELATIONSHIP BETWEEN PRODUCTIVITY AND STANDARDS OF LIVING

There has been a significant slowdown in productivity—in output per hour—and real wages have actually declined during the past two decades. At the same time, as Figure 25.14 shows, real family income has increased slightly since the 1970s, though it took a big dip between 1978 and 1982, when the country entered a major recession.[8] How do we account for the discrepancy between these two statistics?

The answer has largely to do with the increased fraction of women who are working. To put it another way, while pay per hour has declined slightly, when we add up the working time of the husband and wife, the average *family* now works more hours. This is but one example of several that demonstrates that GDP per capita may not adequately reflect either changes in standards of living over time or differences in standards of living across countries. If incomes go up simply because people work more, does this really represent an improvement in standards of living?

---

[8] The data in the figure represent *median* family income; that is, half the families in the country had incomes higher than the amount shown for any particular year, and half the families in the country had lower incomes.

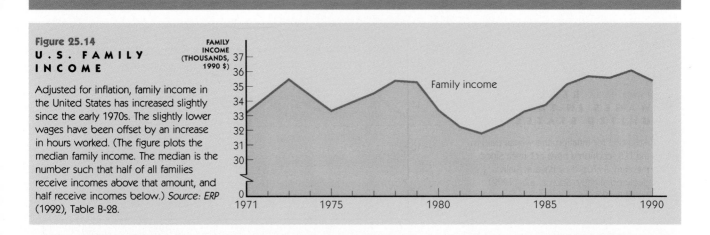

Figure 25.14
U.S. FAMILY INCOME

Adjusted for inflation, family income in the United States has increased slightly since the early 1970s. The slightly lower wages have been offset by an increase in hours worked. (The figure plots the median family income. The median is the number such that half of all families receive incomes above that amount, and half receive incomes below.) *Source: ERP* (1992), Table B-28.

Most of the changes in our environment—which can have enormous effects on standards of living, including life spans—are not reflected well in GDP statistics. For instance, if the government requires steel producers to install devices that reduce their smoke emissions, and the steel producers pass on the price increases to customers, it will appear as if the steel industry has become less productive; more resources are required to produce a ton of steel. The benefits—the improvement in the quality of air—do not show up anywhere in the statistics.

CONNECTING THE VARIABLES

Often the three major macroeconomic variables move together. For example, when the economy is in a recession, as it was in 1982, unemployment tends to be higher and inflation tends to be lower. These connections should make some sense; after all, when the economy is suffering tough times, businesses reduce their output, lay off workers, and do not hire new workers. In addition, businesses that are having a hard time selling products in a competitive market are less likely to raise prices.

FLOWS AND STOCKS

GDP, GNP, and NDP are all measures of output *per year*. Rate measurements such as these are called **flows**. When a news report says, "The quarterly GDP statistic, just released, shows that GDP was $4 trillion per year," it does not mean that $4 trillion of goods and services was produced during the quarter; rather, it means that $1 trillion was produced during the quarter, so that if that rate of production were maintained for a whole year, the total value of goods and services would be $4 trillion.

Flow statistics need to be contrasted with **stock** statistics, which measure some item at a single point in time. Among the most important stocks is the capital stock, the total

Gross domestic product is an approximation, a way of adding up the millions of goods and services in an economy into a single number. But creating that single number requires making some difficult decisions. Here are some of the problems:

Measuring Quality Changes   A tomato today is very similar to a tomato fifty years ago, but an airplane trip or an automobile today is very different than either was even twenty years ago. With some products, the quality (and the price) changes almost every year.

Consider the problem posed by the rapid improvement in computers. If those calculating GDP simply use market prices, they might get the idea that the output of computers is rising only slowly or perhaps even declining, since the price has fallen so rapidly. But one would not want simply to compare the *number* of computers, for that would not allow for how much more powerful the new computers are than the old. A measure of the *real* output of the computer industry must take into account the improvement in quality. If insufficient adjustment is made, it will appear as if output is growing more slowly than it really is.

Or consider the problem posed by the improvement in the quality of medical care. Given the new medical technologies that are available today, how can economists compare the output of the medical care industry today with that of several decades ago?

GDP statisticians are aware of these problems and try to make some adjustments for changes in quality. For example, when antipollution devices were first required in automobiles in the early 1970s, the price of cars rose. Statisticians had to decide whether the increased cost should be counted as a simple price rise and thus a contributor to inflation, or whether it was a quality improvement and effectively adding to real output, since consumers were buying a "better" car. They decided on the second approach. Users of the statistics need to bear in mind, however, that all such adjustments are necessarily imperfect.

Measuring Government Services The standard GDP calculation measures price and quantity at the point of sale. But what about goods that are not sold, at least not directly?

One important category of such goods is government-produced services. Imagine that state government bureaucrats become more efficient and are able to process automobile registrations faster. This might mean that the state can hire fewer workers to do the same job. But the price of registrations is not determined in a competitive market. Taxpayers pay taxes for the salaries of these government workers. And the GDP statistics simply reflect the number of hours worked by government officials. If the government becomes more efficient, measured GDP might go down, even though actual output—the number of registrations—increases.

Measuring Nonmarketed Goods Nonmarketed goods and services, like housework done by family members, present similar problems for the national income statistician. The statistics underestimate the true level of production in the economy, because they ignore such economic activity. For example, if one spouse stays at home and cleans and cooks, that would not be measured in GDP. However, if that spouse leaves home to take a job and hires someone else to do the cleaning and cooking, then both the spouse and the housekeeper would be measured in the GDP.

Importance of Statistical Problems Some economists say that even if GDP is measured imperfectly—which it certainly is—at least these imperfections are roughly the same over time, so economists can still use the figures (with only a bit of hesitation) as a representation of the size of the economy. Over the short run of a few years, this argument holds up fairly well.

But as the structure of the economy changes over time, these biases in the measurement of GDP also change, and hence the measures of growth in output and productivity may be greatly distorted. For example, as more and more women have taken paid jobs outside the home in the past few decades, and in turn have hired more housekeepers and purchased more meals at restaurants, it may be that the previous *under*estimate of GDP is being reduced, and thus some of the growth in GDP is apparent rather than real. Alternatively, if the government sector grows relative to the rest of the economy, and if the way that GDP is measured systematically ignores productivity growth in the public sector, then it may *appear* as if there has been a slowdown in productivity growth in the economy when there has not been.

value of all the buildings and machines that underlie the productive potential of the economy.

There are simple relationships between stocks and flows. The stock of capital at the end of 1991 consists of the stock of capital at the end of 1990 plus or minus the flows into or out of this stock. Investment is just the flow into the capital stock, and depreciation is the measure of the flow out of the capital stock.

Similarly, we can look at the *number* of unemployed individuals as a stock. This number at the end of 1991 consists of the number at the end of 1990 plus or minus the flows into or out of the unemployment pool. New hires represent flows out of the unemployment pool; layoffs, firings, and resignations represent flows into the unemployment pool.

MACROECONOMIC POLICY AND INCOME DISTRIBUTION

This chapter has focused on the macroeconomic objectives of the government—full employment, stable prices, and rapid growth—and discussed how performance in each area is measured. But these macroeconomic goals have to be kept in perspective with other goals and objectives of government, such as the distribution of income and reducing poverty. To a large extent, the successful pursuit of the macroeconomic goals will have important side effects in reducing poverty. When there are more jobs, there are fewer people in poverty. When the economy grows rapidly, there are more goods to go around; the size of the pie is larger, and normally even the poorest segments in society get a larger piece.

But sometimes conflicts do arise. In 1991, with the economic slowdown having lasted more than a year, many people found themselves without unemployment benefits, which normally expire after twenty-six weeks. President Bush and Congress battled over a measure to extend the benefits. The president argued that the higher expenditures would increase the government's deficit and perhaps fuel inflation. Eventually, the legislation was signed into law. To stimulate growth, President Bush advocated a cut in the capital gains tax (the tax imposed on the income a person receives when she sells, say, some shares of stock at a price higher than what she paid), the *direct* benefits of which would be received mainly by upper-income individuals. While tax cuts to the poor might serve as well to stimulate the economy and reduce unemployment, he argued that they would not have the long-term growth benefits of a capital gains tax cut.

Thus, while in this part of the book we focused on aggregates—on output, employment, and inflation—behind those aggregate statistics are individuals, and how different individuals are affected by different government actions is a central concern of macroeconomic policy.

REVIEW AND PRACTICE

SUMMARY

1. The three central macroeconomic policy objectives of the government are low unemployment, low inflation, and high growth. Macroeconomics studies how these aggregate variables change as a result of household and business behavior, and how government policy may affect them.

2. Unemployment imposes costs both on individuals and on society as a whole, which loses what the unemployed workers could have contributed and ends up supporting them in other ways.

3. Seasonal unemployment, such as construction in the winter months of northern parts of the country, occurs regularly depending on the season. Frictional unemployment

results from people being in transition between one job and another. Structural unemployment refers to the unemployment generated as the structure of the economy changes, with the new jobs being created having requirements different from the old jobs being lost. Cyclical unemployment increases or decreases with the level of economic activity.

4. The inflation rate is the percentage increase of the price level from one year to the next. U.S. inflation was low through most of the early part of this century, rose sharply in the 1970s and early 1980s, and then fell somewhat in the later 1980s. In different countries at different times, inflation has sometimes been very high, with prices increasing by factors of tens or hundreds in a given year.

5. The amount of inflation between two years is measured by the percentage change in the amount it would cost to buy a given basket of goods in those years. Different baskets define different price indexes, such as the consumer price index, the producer price index, and the wholesale price index.

6. Gross domestic product (GDP) is the typical way of measuring national output. To derive real GDP, we simply divide nominal GDP by the price index.

7. GDP can be calculated in three ways: the final goods approach, which adds the value of all final goods produced in the economy; the value-added approach, which adds the difference between firms' revenues and costs of intermediate goods; and the income approach, which adds together all income received by those in the economy. All three methods should reach the same answer.

8. One indicator of the standard of living is GDP per capita, which is found by dividing real GDP by population. Productivity, or GDP per hour worked, is found by dividing real GDP by an estimate of the number of hours worked in the economy.

9. Economists seek to understand why many macroeconomic variables seem to move together. For example, in a boom, unemployment tends to fall, inflation tends to rise, productivity tends to rise. In a recession, the reverse happens.

KEY TERMS

unemployment rate
discouraged workers
labor force
   participation rate
inflation rate
price index
consumer price index
deflation
producer price index
wholesale price index

gross domestic product
   (GDP)
real GDP
GDP deflator
potential GDP
boom
recession
gross national product
   (GNP)

depreciation
net domestic product
   (NDP)
GDP per capita
productivity, or GDP
   per hour worked
flow statistics
stock statistics

REVIEW QUESTIONS

1. What are the three main goals of macroeconomic policy?

2. What is the difference between frictional unemployment, seasonal unemployment, and structural unemployment?

3. When there is a reduction in the number of hours worked in the economy, is this normally shared equally by all workers? Are workers in some groups more impacted by increased unemployment than those in other groups?

4. When the prices of different goods change at different rates, how do we measure the rate of inflation?

5. Are all groups of people affected equally by inflation? Why or why not?

6. What is the difference between nominal GDP, real GDP, and potential GDP?

7. What is the difference between the final outputs approach to measuring GDP, the value-added approach, and the income approach?

8. Why is real GDP per capita a better indicator of a country's standard of living than real GDP alone?

9. How is productivity growth related to growth in a nation's standard of living? Will growth in real GDP per hour worked and growth in GDP per capita be identical? Why might a decline in the rate of growth of productivity be of concern?

10. What is the difference between GDP, GNP, and NDP?

PROBLEMS

1. Which would you expect to fall fastest in a recession, real GDP or potential GDP? Could potential GDP rise while real GDP fell?

2. Explain how these two factors would have different effects on real GDP per capita and real GDP per hour worked:
   (a) people working longer weeks;
   (b) a larger proportion of adults holding jobs.

3. Geoffrey spends his allowance on three items: candy, magazines, and renting VCR movies. He is currently receiving an allowance of $30 per month, which he is using to rent 4 movies at $2 apiece, buy 10 candy bars at $1 apiece, and purchase 4 magazines at $3 apiece. Calculate a Geoffrey price index (GPI) for this basket of goods, with the current price level equal to 100, in the following cases.
   (a) The price of movies rises to $3.
   (b) The price of movies rises to $3, and the price of candy bars falls by $.20.
   (c) The price of movies rises to $3, the price of candy bars falls by $.20, and the price of magazines rises to $4.

4. An increase in the consumer price index will often affect different groups in different ways. Think about how different groups will purchase items like housing, travel, or education in the CPI basket, and explain why they will be affected differently by increases in the overall CPI. How would you calculate an "urban CPI" or a "rural CPI"?

5. Given the information below about the U.S. economy, how much did real U.S. GDP grow between 1965 and 1975? between 1975 and 1985?

	1965	1970	1975	1980	1985	1990
Nominal GDP (billions)	$700	$1,000	$1,600	$2,700	$4,000	$5,500
Consumer price index	100	115	160	250	320	415

6. Much of this chapter has discussed how economists often adjust the data to find what they want to know—for example, by adjusting for inflation or dividing by the population level. What adjustments might you suggest for analyzing education expenditures? Social Security expenditures?

26

AN OVERVIEW OF MACROECONOMICS

hapter 25 described the measures we use for the principal aggregate variables that make up the economy. The challenge of macroeconomics is to explain the movement of these aggregate variables.

In many ways, the explanations lie in the microeconomic principles already presented. If we want to know about output, we certainly want to think about the household's consumption decision (Chapter 8) and the firm's production decision (Chapter 13). Growth rates are connected to the household's savings decision (Chapter 9) and the firm's investment decision, discussed in Chapters 12 and 13. Explanations of unemployment necessarily involve the household's labor supply decision, covered in Chapter 11, and the firm's demand for labor, discussed as part of the firm's decisions in Chapters 12 and 13. Inflation is a change in prices, and therefore we want to think about how prices are determined, using the demand and supply analysis presented as far back as Chapter 4.

To a great extent, then, macroeconomics sifts through what we know of microeconomics for its answers. The building blocks are the same, but our perspective will change. The differences between micro- and macroeconomics are striking enough that this chapter is devoted simply to introducing the main analytic issues of the latter. It begins with a brief synopsis of the major schools of macroeconomics. Then it turns to the three major aggregate markets—labor, product, and capital—for an initial look at the issues that will occupy us in the chapters to come.

"This is our first recession together."

Key Questions

1. How do economists analyze what determines levels of aggregate output, employment, and inflation?
2. What causes shifts in the aggregate demand and supply for labor? Why may unemployment result if wages fail to adjust in response to these shifts?
3. What are the typical shapes of the aggregate demand and supply curves in the product market? What are the consequences of shifts in the aggregate demand and supply curves for output and the price level?
4. What is the effect of an increase in investment on the aggregate demand and supply curves?
5. How can we use the aggregate demand and supply curves to interpret some of the major macroeconomic episodes of the past fifty years?

The Roots of Contemporary Macroeconomics

Modern macroeconomics traces its origin to that cataclysmic event the Great Depression, which, in the United States, amounted to almost a decade of massive unemployment and underutilization of resources. The dominant group of economists before the Great Depression, referred to as **classical economists,** recognized that the economy might have short periods of unemployment, but believed that market forces would quickly restore the economy to full employment. They believed that the basic competitive model presented in Parts One and Two by and large provided a good description of the economy: prices and wages were sufficiently flexible that the product and labor markets were in equilibrium (that is, supply equaled demand) most of the time. The policy prescription of the classical economists was summed up by the phrase *laissez faire,* French for "let it be." Government intervention was to be avoided; market forces would do the job of guiding the economy.

The Great Depression: Keynes

The depth and length of the Great Depression shattered confidence in this view. The British economist John Maynard Keynes launched the modern subdiscipline of macroeconomics with his 1936 book *The General Theory of Employment, Interest, and*

Money, in which he explained why the economy could get stuck in a situation where it suffered extended periods of output loss and unemployment. He argued in particular that the labor market might be out of equilibrium for long periods of time—that the supply of labor might exceed the demand, with unemployment as the result. Keynes further maintained that the government should use **fiscal policies,** policies that affect the level of government expenditures and taxes, to bring the economy out of an economic downturn. Keynes was one of the most influential thinkers of the twentieth century, and his work has blossomed into a number of schools of thought that all share the name Keynesian. These schools have in common a belief that the economy may, for a variety of reasons, have unemployed labor and underutilized resources for extended periods of time, and that in these circumstances government action can alleviate the economy's ills.

While World War II brought an economic boom, the aftermath of the war provided an opportunity to test some of Keynes' ideas. Historically, most wars had been followed by economic downturns, as government war expenditures decreased. But by cutting taxes rapidly and stimulating the economy in other ways, the government succeeded in averting a major recession immediately after the war. In the next twenty years, Keynesian theory was applied with greater and greater confidence to help the economy recover from economic downturns. The year 1963 is often cited as the high-water mark of Keynesian economics: President Kennedy, openly espousing Keynesian economics, cut taxes to stimulate the economy; with more money in their pockets, people would spend more, and the increased spending, it was hoped, would refuel the economy. The predictions of Keynesian economics were borne out.

In the 1950s and 1960s, for the most part a period of high employment and stable prices, attention among macroeconomists shifted to economic growth. The basic theories of growth that we will learn in Chapter 37 were first developed then, with Robert Solow of MIT playing a leading role, for which he was later awarded the Nobel Prize.

THE 1970s AND 1980s: MONETARIST, NEW CLASSICAL, AND REAL BUSINESS-CYCLE SCHOOLS

In the 1970s, inflation reached double-digit levels, and the economy was faced with a new experience: high inflation accompanied by high unemployment. Out of this experience developed three new schools of thought, all of which held that government intervention was unnecessary and/or undesirable. All three represented modern adaptations of theories that had been prevalent in the years before Keynes and the Great Depression.

The first school tried to explain the causes of inflation by focusing on the government's **monetary policies.** These are the policies that affect the supply of money and credit and the terms on which credit is available to borrowers. Nobel laureate Milton Friedman, then of the University of Chicago, revised and expanded on earlier theories of money, and the modern **monetarist** school of macroeconomics was born.

Keynes had argued that in deep recessions monetary policy was ineffective, but that fiscal policy would stimulate the economy. The monetarists did not deny that fiscal policy could affect the economy, but they argued that the government was more often the problem than the solution; through mistaken monetary and fiscal policies, the government could be the cause of the economy's downturns. Monetarists believed that markets, if left to themselves, had strong forces that ensured that resources would not long be left idle; they favored sharply restricted limits on fiscal and monetary policy.

While monetarists emphasized the central role of money, they did not have a clearly articulated view of how money affected the economy. Providing such an explanation was a major accomplishment of the **new classical economists,** led by Robert Lucas of the University of Chicago; they were called new classical economists because of the similarity of their views to the old, pre-Keynesian classical economists, who had argued that competitive markets would quickly restore the economy to full employment. In the new classical view, the Great Depression was an aberration. From their 1970s perspective, they pointed out that it had been decades since the economy had experienced a major recession. The new classical economists not only provided a theory of why monetary policy sometimes had major impacts on the economy in the short run, they also explained why the responses of firms and households to government actions—to both fiscal and monetary policies—offset those impacts, with the result that government policy was often ineffective.

By the 1980s, a third school of thought, called the **real business-cycle theory,** had taken the new classical viewpoint even further. Led by Robert King and Charles Plosser of the University of Rochester and Edward Prescott of the University of Minnesota, real business-cycle theorists contended that in fact the economy's fluctuations had nothing to do with monetary policy. Money did not matter at all. The state of the economy was determined only by *real* forces—new inventions, droughts, and so on. It was these real shocks to the economy that gave rise to fluctuations.

To real business-cycle theorists, the fact that monetary policy was ineffective was not a problem; they believed even more strongly than the new classical economists that the economy naturally operates at full employment, without any necessity of government intervention. Changes in public financial policy—for instance, raising revenues by taxing as opposed to borrowing—have no real effect. What matters are *real* actions, but even the impact of real actions may be limited. For example, if the government spends more on defense, resources are diverted from other uses. Since the economy is always operating at full employment, decisions concerning government expenditures do not have an effect on unemployment; they only change the composition of output.

THE 1980s: NEW GROWTH AND NEW KEYNESIAN SCHOOLS

Also in the 1980s, economists turned once again to growth. The reasons were clear. In the 1970s, the standard of living of the average American had risen little if at all. Several industries, including steel and automobiles, that had played a vital role in the U.S. economy in previous decades saw themselves losing in the competition against foreign competitors. Economists sought to understand better the basic forces that led the economy to grow fast at one time and slower at another, or that led some economies to grow faster than others. Paul Romer of the University of California at Berkeley was one of the leaders in the **new growth economics,** which studied these issues, building on the foundations that Solow had established a quarter of a century earlier. The new growth economics incorporated more recent advances in economic theory, such as the ideas of imperfect competition and technological change discussed in Chapters 15–18, and recognized the increased importance of international trade.

As in other areas of economics, a controversy developed over the role of government intervention. Noninterventionists such as Robert Barro of Harvard saw government expenditures as diverting resources away from the economy's natural tendency toward high growth. Others, such as Paul Krugman of MIT, argued that there were several reasons why government intervention might help the economy. For instance, high-technology firms produced benefits that emanated well beyond those doing the innovating; interventionists believed that government should support research and development on the grounds that they had attributes of public goods and would be undersupplied in the absence of such support. Selective and effective government intervention had also played a crucial role in the Asian miracle, the rapid growth experienced by Japan, Korea, Taiwan, and other East Asian economies.

Economic events also turned economists' attention in the 1980s back to unemployment. In the early part of the decade, the American economy experienced the most significant recession since the Great Depression. Some areas of the country seemed economically devastated, with factories shutting down and unemployment rates reaching double digits. Matters were worse elsewhere—in some European countries, as many as one out of five workers could not find a job. And while unemployment decreased slowly in the United States during the remainder of the decade, in several European countries, it persisted. This persistent unemployment again focused economists' attention on disequilibrium, in particular on the possibility that the labor market might have been far out of equilibrium, with wages such that supply greatly exceeded demand. Economists sought explanations for the failure of wages and prices to adjust. Because many of the explanations bore a close affinity to the earlier ideas of Keynes, the new theories were referred to as **new Keynesian.**

The leading schools of macroeconomics today are the new Keynesian and new classical schools. They share one basic premise: unlike their predecessors, both new Keynesian and new classical economists insist on relating macroeconomics to microeconomic principles. Both groups believe an understanding of aggregate behavior must rest on an analysis of firms, households, and government interacting in the labor, product, and capital markets.

A WORD ABOUT MACROECONOMIC MODELS

This and the next two parts of this book take up the various theories that economists have used to understand the macroeconomy and to devise policies that will improve the economy's performance. As was emphasized in Chapter 2, economists use different models for different purposes, and so it is not surprising that the models most suited for studying, say, an economy whose resources are fully employed and that faces a problem of inflation might differ substantially from models appropriate for studying an economy in the depth of a depression, with no inflation and 15 or 20 percent of its labor force unemployed.

Parts One, Two, and Three developed a picture of the economy as consisting of three groups of economic agents—households, firms, and government—interacting in three markets. In the labor market, these groups determine levels of employment and the price of labor (the wage). In the product market, they determine output and the price of goods. In the capital market, they determine the availability of funds and their price (the interest rate).

In the basic competitive model analyzed in Part Two, markets always clear. Since there is never any unemployment, if we want to understand unemployment, we will have to make some important changes in the model. Similarly, in the basic model, any firm can sell as much of any good that it wants at the going market price. It never faces a shortage of demand. And any individual can borrow as much as he wants at the going

From Adam Smith's time until the 1930s, much of economics focused on what would today be called microeconomics. Economics was about trade and exchange, about rational, well-informed consumers and profit-maximizing firms, about monopoly and new technology. Attention was focused on how different markets worked. But that changed in the 1930s, as the global economy suffered the collapse that became known as the Great Depression. In the United States, the economy shrank 30 percent from 1929 to 1933; the unemployment rate hit 25 percent in 1933. Unemployment was still above 17 percent in 1939, before the start of World War II. Attention shifted to what determined aggregate variables like the unemployment rate and GDP.

Today even noneconomists have heard the terms "microeconomics" and "macroeconomics." But economists did not actually begin thinking in those terms until the wrecked economy of the 1930s. In 1933, the famous Norwegian economist Ragnar Frisch clearly had the modern conception of these terms in mind when he wrote: "The micro-dynamic analysis is an analysis by which we try to explain in some detail the behaviour of a certain section of the huge economic mechanism, taking for granted that certain general parameters are given. . . . The macro-dynamic analysis, on the other hand, tries to give an account of the whole economic system taken in its entirety."

John Maynard Keynes also expressed the general idea when he wrote in 1936: "The division of Economics . . . is, I suggest, between the Theory of the Individual Industry or Firm and of the rewards and the distribution of a given quantity of resources on the one hand, and the Theory of Output and Employment *as a whole* on the other hand."

But neither of these eminent economists actually used the words "microeconomic" and "macroeconomic." The first known written use of the specific terms is by P. de Wolff, a little-known economist at the Netherlands Statistical Institute. In a 1941 article, de Wolff wrote: "The micro-economic interpretation refers to the relation . . . for a single person or family. The macro-economic interpretation is derived from the corresponding relation . . . *for a large group of persons or families (social strata, nations, etc.).*"

In the 1960s and 1970s, many economists became concerned that macroeconomic thinking had strayed too far from its microeconomic roots. Interestingly, some of the most important economic work of the last twenty years—which will be described in the following chapters—has sought to break down that wall and explain how rational, well-informed consumers and profit-maximizing firms can combine in a way that sometimes creates unemployment, inflation, or fluctuations in growth.

Source: Hal R. Varian, "Microeconomics," in Eatwell, Milgate, and Newman, eds., *The New Palgrave: A Dictionary of Economics* (1987), 3:461–63.

interest rate. But real economies often do not seem to accord well with these features of the basic competitive model, and to understand why we will need to go beyond the basic model.

Macroeconomists want to know, among other things, why the economy fluctuates as much as it does, why some economies grow faster than others, and what causes inflation. These questions also take us beyond the basic competitive model. Even if we believed all of the model's assumptions, we would need to extend and refine it in order to understand these essential macroeconomic questions.

In our study of macroeconomics, we will employ two simplifications. First, we will not (at least initially) try to understand the three major markets simultaneously. In studying unemployment, it is natural to focus on the labor market and the interaction of the demand and supply for labor; Chapter 27 does this. In studying what makes output fluctuate, it is natural to concentrate on the product market, and Chapters 28–32 do this. In studying inflation, it is natural to focus attention on money, credit, and, more broadly, capital markets. This is the aim of Chapters 33–36. Yet, as we saw in Chapter 14, all three markets are interrelated. The demand for and supply of goods affect the labor market, and in particular the demand for workers. The interest rate affects both the product and labor markets. But the world is too complicated to study all of the pieces simultaneously, and that is why we will study only one market at a time. In Part Six, however, which takes up a variety of policy issues, we will explicitly take into account the interactions among the markets.

As we focus on each of the markets, a second simplification will come into play. In focusing on the labor market, for instance, it is natural to ask how wages are determined. As a simplifying assumption, we take the price level as given. In focusing on the product market, it is natural to ask how prices are determined; there, we take wages as given. Are these models—one allowing wages to fluctuate while prices are fixed and the other doing the reverse—inconsistent? Not really. A more complete model would, of course, look at all markets simultaneously, paying careful attention to how changes in one market affect what is going on in other markets. Such an analysis would take us beyond this elementary course, but the principles derived from our simple model remain valid in these more general models.

We begin our analysis by reviewing the functioning of the labor, product, and capital markets from an aggregate perspective, in order to see how the interaction of demand and supply in these three markets provides insights into the basic macroeconomic issues.

THE LABOR MARKET

The aggregate labor market includes all the workers in the economy. Macroeconomic analysis usually begins by looking at such figures as total employment or total number of hours worked in the economy, ignoring the fact that there are important differences among skills of different workers. If we were interested in studying other questions, such as the relative wages received by different workers, we would want to use a model that treated skilled and unskilled laborers as operating in separate (but related) markets. Sometimes, even in macroeconomics, we may want to use models that focus on this distinction. If unemployment were concentrated among unskilled workers, for instance, the "problem" with the economy might be not with the labor market as a whole, but with one part of it, the market for unskilled labor.

EQUILIBRIUM IN THE LABOR MARKET

For now, we focus our attention on the aggregate market for labor, ignoring the differences among workers. Figure 26.1 shows the demand and supply curves for labor. The aggregate demand for labor depends on the wages firms must pay, the prices firms receive for the

Figure 26.1 THE EFFECTS OF A SHIFT IN THE DEMAND FOR LABOR

Equilibrium in the labor market is at the intersection of the aggregate demand and supply curves for labor. If the wage is above w_1, where demand equals supply, there will be unemployment, putting pressure on wages to fall as workers compete to offer their services. Below w_1, there will be excess demand for labor, which will put pressure on wages to rise.

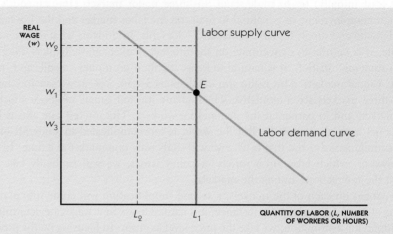

goods they produce, and the prices they have to pay for other inputs, including raw materials and machines. As was just noted, in studying the labor market, we assume for simplicity that the prices of all goods—both the goods that are produced and the other inputs of production—are fixed. With fixed prices, a change in nominal (or dollar) wages is equivalent to a change in *real* wages (wages divided by the price level).

As wages fall, the demand for labor increases for two reasons. First, as wages fall relative to the cost of machines, it pays firms to substitute workers for machines. Second, as the wage falls, labor becomes relatively less expensive compared with the price of the goods it produces, and again employers will want to hire more workers. Thus, the demand curve for labor slopes down, as shown in the diagram.

The figure also shows an aggregate labor supply curve. To simplify matters, we assume that labor supply is inelastic;[1] that is, individuals are either in the labor force, working a full (forty-hour) work week, or they are not. They do not enter and exit the market as wages go up and down, nor do they reduce or increase the hours they work in response to such changes. One advantage of making this assumption is that we can put *either* the number of hours worked or the number of workers hired on the horizontal axis of the figure. The demand and supply of labor hours is simply forty times the demand and supply of workers.

Basic supply and demand analysis implies that market equilibrium should occur at the intersection of the demand and supply curves, point E. The reason for this is simple: if the wage happens to be above the equilibrium wage w_1, say at w_2, the demand for labor will be L_2, much less than the supply, L_1. There will be an excess supply of workers. Those without jobs will offer to work for less than the going wage, bidding

---

[1] Recall the definition of elasticity from Chapter 5: the percentage change in quantity divided by the percentage change in price. Thus, an inelastic labor supply means that a 1 percent increase in price results in a small percentage increase in supply. A perfectly inelastic labor supply curve is vertical; that means the labor supply does not change at all when wages increase.

down the wages of those already working. The process of competition will lead to lower wages, and eventually demand will again equal supply. Likewise, if the wage is lower than w_1, say at w_3, firms in the economy will demand more labor than is supplied. Competing with one another for scarce labor services, they will bid the wage up to w_1.

This is the simple story of the aggregate labor market according to the basic competitive model. Some economists (including the new classical economists) believe that most of the fluctuations in employment can be explained by a slight variant of such a model, where the labor supply curve is upward sloping, and shifts in the demand curve for labor (or the supply curve of labor) will generally result in changes in the equilibrium level of employment. But while this simple story serves to organize the economist's analysis of this market, to most economists, especially Keynesians (both new and old), it has one critical flaw: it does not allow for the kind of persistent unemployment associated with recessions. The next sections describe how economists have expanded on this story to incorporate the fact of unemployment.

ELASTIC LABOR SUPPLY AND VOLUNTARY UNEMPLOYMENT

The preceding analysis assumed that the supply of workers was inelastic, fixed. It is more realistic to think that as wages rise, the number of people who are willing to work increases. This is a particularly likely possibility for married couples, who may decide that at low enough wages it does not pay for both spouses to work. (Indeed, as we saw in Chapter 11, female labor force participation is quite sensitive to the wage.) Figure 26.2 shows that as wages increase, so do the number of individuals who want to work. The labor supply curve is somewhat elastic (rather than perfectly inelastic, as it was in Figure 26.1). The analysis is little changed: equilibrium in the labor market is still at the intersection of the demand and supply curves.

With workers entering and exiting the market, we have **voluntary unemployment.**

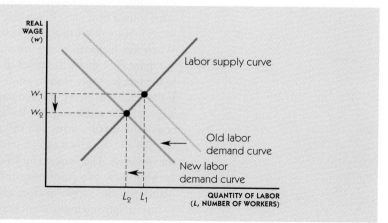

Figure 26.2 THE EFFECTS OF A SHIFT IN THE DEMAND FOR LABOR: ELASTIC LABOR SUPPLY

If the supply curve for labor is relatively elastic, then a leftward shift in the demand curve for labor results in a decrease in employment to L_2 and, if wages are flexible, a decrease in real wages to w_2. But so long as wages are sufficiently flexible that they fall to the point where the demand for labor equals the supply, there is no unemployment. Everyone who wishes to work at the (now lower) going wage can get jobs.

That is, if the wage drops, people will drop out of the labor force; they will not be working—they will be unemployed—by choice. Individuals who *choose* not to work are not included in the unemployment statistics. When economists talk about the "unemployed," they do not mean those who have dropped out of the labor force. To economists, if every worker willing to work at the market wage can find a full-time job, there is full employment.

(This seems simple enough in theory. But in practice, as we saw in Chapter 25, matters are more complicated. There is always some frictional unemployment, as workers move from one job to another. Hence, economists say there is full employment even when there are some workers still looking for a job—the "normal" number of people in the process of making a transition. Economists disagree about what that normal number is and about whether the government can do anything to reduce it significantly. For the remainder of this chapter, we ignore these subtleties and simply assume that full employment means what it says, that everyone who wants a job can get one.)

Consider a shift in the demand curve for labor, depicted in Figure 26.2. As a result of the shift, there is a new equilibrium level of employment in the labor market, L_2. We say that even though employment has fallen from L_1 to L_2, there is still full employment. This is because all labor that is available on the market is purchased. The market clears. *By definition*, when the market clears, there is full employment.

When the labor supply curve is not vertical, as in the figure, there is not a single "full employment" level. At the wage w_1, the economy is fully employed when L_1 workers have jobs; at the wage w_2, the economy is fully employed when the smaller number of workers L_2 have jobs. Though the competitive model assumes that wages will be set so that the demand for labor equals the supply, so there is no unemployment, the level of actual *employment* might be quite low. Wages might be so low that many people are unwilling to accept jobs.

WAGE RIGIDITIES AND INVOLUNTARY UNEMPLOYMENT

Most observers are unwilling to accept the possibility that all unemployment is voluntary. Involuntary unemployment occurs when people willing and able to work at the going wage cannot find jobs. Economic explanations of involuntary unemployment focus on wages that are slow to adjust downward in response to a change in labor market conditions. When this happens, wages are said to be **sticky** downward.

Figure 26.3 shows the effect of sticky wages. The demand curve for labor has shifted to the left; for some reason, employers now demand less labor at every given wage rate. If the wage falls to w_2, the economy will remain fully employed at L_2. However, if the wage is stuck at the original level, w_1, above the wage at which the demand for labor equals the supply, firms will still only hire the amount demanded. More workers will be willing to work than can get jobs at that wage. Those without jobs will be involuntarily unemployed. The demand for labor will only be L_3, while the supply is L_1. The distance between these two points measures the amount of involuntary unemployment. At this high wage, the supply of labor exceeds the demand.

Involuntary unemployment arising from reductions in the demand for labor (combined with wage stickiness) would be much less of a social problem if the impact could be spread over the entire population. Even if the demand for labor were reduced by 10 percent and wages did not fall, the consequences would be limited if each worker worked

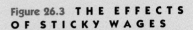
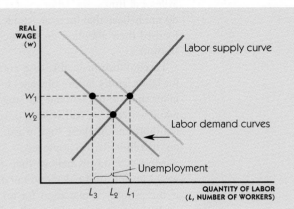

Figure 26.3 THE EFFECTS OF STICKY WAGES

If wages are sticky and do not fall when the demand for labor shifts to the left, unemployment results.

10 percent fewer hours. The problem in that case would be *underemployment:* each person in the economy might work only 36 hours per week, when she wished to work 40 hours.

In the modern industrial economy, the problem is different. Most workers continue to work the same, or only a slightly reduced, number of hours when the labor market goes out of equilibrium, but an unfortunate few will find no full-time job at all at the going wage. This is the problem of unemployment. Whenever the supply of labor exceeds the demand at the going wage, there will be "rationing"—some individuals will not be able to sell all the labor they would like. But the impact of this rationing is not evenly spread in the economy; some workers will manage to sell little if any of their labor services, while others will be fully employed. Many of the social problems associated with a reduced demand for labor result from the fact that the economic burden is so concentrated.

SHIFTS IN THE LABOR DEMAND CURVE, WAGE RIGIDITIES, AND UNEMPLOYMENT

Most economists believe that the labor supply curve, while not perfectly inelastic (or vertical), is relatively inelastic: the supply of labor is relatively unresponsive to wage changes, and the supply curve is *more* like the vertical line in Figure 26.1 than the slanted one in Figure 26.2.

If we look at data on real wages—the wage divided by the price level (the average level of prices of a basket of goods)—we see that wages vary little with economic conditions. Even in the Great Depression, with massive unemployment, they did not fall, or at least did not fall very much. Given the relatively small changes in real wages, the magnitude of the changes in employment that are observed in the economy are greater than can be explained by movements along a fixed, steep labor supply curve. How can we account for such large changes in employment?

There are but two possibilities: either the labor supply curve shifts dramatically or, at least at times, the labor market is not in equilibrium. Because most economists also do not believe that there are sudden dramatic shifts in the labor supply curve, they have focused their attention on the second possibility, that the labor market is not in equilibrium.

Disequilibrium in this case comes about in two steps: a shift in the demand curve for labor, and a failure of wages to adjust. In Figure 26.3, when the demand curve for labor shifts to the left and the wage remains at w_1, firms will employ L_3 units of labor, while workers are still willing to supply L_1. Sticky wages keep the labor market out of equilibrium. At these high wages, the supply of labor exceeds the demand. Workers are involuntarily unemployed.

Most economists believe that a decrease in the demand for labor at each level of wages (a shift in the demand curve for labor) with no corresponding decrease in wages is the primary explanation for an increase in unemployment. This, in turn, focuses attention on two questions: Why do wages not fall? And why would the demand curve for labor shift so suddenly in the first place? Chapter 27 takes up the first question. As for the second, the primary reason for such a shift is a fall in the production of goods by firms, as a result of a decrease in the demand for their products. There is a connection between output levels (as measured, say, by GDP) and the unemployment rate. When output goes up, employment tends to go up as well, and vice versa. Chapters 28–30 will analyze why output might be so variable.

SHIFTS IN THE LABOR SUPPLY CURVE AND UNEMPLOYMENT

The primary explanation for short-run increases in unemployment is that there is a shift in the demand curve for labor. But there is another possible reason: the supply curve for labor could move to the right, as shown in Figure 26.4, so that more people are

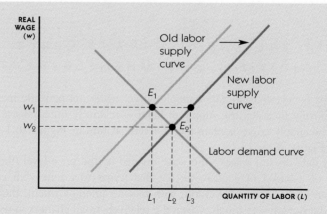

Figure 26.4 A SUPPLY SHIFT IN AGGREGATE LABOR MARKETS

If the aggregate supply of labor shifts out, and wages change, the new equilibrium (E_2) will be at the lower wage w_2 and higher quantity L_2, and no unemployment will exist. If wages do not change, then demand for labor will not change; L_3 will be the new quantity of labor supplied at the original wage w_1, and there will be unemployed people willing to work at the prevailing wage who cannot find jobs.

willing to work at every given wage rate. Though such shifts in the labor supply curve are unlikely to be important in the short run in explaining recessions, over a period of many years they can play and have played an important role. For example, the birthrate in the United States soared in the years after World War II. Some twenty years later, the number of baby boomers was reflected in an outward shift in the labor supply curve. At the same time, the fraction of women working in the labor force increased, also contributing to the rightward shift in the labor supply curve.

A shift in the labor supply curve, unaccompanied by a change in the demand for labor, results in no unemployment if wages adjust enough. In Figure 26.4, if wages fall to w_2, then everyone wanting to work at that wage will be able to do so and employment will rise to L_2. But if real wages fail to fall, the additional labor supply will be unable to find jobs at the going wage w_1, and unemployment of $L_3 - L_1$ will result.

Although the U.S. economy was able to create an enormous number of new jobs in the 1960s and 1970s, more than had been created in any comparable period, the increase in new jobs was not as great as the increased number of job seekers. There were shifts in the labor demand and supply curves like those shown in Figure 26.5; both shifted to the right, but labor supply shifted more than labor demand.[2] If wages had not changed at all but had remained at w_1, unemployment would have been very large. In fact, wages fell, but not enough. There was considerable unemployment, though not as much as there would have been if wages had remained perfectly rigid. Because wages fell and because the demand for labor increased, employment increased. But so did unemployment; employment did not increase as fast as the supply of labor. The figure shows wages falling to w_3, with employment increasing to L_3. But at this wage, the supply of labor is L_4; there is unemployment in the amount $L_4 - L_3$.

[2] When we consider a long-run change, such as here, the assumption of fixed prices is no longer appropriate. With prices freed up, what is relevant for both the demand and supply of labor is the real wage, the wage relative to prices. Thus, it should be understood that this paragraph is referring to real wages.

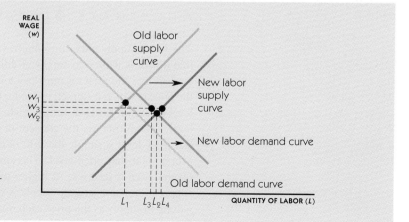

Figure 26.5 DEMAND AND SUPPLY SHIFTS IN THE AGGREGATE LABOR MARKET

Economic growth in the 1970s caused the demand curve for labor to shift out. The entry of new workers into the labor force caused the supply curve for labor to shift out. Since the supply shift was larger than the demand shift, market forces pushed wages down; however, wages fell only from w_1 to w_3, rather than falling all the way to the new equilibrium wage, w_2. The supply of labor L_4 exceeded the demand for labor L_3, and unemployment was the result.

EXPLANATIONS OF UNEMPLOYMENT

Wages failing to adjust downward in response to either of the following events:

(a) A shift in the demand curve for labor

(b) A shift in the supply curve for labor
Even if there were large shifts in the demand and supply curves for labor, no unemployment would result if wages adjusted appropriately.

Basic issues:

(a) What causes shifts in the demand and supply curves for labor?

(b) Why do wages fail to adjust?

(c) Why does disequilibrium take the form of unemployment, rather than a proportionate reduction of hours for all workers?

THE PRODUCT MARKET

Economists begin a macroanalysis of the product market by asking how the output (GDP) of the economy is determined. To answer this question, they use concepts analogous to the familiar demand and supply curves for a particular good. Whereas when we focused on the labor market we assumed that wages were free to change but prices were fixed, here we assume that wages are fixed and prices are free to change.

AGGREGATE SUPPLY

The firm's supply curve introduced in Chapter 4 describes the quantities of a product that a firm is willing to supply at different prices. Given the wage the firm has to pay workers and the prices it must pay for other inputs, it will be willing to supply more as the price at which it can sell its product increases. At higher prices, the profit-maximizing level of output for each firm is higher; it pays to produce more. At the economy-wide level, economists use the concept of an **aggregate supply curve.** Aggregate supply at any price level is simply the sum of the quantities supplied by each of the firms in the economy at that price level. The amount that each firm is willing to supply depends on the price it receives. At higher prices, *keeping wages fixed*, each firm is willing to supply more, so aggregate supply is higher. Tracing out the levels of output firms are willing to supply as the price each one receives increases generates the aggregate supply curve depicted in Figure 26.6. As in the case of any supply curve, rather than asking, what will be the quantity supplied at each price, we can ask, what will be the price that will elicit a particular supply?

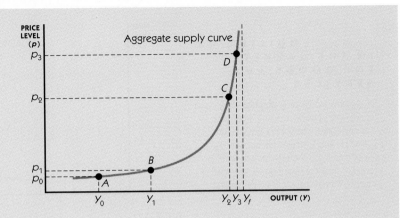

Figure 26.6 THE AGGRE-GATE SUPPLY CURVE

At higher prices, firms are willing to supply more. When output is low (Y_0), there is excess capacity, and a small increase in price elicits a large increase in supply; the supply curve is relatively flat. When output is high (Y_2), the economy is near full capacity, and it takes a large increase in price to elicit a small increase in supply; the supply curve is relatively steep.

The aggregate supply curve masks underlying microeconomic detail. It ignores questions concerning the composition of output. This is deliberate: the objective of macroeconomics is to focus on the important aggregates that describe the economy, such as the level of output and prices. "Output," or quantity, measured along the horizontal axis, is the sum total of the real value of all goods produced in the economy. The best way of thinking about output here is that it is *real* GDP. The vertical axis shows the "Price level." Again, the best way of thinking about this measure is that it represents the average level of prices in the economy, say the GDP deflator, discussed in Chapter 25. If all prices in the economy rise and fall proportionately, then any way of measuring the price level—the consumer price index, the producer price index, the wholesale price index—will give the same result. (In fact, prices of individual goods are constantly changing relative to other goods, and changes in relative prices affect the composition of output. But to focus on aggregate supply, we have to ignore questions concerning the composition of output, and therefore in most of the discussion that follows, we assume that relative prices remain unchanged.)

The aggregate supply curve shown in Figure 26.6 has a typical shape. It is upward sloping, indicating that increases in the price level lead to greater output. Put differently, to elicit increased supply, the price level has to rise. At low levels of output, the aggregate supply curve is relatively flat (or elastic), while at high levels of output, it is relatively steep (or inelastic). The reason for this is as follows. At low levels of output, such as at point A, there is excess capacity in the economy, with underutilized workers and machines. A slight increase in the price level, for instance from p_0 to p_1, would then elicit a very large increase in output, from Y_0 to Y_1.

At very high levels of output, such as at point C, machines and workers are working at close to their capacities, and it is hard to produce much more output. The marginal cost of producing an extra unit may be very large. Accordingly, it takes an enormous increase in the price level, say from p_2 to p_3, to elicit even a small increase in output (from Y_2 to Y_3).

At Y_f, the economy has reached capacity. To produce that level of output with the set of available machines would require everyone in the labor force to be working, and

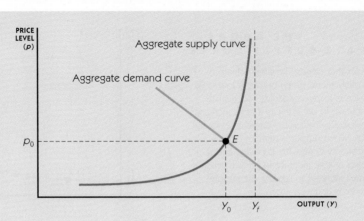

Figure 26.7 EQUILIBRIUM IN THE MARKET FOR GOODS AND SERVICES

A downward-sloping aggregate demand curve and upward-sloping aggregate supply curve intersect at equilibrium price p_0 and equilibrium quantity Y_0. Notice that Y_0, the equilibrium level of output, may be less than Y_f, the level of output that sustains full employment.

expanding output beyond Y_f would require the addition of more labor or more machines. Y_f is sometimes referred to as the economy's **full-employment** or **potential output.** It is the level of output at which all those who wish to work at the going wage are employed.[3] Chapter 31 will provide a more complete analysis of the aggregate supply curve.

AGGREGATE DEMAND

Figure 26.7 combines an aggregate supply curve, like the one shown in Figure 26.6, with an **aggregate demand curve.** The aggregate demand curve relates the total demand for goods by households, firms, government, and foreigners to the price level. Like most microeconomic demand curves, the aggregate demand curve is downward sloping. This curve, like the aggregate supply curve, is drawn under the assumption that wages and relative prices are fixed. Again, the vertical axis shows different price levels; the aggregate demand curve traces out the output that will be demanded at each price level. As prices fall, households can purchase more with the wages they receive; not only can individuals afford more goods, they also feel wealthier. They can purchase more with the money they have. Chapter 31 will also give a more complete derivation of the aggregate demand curve.

AGGREGATE DEMAND AND SUPPLY

Product market equilibrium occurs at the intersection of the aggregate demand and supply curves, point E in Figure 26.7. The argument for why this is the equilibrium should by now be familiar. If the price level is greater than that at which aggregate demand equals aggregate supply, firms are willing to supply more goods than are demanded; there is an excess supply of goods, and this excess supply will cause the overall

---

[3] As a practical matter, things are not so simple, as we saw in Chapter 25. The economy can, at least for short periods of time, have an output greater than Y_f. For instance, during wartime, a country can draw into the labor force people who would not normally be working, or operate machines at full speed without regard to their wear and tear.

price level to fall. The converse argument holds when the price level is below that at which aggregate demand equals aggregate supply.

Much of the discussion in the chapters that follow will be built on information conveyed by the aggregate supply–aggregate demand diagram. It is, therefore, important to understand how the diagram provides us with information about the major macroeconomic issues. First, when there are large rightward movements in output (measured along the horizontal axis) year after year, the economy will have a high growth rate. A single snapshot cannot show us this—it can only show us the level of output. But the level of output is closely connected to another major macroeconomic issue, unemployment, since the demand for labor normally increases as production increases. Finally, just as growth involves changes in output levels year after year, inflation involves a persistent rise in the price level (measured along the vertical axis). Again, the snapshot given in the aggregate demand–aggregate supply diagram cannot trace persistence. Nevertheless, a movement up the vertical axis is evidence of upward pressure on prices that may well lead to inflation. (Chapter 36 will make these connections clear.)

SHIFTS IN AGGREGATE DEMAND

There are various ways of stimulating aggregate demand. We saw in Chapter 25 that what the economy produces could be divided into consumption, investment, government expenditures, and net exports. The government can stimulate aggregate demand by encouraging spending for any one of these components. But we can already see that the outcome of such efforts depends strongly on where the intersection with aggregate supply lies. Along the flat (elastic) portion of the aggregate supply curve, the economy has excess capacity. A shift in demand, say from AD_1 to AD_2 in panel A of Figure 26.8, produces a large increase in output with little effect on the price level. Along the steep (inelastic) portion of the aggregate supply curve, the economy is near capacity. A shift

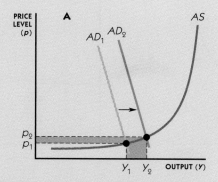 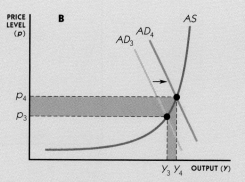

Figure 26.8 DIFFERENT EFFECTS OF SHIFTING AGGREGATE DEMAND

The effect of a shift in aggregate demand on the price level and aggregate output depends on where the initial equilibrium occurs. If the initial equilibrium is along the elastic portion of the aggregate supply curve (as in panel A), a rightward shift in aggregate demand increases output substantially and raises prices by only a little. If the initial equilibrium is along the inelastic portion of the aggregate supply curve (as in panel B), a rightward shift in aggregate demand increases prices substantially but leaves output relatively unchanged.

in demand, say from AD_3 to AD_4 in panel B, produces little change in output but a great increase in the price level. Such repeated upward shifts in the aggregate demand curve, occurring year after year, leading to increases in the price level, help account for the inflationary bouts the economy has experienced.

SHIFTS IN AGGREGATE SUPPLY

Figure 26.9 illustrates a shift in the aggregate supply curve. There are two possible sources of such a shift. Panel A considers the case of an economy-wide increase in investment in plant and equipment, resulting in greater capacity. The aggregate supply will shift to the right, from AS_0 to AS_1. If the economy is operating initially along the steep portion of the aggregate supply curve and aggregate demand is fairly inelastic, as illustrated by the aggregate demand curve AD_1, then the increase in aggregate supply means that the new equilibrium price level may be substantially below the original. On the other hand, if the economy is operating initially along the flat portion of the aggregate supply curve, as illustrated by the aggregate demand curve AD_0, the shift in that curve has little effect. This is because the flat part of the aggregate supply curve represents excess capacity. The new *extra* excess capacity provides little change in either the equilibrium quantity produced or the equilibrium price level.

The other possible source of such a shift is an increase in the price of some input, such as the price of oil purchased from abroad. For firms to be willing to produce the same amount they produced before, they must receive higher prices. The supply curve shifts up, as in panel B. Now the shift in the aggregate supply curve has an effect on the equilibrium price level, even when the economy has excess capacity and is operating along the horizontal portion of the aggregate supply curve.

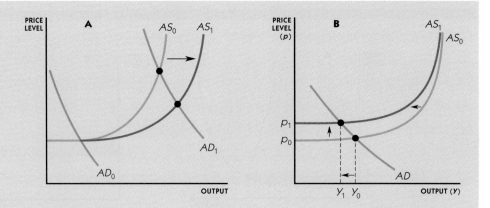

Figure 26.9 A SHIFT IN AGGREGATE SUPPLY

Panel A shows the effect of an increase in capacity. If the economy is operating along the relatively vertical portion of the aggregate supply curve, when the aggregate demand curve is AD_1, equilibrium prices fall and output increases. If the economy is operating along the relatively horizontal portion of the aggregate supply curve, when the aggregate demand curve is AD_0, neither output nor price level is much affected. Panel B shows the effect of an increase in the price of an input purchased from abroad, such as oil. This shifts the aggregate supply curve up, so that the price level increases even if there is excess capacity.

BASIC MACROECONOMIC ISSUES IN THE PRODUCT MARKET

1. What are the shapes of the aggregate demand and supply curves?

2. Where does the intersection of the aggregate demand and supply curves occur—along a horizontal portion of the aggregate supply curve, along a vertical portion, or somewhere in between?

3. What causes shifts in the aggregate demand and aggregate supply curves? Is there anything government can do to shift these curves? Can small disturbances to the economy lead to large shifts in these curves? In particular, when the economy is operating along the horizontal portion of the aggregate supply curve, can shifts in the aggregate demand curve lead to large changes in equilibrium output?

USING AGGREGATE SUPPLY AND DEMAND ANALYSIS

The aggregate demand and aggregate supply framework gives us some insights into a variety of episodes in the history of the U.S. economy.

THE KENNEDY TAX CUT

In 1963, the unemployment rate seemed to be stuck at an unacceptably high level, 5.5 percent. Ten years before, it had been 2.8 percent; by 1959, it was 5.3 percent. President Kennedy's economic advisers, who were of the Keynesian school, believed that a cut in the individual income tax would cause households to consume more. This in turn would lead to a rightward shift in the aggregate demand curve. A shift in the aggregate demand curve, Kennedy's advisers believed, would result in increased output—not higher prices. This is because they believed that the economy had excess capacity, that productive workers and machines were lying idle. In other words, they thought that the aggregate supply curve was relatively flat at the current equilibrium, so that the increase in aggregate demand would be largely translated into increases in output, as shown in Figure 26.10, not increases in the price level.

Increases in output, as we have learned, imply increases in employment. The predictions of Kennedy's advisers turned out to be correct. Unemployment fell to 4.4 percent in 1965 and stayed under 4 percent for the rest of the 1960s. In addition, real GDP grew at the remarkable average rate of 5.5 percent from 1964 to 1966. The success of the Kennedy tax cut is often viewed as one of the great achievements of Keynesian economics.

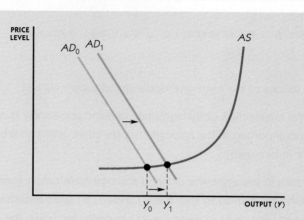

Figure 26.10 THE KENNEDY TAX CUT

The 1963 tax cut shifted the aggregate demand curve to the right and increased output from Y_0 to Y_1, with little rise in prices.

THE JOHNSON INFLATION

In 1965, the economy was operating at close to capacity. In terms of the aggregate demand and supply diagram, the economy was at an equilibrium along a vertical portion of the aggregate supply curve, as shown in Figure 26.11. President Johnson faced a problem: he wanted to fight a war in Vietnam, but he did not want Americans to know how costly such a war might be. As a result, he decided not to raise taxes, at least not enough to pay for the war. In addition, he did not want to cut other government expenditures. On the contrary, he proposed a War on Poverty, with a number of costly

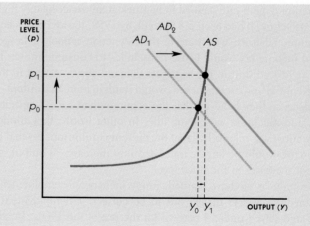

Figure 26.11 THE JOHNSON VIETNAM WAR INFLATION

Following the entry of the United States into the Vietnam War in 1965, inflation increased dramatically. The government stimulated an economy that was already near full employment. The aggregate demand curve shifted to the right, from AD_1 to AD_2. This raised the price level substantially, from p_0 to p_1, without achieving much increase in output.

new social programs. The increase in government expenditures shifted the aggregate demand curve to the right (how it does this will be explored in greater detail in Chapter 28). With this higher level of demand for goods, the old price level jumped up. Inflationary pressures were set off, and the inflation rate, which had been running at between 1 and 2 percent in the early 1960s, climbed to the then staggering rate of almost 6 percent by 1970. Thus began the United States' most serious bout of inflation in half a century.

THE OIL PRICE SHOCK

As spending on the Vietnam War declined in the early 1970s, the U.S. economy was hit by a supply shock. The Organization of Petroleum Exporting Countries (OPEC), consisting mainly of nations in the Middle East, decided in 1973 to use its market power to impose an embargo on the shipment of oil to certain Western nations, including the United States. The original embargo was partially motivated by political concerns, as many OPEC members saw the United States as continually siding with Israel in that country's ongoing dispute with the Arab countries that dominated OPEC. However, they soon realized that they had (at least in the short run) real economic power: the price of oil rose dramatically.

For the U.S. economy as a whole, the higher oil prices raised the costs of production in a large number of industries that had come to rely on oil. The result can be viewed as a shift in the aggregate supply curve, as shown in Figure 26.12. Given the higher cost of oil, the amount that firms were willing to produce at each price level was lowered. The shift in the aggregate supply curve gave rise to inflationary pressures. At the original price level, p_0, the shift meant that there was excess demand for goods. Thus, the inflationary episode that had begun with a rightward shift in the aggregate demand curve as a result of the Johnson inflation was carried forward with an upward shift in the aggregate supply curve as a result of the oil embargo.

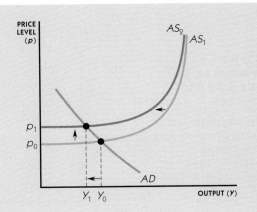

Figure 26.12 THE OIL PRICE SHOCK OF THE EARLY 1970s

In 1973, OPEC raised the price of oil. This shifted the aggregate supply curve up, leading to a higher equilibrium price level, p_1, and lower levels of output.

THE REAGAN PROGRAM

By the time President Reagan took office in 1981, there was a widespread view that something should be done to stop inflation, which was already high and appeared to be moving higher. Our analysis so far would suggest that policies to accomplish this could take one of two forms: they could be designed either to effect a rightward or downward shift in the aggregate supply curve or to cause a leftward shift in the aggregate demand curve.[4]

President Reagan focused on shifting the supply curve. He argued that accelerating the program of deregulation that had begun under President Carter would enable the economy to produce more at the same price level, and that a cut in marginal tax rates would similarly increase the amount people were willing to work at each wage and firms were willing to produce at each price level. The highest tax rates, for instance, were cut in 1981 from 70 percent to 50 percent. Figure 26.13 shows an initial situation with the equilibrium price level p_0. A rightward shift in the aggregate supply curve leads to a lower equilibrium price level. It was Reagan's hope that in practice this would lead to a lower inflation level. Their emphasis on the importance of supply, as opposed to demand, and on shifting the aggregate supply curve as the way to control inflation earned proponents of this view the label "supply-side economists."

The Volcker Victory over Inflation Inflation was brought under control, but the evidence suggests that it was because of a leftward shift in the aggregate demand curve rather than a rightward shift in the aggregate supply curve. We can break down this shift in the aggregate demand curve into two steps. First, Reagan's tax cut stimulated spending throughout the economy, thus shifting the aggregate demand curve to the right. It did this at the same time that it shifted the aggregate supply curve *slightly* to

---

[4] As we learned earlier, inflation is a persistent increase in prices, occurring month after month. The aggregate demand and supply analysis only shows equilibrium prices and output. Still, shifts in the aggregate demand and supply curves that lead to lower equilibrium price levels usually result in reduced inflation; Chapter 36 will explain why this is so.

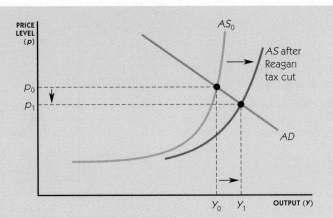

Figure 26.13 SUPPLY-SIDE ECONOMICS UNDER PRESIDENT REAGAN

This figure illustrates how proponents of the Reagan tax cut and other measures such as deregulation intended to encourage production. An outward shift in aggregate supply could result in higher output and a lower price level.

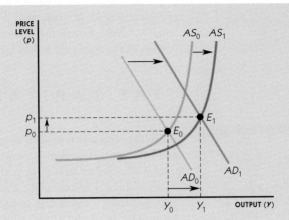

Figure 26.14 1981 TAX CUT

The 1981 tax cut under President Reagan had effects on both the aggregate demand and aggregate supply curves. Both shifted to the right. The shift in aggregate demand was probably larger than the shift in aggregate supply, so that the net effect was to increase excess demand and inflationary pressure. The new equilibrium price level, at E_1, is higher than at E_0.

the right. Since, at least in the year immediately after the tax cut, the aggregate demand effect exceeded the supply effect, the Reagan tax cut actually raised the equilibrium price level, as shown in Figure 26.14.

The second step was taken when the Federal Reserve Board, or Fed (whose responsibility it is to control the monetary system), and particularly its chairman, Paul Volcker, became concerned about these inflationary pressures. The Fed took strong actions to tighten the availability of credit and to raise interest rates—interest rates reached record levels in excess of 20 percent before Volcker deemed inflation defeated. (How the Fed does this and the broader impact of such measures will be the subject of Part Five.) As a result of the Fed's action, firms cut back their investments, and households cut back their purchases of items like cars and houses. This effect far outweighed the effect of

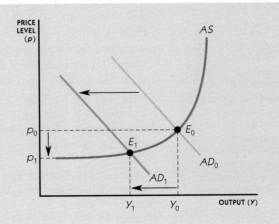

Figure 26.15 MONETARY POLICY CONTROLS INFLATION BUT CAUSES A RECESSION

Beginning in the late 1970s and early 1980s, the Federal Reserve Board acted to restrict credit, and thus consumption and investment, in an attempt to reduce inflation. The resulting leftward shift in aggregate demand reduced the price level but also caused a recession. The effects were so strong that they more than offset the increased inflationary pressures from the 1981 tax cut.

the tax cut. Thus, the aggregate demand curve shifted to the left, as shown in Figure 26.15, and the economy was thrown into a major recession. The national unemployment rate exceeded 11 percent, and climbed as high as 20 percent in certain parts of the country.[5] Note that in the figure, the new equilibrium, E_1, occurs in the horizontal portion of the aggregate supply curve.

THE CAPITAL MARKET

A healthy economy is marked by the full employment of its resources, by price stability, and by sustained economic growth. Unlike the labor or product market, the capital market does not address these goals directly. However, it has a powerful indirect effect on all of them. For example, the availability of credit and the terms on which it is made available have a significant impact on the willingness and ability of firms to invest. Investment in capital goods comprises a major component of the aggregate spending for goods and services, so changes in the capital market affect the aggregate demand curve. We will return to investment spending, and how the capital market influences it, in Chapters 28 and 29. Capital markets are heavily influenced by monetary policy. In Chapters 32–34, we will see how monetary policy operates, in part at least, by affecting the amount of credit banks make available and the terms on which they make loans.

GROWTH

Macroeconomists are interested not only in the short-run performance of the economy—inflation and unemployment—but also in its long-run performance. In the long run, the capital market has an enormous impact. The cumulative effect of investment spending is a long-term rightward shift in the aggregate supply curve: as the productive capacity of the economy is enhanced by new investment, firms are willing to produce more at any given level of wages and prices. As the economy becomes more productive, the production possibilities curve shifts out. A central question with which we will be concerned is, what determines how rapidly it moves out? One important element is the rate of investment.

Panel A of Figure 26.16 shows the production possibilities of the economy, with investment—the output of capital goods—on the vertical axis and consumption on the horizontal. A key objective of short-run macroeconomic policy is to move the economy closer to the production possibilities curve (which represents the full-employment level of output, or the economy's potential output), from a point such as A to a point such as B. Note that in moving from A to B, the economy has increased both its consumption and its investment. Because resources were not being used efficiently, the economy did not face a trade-off.

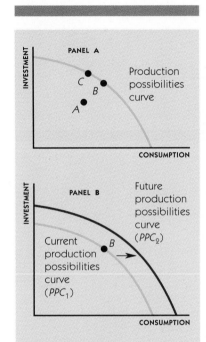

Figure 26.16 CONSUMP-TION, INVESTMENT, AND LONG-RUN GROWTH

Short-run macroeconomic policy aims at assuring that the economy uses all its resources. For example, it tries to stimulate a movement from A (below the production possibilities curve) to B (on the curve) in panel A. Long-run policy focuses on making sure that the production possibilities curve shifts out over time. This may involve a shift from consumption to investment, from B to C. The result will be an outward shift from PPC_1 to PPC_2, as shown in panel B.

---

[5] However, the recession did have the effect of curbing inflation, which fell from over 13 percent in 1980 to just 3.2 percent in 1983. The relationship between unemployment and inflation rates will be discussed in Chapter 36. In the figure, the new equilibrium entails a lower price level than the old. In fact, prices did not fall. But the downward pressure on prices, reflected in the lower equilibrium level, is what brought inflation under control.

CLOSE-UP: TRACING THE RECESSION OF 1990–91 THROUGH THE THREE AGGREGATE MARKETS

Any major macroeconomic event will have ramifications in the aggregate product, labor, and capital markets. The recession of 1990–91 offers a good example.

The Department of Commerce produces quarterly data on GDP. If economic growth is in the range of 2 or 3 percent annually, then quarterly growth should be something in the range of .5 to .8 percent. But from the second quarter of 1990 to the third, while real GDP did rise, it increased by only .06 percent (about one-sixteenth of 1 percent).

Then matters went downhill. From the third to the fourth quarter, real GDP fell by 1 percent. From then to the first quarter of 1991, real GDP fell another .6 percent. And while the economy began growing again in the second quarter of 1991, the increases were small. By the fourth quarter of 1991, real GDP was still smaller than it had been in the first quarter of 1990. The recession was technically over—the shrinkage of the economy had

stopped—but people certainly did not feel a return to robust economic health.

Economists will study and argue over the precise sequence of events leading up to the recession for years, but it seems clear that factors on both the aggregate demand and supply sides contributed. The economy was weak heading into the middle of 1990. The rise in oil prices that followed Iraq's invasion of Kuwait in August 1990 helped turn this weakness into a recession; it shifted aggregate supply for a time. But although oil prices returned to their prewar levels by early in 1991, the recessionary threat they had posed had plunged consumers and businesses into a downward spiral, where low confidence in the future led to reduced spending—a shift in the aggregate demand curve. The reduced spending in turn shrank the economy, confirming the gloomy expectations.

The slowdown in the product market reduced the demand for labor, moving the economy away from full employment. U.S. civilian employment

peaked in May 1990, when 118.4 million Americans held jobs, but then sank to 116.8 million by May 1991. The sluggish recovery in early 1991 prevented the number of jobs from declining still further, but since businesses could not be sure whether the recovery was for real, they were not ready to hire many more workers.

Changes in aggregate capital markets were intimately linked to these changes in the product market. As people grew less confident about their jobs and the economic future, their savings increased sharply. Total personal savings in 1990 were 20 percent higher than the levels in the late 1980s, and remained high into 1991.

However, higher savings rates meant that consumers were not buying. Businesses, seeing their sales falling, hesitated to invest. Banks, concerned about the ability of borrowers to repay, were reluctant to lend. The low levels of consumer spending and business investment contributed to the economy's doldrums. Government policymakers tried to use the capital market to stimulate consumer and investment demand, by attempting to make credit more easily available. But in tough economic times, like late 1990 and 1991, they found it difficult to persuade banks to lend more or to encourage people to buy new homes or businesses to invest in new plant and equipment— at least not enough to restore economic prosperity in short order.

Source: Economic Report of the President (1992), various tables.

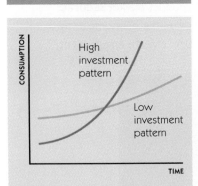

Figure 26.17 INVESTMENT AND GROWTH

If the economy invests a great deal, consumption today will be low, but future output and consumption will be higher.

Once the economy has reached its production possibilities curve, then hard decisions must be faced. Assume we want to move the curve out to PPC_2, as in panel B. One way to do this is to increase the economy's production potential by investing in more new machines and factories. Investment must be increased; the economy must move along the current production possibilities curve shown in panel A from B to C. In doing so, the level of current consumption will be reduced.

Where along the production possibilities curve the economy operates depends on the capital market—on the interaction of the savings decisions of households and the investment decisions of firms (the demand for capital).[6] Decisions have to be made not only about how much to save and invest, but how to allocate these scarce funds. The investment that determines the economy's long-run growth includes, as well as the investments in buildings and machines, investments in human capital and in research and development.

The consequences for consumption, over time, of how much and how well the economy invests are illustrated in Figure 26.17. The figure shows two different possibilities for the economy's consumption over time. In the first, the pink line, there is a high level of consumption today and little investment. In the second, the red line, the economy sacrifices current consumption—more of today's output is invested; that is why initially consumption is lower. But, assuming that the investment dollars are well spent, the economy will grow faster, and eventually the level of consumption will be higher.

[6] See Chapters 9, 29, and 37 for a further analysis of the savings decision; and Chapters 12, 13, 29, and 37 for a further analysis of the investment decision.

MAJOR MACROECONOMIC ISSUES IN THE CAPITAL MARKET

1. What goes on in the capital market can have major effects on the economy in both the short run and the long run.

2. In the short run, the capital market particularly affects the level of investment and consumer purchases of durable goods, and therefore the level of output and employment.

> Issues: Can the government, through monetary policy, affect the level of output? If monetary policy can be used to control the economy, how does the policy exercise its influence? Can monetary policy stimulate the economy in a deep recession as effectively as it can bring about a contraction of the economy?

3. In the long run, to the extent that it affects the level of investment, the capital market can lead to increased growth.

> Issues: How effective is monetary policy in stimulating investment? How important is increased investment in stimulating growth? Does the United States invest or save too little? If so, why? And what can be done about it?

INTERRELATIONS AMONG MARKETS

Chapter 14 made the point that the three major categories of markets are interrelated. We have just seen another example of this, in the way the capital market affects the aggregate demand curve in the short run and the aggregate supply curve in the long run. Then too the demand curve for labor depends on what happens in the product market; and what happens in the labor market—the level of wages and employment—affects the demand for goods in the product market.

In the analysis of later chapters, we will focus on one market at a time. But the big picture, the fact that what happens in one aggregate market affects the other ones, should be kept in mind. Thus, in Chapter 27, we focus on the labor market; but behind the scenes, we know that the demand for labor depends critically on events in the product market. In Chapters 28–31, we focus on the product market, knowing that one of the reasons we are interested in the product market is that when national output is high, so too is employment.

Not only are the interrelations among the labor, capital, and product markets important, but the interrelations between those markets abroad and those markets in the United States are also important. An increase in the price the United States pays for oil shifts the aggregate supply curve and leads to higher prices and lower output. A recession in Europe reduces Europeans' demand for American goods; the resulting shift in the aggregate demand curve leads to lower output in the United States. A fall in prices in the stock market in Japan affects American capital markets, and those effects may reverberate throughout the economy. While we focus on the labor, capital, and product markets within a particular country, again we must keep the bigger picture in mind: the United States is part of a global economy, all the pieces of which are interrelated.

REVIEW AND PRACTICE

SUMMARY

1. Macroeconomics tries to identify the forces that determine the levels of aggregate output, employment, and inflation. It does this by studying what causes changes in the demand and supply curves in the labor, product, and capital markets.

2. To explain unemployment, we need to explain why the aggregate labor market does not clear. If real wages do not adjust to changes in aggregate supply and demand, and either the demand curve for labor shifts to the left or the supply curve for labor shifts to the right, then the quantity of labor supplied will exceed the quantity demanded at the prevailing wage, and unemployment will exist.

3. The demand curve for labor shifts because of a fall in the production of goods by firms, as a result of a decrease in the demand for their products. The supply curve for labor shifts when many workers enter or exit the labor market, as happened when the baby boom generation and women began to enter the labor force in great numbers.

4. In the product market, the aggregate supply curve is relatively flat (elastic) when output is low and a large fraction of the economy's machines are idle. It is relatively steep (inelastic) when output is high and the economy is operating near capacity.

5. If the initial equilibrium is along the elastic portion of the aggregate supply curve, a rightward shift in aggregate demand increases output substantially and raises price by only a little. If the initial equilibrium is along the inelastic portion of the aggregate supply curve, a rightward shift in aggregate demand increases prices substantially but leaves output relatively unchanged.

6. The capital market has powerful indirect effects on the goals of full employment, price stability, and sustained economic growth. Higher levels of investment lead to a shift in the aggregate demand curve and a long-term shift in the aggregate supply curve; as the productive capacity of the economy is enhanced by new investment, firms are willing to produce more at any given level of wages and prices.

KEY TERMS

classical economists

fiscal policies

monetary policies

monetarists

new classical
   economists

real business-cycle
   theorists

new growth
   economists

new Keynesian
   economists

voluntary
   unemployment

sticky wages

aggregate supply
   curve

full-employment or
   potential output

aggregate demand
   curve

REVIEW QUESTIONS

1. What are the three main macroeconomic markets? What is the price called in each market?

2. If the labor market always cleared, would there be any unemployment? What does it mean for the labor market not to clear?

3. If the labor market always cleared, can there be variations in the level of employment?

4. What inferences do you draw from the following two facts?
   (a) The labor supply curve is relatively inelastic.
   (b) Large variations in employment coexist with relatively small variations in real wages.

5. What factors might shift the aggregate demand curve for labor? What factors might shift the aggregate supply curve for labor?

6. Why is the aggregate demand curve downward sloping? Why is the aggregate supply curve upward sloping? What is the characteristic shape of the aggregate supply curve?

7. When will a shift in the aggregate demand curve affect prices little and output a lot? When will the reverse be true?

8. Describe the effects of a shift in the aggregate supply curve.

9. Describe the movement of the economy from a situation where resources are not being fully utilized and unemployment is high to a situation where resources are being fully utilized, in terms of the production possibilities curve. Describe the consequences of an increase in investment when resources are being fully utilized, in terms of a movement along the current production possibilities curve. What does an increase in investment do to next year's production possibilities curve?

10. What is the effect of an increase in investment on the current aggregate demand curve? on the future aggregate supply curve?

PROBLEMS

1. In the 1970s, a large number of new workers entered the U.S. economy from two main sources: the baby boom generation grew to adulthood and the proportion of women

working increased substantially. If wages adjust, what effect will these factors have on the equilibrium level of wages and quantity of labor? If wages do not adjust, how does your answer change? In which case will unemployment exist? Draw a diagram to explain your answer.

2. Soon after Iraq invaded Kuwait in August 1990, many firms feared that a recession would occur. They began cutting back on production and employment. If wages adjust, what effect will this cutback have on the equilibrium level of wages and employment? If wages do not adjust, how does your answer change? In which case will unemployment exist?

3. During the 1980s, government spending and budget deficits rose dramatically in the United States. This had the effect of shifting the aggregate demand curve to the right. What effect will this change have on the equilibrium level of prices and national output? Draw a diagram to illustrate your answer.

4. In the early 1980s, some supply-side economists argued that changes in the tax code would cause people to work hard and entrepreneurs to produce more. If this were to occur, what effect would it have on the equilibrium level of prices and output? Does it make a difference if the economy was initially operating with excess capacity?

5. In the late 1970s, the turmoil in the Mideast that followed the fall of the shah of Iran caused oil prices to rise sharply. What effect would this change alone have on the equilibrium level of prices and national output? Draw a diagram to illustrate your answer.

CHAPTER 27

THE AGGREGATE LABOR MARKET

arge numbers of people collecting unemployment insurance, huge lines at firms that announce they are hiring workers, plants closing down and laying off workers, are all symptoms of an economy in a recession. Though we may regret the loss in output resulting from resources not being fully utilized, and firms will surely miss the loss in profits, the human misery that results from unemployment is far more poignant and underlies the political commitment to limit both the extent and the costs of unemployment in the economy. But if we are to understand how to reduce unemployment, we must first understand its causes.

Since unemployment represents a situation where the supply of labor exceeds the demand, the first place to look when explaining unemployment is at the labor market. We do that in this chapter. The next five chapters take up the product market, which also helps to explain unemployment, because the demand for labor depends in part on the demand and supply for goods.

After an initial look at underlying assumptions, this chapter is divided into four sections. In the first, we address the basic question of whether unemployment is voluntary. This may seem like an odd question, but many economists have suggested that there is at least an element of "voluntariness" in much of unemployment.

Unemployment, as was noted in Chapter 26, is related to the failure of wages to adjust. The second section examines why wages might not adjust quickly to changes either in the demand or supply of labor. The third section argues briefly why unemployment statistics may underestimate the true lack of full utilization of human resources in the economy in periods of recession. The final section considers issues of public policy: if we cannot make wages more flexible, how can we at least reduce the cost of unemployment?

"Since the new flexible working hours began, Seymour, we haven't been able to locate yours."

KEY QUESTIONS

1. What is meant by involuntary unemployment? When does it arise?

2. What are the reasons that wages may not fall even when there is excess supply of labor?

3. What happens to unemployment if a decline in nominal wages is followed by a decrease in prices?

4. What policies might reduce either the extent of unemployment or the costs borne by those who are thrown out of work? What are some of the problems facing the unemployment insurance system?

A WORD ABOUT ASSUMPTIONS

As was noted in Chapter 26, in macroeconomics we are concerned more with the aggregate behavior of the economy than with the parts, though we cannot ignore the parts. Thus, we focus on total employment and unemployment and, for the most part, do not make distinctions between skills and other differences among individuals.

In our systematic analysis of the competitive model in Part Two, we proceeded in three steps. First, we examined each of the decisions of households and firms separately—households' decisions about supplying labor and capital and buying goods and firms' decisions about demanding labor and capital and supplying goods; second, we saw how households and firms interact in the labor, capital, and product markets; finally, we learned that there were important interactions among the markets. In the second stage, in focusing on each market, we kept what was going on in other markets in the background. It was a convenient, almost a necessary device, given the complexity of the possible patterns of interactions. We follow a similar procedure here in our analysis of the aggregate behavior of the economy.

Labor is an input to production—often the most important input—so the demand for labor has much to do with the production decision of the firm. The individual firm will normally demand more labor if the price of its product goes up. Its demand for labor will also depend on the prices of the other inputs used in production. In an economy such as the United States', with millions of firms, each company, in making decisions about how much to pay its workers, believes that those decisions will have no impact on prices in general and therefore on the price level. A manufacturer of pins is unlikely to worry that because it pays its workers more somehow the price it has to pay for the steel used in the pins, or the price it pays for the electricity required to run its pin-making machines, will be altered. In making wage decisions, it makes sense for the company to take those prices as given. Accordingly, in analyzing the firm's labor demand and deriving the aggregate demand for labor, we take the prices facing the firm and the price level facing the economy as given.

This assumption will also allow us to focus on the relationship between wage changes and employment. In this fixed-price situation, changes in wages are equivalent to changes in *real* wages. Real wages, the cost of labor relative to what it produces and relative to the costs of other inputs, are what firms are concerned with in their employment decisions. Workers too focus on real wages—it is not the dollars that compensate them for working hard, but rather the goods they can buy with those dollars.

As we saw in Chapter 25, prices are not perfectly fixed. While the hiring decision of a single firm is unlikely to affect the price level, the hiring decisions (with the accompanying implications for wages) of all firms may eventually affect the price level. In the Great Depression, the price level fell by 10 percent per year. In other periods, prices rise. This complicates, but does not alter in any fundamental way, our short-run analysis. Later in the chapter, we will see how price adjustments may be incorporated into the analysis.

Another simplifying assumption that we will employ for most of this chapter is that each and every person who wishes to work wants a full, 40-hour work week. With this assumption, we can express the demand for or supply of labor either in terms of so many (say, 120 million) workers or in terms of so many (say, 120 million × 40 hours = 4,800 million) work hours. For most of the chapter, our concern is primarily with *unemployment*—with why it is that people who would like to get jobs cannot get them—so it is natural to focus our attention on the demand and supply of workers. Later in the chapter, we will also be concerned with why lower demand for labor results in workers being laid off rather than each employee working shorter work weeks.

Figure 27.1 repeats the demand and supply curves of workers from Chapter 26. There

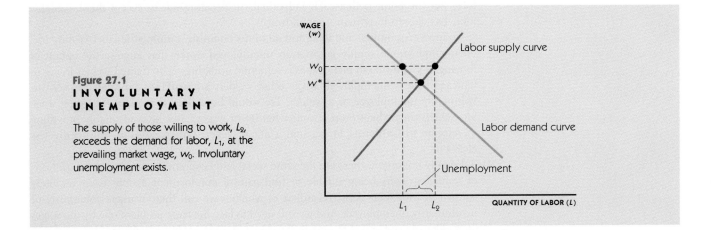

Figure 27.1
INVOLUNTARY UNEMPLOYMENT

The supply of those willing to work, L_2, exceeds the demand for labor, L_1, at the prevailing market wage, w_0. Involuntary unemployment exists.

is an equilibrium wage, w^*, at which the demand and supply are equal. Sometimes, however, it seems that the wage gets stuck, at least for a while, at a level above w^*, such as w_0, so that firms hire fewer workers than want jobs at that wage: there is unemployment. The main issue addressed in this chapter is, why do wages get stuck? First, however, we must ask a more fundamental question.

IS UNEMPLOYMENT VOLUNTARY?

Chapter 25 explained why we do not expect all people to be working all the time: there is seasonal unemployment (gardeners and construction workers in cold climates are likely to be unemployed in the winter) and frictional unemployment (it takes time to move from one job to the next or to get a job when first entering the labor force).

Beyond these two types, there is the unemployment that arises when wages are stuck at a level above that at which the labor market clears. Those who want to work at that higher wage and cannot get employment are said to be involuntarily unemployed. Unemployment is represented in Figure 27.1 by the difference between L_2, the labor supply at wage w_0, and L_1, the labor demand.

The question posed by the classical economists is whether there is really any such thing as involuntary unemployment. In their view, the situation depicted in the figure never arises, or at least arises infrequently and only for brief periods of time. They have advanced two reasons to support their contention.

First, they argue that the unemployed worker could get a job if he would only lower his wage demand to the market-clearing level. By refusing to lower the wage demand, the worker in effect voluntarily makes himself unemployed. The second argument is that there is almost always *some* job a person could get, if he were only willing to make the effort to look for it and then to take it. If the unemployed Chicago welder would move to California and pick grapes, he would have a job. (Of course, if *all* the unemployed decided at the same time that they were willing to accept jobs as low-paid dishwashers, grape pickers, or servers in fast-food restaurants, there might not be enough jobs, but the point is that each individual, in deciding *not* to accept these available jobs, has chosen to remain unemployed.)

To most economists, and to almost all noneconomists, pinning the label "voluntary" on unemployment simply because an unemployed worker has forgone the option of moving to California to pick grapes is semantic quibbling. The trained welder living in Chicago who is unemployed, while other welders are working, considers himself involuntarily unemployed as a welder. He would be willing to work at the going wage for welders (or perhaps even at somewhat lower wages). But he is justifiably unwilling to relocate to California to become a grape picker. Other cases are admittedly less clear-cut.

Equally important, there are the same social and economic consequences of millions of trained workers being unable to find gainful employment at jobs even remotely connected with their skills, regardless of whether we call these workers voluntarily or involuntarily unemployed. And we still need to face the basic problem of why the wages for welders do not adjust to equate the demand and supply for welders.

But the question remains: why don't all workers who are unemployed seek temporary employment at low-wage jobs? Many of them do, but some do not. Several reasons are commonly put forward. First, the available jobs might be in a different geographical area, and the costs of moving would be significant, particularly if the worker thinks (hopes) his unemployment is only temporary. Second, a low-wage job may convey the wrong kind of information to potential future employers. It may suggest that the individual lacks confidence in his abilities and skills. So long as the unemployed welder believes that accepting a job serving hamburgers at McDonald's conveys a negative signal, he will not take such a job unless his assets are sufficiently used up that he has no alternative.

THE WAGE-EMPLOYMENT PUZZLE

It turns out to be difficult to reconcile observed changes in employment (or unemployment) and wages with the basic competitive model. If we applied the basic model to the labor market, which is what classical economists did, we would predict that when the demand for labor goes down, as in a recession, the (real) wage also falls, as illustrated in Figure 27.2. A leftward shift in the demand for labor results in lower wages. If the supply of labor is very unresponsive to wage changes (that is, the labor supply curve is inelastic), as depicted by the steepness of the line in the figure, the reduction in the wage may be quite large.

But this does not seem to happen in the real world. In the Great Depression, when the demand for labor fell, real wages in manufacturing actually rose; one estimate using the consumer price index shows that while unemployment increased from 5.5 percent in 1929 to 22 percent in 1934, real wages *rose* by more than 20 percent. More recently, in the 1980s, real wages rose slightly as the unemployment rate almost doubled, from 5.2 percent to 9.5 percent.

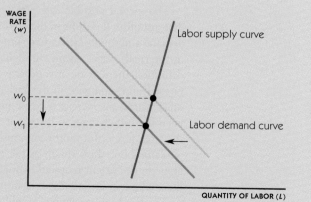

Figure 27.2 CHANGES IN THE DEMAND FOR LABOR AND REAL WAGES

Traditional theory predicts that when the demand curve for labor shifts to the left, real wages fall.

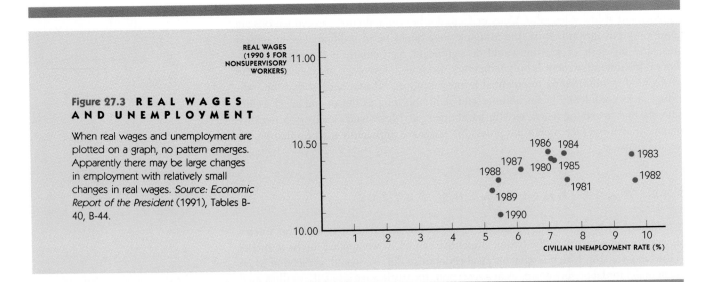

Figure 27.3 REAL WAGES AND UNEMPLOYMENT

When real wages and unemployment are plotted on a graph, no pattern emerges. Apparently there may be large changes in employment with relatively small changes in real wages. *Source: Economic Report of the President* (1991), Tables B-40, B-44.

Figure 27.3, which shows the real wage and unemployment rates during the 1980s, makes clear that real wages have not been much affected by changes in unemployment rates. There are three possible ways to explain the stability of wages in the face of fluctuating employment levels. The first is that the supply curve for labor is horizontal and the demand curve for labor has shifted, as shown in Figure 27.4A. As demand shifts in, the employment level changes with little change in the (real) wage. In this case, the loss in employment does not represent involuntary unemployment by our definition, because the market winds up at an equilibrium point, with demand equaling supply for labor. The labor market has moved along the labor supply curve to a new point of equilibrium. Almost all economists reject this interpretation, because of the huge amount of evidence suggesting that the labor supply curve is relatively inelastic (steep), not flat.

The second possible interpretation is that there are shifts in the labor supply curve that just offset the shifts in the labor demand curve, as depicted in panel B. The shifting demand and supply curves trace out a pattern of changing employment with little change in the (real) wage. Again, the labor market winds up at an equilibrium point, so by definition there is no involuntary unemployment. The reduced employment in the Great Depression was, in this view, due to a decreased willingness to supply labor—in other words, an increased desire for leisure. As we learned in Chapter 26, there have been marked changes in the supply of labor, as women and baby boomers have joined the labor force. But most economists do not see any persuasive evidence that the supply curve of labor shifts much as the economy goes into or comes out of a recession, let alone to the extent required in Figure 27.4B; and they see no reason why shifts in the demand curve for labor would normally be offset by shifts in the supply curve.

The third interpretation, to which most economists subscribe, is that there has been a shift in the demand curve for labor, with no matching shift in the supply curve *and no corresponding change in the wage*, a situation depicted in Figure 27.4C. The labor

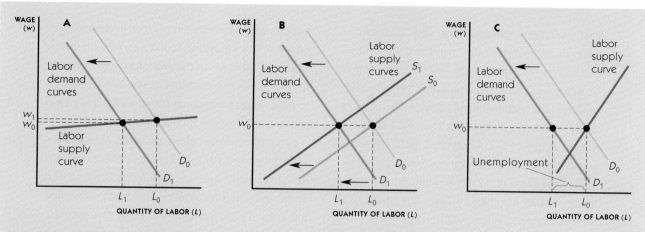

Figure 27.4 WHY WAGES DO NOT FALL WHEN DEMAND SHIFTS

Panel A shows a very elastic labor supply curve. A leftward shift in demand for labor from D_0 to D_1 will decrease employment without affecting wages. Panel B shows a shift in both supply and demand curves. Although the shift in demand for labor from D_0 to D_1 would reduce wages by itself, it is offset by a shift in the supply of labor from S_0 to S_1, leaving the wage level unchanged. In panel c, the demand for labor shifts from D_0 to D_1, but wages do not fall for some reason. Involuntary unemployment results.

market is stuck out of equilibrium: at the wage w_0, the amount of labor that workers would like to supply remains at L_0. But as the demand for labor shifts, the number of workers hired at w_0 falls from L_0 to L_1. The difference, $L_0 - L_1$, is the level of unemployment, and it is *involuntary*. The same argument holds even if there is a slight shift in the labor supply curve and a slight change in the wage: the adjustment in the wage is too small to align demand with supply.

The question posed by panel C is fundamental to macroeconomics: how do we explain the apparent fact that wages do not fall in the face of a shift in the demand curve for labor? Good reasons abound, as we will see in the following sections.

EXPLANATIONS OF WAGE RIGIDITIES

When unemployment is related to wages that fail to adjust sufficiently in response to a shift in the demand or supply curve for labor, economists say that wages exhibit **downward rigidity** or stickiness. There are three major explanations for why wages may not fall enough to eliminate unemployment quickly. First, firms may not be allowed to lower wages, because of either government legislation or union pressure. Second, firms may not choose to lower wages, if lowering wages lowers profits. And third, wages

CLOSE-UP: UNEMPLOYMENT IN EUROPE

Most European nations have had consistently higher unemployment rates than the United States in recent years. For example, the U.S. unemployment rate was below 6 percent from 1988 through 1990, and the recession that started in the second half of 1990 only pushed the rate a bit above 7 percent in early 1992. By contrast, here are some unemployment rates from various European countries at the start of 1992: Belgium, 8.6 percent; France, 9.8 percent; Italy, 10.7 percent; Spain, 15.2 percent; United Kingdom, 9.0 percent.

Perhaps even more interesting are comparisons of what percentage of the unemployed have been out of a job for more than twelve months. In the United States in the late 1980s (before the start of the recession), it was 7.4 percent; in Belgium, 76 percent; Denmark, 26 percent; France, 44 percent; Germany, 49 percent; Italy, 70 percent; Spain, 58 percent; and the United Kingdom, 41 percent.

Why have many European nations had such high and sustained unemployment? Economists have posed several answers. First, unions have far greater power in many European countries; they often embrace half or more of the work force, as opposed to only about one-sixth of U.S. workers. Unions try to raise wages for their members, even if this means higher overall levels of unemployment.

Second, many European countries *have* experienced high growth in wages for people who do have jobs, while average wage levels in the United States (adjusted for inflation) have not risen since the early 1970s. Perhaps the European and U.S. economies are just making different choices, one focusing on higher wages for those with jobs, the other on accommodating more of those who want to enter the labor market.

Third, social insurance programs—from unemployment to publicly provided housing and medical care—are often more generous in European countries, thus giving unemployed workers a reduced incentive to look for work.

Finally, European countries often have laws mak-

ing it difficult to fire workers. While these laws were intended to benefit workers by making their jobs more secure, they also discourage businesses from hiring, since firms know that once they have taken someone on, it will be very difficult to remove him.

Of course, not all European countries exhibit these patterns. Sweden offers a counterexample of particular interest to labor economists. There, the unemployment rate is typically in the range of 2–3 percent, even though the country has powerful unions, generous social insurance programs, and laws that make firing difficult. However, Sweden also devotes large amounts of government money to training and retraining workers, backed by a threat of cutting off those payments eventually if the worker does not eventually succeed in finding a job.

Sources: Supplement to the *OECD Observer* (June/July 1991); Richard B. Freeman, "Evaluating the European View That the United States Has No Unemployment Problem," *American Economic Review* (May 1988), pp. 294–99; "Economic and Financial Indicators," *The Economist,* February 15, 1992, p. 199.

may fall, but prices may fall at the same time and at the same rate, so that *real* wages do not fall. This in fact happened during the Great Depression, as we have seen. These explanations are not mutually exclusive: the reasons for wage stickiness may vary from industry to industry and may overlap.

UNIONS, CONTRACTS, AND GOVERNMENT REGULATIONS

One reason that real wages may not decline much when employment does is that there are contracts and regulations in place that keep them from doing so. In effect, there are wage floors, like the price floors we encountered in Chapter 5. The most conspicuous example is union contracts.

Union Contracts Unions typically negotiate nominal wage contracts—i.e., so many dollars per hour. But remember, in this section we are keeping prices constant, so a wage contract translates directly into *real* wages.

In some industries, labor union power explains wage rigidities. High wages in the U.S. steel industry, for example, have undoubtedly contributed to the high costs of production in that industry, and to the decline of American companies in the world steel market. Average wages in the steel industry in 1982 were $13.96 per hour, 64 percent more than the going wage in all manufacturing industries, but they fell sharply relative to average manufacturing wages after that.

Unions and management share the blame when the high wages called for in their contracts make an industry uncompetitive. In many instances, unions have insisted on high wages even in the face of declining employment. Management has sometimes found it easier to pay the unions what they ask, even if doing so may not be good for the long-term health of the firm, rather than suffer the aggravation of a protracted negotiation or a strike.

Strangely enough, it may be in the interests of those currently employed in unionized industries to make wage demands that significantly reduce the demand for workers. If a union demands ever-higher wages, the employer will have an incentive to reduce the work force. But if the decline in the work force is slow enough, it can be accomplished by natural attrition (that is, by workers who choose to retire or quit). In that case, the job security of those still employed is not threatened, and nonunion workers who would be willing to work for less money are shut out by the union contract and have no way of offering to work for a lower wage.

Unions occasionally accept wage cuts in times of severe economic stress. During the recession of the early 1980s, many companies were faced with bankruptcy or severe cutbacks if they could not reduce their costs. Recognizing this, a number of unions in airlines, automobiles, and steel accepted wage cuts. Whether the unions were able to negotiate so that those cuts were smaller than what they would have been in a perfectly competitive labor market is not clear.

Wage Adjustments   Even if unions do not succeed in the long run in obtaining higher wages for their members, they are probably successful in slowing down the process of adjustment of wages to changed economic circumstances. In some industries, it has been the practice to have a three-year contract. If an economic downturn sets in shortly after the contract has been signed, it may be more than two years before the new economic circumstances are reflected in the wages, when the new contract is negotiated. And by then, it is even possible that the economy is on the road to recovery, so that the workers—in the wages they receive—will have been largely insulated from the economic downturn. If the union and management had expected there to be inflation over the next few years, they might even have built in wage increases. When those price increases fail to materialize because of the economic downturn, the built-in wage increases lead to real wage increases even as the unemployment rate is rising.

When inflation rates are moderate to high, contracts frequently do not rely on built-in wage increases. Rather, wages increase with the cost of living. Contract provisions that allow for such increases, called cost of living adjustments (COLAs), mean that real wages are relatively unaffected by the level of inflation or unemployment.

In the United States, different contracts expire each month—the contracts are staggered, so a relatively small proportion are up for renegotiation at any time. Thus, adjustments of union wages must be slow; wages do not decline rapidly in response to unemployment, even if the unions were sensitive in their wage bargaining to the unemployment rate.

Union contracts, however, cannot provide the full explanation of rigid wages in the United States. This follows from the simple fact that there was high unemployment before unions became important, and there has been high unemployment recently, despite the long-term decline of unions. As the economy went into the Great Depression in 1929, only 7 percent of the labor force was unionized. In the recession of 1982, unemployment hit 10 percent, even though only 18.8 percent of the work force belonged to unions, and this percentage had been falling for the previous thirty years.

Still, while unions cannot be the whole explanation for wage rigidities, it is likely that they have been a contributing factor in particular industries in recent decades. The union membership statistics may understate the influence of unions in determining wages, since many nonunionized firms may base the wages they pay on what unions negotiate for comparable workers. In several European countries, where union bargaining occurs at the national level, and where the fraction of workers belonging to unions is much higher than in the United States—42 percent in Germany, 40 percent in Italy, 85 percent in Sweden—the argument that unions have played an important role in wage rigidities seems more persuasive than it does for the United States.

Implicit Contracts   Union-contract-style wage rigidities may come about even in the absence of a union or an explicit labor contract. There are economic forces at work that may lead to wage rigidities and limit the extent to which an unemployed worker can hope to get a job by offering to accept a lower wage than employed workers, so that wages would not fall by being "bid down."

The relations between an employer and her employees are governed not just by the formal contract, but by a host of implicit understandings developed over time between the firm and its workers. These implicit understandings are referred to as an **implicit contract**.

Workers are generally risk averse; other things being equal, they would like to avoid fluctuations in their income. Many workers have fixed financial commitments like the monthly rent or car payments. They do not want their wages to fluctuate with every change in the demand and supply of labor. Firms can bear these market fluctuations more easily. First, the owners of firms tend to be wealthier, which means that they have a larger cushion for adjusting to variations in income. Second, in the event of a temporary and unexpected shortfall of funds, companies can borrow more easily than can most workers.

Given that firms are less vulnerable to economic fluctuations than individual workers, it pays companies to provide at least some indirect "insurance" to their workers. Workers will be willing to work for a dependable firm that pays a steady wage even if that wage is lower on average than the highly varying wages they could get elsewhere. Such a firm provides a form of insurance to its workers through an implicit contract, an understanding that the wages will not vary with the month-to-month, or even year-to-year, variations in the labor market. That is, the firm behaves *as if* it had a contract with its workers guaranteeing the wage. It is called an implicit contract because it is an understanding, not a formal or explicit contract. The company pays workers a higher wage than it "needs to" in bad periods, but in return workers stay with their firm in good times, even though they are receiving a lower wage than they might obtain elsewhere.

In these circumstances, the wage workers receive can be thought of as consisting of two parts: the "market" wage (the wage the worker could receive elsewhere) plus an adjustment for the implicit insurance component. When the market wage is relatively low, the wage received by the worker may be higher than the market wage; the worker is, in effect, receiving a benefit on the implicit insurance policy. When the market wage is high, the wage received by the worker may be lower than the market wage; the difference is, in effect, the premium the worker pays for keeping wages somewhat more stable.

In many industries in which long-term employment relations are common, implicit contract theory provides a convincing explanation of why wages do not vary much. But while implicit contract theory is useful in explaining why the wages received by workers who are not laid off may not vary much, it does not explain why there are extended layoffs; in fact, the theory predicts that these extended layoffs will not occur. After all, the risk that is of most concern to workers is the complete cessation of their income;

this is far more important than a slight reduction in their weekly paycheck. Thus, implicit contract theory seems to predict that rather than laying people off, firms will engage in **work sharing;** they will reduce the hours each person works. Some firms have in fact experimented with work sharing, but it is not common. Layoffs are.

Proponents of the implicit contract theory have attempted to explain why firms tend to use layoffs rather than work sharing by focusing on the fixed costs associated with employment and on certain details of the unemployment compensation laws. First, they argue that when the work week is reduced below normal levels, productivity is reduced more than proportionately. For example, if a worker works an eight-hour day, the first hour is spent settling into work, the last hour is spent getting ready to leave; the worker has only six productive hours. If the work day is now reduced to six hours, one hour is still spent getting settled into work and one spent getting ready to leave, and there are only four productive hours. Shortening the work day by 25 percent has reduced the actual number of productive hours by 33 percent. This argument holds that the firm loses more in productivity through work sharing than through layoffs. But the argument only suggests that work sharing should take the form of a three- or four-day work week rather than a shortened workday.

Second, proponents of the implicit contract theory point out that the government encourages layoffs, albeit in an indirect way. In most places, individuals are not eligible for unemployment compensation if they are working part time. So if a company just trims the workday, the worker and the company pay the cost, but if the company lays off a worker, the government picks up part of the cost, by paying the worker unemployment compensation. (Several European countries have been sufficiently concerned about this problem that they have changed their laws to allow for unemployment compensation for those who face reductions in their work week.) But these considerations simply suggest that work sharing should take the form of job rotations. That is, one group of workers might be laid off for two months, then another group laid off for two months, and so on. Firms would then avoid the problems of short work weeks, and workers would be eligible for government unemployment compensation. These job rotations would also reduce the major risks of income variability caused by extended layoffs, and resolve the problems posed by productivity losses from shortened days. Job rotations, however, are almost never observed in the real world.

But the most telling criticism of implicit contract theory is that it does not really explain why wages of job seekers should fail to decline when there is unemployment. Even in the deepest recession, the labor market is like a revolving door, with people quitting jobs and some firms hiring new workers. Even if implicit contract theory could explain why some workers are laid off, it does not explain why employers do not decide to pay lower wages to new employees. If the wages paid to new employees fell sufficiently, presumably there would be no unemployment. Wage systems in which new workers are paid lower wages than current workers are called **two-tier wage systems.**

Insider-Outsider Theory   Seeking an explanation for why firms faced with recessionary conditions do not decide to pay lower wages to new employees, economists have devised what is known as **insider-outsider theory.** Insiders in this case are those with jobs at a particular firm, while outsiders are people who want jobs at that firm. The theory assumes that there are contracts, either explicit or implicit.

Insider-outsider theory focuses on the importance of training costs. Each firm needs a labor force trained in the special ways that it operates. Most of the training is done by current employees, the insiders. The insiders recognize that by training new employees, outsiders, they are reducing their bargaining position with the firm. The company can promise to continue to pay them higher wages than the newcomers, but the insiders know this promise could be broken. After all, they are training their own replacements. In future bargaining situations, the employer can use the availability of these lower-wage workers to exert downward pressure on the wages of the current employees. Knowing this, the insiders refuse to cooperate with training the outsiders, unless the new employees' interests are made coincidental with their own. The firm can accomplish this only by offering similar pay, but this results in wage stickiness: the wages offered new workers cannot be lowered to a level at which the demand for new workers equals the supply. Unemployment persists.

Moreover, insider-outsider theory emphasizes that even if the current employees were so foolish as to train new, lower-paid workers, the firm should not take the new workers' willingness to work at a low wage seriously. For once an outsider has been trained, she becomes a trained insider able to extract from the firm higher wages.

There are, in fact, relatively few exceptions to the general principle that firms do not like two-tier wage systems. Most such experiments—such as the contract between Ford and its workers signed in 1982, which provided that new workers be paid 85 percent of what previously hired workers received—are relatively short-lived. The Ford experiment was abandoned in 1984.

Minimum Wages Chapter 5 explained how a minimum wage set by the government could result in unemployment. The minimum wage is a government-enacted price floor. To the extent that workers would accept and firms would offer wages below the minimum if they were allowed to, the minimum wage keeps the demand for labor from equaling supply. Most workers in the United States earn considerably more than the minimum wage, so minimum wage legislation probably has little effect on unemployment for these workers. However, minimum wage legislation probably does contribute *some* to the unemployment of unskilled workers, including teenagers just entering the labor force; how much remains a question of debate. When, in 1990, the government set a special, lower minimum wage for teenagers, relatively few firms availed themselves of this opportunity. They paid their teenaged employees wages that were in excess of the new minimum wage. Still, it is worth noting that in recessions, unemployment rates among unskilled workers and teenagers often increase much more than for the population as a whole.

EFFICIENCY WAGE THEORY

A second reason that wages may not fall enough to eliminate unemployment is that firms may find that they make more profits by paying a wage higher than the one at which the labor market would clear. If paying higher wages leads to higher productivity, then higher wages may improve a firm's profits.

In Chapter 1, we learned that when Henry Ford opened his automobile plant in 1914, he paid his workers the unheard-of wage of $5 per day, more than double the going wage. He wanted his workers to work hard; he knew that with his new technique of production—the assembly line—and hardworking workers, his profits would be higher. Many modern companies apply the same philosophy.

WHY DOES PRODUCTIVITY DEPEND ON WAGES?

Economists have identified three main reasons that firms may benefit if they pay high wages: wages affect the quality of the work force, they affect the level of effort, and they affect the rate of labor turnover. Each of these reasons has been extensively studied in recent years. In each, productivity may depend not just on the wage paid, but also on the wage paid relative to that paid by other firms and on the unemployment rate. The following sections discuss each of the three explanations.

The Quality of the Labor Force   When a firm's demand for workers decreases, it worries that if it cuts wages for all workers, the best employees will be most likely to leave. After all, they will be more confident than their less productive colleagues that they will find a new job at the old (higher) wage. It is all too common for companies to discover after a wage cut that they have lost the best of their workers. Indeed, this is the reason frequently given by firms for not cutting wages. Chapters 6 and 19 introduced the concept of adverse selection. The average quality of used cars offered on the markets is affected by the price of cars, the average riskiness of those wishing to buy insurance is affected (adversely) by increases in the premium. The effect just described is an adverse selection effect: the average quality of those offering to work for a firm is affected adversely by a lowering of the wage.[1]

The Level of Effort   We can easily see that it would not pay any worker to make any effort on the job if all firms paid the market-clearing wage. A worker could reason as follows. "If I shirk—put out a minimal level of effort—I will either be caught or not. If I don't get caught, I get my paycheck and have saved the trouble of making an effort. True, if I am unlucky enough to be caught shirking, I risk being fired. But by the terms of the basic competitive model, I can immediately obtain a new job at the same wage. There is, in effect, no penalty for having been caught shirking."

Firms that raise their wages above the market-clearing level will find that they have introduced a penalty for shirking, for two reasons. First, if their workers are caught shirking and are fired, they will have to take the lower wage being offered by other firms. Second, if many firms offer higher-than-market-clearing wages, unemployment will result, since at the higher wages firms as a whole will hire fewer workers. Now a worker who is fired may have to remain unemployed for a time.

Consider the wage that is just high enough that workers are induced not to shirk. We know that this wage must exceed the wage at which the demand for labor equals the supply. If one of the unemployed workers offers to work for a lower wage at a particular firm, he will not be hired. His promise to work is not credible. The firm knows that at the lower wage, it simply does not pay the worker to exert effort.

The no-shirking view of wages also provides a gloomy forecast for the well-intentioned unemployment benefits policy offered by government. Assume the government, concerned about the welfare of the unemployed, increases unemployment benefits. Now the cost of being unemployed is lower, hence the wage a firm must pay to induce workers to work—that is, not to shirk—is higher. As a result, wages are increased, leading in turn to a lower level of employment. The higher unemployment benefits have increased the unemployment rate.

---

[1] It should be clear that we have now moved away from the assumption that all workers are identical, with which the chapter began.

Higher wages may lead to higher levels of effort for another reason: they may lead to improved worker morale. If workers think that the firm is taking advantage of them, they may reciprocate and try to take advantage of the firm. If workers think their boss is treating them well—including paying them good wages—they will reciprocate and go the extra mile. It is not just the threat of being fired that motivates them to work hard.

The Rate of Labor Turnover   Lowering wages increases the rate at which workers quit. Economists refer to this rate as the **labor turnover rate**. It is costly to hire new workers, to find the jobs that best match their talents and interests, and to train them. So firms seek to reduce their labor turnover rate, by paying high wages. The lower the wages, the more likely it is that workers will find another job more to their liking, either because it pays a higher wage or for some other reason. Thus, while firms may save a little on their direct labor costs in the short run if they cut their wages in a recession, these savings will be more than offset by the increased training and hiring costs incurred as demand rises again and they have to replace lost workers. We can think of what workers produce net of the costs of hiring and training them as their *net* productivity. Higher wages, by lowering these turnover costs, lead to higher net productivity.

DETERMINING THE EFFICIENCY WAGE

If, as we have just seen, net productivity increases when a firm pays higher wages, then it may be profitable for an employer not to cut wages even if there is an excess supply of workers. This is because the productivity of the employer's work force may decline enough in response to a wage cut that the overall labor costs per unit of production will actually increase.

The employer wants to pay the wage at which total labor costs are minimized; this is called the **efficiency wage**. The wage at which the labor market clears—the wage at which the supply of labor equals the demand for labor—is called the market-clearing wage. There is no reason to expect that the efficiency wage and the market-clearing wage will be the same. **Efficiency wage theory** suggests that labor costs may be minimized by paying a wage higher than the market-clearing wage.

If the efficiency wage is greater than the market-clearing wage, it will still pay each profit-maximizing firm to pay the efficiency wage. There will be unemployed workers who are willing to work at a lower wage, but it simply will not pay firms to hire them. The firms know that at the lower wage, productivity will decline enough to more than offset the lower wage.

In some circumstances, the efficiency wage can also be less than the market-clearing wage. In that case, competition for workers will bid up the wage to the competitive, market-clearing level. Firms would like to pay the lower, efficiency wage, but at that wage they simply cannot hire workers. The market-clearing wage thus forms a floor for wages in efficiency wage theory. If the reason that productivity depends on wages is that effort increases with the wage—the shirking view of wages—then the efficiency wage must exceed the market-clearing level.

The efficiency wage for one firm may differ from that of another. If, for instance, it is easy for a particular company to supervise workers, then workers know that if they shirk, they will quickly be caught, and because the penalty for shirking is fairly certain, the firm may not have to pay a very high wage to persuade workers not to shirk. In general, the efficiency wage for any firm will depend on two factors: the wage paid by

Close-up: Efficiency Wages in Tanzania

One of the implications of efficiency wage theory—that employers may be able to get work done more cheaply by *increasing* wages—can lead to some topsy-turvy implications. Or as Alfred Marshall, a famous economist of the late nineteenth and early twentieth centuries put it: "Highly paid labour is generally efficient and therefore not dear labour; a fact which though it is more full of hope for the future of the human race than any other that is known us, will be found to exercise a very complicating influence." The first chapter of this book gave the example of Henry Ford taking advantage of efficiency wage theory by paying higher wages in the automobile industry. But the theory can have striking implications in less developed countries too.

Consider the experience of the east African nation of Tanzania, formed by the union of Tanganyika and Zanzibar in 1964. When the area now known as Tanzania achieved independence in 1961, most wage earners worked on large plantations. Most of the workers were migrants, as is commonly the case in Africa, returning from the plantations to their home villages several times each year. The workers had low productivity and were not paid much. After independence, the government decreed that wage rates for the plantation workers would triple. Plantation owners predicted disaster; such a massive increase in the price they paid for labor, they thought, could only drive them out of business. But the government responded with predictions based on efficiency wage theory, that higher wages would lead to a more productive and stable work force.

The government predictions turned out to be correct. Sisal, for example, is a plant cultivated because it produces a strong white fiber that can be used for cord or fiber. Overall production of sisal quadrupled under the efficiency wage policy. This occurred not because of a change in the overall physical capital available, but because more motivated and highly skilled workers were better employed by the plantation owners. Over several years following the wage increase, however, employment in Tanzania's sisal industry fell from 129,000 to 42,000, thus illustrating how efficiency wages can increase unemployment.

Sources: Mrinal Datta-Chaudhuri, *Journal of Economic Perspectives* (Summer 1990), pp. 25–39; Richard Sabot, "Labor Standards in a Small Low-Income Country: Tanzania," Overseas Development Council (1988).

other firms and the unemployment rate. The wage paid by other firms matters because if other companies pay a lower wage, a firm will find that it does not have to pay quite as high a wage to elicit a high level of effort. Workers know that if they are fired, the jobs they are likely to find will pay less. Thus, the cost of being fired is increased, and this spurs employees on to working harder.

The unemployment rate also comes into play because as it increases, firms will again find that they do not have to pay quite as high a wage to elicit a high level of effort. The workers know that if they are fired, they will have a harder time getting a new job.

Efficiency wage theory also suggests a slow adjustment process for wages. Each firm is reluctant to lower its wages until others do, for several reasons. The company worries that its best workers will be attracted by other firms. It worries that the morale of its workers, and thus their productivity, will be impaired if they see their wage is below that of similar firms. No company wants to be the leader in wage declines, or at least in significant wage reductions. Each therefore contents itself with reducing its wage slowly, and never much below that of other firms. Gradually, as wages in all firms are lowered, employment is increased and unemployment reduced.

These patterns are in contrast to the basic competitive model, which predicts that with a relatively inelastic supply curve for labor, there will be large and quick changes in wages in response to changes in the demand for labor. It is these wage changes that prevent unemployment.

WHY ARE THERE LAYOFFS?

Efficiency wage theory helps explain why wages do not fall, or fall very much, even when there is an excess supply of labor and why, when wages do fall, they fall slowly. Because productivity depends in part on the wages a firm pays relative to those paid by other firms, each firm is reluctant to lower its wages much until others do.

Efficiency wage theory also helps to explain another puzzle of unemployment. If the economy needs a 25 percent reduction in labor supplied, why don't workers simply work thirty hours rather than forty, and save jobs for the 25 percent of their colleagues who otherwise would be laid off? We saw one explanation earlier in this chapter: the fixed costs associated with work. These fixed costs imply that it pays to have workers work a full work day rather than five or six hours. But we also saw that even with fixed costs there can be work sharing, in the form of job rotation. A worker might work one week, his colleague the next, the two of them sharing more fairly the burden of the reduced demand for labor. This does not seem to occur.

According to efficiency wage theory, the reason workers do not just work thirty hours rather than forty is that by reducing work proportionately among its workers, a firm will in effect be reducing overall pay proportionately. The company will fall back into the traps outlined above. If it lowers overall pay, it may lose a disproportionate fraction of its better workers. These workers can obtain offers of full-time work and full-time pay, and they will find this more attractive than a job with 80 percent of full-time work and 80 percent of the pay. They may enjoy the extra leisure, but it will not help meet the mortgage payments. Furthermore, workers now working part time will find that their incentives to exert high levels of effort decline. What they have to lose if they get fired is not so great; losing a part-time job is not as serious as losing a full-time job. This ability to explain concentrated layoffs is one feature that sets efficiency wage theory apart from some of the alternative views of wage rigidity.

THE IMPACT OF UNEMPLOYMENT ON DIFFERENT GROUPS

As noted in Chapter 25, one striking aspect of unemployment in the United States is that it affects different groups in the population very differently. In competitive markets, wages will adjust to reflect productivity; groups with higher productivity will have commensurately higher wage rates, while groups with lower productivity will have lower wage rates. But people in both groups will have jobs. There would be no reason for different groups to have different unemployment rates.

The efficiency wage theory argues that there may be some kinds of laborers, such as part-time workers or those with limited skills, who, at any wage, have sufficiently low productivity that it barely pays a firm to hire them. The labor cost, relative to what the workers produce, is simply too high. These workers are productive, but barely productive enough to offset the wages they receive. Or to put it another way, while they may receive a low wage, the wage is low enough only just to offset their low level of productivity. Paying higher wages would not increase productivity enough to offset the wage increase. And paying lower wages would reduce productivity, making that option unworkable as well.

It is these groups, who lie right at the margin of the hiring decision, who will bear the brunt of the fluctuations in the demand for labor. Chapter 25 pointed out, for instance, that teenagers and young workers not only have higher average unemployment rates, they bear more of the burden of variations in employment. We also saw that when, in 1990, the minimum wage for teenagers was lowered, most firms continued to pay teenagers more than the minimum wage. Presumably firms were worried that were they to cut their wages by 10 percent, productivity would be reduced by more than 10 percent, as they lost their best teenagers and as the remaining workers' effort was reduced.

LIMITS OF EFFICIENCY WAGE THEORY

Efficiency wage theory may provide a significant part of the explanation for wage rigidities in a number of different situations: where training and turnover costs are high; where monitoring productivity is difficult; and where differences in individuals' productivity are large and important, but it is difficult to ascertain them before hiring and training them. On the other hand, in situations where workers are paid piece rates on the basis of how much they produce, or in situations where training costs are low and monitoring is easy, efficiency wage considerations are likely to be less important. These situations may indeed exhibit greater wage flexibility, or at least they might if there are no union pressures, implicit contracts, or insider-outsider considerations.

CHANGES IN THE PRICE LEVEL

For most of this chapter, we have found it convenient to analyze the labor market assuming that prices of goods are fixed. It is now time to drop that assumption, and discover the consequences. We return to the basic supply and demand model with which we began the chapter. There, the demand and supply for labor depended on the wage paid, under the assumption that the prices of all goods were given. Here, we look at what happens if as wages change, prices change too. Since we are dealing with unemployment, the change we will consider is a decline in wages and the price level.

Lower wages might give rise to more employment *if* that were the end of the story.

If workers at a firm were to agree to a cut in their wages, the firm would have a competitive advantage over its rivals; sales would increase (the firm could cut its prices), and so would employment. But when all firms lower wages, the consequences are different. The lower wages have repercussions on the product market.

This is illustrated in Figure 27.5. Panel A shows the aggregate demand and supply curves for labor, and panel B shows the aggregate demand and supply curves for goods. Remember, each curve in panel A is drawn under the assumption of a particular price level, and each curve in panel B is drawn under the assumption of a particular wage level. Initially, the wage is w_0, with the supply exceeding the demand; the resulting unemployment is U_0. Wages fall to w_1. If nothing else happens, unemployment would fall to U_1. But something else is happening in the product market. Lower wages shift the aggregate supply curve for goods to the right—at each price level, firms are willing to supply more goods because wages are lower. The aggregate demand curve may also shift to the left, since workers have less to spend with the lower wages. In any case, the net effect is that prices fall, to p_2 in the figure.

The fall in prices has further repercussions in the labor market. The amount of labor that firms wish to hire at any (nominal) wage depends on the prices at which they can sell what they produce. At lower prices, they demand less labor at each wage. So the demand curve for labor in panel A shifts to D_1, and at the new level of prices, at the wage w_1, the demand for labor is essentially what it was before. Depending on whether prices fall faster or slower than wages, employment may increase or decrease slightly. The basic point is that wage cuts are often ineffective at reducing unemployment or, at best, work slowly because price changes offset the wage changes.

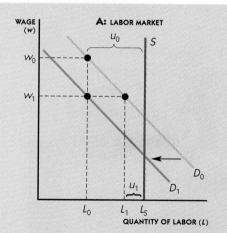 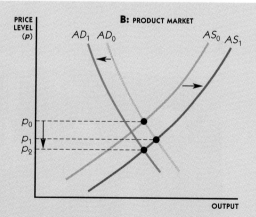

Figure 27.5 PRICE CHANGES OFFSETTING LOWER WAGES

In panel A, the economy begins with wages at w_0, so the supply of labor L_s exceeds the demand for labor L_0, and unemployment exists. The wage begins to decline toward equilibrium and falls to w_1, where firms would be willing to demand L_1. But as panel B shows, the lower wages lead to lower prices. The aggregate supply curve shifts to the right, and the aggregate demand curve shifts to the left; the new equilibrium price level is p_2. This lower price level in turn shifts the demand for labor from D_0 to D_1 in panel A. As a result, the quantity demanded remains at L_0.

CLOSE-UP: IMMIGRATION AND THE AGGREGATE LABOR MARKET

Immigration to the United States has been on the rise. In the 1930s, half a million people legally immigrated to the United States; in the 1940s, the number was 1 million; 1950s, 2.5 million; 1960s, 3.3 million; 1970s, 4.5 million; and 1980s, 5.8 million. Adding those immigrants who arrived illegally would raise the totals for the 1970s and 1980s by several million.

People who would like to reduce immigration tend to see only bad things that can happen with new arrivals. They worry that immigrants are "different" and will not fit into communities. They complain that either immigrants do not find jobs and then become a drain on U.S. taxpayers by receiving welfare payments, or they do find jobs, and by taking those jobs away from Americans, they raise the unemployment rate for those who are already U.S. citizens.

Pure economic logic has little to say about the concern over whether immigrants will change the character of a community, although it is worth noting that many people feel that the quality of their life is improved by having an opportunity to interact with those of different backgrounds. But on the issue of unemployment and welfare, economists do have something to say.

Consider first how immigration might affect unemployment. Many economic models of this subject divide workers into skilled and unskilled labor. Although some immigrants are highly skilled, it is fair to say that the primary effect of immigration is an outward shift of the aggregate supply curve for unskilled labor. If wages are flexible, this shift will lead to lower wages and a higher amount of employment. If wages are not flexible (perhaps because of minimum wage laws, which affect low-skilled workers), it will lead to greater unemployment for low-skilled workers. Either way, less skilled workers as a group are made worse off. Thus, immigration may be one reason why the unemploy-

ment rate for people with less than a college education is about double the rate for those with a college education.

However, skilled laborers and people who receive income from capital are made better off by immigration. Since unskilled labor is a complement in many production processes for skilled labor and capital, a lower wage for unskilled labor will tend to raise the marginal productivity of skilled labor and capital. Moreover, the greater supply of unskilled labor and lower wages will lead to lower prices for many products.

Economic models have shown that the economic gains to society from immigration exceed the losses, but the gains and losses accrue to different parties. To ensure that no individual is worse off as a result of immigration, some economists have proposed allowing immigration, but having the government redistribute income to those who are harmed (low-skilled workers) and away from those who benefit (immigrants themselves, high-skilled workers, and people who receive income from capital).

Sources: Barry R. Chiswick, "Illegal Immigration and Immigration Control," *Journal of Economic Perspectives* (Summer 1988), pp. 101–15; Clark W. Reynolds and Robert K. McCleery, "The Political Economy of Immigration Law: Impact of Simpson-Rodino on the United States and Mexico," *Journal of Economic Perspectives* (Summer 1988), pp. 117–31.

Some economists believe that if wages and prices fell *enough*, the economy would be restored to full employment. They believe, in other words, that as wages and prices fall, the demand curve for labor does not shift down proportionately. One reason it does not is that at very low prices, people feel wealthier; they can buy more with the money they have in the bank. Another reason is that for people to hold the higher *real* supply of money, interest rates must fall, and investment will be stimulated. In both cases, the high demand for goods is translated into an increased demand for labor. But during the Great Depression, wages and prices fell by more than a third, and this seemed to make matters worse rather than better. The reasons for this we take up in Chapters 28–35. What seems clear is that if the economy will indeed be restored to full employment when wages and prices fall enough, this process is too slow and too uncertain for governments to rely on. Clamors for the government to do something about the unemployment will be felt long before the process can work itself out.

OKUN'S LAW

As high as the unemployment statistics sometimes climb, they may not fully reflect the underutilization of human resources. Firms find it costly to hire and train workers. Therefore, when they have a temporary lull in demand, they do not immediately fire workers. They may not even lay them off, for fear that once laid off, the workers will seek employment elsewhere. Firms keep the workers on the job, but they may not fully utilize them. This is referred to as **labor hoarding,** and can be thought of as a form of disguised unemployment. Employees are not really working, though they are showing up for work. Like open unemployment, it represents a waste of human resources.

The importance of this disguised unemployment was brought home forcefully by a study conducted by Arthur Okun, chairman of the Council of Economic Advisers under

President Johnson. He showed that as the economy pulls out of a recession, output increases more than proportionately with employment, and as the economy goes into a recession, output decreases more than proportionately with the reduction in employment. This result is sometimes referred to as **Okun's law**. In Okun's study, for every 1 percent increase in employment, output increased by 3 percent. This was a remarkable finding, for it seemed to run contrary to one of the basic principles of economics—the law of diminishing returns, which would have predicted that a 1 percent increase in employment would have less than a proportionate effect on output. The explanation for Okun's law, however, was quite simple: many of those who were "working" in a recession were not really working. They were partially idle. As the economy heated up, they worked more fully, and this is what gave rise to the increased output.

ALTERNATIVE EXPLANATIONS OF WAGE RIGIDITIES

1. Unions with explicit and implicit contracts prevent wages from falling. Insider-outsider theory explains why firms do not pay newly hired workers a lower wage. Minimum wages explain why wages for very low skilled workers do not fall.

2. Efficiency wage theory suggests that it is profitable for firms to pay above-market wages. This is because wages affect the quality of the labor force, labor turnover rates, and the level of effort exerted by workers.

3. Falling wages may very well be accompanied by falling prices, with the result that there is little change in real wages.

POLICY ISSUES

In this chapter, we have explored a variety of possible reasons why wages do not fall to the market-clearing level, where the demand for labor equals the supply. The truth probably involves a combination of all of these explanations. Minimum wages play a role among very low skilled workers. Unions play a role in some sectors of the economy. In some jobs, firms do not cut wages because of efficiency wage considerations. Lowering wages actually increases labor costs; the firm will get lower-quality workers, workers will not work as hard, and the firm will face higher turnover rates.

Wages do sometimes fall, as in the Great Depression. But what are important for firm decisions are wages relative to prices. Wages do not fall *fast enough* to equilibrate demand and supply. And all of the reasons given in this chapter play a role not only in explaining why wages do not fall, but also in helping us to understand why, when they fall, they fall slowly.

When the labor market does not clear and involuntary unemployment is the result, there may be an economic role for government, and it is worth reviewing government policies that are designed to overcome failures in the labor market. Such policies have centered on three issues: increasing the demand for labor by lowering (real) wages and otherwise increasing wage flexibility; providing income to the unemployed; and increasing the demand for labor by increasing the aggregate demand for the products workers produce. The third of these is the subject of the next three chapters. Here, we discuss the first two policies.

INCREASING WAGE FLEXIBILITY

Those who see wage rigidities as a major cause of unemployment and believe that they are created by unions or implicit contracts have sought ways of increasing wage flexibility. In Japan, for example, large companies have long-term (lifetime) implicit contracts with their workers, but workers receive a substantial fraction of their pay in the form of annual bonuses. In effect, this means that the wage a worker receives varies from year to year depending on the fortunes of the firm. Unemployment in Japan is considerably less variable than in the United States, and many economists believe that flexible wages are an important part of the reason. In his book *The Share Economy*, Martin Weitzman of Harvard University has advocated that U.S. firms adopt a similar system.

Two features make wage flexibility unattractive to workers. First, many workers would have to bear more risk in income fluctuations. Under the current U.S. system, workers who have considerable seniority, and who often dominate union negotiations, face little risk of being laid off during hard times; their incomes are relatively secure, both from year-to-year variation and from the threat of complete cessation. With the bonus system, however, all employees, including the more senior ones, would face considerable risk. And as the discussion of implicit contracts pointed out, the firm is generally in a better position than the worker to bear the risk of economic fluctuations.

Second, workers worry that the firms most likely to be willing to give large profit shares to their employees in exchange for wage concessions may be those firms that expect the smallest profits; by giving up a share of the profit, they are giving the least away. In effect, when the workers' pay depends on the profits of the firm, workers become much like shareholders—what they receive depends on how well the company does. It does no good to own a large share in the profits of a firm that makes no profits.

This second reason makes it clear why unions do not trust wage flexibility systems. Their concern that only firms without profits will offer to share them with their workers proved justified in 1985, when employees of Eastern Airlines actually accepted a pay reduction in return for a share of the profits. The share of profits turned out to be worthless when the airline went into bankruptcy soon after.

Still, the fact is that large segments of Japanese industry employ a system with greater wage flexibility, and that system seems to give rise to less variability in employment. Japan appears to have overcome the obstacles to making wages vary with profits. How this happened, whether it is possible for the United States to move to a system with more flexible wages, and what role government should play in encouraging such a move, remain questions of debate among economists.

REDUCING THE COSTS OF UNEMPLOYMENT

During the past half century, governments have taken it as their responsibility not only to reduce the level of unemployment, but also to reduce the costs borne by those unfortunate enough not to be able to find a job. The difficulty is, how do we do this without giving rise to further economic problems?

UNEMPLOYMENT INSURANCE

The unemployment insurance program is the most important one for reducing the cost to the individual of being unemployed. It was started in 1935 in the midst of the Great Depression with the passage of the Social Security Act; unemployment insurance programs are run by the states, within federal guidelines, and there are some variations between states. The typical program pays up to 50 percent of a person's former salary for twenty-six weeks. In a number of instances, when the unemployment rate has increased, coverage has been extended to thirty-nine weeks or longer. To be eligible for the maximum, workers must have worked for a minimum number of weeks, such as forty out of the previous fifty-two. Thus, new workers are not covered by unemployment insurance.

Critics of the program who claim that unemployment insurance pays too much worry that it reduces the incentive of unemployed workers to search for jobs. There is some evidence for this: the number of people who get jobs just as their unemployment benefits expire is far greater than can be accounted for by chance. Others worry that when high levels of unemployment insurance are available, workers have less incentive to exert effort at any given level of wages and unemployment; after all, given the high level of unemployment compensation, the threat of being fired for shirking is not as fearsome as it would otherwise be. To restore the incentives of efficiency wages, firms must pay higher wages, but when they do, the higher cost of labor induces them to hire fewer workers. By this logic, high unemployment insurance actually contributes to increasing the unemployment rate.

What we have here is another illustration of a familiar basic trade-off—between security (risk) on the one hand and incentives on the other. Economic arrangements that diminish risk also diminish incentives. A person who is guaranteed a job will have little incentive to work. If unemployment insurance were sufficiently generous that it fully replaced whatever income he lost if he were fired, a worker would not find any economic incentives for working. And a worker who is laid off would have no incentive to look for a new job. Thus, some critics of the current unemployment insurance system argue that society has chosen the wrong point on the trade-off curve depicted in Figure 27.6; the gain in increased security at point A is not worth the cost in reduced productivity from attenuated incentives relative to B.

Other critics argue that the current U.S. unemployment system does not provide enough support for either the long-term unemployed or new entrants into the labor force, and provides too much for the short-term unemployed. For a worker who has been employed for a while, insurance for unemployment spells of six or eight weeks may be unnecessary in the eyes of many economists. They argue that people should be able to finance these short-term spells out of savings or by borrowing. One recent

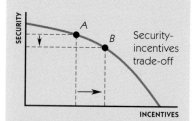

Figure 27.6 TRADE-OFF BETWEEN ECONOMIC SECURITY AND PRODUCTIVITY

Better job security or unemployment insurance provides greater economic security but reduces incentives. There is concern that the present system provides too much security, that it might be possible to get relatively large increases in productivity (through improved incentives) at the cost of small decreases in security, as shown by the movement from A to B.

study calculated that requiring an unemployed worker to wait two weeks before receiving any unemployment payments would save $1.1 billion a year in lower unemployment benefits, while still assuring a steady stream of income to the longer-term unemployed. These economists believe that in general, insurance should be designed to cover *large* losses, against which individuals cannot self-insure.

REVIEW AND PRACTICE

SUMMARY

1. Involuntary unemployment exists when the supply of labor exceeds the demand for labor at the prevailing market wage. This may happen because demand for labor falls but wages do not decline.

2. It has been argued that all unemployment is voluntary, that workers could always find work at a lower wage or in a different field. But the costs of moving to where jobs are available might be significant, and accepting a low-wage job might send the wrong kind of information to potential future employers.

3. The reasons why firms may be unable to reduce wages and thus unemployment include union contracts, insider-outsider theory, and minimum wage laws.

4. Reducing wages may actually lead to an increase in labor costs, because it may result in a lower average quality of workers as the best workers leave; because it may result in lower effort; and because it may result in higher turnover costs.

5. If a decline in nominal wages causes the overall price level to decline, then a fall in nominal wages may not be translated into a fall in real wages, and may not do much to reduce unemployment.

6. Making wages depend more on firm profits might result in less variability in employment. But workers would risk income reductions in hard times, and would worry that the firms most likely to give large profit shares to employees may expect the smallest profits.

7. Unemployment insurance reduces the costs to workers of being laid off, but it also reduces workers' incentives to work hard or to search for a new job. Firms' responses may lead to higher rather than lower unemployment.

KEY TERMS

involuntary unemployment	implicit contract	labor turnover rate
downward rigidity of wages	work sharing	efficiency wage
	insider-outsider theory	Okun's law

REVIEW QUESTIONS

1. Under what conditions will economists argue that involuntary unemployment exists? In what sense could unemployment be considered "voluntary"? Discuss the main arguments for this position and the counterarguments.

2. Make a list of reasons that firms may be unable to reduce wages, and a list of reasons that firms may choose not to reduce wages.

3. True or false: "The prevalence of unions and minimum wage laws is the primary reason for wage stickiness, and therefore for unemployment, in the U.S. economy." Discuss your answer.

4. If an implicit contract is not written down, why would a firm abide by it? Why would a worker?

5. Why does implicit contract theory predict that work sharing is more likely than layoffs?

6. Name three reasons why productivity may depend on the level of wages paid.

7. How does an efficiency wage differ from a market-clearing wage?

8. How does efficiency wage theory help to explain the fact that different groups may have very different levels of unemployment?

9. What trade-off does society face when it attempts to expand economic security for workers with higher unemployment benefits or greater job security?

PROBLEMS

1. In 1990, Congress and President Bush increased the minimum wage. How will this change affect the stickiness of wages and the level of unemployment? In some states, equilibrium wages are already above both the old and the new level of the minimum wage. How would this fact alter your prediction about the effects of the minimum wage in those states?

2. Would you be more or less likely to observe implicit contracts in industries where most workers hold their jobs for only a short time? What about industries where most workers hold jobs a long time? Explain.

3. A number of businesses have proposed a two-tier wage scale, in which the wage scale for new employees is lower than the wage scale for current employees. Using the insights of insider-outside theory, would you be more or less likely to observe two-tier wage scales in industries where a lot of on-the-job training is needed? where not much is needed?

4. The following figures represent the relationship between productivity and wages for the Doorware Corporation, which makes hinges.

Wage per hour	$ 8	$10	$12	$14	$16	$18	$20
Hinges produced per hour	20	24	33	42	52	58	60

Graph the productivity-wage relationship. From the graph, how do you determine the efficiency wage? Calculate output per dollar spent on labor for the Doorware Corporation. What is the efficiency wage?

5. Would you be more or less likely to see efficiency wages in the following types of industries?
   (a) industries where training and turnover costs are relatively low;
   (b) industries where it is difficult to monitor individual productivity;
   (c) industries that have many jobs where individual differences in productivity are relatively large.

APPENDIX: DERIVATION OF THE EFFICIENCY WAGE

Figure 27.7 depicts a curve that represents one possible relationship between productivity and wages. We refer to this curve as the **wage-productivity curve**. Productivity here can be thought of as "the number of pins produced in an hour," or any similar measure of output. There is a minimum wage, w_m, below which the firm will find it difficult, if not impossible, to obtain labor. At a very low wage, w_1, the company can only hire the dregs of the labor market—those who cannot get jobs elsewhere. Worker morale is low, and effort is low. Workers quit as soon as they can get another job, so labor turnover is high.

As the firm raises its wage, productivity increases. The company earns a reputation as a high-wage firm, attracting the best workers. Morale is high, turnover is low, and employees work hard. But eventually, as in so many areas, diminishing returns set in: successive increases in wages have incrementally smaller effects on productivity. The firm is concerned with wage costs per unit of output, not wage costs per employee. Thus, it wishes to minimize not the wage but the wage divided by productivity.

This can be put another way. The company wishes to maximize the output per dollar spent on labor (we are assuming that all the other costs are fixed). Since productivity is defined as the output per unit of time (pins per hour), and the wage is the labor cost per unit of time (dollars per hour), dividing productivity by the wage produces the equation

$$\frac{\text{productivity}}{\text{wage}} = \frac{\text{output/unit of time}}{\text{dollars/unit of time}} = \frac{\text{output}}{\text{dollars spent on labor}}.$$

Thus, a decision to make the ratio of output to dollars spent on labor as high as possible is mathematically equivalent to a decision to make the ratio of productivity to wages as high as possible. To tell what level of wages will accomplish this goal, Figure 27.7 shows the productivity-wage ratio as a line from the origin to a point on the wage-

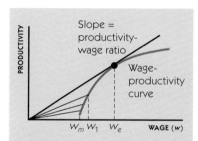

Figure 27.7 THE RELATIONSHIP BETWEEN PRODUCTIVITY AND WAGES

As wages rise, productivity increases, at first quickly and then more slowly. The efficiency wage is the wage at which the ratio of productivity to wage is highest. It is found by drawing a line through the origin tangent to the wage-productivity curve.

Figure 27.8 SHIFTING THE PRODUCTIVITY-WAGE RELATION-SHIP

If unemployment is low, workers have many alternative job possibilities. With the threat of being fired reduced, at each wage workers work less hard, so productivity is lower. In the case shown here, the efficiency wage will be lower when there is high unemployment than when there is low unemployment.

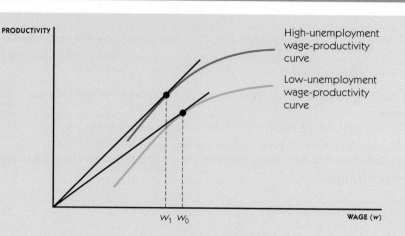

productivity curve. The slope of this line is just the ratio of productivity (the vertical axis) to the wage (the horizontal axis).

As we draw successive lines from the origin to points on the wage-productivity curve with higher wages, the slope first increases and then decreases. The slope is largest for the line through the origin that is just tangent to the wage-productivity curve. The wage at this point of tangency is the wage at which labor costs are minimized: the efficiency wage, w_e.

Changes in unemployment rates may shift the wage-productivity curve, as shown in Figure 27.8. At each wage, the productivity of the labor force is higher at the higher unemployment rate. Also, the efficiency wage—the wage at which the ratio of productivity to the wage is maximized—is lowered slightly: it falls from w_0 to w_1. The change in the efficiency wage may be relatively small, even if the shift in the curve relating productivity to wages is relatively large.

CHAPTER 28

AGGREGATE DEMAND

I n Chapter 27, we focused directly on the labor market. We saw that when the demand for labor decreases, real wages do not fall to allow the labor market to clear, and unemployment is the result. The next question is, what causes the demand curve for labor to shift? The answer lies in the product market. If the level of output (GDP) is high, then employment rates are likely to be high as well. Likewise, declining output is usually accompanied by increasing unemployment. Thus, shifts in the demand for labor are closely related to events in the product market. We therefore need to ask a further question: what determines the level of output?

Output is determined by the interplay of aggregate demand and aggregate supply curves, as we saw in Chapter 26. In this and the next two chapters, our focus will be on the flat range of the aggregate supply curve. This is the portion where the economy has excess capacity, and therefore where shifts in the aggregate demand curve translate primarily into increases in output with little effect on the price level. In this chapter, we make two crucial simplifying assumptions: that the price level is fixed and that there is sufficient excess capacity that producers are willing to produce any output at that price. We are, in effect, pushing questions of aggregate supply and changes in the price level (inflation) aside so that we can focus on aggregate demand. Output, in this simple scenario, is entirely determined by aggregate demand.[1]

---

[1] The analysis is actually broader than this: it encompasses any situation where the price level is fixed and where, at that price level, firms would be willing to increase output if they were able to sell what they produced.

"We could stand a little easing of the crunch down here."

KEY QUESTIONS

1. When the economy has excess capacity, what determines the aggregate level of output?

2. What are the components of aggregate expenditures?

3. How do consumption and imports increase with income?

4. Why, if investment or government expenditures or exports increase by a dollar, does aggregate output increase by more than a dollar? What determines the amount by which it increases?

INCOME-EXPENDITURE ANALYSIS

Aggregate demand, as we learned in Chapter 26, is the total demand for goods and services produced in the economy. There we got a first look at the aggregate demand curve, which gives the level of aggregate demand at each price level.

To know where this curve comes from, we need to understand a new concept, the **aggregate expenditures schedule.** Aggregate expenditures include the total of what households, firms, and governments, both in the United States and abroad, spend on goods produced in the United States. The aggregate expenditures schedule traces out the relationship, at a fixed price level, between aggregate expenditures and national income. By contrast, the aggregate demand curve traces out the levels of output that are demanded at different price levels.[2]

It is natural to think that as consumers' incomes increase, they will want to spend

[2] In Chapter 31, we will analyze what happens to the aggregate expenditures schedule when the price level changes, and then determine the equilibrium level of aggregate demand at each price level. This will enable us to derive the aggregate demand curve.

more. The same pattern holds when all the components of aggregate expenditures are looked at together. Later in the chapter, we will see more precisely how and why increases in income lead to greater expenditure. For now, this rough pattern of aggregate expenditures increasing with income is all we need to form a schedule like the one in Figure 28.1. The vertical axis measures aggregate expenditures, while the horizontal axis shows national income.

There are three critical properties of the aggregate expenditures schedule. First, it is upward sloping—as national income goes up, so do aggregate expenditures. Changes in other variables (like interest rates, tax rates, and exchange rates) cause the aggregate expenditures schedule to shift up or down, and they may even change the slope.

Second, as income increases by a dollar, aggregate expenditures increase by less than a dollar. The reason for this is that consumers save some of their increased income; they do not spend all of it. Figure 28.1 also shows a line through the origin at a 45-degree angle. The slope of this line is unity. Along the line, as we move to the right on the horizontal axis by a dollar, we move up the vertical axis by a dollar. Since aggregate expenditures increase less than dollar for dollar with increased income, the aggregate expenditures schedule is flatter than the 45-degree line.

Third, even if national income were zero, people would still need to spend money to buy goods; they would pay for the goods by borrowing or out of savings. That is one of the reasons why, even when national income is zero, aggregate expenditures are positive. This is reflected in the figure in the fact that the aggregate expenditures schedule intercepts the vertical axis at a positive level, point A. The facts that (a) the aggregate expenditures schedule is flatter than the 45-degree line through the origin and (b) aggregate expenditures are positive, even when income is zero, imply that the aggregate expenditures schedule intersects the 45-degree line, as seen in the figure.

Our objective is to determine the equilibrium level of output in the economy when there is excess capacity. Besides the aggregate expenditures schedule, there are two more concepts we need for our analysis.

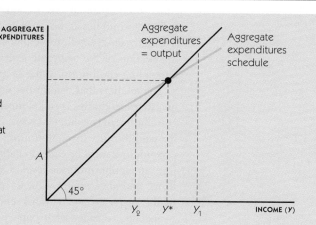

Figure 28.1 THE AGGREGATE EXPENDITURES SCHEDULE AND INCOME-EXPENDITURE ANALYSIS

The aggregate expenditures schedule gives the sum of consumption, investment, government expenditures, and net exports at each level of national income. Aggregate expenditures increase with income. Equilibrium occurs at the intersection of the aggregate expenditures schedule and the 45-degree line. At outputs less than Y^*, such as Y_2, aggregate expenditures exceed output. Goods that are being produced are not being sold; there are unintended inventory accumulations. The reverse is true for outputs greater than Y^*.

THE NATIONAL INCOME-OUTPUT IDENTITY

Chapter 25 showed that national income is equal to national output. This reflects the fact that when a good is purchased, the money that is paid must eventually wind up in someone's pocket—either as wages, in the pockets of workers in the firm that produced the good (or of workers who produced the intermediate goods that were used in the production of the final good); as interest payments, in the pockets of those who have lent the firm money; or as profits, in the pockets of the owners of the firm. The money eventually must show up as someone's income. For simplicity, we will assume that the residents of the country neither receive money (net) from abroad nor pay money (net) abroad, so GNP and GDP coincide. If Y is used to represent national income, this identity can be written

$$GDP = \text{national income} = Y.$$

The identity is useful, because it means that we can interpret the horizontal axis in Figure 28.1 in two different ways: we can say the aggregate expenditures schedule gives the level of expenditures at each level of national *income* or that it gives the level of expenditures at each level of national *output*.

EQUILIBRIUM OUTPUT

Normally, firms will only produce what they believe they can sell. This means that the total output produced by all firms will equal the total demand for output. This is our third necessary concept, and it can be put another way: in equilibrium, aggregate expenditures, which we denote by AE, must equal aggregate output (GDP). Since aggregate output equals national income (Y), we have the simple equation

$$AE = GDP = Y.$$

In Figure 28.1, the 45-degree line through the origin is labeled "Aggregate expenditures = output." The line traces out all points where the vertical axis (aggregate expenditures) equals the horizontal axis (national income, which equals aggregate output).

Equilibrium lies at the point on the aggregate expenditures schedule that also satisfies the aggregate-expenditures-equal-output condition. That is, equilibrium occurs at the intersection of the aggregate expenditures schedule and the 45-degree line. The corresponding equilibrium value of aggregate output is denoted by Y^*.

The analysis that determines equilibrium output by relating income (output) to aggregate expenditures is called **income-expenditure analysis**. We can see that Y^* is the equilibrium in two different ways. First, it is the only point that satisfies the two conditions for equilibrium. In equilibrium, everything produced must be purchased. Aggregate expenditures must be equal to national output (income), as represented by the 45-degree line. In equilibrium, the level of aggregate expenditures must also be what households, firms, and government want to spend in total at that level of national income, given by the aggregate expenditures schedule.

Second, consider what happens at a level of income Y_1, in excess of Y^*. At that point, the aggregate expenditures schedule lies below the 45-degree line. What households, firms, and government would like to spend at that level of national income, as reflected in the aggregate expenditures schedule, is less than national income (output).

More goods are being produced than individuals would like to buy. Some of the goods, like strawberries, cannot be stored. They simply spoil. Other goods can be, and they go into inventories.

Economists distinguish between **planned inventories** and **unplanned inventories**. Planned inventories are inventories firms choose to have on hand because they make business more efficient. They are considered an investment, and their buildup is therefore counted as part of investment spending in the aggregate expenditures schedule. Unplanned inventories come into being simply because firms cannot sell what they are producing. At Y_1, firms find that unplanned inventories are piling up—they are producing goods that cannot be sold, which are either spoiling or increasing inventories beyond the desired level. They respond by cutting back production until they reach Y^*.

Similarly, consider what happens at a level of income Y_2, less than Y^*. At that point, the aggregate expenditures schedule lies above the 45-degree line. At that level of income, households, firms, and government are spending more than national income (output). They are, in other words, purchasing more than the economy is producing. This is possible because firms can sell out of inventories. With planned inventories being depleted, firms increase their production. They continue to do this until equilibrium is restored, with output (income) equal to Y^*.

SHIFTS IN THE AGGREGATE EXPENDITURES SCHEDULE

A variety of changes in the economy could lead households, firms, and government to decide, *at each level of income*, to spend more or less. Such changes give rise to shifts in the aggregate expenditures schedule. Figure 28.2 shows what happens if the level of aggregate expenditures increases at each level of national income by the amount S. The

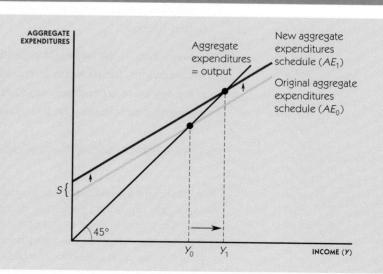

Figure 28.2 EFFECT OF A SHIFT IN THE AGGREGATE EXPENDITURES SCHEDULE

An upward shift in the aggregate expenditures schedule results in an increase in the equilibrium level of output. The magnitude of the increase in equilibrium output from a given upward shift in the aggregate expenditures schedule is greater than the magnitude of the upward shift; that is, $Y_1 - Y_0$ exceeds S, the magnitude of the shift.

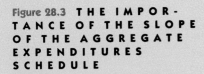

Figure 28.3 THE IMPORTANCE OF THE SLOPE OF THE AGGREGATE EXPENDITURES SCHEDULE

The flatter the aggregate expenditures schedule, the smaller the magnitude of the increase in output resulting from a given upward shift in the schedule.

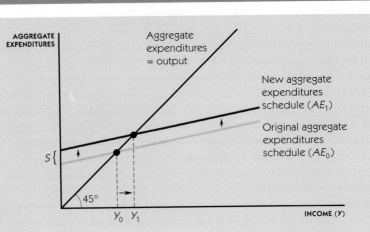

new aggregate expenditures schedule is denoted by AE_1. The equilibrium output increases from Y_0 to Y_1, which is greater than the amount S. How much greater depends on the slope of the aggregate expenditures schedule, as we see in Figure 28.3. Here the aggregate expenditures schedule shifts up by the same amount it did in Figure 28.2. In Figure 28.3, however, the aggregate expenditures schedule is flatter; consequently, the increase in equilibrium output is much smaller.

INCOME-EXPENDITURE ANALYSIS

1. Equilibrium output is at the point where the aggregate expenditures schedule equals output (income).

2. Upward shifts in the aggregate expenditures schedule result in increases in equilibrium output. The increases in equilibrium output are larger than the initial shift in the aggregate expenditures schedule, and become larger when the slope of the aggregate expenditures schedule increases.

We have just learned two of the central principles of macroeconomics: that shifts in the aggregate expenditures schedule determine changes in the equilibrium output of the economy, and that the magnitude of those changes is greater than the magnitude of the shift up or down in the aggregate expenditures schedule and increases with the slope of the aggregate expenditures schedule. The remainder of this chapter, as well as the following two chapters, is devoted to exploring in depth the implications of these principles. Two questions are addressed:

First, what determines the slope of the aggregate expenditures schedule—that is, the extent to which aggregate expenditures increase as income increases? As we have seen, the greater that slope, the larger the increase in output from any upward shift in the schedule.

Second, what causes shifts in the aggregate expenditures schedule? And what, if anything, can the government do to shift the schedule? This is an important question. In the last chapter, we saw that unemployment is created when there is a shift in the demand curve for labor without a corresponding downward adjustment of wages. The primary reason for a shift in the demand curve for labor is a change in the equilibrium level of output: when output is low, the demand for labor is low. If the government can increase the equilibrium level of output by somehow shifting the aggregate expenditures schedule, then it can increase the level of employment.

To answer these questions, we need to take a closer look at each of the components of aggregate expenditures. Recall from Chapter 25 that we can break aggregate expenditures into four components, corresponding to the four final users of the goods produced by the economy: consumption goods, such as food, television sets, or clothes, all of which are purchased by consumers; investment in capital goods, machines or buildings that are bought by firms to help them produce goods; government purchases, goods and services bought either for current use (public consumption) or, like government buildings and roads, for the future benefits they generate (public investment); and net exports.

Exports, the demand by foreigners for American goods, increase the total demand for goods produced in the United States at each level of income. At the same time, we have to remember that some of the demand for goods by consumers, firms, and government is not a demand for goods produced in the United States, but is rather a demand for goods produced abroad. Because we want to know how much will be produced in the United States, we need to subtract off this amount. Thus, in calculating aggregate expenditures we add exports but subtract imports.

Using AE for aggregate expenditures, C for consumption spending, I for investment spending, G for government spending, and E for net exports, we can set out the components of aggregate expenditures in equation form.

$$AE = C + I + G + E.$$

This equation is nothing more than a definition. It says that consumption spending, investment spending, government spending, and net exports add up to aggregate expenditures. Net exports is sometimes written as $X - M$, where X stands for exports and M for imports. These innocuous-looking symbols represent near-astronomical numbers for the U.S. economy. In 1990, AE was \$5,463 billion, of which C was \$3,658 billion, I was \$745 billion, G was \$1,098 billion, X was \$670 billion, and M was \$708 billion.

We now take a brief look at each of these categories.

CONSUMPTION

The most important determinant of consumption is income. On average, families with higher incomes spend more. What they do not consume, they save. And on average, families with higher incomes also save more. Someone with an income of \$20,000 may

Table 28.1 RELATION-SHIP BETWEEN INCOME AND CONSUMPTION

Income	Consumption
$ 5,000	$ 6,000
$10,000	$10,500
$20,000	$19,500
$30,000	$28,500

save a little; someone with $30,000 will save even more. A person with less than $10,000 is likely to dip into savings or borrow (if she can); she has negative savings.

Table 28.1 shows the relationship between consumption and income for a hypothetical family. The same information is depicted graphically in Figure 28.4A, with the amount of consumption given along the vertical axis and income along the horizontal axis. The upward slope of the line indicates that consumption for this family increases as income does. The relationship between a household's consumption and its income is called its **consumption function**. Every family has different consumption patterns because the tastes and circumstances of families differ, but the pattern shown in Table 28.1 is typical.

Aggregate consumption is the sum of the consumption of all the households in the economy. Just as when a typical family's income rises its consumption increases, when

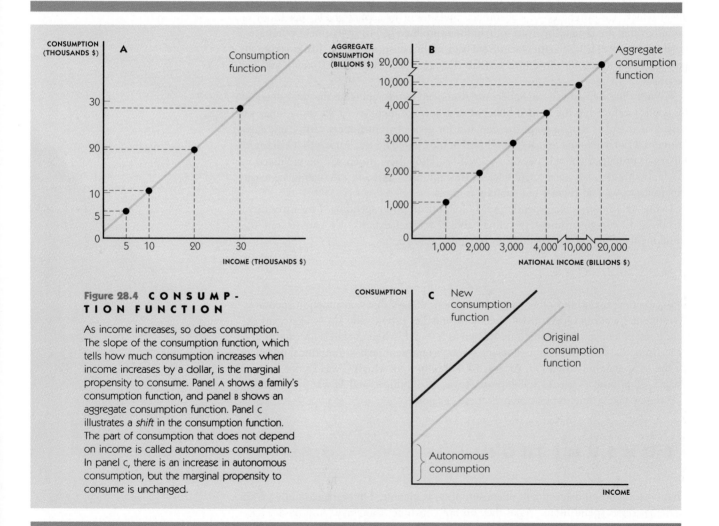

Figure 28.4 CONSUMP-TION FUNCTION

As income increases, so does consumption. The slope of the consumption function, which tells how much consumption increases when income increases by a dollar, is the marginal propensity to consume. Panel A shows a family's consumption function, and panel B shows an aggregate consumption function. Panel C illustrates a *shift* in the consumption function. The part of consumption that does not depend on income is called autonomous consumption. In panel C, there is an increase in autonomous consumption, but the marginal propensity to consume is unchanged.

the total income of the economy rises, aggregate consumption increases. For purposes of macroeconomics, it is the **aggregate consumption function**, the relationship between aggregate consumption and aggregate income, that is of importance. And the measure of income that is important is disposable income, or what people have after paying taxes.[3] The relationship between aggregate consumption and aggregate income is given in Table 28.2, and the aggregate consumption function is depicted graphically in Figure 28.4B.

THE MARGINAL PROPENSITY TO CONSUME

The amount by which consumption increases when disposable income increases by a dollar is called the **marginal propensity to consume** (*MPC*). For the United States as a whole, the marginal propensity to consume in recent years has been somewhere between .9 and .97. That is, of each extra dollar of income households receive, they spend on average between 90 and 97 percent.[4] If aggregate income increases by $100 billion, then aggregate consumption will increase by between $90 and $97 billion. In the hypothetical consumption function illustrated in Figure 28.4B, the marginal propensity to consume is .9: when disposable income goes up by $1 trillion, aggregate consumption goes up by $900 billion.

The slope of the aggregate consumption function conveys important information. It tells us by how much aggregate consumption (measured along the vertical axis) rises with an increase of a dollar of aggregate disposable income (horizontal axis). In other words, the slope of the aggregate consumption function is the marginal propensity to consume. In panels A and B of Figure 28.4, the fact that consumption increases as income rises is reflected in the upward slope of the consumption function, and the marginal propensity to consume is equal to this slope. Flatter slopes would illustrate lower marginal propensities to consume.

John Maynard Keynes stressed the primary role of current disposable income in determining current consumption, and accordingly, the consumption function upon which this chapter focuses is sometimes referred to as the **Keynesian consumption function.** But aggregate consumption depends on other factors besides current disposable income. For example, higher interest rates might cause people to save more (consume less). If people sense hard times on the horizon, they may cut back their consumption now even if their income goes up.

Figure 28.4C shows a shift in the consumption function. The intercept with the vertical axis—the level of consumption that would prevail even if disposable income were zero—is increased. This part of consumption, which does not depend on the level of income, is sometimes called **autonomous consumption**. With the shift depicted in the figure, the marginal propensity to consume remains unchanged; that is, the slope of the consumption function is the same. Sometimes both autonomous consumption and the marginal propensity to consume change. In the late 1980s, the level of autonomous consumption and the marginal propensity to consume both appeared to be higher than in previous decades.

Table 28.2 **AGGREGATE CONSUMPTION AND NATIONAL INCOME (billions of dollars)**

Disposable income	Consumption (C)
$ 1,000	$ 1,050
2,000	1,950
3,000	2,850
4,000	3,750
6,500	6,000
10,000	9,150
20,000	18,150

---

[3] See Chapter 25 for a slightly expanded discussion of disposable income.
[4] In the late 1980s, consumption was sometimes as high as 97 percent of household income. More recently, consumption has been somewhat lower. These statistics give the *average* ratio of consumption to disposable income. The *marginal* propensity to consume is somewhat smaller.

As usual, we have to be careful to distinguish between changes in consumption that result from *movements along a consumption function*—the increase in consumption that results from higher incomes—and changes in consumption that result from a *shift in the consumption function*. Chapter 29 will discuss some of the factors that lead to shifts in the consumption function.

THE MARGINAL PROPENSITY TO SAVE

Individuals have to either spend or save each extra dollar of disposable income, so savings and consumption are mirror images of each other. The definition income = consumption plus savings tells us that when disposable income rises by a dollar, if aggregate consumption increases by 90 cents, aggregate savings increase by 10 cents. The higher level of savings stemming from an extra dollar of income is called the **marginal propensity to save** (MPS). This is the counterpart to the marginal propensity to consume, and the two must always sum to one:

marginal propensity to save + marginal propensity to consume = 1.

The high marginal propensity to consume today means that there is a low marginal propensity to save. Fifty years ago, the marginal propensity to consume was smaller than it is today, somewhere between .8 and .9; of each extra dollar of disposable income, between 80 and 90 cents was spent on consumption. By the same token, the marginal propensity to save was larger; between 10 and 20 cents of each extra dollar of disposable income went into savings.

INVESTMENT

In an exceedingly simple economy—one without government, foreign trade, or investment—the aggregate expenditures schedule would match the consumption function. Aggregate expenditures would consist *only* of consumption, and disposable income would, without taxes, exactly equal total output. The consumption function shown in Figure 28.4B and repeated in Figure 28.5 would then constitute the aggregate expenditures schedule. In this simple economy, the slope of the aggregate expenditures schedule would be just the slope of the consumption function—the marginal propensity to consume.

To make a more realistic case, let us include some level of investment in the aggregate expenditures schedule; to keep matters simple, we continue to ignore government and net exports.

In Chapters 9 and 10, we saw that from the household's perspective, the savings and investment decisions are closely related. But the term "investment" is used in two different ways. Households think of the stocks and bonds they buy as investments—financial investments. These financial investments provide the funds for firms to use to buy capital goods—machines and buildings. The purchases of new machines and buildings represent firms' investments, and we refer to these as *real* investments. In macroeconomics, when we refer to investments, we refer to the real, not the financial, investments. Thus, decisions to invest are made by firms.

Though investment may vary from year to year, we assume the level of investment

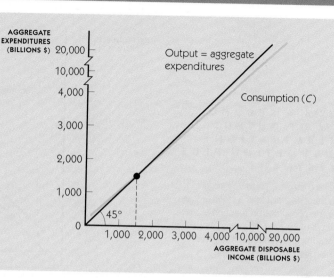

Figure 28.5 A BEGINNING VIEW OF OUTPUT DETERMINATION

In this simplified analysis, aggregate demand consists only of consumption. Equilibrium is at the intersection of the aggregate expenditures schedule (here, just consumption) and the 45-degree line.

is (for the moment) unrelated to the level of income this year. This assumption is made largely to simplify the analysis, but it also reflects the view that investment is primarily determined by firms' estimates of the economic prospects over the future. Accordingly, investment levels are not greatly affected by what happens this year and, in particular, not greatly affected by the level of national income.

Table 28.3 combines the information from Table 28.2 with a fixed level of investment,

Table 28.3 SOME COMPONENTS OF AGGREGATE EXPENDITURES (billions of dollars)

Disposable income (Y_d)	Consumption expenditures (C)	Investment spending (I)	Total aggregate expenditures
$ 1,000	$ 1,050	$500	$ 1,550
2,000	1,950	500	2,450
3,000	2,850	500	3,350
4,000	3,750	500	4,250
6,500	6,000	500	6,500
10,000	9,150	500	9,650
20,000	18,150	500	18,650

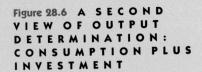

Figure 28.6 A SECOND VIEW OF OUTPUT DETERMINATION: CONSUMPTION PLUS INVESTMENT

Investment is fixed, so the aggregate expenditures schedule is a fixed amount above the consumption function alone. The slope of $C + I$ is the same as that of the consumption function; it is just the marginal propensity to consume.

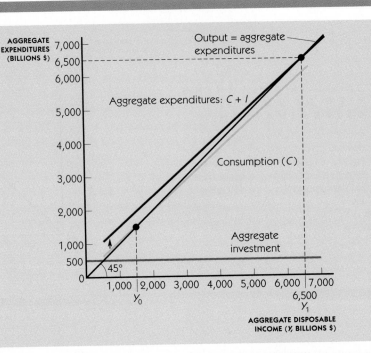

$500 billion. Because we have assumed away government—both taxes and expenditures—disposable income, which we write as Y_d, is the same as national income. The table shows the level of aggregate expenditures for various levels of national income. Now, aggregate expenditures consist of the sum of consumption and investment, shown in the fourth column of the table and plotted in Figure 28.6. Because we assume investment does not depend on current income, the slope of the upper line in the figure is exactly the same as the slope of the consumption function: as income increases, aggregate expenditures increase by the same amount that consumption does, that is, by the marginal propensity to consume. The slope of the aggregate expenditures schedule is still the marginal propensity to consume. The equilibrium—the intersection of the aggregate expenditures schedule and the 45-degree line—is at Y_1 ($6,500 billion).

THE MULTIPLIER

One of the fundamental insights of income-expenditure analysis is that factors shifting the aggregate expenditures schedule will have a compound effect on output. Figure 28.7 depicts the effect of an increase in investment that shifts up the aggregate expenditures schedule. The change in investment, ΔI, produces a greater change in output, the distance from Y_0 to Y_1.

To see why equilibrium output increases by more than the direct increase in investment, consider an economy in which there has been a $1 billion increase in

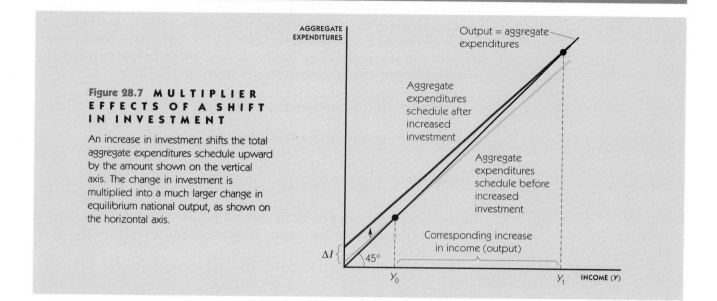

Figure 28.7 MULTIPLIER EFFECTS OF A SHIFT IN INVESTMENT

An increase in investment shifts the total aggregate expenditures schedule upward by the amount shown on the vertical axis. The change in investment is multiplied into a much larger change in equilibrium national output, as shown on the horizontal axis.

investment. We continue to assume that the marginal propensity to consume is .9. The first-round effect of the extra investment spending, shown in Table 28.4, is straight-forward: output increases by $1 billion as firms purchase capital goods. This is only the beginning, however. The value of this increased output is distributed to the members of the economy as income, in the form of either higher wages, higher interest payments, or higher profits that become income to the firms' owners. Given that the marginal propensity to consume is .9, this will lead consumption demand to increase by .9 × $1 billion = $900 million. This second-round effect creates a $900 million increase in output and thus income, which in turn brings on a third-round increase of consumption of .9 × $900 million = $810 million. In the next round, output is increased by .9 × $810,000, then by .9 times that amount, then by .9 times that amount, and so on. In this example, when all the increases are totaled, a $1 billion increase in investment will lead to a $10 billion rise in equilibrium output.

Unfortunately, the multiplier process also works in reverse. Just as an increase in investment leads to a multiple increase in national output, a decrease in investment leads to a multiple decrease in national output. In our example, with an *MPC* of .9, if investment decreases by $1 billion, national output will decrease by $10 billion. The relationship between any change in investment expenditures and the resulting eventual change in national output is called the investment multiplier, or just **multiplier** for short. An increase in government expenditures or net exports has a similar multiplier effect.

The multiplier has a simple mathematical form. It is just $1/(1 -$ marginal propensity to consume). In our example, the marginal propensity to consume is .9; the multiplier is therefore $1/(1 - .9) = 1/.1 = 10$. As the *MPC* increases, $1 - MPC$ gets smaller, and hence the multiplier, $1/(1 - MPC)$, gets larger. Knowing that the marginal pro-

Table 28.4 EFFECTS OF AN INCREASE IN INVESTMENT OF $1 BILLION (millions of dollars)

First round	$ 1,000
Second round	900
Third round	810
Fourth round	729
Fifth round	656
Sixth round	590
Seventh round	531
Eighth round	478
Ninth round	430
Tenth round	387
Eleventh round	349
Sum of twelfth and successive rounds	$ 3,140
Total increase	$10,000

pensity to consume is the slope of the consumption function, we can also see that the lesson of Figure 28.3 is borne out by the multiplier: the steeper the aggregate expenditures schedule, the greater the increase in output resulting from a shift in the schedule.

Now consider the denominator of the multiplier, $1 - MPC$. As we learned earlier, any income an individual does not consume is saved, and an increase of income by a dollar must be spent either on consumption or on savings. Therefore,

$1 - MPC = MPS$, the marginal propensity to save.

This result allows us to rewrite the basic formula for the multiplier:

$$\text{multiplier} = \frac{1}{1 - MPC} = \frac{1}{MPS}.$$

The multiplier is the reciprocal of the marginal propensity to save. If the marginal propensity to consume is .9, the marginal propensity to save is $1 - .9 = .1$, and the multiplier is 10.

THE MULTIPLIER

An increase in investment leads to an increase in output that is a multiple of the original increase.

The multiplier equals $1/(1 - MPC)$, or $1/MPS$.

THE FLATTENING EFFECTS OF TAXES AND TRADE

It is time now to bring government and foreign trade back into the analysis. The basic insights remain the same: changes in government expenditure and net exports lead, through a multiplier, to larger changes in equilibrium output. But as we will see, the value of the multiplier is smaller once the effects of government and trade are taken into account.

THE EFFECTS OF TAXES

Government serves as a double-edged sword in the macroeconomy: its spending increases aggregate expenditures at the same time that its taxes reduce the amount of people's income. Since consumption depends on individuals' disposable income, the amount of income they have available to spend after paying taxes, government taxes also reduce consumption.

Total income equals total output, denoted by Y. Disposable income is simply total income minus taxes, T:

disposable income $= Y - T$.

Taxes do two things. First, since at each level of national income disposable income is lower with taxes, consumption is lower: taxes shift the aggregate expenditures schedule down. Second, when taxes increase with income, the multiplier is lower (the slope of the aggregate expenditures schedule is smaller). This is because when taxes go up with income, when total income increases by a dollar, consumption increases by less than it otherwise would, since a fraction of the increased income goes to government.

Without taxes, when investment goes up by a dollar, income rises by a dollar, which leads to an increase in consumption determined by the marginal propensity to consume. This increase in consumption then sets off the next round of increases in national income. If when income goes up by a dollar government tax collections increase by 25 cents, then disposable income increases by only 75 cents, so the increase in consumption with taxes is one quarter smaller than it is without. If the marginal propensity to consume is .9, then taxes mean that when income goes up by a dollar, consumption increases by $.9 \times (1 - .25) = .9 \times 75$ cents $= 67.5$ cents. Thus, by bringing taxes into the picture, we can see that the consumption function is flatter, as shown in panel A of Figure 28.8.

Because the slope of the aggregate consumption function is flatter, the slope of the aggregate expenditures schedule is flatter, as illustrated in panel B. And because the slope of the aggregate expenditures schedule is flatter, the multiplier is smaller. How much smaller do taxes make the multiplier? With taxes, an increase in before-tax income by a dollar leads to an increase in after-tax income by $(1 - t)$ dollars, where t is the tax rate. An increase in after-tax income increases consumption by the marginal propensity to consume. Hence, the marginal propensity to spend an extra dollar of total income is $(1 - t)MPC$, whereas without taxes, the marginal propensity to spend an extra dollar of total income is just MPC. This means that the multiplier is now $1/\{1 - [(1 - t)MPC]\}$; without taxes, it was just $1/(1 - MPC)$. Thus, with $t = .25$ and $MPC = .9$, the multiplier is $1/[1 - (.75 \times .9)] = 3.08$. By contrast, the multiplier without the income tax is $1/(1 - MPC) = 1/(1 - .9) = 1/.1 = 10$. The difference is significant.

How about government spending? The government's contribution to aggregate expenditures would be much simpler to analyze if its expenditures moved in lockstep with its revenues. We would simply look at the *net* contribution of government to aggregate expenditures, the difference between what it adds as a purchaser of final goods and services and what it subtracts as a consequence of households' reduced consumption. However, the government can spend more than it raises in taxes, by borrowing. When annual government expenditures exceed tax revenues, there is a **deficit**, a commonplace occurrence in many countries in recent years. (When annual government expenditures are less than tax revenues, there is a **surplus**.) There is considerable debate about the effects of deficits, which will be discussed in Chapter 30. For now, we make the simplifying assumption that the deficit has no *direct* effect on either consumption or investment.

We also assume that government expenditures do not increase automatically with

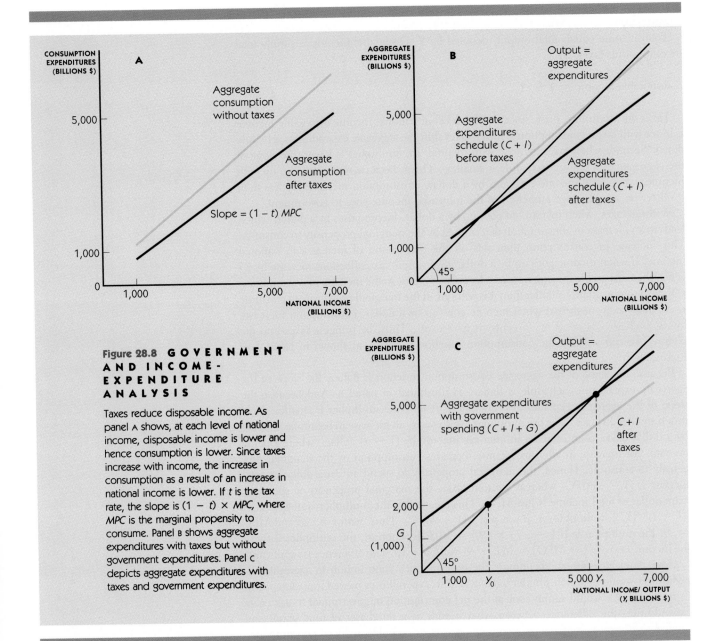

Figure 28.8 GOVERNMENT AND INCOME-EXPENDITURE ANALYSIS

Taxes reduce disposable income. As panel A shows, at each level of national income, disposable income is lower and hence consumption is lower. Since taxes increase with income, the increase in consumption as a result of an increase in national income is lower. If t is the tax rate, the slope is $(1 - t) \times MPC$, where MPC is the marginal propensity to consume. Panel B shows aggregate expenditures with taxes but without government expenditures. Panel C depicts aggregate expenditures with taxes and government expenditures.

the level of income; they are assumed to be simply fixed, say at $1,000 billion. Thus, while taxes shift the aggregate expenditures schedule down and flatten it, government expenditures shift the aggregate expenditures schedule up by the amount of those expenditures, as shown in panel C of Figure 28.8. In this panel, the upward shifts in the aggregate expenditures schedule from government expenditures have been superimposed on the downward shifts in the aggregate expenditures schedule from taxes depicted in panel B. Note that the contributions of investment, I (which are still assumed to be $500 billion), and government expenditures, G, raise the schedule but do not change its slope. The slope in panel C is the same as in panel B, but it is flatter than in an economy with no taxes; as national income increases, the government takes its share in taxes, dampening the increase in consumption. Equilibrium again occurs at the intersection of the aggregate expenditures schedule and the 45-degree line.

The multiplier means that if the government increases its expenditures (keeping taxes fixed), then the effects on national output will be multiplied. Government expenditures can have a powerful effect in stimulating the economy. But if the economy is in a serious recession and the multiplier is low, the government would have to increase expenditures a great deal to raise output to the full employment level. The multiplier also means that changes in investment, autonomous consumption, or net exports can have a strong effect on the economy. A slight decrease in investment results in a drop in national income by a multiple. A low multiplier means that the level of economic activity will be less sensitive to variations in investment.

MULTIPLIER WITH INCOME-RELATED TAXES

$$\text{Multiplier} = \frac{1}{1 - (1 - t)MPC}, \text{ where } t = \text{tax rate.}$$

THE EFFECTS OF INTERNATIONAL TRADE

The analysis so far has ignored the important role of international trade. This is appropriate for a **closed economy**, an economy that neither exports nor imports, but not for an **open economy**, one actively engaged in international trade. Today the United States and other industrialized economies are very much open economies.

International trade can have powerful effects on national output. To begin with, exports expand the market for domestic goods. In recent years, the American economy has exported goods amounting to approximately 7 percent of national output. For smaller countries, exports amount to a much larger percentage of output: 26 percent for the United Kingdom and 12 percent for Japan, for instance.

But just as exports expand the market for domestic goods, imports decrease it. What matters for aggregate expenditures is net exports, and in recent years these have turned sharply negative in the United States. That is to say, imports have exceeded exports. In the late 1980s, net exports amounted to *minus* 2 to 3 percent of U.S. GDP. It is not only that trade has increased in size relative to the economy, but that net exports have changed dramatically, as illustrated in Figure 28.9.

Imports and exports affect the aggregate expenditures schedule in different ways, so it is worth separating them here. First, imports. When households' incomes rise, they not only buy more American-made consumer goods, they also buy more goods from

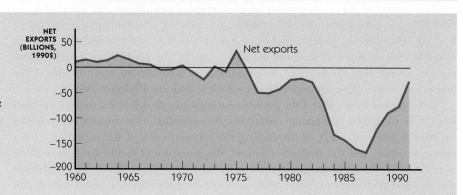

Figure 28.9 U.S. NET EXPORTS SINCE 1960

U.S. net exports were generally positive through the 1960s and 1970s, before turning sharply negative in the 1980s. *Source: Economic Report of the President* (1992), Table B-2.

Table 28.5 IMPORTS AND DISPOSABLE INCOME (billions of dollars)

Disposable income	Imports
$ 1,000	$ 100
2,000	200
3,000	300
4,000	400
5,000	500
10,000	1,000
20,000	2,000

abroad. We can illustrate an **import function** in much the same way that we illustrated a consumption function. (By contrast, we have assumed investment and government expenditures to be fixed, so for now there is no schedule relating either of these to income.) The import function shows the levels of imports corresponding to different levels of income. Table 28.5 shows hypothetical levels of imports for different levels of income. For simplicity, we assume that imports are bought by consumers and that, accordingly, it is disposable income that determines their level. The import function is depicted in Figure 28.10.

Imports increase with income. The **marginal propensity to import** gives the amount of each extra dollar of income spent on imports. If the marginal propensity to import is .1, then if income goes up by $1,000, imports go up by .1 × $1,000 = $100. In Figure 28.10, the marginal propensity to import is given by the slope of the import function.

As for exports, what foreigners buy from the United States depends on the income of foreigners and not directly on income in the United States. Exports may also depend on other factors, such as the marketing effort of American firms and the prices of American goods relative to those of foreign goods. Our focus here is the determination of output in the United States; for simplicity, we assume that these other factors are

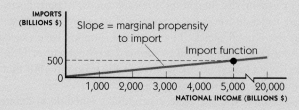

Figure 28.10 THE IMPORT FUNCTION

Imports (*M*) increase steadily as national income (*Y*) rises. The slope of the import function is determined by the marginal propensity to import.

fixed and do not depend on what happens in the United States. In particular, we assume that foreigners' incomes do not depend significantly on incomes in the United States. Hence, the level of exports is taken as fixed at $400 billion, and not dependent on the level of income in the United States.

Exports minus imports are sometimes referred to as the **balance of trade**. Net exports at each level of national income are given in Table 28.6 and shown in Figure 28.11. At very low levels of income, net exports are positive. That is to say, exports exceed

Table 28.6 **NET EXPORTS** (billions of dollars)

Income	Exports	Imports	E (exports — imports)
$ 1,000	$400	$ 100	$ 300
2,000	400	200	200
3,000	400	300	100
4,000	400	400	0
5,000	400	500	− 100
10,000	400	1,000	− 600
20,000	400	1,800	− 1,400

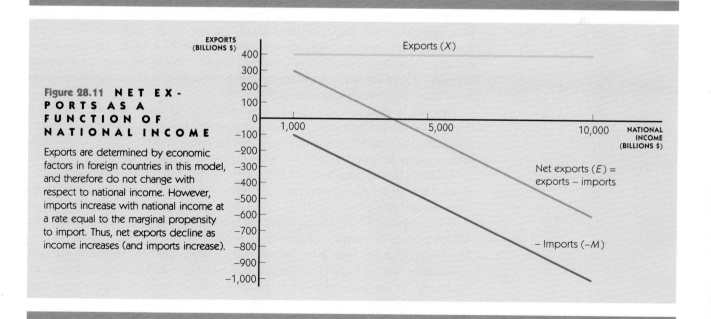

Figure 28.11 NET EX-PORTS AS A FUNCTION OF NATIONAL INCOME

Exports are determined by economic factors in foreign countries in this model, and therefore do not change with respect to national income. However, imports increase with national income at a rate equal to the marginal propensity to import. Thus, net exports decline as income increases (and imports increase).

Table 28.7 AGGREGATE EXPENDITURES SCHEDULE (billions of dollars)

Income	Disposable income	Consumption	Investment	Government	Net exports	Aggregate expenditures
$ 1,333	$ 1,000	$ 1,050	$500	$1,000	$ 300	$ 2,850
2,666	2,000	1,950	500	1,000	200	3,650
4,000	3,000	2,850	500	1,000	100	4,450
5,125	3,844	3,609	500	1,000	16	5,125
5,333	4,000	3,750	500	1,000	0	5,250
13,333	10,000	9,150	500	1,000	− 600	10,050
26,666	20,000	18,150	500	1,000	− 1,400	18,250

Note: The numbers in the table are constructed under the following assumptions: a tax rate of .25, a marginal propensity to consume of .9, and a marginal propensity to import of .1.

imports. As income increases, imports increase, with exports remaining unchanged. Eventually imports exceed exports; the balance of trade becomes negative, as it is now in the United States.

Like taxes, trade has the effect of flattening the aggregate expenditures schedule. This is because as income increases, some of it goes to buy foreign goods rather than domestically produced goods. Hence, aggregate expenditures—spending for goods produced within the country—increase by a smaller amount. When income increases by a dollar in a closed economy, aggregate expenditures increase by the marginal propensity to consume. In an open economy, when income increases by a dollar, aggregate expenditures increase by the marginal propensity to consume *minus* the marginal propensity to import. The difference between the two can be thought of as the marginal propensity to consume domestically produced goods.

This can be seen in Table 28.7, which calculates, for different levels of national income, the level of disposable income, consumption, investment, government expenditures, and net exports. Every time aggregate income increases by $1,333, disposable income increases by only $1,000; and while consumption increases by $900, net exports *fall* (because imports increase) by $100, so the net increase in aggregate expenditures is only $800. In a closed economy with government, aggregate expenditures would have increased by $900.

At an income of $5,333 billion (a disposable income of $4,000), net exports are zero. At higher levels of income, net exports are negative; at lower levels, they are positive. This means that for lower levels of national income, trade has increased aggregate expenditures, and at higher levels of national income, it has decreased aggregate expenditures. At low levels of income, the stimulation provided by exports more than offsets the losses from imports; just the opposite happens at higher levels of income.

In Figure 28.12, the income-expenditure analysis diagram is again used to show how

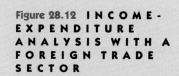

Figure 28.12 **INCOME-EXPENDITURE ANALYSIS WITH A FOREIGN TRADE SECTOR**

Adding exports at a fixed level raises the aggregate demand function. But adding imports makes the slope of the function flatter, since some of national income is now going to buy products produced outside the country. The multiplier is reduced.

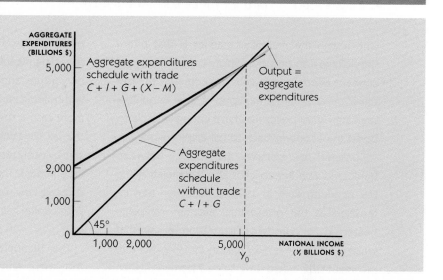

the level of output is determined. As before, the equilibrium condition that output equals aggregate expenditures, $Y = AE$, is represented by the 45-degree line. The aggregate expenditures schedule now sums all of its components: $C + I + G + (X - M)$. The slope of this line is even flatter than in Figure 28.8C, because as income increases, net exports—one of the components of aggregate expenditures—actually decrease. Equilibrium again occurs at the intersection of the aggregate expenditures schedule and the 45-degree line, the output level Y_0 in the figure.

We know that whenever the aggregate expenditures schedule is flattened, the multiplier is lowered. To see precisely how this works in the case of trade, think again about how the multiplier works through various rounds in the economy: the first-round effect of the increase in investment, the second-round effect of the rise in consumption induced by the higher income of those producing the investment goods, the third-round effect of the increase in consumption induced by the higher income of those involved in producing the second round, and so on. But now, when investment rises by $1 billion, the second-round effect is only the increase in consumption of domestically produced goods. If the marginal propensity to consume is .9, the tax rate is .25, and the marginal propensity to import is .1, the increase in *domestically produced* consumption goods is $600 million (not $675 million, as it would be without trade, or $900 million, as it would be without taxes or government).[5] Not only is the second-round effect smaller, so is the third-round effect. The increase of $600 million in the second round leads to increased consumption of domestically produced goods of $360 million in the third round.

[5] Of the $1 billion, the government takes 25 percent, leaving households with $750 million. Households consume 90 percent of this amount, but 10 percent of their income is spent on imports; the implication is that 80 percent of their income is spent on domestically produced consumer goods (.8 × $750 million = $600 million).

CLOSE-UP: MULTIPLIER MUSCLE?

One lesson the multiplier teaches is that critics should take a second look before condemning government efforts to stimulate the economy as "too small." After all, if the multiplier is large enough, a seemingly small policy may have enough muscle to boost the economy back to full employment.

Consider, for example, the conflict between Democrats and Republicans about stimulating the U.S. economy early in 1992, a discussion that intensified as the presidential election campaign heated up. For purposes of illustration, let's say that while U.S. GDP was $5.7 trillion in 1992, full employment GDP would have been 2 percent higher, or an increase of $114 billion.

President Bush fired the first volley in his State of the Union address on January 28. He instructed federal agencies to speed up various federal spending programs, like projects to build roads, as a way of adding $10 billion to the economy during the next six months. He also announced that the amount of federal tax withheld from people's paychecks would be reduced, thus stimulating the economy by another $12 billion over the next six months. Those steps did not require congressional action; they could be taken immediately by the president. Bush then went further and asked Congress to pass tax incentives aimed at investors in real estate, a tax credit for first-time home buyers, a cut in the tax rate on capital gains, and assorted other tax cuts. The president challenged Congress to pass this package by March 20.

Viewed in the rosiest of lights, this package might have totaled about $50 billion. With a multiplier of 2, it would be roughly the right size to move the economy to full employment. But viewed more realistically, many of the provisions packed little

punch. For example, the acceleration in federal spending meant that more would be spent in the near future, and less after that. The reduction in tax withholding meant that taxpayers would have a bit more cash in their hands now, but owe more when the tax bill came due. Since these provisions were so obviously temporary, they seemed likely to have little impact. The tax cuts were also controversial. After all, why did the real estate industry, or people with capital gains, deserve tax cuts more than others?

The Democrat-controlled Congress took over from there. Although it showed a willingness to pass

many of Bush's proposed tax incentives, it also made one major change. It focused the tax breaks on those with annual incomes below $70,000 and raised taxes on wealthier taxpayers. The bill proposed by Congress offered $42 billion in tax cuts—enough with the multiplier to move the economy significantly toward full employment—but then canceled that effect out with $60 billion in tax increases. On March 20, the Congress passed their economic package and sent it to President Bush, who promptly vetoed it, as he had threatened to all along.

In this political waltz, each side blocked the proposals of the other and then sought to blame the other for blocking. But upon close examination, neither side had proposed a package that seemed likely to move the economy toward full employment, not even with the power of the multiplier.

If more of the income generated on each successive round is not spent on goods produced within the country, as is the case here, the multiplier will be smaller. When income generated in one round of production is not used to buy more goods produced within the country, economists say there are **leakages**. Savings and taxes represent leakages in a closed economy. An open economy has three leakages: savings, taxes, and imports.

THE TRADE DEFICIT OF THE 1980s: A CASE STUDY

Income-expenditure analysis can help us understand the effect of a reduction in net exports such as happened in the United States in the 1980s. In 1980, U.S. imports and exports were in very rough balance, as they had been throughout most of the time since World War II. Imports amounted to $294 billion, while exports were worth $279 billion; however, the United States was about to develop a monstrous trade deficit. The level of imports increased dramatically during the 1980s, while exports barely held their own.

By 1985, for example, U.S. exports were $302 billion, only slightly higher than they had been five years before. Imports, on the other hand, had exploded to $417 billion, creating a trade deficit for that year of $115 billion. Some of the rise in imports was due to increased income, but much of it was due to a shift in the import function. At each level of income, Americans were importing more German and Japanese cars, Japanese electronics, Italian and French designer clothes, and so on. By 1990, imports and exports both had continued their climbs, to $625 billion and $550 billion respectively, and the trade deficit was much smaller: $74 billion.

As a result of the decline in net exports in the early 1980s, the aggregate expenditures schedule shifted down, and national output was reduced. If the level of net exports decreases significantly (in the early 1980s, it actually became very negative), the result can be a large reduction in national output and a correspondingly large reduction in employment.

There are two ways of restoring net exports and thus restoring output and employment: increase exports or reduce imports. While there have been efforts in the United States to increase exports—for instance, there have been attempts to persuade the Japanese to make it easier for American firms to sell their goods there—more attention has focused on reducing imports. There have been many proposals to impose tariffs or to restrict imports in other ways, hoping that this action would shift net exports upward. Critics of these proposals argue that they are generally ineffective, because other countries may respond by imposing restrictions on American exports.[6] While tariffs may serve to reduce imports, if foreigners retaliate, tariffs may do the same to exports, and *net* exports may remain relatively unaffected or even be reduced.

This is what happened in the Great Depression. Countries, including the United States, imposed tariffs to reduce their imports in an effort to shift their net export function up. But one country's exports are another country's imports. As other countries responded to the American tariffs by imposing retaliatory tariffs, American exports decreased. These policies aimed at increasing one's national income at the expense of others are often called "beggar thy neighbor" policies. They do not work. The general level of tariffs increases and exports and imports are reduced; however, overall aggregate expenditures are not stimulated and standards of living fall as tariffs stand in the way of each country's taking advantage of its comparative advantage.

There are, however, more constructive ways that government may try to stimulate net exports; they can, for instance, make their products more competitive. Also, throughout this chapter, we have assumed that prices are fixed. The demand by foreigners for American goods depends, of course, on what they have to pay for those goods. What they have to pay is in turn affected by the exchange rate, how many yen or marks or pounds are exchanged for a dollar. Changes in the exchange rate affect net exports. In later chapters, we will learn in more detail how exchange rates affect net exports, and how government policies can affect the exchange rate.

Governments are often faced with the problem of how to stimulate economic activity without worsening the balance of trade. The government might decide to increase aggregate expenditures by increasing government expenditures. But at the higher level of output, net exports may be negative. This is because exports have not changed (they depend on incomes in other countries), but imports have increased as national income has increased.

LIMITATIONS OF THE INCOME-EXPENDITURE APPROACH

This chapter has analyzed the determination of national output by focusing exclusively on the aggregate expenditures schedule, which underlies the aggregate demand curve. But what happened to aggregate supply? Isn't that important too?

Recall that aggregate demand rules the roost when there is excess capacity. That is, changes in aggregate demand alone determine what happens to national output when there are idle machines and workers that could be put to work if only there were sufficient

---

[6] For a more complete discussion of the objections to proposals to restrict trade, see Chapter 3.

demand to purchase the goods they produce. This situation arises when the intersection of the aggregate demand and supply curves occurs along the flat region of the aggregate supply curve. Increases in aggregate demand are translated directly into increases in output, rather than higher prices.[7]

Our analysis has taken the price level as fixed. It has, in other words, calculated the level of output, and aggregate expenditures, at a particular price level. This is appropriate, given our assumption that the economy is operating along the horizontal section of the aggregate supply curve. Increases in aggregate expenditures do not lead to changes in prices. More generally, of course, price levels do change, as the record of inflation makes clear, and in a fuller analysis of the product market we need to know the level of aggregate demand at different price levels. This is what is given by the aggregate demand curve, to which we will return in Chapter 31. There we will see how the analysis of this chapter can be used as a basis for deriving that curve. But before doing so, we need to study more fully the components of the aggregate expenditures schedule—consumption, investment, government expenditures, and net exports. This we do in the next two chapters.

REVIEW AND PRACTICE

SUMMARY

1. Income-expenditure analysis shows how the equilibrium level of output in the economy is determined when there is excess capacity (when the economy is operating along the horizontal part of the aggregate supply curve), so that aggregate demand determines the level of output. Throughout the analysis, the price level is taken as fixed.

2. Equilibrium output is determined by the intersection of the 45-degree line and the aggregate expenditures schedule. The aggregate expenditures schedule shows the level of aggregate expenditures at each level of national income, while the 45-degree line represents the points where aggregate expenditures equal output (income).

3. Shifts in the aggregate expenditures schedule give rise to changes in the equilibrium level of output. The magnitude of the increase in output resulting from an upward shift in the aggregate expenditures schedule depends on the slope of the schedule. Much of macroeconomic analysis focuses on the questions of what determines the slope of the aggregate expenditures schedule, what causes shifts in the schedule, and how government can shift the schedule.

[7] In Chapter 32, we will study another situation in which demand determines output, one involving price rigidities, where the price level is above that at which aggregate demand equals aggregate supply. Firms are willing to produce more, but at the going price level, they cannot sell this increased production. Prices do not decline for some reason, or do not decrease fast enough, so that for a while a situation with excess supply persists. In this situation too, an increase in aggregate demand leads to an increase in output.

4. Aggregate expenditures are the sum of consumption, investment, government expenditures, and net exports. Net exports are the difference between exports and imports.

5. Consumption increases as disposable income increases, and the relationship between income and consumption is called the consumption function. The amount by which consumption increases when disposable income increases by a dollar is called the marginal propensity to consume (MPC). The amount by which savings increase when disposable income increases by a dollar is called the marginal propensity to save (MPS). Since all income must be saved or consumed, the sum of the MPC and MPS must be 1.

6. The multiplier is the factor by which a change in one of the components of aggregate expenditures must be multiplied to get the resulting change in national output. In a simple model without government spending, taxes, or net exports, the multiplier for changes in investment is $1/(1 - MPC)$, or $1/MPS$.

7. Government spending increases aggregate expenditures, and taxes reduce disposable income and therefore consumption. When taxes increase with income, consumption increases by less than it otherwise would, since a fraction of the increased income goes to government. The aggregate expenditures schedule is flatter, and the multiplier is smaller.

8. Exports increase aggregate demand, and imports reduce aggregate demand. Imports increase with income, but exports are determined by factors in other countries. Trade flattens the aggregate expenditures schedule, because as income increases some of it goes to buy foreign rather than domestic goods. As a result, the multiplier is smaller.

KEY TERMS

aggregate expenditures
  schedule
planned and
  unplanned
  inventories
consumption function

marginal propensity to
  consume
autonomous
  consumption
marginal propensity to
  save

multiplier
closed economy
open economy
import function
marginal propensity to
  import

REVIEW QUESTIONS

1. What is the aggregate expenditures schedule? How does it differ from the aggregate demand curve? What are the components of aggregate expenditures?

2. How is the equilibrium level of output determined? Why are points on the aggregate expenditures schedule above the 45-degree line not sustainable? Why are points on the aggregate expenditures schedule below the 45-degree line not sustainable?

3. What is a consumption function? What determines its slope? What is an import function? What determines its slope?

4. What is the consequence of a shift in the aggregate expenditures schedule? Give examples of what might give rise to such a shift.

5. Illustrate the difference between a change in consumption resulting from an increase in income with a given consumption function and a change in consumption resulting from a shift in the consumption function.

6. Why is the sum of the marginal propensity to save and the marginal propensity to consume always 1?

7. Show that the magnitude of the effect of a given shift in the aggregate expenditures schedule on equilibrium output depends on the slope of the aggregate expenditures schedule. What determines the slope of the aggregate expenditures schedule? How is it affected by taxes? by imports?

8. How can changes of a certain amount in the level of investment or government spending have a larger effect on national output? What is the multiplier?

PROBLEMS

1. In the economy of Consumerland, national income and consumption are related in this way:

National income	$1,500	$1,600	$1,700	$1,800	$1,900
Consumption	$1,325	$1,420	$1,515	$1,610	$1,705

Calculate national savings at each level of national income. What is the marginal propensity to consume in Consumerland? What is the marginal propensity to save? If national income rose to 2,000, what do you predict consumption and savings would be?

2. To the economy of Consumerland add the fact that investment will be $180 at every level of output. Graph the consumption function and the aggregate expenditures schedule for this simple economy. What determines the slope of the aggregate expenditures schedule? What is the equilibrium?

3. Calculate the first four rounds of the multiplier effect for an increase of $10 billion in investment spending in each of the following cases:
   (a) a simple consumption and investment economy where the MPC is .9;
   (b) an economy with government but no foreign trade, where the MPC is .9 and the tax rate is .3;
   (c) an economy with an MPC of .9, a tax rate of .3, and a marginal propensity to import of .1.

4. If, at each level of disposable income, savings increase, what does this imply about what has happened to the consumption function? What will be the consequences for the equilibrium level of output?

5. Use the income-expenditure analysis diagram to explain why a lower level of investment, government spending, and net exports all have similar effects on the equilibrium level of output.

6. In a more stable economy (where national output is less vulnerable to small changes in, say, exports), government policy is less effective (changes in government expenditures do not do much to stimulate the economy); in a less stable economy, government policy is more effective. Explain why there is a trade-off between the stability of the economy and the power of government policy.

APPENDIX: THE ALGEBRA OF INCOME-EXPENDITURE MODELS

Many of the ideas presented in this chapter can be expressed using simple algebra. In doing so, we will proceed in steps following those of the text. The first step is to derive an explicit expression for the equilibrium level of income for a simplified economy without government and trade. To do this, we first derive the aggregate expenditures schedule. We can write the consumption function algebraically as

$$C = b + (MPC \times Y),$$

where MPC is the marginal propensity to consume; Y is income (without taxes, "income" and "disposable income" are identical); b is what consumption would be if income were zero—it is the intercept of the consumption function with the vertical axis. (As noted in the text, b is sometimes called autonomous consumption.) Adding the fixed level of investment to consumption, we obtain aggregate expenditures, AE:

$$AE = C + I = b + (MPC \times Y) + I.$$

This relationship says that aggregate expenditures increase as national income rises. More precisely, it says that for each extra dollar of income, aggregate expenditures increase by MPC. If MPC is .9, then if national income rises by \$1 billion, aggregate expenditures increase by \$900 million.

Now we use the national income identity, that income (Y) equals output (GDP), and the equilibrium condition, that aggregate expenditures must equal output ($AE = $ GDP), to obtain

$$Y = b + (MPC \times Y) + I$$
output = aggregate expenditures.

Solving for Y, we obtain

$$Y = \frac{b + I}{1 - MPC}.$$

Notice that for each unit increase in aggregate investment, output will increase by $1/(1 - MPC)$. That is why this figure is called the multiplier.

(To see this, let's evaluate Y at two different values of investment, say \$10 billion and \$11 billion. If Y_0 denotes the first situation and Y_1 the second, we have

$$Y_1 - Y_0 = \frac{b + 11}{1 - MPC} - \frac{b + 10}{1 - MPC} = \frac{1}{1 - MPC}.)$$

Next we introduce government. This increases demand by government expenditures, G, but government taxes mean that disposable income is less than GDP. We rewrite the consumption function to remind us that consumption depends on disposable income:

$$C = b + (MPC \times Y_d),$$

where Y_d is disposable income. For simplicity, we assume the government collects a fixed percentage, t, of income as taxes, so

$$Y_d = (1 - t) \times Y.$$

Using the earlier results, we obtain

$$Y = b + [MPC \times (1 - t)Y] + I + G$$
output = aggregate expenditures;

or, solving for Y,

$$Y = \frac{b + I + G}{1 - (1 - t)MPC}.$$

The multiplier is now $1/[1 - (1 - t)MPC]$.

Finally, we bring in international trade, with exports fixed at X and imports increasing with disposable income:

$$M = MPI \times Y_d$$
$$= MPI \times (1 - t)Y,$$

where *MPI* is the marginal propensity to import. Adding these into aggregate expenditures, we now have

$$Y = b + [MPC \times (1 - t)Y] + I + G + \{X - [MPI \times (1 - t)Y]\}$$
$$= \frac{b + I + G + X}{1 - [(1 - t)(MPC - MPI)]}.$$

An increase in *I* or *G* or *X* will increase *Y* by a multiple amount. The multiplier is now $1/\{1 - [(1 - t)(MPC + MPI)]\}$, lower than in the previous cases.

In our example, with $t = .25$, $MPC = .9$, and $MPI = .1$, the multiplier equals $1/[1 - (.75 \times .8)] = 1/(1 - .6) = 1/.4 = 2.5$. The multiplier is now much smaller than in our first example of a closed economy with no taxes, where the multiplier was $1/(1 - MPC) = 1/(1 - .9) = 1/.1 = 10$; it is even much smaller than in a closed economy with taxes, where the multiplier is

$$1/[1 - (1 - t)MPC] = 1/[1 - (.75 \times .9)] = 1/(1 - .675) = 1/.325 = 3.08.$$

If the tax rate is zero but there are imports, then using the fact that $1 - MPC$ equals the marginal propensity to save, *MPS*, the multiplier becomes simply $1/(MPS + MPI)$, the reciprocal of the *sum* of the marginal propensity to save plus the marginal propensity to import. In our example, the multiplier is $1/(.1 + .1) = 1/.2 = 5$. The multiplier is still large, but smaller than in a closed economy.

CHAPTER 29

CONSUMPTION AND INVESTMENT

Now that we have developed the overall framework of income-expenditure analysis, it is worth taking a closer look at each of the components of aggregate expenditures. Examining them will help us understand both why the level of economic activity fluctuates and what policies the government might pursue to reduce those fluctuations or to stimulate the economy. This chapter takes up consumption and investment; Chapter 30 will consider government spending and net exports.

"You want my opinion. My opinion is that when push comes to shove, it will be more bad news for the consumer."

1. Why may current consumption not be very dependent on current income, and what implications does this have for the use of tax policy to stimulate the economy?

2. What other factors determine the level of aggregate consumption?

3. What are "consumer durables," and why are expenditures on them so volatile?

4. What are the major determinants of the level of investment? What role do variations in real interest rates and the availability of credit play? What role is played by changing perceptions of and the ability and willingness to bear risk?

5. Why is the variability in investment and expenditures on consumer durables so important?

CONSUMPTION

The consumption function presented in Chapter 28 said that the demand for goods and services by households is determined by the level of disposable income: as disposable income goes up, so does consumption. Knowing this year's disposable income, then, an economist can use the consumption function to tell you this year's consumption spending.

This simple consumption function is a good starting point, but it is an incomplete model of consumption behavior. Figure 29.1, which depicts both consumption and income from 1980 to 1991, shows that the relationship between consumption and income is remarkably strong. Income varies from year to year, and so does consumption. If they moved in lockstep as the simple consumption function predicts, however, a straight line could be drawn through all the points in the figure. Clearly, this is not

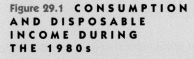

Figure 29.1 CONSUMPTION AND DISPOSABLE INCOME DURING THE 1980s

During the 1980s, there was a remarkably close relationship between disposable income and consumption. *Source: Economic Report of the President* (1992), Tables B-3, B-24.

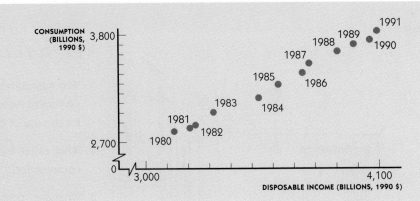

quite possible; further explanation is necessary. Economists have developed several more elaborate theories to explain and predict more precisely changes in consumption. In all of the theories, consumption depends on income, but the theories differ in the exact definition of income that is relevant for determining consumption. They also differ in what other variables besides income are important in determining aggregate consumption.

THE KEYNESIAN CONSUMPTION FUNCTION

The central feature of the Keynesian consumption function is that current consumption depends on current income. To arrive at this conclusion, Keynes took a back-door approach to the question of how much people consume by asking instead what factors cause people to save money. Since savings are by definition what individuals do not consume, he reasoned, figuring out how savings are determined will also show how consumption is determined.

For the most part, people save not simply because the act of saving gives them pleasure. They save because they think they will need the money in the future: for a medical emergency, for retirement, for the down payment on a house, and so on. In short, they save so that they can have more consumption in the future. The decision to save is really a decision of *when* to consume, not whether to consume.

While there are a number of considerations that determine how much an individual saves—whether she is, for instance, saving to send her children through college or to buy a house—in the short run, we can assume that these factors do not change much.[1] Thus, the marginal propensity to save remains constant, which implies that the marginal propensity to consume stays constant as well. To predict changes in consumption from this year to next, we simply need to know the expected change in disposable income,

---

[1] Some of these considerations are discussed at greater length in Chapters 9 and 37.

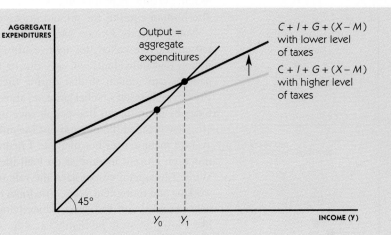

Figure 29.2 A KEYNESIAN CONSUMPTION FUNCTION WITH TAXES

Consumption increases with income. The addition of taxes means that consumption still increases with income, but not as quickly. The 45-degree line shows the points where aggregate expenditures are equal to national output (or income). The figure shows two aggregate expenditures schedules with two different levels of taxes. A decline in taxes raises consumption at each level of national income and hence shifts the aggregate expenditures schedule up.

and we multiply this change in disposable income by the marginal propensity to consume.[2]

The Keynesian consumption function suggests a simple mechanism by which the government can affect aggregate expenditures: it can raise or lower taxes. Figure 29.2 reviews what we learned in Chapter 28. One of the two aggregate expenditures schedules shown corresponds to a high-tax situation. Higher taxes mean lower disposable income, which in turn means lower consumption. The high-tax aggregate expenditures schedule is therefore lower. If the government uses an income tax to raise the additional tax revenue, then there is a further effect: at a higher tax rate, an increase in national income leads to a smaller increase in disposable income and thus a smaller increase in consumption. Accordingly, the aggregate expenditures schedule with higher tax rates is also flatter than the low-tax schedule.

The figure also shows the 45-degree line. The intersection of the aggregate expenditures schedule with the 45-degree line determines the equilibrium level of output. A reduction in taxes leads to an increase in the equilibrium output level from Y_0 to Y_1.

FUTURE-ORIENTED CONSUMPTION FUNCTIONS

In the decades after Keynes' time, many economists questioned Keynes' notion that current consumption depends primarily on current income. They argued that individuals, in making consumption decisions, look to the future. Savings enable a person to

---

[2] In the appendix to Chapter 28, we saw that we could write the Keynesian consumption function as

$$C = b + (MPC \times Y_d),$$

where Y_d is the individual's disposable income, what he has available to spend or save, and b is what consumption would be if income were zero.

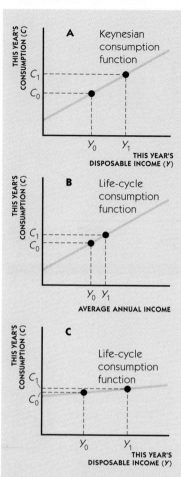

Figure 29.3 EFFECT OF A TEMPORARY INCOME CHANGE IN THE LIFE-CYCLE MODEL

With the Keynesian consumption function, panel A, a temporary change in income results in a large change in consumption. In the life-cycle model, panel B, a temporary change in income has only a small effect on average annual income over a lifetime, and thus leads to only a small change in consumption. Panel C shows how the life-cycle model predicts that consumption will react in response to *this year's income*. Since consumption does not change by much, the life-cycle consumption function is very flat.

make consumption depend not on the vicissitudes of this year's income, but on his total wealth. Wealth here includes not only current capital assets (stocks, bonds, house) but also **human capital**, the present discounted value of expected future wages.

Nobel laureate Franco Modigliani, for instance, emphasized that people save for retirement. He called this motive **life-cycle savings**, a term intended to convey the notion that individuals will save during their working years so that their consumption patterns can remain similar during their retirement years. (See Chapter 9.) Milton Friedman, himself a Nobel laureate, also emphasized how the future affects consumption today by pointing out that people save in good years to carry them through bad years. His view is called the **permanent income hypothesis**. Permanent income is a person's average income over her lifetime. Friedman stressed that consumption depends not so much on current income as on total lifetime income, averaging good years with bad. While Modigliani emphasized the role of savings in smoothing consumption between working and retirement years, Friedman emphasized its role in smoothing consumption between good and bad years. Underlying both views is the notion that people do not like consumption to be highly variable.

These future-oriented theories of savings and consumption have a number of different consequences from the basic Keynesian theory that consumption simply depends on this year's income. Consider an individual who happens to get a windfall gain in income one year—perhaps he wins $1 million in the state lottery. If the marginal propensity to consume is .9, the Keynesian consumption function predicts that he will consume $900,000 of his winnings that year. The future-oriented consumption theories suggest that the lucky winner will spread the extra income over a lifetime of consumption. Similarly, if the government temporarily lowers taxes for one year, the future-oriented consumption theories predict that a taxpayer will not dramatically increase consumption in that year but will spread over his lifetime the extra consumption that the one-year tax reduction allows. They suggest that *temporary* tax changes will be much less effective in stimulating consumption than the Keynesian model predicts.

Figure 29.3 compares the future-oriented consumption function and the Keynesian consumption function for the household. Suppose a household were to have a onetime increase in its disposable income. If consumption responds according to the Keynesian consumption function, it will increase from C_0 to C_1 as shown in panel A.

The future-oriented theories predict that consumption will not change very much. We can see this in two different ways. Panel B shows consumption depending on average disposable income over a person's lifetime. Now the change in this year's income from Y_0 to Y_1 has little effect on average disposable income, and hence little effect on consumption. Panel C puts this year's disposable income on the horizontal axis, as does panel A. The difference between the lines in panels A and C is the difference between Keynes' views and those of the future-oriented theorists. Consumption, in the latter view, is not very sensitive to current disposable income, which is why the line is so flat. Rises in income today increase lifetime income and thus lead to an increase in consumption, but that increase is spread over an individual's life. Today's consumption increases relatively little.

The principle that consumption depends not just on income this year but also on longer-run considerations holds at the aggregate level as well as at the level of the individual. Figure 29.4 shows the implications of future-oriented theories for **aggregate expenditures** and the determination of equilibrium output. Since the relationship between changes in today's income and changes in consumption is weaker than in the Keynesian model, the aggregate expenditures schedule is now much flatter. This in turn has strong implications for the multiplier. An increase in, say, investment, which shifts the aggregate demand curve up, increases equilibrium output by an amount only slightly greater than the original increase in investment. The multiplier is very small.

WEALTH AND CAPITAL GAINS

The future-oriented consumption theories suggest not only that current income is relatively unimportant in determining consumption but also that variables Keynes ignored may be important. For instance, wealthier people consume more (at each level of current income). Since consumption is related to wealth, changes in consumption will be affected by changes in wealth.

The distinction between income and wealth as a determinant of consumption is important. It corresponds to the distinction between flows and stocks. Flows are measured as "rates." Both income and consumption are flow variables. They are measured as dollars *per year*. Wealth is a stock variable.[3] It is measured simply by the total value ("dollars") of one's assets. Future-oriented theories emphasize that there is no reason that an individual's current consumption should be related to his current income. What he consumes should be related to how well off he is, and that is better measured by his wealth.[4] Capital gains, or changes in the value of assets, change an individual's wealth. Thus, these theories predict that when stock or real estate prices rise in value and people expect this change to last for a long time, individuals who own these assets will increase their level of consumption. They will do so because their overall wealth has grown, even if they do not immediately receive any income from the increase in value.

There is some evidence that this is the case. Many economists believe that the stock market crash of 1929, which preceded the Great Depression, contributed to that Depression by generating a downward shift in the consumption function. On the other hand, when the stock market fell by over 22 percent on a single day in October 1987, consumption did not decline sharply in the way one might have expected; people responded only slightly to this capital loss. One reason for this is that individuals respond to changes in wealth only slowly, and in 1987 their consumption had not yet fully responded to the increases in stock market prices that had occurred during the preceding few years. A prolonged and persistent decline in the stock market might, however, have an extremely depressing effect on consumption.

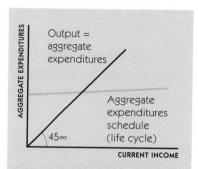

Figure 29.4 THE LIFE-CYCLE MODEL AND DETERMINING NATIONAL OUTPUT

Since changes in today's income have much weaker effects on current consumption in the life-cycle model, the aggregate expenditures schedule is much flatter, which implies that the multiplier is lower.

RECONCILING CONSUMPTION THEORY WITH FACTS

The permanent income and life-cycle hypotheses are convincing theories about how rational households behave. They contain large elements of truth: families do save for their retirement, so life-cycle considerations are important; and households do smooth their consumption between good years and bad, so permanent income considerations are relevant. Nevertheless, household consumption appears to be more dependent on current income than either of these theories would suggest. Two further theories have

[3] Other stock variables in macroeconomics include capital stock; other flow variables include the interest rate.

[4] Future-oriented theories take an expansive view of what should be included in wealth: they include *human capital*, the present discounted value of future wage income. (See Chapter 10 for a discussion of human capital, Chapter 6 for a definition of present discounted value.)

CLOSE-UP: AN EMPIRICAL PUZZLE AND AN INGENIOUS THEORY: FRIEDMAN'S PERMANENT INCOME HYPOTHESIS

The genesis of Milton Friedman's permanent income hypothesis was an empirical puzzle. The story of how he solved it provides a good illustration of insightful economic analysis and the scientific process at work.

When economists plotted aggregate disposable personal income in various years with the corresponding level of aggregate consumption, they obtained a set of points such as those depicted in panel A of the figure. This kind of data suggested a consumption function in which consumption increases roughly proportionately with income. On the other hand, when economists plotted the consumption of different income groups against their current income for any particular year, they obtained a set of points like those depicted in panel B. Households with low incomes consume a much larger fraction of their income than do households

with high incomes. This suggests a consumption function in which consumption increases less than proportionately with income. The two kinds of data thus appear to offer quite different views of the relationship between consumption and income. The problem Friedman set for himself was how to reconcile the data.

His ingenious solution was to say that consumption is related to people's long-term or "normal" income, what he called their permanent income. Friedman observed that people with low incomes included a disproportionate number who were having unusually bad years and were consuming more than one would expect from their one-year income; and correspondingly, those with very high incomes included a disproportionate number having unusually good years and consuming less than one would expect. Individuals having a particularly

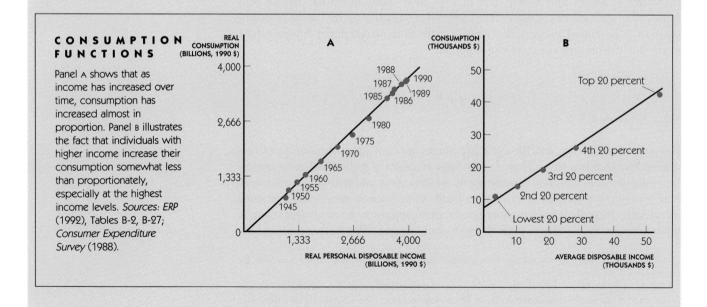

CONSUMPTION FUNCTIONS

Panel A shows that as income has increased over time, consumption has increased almost in proportion. Panel B illustrates the fact that individuals with higher income increase their consumption somewhat less than proportionately, especially at the highest income levels. *Sources: ERP* (1992), Tables B-2, B-27; *Consumer Expenditure Survey* (1988).

bad year did not reduce their consumption proportionately; those having a particularly good year did not increase their consumption proportionately. Friedman was thus able to explain how, over time, aggregate consumption could rise in proportion to income for the population as a whole even though the consumption of any particular household increased less than proportionately with current income.

Stanford University economist Robert Hall has pointed out an unsettling consequence of the permanent income hypothesis. Hall noted that the level of consumption a person chooses depends on permanent income, which incorporates all information about what future expected wages and other income will be. Changes in consumption are accordingly related only to *unexpected* changes. By definition, unexpected changes are random and unpredictable. (If they were predictable, they would be part of expected income.) Thus, the permanent income theory predicts that changes in consumption are largely random and unpredictable, which is not good news for economists trying to understand and forecast such patterns.

been advanced to help reconcile the future-oriented hypotheses with the facts. They have to do first with distinguishing the consumption of durable goods from that of nondurable goods, and second with the likelihood that it may not be as easy for an individual to borrow money as the future-oriented theories would have it.

DURABLE GOODS

The discussion so far has not distinguished between different categories of consumption goods—between refrigerators and groceries, between cars and airplane trips, between furniture and medical insurance. However, the distinction between **durable goods**, refrigerators, cars, and furniture, and **nondurable goods**, groceries, airplane trips, and insurance, is an extremely important one. The purchase of durable goods is more in the nature of an *investment* decision than a consumption decision. These goods are bought for the services that they render over a number of years. If you buy groceries, you eat them in a week. But a refrigerator lasts for years.

What people consume each year of a durable good can be described as the services of the good: one year's worth of transportation by car, one year's worth of a place to live, one year's worth of refrigeration for food, and so on. The decision to buy a durable good is thus affected by the kinds of considerations that are part of any investment decision. Three of these considerations are worth noting here.

1. If the real interest rate increases, it becomes more expensive for people to borrow to buy a car (or other durable good), and this discourages car purchases.

2. If credit becomes less available—if banks, for instance, refuse to make car loans to any but those with the best credit history—again, purchases of cars and other big-ticket items that many consumers buy on credit will decrease.

3. Uncertainty about future income is also extremely important. If individuals think there is some probability of losing work or being laid off, the uncertainty will cause them to be less likely to take on payments for a new car.

Decisions to postpone purchasing a durable good have quite different consequences from decisions not to buy food or some other nondurable. If you do not buy strawberries

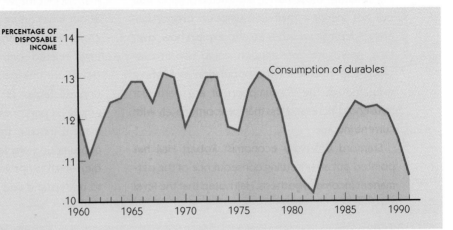

Figure 29.5 VARIABILITY IN PURCHASES OF DURABLE GOODS

The consumption of durable goods fluctuates considerably from year to year, much more than consumption as a whole. *Source: ERP* (1992), Tables B-2, B-25.

today, you will have to do without them. But in most cases, not buying a durable does not mean you will do without the durable. It simply means that you will have to make do with the services provided by an older durable. The costs of postponing the purchase of a new car are often relatively low; you can make do with an old car a little bit longer. However, the benefits of postponing the purchase may be significant.

Given these considerations, it should be no surprise that purchases of durable goods vary a great deal, not only from year to year but also relative to income. Figure 29.5 traces the purchases of durables as a percentage of disposable income during the postwar period. Notice how variable these purchases have been. These fluctuations in purchases of durables, together with the variations in investment, seem to account for much of the variation in economic activity over the business cycle. Meanwhile, variations in the services provided by durable goods—and hence in true consumption—are much smaller.

Thus, when a household's income is temporarily low, rather than borrowing to maintain a steady pattern of purchases of durables, the household simply postpones the purchase of a durable good. This makes aggregate expenditures depend critically on current income.

CREDIT RATIONING

Empirical studies focusing on nondurables show that even nondurable consumption expenditures seem more dependent on current income than the future-oriented theories suggest. These theories, in particular the permanent income hypothesis, assume that when an individual has a bad year, he can maintain his consumption at a steady level. They assume, in other words, either that the household has a large stock of savings to draw on while its income is temporarily low or that the household can easily borrow.

For many people, neither of these conditions is likely to be true. Most individuals, even in the United States, have few liquid assets upon which they can draw. They may have considerable savings tied up in a pension scheme, but they cannot draw upon these until they retire. They may have some equity in their house, but the last thing they want to do is sell their home. Moreover, it is precisely in times of need, when a person is unemployed or a business is doing badly, that banks are least forthcoming with funds. (As the saying goes, banks only lend to those who don't need the money!)

In short, many individuals are credit rationed, meaning that the unavailability of credit limits their options.[5] When their income declines, they have to reduce their consumption. When people have no assets and they are credit rationed, cutting back on consumption when income declines is not a matter of choice. For these individuals, consumption depends heavily on current income.

If people were not credit rationed, short-term unemployment would not be as important a problem as it appears to be. The suffering caused by temporary layoffs would be much less. To see why this is so, we need to look again at the concept of total wealth. Assume, for instance, that a fellow named Evan will work for forty years, that his initial salary is $25,000 per year, that his salary increases in real terms at 5 percent per year, and that 5 percent is the real rate of interest. Then the present discounted value of his lifetime earnings is $1 million. This is his wealth, assuming that he has no unexpected windfall, no inheritance from his great-aunt, and no other assets. Imagine that Evan loses his job and is unemployed for half a year. At first glance, that looks like a personal calamity. But upon closer inspection, we see that it represents a loss of only a bit more than 1 percent of his lifetime wealth.

If Evan could borrow six months' pay, he would have no trouble paying it back, and the period without work would be no tragedy—his life-style would be constrained, but insignificantly. Since he would have to cut expenditures by only a bit more than 1 percent, cutting out a few movies, a fancy restaurant meal or two, and a few other activities would do the trick. However, for most people, losing a job for half a year would in fact be a major disaster, not because of the reduction in total lifetime wealth, but because most individuals face important constraints on the amount they can borrow. Without a job, they cannot obtain loans, except possibly at very high interest rates. Because of these credit constraints, for most lower- and many middle-income individuals, the traditional Keynesian consumption function is all too relevant. When their current income is reduced, their consumption is perforce reduced.

MACROECONOMIC IMPLICATIONS OF CONSUMPTION THEORIES

The alternative theories of consumption we have explored so far have two sets of macroeconomic implications. First, the future-oriented theories of consumption, in arguing that consumption does not depend heavily on current income, maintain that the aggregate expenditures schedule is flat and therefore, as we saw in Chapter 28, the multiplier is low. This is both good news and bad news for the economy. It is good news because the small multiplier means that decreases in the level of investment lead

---

[5] Credit rationing occurs when people are unable to obtain funds at the market rate of interest, which reflects the risks associated with lending to them. We saw in Chapter 21 why there might be rationing in credit markets. Frequently there is limited availability of credit through banks; individuals who might be able to obtain credit from a bank at other times, when credit is more readily available, are turned down. Some of these people could obtain funds from other sources at substantially higher interest rates, and this discourages them from borrowing.

to much smaller decreases in the level of national income than they would if the multiplier were large. It is bad news because it means that government attempts to stimulate the economy through temporary reductions in taxes, or to dampen an over-heated economy through temporary increases in taxes, will not be as effective as they would be if the multiplier were larger.

Second, by identifying other determinants of consumption, future-oriented theories help explain why the ratio of consumption to disposable income may shift from year to year. Expectations concerning future economic conditions, changes in the availability of credit, or variations in the price of houses or shares of stock are among the factors that can give rise to such shifts in the consumption function. These shifts in turn give rise to larger variations in the equilibrium level of national output. Indeed, they help explain how a slight downturn in economic activity can become magnified. With a downturn, consumers may lose confidence in the future. They worry about layoffs, and cut back on purchases of durables. At the same time, banks, nervous about the ability of borrowers to repay loans should the downturn worsen, become more restrictive; even those adventurous souls who are willing to buy a new car in the face of the uncertain future may find it difficult to find a bank willing to lend to them. The net effect is a downward shift in the consumption function, exacerbating the initial decline in national income.

ALTERNATIVE THEORIES OF CONSUMPTION

1. Keynesian consumption function: stresses the dependence of consumption on current income

2. Future-oriented consumption theories: stress the dependence of consumption on total lifetime wealth and the role of savings in smoothing consumption

    a. Life-cycle theory: stresses the importance of savings for retirement
    b. Permanent income theory: stresses the role of savings in smoothing consumption between good and bad years
    c. Implications
        i. Consumption not very dependent on current income: small multipliers
        ii. Consumption sensitive to capital gains and losses

3. Explanations of why consumption seems to be more dependent on current income than future-oriented theories predict

    a. The importance of durable goods
    b. Credit constraints

INVESTMENT

Investment may come second in the $C + I + G + (X - M)$ list of components of the aggregate expenditures schedule, but variations in the level of investment are probably the principal culprit in causing variations in aggregate expenditures, and hence in national output. Just how volatile investment is can be seen in Figure 29.6. In recent years, investment has varied from 13 to 18 percent of GDP.

The investment spending relevant for aggregate expenditures includes three broad categories. The first is firms' purchases of new capital goods, which includes, besides buildings and machines, the automobiles, cash registers, and desks that firms use; these comprise the **plant and equipment** portion of overall investment. Firms also invest in inventories as they store their output in anticipation of sales or store the raw materials they will need to produce more goods. This is the **inventory** portion of investment. The third category consists of households' purchases of new homes. The purchases of previously owned capital goods or houses do not count, because they do not increase output. (Households' financial investments such as stocks and bonds are a related but different concept. Usually when an individual buys, say, a share of stock, she buys it from someone else. She makes an investment, but someone else makes a "disinvestment." There is simply a change in who owns the economy's assets. There is, however, a close relationship between investment in new capital goods and the capital market in general: when firms issue new shares or borrow funds by issuing bonds, they procure the resources with which to purchase new capital goods. This is why the financial investment discussed in Chapter 10 and the *real* investment discussed here are closely linked.)

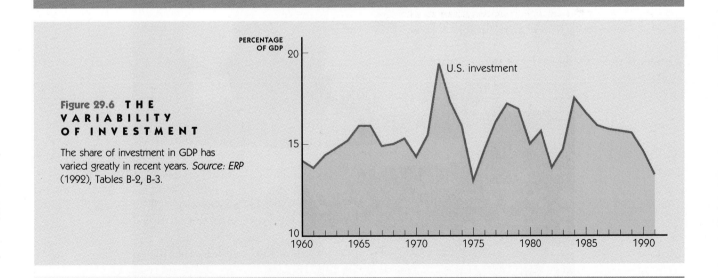

Figure 29.6 THE VARIABILITY OF INVESTMENT

The share of investment in GDP has varied greatly in recent years. *Source: ERP* (1992), Tables B-2, B-3.

CLOSE-UP: THE CORPORATE VEIL

When firms have money left over after paying all their bills, they can either use the funds to pay dividends to stockholders or retain the earnings and invest them. Retained earnings can be thought of as savings done by firms. The table here divides U.S. savings in 1990 into the categories of private (personal and business) and government. Notice that savings done by firms is more than triple the savings of households.

When firms save through retained earnings, they may invest in new plant and equipment, reduce their indebtedness (by paying off loans or buying their own bonds), or buy government securities and those of other firms. But in each case, the future profits of the firm should be higher as it receives a return from this investment, and anticipation of these higher profits should raise the price of shares of stock in the firm. Shareholders should accordingly feel wealthier, and strictly rational shareholders will treat this increase in the value of their stock

the same as they would if they had saved the money personally. It is as if the firm saved on their behalf.

This line of analysis is plausible enough in theory, but it poses a number of questions. Do people in fact perceive what is happening inside the corporation? In the term economists often use, do they see through the "corporate veil"? Do shareholders react so that the prices of shares of stock fully reflect corporate savings? Do the shareholders then incorporate these wealth changes and savings into their overall savings decisions? Recent economic theories have emphasized that shareholders have imperfect information concerning what goes on inside the firm, and it is thus not surprising that they have only blurry vision through the corporate veil.

The extent to which individuals see through the corporate veil is important, because it will affect the size of the multiplier. Assume that the government is successful in stimulating investment. But assume also that firms finance that investment by

increasing their retained earnings, forgoing an increase in dividends. If people do not see through the corporate veil, they may only perceive that their dividends have not increased, without fully realizing that the corporation is putting their money into productive investments. If the low dividends lead individuals to reduce their consumption from what it otherwise would have been, then the total increase in aggregate demand resulting from the increase in investment will be much smaller than predicted by traditional Keynesian theory.

As a final example of the importance of the corporate veil, consider the Tax Reform Act of 1986. This act reduced taxes levied on individuals and increased taxes on corporations by a corresponding amount (roughly $120 billion over a five-year period). Those who believed that people can see through the corporate veil argued that the increase in individuals' disposable income would have little effect, since they would realize that total tax burdens had remained unchanged. However, consumption did seem to increase somewhat, implying that a corporate veil does exist.

Source: Economic Report of the President (1992), Table B-26.

Savings by Sector in 1990

		% of total savings
Gross savings	$711 billion	100
Gross private savings	$850 billion	119
Personal savings	$206 billion	29
Gross business savings	$644 billion	91
Government savings	−$139 billion	−19
Federal	−$165 billion	−23
State	$ 26 billion	4

We restrict our focus in this part of the chapter to the two portions of investment done by business firms. Houses can be viewed as very long-lived durable consumption goods—and the principles discussed earlier in the chapter governing the demand for durables apply equally to consumers' demand for new housing.

Business investment is quite volatile. Since decreases in investment are often the source of an economic downturn, it is no surprise that when the government wishes to increase aggregate expenditures to stimulate the economy and reduce unemployment, it often tries to induce increases in business investment. We are concerned here with three questions: what determines the level of investment, why is it so variable, and how does the government influence it? We direct these questions first to firms' investment in plant and equipment, and then to firms' investment in inventories.

INVESTMENT IN PLANT AND EQUIPMENT

Firms invest in new plant and equipment because they expect that the future production that will result from the investment will earn them a profit. The fact that investments yield their returns over a long period of time gives rise to two problems in firms' investment decisions. The first is that businesses must make predictions about their products: future prices, future demand, and future production costs. They must try to imagine whether changes such as new inventions or new products will make this investment obsolete too quickly. Would the company be better off buying a computer today or waiting to see if a still better computer is marketed next year? If the new product is one that appeals especially to teenagers or to the elderly, how many people will be in that group in the next ten or fifteen years? Forming these judgments is a central part of the responsibility of the firm's management, though they often rely heavily on economic consultants.

The second problem is that firms must evaluate income and expenses occurring at different dates. Chapter 6 showed how to calculate the present discounted value of a project. A dollar today is worth more than a dollar next year or the year after; firms must discount future receipts and costs in their calculations. They also need to look through the illusions created by inflation and figure *real* profits. Accordingly, we can think of firms proceeding in two steps when evaluating the desirability of a project. First, they convert all future expenditures and receipts into dollars of constant purchasing value. Then they calculate the present discounted value, using the *real* interest rate.[6]

In our analysis, we will begin by assuming the firm has some well-defined projects. It knows how much each costs and what the return each year will be. The critical question is whether the firm can obtain the funds to finance the projects, and what it will have to pay for those funds. We then turn to factors that determine the company's forecasts of the returns it will receive in coming years.

CHANGES IN THE REAL INTEREST RATE

Keynes first formulated the income-expenditure analysis we are investigating, so it should come as no surprise that we again begin with Keynes' views. While Keynes focused on disposable income as the primary determinant of consumption, he concentrated on interest rates as the primary determinant of investment.

The **investment schedule** describes the total value of investment that firms would like to undertake at each rate of interest. In general, an increase in the real interest rate, the interest rate adjusted for inflation, decreases the level of investment. This is because of present discounted value. The firm invests money today in the expectation of returns in the future. An increase in the real interest rate means that those future profits, valued as of today, are worth less; to put it another way, in calculating the present discounted value of a project, the future profits of the firm must be divided by a larger number. The present discounted value of the project is reduced.

The interest rate represents the "cost" of funds to the firm. When the interest rate is

---

[6] Recall that the real interest rate is just the nominal interest rate minus the rate of inflation. If banks charge 10 percent interest on their loans and the rate of inflation is 4 percent, then the real interest rate is 6 percent. See Chapter 6.

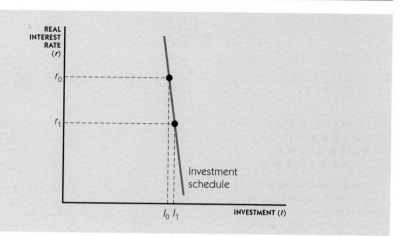

Figure 29.7 THE INVEST-MENT SCHEDULE

The number of investment projects that have a positive present discounted value increases as the real rate of interest falls. As the real rate of interest declines from r_0 to r_1, investment increases from I_0 to I_1. However, at least in recessions and depressions, the relationship is probably inelastic, so that relatively large changes in the real interest rate will have little effect on the level of investment.

higher, it costs the firm more to borrow. Alternatively, when the interest rate is higher, a firm with funds can obtain a higher return simply by buying a government Treasury bill. A higher interest rate represents a higher opportunity cost of funds. When the cost of funds is higher, only the better projects are worth undertaking. In other words, the higher the interest rate, the fewer the investment projects that are worthwhile.

Figure 29.7 depicts the investment schedule. As the real rate of interest declines from r_0 to r_1, investment increases from I_0 to I_1. The difference in the level of investment represents investment in projects that are profitable at the lower interest rate but not profitable at the higher interest rate. The fact that investment depends on interest rates suggests that government can stimulate the economy by lowering interest rates, thereby increasing investment.

Keynes, having recognized the link between investment and the interest rate, also observed that, at least in recessions and depressions, this may be difficult. There are two reasons. First, it may be difficult to lower the *real* interest rate. And second, because the investment schedule is inelastic—as shown in Figure 29.7, the investment schedule is almost vertical—the interest rate must be lowered a great deal to have a big effect on investment and hence on aggregate expenditures.

While they recognize the overall importance of real interest rates, economists have become increasingly skeptical of their role in explaining many of the short-term variations in investment. Indeed, there is little correspondence between interest rate variation and investment. Figure 29.8A shows the real interest rates during the period from 1954 to 1969 that would have been relevant for a firm borrowing for a five-year investment. Note that real interest rates varied little, by not more than 2 percentage points over this period of sixteen years. In the same figure, we see the fluctuations in investment for the same period. The message of this figure is that investment fluctuations were due to factors *other* than the interest rates.

Looking at real interest rates and investment over a broader span of time, as displayed in panel B, we see that real interest rates have fluctuated much more over the longer run, but again, the fluctuations do not appear to be closely linked with changes in

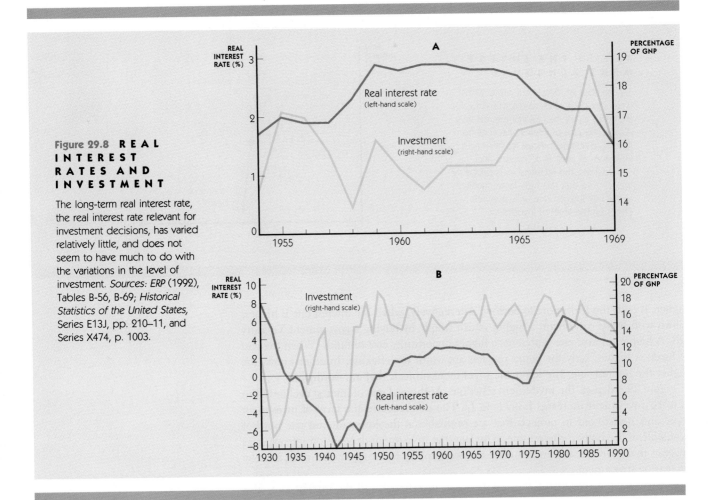

Figure 29.8 REAL INTEREST RATES AND INVESTMENT

The long-term real interest rate, the real interest rate relevant for investment decisions, has varied relatively little, and does not seem to have much to do with the variations in the level of investment. *Sources: ERP* (1992), Tables B-56, B-69; *Historical Statistics of the United States,* Series E13J, pp. 210–11, and Series X474, p. 1003.

investment.[7] Much of the variation in real interest rates falls into three episodes: the Great Depression, the 1940s, and the early 1980s. The variations again seem to bear little relationship to the fluctuation in investment. In particular, relatively high levels of real interest rates in the 1980s do not seem to be associated with especially low levels of investment, and the fluctuations in investment are not well accounted for by changes in the real interest rate.

The fact that small variations in real interest rates have relatively little effect on investment is not surprising; given the uncertainty involved in any investment project, a change in the real interest rate from, say, 5 percent to 4 percent will not alter many investment decisions. To be on the safe side, firms typically require that their rough calculations show a 15 to 25 percent (real) return on an investment project before they are willing to undertake it. They know from sad experience that if they insist on this

---

[7] If we extend the analysis back still further in time, to the nineteenth century, we observe very long periods—decades—with almost no variation in real interest rates.

high level of return, they will in fact be fairly certain of actually obtaining a return of only 8 to 10 percent, enough to compensate them for their time, effort, and resources. A change in the real rate of interest from 5 percent to 4 percent will have little impact on the decision to go ahead with a project yielding 25 percent; at either interest rate, the project will look enormously profitable.

To make matters worse, what is of concern to the firm is not the real interest rate for borrowers for a month or a quarter, but real interest rates over the life of the project. Thus, even were the government temporarily successful in changing the short-term real interest rate, the long-term real interest rate may be little affected. This is what happened in the spring of 1992: the Fed succeeded in lowering short-term interest rates by 1 percentage point, but long-term interest rates hardly budged.

CHANGES IN THE PRICE OF SHARES IN THE STOCK MARKET

Nobel laureate James Tobin of Yale University has argued that what affects a firm's investment is not so much the interest rate, but the price of shares in the stock market relative to the value of its machines and other assets. This ratio is called "Tobin's q." When Tobin's q is high, as in a stock market boom, issuing new shares is an attractive prospect to firms.

In statistical studies conducted over the past decade, this theory has fared only moderately well. True, in general, when Tobin's q is high, investment is high, but the relationship is much weaker than Tobin's theory predicts. Perhaps this is because firms do not rely much on the stock market to raise additional capital.

More troubling is the view that the relationship between share prices and investment is not causal. We learned in Chapter 1 that correlation does not prove causation. Here is a good example. When a firm's prospects are good, investors will bid up the price of its shares. And under the same circumstances, managers are more likely to decide to undertake more investment. Thus, it is not high values of Tobin's q that lead to high investment but, rather, good prospects for the firm that lead to both high stock market prices and high levels of investment.

THE AVAILABILITY OF FUNDS

The fact that changes in real interest rates do not play a large role in determining the level of investment does not mean that government policy is impotent. At times, it can affect the level of investment by varying the availability of funds. Sometimes the government actually gets involved in making loans, for instance to small businesses or to finance housing. Chapter 34 will explore how government monetary policies affect credit availability. For now, we simply observe that to most firms, the availability of funds is often as important as or more important than the interest rate they must pay.

Chapter 21 explained the ways in which the capital market does not match the model of a typical competitive market. It is worth recalling here that most firms simply cannot borrow all they want to at the market rate of interest. Credit is rationed.

Whether because of credit rationing or for other reasons, most firms rely heavily for their investment capital on retained earnings, the funds left over from sales after paying labor, other production costs, interest on outstanding debt, and dividends to shareholders. *If* firms have some very promising projects that cannot be financed out of retained earnings, they may turn to the capital market, and in particular to banks, for additional finance. And when firms do turn to banks for funds, they often bump into credit constraints. They have a list of projects that they believe are profitable and that they would undertake if only they could get the necessary funds, but the banks do not share their view. Thus, when firms are credit rationed, making more funds available will lead to increased investment, while making funds less available will lead to decreased investment.[8]

Economic Downturns   When a firm needs money most is often when it finds money least available. In an economic downturn, revenues decrease far more rapidly than expenses, so retained earnings are likely to fall sharply as well even if dividends are cut (and most firms appear very reluctant to cut dividends). In fact, many firms find they cannot even cover costs, let alone meet the interest obligations on their outstanding debt. It is in such circumstances that the company needs most to borrow—their very survival may depend on getting funds—and it is in these circumstances that the bank is most reluctant to lend.

When firms see the possibility of a credit crunch coming up, they may cut back on investment in plant and equipment, and they may also reduce inventories, either of which strategy will have the same negative effect on aggregate expenditures. Their goal is to have funds available for day-to-day expenses; if sales fall short, revenues decline, and with limited availability of credit, they cannot turn to the banks to meet their obligations. If they do not take actions to keep their funds free, without cash to meet their obligations, they may be forced into bankruptcy.

The response of firms to the perception that they may face a shortage of funds can actually help to bring on or aggravate a recession. After all, we saw in Chapter 28 how a decrease in investment spending leads to multiplier effects on national output. Thus, the pessimism of firms can be self-fulfilling. As firm after firm cuts back on investment and reduces inventories, matters turn out every bit as bad as they feared, and they face the shortfall of funds they anticipated. Managers may congratulate themselves on their foresightedness, but in this case their individually rational actions have combined to bring on the very circumstances they hoped to avoid.

The government may recognize this problem and try to encourage banks to make funds more available to firms. But if banks are sufficiently pessimistic—if the reason they are refusing to make funds available is their fear that, with the economic downturn, borrowers will be unable to repay the loans—then the government may be unsuccessful, as we will see in greater detail in Chapter 33.

Stimulating the Economy   We have seen how a reduction in credit availability—or even the anticipation of one—can exacerbate an economic downturn. The bad news does not stop there. In a prolonged economic downturn, firms may become pessimistic about future prospects and be unwilling to undertake many investment projects, even at low real interest rates. An increase in credit availability at this point may be ineffective in stimulating investment. There is an old expression, "You can lead a horse to water,

---

[8] Chapter 21 also explained why firms that cannot obtain funds from banks may not be able to raise funds in other ways, for instance by issuing bonds or new shares. In fact, American firms make relatively little use of bonds or shares in raising new funds.

but you can't make him drink." Making more funds available for investment need not lead to more investment, particularly if what is limiting the firm's investment is not the lack of availability of credit but the lack of investment projects that look profitable.

Economic Booms Just as the lack of credit availability exacerbates economic downturns, economic booms may be sustained in part by the flow of profits (and with them, retained earnings) they generate. There is another old adage, "Nothing succeeds like success." Firms and countries that find themselves in a strong financial position (whether as a result of luck or foresight) will have high levels of investment, which will, at least for a while, sustain and expand the high level of prosperity. In the late 1970s, for example, many oil companies found themselves in a cash-rich position. The price of oil had soared, creating an unexpected bonanza for these firms. Given their high level of retained earnings, they were willing to undertake investments they could not or would not have attempted in leaner days.

THE PROFITABILITY OF PROJECTS

Theories having to do with the cost and availability of funds address one side of the firm's investment decision. On the other side are the expected returns of the projects to which those funds will be applied. We turn now to this side, noting three circumstances in which firms will be induced to invest: if they anticipate that demand for their products will rise, if the investment project will lower the firm's overall costs of production, and if the price of the investment project goes down because of favorable tax treatment.

Demand Forecasts and the Investment Accelerator If firms believe that the demand for their products will increase in the near future, this will heighten their willingness to invest today, so as to be able to meet this expected increase in demand. A major determinant of the level of demand facing any firm is the overall level of national income. Some economists have argued that this relationship gives rise to an investment **accelerator**. That is, investment doubles back: the increased output to which it gives rise produces still more investment. If for some reason, such as a rise in government expenditures, aggregate output increases, firms will increase their investment. This in turn will lead to further growth in output.

Since the ratio of capital to annual output in the economy is fairly high (around 2:1), if a firm believes that it faces a level of demand that, valued at today's prices, will be higher by $100,000 per year, it will wish to invest roughly $200,000 more in plant and equipment today in order to fully meet this expected demand. The $200,000 increased investment will lead, through the multiplier, to a much greater increase in output. If the multiplier is 5, then output will rise by $1 million. But if the firm expects this $1 million increase in output to be permanent, it will want to increase investment by $2 million. Through the multiplier, this will lead to a $10 million increase in output, and so on. We now see why the increased investment is called an accelerator: the economy spirals upward and onward, like a car going faster and faster, until it eventually runs into constraints—limitations posed by the available labor and capital.

In recent years, however, economists have paid less attention to the investment accelerator. After all, investment decisions are based on long-run considerations, not just on unexpected events of this year. Only the most naive business would simply assume that a change in demand this year will persist forever. Moreover, firms in the simple accelerator model never seem to have anticipated the increase in output; for if they had, they would already have set in place the investment that that higher level of sales called forth.

Increased sales may lead to greater investment for a quite different reason from the accelerator. When sales increase, firms earn more and can therefore retain more earnings for investment. If investment had been limited by the unavailability of funds during a recession, firms will now respond to the wider availability of funds by increasing investment, undertaking some of the investments that were earlier postponed. Moreover, the more favorable financial positions firms find themselves in as a result of the increased sales make them both more willing to undertake the risks associated with investment and more attractive to banks and other lenders. Finally, as the economy recovers from a recession and output increases, the uncertainties associated with how long the recession would last are removed, and this reduction in macroeconomic uncertainty also serves as a stimulus for investment.

Production Costs　A second consideration in the expected-returns calculation is a forecast of costs of production. While all production costs are variable, firms often focus on labor because it represents such a large fraction of total costs. Increases in real wages affect the level of investment, although the effect is ambiguous. Higher (real) wages make it more attractive to use machines rather than laborers, and thus provide an incentive for investing in more machines. On the other hand, higher wages may make some labor-intensive investment projects unprofitable, thus discouraging investment. Finally, higher real wages may reduce the amount of retained earnings that firms have available for investing.

Lowering the Cost of Investment: Taxes　In the past sixty years, taxes have played a central role in determining the level and timing of firms' investments. The government has encouraged investment at various times—most recently, until 1986—by providing an **investment tax credit (ITC).** The ITC works this way. Firms making long-term investments subtract from their tax bill 10 percent of the value of their investment. The federal government in effect pays 10 percent of the cost of the new machine or project. By reducing the effective costs of investments, the ITC makes more investment projects profitable and thus stimulates investment. But the ITC's effect is even greater when it is temporary. If the government announces that a tax credit will apply only for investments made in one particular year, it encourages firms to invest in that year—to bring forward investments they would have made later and to postpone investments they would have made earlier. The effect is the same as that of a nationwide "sale" on machines, with prices marked down by 10 percent.

RISK AND INVESTMENT

Firms do the best they can to forecast sales and costs and thus to determine the profitability of new investments. But try as they might, they can predict the future only imperfectly. Even the best managers' crystal ball is cloudy. There is therefore considerable risk associated with any investment decision. Firms are, for the most part, risk averse; when they perceive the risk associated with an investment project to be particularly high, they will not undertake the project unless the expected returns are sufficiently high to compensate them for bearing the risk. Thus, when the economy goes into a downturn, not only may expected returns decline, the risk associated with investment may increase. This increased risk further discourages investment.

There is another important way that risk enters the firm's investment decision. The issue frequently facing a company is not so much whether to invest but when to invest. An investment opportunity once undertaken cannot be wholly reversed, and investing in even a good project at the wrong time can have disastrous effects. This is because many firms operate on a small margin—costs may be 90 percent or more of revenues. A slight increase in costs or a slight decrease in revenues can have a huge effect on profits, which are the difference between revenues and costs. When costs are 90 percent of revenues, a 1 percent increase in costs can reduce profits by 10 percent. If a firm with such costs should take the risk of investing and a lengthy recession does hit, it may face bankruptcy. Nothing so dire faces the firm if it simply postpones its decision. The company may lose some profits by delaying an investment; it may, for instance, have to get along with an aging machine. But often this possibility of a loss of profit is a small price to pay for the option of waiting to see how economic events unfold.

As firms' perception of risk may change when the economy goes into a downturn, so too may their willingness to bear risk. Firms' willingness to undertake risks depends in part on their financial position. If companies have a strong balance sheet—if they have an ample supply of cash and other liquid assets on hand—then they are more willing to take risks. Even if things turn out badly, they will not go bankrupt. When an economy goes into a downturn, however, firms often face large losses, as sales that had been counted upon fail to materialize. Firms' financial positions deteriorate, making them less willing to undertake the risks associated with investment.

Thus, the risk factor contributes yet another explanation of the volatility of investment. Economic downturns are associated with both a perception of increased risk and a reduced willingness and ability to bear risks. They both contribute to a decline in investment, which, through the multiplier, leads to further declines in national income and exacerbates the economic downturn.

PRINCIPAL DETERMINANTS OF INVESTMENT

1. The cost and availability of funds. Although investment may be influenced by (real) interest rates, it is also influenced by the availability of funds, both through retained earnings and through capital markets, and both sources may be limited.

2. The expected profitability of the investment project. Firms take into account anticipated future demand for their products, the degree to which the project will reduce their costs of production, and the after-tax cost of the project.

3. Firms' willingness and ability to take on risk. Firms may reduce risk with little effect on expected profitability by delaying an investment project. In an economic downturn, firms' perception of risk increases and their willingness to bear risk decreases, both factors contributing to a downturn in investment.

THEORIES OF INVENTORY INVESTMENT

Investment in plant and equipment, which has been our focus so far, is not the only category of investment. Another category, inventory investment, is a major contributor to fluctuations in aggregate expenditures. To understand inventory investment, we need to understand first the function that inventories serve. Inventories consist of materials that are being held in storage, either awaiting use in production or awaiting sale or delivery to customers.

Inventories are typically very large. In 1990, for example, the value of inventories was $1,100 billion, while the value of monthly final sales of business was only $394 billion. In other words, there were almost $3 worth of goods in storage for every $1 of goods sold each month.

There is a cost to holding inventories. If firms borrow funds to finance their inventories, planning to pay back the loans after selling the inventoried products, they must pay interest on these funds while the products remain unsold. If a company finances the inventories itself, it faces an opportunity cost: the funds that pay for the inventory could be used for other purposes. Beyond the cost of inventory, storage space costs money, and frequently goods spoil or deteriorate in the process of storage.

Given the costs, why do firms hold so much in inventories? One reason is that inventories on the input side facilitate production. This is called the **production-facilitating function** of inventories. It is very costly, for instance, for a printing plant to run out of paper and have workers and machines standing idle until more arrives. On the output side, customers often rely upon the producer to supply the good to them when they need it. To do that, the producer must maintain inventories sufficient to meet anticipated sales. If there are long delays in fulfilling an order, the customer may well turn elsewhere.

Inventories also enable firms to save money by producing at a steady rate. It is expensive to let sales dictate the level of production. There would be too much variation from day to day or even month to month; workers and machines might be left idle or forced to work overtime. Thus, firms should prefer to set a steady level of production, which, when combined with the unsteady demand for their products, produces inventory. To smooth production, firms put goods into inventories in slack periods and take them out of inventories in peak times. This is called the **production-smoothing function** of inventories.

In the production-facilitating explanation, inventories are positively correlated with the level of output and aggregate expenditures: inventories increase when the level of output is high. In the production-smoothing explanation, inventories are negatively correlated with aggregate expenditures: they go up when expenditures go down. The latter explanation would seem to suggest that inventories reduce fluctuations in national output, by allowing firms to keep an even level of production.

In fact, inventories vary far more than output, and as was mentioned earlier, they seem to be a major contributing factor to fluctuations in aggregate expenditures. Rather than serving to dampen business fluctuations, they seem to exacerbate them. This is true even for inventories of consumer goods, which should be serving a smoothing role.

One reason for the variability of investment in inventories may again have to do with the risk-averse behavior of firms and the availability of credit. When the economy enters a recession, firms often find that their net worth is decreased. They are less willing to

Simmons is the firm that makes the well-known "Beautyrest" line of mattresses. But in the mid-1980s, the company was anything but relaxed. It was operating a network of 19 manufacturing facilities and 67 warehouses, linked together by 128 truck tractors and 250 trailers. The costs of inventories were high; the company's freight bill alone was 6 percent of total sales; and it was past time to cut costs. The solution? A "just-in-time" manufacturing system. Instead of delivering from factories to warehouses and then from warehouses to retail stores, the company determined that it would only produce *after* receiving an order. The challenge was then to design a system in which customers would receive their orders within four days.

Simmons reorganized the company to eliminate all its warehouses and five of its plants. After careful planning, it now uses only 85 tractors to make its deliveries. As a result, the company saved money that had been tied up in facilities and extra trucks. In the process, it added 4 percentage points to its market share.

The Simmons plan was based on the just-in-time inventory system pioneered by Toyota in 1972. The idea was to hold inventories to a bare minimum by providing inputs only when they were immediately needed. Toyota, like many large manufacturers, faced a basic inventory dilemma. On one hand, running out of some input to production could shut down a factory. On the other hand, keeping large stockpiles around means paying for them in advance and maintaining a large storage area. Besides, some products do not keep especially well if stored for too long.

In a just-in-time inventory system, many small deliveries of materials are made throughout a working day, rather than a few large deliveries that need to be stored for days or weeks. The goal is to have supplies arrive just in time to be used, rather than go into storage. After being adopted at Toyota in 1972, the system spread throughout the Japanese industry during the rest of the 1970s. During the 1980s, it was adopted in the United States, with big companies like General Motors, IBM, Hewlett-Packard, General Electric, and Black and Decker among those who tried it out first.

Besides saving on the costs of carrying inventory, just-in-time systems seem to help companies modernize in many other ways. *The Economist* magazine described it this way: "A favorite analogy is with water in a river. When the level of water falls, rocks start to appear. The rocks can be removed rather than hit." In other words, carrying big inventories can allow a company to cover up a variety of other organizational problems. Thinking about how to

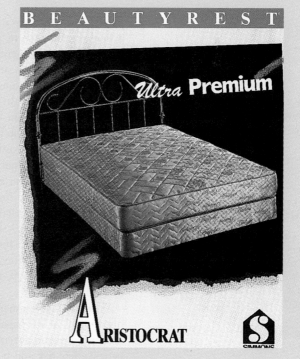

organize matters so inventories do not stand around or accumulate can be a powerful tool to thinking about the overall efficiency of the organization.

If just-in-time systems were widely adopted across the entire economy, the overall stability of the economy would tend to be enhanced. When sales dip, a business with large inventories may cut off purchases of inputs altogether for a time, de-

pleting inventories. A business with just-in-time inventories will reduce purchases only a little, and will cut production just by the amount of the reduction in sales.

Sources: The Economist, April 25, 1987, p. 68; Richard J. Schonberger, "The Transfer of Japanese Manufacturing Management Approaches to U.S. Industry," *Academy of Management Review* (1982) 7:479–87; "Bringing JIT's Benefits to the Bottom Line," *Traffic Management* (November 1991), p. 57.

make any kind of investment, including inventory investment. Where possible, they would like to "disinvest," or convert their assets back into cash. The easiest kind of disinvestment is to sell off inventories, rather than, say, a factory. Moreover, when a business faces credit rationing, it may be forced to sell its inventories to raise the requisite capital. And even if it is not yet forced to sell off its inventories, it may fear future credit rationing and, in anticipation, seek to reduce its inventories.

VARIABILITY OF INVESTMENT

Now that we have investigated the main determinants of investment, we can understand better why investment is so volatile. Furthermore, the multiplier explains why the variability of investment translates into even greater volatility in output.

Firms' investments are determined by their ability to raise funds, their perceptions of the profitability of new projects, and their willingness to undertake risks. All of these can change dramatically within a short period of time. An economic decline—or rumors of an economic decline—may lead a firm to be more pessimistic about sales and prices, and therefore about profits. Lower sales or prices may result in losses for the company, thus eroding its net worth and its willingness to undertake risks. The lower flow of funds impairs its ability to finance investment out of retained earnings. Pessimism is contagious; in these same circumstances, banks are reluctant to lend funds (at least on terms that are acceptable to the firm).

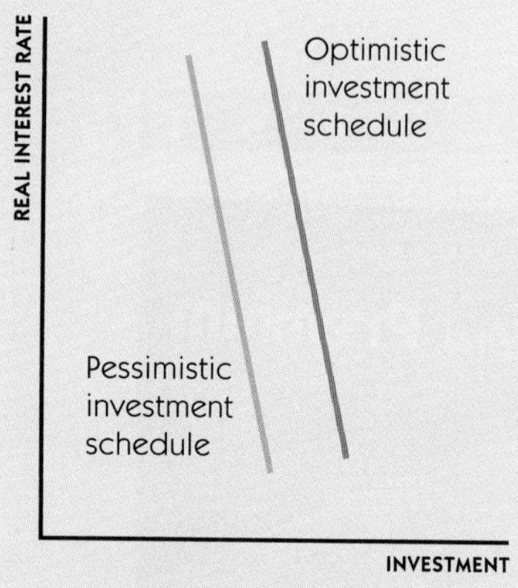

The factors that determine investment can be represented as *shifts* in the investment function. Figure 29.9 shows "pessimistic" and "optimistic" versions of the investment schedule first shown in Figure 29.7. Since real interest rates have not varied much, most of the fluctuations in investment are due to shifts of the investment schedule as shown in Figure 29.9, rather than movements along the investment schedule as seen in Figure 29.7.

While the government cannot control all of these determinants, it has a variety of instruments at its disposal that may affect investment. If the business community is convinced of the government's commitment to economic stability, businessmen may perceive less risk and be more willing to invest. But predicting, let alone controlling, the psychology of business executives is at best a tricky business.

Figure 29.9 **SHIFTS IN THE INVESTMENT FUNCTION**

The investment function will shift in, resulting in less investment at every level of real interest rates, if firms perceive greater riskiness, if the tax code is less favorable to investment, and for other reasons.

Temporary tax changes like the investment tax credit are more reliable, but they are a cumbersome tool, because they require action by Congress and the president. Temporary tax changes may also distort how resources are allocated, though the macroeconomic gains—in higher levels of output—may well be worth the microeconomic losses from these distortions.

For the most part, however, the government relies on monetary policy that affects both the availability of credit and the terms on which firms can borrow. Firms raise funds through the capital market. How and when the government, through the monetary authorities, affects the capital market are questions of sufficient importance and complexity that most of the next part of the book is devoted to exploring them. For now, it is simply worth observing that what goes on in the product market (the determination of the equilibrium level of output) affects the labor market (the level of unemployment in the economy), and what goes on in the capital market (the availability of credit) affects investment and thus the product market.

WAYS OF STIMULATING INVESTMENT

1. Increasing business confidence: government demonstrating a commitment to maintaining high levels of employment and output

2. Lowering the cost of investment: subsidies to investment through the tax system

3. Increasing the availability of credit or making it available on more attractive terms (monetary policy; direct government lending programs)

REVIEW AND PRACTICE

SUMMARY

1. The Keynesian consumption function stresses the importance of current disposable income in determining consumption. In contrast, the life-cycle hypothesis says that people save during their life so that they can spend after retirement. The permanent income hypothesis argues that people save in good years to offset the bad years.

2. In the Keynesian consumption function, the government could manipulate this year's consumption by changing this year's tax rate. In the future-oriented theories, temporary tax reductions would have a limited effect in stimulating consumption, since people are considering a longer horizon than this year for their consumption decisions.

3. Both the life-cycle and permanent income models predict that consumption will depend on lifetime wealth, and that capital gains will therefore affect consumption.

4. Household consumption appears to be more dependent on current income than either the life-cycle or permanent income theory suggests. Consumers can easily postpone the purchase of durables when current income falls. Also, limitations on their ability to borrow (credit rationing) may keep the consumption of many people with little savings close to their current income.

5. Future-oriented theories of consumption suggest that the aggregate expenditures schedule is flat and the multiplier is low; they help explain why the ratio of consumption to disposable income may shift from year to year; and they imply that temporary changes in disposable income may have only a slight effect on consumption.

6. Variations in the level of investment are probably the principal reason for variations in total aggregate expenditures. The three main categories of investment are firms' purchases of plant and equipment, firms' increase or decrease of inventories, and households' purchases of new homes.

7. Historically, short-term variations in real interest rates have often proved relatively unimportant in explaining variations in investment.

8. The availability of funds is an important determinant of variations in investment. Most firms finance much of their investment out of retained earnings. They also borrow when possible, although they sometimes face credit constraints. Relatively little use is made of equity markets (selling shares) to finance investments.

9. Firms will be induced to invest if they anticipate that demand for their products will rise, if the investment project will lower the firm's costs of production, or if the price of the investment project goes down, for instance because of favorable tax treatment.

10. In an economic downturn, firms are less willing to bear risk, and this contributes to a downturn in investment.

KEY TERMS

life-cycle hypothesis	durable goods	investment tax credit
permanent income	investment schedule	(ITC)
hypothesis	accelerator	

REVIEW QUESTIONS

1. What is the difference between the Keynesian model of consumption, the life-cycle model, and the permanent income model?

2. Why do the life-cycle and permanent income hypotheses predict that temporary tax changes will have little effect on current consumption?

3. What factors affect consumer expenditures on durables? Why are these expenditures so volatile?

4. How will the existence of credit rationing make consumption more dependent on current income than the future-oriented consumption theories would suggest?

5. What are the possible sources of funds for firms that wish to invest? Which is used most often, and least often?

6. What is the investment accelerator?

7. Why does an investment tax credit stimulate investment?

8. How might changes in perceptions of economic risk affect investment levels?

9. Why might firms' willingness to bear risk decrease in a recession?

10. What are the costs and benefits to the firm of holding inventories? Why might inventory investment be as volatile as it is?

PROBLEMS

1. Under which theory of consumption would a temporary tax cut have the largest effect on consumption? Under which theory would a permanent rise in Social Security benefits have the largest effect on consumption? Under which theory would permanently higher unemployment insurance benefits have the largest effect on consumption? Explain.

2. Which theory of consumption predicts that aggregate savings will depend on the proportion of retired and young people in the population? What is the relationship? Which theories predict that consumption will not vary a great deal according to whether the economy is in a boom or recession? Why?

3. If the government made it easier for people to borrow money, perhaps by enacting programs to help them get loans, would you expect consumption behavior to become more or less sensitive to current income? Why?

4. How would you predict that a crash in the stock market would affect the relationship between consumption and income? How would you predict that rapidly rising prices for homes would affect the relationship between consumption and income? Draw shifts in the consumption function to illustrate. How do your predictions differ depending on whether the consumer is a Keynesian, life-cycle, or permanent income consumer?

5. A company that expects the long-term real interest rate to be 3 percent is considering a list of projects. Each project costs $10,000, but they vary in the amount of time they will take to pay off, and in how much they will pay off. The first will pay $12,000 in two years; the second, $12,500 in three years; the third, $13,000 in four years. Which projects are worth doing? If the expected interest rate was 5 percent, does your answer change? You may assume that prices are stable.

6. Take the projects in problem #5 and reevaluate them, this time assuming that inflation is at 4 percent per year and the payoffs are in nominal dollars at the time they occur. Are the projects still worth doing?

7. Draw a diagram to show how investment is affected in each of the following situations.
   (a) The government passes an investment tax credit.
   (b) Businesses believe the economic future looks healthier than they had previously thought.
   (c) The government reduces the real interest rate.

8. Imagine that the government raises personal income taxes, but also enacts an investment tax credit for a corresponding amount. Describe under what circumstances this combination of policies would be most effective in stimulating aggregate demand. Consider differing theories of consumption, and the choice between permanent and temporary changes in the tax code.

APPENDIX: THE INVESTMENT-SAVINGS IDENTITY

We typically think of savings and investment together. Both are virtues: "A penny saved is a penny earned." Increased investment enhances the future productivity of the economy. In recent years, there has been concern about the level of investment in the U.S. economy. It has frequently been suggested that Americans should encourage savings, the presumption being that savings are automatically converted into investment.

When the economy is operating along its production possibilities curve, with all resources fully utilized, increased savings—reduced consumption—mean that more capital goods can be produced. But when the economy is operating below its production possibilities curve, increased savings—reduced consumption—may simply push the economy further below the curve.

In *open* economies, savings and investment do not have to change together even when the economy is on its production possibilities curve. The economy can undertake investment, even when there is little domestic saving, by borrowing from abroad. The consequences of this are discussed in later chapters.

The income-expenditure analysis of Chapter 28 focused on the relationship between aggregate expenditures and income. Equilibrium occurs when aggregate expenditures equal national income. An alternative way of describing how national output is determined focuses on savings and investment. We look at a simple model first, in which disposable income equals national income. For this to be the case, we assume that taxes are zero and all of a firm's profits are paid out as dividends. To simplify further, we assume there are no government savings or dissavings, or flow of funds from abroad. Later we will loosen up these assumptions and get a fuller picture.

Individuals can either spend their income today or save it, either to consume later or to leave as a bequest to their children. This is true by definition:

$$\text{income} = \text{consumption} + \text{savings}. \tag{29.1}$$

With no government purchases or net exports, we know from the components of aggregate expenditures that firms can produce only two kinds of goods: consumer goods and investment goods. Thus, output, Y, can be broken into its two components:

$$Y = \text{consumption} + \text{investment}. \tag{29.2}$$

These two identities can be combined to form a new one. Since the value of national output equals national income,

$$Y = \text{income}, \tag{29.3}$$

we can use the right-hand side of (29.1) and (29.2) to get

$$\text{consumption} + \text{savings} = \text{consumption} + \text{investment}. \tag{29.4}$$

Subtracting consumption from both sides of the equation leaves the equation

$$\text{savings} = \text{investment}. \tag{29.5}$$

In short, savings must equal investment. This is a simple matter of definition.

One way to understand this identity is to think of firms as producing a certain amount of goods, the value of which is just equal to the income of the individuals in the economy (because everything firms take in they pay out as income to someone in the economy). The income that is not consumed is, by definition, saved. On the output side, firms either sell the goods they produce or put them into inventory for sale in future years. Some of the inventory buildup is planned, because businesses need inventories to survive. Some of it is unplanned—businesses may be surprised by an economic downturn that spoils their sales projections. Both intended and unintended inventory buildups are considered investment. The goods that are not consumed are, by definition, invested. After all, inventory accumulation consists of goods that are produced not for current consumption but presumably for future consumption.

This identity (29.5) can be transformed into an equation determining national output, once it is recognized that in equilibrium firms will cut back production if there is unintended inventory accumulation. Because firms will cut back, in equilibrium the amount companies invest is the amount they wish to invest (including inventories), given current market conditions. That is, in equilibrium, firms do not suffer unpleasant surprises. The equilibrium condition, then, is that

$$\text{investment} = \text{desired investment}. \qquad (29.6)$$

Now switch over to the savings side of the identity (29.5). The consumption function presented earlier tells how much people wish to consume at each level of income. But since what is not consumed is saved, the consumption function can easily be transformed into a savings function, giving the level of savings at each level of income. Savings is just income minus consumption:

$$\text{savings} = \text{income} (Y) - \text{consumption}. \qquad (29.7)$$

Figure 29.10 shows the savings function. The slope of this curve, the amount by which savings increase with income, is the marginal propensity to save, which is just 1 minus the marginal propensity to consume.

Figure 29.10 THE SAVINGS FUNCTION AND NATIONAL INCOME

As income increases, the amount individuals desire to save increases. The amount by which savings increases as the result of a $1 increase in income—the slope of the savings function—is called the marginal propensity to save. In equilibrium, savings equal investment. Thus, equilibrium occurs at the intersection of the savings function and the level of investment.

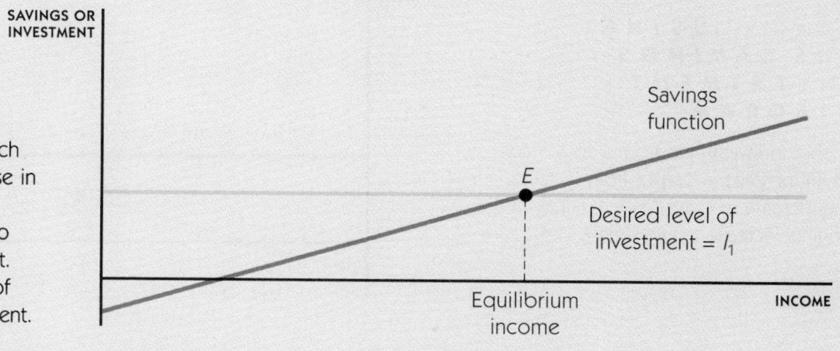

SAVINGS OR INVESTMENT

Savings function

E

Desired level of investment = I_1

Equilibrium income

INCOME

Since savings must equal investment, and in equilibrium investment must equal desired investment, then in equilibrium

$$savings = desired\ investment. \tag{29.8}$$

The figure shows a fixed level of desired investment, I_1. Desired investment is horizontal because investment is assumed to be unaffected by the level of income. Equilibrium occurs at the intersection of the desired investment curve and the savings curve, point E.

As with income-expenditure analysis, savings-investment analysis shows how an increase in investment leads to an increase in output that is a multiple of itself. Figure 29.11 shows that as investment shifts up from I_1 to I_2, the equilibrium shifts from E_1 to E_2, and output increases from Y_1 to Y_2. The change in investment, ΔI, is again smaller than the change in output. This should not surprise us, since income-expenditure analysis and savings-investment analysis are two ways of looking at the same thing.

The Paradox of Thrift   We can use a similar diagram to illustrate what may seem to be a paradoxical result: when the economy's resources are not fully employed, an increase in thrift—the level of savings at each level of income—may have no effect at all on the equilibrium level of savings or investment. The only effect of greater thrift is to lower national income and output. Figure 29.12 shows the effect of an upward shift in the savings function—at each level of income, savings are higher. But in equilibrium, savings equal investment. With investment fixed, savings too, in equilibrium, must be the same; and to attain that level of savings (equal to the level of investment), income must be lowered from Y_1 to Y_2.

Government Savings, Business Savings, and Borrowing from Abroad   What happens when government purchases and net exports are allowed to enter the picture? Again, savings equal investment. Now, however, there are three additional sources of investment funds, along with the household savings we have considered so far (denoted by the symbol S_h). Funds can be obtained from abroad (S_x) or from the government

Figure 29.11 USING THE SAVINGS-INVESTMENT DIAGRAM

A shift in investment from I_1 to I_2 leads to an increase in output from Y_1 to Y_2; the increase in output is a multiple of the original increase in investment.

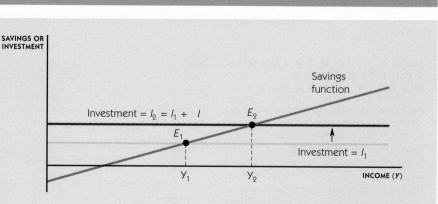

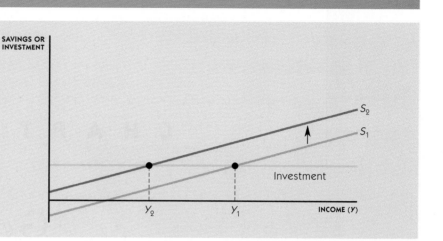

Figure 29.12 THE SAVINGS FUNCTION AND THE PARADOX OF THRIFT

Given a level of investment fixed by other factors, increased thriftiness, reflected in an upward shift in the savings function, lowers output from Y_1 to Y_2, but leaves savings unchanged.

(S_g). Just as household savings are the difference between the household's income and its consumption, government savings are the difference between its income (tax revenues) and its expenditures. In recent years, government savings have been negative—the government has been spending more than its income. Finally, businesses save too, when their receipts exceed what they pay out as wages, taxes, interest, and dividends,[9] and these savings (S_b) are another source of investment funds. Thus,

$$S_b + S_h + S_g + S_x = I. \tag{29.9}$$

We frequently combine business and household savings together, as private savings (S_p):

$$S_p = S_h + S_b. \tag{29.10}$$

The new savings-investment identity is

$$S_p + S_g + S_x = I. \tag{29.11}$$

Investment must equal the sum of private savings, government savings, and borrowing from abroad.

In the 1980s, the rate of private savings was very low and the rate of government savings was actually negative. However, borrowing from abroad dramatically increased. Thus, there were large changes in the sources of savings. The explanation for these changes, and their long-run consequences, are questions we will take up in Chapter 38.

[9] Additions to inventory are included in the firm's books as if they were sales; the firm records a "profit" even though there is no cash to show for it. This profit is saved, and is reflected in statistics on business savings.

CHAPTER 30

GOVERNMENT
EXPENDITURES
AND TRADE

 ow we take a closer look at the two other major components of the aggregate expenditures schedule: government expenditures and net exports. As with the study of consumption spending and investment in Chapter 29, our objective is twofold: to understand why aggregate expenditures fluctuate, and to understand how government policy can affect these fluctuations.

"As I see it, every billion dollars spent on the MX missile is a billion dollars not spent on the salted peanuts industry."

KEY QUESTIONS

1. What is the consequence of an increase in government expenditures matched by an increase in taxes?

2. What is the fiscal deficit? the full-employment deficit? What are the consequences of these deficits?

3. When do government expenditures crowd out private expenditures? Why is crowding out important?

4. How has the role of foreign trade in the economy changed in recent years? What explains the large increase in imports relative to exports?

5. How does the fact that the United States is an open economy affect the conduct of macroeconomic policy?

6. Why is protectionism unlikely to be a good solution to the problem of a trade deficit?

GOVERNMENT EXPENDITURES

Like consumers and business firms, the government stimulates the economy when it spends money. Consumers and business firms, however, get the money they spend by selling their services and goods, while government gets most of its money through taxes. Taxes give government funds to spend, but they take an equal amount away from the private sector.

There is one complication to the analysis of fiscal policy that merits a brief mention. While we based the analysis of investment, for instance, on the idea that firms maximize profits or market value, we will not look closely here at the motivations of government officials. For most of this chapter, we simply ask what would happen if the government increased expenditures or reduced taxes. There are economists, however, such as Nobel laureate James Buchanan of George Mason University, who believe that the government should be analyzed as an economic organization, like households and firms.[1] They believe that the behavior of government can (and must) be explained in much the same way that the behavior of households and firms can be explained, and that the politicians and bureaucrats who make government decisions respond rationally to the incentives

---

[1] The discussion of public choice in Chapter 23 gives some insights into these motivations.

Figure 30.1
GOVERNMENT POLICIES AND AGGREGATE OUTPUT

In panel A, an increase in government expenditures increases equilibrium output from Y_1 to Y_2. Panel B shows the imposition of taxes as lowering disposable income at each level of national income, and thus the level of consumption. The $C + I + G + (X - M)$ line shifts down and becomes flatter.

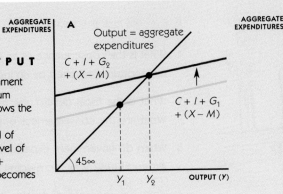

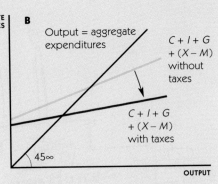

they face. Just as changes in economic conditions (an increase in disposable income, for example) lead households to change their consumption decisions or cause firms to change their investments, changes in economic and political conditions can, in this view, predictably be related to changes in the behavior of the government. In some circumstances, the incentives facing politicians may actually lead the government to contribute to the volatility of the economy.

In Chapter 28, we learned that government spending serves to increase aggregate expenditures, shifting the aggregate expenditures schedule up, as in Figure 30.1A. At the same time, taxes reduce disposable income and therefore reduce aggregate expenditures. Moreover, taxes that increase with income make the aggregate expenditures schedule flatter than it is in the absence of government. Thus, government makes the multiplier smaller, as illustrated in panel B. We now take a closer look at the relationship between taxes, government expenditures, and multipliers.

BALANCED BUDGETS

An old-fashioned view of the government (one that is currently enjoying a revival) holds that government should keep its revenues and its expenditures in balance. If defense, Social Security, education, and other government programs are going to cost $1 trillion this year, then taxes should be set so as to generate $1 trillion in revenues.

Even in this simple (simple to explain, not to achieve) scenario, the balanced budget increase in expenditures stimulates output. But the multiplier is greatly reduced; in fact, normally aggregate output and income will go up just by the amount of the increased government expenditures and taxes.

How is it possible that when the government is reducing private income through taxes by the same amount that it increases public spending, aggregate expenditures are nonetheless increased? Assume that some fraction, say 90 percent, of all disposable income is consumed. The remaining 10 percent is saved. If taxes are raised by $1,000, consumption will be reduced by $900. However, government expenditures will have also increased by $1,000, so the first-round effect of the tax rise is to increase overall expenditures (public and private) by $100. This increased expenditures income leads to greater consumption, and then to further increases in income, by the usual multiplier analysis. Thus, the government *can* still play an active role in stabilizing the economy even if it is committed to having balanced budgets. But to stimulate the economy will require much larger variations in government expenditures.

This is illustrated in Figure 30.2, a standard income-expenditure analysis diagram. The initial equilibrium is at Y_0. We can think of a balanced budget increase in expenditures as a two-step process. First, government expenditures are increased from G_0 to G_1. This increases output from Y_0 to Y_1. Then the government raises tax rates to pay for the increased expenditures. The higher tax rates reduce consumption at each level of income, and the aggregate consumption function is flatter. The new equilibrium is at Y_2, much lower than output would have been had taxes not been raised, but still higher than in the initial situation.

A numerical example will help illustrate why this is so. Assume that national output is at $4 trillion, and the government calculates that to attain full employment will necessitate increasing national output to $4.4 trillion. That is to say, output is $400 billion short of its full-employment potential. If the multiplier is 5 and the government wants to increase expenditures but leave taxes unchanged, it needs to increase its expenditures by $80 billion ($400 billion ÷ 5)—still a considerable sum, but easier to achieve than $400 billion. If the government is committed to having a balanced budget, however, it will have to increase its expenditures by much more than that amount, as increased taxes offset the effects on consumption of increased income.[2] In effect, the

[2] The exact amount government will have to increase expenditures depends on how it raises the tax revenues. If the government raises the taxes on households, then to raise output by $400 billion, the government would have to raise government expenditures, and taxes, by a full $400 billion. Income after taxes—disposable income—would, accordingly, remain unchanged, so consumption would remain unchanged. Thus, aggregate expenditures—C + I + G (ignoring net exports)—would increase simply by the increase in government expenditures. There is no multiplier at work.

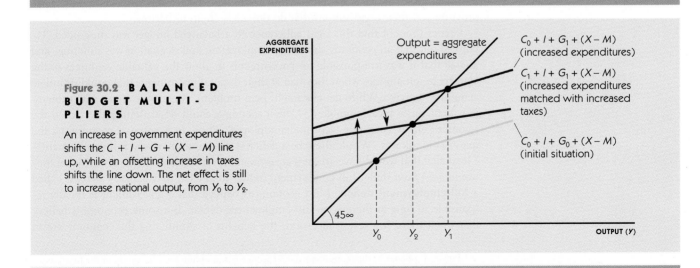

Figure 30.2 BALANCED BUDGET MULTI-PLIERS

An increase in government expenditures shifts the C + I + G + (X − M) line up, while an offsetting increase in taxes shifts the line down. The net effect is still to increase national output, from Y_0 to Y_2.

AGGREGATE EXPENDITURES

Output = aggregate expenditures

$C_0 + I + G_1 + (X - M)$ (increased expenditures)

$C_1 + I + G_1 + (X - M)$ (increased expenditures matched with increased taxes)

$C_0 + I + G_0 + (X - M)$ (initial situation)

45∞

Y_0 Y_2 Y_1

OUTPUT (Y)

multiplier for an increase in expenditures matched by a corresponding increase in taxes will be small. Indeed, there may be no multiplier, in which case the government would have to increase expenditures by $400 billion. It is unlikely that the government will find good uses for those extra funds, and so it is unlikely that such an increased level of expenditures would be politically acceptable.

The political climate of recent years has called for strict limits on government expenditures, and that attitude, combined with a commitment to a balanced budget, severely limits the scope of the government to use fiscal policy to stabilize the economy. This is a marked reversal of the views of the decades immediately following World War II, when governments were committed to using fiscal policy to stabilize the economy.

THE FULL-EMPLOYMENT DEFICIT

The government can stimulate the economy even more if it increases expenditures without raising taxes at the same time, a situation known as **deficit spending**. Deficit spending requires that the government borrow what it does not raise in taxes. It borrows money by selling Treasury bills and bonds to investors; in effect, the investors are lending the government money it can spend today in exchange for a promise of repayment with interest in the future. Because the stimulus provided by government spending is not offset by the reductions in consumer spending that would result from increased taxes, increases in government expenditures financed by deficits, as opposed to taxes, have multiplier effects.[3]

Budget deficits may seem almost unavoidable today, but the very idea of financing government expenditures through deficits on a regular basis was another of the revolutionary insights produced by John Maynard Keynes. Early in this century, many economists held as a basic tenet that responsible governments should always maintain a balanced budget. Some governments that had borrowed heavily from abroad found themselves unable to pay their debts. They had, in effect, gone bankrupt, an experience that has almost been repeated in the last decade by some governments in Latin America. Within the United States in the nineteenth century, several state governments were put into bankruptcy by their creditors, which is one of the reasons why some states have provisions in their constitutions that do not allow them to borrow.

Keynes thought that this rigid adherence to a balanced budget was misguided. He pointed out that an economy sunk in unemployment and stagnation was suffering, and argued that it was irresponsible for governments to allow the valuable resources of the country to remain idle when they had at their disposal instruments that could stimulate economic activity. While deficits might be a problem, there were times when unemployment was a greater problem. Deficit spending could be a useful policy when the resources of the economy were underemployed. Thus, to Keynesian economists, the question to ask was "Would there be a deficit if the economy was at full employment?" The deficit that would have arisen if government revenues and spending were what they *would have been* under full employment (rather than what they actually were) is called a **full-employment deficit**. Most economists believe that a government is fiscally responsible so long as there is no full-employment deficit. But some economists believe that when there is a severe recession, the benefits of stimulating the economy are so

---

[3] Provided, of course, that consumers do not reduce consumption in anticipation of the future taxes they will have to pay to finance the higher government debt.

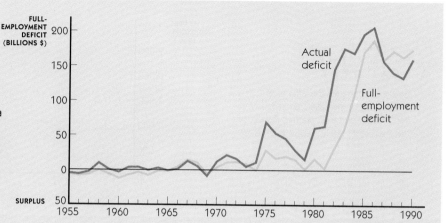

Figure 30.3 FULL-EMPLOYMENT AND ACTUAL DEFICITS

The full-employment deficit is normally less than the actual deficit. When unemployment is high, as in 1982, adjusting for full employment can make a seemingly large deficit fade away. But when unemployment is lower, as in 1984, even adjusting for full employment leaves the deficit very large. Sources: Robert Eisner, *How Real Is the Federal Deficit?* (1986), p. 84; *Survey of Current Business* (1983–91).

great that it may be desirable for the government even to have a full-employment deficit.

Figure 30.3 gives the full-employment and actual deficits since 1955. When the economy is booming, the actual and full-employment deficits are roughly the same, as they were in 1965 and 1969. When the economy is not in a boom, the full-employment deficit is smaller than the actual deficit: for example, in 1982, while the actual deficit was almost 5 percent of GDP, the full-employment deficit was around 1 percent of GDP. It is even possible for there to be a full-employment surplus and an actual deficit. This happened in 1961 and 1962. The target of a zero full-employment deficit was attained in 1958, though the actual deficit that year was more than 2 percent of GDP.

The difference between the actual deficit and the full-employment deficit arises because during periods of unemployment, tax revenues are lower and some types of expenditures (such as welfare payments and unemployment insurance) are higher than they would be if the economy were fully employed.

Until 1975 (with the exception of war years), the actual deficits in the United States were always sufficiently small that there was either a full-employment surplus or a negligible full-employment deficit. Since then, the actual deficit has been so massive that there have been substantial full-employment deficits in most years.

Use of the full-employment deficit as a measure of fiscal responsibility is now widespread. In recent legislation aimed at eliminating the huge deficits of the 1980s, the targets Congress has set for itself each year are expressed in terms of a full-employment deficit. The legislation calls for eventually attaining the target of a zero full-employment deficit. But this goal allows for an actual deficit, should the economy be in a recession.

THE DEBT AND THE DEFICIT

It is important to distinguish between deficits and government debt. The deficit measures a shortfall in any given year. The debt is the total of unpaid deficits; it measures what the government owes from past years. Figure 30.4 traces the government's debt from

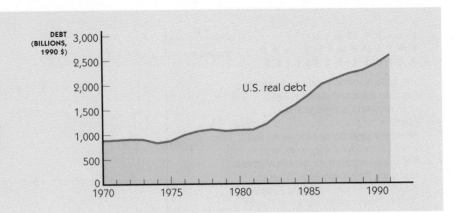

Figure 30.4 THE REAL DEBT

Even correcting for the effects of inflation, debt increased enormously in the 1980s. *Source: Economic Report of the President* (1991), Tables B-57, B-82.

1970 to 1990. Note in particular how it has increased dramatically since 1980. The figures are adjusted for inflation and thus measure the real debt.

The real budget deficit can be defined as the change each year in the real level of total accumulated government debt. If inflation erodes the value of the total debt by more than the government borrows in a particular year, there may be a real budget surplus, even though it may appear to be a nominal dollar deficit. This happened in the late 1970s. The government had a small deficit, but inflation was running at more than 8 percent. As a result, the real indebtedness declined; there was a real surplus. The budget deficits during the 1980s appear even more remarkable when we see that the economy switched from real surpluses to huge real deficits.

CROWDING OUT

The analysis behind deficit spending—whatever measure one uses—may overestimate the power of the government to stimulate the economy, because increased government expenditures or deficits may lead to reduced investment. If the government increases its expenditures without at the same time raising taxes, the resulting budget deficit will result in more borrowing by the government. This in turn will reduce the supply of funds available for the private sector to borrow. Economists say that government borrowing will **crowd out** private investment.

Proponents of the crowding out view remind us that government competes with private firms and individuals in the capital market. If there is a fixed amount of funds available, then for the government to obtain more funds (to finance the deficit), firms will have to get less funds. In the extreme case, an increase in government expenditures (with taxes fixed) crowds out investment on a dollar-per-dollar basis: the more deficit spending the government does, the less investing private firms do, and the increase in government expenditures does not stimulate the economy at all.

In fact, the U.S. government is just as likely to do its borrowing from the Japanese and other lenders from outside the economy as it is from U.S. citizens. The other extreme case is that of an international capital market where the country can borrow as much as it would like at a fixed rate of interest. Then, instead of crowding out domestic investment, government borrowing simply leads to a flow of funds from abroad, as we will see in greater detail in Chapter 38.

Reality lies somewhere in between: as the government tries to get more funds, some additional funds are attracted from abroad and some individuals save more than they otherwise would, and so there is some increase in the total available funds. At the same time, some investment is crowded out, so that the total stimulus provided to the economy by the increased government expenditures is less than the simple model of Chapter 28 would suggest.

The magnitude of crowding out is also likely to depend on whether or not the economy has a lot of excess capacity. In this chapter, as in the preceding two, we are focusing on the situation where the economy is operating along the horizontal part of its aggregate supply curve, as shown in Figure 30.5A. It is in such situations that the actual level of output produced by the economy is determined by aggregate demand. And it is possible for the economy to increase government expenditures without reducing the output of other goods. On the other hand, if the economy is operating along the vertical part of the aggregate supply curve, as in panel B, where output cannot be increased by much, increases in government expenditures must be offset by decreases in some other component of national output: there must be some crowding out.

There is an important lesson in all of this: the fact that at times there must be crowding out should not mislead us into thinking that there will always be crowding out. The situations with which we are concerned here, where the economy is not fully utilizing its resources, where some government intervention may be required to restimulate the economy, are precisely those situations in which crowding out is least likely to occur.

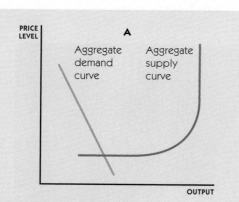
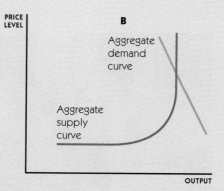

Figure 30.5 **CROWDING OUT**

Panel A shows a situation where initially the economy is operating along the horizontal part of the aggregate supply curve. Increases in government expenditures are likely to increase aggregate demand and thus equilibrium output; there will be at most limited crowding out. Panel B shows a situation where initially the economy is operating along the vertical part of the aggregate supply curve. Since total output cannot increase, increases in government expenditures must come at the expense of some other component of aggregate demand; government expenditures may, for instance, crowd out investment.

The permanent income and life-cycle theories emphasize that current consumption depends not only on today's income, but also on income that is expected to be received in the future. If disposable income goes up today but is expected to go down next year by a corresponding amount, consumption should remain unchanged. This observation has potentially profound implications for the ability of the government to use tax policy to stabilize the economy.

If the government reduces income taxes this year but keeps expenditures unchanged, the budget deficit will increase. This deficit is a liability for taxpayers; in the future, taxes will have to be increased (from what they otherwise would have been) to pay interest on the debt and to repay the debt. If individuals have their taxes reduced this year but know that they will have to pay for it with higher taxes in the future, their total lifetime income will remain unchanged. In that case, a tax cut—keeping government expenditures fixed—will have no effect on aggregate consumption. Clearly, this view

goes beyond the permanent income and life-cycle models introduced earlier, which said a temporary tax cut would have a small effect on total lifetime wealth, and therefore have a small effect on today's aggregate consumption.

The view that whether the government finances a given level of expenditures by taxes or borrowing makes *no* difference to current consumption—the two are perfectly equivalent—is sometimes called the Ricardian equivalence view, in honor of David Ricardo, the nineteenth-century English economist who also discovered the principle of comparative advantage. Ricardo described the equivalence theory, then dismissed it as impractical in the real world. In recent years, the view has been resurrected and promoted by Robert Barro of Harvard University.

The theory of Ricardian equivalence suggests that the huge increase in government borrowing in the 1980s should have led to a huge increase in private savings. After all, when people see deficits, they should expect that taxes will increase at some time

in the future, and begin setting aside funds to pay the bills. But instead of increasing, private savings rates in the United States continued at their low levels in the 1980s.

The reasons why Ricardian equivalence does not hold are not completely understood, but they are summarized by the idea of the "public veil." If rational individuals could see through the public veil—that is, if they could look at government borrowing, forecast their future tax liabilities, and act accordingly—then Ricardian equivalence would hold. But people do not seem to see through the public veil, at least not with complete clarity.

Some economists say that this is because most people simply spend most of what they earn and do not adjust to whether the government is saving more or less. Other economists argue that even if taxes do need to be raised in the future, there is uncertainty about when this will happen and who will pay at that time. If the burden of repaying the public debt can be passed on to future generations, and if parents do not fully adjust bequests to their heirs to reflect this, then the tax reduction does represent an increase in the current generation's lifetime wealth, and accordingly aggregate consumption should rise for this generation.

AUTOMATIC STABILIZERS

Chapter 28 pointed out that income taxes flatten the aggregate expenditures schedule, thus reducing the multiplier. The fact that the multiplier is smaller has two implications that should be familiar: it means the economy is less sensitive to variations in, say, the level of investment; but it also means that the economy responds less to attempts by the government to stimulate the economy by increasing expenditures.

In effect, the income tax builds a stabilizing mechanism into the economy. As the economy slows down and national income is reduced, the government takes less away from individuals in taxes. Disposable income is reduced by less than total national income. Such mechanisms are called **automatic stabilizers** and are important because they start to work as soon as the economy goes into a downturn. No political debate is required before they can be put to work.

Other government programs in which expenditures increase automatically as national income declines also serve as automatic stabilizers. For example, when incomes decline, unemployment insurance benefits increase; Social Security benefits tend to rise slightly, as people retire earlier than they otherwise would; and food stamp and other welfare expenditures increase. These government programs are already in place, cushioning the effects of a decline in national income from, say, a decrease in net exports or investment.

By the same token, not only do individual income taxes increase as incomes rise, but so do sales tax revenues, corporate income tax revenues, and excise taxes (taxes on telephone service, airlines, gasoline, and so on). If the economy is growing very rapidly, these mechanisms automatically help to slow it down.

STATE AND LOCAL GOVERNMENTS

Though the discussion of government expenditures so far has focused on the taxes and expenditures of the federal government, approximately one-third of U.S. government expenditures are at the state and local levels. These expenditures and the taxes that

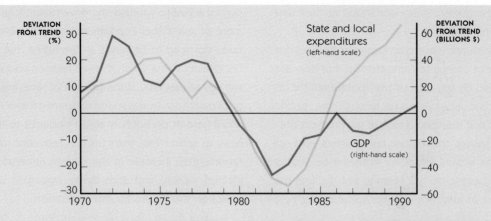

Figure 30.6 EXPENDITURES BY STATE AND LOCAL GOVERNMENTS

The figure shows expenditures of state and local governments, relative to their trend. These expenditures tend to increase in booms and decrease in recessions, thus contributing to the volatility of the economy. (State and local expenditures have on average been increasing in recent decades. The "trend" is the average rate of increase over a period. The figure shows that in boom years the expenditures are greater than this average, while in recessions they are much less.) *Source: ERP* (1992), Tables B-2, B-77.

finance them are governed by quite different considerations from those that prevail at the national level. The states do not see stabilizing the economy and maintaining full employment as their responsibility. Indeed, the fluctuations in their expenditures have probably contributed to the fluctuations in the aggregate level of economic activity, as shown in Figure 30.6. Many state constitutions require a balanced budget; that is, they limit expenditures to the amount collected in taxes. Local governments are often restricted in their borrowing, and any borrowing has to be approved directly by voters. Moreover, states often find it difficult (or at least politically inopportune) to raise tax rates, particularly in bad times.

Thus, when the economy goes into a recession, states and localities often find their revenues reduced, and they respond by reducing their expenditures. They are in effect cutting back on the fiscal stimulus at just the time it is most needed. The situation is identical to that of a balanced budget reduction in government expenditures, the outcome of which is reduced national output.

THE DEFICIT AND STABILIZATION POLICY

The huge deficits of the last decade have placed the subject of deficits at the center of the stage of political debates. Who is to blame? What are the consequences? What should be done? These are questions we will pursue in greater detail in Chapter 38. Here we ask, what are the implications for government stabilization policy?

In 1988, President Bush ran on the slogan "Read my lips: No new taxes." Nevertheless, two years later, his concern about the consequences of the unbridled deficits and his recognition of the seeming impossibility of cutting expenditures led him to propose tax increases. Even with the tax increases, the downturn in economic conditions resulted

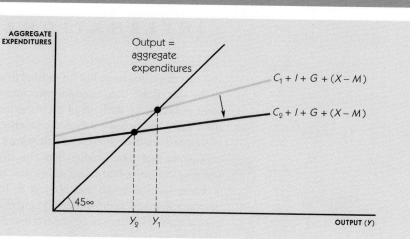

Figure 30.7 THE EFFECT OF THE BUSH ADMINISTRATION TAX INCREASE

In an attempt to reduce the deficit, the government increased taxes in 1990, shifting the $C + I + G + (X - M)$ line down and thus perhaps contributing to the incipient recession.

in record deficits, as the automatic stabilizers went to work producing lower tax revenues and higher expenditures.

The tax increases may have had another deleterious effect on the economy. Earlier we distinguished between situations where the economy is at full employment—on the vertical portion of its aggregate supply curve—and where it is in the flat, excess-capacity range. An increase in taxes shifts the aggregate demand curve to the left, reducing national output. In 1990, at the time the tax increase was enacted, the economy already appeared to have some excess capacity. There was concern that the tax increase was timed at almost the worst possible moment; rather than offsetting what appeared to be an incipient recession, fiscal policy may have been abetting it. Figure 30.7 shows the downward shift in the $C + I + G + (X - M)$ schedule caused by the tax increase, and the resulting reduction in national income from Y_1 to Y_2.

More generally, the large deficits of the 1980s, and the evident difficulty in reducing them, are likely to impair for years to come the government's ability to use fiscal policy to help stabilize the economy.

DEFICITS

1. Whether deficits are good or bad depends on the state of the economy. Deficits may help restore the economy to full employment.

2. While deficits may crowd out some private investment, they will nevertheless have a stimulative effect so long as the economy has many underutilized resources. Crowding out is less likely if the country can borrow abroad.

INTERNATIONAL TRADE

It seems surprising now, but for most of this century, the level of foreign trade in relation to the size of the U.S. economy was so small that foreign trade could be ignored, for most purposes, by students of the American economy. Appropriately, they considered the United States to be a closed economy, or one that did not trade, for the purposes of simplicity in their analysis. Trade was an issue relevant to the study of those European economies that were smaller than the United States and close together, or those developing countries that relied on outside suppliers for technology and materials.

Today sales of goods and services to foreigners represent a major portion of U.S. aggregate demand: approximately $1 out of every $10 of what the U.S. economy produces goes abroad. The amount of imports that America purchases from abroad is even larger. The U.S. economy is an open one, and the foreign sector is critical to any consideration of policy. The following sections describe the growing importance of trade in the U.S. economy and how it fits into the macroeconomic analysis presented so far.

THE GROWING TRADE DEFICIT

Figure 30.8 shows how dramatically imports and exports have increased as a share of GDP between 1960 and 1990. Its clear message is that the U.S. economy is no longer so self-sufficient that foreign production can be ignored. Figure 30.9 illustrates the fact that foreign trade looms even larger in the economy of other countries.

Chapter 3 discussed the reason for all of this trade: it allows each country to make the most of its comparative advantage, to specialize in its strengths. International trade is mutually advantageous—all countries gain.

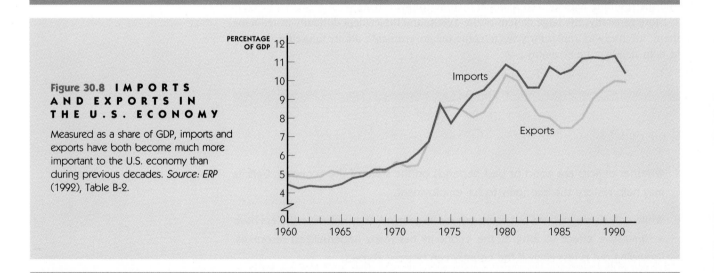

Figure 30.8 IMPORTS AND EXPORTS IN THE U.S. ECONOMY

Measured as a share of GDP, imports and exports have both become much more important to the U.S. economy than during previous decades. *Source: ERP* (1992), Table B-2.

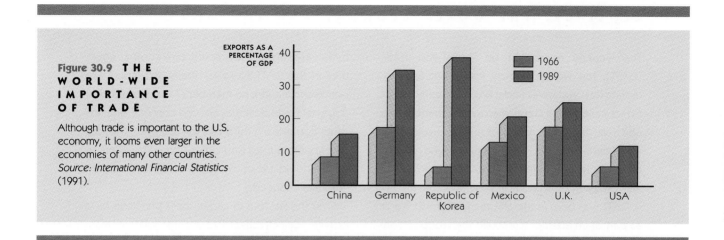

Figure 30.9 THE WORLD-WIDE IMPORTANCE OF TRADE

Although trade is important to the U.S. economy, it looms even larger in the economies of many other countries. *Source: International Financial Statistics* (1991).

But in the midst of these advantages, there is a small dark cloud. As explained in Chapter 3, when exports fall short of imports, there is a trade deficit. There was a dramatic increase in U.S. trade deficits during the 1980s. This climb was matched in magnitude by the advancing federal budget deficits of the same period, and was the cause for at least as much alarm. The connections between the trade and budget deficits will be discussed in Chapter 38. For now, we will examine the trade deficits alone.

One gets a sense of how quickly the U.S. trade situation has changed by noting that in the years immediately after World War II, there was worry that U.S. trade surpluses might be too large. If we look closely at today's large trade deficits, we find that the aggregate deficit statistics are focused primarily in a handful of industries. In the first half of the 1980s, car imports rose from $16.8 billion to $36.5 billion. Machinery imports increased from $32.3 billion to $75.3 billion. Imports likewise rose in the steel, textile, shoe, even sophisticated computer chip industries. As imported products gained market share in these and other industries, regions in the United States where steel, cars, textiles, and so on were produced began to suffer unemployment or slower economic growth. Foreign imports took the blame for the hard times. While the country as a whole may have benefited from the increase in trade, some regions of the country were seriously hurt.

PROTECTIONISM, 1980S STYLE

The trade deficits of the 1980s fed a cascade of fearful rhetoric. Those foreigners, it was often said, were refusing to buy American products, which was why exports were not increasing. A common theme in public debates over trade policy, though not one favored by most economists, is protectionism, the view that policies should be pursued to protect domestic producers from competition from imports. The contrasting view, favoring no barriers to international trade, is known as **free trade**. A spirit of protectionism grew in hopes that protectionist policies would save American workers and jobs from the threat posed by imports. During the 1980s, for example, while President

CLOSE-UP: THE WORLD ECONOMY AND THE GATT

The General Agreement on Tariffs and Trade (GATT), the world's primary instrument for promoting free trade, was under fire in the early 1990s. Cynics called it the Gentleman's Agreement to Talk and Talk. The latest round of talks to update the agreement—the so-called Uruguay round, named after the host country—had started in 1986 but was dragging on without a resolution.

GATT was born in the aftermath of World War II, as part of an attempt to rebuild the world's economy. Participants from many countries remembered the destructive trade battles of the 1930s, when countries restricted imports in an attempt to protect their own economies, only to find that when all countries restrict imports, their exports suffer too. The strangulation of world trade was one of the factors contributing to the Great Depression.

GATT began with twenty-three countries as members and three guiding principles for reducing trade barriers. One principle was *reciprocity*: if one country lowered its tariffs, it could expect other countries in the GATT to lower theirs. A second was *nondiscrimination*: no member of GATT could offer a special trade deal that favored only one or a few other countries. A third was *transparency,* the idea that import quotas and other nontariff barriers to trade should be converted into tariffs and then gradually reduced.

Over the last four decades, these principles have proved very effective. The average tariff on manufactured goods was 40 percent in 1947; it is less than 5 percent today. The volume of world trade has grown twice as quickly as the world economy, making national economies more stable and more interdependent. Today, about one hundred nations are members of GATT.

But despite these accomplishments, most of what has been written about GATT in the last few years has a tone of frustration, even defeatism. The main goal of the Uruguay round was to extend the trade

agreement so that industrialized nations would reduce protectionism for their own farmers and textile industries, thus offering new opportunities for imports from the world's poorer countries. However, new trade rules would also allow industrialized nations to export their service industries, such as financial services, to the poorer nations, and to protect their inventors from patent violators in the Third World. Although the deal seemed to offer something for every nation, Europe's heavily protected farmers lobbied hard against it and produced a stalemate.

But the problems of GATT went beyond the particular issues of the Uruguay round. Although GATT has been very successful at reducing tariffs, it is ill-equipped to address many of the other barriers to free trade.

Massive changes in exchange rates during the 1980s made many countries fearful that their economies could be exposed to violent fluctuations from foreign trade, not because of any fundamental change in the markets for the goods they were producing, but simply because of events in financial markets. This fear led many countries to impose import quotas and other ways of limiting the quantity of imports. Clearly, this works against the GATT principle of transparency. Moreover, countries in both Europe and North America were negotiating to form free-trade zones, where countries within the zone would be treated differently from those outside; these agreements may threaten the GATT principles of reciprocity and nondiscrimination.

Like all treaty arrangements, GATT does too little for the satisfaction of some parties. But its successes should serve as a reminder that it remains a useful tool for preventing a cycle of trade restrictions that could reduce the wealth of all nations.

Source: "World Trade: Jousting for Advantage," The Economist, September 22, 1990.

Reagan talked about the importance of free markets, American protectionism soared. A study by the International Monetary Fund concluded that America's trade barriers against importing cars, textiles, and steel were the equivalent of a 25 percent tariff on those products.

By the late 1980s, about 40 percent of Japan's exports to the United States were limited by some form of U.S. protectionism. The United States had persuaded Japan to restrict its exports of cars. The United States had also restricted the imports of Japanese computer chips, accusing Japan of dumping their chips (that is, selling their chips at below the cost of production) on the American market in an effort to drive U.S. firms out of business. New trade legislation was enacted in 1988, giving the president strong powers to take actions against countries deemed to be engaged in unfair trade practices.

All told, the decade of the 1980s produced a dramatic rise in trade barriers. While about one-eighth of all U.S. imports were affected by protectionism in 1980, by the end of the decade the figure was one-quarter. It is estimated that trade barriers may prevent consumers and businesses from buying as much as $50 billion in imports they would otherwise have purchased. Clearly, the United States is no angel of free trade; it has plenty of trade barriers to shut out products from other countries.

While charges of unfair competition and trade practices in the 1980s struck a sympathetic chord with the public, most economists believed that clever or unscrupulous foreign traders were not at the root of America's trade problems. One can always point to examples of foreign trade practices that seem unfair. But the trade deficits of the

1980s developed rapidly: the deficit doubled in 1983, doubled again in 1984, almost doubled again in 1985, and continued to increase in succeeding years. It is simply not plausible that this happened just because tricky foreigners rapidly increased the extent to which they engaged in unfair practices in those years. Instead, most economists argued that the trade deficit and the resulting economic dislocations were a symptom of a deeper illness in the American economy. Protectionism was not the appropriate cure; in fact, it was not a cure at all. It might not create jobs, and, more important, it would interfere with the ability of the economy to use its comparative advantage, thus making everyone worse off.

An increase in the trade deficit can come about for two reasons. First, with given exports and a given import function, an increase in national income—caused, for example, by an increase in government expenditures or investment—will result in a higher trade deficit. This is simply because as income increases, imports increase, while exports remain unchanged. Second, there could be an upward *shift* in the import function, so that at any given level of income the country imports more. In either case, *net* exports at any given level of income will be lower. Such shifts do put a major drag on the economy, as Figure 30.10 shows. In panel A, an income-expenditure analysis diagram, the initial equilibrium lies at the intersection of the aggregate expenditures schedule with the 45-degree line. If net exports decline to $X_2 - M_2$, national income will decline to Y_2, and employment will also go down.

There are several reasons that protectionism may not create jobs. One likely result of protectionism is that foreigners will retaliate against it. If this happens, then while protectionism may reduce U.S. imports, it will also reduce U.S. exports; net exports could therefore be even further reduced, and national output further decreased. Thus, in panel B, the reduction of net exports from $X_2 - M_2$ to $X_3 - M_3$ lowers equilibrium output from Y_2 to Y_3, with a corresponding further reduction in employment. As noted earlier, policies that try to increase national income by reducing imports are referred to as beggar-thy-neighbor policies, because one country's economy is helped at the expense of others'. In the Great Depression, many countries followed these beggar-thy-neighbor protectionist policies, with all countries suffering as a result.

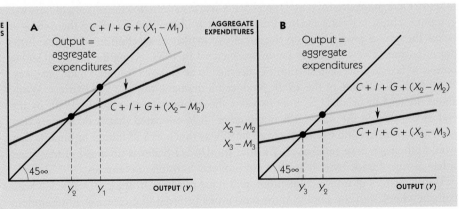

Figure 30.10 NET EXPORTS AND NATIONAL OUTPUT

In panel A, a reduction in net exports shifts the $C + I + G + (X - M)$ schedule down and lowers national output from Y_1 to Y_2. Panel B shows that trade restrictions may not be effective. While they reduce imports, if foreigners retaliate, exports are also reduced. The net effect may be a reduction in net exports and a further decrease in output from Y_2 to Y_3.

THE DETERMINANTS OF NET EXPORTS

To understand the marked changes in net exports that have occurred, we need to study more closely the determinants of net exports. Exports are determined by the prices of goods produced by other countries relative to the prices of American goods, as well as the level of incomes abroad and foreigners' tastes for American goods. Imports are also determined by relative prices, as well as the level of income in the United States and Americans' tastes for foreign goods. The first section below takes up changes in tastes; the second, changes in relative incomes; and the third, changes in relative prices.

CHANGES IN TASTES

In the years following World War II, "Made in America" became a label coveted around the world, as American songs, American dress, and a whole range of American products made great inroads into foreign markets. At each level of income, net exports increased. This is illustrated in Figure 30.11, which gives the level of net exports at each level of income, by the upward shift from $X_1 - M$ to $X_2 - M$. We refer to this as the **net export function**. An increase in exports leads to an upward shift in the net export function and in the aggregate expenditures schedule, as seen in Figure 30.12—the familiar income-expenditure analysis diagram—increasing national income.

Reebok athletic shoes, Christian Dior designer clothes, Mercedes-Benz cars: such high-priced imported goods have long had a certain cachet with American consumers. They have been a symbol of luxury. But in the 1970s and 1980s, middle-class Americans began buying these brand-name imported goods on a massive scale. Some of the changed demand could be traced to changed economic circumstances: the high price of oil led Americans to desire the small cars that Japan had learned to produce more efficiently than General Motors or Ford. But some of the changed demand was simply a change in tastes.

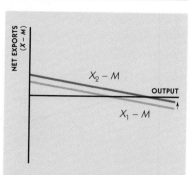

Figure 30.11 HOW FOR-EIGNERS' TASTES FOR AMERICAN GOODS SHIFT THE NET EXPORT FUNCTION

A shift in tastes by foreign buyers that leads to the purchase of more U.S. exports shifts the net export function up, as shown by the shift from $X_1 - M$ to $X_2 - M$.

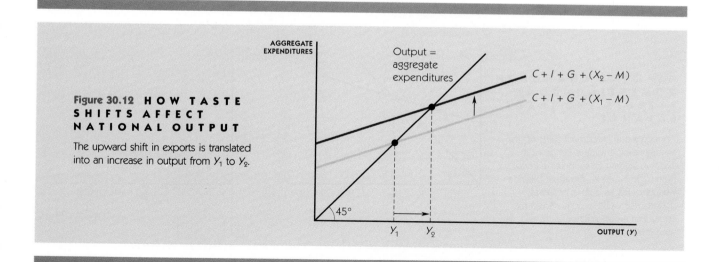

Figure 30.12 HOW TASTE SHIFTS AFFECT NATIONAL OUTPUT

The upward shift in exports is translated into an increase in output from Y_1 to Y_2.

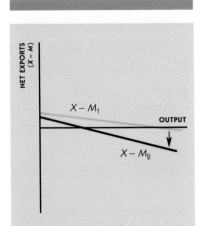

Figure 30.13 HOW TASTES FOR IMPORTS SHIFT THE NET EXPORT FUNCTION

A shift in tastes by U.S. consumers in favor of buying more imports increases the level of imports at each level of income as well as the marginal propensity to import. As a result, the net export function shifts down, from $X - M_1$ to $X - M_2$. Moreover, the larger marginal propensity to import makes the net import function steeper.

The increased level of imports at each level of income reduced net exports at each level of income; this is shown in Figure 30.13 by the reduction from $X - M_1$ to $X - M_2$. The figure assumes not only that Americans import more at each level of income, but that their **marginal propensity to import** has also increased. Out of each extra dollar of income Americans have to spend, they spend more of it on imports. That is why the net export function has become steeper. This downward shift in the net export function decreases aggregate expenditures at each level of national output, and as we saw in Chapter 28, the increased marginal propensity to import reduces the multiplier. Increases in government expenditures will be less effective in stimulating the economy than they were when imports were less important.

CHANGES IN RELATIVE INCOMES

Chapter 28 showed how a rise in income in the United States would increase imports. By the same token, higher incomes in foreign countries increase *their* imports—U.S. exports. If incomes in the United States and abroad rise together, then imports increase with exports and trade remains balanced. The United States began its recovery from the worldwide recession of the early 1980s around 1983. Europe was much slower to recover, and this accounts for some—but only some—of the growth in the trade deficit that occurred in those years.

Figure 30.14 focuses on what happens to the trade deficit if incomes abroad remain unchanged but incomes in the United States rise; this could be the result of an increase, for instance, in investment. Panel A shows the initial level of aggregate expenditures (at each level of income), with the equilibrium output at Y_1. Now assume investment increases, shifting the aggregate expenditures schedule up to $C + I_2 + G + (X - M)$. As a result, the level of national income rises to Y_2, for the usual reasons.

The effect this has on the trade deficit is shown in panel B, which depicts the net export function. (Remember, while exports are assumed not to depend on income, imports are, and that is why net exports decrease as income rises.) In the initial situation,

Figure 30.14 A CHANGE IN DOMESTIC INCOME AFFECTS THE TRADE BALANCE

An increase in investment shifts up the aggregate expenditures schedule in panel A, leading to an increase in output from Y_1 to Y_2. At Y_1, the trade balance was zero. But as output increases, imports rise while exports remain the same, and a trade deficit is created, as seen in panel B.

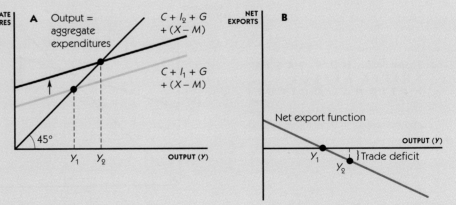

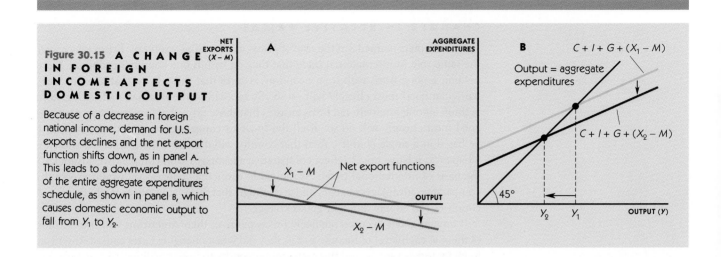

Figure 30.15 A CHANGE IN FOREIGN INCOME AFFECTS DOMESTIC OUTPUT

Because of a decrease in foreign national income, demand for U.S. exports declines and the net export function shifts down, as in panel A. This leads to a downward movement of the entire aggregate expenditures schedule, as shown in panel B, which causes domestic economic output to fall from Y_1 to Y_2.

with income (output) equal to Y_1, exports balance imports: net exports are zero. The higher level of income then produces an increase in imports. Incomes abroad remain unchanged, however, so exports remain unchanged.[4] Thus, the higher income produces a trade deficit at Y_2.

The effect of a decline in incomes abroad can be seen in Figure 30.15A, which shows the net export function shifting down from $X_1 - M$ to $X_2 - M$: at each level of income in the United States, the level of net exports is now lower. Panel B then shows how this results in a lower level of income (output) in the United States, as the level of aggregate expenditures at each level of income decreases. One message of the figure is that recessions are a contagious disease in the international economy: a decline in income in one country gets transmitted to others.

The concept of income elasticity of demand can be used to make very rough calculations of the effect of different growth rates of incomes in the United States and Europe on the trade deficit. The assumption behind Figure 30.14B, that in the initial situation exports equal imports, is not a bad assumption for the U.S. economy at the start of the 1980s. Now, if incomes in the United States grow 5 percent while those abroad stagnate, and if the income elasticity of demand for imports is 1 (that is, a 1 percent increase in income leads to a 1 percent increase in imports) and relative prices are fixed, then exports will remain stagnant while imports grow by 5 percent. Since initially imports equaled exports, now imports exceed exports by 5 percent.

But as the evidence presented earlier shows, U.S. imports increased by nearly 100 percent in five years, and U.S. incomes did not increase by enough to account for that sort of growth. Calculations like these lead most economists to believe that the differences in growth rates of incomes between the United States and Europe, while they could account for some of the increase in the trade deficit, played a relatively small role.

---

[4] Of course, increased U.S. imports mean increased exports for Europe; if not offset by other factors, these increased European exports will raise incomes in Europe. Europe will then import more. Some of those imports will be from the United States. So increased U.S. imports may eventually lead to some increase in U.S. exports.

CHANGES IN RELATIVE PRICES

Earlier chapters pointed out the role of prices in allocating resources. Prices play exactly the same role in international trade that they do within one country's economy. Competition among firms within an economy ensures that those firms that can produce a particular good most cheaply will do so. So too within the international setting: competition among international firms ensures that those firms that can produce a particular good most cheaply will do so. If all the low-cost companies in an industry happen to be based in a single country, then that country will dominate the market. As shown in Chapter 3, relative prices reflect comparative advantages, and comparative advantage is the basis of international trade. As the world economy changes, we would expect that comparative advantages change, and accordingly that the relative prices at which different countries can supply different goods change.

If foreign goods become relatively less expensive, then Americans will import more of them at each level of income just as they did when changing tastes caused Americans to prefer foreign goods; and the marginal propensity to import will increase as well. The import function, giving the level of imports at each level of income, will shift up, as in Figure 30.16A, and the marginal propensity to import will increase. At the same time, American firms will find it increasingly difficult to sell their goods abroad. As a result, exports will be reduced. Net exports will thus decline from $X_1 - M_1$ to $X_2 - M_2$, as shown in panel B. This in turn means that the aggregate expenditures schedule will drop. Panel C traces out the effect of the shift in the net export function on the level of aggregate expenditures—it shifts down—and hence on the level of equilibrium output, which falls from Y_1 to Y_2. And the flatter slope of the aggregate expenditures schedule means that the multiplier has been reduced as well.

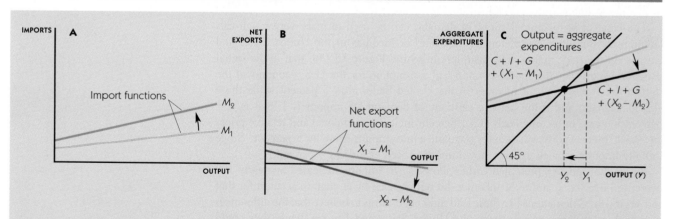

Figure 30.16 CHANGES IN RELATIVE PRICES AFFECT AGGREGATE DEMAND

If foreign goods become less expensive relative to U.S. products, then the import function shifts up, as shown in panel A. Since foreign goods are also now relatively less expensive in their home countries, it becomes more difficult to export, and the net export function shifts down, as in panel B. These combined changes result in a downward shift in the aggregate expenditures schedule and a resulting decrease in the equilibrium level of output, depicted in panel C.

The price of American goods relative to those produced abroad depends on the **exchange rate**. The exchange rate measures the cost of one currency in terms of another, in this case the rate at which American dollars can be exchanged for Japanese yen, German marks, British pounds, and other currencies. If a bottle of good French wine costs 50 francs in Paris and if the exchange rate is 5 francs to the dollar, an American can buy the bottle for $10. But if the exchange rate should change, as it did in the early 1980s, so that there are 10 francs to the dollar, an American can buy that same bottle for $5. If Japanese yen become more expensive in terms of dollars, then Japanese goods simultaneously become more expensive to Americans.

The expression "There are two sides to every coin" applies with particular force to international exchange. A change in the exchange rate—say, from 5 francs to the dollar to 10 francs to the dollar—that makes foreign goods look less expensive to Americans makes American goods look more expensive to foreigners. This kind of change is called a **depreciation** in the value of the franc (the franc is worth less in terms of dollars) or an **appreciation** in the value of the dollar (the dollar is worth more in terms of francs). When the franc depreciates against the dollar, we say the dollar is stronger and the franc is weaker; conversely, when the franc appreciates against the dollar, we say the dollar is weaker and the franc is stronger.

Changes in exchange rates, like changes in any other relative price, are not necessarily good or bad. It is not necessarily "good" that the dollar becomes stronger or bad that it becomes weaker, though some countries view the strength of their currency as a source of national pride. Like any change in relative prices, some people benefit and some people lose. A strong dollar is good for American consumers, who find they can buy French goods more cheaply, and good for French exporters, who find they can sell their goods more easily. It is bad for American exporters, who find their markets for foreign goods disappearing, and bad for French consumers, who find they can no longer afford American goods. Thus, when the dollar appreciates, U.S. imports increase and exports decrease; when the dollar depreciates, U.S imports decrease and exports increase.

Relative prices also depend on relative rates of inflation. If Britain has 10 percent inflation while the United States has 5 percent, then even if exchange rates stay the same, the *relative* price of British goods will increase by 5 percent. Likewise, the international demand for U.S. goods declines when (at a given exchange rate) inflation in the United States outpaces that in other countries.

Changes in the prices of American goods relative to those produced abroad depend, then, on three factors: changes in the exchange rate; changes in the prices of American goods (in terms of dollars), that is, the rate of inflation in the United States; and changes in the prices of goods produced in foreign countries (in terms of their own currencies), that is, the rate of inflation in each of the producing countries. The exchange rates adjusted for the changes in price levels in each country are called **real exchange rates**. We postpone until Chapter 35 the discussion of the relationship between inflation and exchange rates. The remainder of this chapter assumes prices in each country are fixed (or rising at the same rate, so the differential is zero), and focuses attention on changes in the exchange rate. (Under these assumptions, changes in the exchange rate and changes in the real exchange rate are equivalent.)

What determines the exchange rate is a complicated matter, which we also take up in Chapter 35. For now, we simply ask, what are the *consequences* of changes in the exchange rate? How much imports and exports change when exchange rates change depends on the price elasticity of demand, the percentage change in the demand for imported goods as a result of a 1 percent change in the price. Consider a situation where the value of the dollar increases by 40 percent relative to other currencies; Americans find foreign goods 40 percent cheaper than they were before, foreigners find U.S. goods 40 percent more expensive than they were before. Assume that the price elasticity of exports is 1.5 and the price elasticity of imports is similarly 1.5; that is, a 1 percent increase in the price results in a 1.5 percent decrease in the quantity demanded. To make the calculations easy, assume that initially there was $200 billion in exports and $200 billion in imports.

Because of the shift in exchange rates, the quantity of U.S. exports demanded by foreigners will decline by 60 percent, or $120 billion. At the same time, the *quantity* of imports (at any given level of income in the United States) will increase by 60 percent, but because the dollar is worth 40 percent more, Americans will only have to spend 20 percent more (in terms of U.S. dollars) to increase their demand by 60 percent.[5] Hence, in terms of dollars, imports will rise to $240 billion. Thanks to the change in exchange rates, the trade deficit will grow from zero to $160 billion. This is a downward shift in the net export function—it is the change in net exports at a particular level of income. The shift in the net export function will, if not offset, give rise to a change in equilibrium output.

SOURCES OF DOWNWARD SHIFTS IN THE NET EXPORT FUNCTION

1. A change in tastes for imported goods

2. An increase in income in the United States relative to incomes abroad

3. An increase in the prices of American goods relative to those of foreigners, caused by either an appreciation of the dollar or a higher rate of inflation in the United States than abroad

Changes in the Exchange Rate in the 1980s Some of the growth in the U.S. trade deficit in the early 1980s can be traced to the enormous change in the exchange rates during that period. Figure 30.17 illustrates these changes over the past two decades, showing how much the Japanese yen, the German mark, and the Canadian dollar have been worth in terms of the U.S. dollar. (By comparing the ratios with each other, you

---

[5] Note that if Americans' demand for foreign goods is relatively inelastic—say the price elasticity is .2—then the appreciation of the dollar will actually reduce what Americans spend abroad. The 40 percent decline in price will give rise to an 8 percent increase in U.S. imports; so expenditures, measured in dollars, will decline by approximately 32 percent. If foreigners' demand for U.S. goods is inelastic, with a price elasticity of .2, then exports will decline by a relatively small amount—the 40 percent price increase facing foreigners will lead to an 8 percent decrease in U.S. exports. Thus, in this case, imports (measured in dollars) will decrease *more* than exports. The appreciation of the dollar will shift the net export function up. This, however, is not the typical case; normally we expect a dollar appreciation to shift the net export function down, a depreciation to shift it up.

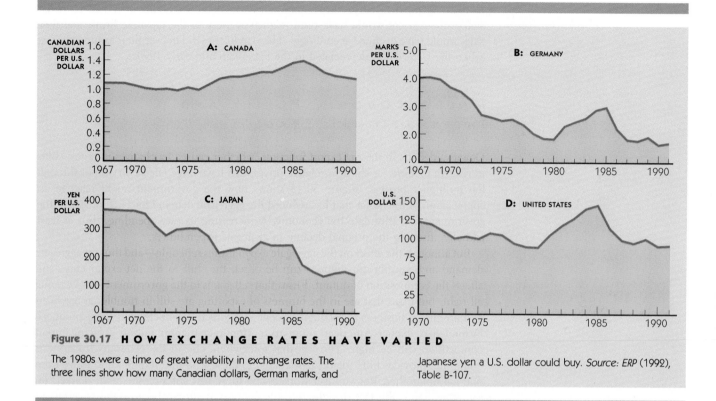

Figure 30.17 **H O W   E X C H A N G E   R A T E S   H A V E   V A R I E D**

The 1980s were a time of great variability in exchange rates. The three lines show how many Canadian dollars, German marks, and Japanese yen a U.S. dollar could buy. *Source: ERP* (1992), Table B-107.

can also tell how much any one of those currencies is worth in terms of any other one.) Sometimes you may see a reference to one currency, perhaps the dollar, becoming "stronger" or "weaker" with no particular reference to another currency. In that case, the analyst is discussing the dollar in terms of some average of the currencies of U.S. trading partners. These averages are generally weighted to match the trading relationships, so that the value of currencies of major trading partners like Canada, Mexico, and Japan receive a greater weight than the currencies of countries that have a smaller amount of trade with the United States. Panel D shows the movements in the trade-weighted exchange rate.

When the dollar-mark exchange rate shot up by more than 60 percent between 1980 and 1985, for American consumers it was as if German goods were on sale, marked down by 60 percent, and as if a 60 percent tax had been placed on all American exports.[6] With a sale this big, it is little wonder either that U.S. expenditures on imports soared or that those in other countries found it unattractive to buy American products. America's trade problems in the early 1980s were primarily macroeconomic, in the sense that they affected all sectors of the economy. American industries that were not keeping up with foreign competition—whose costs of production were, for instance, not declining as fast

---

[6] Actually, in many manufacturing industries, such as automobiles, the Germans absorbed a significant fraction of these changes. This may be explained in terms of the theories of imperfect competition discussed in Chapters 15–16.

as those in Japan—had a deeper problem: even if the exchange rates had remained stable, their prices would have risen relative to those of the Japanese firms, and their sales would have declined accordingly. These industries did not see their fortunes reverse when the U.S. dollar depreciated in the late 1980s and early 1990s.

MACROECONOMIC POLICY AND INTERNATIONAL TRADE

Downward shifts in the net export function, whether caused by changes in tastes, shifts in relative income, or shifts in relative prices, can have large effects on output through the multiplier process. Figure 30.18 shows how the government might react to an appreciation of the dollar that has reduced the aggregate demand for U.S. products: the government can stimulate the economy by increasing its own spending, thus at least partially offsetting the original decline in aggregate expenditures.

But although the effect on the aggregate expenditures schedule—and thus on aggregate demand and equilibrium output—can be offset, the shift in the net export curve still affects the composition of output. Firms that sell goods to the government may be doing all right, but firms that are in the business of exporting are still in trouble, as are firms that are in the business of producing goods that directly compete with those produced by foreigners, such as American automakers. Unemployment in industries facing import competition will be high. The fact that somewhere else in the economy someone is doing well provides little solace, particularly to those who find it difficult to move from one job to another. For younger workers and those just entering the labor market, on the other hand, the fact that the overall economy is strong (because the government has taken actions to counteract the effects of the appreciation of the dollar) makes a big difference. They are in a good position to seek out the new jobs being created.

There is another consequence of the government's attempt to restore the economy's output: the trade deficit will increase. Remember, what initiated the problem was a shift in the net export function, so that at each level of income net exports are lower.

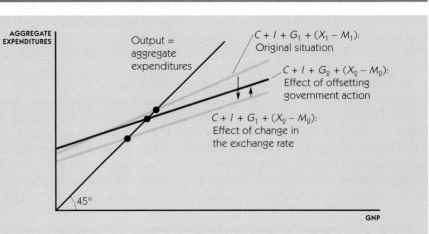

Figure 30.18
MACROECONOMIC POLICY TO OFFSET SHIFTS IN FOREIGN EXCHANGE

Macroeconomic policy can offset changes in exchange rates. If the dollar appreciates, for example, the aggregate expenditures schedule will shift down as imports increase and exports fall. But government policies to stimulate the economy, whether by encouraging consumption or investment or spending more directly, can shift the aggregate expenditures schedule back up again.

AGGREGATE EXPENDITURES

Output = aggregate expenditures

$C + I + G_1 + (X_1 - M_1)$: Original situation

$C + I + G_2 + (X_2 - M_2)$: Effect of offsetting government action

$C + I + G_1 + (X_2 - M_2)$: Effect of change in the exchange rate

45°

GNP

If the government succeeds in restoring output to the level where it was before the downward shift in the net export function took place, the trade deficit will have increased by the full amount of the downward shift in the net export function (assuming the exchange rate remains unchanged).

LOOKING AHEAD: EXCHANGE RATES AND GOVERNMENT POLICIES

Exchange rates adjust in response to government policies, and how they respond may either decrease or increase the effectiveness of the government policy.

Consider, for instance, the problem posed earlier in this chapter: the effectiveness of protectionism in creating American jobs. If the United States imports less from, say, Japan, as a result of tariffs or other trade barriers, Americans will demand fewer Japanese goods and therefore fewer yen, since they will need fewer yen to purchase Japanese goods. With less demand for yen, it would not be surprising to see the yen depreciate—become less valuable relative to the dollar. But we have already analyzed the effects of such a change in the exchange rate: an appreciation of the dollar (this corresponds to the depreciation of the yen) shifts the net export function down. Thus, changes in the exchange rate may offset the effect of protectionism. Indeed, these changes may be so powerful that they fully offset the effects of protectionism: imports are not actually reduced in total, and jobs are not created.

Changes in the exchange rate may also offset government attempts to stimulate the economy through increasing government expenditures. In the discussion of government expenditures in the first part of this chapter, we learned that government policies may be less effective in stimulating the economy than was suggested by the basic model of Chapter 28; increased government expenditures may crowd out private investment, and the net effect on the economy may be quite small.

In an open economy, changes in the exchange rate can either dampen or amplify the effectiveness of government attempts to stimulate the economy, depending on whether they lead to an appreciation or depreciation of the dollar. If increased government expenditures lead to an appreciation, then the net export function will shift down, offsetting the stimulating effect of the increased government expenditures. Chapter 35 will discuss the circumstances in which increased government expenditures may lead to an appreciation or depreciation of the dollar.

PRINCIPLES OF MACROECONOMIC POLICY IN OPEN ECONOMIES

1. In determining macroeconomic policy in an open economy, the government must pay careful attention to what is happening to the exchange rate, for any changes will not only determine how effective government policy will be, they will also determine how different policies affect different individuals within the economy.

2. In an interconnected world economy, unemployment and recessions are like contagious diseases. Downturns in one economy can spread to others.

3. Upward shifts in the net export function can stimulate the economy, just as downward shifts in the net export function can drag it down.

4. Changes in the exchange rate, by affecting imports, may affect not only the *level* of national income but also the magnitude of the multiplier. This is because spending on imports represents a leakage. Changes in the exchange rate affect the fraction of each additional dollar of income that is spent abroad.

5. Protectionism is not a good solution to macroeconomic problems, even when the unemployment is due to a shift in the net export function. Beggar-thy-neighbor policies may not succeed in restoring net exports, since the reduction in imports is met by retaliation from abroad, which reduces exports; and changes in exchange rates may simply offset any benefits from the protectionist policies. Most important, protectionism is costly because it interferes with countries' ability to use their comparative advantage.

REVIEW AND PRACTICE

SUMMARY

1. If the government simultaneously increases (or decreases) taxes and expenditures by the same amount so that the budget is balanced, aggregate expenditures in the economy still increase.

2. The magnitude of the fiscal stimulus provided by the government is sometimes measured by the full-employment deficit, the deficit that would have arisen if the economy were at full employment. When the economy is below full employment, the full-employment deficit is smaller than the actual deficit.

3. The government debt is the accumulation of annual budget deficits. The real debt takes into account the effects of inflation. The real deficit is the change in the real debt. In some years, while there has been a nominal deficit, real debt has been reduced.

4. If government and private investors are competing for the same fixed pool of capital, then government borrowing to finance the deficit may crowd out private investment. Crowding out is most likely when the economy is near the full-employment level of output and least likely when the economy has excess capacity; it is also less likely in open economies.

5. Some government programs act as automatic stabilizers. They increase expenditures and reduce taxes as the economy goes into a recession, and cut expenditures and raise taxes as the economy expands, thus reducing the value of the multiplier and the instability of the economy.

6. State and local governments also tend to increase their spending in booms and reduce it during recessions, thus contributing to the fluctuations of the economy.

7. In recent years, foreign trade has become much more important to the U.S. economy. In addition, the United States began to run large trade deficits in the 1980s, as imports increased sharply.

8. Shifts in the net export function, which gives the level of net exports at each level of income, give rise to shifts in the aggregate expenditures schedule and hence to variability in the equilibrium level of output. Possible reasons for these shifts include changes in consumer preferences for imported goods in the United States and abroad, changes in relative incomes in the United States and abroad, and changes in relative prices in the United States and abroad.

9. Such macroeconomic policies as increased government expenditures can offset the effect of changes in the net export function. However, there is no assurance that the government stimulus for the economy will help those who were hurt by declining exports and increased imports.

KEY TERMS

deficit spending
full-employment
  deficit
crowding out

net export function
marginal propensity to
  import

exchange rate
depreciation
appreciation

REVIEW QUESTIONS

1. Is it possible for the government to stimulate the economy without changing the size of its budget deficit? Explain.

2. How is a full-employment deficit calculated? Will it be higher or lower than the actual deficit? Why?

3. What is the difference between the deficit and the debt?

4. If complete crowding out occurs, how much will running a larger budget deficit stimulate the economy? Explain. What are the factors that make crowding out more likely? less likely?

5. Name at least two automatic stabilizers, and describe how they work.

6. How might the federal government contribute to economic instability? How might state and local governments contribute to economic instability?

7. What are the major determinants of shifts in the net export function? Explain how each one can work in each direction.

8. How can recessions be contagious in the world economy?

9. If exchange rates do not change, why is a government stimulus of the economy likely to lead to a trade deficit?

PROBLEMS

1. Suppose that while pursuing your favorite pastime in the dormitory of arguing over economic issues, someone says that the budget deficit rose from $128 billion in 1982 to $270 billion in 1992. How might you adjust these figures to get a more accurate picture of the economic impact of the deficit?

2. Imagine that Japanese products go out of fashion in the United States. How would this affect Japan's net export function and aggregate expenditures schedule? Draw two diagrams to illustrate.

3. Imagine that U.S. consumers begin to believe that imports are often of better quality than American-made products. How will this affect the U.S. net export function and aggregate expenditures schedule? Draw two diagrams to illustrate.

4. Assume that exports equal imports, and both equal $100 billion. America's income elasticity for foreign imports is 1.5, while foreigners' income elasticity for American imports is also 1.5. If foreign exchange rates do not change, what happens to America's imports if income in the United States increases by 10 percent? What happens to American exports if foreigners' income increases by 10 percent? If both incomes increase, is there a trade deficit? If foreign incomes had increased by only 5 percent (all else remaining the same), what would the trade deficit be? If the income elasticity of demand for American goods was only 1 (all else remaining the same), what would the trade deficit be?

5. Explain whether each of the following would prefer to see the dollar appreciate or depreciate:

    (a) a U.S. tourist in a foreign country;

    (b) a U.S. consumer shopping for a car;

    (c) a European consumer shopping for a car;

    (d) a Japanese consumer electronics business;

    (e) a U.S. steel mill;

    (f) a foreign tourist visiting the United States.

6. Assume initially that exports equal imports, and both equal $100 billion. Suppose that America exports goods (like grains) for which the price elasticity is low, say .5, and imports goods (like luxury cars) for which the price elasticity is high, say 2. Assuming that incomes in the United States and abroad do not change, what are the consequences of a 10 percent appreciation of the dollar?

7. Again, begin by assuming that exports equal imports, and both equal $100 billion. Prices in the United States increase by 10 percent, while prices abroad increase by only 5 percent. If the price elasticity of both U.S. and foreign consumers is 2 and the exchange rate does not change, how does the divergence in inflation rates affect exports, imports, and the trade deficit? How large a currency devaluation would be required to restore the trade balance?

8. If foreigners' demand for American exports is inelastic and Americans' demands for foreigners' goods is inelastic, explain how it is possible that a devaluation could actually make the trade deficit worse.

CHAPTER 31

AGGREGATE DEMAND AND SUPPLY

W e have seen how income-expenditure analysis can be used to show how the equilibrium level of output is determined when there is excess capacity—that is, when the economy is operating along the horizontal portion of the aggregate supply curve. In such a situation, a shift in the aggregate expenditures schedule leads to a higher level of output rather than higher prices.

In wartime and in economic booms, the economy finds itself on the vertical portion of its aggregate supply curve. Here, what limits output is not demand but supply. An increase in aggregate demand simply pushes the economy up the aggregate supply curve. The price level rises, but output does not change much. For output to increase, the aggregate supply curve has to shift; the productive capacity of the economy must increase.

When the economy is operating in between the horizontal and vertical portions of the aggregate supply curve, shifts in the aggregate demand curve have effects on both output (employment) and the price level. In this region, goals of price stability and output (employment) may conflict: if the government can shift the aggregate demand curve up, it can increase output and employment, but only at the expense of a higher price level.

These cases can be illustrated by our familiar aggregate demand and supply diagram. Figure 31.1A shows the situation that was the focus of Chapters 28–30, where the intersection occurs along the horizontal portion of the aggregate supply curve. A rightward shift in the aggregate demand curve simply changes the level of output. In panel B, the intersection is along the vertical portion of the aggregate supply curve, and now the shift in the aggregate demand curve has no effect on output. In panel C, where

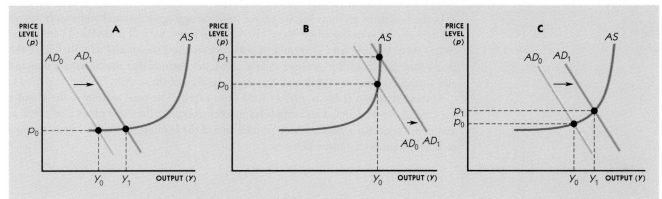

Figure 31.1 PATTERNS OF EQUILIBRIUM

Panel A shows that when the economy is operating along the horizontal portion, a rightward shift in the aggregate demand curve leads to an increase in output with little change in the price level. When the economy is operating along the vertical portion, as in panel B, a rightward shift in the aggregate demand curve leads to an increase in the price level, with little change in output. Panel c shows that in the in-between cases, a shift can lead to some increase in the price level and some increase in output.

the intersection is between the horizontal and vertical portions, a rightward shift in the aggregate demand curve leads to a higher level of both output and prices.

It is apparent that a fuller analysis of the economy needs to bring in both the aggregate demand and supply curves. We need to know the shape of each of these curves, and what makes them shift. What, for instance, can the government do to shift them? Is the aggregate demand curve relatively steep—do even large changes in the price level have small effects on aggregate demand? Figure 31.2 shows that with an inelastic

Figure 31.2
IMPLICATIONS OF AN INELASTIC AGGREGATE DEMAND CURVE

If the aggregate demand curve is relatively inelastic, a leftward shift in the aggregate supply curve results in a large increase in the equilibrium price level.

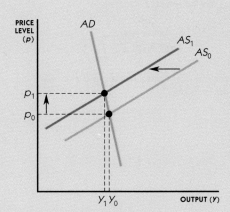

aggregate demand, a slight leftward movement in the aggregate supply curve results in a large increase in the equilibrium price level.

In the first three sections below, we see how the aggregate demand and supply curves are derived. By knowing where these curves come from, we will understand better what causes them to shift, how government policies can affect them, and why they have the shape they do. The third section then reviews the reasons that the aggregate demand and supply curves might shift and the consequences of those shifts.

Macroeconomics today is a lively field of research. The final section of the chapter uses the aggregate demand and supply framework to explore the views of the new classical and new Keynesian schools, which provide two of the leading alternative interpretations of how the macroeconomy behaves.

"What the economy needs is a depression. Just a small one, and present company excepted, of course."

KEY QUESTIONS

1. How do we use the income-expenditure analysis developed in Chapters 28–30 to derive the aggregate demand curve? Why might the aggregate demand curve be inelastic?

2. How do we derive the aggregate supply curve, and what determines its shape?

3. What determines *shifts* in the aggregate demand and supply curves, and how can these lead to a recession?

4. What are the interactions over time between the goods market (aggregate demand and supply) and the labor market (the demand and supply for labor)? Why might these interactions slow down the adjustment of the economy?

5. What role do expectations play in determining aggregate supply? Why might the aggregate supply curve look different in the long run and in the short run? Why might it appear to be vertical in the long run?

6. What are rational expectations? Why do some economists who believe in rational expectations believe that government policy is ineffective? Why do new Keynesian economists dispute this conclusion?

DERIVING THE AGGREGATE DEMAND CURVE

The aggregate demand curve shows the level of aggregate demand at each price level. It gives us, in other words, what the equilibrium output would be at each price level if there were sufficient capacity in the economy to produce that output.

The objective of income-expenditure analysis, upon which we have focused for the last three chapters, is to calculate what the equilibrium output would be at any price level under the assumption that the economy has excess capacity. The income-expenditure analysis diagram is, accordingly, the basic tool we use in deriving the aggregate demand curve and in understanding its shape. It focuses on the demand side of the economy—what people would like to spend—ignoring (for the moment) all considerations of supply.

Before undertaking the task of using the income-expenditure analysis diagram to construct the aggregate demand curve, we should clarify one further set of assumptions we have been making. In the last three chapters, not only were prices fixed, so were current wages. Expectations about future prices and wages—which form the basis of decisions about consumption and investment—were also given. Likewise, interest rates, the availability of credit, and foreign exchange rates were taken as given. With all these factors fixed, income-expenditure analysis tells us how the components of aggregate expenditures vary with respect to one variable: national income.

To derive the *short-run* aggregate demand curve, which gives the level of aggregate demand at each price level, we loosen up one of these restrictions: we allow prices *today* to vary. We continue for now with the assumption that all other determinants (future prices, interest rates, credit availability, and exchange rates) are unchanged. (These assumptions too will be relaxed in the sections below, when we derive the *long-run* aggregate demand and supply curves; there, expectations of future prices and wages are also allowed to vary, along with current prices and wages. But for now, our focus is on the short run.)

At each level of prices, the level of output can be calculated by the techniques set out in Chapter 28. That is, we use the income-expenditure analysis diagram to establish the point on the aggregate expenditures schedule where aggregate expenditures equal the actual level of goods produced: the intersection of the aggregate expenditures schedule and the 45-degree line. Such a calculation is shown in Figure 31.3A. As the price level decreases, the aggregate expenditures schedule shifts up, for reasons that will be explained shortly. Chapter 28 demonstrated that whenever the aggregate expenditures schedule shifts up, the equilibrium level of output increases. This is true here as well, when the reason for the upward shift in the aggregate expenditures schedule is a fall in the price level.

Thus, we can draw a diagram like the one shown in panel B, which plots for each price level on the vertical axis the corresponding level of output along the horizontal axis. The level of output that we identified as the equilibrium level of output in our income-expenditure analysis (drawn for any particular price level) is the one that, in the aggregate demand curve, corresponds to that particular price level. By using the income-expenditure analysis diagram at a succession of price levels to learn the cor-

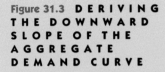

Figure 31.3 DERIVING THE DOWNWARD SLOPE OF THE AGGREGATE DEMAND CURVE

A decrease in the price level shifts up the aggregate expenditures schedule, as shown in panel A. Thus, a lower price level leads to a higher level of national output, which produces the downward-sloping aggregate demand curve in panel B.

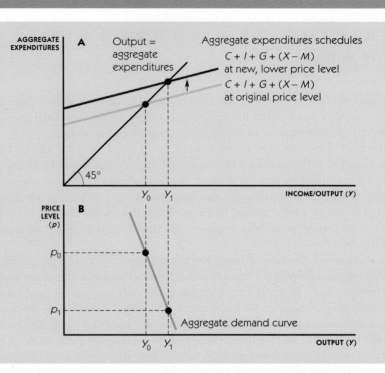

responding outputs, an aggregate demand curve emerges, as shown in panel B. This is the same aggregate demand curve that was originally discussed in Chapter 26.

The aggregate demand curve shown in the diagram is downward sloping. The reason for this becomes clear by looking at what happens to the demand for consumption, investment, and net exports at lower levels of prices. We ask, at each level of income, what happens to consumption, investment, and net exports with a change in the price level.[1] Economists have identified a number of ways in which a change in the price level leads to a change in these components of aggregate expenditures. Here we focus on only the most widely discussed. Other explanations of how price changes affect consumption and investment are presented in the Chapter Appendix.

The net effect of, say, a lowering of the price level is only a slight upward shift in the aggregate expenditures schedule. Any upward shift in the schedule has a larger effect on the change in output because of the multiplier, first introduced in Chapter 28. But as we saw in Chapters 28–30, the multiplier may not be very large—consumption decisions are future-oriented, and so consumption may not increase much with income.

---

[1] We continue with our assumption that *real* government expenditures are fixed. One of the objectives of our inquiry is to understand the role of government in stabilizing the economy; that is, what happens to national income at each level of real government expenditures. Chapter 30 explores more closely alternative perspectives on government expenditures.

And the fact that taxes and imports increase with income is a further reason that the aggregate expenditures schedule is relatively flat, so that the multiplier is relatively small. Because the multiplier is small and a lowering of the price level has only a slight effect on the aggregate expenditures schedule, the increase in output (the intersection of the aggregate expenditures schedule and the 45-degree line) is small. That is why the aggregate demand curve is likely to be relatively inelastic.

CONSUMPTION

We begin with the first component of the aggregate expenditures schedule, consumption. Chapter 28 introduced the consumption function, which shows that consumption increases with income. Chapter 29 elaborated on the consumption function, explaining the various factors that determine both the level of consumption at each level of disposable income and how consumption changes when disposable income changes. We saw that among the determinants of an individual's consumption is his wealth. A wealthier person of a given age and income need, for instance, save less for his retirement. He will accordingly consume more.

More generally, at any given level of income, the higher the level of wealth—not wealth valued in dollars but real wealth, what the individual's bonds and stocks will buy—the higher the level of the consumption function. As prices fall, the *real* value of people's holdings of money (and other assets whose value is fixed in terms of money) increases. People are wealthier. This effect is called the **real balance effect**, because people's financial balances have gone up in real terms, and their increased wealth leads them to consume more. Figure 31.4 shows the real balance effect in action. A fall in the price level has shifted the aggregate consumption function up. This upward shift causes the kind of upward shift in the aggregate expenditures schedule depicted in Figure 31.3A, and this leads in turn to an increase in the equilibrium output.

The real balance effect was stressed by the late Cambridge University economist A. C. Pigou and continues to be emphasized by Donald Patinkin of Hebrew University. Today most economists believe that, while present, this effect is small at best. Most estimates suggest that a 10 percent increase in overall real wealth increases consumption by around .6 percent. However, only money, government bonds, and other similar dollar-dominated assets are affected by a change in the price level. Such assets represent less than a quarter (25 percent) of overall wealth. Hence, a 10 percent decrease in the price level, which implies the same increase in the value of money and government bonds, represents less than a 2.5 percent increase in the value of total wealth, and leads to an increase in consumption of less than .15 percent (.6 × 2.5 percent). During the Great Depression, the period in this century when prices fell most rapidly, prices fell by about a third, inducing an increase in consumption by at most .5 percent—hardly enough to get the economy out of its troubles.

There are several other effects of changes in the price level, involving redistributions of income and wealth and changes in the patterns of consumption over individuals' lives; these are briefly discussed in the Chapter Appendix. The general consensus of most economists, however, is that these effects, while partially offsetting each other, are in total small.

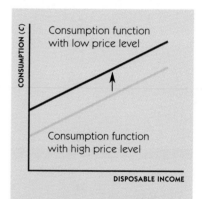

Figure 31.4 THE REAL BALANCE EFFECT

A lower price level shifts the aggregate consumption function up; at each level of disposable income, consumption is higher.

INVESTMENT

Lower prices may lead to higher investment in capital goods primarily through changes in interest rates. Whether, how, and when lower prices lead to lower interest rates is the subject of Part Five. When lower prices do lead to lower interest rates, this results in higher aggregate demand, since at a lower interest rate firms find it more attractive to invest. For simplicity, we refer to this as the **interest rate effect**.

The significance of this effect has been questioned on several grounds, which will be discussed further in Part Five. First, what is relevant for investment is the *real* interest rate (the nominal interest rate minus the rate of inflation), not the nominal interest rate. Many economists question whether lower prices lead to lower *real* interest rates. But even if they do, questions remain about the importance of variations in real interest rates in explaining variations in investment. In recessions, in particular, investment may be relatively insensitive to changes in real interest rates.

There are other reasons that a lower price level, even were it to lead to lower real interest rates, might not result in significant increases in investment. Firms may not be able to increase their investment even if they would like to. We saw in Chapter 29 that many firms may face credit constraints. Hence, for investment funds, these firms must rely on retained earnings. When prices fall, particularly when they fall unexpectedly, the revenue entering a firm goes down, while some of its costs, such as what it owes on money it had previously borrowed, remain unchanged. As a result, the funds a firm has available for investing decrease, and investment falls. This we refer to as the **credit constraint effect**.

Second, even if there are no constraints on the firm's ability to increase investment, it may not be willing to do so. Given the lower level of prices that companies are receiving for their goods, each firm's profits and net worth will fall, especially if the lower prices were not anticipated. If firms are risk averse, then they will be less able to accommodate an economic downturn, and accordingly will be less willing to undertake the risks associated with investment. This effect we refer to as the **firm wealth effect**.

The net result of all this is that investment is probably not stimulated much—and may even be discouraged—by a fall in the price level. For small- and medium-sized firms, the credit constraint and firm wealth effects seem particularly important, and these firms may well decrease their investments. For larger companies, neither the firm wealth effect nor the credit constraint effect may be important, and the interest rate effect may predominate.

NET EXPORTS

We come now to the final component of aggregate expenditures. Lower prices in the United States (at a fixed exchange rate) make American goods more attractive, both to American consumers and to foreign consumers. Hence, exports increase and imports decrease. Net export spending increases.

The net export function, giving the level of net exports at each level of national income, shifts up to the left, as seen in Figure 31.5. The shift in net exports shifts up the aggregate expenditures schedule, as in Figure 31.3A, again leading to a higher level of equilibrium output. Thus, at lower prices, aggregate demand is higher.

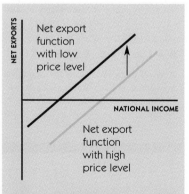

Figure 31.5 THE EFFECT OF LOWER PRICES ON EXPORTS

Lower prices make U.S. goods cheaper to both Americans and foreigners. Exports increase, and the net export function shifts up.

While the net export function does shift up with a fall in the price level, net exports are a reasonably small fraction of total aggregate expenditures in the United States.[2] Accordingly, even a substantial percentage change in net exports translates into a relatively small upward shift in the aggregate expenditures schedule, and thus into a relatively small shift in the aggregate demand curve.

SUMMING UP

A lower price level causes the aggregate expenditures schedule to shift up slightly, as depicted in Figure 31.3A, but only slightly. Accordingly, even with the multiplier effects taken into account, the equilibrium level of output increases only slightly. Thus, the aggregate demand curve is normally relatively inelastic, or quite steep.

The fact that the aggregate demand curve is relatively inelastic means that when the economy is in the excess capacity range, changes in prices have a relatively small effect on equilibrium output. Though our analysis in Chapters 28–30 focused on calculating the equilibrium output at any particular price level, the equilibrium would not have been much different if we had calculated it at a slightly higher or lower price level.

THE EFFECT OF LOWER PRICES ON AGGREGATE DEMAND

Consumption

Real balance effect—positive but small.

Investment

Interest rate effect (firms' cost of obtaining capital)—positive, but possibly small, particularly in recessions.

Credit constraint effect (firms' ability to invest)—for small and medium firms, negative.

Firm wealth effect (firms' desire to bear risks of investing)—for small and medium firms, negative.

Net exports

With exports a small fraction of GNP, even if exports increase by a large percentage, the percentage increase in aggregate demand may be small.

Overall effect: positive but small.

---

[2] We are assuming that the exchange rate remains the same. It would be more realistic to assume that it changes in a way that partly offsets the effect of the lower price level.

DERIVING THE AGGREGATE SUPPLY CURVE

While the construction of the aggregate demand curve was rather complex, that of the aggregate supply curve is a more straightforward extension of the kind of analysis used in Chapter 13. The market supply curve was shown there to be the sum of the supply curves of each of the firms in an industry. The supply curve of the typical firm consists of two parts: (1) If the price is too low, it simply does not pay to produce; it is better to shut down. Figure 31.6A denotes this price by p_0. (2) For prices beyond p_0, the higher the price, the more the company produces, up to some capacity level (Q_c in the figure). No matter what the price, the firm cannot produce beyond that capacity level. Since most plants are designed to produce a particular capacity, the firm's supply curve for prices above p_0 is relatively inelastic, as in the figure.

The market supply curve is formed by adding up the amounts each firm is willing to supply at each price, as in panel B. If all firms had the same supply curves (which they would if they all faced the same technology and costs), then the market supply curve would consist of two parts—a flat portion at p_0 and a rising portion beyond p_0. At p_0, production is increased simply by operating more and more plants.

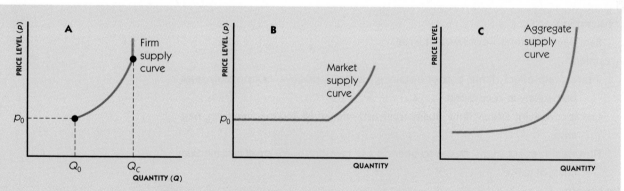

Figure 31.6 DERIVING THE AGGREGATE SUPPLY CURVE

Panel A shows a typical firm supply curve. There is a critical price, p_0, below which the firm will not produce. At that price, there is a minimum scale, Q_0, at which the firm can efficiently operate. At higher prices, output increases until the capacity of the firm, Q_c, is reached. As output gets near Q_c, the firm's supply curve becomes vertical.

Panel B shows a market supply curve, formed by adding up the supply curves of the firms within an industry. At p_0, the curve is flat.

Output is increased by raising the number of firms operating. When all firms are operating, further increases in output require a rise in price. Higher prices elicit greater supply, until the industry capacity is approached.

Panel C shows the aggregate supply curve, whose shape reflects the shape of the market supply curve—a flat portion when there is excess capacity and a vertical portion as the economy approaches full capacity.

On an intuitive level, most people find it sensible that consumer expectations about the future rise and fall in response to events. But social scientists insist on having data to test their conjectures. One of the most commonly cited surveys of consumer confidence is done by the Consumer Research Center of the Conference Board, a nonprofit research organization.[1] The survey covers five thousand consumers during the first two weeks of each month and includes questions about the present situation and the future.

Some typical questions are: Do you perceive business conditions as good, bad, or normal? Are jobs plentiful, not so plentiful, or hard to get? Are business conditions going to get worse, get better, or remain the same? What will be the inflation rate and the likely movement in interest rates and stock prices over the next twelve months? The survey

1. The other often-cited survey is done by the Institute for Social Research at the University of Michigan.

also asks about whether the consumer plans to buy a new home, car, or major appliance in the next six months, or plans to take a vacation.

A detailed breakdown of the answers to these questions is available, but the number more commonly reported in the newspapers is an index number, which is calculated in relation to an arbitrarily set level of confidence of 100 for 1985. As one would expect, the path of consumer expectations varies with the course of the economy. In July 1989, as the economy continued to perform reasonably well, the consumer confidence level measured 120. But in July 1990, at the start of the recession, it was down to 101, back to the level of 1985.

By February of 1991, with the recession continuing and the war against Iraq in progress, confidence in the economy was down to 60. With the end of the war in March, consumer confidence bounced back to 81, but then gradually slumped through the rest of the year as the economy failed to rebound with any vigor. At the start of 1992, the

index of consumer confidence was below 50, the lowest it had been since the deep recession in 1974.

Changes in consumer confidence are a fairly good predictor that the course of the economy will soon change. When consumer confidence starts turning down, the economy often follows a few months later. When consumer confidence starts turning up, the economy often does the same. One connection may be that businesses watch the survey results closely. When they see that consumers are more likely to spend, they become more willing to invest.

Sources: "Consumer Confidence Survey," Conference Board (March 1992 and various issues); Gary E. Clayton and Martin G. Giesbrecht, *A Guide to Everyday Economic Statistics* (New York: McGraw-Hill, 1990), pp. 73–75.

The aggregate supply curve can be derived in the same way, and is illustrated in panel C. The output of the economy is nothing more than the sum of the outputs of each of the different industries. And accordingly, the shape of the aggregate supply curve has the same shape we have seen throughout this and earlier chapters: at low levels of output, it is relatively flat; at higher levels of output, relatively steep.

The fact that not all firms are identical means that they do not all shut down their production at exactly the same price. The supply curve, therefore, is not perfectly flat. But still, when the economy is operating with considerable excess capacity, a slight increase in price is much more likely to elicit a considerable increase in production than when the economy is operating at capacity.

We need to note two simplifications in our analysis. The first concerns what we are holding constant in the background. Since our aggregate demand and supply analysis focuses on the market for goods currently being produced, the aggregate demand curve is drawn with the assumption that wages and expectations of future prices and wages are fixed. The aggregate supply curve is drawn under the same assumptions. (This parallels the firm and market supply curves of Part Two, where a market supply curve gave the quantity of a good that the industry would supply at each price, taking all other wages and prices, including future wages and prices, as fixed. Later in this chapter, we will see how the long-run supply curve allows expectations of future wages and prices to adjust.)

The second simplification is that this analysis of the aggregate supply curve assumes that product markets are competitive. Many markets are not perfectly competitive, as we saw in Chapters 15–18. Imperfectly competitive firms face downward-sloping demand curves. They decide at which point along their demand curve to operate, choosing price and output levels. For imperfectly competitive industries and firms, we cannot define a supply curve in the way we did for competitive industries and firms. But we can ask, what is the equilibrium price we will observe firms charging at each level of output? (Imperfectly competitive firms get to *choose* their price.) The resulting curve is called the aggregate price-quantity curve, to avoid confusion with the competitive aggregate supply curve.

A simple hypothesis about how firms in imperfectly competitive markets behave is that they mark up prices over marginal costs by a fixed percentage. Since where there is considerable excess capacity the marginal cost of producing more is relatively constant, the price charged by firms will be relatively constant within the excess capacity range.

On the other hand, as firms reach their capacity constraints, the marginal costs of producing more increase greatly, so that the price charged by firms will rise rapidly. In this range, the aggregate price-quantity curve will accordingly be very steep. Thus, the aggregate price-quantity curve with imperfect competition is the shape we are familiar with: a flat, horizontal portion at high excess capacity and a vertical portion as the economy reaches capacity. The results would be quite similar even if the markup (the relationship between price and marginal cost) was not constant, so long as it did not vary greatly.[3]

SHIFTS IN AGGREGATE DEMAND AND SUPPLY

The economy is characterized by booms and recessions. There are good years and there are bad years. Chapter 25 showed how variable output and employment were in the United States, and similar patterns hold for other countries as well. In recessions, machines and workers remain idle. In booms, they are stretched to capacity. There is real economic waste in leaving resources idle during long recessions. Is there a way of running the economy so that resources are not periodically left idle? To begin to answer this question, we must understand how aggregate demand and aggregate supply curves shift.

SHIFTS IN THE AGGREGATE DEMAND CURVE

We already know why the aggregate demand curve might shift. The reasons were laid out in Chapters 28–30. Anything that makes the aggregate expenditures schedule shift up or down at a given price level also makes the aggregate demand curve shift up or down. The major culprits that give rise to demand volatility are consumer purchases of durable goods, investment demand (particularly inventories and construction), net

---

[3] The markup model (with a constant markup) can be shown to correspond to the profit-maximizing behavior of an imperfectly competitive firm facing a demand curve with constant elasticity.

From Chapter 15, we know that an imperfectly competitive firm sets marginal revenue equal to marginal costs. The exact relationship between price and marginal revenue is described by the equation

marginal revenue = $p[1 - (1/\text{elasticity of demand})]$.

When the elasticity of demand is infinite—that is, when the demand curve is horizontal—marginal revenue equals price, as the equation says. Accordingly, an imperfectly competitive firm sets its price so that

$p[1 - (1/\text{elasticity of demand})]$ = marginal costs,

or

price = marginal cost/$[1 - (1/\text{elasticity of demand})]$.

If the elasticity of demand is constant, then price is a constant markup over marginal cost, where the markup is $1/[1 - (1/\text{elasticity of demand})]$.

exports (as a result of changes in the exchange rate), and government expenditures. Usually government expenditures are undertaken in an attempt to stabilize the economy. However, they have not always had a stabilizing effect; the increases in expenditures as the country goes into a war (not offset by tax increases) and the reduction in expenditures as the war ends (not offset by tax decreases) have contributed to the economy's volatility.

The new aggregate demand curve resulting from, say, an increase in real government expenditures is constructed in exactly the same way that the old one was; at each price level, we draw the aggregate expenditures schedule, and then look for the intersection of that schedule with the 45-degree line in the income-expenditure analysis diagram. Figure 31.7 shows an upward shift in the aggregate expenditures schedule. The shift means that at each price level, the level of aggregate demand is higher. In fact, because of the multiplier, the increase is a multiple of the initial increase in real government expenditures. Thus, in panel B, the point on the aggregate demand curve corresponding to the initial price level p_0 is shifted to the right.

The consumption, investment, or net export component of aggregate demand can change for any of the reasons discussed in Chapters 28–30—for instance, because of changes in interest rates or the availability of credit—and the consequences can be traced out in exactly the same manner as for a change in government expenditures.

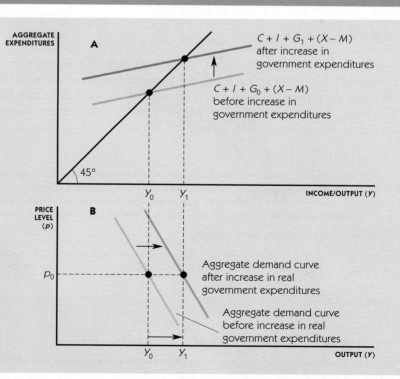

Figure 31.7 A SHIFT IN THE AGGREGATE DEMAND CURVE

If, *at any given price level*, the aggregate expenditures schedule ($C + I + G + [X - M]$, at each level of real income) shifts up, then at that price level the intersection of the schedule with the 45-degree line will increase. There will be a shift in the aggregate demand curve.

SHIFTS IN THE AGGREGATE SUPPLY CURVE

The explanation of shifts in the aggregate supply curve begins by looking at the underlying supply curves of firms: at any given price level, firms are willing to supply a different quantity of output. A shift in the aggregate supply curve resulting from an increase or decrease in the capacity of the economy has a major impact on the portion of the curve we have been calling the full-capacity range, the vertical portion. For instance, additional capital in the economy will shift the vertical portion of the aggregate supply curve to the right, as in Figure 31.8A.

There are, of course, some circumstances in which the flat portion of the aggregate supply curve may shift. If workers suddenly became more efficient, then firms would be willing to sell their goods at a lower price—even with wages remaining unchanged. The flat portion of the aggregate supply curve would shift down, as in panel B.

While many of the causes of major shifts in the aggregate demand curve, such as the simultaneous buildup of expenditures to fight the Vietnam War and the War on Poverty, are easy to see, many of the causes of shifts in the aggregate supply curve are harder to identify. Five possibilities are worth mentioning. Most of them correspond to the sources of shifts in market supply curves discussed in Chapter 4.

Natural and Man-Made Disasters The most dramatic shifts in aggregate supply result from a natural or man-made disaster. An earthquake or a wartime bombing may greatly reduce the amount of capital in the economy, and as a result, the amount of output that can be produced with any amount of labor will be reduced. This generates a leftward shift in the aggregate supply curve. However, if a war had devastated the economy, you would not need an economist to explain why output had decreased. Natural or other man-made disasters, while they may affect one or another part of the American economy, are usually too small to have much affect on the *aggregate* output.

Figure 31.8 SHIFTS IN THE AGGREGATE SUPPLY CURVE

In panel A, an increase in the number of machines will increase the economy's productive capacity, shifting the aggregate supply curve out to the right. In panel B, an increase in the efficiency of labor (without changing the capacity of plant and equipment) will shift the minimum price firms need in order to be willing to produce. The aggregate supply curve will shift down, but the vertical portion will remain unchanged.

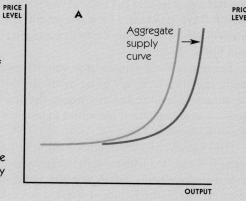

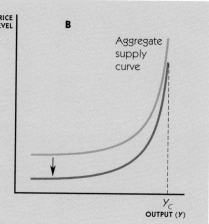

Thus, economists do not spend much of their time studying policies to mitigate the effects of such disasters.

Technology Shifts Another possible cause of a shift in the aggregate supply curve might be a change in technology, increasing the amount that could be produced from any given combination of inputs. But although technology does change frequently, these changes are seldom sudden and they take years to disseminate through the economy. Not only must the knowledge diffuse through businesses, but new machines, making use of the new technology, must be installed. All of this takes more time than can explain one year's recession or boom. Moreover, since technology is almost always improving, the effect of a technological improvement is to move the aggregate supply curve to the right. In studying downturns, economists are interested in shifts of the aggregate supply curve to the left.

Changes in Prices of Imported Goods A more likely cause of a sudden shift in the aggregate supply curve is a change in import prices. The amount firms are willing to produce depends on the price they receive relative to the cost of what they must buy in order to produce. Oil is a major input to production in the United States, and about half of it is imported. An increase in the price of oil (like an increase in wages) thus decreases the amount American producers are willing to produce at any given price. In 1973, the price of oil rose dramatically, by 45 percent in real terms; in 1979, it increased once again, by an even larger percentage—51 percent in real terms; and then in 1985, it fell in an equally dramatic way, by 47 percent in real terms. Each of these changes can be thought of as inducing shifts in the aggregate supply curve.

Changes in Perception of or Willingness to Bear Risk There are always risks associated with production. As the economy goes into a recession, these risks increase, and the willingness and ability of firms to bear risks decrease. For instance, the managers of firms do not know how long the recession will last, or if an upturn will restore the demand for the particular goods they produce. If the downturn is unexpected or un-expectedly long, firms will have excess inventories—more reserves than they would like to have. They will have paid their workers to produce these goods, but they will not yet have received any cash in return for their sale. And they still have other obligations to meet—they have to pay interest on their debt, and there may be some loans coming due. If they cannot meet these obligations, they may be forced into bankruptcy. Firms know that if they continue to produce and sales remain at a low level, their cash position will further deteriorate.

Because of these dangers, a general increase in economic uncertainty makes firms more cautious. One way to be more cautious is to cut back on production and in-ventories—to reduce, in other words, the amount the firm is willing to supply at any price. The amount firms are willing to supply will therefore be reduced as the economy enters a recession.

This has one important implication, illustrated in Figure 31.9. An economic down-turn, initiated by a leftward shift in aggregate demand (the shift from AD to AD_1), may give rise to a leftward shift in aggregate supply (the movement from AS to AS_1), so that there will be relatively little downward pressure on prices. Indeed, in the figure, new aggregate demand equals new aggregate supply at the original price—but output has been greatly reduced.

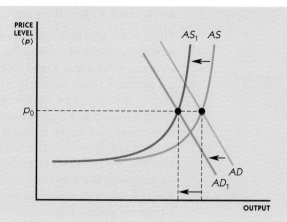

Figure 31.9 **THE RISK CONNECTION BE-TWEEN AGGREGATE DEMAND AND SUPPLY**

A shift in the aggregate demand curve from AD to AD_1 is accompanied by an increased perception of risk, which can lead aggregate supply to shift from AS to AS_1. As drawn here, the result is that the price level remains the same but output is substantially reduced.

Changes in Wage Rates The aggregate supply curve, like the aggregate demand curve, is drawn under the assumption that wages are given. Changes in wage rates will, accordingly, shift the aggregate supply curve. For example, at lower wages, firms will be willing to supply more of their products at any given price level; lower wages will result in a shift to the right of the aggregate supply curve.

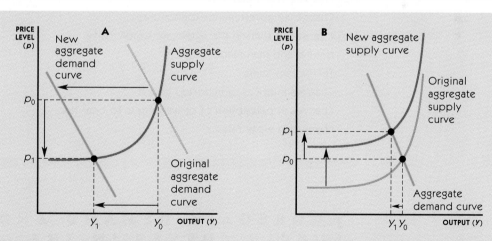

Figure 31.10 ECONOMIC DOWNTURNS AND SHIFTING AGGREGATE DEMAND AND SUPPLY CURVES

Shifts in the aggregate demand and supply curves may move the economy from a situation where it is initially operating along the vertical portion of the aggregate supply curve to one where it is operating along the horizontal portion. In panel A, a leftward shift in the aggregate demand curve moves the economy along the aggregate supply curve. In panel B, an upward shift in the aggregate supply curve moves the economy along the aggregate demand curve.

CONSEQUENCES OF SHIFTS IN THE AGGREGATE DEMAND AND SUPPLY CURVES

Shifts in the aggregate demand and aggregate supply curves contribute to the variability in output. Figure 31.10 shows two kinds of shifts that can lead to low levels of output. In both panels A and B, the economy is initially operating along the steep portions of the aggregate supply curve. In panel A, a large leftward shift in the aggregate demand curve results in a new equilibrium in the horizontal portion of the aggregate supply curve. In panel B, a large upward shift in the aggregate supply curve also results in a new equilibrium in the relatively flat portion of the aggregate supply curve. However, of the major downturns that the economy has experienced over the past half century, only two are attributed by general consensus to a shift in the aggregate supply curve: the recessions that took place in the aftermath of the oil price shocks in 1973 and 1979. It is more likely that a shift in the aggregate supply curve will play a role in perpetuating a recession once it begins than that such a shift will set one off in the first place.

SHIFTS IN THE AGGREGATE DEMAND AND SUPPLY CURVES

Major causes of shifts in the aggregate demand curve

    Changes in consumer purchases of durable goods

    Changes in investment demand (particularly inventories and construction)

    Changes in net exports

    Changes in government expenditures

Major causes of shifts in the aggregate supply curve

    Natural and man-made disasters

    Technology shifts

    Changes in prices of imported goods

    Changes in perception of or willingness to bear risk

    Changes in wage rates

AGGREGATE DEMAND AND SUPPLY CURVES IN THE SHORT RUN AND LONG RUN

The aggregate demand and supply curves analyzed thus far were based upon the assumption that wages today, and expectations of wages and prices in the future, are fixed. These assumptions parallel those we made for the demand and supply curves in Parts One, Two, and Three, and they are natural simplifying assumptions, given our focus here on the product market. Two variables that have so far been held fixed will now be permitted to move: wages will change, as will expectations about both wages and prices in the future. Keeping them fixed has been a convenient simplifying assumption, but in some cases these assumptions may give misleading results.

SHIFTING AGGREGATE DEMAND AND SUPPLY CURVES

Consider a situation that might describe the Great Depression: initially the economy is at a point where aggregate demand equals aggregate supply, at a point of excess capacity, as depicted in Figure 31.11A. The initial price level is p_0, and the initial output is Y_0. At the same time, in panel B, the wage, w_0, is such that the demand for labor at that wage, L_0, is less than the supply, L_1; this illustrates the labor market as described in Chapter 27. For simplicity, the labor supply is drawn as a vertical line; it is assumed to be unresponsive to changes in real wages. The results, however, would remain unchanged even if the labor supply responded to changes in real wages.

The excess supply of labor means that wages will fall. As wages fall, income falls; in turn, aggregate demand at any price level falls. This is because consumers can afford to purchase fewer consumption goods.[4] The new aggregate demand curve is to the left

---

[4] At any level of *real* income, a fall in wages implies an increase in profits. This increase may induce more spending, but the spending is still likely to be smaller than the reduced consumption from lower wages, especially during recessions.

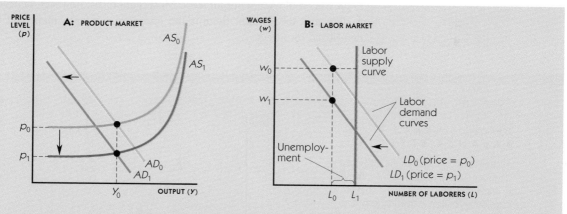

Figure 31.11 OFFSETTING CHANGES IN WAGES AND PRICES

The economy begins in a situation where aggregate demand equals aggregate supply along the horizontal portion of the aggregate supply curve, with price level p_0 and output level Y_0, as shown in panel A. In the labor market (panel B), wages are fixed at w_0, with the supply of labor, L_1, exceeding the demand, L_0. The excess supply of labor causes wages to fall from w_0 to w_1. Returning to panel A, lower wages shift aggregate demand to the left, to AD_1,

and aggregate supply down, to AS_1. As a result of both curves changing, the price level falls to p_1 but output remains at Y_0. In panel B, the lower price causes the demand for labor to shift left from LD_0 to LD_1, since firms are receiving lower prices for their output. Although the wage has fallen from w_0 to w_1, unemployment remains the same. Thus, wages and prices have fallen while output and employment are unaffected.

of the old, and is labeled AD_1 in panel A. Meanwhile, the aggregate supply curve shifts because firms find their production costs are lower. The amount firms are willing to supply depends on what they get for selling their products—prices—relative to the costs of production. The costs of production are basically wages and the prices of other goods used as inputs. The new aggregate supply curve is labeled AS_1. Panel A shows that even though prices have fallen because of the shifts in the aggregate demand *and* supply curves, the new equilibrium entails the same output at a new, lower price. The fall in prices has failed to stimulate output. At the new price, p_1, output remains Y_0.

Now look again at the demand and supply for labor in panel B. The demand for labor has not received any stimulus from an increase in output. Because prices have fallen, at each wage the demand for labor is lower—the demand curve for labor has shifted from LD_0 to LD_1. The supply of labor remains unchanged at the same vertical position, so even though the wage has fallen from w_0 to w_1, the gap between labor supply at L_1 and labor demand at L_0 remains unchanged. The level of employment remains virtually unchanged. In this example, the interaction between the product market (aggregate demand and supply) and the labor market is such that as wages and prices fall, output and employment remain relatively unaffected.

Historically, nominal wages and prices have tended to move in tandem. As we have seen, falling wages shift both the aggregate demand and supply curves, leading to lower price levels. Lower price levels shift the demand for labor to the left, thus offsetting the gains from the originally lower wages. In these cases, falling wages and prices do very little to restore the economy to full employment.

Economists who believe that the real balance effect is important believe that the shift in the aggregate demand curve is less than the offsetting shift in the aggregate supply curve, so that there is an increase in the equilibrium output, as illustrated in Figure 31.12 by the movement from Y_0 to Y_1. *Eventually*, they argue, output will be restored to the full employment output level. Most economists, however, believe that this process is slow; and meanwhile, there is the misery of unemployment and the waste of underutilized resources.

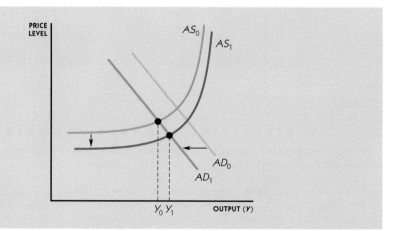

Figure 31.12 REAL BALANCE EFFECTS

As wages fall, the shift in the aggregate demand curve may be less than the shift in the aggregate supply curve, so that equilibrium output increases from Y_0 to Y_1. This may be because the real balance effect—the higher value of consumers' real wealth—induces them to buy more. Still, the net effect on output is small; output is restored to the full-employment level only slowly.

EXPECTATIONS AND THE LONG-RUN AGGREGATE SUPPLY CURVE

So far, we have seen what happens to the aggregate demand and supply curves when wages fall. We have seen that changes in wages lead to changes in prices. Quite naturally, if this pattern persists, individuals and firms will come to expect future wages and prices to be different from current wages and prices. Such expectations may affect what they are willing to spend or what they are willing to supply at any given level of *current* prices. We focus here, in particular, on how these expectations affect the aggregate supply curve.

When firms expect wages and prices to move together, output will not be very responsive to changes in the price level. And if workers can correctly foresee future prices, it is reasonable to assume that wages will indeed move with prices. If they anticipate prices rising by 10 percent next year, their bargaining position for wages to be paid next year will reflect this. We refer to the aggregate supply curve that has today's wages as well as future wages and prices moving with the current price level as the long-run aggregate supply curve.

If nominal wages move in tandem with prices, the real wages facing firms will remain the same. If the prices of what they sell and the costs of production rise together, firms have no incentive to change their production level. Only if price changes outpace costs will their supply increase. Thus, if every change in the price level is accompanied by an exactly offsetting change in the wage level, the level of output at each price level will be the same. (Remember, wages change because the change in the price level was anticipated.) Under our new assumptions concerning wage and price expectations, the long-run aggregate supply curve will be vertical, as illustrated in Figure 31.13.

The figure illustrates one very strong implication of the vertical long-run aggregate supply curve. Earlier we learned that if the intersection of the aggregate demand and

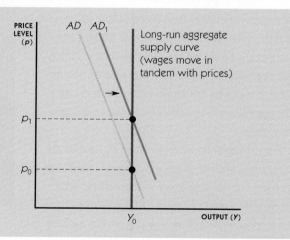

Figure 31.13 VERTICAL AGGREGATE SUPPLY

Some economists believe that the aggregate supply curve is vertical. If this is true, then shifts in the aggregate demand curve can affect only the price level, not the level of output.

CLOSE-UP: COMPUTER TECHNOLOGY AND AGGREGATE SUPPLY

At the start of the 1980s, it was rare for a student to use a computer, at least in any class not related to statistics or computer science itself. Papers for other classes were typed out on typewriters. By the start of the 1990s, however, many college students went off to school with a computer of their own, and instead of running out of typing paper at 3:00 A.M.—the old problem—students panicked at the last minute because their diskette did not seem to work when they tried to print out their papers.

Computers invaded the entire economy, in fact, in industries from manufacturing to banking and finance. Yet even as these technological miracles spread like wildfire to desktops and the inside of machines, productivity growth remained perplexingly low for the U.S. economy. Robert Solow of MIT once summed up the paradox by saying, "We see computers everywhere except in the productivity statistics."

Has the so-called computer revolution actually contributed little to growth in productivity? If so, how can its seeming failure to spur growth be explained? One set of explanations emphasizes that in many companies, computers may have led to more paperwork rather than more output at lower cost. In this view, too many businesses bought computers because it seemed like the fashionable thing to do, not because they had a real idea of how to use the computers to improve productivity. As a result, computers diverted energy from more productive tasks.

A second explanation, formulated by Paul David of Stanford University, is no less gloomy about the short term, but considerably more optimistic about the long term. David points out that available computer technology is still very young. In the case of the invention of the dynamo, for example, which is used for generating electrical power, it took decades for factories to figure out how to use this new technology and to rebuild their plants and redesign their operations accordingly. David warns against the impatient belief that a new invention immediately jolts the economy forward; the diffusion and use of a new invention has always been a process that takes years, if not decades.

A third explanation is that the productivity statistics themselves are misleading. Consider, for example, the case of automatic teller machines at banks, which offer twenty-four-hour access to deposits and allow tellers inside the bank to concentrate more on other services. This new range of services will not necessarily mean an expanded banking industry—they simply will not be captured by the GDP statistics.

There is some evidence that productivity statistics are not especially accurate in many service-related

supply curves occurred along a vertical portion of the aggregate supply curve, then a shift in aggregate demand would *only* have an effect on the price level. A vertical long-run aggregate supply curve means that in the long run an increase in aggregate demand from AD to AD_1 has the same result. It has no effect on aggregate output, which remains at Y_0 (and similarly no effect on aggregate employment). It only affects price levels.

It is important to remember that the aggregate demand and supply curves depicted in Figure 31.13 differ from those drawn in Parts One to Three, Chapter 26, and earlier in this chapter. The earlier curves were drawn on the assumption that current wages and expected wages and prices were kept fixed. The curves in the figure are drawn on the assumption that all wages and prices (current and future) move together. To remind us of this important difference, the expectations-adjusted aggregate supply curve will always be referred to as the long-run aggregate supply curve.

RATIONAL EXPECTATIONS

We have seen that the shape of the long-run aggregate supply curve depends in part on the expectations that firms and individuals have about what will happen in the future.[5] There is some controversy, however, about how individuals form their expectations of future conditions.

One hypothesis is that changes in current prices or wages have no effect on future expected wages and prices. In that case, if prices are lowered today, then today is a good time to buy goods. Under a second hypothesis, households and firms extrapolate any observed price and wage changes and predict that they will continue into the future. The extrapolation principle takes several different forms. In one form, today's lower prices are expected to continue into the future; the change in the price level today makes it neither more nor less attractive to buy today. This is called **static expectations**. In a second form, consumers might extrapolate not the level of prices but the rate of change of prices. Consumers might believe that if prices are lowered today they are going to be even lower in the future. They expect the trend to continue, and accordingly may

---

[5] The Chapter Appendix also discusses how aggregate demand may depend on expectations.

decide to postpone their consumption. This is called **adaptive expectations**. The difference between the consumer's responses under the static expectations and adaptive expectations hypotheses shows the important role that expectations play in the analysis of how aggregate demand changes with a change in the price level. It plays an equally important role in supply responses.

Some economists, such as John Muth of Indiana University and Robert Lucas of the University of Chicago, have argued for another form of expectations. In their view, the static expectations and adaptive expectations hypotheses are naive. Lucas and Muth have emphasized that just as people are rational in their decisions concerning what goods to buy, they are rational in forming expectations; that is, they use all the information that is available to them in forming their expectations concerning the future course of events. Expectations formed in this way are referred to as **rational expectations**.

Every year, retailers mark down their wares right after New Year's Day. Let's consider how three different consumers, each in the market for a new CD player, respond to these holiday discounts. Marie, who has static expectations, is just as likely to buy in either December or January. Prices, she reasons, will stay the same from December into January. Will, who has adaptive expectations and has already postponed his purchase until January, will be tempted to postpone his consumption until February, thinking that the price decline will continue. But there is a sense in which neither of these ways of forming expectations is fully rational. People know that every year there is a sale in January. It is not rational to ignore this information. Paula has rational expectations; unless she strongly wishes to have the CD player in December (perhaps to give as a Christmas present), she will deliberately postpone the purchase until January because she knows that every year there are holiday season sales.

In a sense, one can say that each of these individuals is extrapolating from the past. Marie's extrapolation assumes that next month is like this month; Will's extrapolation assumes that the change between next month and this month is like the change between this month and last month; and Paula's extrapolation assumes that the pattern of prices over the year will be the same from one year to the next. We say the third method is "rational" because it uses all of the relevant information, whereas the first two methods ignore some of it.

In this example, forming rational expectations was easy. But often it is extremely difficult to know what is relevant when making one's forecast of the future. Events like the Great Depression do not, fortunately, occur every year or even every decade. They are once- or perhaps twice-in-a-lifetime events. If prices start to fall, will consumers extrapolate, believing that they will continue to fall? Do they have any better principle on which to base expectations? These are questions about which there continues to be debate among economists. And as we will see, alternative expectations have very important consequences.[6]

Policy Implications of Rational Expectations The principle of rational expectations has some important lessons to teach. If the government announces that in order to

[6] Many of the simpler rational expectations models have been criticized for their assumption that all individuals are identical and, in particular, have the same expectations. Under the rational expectations assumption, if all individuals had the same information, they would have the same expectations. But, of course, people do not all have the same information, so that the observed differences in opinions may be consistent with the rational expectations view.

reduce the demand for cars it will increase the automobile tax beginning next January, individuals "rationally" know that the cost of purchasing a car will rise next January, and those who were planning to buy a car in January or February will buy it in December. The government, in making its revenue projections, ought to take these responses into account.

The shift in the timing of the purchase of cars from January to December is an unintended but perfectly anticipatable consequence of the government policy. This response will subvert the success of the program in the short run. But in the long run, the higher tax on cars will indeed reduce car purchases—the government policy will succeed.

Some economists, however, believe that rational expectations responses to government policies frequently subvert those policies, making them almost totally ineffective.

THE NEW CLASSICAL AND NEW KEYNESIAN SCHOOLS OF MACROECONOMICS

Any reader of the newspaper will know that economists do not always agree about what the government should do about the macroeconomic problems facing the economy. Some economists believe that when the economy is facing unemployment, the government should move aggressively to stimulate the economy, and increase aggregate demand by either cutting taxes or increasing government expenditures. Others, more worried about the longer-run consequences of these deficits or about the possible effects that the increased aggregate demand will have on the price level, urge a more cautious course. Later, in Chapter 39, we will look more thoroughly at disagreements about the extent to which government intervention is needed, whether there are any effective tools government can use, and whether government intervention, for the most part, makes matters better or worse.

Underlying these differences in views about government policy are differences in views about the economy. At this point, it will be useful to see how our aggregate demand and supply analysis helps shed light on some of the important differences.

RATIONAL EXPECTATIONS AND POLICY INEFFECTIVENESS

For the most part, economists who study macroeconomic issues today toil either in the classical or in the Keynesian tradition. What distinguishes new classical and new Keynesian economists from their forebears is a common interest in tracing macroeconomic phenonema back to their microeconomic underpinnings, and the explicit attention they pay to the manner in which expectations are formed.

They differ in several respects, which will be discussed in later chapters. But one of the important differences is the extent to which they are willing to push the rational expectations argument. Robert Lucas, one of the leaders in the new classical school of economics, has emphasized the importance to the aggregate supply curve of the relationship between the expected price and the actual price that will be realized in the market in the future. Assume, for instance, that workers make wage agreements with employers based on particular expectations of future prices. If prices are expected to be 10 percent higher, wages are increased in tandem. Once the wage is set, then the higher the price level turns out to be, the larger the amount of goods firms are willing to supply. Higher prices mean lower real wages.

Thus, according to Lucas, the short-run supply curve is upward sloping, as depicted in Figure 31.14. But the real wages are low only because the increase in prices was not fully anticipated. If workers and their employers throughout the economy anticipate price changes correctly, then higher price levels will bring forth only higher wages and no corresponding increase in output. The long-run supply curve, then, is close to vertical. Output will be fixed at Y_L, regardless of the actual level of prices. Lucas argues that normally wages increase in tandem with prices, since with rational expectations workers will anticipate those price increases, and therefore most of the time the relevant supply curve is the vertical one.

Figure 31.14 shows both the long-run and short-run aggregate supply curves. The vertical portion of the short-run aggregate supply curve is drawn slightly to the right of the vertical long-run aggregate supply curve. In Lucas' view, the reason that the short-run aggregate supply curve is upward sloping is that people do not fully anticipate price changes. We saw earlier (in Chapters 25 and 26) that for short periods of time, such as wartime, people can be induced to work more and firms to produce more than they would at other times, so that output can exceed the "normal" capacity of the economy. Similarly, by not fully anticipating price changes, they may be "tricked" into producing more than they would if they had anticipated the changes.

The new classical economists draw a very strong conclusion from the long-run vertical supply curve. Since the long-run level of output in the economy is effectively determined by aggregate supply, which is inelastic, trying to manipulate aggregate demand at most simply changes the price level, as was shown in Figure 31.13. This conclusion, known

Figure 31.14 LONG-RUN AND SHORT-RUN AGGREGATE SUPPLY CURVES

While in the long run the aggregate supply curve may be vertical, in the short run aggregate supply may increase with the price level.

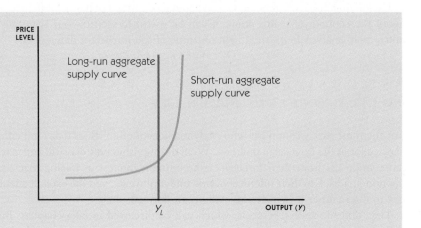

as the **policy ineffectiveness proposition**, has been criticized by new Keynesian economists. They note that the conclusion that policy is ineffective is a consequence of the vertical supply curve *combined* with the assumption that the economy is operating at the intersection of the aggregate demand and supply curves.

MARKET CLEARING

A second main difference between the two groups of economists is the assumption of the new classical economists that all markets clear; when applied to the labor market, this assumption precludes the possibility of involuntary unemployment. Changes in the economy can lead to changes in real wages, which affect the level of unemployment (as we saw in Chapters 26 and 27), but in the new classical perspective, involuntary unemployment simply is not a problem. Moreover, the assumption that the product market always clears means that all firms can sell as much as they would like at the going prices, even in the midst of the worst recession. New Keynesians think that wages may be sticky, so that the labor market may not always clear—at times, such as the Great Depression, there really is a problem of involuntary unemployment. And, as we will see in the next chapter, most new Keynesians think that prices may also be sticky, so that the product market too may not clear.

The differences between new classical and new Keynesian economists can be seen as differences in assumptions concerning speeds of adjustment. New classical economists believe that expectations are revised quickly, after making use of all relevant information, and that markets adjust quickly, so that the labor market essentially always clears. New Keynesian economists believe that under certain circumstances, expectations may be slow to be revised and that wages may adjust slowly, so that unemployment may persist for extended periods of time. The new Keynesian economists concede that the new classical economists may be correct in the long run: eventually the economy *may* adjust (but even that is a matter to be established, not assumed), and in the long run it may operate along a vertical supply curve. Thus, shifting the aggregate demand curve may do no good in the long run. The critical question then becomes "How long do we have to wait for the long run?" Keynes dismissed the optimistic assertion that in the long run the economy would restore itself to full employment with the retort "In the long run, we are all dead."

The new Keynesians believe that in the short run, the aggregate supply curve is not vertical, largely because the new classical economists' assumptions of expectations have been questioned. It was the (rational) anticipation of price changes that led wages to change in tandem with prices, so that changes in the price level had no effect on aggregate supply. Many new Keynesians argue that the vagaries of the economy are so great as to make the assumption of rational expectations, in the short run, questionable. As we have seen, it is not clear what it means to have rational expectations concerning events that happen but once or twice in a lifetime. What inferences were to be made about the future consequences of the decline in the stock prices that occurred in October 1987, a larger percentage decline in the value of stocks than had ever occurred? Analogies with earlier periods are at best just that: analogies. There have been enormous changes in the institutions of the economy and its structure since the last major crash of the stock market, in October 1929.

According to new Keynesian economists, even if one believes that firms and households cannot consistently be wrong in their expectations—that eventually expectations become rational—it may take some time for expectations to adjust; and in the interim, the supply curve will be upward sloping.[7] And so long·as the short-run aggregate supply curve is not vertical, even if prices adjust quickly so that aggregate demand equals aggregate supply, shifting the aggregate demand curve can lead to increased equilibrium output, as illustrated in Figure 31.15. The short-run aggregate supply curve is not vertical; wages are not assumed to move completely in proportion to prices. The intersection is at an output of Y_0 and a price p_0.

The fact that the aggregate supply curve is less elastic in the long run than in the short run means that the gains to output and employment are less in the long run than in the short run. This is also illustrated in Figure 31.15. The increase in output in the long run, $Y_2 - Y_0$, is smaller than it is in the short run, $Y_1 - Y_0$. The corresponding changes in employment are also smaller in the long run.

The policy ineffectiveness proposition, if confirmed, would be cause for concern to anyone who feels that markets might fail to keep the economy running efficiently and at capacity. But to the new classical economists, who believe that output is determined by aggregate supply, the ineffectiveness of policies attempting to stimulate output by increasing aggregate demand is not much of a worry: they believe that the economy almost always operates efficiently, with labor markets clearing, so there is no unemployment. There is little to be gained from policies aimed at controlling aggregate demand to maintain the economy at full employment. And there is much to be lost: by attempting to stimulate demand, such policies simply induce higher prices.

[7] The assumption that rational expectations *necessarily* imply that a fall in the price level must be accompanied by a proportionate fall in wages has also been questioned. The analysis is sufficiently technical to be beyond the scope of this text.

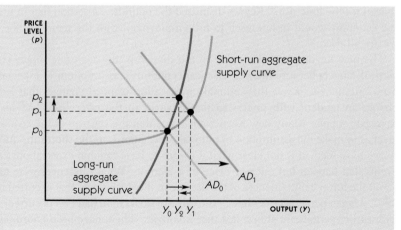

Figure 31.15 EFFECT OF SHIFTS IN AGGREGATE DEMAND WITH A NONVERTICAL SHORT-RUN AGGREGATE SUPPLY CURVE

So long as the short-run aggregate supply curve is not vertical, a shift in the aggregate demand curve can lead to increased output, from Y_0 to Y_1. In the long run, the aggregate supply curve is less elastic, so over time output may fall from Y_1 to Y_2.

New Classical versus New Keynesian Economists

NEW CLASSICAL ECONOMISTS

In the long run, because of rational expectations, the aggregate supply curve is vertical, so that shifts in the aggregate demand curve only affect the price level (policy is ineffective).

The short-run, nonvertical aggregate supply curve, if it applies at all, applies only for very short periods.

Equilibrium, in which wages adjust to clear the labor market and there is no involuntary unemployment, is attained very quickly.

NEW KEYNESIAN ECONOMISTS

In the long run, we are all dead. While rational expectations may be relevant in the long run, they are not in the short run. So for extended periods of time, the aggregate supply curve may be nonvertical, and shifts in the aggregate demand curve have significant effects on output.

There may be extended periods of time during which wages fail to adjust to clear the labor market; unemployment may be persistent.

REVIEW AND PRACTICE

SUMMARY

1. The aggregate demand curve is derived using income-expenditure analysis. The intersection of the 45-degree line with the aggregate expenditures schedule *for a particular price level* determines the point on the aggregate demand curve corresponding to that price level.

2. Lowering the price level shifts the aggregate expenditures schedule up and increases the equilibrium level of output. Accordingly, the aggregate demand curve is downward sloping.

3. Lower prices may lead to a slight upward shift in the aggregate expenditures schedule because consumption increases (the real balance effect), because investment increases (the interest rate effect), or because exports increase. Because the shift is only a small one, the aggregate demand curve may be relatively steep, which means that when the

economy is in the excess capacity range (where actual output is determined by aggregate demand), changes in price have a relatively small effect on equilibrium output.

4. The aggregate supply curve is derived from the sum of industry supply curves. At lower levels of output, when there is excess capacity, it is relatively flat; at higher levels of output, it is relatively steep. Causes of shifts in the aggregate supply curve include disasters, technology shifts, changes in import prices, and changes in the perception of risk.

5. A decline in prices shifts the demand curve for labor to the left, leading to lower wages. Lower wages may shift the aggregate supply curve to the right and down and the aggregate demand curve to the left, resulting in a new equilibrium with lower prices but relatively unchanged output. If wages and prices fall in tandem, then real wages will not fall and there will be little change in either the demand or supply for labor.

6. In the long run, rational expectations of prices and wages mean that higher current prices will be anticipated, followed by higher wages and higher expectations of prices and wages in the future. Then, a rise in prices does not affect aggregate supply, since firms expect that the prices of their inputs—including labor—will rise by the same amount, and the aggregate supply curve is vertical.

7. If the aggregate supply curve is vertical and equilibrium occurs at the intersection of the aggregate demand and supply curves, aggregate demand cannot affect the level of output; rightward shifts in the aggregate demand curve only lead to increases in the price level.

8. New classical economists believe that expectations are rational and therefore the aggregate supply curve is vertical, and that the labor market quickly adjusts so that the economy normally operates at full employment. Policy is ineffective. New Keynesian economists believe that the aggregate supply curve is not vertical and that the labor market may not clear quickly—there may be extended periods of unemployment. Shifts in the aggregate demand curve can have real effects on output and employment.

KEY TERMS

real balance effect
interest rate effect
credit constraint effect

firm wealth effect
static expectations
adaptive expectations

rational expectations
policy ineffectiveness
proposition

REVIEW QUESTIONS

1. How is income-expenditure analysis used to derive the aggregate demand curve?

2. Why is the aggregate demand curve downward sloping? What are reasons that a lower price level would shift the aggregate expenditures schedule? Why might the aggregate demand curve be relatively inelastic?

3. How is the aggregate supply curve related to the supply curve for a firm? What is the characteristic shape of the aggregate supply curve?

4. What factors can shift the aggregate demand curve? What factors can shift the aggregate supply curve?

5. What effects do lower wages have on aggregate demand and supply? What effects do lower prices have on the demand and supply for labor? What implications do these interactions have for the adjustment of the economy?

6. What are rational expectations? adaptive expectations? static expectations? What is the role of expectations in determining the slope of an aggregate supply curve? Why might the aggregate supply curve be vertical in the long run? What are the consequences of a vertical aggregate supply curve?

7. What problems does the rational expectations hypothesis face, particularly in explaining behavior in the short run?

8. How do the new classical economists and the new Keynesian economists differ in (a) their assumptions about how the economy functions and (b) their views of the need for and effectiveness of government intervention?

PROBLEMS

1. Below are data for aggregate supply and demand curves. The price level is an index number, and aggregate demand and supply are expressed in trillions of dollars.

Price level	100	105	110	115	120	125	130
Aggregate demand	6.4	6.2	6.0	5.8	5.6	5.4	5.2
Aggregate supply	3.0	4.0	5.0	5.4	5.6	5.8	5.8

Plot the aggregate demand and supply curves, putting *real* output on the horizontal axis.

2. Consider the problem of a firm that has just seen the price of what it produces rise. The firm will reconsider its production plans based on one of the following expectations.
   (a) It expects that the wages it pays and the prices of its inputs will not increase.
   (b) It expects that the wages it pays and the prices of its inputs will increase by the same amount as the rise in price, but this will take several years.
   (c) It expects that the wages it pays and the prices of its inputs will quickly increase by the same amount as the rise in price.
For which set of expectations will the firm make a small change in the amount it supplies? a large change? When will the change be temporary? Explain.

3. Use aggregate demand and supply diagrams to explain why the expansionary, fiscal policies of the Johnson administration in the late 1960s, when the economy was close to full employment, did not have the same effect as the expansionary fiscal policies of the Kennedy administration in the early 1960s, when there was excess capacity in the economy.

4. The price of imported oil fell sharply in the early 1980s, from about $24 a barrel in 1985 to about $12 a barrel in 1986. Using an aggregate demand and supply diagram, predict how this might affect national output and the price level. Is the effect of the price decrease symmetric with the effect of the rise in oil prices that occurred in 1973 and 1979? (In each case, assume that initially the economy was in equilibrium, at the intersection of the aggregate demand and supply curves. How is your answer affected by whether the economy was operating at first along the horizontal or the vertical portion of the aggregate supply curve?)

APPENDIX: ALTERNATIVE EXPLANATIONS FOR THE DEPENDENCE OF CONSUMPTION AND INVESTMENT ON PRICE

In the text, we learned several of the reasons that a change in the price level may affect consumption or investment. Following are some other reasons economists have given.

EFFECTS OF CURRENT PRICE CHANGES ON AGGREGATE DEMAND

What would you do if you saw prices today were very low, but you expected them to be much higher in the future? It would be as if there were an economy-wide sale! You would take advantage of the low prices to buy more consumption goods today. This is called the **intertemporal substitution effect**. "Intertemporal" means over time, and the intertemporal substitution effect is the substitution of consumption at one point in time for consumption at another point. In this case, people substitute consumption when prices are low for consumption when prices are higher.

There is another reason that a decrease in the price level may affect the level of consumption. At any moment, some individuals owe money to other individuals. Some people have borrowed money to buy a variety of consumer goods; others have borrowed money to buy houses. When prices fall, the *real* value of what debtors (those who owe money) owe to creditors (those who lend) has increased. Debtors are worse off; creditors are better off. Debtors will accordingly decrease their demand for consumption goods; creditors will increase their demand. If debtors, on average, respond by decreasing their consumption by more than creditors increase their consumption, aggregate consumption will be reduced. Since debtors are by and large poorer than creditors, one might expect that this in fact happens. This is called the **wealth redistribution effect**. A reduction in the price level shifts wealth in the population, with the ultimate result that aggregate consumption goes down. Thus, the wealth redistribution effect may somewhat offset the real balance and intertemporal substitution effects, both of which lead to higher consumption at lower prices.

Another effect, the **income redistribution effect**, also serves to increase consumption slightly when prices fall (at fixed wages). The increase in real wages lowers profits at the same time that it raises workers' real incomes. Those who depend on profits reduce their consumption, while workers increase theirs. The latter consequence is probably greater than the former.

How significant are these effects? Most economists think their significance is relatively small. There is thus some presumption that their net effect combined with the real balance effect is that a reduction in prices does increase consumption, but not by a great deal.

Firms also enjoy the intertemporal substitution effect. When the cost of capital goods has decreased relative to the price of the goods that those machines will produce in the future, firms will want to increase their investment.

EFFECTS OF EXPECTED PRICE CHANGES ON AGGREGATE DEMAND

The impact of a decline in both prices and wages depends on whether households and firms expect such changes to continue. Their expectations are important because they affect the magnitude, and possibly even the direction, of the intertemporal substitution effect. If expectations concerning future prices are fixed, then if the price today is lowered, it is cheaper to buy the good today rather than wait until tomorrow, and this intertemporal substitution effect leads to increased consumption and investment today. But if lowered prices today lead consumers and firms to expect that prices will be even lower tomorrow, then they will postpone their purchases. Lower prices may then actually lead to lower sales.

Thus, as prices fall, if wages fall and expected future prices also fall, aggregate demand is not likely to increase as much as it would have had wages and expected future prices not declined. The weakened intertemporal substitution effect is only one reason. A second reason is that with fixed wages, a decline in prices represents an increase in real wages, and the consequent redistribution of income may slightly increase consumption. With wages falling with prices, there is no income redistribution effect. Third, if the exchange rate changes to offset the change in prices, then there will be no effect on net exports.

Fourth, if the prices at which firms can sell the goods they produce in the future is anticipated to be lower, lower prices of investment goods today will not stimulate more investment; if prices in the future are expected to fall more, investment will be discouraged. Finally, the wealth redistribution effect—the fact that lower prices make creditors better off (since they are being repaid with dollars that are worth more) and debtors worse off—is no longer present, since when the price changes are anticipated, the loan contracts will take these price changes into account. A similar argument holds for what was called the firm wealth effect. Both of these effects depend on the price change being unanticipated.

In short, the main remaining effect on aggregate demand of a decline in prices is the real balance effect, an effect that is at best relatively small. In the text, we saw that the aggregate demand curve is relatively inelastic. When a lower price level is accompanied by a corresponding decline in wages and future expected prices, the aggregate demand curve is even more inelastic. Changes in the price level may do little to restore the economy to full employment. To increase output (and employment), the aggregate demand curve must be shifted.

32

STICKY PRICES[1]

T he discussion of aggregate demand and aggregate supply in Chapter 31 assumes that prices are flexible. When they are, the output of the economy is determined by the intersection of the aggregate demand and supply curves. In Chapter 27, we learned why wages might be rigid, or sticky. The consequence of sticky wages is that the demand for labor might not equal the supply of labor; involuntary unemployment may be the result. It turns out that there are good reasons to think that prices too might not adjust in the speedy way envisioned by the basic competitive model. If they do not, then the economy might get stuck away from the point of intersection of aggregate demand and supply. This has potentially important consequences, for both the behavior of the economy and the role of government intervention. The objective of this chapter is to explore the causes and consequences of sticky prices.

[1] This chapter may be omitted without affecting the understanding of later chapters.

"We are, of course, unable to reprint menus to accurately reflect our constantly changing food costs. In strict accordance with price regulations, a small charge will be added to the menu items to cover our actual increased purchasing price. We ask that you bear with us during this difficult period."

KEY QUESTIONS

1. How is output determined when prices are sticky and so do not adjust to the level at which aggregate demand equals aggregate supply?

2. Why might sticky prices give rise to low levels of output, regardless of whether they are stuck at a level that is too low or too high?

3. How does the level at which prices are stuck affect the appropriate remedy for increasing output?

4. How do new classical and new Keynesian economists differ in their views about the importance of sticky prices, and what policy implications follow from these differences in views?

5. What are the principal reasons that prices may be sticky?

STICKY PRICES: THE DEMAND AND SUPPLY RANGES

In Chapter 5, we studied the effect of price floors (for example, minimum wage legislation) and price ceilings (rent control). Since no firm can be forced to produce more than it wishes, the amount actually produced and consumed when there is a price ceiling, when prices are kept below the market-clearing level, is the quantity firms are willing to supply. Since at the price ceiling demand exceeds supply, after firms produce the amount they are willing to supply, some demand will be left unsatisfied. Likewise for price floors: since no consumer can be forced to consume more than she wishes, the amount actually consumed when prices are above the market-clearing level is just the amount consumers are willing to purchase and lower than the quantity firms are willing to produce. Firms are not irrational. Knowing that demand will be artificially low when there is a price floor, they cut back production. The amount they actually produce then will be less than the amount they would be willing to produce at the given price (and wage), if only there were a demand for their goods.

The same principles apply when the economy gets stuck at a point away from the intersection of aggregate supply and aggregate demand. If the price level is stuck above the level at which aggregate demand equals aggregate supply, so that aggregate demand is less than aggregate supply, then output will be the level of aggregate demand at that price. If the price level is stuck below the intersection of aggregate supply and demand, so that aggregate supply is less than aggregate demand, output will be the level of aggregate supply at that price. The first case is called a **demand-constrained equilibrium**, because what constrains output is demand; the second is called a **supply-constrained equilibrium**, because what constrains output is the amount firms are willing to supply at the given price. Let's look at these equilibria in more detail.

DEMAND-CONSTRAINED EQUILIBRIUM AND KEYNESIAN UNEMPLOYMENT

In Figure 32.1, aggregate demand and supply intersect at a price level p^*. Output at that price level is Y^*. In the diagram, the intersection occurs along the vertical portion of the aggregate supply curve. If prices were flexible and the economy operated at this intersection, it would be operating at full capacity, with all of its resources fully utilized. There would be full employment.

If for some reason prices were stuck at a higher level, say p_0, then the amount produced would only be Y_0, the level of output along the aggregate demand curve corresponding to that price level. It does not pay firms to produce unless there are buyers for their goods, regardless of whether they would make a profit *if* a buyer were available at the going market prices. Firms produce only what they can sell.

Accordingly, when at a given, fixed price level demand is less than the amount firms are willing to supply, the level of output is given by the demand curve. If this level of output is less than that associated with full employment, the resulting unemployment

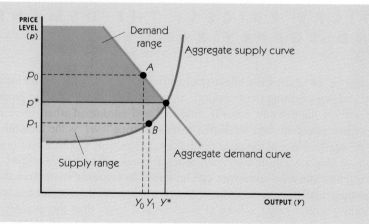

Figure 32.1 DEMAND- AND SUPPLY- CONSTRAINED EQUILIBRIUM

If prices are above the intersection of aggregate demand and supply (at p_0), the economy will only produce the amount *demanded*, at point A. If prices are below the intersection of aggregate demand and supply (p_1), the economy will only produce the amount firms are willing to *supply*, at point B.

is called **Keynesian unemployment;** it was the great British economist Keynes who first enunciated the idea that what often limits production—and consequently employment—is the demand for output, the willingness of individuals, business firms, and the government to purchase goods.

SUPPLY-CONSTRAINED EQUILIBRIUM AND CLASSICAL UNEMPLOYMENT

Just as prices might be fixed at a level *above* the point where aggregate demand equals aggregate supply, so too can they be below that point. In this case, when prices are fixed at a point above the intersection of aggregate demand and aggregate supply, firms only produce what they are willing to produce; some customers are left unsatisfied. The reason firms are not willing to produce more is that prices are low relative to wages, and seeing these low prices, firms are unwilling to hire additional workers.

Figure 32.1 illustrates a supply-constrained equilibrium as well. When the price level is stuck at p_1, below the equilibrium price level p^*, the level of output will be Y_1, less than the full-employment level Y^*.

In the 1800s and early 1900s, many economists thought that most of the time the economy operated at full employment. They argued that there were strong economic forces that came into play whenever there was unemployment, which would ensure that the unemployment was only temporary. These economists, as was noted earlier, were referred to as classical economists. In their view, the major cause of unemployment was high real wages (low prices relative to the given level of nominal wages)—the case we have just seen. For this reason, this kind of unemployment is referred to as **classical unemployment**.

In the 1970s, there was a strong revival of this line of thought. The new classical economists, whom we encountered in Chapter 31, while agreeing with the earlier classical economists that most of the time the economy was at full employment, sought explanations of why real wages might temporarily be too high. For instance, if workers and employers had overestimated the rate of increase in prices and workers had succeeded in getting wage increases based on those higher price expectations, then real wages would be (temporarily) high.

Figure 32.1 illustrates the demand- and supply-constrained equilibria. There are two regions: at prices below p^*, output is determined by aggregate supply (the supply-constrained range), and at prices above p^*, output is determined by aggregate demand (the demand-constrained range).

CONTRASTING IMPLICATIONS OF DEMAND- AND SUPPLY-CONSTRAINED EQUILIBRIA

The distinction between situations in which demand limits output and those in which supply limits output has important policy implications.

Changes in Prices First, consider the effects of an increase in prices (at fixed wages). In the demand-constrained equilibrium (at p_0 in Figure 32.1), as prices rise, output and employment fall because demand falls. This is in spite of the fact that real wages

In a supply-constrained equilibrium, prices are stuck below the level where aggregate supply meets aggregate demand. As a result of the low prices, suppliers are not willing to meet the demand. Shortages and waiting in lines are common.

This was the situation that the economies of Eastern Europe faced for decades following the Communist takeovers after World War II and even into the period of transition to a market economy in the early 1990s. Under Communism, in countries such as Poland, Hungary, Czechoslovakia, and the former East Germany, most consumer prices were fixed by law. Upon winning their political independence in the late 1980s and early 1990s, many of these countries decided to make their producers autonomous and allow them to compete. However, many of the price controls remained in place.

If these nations do not allow prices to move, then suppliers will not expand their production. The lines and shortages will remain. If prices are allowed to increase, then a sizable burst of inflation seems likely, which raises several problems. If the price level jumps by, say, 30 or 40 percent, then the value of everyone's savings in the entire economy will be reduced by that amount. Many pensions and wage levels are not indexed against inflation and are not high to begin with, so many people will suffer from the increase in the price level.

The natural instinct of governments, when besieged by voters angry at being worse off, is to legislate raises in pay to offset the rise in prices. But higher wages will cause aggregate supply to shift back, resulting in additional pressure from business for still higher prices. If a scenario unfolds in which price rises increase the wage level and wage rises increase the price level, then a destructive cycle of accelerating inflation can begin.

A supply-constrained equilibrium offers no escape from these hard choices. One possible option, the one adopted by Poland and other countries, is to allow a onetime price rise, but then to use fiscal and monetary policy to avoid continuing inflation and social programs to alleviate poverty. Those who find the value of their wages or savings diminished, at least in an economy that has escaped the supply-constrained equilibrium, will be able to purchase goods with the money they have left. A major drawback of this solution is the high unemployment that may (in the case of Poland, did) result from policies designed to control inflation.

(wages divided by prices) have fallen. At lower real wages—at higher prices—firms are willing to supply more. That is why the aggregate supply curve is upward sloping. But what is limiting output is demand, not supply, and at the higher prices, demand is lower.

By contrast, in the supply-constrained equilibrium (at p_1 in the figure), as prices rise, output and employment rise (again, assuming wages are fixed). The reason that high price levels lead to greater employment is that with fixed wages, at higher prices, firms are willing to produce more; and to produce more, they must hire more labor. In the supply-constrained equilibrium, they can always sell what they produce; what is limiting production is not sales but the profitability of further production.

Changes in Wages Classical economists focused on high real wages as the cause of unemployment. Thus, they argued that a lowering of wages would increase the amount that firms are willing to produce at each price level—the aggregate supply curve would shift, as in Figure 32.2. If the economy is in a supply-constrained equilibrium—with the price level at p_1 below that at which demand equals supply—this can have a large effect on the amount produced, increasing production from Y_0 to Y_1.

While the classical economists argued that a (real) wage cut was all that was required to restore full employment, Keynes, focusing on a demand-constrained equilibrium rather than a supply-constrained equilibrium, argued that reductions in wages might actually be harmful; workers, receiving lower wages, would reduce their demand, thus shifting the aggregate demand curve to the left, as illustrated in Figure 32.3. Keynes ignored the effect of wage changes on aggregate supply, because he thought that what limited production was aggregate demand. He thought that typically when there was unemployment, the price level was high, such as p_0 in the figure, above the level at which aggregate demand equaled aggregate supply. The lower wages shift aggregate demand to the left and thus *decrease* output and employment. Keynes argued that the remedy to the problem of low output and high unemployment advocated by the classical economists would actually exacerbate the economy's problems, not alleviate them.

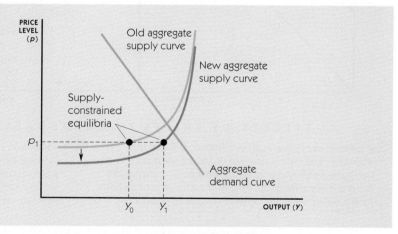

Figure 32.2 EFFECTS OF LOWERING WAGES: SUPPLY-CONSTRAINED EQUILIBRIUM

Lower wages cause the aggregate supply curve to shift down. In the supply-constrained equilibrium, this increases output from Y_0 to Y_1.

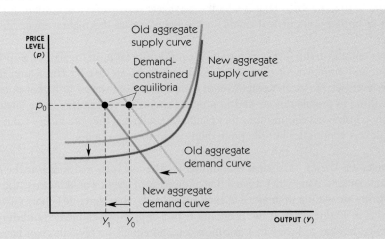

Figure 32.3 EFFECTS OF LOWERING WAGES: DEMAND-CONSTRAINED EQUILIBRIUM

In the demand-constrained equilibrium, lowering wages shifts the aggregate demand curve to the left. This lowers national output from Y_0 to Y_1. Though there is also a shift in the aggregate supply curve, this is irrelevant, since what determines output is aggregate demand, not supply.

Shifts in the Aggregate Demand Curve Keynes thought that government should respond to economic downturns by stimulating aggregate expenditures somehow. Figure 32.4 reviews how this is done, beginning with the familiar income-expenditure analysis diagram. By lowering taxes, increasing expenditures, or stimulating investment or ex-

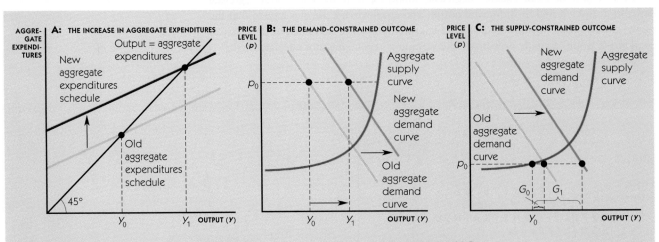

Figure 32.4 EFFECTS OF SHIFTS IN AGGREGATE DEMAND

In panel A, an increase in government expenditures shifts the aggregate expenditures schedule up (at any given price level), leading to a higher level of output. As a result, the aggregate demand curve shifts to the right, as depicted in panels B and C. Panel B shows that in the demand-constrained equilibrium, if the government can shift the aggregate demand curve to the right, it can increase output and employment. Panel C shows that in the supply-constrained equilibrium, an increase in aggregate demand has no effect on output; it only increases the gap between aggregate demand and aggregate supply from G_0 to G_1.

ports, the government shifts the aggregate expenditures schedule upward (panel A), so that at each level of income aggregate expenditures are higher. Thus, an upward shift in the aggregate expenditures schedule means that at the given price level, equilibrium output is higher. The resulting rightward shift in the aggregate demand curve is illustrated in panel B, which shows the case of a demand-constrained equilibrium, with the resulting increase in output (at the given price level) from Y_0 to Y_1.

By contrast, if the economy is in a supply-constrained equilibrium, as in panel C, the shift in the aggregate demand curve is completely irrelevant. What limits production is supply; and the shift in demand does nothing but increase the gap between demand and supply, from G_0 to G_1.

Shifts in the Aggregate Supply Curve   A completely symmetric argument applies to shifts in the aggregate supply curve. Assume somehow the government could, say through a cut in tax rates, engineer a rightward shift in the supply curve, as illustrated in Figure 32.5. In the demand-constrained equilibrium of panel A, this shift in the aggregate supply curve has no effect. In the supply-constrained equilibrium of panel B, the shift leads to increased output.

Economic Policy   In effect, Keynes and the classical economists focused on two different sides of the supply and demand scissors. The classical economists ignored the effect of wage changes on aggregate demand, because they thought that what limited production was aggregate supply. Wage changes were, in their view, desirable, because they shifted the aggregate supply curve and led to higher levels of output and employment. Keynes argued that cutting wages was counterproductive because it reduced aggregate demand, and it was aggregate demand that limited output. And since it was aggregate demand that limited output, Keynes thought that government actions to stimulate aggregate demand were effective in increasing national output. The classical economists, focusing on supply-constrained situations, argued that increasing aggregate demand would do no good.

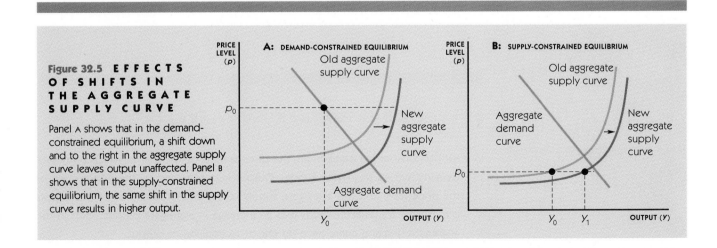

Figure 32.5 EFFECTS OF SHIFTS IN THE AGGREGATE SUPPLY CURVE

Panel A shows that in the demand-constrained equilibrium, a shift down and to the right in the aggregate supply curve leaves output unaffected. Panel B shows that in the supply-constrained equilibrium, the same shift in the supply curve results in higher output.

A: DEMAND-CONSTRAINED EQUILIBRIUM

PRICE LEVEL (*p*)

Old aggregate supply curve

p_0

New aggregate supply curve

Aggregate demand curve

Y_0 OUTPUT (*Y*)

B: SUPPLY-CONSTRAINED EQUILIBRIUM

PRICE LEVEL (*p*)

Old aggregate supply curve

Aggregate demand curve

New aggregate supply curve

p_0

Y_0 Y_1 OUTPUT (*Y*)

WHO RULES THE ROOST: DEMAND OR SUPPLY?

When we combine the analysis of this chapter with that of the preceding chapters, we see that there are two situations where demand rules the roost: when prices are flexible and the economy finds itself along the horizontal, excess-capacity section of the aggregate supply curve; and when prices are sticky and set at a level above that at which aggregate demand equals aggregate supply. Under either of these circumstances, changes in demand translate directly into changes in output.

Likewise, there are two situations where supply rules the roost: when prices are flexible and the economy operates along the vertical section of the aggregate supply curve; and when prices are sticky and set at a level below that at which aggregate demand equals aggregate supply. Under either of these circumstances, changes in demand are irrelevant, but shifts in the supply curve determine what happens to output.

DEMAND-CONSTRAINED EQUILIBRIUM

In a demand-constrained equilibrium, the price level is above that at which aggregate demand equals aggregate supply. Output is determined by the intersection of the price level and the aggregate demand curve; an increase in aggregate demand is therefore translated directly into an increase in aggregate output. Shifts in the aggregate supply curve have no effect on equilibrium output.

SUPPLY-CONSTRAINED EQUILIBRIUM

In a supply-constrained equilibrium, the price level is below that at which aggregate demand equals aggregate supply. Output is determined by the intersection of the price level and the aggregate supply curve; an increase in aggregate supply is therefore translated directly into an increase in aggregate output. Shifts in the aggregate demand curve have no effect on equilibrium output.

THE SHAPES OF THE CURVES AND THE ROLE OF PRICE RIGIDITIES

In Chapter 31, we saw that the aggregate demand curve is normally fairly inelastic, while the aggregate supply curve has two portions, a relatively flat initial range and a relatively steep range as the economy approaches its capacity. The shapes of these curves have some interesting implications.

We have already seen one of these: when the initial equilibrium lies along the almost horizontal portion of the aggregate supply curve, then shifts in the aggregate demand curve have an effect only on output. Figure 32.6A shows the effect of a leftward shift in this situation. If prices are flexible, they fall from p_0 to p_1, and output falls from Y_0 to Y_1. If prices are sticky and remain at p_0, then output falls only slightly more, to Y_2. Whether prices are rigid or not makes little difference.

Now let's look at what happens when the initial equilibrium is in a steeper portion of the aggregate supply curve, as shown in panel B. The shift in the aggregate demand curve leads to a larger reduction in the price level. Because of the large price change, price rigidity now has important consequences for output. The difference between the output with flexible prices, Y_1, and the output with price rigidities, Y_2, is much larger; price rigidities here are responsible for much of the output decrease.

Thus, the inelasticity of aggregate demand has important consequences for prices but not output when the initial situation occurs in the vertical portion of the aggregate supply curve, as Figure 32.7 shows. A relatively small shift in the aggregate demand curve to the right can lead to a large increase in the price level but have little effect on output.

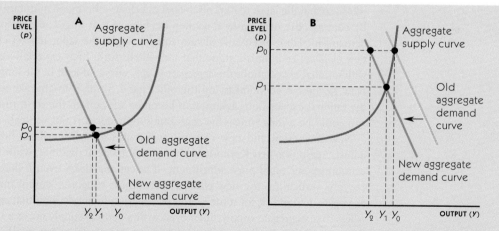

Figure 32.6 **SHAPES OF THE AGGREGATE DEMAND AND SUPPLY CURVES AND THE ROLE OF PRICE RIGIDITIES**

In panel A, the initial equilibrium is along the relatively horizontal portion of the aggregate supply curve; there is little difference between the effect of a leftward shift in the aggregate demand curve when prices are flexible and when they are sticky. In panel B, where the aggregate supply curve is very inelastic (steep), there is a large difference in the change in the level of output induced by a shift in the aggregate demand curve to the left, depending on whether prices are flexible or sticky.

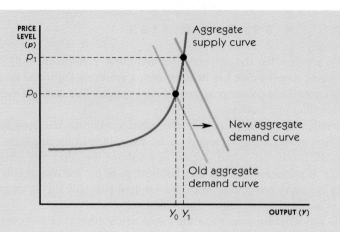

Figure 32.7 VERTICAL AGGREGATE SUPPLY CURVE AND PRICE RIGIDITIES

If the initial equilibrium occurs in the portion of the aggregate supply curve that is nearly vertical, then a rightward shift in the aggregate demand curve will have little effect on output, even if prices are perfectly flexible. The change in the price level, however, may be very large.

PRICE RIGIDITIES AND NEW CLASSICAL AND NEW KEYNESIAN ECONOMISTS

In Chapter 31, we saw that new Keynesian economists believe that wages are often sticky, so that the labor market often does not clear—there is involuntary unemployment. By contrast, the new classical economists believe that wages adjust rapidly, so that the demand for labor essentially always equals supply; the labor market clears. Similarly, new classical economists argue that individuals form their expectations rationally, and with rational expectations the aggregate supply curve, at least in the long run, is vertical. New Keynesian economists, on the other hand, think it might take some time before the rational expectations assumption becomes relevant; in the short run—and the short run could be a long time—the aggregate supply curve is not vertical.

New Keynesian and new classical economists also differ about how rapidly prices adjust. Again, the new Keynesians line up on the side of rigidities, while the new classical economists see rapid price adjustment. If prices are sticky, even if the aggregate supply curve is vertical (as the new classical economists suppose), output may be limited by aggregate demand. If for some reason prices are sufficiently high that aggregate demand is less than aggregate supply, then even with a vertical supply curve a shift in aggregate demand can be effective in increasing output and employment, as illustrated in Figure 32.8. At the price p_0, a rightward shift in the aggregate demand curve increases output from Y_0 to Y_1.

Our earlier analysis of market equilibrium suggested that when, at the going market price, supply exceeds demand, there are forces at work to lower prices. Firms that would like to supply more but cannot sell their goods try to undercut other firms. The same principle applies at the aggregate level. When prices are in the demand-constrained range, where supply exceeds demand, there are forces at work to lower prices. Some

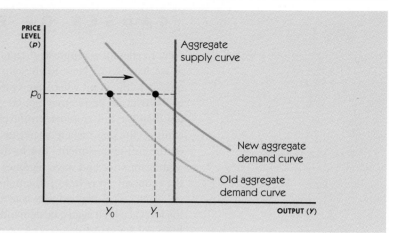

Figure 32.8 VERTICAL AGGREGATE SUPPLY CURVE AND SHIFTS IN AGGREGATE DEMAND

If prices are sticky at a level above that at which aggregate demand equals aggregate supply, then a rightward shift in aggregate demand will lead to an increase in output, even if the aggregate supply curve is perfectly vertical.

of the reasons why prices may not adjust quickly or at all are discussed below.

The Keynesian conclusion—that shifting the aggregate demand curve may be an effective way of stimulating the economy—is correct so long as prices do not adjust instantaneously. If prices are slow to adjust, then the government may be able to shift the aggregate demand curve, increasing aggregate output by a considerable amount, before the vertical supply constraints become binding. There is more than just an effect on the price level, even though the aggregate supply curve is vertical: output and employment may be increased.

NEW CLASSICAL AND NEW KEYNESIAN ECONOMISTS AND STICKY PRICES

NEW CLASSICAL ECONOMISTS

Prices are flexible, so that equilibrium always occurs at the intersection of the aggregate demand and supply curves. With a vertical aggregate supply curve, output is determined in effect by aggregate supply; shifts in aggregate demand only affect the price level.

NEW KEYNESIAN ECONOMISTS

Prices are sticky, so that equilibrium may not be at the intersection of the aggregate demand and aggregate supply curves. If the price level is above that at which aggregate demand equals aggregate supply, output is determined by aggregate demand, and increases in aggregate demand increase output, even if the aggregate supply curve is vertical.

CAUSES OF PRICE RIGIDITIES

New Keynesian economists disagree with new classical economists on several counts, as we have seen. New Keynesians believe that even if prices are flexible and adjust quickly to the point where aggregate demand equals aggregate supply, the supply curve in the relevant period may not be vertical, and the equilibrium level of output may be less than the full-employment level of output. Price flexibility—the ability of prices to adjust to the point where aggregate demand equals aggregate supply—by itself does not ensure full employment. But further, new Keynesian economists see the existence of significant price and wage rigidities, which, as we have seen, may keep output low and the economy away from full employment.

Chapter 27 explained why wages may be rigid. But why do prices not quickly fall to the level at which aggregate demand equals aggregate supply? New Keynesian economists have put forward three groups of explanations. All the explanations are based on the hypothesis that at least in the short run, the rules of imperfect competition—in which firms have some control over the prices they charge—rule the economy. That is, if businesses raise their prices a little bit, they will not lose all of their customers, and if they lower their prices a little bit, they will not capture all of the market. Several of the theories are complementary; they emphasize different aspects of the price-setting decision facing firms.

MENU COSTS

The first explanation for price rigidities emphasizes the costs of changing prices. When firms change their prices, they must print new menus and price lists or otherwise convey the change in prices to their customers. Changing prices costs money, and these costs are referred to as **menu costs**. Menu costs may be large, but advocates of the menu-cost explanation of price rigidities, who include Gregory Mankiw of Harvard University and George Akerlof and Janet Yellen of the University of California at Berkeley, point out that even small costs can have big effects.

Let's use an analogy from physics. A ball rolling on a frictionless plane will roll on forever. Just as a small amount of friction has a big effect on how the ball behaves—it eventually will stop—so too if each firm in the economy is slow to adjust its prices because of menu costs, even if these costs are small, the cumulative effects could still be significant. There could be powerful aggregate price rigidities.

RISK AND IMPERFECT INFORMATION

A second explanation has to do with risk. When the economy goes into a downturn, firms face a shift in their demand curve. They must decrease either their price or their output. Businesspeople must make decisions about how much to cut each. In many industries, businesses focus most of their attention on adjusting output rather than price because the uncertainties associated with changing prices may be much greater than those associated with changing output.

CLOSE-UP: MENU COSTS AND MAGAZINES

In January 1982, a copy of *Business Week* cost $2. In February 1991, it still cost $2. But during that time, prices in general increased by about 50 percent, which means that the real price of the magazine had actually fallen sharply. Surely *Business Week* knows the rate of inflation. So why was the price of the magazine so sticky? Why didn't it move at all for nine years?

Business Week is not alone in this pattern. One study analyzed price changes of thirty-eight magazines from 1950 to 1980 and found that magazines allow inflation to erode their cover prices by nearly one-fourth, on average, before raising their price. Over the time of this study, about one-third of all magazines were sold in the form of single copies, rather than by subscription.

This pattern of sticky prices is not unique to magazines, and it makes the point that choosing or changing a price can be among the toughest decisions for a business. In economists' usage, "tough" means costly. As Gregory Mankiw of Harvard University has written, "The act of altering a posed price is certainly costly. These costs include such items as printing new catalogs and informing salesmen of the new price. . . . More metaphorically and more realistically, these menu costs include the time taken to inform customers, the customer annoyance caused by price changes, and the effort required even to think about a price change."

No one denies that menu costs exist or that they provide a reason for individual companies to wait for a time before altering prices, rather than raising prices a bit each year. However, economists remain divided over whether menu costs are a powerful enough factor, taken alone, to explain economy-wide price stickiness.

Sources: N. Gregory Mankiw, "Small Menu Costs and Large Business Cycles: A Macroeconomic Model of Monopoly," *Quarterly Journal of Economics,* pp. 529–37; Mankiw, "A Quick Refresher Course in Macroeconomics," *Journal of Economic Literature* (December 1990), pp. 1645–60; Stephen G. Cecchetti, *Journal of Econometrics* (1986), pp. 255–74.

There are several reasons for this. When a firm lowers its price, whether sales increase or not depends on how other firms in the industry respond and how its customers respond. Customers may think that this is just the first of several price decreases, and decide to postpone purchases until prices get still lower. (In Chapter 31, we saw how expectations of future prices affect households' decisions about when to buy goods.) Customers may simply decide to wait to see how other firms behave. On the other hand, when a firm cuts back on its production, provided it does not cut back too much, its only risk is that its inventories will be depleted below normal levels, and that the firm will have to increase production next period to replace the lost inventories. But if production costs are likely to be approximately the same in both periods, there is little extra cost—and little extra risk—to this strategy.

KINKED DEMAND CURVES

A third group of explanations attribute price rigidities to the shape of demand curves facing firms under imperfect competition. Recall that with perfect competition, a firm faces a horizontal demand curve. With imperfect competition, a firm faces a downward-sloping demand curve; in particular, the demand curve may have a kink, as illustrated in Figure 32.9.[2] The kink means that firms lose many more sales when they raise prices above p_0 than they gain when they lower prices below p_0.

There are two reasons why the demand curve may be kinked—that is, why there are very different responses to price increases and price decreases. One is that companies believe that if they raise their prices, their own customers will immediately know it and will start searching for stores selling the good at a lower price; but if they lower their prices without heavy expenditures on advertising, customers at other stores may not find out about their lower prices, so they gain few new customers.

Another reason is that firms worry that if they raise their prices their rivals will not match the increase, and hence they will suffer from their relatively uncompetitive prices.

[2] See Chapter 16 for a review of kinked demand curves.

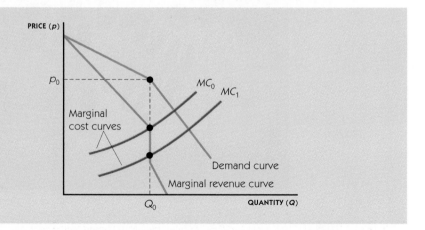

Figure 32.9 KINKED DEMAND CURVES AND PRICE INFLEXIBILITY

If firms lose many more sales from price increases than they gain from price decreases, their demand curve will be kinked. When the demand curve is kinked, the marginal revenue curve has a vertical section, and small changes in marginal cost will not lead to any change in price or output.

But if they lower their prices, rivals will view this as a threat and will match the decrease, and the firm will gain little from its attempt to beat the market.

Kinked demand curves have one dramatic implication: small changes in marginal costs may have no effect on the price firms charge. Even if the company's costs go down, it will continue to charge the price at the kink, p_0 in Figure 32.9. Firms worry, for instance, that if they cut their price in response to the lower marginal cost, other firms will simply match them and they will be no better off. Thus, kinked demand curves give rise to price rigidities: small changes, perhaps resulting from a fall in wages, have absolutely no effect on either the output or pricing decisions of the firm.[3]

REVIEW AND PRACTICE

SUMMARY

1. If the price level is stuck above the level at which aggregate demand equals aggregate supply, then demand is less than supply, output equals aggregate demand, and the economy is in a demand-constrained equilibrium. If the price level is stuck below the level at which aggregate demand equals aggregate supply, then supply is less than demand, output equals aggregate supply, and the economy is in a supply-constrained equilibrium.

2. Unemployment in the demand-constrained equilibrium, referred to as Keynesian unemployment, is reduced when the aggregate demand curve shifts to the right. Shifts in the supply curve have no effect on output. Unemployment in the supply-constrained equilibrium, referred to as classical unemployment, is reduced when the aggregate supply curve shifts to the right. Shifts in the aggregate demand curve have no effect on output.

3. If the economy is operating in the flat portion of the aggregate supply curve, then shifts in aggregate demand and supply will have approximately the same impact on national output whether prices are flexible or not. When the economy is operating in the upward-sloping portion of the aggregate supply curve, then price rigidity makes a difference: for instance, a leftward shift in the aggregate demand curve has a much larger effect on output if prices are flexible than it does if prices are rigid.

4. New Keynesian economists believe that prices are sticky, and if they are stuck above the level at which aggregate demand equals aggregate supply, aggregate demand rules the roost. New classical economists believe that prices are flexible and the aggregate supply curve is vertical, so that output is determined by aggregate supply.

[3] To see this more formally, we have to look carefully at the marginal revenue curve. Marginal revenue—the extra revenue a firm receives from selling an extra unit—has a jump at the output corresponding to the kink. The firm gains less revenue from lowering its price than it loses when it raises the price. When there is a jump in marginal revenue, we replace the condition that "marginal revenue equals marginal cost" with a new one: marginal revenue from increasing output must be less than marginal cost (it does not pay to expand output); and the marginal revenue from the last unit produced must exceed the marginal cost (it does not pay to reduce output). With the marginal cost curve MC_0, the firm depicted in Figure 32.9 is in equilibrium, producing Q_0 units of the good and selling these units at price p_0. The marginal revenue for increases in output are less than marginal costs: it does not pay to expand production. And for decreases in output, the marginal revenue is greater than marginal costs. It does not pay to reduce production, since the loss in revenue would exceed the reduction in costs. Output remains unchanged even when marginal cost shifts to MC_1.

5. New Keynesian economists have proposed three reasons why prices may be slow to adjust to the level at which aggregate demand equals aggregate supply. Firms may face menu costs; firms may adjust output rather than prices during a recession because the uncertainties associated with changing prices may be greater; and firms may face kinked demand curves, and with kinked demand curves they may not change prices even when marginal costs change.

KEY TERMS

demand-constrained
  equilibrium
supply-constrained
  equilibrium

Keynesian
  unemployment

classical
  unemployment
menu costs

REVIEW QUESTIONS

1. What is a demand-constrained equilibrium? a supply-constrained equilibrium? What is Keynesian unemployment? new classical unemployment?

2. How do new Keynesian and new classical economists differ in their views about the consequences of changes in prices and wages and shifts in the aggregate demand and aggregate supply curves? How do they differ in their views about policies to help reduce unemployment?

3. What are the two situations in which demand rules the roost? in which supply rules the roost?

4. Under what circumstances does the fact that the aggregate demand curve is inelastic make a difference? Are the consequences of price stickiness different depending on whether the economy is operating along the horizontal or the vertical portion of the aggregate supply curve? Explain.

5. How are new classical and new Keynesian economists' views about price stickiness different? What are the implications of those differences in views?

6. Name and explain three reasons why prices in the aggregate market for goods and services may be slow to adjust.

PROBLEMS

1. Suppose the economy begins in equilibrium between aggregate demand and supply, but the price level does not change. Illustrate the fact that a rightward shift and a leftward shift in aggregate demand will not have symmetric effects. Will a rightward shift and a leftward shift in aggregate supply have symmetric effects? Why or why not?

2. There are two ways in which the aggregate supply curve can shift: increased excess capacity can lead to rightward shifts, and reduced wages can lead to downward shifts.

Under what circumstances will the consequences of these two forms of shifts be the same? Under what circumstances will they be different?

3. Imagine that the aggregate market for goods and services begins in a demand-constrained equilibrium, but the price level begins to adjust and moves the economy toward equilibrium. Assume that the supply curve for labor is inelastic. Draw a diagram to show what the falling price level does to the demand curve for labor. Why will the fall in prices put downward pressure on the level of wages?

Assume that this change in the price level alters wages by the same amount. Explain how this resulting change in wages will affect aggregate supply and demand, and how it is possible that the economy may end up at the same level of output as when it started.

4. Under what circumstances would you recommend a reduction in wages as a cure for unemployment? When would such a wage reduction be counterproductive? When might it have little if any effect?

5. Compare the discussion of sticky prices in this chapter with the discussion of wage rigidities in Chapter 27. When wages are above the equilibrium level, at which demand equals supply, what determines the employment level? When prices are above the equilibrium level, what determines output? When wages are above the equilibrium level, what are the consequences of a shift in the demand curve for labor? in the supply curve for labor? When prices are above the equilibrium level, what are the consequences of a shift in the aggregate demand curve? in the aggregate supply curve?

PART FIVE

Money's Role

O ne of the lessons we learned in Chapter 14 is that all of the markets in the economy are interrelated. What goes on in one market can have important effects on other markets. Nonetheless, to develop our understanding of what goes on in the economy, we need to study one market at a time. That is why in Part Four we concentrated on the labor and product markets, making only passing reference to the capital market.

One of the principal determinants of the level of output is the level of investment. This in turn is affected by the capital market, by the availability of funds for investment and the terms (including interest rates) at which firms can obtain those funds. Indeed, one of the main ways by which the government attempts to affect the level of economic activity is through monetary policy, which affects interest rates and the availability of funds.

There is another important reason for focusing attention on the capital market. The central policy concern of Part Four was unemployment. But another major policy concern is inflation, and inflation too is intimately linked to monetary policy.

This part consists of four chapters. Chapter 33 explains what money is, why people hold money, and how the government uses monetary policy to control the money supply. Chapter 34 takes up the question of how and when monetary policy affects the economy in the simple case where the rest of the world can be ignored. Chapter 35 turns to the more realistic situation of monetary policy in an international context. Finally, Chapter 36 focuses on the policy issue of price stability and inflation. It asks, what causes inflation, what are the costs of inflation, and what are the costs of fighting inflation?

33

MONEY, BANKING, AND CREDIT

Some say money is the root of all evil. Some say money makes the world go 'round. Actually, in one sense, money does not *do* anything. Money is not a factory or a new invention or a skill that can be taught. While part of the economy is made up of real people working with real machines to make goods that satisfy needs directly, for the most part money is just dumb paper and a ledger mark in a bank account that satisfies needs only indirectly, when it is spent. Yet controlling the supply of money is considered an important function for the government of every industrialized country, and failure to exercise that control has been blamed for inflations and depressions. How can money have such importance? This chapter and the next two will explain what money is from an economist's point of view, why money is important, and why it is sometimes given too much credit or blame for what happens in the economy and in people's lives.

KEY QUESTIONS

1. What *is* money? What economic functions does it serve?

2. What is meant by the money supply, and how is it measured?

3. What institutions in our economy are responsible for controlling the money supply and determining monetary policy?

4. How do modern economies create money through the banking system? How do monetary authorities affect the creation of money and the availability of credit? How do they, in other words, affect the supply of money and credit?

MONEY IS WHAT MONEY DOES

The term "money" is used in a variety of ways, and not just to mean currency and coins. When someone asks you how much money you make, he means what is your income. When someone says, "He has a lot of money," she means he is wealthy, not that he has stashed away lots of currency. When someone accuses corporations of being "interested only in making money," what she really means is that the corporations are interested only in making profits.

Economists use the term "money" in a much narrower sense. Their definition begins with the paper and metal, the currency and coins, that people exchange for goods and services. But these dollar bills and nickels represent only a fraction of what economists call money. They define money by the functions it serves, and it is necessary to look first at these functions before learning a formal definition of money.

MONEY AS A MEDIUM OF EXCHANGE

Trade that occurs without money is called **barter**. Barter involves a simple exchange of one good or service for another. Most examples of barter are fairly simple: two families agree to take turns baby-sitting for each other, or a doctor and a lawyer agree to trade consultations. Nations sometimes sign treaties phrased in barter terms; a certain amount of oil, for example, might be traded for a certain amount of machinery or weapons.

Barter works best in simple economies: one can imagine an old-style farmer bartering with the blacksmith, the tailor, the grocer, and the doctor in his small town. For simple barter to work, however, there must be a **double-coincidence of wants**. That is, one individual must have what the other wants, and vice versa. Henry has potatoes and wants shoes, Joshua has an extra pair of shoes and wants potatoes; by bartering they can both be made happier. But if Henry has firewood and Joshua does not need any of that, then bartering for his shoes becomes very difficult, unless Henry and Joshua go searching for more people in the hope that they will be able to make a multilateral exchange. Money provides a way to make multilateral exchange much simpler; Henry sells his firewood to someone else for money and uses the money to buy Joshua's shoes. The convenience of money becomes even clearer when one considers the billions of exchanges that take place in a modern economy. The use of money to facilitate exchange is called the **medium of exchange** function of money.

A wide variety of items have served the medium of exchange function. Indeed, to a large extent, the item chosen as "money" can be thought of as a social convention: the reason that you accept money in payment for what you sell is that others will accept it for things you want to buy. Different cultures in different times have used all sorts of items as money. American Indians used wampum, while on some South Sea islands cowrie shells serve as a medium of exchange. In World War II prisoner-of-war camps and in many prisons of today, cigarettes serve as a medium of exchange.

Any easily transportable and storable good could, in principle, be used as a medium of exchange. For a long time, gold was the major medium of exchange. However, gold has some problems. The value of a gold coin depends on its weight and purity, as well as on the supply and demand for gold in the gold market. It would be expensive to weigh and verify the quality of gold every time you engaged in a transaction. So one of the early functions of governments, up until the twentieth century, was to mint gold coins, certifying their weight and quality. But because gold is soft, it wears with usage. Criminals have also profited by shaving the edges off gold coins. The ridges on U.S. dimes and quarters are a carryover from coins developed to deter this practice.

Today all the developed countries of the world use pieces of paper for money. These are printed by the government specially for this purpose. However, most business transactions use not currency but checks drawn on banks, credit cards whose balances are paid with checks, or funds wired from one bank to another. Economists consider checking account balances to be money, just as currency is, because they are accepted as payment at most places and thus serve the medium of exchange function. Since most people have much more money in their checking account than they do in their wallets, it should be evident that the economists' measure of the money supply is much larger than the amount of coins and currency in circulation.

MONEY AS A STORE OF VALUE

People will only be willing to exchange what they have to sell for money if they believe that they can later exchange the money for the goods or services they wish to purchase. Thus, for money to serve its role as a medium of exchange, it must hold its value, at least for a short while. This function is known as the **store of value** function of money. There was a time when governments feared that paper money by itself would not be

CLOSE-UP: WHEN ATLANTA PRINTED MONEY

In the nineteenth and early twentieth centuries, it often happened in the rural South and West that there was a shortage of cash for everyday transactions. Workers could not shop for food or clothing, bills were not paid, and the local economy lurched sideways or backward.

It was common in such cases for towns, private companies, and sometimes states to print their own currency, known politely as "scrip" and less politely as "soap wrappers," "shinplasters," "doololly," and many less printable names. The idea was that issuing scrip could keep the local economy circulating until official currency became available again, at which point people could cash in their scrip.

The last major issue of scrip in the United States came during the Great Depression of the early 1930s. Banks were crashing right and left, and bank runs were a daily occurrence. Remember, these were the days before deposits were insured. When President Franklin Roosevelt took office early in 1933, one of his first major actions was to declare a "bank holiday" for the week of March 6–12. In short, he closed all the banks for a week to give everyone time to relax and get their bearings.

But these were also the days before checking accounts had become widespread, when workers were paid weekly, in cash. If firms could not get to the bank, they could not pay their workers. How could the local economy react to these sorts of financial disturbances?

Each area adapted in its own way; let's consider what happened in Atlanta. The city issued about $2.5 million in scrip, in eight different issues made during the first half of the 1930s. One of the first payments was to schoolteachers, and the city made sure that Rich's, a prominent local department store, would take the scrip at full face value. Many other stores, however, would only count the scrip at 75 percent or less of face value. Notice that by taking scrip, which it would later turn in to the city for cash, stores were effectively loaning money to the city that issued the scrip.

Such stories of scrip may sound antiquated today (though in its 1992 financial crisis, California paid its workers with something akin to scrip). But they emphasize the fact that without something to serve as a medium of exchange, a yardstick for measurement, and a (short-term) store of value, an economy simply cannot function. Today the Federal Reserve acts to ensure that currency is available. But in the 1930s, issuing scrip was one thing a city could do on its own to cushion the ravages of the Great Depression.

Source: William Roberds, "Lenders of the Next-to-Last Resort: Scrip Issue in Georgia During the Great Depression," *Economic Review of the Federal Reserve Bank of Atlanta* (September–October 1990), pp. 16–30.

accepted at some time in the future and so paper money was not as good a store of value as gold. People had confidence in paper dollars only because they were backed by gold (if you wished, you could exchange your paper dollars for gold).

Today, however, all major economies have **fiat money**, money that has value because the government says it has value and because people are willing to accept it in exchange for goods. The dollar bill in your pocket recognizes this need for security with its message: "This note is legal tender for all debts, public and private." The fact that it is legal tender means that if you owe someone $100, you have fully discharged that debt if you give her a hundred-dollar bill. The view that anything, even money, will retain its value just because the government says so flies in the face of the economic theory of demand and supply. One of the important functions of monetary policy, as we will see in Chapter 34, is to maintain the value of fiat money.

There are many other stores of value. Gold, which is no longer "money" because it no longer serves as a medium of exchange, nevertheless continues to serve as a store of value. In India, for instance, people hold much of their savings in the form of gold. The gold in Fort Knox is still there and worth billions of dollars. Land, corporate stocks and bonds, oil and minerals, are all stores of value. Of course, none of them is perfectly safe, in the sense that you cannot be precisely sure what they can be exchanged for in the future. But currency, checking account balances, and other forms of money are not a perfectly safe store of value either. If prices change, then the dollars in your pocket or your bank account will be able to buy less or more.

MONEY AS A UNIT OF ACCOUNT

In performing its roles as a medium of exchange and a store of value, money serves a third purpose: it is a way of measuring the relative values of different goods. This is the **unit of account** function of money. If a banana costs 25 cents and a peach 50 cents, then a peach is worth twice as much as a banana. A person who wishes to trade bananas for peaches can do so at the rate of two bananas for one peach. Money thus provides a simple and convenient yardstick for measuring relative market values.

Imagine how difficult it would be for firms to keep track of how well they were doing without such a yardstick. The ledgers might describe how many of each item the firm bought or sold. But the fact that the firm sold more items than it purchased would tell you nothing. You need to know the value of what the firm sells relative to the value of what it purchased; money provides the unit of account, the means by which the firm and others take these measurements.

We are now ready for the economic definition of **money**. Money is anything that is generally accepted as a medium of exchange, a store of value, and a unit of account. Money is, in other words, what money does.

MEASURING THE MONEY SUPPLY

The quantity of money is called the **money supply**, a stock variable like the capital stock. Most of the other variables discussed in this chapter are stock variables as well, but they have important effects on the flow variables (like the level of economic activity, measured as dollars *per year*).

We have already seen that measuring the supply of money is not so simple as counting

One of the problems in defining money is that there are many assets that are not directly used as a medium of exchange but can be readily converted into something that *could* be used as a medium of exchange. Should they be included in the money supply? There is no right or wrong answer. The definition of money is not God-given. Below are definitions of nine terms, some of which were defined in earlier chapters. Each of these assets serves, to some extent, the function of money.

Currency and coins	One-, five-, ten-, twenty- (and so on) dollar bills, and pennies, nickels, dimes, quarters, half dollars.
Traveler's checks	Checks issued by a bank or a firm such as American Express that you can convert into currency upon demand.
Demand deposits, or checking accounts	Deposits that you can withdraw upon demand (that is, convert into currency upon demand), by simply writing a check.
Savings deposits	Deposits that technically you can withdraw only upon notice; in practice, banks allow withdrawal upon demand (without notice).
Certificates of deposit	Money deposited in the bank for a fixed period of time (usually for periods of six months to five years), with a penalty for early withdrawal.
NOW (negotiable order of withdrawal) accounts	A kind of account that breaks through legislative loopholes to allow customers to write checks on interest-bearing deposits.
Money market accounts	Another category of interest-bearing bank checking accounts, often paying higher interest rates but with restrictions on the number of checks that can be written.
Money market mutual funds	Mutual funds that invest in Treasury bills, certificates of deposit, and similar safe securities. You can usually write checks against such accounts; they are thus similar to NOW and other interest-bearing bank checking accounts.
Eurodollars	U.S. dollar bank accounts in banks outside the United States (mainly in Europe).

the number of dollars of currency and coins in circulation. The question is, what should be included in the money supply? A variety of items serve some of the functions of money, but not all of them. For example, the chips issued in casinos for gambling serve as a medium of exchange inside the casino and perhaps even in some nearby stores and restaurants, but no place outside the casino is obligated to take them; they are neither a generally accepted medium of exchange nor a unit of account.

The economists' measure of money begins with the currency and coins that we carry around. Economists then expand the measure of money to include anything else that serves the three functions of money as well as they do. Checking accounts, or **demand deposits**, are included in the money supply as are some other forms of bank accounts.

But if anything that serves the three functions of money is included in the money supply, then what are the limits? There is a continuum here, running from items that everyone would agree should be called money to items that can work as money in many circumstances, to items that can occasionally work as money, to items that would never be considered money. Some of the more common items are given in the Close-up on page 884.

Economists have thus developed several measures of the money supply. The narrowest, called **M1**, is the total of currency, traveler's checks, and checking accounts. In other words, M1 is currency plus items that through the banking system can be treated like currency. In late 1990, M1 totaled $822 billion.

A broader measure, **M2**, includes everything that is in M1 plus some items that are *almost* perfect substitutes for M1. Savings deposits of $100,000 or less are included. So are certificates of deposit (deposits put in the bank for fixed periods of time, between six months and five years); money market funds held by individuals; and Eurodollars, U.S. dollars deposited in European banks. In late 1990, M2 totaled $3,319 billion.

The common characteristic of assets in M2 is that they are very *liquid*, or easily convertible into M1. You cannot just tell a store that the money it requires is in your savings account, but if you have funds in your savings account it is not hard to turn those into something the store will accept. You can transfer funds from your savings account into your checking account or withdraw them as currency.

A third measure of the money supply, **M3**, includes everything that is in M2 (and thus everything that is in M1) plus large-denomination savings accounts (over $100,000) and institutional money market mutual funds. M3 is just about as liquid as M2. In late 1990, M3 totaled $4,092 billion.

Figure 33.1 shows the relative magnitude of the different measures of the money

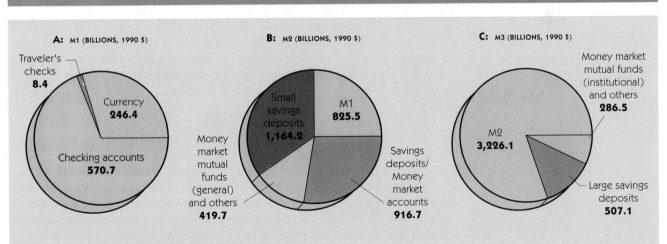

Figure 33.1 THE MEASURES OF MONEY

The money supply can be measured in many ways, including M1, M2, and M3. *Source: Economic Report of the President* (1992), Table B-66.

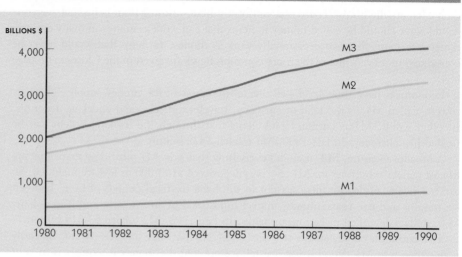

Figure 33.2 GROWTH OF THE MONEY SUPPLY

It makes a difference which measure of the money supply is used. Different measures grew at different rates during the 1980s. *Sources: Federal Reserve Bulletin (December 1991), World Almanac (1991).*

supply, while Figure 33.2 shows that during the past decade the different measures have grown at different rates.

Recent changes in financial institutions such as the growth of mutual funds, the more extensive use of credit cards, and home equity loans have made it even more difficult to answer the question of what to include in the money supply. For instance, many people own shares in money market mutual funds (which invest assets in certificates of deposit and government bonds) that provide check-writing privileges. When an individual writes a check on a bond mutual fund, the mutual fund sells just the value of bonds required to transfer the amount of the check into the bank account. The funds go into and out of the bank account in a split second. Thus, the bond mutual funds with check-writing privileges function just like money. And yet they are not included within the money supply, while money market mutual funds are.

MONEY AND CREDIT

One of the key properties of money is that it is a medium of exchange. However, many transactions do not entail the use of any of the measures presented so far: M1, M2, or M3. They involve credit, not money. In selling a suit of clothes or a piece of furniture or a car, stores often do not receive money, but rather a promise from you to pay money in the future. Credit is clearly tied to money: what you owe the store is measured in dollars. You want something today, and you will have the money for it tomorrow. The store wants you to buy today and is willing to wait until tomorrow or next week for the money. There is a mutually advantageous trade. But because the exchange is not *simultaneous*, the store must rely on your promise.

Promises, as the saying goes, are often broken. But if they are broken too often, stores will not be able to trust buyers, and credit exchanges will not occur. There is therefore an incentive for the development of institutions, such as banks, to ascertain who is most likely to keep economic promises and to help ensure that once such a promise has been made it is kept.

When banks are involved, the store does not need to believe the word of the shopper; rather, the shopper must convince the bank that he will in fact pay. Consider a car purchase. Suppose a bank agrees to give Luke a loan, and he then buys the car. If he later decides to break his promise and does not pay back the loan, the car dealer is protected. It is the bank that attempts to force Luke to keep his commitment.

As technology has changed, modern economies have increasingly relied on credit as a basis of transactions. Banks have a long tradition of extended **lines of credit** to firms; this means that a bank agrees to lend a business money automatically (up to some limit), as it is needed. With Visa and MasterCard and the variety of other national credit cards that came into widespread use in the 1970s and 1980s, lines of credit have been extended to millions of consumers, who now can purchase goods even when they have no money on hand, in the form of either currency or checking account balances. Today individuals can also easily get credit based on the equity in their houses (the difference between the value of the house and what they owe on their mortgage, the loan taken out to buy the house). These are called home equity loans. When house prices increased rapidly in the 1980s, they provided a ready source of credit for millions of home owners.

These innovations make it easier for people to obtain credit. But they have also altered the way economists think about the role of money in the economy, blurring definitions that once seemed quite clear.

THE FINANCIAL SYSTEM IN MODERN ECONOMIES

Broadly speaking, a country's **financial system** includes all institutions involved in moving savings from households and firms whose income exceeds their expenditures and transferring it to other households and firms who would like to spend more than their income and liquid assets allow. Here we take a closer look at the most important of these institutions.

The financial system in the United States not only allows consumers to buy cars, televisions, and VCRs even when they do not have the cash to do so, it also enables firms to invest in factories and new machines, to enhance the productivity of the economy and provide jobs for those entering the labor force. Sometimes money goes directly from, say, a household doing some saving to a firm that needs some additional cash. For example, when Ben buys a new bond from General Motors promising to pay a fixed amount in 90 or 180 days, or in 5 or 15 years, he is lending money directly to GM.

But most of the funds flow through **financial intermediaries**. These are firms that stand in between the savers, who have the extra funds, and the borrowers, who need extra funds. The most important group of financial intermediaries is the banks, but the

CLOSE-UP: A GLOSSARY OF FINANCIAL INTERMEDIARIES

There are a variety of financial intermediaries that take funds from the public and lend them to borrowers or otherwise invest the funds. Though there are many legal differences between these institutions, the principal differences relate to the kinds of loans or investments they make. The following list is ranked roughly by the asset size of each intermediary.

Commercial banks — Banks chartered by either the federal government (national banks) or a state (state banks) to receive deposits and make loans.

Life insurance companies — Companies that collect premiums from policyholders out of which insurance payments are made.

Savings and loan associations (S & L's, or "thrifts") — Institutions originally chartered to receive deposits for the purpose of making loans to finance home mortgages; in the early 1980s, they were given more latitude in the kinds of loans they could make.

Credit unions — Cooperative (not for profit) institutions, usually organized at a place of work or by a union, that take deposits from members and make loans to members.

Mutual funds — Financial intermediaries that take funds from a group of investors and invest them. Major examples include stock mutual funds, which invest the funds in stocks; bond mutual funds, which invest in bonds; and money market mutual funds, which invest in liquid assets such as Treasury bills and certificates of deposit. Many mutual funds allow you to write checks against the fund.

Institutional money market mutual funds — Money market mutual fund accounts held by institutions.

CMA™ accounts (cash management accounts) — Accounts at a brokerage firm (the name was given to the first such accounts, established by Merrill Lynch) that enable people to place stocks, bonds, and other assets into a single account, against which they can write checks.

Close-up above makes clear that there are many other groups of financial intermediaries as well. All are engaged in looking over potential borrowers, ascertaining who are good risks, and monitoring their investment and loans. The intermediaries take "deposits" from consumers and invest them. By putting the funds into many different investments, they diversify and thus reduce the risk. One investment might turn sour, but (with some important exceptions) it is unlikely that many will, and this provides the intermediary with a kind of safety it could not obtain if it put all its eggs in one basket. The different financial institutions differ in who the depositors are, where the funds are invested, and who owns the institutions.

FEDERAL RESERVE SYSTEM

Just as there is a continuum from currency and demand deposits to money market accounts that serves in varying degrees the functions of money, so too is there a continuum of financial intermediaries that perform in varying ways the functions that banks perform. For instance, savings and loan associations accept deposits and make loans today in a way that is almost identical to that of banks. While at one time S & L's were restricted to making real estate loans, this is no longer true. Financial intermediaries play an important role in our financial system. Their actions affect the supply of money (particularly money in the broader definitions, such as M2 and M3). Nevertheless, the discussion here focuses on commercial banks and the narrower definition of money, M1. Traditionally, banks have been the most important way in which businesses raise capital and by which the government attempts to control the level of investment and hence the level of national economic activity.

Governments today have two objectives in their involvement with the bank portion of the financial system. One objective is to protect consumers: when banks go bankrupt, depositors stand to lose their life's savings. The typical saver is not in a position to audit a bank's books to see whether it is really sound. During the Depression of the 1930s, hundreds of banks closed, leaving thousands destitute. Today banks are more tightly regulated. In addition, depositors are insured by government agencies, to limit their losses should a bankruptcy occur.

The second objective of government involvement in the banking system is to stabilize the level of economic activity. We have seen the important role that the banking system provides in taking funds from savers and providing them to investors. When the banking system collapses, firms cannot obtain funds to make their investments, and the entire economy suffers. More broadly, the banking system, by its actions, affects the level of investment, and this affects the level of economic activity. Sharp declines in investment can throw the economy into a recession; sharp increases can set off an inflationary spiral.

CENTRAL BANK

Different economies have developed a variety of institutions and laws for accomplishing these twin objectives. The most important institution in each country is its **central bank**. The central bank is a bank from which other banks can borrow. But it is more than a banker's bank. In each country, the central bank has two main objectives: to stabilize the level of economic activity by controlling the money supply and the availability of credit, and to regulate the banking system to ensure its financial health. In the United States, the central bank is called the **Federal Reserve**, which was established in 1913. The Federal Reserve consists of a Board of Governors, also known as the **Federal Reserve Board**, that supervises a system of twelve regional **Federal Reserve banks** that in turn monitor the operations of six thousand member banks. The collection of governors and Federal Reserve banks, often simply referred to as the "Fed," is at the heart of the **Federal Reserve System**, which includes all of the member banks.[1]

The structure of the system is depicted in Figure 33.3. The Board of Governors

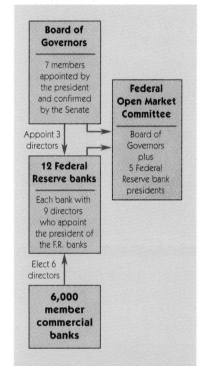

Figure 33.3 STRUCTURE OF THE FEDERAL RESERVE SYSTEM

The Federal Reserve operates at both a national level and a district level. The Board of Governors are appointed by the president; the district level includes some directors appointed nationally and some from within the district; the Open Market Committee also includes both presidential appointees and representatives from the district banks.

---

[1] While the Federal Reserve banks are officially "owned" by the member banks and therefore in a technical sense are not really part of the government, most of the profits of the Fed—which generally amount to a little under $20 billion a year—are turned over to the U.S. Treasury.

consists of seven members appointed by the president and confirmed by the Senate.[2] But while in theory each member of the Board of Governors has one vote, the chairman of the board has traditionally wielded enormous power. The chairman is appointed by the president to serve a four-year term, with that term of office intentionally set so as not to coincide with the term of the president—it is not a political appointment. Once appointed, the chairman is theoretically fully independent of the president or Congress. Indeed, because the funding of the Fed comes from the profits it earns on its operations, Congress and the president cannot even threaten to reduce the Fed's funding. Still, the Fed pays careful attention to the views of the president and Congress.

CONTROLLING THE MONEY SUPPLY

The country is divided into twelve Federal Reserve districts, as shown in Figure 33.4, each with its own bank. But responsibility for controlling the money supply is not left up to the separate Federal Reserve banks in each district; it is vested in a committee of the Federal Reserve Board called the **Federal Open Market Committee**. This committee consists of the Board of Governors plus five of the twelve Federal Reserve bank

[2] The official length of the term is fourteen years, but the average length of service is about seven years.

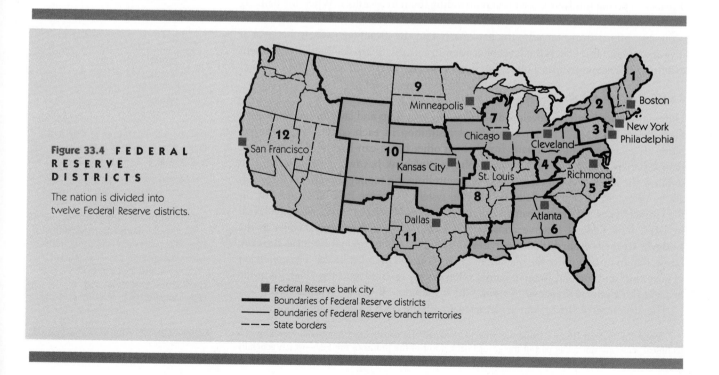

Figure 33.4 FEDERAL RESERVE DISTRICTS

The nation is divided into twelve Federal Reserve districts.

■ Federal Reserve bank city
▬ Boundaries of Federal Reserve districts
— Boundaries of Federal Reserve branch territories
--- State borders

presidents. The name comes from the way the committee operates. The Fed engages in **open market operations**, so called because they involve the Fed entering the capital market directly much as a private individual or firm would, buying or selling government bonds. (Later in the chapter, we will see how these actions translate into changes in the money supply, and look at other ways that the Fed controls the money supply.) Once the Open Market Committee has set its goals, its operations are carried out by the Federal Reserve Bank of New York because of that bank's proximity to the huge capital markets in New York. As a result, the Federal Reserve Bank of New York is by far the most powerful of the twelve Federal Reserve banks.

REGULATING BANKS

The other primary objective of central banks is ensuring the financial soundness of banks. To open its doors, a U.S. bank must receive a charter, from either the federal government or one of the states. Figure 33.5 shows that almost two-thirds of all banks are state-chartered. All the federally chartered banks, and some of the state-chartered banks, belong to the Federal Reserve System; they are called **member banks**, as opposed to **nonmember banks**, which do not belong to the Federal Reserve System. Depositors in virtually all U.S. banks, whether they belong to the Federal Reserve System or not, are insured by the Federal Deposit Insurance Corporation for deposits up to $100,000.

Most banks are state-chartered and do not belong to the Federal Reserve System, but these are (for the most part) small banks. A few large banks control most of the assets within the banking system; 3 percent control more than 70 percent of the assets. The smallest 60 percent control less than 8 percent of the assets. The sixteen largest banks,

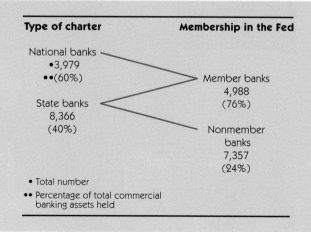

Figure 33.5 WHERE BANKS ARE CHARTERED

Two-thirds of banks are state-chartered. All federally chartered banks and some state-chartered banks are members of the Federal Reserve System. Depositors in almost all banks, whether state or federal, are insured by the Federal Deposit Insurance Corporation. *Source: Statistics on Banking* (1990), Table 104.

Type of charter

National banks
• 3,979
•• (60%)

State banks
8,366
(40%)

• Total number
•• Percentage of total commercial banking assets held

Membership in the Fed

Member banks
4,988
(76%)

Nonmember banks
7,357
(24%)

The savings and loans are not the only financial intermediaries facing troubled times. The U.S. banking industry too has been on the skids for the past few years. Profit levels have been falling, and the number of bank failures was ten times higher in the 1980s than the average for the decades of the 1950s, 1960s, and 1970s. By early in 1992, the Bank Insurance Fund of the Federal Deposit Insurance Corporation was almost completely out of money, raising the possibility that just about when taxpayers finished paying off depositors in savings and loans, they might have to start paying off depositors in banks as well.

A number of factors contributed to the banks' downturn. Some banks had made massive loans to nations like Mexico or Peru, which these countries either did not or could not repay. Others had loaned heavily in Texas and the Southwest and were caught by the rash of business failures caused by the downturn in oil prices in the early 1980s.

Still others seemed to believe that it was impossible to lose money if it was loaned to buy real estate, but the value of real estate in New England, the Southwest, and parts of California slumped in the early 1990s.

Banks faced considerable new competition in the 1980s: mutual funds offered new competition for deposits; credit cards and auto companies competed to offer loans to consumers; and the bond market offered an alternative source of finance for business.

Banks as a group were more diversified than the savings and loan industry, and thus did not go under as quickly. But once they did start sinking, their failures were compounded by the vicious cycle of moral hazard. Managers of banks that were about to go under knew that the only way to save the bank was to raise some quick money by making high-risk loans. If the loans succeeded, the bank was saved. If they failed, the bank was no worse

off: it would still go out of business.

Early in 1991, at the request of President Bush, the Department of the Treasury put forward a plan for reforming the nation's banking system, which is primarily governed by laws passed during the Depression of the 1930s. The plan had a number of elements. Among them:

1. Allow full interstate banking. Banks have generally been allowed to do business in only one state. As a result, they are not as diversified as they could be, and are vulnerable to a downturn in the local economy.

2. Allow banks to affiliate with other financial companies, like insurance companies, so that if the bank has a bad year, another company, rather than the deposit insurance fund, can help out.

3. Allow commercial firms to own banks directly, thus providing another source of funds if the bank has a tough time.

4. Reduce the discretion of bank regulators, so that if a bank finds itself in a precarious situation, regulators are required to limit its operations or shut it down right away, regardless of political pressure.

5. Reform the deposit insurance system in a number of ways. One way would be to require banks to hold a greater amount of capital so that they are more likely to have their own capital at risk. Another would be to protect only those deposits under $100,000, rather than all accounts.

Most of these proposals are controversial. For example, while most economists support the idea of allowing interstate banking, banks in small states fear the new competition from their large-state neighbors. Allowing banks to own or be owned by other companies raises difficult questions of how to separate bank business from other business, so that an unhealthy insurance company, say, does not cause a bank to go broke. Removing the discretion of regulators may mean that some banks that might have recovered on their own will not be given a chance to do so.

Although President Bush had announced that bank reform was his top legislative priority for 1991, the bank reform bill never quite made it through Congress that year. It is not necessary to swallow the Treasury plan whole, but without some reform of banking and deposit insurance, the bank industry may continue to sink.

Sources: William R. Keeton, "The Treasury Plan for Banking Reform," *Economic Review of the Federal Reserve Bank of Kansas City* (May/June 1991); Frederic Mishkin, "An Evaluation of the Treasury Plan for Banking Reform," *Journal of Economic Perspectives* (Winter 1992), pp. 133–53.

each with assets of over $20 billion, control one-third of the assets in the entire banking system.

The banks that are members of the Federal Reserve System are subjected to three layers of regulation. The U.S. Treasury, through the comptroller of the currency, the Federal Deposit Insurance Corporation, and the Federal Reserve itself all share the job of supervision. Nonetheless, in the late 1980s and early 1990s, a rash of bankruptcies and near bankruptcies, some in fairly large banks, raised questions about the adequacy of the banking regulations.[3]

[3] The bankruptcies increased to the point that there were doubts about whether the FDIC had sufficient funds to honor its obligations. The extent of these bankruptcies, however, came nowhere near that associated with the S & L's.

CREATING MONEY IN MODERN ECONOMIES

In order to understand how the Fed goes about its task of controlling the money supply, we need to know more about how a bank runs its business, particularly how banks create money. Surprisingly to many, the money supply of today is created not by a mint or printing press but largely by the banking system. When you put money into the bank, the bank does not simply take the currency down to its vault, put it into a little slot marked with your name, and keep it there until you are ready to take it out. Any bank that did that would be foolish. Instead, banks realize that not all of their thousands of depositors will withdraw their money on any given day. Some will come by next week, some in two weeks, and some not for a year. In the meantime, the bank can lend out the money deposited in the vault and charge interest. The more money the bank can persuade people to deposit, the more can be loaned out and thus the more money the bank will earn. To attract depositors, the bank pays interest on its deposits, effectively passing on (after taking its cut) the interest earned on its loans.

The question is, how much can safely be lent out? Money retained by a bank in case those who have deposited money want it back is called its **reserve**. How much needs to be kept as reserves? Should the bank keep reserves of 5 percent of deposits? 20 percent of deposits? The less it keeps as reserves, the more money it can earn, but the greater the possibility that it will not have enough funds on hand if by chance a large number of depositors should want their deposits back at the same time. To understand how these reserves work and how they affect the supply of money and credit available in the economy, we need to take a close look at a bank's balance sheet.

THE BANK'S BALANCE SHEET

Bankers see the world backward. Where else would loans be called "assets" and deposits be called "liabilities"? This is the perspective shown on a bank's **balance sheet**. Like any firm's balance sheet, it describes the bank's **assets** and **liabilities**. Assets are what the firm owns, including what is owed to it by others. That is why the bank's loans appear as assets on its balance sheet. Liabilities are what it owes to others. We can think of the bank's depositors as having loaned money to the bank; they can get their money back when they wish. That is why deposits are treated by the bank as liabilities.

Table 33.1 shows the balance sheet of AmericaBank. Its assets are divided into three categories: loans outstanding, government bonds, and reserves, including cash in the vault. Loans outstanding consist of loans to business firms, real estate loans (mortgages), car loans, house-remodeling loans, and so on. Banks hold some government bonds because they are more secure than loans to households or firms. Most banks' holdings of government bonds are typically concentrated in Treasury bills (or T-bills), short-term bonds maturing in thirty, sixty, or ninety days after the date of issue.[4] Most secure are the cash in the vault and the reserves that are held on deposit at the "banker's bank," the local Federal Reserve bank.

---

[4] As Chapter 10 explained, long-term bonds are volatile in price, because their price changes with changes in interest rates. Banks hold short-term government bonds because the risk of such changes over a relatively short period of time is low, and the banks wish to avoid risk.

Table 33.1 AMERICABANK BALANCE SHEET

Assets		Liabilities	
Loans outstanding	$28 million	Deposits	$30 million
Government bonds	$ 2 million		
Reserves	$ 3 million	Net worth	$ 3 million
Total	$33 million	Total	$33 million

Chapter 28 explained that the amount of money people need to set aside for a rainy day depends (in part) on how easily they can borrow. The same is true for banks. If they can easily borrow from other banks to meet any shortfall of reserves, then they need to keep very little in reserves. In the United States, the Federal Reserve banks act as the banker's bank, lending money to other banks when they need it. (Banks do not, however, have an automatic right to borrow; they are rationed in how much they can borrow from the Fed.) The Fed imposes reserve requirements on banks. Thus, today the amount of reserves banks hold is dictated as much by regulations as by the banks' own perceptions of what is prudent. And the level of reserves required by the Fed is designed primarily from the perspective of controlling the money supply and thereby the level of economic activity. Table 33.2 shows the level of current reserve requirements. The system of banking in which banks hold a fraction of the amount on deposit in reserves is called the **fractional reserve system**.

The liability side of AmericaBank's balance sheet consists of two items: deposits and net worth. Deposits can take on a variety of forms: these include checking accounts, which are technically known as demand deposits, and the variety of forms of savings accounts, which are technically known as time deposits. The bank's net worth is simply

Table 33.2 REQUIRED RESERVES

Type of deposit	Minimum reserve required (percentage of deposits)
Very large checking accounts (over $42.2 million)	3
Other checking accounts (under $42.2 million)	10
All other deposits	0

Source: Federal Reserve Bank of San Francisco (1992).

the difference between the value of its assets and the value of its liabilities. In other words, if the bank's assets were sold and its depositors paid off, then what remained would equal the net worth of the bank.

Since net worth is *defined* as the difference between the value of the liabilities and the value of the assets, it should be clear that the numbers on both sides of the balance sheet should balance.

How Banks Create Money

Who creates money? Banks do. As we have seen, the coins and currency manufactured by the Treasury are a relatively small part of the money supply.

To see how banks create money, let's figuratively lump all 13,000 U.S. banks into a big pile and consider them as one huge superbank. Assume that the Fed is requiring that reserves be 10 percent of deposits. Now suppose that a wealthy individual deposits $1 billion in currency in his account.

The bank reasons as follows. It knows it must keep a reserve-to-deposit ratio of 1 to 10. It has a long line of loan applicants. When the bank makes a loan, it credits the borrower with funds in her checking account; it does not actually give her currency. What it does is simply place an entry into its books on both the left- and right-hand side of the ledger: there is a loan on the asset side and a deposit on the liability side. If it makes $9 billion worth of loans, its liabilities will have gone up $10 billion (the $1 billion original deposit plus the $9 billion worth of loans). On the asset side, the bank takes the $1 billion in currency to the Fed and is credited with the amount, so that it now has $1 billion in reserves. Thus, its reserves have increased by $1 billion, its deposits by $10 billion; it has satisfied the reserve requirement.

We can reach the same result by a slower route, as shown in Table 33.3. The bank might reason, now that its deposits have gone up by $1 billion, that it must send $100 million to the Federal Reserve as part of its reserve requirements. But it can lend out the remaining $900 million (.9 × $1 billion). This is the first-round balance sheet that appears in the table. Deposits have increased $1 billion (compared with the initial situation), loans have increased $.9 billion, and reserves have increased $.1 billion.

For the sake of argument, let's assume that the loan is all made to one customer: Desktop Publishing borrows $900 million so that it can purchase new computers from ComputerAmerica. When Desktop pays $900 million for the computers, ComputerAmerica deposits the money in its account. Thus, the loan of $900 million is reflected in the addition of $900 million in deposits. This is shown on the right-hand side of the second-round balance sheet in the table, where deposits have now risen from $101 billion to $101.9 billion.

But with the $900 million additional deposits, the bank is allowed to increase its lending by .9 × $900 million, or $810 million, putting $90 million into reserves. These changes are shown in the left-hand side of the second-round balance sheet. Assume that all $810 million is lent out to various companies, each of which uses the money to purchase new goods. In each case, some other firm will sell its good and will put these new funds into the superbank. As a result, new deposits at the superbank will again grow by $810 million. As the third round begins, deposits are once again increased.

But the bank is still not in equilibrium. Because of the increase in deposits of $810 million, it can lend out .9 × $810 million = $729 million. And so the process continues.

Table 33.3 SUPERBANK BALANCE SHEET

Before-deposit equilibrium			
Assets		**Liabilities**	
Loans outstanding	$ 91 billion	Deposits	$100 billion
Government bonds	2 billion		
Reserves	10 billion	Net worth	3 billion
Total	103 billion	Total	103 billion

First round (Add $1 billion deposits, $.9 billion loans)			
Assets		**Liabilities**	
Loans outstanding	$ 91.9 billion	Deposits	$101 billion
Government bonds	2 billion		
Reserves	10.1 billion	Net worth	3 billion
Total	104 billion	Total	104 billion

Second round (Add $.9 billion deposits, $.81 billion loans to previous round[a])			
Assets		**Liabilities**	
Loans outstanding	$ 92.71 billion	Deposits	$101.9 billion
Government bonds	2 billion		
Reserves	10.19 billion	Net worth	31 billion
Total	104.9 billion	Total	104.9 billion

Third round (Add $.81 billion deposits, $.73 billion loans to previous round[a])			
Assets		**Liabilities**	
Loans outstanding	$ 93.44 billion	Deposits	$102.71 billion
Government bonds	2 billion		
Reserves	10.27 billion	Net worth	3 billion
Total	105.71 billion	Total	105.71 billion

After-deposit equilibrium (Add $10 billion new deposits, $9 billion new loans to original equilibrium)			
Assets		**Liabilities**	
Loans outstanding	$100 billion	Deposits	$110 billion
Government bonds	2 billion		
Reserves	11 billion	Net worth	3 billion
Total	113 billion	Total	113 billion

[a] In each subsequent round, new deposits equal new loans of the previous round; new loans equal .9 × new deposits.

Notice that on each round, the increase in deposits is smaller than in the previous round. In the second round, the increase in deposits was $900 million, in the third round $810 million, and so on. The after-deposit equilibrium balance sheet in the last part of the table shows that the bank has increased its deposits by ten times the original deposit ($100 billion to $110 billion) and increased its lending by nine times the original deposit ($91 billion to $100 billion). The $1 billion injection into the banking system has turned into a $10 billion increase in the money supply.

In the new situation, the banking system is in equilibrium. Its reserves of $11 billion are precisely equal to 10 percent of its $110 billion deposits. It cannot lend out any more without violating the reserve requirements.

In this way, any new deposit into the banking system results in a multiple expansion of the number of deposits. This is the "miracle" of the fractional reserve system. Deposits increase by a factor of 1/reserve requirement. In the superbank example, the reserve requirement was 10 percent; 1/reserve requirement is 10. If the reserve requirement had been 20 percent, deposits would have increased by 1/.2, or 5. Note that as the deposits increased, so did the supply of outstanding loans.

In this example, there were no "leakages" outside the system. No one decided to hold currency rather than put her money back into the bank. Whenever sellers were paid, they put what they received into the bank. With leakages, the increase in deposits and thus the increase in money will be smaller. These leakages are large; the ratio of M1 to reserves is only around 3, and even for M2 the ratio is only between 11 and 12. Nevertheless, the increase in bank reserves will lead to some multiplied increase in the money supply. This relationship between the change in reserves and the final change in deposits is called the **money multiplier**. [5]

MONEY MULTIPLIERS WITH MANY BANKS

The lesson of the money multiplier works just as well when there is more than one bank involved. Assume that Desktop Publishing and ComputerAmerica have their bank accounts in two separate banks, BankNational and BankUSA, respectively. When Desktop Publishing writes a check for $900 million to ComputerAmerica, $900 million is transferred from BankNational to BankUSA. Once that $900 million has been transferred, BankUSA will find that it can lend more than it could previously. As a result of the $900 million increase in deposits, it can lend .9 × $900 = $810 million. Suppose it lends the $810 million to the NewTelephone Company, which uses the money to buy a machine for making telephones from Equipment Manufacturing. If Equipment Manufacturing has its bank account at BankIllinois, after Equipment Manufacturing has been paid, BankIllinois will find that because its deposits have increased by $810 million, it can lend .9 × $810 = $729 million. The process continues, until the new equilibrium is identical to the one described earlier in the superbank example, where there is a $10 billion increase in the money supply. The banking system as a whole

---

[5] This multiplier should not be confused with the multiplier introduced in Chapter 28. That multiplier showed that an increase in investment or government expenditures leads to a multiple increase in the equilibrium level of aggregate expenditures. There are clearly some similarities in the way we go about calculating these multipliers.

will have expanded the money supply by a multiple of the initial deposit, equal to 1/reserve requirement.

It should be clear that when there are many banks, no individual bank can create multiple deposits. Individual banks may not even be aware of the role they play in the process of multiple-deposit creation; all they see is that their deposits have increased and that therefore they are able to make more loans.

The process of multiple-deposit creation may seem somewhat like a magician's pulling rabbits out of a hat: it seems to make something out of nothing. The process of creating deposits is a real physical process. Deposits are created by making entries in records; today electronic impulses create records on computer tapes. The rules of deposit creation are rules specifying when you may make certain entries in the books. It is these rules—in particular, the fractional reserve requirements—that give rise to the ability of the system to create multiple deposits.

MONEY MULTIPLIER

An increase in reserves by a dollar leads to an increase in total deposits by a multiple of the original increase.

THE INSTRUMENTS OF MONETARY POLICY

Most changes in the money supply are not the result of someone depositing a billion dollars of currency in a bank. No longer do they involve someone selling gold to or depositing gold in a bank. Instead, they are the result of actions by the Federal Reserve Board. The Fed creates reserves. It does so deliberately, in order to increase the supply of money and credit. By such action, the Fed affects the level of economic activity. The connections between the actions the Fed takes and their effect on the level of economic activity are the subject of the next two chapters. Here, our concern is simply with the supply of money and credit. Money and credit, as we have seen, represent the two sides of a bank's balance sheet: when deposits (money) increase, either bank loans (credit) or bank holdings of T-bills must increase. Frequently both will. Though ultimately our concern will be with bank lending, bank lending is not directly under the control of the Fed. The money supply is more directly under its control. The Fed has three tools with which it can change the money supply, and which form the subject of the next three sections.

RESERVE REQUIREMENTS

The simplest tool available to the Fed is to alter **reserve requirements**. The Fed sets the minimum amount of money each bank is required to hold in reserves. While in principle the government could require banks to hold reserves in a variety of forms (cash, government bonds, gold), the Fed requires that the reserves be held as deposits with the Federal Reserve, partly because this stipulation facilitates monitoring of the reserve requirement. The existence of reserve requirements gives the Federal Reserve a powerful tool with which to influence the amount of money and credit in the economy, though it is a tool the Fed seldom uses.

Assume that banks are initially required to maintain reserves equal to 10 percent of deposits, and consider what happens if reserve requirements are lowered to 5 percent. Each bank will find that it now has **excess reserves** or **free reserves**—reserves in excess of the amount required; that is, each bank will be in a position to lend more. Where a lack of funds may have caused the bank to reject loans to projects it considered worthy, now it will make these loans. The new loans get spent, creating new deposits and allowing still further loans, and the multiplier process is once again set in motion.

DISCOUNT RATE

The second tool of monetary policy is the **discount rate**. As explained earlier in this chapter, the Federal Reserve banks are called the banker's bank because they lend money to banks and hold their deposits. The interest rate banks must pay when they borrow from the Federal Reserve banks is called the discount rate. When the discount rate is high, interest rates charged by banks tend to be high, and banks make loans less available.

Consider an aggressive bank that always keeps just the minimum amount of reserves. It lends out all the funds that are not kept in reserves. If a major depositor suddenly wishes to withdraw funds, the bank is forced to borrow funds, either from other banks or from the Federal Reserve banks. When the discount rate increases, the interest rate the bank must pay for borrowing from other banks increases in tandem. The discount rate affects this bank as a direct cost of doing business. If it has to pay the Fed more to borrow itself, it must charge its own customers more.

If the bank pursues a less aggressive policy and holds more funds in the form of Treasury bills or other liquid assets, a large deposit withdrawal causes only a minor adjustment: the bank simply sells some of its liquid assets. Raising the discount rate makes it more expensive to call upon the Fed in the event of a shortfall of funds, and this induces banks to hold more liquid assets, which in turn means that the bank will be lending less.

The Fed not only uses a higher discount rate to discourage banks from lending, it also rations access to the discount "window." That is, it may refuse to lend to a bank, even at the announced discount rate; this action forces the bank to take more costly remedial actions to satisfy the reserve requirements set by the Fed.

The discount rate is the only interest rate the Fed directly sets. All other interest rates are set in the market, by the forces of demand and supply. But as the Fed affects banks' willingness to lend, it may at the same time affect the interest rates they charge and the rates they pay depositors. The interest rates the government pays on both short-term borrowing (T-bills) and longer-term borrowing are also determined in the market. The Fed's actions affect these interest rates only indirectly.

The Fed often uses the discount rate not so much for its direct effects but as a signal of its intentions. When the Fed lowers the discount rate, the market knows the Fed is serious about making credit more available in the economy, and conversely when it raises the discount rate. On the other hand, often the discount rate is changed to reflect changes in interest rates that have already occurred. If market interest rates have risen but the Fed has failed to increase the discount rate in tandem, the difference between the discount rate, the rate banks have to pay to obtain funds from the Fed, and the rate they can receive on loans may be large; this will tempt banks to try to borrow excessively from the Fed. Thus, while changes in the discount rate sometimes signal a change in policy, at other times the changes just reflect the Fed's catching up with the market.

OPEN MARKET OPERATIONS

Open market operations are the most important instrument the Fed uses to control the money supply. In open market operations, the Federal Reserve enters the market directly to buy or sell government bonds. Imagine that it buys $1 million of government bonds from wealthy Joe Brown (or from a thousand different Joe Brown families), paying him with a $1 million check. Joe Brown takes the check down to his bank, AmericaBank, which credits his account with $1 million. AmericaBank presents the check to the Fed, which credits the bank's account with $1 million. AmericaBank now has $1 million of new deposits, $1 million in new reserves, and it can accordingly lend out an additional $900,000. A money multiplier goes to work, and the total expansion of the money supply will be equal to a multiple of the initial $1 million increase in deposits. And credit—the amount of outstanding loans—has also increased by a multiple of the initial increase in deposits.

The purchase of bonds from Joe Brown by the Federal Reserve has a quite different effect from a purchase of the same bonds by a private citizen, Jill White. In the latter case, Jill White's deposit account goes down by $1 million, and Joe Brown's deposit account goes up by $1 million. The funds available in the system as a whole remain unchanged. The money multiplier goes to work only when funds enter from "outside," and in particular from the Federal Reserve banks.

Thus, the Fed has three indirect ways in which it controls the money supply and credit-creating activities of banks. Through open market operations, it affects the supply of reserves. Through reserve requirements, it affects the amount of reserves that banks must have, relative to their deposits. Through the discount rate, it affects the cost of having too few reserves. By changing the supply of reserves, the required amount of reserves, or the cost of not having sufficient reserves, the Fed affects the amount that banks can lend, and the attractiveness to banks of making loans as compared with holding their assets in a liquid form, such as T-bills.

INSTRUMENTS OF MONETARY POLICY

1. Open market operations—by buying and selling Treasury bills, the Fed changes the supply of reserves and thus the money supply.

2. Reserve requirements—the required ratio of reserves to deposits. The Fed can change the reserve requirement to change the amount that banks must hold as reserves.

3. Discount rates—the rate the Fed charges for loans made to member banks. The Fed can change the discount rate and thus change the amount that banks wish to hold as reserves.

SELECTING THE APPROPRIATE INSTRUMENT

Of the three instruments, the Federal Reserve uses open market operations most frequently. Changes in discount rates and in reserve requirements are viewed to be blunt tools, compared with the fine-tuning that open market operations make possible. Thus, changes in reserve requirements and in discount rates are used to announce major shifts in monetary policy, but not on a regular basis. Such changes signal tighter credit (that is, changes in monetary policy that entail higher interest rates and reduced credit availability) or looser credit (that is, changes in monetary policy that have the reverse effect). They can be quite effective: for instance, banks, foreseeing a tightening of credit, may cut back their lending, and firms may put plans for investment onto the shelf.

THE STABILITY OF THE U.S. BANKING SYSTEM

The fractional reserve system explains how banks create money, and it also explains how, without the Fed, banks can get into trouble. Well-managed banks, even before the advent of the Fed and its reserve requirements, kept reserves equal to some average expectation of day-to-day needs. A bank could get into trouble in a hurry if one day's needs exceeded its reserves.

If (for good reasons or bad) many depositors lose confidence in a bank at the same time, they will attempt to withdraw their funds all at once. The bank simply will not have the money available, since most of the money will have been lent out in loans that cannot be called in instantaneously. This situation is called a **bank run**. Bank runs were as common in nineteenth-century America as they were in the old Western movies, where customers in a small town would line up at the bank while it paid out what reserves it had on a first-come, first-served basis.[6] People who showed up and asked for their money got it until there was no more left. Even if a bank was fairly healthy, such a run could quickly drive it out of business. After all, if a rumor spread that a bank was in trouble and a few savers ran to the bank to clean out their accounts, then other investors would feel they were foolish to sit back and wait. Only by running down to the bank themselves could they protect their deposits. Rumors could easily snowball into panic, and other banks could also be drawn into a run. As a result, one vicious rumor could lead to a healthy bank's having to shut down, thus destabilizing the banking system and the local economy.

REDUCING THE THREAT OF BANK RUNS

Bank runs and panics have periodically afflicted the American banking system. In fact, one reason the Fed was set up in 1913 was to make them less likely. In this it has largely been successful; the last major panic occurred in the midst of the Great Depression in 1933. To stop it, President Roosevelt declared a "bank holiday" and closed all banks. But since then, the modern banking system has evolved a variety of safeguards that have ended, or at least reduced, the threat of bank runs for most banks. There are three levels of protection.

First, the Fed sets reserve requirements and serves as a banker's bank, as we have seen. Even those bank executives who might like to live recklessly, getting along on minuscule reserves, are unable to do so. Moreover, if the only problem facing the bank is one of short-term liquidity—having the cash on hand to meet depositors' demands—it can now borrow from the Fed. The Fed is therefore referred to as "the lender of last resort." But the problem with being the lender of last resort is how to distinguish between banks that face only a liquidity problem and those that are truly insolvent, that should be shut down because their loans have turned bad and they owe more to depositors than the value of their assets. In the Great Depression, the Fed refused to lend to many banks, and they were forced to shut down.

The second level of protection is provided by the owners of the bank. Most banks are started by investors who put up a certain amount of money in exchange for a share of ownership. The net worth of the firm—the difference between the bank's assets and its liabilities—is this initial investment, augmented or decreased over time by the bank's profits or losses. If the bank makes bad investment decisions, then these shareholders can be forced to bear the cost, not the depositors. This cushion provided by shareholders not only protects depositors, it also encourages the bank to be more prudent in its loans. If the bank makes bad loans, the owners risk their entire investment. If the owners' net worth in the bank is too small, the owners may see themselves in a "Heads I win, tails you lose" situation: if risky investments turn out well, the extra profits accrue to the bank; if they turn out badly, the bank goes bankrupt, but since the owners had little at stake, they have little to lose. Thus, the government has imposed **capital requirements** on banks: banks must maintain a certain ratio of net worth to deposits. Capital requirements protect against insolvency; they mean that if the bank invests badly and many of its loans default, the bank will still be able to pay back depositors. (By contrast, reserves and the ability to borrow from the Fed protect against illiquidity; they ensure that if

---

[6] One famous fictional bank run occurred in the popular 1946 Frank Capra movie *It's a Wonderful Life.*

CLOSE-UP: HISTORICAL PERSPECTIVES ON MONEY CREATION

We have seen that today most money is created within the banking system. But this has not always been the case. When money consisted primarily of gold and silver, the money supply was determined by accidents of fate: the discovery of new sources of these metals. The discovery of the New World, for instance, with its stocks of gold and silver, greatly increased the money supply of Europe in the sixteenth and seventeenth centuries.

With the advent of fiat money, expansion of the money supply was a government decision: how fast should the printing presses be run? When the government's revenues fell short of its expenditures and it could not borrow or found borrowing to be too expensive, it paid for expenditures with newly printed money. This is how the Second Continental Congress paid for some of its expenditures from 1776 to 1789 (the period between the writing of the Declaration of Independence and the establishment of the U.S. Constitution). Many people did not think much of these pieces of printed paper and were unwilling to take them as a form of exchange; a popular phrase of disparagement was that something was "not worth a Continental."

In the late nineteenth century in the United States, questions of money supply became the center of a heated political debate. The period was marked by deflation; the price level was actually falling. Lenders like deflation and dislike inflation: they prefer to be paid back with dollars that are worth more than at the time the loan was made. By the same token, debtors dislike deflation, for it means they have to pay off their loans with money that is worth more. The divergence of views between farmers and others who were in debt and the banks to which they owed money is what made the political debate then so heated.

Increasing the money supply would, it was thought, stop the deflation. One way to do this would be to include in the money supply not only gold but also silver, which was much more plentiful. Silver would be minted into coins, and the price of silver would be fixed not by the law of supply and demand but by legislation. People could pay off any debts with silver at the officially determined value. One of the most famous lines from any presidential campaign was said in 1896 by William Jennings Bryan (who was defeated by William McKinley) at the Democratic National Convention in Chicago: "You shall not press down upon the brow of labor this crown of thorns; you shall not crucify mankind upon a cross of gold." That campaign gave the money supply an unusually high profile. In recent years, while issues of monetary policy have been important, they have not elicited the passions that they did a century ago.

depositors want cash, they can get it.) On occasion—more frequently in recent years—a bank will make so many bad loans that it fails to satisfy the capital requirements.

As a third and final backstop, the government introduced the Federal Deposit Insurance Corporation (FDIC) in 1933. Federal banks and savings and loans have had to purchase insurance, which ensures that depositors can get all their money back, up to $100,000 per account. Since deposits are guaranteed by the federal government, depositors fearing the collapse of a bank have no need to rush to the bank. They can walk to the bank rather than run. The deposit insurance thus not only protects depositors, it has an enormous impact in increasing the stability of the banking system. The beauty of deposit insurance lies in the fact that because it exists, the threat against which it insures is much less likely to occur. It is as if life insurance somehow prolonged life dramatically.

Critics of deposit insurance point to an offsetting disadvantage: depositors no longer have any incentive to monitor banks, to make sure that they are investing the funds safely. Regardless of what the bank does with their funds, they are protected. While many economists are not convinced that depositors themselves could effectively monitor banks, the system of deposit insurance creates some peculiar incentives. Depositors have an incentive to put their money with whatever bank offers the highest returns. To earn high returns requires the bank to undertake greater risk. But greater risks make it more likely that the bank will fail and need to call on its federal guarantees. The fact that depositors are protected against the risk of a bank becoming insolvent makes it more likely that bankruptcy will occur.

Since depositors have no incentive to monitor the banks—and might not do a very effective job even if their incentives had not been removed by depositor insurance—the burden of monitoring the banks rests on the Fed and other government agencies. This regulation goes beyond just reserve and capital requirements: it limits the kinds of investments that banks can make. A part of the blame for the collapse of the S & L's (see Chapter 6) lies in a loosening of those restrictions; some S & L's took advantage of their greater freedom to make high-risk investments and loans.

Deposit insurance is also blamed for the precarious state in which the U.S. banking system currently finds itself. During the 1920s, before the creation of the FDIC, banks failed at an average rate of 600 per year, and during the Depression from 1930 to 1933, at the incredible rate of 2,000 per year. The regulatory structure established by the FDIC at first seemed to do the trick. From 1960 to 1974, there were on average only 6 bank failures a year, while from 1975 to 1981 there were on average only 11 a year. And most of the failures that did occur were small and insignificant banks. But as Figure 33.6 makes clear, since then bank failures have skyrocketed, and a still larger number of banks are in a precarious financial position.

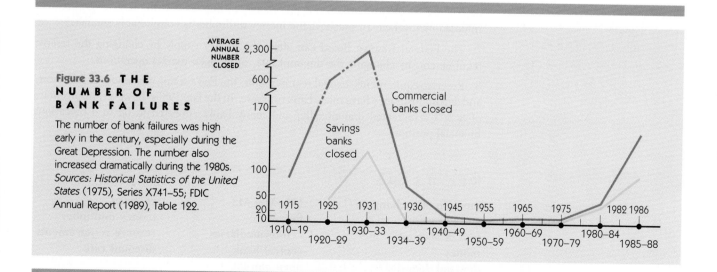

Figure 33.6 THE NUMBER OF BANK FAILURES

The number of bank failures was high early in the century, especially during the Great Depression. The number also increased dramatically during the 1980s. *Sources: Historical Statistics of the United States (1975), Series X741–55; FDIC Annual Report (1989), Table 122.*

The weakening financial position of the U.S. banks was thought to have contributed to the economic recession that began in 1991. Banks were unable or unwilling to lend, and the restriction in credit led to reduced investment. Chapter 34 takes a closer look at the relations between monetary policy, the financial position of banks, money and credit, and the level of economic activity.

REVIEW AND PRACTICE

SUMMARY

1. Money is anything that is generally accepted in a given society as a medium of exchange, store of value, and unit of account.

2. There are many ways of measuring the money supply, with names like M1, M2, and M3. All include both currency and checking accounts. They differ in what they include as assets that are close substitutes to currency and checking accounts.

3. A buyer does not need money to purchase a good, at least not right away, if the seller or a financial institution is willing to extend credit.

4. Financial intermediaries, which include banks, savings and loans, mutual funds, insurance companies, and others, all have in common that they form the link between savers who have extra funds and borrowers who desire extra funds.

5. Government is involved with the banking industry for two reasons. First, by regulating the activities banks can undertake and providing deposit insurance, government seeks to protect depositors and ensure the stability of the financial system. Second, by influencing the willingness of banks to make loans, government attempts to influence the level of investment and overall economic activity.

6. By making loans, banks can create an increase in the supply of money that is a multiple of an initial increase in the banks' deposits. If every bank loans all the money it can and every dollar lent is spent to buy goods, purchased from other firms who deposit the check in their account, the money multiplier is 1/ the reserve requirement imposed by the Fed. In practice, the money multiplier is considerably smaller.

7. The Federal Reserve Board can affect the money supply by changing the reserve requirement, by changing the discount rate, or by open market operations.

8. Reserve requirements, capital requirements, the Fed's acting as a lender of last resort, and deposit insurance have made bank runs rare. In the late 1980s, however, insolvencies of S & L's increased dramatically, and many banks appeared to be in a precarious financial position.

KEY TERMS

medium of exchange	M1, M2, M3	reserve
store of value	financial	money multiplier
unit of account	intermediaries	reserve requirements
money	central bank	discount rate
demand deposits	open market	
	operations	

REVIEW QUESTIONS

1. What are the three characteristics that define money?

2. What are the differences between M1, M2, and M3?

3. When consumers or businesses desire to make a large purchase, are they limited to spending only as much as the M1 money that they have on hand? Explain.

4. What is the Federal Reserve System?

5. What are the two main reasons for government involvement in the banking system?

6. What are three ways for the Federal Reserve to reduce the money supply?

7. What has the government done to make bank runs less likely?

PROBLEMS

1. Identify which of money's three traits each of the following assets shares, and which traits it does not share:
   (a) a house;
   (b) a day pass for an amusement park;
   (c) German marks held by a resident of Dallas, Texas;
   (d) a painting;
   (e) gold.

2. How might bank depositors be protected by legal prohibitions on banks' entering businesses like insurance, or selling and investing in stocks or venture capital? What are the possible costs and benefits of such prohibitions for depositors and for the government?

3. Down Home Savings has the following assets and liabilities: $6 million in government bonds and reserves; $40 million in deposits; $36 million in outstanding loans. Draw up a balance sheet for the bank. What is its net worth?

4. What factors might affect the value of a bank's loan portfolio? If these factors are changing, explain how this would complicate the job of a bank examiner trying to ascertain the magnitude of the bank's net worth. Why would the bank examiner be concerned about the value of the net worth?

5. While gardening in his backyard, Lucky Bob finds a mason jar containing $100,000 in currency. After he deposits the money in his lucky bank, where the reserve requirement is .05, how much will the money supply eventually increase?

6. Why is it that if the Fed sells Treasury bonds the money supply changes, but if a big company sells Treasury bonds (to anyone other than the Fed) the money supply does not change?

7. "So long as the Central Bank stands ready to lend to any bank with a positive net worth, reserve requirements are unnecessary. What underlies the stability of the banking system is the central bank's role as a lender of last resort, combined with policies aimed at ensuring the financial viability of the banks—for instance, the net worth requirements." Comment.

34

MONETARY THEORY AND POLICY

I n Chapter 33, we saw the close link between the creation of money and credit (loans). This chapter explains why the money supply and the availability of credit are important to the economy. Knowing this, we can interpret monetary policy, the collection of policies aimed at affecting the money supply and the availability of credit. As was pointed out in Chapter 26, monetary and fiscal policy are the two main instruments the government uses to pursue its goals of economic growth, stable prices, and full employment.

In Chapter 33, we saw how the Fed, through reserve requirements, changes in the discount rate, and open market operations, can affect both the supply of money and the amount of credit (loans) that banks make available to borrowers. This chapter attempts to answer the questions of *how* and *when* the Fed's actions have significant effects on the level of economic activity.

Changes in the money supply and changes in the availability of credit are two sides of the same coin. Different economists have focused on each side. We begin by looking at the Fed's direct effects on the money supply, then turn to its effects on credit availability.

"O.K., folks, let's move along. I'm sure you've all seen someone qualify for a loan before."

1. What determines the demand for money? How and why does it depend on the interest rate and the level of income?

2. How is the demand for money equilibrated to the supply of money?

3. What are the consequences of changes in the supply of money? Under what circumstances will a change in the money supply simply lead to a change in the price level? When will it lead to a change in real output? When will it largely lead to a change in the amount of money that individuals are willing to hold?

4. What are the channels through which monetary policy affects the economy? What role is played by changes in the real interest rate? the availability of credit?

5. What are the different schools of thought concerning the extent to which monetary policy affects the economy? What are the underlying sources of their disagreements? What are some of the important ways that they differ in their policy recommendations?

MONEY SUPPLY AND ECONOMIC ACTIVITY

If the Fed increases the money supply, three different results are possible. First, people who get the additional money could just hold on to it. Nothing would happen to the rest of the economy, only these people's bank balances would be increased. This outcome is most likely when the economy is in a deep recession, such as the Great Depression, in which case monetary policy will be relatively ineffective.

Second, those who get the additional money could try to spend it. By bringing that new money to the market, they might increase aggregate expenditures and shift the aggregate demand curve to an intersection with aggregate supply at a higher output level, as seen in Figure 34.1A. This is more likely to occur if initially there was considerable excess capacity.

The third result is that those who get the additional money also spend it, but this time the economy is originally in a situation where there is no excess capacity, as in panel B. The initial intersection of the aggregate demand and aggregate supply curves occurs along the vertical portion of the aggregate supply curve. Instead of output increasing, only prices increase.

What actually happens when the money supply is increased is some combination of the three possibilities—changed holdings of money, changed output, and changed prices. Which outcome is more likely to occur depends, as noted, on economic circumstances.

What policies the government wishes to pursue will also depend on economic circumstances. When the economy is in a recession and has excess capacity, the government wants to stimulate the economy. In this case, the question is whether or under what circumstances monetary policy can be used to stimulate the economy. On the other hand, when all of the resources of the economy are fully utilized, attention is switched to the problem of inflation and the role of monetary policy in reducing aggregate demand and thus reducing those inflationary pressures.

In Chapter 33, we learned several different ways of measuring the money supply— M1, M2, and M3. For much of our discussion, we do not have to be very precise about which supply of money we have in mind. But it is natural to focus our attention on M1, for two reasons. First, M1 is the supply of money most directly under the control of the Fed. M2 and M3 include such items as money market mutual fund balances, which are not directly related to the banking system, and it is through the banking system that monetary policy most directly has its impact. Second, the key attribute of money upon which we will focus is its role as a medium of exchange; money facilitates

Figure 34.1 EFFECT OF INCREASING THE MONEY SUPPLY

If individuals decide to spend some of the extra money rather than just holding it, then increasing the money supply shifts aggregate demand to the right. If the economy is far from full employment, on the horizontal portion of the aggregate supply curve, as in panel A, then the shift raises output with little effect on the price level. But if the economy is near full employment and on the vertical portion of the aggregate supply curve, as in panel B, then this shift affects only the price level, not output.

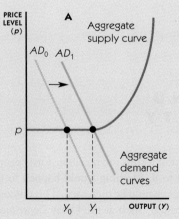

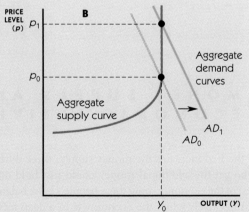

transactions. And M1, which includes checking accounts and currency, is the definition of money most directly related to its use as a medium of exchange.

Within M1, we will focus on the portion most directly under the Fed's control: demand deposits and other checking-account deposits. This is also appropriate because they are more important—they comprise more than 70 percent of the M1 total.

THE VELOCITY OF MONEY

As important to monetary policy as the money supply itself is its **velocity**, the speed with which money circulates in the economy. In a bustling city, money changes hands quickly, and thus a given money supply supports many more transactions there than it would in a depressed city where people do not make exchanges as often. If individuals as a whole keep money under the mattress for weeks after being paid, money may circulate very slowly. The velocity of money is formally defined as the ratio of GDP or GNP to the money supply. (In this chapter, the distinction between GNP and GDP will play no role.) If Q represents the quantity of goods produced in the economy and p is a weighted average of their prices, pQ is equal to GDP (which, you will recall, equals income), represented by the symbol Y. Using the symbol V to denote velocity and M as the money supply, we get

$$V = pQ/M = Y/M.$$

To see how velocity is calculated using this equation, assume that Y is $5 trillion per year and the money supply is $500 billion; the velocity would be 10 (per year). If producing a dollar of output required only one transaction, then the average dollar would have to circulate 10 times every year to produce an output of $5 trillion. If the money supply were only $50 billion, then every dollar would have to circulate 100 times each year, or ten times faster, to produce an output of $5 trillion.

The variable p was called a weighted average of prices. This is the same as calling p the price level. Let's use the velocity equation to look again at what happens when the money supply increases. If M increases, either V must be lowered, Q must increase, or p must increase. This result matches the three possible consequences of an increase in the money supply with which we began the chapter: individuals could simply hold the extra money, which would decrease velocity; the amount bought, Q, may increase; or the price level, p, may rise.

The essential problem of monetary theory is to understand when each of these outcomes will result. While the extreme cases, where only one of the three possibilities occurs, are instructive for understanding what is going on, they can be misleading. When the *only* effect is on prices or on money holdings, monetary policy is completely ineffective in stimulating aggregate output and employment. But if there is *some* effect on output as well, then monetary policy can be a useful instrument in stimulating the economy. It may take a larger dose of the medicine—a larger increase in the money supply—to achieve any desired goal.

POSSIBLE CONSEQUENCES OF INCREASED MONEY SUPPLY

Increased money holdings (decreased velocity)
Changes in quantities produced and sold
Changes in prices

To solve this problem, we need to ask two questions. First, to what extent will a change in the money supply lead to a change in velocity or a change in income, pQ? And second, how will any change in pQ be divided into a change in price level, p, and change in output, Q?

The second question is easy to answer, given what we have already learned about aggregate demand and supply curves. If the economy is operating along the horizontal portion of the aggregate supply curve, with excess capacity, then the price level will be unaffected when aggregate demand increases; only output will change. But if the economy is operating along the vertical portion of the aggregate supply curve, where output cannot change, then only the price level will be affected when aggregate demand increases.

We now turn to the first question. To keep the discussion simple, we focus on the situation where the economy is in the excess-capacity region, so that the price level is fixed.

THE DEMAND FOR MONEY

The velocity of money—how fast money circulates through the system—depends on how willing people are to hold, or keep, money. You may remember the game of hot potato, in which a hot potato is passed rapidly among people in a group. In a way, money is like a hot potato. Currency is an asset that bears no interest. Since people would usually prefer to earn interest, they have an incentive to pass their currency along to someone else, exchanging it for either goods or an interest-bearing asset like a Treasury bill. Why do they hold money at all? Because it is convenient. You can buy groceries with currency. You cannot buy groceries with a T-bill; you would have to convert your T-bill back into currency, and there are costs (transactions costs) of doing so.

Thus, people's willingness to hold money is a result of their balancing the benefits of holding money—the convenience—against the *opportunity* cost, the forgone interest. The benefits of holding money are related to money's use as a medium of exchange. The more transactions people engage in, the more money they will want to hold. The demand for money arising from its use in facilitating transactions is called the **transactions demand for money**. This demand for money rises with *nominal* income: higher incomes mean that the value of goods bought will be greater, which implies that the value of transactions will be greater. In fact, the demand for money increases proportionately with the nominal value of output, pQ; if prices double, then other things being equal, people will need to have twice the amount of money to engage in the same transactions.

The basic elements of monetary economics we have learned so far are agreed upon by most economists: the government controls (or at least affects) the money supply—through open market operations, reserve requirements, and changes in the discount rate—and the demand for money increases with the level of nominal income. But there is some disagreement about whether the ratio of money demand to income—the velocity of circulation—is constant, or even predictable; and the extent to which the demand for money, at any income level, depends on the interest rate. We will now explore the reasons for these differences in views, and their consequences.

COMMONLY ACCEPTED INGREDIENTS OF MONETARY THEORIES

1. Government controls (or affects) the money supply through open market operations, reserve requirements, and changes in the discount rate.

2. Money demand depends on nominal income.

KEYNESIAN MONETARY THEORY

Keynesians have traditionally emphasized that the demand for money may be dependent on the rate of interest. The cost of holding money is the interest that could have been earned if the money in your checking account (or in your pocket) had been invested in some other asset. If checking deposits pay interest of 0 percent and very short-term government bonds (Treasury bills) pay 4 percent, then the cost of holding money is 4 percent per year. Today checking accounts pay interest, so the opportunity cost of holding funds in them is lower than it used to be. Nevertheless, the difference between the interest paid on checking accounts and the return to other assets deters people from holding money. We focus on the interest rate paid on T-bills for a simple reason: they are just as safe as money. The only difference is that T-bills yield a higher interest rate, but money is better as a medium of exchange.

The demand for money is much like the demand for any other good; it depends on the price and on people's incomes. The price of a good tells us what a person has to give up of other goods to get an additional unit of this good. The price also measures the opportunity cost of consuming an additional unit of the good. The interest rate (r)

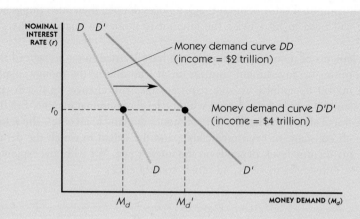

Figure 34.2 DEMAND CURVE FOR MONEY

The quantity demanded of money slopes down as the opportunity cost of holding funds—that is, the interest rate—increases. An increase in income causes a shift in the money demand function from DD to $D'D'$.

the individual could have earned on a government bond can be thought of as the price of money, since it measures the opportunity cost of holding money. As the interest rate rises, the amount of money demanded declines.

Another way to think about this is to remember that the velocity of circulation measures how fast money moves through the economy—that is, how frequently a given dollar bill circulates. The lower the interest rate, the lower the velocity of circulation. It is costly to hold on to money—people must forgo interest that they could otherwise be earning. The higher the interest rate, the more costly and therefore the more quickly they pass it on to someone else after receiving it, by buying goods or investing it in an asset yielding a higher return.

To see how the demand for money depends on people's incomes, consider Table 34.1, which shows a hypothetical example. These are the numbers plotted in Figure

Table 34.1 DEMAND FOR MONEY

Nominal interest rate	Income: $2 trillion	$4 trillion
2%	412	824
4%	404	808
6%	396	792
8%	388	776
10%	380	761

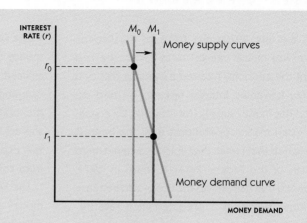

Figure 34.3
EQUILIBRIUM INTEREST RATES

The interest rate adjusts to make the demand for money equal the supply. In this diagram, a government-induced shift in the supply of money from M_0 to M_1 has a large effect on the interest rate, since the demand for money is relatively inelastic with respect to the interest rate.

34.2. With an income level of $2 trillion, the demand for money is given by the curve on the left. The table and figure illustrate the two basic properties of the demand for money: it decreases as the interest rate rises, and increases, at a fixed interest rate, in proportion to income. Doubling the income level to $4 trillion at any fixed interest rate shifts the demand curve for money out.

In equilibrium, the interest rate adjusts to make the demand for money equal the supply. Figure 34.3 shows supply curves for money as well as a demand curve. The supply of money is controlled by the government (the Fed), through the instruments described in Chapter 33. The amount of money the government makes available does not depend at all on the interest rate. That is why the supply curves are vertical. The equilibrium interest rate with money supply M_0 is r_0.

The principles described in this section—that the nominal interest rate is the opportunity cost of holding money, the demand for money decreases as the interest rate rises, and the interest rate is determined to equate the demand and supply of money—are together called **Keynesian monetary theory**. Keynes used this theory to explain how monetary policy works when it works, and why it sometimes does not work. To do this, he traced out the effects of a change in the supply of money on the interest rate, the effects of a change in the interest rate on investment, and the effects of a change in investment on the level of national income. We now take a closer look at each of the steps in this analysis.

HOW MONETARY POLICY MAY AFFECT THE ECONOMY THROUGH CHANGING INTEREST RATES

Figure 34.3 can also be used to show how changes in the money supply can lead to changes in the interest rates. Initially, the money supply is at M_0 and the equilibrium interest rate is r_0. When the government increases the money supply to M_1, the interest

Before the late 1970s, the focus of the Federal Reserve was mainly interest rates. When the Fed thought the economy needed a boost, it decided how low it wanted interest rates to go, and expanded the money supply (for instance, by engaging in open market operations) until the interest rate reached that target. Paul Volcker, when named chairman of the Federal Reserve Board in 1979, announced that henceforth the Fed would increase the money supply at a predetermined rate, regardless of what happened to the interest rate. He shifted the "target" from controlling the interest rate to controlling the money supply. The chosen rate of expansion of the money supply was sufficiently low to bring down the rate of inflation, which had climbed from 6.7 percent in 1977 to 9.0 percent in 1978 and 13.3 percent in 1979.

Volcker's policy was based on the theory that velocity was constant (or at least predictable). If the money supply increased at a steady pace, enough to accommodate the increased production of goods (and any anticipated change in velocity), then the price level would be steady. Recall the definition of velocity (V): $V = pQ/M$.

The Fed pursued this policy vigorously. When the money supply started to increase faster than the amount targeted, the Fed engaged in open market operations, selling government bonds. Growth in the money supply was reduced, but interest rates soared to 10, then 15, then 20 percent, pushing the economy into a serious recessionary period from early 1980 through the later part of 1982.

The Fed abandoned this policy of targeting the money supply, for two reasons. First, the rate of inflation tumbled sharply, falling to 3.8 percent in 1982. With inflation much lower and the economy in a recession, it became important to try to stimulate the economy rather than harness inflation. Moreover, it became increasingly evident that the velocity of circulation was not constant, and the rapidly changing financial institutions also made the appropriate definition of money less and less clear. Saying that the money supply should expand at a constant rate was one thing, but in practice did that mean M1, M2, or M3? Today the monetary authorities keep an eye on interest rates and all of the indicators of the money supply, and attempt to develop a feel for what these sometimes conflicting indicators are telling them.

rate falls to r_1. In the figure, the demand for money is relatively inelastic, so that an increase in the supply of money at a given level of income causes a large decrease in the interest rate. If inflationary expectations remain unchanged, then the change in the nominal interest rate is translated into a change in real interest rates (the nominal interest rate minus the rate of inflation). As interest rates fall, investment rises. As investment spending increases, income (which is the same as output) rises via the multiplier.

The increase in investment shifts the aggregate expenditures schedule up, as depicted in Figure 34.4A, and results in a higher equilibrium level of output. Output increases from Y_0 to Y_1.

The aggregate expenditures schedule assumes a particular price level. A similar effect occurs at each price level. Accordingly, the aggregate demand curve shifts to the right, as shown in Figure 34.4B. Here we are focusing on a situation where in the initial

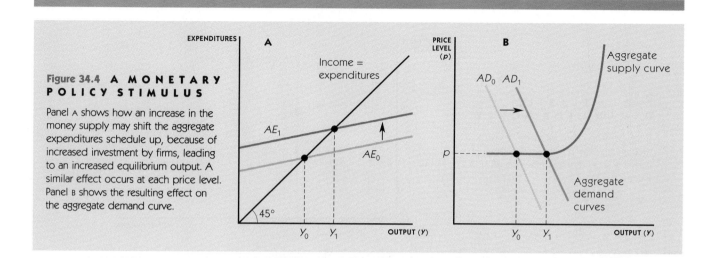

Figure 34.4 A MONETARY POLICY STIMULUS

Panel A shows how an increase in the money supply may shift the aggregate expenditures schedule up, because of increased investment by firms, leading to an increased equilibrium output. A similar effect occurs at each price level. Panel B shows the resulting effect on the aggregate demand curve.

equilibrium there is excess capacity; that is, the intersection of the aggregate demand and aggregate supply curves occurs along the horizontal portion of the aggregate supply curve. Thus, the effect of the shift in the aggregate demand curve is to increase output, with no change in prices.

When income increases, the money demand curve shifts to the right, as shown in Figure 34.5. Thus, the eventual equilibrium attained will involve a smaller decrease in the rate of interest than r_1. The new equilibrium interest rate will lie somewhere between r_0 and r_1; in the figure, it is r_2.

Figure 34.5 SECOND-ROUND EFFECTS OF INCREASED MONEY SUPPLY

In the first round, the increased money supply led to lower interest rates (Figure 34.3), which led in turn to higher levels of national income (Figure 34.4). This higher level of income now shifts the money demand curve up (since the demand for money at each interest rate is higher). The equilibrium interest rate is r_2.

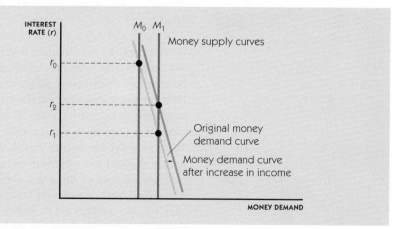

Figure 34.6 ELASTIC DEMAND FOR MONEY

If the demand curve for money is elastic, then an increase in the money supply causes a small change in the rate of interest.

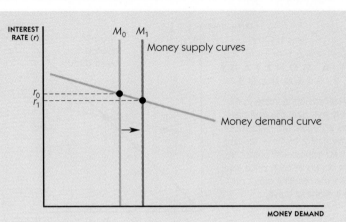

MONETARY POLICY IN DEEP RECESSIONS AND IN PERIODS OF FULL EMPLOYMENT

Figure 34.6 illustrates a situation that Keynes thought was prevalent in an economy suffering from deep recession: the demand curve for money is relatively elastic, so that changes in the supply of money have a negligible effect on the interest rate. In an extreme case, the demand curve for money would be perfectly horizontal. Then the only effect of an increase in the money supply would be that people would hold more money. Although this extreme case is not likely to occur, in deep recessions even large changes in the supply of money may induce relatively small changes in the interest rate.

Not only did Keynes think increasing the money supply would have little effect on interest rates, he also thought that in a recession any changes in the interest rate that did occur would have little effect on aggregate expenditures, since investment would be relatively unresponsive to changes in interest rates. Consumers would also respond little to reductions in the interest rate. Hence, in Keynes' view, increases in the money supply did not cause increases in output when they were most needed. Money supply changes did not move the aggregate expenditures schedule upward by much, and as a result they did not induce much of a change in the aggregate demand curve. They mostly changed the velocity of circulation.

Keynes' theory of monetary policy can easily be extended to situations where the economy is not in a recession but is operating along the vertical portion of the aggregate supply curve, as depicted in Figure 34.7A. The lower interest rate shifts the aggregate demand curve to the right, as we have seen before. But now the shift only results in an increase in the price level. It has no effect on output.

In between the two extremes are cases where the economy is operating along the

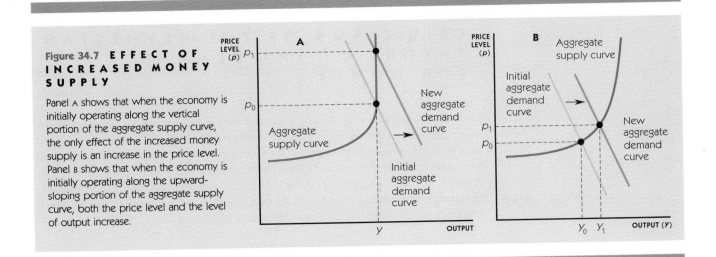

Figure 34.7 EFFECT OF INCREASED MONEY SUPPLY

Panel A shows that when the economy is initially operating along the vertical portion of the aggregate supply curve, the only effect of the increased money supply is an increase in the price level. Panel B shows that when the economy is initially operating along the upward-sloping portion of the aggregate supply curve, both the price level and the level of output increase.

upward-sloping portion of the aggregate supply curve, seen in panel B. Then the increase in money supply will lower interest rates, shift the aggregate demand curve, and result in both a higher output and a higher price level.

KEYNESIAN MONETARY THEORY

The nominal interest rate is the opportunity cost of holding money.

The demand for money decreases as the interest rate rises.

The interest rate equates the demand and supply for money.

KEYNESIAN THEORY OF MONETARY POLICY

When monetary policy is effective in generating increased output, it is because the policy induces a lower interest rate.

Monetary policy is ineffective in deep recessions, because

1. the money demand curve is elastic, so changes in the money supply induce only small changes in interest rates; and

2. even large changes in the interest rate induce little change in investment and hence in aggregate demand.

CRITICISMS OF THE KEYNESIAN THEORY OF THE DEMAND FOR MONEY

In the Keynesian monetary theory, there is a simple mechanism by which monetary policy affects the economy: when the government increases the supply of money, interest rates must fall in order for the demand for money to equal the supply; and lower interest rates induce more investment and consumer purchases of durables, stimulating aggregate demand. In recent years, changes in the U.S. financial system have led to a reexamination of this theory. Both its premises and its conclusions about the mechanisms by which monetary policy affects the economy have been questioned.

RELATIONSHIP BETWEEN MONEY AND INCOME

Economists have raised several questions concerning the demand function for money underlying the theory. Some questions focus on the relationship between the demand for money and income, others on the effect of interest rates on the demand for money.

Earlier we saw that what particularly distinguishes money from other assets such as government Treasury bills is its role as a medium of exchange in facilitating transactions. The Keynesian monetary theory implies that the higher their income, the more money people will want to hold. There is a simple relationship between the volume of transactions and the level of income. This would be the case if most transactions were directly related to output—employers paying wages and buying goods from suppliers, customers buying goods from firms, and so on.

But in fact, in terms of their dollar value, most transactions are for exchanges of financial assets, not the purchase of goods and services. One individual thinks General Motors stock is going to go down, and so he sells his shares. Another person thinks it is going up, and so she buys shares. The relationship between the volume of these financial transactions has virtually no direct bearing on national output and income. Indeed, the *ratio* of these transactions to national income may change markedly with economic conditions. When there is greater uncertainty and change, there may be more financial exchange, as people take differing views of what the future holds and as individual circumstances change rapidly.

In the longer run, there are a number of other factors that affect the relationship between money and income. For instance, not all transactions require payment by cash or check; today most transactions are made with credit. You need neither have money in a bank account nor have currency in your pocket to buy a car or a vacation in Hawaii, so long as you can get credit. You can pay with a credit card or write a check against your home equity credit line. Of course, some kinds of transactions are not easily done with credit; in most cities in the United States, you still have to pay for taxis with cash. But in Australia, taxis accept Visa, MasterCard, and American Express. The transactions that require money at the point of sale represent a relatively small and shrinking proportion of all transactions in the modern economy.

Similarly, technology has altered the whole idea of the velocity of money. With electronic fund transfers, in which computers can transfer funds from bank to bank or from account to account almost instantaneously, the velocity of circulation can become extremely high, even close to infinite for a few moments.

One might have thought that the increased use of credit and new technologies would have led to a higher velocity, a reduced ratio of money to income. In fact, the upward trend of velocity in the previous forty years has been reversed since 1980. There are no widely accepted explanations for these changes,[1] and they appear to have had little effect on the economy. Nevertheless, to the extent that they indicate that the money demand curve moves in ways that are not totally predictable, the ability to rely on monetary policy has been thrown into doubt.

RELATIONSHIP BETWEEN INTEREST RATES AND THE DEMAND FOR MONEY

Another set of criticisms of Keynesian monetary theory relates to the relationship between interest rates and the demand for money. Today demand deposits, which constitute the bulk of the money supply, pay interest. Thus, the opportunity cost of holding money is now the *difference* between the return to holding a government bond, for example, and the return to keeping one's money in a checking account; and that difference is small and may relate primarily to the bank's cost of running the checking account. Interest-bearing checking accounts were largely unavailable in the early part of this century, when the Keynesian theory of money demand was set forth. Their existence today calls into question the extent to which the demand for money will rise or fall in response to changes in interest rates.

But the Keynesian version of monetary theory has been criticized not only because the underlying assumptions concerning the demand for money are unpersuasive. Equally important, its conclusion, that monetary policy operates through changes in the interest rate, has been questioned. It is the real interest rate that matters most to firms, but it is the nominal interest rate that the Fed controls. The link between nominal and real interest rates may be tenuous. Changes in nominal interest rates translate directly into changes in real interest rates only if they produce no change in inflationary expectations. However, this is unlikely. By and large, higher nominal interest rates are associated with higher rates of inflation. And the data discussed in Chapter 29 showed that for long periods of time real interest rates varied relatively little.

Not only has the link between monetary policy and real interest rates been questioned, so has the link between real interest rates and investment. The data presented in Chapter 29, showing little relationship between changes in real interest rates and investment, suggest that much of the time the interest rate is not the only or primary mechanism through which monetary policy operates.

---

[1] One hypothesis is that there is a growing "underground" economy—drug dealers and others wishing to avoid paying income taxes. These individuals hold money as a store of value. But many observers think that the magnitude of the shift is too large to be simply accounted for by the development of the underground economy.

MONEY AND KEYNESIAN MONETARY THEORY: SOME PROBLEMS

There is no simple relationship between the demand for money and income.

Most transactions involve not goods and services (output) but the exchange of assets. The connection between transactions related to output and those related to exchange may not be stable.

Transactions do not necessarily need money; credit will do.

Changes in technology have allowed more extensive use of credit and make possible much higher velocities.

Real interest rates may not be directly affected by monetary policy.

Today most money takes the form of demand deposits and is interest-bearing. Thus, the opportunity cost of holding money is low and is not directly related to the nominal interest rate.

The opportunity cost is the nominal interest rate; investment is affected by real interest rates.

Fluctuations in investment are not closely linked with changes in real interest rates.

ALTERNATIVE WAYS THAT MONETARY POLICY WORKS

Economists dissatisfied with the interest rate links between money supply and output, but nonetheless convinced that there *is* a link between money and output, have looked for alternative ways that monetary policy exerts its effects. One important channel, through exports and imports, will be discussed in Chapter 35. Here we look at three other theories.

The first theory argues that investment is affected not so much because monetary policy changes the interest rate, but rather because it changes the prices of shares. The second extends this argument and maintains that as monetary policy increases the prices of shares and long-term bonds, people feel wealthier and are induced to consume more. The third provides an alternative explanation for why interest rates may fall when the government engages in open market operations; it focuses not on households' demand for money but on the behavior of banks.

INVESTMENT AND PORTFOLIO THEORY

Portfolio theories, which draw attention to stock market prices, focus on the store of value role of money.[2] Individuals, in deciding on their portfolios, look at the returns afforded by different assets—by Treasury bills, long-term government and corporate bonds, and stocks. Money is an asset that has similar properties to Treasury bills, except that it is also a medium of exchange and yields a lower return.

Nobel laureate James Tobin, of Yale University, focuses on the fact that when interest rates are low, individuals will shift their wealth toward stocks. This will drive the price of stocks up. At the higher price of shares, firms will engage in more investment. This theory is important in that it emphasizes the fact that firms do not look solely at the rate of interest on government bonds in deciding their investment. But it probably overemphasizes the role of the price of shares in determining firms' investment decisions, particularly since even in the best of times new equity issues finance a relatively small proportion of all investment.[3]

CONSUMPTION AND WEALTH EFFECTS

Another theory points out that the higher prices of shares and long-term bonds resulting from lower interest rates may make people feel wealthier. And when they feel wealthier, they consume more. It is not clear, however, how significant this effect is in the short run. As we saw in Chapter 29, individuals do not adjust their consumption quickly to changes in market values of their stocks and bonds, and even when they do, the increase in consumption is limited.

Still another set of theories pays less attention to households and firms and more attention to banks, but with much the same result in terms of national output. Open market operations result in banks' having more reserves. Earlier we saw how non-interest-bearing money is like a hot potato: it yields a zero return, so that apart from any convenience it might yield in facilitating transactions, you would like to get rid of it as fast as you can, to get an asset that yields a return. Today, since money yields a return, it is less like a hot potato. But to banks, reserves are really like hot potatoes, since they do not yield a return.[4] Banks hold reserves only because they are required to. The reserves are not required for "safety," since holding Treasury bills is as safe as holding reserves.

Consider what happens when the Fed creates some reserves through open market operations. Suppose the Fed buys a $10,000 Treasury bill from Rosa Diaz, who takes her check drawn against the Fed down to her local bank and deposits it. The Fed credits the bank with additional reserves. Reserves have gone up by $10,000 and so have deposits. The bank now has excess reserves and wants to invest them. It lowers its interest rates to attract more loan applicants, or it buys Treasury bills. As it tries to buy T-bills,

---

[2] For a fuller discussion of how individuals choose their portfolios, see Chapter 10.

[3] Moreover, empirical studies show the relationship between investment and the price of shares to be much weaker than Tobin's theory suggests. See Chapter 29 for a fuller discussion, including why even the weak relationship that has been observed can be interpreted in a quite different way.

[4] In some European countries, reserves do yield a return.

the price of T-bills goes up, and again the interest rate falls. And as the interest rate falls, stock and bond prices rise, and investment may increase because of either the lower interest rates or higher stock market prices. But, as we have seen, many economists are skeptical about the significance of these effects, and they look to an alternative mechanism, the availability of credit.

ALTERNATIVE MECHANISMS BY WHICH MONETARY POLICY MAY WORK

1. An increased money supply leads to lower interest rates and may also lead to higher prices of shares, which induce greater investment.

2. Higher prices of shares and long-term bonds may result in more consumption.

3. Open market operations may lead to lower interest rates and higher prices of shares and bonds because of the way banks respond to increased reserves.

MONETARISTS

One group of economists who were particularly influential in the late 1970s and early 1980s are the monetarists, whom we first encountered in Chapter 26; Nobel laureate Milton Friedman is perhaps the most well-known. Monetarists emphasize that what is important is not *how* monetary policy exerts its effects, but the simple fact that it *does* exert effects—that there is a systematic and predictable relationship between the money supply and the level of national income, or output.

The simplest version of this theory returns to the basic definition of velocity:

$$V = pQ/M.$$

Now let's assume that velocity is constant and use an asterisk to signify this. We can rewrite the equation as

$$MV^* = pQ.$$

If V^* is a constant and M doubles, pQ, the value of income, must also double. The theory that holds that velocity is constant so that increases in the money supply are reflected simply in proportionate increases in income is called the **quantity theory of money**.

We have repeatedly seen that whether p increases or Q increases, or a little bit of

Milton Friedman did not invent monetarism; the basic ideas had been around for quite some time. But he returned intellectual respectability to these ideas. In describing Friedman's contributions to economics in the 1987 *New Palgrave Dictionary of Economics,* Alan Waters, who served as principal economic adviser to the United Kingdom's prime minister Margaret Thatcher in the 1980s, wrote:

> In the late 1950s, to anyone subjected to the Anglo-Saxon schools of economics during the previous two decades, any attempt to revive monetary economics appeared to be foolhardy, like flogging a decomposing horse. The Radcliffe committee, advised by the most eminent economists, had reported in 1959 that the quantity of money was of little or no interest since the velocity of circulation had no limits. The quantity theory of money was subject to particular scorn as a mere identity without content. As Friedman was to point out, however, all theory consists of tautologies; all that theory does is to rearrange the implications of the axioms to produce interesting, even surprising, consequences.

To sum it up in two words, Friedman argued that "money matters." His studies maintained that in the short run, changes in the money supply could affect real economic growth and employment. In the long run, though, money affected only the price level. In the late 1940s and early 1950s, before he and his colleagues at the University of Chicago pushed these arguments, many, perhaps most, economists would have disagreed with the notion that money matters. By the late 1960s and 1970s, monetarism was at the center of policy discussions. In many countries, central banks announced that they would follow a monetarist philosophy.

But in the 1980s, as the velocity of money shifted unpredictably and the character of the financial system was changed by upheavals in the banking and finance industry, the confidence many economists felt in monetarism subsided. While a majority still believe that money matters, they are no longer certain of exactly how or why it matters. In fact, economists who subscribe to the real business-cycle view of economics have argued that changes in the money supply affect only inflation, but nothing in the *real* economy.

both, depends on whether the economy is initially operating along the horizontal, vertical, or upward-sloping portion of the aggregate supply curve. Consider, in particular, what happens if the economy is operating along the vertical portion, so that output cannot change. Then if M increases, the price level must increase proportionately. Consider what would happen if one night an elf went around doubling the money in everyone's pocket. Stores, acting perfectly efficiently, knowing that there is a fixed supply of goods available and knowing that the money supply had doubled, would immediately double their prices. Nothing *real* would happen.

How does an increase in the money supply have this effect on the price level? How does it lead to a shift in the aggregate demand curve? Some monetarists believe the answer is very simple: with more money chasing the same number of goods, prices must rise, just as though there were an elf. Others think the process may be more complicated. But monetarists all agree on the outcome: if money supply goes up and the economy is at full capacity, the price level must go up proportionately.

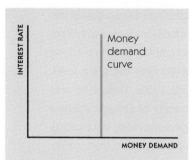

Figure 34.8 INELASTIC DEMAND CURVE FOR MONEY

Monetarists believe that the interest elasticity of the demand curve for money is essentially zero, which means that it is a vertical line.

A MONEY DEMAND CURVE INTERPRETATION

If velocity were constant, then individuals' willingness to hold money would not be sensitive to the interest rate. That is, the demand curve for money is perfectly inelastic, as depicted in Figure 34.8. The demand for money, M_d, is simply proportional to income:

$$M_d = k(pQ),$$

where k is a proportionality constant. In equilibrium, the demand for money must equal the supply, M_s:

$$M_s = M_d = k(pQ).$$

When velocity is constant, changes in the interest rate cannot balance the demand and supply for money. The only way that the demand and supply of money can be in equilibrium is through changes in the level of income. The demand for money is simply proportional to income, so that if the supply of money is increased by 10 percent, for the demand for money to equal supply, national income must rise by 10 percent. If the supply of money is decreased by 10 percent, then national income must fall by 10 percent.

MONETARISM AND MONETARY POLICY

Monetarists see a clear prescription for economy policy: let the money supply grow at the rate of growth of full-employment output. When the economy is operating along the vertical portion of the aggregate supply curve (there is no excess capacity), then such a policy ensures that prices will be stable. If output grows by 3 percent and the Fed increases the money supply by 3 percent, the price level will remain unchanged. At a faster rate of growth of the money supply, the price level will have to increase.

When the economy is operating along the horizontal portion of the aggregate supply curve, a decrease in the money supply can have devastating effects on the level of national income. In situations with excess capacity, we can take the price level as fixed. Thus, changes in the money supply result in proportionate changes in output. Monetarists like Milton Friedman believe that contractions of the money supply are largely responsible for many of the major downturns in the economy, including the Great Depression.

While Keynes focused on one extreme case, where the demand for money is highly sensitive to the interest rate, the monetarists focus on the other extreme, where the demand for money does not depend at all on the interest rate. More generally, the effectiveness of monetary policy depends on two variables: the elasticity of the demand curve for money (how sensitive the demand for money is to interest rates) and the interest elasticity of investment (how sensitive investment is to interest rates). Both of these elasticities can change with economic circumstances. Except in the extreme cases upon which Keynes focused, we would expect to see some relationship between the money supply and the level of economic activity, and there clearly is such a relationship. Figure

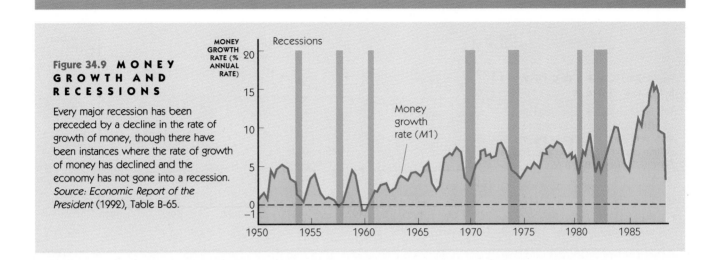

Figure 34.9 MONEY GROWTH AND RECESSIONS

Every major recession has been preceded by a decline in the rate of growth of money, though there have been instances where the rate of growth of money has declined and the economy has not gone into a recession. *Source: Economic Report of the President* (1992), Table B-65.

34.9 shows the rate of growth of the money supply. The shaded areas represent recessions. It is apparent that every major recession has been preceded by a decline in the rate of growth of the money supply (though there have been instances where the rate of growth of money has declined and the economy has not gone into a recession).

VARIATIONS IN VELOCITY

A closer look at the data helps us see more clearly the nature of the money-income relationship. Figure 34.10 shows the velocity since 1920, and Figure 34.11 shows a close-up of the patterns since 1960. Three conclusions emerge.

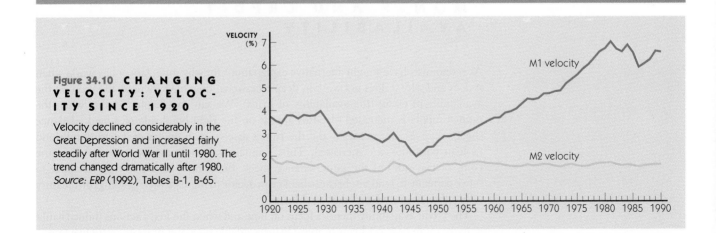

Figure 34.10 CHANGING VELOCITY: VELOCITY SINCE 1920

Velocity declined considerably in the Great Depression and increased fairly steadily after World War II until 1980. The trend changed dramatically after 1980. *Source: ERP* (1992), Tables B-1, B-65.

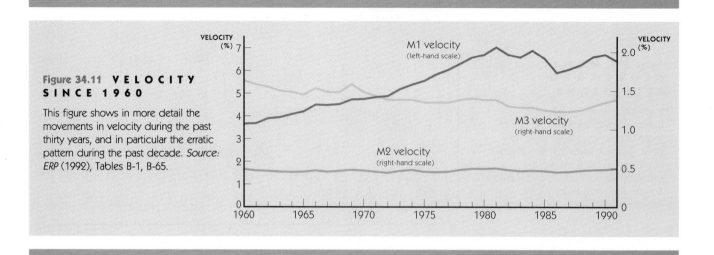

Figure 34.11 VELOCITY SINCE 1960

This figure shows in more detail the movements in velocity during the past thirty years, and in particular the erratic pattern during the past decade. *Source: ERP* (1992), Tables B-1, B-65.

First, in the one major economic downturn of this century, the Great Depression, velocity changed significantly.

Second, in the post–World War II period until the 1980s, the dominant feature of the velocity of M1 was its steady upward trend. This trend was slowed down in recessions. The relatively slight effect of these recessions on velocity could be for two reasons. One is that nominal interest rates in fact changed relatively little—that after an initial downturn they quickly returned to their previous level. The other reason is that the demand for money is relatively insensitive to changes in nominal interest rates.

The third conclusion is that since 1980, there has been a significant decline in velocity, and its behavior appears to be erratic. At the very least, the monetarist idea of a constant or predictable money-income relationship has to be looked at with suspicion.

MONEY AND CREDIT AVAILABILITY

As economists have sought alternative explanations for why monetary policy works when it does and why it does not work in deep recessions, they have focused attention on the availability of credit (the availability of loans). We saw in Chapter 33 that when the money supply is increased (deposits appear on the right-hand side of a bank's balance sheet), reserves are increased and the bank's assets—its holdings of Treasury bills and its loan portfolio—are increased. Thus, money and credit are two sides of the same coin, or two sides of the same balance sheet. But money and credit do not have to move perfectly in tandem, because banks can decide to increase their holdings of Treasury bills rather than making additional loans.

The credit availability theories focus on how and when the Fed's actions induce banks to make more or fewer loans or make loans available on easier or more restrictive terms.

These changes in credit availability have a direct effect on economic activity: if credit is more available, or available at better terms, firms will undertake more investments and consumers may buy more goods, particularly durables. There is an important proviso, however: the Fed's credit-making powers will only be effective in stimulating the economy when firms' investment and household purchases are limited only by the availability of credit or the terms at which credit is available.

We saw earlier that changes in the interest rate may not induce much additional investment. Even if banks announced that they were willing to lend money at a zero interest rate to any project that could persuade the loan officers that it had at least a 95 percent chance of being repaid, few additional loans might be made: if prices were falling at the rate of 10 percent a year (as they did in the Great Depression), the real interest rate would be 10 percent, and given the terrible economic conditions, firms might not be willing to undertake much investment at that high real interest rate.

INDUCING BANKS TO LEND MORE

The first question in the credit availability approach to monetary policy is, how does the Fed induce banks to lend more? One way is to engage in open market operations. That is, the Fed buys a Treasury bill. We saw in Chapter 33 that when the check the Fed uses to buy the Treasury bill is deposited in a bank, the deposits in the banking system increase, as do the reserves. Banks then want to invest more either in Treasury bills or in loans. If there are good loan opportunities, banks will lend more. Another way the Fed gets banks to lend more is to lower its reserve requirements. Since a bank will then have excess reserves, it can either lend more or buy more T-bills.

In either case, it may take banks a while before they can lend out additional funds. Meanwhile, they will invest funds in Treasury bills. Thus, in the short run, the demand for Treasury bills will increase, raising their price and lowering the rate of interest. In the longer run, the interest rate effect on T-bills will be reduced as banks find good loan opportunities and buy fewer T-bills; but banks may still decide to hold some of their increased assets in the form of T-bills, so that even in the longer run interest rates on T-bills may be slightly lower.

Fed policies affect the banks' ability to lend. As the expression goes, however, you can lead a horse to water, but you cannot make him drink. The Fed cannot *force* banks to lend. Banks decide whether to lend more or to buy Treasury bills. And there are three problems banks might have with lending. First, when default rates are high, banks are more likely to be content with a low return on Treasury bills rather than risk a loss on a loan. Second, their ability and willingness to bear these risks depend on their financial positions. If their net worth has been greatly reduced by defaults on earlier loans, then they will be less willing to make loans. They have no cushion to absorb any further losses. Third, the capacity and willingness of the banking system as a whole to make loans may be adversely affected when many banks have gone bankrupt. Each bank has specialized information about those firms to which it normally lends money. They have information about the prospects of these firms, and know how much they can safely lend. If one bank fails, other banks, lacking this information, will be reluctant to step in.

All three of these problems were present in the Great Depression: the high default rate made lending seem particularly risky; the huge losses banks had experienced meant that many of them had no cushion to bear further losses; and the huge bankruptcy rates among banks further diminished the system's capacity to make loans.

Each of these problems appeared again in somewhat muted form in the recession that began in 1991. While attention was focused on the S & L crisis, in which there were massive bankruptcies, the banking system itself was not in great shape. Banks too had encountered huge losses in real estate loans. The decrease in the price of oil in the mid-1980s had also led to large defaults on oil and gas loans. Finally, the banks had lent billions of dollars to Brazil, Argentina, Mexico, and other less developed countries, and several of these countries found their debt burden beyond their capacity to repay. There were some major bankruptcies: the Bank of New England, the largest bank in the Northeast, went belly-up in 1991 as a result primarily of large real estate losses. Deposit insurance combined with effective actions of the Fed and others limited the damage. Nonetheless, the banking system as a whole seemed reluctant to make loans.

LENDING RATES AND CREDIT RATIONING

While the Treasury bill rate is important to banks and may be an important determinant of the demand for money, firms are concerned with the interest rates they have to pay to borrow funds. In 1991, however, interest rates on loans did not change much even as the T-bill interest rate fell.

Chapter 22 explained why this might be so. As interest rates rise, the best borrowers, those most likely to repay their loans, decide not to borrow. And those who do borrow attempt to offset the effect of higher interest rates by getting a higher return, but to do that, they must undertake greater risks. As a result, there is a greater chance that they will be unable to meet their commitments to repay. Increased interest rates have an adverse selection effect on the mix of those taking loans and an adverse effect on incentives (from the banks' perspective).

Figure 34.12 shows the result of both of these effects. The expected return to the bank—which takes into account the increased rate of default—may actually decline as the interest rate charged by the bank increases beyond r^*. Therefore, banks do not raise the rate of interest they charge beyond r^*, even if there is an excess demand for credit at that interest rate. They simply ration credit. And changes in the T-bill rate or the interest rate banks must pay depositors may similarly have little or no effect on the interest rate banks charge.

The prevalence of credit rationing has serious implications for monetary policy. Consider a situation where at r^* there is an excess demand for loans. But banks do not respond by raising the interest rate, since doing so would only reduce the expected returns to the loans. Now, assume that the Fed lowers the reserve requirements or engages in open market operations, making it possible for banks to lend more. More loans are made, at the same interest rate. Monetary policy has its effects, not because it leads to a large change in the real interest rate charged on loans, but because it leads to changes in the availability of credit. The same process works in reverse. If the Fed tightens credit by raising reserve requirements or engaging in open market operations, banks reduce the number of loans; they may not raise the interest rate, or may raise it only a little.

When banks tighten or loosen credit, with minimal changes in interest rates, they

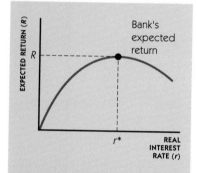

Figure 34.12 INTEREST RATES AND EXPECTED RETURN

Charging too high a rate of interest may actually lower the expected return, because the higher interest rate will tend to drive away prudent borrowers who would have been careful to repay. The bank's expected return is maximized at r^*, and charging a higher interest rate would reduce the bank's return.

Figure 34.13 EFFECT OF MONETARY POLICY WITH CREDIT RATIONING

If monetary policy succeeds in making credit more available, then investment may increase. The aggregate demand curve shifts to the right and, if initially there is excess capacity, aggregate output increases.

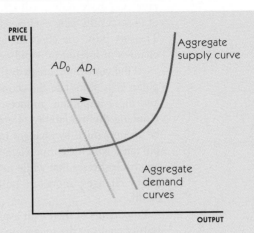

may nonetheless alter other terms of the credit contract. They may, for instance, increase their collateral requirements, the assets that borrowers have to put up when they take a loan and that will be forfeited in the event of a default. Higher collateral requirements both preclude some borrowers from borrowing—those with insufficient collateral to get loans—and make borrowing less attractive to other borrowers, who now have more to lose.

Figure 34.13 shows the effect of monetary policy. As banks make credit more available, investment increases. The aggregate demand curve therefore shifts to the right, and equilibrium output increases.

OTHER CREDIT AVAILABILITY INSIGHTS

Credit availability theory provides several explanations other than credit rationing for why monetary policy is sometimes effective and sometimes not. Monetary policy will be ineffective under two circumstances. First, even if banks are willing (at the initial interest rates) to lend more, it may be hard to induce firms to borrow more. Firms may have an inelastic investment curve, as was pointed out in Chapter 29; as banks compete for borrowers, interest rates fall but little additional investment results. Second, the Fed may have difficulty inducing additional lending.

Thus, those holding credit availability theories come to much the same conclusion as Keynes did: in severe recessions, monetary policy may be of limited effectiveness. Keynes and the credit availability theorists only partially agree on the reasons. Both believe that it may be hard to get firms to invest more or consumers to purchase more, through monetary policy. Both believe that there may be small changes in the interest rate. In Keynes' theory, the small change in the interest rate is caused by an elastic demand for money. In the credit availability theories, the small change in the interest rate is caused by the fact that it does not pay banks to lower the interest rate they charge on loans. Both believe that small—or, in a depression, even large—changes in interest rates may have only small effects. In the prolonged recession that began in 1990, all of these results were evidenced. While the Fed succeeded in lowering interest rates on Treasury bills, the effect on lending rates and credit availability was small; and what changes in interest rates did occur did not stimulate much additional investment.

At the same time, credit availability theorists believe that in mild recessions, monetary policy may stimulate the economy by increasing the availability of credit. Conversely, and more important, monetary policy may lead to a contraction of the economy, by reducing the availability of credit. These expansions or contractions may or may not be accompanied by changes in interest rates. There may well be changes in Treasury bill rates, which are much larger than changes in lending rates. But the credit availability approach stresses that while interest rate changes may frequently accompany monetary policy changes, monetary policy works largely through effects on the availability of credit.

Proponents of the credit availability approach warn, further, that the Fed's ability to restrict credit in the longer run may be limited: it can reduce the amount of credit that banks can extend, but borrowers can find substitute sources of credit. Some big firms, like General Electric, can borrow directly by issuing what is called commercial paper; they do not have to use banks or any other financial intermediaries. Other borrowers can switch from banks to one of the other financial intermediaries discussed in Chapter 33. In the longer run, the net contraction in credit may be less than the contraction in bank credit. Still, at least in the short run, borrowers cannot quickly find substitute sources of finance, so that credit restrictions take their toll.

CREDIT AVAILABILITY THEORIES

1. The role of credit availability should be the focus rather than money supply directly or interest rates.

2. Increases in money supply may not lead to increases in credit, particularly in severe recessions, if banks decide to invest in government bonds.

   Increased bank lending is likely to be limited if
   a. banks are pessimistic about returns on loans and view them as particularly risky;
   b. banks have lost a substantial amount of their net worth as a result of defaults, and so are unwilling or unable to bear high risks;
   c. many banks have gone into default.

3. Interest rates charged borrowers may not change much in response to credit availability; other terms of credit may adjust.

MONEY AND CREDIT: COMPETING OR COMPLEMENTARY THEORIES?

Money affects the economy for a variety of reasons and in a variety of ways. Advocates of different monetary theories argue not that theirs is the only way that money affects the economy, but that focusing on their particular approach provides a best "first picture" of what is going on. As we have seen, money and credit are two sides of the same coin, or of a bank's balance sheet.

The different theories provide a simple and intuitive explanation not only for why there should be a relationship between credit or money and output, but also for the fact that increases in credit or money occur before increases in production. When firms plan to expand their production and sales, they take out loans, which increase the measures of both credit and money. That is why measures of credit increase before Christmas, just as does the money supply.

This example provides another dramatic illustration of the difference between correlation and causation. The fact that the money supply or credit increases before the huge increases in sales at Christmastime would not fool many people into thinking that the money supply *causes* the increased sales at this time. On the contrary, it is the huge anticipated increases in sales at Christmas that lead merchants to borrow more to buy goods to stock their shelves. But while the increased credit does not cause the rise in sales, if the Fed were to try to contract credit before December, it could have a disastrous effect on Christmas sales.

For many purposes, the exact mechanism by which monetary policy affects the economy may make little difference. In fact, since increases in the money supply and bank loans are closely connected, changes in the money supply may provide a good measure of the tightness of credit. Indeed, they may provide a better measure than looking at the interest rates at which banks make loans. Interest rates, as the credit availability theories emphasize, may not change much even when credit is significantly tightened.

There are situations where the different theories have different implications: credit availability theories suggest that changes in the credit institutions of the economy may alter earlier stable relationships between income and credit, and may even affect the efficacy of monetary policy. If many or most borrowers can easily find close substitutes for banks for raising capital, attempts by the Fed to restrict credit may have limited effects. On the other hand, the theories that focus on the role of money in transactions suggest that changes in the institutions by which transactions are conducted (like credit cards) may have large effects on the relationship between money and income.

DIFFERING VIEWS ON THE ROLE AND MECHANISMS OF MONETARY POLICY

We have seen in this chapter the different effects that monetary policy may have and the different channels through which it may operate. In spite of a variety of sources of disagreement, today most economists would agree with the following conclusions.

CLOSE-UP: WHO SHOULD CONTROL MONETARY POLICY?

There are many possible answers to the question of who should control monetary policy. At one extreme, the monetary authorities may be given a single goal, like controlling inflation, and then be given the authority to pursue that goal with minimal political interference. At the other extreme, monetary authorities may be subject to considerable political control and thus come under pressure to stimulate the economy, even if it means allowing greater inflationary pressure.

Germany and Switzerland have exceptionally independent central banks. In Germany, the law explicitly states that the central bank has the "assigned task of preserving monetary stability" and "shall be independent of instructions from the federal government." Perhaps not surprisingly, both countries have had relatively low rates of inflation—about 3.5 percent since 1975. The flip side is that monetary policy is not often used to stimulate the economy in the face of an economic downturn.

In the United Kingdom and Italy, the monetary authorities have relatively little independence from political control. In the United Kingdom, for example, the Bank of England is by law subordinate to the Treasury Department and must make short-term loans to the Treasury whenever they are requested. As a result, the bank is often under pressure to increase the money supply and stimulate the economy, and the average inflation rate in Britain has been 12.4 percent since 1975.

The United States and Japan are countries with intermediate systems, whose central banks have considerable independence but are still under some political pressure. A famous sparring match occurred in the late 1950s between the chairman of the Federal Reserve Board, William McChesney Martin, and President Eisenhower; the exchange between the two became so heated that Eisenhower threatened to try to remove the Fed's autonomy. More recently, during the recession beginning in 1990, the Bush administration prodded the Federal Reserve to cut interest rates more rapidly than it was doing.

Whether the central bank should be put under tighter control is an ongoing political issue. Many observers believe that questions of monetary policy are better kept out of the political process. They point out that some of the sparring between the Federal Reserve Board and the politicians may be for show. For example, a president might secretly approve of the Fed's tight monetary policy, but would rather have the Fed blamed for unemployment than take the rap himself. Countries like New Zealand and Chile have recently put laws into place to give their central banks greater independence from political intervention.

Others believe that in a democracy, any matter of such importance to the functioning of the economy should be controlled by elected representatives. They worry that the Federal Reserve Board may reflect too much the views of bankers and the business community, rather than a more balanced perspective of the economy as a whole. Of course, elected representatives are subject to pressures from still other special interests.

Source: Sun Bae Kim, "The Independence of Central Banks," *Federal Reserve Bank of San Francisco Weekly Letter,* December 13, 1991.

1. When the economy is operating close to capacity, looser monetary policy is likely to lead to increased prices.

2. A major tightening of money and credit may so reduce aggregate demand, as illustrated in Figure 34.14, that the economy shifts from being close to full employment to having substantial unemployment. This is the common interpretation of what happened in the early 1980s. (See Chapter 26.)

3. When the economy has excess capacity, a loosening of credit may shift the aggregate demand curve out, leading to an increase in output (not in prices).

4. When the economy is in a deep recession, monetary policy may be relatively ineffective. Drastic actions may be required to stimulate the economy. (Economists disagree whether even then monetary policy will be effective.)

This is a good time to ask how the different schools of thought we have encountered in this book—real business-cycle theorists, new classical economists, new Keynesians, and monetarists—view the role of monetary policy.

For real business-cycle theorists, the answer is easiest: they believe that monetary policy has no effect on the level of economic activity. Real variables such as real output and real wages are, in their view, determined by real forces like changes in technology, not by money. Monetary policy affects the price level, but nothing more. In effect, with a vertical aggregate supply curve, all that monetary policy can do is change the level of prices or the rate of inflation. At the same time, monetary policy is not responsible for recessions. The lack of effectiveness of monetary policy is of no great concern to real business-cycle theorists. They believe that the competitive model described in Part Two provides a good description of the economy. Accordingly, they believe that markets are efficient without government intervention. They do not believe that unemployment is a serious economic problem.

Monetarists tend to agree with real business-cycle theorists that in the long run the main impact of monetary policy is on the price level. However, for monetarists, money can have real effects on output in the short run. They believe that velocity is not very

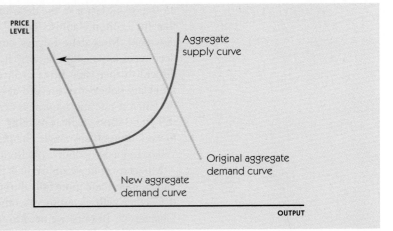

Figure 34.14 LARGE CHANGES IN MONETARY POLICY

With large enough changes in monetary policy, the aggregate demand curve can be shifted far to the left, moving the economy from where the equilibrium is along the vertical portion of the aggregate supply curve to where the equilibrium is along the horizontal portion. Output is greatly reduced.

PRICE LEVEL

Aggregate supply curve

Original aggregate demand curve

New aggregate demand curve

OUTPUT

sensitive to changes in the interest rate, so that changes in the money supply will be reflected in changes in nominal national income. Recall the basic quantity theory equation: $MV = PQ$. The right-hand side, PQ, is the nominal value of national income. With V fixed, a decrease in M is immediately translated into a corresponding decrease in PQ. Unlike real business-cycle theorists, monetarists believe that the price level may not immediately adjust downward, in response to a decrease in the money supply. If prices do not immediately adjust downward, the only way that national income can fall is for output to fall. Monetarists are not specific about the mechanism by which a change in the money supply is translated into a change in nominal income, nor about why prices do not quickly adjust.

New classical economists also believe that in the long run monetary policy can only affect the price level. Their major contribution has been their emphasis on rational expectations: in the long run, firms and consumers understand exactly what the government is doing with the money supply and therefore translate money supply changes into price level changes. In some cases, firms and consumers may see straight through a policy change, and the price adjustment may be instantaneous. In other cases, however, firms or consumers may have difficulty distinguishing between real and nominal changes, and so in the short run prices may not adjust fully to an increase or decrease in the money supply.

While monetarists and new classical economists thus believe that monetary policy can affect the economy in the short run, they are not in favor of government intervention, for two reasons. First, the short run is short: an increase in output induced by an expansionary monetary policy quickly leads to price increases. The reductions in unemployment resulting from an expansionary monetary policy are thus short-lived in their view, but the price increases to which it gives rise may be persistent.

Second, the two schools emphasize that bad government policy can cause a recession. In fact, they see the major fluctuations in the economy as being caused by bad monetary policy. As a result, they prefer the government to follow simple rules, like expanding the money supply at a constant rate. While such rules preclude the government from taking an active role in stabilizing the economy, they serve the more important function of preventing the government from messing things up.

Finally, new Keynesians take an eclectic view. They too believe that money can be an important factor in the determination of national income. They share Keynes' view that the economy adjusts slowly, so that there may be extended periods with unemployment. Most share Keynes' conclusions about monetary policy being ineffective in deep recessions, either because it is difficult to get banks to lend more or because it is difficult to persuade firms to invest more. But they differ in their views about how monetary policy may succeed at other times in stimulating output. Some believe that the interest-rate mechanism is central, others emphasize the portfolio theories, while still others stress credit availability. Indeed, there is no reason that monetary policy needs to work through any single channel; it may work through many different mechanisms. When monetary policy is ineffective, all of the mechanisms become weak.

Monetary policy is only one of the instruments that the government has at its disposal, and to understand more fully the appropriate role of monetary policy, we have to consider it together with government's other principal set of tools, fiscal policy. This we do in Chapter 39. But first we need to see how monetary policy operates in a world in which Americans can borrow not only from American banks, but also from Japanese and other foreign sources (Chapter 35). And second, we need to complete our discussion of the major objectives of macroeconomic policy, price stability (preventing inflation) and growth, to which we turn in Chapters 36 and 37.

ALTERNATIVE VIEWS OF MONETARY POLICY

School	Effect of monetary policy	Desirability of active monetary policy
Real business cycle	Unemployment is not a serious economic problem. Money only has an effect on the price level, and no effect on output.	Monetary policy is largely irrelevant, other than for determining the price level. Monetary policy is not responsible for recessions.
Monetarist	Money is central to the determination of national income. In the short run, money can affect the level of output. In the long run, it affects mainly the price level.	Misguided monetary policies are largely responsible for recessions. Policy should be limited to a simple rule, such as a constant rate of increase in the money supply.
New classical	Firms and consumers with rational expectations see through monetary policy, at least in the long run, and translate money supply changes into price level changes.	Same as monetarists.
New Keynesian	Money is one of the central factors in the determination of national income. The economy may be at less than full employment for extended periods of time.	Monetary policy may exercise its effects through a variety of channels: the interest rate, credit availability, and portfolio effects. When the economy is in a deep recession, monetary policy is ineffective, either because it is difficult to induce banks to lend more or because it is difficult to persuade firms to invest more.

REVIEW AND PRACTICE

SUMMARY

1. Theories concerning the effect of monetary policy on the economy focus on the two sides of the banks' balance sheet, on money and on credit.

2. Changes in the supply of money can cause some combination of three effects: changes in holdings of money, changes in output, or changes in prices. When the economy is at full capacity, then an increased supply of money will affect mainly the price level. When the economy has considerable excess capacity, normally output will increase; in deep recessions, the effect on output may be minimal.

3. Keynesian theories of the demand for money focused on its dependence on the (nominal) rate of interest and on the level of income. Equilibrium required the demand for money to be equal to the supply. Changes in the supply of money resulted in changes in the interest rate and, through changes in the interest rate, in the level of aggregate expenditures and equilibrium output.

4. Keynes argued that in severe recessions, the interest elasticity of the demand for money was high and the interest elasticity of investment was low, so monetary policy was ineffective.

5. The quantity theory of money holds that the demand for money does not depend on the interest rate, and accordingly that the velocity of money is constant. Increases in money supply then result in proportionate increases in national income.

6. There are many difficulties with the traditional monetary theory. Money is not used for many transactions, and many transactions involve exchanges of assets, which have little to do with income generation. Changes in technology and the structure of the economy may alter the money-income relationship. Most money bears interest, and the opportunity cost is only the difference between the interest rate it pays and the interest rate on government Treasury bills. Finally, the link between changes in the nominal interest rate and the real interest rate is tenuous, and depends on inflationary expectations; and the link between real interest rates and investment appears weak. In recent years, velocity has changed in relatively unpredictable ways.

7. Portfolio theories stress the effect of changes in monetary policy on the demand and supply of various assets and the resulting effect on prices of assets.

8. Credit availability theories stress the effects of monetary policy on the availability of credit by banks. The Fed may, in some recessions, have a hard time inducing the banking system to lend more if banks view commercial loans as highly risky, if as a result of previous defaults banks' net worth and thus their ability to bear risk has been eroded, or if a number of banks have gone into bankruptcy.

KEY TERMS

velocity
transactions demand
  for money

portfolio theories
quantity theory of
  money

REVIEW QUESTIONS

1. What are the three things that might happen in response to a change in the money supply?

2. Is it possible for a change in the money supply to affect neither the price level nor the output level in the economy? Explain.

3. What is the most likely effect of an increase in the supply of money when the economy is at full capacity?

4. Why does demand for money fall as the interest rate rises? What is the opportunity cost of holding money that pays interest (such as demand deposits)?

5. What might cause changes in the relationship between the demand for money and income besides changes in the interest rate?

6. Why might changes in the money supply not lead to increases in the level of investment in a severe recession?

7. What assumptions are involved in the quantity theory of money? What conclusion can be drawn on the basis of those assumptions? What is the evidence concerning the constancy of the velocity of circulation?

8. What are the mechanisms by which portfolio theories suggest that monetary policy affects the economy?

9. Describe how monetary policy might affect investment or consumption, *even if monetary policy has no effect at all on interest rates*.

10. Why might a bank refuse to charge the interest rate determined by the intersection of supply and demand for credit, and instead insist on offering loans only at a lower interest rate?

11. Why might the Fed have a hard time expanding credit?

PROBLEMS

1. If GDP is $4 trillion and the money supply is $200 billion, what is velocity? How does your answer change if GDP rises to $5 trillion while the money supply remains the same? If GDP remains at $4 trillion while the money supply increases to $250 billion, how does velocity change?

2. Graph the money demand curve from the following data, with quantity of money demanded given in billions of dollars.

Interest rate	7%	8%	9%	10%	11%	12%
Money demand	900	880	860	840	820	810

How do changes in national income affect the demand curve?

3. Using money supply and demand diagrams, explain how the elasticity of the money demand curve determines whether monetary policy can have a substantial effect on the interest rate.

4. Explain how the elasticity of investment with respect to interest rates determines whether monetary policy can have a substantial effect on aggregate demand.

5. Explain how each of the following might affect the demand for money:
    (a) interest is paid on checking accounts;
    (b) credit cards become more readily available;
    (c) electronic fund transfers become common.
Would the changes in the demand for money necessarily reduce the ability of the Fed to use monetary policy to affect the economy?

6. Explain how the Fed can reduce the amount of credit in an economy where credit rationing is common without affecting the interest rate.

APPENDIX: AN ALGEBRAIC DERIVATION OF EQUILIBRIUM IN THE MONEY MARKET

The money demand equation can be written

$$M_d = M_d(r, Y),$$

where M_d is the demand for money and $Y = pQ$, the value of national income. If M_s is the money supply, then the equilibrium condition that the demand for money equals the supply can be written

$$M_s = M_d(r, Y). \tag{34.1}$$

From Chapter 28, we know that

$$Y = C + I + G,$$

where I (investment) depends on the interest rate, r, and G (government expenditures) is assumed to be fixed. If consumption is just $(1 - s)$ times income, Y, then

$$Y = (1 - s)Y + I(r) + G,$$

or

$$Y = [I(r) + G]/s. \tag{34.2}$$

Equations (34.1) and (34.2) provide us two equations in two unknowns. The solution gives us the equilibrium income and interest rate. An increase in the money supply results in a new solution, with a lower interest rate and a higher level of national income.

MONETARY POLICY: THE INTERNATIONAL SIDE

I n economies that are open to international trade, monetary policy may induce changes in the exchange rate and in the flow of capital from abroad. Thus, the channels by which monetary policy affects the economy in an international setting may be quite different from those in an economy closed to international trade and capital movements. This chapter traces out the channels by which monetary policy affects exchange rates, capital flows, and ultimately the level of economic activity in an open economy.

"What's your thinking on cracking the Pacific Rim markets?"

KEY QUESTIONS

1. Increasingly, we live in a world in which all economies are interrelated. How does this fact affect the workings of monetary policy?

2. What determines the exchange rate? And how does monetary policy affect the exchange rate?

SOME TERMINOLOGY

International financiers often seem to speak in a foreign language of jargon and abstruse technical terms. Nevertheless, out of this vocabulary, there are a few key terms we will need if we are to understand how monetary policy works in an open economy.

The first we have already encountered: the exchange rate, the rate at which dollars are exchanged for yen, or marks for pounds. The **foreign exchange market** is the market in which currencies are bought and sold. When the Japanese yen becomes more valuable relative to the U.S. dollar, then we say that the yen has appreciated and the dollar has depreciated. If there used to be 300 yen to the dollar and now there are 150 yen to the dollar, the yen has appreciated; you need fewer of them to get a dollar now than you did before.

Systems in which exchange rates are determined by the law of supply and demand, without government interference, are called **flexible** or **floating exchange rate systems**. Governments often do intervene in foreign exchange markets, and later in the chapter we will look at the different forms government intervention takes. But first we need to learn what determines the exchange rate in flexible exchange rate systems.

DETERMINING THE EXCHANGE RATE

Consider a world consisting of only two countries, America and another country we will call Europa, whose currency is called the Euro. Americans and Europans exchange dollars for Euros. There are three reasons that Europans might want dollars, and might therefore supply Euros to the foreign exchange market: to buy American goods (American exports, or imports into Europa), to make investments in the United States, or for speculative purposes—that is, if Europans think the dollar is going to become more valuable relative to the Euro, they might want to hold dollars in order to reap that increase in value, called a capital gain. Similarly, there are three reasons that Americans might want Euros, and might accordingly supply dollars to the foreign exchange market: to buy Europan goods, to make investments in Europa, and for speculative purposes, if they think that the Euro is going to become more valuable relative to the dollar. The question is, how many Euros will an American get in exchange for a dollar, or equivalently, how many dollars will a Europan get in exchange for her Euros? The exchange rate can be thought of as nothing more than the *relative price* of dollars and Euros.

In competitive markets, prices are determined by demand and supply. We can view the exchange rate in this two-country example as being determined from the perspective of either the demand and supply of dollars or the demand and supply of Euros. The two are equivalent. The Europan supply of Euros on the foreign exchange market is equivalent to Europans' demand for dollars. The U.S. supply of dollars is equivalent to Americans' demand for Euros.

The three reasons why Europans might want dollars and that Americans might want Euros are the three main factors that determine the exchange rate. The first factor is the demand and supply of exports and imports, to which we now turn.

EXCHANGE RATES WITH NO BORROWING

Figure 35.1A shows a demand and supply diagram for U.S. dollars. The vertical axis is the exchange rate, the "price" of dollars, expressed in this example as Euro/dollar. When the exchange rate is 1,000 Euros to the dollar, the dollar is very expensive; when it is 300 Euros to the dollar, the dollar is relatively cheap. The figure shows a downward-sloping demand curve and an upward-sloping supply curve, and the intersection represents the equilibrium exchange rate. A rightward shift in the supply curve (panel B) or a leftward shift in the demand curve (panel C) leads to a depreciation of the dollar. The value of the dollar relative to Euros is then lower.

While thinking about exchange rates in terms of demand and supply is helpful, it pushes the question back still one more step. Why do demand and supply curves for foreign exchange have the shape they do? What might cause them to shift and thus the exchange rate to change?

EXPORTS AND IMPORTS

Let's return to our two-country example. Suppose Europa was a country that trusted no one and that no one trusted. No Europan would be able to borrow abroad, because

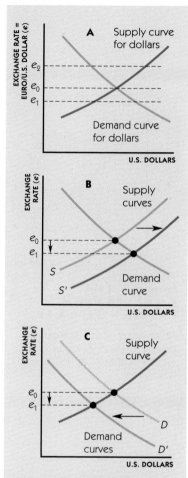

Figure 35.1 THE EXCHANGE RATE

In equilibrium, the exchange rate is determined where the demand for dollars equals the supply, as in panel A. A rightward shift in the supply curve of dollars (panel B) or a leftward shift in the demand curve for dollars (panel C) results in a lower exchange rate; that is, the dollar depreciates.

potential lenders would fear that the loan would not be repaid. Similarly, the country would refuse to loan out any money to foreigners. Europa's exports must precisely equal its imports.

When U.S. producers sell products in Europa, they receive Euros, and they want to convert those Euros immediately into dollars. After all, if they do not convert the Euros into dollars, they will have to deposit them in a bank or investment in Europa—they will have to *lend* the Euros to Europa—and they do not trust Europa enough to do that. Similarly, when producers from Europa sell in the United States, they receive U.S. dollars, and they want to exchange those dollars immediately into Euros. In short, this situation has parties who want to trade Euros for dollars and parties who want to trade dollars for Euros. Clearly, there are possibilities for mutually beneficial exchange. At a low exchange rate, like e_1 in Figure 35.2, the demand for dollars exceeds the supply. At a high exchange rate, like e_2, the supply of dollars exceeds the demand. The point at which the demand for dollars equals the supply is the equilibrium exchange rate. In the figure, this point is e_0.

We can also see how the exchange rate is determined by focusing directly on exports and imports. In the absence of borrowing or lending, the value of exports must equal the value of imports. Americans might like to import more from Europa than they export, but unless they sell goods to Europa, they will not have the money (the Euros) with which to buy Europan goods. And since Europans are skeptical about whether Americans will repay any loans, they will not deliver the goods without receiving the money first. There are no credit sales.

At a high value of the dollar, U.S. exports will be low. Europans must give up a lot of their currency to buy American goods. Europans' demand for imports will translate directly into a supply of dollars. A high value of the dollar is equivalent to a low value of the foreign currency (here, Euros). From the perspective of Americans, foreign goods are cheap, and Americans will want to buy them. Their demand for imports will be high. To buy these goods, they have to pay the Europans in their own currency, Euros. So American importers supply dollars to be exchanged for Euros on the foreign exchange market.

Figure 35.3A and B shows how imports increase and exports decrease as the exchange rate increases (as the dollar becomes "more expensive"). The exchange rate at which exports equal imports is the equilibrium exchange rate. In the U.S.–Europa example, a decrease in the exchange rate has one of two causes: either a reduction in the demand for U.S. exports *at any exchange rate*, which will translate into a leftward shift in the demand curve for dollars, or an increased U.S. demand for imports *at any exchange rate*, which will translate into a rightward shift in the supply of dollars. These are illustrated in panel C.

In this simple model, changes in the exchange rate can be related to shifts in the U.S. demand for imports (at any exchange rate) or foreigners' demand for U.S. goods. For instance, shifts in the demand curve for imports played a role in the recession of the early 1980s. First, the shift of American tastes to smaller, foreign-made cars can be thought of as an increase in the demand for imports (a rightward shift of the supply curve of the dollar), at each level of national income. Figure 35.3A illustrates this shift in the demand curve for imports. Panel C shows how the shift translates into a shift in the supply curve of dollars. The increased supply of dollars would, if nothing else had happened, have led to a depreciation of the dollar—that is, to a lower exchange rate—as illustrated in the figure. The depreciation of the dollar means that foreign imports would be smaller and exports larger than they would have been had exchange rates

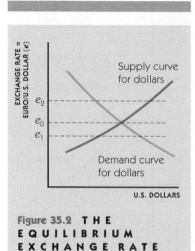

Figure 35.2 THE EQUILIBRIUM EXCHANGE RATE

At the exchange rate e_2, supply exceeds demand. At e_1, demand exceeds supply. At e_0, equilibrium is achieved.

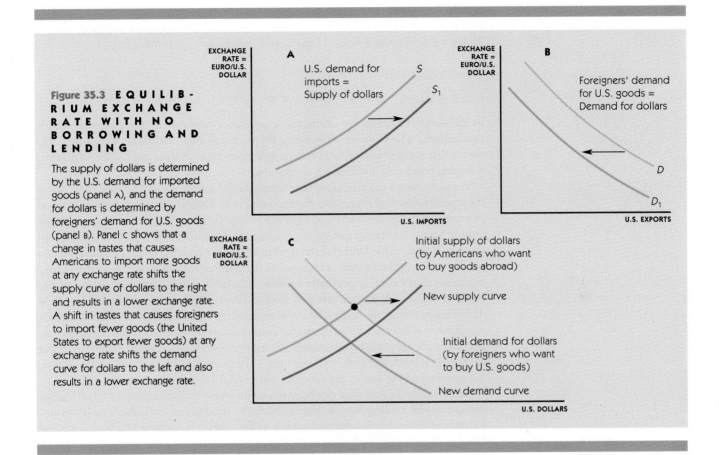

Figure 35.3 EQUILIB-RIUM EXCHANGE RATE WITH NO BORROWING AND LENDING

The supply of dollars is determined by the U.S. demand for imported goods (panel A), and the demand for dollars is determined by foreigners' demand for U.S. goods (panel B). Panel C shows that a change in tastes that causes Americans to import more goods at any exchange rate shifts the supply curve of dollars to the right and results in a lower exchange rate. A shift in tastes that causes foreigners to import fewer goods (the United States to export fewer goods) at any exchange rate shifts the demand curve for dollars to the left and also results in a lower exchange rate.

remained fixed. Thus, with flexible exchange rates, the decline in net exports at each level of national income was *smaller* than it would have been if exchange rates had not changed. The adjustments in the exchange rate helped to stabilize the economy.

As the economy recovers from a recession (as it did in the period after 1982), incomes in the United States rise, and at any exchange rate the demand for imports increases. Exports at any exchange rate are unaffected, since they depend on the incomes of foreigners. Thus, higher levels of income induce a shift in the demand curve for imports, or equivalently a shift in the supply curve of dollars. Again, this leads to a depreciation of the dollar, the effect of which is to *enhance* the recovery.

In each of these cases, the change in the exchange rate dampens the increase in imports from what it would have been had exchange rates been fixed. That is, as a result of the change in tastes or change in national income, imports are higher than they would have otherwise been *at any exchange rate*. The resulting devaluation of the dollar reduces imports, although they are still larger than they were in the initial situation. As always, we have to be careful to distinguish shifts in demand and supply curves from movements along those curves. However, these changes do not explain why the value of the dollar should have increased sharply in the first half of the 1980s, and they are not large enough to account for the dollar's fall since then.

The model of trade without foreign lending or borrowing made more sense a few decades ago, when international financial markets were not widely developed and so exchange rates were primarily shaped by the supply and demand for imports and exports. Today we need to look beyond exports and imports to capital markets.

FOREIGN BORROWING AND LENDING

In the world of Europa and Euros, there is never a trade deficit. The values of exports and imports, when compared by using the exchange rate, are always the same. This means that the problem of trade deficits will never arise. A trade deficit can only occur if foreign borrowing and lending are possible.

Today there is a massive amount of international borrowing and lending, and this is the second factor that determines the exchange rate. Capital markets today, the markets in which funds are borrowed and lent, are global. Investors in Japan, Europe, and the United States, constantly seeking to maximize their returns, will shift their funds from Japan or Europe to the United States if returns there are highest. When investors respond quickly and shift their funds in response to slight differences in expected returns, economists say that capital is **perfectly mobile**. In today's world, capital is highly but not perfectly mobile. American investors may still feel slightly more comfortable keeping their money within the United States than sending it abroad; they may feel relatively uninformed about changes in economic conditions or tax conditions that could quickly and adversely affect their investments. Foreign investors may feel the same way about keeping their funds within their own country. The more stable the political and economic environment of the world, the more mobile capital becomes across countries.

Determining the exchange rate becomes considerably more complicated when foreign borrowing and lending are introduced. Now the equilibrium exchange rate is not just a matter of balancing imports and exports as they occur; it is affected by borrowing and lending decisions as well. Figure 35.2 can be modified to incorporate these effects. Foreigners who want to invest in the United States will want dollars to make their purchases of American assets. This increases the demand for dollars. On the other hand, some Americans may want to make investments abroad. They want to sell dollars to get foreign currency with which to make these investments. How these investments affect the exchange rate depends on whether foreigners want to invest more in the United States than Americans want to invest abroad.

Figure 35.4 shows the demand and supply curves for dollars both with and without foreign borrowing and lending. Some Americans want to invest abroad, and hence the supply of dollars at any exchange rate is greater than it would have been without foreign investment; and some foreigners want to invest in the United States, and so the demand for dollars is greater than it otherwise would have been. In this example, however, the amount foreigners want to invest in the United States is much greater than the amount Americans want to invest abroad. The demand curve for dollars shifts more to the right than does the supply curve for dollars. As a result, the exchange rate increases.

Normally, if investments in the United States become more attractive, Americans will decide to leave more of their wealth at home rather than investing abroad. Then the supply of dollars will shift to the left, as in Figure 35.5. At the same time, foreigners will decide to invest more in the United States, shifting the demand for dollars to the right. Both of these effects work to increase the value of the dollar relative to other currencies.

This helps to explain what caused the changes in the exchange rate in the 1980s. In

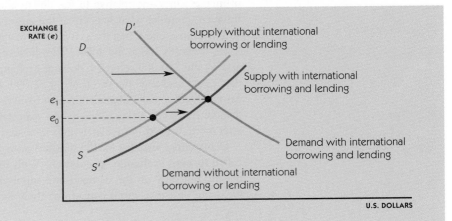

Figure 35.4 EQUILIBRIUM EXCHANGE RATE WITH BORROWING AND LENDING

When Americans want to invest abroad and foreigners want to invest in the United States, the supply of and demand for dollars are greater than they otherwise would have been. In the figure, more foreigners want to invest in the United States than Americans want to invest abroad, so the demand curve for dollars shifts more to the right than does the supply curve for dollars. As a result, the exchange rate increases.

the early part of the decade, foreign investment in the United States surged, which resulted in an appreciation of the dollar, lower exports, and higher imports. The increase in foreign investment continued through the mid-1980s and then declined, and the dollar fell in the late 1980s.

SPECULATION

The third factor that is important in determining the exchange rates today is speculation. In Chapter 6, we saw that the demand for any asset depends on beliefs about what that asset could be sold for in the future; it depends on expectations. Money in any country

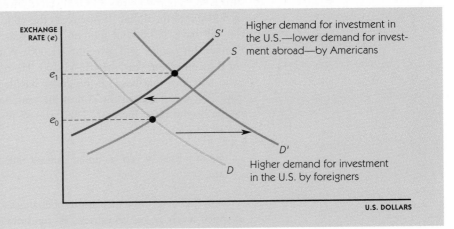

Figure 35.5 INCREASED ATTRACTIVENESS OF INVESTING IN THE UNITED STATES

As some Americans decide not to invest abroad, the supply curve of dollars shifts to the left. As more foreigners wish to invest in the United States, the demand curve shifts to the right. Both shifts serve to increase the equilibrium exchange rate.

is an asset, as we saw in Chapter 34. If Americans believe that the Japanese yen is going to increase in value relative to the dollar, they may want to hold Japanese yen. For instance, consider what happens if the current exchange rate is 200 yen to the dollar and investors believe that the yen is going to appreciate, so that by the end of the month it will be worth 100 to the dollar. They believe, in other words, that if they took $1,000 and bought 200,000 yen (each dollar is exchanged for 200 yen), at the end of the month they could exchange the yen back for $2,000. By holding yen for a month, they would earn a phenomenal 100 percent return. American investors with such a belief will want to hold more yen today. This is how expectations about future changes in exchange rates are translated immediately into increased exchange rates today.

Demanding currency for the possible gains from the appreciation of the currency is called **foreign exchange speculation**. With speculation, exchange rates in the market depend not only on the demand and supply for exports and imports and investment today but on expectations concerning those factors in the future.

EXPECTATIONS

Expectations about changes in the exchange rate in fact play a role in all overseas investments. Consider the Japanese investor who is planning to convert his yen into dollars and invest it in the United States. He will want to bring his profits back to Japan, and he may even decide eventually to sell his investment and bring his money back home. In either case, he will have to convert his dollars back into yen at some later date. The question is, how many yen will he get for his dollars? If he believes that the dollar is going to become weaker, then he believes that he will get fewer yen when he exchanges his dollars in the foreign exchange market. If he thinks that the dollar will become stronger in the future, investment in the United States appears more attractive.

American investors thinking about investing abroad will be equally concerned about changes in exchange rates. But for Americans, expectations that the dollar will become *weaker* in the future make investment abroad more attractive.

Now let's suppose our Japanese investor is thinking about buying a U.S. Treasury bill. He will not want to put his money in a T-bill that yields a 10 percent return, even if bonds issued by the Japanese government yield only 5 percent, if he believes that the dollar is going to decrease in value by more than 5 percent during the year. To see why this is so, suppose he has 300,000 yen to invest, and assume the current exchange rate is 300 yen to the dollar. If he invests the 300,000 yen in a Japanese government bond, he will have 315,000 at the end of the year. But if he takes the 300,000 yen to his banker, his banker will give him $1,000. With that $1,000, he buys a Treasury bill. At the end of the year, he has $1,100. He now takes this $1,100 back to his banker, who tells him that because the dollar has depreciated in value, each dollar is worth, say, 250 yen. Thus, at the end of the year, he has only 275,000 yen, fewer yen than at the beginning of the year. The Japanese investor's expected returns can be summed up in a formula:

rate of return in yen = dollar interest rate − expected rate of change in exchange rate.

Over the long run, expectations of changes in the exchange rate are linked to changes in price levels across countries. To see how this works, we focus on the case of two countries, the United States and Japan, in which the rates of inflation differ.

INFLATION

If two countries differ in their rates of inflation, over the long run there will be changes in exchange rates that offset those inflation rates. For example, if the rate of inflation in the United States is 3 percent and there is no inflation in Japan, the dollar is becoming less valuable—each year people can purchase 3 percent fewer goods with a dollar bill—while the value of the yen is unchanged. Thus, the exchange rate might be expected to change; the dollar will depreciate 3 percent against the yen each year.

In a world with perfect capital mobility, interest rates will have to adjust quickly to reflect differences in inflation rates and changing exchange rates. If the interest rate in Japan is 5 percent, the interest rate in the United States should be 8 percent; the extra 3 percent reflects the higher rate of inflation. Notice that if this is the case, the *real* interest rate in Japan and the United States will be the same (5 percent). Moreover, a Japanese investor will be indifferent between investing in the United States or in Japan; his real return will be the same, even though he earns a higher nominal return in the United States.

These adjustments in interest rates and exchange rates just offset the effects of inflation: they mean that Americans find Japanese products become no more or less attractive over time, and Japan's consumers find American products become no more or less attractive over time. Like the real wages and real interest rates, economists use the term **real exchange rate** to indicate the exchange rate adjusted for changes in the relative price levels in two countries. That is, if the inflation rate is 3 percent higher in the United States than in Japan and the nominal exchange rate has changed so that the dollar is worth 3 percent less relative to the yen, the real exchange rate has remained unchanged; the changes in the nominal exchange rate are just those required to offset the changes in relative price levels. Similarly, in spite of differences in nominal returns, investors find real returns to be the same. Figure 35.6 contrasts movements in the real and nominal exchange rates between the United States and Japan during the 1980s.

Figure 35.6 REAL VERSUS NOMINAL EXCHANGE RATES

Real exchange rates vary from nominal exchange rates because they take account of changes in price levels. *Source: Economic Report of the President* (1991), Table B-109.

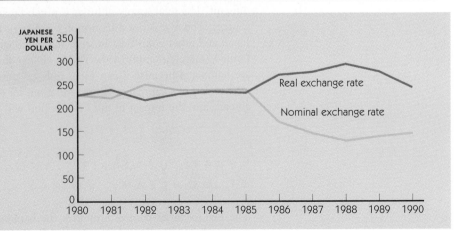

WHAT DETERMINES THE EXCHANGE RATE?

The U.S. exchange rate today is determined by supply and demand for dollars. Foreigners' demand for U.S. dollars and Americans' supply of dollars is determined by

1. underlying trade factors: the demand for U.S. goods (U.S. exports) and Americans' demand for foreign goods (imports);
2. underlying investment factors: the returns to investments in the United States and abroad;
3. speculation based on expectations concerning future changes in the exchange rate.

A shift in tastes for foreign goods or an increase in income in the United States will lead to a depreciation of the dollar.

Improved attractiveness of investment in the United States will also lead to a depreciation of the dollar.

MONETARY POLICY IN AN OPEN ECONOMY

The global capital market makes the Fed's job of controlling the economy much more difficult. The total supply of funds is much broader than the supply of funds from U.S. sources. Today it is not uncommon for American firms to borrow funds from banks in Japan and other countries. Indeed, many foreign banks even have branches within the United States. Attempts by the Fed to change the interest rate or total credit availability are hampered because it can focus only on domestic banks. If it tries to raise interest rates as part of a campaign against inflation, for example, Americans will simply borrow abroad, and the impact of the Fed's action will be dramatically dampened.

SUBSTITUTABILITY AND THE EFFECTIVENESS OF MONETARY POLICY

The Fed exercises control only over the banking system. Through open market operations, changes in the reserve requirement, and changes in the discount rate, it affects the money supply and the availability of bank credit. But its actions touch other financial institutions and eventually reverberate throughout the entire economy. The extent of the effects of monetary policy depends largely on whether there are substitutes for the credit, transaction, and other services provided by the banking system. If there are, monetary policy may have limited effects.

As we have seen, Americans can borrow abroad if the Fed reduces the availability of credit. Not everyone has easy access to foreign credit, but large American firms like General Motors and Ford, which operate in countries around the world, can easily obtain funds elsewhere. This alone is enough to seriously weaken the effectiveness of monetary policy. If enough firms borrow abroad, then it will take an enormous reduction in credit availability in the United States to have significant effects on spending by firms and individuals.

In Chapter 34, we observed two other examples of substitution: other sources of credits are a substitute for bank credit; and other financial institutions provide close substitutes for money.

The fact that monetary policy may be less effective in the context of global capital markets in limiting credit availability or changing the interest rate does not mean that monetary policy is completely ineffective. This is because in practice, international capital markets are far from perfect. Accordingly, when the Fed acts to tighten monetary policy (by raising reserve requirements or through open market operations), interest rates within the United States may indeed rise and credit may become less available. Investment and purchases of consumer durables are likely to be dampened.

To some extent, the global situation today mirrors the relationship among the individual states of the United States. It is difficult to conceive of a small state like Delaware or Rhode Island having an independent monetary policy. Any attempt at a change in the availability of credit or interest rates in Delaware would be quickly dampened as funds flowed in from the rest of the country. As the United States becomes part of a larger international community, with countries lending to and borrowing from each other, it may be increasingly difficult for the United States to change interest rates or credit availability within the country.

There is, however, one important difference between the relationship of the United States with other countries and the relationships of the different states with one another: there is a common currency within the United States, while different countries have different currencies. With different currencies, exchange rates can change, and these changes in the exchange rate can have large, real effects.

CHANGES IN EXCHANGE RATES

Assume that the Fed succeeds in increasing interest rates in the United States, and Japan and other countries do not match the interest rate changes. Then the higher yields in bonds in the United States make these more attractive to both foreigners and Americans. The result can be seen in Figure 35.7. Americans' supply of dollars (at any exchange rate) shifts to the left, and foreigners' demand for dollars shifts to the right; there is a new, higher equilibrium exchange rate.

The higher exchange rate discourages exports and encourages imports. The aggregate expenditures schedule shifts down, as in Figure 35.8A, yielding (at any price level) a lower level of output. Correspondingly, the aggregate demand curve shifts to the left, as illustrated in panel B. Thus, monetary policy succeeds in dampening aggregate

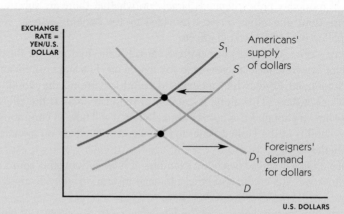

Figure 35.7 MONETARY POLICY IN OPEN ECONOMIES

If the Fed succeeds in increasing interest rates in the United States, the demand by foreigners to invest there may increase, and hence the demand curve for dollars will shift to the right. Similarly, fewer Americans will find it attractive to invest abroad, so the supply curve of dollars will shift to the left. Both shifts lead to an appreciation of the dollar.

demand, not so much by restricting credit availability and reducing investment as by discouraging exports and encouraging imports.

Monetary policy may also affect expectations concerning future exchange rates. Changes in those expectations may either reinforce or dampen the effects described so far. How expectations are formed and how they are affected by monetary policy are complicated matters, and it may therefore be difficult to predict the precise effect of monetary policy.

Earlier, we saw that one ingredient in determining expectations of changes in the exchange rate are expectations concerning inflation. If tighter monetary policy leads investors to believe that inflation will be reduced (that is, if investors believe that monetary

Figure 35.8 EFFECTS OF DOLLAR APPRECIA-TION ON ECONOMIC ACTIVITY

At a higher value of the dollar, imports are increased and exports are reduced. With lower net exports, the aggregate expenditures schedule shifts down, leading to a lower level of equilibrium output as shown in panel A. Panel B shows the same result in terms of the aggregate demand and supply framework. At each price level, aggregate demand is lower.

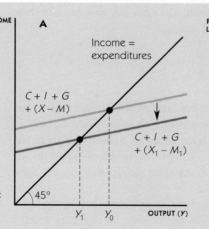

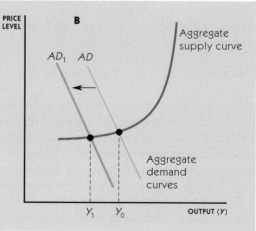

policy actually works to shift the aggregate demand curve to the left), then they may believe that the dollar will become stronger (the exchange rate higher) than it otherwise would have been. In that case, it becomes even more attractive to invest in the United States; the dollar appreciates even more, and exports are discouraged and imports are encouraged more than they would have been in the absence of these changed expectations.

Changed expectations induced by changes in monetary policy may have large and immediate effects on exchange rates. If investors believe that the Fed will succeed in lowering the inflation rate by 2 percent over the course of the next year and therefore the dollar will be 2 percent stronger relative to other currencies, then that will have an immediate effect on today's exchange rate. The reason for this is simple. If investors think that the dollar is going to be worth 2 percent more tomorrow, then they will want to buy it today, to realize the capital gain; hence it will go up 2 percent today.

But the fact that exchange rates may adjust quickly does not mean that exports and imports adjust as rapidly and thus that monetary policy has quick effects through this channel. For instance, German and Japanese automakers responded very slowly to changes in the exchange rate that occurred in the 1980s; they changed the prices they charged in the United States only gradually, so automobile imports decreased slowly as the dollar depreciated.

MONETARY POLICY IN AN OPEN ECONOMY

In an open economy, the effect of monetary policy on domestic spending is dampened by the ability of Americans to borrow abroad. But it is strengthened because it may affect exchange rates and, through exchange rates, the level of economic activity.

EXCHANGE RATE MANAGEMENT

As the link between monetary policy and exchange rates has become increasingly clear, monetary authorities in many countries have attempted to "manage" the exchange rate. In some cases, they have simply tried to smooth out day-to-day fluctuations in exchange rates. In other cases, they have tried to move the exchange rate permanently higher or lower.

FIXED EXCHANGE RATE SYSTEM

The current international system of flexible exchange rates, in which exchange rates are determined by demand and supply, has been in practice for only two decades. Previously, the world had a **fixed exchange rate system**, in which exchange rates were pegged at a particular level. If, as in Figure 35.9, the market equilibrium exchange rate (e^*) was below the pegged level (e_f), then the government intervened; it bought dollars, selling gold or foreign currencies that it held in reserve, shifting the demand curve up.

Sometimes government intervention was not needed. If investors believed that the government was going to succeed in sustaining the pegged rate, they helped the government. If the exchange rate drifted slightly below the pegged rate, they knew that sooner or later the government would intervene and increase the exchange rate. Hence, foreign speculators believed that if they bought dollars they would reap a capital gain. These expectations led them to demand dollars, to the point where the exchange rate was driven up to the pegged level.

A problem arose when investors believed that the equilibrium exchange rate was far different from the pegged rate. Recall that the way the government attempted to sustain the exchange rate was to buy dollars, selling gold or foreign currencies. But if the government had insufficient gold or foreign currencies and investors believed that the government could not or would not sustain the exchange rate at the pegged level, the results were disastrous.

When the government announces that there will be a new, lower exchange rate under the fixed exchange rate system in order to stimulate exports and help industries that face competition from foreign imports, then it is said to **devalue** the currency. When investors believe that the dollar is about to be devalued, they will not want to hold dollars. Americans, by holding foreign currencies, can reap large capital gains. As we saw in an earlier example (p. 948), they can convert their dollars to a foreign currency and then reconvert to dollars the next day. The result is that the supply of dollars increases enormously. The gap between supply and demand at the original pegged exchange rate becomes enormous. The task of the government in sustaining the exchange rate becomes impossible.

Many governments have attempted to maintain the exchange rate at a rate higher than what would have prevailed in a free market; in such cases, the currency is said to be **overvalued**. The government may take such action for a variety of reasons. In some cases, the exchange rate is a source of pride. A depreciation of the currency is taken to reflect negatively on the country or the government's ability to manage its economic

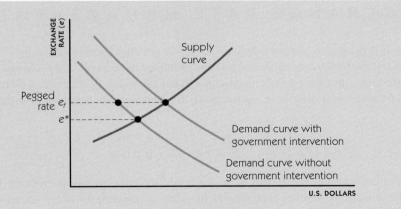

Figure 35.9 GOVERNMENT INTERVENTION IN THE FIXED EXCHANGE RATE SYSTEM

If the "fixed" rate under the fixed exchange rate system, e_f, exceeds the market equilibrium rate, e^*, then to sustain the fixed exchange rate requires government intervention. Government enters the foreign exchange market demanding dollars (supplying foreign exchange) to the point where the equilibrium exchange rate is the pegged rate.

EXCHANGE RATE (e)

Supply curve

Pegged rate e_f

e^*

Demand curve with government intervention

Demand curve without government intervention

U.S. DOLLARS

CLOSE-UP: BRITAIN JOINS THE EMS

In October 1990, after an acrimonious debate between and within its political parties, Great Britain joined the European Monetary System. In joining, Britain promised to stabilize the foreign exchange value of the pound relative to the average of the other European currencies, limiting fluctuations to 3 percent, plus or minus. The primary controversy was whether Britain had surrendered control over its own monetary policy. To some extent, it had.

Here's why. To stabilize the value of the pound, the Bank of England must avoid extremes of inflation (which would depreciate the currency) and high real interest rates (which would tend to appreciate the currency). Either too loose or too tight a monetary policy could easily push exchange rates out of their agreed-upon range. Thus, unless all the rest of Europe decides to pursue a loose monetary policy, Britain will not be able to do so. And since Germany, the largest European economy, has traditionally held inflation in check by running a tight monetary policy, Britain will be compelled to do the same.

But those who favored joining the EMS argued that limiting the power of the central bank was a good thing. They argued, for instance, that the promise of a relatively stable currency will allow British businesses to make long-term plans for investing in the rest of Europe, and European businesses to make long-term plans for investing in Britain.

During August and September 1992, with Germany maintaining high interest rates to combat inflation and Britain trying to keep interest rates low to stimulate its sluggish economy, the high demand for German marks relative to the British pound led to a higher "equilibrium" exchange rate. To maintain the exchange rate within the agreed-upon limits required more government intervention, to buy pounds and sell marks. As speculators and investors became convinced that the exchange rate could not be maintained, the demand for marks and the supply of pounds became still greater, requiring further intervention. Finally, the week of September 14, the pound fell, and Britain withdrew, at least temporarily, from the EMS.

Source: "Going for It," *The Economist,* October 13, 1990, pp. 14–15.

affairs. Sometimes the government attempts to keep a high exchange rate to enable it to buy foreign goods such as expensive luxury imports for the ruling elites or expensive machines for new factories at a lower cost in terms of domestic currency.

GOVERNMENT INTERVENTION IN FLEXIBLE EXCHANGE RATE SYSTEMS

Today, while governments do not peg the exchange rate at a particular value, they frequently intervene in the foreign exchange markets, buying and selling currencies, in an attempt to reduce the day-to-day variability in exchange rates. Economists sometimes refer to this as a **"dirty float" system**. As we will see, exchange rate variability may have a dampening effect on the economy, exposing both export and import sectors to considerable risk.

VOLATILITY OF EXPECTATIONS

Many economists have been concerned with the high degree of volatility in exchange rate markets. Exchange rates have fluctuated greatly, both on a day-to-day and on a longer-term basis, as illustrated in Figure 35.10. The French franc went from 4.2 francs to the dollar in 1980 to 9.0 francs in 1985, and back to 6.9 francs in 1986. The dollar has had single-day declines of more than 1 percent against the German mark (February 18, 1985), and more than 1 percent against the Japanese yen (October 14, 1987). This may not seem like a lot, but if there were a 1 percent decline every business day for a year, it would mean that the exchange rate would have declined by more than 240 percent within a year. Many of these gyrations, particularly the ones that happen from day to day, cannot be explained by any correspondingly large changes in the economy. They only seem explainable in terms of large shifts in expectations.

As was noted above, dollars or yen are assets. That is why the value of the exchange rate today depends on what they expect the exchange rate will be next year. Thus, the

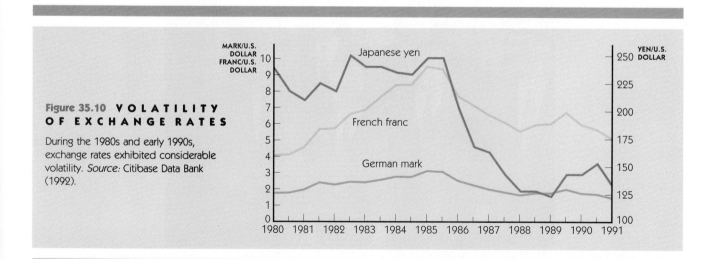

Figure 35.10 VOLATILITY OF EXCHANGE RATES

During the 1980s and early 1990s, exchange rates exhibited considerable volatility. *Source:* Citibase Data Bank (1992).

stability of the exchange rate depends on the stability of the expectations of investors. For instance, when the dollar is lower, foreign investors might expect it to rise again. In that case, as the value of the dollar declines, the expected return to holding dollars increases because investors believe that it is likely to appreciate and that they will benefit from a capital gain when the dollar does appreciate. In this case, expectations help stabilize the market, since foreign investors may help to limit any decline in the dollar by buying it as it falls.

But if as the dollar depreciates foreign investors expect further depreciation, then their willingness to invest in America may actually decrease as the dollar falls in value. In that case, an initial decline in the value of the dollar in effect shifts the demand curve for dollars down, leading to further decreases in the value of the dollar.

Chapter 10 presented the notion that prices of assets move like a random walk. If there were predictable patterns, investors would discover them and, by their resulting bidding actions, eliminate them. Dollars, pounds, yen, francs, marks, are all assets. If it were the case that normally when the dollar depreciated with respect to the yen, it recovered, then investors would know that under these circumstances the dollar was a good buy. They would bid for dollars, driving up the exchange rate. In equilibrium, then, investors must believe that whatever the exchange rate is today, it must have a roughly equal chance of going up or down. Exchange rates that do not move in this way cannot be consistent with rational expectations. While the empirical evidence casts some doubt on whether foreign exchange markets are well described by a random walk, it is nonetheless clear that it is extremely difficult to predict how exchange rates will move.

Whatever their cause and whatever the nature of expectations concerning future movements, these huge swings in exchange rates add to the risk of doing business in the world market and thus discourage businesses and countries from pursuing their comparative advantages. If the exchange rate appreciates greatly, exporters suddenly find that the market for their goods has dried up, unless they drastically cut prices; either way, profits are dramatically reduced. Even American firms that produce only for the American market face huge risks as a result of exchange rate fluctuations. Shoe manufacturers may find the American market flooded with cheap Brazilian shoes if the dollar appreciates relative to the Brazilian cruzado; again, they either lose sales or must cut their prices, and in either case, profits fall.

There are ways that exporting and importing firms can mitigate the effects of foreign exchange risks in the short run, say the next three to six months. Consider an American firm that exports abroad. It has a contract to deliver so many ball bearings to France at so many francs per ball bearing. But it pays its workers in dollars, not francs. If the franc depreciates, when the firm takes the francs it receives and converts them into dollars, its revenues will fall short of the dollars it has already paid to workers. It can insure itself by making a contract (with either a bank or a dealer in the foreign exchange market) for the future delivery or sale of those francs at a price agreed upon today. It can thus avoid the risk of a change in the foreign exchange rate. However, firms cannot easily buy or sell foreign exchange for delivery two or three years into the future. Since many investment projects have a planning horizon of years or even decades, investors are exposed to foreign exchange risks against which they cannot get insurance. But even firms that do not buy or sell in foreign markets are exposed to risks from foreign exchange rate fluctuations: American firms cannot buy insurance against the longer-term risk that the American market will be flooded with cheap imports as a result of an appreciation of the U.S. dollar.

STABILIZING THE EXCHANGE RATE

Given the costs of exchange rate instability, there have been demands that the government should actively try to stabilize the exchange rate. What producers are particularly concerned with is stabilizing the real exchange rate, so that if inflation in the United States is higher than in foreign countries, American exporters can still sell their goods abroad. As Figure 35.11 shows, there have been large movements in real exchange rates, just as there have been in nominal exchange rates.[1]

There are three requirements facing any government program to stabilize the (real) exchange rate. First, they must choose what the exchange rate should be. Second, they must have a mechanism for keeping real exchange rates at that value. For example, if the dollar seems to be climbing too high against the yen, a plan might propose that the Fed sell dollars and buy yen, thus pushing up the demand for yen and increasing the supply of dollars. Producers in the United States may be delighted by this move; demand for exports will increase, as will demand for goods that compete closely with imports. But producers in Japan will feel just the opposite. If the Japanese government, responding to these pressures, were to intervene simultaneously and start selling yen and buying dollars, the two efforts would offset each other. In effect, it would be as if the U.S. government sold dollars in exchange for yen directly to the Japanese government, with private markets unaffected.

This brings up a third requirement of exchange-rate-stabilization proposals: there must be some degree of cooperation among countries. This is particularly true in the modern world economy, where no single country is dominant. There are several big players—Japan, Germany, and the United States—and setting exchange rates requires these governments to work together.

[1] The figure shows the trade-weighted value of U.S. dollars, with (real) and without (nominal) adjustments for inflation in different countries.

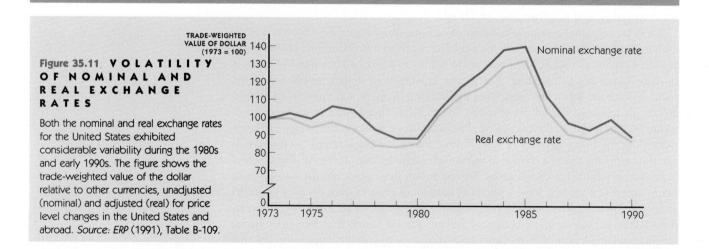

Figure 35.11 VOLATILITY OF NOMINAL AND REAL EXCHANGE RATES

Both the nominal and real exchange rates for the United States exhibited considerable variability during the 1980s and early 1990s. The figure shows the trade-weighted value of the dollar relative to other currencies, unadjusted (nominal) and adjusted (real) for price level changes in the United States and abroad. *Source: ERP* (1991), Table B-109.

INTERNATIONAL COOPERATION

Following World War II, the major countries, including Britain, France, and the United States, recognized their economic interdependence and the importance of orderly foreign exchange markets for the conduct of international trade. In a famous 1944 meeting at Bretton Woods, New Hampshire, at which Keynes was a leader, they signed an agreement that called for fixed exchange rates between countries and that set up the **International Monetary Fund (IMF)**. Just as the Federal Reserve was set up as a central or banker's bank, providing a source that U.S. banks could borrow from in times of need, the IMF was to serve as the bank for the various central banks of the world. In the United States, a bank could borrow from the Fed in the case of a bank run, and the knowledge that a bank could do so was supposed to reduce the likelihood of a run. Likewise, a central bank could borrow from the IMF, and this was supposed to protect the country against runs on its currency and help it maintain the agreed-upon exchange rate.

In the years after World War II, the countries of the world tried to maintain exchange rates within fairly narrow bands. To do this required governments' buying and selling money and gold out of their reserves. To keep the dollar at the desired level, the United States would have to buy dollars and sell German marks, Japanese yen, and whatever other currencies were gaining strength against the dollar. During the first two decades after the war, the American economy dominated the world scene, and it was easy for the United States to take on the responsibility of stabilizing exchange rates—buying and selling dollars, foreign currencies, and gold to do so. Everyone wanted American goods, and the United States exported much more than it imported. The Fed accumulated vast amounts of foreign currency. Thus, if it looked like the demand for marks at the fixed exchange rate exceeded the supply, the Fed would simply sell some of the marks out of its horde. But what happens when the Fed runs out of its reserves, when it has no more marks or yen to sell?

If the demand for dollars is weak, the dollar's exchange rate will not be able to be sustained at the desired value. Foreign central banks could intervene. The German Bundesbank might, for instance, buy dollars and sell marks, and the increased demand for dollars would allow the exchange rate to be maintained. But the German bank might not want to do this. If it believes that the dollar cannot be sustained at the pegged value, then the Germans will be left holding dollars that are about to decrease in value. This seems like bad business. Why should they pay the price for America's problems?

Although the Fed could borrow from the IMF, this may only postpone the eventual day of reckoning. Try as they might, governments cannot support forever an exchange rate that differs from the one that would have emerged without government intervention in the market. Under the Bretton Woods system, Britain, France, and other countries found from time to time that they simply had to devalue their currencies.

The end of the system of fixed exchange rates can probably be dated to 1971, when the United States, which had been the pillar of the system, found it increasingly difficult to support the value of the dollar. The United States (with the rest of the world quickly following) switched to a system of flexible exchange rates. Advocates of flexible exchange rates say that it is better to have frequent small changes in response to market forces rather than the large, disruptive changes that characterize a fixed exchange rate regime. Even with flexible exchange rates, however, there are still heavy doses of government intervention, requiring continuing cooperation among the countries of the world. Every year there is an economic summit of the leaders of the major industrialized countries, and one of the topics frequently discussed is exchange rate management. The United States has been concerned with not only the volatility of the dollar, but also its level.

Especially in the mid-1980s when the dollar was flying high, it was often argued that the dollar is overvalued, making it difficult for the United States to export and for American producers to compete with foreign imports. Most of the leaders of the other countries have been only mildly sympathetic. They believe that in the long run the exchange rate is determined by basic economic forces. Most economists share this view. The high value of the dollar in the mid-1980s was caused by the huge flow of capital to the United States; this in turn was caused by the high interest rates paid in the United States, which in turn was related to the huge amount of borrowing on the part of the federal government. The governments of America's major economic partners have contended that there is little that can be done about the overall level of the exchange rate unless the United States first takes serious steps to cut its budget deficit. Cooperation may still have a role in maintaining short-run stability in exchange rates.

CAN GOVERNMENTS STABILIZE EXCHANGE RATES?

Some economists are skeptical about the ability of the government to stabilize the exchange rate even in the short run. If the current exchange rate between the franc and the dollar is 6 francs to the dollar, and if the market knows that the exchange rate must change in the near future to 6.6 francs to the dollar, it will be futile for the government to try, in the short run, to maintain the current exchange rate. French investors, believing that there will be a devaluation of the franc, know that the return to holding assets in dollars will be enormous. By converting their francs to dollars and holding them for the short period until the franc is devalued, they obtain a large return.

There will be what is referred to as a run on the franc, as those holding assets denominated in francs seek to sell them now. This run will be too large for the French government to stop by buying francs and selling dollars. There are more private individuals willing to sell francs and buy dollars than the French government has resources to cope with. The government may be successful in postponing the fall of the franc for a few days, but to do that it must pay a huge price. It would have obtained the capital gain on the dollars that it held if it did not sell dollars for francs; instead, the capital gain is earned by private individuals. If the government spends $1 billion trying to support the franc and the franc goes down 10 percent (as in our example), the cost of the short-run support is more than $100 million.

Critics of government stabilization programs make several other points. First, they stress the difficulties in determining the equilibrium exchange rate that is supposed to be stabilized. Is there any reason, they ask, to believe that government bureaucrats are in a better position to make judgments about the equilibrium exchange rate than the thousands of investors who buy and sell foreign exchange every day? If the government makes mistakes, as it is almost bound to do, it can actually contribute to destabilizing the exchange rate rather than stabilizing it.

Exchange rates often need to change. For example, if one economy grows faster than another or has higher inflation than another, the exchange rate will have to compensate.

Investors face two major problems in forming expectations about what exchange rates will be in the future. One problem is that even if an investor can make a reasonably confident prediction about what the exchange rate ought to be, she cannot be sure of how long it will take the market to reach that particular value. Thus, an investor might have said in 1982: "The dollar has increased in value by one-third in the last two years, and it's higher than at any time in the 1970s. I'm sure it will go down."

Indeed, by 1987 that prediction had come true; the dollar was actually lower in value than it was in 1982. But in the interval, it had increased by an additional one-third above its 1982 value before beginning to fall. An investor who had bought other currencies, planning to cash them back into dollars when the dollar fell, could easily have gone broke during this time. Investors cannot always wait for the long run; they have to worry about losing money in the short run too.

The second problem investors face is even more fundamental. How can they tell what the equilibrium exchange rate will be? Any government that decides its currency is too high or too low and wants to alter its value will face a similar problem of deciding what the "correct" value should be.

The purchasing power parity theorem offers a way of tackling this question. This theorem holds that in equilibrium, the value of different currencies should be such that one could purchase a roughly equivalent bundle of goods for the same amount of money in different countries. For example, consider a bundle of goods made up of wheat, oil, steel, cars, computers, and other internationally traded goods. If it costs $1 million to purchase this bundle in the United States, then the purchasing power parity exchange rate will be determined by how many yen or marks or pounds or francs it takes to buy that same bundle in another country.

The theorem does *not* say that the price of individual goods must be the same in different countries, only that the price level of internationally traded goods, taken as a group, should be equal. After all, if all tradable goods were, on average, much more expensive in one country than another, then that country would have a very difficult time exporting at all! The purchasing power parity theorem is thus based on the premise that in the long run, countries will not continually be borrowers or lenders.

Tourists traveling in other countries may feel that purchasing power parity cannot be right since hotels, meals, and trips often are either cheaper or more expensive in other countries. But most of what tourists buy when they visit a country are goods and services that are not internationally traded, like a hotel room, and the purchasing power parity theorem has nothing to say about such prices.

Businesspeople and investors concerned with the currency market usually keep the purchasing power parity exchange rate in their peripheral vision. But they know that the economy may take years to converge to that rate. In the meantime, they tend to focus their attention on trying to understand and predict the short-term determinants of exchange rates, like government actions, the course of inflation, and the expectations of other investors.

How will a scheme for stabilizing exchange rates let them adjust naturally while controlling them at the same time?

Second, critics of government stabilization programs question whether international economic cooperation is achievable. Running domestic economic policy is difficult enough. For example, will a country take steps to raise its exchange rate and thus hurt its exporters to keep a political agreement with foreign countries?

Thus, there are questions about whether stabilizing the currency is possible either economically or politically.

REVIEW AND PRACTICE

SUMMARY

1. Exchange rates are determined by the forces of demand and supply. The demand and supply for dollars is determined by exports and imports, foreigners' demand for investment in the United States and Americans' demand for investment abroad, and by speculators, whose demands for various currencies are based on expectations concerning changes in exchange rates.

2. In an open economy, government monetary policy is likely to have a smaller effect on interest rates and credit availability than it otherwise would. If the Fed attempts to restrict credit or raise interest rates, capital can flow in from abroad.

3. To the extent that monetary policy leads to flows of capital into the country, it also normally leads to an appreciation of the dollar, reducing exports and increasing imports.

4. It may not be possible for the government to stabilize exchange rates effectively. It is difficult to determine the equilibrium exchange rate that is supposed to be stabilized, and international economic cooperation may not be achievable.

KEY TERMS

flexible or **floating** exchange rate system	**perfectly mobile** capital **real exchange rates**	**fixed exchange rate** system **devaluation**

REVIEW QUESTIONS

1. Why is monetary policy, whether tight or loose, likely to have less of an effect on interest rates or on the supply of credit in an open economy?

2. Name three factors that cause exchange rates to shift.

3. How does monetary policy affect output in an open economy?

4. Why are expectations concerning changes in the exchange rate important? How do relative rates of inflation affect those expectations?

5. What are the costs of exchange rate stability? How might the government attempt to reduce instability in exchange rates? What are the obstacles to doing so? Why is international coordination important? What problems might result from government attempts to stabilize the exchange rate at a nonequilibrium level?

6. Why would you be surprised to find obvious patterns in movements of foreign exchange markets? (Hint: Review the discussion in Chapter 10 on random walks.)

PROBLEMS

1. Tell whether each of the economic actors in the following list would be suppliers or demanders in the foreign exchange market for U.S. dollars:
   (a) an American tourist in Europe;
   (b) a Japanese firm exporting to the United States;
   (c) a British investor who wants to buy U.S. stocks;
   (d) a Brazilian tourist in the United States;
   (e) a German firm importing from the United States;
   (f) a U.S. investor who wants to buy real estate in Australia.

2. Explain whether each of the following changes would tend to appreciate or depreciate the U.S. dollar, using supply and demand curves for the foreign exchange market to illustrate your answers:
   (a) higher interest rates in Japan;
   (b) faster economic growth in Germany;
   (c) a higher U.S. rate of inflation;
   (d) a tight U.S. monetary policy;
   (e) an expansionary U.S. fiscal policy.

3. Suppose that at the start of 1991, a U.S. investor put $10,000 into a one-year German investment. If the exchange rate was 1.5 marks per dollar, how much was this in marks? Over the course of the year, the German investment paid 10 percent interest. But when the investor switched back to dollars at the end of the year, the exchange rate was now 2 marks per dollar. Did the change in exchange rates earn the investor more or less money? How much? How does your analysis change if the mark had fallen to 1 per dollar?

4. If the government wanted to reduce its trade deficit by altering the exchange rate, what sort of monetary policy should it employ? Explain.

5. If the government succeeds in raising the exchange rate, who benefits and who is injured?

CHAPTER 36

PRICE STABILITY

I t is an axiom of political rhetoric that inflation is bad. Popular sentiment runs so strongly against inflation that it is usually taken for granted that the government should do something about it. This is especially true when, for example, the price level doubles every month; no one would then dispute the view that the economy is in some way sick. Such extremely high rates of inflation, called **hyperinflation**, have plagued many countries in recent years, including Brazil, Argentina, Bolivia, and Israel. With these rates of inflation, money no longer serves its primary functions very well; it is no longer a good store of value or a unit of account, and it may not even be used widely as a medium of exchange. In certain Latin American countries, the rate of inflation has been so high at times that people have preferred not to use their own national currency; instead, they often use U.S. dollars, whose value is relatively stable.

For the past two centuries, the United States has been spared these extremes of inflation. But even far lower rates have given rise to concern, as when the inflation rate climbed to 1 percent per month in the late 1970s and early 1980s. It is less clear that these relatively low rates of inflation portend any serious problems for the economy. If incomes go up as rapidly as prices do, then the family's opportunity set remains the same. Under these circumstances, is there any harm in (moderate) inflation? More generally, what causes inflation and what can or should be done about it? No inflation may be preferable to even moderate inflation, but with a better understanding of the causes and remedies, we will see that the cure may be as bad as or worse than the disease.

"Well, gentlemen, how much do we raise the cost of living this time?"

LIVING WITH MODERATE INFLATION

Inflation is much maligned, but most of the economic costs of inflation disappear when it is anticipated. Workers who know that the consumer price index will be rising by 10 percent this year may negotiate wages that rise fast enough to offset the inflation. If inflation drives up a producer's costs but boosts the price he receives for his product by a similar amount, then the producer is no worse off (and no better off) on account of inflation.

The formal linking of any payment to some measure of inflation is called **indexing**. To see how indexing works, consider the provisions called cost of living adjustments, or COLAs, that appear in many labor contracts. Collective bargaining agreements (the contract) often cover three years or so. To be sure that the wages negotiated today for three years from now will have the purchasing power agreed to, a COLA is often added. This provision contains a formula that will further increase the (nominal) wage if inflation has occurred. Thus, a worker with a COLA is relatively immune to the effects of inflation (but she should also remember that a COLA raise will not buy her more groceries or a larger car). Likewise, Social Security payments, interest rates, and tax rates have been indexed in recent years, and this has eased the economic cost of inflation throughout the economy.

WHO SUFFERS FROM INFLATION?

While indexing goes a long way toward softening the effects of inflation, it is far from complete. So who suffers today from inflation? Many people may suffer a little, since indexing does not fully protect them, but some are more likely to suffer than others. Among the groups most imperfectly protected are lenders, taxpayers, and holders of currency.

Lenders Since most loans are not fully indexed, increases in inflation mean that the dollars that lenders receive back from borrowers are worth less than what they lent out. We often think of bankers as the country's major lenders, and making bankers worse off is hardly likely to evoke an outpouring of sympathy. But many people put a large part of their savings for their retirement into bonds or other fixed-income securities. These people will suffer if an inflationary bout comes between them and their nest eggs. The extent to which they will suffer depends in large measure on whether the price changes were anticipated. After World War II, many people bought bonds yielding a 3 or 4 percent annual return. They did not anticipate much inflation. When inflation reached double-digit levels in the late 1970s, they were badly hurt; the rate of interest they received did not even come close to compensating them for the reduced value of the dollars. In real terms, they received a negative return on their savings. If the inflation had been anticipated, the interest rate would have reflected it.

Taxpayers Our tax system is only partially indexed, and inflation frequently hurts investors badly. All returns to investment are taxed, including those that do nothing more than offset inflation. Consequently, real after-tax returns are often negative. Consider a rate of inflation of 10 percent and an asset that yields a return of 12 percent before tax. If the individual has to pay a 33 percent tax on the return, his after-tax yield is 9 percent—not enough to compensate him for inflation. His after-tax real return is minus 1 percent.

Holders of Currency Inflation also makes it expensive for people to hold currency because as they hold it, the currency loses its value. Since currency facilitates a variety of transactions, inflation interferes with the efficiency of the economy by discouraging the holding of currency. The fact that inflation takes away the value of money means that inflation acts as a tax on holding money. Consequently, economists refer to this distortionary effect as an **inflation tax**.

This distortion is not as important in modern economies, where even transactions that use money more frequently entail the use of checking accounts, and checking accounts typically pay interest. As the rate of inflation increases, the interest rate they pay normally increases. Even in Argentina in the 1970s, when prices were rising at 800 percent a month, bank accounts yielded more than 800 percent a month. Still, poorer individuals who do not have checking accounts and therefore must hold much of what little wealth they have in the form of currency are adversely affected.

Following World War I, Germany was required by the victorious Allied nations to make substantial "reparation" payments. But the sheer size of the reparations, combined with the wartime devastation of German industry, made payment nearly impossible. John Maynard Keynes, then an economic adviser to the British government, was among those who warned that the reparations were too large. To finance some of Germany's financial obligations, the German government started simply printing money.

The resulting increases in both the amount of circulating currency and the price level can be seen in the figure. From January 1922 to November 1923, the average price level increased by a factor of almost 20 billion.[1] People made desperate attempts to spend their currency as soon as they received it, since the value of currency was declining so rapidly. One story often told by Keynes was how Germans would buy two beers at once, even though one was likely to get warm, for fear that otherwise, when it came time to buy the second beer, the price would have risen.

1. Thomas Sargent, "The Ends of Four Big Inflations," in Robert Hall, ed., *Inflation* (Chicago: University of Chicago Press, 1982), pp. 74–75.

At an annual inflation rate of 100 percent, money loses half its value every year. If you save $100 today, in five years it will have buying power equal to only 3 current dollars. It is possible for nominal interest rates to adjust even to very high inflation rates. But when those high inflation rates fluctuate in unanticipated ways, the effects can be disastrous.

Periods of hyperinflation create a massive redistribution of wealth. If an individual is smart or lucky enough to hold assets in a form such as foreign funds or land, then the hyperinflation will do little to reduce that person's actual wealth. Those who cannot avail themselves of these "inflation-proof" assets will see their wealth fall.

THE GERMAN HYPERINFLATION

Inflation in Germany during the 1920s reached levels that may seem unbelievably high. At the end of 1923, prices were 10 billion times higher than they were two years earlier.

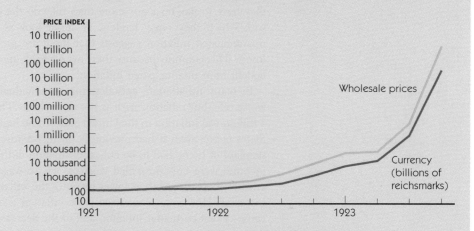

The Economy The economy as a whole suffers from inflation for two reasons. The first has to do with relative prices. Normally increases in the rate of inflation lead to a greater variability of relative prices. If the shoe industry makes price adjustments only every three months, then in the third month, right before its price increase, shoes may be relatively cheap, while right after the price increase, shoes may be relatively expensive. On the other hand, the prices of groceries might change continually throughout the three-month period. Therefore, the ratio of the price of groceries to the price of shoes will continually be changing. Price increases are never perfectly coordinated. When the average rate of inflation is only 2 or 3 percent per year, this does not cause much of a problem. But when the average rate of inflation is 10 percent per month, this can be serious. At rates this high, inflation causes real distortions in how society allocates its resources.

The second economy-wide cost of inflation arises from the risk and uncertainty that inflation generates. If there were perfect indexing, the uncertainty about the rate of inflation would be unimportant. But indexing is, as has been noted, far from perfect, and the resulting uncertainty makes it difficult to plan. Lenders cannot charge interest rates that would take into account fully the fact that the dollars paid back will be worth less than the dollars lent. People saving for their retirements cannot know what to put aside. Business firms borrowing money are uncertain about the price they will receive for the goods they produce. Firms are also hurt when they build wage increases into multiyear contracts to reflect anticipated inflation. If for any reason a firm finds that the prices it can charge increase less rapidly than what was anticipated in the contract, the employer suffers.

PERCEIVED COSTS OF INFLATION

Before leaving the subject of inflation's costs, we would do well to review some of the perceived costs, and how economists weigh them. While some people gain from inflation and some lose, more individuals *perceive* that they are losers. If a poll were conducted asking people whether they were hurt or helped by inflation, most would say they were hurt. Much of this is simply perception. People "feel" price increases much more vividly than they do the corresponding income increases. They "feel" the higher interest rates they have to pay on loans more than they do the decrease in the value of the dollars with which they repay lenders. A closer look at who benefits and who loses from unanticipated inflation suggests that there are probably more gainers than there are losers. This is simply because there are probably more debtors than lenders, and debtors benefit from unanticipated inflation.

In many inflationary episodes, many individuals not only *feel* worse off, they *are* worse off—but inflation itself is not the culprit. The oil price increases of 1973 set off a widespread inflation in the United States. The higher price of oil also made the United States poorer than it had previously been, because it was an oil importer. Someone's standard of living had to be cut, and inflation did the cutting. Frequently those whose incomes were cut—unskilled workers, whose wages did not keep pace with prices—cited as the *cause* of their lower incomes the inflation that accompanied the oil price increases. However, generalized price inflation was only a symptom. The underlying cause of that particular inflation and of the decreased real incomes was a sharp rise in the price of oil.

It is clear that the costs of inflation are different, and undoubtedly lower, than they were before indexing was so extensive. Today economists are not agreed on how seriously to take inflation. Given the popular concern about inflation, most economists would say that it would be worth reducing inflation, if it were relatively costless to do so. But if the costs of fighting inflation are high and if the benefits are low, then it may not pay to fight at least the moderate kind of inflation that the United States has experienced in the past half century. To ascertain the costs of fighting inflation, we have to understand something about its causes, a question to which we now turn.

COSTS OF INFLATION, ACTUAL AND PERCEIVED

Real costs
  Variability in relative prices
  Increased uncertainty

Misperceptions
  Failing to recognize offsetting increases in income
  Blaming losses in real income that occur during inflationary episodes on the inflation

WHY THE PRICE LEVEL CHANGES

The discussion of the goods market in Part Four focused on situations where there is excess capacity, where the intersection of the aggregate demand and supply curves occurs along the horizontal portion of the aggregate supply curve. In such cases, changes in aggregate demand lead to changes in output levels, with no change in the price level. Here, we focus on situations where there is no excess capacity, where the intersection of the aggregate demand and supply curves occurs along the vertical portion of the aggregate supply curve; this is the condition in which inflation most frequently occurs. Because inflation is the process of prices rising over an extended period of time, not a once-and-for-all change in the price level, we break the analysis of inflation down into two parts: what causes the inflation, and what perpetuates it. This section is concerned with the first part.

Figure 36.1 shows an economy initially in equilibrium, with aggregate demand equal to aggregate supply, at a point where the economy is operating at capacity. The machines are all humming at top speed, and workers are all employed. Panel A shows a cause of

CLOSE-UP: HYPERINFLATION IN ARGENTINA IN THE 1980s

Argentina was an economic basket case during most of the 1980s, with annual inflation rates *averaging* 450 percent, topped off with a spurt of 20,000 percent inflation for the twelve months ending early in 1990. In that atmosphere, the main goal of economic activity was simply to avoid letting inflation eat you up. Writer V. S. Naipaul visited Argentina recently and spoke with Jorge, an Argentine businessman and an insightful survivor of the inflationary times. Jorge told Naipaul:

Inflation keeps you on your toes.

Our company is in an industry where we can let you have only about four or five days' credit. Otherwise, with the kind of inflation we have, working capital gets murdered. . . .

Another negative aspect of inflation is that you cease to worry about productivity and even technology. Now that is the secret of all progress: productivity. But you really can get no more than 3 or 4 percent per annum improvement in productivity anywhere in the world. With inflation like ours you can get 10 percent *in one day,* if you know when and where to invest [nominal return, of course!]. . . . It is much more important to protect your working capital than to think about long-term things like technology and productivity—though you try to do both. . . .

This is the inevitable result of inflation, which is the monetary disease. Your money is disintegrating. It's like a cancer.

You live day by day. That's all you can do when you have inflation of more than 1 percent a day. You cease to plan. You're just happy to make it to the weekend. And then I stay in my flat in Belgrano and read about ancient cricket matches.

We are now 25 percent poorer on a per capita basis than we were in 1975. The people who are really suffering are the people you won't see—the poor, the old, the young. These people get washed up at the big railway termini. . . . The flotsam and jetsam of Argentine life—like spray from the sea, these people.

inflation known as a **demand shock**. In a full-capacity economy, if there is a rightward shift in the aggregate demand curve, from AD_0 to AD_1, then at the initial price level p_0 there is excess demand. We say there is "inflationary pressure." With the demand for goods exceeding the supply, prices tend to rise, in this case to p_1.

Panel B shows another cause of inflation, called a **supply shock**. Here, it is the aggregate supply curve that shifts. This upward shift leaves capacity unchanged—that is why the vertical portions of the two curves coincide. But firms require higher prices to be willing to supply any given level of output. Again, there is excess demand at the original price level p_0. Like demand shocks, supply shocks introduce inflationary pressure.

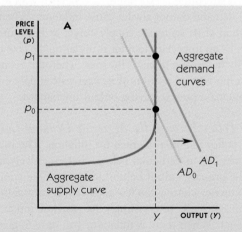
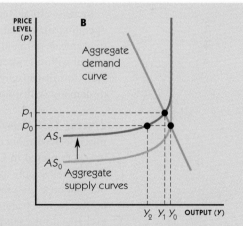

Figure 36.1 HOW SHIFTS IN AGGREGATE DEMAND AND SUPPLY CAN CAUSE INFLATION

In panel A, a rightward shift in the aggregate demand curve from AD_0 to AD_1 leads to an increase in the equilibrium price level when the equilibrium is already near full employment. Panel B shows that an upward shift in the aggregate supply curve from AS_0 to AS_1 leads to an increase in the equilibrium price level. At the original price level, p_0, aggregate demand, Y_0, exceeds the level of aggregate supply, Y_2.

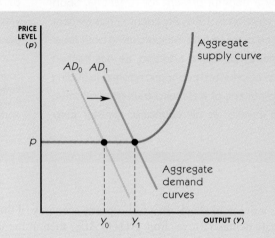

AGGREGATE DEMAND SHOCKS

What might cause the aggregate demand curve to shift? We know that aggregate demand is the sum of consumption, investment, government expenditures, and exports minus imports; it can shift because of an increase in any one of these four components. For example, the inflationary episode that began in the United States in 1966 is generally attributed to the increased government expenditures associated with the Vietnam War.

Increases in aggregate demand do not always cause inflation. When the economy is operating in the flat portion of its aggregate supply curve, as in Figure 36.2, increases in aggregate demand can be an important tool for stimulating the economy—increasing output without necessarily increasing prices. However, when the economy is operating close to full capacity, in the vertical portion of its aggregate supply curve, an increase in demand will simply increase prices, leaving output unchanged.

Tracing Out Monetary Policy Through the Aggregate Demand Curve   Money and misconceived monetary policy are often blamed for inflation. The monetarists, whom we encountered in Chapter 34, in particular believe that excessively rapid increases in the money supply are the primary culprit behind inflation. One common description of inflation is "too much money chasing too few goods." It is natural that money should be the focus of attention: after all, prices simply tell us how much money must be exchanged for each product. When there is inflation, you have to give up more dollar bills to buy a soda. From the point of view of the seller, inflation means giving up fewer sodas to receive a dollar.

Just as an increase in the supply of fruit juices relative to that of sodas will lead to an increase in the price of sodas relative to the price of fruit juices, an increase in the supply of money relative to that of sodas will result in an increase in the price of sodas relative to money; sodas become more expensive.

To take an example from an earlier period, the influx of gold from the New World in the sixteenth century increased the money supply in Europe and set off an inflationary episode. Those who brought the gold to Europe wanted to exchange it for goods. And with only a given supply of goods, the amount of gold required to obtain any item increased—the price of goods in terms of gold increased. The increase of aggregate demand as a result of an increase in the money supply is a particular example of a demand shock, and is referred to as a **monetary shock**.

Likewise, in wartime, governments often simply print money to make up for the gap between what they want to spend and what taxes bring in. Though we can look at the resulting inflation as too much money chasing too few goods—we can say the inflation was due to a monetary shock—we can also look at inflation as simply a problem of excess aggregate demand: the combination of households' demand for consumer goods, firms' demand for investment, government demands for goods and services (including those required to fight the war), and foreigners' demand for net exports simply exceeds the available supply of goods.

In modern economies, governments usually do not simply print money. But they can have the same effect on aggregate demand through their monetary policies. If the monetary authorities pursue a loose monetary policy and lower interest rates, banks find it easier and more attractive to make loans; credit becomes more readily available on easier terms, so investment and consumer purchases of durables are stimulated. Lower interest rates also lead to an outflow of funds from the United States to abroad, resulting in a lower value of the dollar, higher exports, and lower imports. Aggregate demand will shift to the right, and if the economy is operating along the vertical portion of its aggregate supply curve, near full capacity, the price level will rise, as illustrated earlier in Figure 36.1A.[1]

Monetarists place particular stress on the role of the monetary authorities in causing inflation. The monetarists, you will recall, typically believe that the economy is close to full employment—on the vertical section of the aggregate supply curve—and that velocity is close to constant, so that increases in the money supply in excess of the growth in output must necessarily be translated into higher prices.[2] In their view, the exact channel by which the increased money supply raises prices—whether the shift in aggregate demand is a result of increased investment, increased exports, or increased consumption—is not so important as the fact that inevitably prices must rise.

AGGREGATE SUPPLY SHOCKS

Other inflationary episodes have been attributed to supply curve shifts, or supply shocks. In 1973 as a result of the Arab oil embargo, the price of oil rose by 35 percent. The increase in the cost of any important input will result in an upward shift in the supply curve, as illustrated earlier in Figure 36.1B. This is because the price firms must receive to make them willing to supply any given quantity is increased. At the old price level,

---

[1] The increased investment *eventually* may choke off the rise in the price level through its impact on the aggregate supply curve, as the economy's productive potential increases. However, the effects on aggregate demand come first.

[2] On the other hand, most monetarists believe that large *negative* shocks to the money supply can move the aggregate demand curve down so much that they can, in the short run, induce substantial unemployment.

p_0, there is a gap between aggregate demand, Y_0, and the new level of aggregate supply, Y_2; the excess of aggregate demand over aggregate supply gives rise to inflationary pressures. The price level at which aggregate demand equals aggregate supply, p_1, is higher than the initial level, p_0.

WHY INFLATION PERSISTS

The analysis so far has sketched how a shock to the economy can shift the aggregate demand or supply curve, leading to a new, higher equilibrium price level. But inflation is not a onetime change in the price level; it is a persistent increase in the price level, month after month. In most modern industrialized economies, inflation tends to have inertia. Much like a skater, who will continue to glide on the ice after an initial push, an economy that has an inflation rate of 5 percent will continue to experience an inflation rate of 5 percent unless something dramatic happens.

The reason for this is that if most people in the economy expect the same rate of inflation, then these inflationary expectations will be built in to the economy's institutional practices. We then say that the economy has entered into an **inflationary spiral**. Laborers bargaining with managers will make sure that their wages keep pace with price increases so that their *real* wages will not fall. Bankers, in giving out loans, will want to guarantee themselves a certain *real* rate of return, and accordingly will demand interest rates that take into account the fact that the dollars they will receive at the end of the year will be worth less than the dollars they lend out at the beginning. These expectations are self-fulfilling. And because they are realized, there is no reason for anyone to revise them.

The essential property of an inflationary spiral is that it is self-perpetuating. It matters little what causes the inflation. It could be initiated by an increase in aggregate demand. For example, there could be an increase in government expenditures to fight a war when the economy is already at full employment; as a result, the price level rises, and this in turn leads workers to negotiate wage increases simply to keep up with changes in the price level. This kind of inflation is referred to as **demand-pull**.

On the other hand, there are situations in which wage increases and other higher costs of production can be thought of as a cause of inflation. For example, strong unions sometimes demand wage increases that are far in excess of productivity or price level increases. These higher wages induce an upward shift in the aggregate supply curve; automobile firms will be willing to supply a given quantity only if they receive a higher price.[3] The effect of this shift in the supply curve is exactly the same as a shift in the supply curve caused by any other increase in cost. If the economy is initially in equilibrium, then after the supply shift at the old level of prices, there will be an excess demand for goods. This will lead to higher prices, which may in turn create another increase in wage demands and upward shift in the aggregate supply curve, and the inflationary spiral is perpetuated. When increases in wages or other costs of production,

---

[3] It is no coincidence that many of the industries that decide to pay large wage increases are far from competitive. They are price makers, rather than price takers. When they set their price to maximize their profits, they will raise prices to offset cost increases, thus passing on part of the wage increases to their customers.

such as the price of oil, are the initial cause of the inflation, the inflation is known as **cost-push** inflation, which refers to the increased production costs that push up prices.[4]

Unfortunately, it is difficult to tell in many circumstances whether the inflation is cost-push or demand-pull. It is like asking which came first, the chicken or the egg. Price levels rise because wages increase; and wages increase because price levels are rising.

Once the inflation starts, the two processes (demand-pull and cost-push) look essentially the same. And the inflation can perpetuate itself even after the initial cause of the inflation, whether it was demand or costs, has disappeared. When workers expect prices to go up, they will insist on higher wages, which increase firms' costs, and these in fact lead to higher prices.

ACCOMMODATING INFLATION

As price levels rise, firms will need to have access to more credit to finance the same level of real investment. The demand for money and credit, in nominal terms, by both households and firms will rise with the price level. The Federal Reserve then must decide whether to allow an expansion of money and credit to "accommodate" the inflation. If it does not, then credit, in real terms, will become tighter, real interest rates may rise, investment will be discouraged, and aggregate demand will decrease. The decrease in aggregate demand will reduce inflationary pressures. But at the same time, the decrease in aggregate demand may reduce the *real* level of output and employment if the decrease is large enough to move the aggregate demand curve far enough to the left so that the new intersection of the aggregate demand and supply curves is *not* on the vertical portion of the aggregate supply curve.

The Fed is often blamed for causing inflation. But just as it is difficult to distinguish cost-push from demand-pull inflation, it is often difficult to distinguish situations where excessively loose credit starts an inflationary episode from those in which monetary policy simply accommodates the inflation. In the latter cases, when the inflation results from, for instance, a demand shock from higher government spending or a supply shock from oil prices, the Fed simply lets money and credit expand with the price level.

While inflation can be fought by identifying and attacking its cause, inflation from any cause can often be checked by a sufficiently large decrease in aggregate demand, whether that happens through a decrease in government expenditure, an increase in taxes, or a tightening of monetary policy. While several factors may have contributed to the high rates of inflation of the 1970s (the oil price shock, government expenditures on the Vietnam War, excessive union wage increases) and while the tax cut of 1981 might have fueled the inflationary fires even more, the extremely tight monetary policy of the Fed in the early 1980s was successful in reining in inflation.

This process is illustrated in Figure 36.3. Initially the economy is in equilibrium at price level p_0 and output Y. Then there is a shift in aggregate demand, caused, for

---

[4] Remember that the aggregate demand and supply curves give the levels of aggregate demand and supply at each price level *given* the level of wages. An increase in wages shifts the aggregate supply curve up; to elicit the same aggregate supply, prices have to be higher. It also typically shifts the aggregate demand curve to the right; because workers have higher incomes, the amount they are willing to spend, at each price level, is increased. (Higher wages, at any price level, imply that profits are lower; this may reduce the consumption level of owners of firms and may even reduce investment, but it is usually thought that this effect is smaller than the stimulation to workers' consumption.)

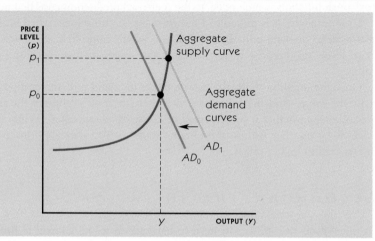

Figure 36.3 MONETARY POLICY TO FIGHT INFLATION

If the economy is at AD_1, facing excess demand at the price level p_0, tighter monetary policy will shift aggregate demand to the left, to AD_0, eliminating the excess demand and the inflationary pressure.

example, by increased government expenditures to fight a war not financed by a tax increase. This is reflected in the rightward shift in aggregate demand to AD_1. At the initial price level, there is excess demand; there are inflationary pressures to drive the price level up to p_1. Then the Fed steps in, tightening monetary policy. This reduces investment and consumer purchases of durables, and aggregate demand shifts back to AD_0. The inflationary pressure has been eliminated. The original source of the inflationary pressure has not been eliminated; but the higher level of government expenditures is balanced by a lower level of investment and consumer purchases of durables.

INITIATING AND PERPETUATING INFLATION

Initiating inflation
    Shift in aggregate demand (up and to the right) when the economy's resources are
        already fully employed, from an increase in consumption, investment, govern-
        ment expenditures, or net exports: demand-pull
            May be induced by monetary policy
    Upward shift in aggregate supply from an increase in wages or the price of imports
        (e.g., oil): cost-push

Perpetuating inflation
    Price increases lead to wage increases, which lead to further price increases: infla-
        tionary spiral

Role of monetary policy

   May initiate inflation by causing a shift in the aggregate demand curve

   May perpetuate inflation by increasing the money and credit supply—accommodating inflation

   May choke off inflation by refusing to accommodate, shifting the aggregate demand curve to the left

THE COSTS OF FIGHTING INFLATION

The Fed's success in reining in inflation in the early 1980s came at the cost of a major recession. Thus, while inflation certainly causes problems in a world of uncertainty and imperfect indexing, taming inflation often has costs too. To get less inflation, an economy may have to take on more unemployment; and to get less unemployment, the economy may have to take on more inflation.

THE PHILLIPS CURVE AND THE UNEMPLOYMENT-INFLATION TRADE-OFF

To fight unemployment, the government often seeks to stimulate the economy. As it reduces unemployment toward the full-employment level, the labor market becomes tighter. More and more firms find it difficult to obtain the labor they want, and so as they compete for workers, wages get bid up. (Conversely, when the unemployment rate is very high, there are many more job seekers than jobs, and there is little pressure to increase wages.) Accordingly, less unemployment results in more rapid increases in wages, which in turn result through the inflationary spiral in more rapid increases in prices.

There is thus a trade-off between unemployment and inflation: lower levels of unemployment will be associated with higher levels of inflation. This relationship is called the **Phillips curve**, after A. W. Phillips, a New Zealander teaching in England in the 1950s who discovered the historical relationship between the unemployment and inflation statistics for Great Britain.

Figure 36.4A depicts the curve that Phillips fitted to British data. Since Phillips was focusing his attention on the labor market, he put the unemployment rate on the horizontal axis and the rate of increase in wages on the vertical axis. Because wage increases implied price level increases, there was a link between unemployment and inflation. His study suggested that lower inflation rates could be achieved, but there would be a cost: higher unemployment rates.

In the data Phillips analyzed, wages (and hence the price level) were stable when there was 5.5 percent unemployment. When the unemployment rate is anywhere near

Figure 36.4 THE PHILLIPS CURVE

The Phillips curve shows that as the level of unemployment falls, the rate of inflation rises. The intercept of the curve with the horizontal axis gives the unemployment rate at which inflation is zero, which is called the natural rate. Panel A shows the curve A. W. Phillips actually plotted in 1958 for the British economy. Panel B depicts the Phillips curve relationship for U.S. data in the 1960s, early 1980s, and late 1980s. Panel C gives the Phillips curve for Japan for 1974–90. *Source: Economic Report of the President* (1992), Tables B-37, B-59, B-105, B-106.

0 percent, the inflation rate is very high. The rate of unemployment at which inflation is zero has come to be called the **natural rate**, but the name should not confuse you; just as natural foods may or may not be good for you, the natural rate of unemployment may or may not be good for the economy. All the natural rate signifies is that wages and therefore the price level are stable at that rate of unemployment.[5] With less unemployment, the price level would rise; with more, the price level would decline. Whether it is desirable to attain the natural rate depends on how much extra inflation results if unemployment is reduced below the natural rate, on who bears the costs of the inflation or unemployment, and on how one weighs these various costs.

Policymakers weighing these costs need to know the shape and position of the Phillips curve. They need to know the unemployment-inflation trade-off—how much *extra* unemployment they must absorb if they want to reduce inflation by 1 percent, and how much inflation will increase if they want to reduce unemployment. If the Phillips curve is very steep, then the cost is high; that is, reducing the unemployment rate a little results in a large increase in the inflation rate, and, conversely, a government decision to fight inflation may lead to a higher rate of unemployment. A comparison of panels A, B, and C of Figure 36.4 shows that the shape and position of the Phillips curve can vary in different countries and within the same country at different times.

THE PHILLIPS CURVE

1. There is a trade-off between inflation and unemployment.

2. When the rate of inflation is zero, the rate of unemployment is greater than zero. This rate is called the natural rate of unemployment.

SHIFTS IN THE PHILLIPS CURVE

Chapter 4 distinguished between movements along a curve and shifts in the curve. We saw how the demand curve gives the quantity demanded at each price; but that when incomes, tastes, or a variety of other circumstances change, the demand curve shifts. The same basic principle applies to the Phillips curve. The curve gives the rate of inflation corresponding to any level of unemployment, but there are a number of changes in economic circumstances that lead to shifts in this relationship.

The distinction between shifts in and movements along the Phillips curve is important. Figure 36.5A shows a movement from point A on an old Phillips curve to point B on

[5] That the natural rate of unemployment is not zero but rather some positive amount may seem to contradict the model of how labor markets clear. After all, if there are unemployed workers, won't wages be bid *down*? In the real economy, however, not every worker is qualified to do every job. There may be unemployment in Detroit and vacancies in Seattle; but unemployed autoworkers in Detroit cannot simply walk into jobs making airplanes in Seattle.

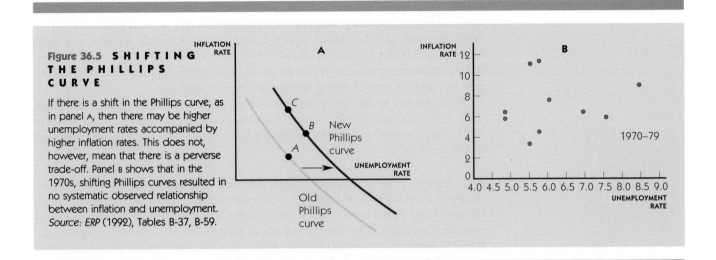

Figure 36.5 SHIFTING THE PHILLIPS CURVE

If there is a shift in the Phillips curve, as in panel A, then there may be higher unemployment rates accompanied by higher inflation rates. This does not, however, mean that there is a perverse trade-off. Panel B shows that in the 1970s, shifting Phillips curves resulted in no systematic observed relationship between inflation and unemployment. *Source: ERP* (1992), Tables B-37, B-59.

a new Phillips curve. Because the Phillips curve has shifted up, at *B* there is more unemployment and more inflation than at A. It appears as if there is a perverse trade-off. But that is wrong. If, at the later date, unemployment had been reduced to the level that it was at A (to point C), inflation would have been even higher.

In the 1970s and early 1980s, the Phillips curve shifted considerably. Panel B contains the data for this period, which by themselves show no evidence of a systematic trade-off. There was more inflation along with more unemployment, a situation that was dubbed **stagflation**. By the mid to late 1980s, a more stable relationship seems to have emerged, as illustrated earlier in panel B of Figure 36.4.

What causes the Phillips curve to shift? And what, in particular, happened in the 1970s to lead to such decisive shifts? The two most important causes are changes in the structure of the labor market, referred to as *real* factors, and expectations.

Real Factors   One real factor that can shift the Phillips curve is the size and composition of the labor force. In the 1970s, the number of workers expanded dramatically, for two reasons. First, the working-age population soared as the post–World War II baby boomers (born between 1945 and 1960) entered the labor force. Second, the percentage of working women rose dramatically as millions more women entered the labor force than had previously done so. Younger workers change jobs more frequently than older workers do. So do new entrants to the labor force, as they explore various jobs to find out what they like and what they are well suited for. Thus, if the fraction of workers that are young or that are new entrants increases, as it did in the 1970s, the level of frictional unemployment may increase. This shifts the Phillips curve and raises the natural rate of unemployment, as we saw in Figure 36.5A.

A second factor is how fast individuals move between jobs, which also affects the level of frictional unemployment. If workers receive generous unemployment compensation, this may reduce their incentives to search for a job or accept a job, and thus extend the length of time during which they remain unemployed. Also, if there are laws that make it more difficult or costly for firms to lay off or fire workers, then firms will be reluctant to hire new workers. The effect will be to slow down the process of workers moving from areas where there is an excess supply to areas where there is an excess demand, and the natural rate of unemployment will shift. Finally, as a third factor, if skills become more specialized through advances in technology, it will be more difficult to substitute those workers who are in excess supply for those who are in excess demand, and the natural rate of unemployment will again rise.

These changes in the size of the labor force, in government programs that reduce the cost of being unemployed, and in technology probably contributed to the increase in the natural rate of unemployment and the kind of shift in the Phillips curve depicted in Figure 36.5A.

Expectations   Most economists believe that the relationship between inflation and unemployment depends at least in part on expectations of inflation, and these expectations depend on the experiences of the economy. If an economy with unemployment operates at any level below the natural rate of unemployment, inflation is engendered. It is not rational to ignore this inflation. Rather, it is rational for everyone to incorporate expectations of inflation into her behavior. And these expectations themselves shift the Phillips curve. The combinations of inflation and unemployment that are available to the economy in the long run are different from those in the short run, when expectations are assumed to be fixed. It is useful, therefore, to distinguish between a long-run and a short-run Phillips curve. The most dramatic interpretation of the long-run Phillips curve is that fully rational expectations make it vertical, as in Figure 36.6. When economists draw the curve as a vertical line, they mean that no trade-off exists that will bring unemployment below the natural rate. The so-called **natural-rate proposition** argues that if the government attempts to reduce unemployment below the natural rate, it simply induces an increase in the inflation rate. At best, the gains in reduced unemployment are only temporary.

To see how shifting expectations can give rise to a vertical long-run Phillips curve, consider what happens if the government attempts to lower the unemployment rate below the natural rate, from U^* to U_1 in the figure. The inflation rate rises to i_1. But

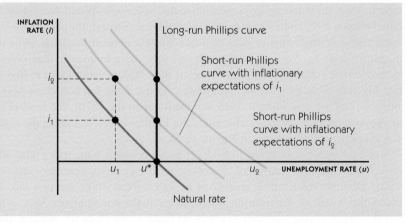

Figure 36.6 A VERTICAL LONG-RUN PHILLIPS CURVE

If the government tries to lower the unemployment rate below U^* (the natural rate) to U_1, by moving along a Phillips curve, the resulting inflationary pressure will lead workers to demand higher wages. The short-run Phillips curve will shift up, and the eventual result is that inflation will increase. If the government repeats its policy and attempts to reduce unemployment, it will find in the long run that the inflation level will be still higher. If the government then wishes to reduce inflation and thereby shift the Phillips curve down, it will have to increase the unemployment rate considerably, here to U_2.

if workers come to believe that this new inflation rate will persist, then the Phillips curve will shift upward. This is because all workers insist on wage increases just to offset the effects of inflation, so that the inflation rate at U^* is not zero but the rate that the economy has been experiencing, i_1. The inflation rate corresponding to U_1 is now even higher at i_2. But if the government persists in maintaining the low unemployment rate and workers believe that this new, higher rate of inflation will persist, the Phillips curve will shift up even more.

The government faces an uphill battle. It can, in the short run, get the economy to an unemployment rate below the natural rate, but it can do so for an extended period only at the cost of higher and higher rates of inflation. And the economy may pay a very high price, even for a short-run reduction in unemployment. This is because inflationary expectations may be stuck even if the government decides to abandon its policy of trying to force an unemployment rate below the natural rate. The economy will have purchased a low level of unemployment for one period at the price of a persistent rate of inflation. If the government then wants to restore price stability, it again has to pay a high price: it must increase unemployment to a level high enough to bring inflation down and thus inflationary expectations down. If inflationary expectations are at i_2, unemployment must increase up to U_2. Given the shape of the Phillips curve, the increase in unemployment required to wring out inflationary expectations may be much larger than the initial decrease in unemployment.

In the late 1970s, many economists became convinced that the long-run Phillips curve was, if not vertical, in any case quite steep. The evidence of the 1980s was different, however. Higher unemployment rates coincided with lower inflation rates. This restored the faith of many economists not only in the existence of a trade-off relationship between unemployment and inflation, but even in the stability of the relationship between the two: the economy can have lower rates of unemployment at the cost of higher inflation rates. In the long run, the Phillips curve might be vertical. But nonetheless, there may exist a long period during which there is a trade-off between inflation and unemployment.

Shifts in the Phillips Curve

Causes
> Real factors: changes in the size and composition of the labor force, the speed with which workers move between jobs, changes in technology
>
> Expectations of inflation

Consequences
> There may be stagflation, with higher unemployment *and* inflation.
>
> The long-run Phillips curve may be essentially vertical; there may be no trade-off between inflation and unemployment in the long run.
>
> There may still be a short-run trade-off.

GOVERNMENT POLICIES TOWARD INFLATION

Governments have long sought to control the rate of inflation. In the late Middle Ages in Europe, there was an episode in which several governments attempted to limit inflation by imposing price and wage controls; these were enforced in one instance by the threat of having one's ears cut off. Today there are two major differences in perspectives about how important it is to fight inflation, and how best to go about it. For simplicity, we can group these different views into those of the monetarists and those of the Keynesians and new Keynesians.

THE MONETARIST PERSPECTIVE

The monetarists stress the costs of inflation, particularly the uncertainty it induces and the distortions to the economy that result from the inflation tax. Perhaps most important, they believe in a vertical Phillips curve, at least in the long run, so that any gains that come from pushing unemployment below the natural rate are only temporary. With a vertical Phillips curve, there is no trade-off: one does not purchase less unemployment with a higher inflation rate. Thus, while there are costs in *attempting* to lower the unemployment rate below the natural rate, the benefits if any are but temporary.

For fighting inflation, the monetarists have a simple prescription: the Fed should simply increase the money supply at a constant rate, the rate chosen to ensure that in the long run prices will be stable. If real output is increasing on average at 3 percent per year and if the money supply is increasing at 3 percent and velocity is constant, then prices will be stable. If real output is increasing at 3 percent per year and changes in technology enable velocity to increase at 1 percent per year, then the monetary authorities should ensure that the money supply increases at a steady 2 percent per year.

Monetarists believe that this prescription will ensure that monetary shocks will not initiate an inflationary episode, and that monetary policy will not accommodate an inflationary episode. Whatever the source of the inflation, such a policy will choke the inflationary pressures off.

THE MONETARIST PERSPECTIVE

1. Inflation is costly.

2. The Phillips curve is vertical.

3. The best way to fight inflation is to control the money supply.

The Keynesian Critique of the Monetarist Perspective Keynesians and new Keynesians believe that monetarists overemphasize the costs of inflation, particularly in modern economies with extensive indexing. And they believe that monetarists, by assuming a vertical Phillips curve, underestimate the costs of *fighting* inflation. With a vertical Phillips curve, there is no trade-off; fighting inflation does not give rise to increased unemployment, since no matter what the government does, the unemployment rate will be stuck at the natural unemployment rate. But Keynesians believe that there are real costs, in terms of increased unemployment, to fighting inflation and that at least in the short run, the Phillips curve is not vertical.

Keynesians also point out that the burden of fighting inflation is concentrated among those who are thrown out of work rather than spread among the population as a whole. Furthermore, those who lose their jobs are disportionately the unskilled, whose income in any case is low and whose ability to bear the burden of even temporary unemployment is limited. By contrast, inflation for the most part hurts lenders, who are repaid with dollars that are worth less. Thus, fighting inflation benefits disproportionately the rich.

As for the monetarist prescription for fighting inflation, Keynesians have three objections. The first is the focus on monetary policy. Keynesians believe that the government needs to make use of all the instruments in its arsenal, not just monetary policy. The second objection is that the reliance on a rule—such as the expansion of the money supply at a fixed rate—amounts to the abandonment of the use of **discretionary policy**, the ability to use monetary policy to respond to economic circumstances.

The third source of dispute is the particular rule that monetarists tend to advocate, which is a constant expansion of the money supply. Such policies, called **money target policies**, were widely adopted toward the end of the 1970s and early 1980s. These policies led to extremely volatile and at times extremely high interest rates. Part of the difficulty with such policies is the instability in velocity during the past decade. With velocity being unstable, the effect of a constant rate of change in the money supply on inflation is uncertain. Thus, money target policies may actually contribute to uncertainty rather than reduce it. Today almost all governments that adopted these simple policies have abandoned them. Still, monetary authorities continue to eye closely the rate of increase of money and credit, and they have become more sensitive to their role in perpetuating inflation by accommodating to it.

THE KEYNESIAN POLICY PRESCRIPTION: MOVING ALONG THE PHILLIPS CURVE

Keynesian policies for fighting inflation can be grouped into two categories, those intended to move the economy along the Phillips curve and those intended to shift the Phillips curve.

To move the economy down along the Phillips curve requires reducing aggregate demand, so that the aggregate demand curve shifts to the left. The government can accomplish this through tight monetary policy, through a decrease in its level of expenditures, or through an increase in taxes, which leads consumers to spend less. One way of thinking about these choices in reducing aggregate demand is that inflation results when the sum of claims on national output—by consumers, firms, and government—exceeds the output available. These three methods, in effect, attempt to reduce the claims of one or more of the claimants. The difficulty for government is to decide who should receive less—those who benefit from government spending (by reducing government expenditures), consumers (by increasing taxes, reducing after-tax income), or future generations (whose incomes will be lower as a result of reduced investment).

Reductions in aggregate demand lessen inflationary pressure because they reduce the gap between the demand and supply of goods. But they also lead to reductions in the demand for labor and thus more unemployment. And when the level of unemployment rises, the pressure for wage increases is reduced. Thus, whether one believes in demand-pull or cost-push inflation, reductions in aggregate demand may be an effective instrument in fighting the inflation.

THE KEYNESIAN POLICY PRESCRIPTION: SHIFTING THE PHILLIPS CURVE

When the economy fights inflation by moving along the Phillips curve, it pays a high price: increased unemployment. But if government policy can shift the Phillips curve, then it can achieve lower inflation without increasing unemployment. The government can attempt to do this by affecting real factors, using wage and price controls, using moral suasion, or changing expectations.

Real Factors   One of the reasons that the natural unemployment rate may be high is that it takes time to find a new job. Government has an ambiguous effect on job mobility: while government job-placement services facilitate labor mobility, unemployment insurance may actually encourage people to search longer for a job after they are thrown out of work. In Europe, where unemployment rates remained persistently high through the 1980s, there is concern that legislation that was intended to increase workers' job security (by making it more difficult for employers to fire them) has had the side effect of making employers more reluctant to hire new workers, and has thus impeded the process of job transition. Changing these laws may shift the Phillips curve.

An alternative way of shifting the Phillips curve, in the short run at least, is to shift the aggregate supply curve down and out, as illustrated in Figure 36.7. This increases output and the employment level, and thus reduces inflationary pressure. One way of shifting the aggregate supply curve is to reduce regulation. Deregulating airlines, trucks, and natural gas prices, for example, leads to lower prices as competitive forces come into play. And these lower prices have a ripple effect as they spread their way throughout the economy; industries that use trucks and natural gas as inputs lower their prices, and sectors that use those industries' products in turn are able to lower their own prices. Such a policy was initiated by President Carter and continued by President Reagan.

Most economists, whether Keynesian or not, applauded these initiatives of Presidents Carter and Reagan because they would increase the efficiency of the economy. However, many Keynesians and new Keynesians questioned both the magnitude of the effects and the speed with which they would come into play. Many economists think the time it takes for supply reactions to occur, if they do occur, is too long to make supply-side policies effective instruments for short-term inflation control. Thus, it appears that the government has a limited ability to shift the Phillips curve through real factors.

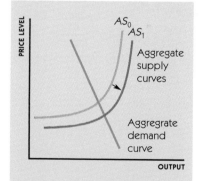

Figure 36.7 SUPPLY-SIDE POLICIES AND INFLATION

If the government could enact policies to shift out the aggregate supply curve, this would be an effective method of fighting inflation.

Wage and Price Controls   Perhaps the most direct, but by no means the best, response to inflation is simply to outlaw price (and wage) increases. This amounts to attempting to legislate a shift in the Phillips curve. Governments often resort to **wage and price controls**, as such policies are known, during periods of war. Such controls have been tried in peacetime only once in the United States, under President Nixon. The story begins in the early 1960s, when the inflation rate began to climb—from a 1 percent increase in the consumer price index in 1961 and 1962 to a 1.3 percent rate in 1963 and 1964. The rate was 1.6 percent in 1965, but jumped to 2.9 percent in 1966, 3.1 percent in 1967, 4.2 percent in 1968, 5.5 percent in 1969, and 5.7 percent in 1970. There were fears then that the rate would continue to rise. Despite his free-market sympathies, Nixon decided to put a halt to it.

In August 1971, Nixon imposed a three-month wage and price freeze on the entire U.S. economy. In November, what was called phase II began. Most prices were required to be kept under certain ceilings, but exceptions were allowed for goods like fresh vegetables and corporate stocks. For other goods, the price ceilings were to be adjusted by complex and not particularly clear formulas that combined an overall target rate of inflation with special allowances for increasing costs and changes in productivity. Any company that broke the guidelines could be taken to court.

At first, Nixon's program did have a powerful effect in holding down prices. Between mid-1971 and mid-1972, prices rose by only 3.2 percent. Economist Herbert Stein, then on the President's Council of Economic Advisers, wrote: "The freeze was an amazing accomplishment in decision-making and administration, and also in the provision of voluntary support and compliance by the American people."

But while the freeze and the price control guidelines succeeded in bottling up inflationary pressures in the short run, it could not hold them back indefinitely. In the first three months of 1972, even with the price ceilings in effect, prices were already rising at a 6 percent annual rate. As the controls were phased out later that year, inflation continued to rise: it hit 11 percent in 1974. One major reason for the price increase in 1974 was the sharp rise in oil prices that resulted from the OPEC oil embargo, but another reason was surely that after voluntarily restraining prices for a time, businesses and workers felt a need to catch up. Double-digit inflation had returned for the first time since World War II.

Most economists oppose price controls because they do not attack the underlying problems, such as the excess demand for goods. Also, such controls are difficult to administer and frequently result in a variety of inefficiencies. For instance, when wage controls are imposed, employers can get around them by reclassifying jobs. It may be illegal to increase the salary of a secretary, but it is not illegal to promote the secretary to a "new" job, perhaps administrative assistant, and pay a new wage. Similarly, a firm may not be able to increase the price it charges for its washing machine model 70237, but it can phase out that model, introduce "new" model 70238 with some minor variations, and increase the price. Or the firm could keep the price the same but strip some features from the model, providing in effect a lower-quality machine at the same price. The manufacturer may claim, of course, that it has increased the quality by improving the design. The sheer weight of bureaucracy makes it virtually impossible for the government to rule on each of the myriad of resulting cases.

There is another difficulty with enforcing price controls. Inflation, remember, is the price of all goods taken together, not the price of each good separately. Even when there is little or no inflation in the overall price level, relative prices of different goods are constantly changing. The prices of computers have declined and the prices of haircuts have increased over the last twenty years. If price controls are to remain in force for any extended period of time, they must allow for these changes in relative prices. If they do not, shortages will develop of those goods whose prices are kept below their equilibrium level.

This happened during the Nixon price controls, when there was suddenly a shortage of chickens. Price controls were more effective in limiting the prices chicken producers could charge than in limiting the prices they had to pay for their inputs, such as feed. As a result, at the fixed prices that they were able to sell their chickens, it simply did not pay them to produce the quantity of chickens that Americans demanded at that price. Socialist economies, where price controls are universal, are constantly experiencing shortages and surpluses of one good or another. In short, the price controller simply cannot make allowances for all the needed changes in relative prices.

Moral Suasion   Another way that governments have fought inflation is through informal wage and price controls. Rather than controlling prices and wages directly, the government might use tactics that have been called **moral suasion** or **jawboning**, in which it tries to *persuade* firms and workers not to raise prices and wages. The government sets wage and price guidelines, with which it hopes workers and firms will comply. The government often has considerable leverage beyond its appeal to moral rectitude because it can threaten not to buy from firms that violate its suggestions. There have been some dramatic episodes where such jawboning appears to have worked. President Kennedy, concerned that a proposed increase in prices by U.S. Steel would set off an inflationary spiral, successfully jawboned the company into rolling back the price increases.

Changing Expectations   When moral suasion has worked, it has been largely because this method served to break the inflationary psychology, the expectations that can play such an important role in perpetuating inflation. If unions and firms believe that everyone else will be jawboned successfully, they will be willing to moderate their wage demands and price increases. But that is precisely why jawboning is an unreliable instrument: it is difficult to predict the market psychology reaction.

Some economists think that a major role of monetary policy is also persuasion, as when the Federal Reserve attempts to convince everyone that it will be tough on inflation. If the Fed is successful, inflationary expectations are broken, wage increases are lowered, and the wage-price spiral may be broken. The Fed's success is self-confirming: given that inflation has been broken, it does not have to take actions like tightening credit, which would have adverse effects on output and employment.

If people believe that any of the actions government takes to break inflation will be successful, these expectations themselves will help dampen inflation. The government policy will succeed in part because people believe it will do so. On the other hand, if they do not believe the policy is going to work, inflationary expectations will not be broken and inflation is likely to persist.

How sensitive the rate of inflation and people's expectations are to government policy is the subject of considerable debate among economists. If there is a shock to the economy, such as a change in government policy, and individuals continue to base their inflationary expectations on past inflation rates, then the economy will be stuck with its inflation rate for a long time. Severe, protracted shocks to the economy will be required to change people's inflationary expectations.

With slowly changing expectations, there will be a trade-off between unemployment and inflation, extending over a considerable length of time. Slowly changing expectations make it relatively easy for the government to reduce unemployment without setting off rapid inflation. But once inflationary expectations have been developed, it is difficult to stop inflation. Even if the unemployment rate is high, the rate of inflation will be high. To break the back of inflation will require high unemployment rates over long periods of time.

On the other hand, with rapidly adapting expectations, the Phillips curve will be close to vertical, even in the short run. This has both its positive and negative sides. If individuals react to certain changes in government policy by immediately changing their expectations of future inflation, inflation's back can be quickly broken. The costs of fighting inflation will be quite small, only requiring an appropriate government policy. On the negative side, rapidly changing expectations make it relatively easy to set off an inflationary spiral if an attempt is made to reduce unemployment below the natural rate.

Economists who believe that expectations adapt slowly point to the difficulty involved in reducing the high inflation rates of the 1970s. Those who believe that expectations adapt quickly concentrate their attention on historical periods of extremely high inflation, like the German hyperinflation of the 1920s, when phenomenally high rates of inflation were brought quickly under control. Both views may be right: whether expectations adapt slowly or quickly depends on the situation.

THE KEYNESIAN PRESCRIPTION FOR FIGHTING INFLATION

Movements along the Phillips curve
    Limiting aggregate demand by tightening monetary policy, decreasing government
        expenditures, or increasing taxes

Shifts in the Phillips curve
    Changing real factors
        Facilitating job mobility
        Shifting the aggregate supply curve
    Wage and price controls
    Moral suasion (jawboning)
    Changing expectations
        Any policy that is believed to be effective may be effective.
        Slowly adjusting expectations mean that there is a short-run unemployment-in-
            flation trade-off, but inflationary expectations, once built in, are hard to
            reverse.
        Quickly adjusting expectations mean that the Phillips curve may be close to vertical
            even in the short run, but inflation is easy to reverse because inflationary
            expectations are easy to reverse.

REVIEW AND PRACTICE • 989

REVIEW AND PRACTICE

SUMMARY

1. Most of inflation's effects can be lessened through indexing—adjustments in wages, Social Security payments, interest rates, and tax rates—to changes in the price level. Unanticipated inflation without indexing tends to injure lenders, taxpayers, and holders of currency.

2. Inflation can be caused either by a demand shock—excess demand for goods shifting the aggregate demand curve to the right; or by a supply shock—sharp increases in costs shifting the aggregate supply curve upward. Regardless of the initial cause, a spiral of higher wages and prices may be created.

3. Monetary policy may increase the supply of money and credit, thereby accommodating the inflation, or it may refuse to accommodate the inflation and thus shift the aggregate demand curve to the left.

4. Lower levels of unemployment are associated with higher levels of inflation, a trade-off depicted by the Phillips curve. The Phillips curve can shift because of real factors (changes in the structure of the labor market) and expectations.

5. Monetarists contend that the costs of inflation are high, that the Phillips curve is vertical (so that any *attempt* to reduce unemployment below the natural rate will lead to higher inflation), and that the best method of fighting inflation is limiting the growth of the money supply.

6. Keynesians contend that with indexing, the costs of inflation are not that high; that for an extended period of time, at least, the Phillips curve is not vertical, and fighting inflation results in higher unemployment; and that those who lose their jobs are disproportionately the unskilled.

7. Keynesians believe that the government can limit aggregate demand and move down along the Phillips curve by tightening monetary policy, decreasing government expenditures, or increasing taxes. The government can attempt to shift the Phillips curve by changing real factors, using wage and price controls, using moral suasion, or changing expectations.

KEY TERMS

indexing

inflation tax

inflationary spiral

demand-pull inflation

cost-push inflation

Phillips curve

natural rate of
unemployment

REVIEW QUESTIONS

1. What difference does it make whether inflation is anticipated or unanticipated? What difference does it make whether there is indexing or not?

2. How do lenders, taxpayers, and holders of currency suffer from inflation? To what extent are retired individuals hurt by inflation today? How is the economy as a whole adversely affected by inflation?

3. How does an inflationary spiral perpetuate itself?

4. What is the difference between cost-push and demand-pull inflation?

5. What is the relationship between monetary policy and inflation?

6. What is a Phillips curve?

7. What are the reasons that a short-term Phillips curve might shift? When the Phillips curve shifts, what might be the observed patterns of unemployment and inflation?

8. Why might the long-run Phillips curve be vertical?

9. What are the principal differences between monetarists and Keynesians over the costs of inflation, the costs of fighting inflation, and how best to fight it?

10. What are the various policies that might induce a movement along the Phillips curve? a shift in the Phillips curve?

11. What are the costs of using wage and price controls to fight inflation? How might companies circumvent such controls?

PROBLEMS

1. Priscilla earns $40,000 per year, but her wages are not indexed to inflation. If over a period of three years inflation is at 5 percent and Priscilla receives raises of 2 percent, how much has the actual buying power of her income changed over that time?

2. Patrick receives a gift of two $100 bills for his birthday. Because he likes having the bills around to admire, he does not spend them for a year. With an inflation rate of 6 percent, what inflation tax does he pay?

3. "It is unfair to tax capital gains—the increases in the value of stocks and bonds—at the same rate as ordinary income in inflationary situations." Discuss.

4. There have been proposals to increase Social Security benefits with the wages received by current workers, so that retired individuals do not fall behind those who are employed. What would be the consequences of increasing Social Security benefits *both* to compensate for increases in the price level and to match salary increases of the currently employed?

5. Use aggregate supply and demand curves to explain whether (and when) the following events are likely to trigger inflation:
    (a) an increase in business confidence;
    (b) an increase in the discount rate;
    (c) the development of important new technologies;
    (d) an increase in the price of imports;
    (e) an increase in government spending.

6. What would be the effect on the Phillips curve of falling oil prices?

7. While playing around with old economics data in your spare time, you find that in 1963, unemployment was 5.5 percent and inflation was 1.3 percent; in 1972, unemployment was 5.5 percent and inflation 3.2 percent; in 1979, unemployment was 5.8 percent and inflation 11.3 percent; in 1988, unemployment was 5.5 percent and inflation 3.6 percent. Does this evidence necessarily imply anything about the shape of the short-run or long-run Phillips curve? How might you interpret this data?

APPENDIX: THE INFLATIONARY SPIRAL: A DIAGRAMMATIC ANALYSIS

The inflationary spiral can be illustrated in diagrams describing demand and supply in the labor market and the product market. In Figure 36.8A, initially the economy is in equilibrium at point E on the relatively steep portion of the aggregate supply curve. Now consider a shift in the aggregate demand curve from AD_0 to AD_1. This shift leads to excess demand at the initial price level p_0, and prices consequently rise to p_1.

Panel B shows the implications of these changes for the labor market. For simplicity, we assume that the supply of labor is inelastic. The number of people who wish to work remains unchanged, at least with small changes in wages and prices. Firms are willing

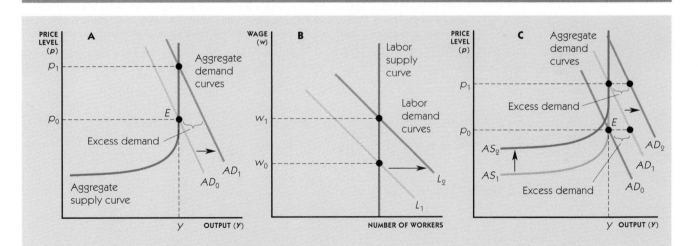

Figure 36.8 AN INFLATIONARY SPIRAL

In panel A, the shift in aggregate demand from AD_0 to AD_1 increases the price level from p_0 to p_1. This causes an increase in nominal wages, shown in panel B, because the increase in the price level shifts the demand for labor to the right. In panel C, higher wages then shift the aggregate supply curve up from AS_1 to AS_2, while also shifting the aggregate demand curve to the right from AD_1 to AD_2. Again there is excess demand for goods. The resulting higher prices will again lead to higher wages.

to employ workers as long as the real wage they pay is less than or equal to the marginal output new workers produce. Given that the labor market was initially in equilibrium at wage rate w_0, with this new increase in the price level and no change (yet) in the wage rate, the real wage falls and employers demand more labor at this wage. The labor demand curve shifts to the right, to L_2. The new equilibrium wage, w_1, is higher.

To see what this implies, let's return to the goods market in panel C. The aggregate demand and supply curves are drawn on the basis of a given level of wages. The higher wage rate means that people have more income, leading to greater consumption and hence increased aggregate demand, and the aggregate demand curve shifts from AD_1 to AD_2. At each price level, aggregate demand is higher. Similarly, the aggregate supply curve shifts up from AS_1 to AS_2 because the higher wages mean that firms must receive a higher price to induce them to supply any given quantity. At the new price level p_1, the gap between the new aggregate demand curve AD_2 and the new aggregate supply curve AS_2 remains. Again we are left with excess demand for goods, leading to further price increases, setting off another increase in wages, and so on.[7] The inflationary pressure keeps cycling through the economy.

It makes little difference to this analysis whether the initial disturbance that set off the inflationary episode was an increase in aggregate demand or a decrease in aggregate supply. Both will result in an excess demand for goods at the original price level. Once inflationary expectations are built in to wage- and price-setting behavior, inflation may persist. Note too that the story of the inflationary spiral would have been exactly the same if the initial impetus to the inflation had occurred in the labor market.

---

[7] Some economists argue that this process could not go on indefinitely. They point to the real balance effect described in Chapter 31. With these increased prices, the government bonds that individuals hold would be worth less; people would experience a decline in their wealth and would consequently cut back on their demand, shifting back the aggregate demand curve. The effect of real balances in modern economies is empirically small and is therefore unlikely to make much of a difference at low levels of inflation.

PART SIX

POLICIES FOR GROWTH AND STABILITY

U nemployment and inflation, the subjects of Parts Four and Five, are not the only economic concerns that make the news. Deficits in the United States, starvation in Ethiopia, the economic crises in the formerly Communist countries of the Soviet Union and Eastern Europe, are among other events that have grabbed headlines in the past decade. In this part of the book, we use the principles and insights developed in the preceding chapters to take a look at these and other current public policy issues.

Chapter 37 discusses a major problem facing the United States: the slowdown in its rate of economic growth. The country is growing neither as fast as it did in earlier decades nor as fast as some of its major economic rivals. We ask, what causes economic growth, and what can be done to stimulate it?

Chapter 38 focuses on two deficits. The fiscal deficit has been at the center of public concern now for almost a decade, and has persisted despite seeming efforts to reduce it. The trade deficit—the excess of U.S. imports over exports—has also persisted for more than a decade. We learn why the two deficits are, in fact, closely related.

The economy seems to have its ups and downs. There are boom years and bust years. Having developed an understanding of what causes unemployment and inflation, we ask, is there a reason that the economy fluctuates so greatly? Is there no way of maintaining a more even course? As we will see in Chapter 39, the various macroeconomic schools we have encountered look at this question from different perspectives and provide different answers about what the government should do.

The collapse of the Soviet empire is undoubtedly one of the biggest events of the twentieth century, just as its rise was, in the aftermath of World War I. The Soviets established an alternative economic system that they believed would eventually dominate capitalism. In Chapter 40, we look at what the system's basic tenets were, why it failed, and the problems these countries face today in making a transition to capitalism.

Most of the world lives in countries where incomes are but a fraction of those in the United States, Western Europe, Japan, and the other developed countries. By the standards in these less developed countries, referred to as the Third World, most people who consider themselves poor in the more developed countries are indeed well off. In Chapter 41, we learn some of the major differences between the developed and less developed countries. We also ask, what are some of the major issues facing these poorer countries as they struggle to grow and raise themselves out of the mire of poverty in which they have remained for centuries?

CHAPTER 37

GROWTH AND PRODUCTIVITY

I t is hard to comprehend fully the changes that have taken place in the U.S. standard of living during the past century. In 1900, Americans' level of consumption was little higher than that of the average citizen in Mexico or the Philippines today. Life expectancy was low, in part because diseases like smallpox, diphtheria, typhoid fever, and whooping cough were still common. You were fifteen times more likely to catch measles in 1900 than you would be today. Though the abundance of land in the United States meant that relatively few Americans were starving, luxuries were scarce. People worked as long as they could, and when they could no longer work, they became the responsibility of their children; there was no easy period of retirement.

During the nineteenth century, the standard of living in England and a few other European countries was comparable, perhaps slightly higher than that of the United States; for the time, these countries' standard of living was the highest in the world. Even within Europe, there were periodic famines. In the most famous of these, the Irish potato famine of 1845–48, more than a tenth of the population is estimated to have died, and more than another tenth migrated to the United States. And for those living in Asia, Africa, and Latin America, as the vast majority of people did then and do now, life was even harder.

Chapter 25 set out the various ways in which increased standards of living could be measured, such as higher per capita incomes and longer life expectancy. But higher standards of living are also reflected in shorter working hours and higher levels of education. The improved education is both a benefit of a higher standard of living and one of its causes. Table 37.1 sets forth a comparison between the United States today and at the turn of the century.

Table 37.1 THE UNITED STATES IN 1900 AND 1990

	1900	1990
Population	76 million	251 million
Life expectancy	47.3 years	75.6 years
GNP (in 1990 dollars)	$327 billion	$5,463 billion
GNP per capita (in 1990 dollars)	$4,309	$21,730
Average hours worked each week in manufacturing industry	59 hours	41 hours
Average hourly pay in manufacturing industry (in 1990 dollars)	$3.79	$10.84
Total telephones in country	1.3 million	160 million
Total bachelor's degrees conferred	29,375	1,017,667
Total doctoral degrees conferred	382	35,759
Average days of primary or secondary school attended per year	99	160
Percentage of those age 5–19 enrolled in school	50.5 percent	91.4 percent

Sources: Economic Report of the President (1990); Statistical Abstract of the United States (1990).

Underlying all of these changes is an increase in the output of each hour worked, what Chapter 25 identified as productivity. A major concern of this chapter is to understand what causes productivity to increase.

There is a second objective. In the last two decades, confidence in America's technological leadership has declined. Americans are no longer certain that their wages and standard of living will continue to rise as they have for over a century. Behind these concerns is the sudden slowdown in the rate of increase of productivity during the past two decades. What caused this sudden slowdown, and what can be done to reverse it?

"The United States Congress is urging all of us to produce more."

KEY QUESTIONS

1. What are the principal determinants of the growth of the economy?

2. What factors might account for the slowdown of growth in the United States? What, for instance, might explain the low savings rate or the low investment rate?

3. Are there any policies available to the government that might stimulate the country's economic growth?

THE U.S. PRODUCTIVITY SLOWDOWN

For almost a century, the United States has been at the center of the technological advances that have changed the face of the world. Though the automobile was not actually invented in the United States, the techniques of mass production (like the assembly line) that made the car almost universally affordable were developed in the United States. The airplane, from its inception at the hands of the Wright brothers to the development of the jet engine and the modern commercial aircraft, has a "Made in the USA" stamp on it. The telegraph, the telephone, atomic energy, the laser, the transistor . . . the list of America's technological achievements goes on and on. This is meant to deny neither the importance of technological developments that happened in other parts of the world—for example, Italy's Guglielmo Marconi and the radio or Britain's Sir Alexander Fleming and penicillin—nor the importance that foreigners have

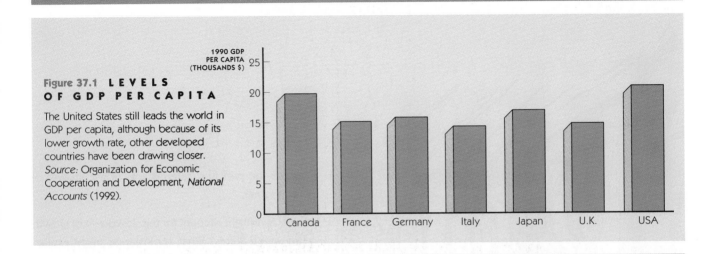

Figure 37.1 LEVELS OF GDP PER CAPITA

The United States still leads the world in GDP per capita, although because of its lower growth rate, other developed countries have been drawing closer. *Source:* Organization for Economic Cooperation and Development, *National Accounts* (1992).

played in America's breakthroughs. The team that developed atomic energy, for instance, was based in the United States but it was truly international. All told, however, it is fair to say that America has been on the technological frontier during the twentieth century, and the country has reaped a huge reward: levels of productivity and thus living standards increased continually, so that by the end of World War II they were among the highest in the world.

Today that leadership in technology and growth is being challenged. As the twentieth century draws toward its close, living standards in the United States are still among the highest in the world, as shown in Figure 37.1. The figure also shows, however, that other countries also enjoy comparable living standards. And in several key industries,

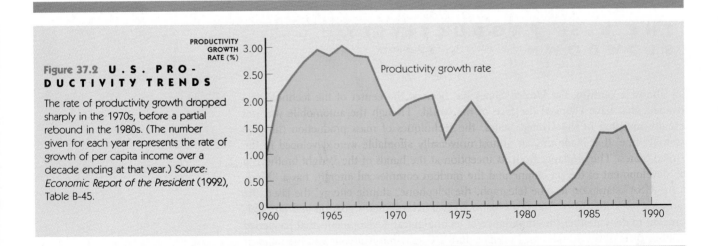

Figure 37.2 U.S. PRODUCTIVITY TRENDS

The rate of productivity growth dropped sharply in the 1970s, before a partial rebound in the 1980s. (The number given for each year represents the rate of growth of per capita income over a decade ending at that year.) *Source: Economic Report of the President* (1992), Table B-45.

the formerly dominant U.S. position seems to be slipping. This is true not only in the heavy industries like steel, cars, and shipbuilding, but in more technologically oriented industries such as electronics and computers. For instance, though the United States has continued to be in the forefront in developing new and better computers and computer chips, most of the personal computers (whether assembled in the United States or not) consist mostly of foreign-made parts.

The U.S. rate of growth of productivity slowed remarkably in the late 1960s and early 1970s, as illustrated in Figure 37.2. By the mid-1970s, the growth rate was less than half what it was in the 1950s and 1960s. There appears to have been a small rebound in the 1980s, but nothing like a return to the earlier levels.

THE IMPORTANCE OF THE PRODUCTIVITY SLOWDOWN

A skeptic might question whether the percentages shown in Figure 37.2 make much difference. So the average rate of productivity growth used to be slightly in excess of 2 percent, and now it is slightly in excess of 1 percent—what's so important about a difference of only 1 percent? The answer is that the percentage point difference compounds over time. Consider this simple calculation. Two countries start out equally wealthy, but one grows at an average annual rate of 2.5 percent while the other grows at an average annual rate of 3.5 percent. The difference would be barely perceptible for a few years. But after thirty years, the slower-growing country would be only three-quarters as wealthy as the faster-growing one. Slow growth can move a country from relative wealth to relative poverty in a few generations. Some argue that the United States, after more than a decade of slow growth, may be locked into this low-growth pattern. America's lower growth compared with the growth of other developed countries in the last two decades, shown in Figure 37.3, explains why many countries have almost caught up to the United States.

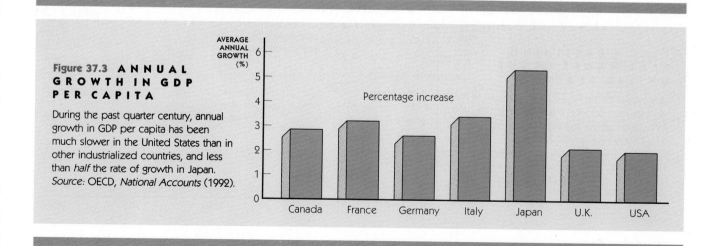

Figure 37.3 ANNUAL GROWTH IN GDP PER CAPITA

During the past quarter century, annual growth in GDP per capita has been much slower in the United States than in other industrialized countries, and less than *half* the rate of growth in Japan.
Source: OECD, *National Accounts* (1992).

Lower growth in productivity means lower growth (on average) in standards of living. Incomes will be lower than they would have been had productivity grown more rapidly. On average, people will have less of everything—not only fewer consumer goods, but also less medical care, less education, less travel, and fewer government services for the poor. If America's rate of growth of productivity remains below that of other countries, other countries will eventually catch up to and outstrip the United States in their standard of living, which means that the middle class in other countries will be able to afford new products and services that only wealthy U.S. citizens can now afford.

The symptoms of the U.S. productivity slowdown are already showing. Over the long run, wage rates tend to change with productivity increases. Unless productivity continues to grow, wages cannot continue to grow. From this perspective, the fifteen years beginning in 1973 were a disaster: average *real* wage rates actually declined, and the decline was greater for lower-skilled workers. Figure 37.4 illustrates the movement of real wages for prime-aged men for the upper 40 percent and for the lowest 10 percent, relative to what they were in 1970. By 1989, relative wages of the bottom 10 percent were down more than 30 percent, while wages of the upper 40 percent had barely increased at all. (However, the *incomes* of American families did not decline, mainly because as women became more active in the labor force, the total number of hours worked by the members of each household increased.)

Some economists believe that measurement problems exaggerate the magnitude of the slowdown in productivity, for the reasons discussed in Chapter 25. For instance, the measure of output ignores the improvement in the quality of the air and water during the past two decades and the degradation of the environment that occurred in earlier decades. Still, even when account of these measurement problems is taken, there is a general consensus that there has been some slowdown in productivity.

The question is, what is the prognosis for the future? To answer this question, we need to know what causes growth and increases in productivity, and to see what factors can account for the productivity slowdown.

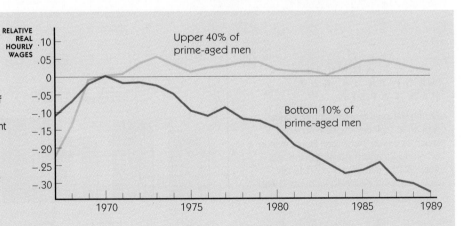

Figure 37.4 DECLINING REAL WAGES IN THE UNITED STATES

Real wages for the lowest 10 percent of workers have declined markedly since 1970, and even for the upper 40 percent they have barely increased. *Source:* C. Juhn, K. Murphy, and R. Topel, "Why Has the Natural Rate of Unemployment Increased over Time?" *Brookings Papers on Economic Activity* (1991).

CLOSE-UP: THE PRODUCTIVITY SLOWDOWN AND INCREASED INEQUALITY

The years following 1970 were marked not only by a slowdown in the rate of growth of productivity, but also by an increase in income inequality. Economists have speculated about whether, and in what ways, these two phenomena are interrelated.

Figure 37.4 depicted the movement of real hourly wages for prime-aged men in the lowest 10 percent and the upper 40 percent of the labor force. The lowest 10 percent shows a significant decrease in real wages—real wages today are a third lower than they were two decades ago. This wage gap is reflected in increased income inequality. The figure here shows that while the richest 20 percent have increased their share of national income from slightly more than 40 percent in 1970 to about 45 percent today, the share of the poorest 20 percent has decreased from around 5.6 percent in 1970 to 4.6 percent today. The widening gap reflects the increased return to education.

Some economists look to supply-side explanations, particularly for the decrease in real wages among the lowest decile. They see the "television era" in particular, and the decreased quality of education in general, as having increased the number of functionally illiterate and semiliterate workers. They also see life-style changes—the drug culture, the larger number of broken homes, the increased fraction of homes in which both parents are out working—as having played some role.

Other economists focus on demand-side explanations. They see technological change as having decreased the demand for unskilled workers and increased the demand for highly skilled workers, such as those who work with computers.

While the immigration of unskilled workers, particularly from Latin America, may also have driven down the real wages of unskilled workers, the flow of imports may have had its effects: to compete with these cheap imports, workers in some industries had to accept wage cuts or be content with smaller than usual wage increases. Meanwhile, high-wage industries like steel and autos faced a decline in employment, as they modernized—or faced rapid decline—in the face of the competition.

INCREASING INCOME INEQUALITY

Increasing wage inequality has contributed to greater income inequality. Today the share of national income going to the richest 20 percent is much higher than it was a quarter century ago, and the share of national income going to the poorest 20 percent is lower. *Source:* "Why Has the Natural Rate of Unemployment Increased over Time?"

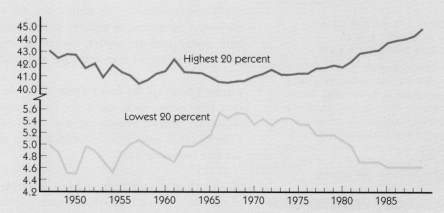

THE SOURCES OF PRODUCTIVITY GROWTH

Economists have studied the sources of economic growth for a variety of reasons. One reason is historical, to understand what changes in the latter half of the nineteenth century allowed for the remarkable increase in productivity that began then. Another reason is to understand why different countries have had different rates of growth. A third reason is to help in formulating policies to encourage growth. Economists have found that there are four major causes of increases in productivity: increases in the accumulation of capital goods (investment), a higher quality of the labor force, greater efficiency in allocating resources, and technological change.

Increases in the Accumulation of Capital Goods (Investment)   If workers in one country have more capital goods with which to work than do their counterparts in other countries, their productivity will normally be higher. Even a relatively simple device like an electric screwdriver has increased the productivity of workers in the construction industry enormously. As agriculture became more mechanized, beginning in the late nineteenth century, productivity soared. In the less developed economies, farmers often grow barely enough to support their own families, while in the United States, the 3 percent of the population currently employed in agriculture produce more than Americans can eat. Even after the United States has exported a large share of its agricultural production, there are still surpluses of major crops. Much of this increase in productivity is due to the mechanization of American agriculture. Tractors, combines, and other equipment allow U.S. farm workers today to do in an hour what might have taken them a week fifty or seventy-five years ago.

The effect of an increase in capital goods per worker is shown in Figure 37.5. Chapter 12 introduced the concept of a production function, which relates the level of inputs (capital goods, labor, and raw materials) to the level of output. More inputs obviously imply greater output. By the same token, the more capital goods *per worker*, the greater the output *per worker*, as depicted in the figure. But while output per worker increases with capital goods per worker, the law of diminishing returns also applies. Successive increments in capital lead to smaller and smaller increments in output per worker.

Higher Quality of the Labor Force   The United States invests, publicly and privately, over $300 billion each year in the formal education of its youth. Investments in individuals are referred to as investments in human capital, a term that was introduced in Chapter 11. A more educated work force is an important element contributing to the increase in productivity.

Reallocating Resources from Low- to High-Productivity Sectors   As the economy shifts resources such as labor from sectors in which they are less productive (like traditional agriculture) to modern manufacturing industries in which they are more productive, the *average* productivity of the economy goes up. The last hundred years have been marked by enormous shifts. In 1870, 50 percent of the work force was employed in

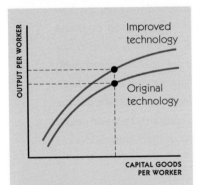

Figure 37.5 CAPITAL GOODS AND PRODUCTIVITY

As the amount of capital goods available to each worker increases, output per worker increases. But the existence of diminishing returns means that each successive increment to capital goods adds less and less to output per worker. An improvement in technology would shift the entire production function upward.

agriculture. As recently as 1960, about 10 percent of the labor force was employed in agriculture; today the share is less than one-third that amount.

Technological Change   The past century has seen a myriad of technological improvements, manifested in better products, better ways of producing goods, and better ways of organizing production. Henry Ford's exploitation of the assembly line increased productivity several fold within a year. Technological change shifts the production function, meaning that at each level of inputs, more output can be produced. In particular, at each level of capital goods per worker, output per worker is increased, as illustrated in Figure 37.5. The upper line represents the higher level of productivity at each capital goods–labor ratio resulting from technological change.

These four sources of productivity growth are interrelated. For example, the invention of a new machine (technological change) may also require new investment (increases in capital goods) in order to enter the economy. The idea of a jet engine does not increase productivity until the new jet engines are actually produced. New ideas do not simply happen; it takes researchers, engineers, and good managers to bring them about. This in turn requires a high level of human capital. Though the movement from agriculture to industry was reflected in an increase in average productivity, that movement would not have been possible without the innovations that increased productivity in agriculture so enormously.

Though all four factors are important and intertwined, economists have tried to measure their relative importance. The classic study in this area is by Robert Solow of MIT, who received the Nobel Prize for his work on growth theory. He estimated that increases in the supply of capital goods have accounted for approximately one-eighth of the increases in productivity. The rest of the growth was due to the other three factors. Edward Denison of the Brookings Institution has concluded that while human capital is important, technological change has played the predominant role.[1] The sections that follow take a closer look at each of the four sources of productivity growth.

INCREASES IN THE ACCUMULATION OF CAPITAL GOODS (INVESTMENT)

Economists dispute exactly how important the accumulation of capital goods is, but there is no disagreement about two simpler propositions: no country has gone from being less developed to more developed without the accumulation of a considerable amount of capital goods, and countries that fail to maintain their level of capital goods per worker suffer decreases in productivity. Thus, countries that have rapidly growing populations must invest a great deal just to provide new entrants to the labor force with the machines required to sustain their productivity. The United States does not have a rapidly growing population, but during the 1970s it had a rapidly growing labor force, as more and more women decided to work outside the home. Given the low rate of accumulation of capital goods in the United States during the 1970s, this entry of new

---

[1] Just as measurement problems make it difficult to obtain a precise estimate of the rate of growth of productivity, they also make it difficult to obtain a good estimate of the relative importance of various sources of economic growth. Dale Jorgenson of Harvard University, for instance, claims that most of the increase in productivity can be attributed to increases in capital goods.

workers is one reason that measured productivity slowed down at about this time.

Investment is also required to implement new technologies. Without high rates of investment, American industry will fall behind technologically. To take one example, even by 1984 Japan had more than three times the number of industrial robots that the United States had.

WHY INVESTMENT (CAPITAL GOODS) IS IMPORTANT

1. It provides new entrants into the labor force with machines to make them productive.

2. It provides existing workers with more machines, to increase their productivity.

3. It implements new technologies.

HOW IMPORTANT ARE DIMINISHING RETURNS?

Figure 37.5 showed that as the capital goods per worker increase, diminishing returns set in, so that successive increments in capital goods have less and less effect on output per worker. This has one extremely important implication. Higher investment rates (that is, the fraction of national output that is invested) cannot sustain higher *rates of growth* in the economy forever, though they can lead to a sustained increase in the *level* of per capita income. As the economy's per capita capital goods stock increases, a higher investment rate is required simply to sustain that higher level, to give new workers the machines with which to work and to replace old machines as they wear out. Higher investment rates can help provide a short-term spur to the economy.

If increases in the amount of capital goods per worker were the only, or primary, source of increases in productivity—in output per worker—then we would expect diminishing returns eventually to set in, no matter how high the investment rate. The higher *rates of growth* of productivity could only be sustained by higher and higher investment rates. Figure 37.6 shows the movements in the rate of growth of productivity in the United States since 1839. Note that from 1879 to 1959 the rate of growth of productivity increased—during a period in which there was an enormous accumulation of capital goods. The United States was able to sustain a high and in fact increasing rate of productivity growth for long periods of time without diminishing returns seeming to set in.

Similar patterns have been observed elsewhere. Japan, for the past quarter century, has had huge investment rates, resulting in large increases in capital goods per worker. Yet the rate of productivity growth has not decreased in the way that one would have expected on the basis of diminishing returns.

The reason that diminishing returns did not seem to set in in these instances is that the technological change more than offset the effects of diminishing returns. The high rate of technological progress accompanying the high rate of investment may not have

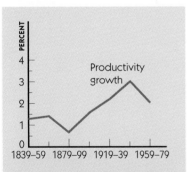

Figure 37.6 LONG-RUN U.S. PRODUCTIVITY GROWTH

Productivity growth increased sharply during the first part of the twentieth century, a period of rapid capital goods accumulation, before declining in the last few decades. *Source:* Paul M. Romer, "Capital Accumulation in the Theory of Long-Run Growth," in Barro, ed., *Modern Business Cycle Theory* (1989).

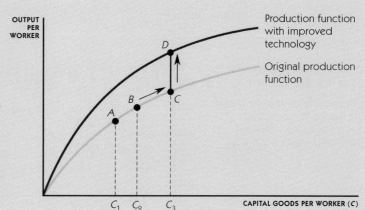

Figure 37.7 EXPLAINING THE FAILURE TO OBSERVE DIMINISHING RETURNS

With a given production function, the increase in capital goods per worker from C_2 to C_3 would result in a smaller increase in productivity than the corresponding increase from C_1 to C_2. But as the economy increases its capital goods per worker, the production function shifts. Rather than moving from B to C, the economy moves from B to D. The proportionate increase in output per worker may be as large as or even larger than the movement from A to B.

been a mere accident. There is, in fact, a double link between investment and technological change. Higher rates of technological change increase investment, because the new technologies provide better investment opportunities; at the same time, higher rates of investment provide manufacturers of machines greater incentives to develop new, improved machines. The consequences of investment accompanied by technological change can be seen in Figure 37.7. As the economy invests more, the production function shifts up enough to offset the effects of diminishing returns. Thus, the output per worker increases proportionately as capital goods per worker increase.

THE LINK BETWEEN SAVINGS AND INVESTMENT: CLOSED VERSUS OPEN ECONOMIES

In a closed economy, the level of investment is determined by the domestic level of savings. Investment equals savings, and investment cannot be increased without greater savings. In an open economy, the link between the two is loosened, since a country can borrow from abroad to finance its investment. Chapter 38 will explore the enormous amount of foreign borrowing that the United States has done during the 1980s. But by and large, it remains true that savings and investment within a country have tended to move together, as shown by data for the United States in Figure 37.8.[2]

This might be so for a number of reasons. One possibility is that so much of investment in modern economies is done within large corporations, which finance much of their investment out of retained earnings, and which save more when they see better investment opportunities.

Although savings and investment do tend to move together, each one responds to different stimuli; and understanding the spurs to each will help policymakers in their goal of improving productivity.

[2] The close link between savings and investment even for economies that are supposedly open was noted in a famous paper by Martin Feldstein and Charles Horioka in the *Economic Journal* (June 1980), vol. 90, no. 358. There is by now a large literature that tries to explain this puzzling finding.

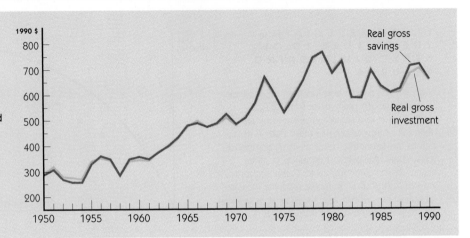

Figure 37.8 SAVINGS AND INVESTMENT

Savings and investment within the United States have tended to move closely together, as is true of most countries. *Source: ERP* (1992), Tables B-2, B-3.

WHY ARE U.S. SAVINGS SO LOW?

There are three sources of savings: personal (or household) savings, business savings, and government savings (the fiscal surplus, when the government has one). Figure 37.9 shows how each of these as well as total savings has changed over time. Total U.S. savings were extraordinarily low in the 1980s. We can also see this in Figure 37.10, which compares the savings in the United States with those of other countries. The U.S. savings rate is less than one-seventh that of Japan.

Figure 37.9 makes clear that the low level can be attributed to the huge government

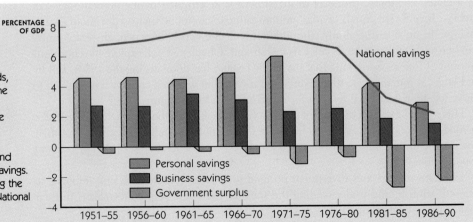

Figure 37.9 THE DECLINE IN U.S. SAVINGS

Savings can come from households, business, or government. During the 1980s, total national savings were exceptionally low. Though all three components were low, the most significant decline arose from government savings, and the second most significant from household savings. *Source:* John Shoven, "Determining the Future of America: Pensions and National Saving" (unpublished, 1991).

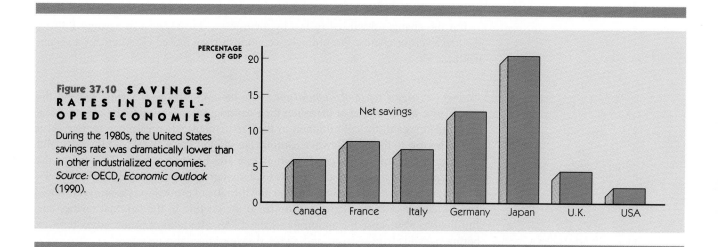

Figure 37.10 SAVINGS RATES IN DEVELOPED ECONOMIES

During the 1980s, the United States savings rate was dramatically lower than in other industrialized economies. *Source:* OECD, *Economic Outlook* (1990).

deficits and a remarkably low level of household savings of recent years. What gave rise to the government deficits will be discussed in Chapter 38. Here, the focus is on household savings.

The low household savings rate and its decline in recent years is partially explainable in terms of the motives for saving and changes in the American economy in recent decades, though the extent of the decline is both disturbing and puzzling. Chapters 9 and 29 identified several motives for saving: people save for retirement (life-cycle savings) and to buy a home, to pay for their children's college education or to meet certain other needs (target savings); people save for emergencies, for a rainy day, for periods in which their incomes may be low either because they are laid off from their job or because they are sick (precautionary savings); and people save to leave something to their children (bequest savings). Furthermore, we saw that savings can be analyzed like any other consumption choice. The price (with savings, this is the interest rate) and the public's "taste" for savings—their attitudes about the future—also influence rates of saving.

During the past two decades, virtually all of the motives and incentives for saving changed in a way to discourage saving. Improved Social Security (particularly during the 1970s) reduced the need for savings for retirement; improved capital markets and insurance—provided by both government and employers—meant that people did not have to save as much for emergencies; improved capital markets also meant that people did not have to save as much for a down payment for a house; and improved government student-loan programs meant that parents did not have to save as much for their children's education.

On the other hand, there were some changes that should have stimulated savings. We saw in Chapter 9 that what is relevant for savings is the real after-tax return. This return can increase if either tax rates are lowered (so that the individual gets to keep more of the return) or real before-tax returns rise. In the 1980s, taxes on the return to capital, particularly for upper-income levels, plummeted—from 70 percent in 1980 to 28 percent in 1986—and real before-tax returns soared. Nevertheless, savings fell. This should not come as too much of a surprise: we also learned in Chapter 9 that the effect of changes in real after-tax interest rates on savings, while positive, is probably small.[3]

But the changes discussed so far, by themselves, do not seem to account fully for the low levels of savings. Accordingly, economists have looked elsewhere for an explanation.

Changes in Age Profile of Population   The life-cycle theory of savings suggests that people save in the period of life when their earnings are relatively high (ages 45–65) to accumulate wealth for consumption in their retirement, when earnings are low. Also, people borrow in their youth when earnings are still low (ages 21–44), yet their demands for expensive consumption goods such as cars and houses are high. This means that the age profile of the population affects total savings. Since the middle 1970s, the 45–65 age group has grown relatively smaller and the ratio of prime savers to prime borrowers has decreased, with a pattern very similar to the decline in the personal savings rate. But there is also cause for optimism: in the 1990s, the ratio of prime savers to prime borrowers is likely to recover, and personal savings may also increase.

Changes in Personal Values   Many economists believe that changes in attitudes and values are more responsible for the decline in the savings rate in the United States than the changes in economic conditions and institutions. What is sometimes referred to as the "Me" generation wants immediate gratification; its willingness to defer consumption to a later date is very low. In nineteenth-century discussions of the rise of capitalism, writers like Max Weber placed considerable stress on the importance of the "work ethic" and savings, with these values being particularly associated with certain religious beliefs. The weakening of religious beliefs during recent decades may have been accompanied by a corresponding weakening in these values.

Other changes in cultural patterns have reduced the level of bequest motive savings. Social changes have loosened the links among family members. Just as Social Security has meant that children take less responsibility for their parents as they age, parents may increasingly feel that aside from being entitled to a good education, children should be responsible for themselves. Such changes in cultural attitudes would be reflected in a lower level of bequests.

Statistical Confusion   Another view is that the statistics underestimate savings and thus overestimate the extent of the savings problem. From the perspective of the individual, savings can be thought of as an increase in wealth. Savings, in this view, should include not only new investments but also "unrealized" capital gains. After all, people care about the total return they get from an asset, the capital gain plus the dividend or interest, and accordingly both should be treated as part of income, and any capital gains that are not "realized" by selling the asset should be treated as part of savings.

During the 1970s and 1980s, the price of houses increased enormously. In effect, individuals were increasing their wealth simply by holding on to their houses; they were saving, not by taking a part of their paycheck down to the bank, but simply by letting their houses appreciate in value. They could, of course, have tried to borrow against

---

[3] There, we saw that while the *substitution* effect leads to increased savings, the *income* effect results in reduced savings. While on theoretical grounds the *net* effect is ambiguous, the evidence supports a small positive effect.

Close-up: Accounting for Growth

Many economists have attempted to quantify the role played by capital accumulation, improvements in education, shorter working hours, and technological change. One of the most widely cited studies is by Edward Denison of the Brookings Institution. In his calculations, 20 percent of the total increase in productivity is due to increases in capital, and 27 percent is due to increases in human capital, as shown in the table.

At the bottom of the table is a category labeled "Residual"—the part of increased productivity that cannot be explained by other factors. Most of the residual is interpreted as being technological change. But the residual could also include the myriad of other factors discussed in this chapter, such as the legal and regulatory environment. Since some of these factors have actually worked against productivity, the role of technological progress, of innovation, may be even more important than these calculations suggest.

The major controversy in these numbers is as-sociated with the role of capital accumulation. Some economists believe that capital accumulation is far more important than these numbers would suggest, partly because without new investment there would not be learning by doing, new techniques would not be introduced into the economy, and the spur to R & D would be reduced.

THE SOURCES OF ECONOMIC GROWTH

Fraction of increases in output per worker accounted for by	
Capital accumulation	20%
Human capital	27%
Shorter hours	−12%
Reallocation of resources	16%
Economies of scale	18%
Residual	31%

Source: Edward F. Denison, *Trends in American Economic Growth, 1929–1982* (Washington, D.C.: Brookings Institution, 1985).

their houses. They could have consumed more than their wages and interest income. But they chose not to; they chose to save their capital gains. Conventional statistics measuring savings as a fraction of national income or GDP do not include capital gains. In this view, then, America does not have a problem with the *level* of household savings, but with the form the savings take. Savings are largely in the form of capital gains for housing, which do not allow for a flow of resources into manufacturing and production.

This problem has plagued many poorer countries, where savings have gone into purchases of land or holdings of gold rather than uses that would have a greater effect on increasing productivity. Those who believe that most savings are in the form of capital gains put some of the blame on government: tax policies have encouraged investment in housing. They believe that removing these tax preferences would induce a flow of resources elsewhere.

Still, while the capital gains on housing may provide part of the explanation of the low savings rate (as conventionally measured), it probably does not account for all of it. And it does not resolve the basic problem: how to increase the flow of funds available to be invested in the new machines and new enterprises that would increase the productivity of the economy.

Stymied by a Low Savings Rate All in all, both government officials and economists feel somewhat stymied by the low level of savings. The price-related tools that economists like to work with best, like changes in real after-tax interest rates, are not likely by themselves to prove effective. Savings do not seem to be very sensitive to real after-tax interest rates.[4] It would prove difficult, to say the least, to substantially reduce Social Security or medical insurance or to make it more difficult for people to borrow, all in the name of increasing the savings rate! In fact, few seriously advocate such steps.

Thus, microeconomic instruments to stimulate household savings are likely, at best, to have small effects. The other major reason for low national savings is the huge government deficits. While the government may be ineffective in stimulating private savings, it might be able to get its own house in order. But doing that, as we will see in the next chapter, is perhaps easier said than done.

THE PUZZLE OF THE LOW AMERICAN SAVINGS RATE

Factor that increases the savings rate
    High real after-tax interest rates
Factors that decrease the savings rate
    Reduced need for life-cycle savings: improved Social Security
    Reduced need for precautionary savings: better insurance and easier access to
        the capital market
    Reduced bequest motive savings: changes in social attitudes
    Changes in age profile of the population
    Underestimates of savings as a result of unrealized capital gains from home own-
        ership

THE LEVEL AND ALLOCATION OF INVESTMENT

There are two concerns about investment in the United States: that the level of investment is too low, and that too much investment has gone into areas—like real estate—that do not contribute much to long-run productivity growth.

A Bad Investment Climate: High Risk and Problems in Obtaining Finance A number of factors contributed to the relatively low level of investment in the 1980s, including high costs of capital, a heightened sense of uncertainty, and increased government regulations.

The cost of obtaining funds was substantially higher in the United States than in Japan, and the real interest rates in the United States during the 1980s were very high,

---

[4] As noted earlier, income and substitution effects work in the opposite direction.

and highly variable, by historical standards. By the same token, funds for investment in new machines, new ventures, and research and development seemed to be less available, as Wall Street focused its energies on high-profile takeovers and corporate reorganizations. Funds became even less available in the late 1980s and early 1990s; as their real estate and other loans went sour, many banks responded to severe economic problems by tightening credit standards, and as many of the supposedly great deals of the early and mid-1980s wound up in bankruptcy, many investors became more skeptical of new security issues.

Frequent changes in tax laws, highly variable interest rates, and extreme fluctuations of exchange rates all contributed to a sense of business uncertainty. As we learned in Chapter 35, exchange rate volatility, for instance, means that exporters do not know whether they will be able to sell their goods abroad (at a price at which they can recover their costs), and domestic producers worry about the threat of foreign competition. This uncertainty has discouraged firms from making the long-term commitments that are associated with investment.

The Effect of Rules and Regulations on Investment   Government rules and regulations can affect investment too. Changes in regulations during the past two decades may have contributed to the productivity slowdown, by both discouraging investment and forcing investment to take forms that do not show up directly in the national income statistics.

There is concern, for instance, that laws aimed at protecting the environment force businesses to put too much of their money into clean air rather than into more efficient methods of production. The improved quality of air benefits the standard of living, of course, but is not reflected in GDP statistics or hence in productivity measures. Investment in the electric power industry, particularly in nuclear power plants, has been dominated by environmental concerns. Billions of dollars were invested in nuclear power plants around the United States, but in some cases plants were never put into production. The investments were, in effect, lost. Even when some plants did go into operation, the delays caused by environmental concerns added much to the cost.

People in the construction industry often point to the myriad of regulations that raise their costs and decrease their productivity. For instance, obtaining approval of plans leads to delays, and these delays bring large costs. In some places where the delays may be particularly long, like New York City, those in the industry claim that they raise the cost of construction by as much as a third.

Misallocating Investment   Taxes affect both the level of investment and its allocation. In the early 1980s, the tax laws gave extremely favorable tax treatment to commercial real estate such as office buildings. These laws, combined with a widespread belief that they were too generous to be permanent, spurred a boom in commercial real estate, which by the mid-1980s had resulted in oversupply. Vacancy rates for commercial real estate were as high as 20–30 percent in many urban areas. The anticipation that these benefits were only temporary was correct: the Tax Reform Act of 1986 took most of the special treatment away.

Tax changes in 1981 also contained special provisions intended to encourage investment in "smokestack America," the heavy industries like steel and automobiles. The provisions were successful in some cases; with these tax breaks and additional indirect subsidies from trade protectionism, the automobile industry retooled and once again became competitive (at least for a while). But in other industries, such as steel, even the combination of tax breaks and trade protectionism did not seem to be enough.

A broad intent of the 1986 Tax Reform Act was to provide a more "level" playing field, so that scarce investment resources would be used where their productivity was highest, not where tax benefits were the greatest. In this it was only partially successful. For instance, the special, favorable treatment of the oil and gas industries was retained. In addition, housing continues to receive favorable treatment. Interest paid on a home mortgage loan is deductible from income subject to tax, and there are a variety of provisions in the tax laws that assure that most of the gains in the value of housing escape the capital gains tax.

Investment in Infrastructure The U.S. interstate highway system has been called the eighth wonder of the world. This system together with others such as airports, bridges, and sewer lines form an infrastructure that allows the economy to operate. These physical investments are of real importance to the sustained productivity of the economy. There is a growing concern that the government's failure to maintain this infrastructure at an adequate level, and to improve it to keep pace with the potential growth of the economy, will act as a dampening force on future economic growth. For instance, the nation's airports have not been able to keep up with the increase in air traffic; and the interstate highway system that was created in the 1950s is, at critical points, not up to the burden of the 1990s.

Encouraging Investment Encouraging investment is not much easier and may be more problematic than encouraging savings. Most economists would agree that government should provide more of the basic infrastructure, such as roads and airports, which are its responsibility, and reduce unnecessary regulatory interference. The disagreement arises in trying to figure out which of the regulations could be eliminated or simplified without serious harm to the objectives for which the regulations were adopted. Though few would advocate stripping away all environmental and safety regulations, many economists think that some of the regulations yield at best marginal benefits at huge costs.

The government can use tax policy to encourage investment—for instance, by providing investment tax credits (see Chapter 29). But in the past, at least, its policies have led as much to a misallocation of investment, by stimulating tax-favored investments at the expense of others, as they have to an overall increase in the level of investment.

Looser monetary policies (lower interest rates) can encourage investment. To offset the inflationary pressures to which such policies may give rise, government may need to have tighter fiscal policies—it may have to limit government expenditures and increase taxes on households. In fact, during the 1980s, the government pursued exactly the opposite pair of policies: tight monetary policies combined with large government deficits. Only the huge inflow of funds from abroad prevented this combination of policies from having disastrous effects on U.S. investment.

HIGHER QUALITY OF THE LABOR FORCE

A second source of productivity growth is the quality of the labor force. If workers become more efficient, so that a worker can do in one hour what used to take two, productivity will increase. Many factors contribute to the productivity of labor. Good nutrition and health are obviously important, and the last century has made great strides in this direction. Shorter work weeks may enable workers to be more productive while they are working, and thus may contribute not only to the quality of life but also to the quality of work. In 1947, the typical work week was 40.3 hours; by 1990, it was 34.5 hours.

Recent discussions of the quality of the labor force have focused on workers' skills. The more skilled the labor force, the higher will be the economy's productivity. There is a general consensus that it would be difficult if not impossible to run a modern industrial economy without a well-educated labor force. In addition, an economy on the cutting edge of technological change needs trained engineers and scientists to discover and shape those innovations. There is concern that the United States has been falling behind both in providing a basic core education to everyone and in training enough engineers and scientists.

THE SYMPTOMS OF A HUMAN CAPITAL PROBLEM

Judging from the well-publicized decline in scores on Scholastic Aptitude Tests and similar tests from the late 1960s through the early 1980s, high schools may be failing to educate students in the basic areas of knowledge. News stories often report high levels of illiteracy in the United States, or report that students in other countries do far better on tests of mathematical or science aptitude than do U.S. students. Figure 37.11 shows that in 1988 American students performed more poorly in math tests than students in Ireland, South Korea, Spain, or the United Kingdom, and more poorly in the science exam than students in all of the countries except Ireland. Figure 37.12 suggests a growing problem at the secondary school level. While declines in science proficiency during the seventies were slight among 9-year-olds, they were significant among 17-year-olds. Of course, these standardized tests are imperfect and limited; one of many problems with them is that they do not measure creativity. But the tests do measure success in certain objectives of education, such as mastery over basic skills, and the poor performance of American students is accordingly disturbing.

Similarly, while America remains unique in the large fraction of its youth that go on from high school to college, the proportion of the population that chooses to study

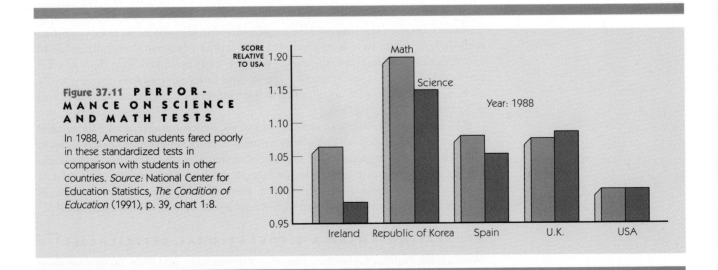

Figure 37.11 PERFORMANCE ON SCIENCE AND MATH TESTS

In 1988, American students fared poorly in these standardized tests in comparison with students in other countries. *Source:* National Center for Education Statistics, *The Condition of Education* (1991), p. 39, chart 1:8.

SCORE RELATIVE TO USA

Math

Science

Year: 1988

Ireland   Republic of Korea   Spain   U.K.   USA

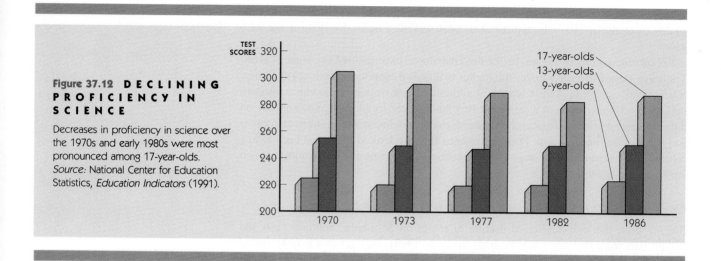

Figure 37.12 DECLINING PROFICIENCY IN SCIENCE

Decreases in proficiency in science over the 1970s and early 1980s were most pronounced among 17-year-olds. *Source:* National Center for Education Statistics, *Education Indicators* (1991).

engineering or science or math is declining. The result is that today, while there are 65 researchers per 10,000 workers in the United States, Japan has almost a quarter more, 79.

THE STRENGTHS OF AMERICA'S EDUCATIONAL SYSTEM

While America's elementary and secondary schooling has come under extensive criticism, its educational system as a whole has some distinct strengths. One is the greater commitment to egalitarianism. For instance, young children are not assigned particular schools that will determine whether or not they can go on to college. Early "tracking" of this sort, based on test scores, gives a distinct advantage to children with more educated parents.

Another great strength is the U.S. system of junior colleges and state universities, many of which provide a high-quality education to those who could not afford to go to private schools or who may not have performed well in high school. In many countries, such students would have been precluded from further education. Ironically, while in many respects the American educational system is more egalitarian than those of other developed countries, in one respect it is less so: most European countries charge virtually no tuition to students who are admitted to their universities, and some actually pay all or part of students' living costs.

A third strength is America's universities overall, which number among the greatest in the world. Students from virtually every other country come to the United States to study, as both undergraduates and graduate students. The discoveries and innovations flowing out of the universities' research laboratories have been an important basis of America's technological superiority. Indeed, the success of the universities, in light of the problems at the elementary and high school levels, appears almost paradoxical.

ADDRESSING AMERICA'S EDUCATIONAL DEFICIENCIES

What are the sources of America's educational deficiencies, and what can be done about them? To some, the sources lie not so much in the educational system itself as in society more broadly. The University of Chicago's James Coleman has, for instance, expressed concern that with fewer women staying at home with children, there is less education going on at home; and this home education is an important complement to what schools provide. Indeed, Coleman's statistical studies show that school performance is better explained by these "home factors" than by differences in expenditures in the schools.

Other changes in society have increased the challenges facing elementary and secondary schools. There is strong evidence of a decline in the quality of teachers, particularly in the sciences. One reason is that as job opportunities for women have increased, many of the able women who formerly would have gone into teaching because of the circumscribed opportunities elsewhere are now seeking employment in higher-paying jobs.

One of the educational system's great strengths—its commitment to egalitarian education—may impair one of its basic objectives, to provide the most able students with the skills required to help the country sustain technological superiority. An increasing commitment to egalitarianism means that a larger proportion of the available resources go into raising slower learners up to a minimal level than into helping faster learners cover as much material as they can. At the same time, several states have actually imposed limits on the expenditures of richer school districts—an approach to equality that its critics call leveling down rather than leveling up.

While there is a consensus that America's educational system has its problems, there is no consensus on what should be done. It seems clear that more resources would help. For one thing, improving teachers' pay would improve the quality of teachers. But how much extra funds would help is much debated—expenditures per pupil increased significantly over the past fifteen years, and they are considerably higher in the United States than in other countries that seem to consistently outperform the United States. There is a general view that money only is not the solution. In any case, in the prevailing mood of financial stringency, substantial expenditure increases seem unlikely.

Recent discussions have focused on reorganizing the educational system, in ways that would elicit more involvement from parents and more commitment from teachers. One proposal would decentralize public schools, giving more discretion to the principal in the running of her school. Another advocates more competition between private and public schools. In one widely discussed plan, the government would provide educational vouchers that parents could use to enroll their children at either public or private schools. A more limited proposal would let students enroll at any public school within a certain district. Advocates of proposals like these, which were endorsed by President Bush in 1991, believe that competition among schools will improve their quality, and the process of choice will enhance commitment and involvement of all participants in the educational process.

THE CHANGING MIX OF THE WORK FORCE

The productivity of the work force is affected by the mix of workers of which it is composed. Very young workers, for instance, are less productive, because they have not yet acquired the range of skills that can only be obtained by experience. And very old workers are often less productive, both because the skills they have acquired may have become obsolete and because of health problems. Historically, women have been less educated and have remained out of the labor force during their childbearing years; they therefore lacked the productivity-enhancing job experiences of their male counterparts. Today these differences have become much less important.

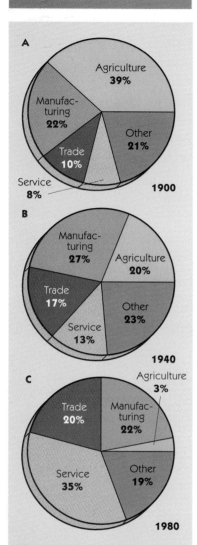

Figure 37.13 **SECTORAL SHIFTS**

Employment in the U.S. economy shifted from agriculture to manufacturing industries in the first half of this century and from manufacturing to services in the second half. *Sources: Historical Statistics of the United States* (1975); *Survey of Current Business* (1981).

As we have seen, there were important changes in the composition of the labor force in the 1970s and 1980s, from the influx of baby boomers who reached working age and the dramatic increase in the fraction of women who sought employment outside the home. To the extent that new workers in the labor force are actually less productive than those already *in* the labor force, the new workers will tend to bring down the average productivity as measured by standard productivity statistics. However, if new workers are nonetheless more productive in the job market than they used to be when they were not in the job market, then the true productivity of the economy will increase. This increase, however, will not be captured in the productivity statistics.

By the same token, early retirement has become much more of a possibility in recent years. In 1900, 68 percent of men over age sixty-five were holding jobs or looking for jobs, while in 1988 the figure had fallen to 11.5 percent. However, these late working years that have been cut off are (on average) among a worker's least productive years, and thus early retirement has probably helped create a work force that is *more* productive on average.

Finally, it appears that unemployment may have a long-term effect on the quality of the labor force. In general, sustained work experience makes workers more productive over time. In a deep recession, though, when unemployment climbs near 10 percent or even higher, a large number of workers are not adding any experience. In fact, some of their work skills may atrophy. In this way, a deep recession can mean a reduction not only in current output but in the growth of future output as well.

The changing composition of the labor force and periods of unemployment, while they play an important role in determining changes in productivity in the long run, are probably not that important in explaining the productivity slowdown. On the other hand, a deterioration in the quality of schools—a lower level of human capital—may play a role, the quantitative significance of which is hard to ascertain.

REALLOCATING RESOURCES FROM LOW- TO HIGH-PRODUCTIVITY SECTORS

During the past century, the United States has evolved from an agricultural economy to an industrial economy to a service economy. Figure 37.13 shows this dramatic structural change. The service sector, broadly defined, includes not only traditional services such as haircuts and restaurant meals but also the services provided by doctors and lawyers, educational institutions, secretaries, accountants, and computer programmers. The medical sector alone has grown to the point where today it accounts for more than 11 percent of GDP.

The movement out of agriculture and into industry explains much of the productivity increase in the early part of the century. While the level of productivity in agriculture was increasing rapidly, it remained lower than the level in industry. Thus, as workers shifted out of low-productivity jobs in agriculture into high-productivity jobs in manufacturing, average productivity in the economy increased.

TECHNOLOGICAL CHANGE

This final source of productivity growth may be the most important. One of the major ways that the economy today is different from what it was at the start of this century is that the modern economy has made change routine: it has created systematic processes by which knowledge is acquired, translated into uses, and applied. The prototype of the nineteenth- and early twentieth-century inventors were men like Thomas Edison and Alexander Graham Bell—lone individuals, working by themselves or with a small number of collaborators. By contrast, the prototype of a modern research effort might be something like the U.S. program to put a man on the moon, in which thousands of scientists worked together to accomplish in the space of a few short years what would have been almost unimaginable a short time before. Modern research is centered in huge laboratories, some of them employing thousands of people. While some of these laboratories are run by the government, such as the Brookhaven, Argonne, and Lawrence laboratories, which carry out research in basic physics, many are private, like Bell Labs (part of AT&T), where the transistor and laser were developed. Indeed, most major firms have research departments and spend approximately 3 percent of their gross revenues on research and development.

Although much of the research today requires capital expenditures that far exceed the means of any individual, small entrepreneurs and innovators do continue to play a role in developing new products. The computer industry in particular has been marked by a disproportionate number of major innovations created by relatively small firms, as compared with those developed by the industry leader, IBM.

The current level of technological progress has become so expected that it is hard to believe how different the view of reputable economists was in the early 1800s. After all, by then the real wages of workers were little higher than they had been five hundred years earlier, when the bubonic plague destroyed a large part of the population of Europe and thereby created a great scarcity of labor. After half a millennium of at best slow progress, it is no wonder that economists writing in the early nineteenth century had such a gloomy view of the future! Thomas Malthus, one of the greatest economists of that time, saw population expanding more rapidly than the capacity of the economy to support it. What was missing from these dismal forecasts was technological change.

But while we have come to expect technological progress, confidence in America's technological superiority has eroded during the past two decades. *Some* of the observed decline in the rate of productivity growth is related to the changes in the composition of output noted earlier.

Some economists, such as William Baumol of New York and Princeton universities, contend that the decline in heavy industry—in steel, automobiles, and manufacturing in general—and relative growth in the service sector help explain the recent slowdown in productivity growth. They worry that the opportunities for innovation in the service sector are lower than in manufacturing or agriculture. They cite haircutting as an example: the only major innovation in this field in the past hundred years has been the electric hair clipper. Other economists are more hopeful. They cite the development by McDonald's of more efficient ways of delivering "fast food" and improvements by many of the country's major retailers that have reduced the markup of retail prices over wholesale costs. In addition, the computer revolution continues to open up new technological possibilities in service industries such as banking, insurance, accounting, and design.

But there is more to the productivity slowdown than just the change in the composition of output. One indicator of technological leadership is the number of patents. Figure 37.14 shows that today, relative to the size of the population, the United States is performing more poorly (by this indicator) than Japan, the United Kingdom, and Germany.

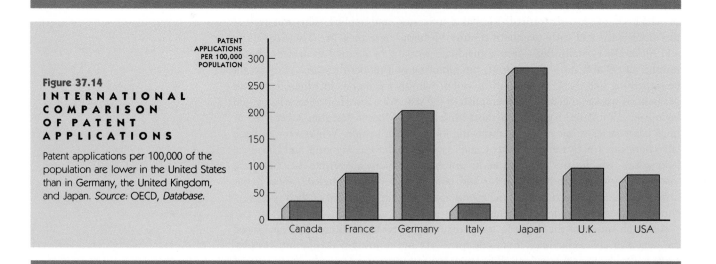

Figure 37.14
INTERNATIONAL COMPARISON OF PATENT APPLICATIONS

Patent applications per 100,000 of the population are lower in the United States than in Germany, the United Kingdom, and Japan. *Source:* OECD, *Database.*

SOURCES OF TECHNOLOGICAL PROGRESS

While technological progress in modern industrialized society is largely the result of searches for new ideas, new products, and better ways of producing, some of it happens through experience. As we learned in Chapter 18, this is called learning by doing: in the process of production, firms learn how to produce their goods more efficiently. The learning curve describes how costs come down with experience. Figure 37.15 shows the learning curve for building air frames (the basic bodies of airplanes) during World

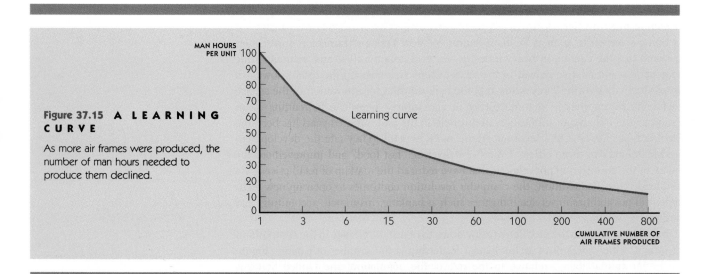

Figure 37.15 A LEARNING CURVE

As more air frames were produced, the number of man hours needed to produce them declined.

War II. As more and more air frames were constructed, better and better ways of organizing the production were discovered, and costs of production fell dramatically.

There is often an intimate connection between progress resulting from R & D expenditures and progress resulting from learning by doing. Firms learn more if they systematically study their production experiences. For instance, they can experiment with different ways of organizing a production process, or give some employees the primary responsibility of thinking about how productivity can be improved. In Japan, about 10 percent of the labor force in manufacturing consists of engineers who are directly involved in production and whose task is to make constant incremental improvements in production processes.

While discussions of technological progress often focus on manufacturing, and particularly on dramatic inventions such as transistors and lasers, no less important are those smaller innovations that year by year lead to steadily higher levels of productivity. This has been particularly evident in agriculture. The output of U.S. farms per worker has increased eightfold in the last forty years. Productivity increases like these have enabled a relatively small fraction of the population to provide all the food requirements for the whole country. Various government programs prohibit or discourage farmers from planting all they can, but even so, the United States exports roughly one-third of its agricultural produce. These rapid advances in agricultural productivity have resulted from mechanization (the use of the tractor), the development of better fertilizers, new techniques of planting, new seeds, and a better adaptation of seeds, fertilizers, crops, and farming patterns to local conditions.

POLICIES TO INCREASE THE RATE OF TECHNOLOGICAL CHANGE

There are some important connections between government programs to stabilize the economy and the economy's rate of technological progress. If the government is successful in sustaining the economy near full employment, it will at the same time stimulate productivity growth. In a recession, national economic output actually declines, which means that the amount of "doing," and hence the amount of learning by doing, in the economy falls as well. Furthermore, when profit margins are squeezed to the bone in a recession, firms are less likely to take the risk of trying out slightly new production processes or undertaking the risks of research and development expenditures. These are among the expenditures that are cut in an economic downturn. Macroeconomic policies that maintain the economy at a high level of output and employment are therefore one important way that the government can help promote growth.

There are also a variety of "microeconomic" government policies that affect the rate of technological progress. Unfortunately, the link between these policies and technological progress is often difficult to perceive, since the benefits from increased productivity may be felt only years later. Because the consequences of cutbacks in R & D are not felt immediately, they are an obvious target when either the government or private firms are in a period of financial stringency. By the same token, it may be years before the effects of the low expenditures of the 1980s show up in the productivity statistics. To the extent that the productivity slowdown in the 1970s was due to decreased expenditures on research, it would have been due to a decrease in expenditures in the 1950s and 1960s. But the 1960s in particular were a period of high spending on research; some economists are therefore skeptical about the role of the levels of expenditures on research in explaining the *current* U.S. productivity slowdown.

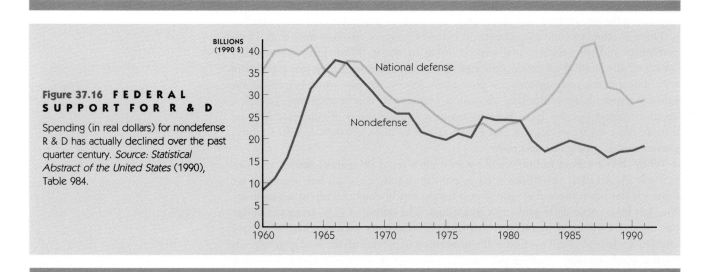

Figure 37.16 FEDERAL SUPPORT FOR R & D

Spending (in real dollars) for nondefense R & D has actually declined over the past quarter century. *Source: Statistical Abstract of the United States* (1990), Table 984.

Direct Expenditures: Military and Civilian Not only is the U.S. educational system producing too few scientists and engineers, the human resources required for innovation and invention, the government has diverted a large fraction of what scientists there are into military research. While the Department of Defense points with pride to the many civilian benefits of military research, presumably engineers who were focused on non-military problems would have generated even greater benefits for the civilian economy. Thus, from the 1960s through the 1980s, while Japanese scientists and engineers were devoting their efforts to building better consumer products, a disproportionate fraction of America's scientists and engineers were devoting their efforts to building better bombs, missiles and other weapons.

To be sure, the government does provide considerable direct support of R & D. Some of the government's funding is for research in the basic principles of science, what can be thought of as the underlying intellectual infrastructure.[5] Still, most of government research support has been in defense-oriented work, which naturally tends to focus on the breakthroughs that would be most helpful in producing weapons, not those that increase overall economic productivity. Indeed, as Figure 37.16 makes clear, actual spending (in constant dollars) on nondefense R & D has actually declined in the past quarter century. As a percentage of GDP, the decline has been even more dramatic.

Furthermore, Figure 37.17 shows that while in terms of total R & D (relative to the size of the economy) the United States does not fare badly—only Japan spends more—once we subtract military R & D, government support in the United States is much weaker than in many developed countries.

---

[5] Chapter 18 explained why basic research is normally the responsibility of government. Basic research is a public good, the benefits of which accrue to many firms, often in many different industries, and to their consumers. Research also has large positive externalities. If the responsibility was left to the private sector, there would be too little research.

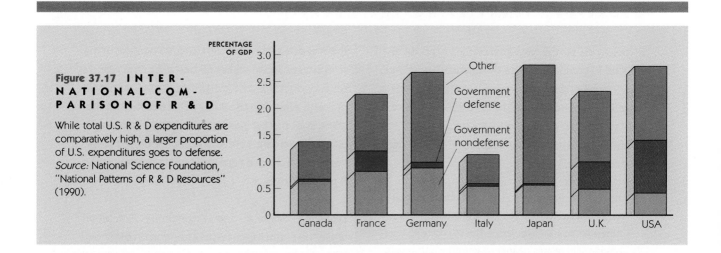

Figure 37.17 INTER-NATIONAL COMPARISON OF R & D

While total U.S. R & D expenditures are comparatively high, a larger proportion of U.S. expenditures goes to defense. *Source:* National Science Foundation, "National Patterns of R & D Resources" (1990).

Taxes   Taxes that reduce the return to investments in general also reduce the return to investments in research and development and thus discourage R & D. The Tax Reform Act of 1986 included higher taxes on capital gains. Since a large part of the return obtained by entrepreneurs takes the form of capital gains—when a high-tech company is successful, its shares soar in value—there was considerable concern that this tax increase would discourage R & D.

Many government policies to encourage R & D are similar to those used to encourage other forms of investment.[6] The government has one tax program directed specifically at research and development: R & D tax credits. Through these credits, the government in effect pays part of the costs of R & D.

The Legal and Regulatory Environment   There has been concern that changes in the U.S. legal environment have had an adverse effect on innovation. When a firm develops a new product, there is always some danger that even after it has been well tested, there may be some adverse effects. For example, some drugs may have unanticipated side effects that show up only years later. Courts in recent years have provided huge awards to compensate victims of such drugs. While these suits have encouraged producers to be more careful, they have also made them more reluctant to bring out new products. Valuable new drugs have been developed that no manufacturer is willing to sell in the United States. As a result, there are currently proposals to limit **product liability** (the obligation of a producer to compensate victims of a defective product that has injured them) in the case of new drugs.

Other aspects of the regulatory environment may also affect the pace of R & D. The long and extensive testing of drugs and the long delays in gaining approval for their production undoubtedly have a dampening effect. There is clearly a problem of weighing and balancing costs and benefits.

[6] See Chapter 18 for a more thorough discussion of these alternative policies.

In response to the growing concerns about the decline in competitiveness of American industries, the Council of Competitiveness was formed. It is a private group, headed by John A. Young, chief executive officer of Hewlett-Packard, one of the country's leading innovating firms. The council concluded:

> There is no question that the United States enjoys significant strengths in science and technology. . . . America's primary problem in the science and technology field relates neither to entrepreneurship, research nor the performance of its universities, but to the commercial application of technology. Considerable evidence suggests that America is failing to commercialize the kinds and quality of technology that the market demands.
>
> The problem is relatively new. For many years, particularly in the two decades following World War II, U.S. firms dominated the commercial application of technology in most industries. Over time, however, foreign companies assimilated state-of-the-art technology, often American in origin; improved it; generated their own products and processes; and brought them skillfully to market.

Declining Market Share in Technology Industries
One piece of evidence for the council's conclusion was the decline in technology industries in the United States. American producers' share of the U.S. consumer electronics market has fallen from 100 percent in 1970 to less than 5 percent today. U.S. companies make only 10 percent of the color televisions sold in the country, only 1 percent of the videocassette recorders, only 25 percent of the telephones. Japan makes 65 percent of the world's semiconductors, and the United States makes 35 percent. American producers' share of the U.S. machine tool market has fallen from 100 percent to about 35 percent. In recent years, the United States has imported more high-technology products than it has exported.

Declining Science and Engineering Education
While the council focused its attention on the problem of commercialization, it was also concerned with the declines in science and engineering education. By one estimate, the nation will be 500,000 engineers short in two decades. The percentage of American students choosing engineering is declining, and 40 percent of graduate students in engineering in the United States come from foreign countries. In addition, there is a shortage of teachers of math, science, and engineering. The National Science Foundation estimates that with the increased number of students, the United States will need an additional 300,000 secondary-school math and science teachers by 1995. At the college level, engineering faculty are taking jobs in private industry.

Low Levels of R & D Spending The failure of the United States to support *non-defense*-related research was also cited as a major problem. As already noted, while most countries focus their R & D effort on helping commercial industry, the United States focuses on its defense industry.

Patent and Antitrust Policies   Patent policies, which enable an inventor to appropriate the returns to his innovative activity, are another major aspect of government policies affecting R & D. By and large, "stronger" patents—patents that are broader in coverage and longer in duration—provide greater incentives for R & D. Antitrust policies, which prohibit firms from colluding, also impede them from cooperating in research ventures, though recent legislation has made such ventures easier than previously. Here too, the government must balance the losses from reduced competition with the gains from increased innovation.

THE COSTS OF ECONOMIC GROWTH

There is a widespread faith in the virtues of economic progress. Even among people who have serious doubts about certain technologies, few will openly embrace the alternatives of economic stagnation and a relatively lower standard of living for the United States in comparison with other developed countries. However, this acceptance of technological progress should not blind anyone to its real costs.

In the early 1800s, English workmen sometimes destroyed labor-saving machinery rather than see it take over their jobs. They were referred to as **Luddites,** after their leader Ned Ludd. (Ludd's role may have been largely mythical, but the term still bears his name.) Concerns about workers who are thrown out of their jobs as a result of some innovation are no less real today, although those fighting against technological change today have their unions to help, and they are more successful than the Luddites were. For example, the plumbers' union got many communities to forbid the use of plastic pipes, which, while cheaper and better for some uses than metal pipes, require less skill to install. Similarly, pilot unions have insisted on crews of three even for planes designed for crews of two.

Technological progress creates jobs as it destroys them. Earlier this century, jobs for blacksmiths were replaced by jobs for automobile mechanics. Today a computerized "brain" in a machine may mean that fewer automobile workers are needed on the assembly line, but new jobs are created in the computing industry. The adjustment of the economy, however, is more complicated than the simple conversion of an assembly-line worker into a computer programmer. It is better to think of the new computer-programming job as setting off a chain. Had the new job not come along, the computer programmer would have taken a slightly less skilled job; by taking this new position, he frees up the less skilled job. This less skilled job is grabbed by a worker who otherwise would have had a still less skilled job—say, a semiskilled job. But this creates a vacancy at the semiskilled job, and so on down the chain. The assembly-line worker may find that there is thus a job requiring only slightly more skills than he presently has, skills that, with an appropriate job-training program, he can readily acquire.

Of course, it can be hard to teach an old dog new tricks, so a middle-aged or older worker who loses her job may have real difficulty in getting another that is even nearly as good. She may have to content herself with taking an unskilled job, with a commensurately lower wage. How much sympathy this displaced worker should receive is a matter on which reasonable people can disagree. Does a worker who is used to a certain wage deserve not to have it changed? Should we pay more attention to the costs to the worker who loses a job than to the benefits to a worker in the new industry who gets a better job?

Not surprisingly, then, technological progress frequently meets with resistance. The loss of any jobs as a result of technological progress gives rise to fear and insecurity, even among people who are not immediately threatened with losing their own jobs. The pleas of those affected to "stop" or at least slow down the pace of innovation strikes a concordant note in others, and the government often responds positively to the pleas for its intervention. We have already noted the sometimes successful attempt by plumbers to incorporate into building codes restrictions against plastic piping. There are many more instances throughout the economy.

Most economists believe that these self-serving restrictions are harmful when judged from an overall perspective. The cost to society exceeds the gains to the protected groups. On the other hand, the concerns of the displaced cannot be simply ignored. The objective of the government should be to design programs that assist in the transition of people displaced by technological change. Such programs can be thought of as a form of insurance. Most workers face the possibility that their jobs will be made technologically obsolete. Knowing that if they are thrown out of work for this reason they will be at least partially protected adds to a sense of security, something most risk-averse workers value highly. In the long run, such programs can actually help increase the rate at which technological changes are adopted by making job loss a less fearful prospect.

ARE THERE LIMITS TO ECONOMIC GROWTH?

As we learned earlier, technological progress was not taken for granted in the early 1800s as it is today. Thomas Malthus envisioned the future as one in which more and more workers would crowd themselves into a fixed supply of land. The ever-increasing labor force would push wages down to the subsistence level, or even lower. Any technological progress that occurred would, in his view, raise wages only temporarily; as the labor supply increased, wages would eventually fall back to the subsistence level. The capitalists, who owned the land and factories and machines, would eventually receive any gains from technological improvements.

Over the past century, there has been a decrease in the rate of population growth, and this phenomenon, which was also unforeseen, is perhaps as remarkable as the increase in the rate of technological progress. One might have thought that improved medicine and health conditions would have led to a population explosion, but the spread of birth control and family planning has had the opposite effect, at least in the more developed countries. Today family size has decreased to the point where in many countries population growth (apart from migration) has almost halted. Those who worry about the limits to growth today usually describe the future not as a case of more and more people crowding onto a plot of land, but rather a case of some natural resource such as oil, natural gas, phosphorus, or potassium running out. They believe that *exhaustible* natural resources like these may pose a limit to economic growth as they are used up in the ordinary course of production.

However, most economists believe that markets do provide incentives for wise use of most resources. They believe that as any good becomes more scarce and its price rises, the search for substitutes will be stimulated. Thus, the rise in the price of oil led to smaller, more efficient cars, cooler but better insulated houses, and a search for alternative sources of energy like geothermal and synthetic fuels, all of which resulted in a decline in the consumption of oil.

Since the time of Malthus, an unending string of doomsayers have worried that the world was about to run out of something or other. There were predictions that when Pennsylvania ran out of oil, economic growth would stop. Someday these dire predictions may come true. But for now, the prospects look about as good as they always have. There appears to be a sufficient supply of fossil fuel for decades to come. As these fuels become more scarce and thus more expensive, perhaps new technologies like solar power or nuclear fusion will provide an almost limitless supply of cleanly produced energy. This argument, that rising prices encourage both greater conservation and a search for substitutes, applies to other exhaustible natural resources as well.

Still, there is one area in which the price system does not work well—the area of externalities, discussed in Chapter 23. Without government intervention, producers do not have incentives to worry about air and water pollution. And in our globally connected world, what one country does results in externalities for others. Cutting down the rain forest in Brazil, for example, may have worldwide climatic consequences. The less developed countries feel that they can ill afford the costs of pollution control, when they can barely pay the price of any industrialization. They feel it is unfair to ask them to pay the price of maintaining the environment, when the major industrialized economies are the major source of the environmental degradation. Environmentalists argue that we are all in the same boat together. And if global warming occurs, it could have disastrous effects on all of us, in both the less and more developed countries. While the scientific community is not in agreement about the significance of these concerns, most economists do not believe that we face an either/or choice: we do not have to abandon growth to preserve our environment. Nevertheless, a sensitivity to the quality of our environment may affect how we go about growing.

THE PROGNOSIS

It is too soon for any final judgment as to whether the productivity slowdown in the United States is permanent or only a temporary aberration. Though this century has been marked by large increases in productivity, the rate of productivity growth has not been steady. There have been periods of relative stagnation as well as periods in which the economy has burst forth with energy and growth. The hopeful interpretation of the decline in productivity growth is that it is just a passing phase.

A less optimistic view is that the high rates of productivity growth the United States experienced during the 1950s and 1960s were the aberration. Some economists believe that various possibilities for economic growth were bottled up during the Great Depression of the 1930s and World War II in the early 1940s, and the realization of those postponed opportunities resulted in the productivity boom of the 1950s and 1960s. From this point of view, the loss in the United States' dominant technological position is not surprising.

After all, the United States has no monopoly on ideas or on the ability to do research, and it was only a matter of time before some countries would catch up.

The analysis of this chapter suggests that there are grounds for both pessimism and optimism. There is no quick or easy reversal of many of the factors hampering productivity growth, such as the low rate of savings; the failure of the U.S. educational system to provide the kind of education required in a competitive, technologically oriented world; and the changing structure of the American economy, with the low-productivity service sector growing more rapidly than other parts of the economy.

Some of the factors hampering productivity growth could more easily be altered. These include the failure of government to improve the economy's infrastructure; the distortion of taxes and regulation; and the low level of expenditures on research and development, at least expenditures directed at improving the economy's productivity rather than increasing military prowess.

Thus, while most economists think it unlikely that the United States will ever again be in the position of technological superiority that it held for so long, there is widespread optimism that the U.S. economy can return to a higher level of productivity growth, provided the right government policies are pursued.

AN AGENDA FOR ECONOMIC GROWTH

Factors that stimulate savings
    Lower federal government budgetary deficits
    Tax breaks for savers
Factors that stimulate investment
    Improved economic environment: less regulation, lower cost of capital, less risk with stable economy operating at full employment
    Tax breaks for firms that invest
Factors that improve human capital
    More funds for education
    Reorganization of education—more decentralization, more competition, more choice
Factors that stimulate technological change
    Tax breaks—reducing capital gains taxation for R & D projects
    More funds for training scientists and engineers
    More support for civilian (including basic) research, rather than military
    Improved economic environment
        Reduced regulation
        Reduced legal barriers
    Ensuring that antitrust policies do not act as impediments

REVIEW AND PRACTICE

SUMMARY

1. The United States experienced a marked slowdown in the rate of productivity growth in the late 1960s and early 1970s, compared with the preceding two decades. Even seemingly small declines in the rate of increase in productivity will have a powerful adverse effect on the standard of living over a generation or two.

2. There are four major sources of productivity growth: increases in the accumulation of capital goods (investment); a higher quality of the labor force; greater efficiency in allocating resources; and technological change.

3. The rate of savings in the United States has declined in recent years. Some of the reasons are improved government retirement programs, more extensive insurance coverage and greater ease in borrowing, changes in social attitudes, the fact that the proportion of the population in their prime savings years during the 1980s was relatively low, and the fact that people are choosing to save by building up equity in houses, rather than by setting aside income.

4. The most plausible way to achieve an immediate increase in overall national savings would be to reduce the government deficits.

5. Investment levels were low in the United States during the 1980s. Possible reasons include the high costs of capital, the impact of government rules and regulations, and uncertainty about the future, including changes in taxes and interest rates.

6. The government has several policies available to stimulate investment: spending money on infrastructure projects like roads and bridges; monetary and fiscal policies to keep credit available and interest rates low; and incentives like the investment tax credit.

7. There are serious concerns about the quality of education American students are receiving in preparation for the labor force and about the number of scientists and engineers being trained. While allocating more money to training and education may help, educational reorganization may also be needed.

8. The twentieth century has been marked by shifts in the U.S. economy from an agricultural base to an industrial base and more recently to a service base. Some economists think that the potential for technological progress is less in the service sector than in the industrial sector, and this accounts for part of the productivity slowdown.

9. Government supports R & D through both direct spending and tax incentives, though direct support for R & D that is not defense-related has actually declined during the past quarter century.

10. There has long been concern that certain natural resources (like oil) will someday run out, causing economic growth to halt. However, most economists would argue that the price of resources will increase as they become more scarce, and this will encourage both greater conservation and a search for substitutes.

KEY TERMS

product liability   Luddites

REVIEW QUESTIONS

1. True or false: "Since growth-oriented policies might have an effect of only a percent or two per year, they are not worth worrying much about." Explain.

2. What are the four possible sources of productivity growth?

3. What are the components of overall U.S. savings, and how did they change in the 1980s?

4. What are some reasons for the decrease in savings during the 1980s?

5. Will government policies to raise the rate of return on savings necessarily lead to increased savings? (Hint: You may wish to review the discussion of income and substitution effects in Chapter 9.)

6. What are some of the factors that contribute to a low level of investment?

7. How might a recession contribute to a slowdown in productivity several years later?

8. What policies might the government use to increase investment in R & D?

9. What are some costs of economic growth? Short of seeking to restrain growth, how might government deal with these costs?

PROBLEMS

1. Will the following changes increase or decrease the rate of household savings?
   (a) The proportion of people in the 45–64 age bracket increases.
   (b) Government programs provide secure retirement benefits.
   (c) Credit cards become much more prevalent.
   (d) The proportion of people in the 21–45 age bracket increases.
   (e) Government programs to guarantee student loans are enacted.

2. Explain how the following factors would increase or decrease the average productivity of labor:

   (a) successful reforms of the educational system;
   (b) the entry of new workers into the economy;
   (c) earlier retirement;
   (d) high unemployment rates during a recession.

3. Suppose a firm is considering spending $1 million on R & D projects, which it believes will translate into patents that it will be able to sell for $2.5 million in ten years. Assume that the firm ignores risk. If the interest rate is 10 percent, is the firm likely to attempt these R & D projects? If the government offers a 20 percent R & D tax credit, how does the firm's calculation change?

4. Explain why a rapid influx of workers would result in a lower output per worker (a reduction in productivity). Would the effect on productivity depend on the skill level of the new workers?

5. Explain, using supply and demand diagrams, how a technological change such as computerization could lead to lower wages of unskilled workers and higher wages of skilled workers.

6. Consider the growth agenda set forth on page 1024. Discuss the relative importance of the various items. Which are most likely to have a significant effect on growth?

THE PROBLEM OF THE TWIN DEFICITS

E ach decade seems to have a particular economic theme. The major economic phenomenon of the 1960s, for example, is generally taken to be the decision of President Johnson to pursue a "guns and butter" economic policy, simultaneously fighting a war in Vietnam and a War on Poverty in the United States. The result, as explained in Chapter 26, was a surge of inflation. The major economic events of the 1970s were the dramatic increases in the price of oil in 1973 and 1979.

In the 1980s, the most prominent economic themes were the lagging growth in productivity, discussed in Chapter 37; the huge fiscal, or budget, deficit of the U.S. government, with spending far exceeding tax revenues; and the huge trade deficit, with America's imports far exceeding its exports. Both deficits set new records and became a cause for concern.

This chapter inquires into the causes and consequences of the twin deficits. How might they be related? And are they a genuine cause for alarm?

"If you ask me, this thing is going to get a whole lot worse before it gets better."

KEY QUESTIONS

1. What gave rise to the fiscal deficit? And why is it so difficult to reduce?

2. What gave rise to the trade deficit? What is the relationship between the fiscal deficit and the trade deficit? Why is it so difficult to reduce the trade deficit? Why are protectionist policies aimed at keeping out foreign imports unlikely to reduce the trade deficit, and why are they likely to have harmful effects?

THE GROWTH OF THE BUDGET DEFICIT

The combination of the tax and spending policies pursued by Congress and the Reagan and Bush administrations in the 1980s was extraordinary. Government spending rose slightly during the 1980s, from 23.0 percent of GDP in 1981 to 23.3 percent of GDP in 1991. But taxes failed to rise with this boost in spending—in fact, federal taxes were cut from their 1981 levels—and as a result, the government had to borrow huge sums of money. While taxes were 21.1 percent of GDP in 1981, in 1991 they were only 19.7 percent. The annual deficit, that is, the amount by which expenditures exceeded tax revenues, was enormous, whether measured in real terms, as a ratio of GDP, or as a percentage of government expenditures.[1] The total federal debt, which is the accumulated sum of the deficits, was also huge, no matter how it was measured.

Figures 38.1 and 38.2 show this impressive increase in deficit and debt, each measured

---

[1] Chapter 30 noted two other ways of measuring the deficit that makes the *change* in the deficit appear to be even more dramatic. One measure is defined as the difference between the real value of the outstanding deficit at the beginning of the year and at the end; it takes account of the change in the real value of the outstanding debt as a result of inflation. The other, the full-employment deficit, takes account of the level of economic activity in the economy; that is, it asks what the actual deficit would have been had the economy been operating at full employment.

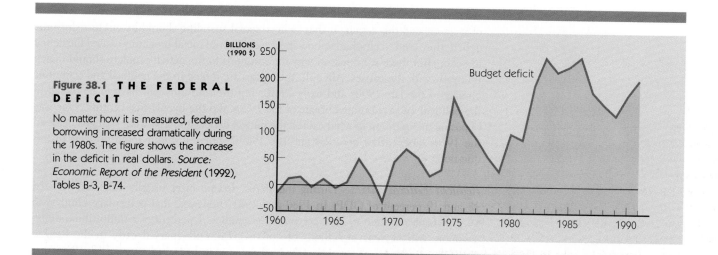

Figure 38.1 THE FEDERAL DEFICIT

No matter how it is measured, federal borrowing increased dramatically during the 1980s. The figure shows the increase in the deficit in real dollars. *Source: Economic Report of the President* (1992), Tables B-3, B-74.

in 1990 dollars. Figure 38.1, which expresses the annual deficit in real dollars, makes clear why there is concern about the deficit: it skyrocketed in the 1980s and early 1990s. Figure 38.2 shows that the real debt was very large at the end of World War II; much of the war had been financed by borrowing. What was remarkable about the deficits of the 1980s was that they occurred in peacetime, and indeed in a period in which the economy was experiencing relative prosperity. Large deficits had previously only arisen in times of war and depression. After World War II, the government struggled to reduce the deficit that had accumulated during the war; but by 1991, the debt had set a new high, a record of dubious distinction.

Isolating the cause of the explosive increase in the budget deficits during the 1980s is a tricky business, because most analysts have an axe to grind. If people believe that

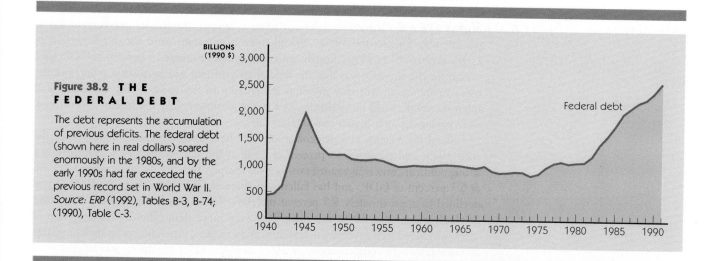

Figure 38.2 THE FEDERAL DEBT

The debt represents the accumulation of previous deficits. The federal debt (shown here in real dollars) soared enormously in the 1980s, and by the early 1990s had far exceeded the previous record set in World War II. *Source: ERP* (1992), Tables B-3, B-74; (1990), Table C-3.

taxes should be raised to reduce the budget deficit, they tend to argue that the lowering of taxes created the deficit. If they believe social spending should be cut to reduce the deficit, they tend to emphasize how increases in some social programs caused the deficit to occur. But there is no reason why the solutions to the deficit problem should match up neatly with the causes. After all, the causes are rooted in the political and economic climate of the late 1970s and early 1980s, but the solutions will have to be rooted in the political and economic climate of the 1990s and the twenty-first century. One way of posing the question of what caused the budget deficit is to ask, what changed between the 1970s (and earlier decades) and the 1980s? There are four main answers to this question.

Reduced Federal Taxes During the 1970s, federal taxes usually collected between 18 and 19 percent of GDP. In 1980 and 1981, however, that percentage climbed to 20.4 percent and then to 21.1 percent. (Remember, 1 percent of a multitrillion-dollar economy will be tens of billions of dollars.) Tax cuts enacted early in the Reagan presidency pushed the federal tax take back down to its historical range of 18–19 percent of GDP. The tax cuts, like all tax cuts, were politically popular, but they clearly contributed to the deficit problem.

Higher Defense Spending Federal defense spending fell during the 1970s, as the Vietnam War came to an end, from 8.4 percent of GDP in 1970 to 4.9 percent of GDP in 1979. In 1979, though, the Soviet Union invaded Afghanistan, and President Carter called for a large defense buildup. After Ronald Reagan was elected president in 1980, he followed through on these plans. From 1983 to 1988, defense spending exceeded 6 percent of GDP.

Higher Social Spending on the Elderly As the number of elderly people in the United States has grown, federal expenditures on programs like Social Security and Medicare have expanded dramatically. These programs averaged 5.0 percent of GDP in the 1970s, but increased to over 6 percent of GDP by 1980 and close to 7 percent by 1982. By the end of the decade, they constituted once again just slightly more than 6 percent of GDP.

Higher Interest Payments Like any other borrower, the federal government has to pay interest. During the 1970s, federal interest payments were about 1.5 percent of GDP. From 1983 to 1990, though, interest payments exceeded 3 percent of GDP. One reason for the increase was that the federal government was borrowing more. But the other main reason was that inflation fell sharply in the early 1980s, while nominal interest rates declined more slowly. As a result, borrowers (like the federal government) were paying a much higher real interest rate.

Federal tax receipts as a percentage of GDP have been increasing slightly since the early 1980s and exceeded 19 percent of GDP at the start of the 1990s, but there is a strong political consensus against raising taxes sharply. Defense spending peaked in 1986 at 6.5 percent of GDP, and has fallen as a share of GDP since then. By 1990, it had declined to approximately 5.7 percent of GDP. These changes helped to bring down the budget deficit in 1990, but the effects were more than offset by the recession of 1991, which reduced government revenues and increased expenditures for such programs as unemployment compensation; in fact, a new record for the deficit was set. But even without the recession, the slightly higher taxes and decreased defense spending would

While there is little doubt that the deficits of the 1980s and early 1990s are huge, exactly how huge is a matter of some dispute. The official federal deficit for the 1991 fiscal year reported by the Office of Management and Budget, the government agency responsible for keeping track of such matters, was $269 billion.

Congressional legislation requires that Social Security and the U.S. Postal Service be kept separate from the other activities of the government. But when the Office of Management and Budget reports the deficit, it reports them together. Social Security currently has a surplus of funds, which are supposed to pay benefits for the huge number of baby boomers who will begin to retire around the year 2010. Excluding the accounts for Social Security and the Postal Service, the 1991 deficit was $321 billion.

The deficit was higher than it would have been had the economy been at full employment. The full-employment deficit—the deficit that would have prevailed if the unemployment rate had been 5.5 percent—is estimated to have been approximately $78 billion smaller.

Of the deficit, $67 billion went to pay for the S & L bailout. Many people like to exclude this expenditure from the deficit. Some say that it is just a transfer payment (but so are lots of other government expenditures). Some say that the "real" expenditure occurred when the government provided the deposit insurance and did not charge appropriate premiums. Others say that the payment is nothing more than the formal recognition of a debt already incurred, when the government provided the deposit insurance and the S & L's went bankrupt.

Robert Eisner of Northwestern University has suggested several other adjustments in the calculation of the deficit, the effect of which is to make the deficit still smaller. Since inflation means that the real value of the outstanding debt is smaller, Eisner estimates that inflation reduces the real value of the debt by $85 billion. Furthermore, of the government expenditures, $70 billion represent net investment. Making these two adjustments to the $269 billion consolidated budget deficit leaves a deficit of $114 billion—still large, but much smaller. Making the further adjustments for unemployment and the S & L bailout turns up a surplus of $31 billion. Economists can do marvelous things with statistics, even turn a seemingly huge deficit into a surplus!

The real point that Eisner stresses is that while the deficits may or may not be large, the losses from having the economy run below full employment are enormous. He calculates that during the 1991 recession, the economy, by not using its resources fully, was in effect throwing away output at the rate of $300 billion per year—dollars that may never be recovered. These are real costs, and they bring real suffering.

not have helped enough to bring the government's budget into balance. And unless something dramatic happens, large deficits loom for the foreseeable future.

We saw in Chapter 28 that government expenditures stimulate the economy, while taxes reduce aggregate demand. When expenditures exceed taxes, as they did throughout the 1980s, the net effect is positive. The U.S. economy grew steadily from the start of 1983 through 1990, one of the longest economic expansions on record. In fact, given the size of the stimulus, one might think that fiscal policy would have given rise to an inflationary episode. We will return to this puzzle at the end of the chapter.

Figure 38.3 **BUDGET AND TRADE DEFICITS**

Increases in government deficits in the early 1980s were accompanied by increases in foreign borrowing. The correlation does not prove causality, but it is suggestive. *Source: ERP* (1992), Tables B-1, B-3, B-77.

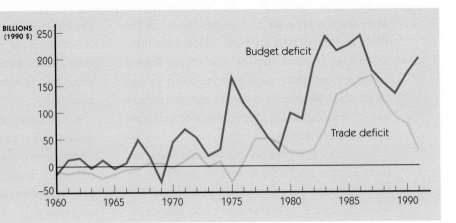

THE GROWTH OF THE TRADE DEFICIT

The U.S. trade deficit exploded onto the international economic scene in the early 1980s. The United States ran a trade deficit of about $20 billion a year from 1977 to 1982, but then the trade deficit increased in nominal dollars to $51 billion in 1983, $103 billion in 1984, and finally $143 billion in 1987. The trade deficit declined each of the next four years, reaching $27 billion in 1991. A closer look is given in Figure 38.3, which shows the deficit in real dollars.

Figure 38.3 also shows the fiscal deficit, and we can see that both deficits increased together during the 1980s. This is no accident: the fiscal deficit and the trade deficit are in fact closely related.

THE BURDEN OF GOVERNMENT BORROWING

During the 1980s, Americans consistently rated the federal budget deficit as the biggest economic problem facing the country. For one thing, deficits involve borrowing, and borrowing has a bad name. In the Middle Ages, the payment of interest was condemned as the sin of usury. Even today, some segments of the Islamic religion forbid the payment of interest. And remember the fatherly advice that Polonius gives to Laertes in Shakespeare's *Hamlet:*

> Neither a borrower nor a lender be;
> For loan oft loses both itself and friend,
> And borrowing dulls the edge of husbandry.

Economists have traditionally argued that government borrowing, just like individual borrowing, makes sense or does not make sense according to the purpose for which the money is used. It makes some sense to borrow to buy a house that you will live in for many years or a car that you will drive for a few years. In that way, you spread out paying for the item as you use it. It makes economic sense to borrow money for an educational degree that will lead to a higher-paying job in the future. But if you are paying this year for the vacation that you took two years ago, maybe you should think about chopping up your credit cards!

Countries are in a similar situation. Borrowing to finance a road or a school or an industrial project that will be used for many years may be quite appropriate. Borrowing to pay for projects that are never completed (or perhaps are never even started) or borrowing to finance this year's government salaries poses real problems. Over time, many governments have taken on more debt than they could comfortably pay off. Many countries have had to raise taxes sharply and reduce their standard of living to pay off their debts. Others have simply failed to repay, jeopardizing their ability to borrow in the future. Mexico, Brazil, Argentina, the Philippines, and several other countries faced this harsh choice in the 1980s.

HOW FUTURE GENERATIONS ARE AFFECTED BY THE DEFICITS

Government debt does differ from private debt in some ways. A child generally has no legal obligation to repay the debts of a parent, but the obligation to repay government debt rests on everyone in the country, including future generations. There are three distinct ways that the debt produced by federal fiscal deficits imposes a burden on future generations.

Direct Shifting First, when resources are devoted to public expenditures (to fight a war, for example), resources have to be diverted away from other uses, from private consumption in particular. The question is, whose private consumption is reduced? By borrowing, the government places the burden of this reduced consumption on future generations. The U.S. government partly financed World War II by borrowing rather than raising taxes. Though the resources were indeed spent during the war, those who have had to forgo consumption to pay the bill were not (only) those working at that time.

Typically, governments borrow by issuing bonds. Suppose that the government decides to issue bonds to finance a war and these bonds are purchased by forty-year-old workers. Then thirty years later, as these forty-year-olds enter retirement, the government decides to pay off the bonds by raising taxes on those who are then in the labor force. In effect, the government is transferring funds from these younger workers to those who *were* the workers during the war, who are now seventy and retired. Thus, part of the cost of the war is borne by the generation who entered the work force after the war. The lifetime consumption of the original forty-year-olds is little affected. They might otherwise have put their savings into stocks or bonds issued by firms; the war (to the extent it is financed by debt, or bonds) affects the form of their savings, but not the total amount they have to spend over their lifetime.

Decline in Investment   The burden of government debt also affects future generations by leading to a decline in investment in capital goods. As we have just seen, when the government borrows, the current generation puts their savings into government bonds rather than leaving the funds available for private companies to borrow for productive investments. In effect, the government borrowing crowds out private investment (see Chapter 29). If the government invests the money itself (perhaps in schools, research and development activities, or highways and bridges), then the government debt may not affect future levels of economic output. However, if the government spends or invests the money in ill-conceived projects, the result will be less human and physical capital in the economy, which in turn means that output and wages in future years will be lower than they might otherwise have been.

Foreign Indebtedness   In Chapter 30, we saw that as the world economy has become more open, concerns about government borrowing crowding out investment have become less acute. Rather than reducing investment, the government simply borrows from abroad. Instead of selling bonds to U.S. citizens, the government has increasingly financed its budget deficits by selling them to foreign investors. When it comes time to repay these bonds, the buying power will be transferred out of the country. An ever-increasing fraction of national output will have to be sent overseas to pay interest on what is owed to foreigners. The net income levels, what is left over after paying foreigners interest on their capital, of future generations will be lower.

If we look at who has bought the additional bonds the government has been issuing in recent years, we note that some but not all of the higher deficit has been financed by foreigners. But the consequences are equally or even more disturbing if they do not *directly* finance the deficit. The government can increase foreign debt directly by borrowing directly from abroad, or it can increase foreign debt indirectly by sopping up available domestic savings so that Americans no longer have the money to invest in U.S. businesses and foreigners come in to fill the gap. Some economists have described the latter situation by saying that government borrowing can "crowd in" foreign investment. In either case, whether the foreigners' funds have gone directly to finance the debt or have gone to buy American stocks and real estate, releasing funds for Americans to finance the deficit, the aggregate indebtedness of the country to foreigners has increased. Americans, in total, will be making payments to foreigners for some time, reducing future standards of living.

The "Debt Does Not Matter Because We Owe It to Ourselves" Argument   It used to be argued in the United States that the fiscal deficit does not matter because we simply owe the money to ourselves. The budget deficit was compared to the effect of one brother borrowing from another on the total welfare of the family. One member of the family may be better off, another worse off, but the indebtedness does not really matter much to the family as a whole. Financing government expenditures by debt, it was argued, clearly could lead to a transfer of resources between generations, but this transfer would still keep all the buying power in the hands of U.S. citizens.

We now recognize that this argument is wrong on two counts. First, even if we owe the money to ourselves, the debt affects investment and thus future wages and productivity, as noted. And second, today we do not in fact owe the money to ourselves: the United States is borrowing abroad. It is becoming indebted to foreigners. The consequences of the country spending beyond its means are no different from those of a family spending beyond its means: eventually it has to pay the price of the consumption binge. In the case of a national consumption binge, it is future generations that may have to pay the price.

CONSEQUENCES OF GOVERNMENT FISCAL DEFICITS

1. Some of the burden of current expenditures is shifted to future generations directly.

2. Issuing bonds may decrease investment and thus make future generations worse off indirectly.

3. Foreign indebtedness may increase, reducing future standards of living.

THE TRADE DEFICIT

A trade deficit (or surplus) is simply the difference between the value of imports and the value of exports. As we learned in Chapter 35, some of the large increase in the trade deficit during the 1980s may be because incomes grew more rapidly in the United States than in other countries, leading imports to increase faster than exports. It also may have resulted from a shift in the demand curve for imports. But most of the increase in the trade deficit, at least in the early 1980s, appears to have been due to the change in the exchange rate. The U.S. dollar appreciated relative to foreign currencies, making American goods more expensive to foreigners and foreign goods less expensive to Americans. This quite naturally led to reduced exports and increased imports.

But why did the dollar appreciate? Largely because of an increased desire on the part of foreigners to invest in the United States. Investors base their investment decisions on relative returns. If the returns to investing in the United States rise, relative to returns to investing elsewhere, capital will flow to the United States from foreign investors, and the value of the dollar will rise. In the international capital markets of the modern economy, investors are willing to shift their investments from country to country in response to relatively small changes in returns. Such shifts are particularly attractive if a country with high interest rates also has a stable government. Thus, the relatively small increase in the return to investing in the United States that occurred in the 1980s induced fairly large capital flows, explaining the change in the value of the dollar and the resulting trade deficit.

Figure 38.4 depicts demand and supply curves for dollars that depend on the exchange

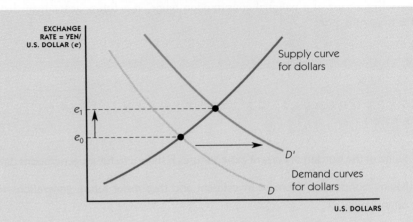

Figure 38.4 HOW HIGHER INTEREST RATES AFFECTED THE DOLLAR

Higher interest rates during the 1980s made investment in the United States more attractive. The demand curve for dollars shifted out, so there was a new, higher equilibrium exchange rate. The higher exchange rate discouraged exports and encouraged imports.

rate between dollars and yen. The initial exchange rate is e_0. The shift in the demand curve for dollars, caused by foreigners wishing to invest in the United States, results in the exchange rate rising to e_1. The dollar is worth more yen. This means that a Japanese firm wanting to buy, say, a computer in the United States for $10,000 must give up more yen. In terms of the foreign country's currency, the computer is more expensive. Not surprisingly, the demand for American products decreases.

CAPITAL FLOWS

The fact that capital flows to the United States accompanied the trade deficit is no accident or coincidence; in fact, it is a matter of definition. Let's trace what happens when an American decides to buy a German car. To buy the car, he needs German marks. So he goes to a German bank and exchanges his dollars for marks. But the bank is not simply going to hold those dollars. It will eventually sell them, either to someone wanting to purchase U.S. goods or to someone wanting to invest in a dollar-denominated asset. Thus, every dollar an American spends to buy a foreign import eventually comes back, either to buy American exports or to buy an investment in the United States.

We can express this relation by a simple equation:

imports into the United States = exports + foreigners' investment in the United States, or capital inflows.

If foreigners invest nothing in the United States, then this equation tells us that imports will equal exports. But if some of the money earned by foreign producers goes to buy investments in the United States, then the equation shows that the value of American imports will exceed the value of American exports. This is by definition a trade deficit. The magnitude of the trade deficit will be exactly equal to the amount invested in the United States. A trade deficit and an inflow of foreign capital are really two ways of saying the same thing. This can be put another way: the only way that American consumers and businesses can import more from abroad than they export abroad is if foreigners are willing to make up the difference by lending to or investing in the United States.

This international borrowing and lending often takes place through financial intermediaries. For example, Toyota might accept payment for its cars in dollars, knowing that a Japanese businessman who is interested in buying an apartment building in Los Angeles, an office building in Manhattan, shares in an American company, or a U.S. government bond is willing to trade his yen to Toyota for Toyota's dollars. Although the two might make the exchange directly, it is more likely that Toyota will exchange its dollars for yen at the bank (or equivalently, Toyota might insist on being paid in yen, in which case the American buyer would take her dollars to the bank to buy yen) and that the Japanese businessman will go to the same bank and exchange his yen for Toyota's dollars. And then the businessman will return his dollars to the United States as he makes his investment there.

In a world of multilateral trade, the accounts between any particular company or country and the United States do not have to balance. Toyota may sell the dollars it earns not to a Japanese businessman, but to a German or French investor. But what must be true for any country is that imports minus exports (the trade deficit) equal capital inflows. What are important are *net* inflows, the difference between what foreigners invest in the United States and what Americans invest abroad.

This is the basic trade identity:

trade deficit = imports − exports = capital inflows.[2]

Capital flows are a shorthand way of summarizing all the borrowing and lending that goes on. American firms invest in Japan; Japanese firms invest in the United States. To calculate the net capital flows between the United States and Japan, we add up all the dollars lent by Japan to the United States, all the investment by Japan in the United States, all the Japanese purchases of bonds, and the increase in Japanese holdings of U.S. dollars and then subtract the corresponding numbers on the American side.

As noted earlier, since we live in a world of multilateral trade, the U.S. trade deficit with Japan does not necessarily have to equal capital flows from Japan. Assume Japan and Europe are in trade balance and the United States and Europe are in trade balance, but Japanese investors like to put their money into Europe and Europeans like to invest in the United States. Europe has zero net capital flows, with a positive capital flow from Japan offset by a capital flow to the United States. In this situation, the U.S. trade deficit with Japan is offset by a capital flow from Europe.

The basic trade identity can describe a capital outflow as well as a capital inflow. In the 1950s, the United States had a substantial trade surplus, as the country exported more than it imported. Europe and Japan did not receive enough dollars from selling exports to the United States to buy the imports that they desired, and they borrowed the difference from the United States. There was a net capital outflow from America, which gradually accumulated.

Japan is now in a situation analogous to that of the United States in the 1950s. Japan exports more than it imports, and the difference is equal to its capital outflows. The

---

[2] This equation is exactly the same as the equation given earlier; simply subtract exports from both sides of the earlier equation.

CLOSE-UP: THE DOLLAR AND THE TRADE DEFICIT IN THE 1980s

The average value of the dollar on foreign exchange markets strengthened by 50 percent between 1980 and 1984. From the standpoint of the basic supply and demand model, it made complete sense that this rise in the dollar should be reflected in lower exports, higher imports, and a rising trade deficit. But between 1985 and 1987, the dollar reversed nearly all of its earlier rise, returning almost to the level it was in 1980. Economists have been puzzled as to why the fall of the dollar did not largely eliminate the trade deficit. Why didn't U.S. exports respond to the fall in the dollar in the late 1980s in the way that foreign exports responded to the rise in the dollar in the early 1980s?

Several explanations have been put forward. One emphasizes lags in the response of exporters and importers. Most international trade is in manufactured goods, which differ in characteristics and qualities. A Citroën is not just like a Chevy, and a British Shetland sweater is different from a Benetton sweater. Markets for these goods have to be cultivated, and this takes time. By the same token, it takes time to lose markets. When the dollar rose, U.S. consumers did not immediately shift to foreign goods, nor did foreign buyers shift away from U.S. goods. Many exports are *intermediate* goods, used to produce final goods. These intermediate goods must be manufactured to exact specifications, and it takes time to find alternate sources of supply.

Even in the case of goods like oil and wheat, much trade occurs under long-term contracts, slowing down the process of adjustment.

In this view, then, had the dollar not fallen, the trade deficit would have grown even worse as these adjustments continued. The devaluation of the dollar prevented any additional decline, but it takes years to recover markets already lost. In effect, the short-run elasticity of demand for American exports may be very low. In support of this hypothesis, U.S. exports increased sharply in the later part of the 1980s, rising from $227 billion in 1986 to $420 billion in 1991, and leading to a substantial fall in the trade deficit by the early 1990s.

A second explanation hypothesizes a decline in the competitiveness of U.S. industry. This view holds that even though exchange rates declined enormously from their peak in 1985, they have not declined enough, given a weakened competitive position for the United States.

A final explanation emphasizes the overall lesson of the national income identity. If the United States as a whole saves less and consumes more—whether because of higher government borrowing or a low level of individual saving—then the nation must borrow from abroad and buy from abroad. From this point of view, exchange rates will adjust to reflect the underlying balance between national savings and investment.

capital outflows take the form not only of direct lending of money to Americans to pay for Japanese exports, but also of Japanese purchases of apartment buildings in Los Angeles, purchases of American tire companies, and investment in American stocks.

The basic trade identity is *only* an identity: it only provides a framework for looking for an explanation. It says that if we observe a change in one part of the identity, we will always see corresponding changes in some other part. But the identity alone does not allow us to differentiate between explanations. It does not explain whether the U.S. trade deficit was caused by an increase in the demand for imports, with foreign firms accommodating that increase by lending Americans the money to buy those goods; whether the foreign taste for American exports suddenly declined; or whether there was an increase in the amount foreigners wanted to invest in the United States, which led to an exchange rate (dollar) appreciation, which in turn resulted in the trade deficit. To determine what actually happened in the 1980s, it is necessary to look more closely at how the trade deficits developed.

While it is theoretically possible that the trade deficits developed because of a substantial shift in the American demand curve for imports or a shift in the foreign demand curve for American exports, the much likelier reason is higher interest rates in the United States, which attracted foreign investment, raised the value of the dollar, and thus made imports appear cheaper and exports more expensive. That is, as Figure 38.4 showed, there was a shift in the demand for dollars, which led to an appreciation of the dollar; this was caused not by a change in tastes but by a demand for funds to invest in the United States.

Foreigners wanted to invest in the United States because the returns to their investments were relatively higher. But the cause of these higher returns does not seem to have been the prosperity of the country. Although the United States was growing faster than most European countries, it was not doing any better than Japan. Rather, the high interest rates reflected the high demand for borrowed funds in the United States. The demand for borrowing increased sharply in the early 1980s largely as a result of the increase in federal government borrowing. The one really large change between the 1980s and the preceding years was the federal budget deficits. The fact that the trade and budget deficits have increased together is no accident: large fiscal deficits lead to higher exchange rates, which lead to trade deficits. In this sense, the fiscal deficit is responsible for trade deficit. We can see this more clearly if we take a closer look at savings and investment in the U.S. economy.

THE SAVINGS-INVESTMENT IDENTITY FOR AN OPEN ECONOMY

In an economy without trade, where government does not borrow or lend, private (household and business) savings must equal private investment, as we learned in Chapter 29. However, in an economy with international borrowing and lending, private savings might be loaned out abroad and foreign savings might be borrowed to finance private investment. Private savings need not equal private borrowing. These considerations lead to an expanded formulation of the savings-investment identity:

$$\begin{array}{l} \text{private (household and business) savings} \\ \text{+ capital flows (borrowing) from abroad} \end{array} = \begin{array}{l} \text{investment in machines and equipment} \\ \text{+ federal budget deficit.} \end{array}$$

Private savings and capital flows from abroad can be thought of as the "sources" of funds; and investment and budget deficits can be thought of as the uses of funds. A slightly different approach is to think of the fiscal deficit as dissaving, or negative savings. Just as when a household spends less than its income it is saving, and when it spends more than its income it is dissaving, so too with government. The savings-investment identity can thus be rewritten:

private savings + government savings + capital flows from abroad = investment.

In the latter half of the 1970s, gross private savings were relatively low, at about 18 to 19 percent of GDP.[3] Gross private investment was also low by historical standards, at about 18 percent of GNP in 1978 and 1979. There was a moderate federal budget deficit matched by a moderate trade deficit (capital flows from abroad). But then the budget deficits exploded, and their increase meant that at least one of four things had to happen. Either private savings or borrowing from abroad had to increase to provide more money; or either investment or the deficit had to be reduced. This is what the basic identity tells us. The identity does not tell us which of these four possibilities will occur. As it happened, the main factor that adjusted was foreign capital flows.

The savings-investment identity says that if there is an increase in the deficit and if private savings and investment are unchanged, capital flows from abroad must increase and foreigners must end up holding more American assets. But the identity does not specify which assets they will hold. It does *not* say, for example, that the link between the trade deficit and the fiscal deficit is that foreign investors are buying U.S. government bonds. That may be true, but it is only part of the story. Foreign investors may be buying American companies, and Americans may be holding U.S. government bonds.

REVERSING THE TRADE DEFICIT

Some of the agitation that is heard about the trade deficit is often self-interested, from producers who are forced to compete with imports and would like protection or from those in the export sector who would like government subsidies. But there is also genuine reason to be concerned that huge trade deficits are not in the long-run interests of the United States.

WHY THE TRADE DEFICITS ARE A PROBLEM

Borrowing from abroad is not necessarily bad, any more than borrowing in general is necessarily bad. In its first century, America borrowed heavily from abroad; for most of this century, the United States has loaned out more money to foreign countries and investors than it has borrowed. This pattern is typical: in the early stages of development, countries borrow, use the money to build up their economies, and repay the loans with a portion of their economic gains. More mature economies, on the other hand, typically lend capital.

But as we have seen, the enormous U.S. trade deficits in the 1980s have reversed this pattern. Just as when the government borrows year after year the cumulative budget deficits lead to a high level of government debt, when the country borrows from abroad

---

[3] Remember that gross private savings include not only savings by households but also savings by firms. Household savings were much smaller, in the range of 3 to 6 percent.

year after year, the cumulative trade deficits (cumulative capital inflows) also lead to a high level of debt to foreigners.

The effect of the trade deficits of the 1980s was to convert the United States from the world's largest creditor nation at the beginning of the 1980s to the world's largest debtor nation by the end of the 1980s. Indeed, the sum of U.S. indebtedness equals the combined amount owed by the three huge Latin American debtor countries, Mexico, Brazil, and Argentina—although America's ability to meet these obligations is also far greater. Figures on how much private parties in one country owe or have borrowed from another country are not fully reliable, yet it is clear that the U.S. debt is huge and growing.

Figure 38.5 shows that it was in the mid-1980s that the United States slipped from being a creditor nation to being a debtor nation. Before 1987, the net international investment position of the United States—the value of all of America's assets abroad plus what others owe it minus the value of all assets within the United States owned by foreigners minus what it owes others—was positive.[4] But the cumulative effect of the trade deficits was to make this position negative. As a result, the U.S. economy will have to pay interest, dividends, and profits to foreign investors each year.

The consequences for the nation are little different from those you would experience as an individual if you borrowed a large amount from the bank. In the future, unless you used the borrowed funds to make an investment that yielded a return at least equal to the interest you had to pay, you would be unable to consume as much as you would otherwise; your consumption must be less than your income, as you must pay the bank interest as well as the principal. Consider this rough calculation: if the nation's debt to foreign investors reaches $1 trillion by the mid-1990s and the average rate of interest is 6 percent, the interest payments alone work out to over $200 for every man, woman, and child in the United States *every year*.

---

[4] One has to be careful about interpreting the figures. Critics of such figures point out that many of the assets that the United States owns abroad have greatly increased in value since it obtained those assets, but the data do not adequately reflect these increases. Still, there is little doubt about the general picture—there is a definite deterioration in America's net investment position.

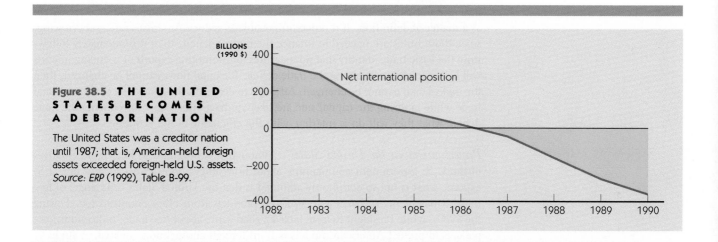

Figure 38.5 THE UNITED STATES BECOMES A DEBTOR NATION

The United States was a creditor nation until 1987; that is, American-held foreign assets exceeded foreign-held U.S. assets. *Source: ERP* (1992), Table B-99.

BILLIONS (1990 $)

Net international position

In a world of international trade, the fiscal deficit is a problem because unless private savings increase commensurately or private investment decreases commensurately, it leads to a trade deficit and foreign borrowing. The trade deficit in turn means that in the future, the U.S. economy will have to send abroad a part of what it produces at home to pay off this debt.

The trade identity and the savings-investment identity provide a framework for thinking about what might be done about the trade deficit. One policy option is to try to affect trade directly, by stimulating exports or decreasing imports; another option is to try to affect the capital flows, by making capital flows to the United States less attractive. We now take a closer look at these options, to see if either is viable.

TRADE POLICIES

Surely, by subsidizing exports and imposing tariffs on imports, it is possible to increase exports and reduce imports. Isn't that the basic lesson of economics—that markets respond to prices? But this situation is complicated by an important factor: the exchange rate.

Assume that export subsidies are successful in shifting the supply function for U.S. exports; the supply curve for exports shifts out, as U.S. exporters are willing to supply more goods to foreigners at any given price. The exporters then receive more foreign currency than they would have otherwise, which they try to trade for dollars. The increased supply of foreign currency will tend to make foreign currency relatively less valuable and dollars more valuable on foreign exchange markets. But because the dollar is more valuable, the market for U.S. exports will be reduced; the changes in the exchange rate will partially offset the export subsidies. Subsidies do distort the efficiency of the economy. The export industries that are lucky or powerful enough to get government subsidies will be a little better off; the export industries that do not get subsidized will be hurt by the increased exchange rate.

The same story will hold, in reverse, for attempts to restrict imports. The exchange rate will change in a way that offsets at least part of the import restriction.

It may seem paradoxical to say that policies intended to restrict imports or subsidies to encourage exports will be offset by changes in the exchange rate. But remember the lesson of the basic trade identity, which says that capital inflows equal the trade deficit as a matter of definition. If it proves impossible to reduce America's foreign borrowing, since those funds are needed to finance the budget deficit, then it immediately follows from the basic trade identity that no measures for promoting exports or reducing imports will be successful in reducing the trade deficit. If capital flows cannot be changed, then the trade deficit cannot be changed. Attempts to deal with the goods side of international trade while ignoring the capital side are likely to have little effect in reducing the trade deficit; what they will do is interfere with the efficiency of the economy.

Protectionism in the United States Although it is common to hear representatives of the U.S. government complaining about how other countries act to shut out U.S. exports, what is not so commonly admitted is that the United States is no angel of free trade; it has plenty of barriers to shut out products from other countries too. During the 1980s, while President Reagan talked a good game about free trade, protectionism—policies to protect American producers from foreign competition—soared. A study by the International Monetary Fund concluded that America's trade barriers against importing cars, textiles, and steel were the equivalent of a 25 percent tariff on those products. By the late 1980s, about 40 percent of Japan's exports to the United States were limited by some form of U.S. protectionism. About one-eighth of all U.S. imports were affected by protectionism in 1980; by the end of the decade, the figure was one-quarter.

In fact, when all America's trade barriers are added up, they may prevent consumers and businesses from buying as much as $50 billion in imports they would otherwise have purchased. The cost to American consumers is enormous. Not only are they unable to purchase the goods they would like, but U.S. producers, freed from the pressure of foreign competition, charge higher prices. The total magnitude of these higher prices may be over $30 billion, or over $400 for the average family. America's trade barriers probably do as much or more to shut out imports than the trade barriers of other countries do to shut out American products. And they have done nothing to solve the trade deficits.

Protectionism has always had some popular support in the United States, and it only increases when Americans are thrown out of jobs as a result of foreign competition. Economists have long waged a battle against protectionism on the grounds that (1) such policies do not in general succeed in creating jobs and (2) such policies interfere with the efficiency of the economy; when they do create jobs, they create them at a high cost.

Such policies do not create jobs not only because their effects may be offset by exchange rate changes. When America acts to shut out imports from other countries, those other countries often retaliate by shutting out American exports. For example, if the United States limits automobiles and electronics products from Korea, Korea might act to shut out U.S. farm exports. In trying to save jobs in one industry, protectionism often creates a reaction that makes other American workers worse off. Industries (like automobiles) that have strong competition from imports might well benefit from a ban on imports, but industries (like farming) that rely on exports would suffer considerably.

Economists' second objection is that when protectionism does save jobs, the evidence suggests it does so at a high cost. Consider what happened in the automobile industry. Threatened by Japanese imports, American car producers in 1981 persuaded the U.S. government to negotiate what were called "voluntary export restraints." Under these restraints, the Japanese "voluntarily" agreed to reduce their auto sales in the United States (with the knowledge that if they did not agree, the United States would impose them anyway). Shutting out less expensive imports of cars will certainly help U.S. workers in the automobile industry. But limiting the competition from imports forces American consumers to pay higher prices for a car that would perhaps have been only their second choice. Import restrictions have imposed costs on consumers that amount to as much as $100,000 or more in higher prices for every job that is saved in the protected industry.

More generally, protectionism results in the U.S. economy becoming less efficient. There is a loss of gains from trade: less specialization, less ability to take advantage of comparative advantage, and less competition. With less competition, not only can U.S. producers charge higher prices, firms have a reduced incentive to be efficient and become more productive and competitive. In the long run, these factors can also lead to slower growth of productivity. Most economists would argue that the negative effects of trade, such as putting people or businesses out of work, should be countered directly by helping businesses become more productive and helping workers find new jobs, not by trying to freeze the economy in one place.

Mercantilism is the name economists have given to the school of economic thought that was most prevalent in Europe between about 1500 and 1800. Mercantilists focused on building the power and wealth of the state, two attributes they felt to be interrelated. For example, they supported a policy to build up a country's wealth by making it illegal to ship gold and silver out of the country. In 1693, Josiah Child, one of the better-known of the mercantilist writers, summed it up this way: "Foreign trade produces riches, riches power; power preserves our trade and religion."

The policies of the mercantilists were to export wherever possible, unless those exports might help other nations militarily. Imports were to be discouraged, unless they were imports of the sort of raw materials that could be processed and immediately reexported. To have lots of products left over for export, the nation had to produce more than it consumed, so the citizens were exhorted to work hard for low wages. By selling items to foreign purchasers for gold and silver but avoiding buying from foreign producers whenever possible, a nation could build up its economic wealth and thus its power.

The mercantilist philosophy should sound familiar, because it is very similar to a philosophy that is still popular in the United States and throughout the world. One often hears people talking of how their country should strive for self-sufficiency and avoid becoming dependent on other nations. They argue that if foreign producers are allowed to sell in the United States, they will take jobs from U.S. workers. Thus, imports should be restricted and cut back.

Nations like Japan and South Korea have built their wealth in modern times by selling products to other countries and using the money received to build up the industrial base of the country. One will often hear of state and federal attempts in the United States to promote exports, sometimes by giving subsidies to other countries to buy American products. In this philosophy, products become projections of national power. If U.S. products invade foreign shores successfully, America wins. If foreign products invade American shores, the country loses.

Adam Smith provided an answer to the mercantilists and a different version of how to think about the wealth of nations in his classic book *The Wealth of Nations.* This short passage gives the flavor of his argument:

A rich country, in the same manner as a rich man, is supposed to be a country abounding in money; and to heap up gold and silver in any country is supposed to be the readiest way to enrich it. For some time after the discovery of America, the first enquiry of the Spaniards, when they arrived upon any unknown coast, used to be if there was any gold or silver to be found in the neighborhood. By the information which they received, they judged whether it was worth while to make a settlement there, or if the country was worth the conquering. Plano Carpino, a monk sent ambassador from the king of France to one of the sons of the famous Gengis Khan, says that the Tartars used frequently to ask him if there was plenty of sheep and oxen in the kingdom of France. Their enquiry had the same object with that of the Spaniards. They wanted to know if the country was rich enough to be worth the conquering. Among the Tartars, as among all other nations of shepherds, who are generally ignorant of the use of money, cattle are the instruments of commerce and the measures of value. Wealth, therefore, according to them, consisted in cattle, as according to the Spaniards it consisted in gold and silver. Of the two, the Tartar notion, perhaps, was the nearest to the truth.

Smith's fundamental answer to the mercantilists was that the wealth of a nation was not properly measured by gold and silver, but by the physical characteristics of the country. Smith pointed out that even from the standpoint of national power, a nation's army does not run on gold and silver, but on physical products like ships, food, clothing, and weapons. That is why Smith said that the Tartars, who focused on real items like sheep and oxen, may have understood wealth more clearly than the Spaniards did.

Smith also emphasized the advantages of both buying and selling. In his view, foreign trade offered two major advantages. First, if another nation could make a product more efficiently, then people of the first nation benefit from being able to buy that cheaper product. Second, by allowing companies to sell throughout the world, trade allows expanded production, which in turn encourages greater division of labor. Thus, rather than seeing foreign trade as a matter of invasions of goods, Smith argued that foreign trade allowed people to produce more as workers and get the best deal the world could offer them as consumers.

Smith's answer to the mercantilist argument should also sound somewhat familiar, because it is the great-great-grandfather of today's arguments for free trade between nations. In effect, Smith told the businessmen of his day, who were arguing for promoting their export sales and preventing import competition, that restrictions on competition might benefit them, but that free trade would be beneficial for society as a whole.

Sources: Adam Smith, *The Wealth of Nations,* Book IV, Chapter 1, pp. 450–51; William R. Allen, "Mercantilism," in the *New Palgrave Dictionary of Economics* (1987).

Export Subsidies   Besides restricting imports, another way of reducing the trade deficit is to increase exports. Firms in exporting industries often argue that the government should subsidize them, to enable them to sell more abroad. The government does provide direct subsidies for agricultural exports and hidden subsidies, through loan guarantees and favorable credit terms, to a variety of other industries.

But export subsidies suffer from the same problems that protectionist policies do. Changes in the exchange rate reduce their effectiveness. Foreign governments frequently match whatever export subsidies are being offered. American producers thus do not gain at the expense of foreign producers, though more of the subsidized product will be purchased than would have been the case if it were not subsidized. Finally, even when such policies do create jobs, the cost of creating them is extremely high. The whole economy pays a high price for the inefficiencies these policies induce.

Of course, people in the export industry and in industries that compete with imports see things differently. There is little doubt that many individual industries and workers could benefit, at the expense of the rest of the U.S. economy, from export subsidies. Industries asking for protection often talk about the pain they are suffering, but downplay or ignore the costs that protectionism would impose on the rest of the economy. Those in the export industry see the extra profits they obtain if they can sell more exports, possibly with the help of government subsidies, and it is natural for them to feel that it is important to the country that their particular business do well. They too often fail to account for the costs that these subsidies impose on the nation as a whole.

The case for free trade is not that it is a favor the United States does for foreign countries. Trade is not aid; it is not a giveaway. Even from the point of view of America's own narrow self-interest, free trade is a favor the United States can do for itself.

Changing the Exchange Rate There is one other way that the government may attempt to reduce the trade deficit, a way that does not discriminate against or favor particular industries: it can try to change the exchange rate. If the government can do something that leads to a depreciation of the dollar, imports will be more expensive and foreigners will view American goods as less expensive, so that exports will increase.

Sometimes monetary policy can achieve this effect, at least in the short run. Monetary policy can drive down interest rates, making it less attractive for foreigners to invest in the United States. The demand curve for dollars (to be used to purchase investments in the United States) shifts down, and this in turn leads to a depreciation of the dollar. In the longer run, however, changes in the exchange rate will be related to the magnitude of underlying capital flows, to which we now turn.

WHY TRADE RESTRICTIONS ARE INEFFECTIVE AND UNDESIRABLE

1. The exchange rate adjusts in such a way as to offset the effects of export subsidies and import duties.

2. They may lead to retaliation from other countries, so that the United States loses exports as it reduces imports.

3. They succeed in shutting out particular imports, but the country loses its gains from trade, the ability to take advantage of specialization, comparative advantage, and competition.

4. The insulation of American producers from foreign competition may reduce the efficiency of American firms.

REDUCING CAPITAL FLOWS

If trying to affect imports and exports will not succeed in reducing the trade deficit, what will? The basic trade identity provides another answer: reducing capital flows. The savings-investment identity suggests how this might be done. In an open economy, capital flows equal investment plus the fiscal deficit minus private savings. So to decrease capital flows, it is necessary either to reduce the budget deficit, to increase private savings, or to decrease investment in machines and equipment by U.S. firms. Some of these possibilities are self-evidently bad policy. For example, decreasing investment would have terrible consequences for the growth of the economy. Indeed, an objective of growth-oriented policies is to *increase* the rate of investment.

What about increasing household savings? For savings to be increased, consumption must be reduced. In a sense, this is the nub of the problem: the United States has been living beyond its means.

If it were possible to stimulate household savings, there is general agreement that it would be desirable to do so. U.S. savings rates are lower than those of almost any other industrialized country—much lower than Japan's. But as we saw in Chapter 37, experts in savings behavior are generally pessimistic concerning the government's capacity to stimulate the savings rate in the near future.

Business savings might be increased if after-tax corporate profits were higher. (Indeed, the extra funds would likely stimulate further firm investment as well.) But beyond increasing the general level of economic activity (when the economy is operating at a high level, profits tend to be high), the only way to increase after-tax corporate profits is to lower the tax rate on corporations, and doing so would only add to the federal budget deficit. Thus, while business savings would be increased, government savings would be reduced and the overall picture would remain unchanged.

The only remaining way—the only practical way—to decrease capital flows and reduce the trade deficit is to reduce the government's fiscal deficit. The twin deficits are indeed intimately interlinked.

REDUCING THE TRADE DEFICIT, USING THE SAVINGS-INVESTMENT IDENTITY

1. Reduce investment.

2. Increase household savings.

3. Increase business savings.

4. Reduce the federal budget deficit.

THE BUDGET DEFICIT

During the 1960s and 1970s, most economists focused their attention on the trade-off between unemployment and inflation as reflected in the Phillips curve. At the time, many would have predicted that if the federal government chose to run extraordinarily large budget deficits, the result would be higher employment (if only in the short run) followed by higher inflation. In effect, the huge deficits would shift the aggregate demand curve to the point where it intersected the aggregate supply curve on the steep upward-sloping portion, illustrated in Figure 38.6A. The rightward shift in the aggregate demand curve from AD_0 to AD_1 would result in a significant increase in the equilibrium price

Figure 38.6 BUDGET DEFICITS AND INFLATION

Heading into the 1980s, many economists would have predicted that huge budget deficits would have shifted aggregate demand and triggered a surge of inflation, as in panel A. But the economy proved more open to foreign goods and capital than many had predicted. The aggregate supply curve turned out to be flatter than expected, as in panel B. While federal borrowing led to a trade deficit and U.S. indebtedness, it did not cause inflation.

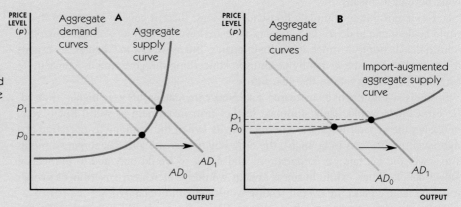

level, and many economists would have predicted that this would set off an inflationary spiral.

As the experience of the 1980s has made clear, that view of government budget deficits rested on an assumption that the economy was largely closed to foreign capital and foreign goods. In the 1980s, the economy was able to consume more without moving past the full-employment portion of the aggregate supply curve to where inflation would be increased sharply. Thus, an open economy appears more able to absorb an increase in aggregate demand without inducing inflation. In effect, the import-augmented aggregate supply curve—the total supply of goods available to the economy, produced both at home and abroad—is relatively flat, as illustrated in panel B. Therefore, the shift in the aggregate demand curve need not give rise to much inflationary pressure.

However, avoiding one trade-off led to another in the 1980s. The inflow of foreign capital and the U.S. status as a debtor nation mean that a share of U.S. output must be repaid to foreign investors, with interest. In effect, the money borrowed from abroad during the 1980s was not invested in projects that will yield greater economic growth in the future, but rather went to finance increased military expenditures, reduced tax burdens (allowing taxpayers to enjoy higher levels of consumption than they otherwise would have), and high levels of Social Security and Medicare benefits to the aged. As desirable as any of these expenditures may have been, they are not like expenditures on new factories: they do not themselves generate the returns that will pay back these loans with interest.

This means that it will not be possible to repay the foreign borrowing with a portion of the fruits of economic growth; instead, repayment will require Americans to have a lower standard of living than they otherwise would have. Even if the standard of living is only a few tenths of a percent lower, that accumulates in a generation into a heavy burden. The fact that for a decade, beginning around 1973, real wages did not rise at all, and even since then real wages have increased but slowly, has shaken the long-standing confidence that come what may, incomes and living standards will always be rising. If an increasing proportion of these slowly rising incomes has to go abroad to repay the debts of the 1980s and 1990s, then living standards may indeed have to fall.

REDUCING THE BUDGET DEFICIT

We have seen that the only practical way to reduce America's ever-increasing indebtedness to foreigners resulting from its trade deficit is to reduce the federal budget deficit. While politicians of all parties and persuasions seem agreed upon this objective, it has become a seemingly unobtainable one. When George Bush ran for the presidency in 1988, not only did he say, "Read my lips: no new taxes," he also promised to eliminate the fiscal deficit. The first promise was broken in 1990, when taxes were raised as the only feasible way of making any headway at all on the deficit problem. The downturn of the economy starting in 1990 reduced tax revenues below the optimistic projections that were made in the beginning of the Bush administration and led to further increases in the deficit, which reached record high levels. There is a popular impression that eliminating the deficit should be an easy matter—all that is required is to cut out the fat in government spending. Surely there are inefficiencies in government, just as there are inefficiencies in the private sector. But almost a decade of lean years for most government departments has eliminated much of the fat, and yet the country is little closer to solving the deficit problem.

The budgetary process was also blamed for the persistent deficits, and there was a call for a reform in that process. Traditionally, the president sends a budget proposal to Congress, but then each of the various committees in Congress takes responsibility for the part of the government that falls within its purview. There are committees in both the Senate and House concerned with defense, health care, agriculture, and the other major activities of government; each argues for the merits of its charges. But none is able to balance off in an objective manner the merits of its claims with those of others. The total budget recommended by the committees exceeds the revenues of the government, and even after being whittled down a large gap remains.

Congress, concerned about these procedures, has instituted a number of reforms. For example, at the beginning of the year, an agreement is made on the overall dimensions of the budget—how much money should go to defense, how much to other broad categories, how much should be raised in new taxes. A much more dramatic effort, the Gramm-Rudman-Hollings Bill, named after its sponsors and passed in 1986, called for specific deficit targets that would lead (it was hoped) to a balanced budget in 1991. Under the bill, if the planned expenditures exceeded the targets, there was a simple formula by which expenditures in each program were to be scaled back. After the Supreme Court held as unconstitutional the procedures by which these automatic cuts were to be implemented, Congress enacted alternative procedures in 1987, and at the same time postponed until 1993 the target date for balancing the budget.

Then, in 1990, Congress and President Bush could not reach an agreement on a budget that would satisfy the deficit targets. In the absence of an agreement, the president refused to sign bills authorizing the temporary continuation of expenditures for the new fiscal year at their previous level. And in the absence of that authorization, government offices and services would have to be shut down. There were fears of wide-ranging effects; for instance, without federal air controllers, the nation's airlines would have to shut down.

With the threat of a government shutdown in the background, congressional leaders and the White House worked out an agreement, but it was rejected by Congress. Eventually a new agreement was reached: the Gramm-Rudman-Hollings target of a balanced budget was postponed until 1995, and the budgetary procedures were reformed. Among the reforms, targets were now expressed in terms of "full-employment deficits"— what the deficit would be if the economy were at full employment.

This change was important for the role of fiscal policy in stabilization. When there is a downturn in the economy, tax revenues are reduced. Under the Gramm-Rudman-Hollings Bill, when this happened, government expenditures would be reduced commensurately. But we saw in Chapter 30 that a reduction in expenditures, matched by a reduction in taxes, leads to a lower level of aggregate demand. Thus, this response of the government to the economic downturn would automatically exacerbate it.

The new law is, in this respect, far better. But if it works, it will effectively prohibit the government from taking an *active* policy in stabilizing the economy. Under the law, when the economy goes into a downturn, government expenditures do not have to be cut. But the government cannot try to stimulate the economy *further* by either cutting taxes or increasing expenditures. It is only permitted to stimulate the economy by increasing taxes and expenditures together, by an equal amount. And given the difficulty of increasing taxes at any time, let alone in a recession, this means that the government has effectively forsworn the use of discretionary fiscal policy. But the experiences of 1987 and 1990—with Congress and the president abandoning the commitments to a balanced budget as soon as they posed serious political problems—suggest that this new agreement may not be worth a great deal!

A closer look at how government spends its money makes clear why eliminating the deficit has proved so difficult. Figure 38.7 breaks down federal government expenditures into different categories. Some of these expenditures cannot be cut in the short run— they are nondiscretionary. For example, the government must meet the interest obligations on the bonds it has issued to finance the deficit; as government debt has increased, these interest payments have soared to the point where they now account for 16 percent of the federal budget. Other expenditures are for entitlement programs like Social Security and Medicare. These social insurance programs constitute nearly a third of the budget. Given the rules for Social Security, expenditures simply increase as the number of

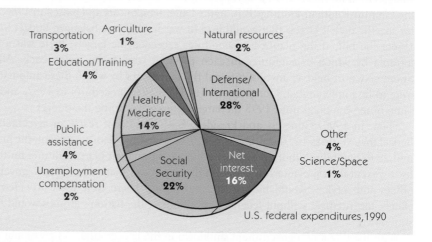

Figure 38.7 THE CHALLENGE OF REDUCING FEDERAL SPENDING

A large proportion of federal spending is devoted to three programs: defense, entitlement programs, and interest payments. To reduce federal spending, large cuts must be made in at least some of these categories, since other areas of spending are simply not large enough to make much difference. *Source: ERP* (1992), Table B-70.

Transportation 3%
Agriculture 1%
Natural resources 2%
Education/Training 4%
Defense/International 28%
Health/Medicare 14%
Public assistance 4%
Social Security 22%
Net interest 16%
Other 4%
Science/Space 1%
Unemployment compensation 2%

U.S. federal expenditures, 1990

people eligible for Social Security increases. The only way to cut these expenditures is to change the rules. And no one seems to want to cut back on the programs for the aged.

There is some scope for cutting back on Medicare expenditures (expenditures for medical care for the aged), by cutting back on costs—paying doctors less, trying to ensure that patients stay in hospitals no longer than necessary, and so on. These savings, however, will only make a small dent in the deficit. And, if anything, there are strong political pressures to increase expenditures on medical care as deficiencies in the American medical care system, such as the large number of unemployed people not covered by insurance, become more evident.

The largest single component of government expenditures is for defense. If we add up the total of interest payments, defense expenditures, and entitlement programs, we have accounted for three-fourths of federal expenditures. The deficit during the 1980s was running at 15 to 20 percent of government expenditures. No wonder, then, that with a commitment not to increase taxes, the deficit problem could not be solved. It would have required cutting all the remaining areas of government expenditures—from the costs of running the government itself to its road programs, expenditures on R & D, public assistance, and housing—by between one-third and two-thirds. This was an amount that most economists believe would have had disastrous consequences and that most politicians found completely unacceptable.

Events in 1990 and 1991 held open the possibilities of obtaining a more balanced budget. The ending of the Cold War resulted in what came to be called the "peace dividend," the possibility of substantially reduced defense expenditures. The Bush administration's abandonment of its commitment to no new taxes opened up the possibility of increasing revenues as an alternative way of reducing the deficit. But those who view the twin deficit problem as a serious threat to America's long-run economic strength want more of both: more tax increases and more defense cuts. Without these, there seems to be no possibility of making serious inroads into a problem that has plagued the country for more than a decade.

REDUCING THE BUDGET DEFICIT

Basic problem: large fraction of total expenditures that are nondiscretionary, such as interest payments and entitlement programs

Two major alternatives

1. Increase taxes.

2. Reduce defense spending.

3. Contain costs of other government programs.

REVIEW AND PRACTICE

SUMMARY

1. The early 1980s were marked by a surge in the size of federal budget deficits. There appear to be four main causes for the increase: lower taxes, higher defense spending, higher spending on support for the elderly, and higher interest payments.

2. The 1980s were also marked by a large increase in the U.S. trade deficit, and by a sharp increase in U.S. borrowing from abroad. In the mid-1980s, the United States changed from being a creditor to a debtor nation.

3. Government borrowing can be an economic burden for future generations in several ways. First, future generations may have to bear the burden of paying off the borrowing; there is a transfer from one generation to another. Second, government borrowing can crowd out investment, which will reduce future output and wages. Third, when the money is borrowed from foreign investors, then Americans as a whole must pay some of their national income each year to foreigners just for interest, resulting in lower standards of living.

4. A country's trade deficit is equal to the difference between its imports and exports, which is also equal to its capital inflows. Thus, a trade deficit and borrowing from abroad are two ways of describing the same pattern.

5. The savings-investment identity for an open economy says that the sum of private savings, capital flows from abroad, and government savings are equal to investment. This identity implies that a change in any one factor must also involve offsetting changes in the other factors.

6. Policies that aim to reduce the U.S. trade deficit and foreign borrowing by blocking imports or subsidizing exports encounter several problems: the exchange rate will adjust in a way that offsets the policy; other countries are likely to retaliate; restricting imports means that foreigners will buy less from U.S. exporters; the economy loses its gains from trade.

7. Other policy options for reducing the U.S. trade deficit and foreign borrowing include decreasing investment (a bad idea for long-term growth), increasing household and business savings (a good idea if the government could do it), or reducing the federal budget deficit.

8. Reducing the federal budget deficit has proved to be politically difficult. Three-quarters of federal spending goes to defense, entitlement programs, and interest payments. Without tax increases or large cuts in these areas, the deficit cannot be easily reduced.

REVIEW QUESTIONS

1. What happened to the size of the budget deficits in the 1980s? Had there ever been such large deficits in peacetime?

2. Name four fiscal changes that contributed to the large budget deficits of the 1980s.

3. What is the relationship between the deficits and the U.S. government debt?

4. What happened to the trade deficit during the 1980s? How did the foreign indebtedness of the U.S. economy change during the 1980s? What is the relationship between these two changes? What is the relationship between the trade deficit and an inflow of foreign capital?

5. How can borrowing from abroad affect future generations for the better? How can it affect future generations for the worse?

6. What is the argument that "the debt doesn't matter, since we owe it to ourselves"? What is wrong with this argument?

7. What is the savings-investment identity for an open economy?

8. Why may protectionism fail to save jobs? Why is protectionism costly?

9. Using the savings-investment identity for an open economy, list the various ways that capital flows from abroad might be reduced. Evaluate each of these alternatives.

10. Since it is politically or legally difficult to cut defense spending, entitlement programs, and interest payments, why can't federal spending be cut substantially by focusing on all the other federal programs?

PROBLEMS

1. U.S. foreign indebtedness is greater than that of Mexico, Brazil, and Argentina combined. But does this necessarily mean that the United States has a larger debt problem than those countries? Why or why not? Can you think of a situation in which an individual with debts of larger value may actually have less of a debt problem?

2. True or false: "Government borrowing can transfer resources from future generations to the present, but it cannot affect the overall wealth of the country." Discuss.

3. If Congress were to pass a law prohibiting foreigners from buying U.S. Treasury bills, would this prevent government borrowing from leading to capital inflows? Discuss.

4. Japan had large trade surpluses during the 1980s. Would this cause Japan to be a borrower or a lender in international capital markets?

5. If a nation borrowed $50 billion from abroad one year and its imports were worth $800 billion, what would be the value of its exports? How does your answer change if, instead of borrowing, the nation loaned $100 billion abroad?

6. Suppose a certain country has private savings of 6 percent of GDP, foreign borrowing of 1 percent of GDP, and a balanced budget. What is its level of investment? If the budget deficit is 1.5 percent of GDP, how does your answer change?

7. Imagine that a nation's budget deficit increases while its foreign borrowing remains unchanged. What factors would you expect to change in this situation?

8. Since other countries benefit from exporting their products to the United States, why shouldn't the U.S. government charge them for the privilege of selling in the United States?

9. Explain how reducing the budget deficit would contribute to long-term growth, using the savings-investment identity.

DIFFERING
APPROACHES TO
MACROECONOMIC
POLICY

T he making of government economic policy often seems like walking a tightrope. Lean too far to one side, and the economy faces growing unemployment. Lean too far to the other, and there is inflation. While it may be difficult to reach the best of all possible worlds, it does seem possible to have the worst of all worlds: simultaneous inflation, unemployment, and slow growth.

Many of the basic macroeconomic problems arise out of the variability in the level of economic activity. When the economy seems to be dragging along, a jump start may be required to reignite it. But when the economy is racing along, unless something is done to slow it down, inflation may loom ahead. Both unemployment and inflation cause economic hardship to large segments of the population. Unemployment particularly affects the young, who have no cushion of accumulated savings to fall back upon, as well as blacks, Hispanics, and unskilled workers. Inflation takes its toll among retired individuals, who may suffer because their incomes do not rise commensurately with inflation.

It should come as no surprise that with a subject as vital as the economic health of the nation, there is much disagreement even among experts. This chapter begins by reviewing the evidence concerning economic fluctuations and how that evidence has been interpreted. We then look at the related question of what government can do about economic fluctuations. We will see that the major macroeconomic schools can be divided into two categories: those who favor government intervention and those who do not. For economists who favor intervention, the question becomes how best to do so, and the final section of the chapter reviews the major policy instruments and the criteria that should be used in choosing among them.

"Ferguson claims he's being whipsawed by inflation and taxes. Whoops! There he goes now!"

KEY QUESTIONS

1. What are the alternative explanations of the pronounced fluctuations in the level of economic activity in the economy? Why does the economy periodically experience a downturn in which unemployment is high, growth slows down, and output actually falls?

2. Why do some economists believe that the government should not intervene to stabilize the economy? Why do they believe that such intervention is unnecessary, ineffective, or more likely to do harm than good? And why do other economists believe that intervention can at times be helpful?

3. If intervention is desirable, what are the different instruments that are available to government? What are their different impacts? What are the criteria for choosing among them?

BUSINESS FLUCTUATIONS

The recession that began in 1990 closed the door on the longest peacetime expansion in U.S. history. There had been seven years of uninterrupted economic growth, 1983–1990. Some of the growth was simply the recovery from the worst recession since World

War II, which had gripped the economy in the years immediately prior to 1983. But even taking that into account, the record was impressive. Most economists believed the expansion would not continue forever, and they were right; the economy went into a downturn in the fall of 1990.

All modern economies experience ups and downs in the level of economic activity. There are periods of faster growth and higher employment, followed by periods of slower growth. Figure 39.1A shows the movement of U.S. economic output over the past fifty years. A smooth line has been drawn through the data, tracing out the path that the economy might have taken had it grown at a steady rate. This line represents the economy's **long-term trend**. The figure makes clear that while the long-term trend is upward, the economy is sometimes above the trend line and sometimes below. Panel B shows the percentage by which the economy has been below or above that trend line. It also shows the unemployment rate, to illustrate the negative correlation between these deviations of output from trend and unemployment.

It is apparent from the figure that the economy fluctuates. Sometimes it grows faster than at other times. The term "recession" is reserved for periods in which output actually declines, but even growth at a substantially lower rate represents an economic slowdown, with significant consequences. To take one important example, jobs will likely not be

Figure 39.1
ECONOMIC FLUCTUATIONS: OUTPUT

Panel A shows how output has moved above and below a long-term trend line over the past fifty years. Panel B compares the deviation of GNP from its long-term trend with the unemployment rate. Notice that when GNP is above its long-term rate, unemployment tends to be low; and when GNP is below its long-term rate, unemployment tends to be higher. *Source: Economic Report of the President* (1992), Table B-1; (1991), Table B-1.

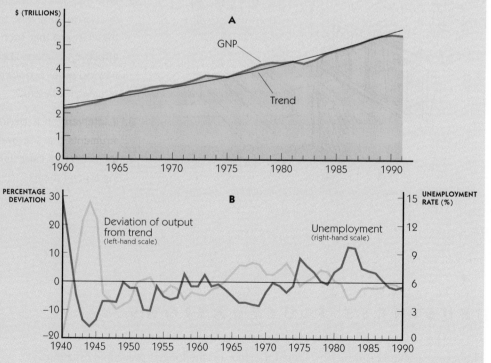

created at a rate that will allow new workers to be absorbed into the labor force, so unemployment will rise.

There are four principal views on the nature of these fluctuations in the level of economic activity, often referred to as business cycles. The traditional business-cycle theory argues that there are built-in forces within the economy that give rise to fluctuations. The real business-cycle theory argues that the fluctuations are nothing more than the result of random and unpredictable shocks. Monetarists and new classical economists see the fluctuations as largely the consequence of misguided monetary policy. And new Keynesians see the fluctuations as originating from a variety of sources both inside and outside the economy, but believe that built-in characteristics of modern economies amplify some of the disturbances and make their effects persist.

THE TRADITIONAL BUSINESS-CYCLE VIEW

The traditional view of business cycles held that there are regular and predictable fluctuations in economic output, and it is the structure of the economy that gives rise to them. In this view, the source of the fluctuations is **endogenous**, that is, within the economy itself; if this is the case, then the upswings and downswings of the economy are to a large extent predictable.

THE MULTIPLIER-ACCELERATOR

To see how internal forces cause fluctuations, assume that the economy is initially in a recession but output begins to increase, as was the case in 1983. Suppose the upturn is initiated by an additional $100 million of exports, and the multiplier is 2.5. Then national income increases by $250 million. With higher sales of $250 million, firms believe that they need to install additional capacity, or capital goods. If the accelerator is 2 (the accelerator is the increase in capital goods—the investment—required to produce greater output), then the increased sales of $250 million lead to increased investment of $500 million. Now, the increased investment of $500 million leads, through the multiplier process, to a greater output of $1.25 billion ($500 million × 2.5). The higher sales reinforce firms' optimism. Wanting to keep pace with their sales, they increase investment by $2.5 billion (output is now up by an additional $1.25 billion, so they think they need $2.5 billion of new capital goods). And this greater investment leads to a still larger output.

Eventually the economy hits constraints; for example, shortages of labor may impose a limit on the expansion of the economy. Once these constraints are hit, the economy stops expanding, or at least stops expanding as fast. But when the economy expands at a slower rate, the demand for investment decreases. And because of the multiplier effects, this reduces aggregate demand. A downturn in the economy thus begins. As output declines, investment drops lower, further accentuating the decline. Investment comes to a standstill. But eventually the old machines wear out or become obsolete. Even to produce the low level of output associated with the recession, new investment is required. This new investment stimulates demand, which in turn stimulates investment; the economy turns up.

This way of relating business cycles to the internal working of the economy is called the **multiplier-accelerator model** and was first developed by Nobel laureate Paul

Samuelson of MIT.[1] The term reflects the model's two major ingredients: the multiplier discussed in Chapter 28 and the accelerator, based on the relationship between capital and output, discussed in Chapter 29.

THE REAL BUSINESS-CYCLE VIEW

By contrast with the traditional business-cycle theory, which sees cycles as regular and predictable, the real business-cycle view considers fluctuations in economic output to be random and unpredictable. Among its leading advocates are Charles Plosser and Robert King, both of the University of Rochester. In this view, if the economy has been growing by 4 percent, it is as likely to grow by 5 percent next year as it is to grow by 3 percent. If the economy is growing at 2 percent, it is as likely to decline by 1 percent next year as it is to grow by 3 percent. Where the traditional business-cycle school finds the cause for fluctuations in the internal forces of the economy, such as the working of the multiplier and accelerator, this school pins the blame on real, external events such as a change in the price of an important input like oil, natural disasters, and especially shocks to technology such as new inventions. These shocks all come from outside the economy, or at least outside the part of the economy upon which we are focusing; they are **exogenous** events. Because they are exogenous, they are outside the control of policymakers.

The shocks real business-cycle theorists focus on are those to the supply side of the economy, to what firms are willing to produce at any given set of wages and prices. Real business-cycle theorists thus stand in stark contrast to the other economic schools, which emphasize the importance of shocks to aggregate demand as being a major source of disturbances to the economy. Real business-cycle theorists also tend to believe that markets respond quickly and efficiently to these supply-side shocks, so they do not see economic fluctuations as a major problem.

"Cycle" is something of a misnomer here, since the real business-cycle school sees nothing as predictable as a cycle in its observation of economic fluctuations. But what about the patterns that we saw in Figure 39.1, the ups and downs that look like cycles? Real business-cycle proponents see these as illusions. They observe that when someone flips a coin several hundred times, she may come up with some streaks of heads or tails just by blind chance. Some fifty years ago, the great Russian mathematical economist Eugen Slutsky demonstrated that what might appear to be regular cycles could have been generated simply from random events. Figure 39.2A shows how totally random occurrences can add up to a picture that looks remarkably like the cyclical fluctuation of consumer durable sales shown in panel B.

Some economists have criticized real business-cycle theories because of their failure to identify the large exogenous disturbances that could account for the magnitude of the fluctuations the economy has experienced. Even the largest shocks in recent decades, such as the increase in the price of oil in the 1970s, are quite small when viewed from the perspective of the economy as a whole. For example, oil imports account for a fairly small share of GNP. If the cost of oil doubled and nothing else happened, the effect would be the same as a reduction in aggregate income of a commensurately small amount. When the price of oil increased sharply in the early 1970s, the total value of

---

[1] In the simple version of the model Samuelson developed, the full-employment constraint on the economy does not play a role. He showed that one could have a business cycle without relying on such constraints. However, the importance of these constraints was emphasized by Richard Goodwin, an American teaching in Cambridge, England, and by Nobel laureate Sir John Hicks of Oxford University.

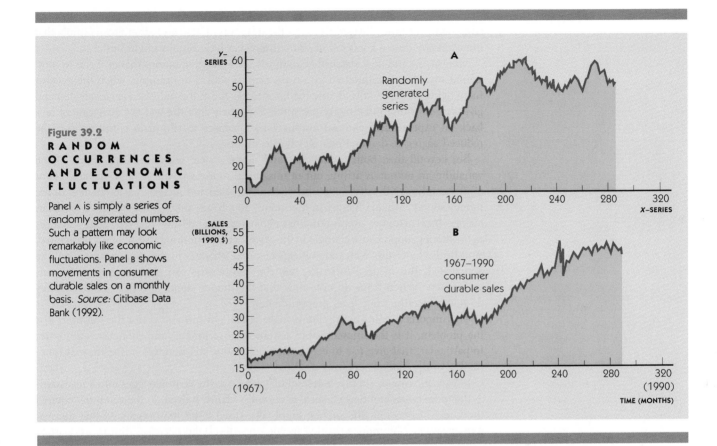

Figure 39.2
RANDOM OCCURRENCES AND ECONOMIC FLUCTUATIONS

Panel A is simply a series of randomly generated numbers. Such a pattern may look remarkably like economic fluctuations. Panel B shows movements in consumer durable sales on a monthly basis. *Source:* Citibase Data Bank (1992).

U.S. oil imports climbed from $7.6 billion in 1973 to $24.8 billion in 1975. A large increase to be sure, but since the increase of $17.2 billion was only about 1 percent of 1975 GNP, one might think it would have only a small effect.

Critics also maintain that supply-side shocks do not have immediate effects. It takes years for a major new innovation like computers or lasers or transistors to be absorbed into the economy. Equally important, real business-cycle theory has failed to explain the major downturns in the economy. There has been no convincing interpretation of the large negative shocks that real business-cycle theorists claim are responsible for economic fluctuations: what set off the Great Depression or, even more recently, the recession that began in 1990?

MONETARIST AND NEW CLASSICAL VIEWS

Monetarists such as Milton Friedman and new classical economists such as Robert Lucas share the real business-cycle view that for the most part the economy responds quickly and efficiently to disturbances, which are unpredictable. But they differ in their opinion of the source of the disturbances. In their view, it is not changes in technology that are the culprits; there simply are not large enough exogenous shocks to the economy to account for the magnitude of the observed variations. Indeed, these economists believe that if left to itself, the economy would not be highly variable. People smooth consumption over time. Investors look to the long run. These and other factors imply that the economy does a good job of smoothing what little bumps might buffet it.

Monetarists and new classical economists blame the big bumps that give rise to most significant economic fluctuations on the government. For example, when the government fights a war but fails to raise the taxes to pay for it, the increased aggregate demand gives rise to strong inflationary pressures; and when after the war the government cuts back on expenditures without cutting back on taxes to stimulate consumption, the reduced aggregate demand can set off a recession.

But beyond this, both monetarists and new classical economists see much of the variability in output as arising out of misguided monetary policy. New classical economists emphasize the distinction between anticipated and unanticipated changes in the money supply. When changes in the money supply are anticipated, the price level can change; the real money supply remains unchanged, and nothing "real" happens. Changes in the money supply cause changes in the price level and nothing else; policy is ineffective. And in the long run, with rational expectations, changes in the money supply will be anticipated. But in the short run, monetary authorities can act in ways that are unanticipated. When firms do not know that the money supply has been reduced, they do not reduce the price level proportionately.

The important point both schools make is that government is not the solution, it is the problem; it is the unpredictable actions of government, and monetary authorities in particular, that give rise to economic fluctuations and interfere in the normal functioning of the market economy.

In fact, the money supply does tend to decrease as the economy goes into a recession, as the monetarists and new classical economists claim. Indeed, as the economy entered the Great Depression, the money supply decreased faster than prices, so that the real money supply (the money divided by the price level) did decrease. But as we learned earlier, one has to be careful in distinguishing between causality and correlation. The real money supply always increases before Christmas, yet few would claim that the higher sales at Christmas are due to the larger money supply; rather the larger money supply is a response to the anticipated increase in sales. Critics of the monetarist analysis of the Depression suggest that a similar argument applies here: the lower money supply was not the cause but the consequence of the Depression. (Even the somewhat weaker contention, that while the Fed may not have caused the Depression it should have done more to reverse it, is disputed; as we have seen, there are reasons to believe that in a deep recession monetary policy may be relatively ineffective.)

NEW KEYNESIAN VIEWS

Between the traditional business-cycle theory and the real business-cycle theory is a view held by new Keynesians that there are processes in the economy that amplify a variety of small- and medium-sized external, unpredictable shocks and transform them into large fluctuations. And the economy not only amplifies the shocks, it makes their effects persist long after the initial disturbance has disappeared. In this view, the sources of the disturbances are exogenous, but there are endogenous forces that make the fluctuations significant and make the effects of disturbances persist.

New Keynesians include as possible sources of disturbances to the economy both the kinds of supply-side disturbances emphasized by the real business-cycle theorists and the monetary disturbances emphasized by the monetarists and new classical economists.

Deciding when a recession begins is a tricky business with major political consequences. A look at the two most recent downturns, in 1980–82 and in 1990–91, shows the finger-pointing that accompanies the dating process.

The typical definition of a recession is two successive quarters in which GDP does not rise. By this definition, there were two recessions in the early 1980s. One started in January 1980 and ended in July 1980. The other began in July 1981 and ended in November 1982. But many people (including many economists) merge the two into a single downturn with a plateau in the middle. Some call it a "double-dip" recession.

Considerable politicking has surrounded this dating question. If the two recessions are considered as one, then the mega-recession started while President Carter was in office, and the nation pulled out of it early in President Reagan's term. Republicans who take this line describe the Reagan presidency as an uninterrupted period of economic growth. On the other side, if a brand-new recession began in July 1981, Democrats can blame it on the new budget policies Reagan announced when he took office.

The truth is probably that neither president played a particularly powerful role in causing the recession of the early 1980s. The main causes seem to be the increase in oil prices when the government of Iran fell in 1979 and the determination by the Federal Reserve to choke off inflation, even if it meant choking the economy as well. But like the coach of a sporting team, the president tends to get too much credit when the economy performs well and too much blame when it does badly.

Ten years later, another recession provoked another political debate. This time the question was not whether there had been one recession or two, but precisely when did the recession begin?

In April 1991, a committee of the National Bureau of Economic Research chose July 1990 as the month that the recession had started. The government's explanation was that it had been triggered by Saddam Hussein's invasion of Iraq in August 1990, which caused oil prices to skyrocket for several months. That rise in oil prices led to a decline in consumer and business confidence that fed on itself and became a recession. This explanation implies that President Bush could not have prevented the recession. In fact, the president could argue that the war helped bring oil prices back down and thus shorten the recession.

But Hussein did not invade Iraq until August. When the NBER targeted July as the start of the recession, the date was taken by hopeful Democrats as a sign that the economy was already in reverse before the invasion, and Bush administration policies could therefore be blamed.

They differ from these groups in that they do not believe that the market economy is *always* able to absorb and respond to shocks so that full employment is maintained. On the contrary, they believe that there are times in which the economy actually amplifies a shock and makes its effects persist.

To new Keynesians, what is important is not so much the source of shocks—the economy is frequently disturbed, sometimes from the demand side, sometimes from the supply side—but how the economy responds to them. Historically, the length and depth of the Great Depression in the United States provided the strongest evidence of the weak nature of the economy's restorative forces; further evidence has been provided more recently by the persistently high levels of unemployment in many European countries. Critics of this perspective argue either that these are exceptions and that economics should focus on the normal case, or that in these cases government policy interfered with the normal restorative process of the market—for instance, by repeatedly reducing the real money supply during the Great Depression.

Amplification To understand the new Keynesian perspective, we need to understand how the economic system can amplify disturbances. The model of the economy analyzed in Parts Four and Five shows how this can occur. Any change in investment has a multiplied effect on national output. In a credit-constrained economy, reduced sales and lower prices eat up firms' cash reserves and reduce their ability to fund investment projects and their willingness to undertake the risks associated with investment. Hence, a reduction in a firm's sales today, for any reason, may lead to a more than corresponding reduction in investment, and this, through the multiplier process, has an even larger effect on national output.

The same process works in reverse. A positive shock to the economy—for example, an increase in the demand for exports—results in higher profits, allowing firms to increase their investment and stimulating the economy further. This view of a positive shock is similar to the multiplier-accelerator approach of traditional business-cycle theory, with one important difference. While that theory emphasizes the fact that a positive shock to the economy leads to more optimistic expectations for the future, and thus to increased demand for machines and buildings and thus to higher levels of investment, the new Keynesian theories emphasize the effect of positive shocks on the availability of funds for investment (profits). In reality, both effects undoubtedly play a role.

Persistence Not only might the economy amplify external shocks, but it might respond only slowly to the economic forces that restore it to health. As recession-mired firms pursue their conservative production and investment strategy, their financial position improves, but only gradually. As machines wear out, it becomes more and more expensive to postpone making new investments. Eventually investment starts to recuperate. As this happens, output increases. As output increases, investor confidence is restored, and firms' financial position improves further and faster. The economy does recover, but the process of recovery may take months or years.

Recessions also sometimes seem to have long-lasting effects on the rate of economic growth, with the economy taking years to get to where it would have been in the absence of the recession. Two recent recessions, one in 1973–74 and the other in the early 1980s, are cases in point. They pushed the economy down to the point that even by 1990, when the most recent expansion ended, the economy did not seem to have bounced back to what would have been expected by extrapolating the trend of growth that existed in the late 1960s and early 1970s. In this new Keynesian view, the costs of the economic downturn are not just the lost output from the idle resources, shown in Figure 39.3A as the shaded area, but also the lower output that the economy experiences from then on, shown as the shaded area in panel B.

One possible reason for these long-run effects is that workers who are thrown out of work or do not manage to get jobs in the several years of a deep recession may lose experience and job skills so that they are less productive for the rest of their working lives. A second reason is that in recessions, firms not only invest less in machines and factories, they also invest less in R & D.

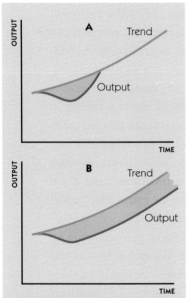

Figure 39.3 THE LINGERING COSTS OF A DOWNTURN

A downturn pushes the economy off its trend line, as shown in panel A. Even when resources are put back to work at the end of the recession, however, the economy may find itself on a new trend line, as shown in panel B. In this interpretation, the costs of the original recession are much larger, as we can see by comparing the shaded areas in the two panels.

DIFFERING VIEWS OF BUSINESS FLUCTUATIONS

SCHOOL	REGULARITY OF FLUCTUATIONS	SOURCE OF FLUCTUATIONS
Traditional business cycle	Fluctuations are regular and predictable.	Arise from endogenous forces as exemplified by the multiplier-accelerator process.
Real business cycle	Fluctuations are largely irregular and unpredictable.	Arise from exogenous shocks, mainly on the supply side, and there mainly through changes in technology.
Monetarist/New classical	Fluctuations are largely irregular and unpredictable.	Arise mainly from shocks to aggregate demand that result from changes in monetary policy.
New Keynesian	Fluctuations are largely irregular and unpredictable.	Arise from shocks to both aggregate demand and aggregate supply; the effect of exogenous shocks are amplified and persist as a result of the structure of the economy.

DIFFERING APPROACHES TO ECONOMIC POLICY

The alternative views described in this chapter of the source of the economy's fluctuations are important because they have different implications for government policy. If the source of fluctuations is exogenous disturbances to which the economy quickly adapts, as the real business-cycle theorists claim, there is no role for government; the market will provide the best possible solution to any change in the economic environment. If, on the other hand, as the new Keynesian theories contend, the economy amplifies disturbances, allowing them to have large and persistent effects, then there is a *potential* role for the government: it *might* be able either to offset the initial disturbance, or to alter the structure of the economy in such a way that the effects of the disturbance are less amplified, less persistent. If the government is the cause of the problem, as the monetarists and new classical economists argue, then one really needs to rethink the whole question of the role of government in stabilizing the economy.

We can oversimplify matters slightly and group economists into two categories: those who believe in strong discretionary government intervention to regulate the macro-economy (the "interventionists") and those who believe that by and large discretionary government intervention should not be allowed (the "noninterventionists"). The non-interventionists include real business-cycle theorists, who view government intervention as futile; and monetarists and new classical economists, who feel that policy does have effects but mainly negative ones, and that government should therefore be bound by policy rules. The interventionists consist largely of traditional business-cycle theorists and new Keynesian economists. We now take a closer look at what these different schools have to say about economic policy.

THE REAL BUSINESS-CYCLE APPROACH

The position of the real business-cycle theorists is the easiest to explain. As has been pointed out, they believe that the source of economic fluctuations is exogenous shocks to the economy, to which the economy quickly and efficiently responds. The fluctuations do not require government intervention because the market economy will give the best possible solution. Even the variability in income to which fluctuations give rise is not a problem; people acting rationally will have put aside savings to protect themselves against hard times. And unemployment, according to real business-cycle theorists, is more apparent than real. Individuals who want jobs could get them if only they lowered their expectations as to wage and nonpecuniary remuneration. It is better to encourage them to do this and move quickly to new jobs than to prolong the agony by allowing them not to face the facts.

While monetary policy is unnecessary to real business-cycle economists, it is also largely ineffective. If firms see that the government has increased the money supply, they simply increase prices proportionately. And individuals and firms protect themselves against the effects of change in the price level through indexing. There are no *real* effects. The real money supply and the real credit supply are unchanged. A distinctive lesson of the real business-cycle view is that while the government can offer no relief, it can also do no harm.

In the form just presented, the real business-cycle theory may seem too extreme—monetary policy has no effect, inflation has no consequences, unemployment is not important. Still, many economists believe that its basic lesson is still correct: by and large, economic fluctuations are a result of real disturbances, to which the economy adjusts relatively efficiently, and government policy is unlikely to speed or improve the adjustment.

While monetary policy has no effect according to the real business-cycle theory, fiscal policy does. The effect is simple and straightforward: government expenditures divert resources from private consumption to the government. But fiscal policy does not have any effect on the real unemployment rate since there is, in real business-cycle theorists' perspective, no unemployment.

This view of fiscal policy is different from that found in traditional Keynesian analysis. To Keynesians, the government expenditure level has a direct effect in stimulating the economy. Taxes have exactly the opposite effect, and much of their focus is on the difference between expenditures and revenues—the deficits. Deficits stimulate the economy. Real business-cycle theorists deny this. They believe that only the expenditures matter; deficits are as irrelevant as monetary policy. If the government borrows to pay for current expenditures (deficit spending), taxpayers know that eventually they will have to pay, so they set aside the appropriate amount. Savings rise to match the deficit. The failure of household savings to rise in response to the huge government deficits of the past decade has provided the most telling criticism against this aspect of real business-cycle theory.

THE NEW CLASSICAL AND MONETARIST APPROACH

The new classical and monetarist theories have much in common with real business-cycle theories. All three believe that markets respond quickly to changes in the economy. To a great extent, all three agree that the economy adjusts quickly enough to government policy to make it *largely* ineffective. The view that government policy is largely ineffective has been a long-standing one among monetarists and classical (old and new) economists. They believe that private actions may offset government actions, thus impairing the effectiveness of policy instruments.

This view, most effectively articulated by the new classical economists, is known as the policy ineffectiveness proposition. Its adherents hold, with Abraham Lincoln, that while you can fool all the people some of the time and some of the people all the time, you can't fool all the people all the time. The market learns what the government is doing and "undoes" it. If the government attempts to stimulate the economy by monetary policy, the market, with its rational expectations of government policy, figures this out and raises prices. There will then be no real effects—no effects on the amount of goods produced or on the level of employment.

Monetary Policy and Inflation   Monetarists and new classical economists believe that expansionary monetary policy can cause inflation. They do not consider inflation as innocuous as the real business-cycle theorists or many new Keynesian economists do. The economy is only partially indexed against inflation, as we saw in Chapter 36; and so long as this is the case, inflation can take its toll. They believe, moreover, that the uncertainty to which inflation gives rise has further debilitating effects on the economy. They also believe that the Phillips curve is vertical, so that when the government attempts to stimulate the economy by monetary policy, *all* it does is increase the price level—it gets nothing in return. The policy prescription is clear. Do not try to use monetary policy to stimulate the economy; use it only to maintain a stable price level.

Fiscal Policy   New classical economists and monetarists agree for the most part with real business-cycle theorists that the main effect of fiscal policy—of an increase in government expenditures—is to divert resources away from the private sector and toward the public sector. Since most of the time the economy's resources are fully employed, only movements along the production possibilities curve are possible: more of one good can be produced only by producing less of another; more public goods can be produced only by producing fewer private goods.

This conclusion is not affected by the presence of some unemployment. To new classical economists and monetarists, there is a *natural* rate of unemployment—a level of unemployment that arises as workers move between jobs and as new jobs are created, replacing old jobs that are destroyed as new technologies develop. In Chapter 36, we saw how some economists, such as new classical economists, believe the long-run Phillips curve is vertical at the natural rate of unemployment. In their view, it is not possible for the unemployment rate to be lowered permanently below this level. Attempts to do so simply lead to higher and higher rates of inflation.

The conclusions of new classical economists and monetarists concerning the use of fiscal policy to stabilize the economy parallel those concerning monetary policy. At most, the government might be able to reduce the unemployment rate below the natural rate for a short period of time. But the cost in terms of increased inflation may be enormous, and in all likelihood the government will mess up in its timing and stimulate the economy precisely at the time when it should be doing the reverse.

Perverse Effects of Government Intervention   The new classical and monetarist economists depart from the real business-cycle theorists in one important way. For the new classical and monetarist economists government policy is not *completely* ineffective. Government policy, particularly its monetary policy, has at times had large *real* effects on output and employment. The trouble is that well-intentioned government policy is just as likely to do harm as to do good. In the view of one monetarist, Milton Friedman, monetary authorities were the primary culprit in causing the Great Depression. They contracted the money supply too much. More recently, monetarists have blamed contractionary monetary policy for the downturns of 1979 and 1982.

Friedman's reason for why monetary policy has real effects on output and employment is that the price level does not adjust instantaneously to undo the effect of decreases in the money supply. The new classical economist Robert Lucas provides one explanation for why prices do not adjust. In Lucas' theory, producers are unable to distinguish whether a decrease in demand is the result of monetary policy—to which the appropriate response would be an equal offsetting decrease in prices—or the result of a shift in demand toward the particular products they produce. And because of these limitations on their information, producers tend not to offset fully changes in the money supply. Because prices do not adjust fully to changes in the money supply, these changes can have real effects. They can affect the level of aggregate demand; a decrease in the money supply can cause an economic downturn.

While monetarists and new classical economists thus contend that monetary policy may have real effects, they believe there are innate reasons why government cannot use these powers to stabilize the economy. The first is that government has only a limited ability to forecast accurately, and there are long lags in implementing policies and in policies having effects. Thus, it is impossible for the government to intervene in a timely way. By the time the government has recognized a problem and taken an action and the action has had time to have its effects, it is likely that what is required is something quite different. For instance, if the government finally sees the economy in a recession, by the time it acts to stimulate the economy and that action has had time to have its effects fully felt, the economy may be well on the way to recovery on its own. The

CLOSE-UP: THE POLITICAL BUSINESS CYCLE

Several economists, such as Bruno Frey of the University of Zurich and William Nordhaus of Yale University, have argued that there is an intimate connection between the electoral process and the economy's fluctuations.

First, they note that the electorate is very sensitive to economic conditions. When unemployment is high, people tend to vote against the incumbents, blaming them for the bad economic conditions. Political scientists and economists have done a remarkably accurate job using these economic factors to predict, for instance, the fraction of seats in the House of Representatives that will change.

Second, these economists note that politicians are aware of this. Since politicians like to get reelected, they plan for economic policies to be favorable at the time of election.

The third part of the theory maintains that the electorate is short-sighted. The economists argue that it pays politicians to overstimulate the economy as elections approach, even though this may (and systematically does) have adverse effects *after* the election. The overheated economy generates inflation; to quell the inflation, after the election, the government slows down the economy, causing unemployment. But voters' memories are limited. They do not hold grudges. So long as the economy has recovered by the time of the *next* election, they are forgiving. In this view, then, the electoral process is a primary source of economic fluctuations.

---

main effect of the government stimulation may then simply be to bring on inflationary pressures.

The interplay between politics and economics, with governments excessively stimulating the economy shortly before an election in order to win more votes, also results in government destabilizing the economy rather than stabilizing it.

Rules versus Discretion   Monetarists such as Milton Friedman who have grave doubts about the government's ability to stabilize the economy argue that the government should not have discretion in setting economic policy. It should be bound by policy rules. For instance, the money supply should increase at a fixed rate per year, or at a rate proportional to the increase in last year's income. Such rules, they contend, would allow the economy to grow, fully utilizing its resources, without inflation.[2]

Government expenditures should likewise be limited to a fixed proportion of national income. Deficits should be zero or limited to some share of GDP. In recent years, several amendments to the U.S. Constitution have been proposed that would impose such rules on the federal government. Those who advocate the use of policy rules argue further that doing so will eliminate a major source of uncertainty in the economy; the future course of policy would be known.

[2] Recall that the relationship between velocity, V, money supply, M, the price level, p, and output, Q, is given by $MV = pQ$. Thus, if velocity is increasing at a steady rate of 3 percent and the full employment output of the economy is increasing on average at 4 percent, then if money supply increases at the rate of 1 percent, the price level can remain on average constant.

NEW KEYNESIAN AND TRADITIONAL BUSINESS-CYCLE THEORIES

New Keynesians as well as traditional business-cycle theorists disagree with virtually every one of the presumptions underlying the noninterventionist theories, with the new Keynesians taking the lead in recent debates. First, they believe that markets often do not adjust quickly, so that there may be periods of extended unemployment. As evidence, they cite the Great Depression in the United States and the extended period of high unemployment in Europe during the 1980s. The economic misery of recessions cannot be ignored. Government can and should do something about it.

Policy Effectiveness   New Keynesians also believe that even with rational expectations, some government policies can have large effects. For instance, there is strong evidence that the effects of monetary policies have not always been offset by changes in the price level. The recession of the early 1980s, generally attributed to the tight monetary policy pursued by Federal Reserve chairman Paul Volcker, persuaded most economists that monetary policy can have large real effects (see Chapter 26). And the effects of the increased government deficits during the 1980s certainly did not seem to be offset by *increases* in private savings.

New Keynesians agree that the new classical and monetarist economists have made an important contribution in emphasizing that private actions may offset public policies. Government needs to take into account the responses of the private sector to its actions. Frequently the reactions of private individuals, who have rational expectations, do partially offset the government actions. Occasionally they might even fully offset government actions. But to new Keynesians, the contention that they always will do so seems incorrect.

For one thing, theories that the private sector will always offset public sector actions assume that prices and wages are more flexible than they really are (recall the discussion of price rigidities in Chapter 32). For another, some of the assumptions underlying the rational expectations theories, that households and firms will quickly respond to any government action by undoing it, are, to say the least, questionable. Most observers are skeptical that people can quickly learn what the government has done, know enough about the structure of the economy to be able to undo government policy, and believe that everyone else will behave similarly.

Even if there are some policies for which the private sector can and will take offsetting actions, there are other policies for which this is not true. Tax policies affect the prices individuals and firms face. Investment tax credits affect the cost of investment. Changes in the tax rate on interest income or on bequests affect the incentives to save. The responses of households and firms to these policies may just as well augment as offset them. An increase in the interest income tax may not only induce more consumption directly, but will produce more government revenue and thus reduce the deficit. This in turn may stimulate consumption as well, as taxpayers realize that their future tax liabilities for paying off the deficit are reduced. Similarly, consumers, knowing that their future incomes will be higher as a result of the investment stimulated by an investment tax credit, may, with these rational expectations, decide to enjoy some of these future benefits today; they may increase consumption today, further stimulating the economy.

Policy Successes   Finally, new Keynesians believe that on balance the government has done more to stabilize the economy than to destabilize it. They point to successes like the Kennedy tax cut in 1963, which, you may recall from Chapter 26, did exactly what macroeconomic theory said it should to stimulate the economy.

New Keynesians disagree with those who assign to the government the blame for many downturns. For instance, while they agree that the real money supply decreased in the Great Depression, they believe that the underlying source of the economic downturn lay elsewhere. Indeed, the decrease in the real money supply was largely a consequence of the low levels of economic and lending activity, rather than a cause. The Fed tried to increase lending activity but met with only limited success. Perhaps it should have tried harder, but there is no reason to believe that there was much it could do. Unfortunately, the historical evidence is sufficiently ambiguous that in many cases the debates will continue indefinitely.

Rules versus Discretion: The New Keynesian Perspective   Thus, new Keynesians see a need for government action because of the failure of markets to adjust by themselves sufficiently rapidly to maintain full employment, and they believe that government action can be and has been effective. They also believe that government should not bind itself to fixed rules, such as increasing the money supply at a fixed rate, but should use discretionary policies. Changing economic circumstances require changes in economic policy, and it is impossible to prescribe ahead of time what policies would be appropriate. While there are common patterns to all economic downturns, most have distinctive characteristics. The 1973 recession was initially the result of an increase in the price of oil. The collapse of the S & L's in the late 1980s, the fall in real estate prices, and the precarious position of many banks posed their own particular problems in the recession that began in 1990.

New Keynesians not only argue that discretionary policies can be helpful and effective, they question whether the government could really commit itself to following a set of rules. It is all well and good, they point out, for academics to talk about the government pursuing noninterventionist policies. The reality is that no government can stand idly by as 10, 15, or 20 percent of its workers face unemployment.

Accordingly, there is no way really to remove the uncertainty associated with changes in government policy. Even if lawmakers and policymakers say they will follow a particular rule, such as expanding the money supply at a constant rate, what is to prevent them from altering their behavior should it prove desirable to do so? In 1985, the federal government made a commitment to attain a balanced budget by 1991; by 1987, it became apparent that the goal could not easily be attained, so the government simply abandoned that commitment. It then made a commitment to attain a balanced budget by 1993; but by 1990, it was again clear that this goal could not easily be reached, and the government again abandoned its pledge. The government made a new commitment in 1990, no more likely to be fulfilled than the previous two.

The problem of whether the government will actually carry out a promised course of action is called the problem of **dynamic consistency.** The government may announce that a particular tax change is permanent—and it might even deceive itself into believing that the tax change *is* permanent. But when circumstances change, policies will change. And the fact that policies will change (or that individuals and firms expect them to change) has enormous consequences for the behavior of individuals and firms. In 1981, for instance, new legislation gave special tax breaks to the real estate industry. These breaks were intended (by the legislation) to be permanent. A real estate boom began that year, with construction of commercial real estate rushing ahead even when there were vacancy rates of 20 and 30 percent in already constructed buildings. The boom is sometimes attributed to the fact that builders did not believe that the tax breaks would last. As it turned out, they were right: the tax advantages were repealed in 1986.

New Keynesians contend is that if the unemployment rate becomes high, government must and will do something, regardless of what it has said. The role of economists is to advise the government on the policies most likely to be effective.

New Keynesian economists also believe that it is virtually impossible to design rules that are appropriate in the face of a rapidly changing economy. When velocity fell unexpectedly in the 1980s, the rule of expanding the money supply at a constant rate, had it been adopted, might well have gotten the economy into serious trouble. If the monetary authorities had restricted the increase of the money supply to, say, 3 percent, with the associated increase in credit, the economy might have been thrown into a major recession.[3]

The argument of the monetarists and new classical economists that the government has at times contributed to the economy's fluctuations has had a profound effect on new Keynesian views concerning the scope of government intervention. New Keynesians believe that society can learn from these historical experiences how to improve the effectiveness of fiscal and monetary policy. Most new Keynesians are not as optimistic as their Keynesian forebears about the ability of the government to "fine tune" the economy, keeping the economy humming along with full employment and no inflation. They tend to agree with monetarists and new classical economists that by attempting to do too much, the government may do worse than it would if it were less ambitious.

Automatic Stabilizers   At the same time, new Keynesians and traditional business-cycle theorists believe that there are some policies or rules that will enhance the stability of the economy and make it more likely that shocks to the economy will have less adverse effects. Indeed, one of the major objectives of traditional business-cycle theory, which emphasizes the endogenous nature of cyclical fluctuations, is to find policies that will reduce the endogenous forces that give rise to cycles. These policies are called automatic stabilizers, and were discussed in Chapter 30. Unemployment insurance payments, for example, automatically increase when unemployment rises; and when income falls, the average tax rate drops because of the progressive tax structure in the United States.[4]

---

[3] Note 2 recalled the basic relationship between M, the money supply, V, velocity, p, the price level, and Q, aggregate output: $MV = pQ$. This implies that if the government anticipates an increase in velocity of 3 percent per year and an increase in full employment output of 4 percent per year, then the appropriate rule for stabilizing the price level is a 1 percent annual increase in the money supply. But in the 1980s, velocity suddenly started to decrease. If, instead of the 3 percent increase in velocity that had been anticipated, velocity fell 3 percent, prices would have to fall 6 percent if output was to continue to grow at the desired rate. If prices did not fall, output would have to fall.

[4] The tax system is supposed to be an automatic stabilizer, but in periods of stagflation, when prices rise though unemployment is high (as they did in the late 1970s and early 1980s), it contributes to the downturn. Prior to 1981, the tax system was not indexed; that is, the income levels at which various tax rates came into play were not adjusted for changes in price levels. With stagflation, there was unemployment as well as inflation. Though "real" output and employment were declining, "nominal" output (measured in terms of dollars) was increasing, and hence the tax system imposed higher and higher taxes, further depressing the economy.

DIFFERING VIEWS OF ECONOMIC POLICY

NONINTERVENTIONIST THEORIES

Markets respond quickly to economic disturbances, so that resources are fully and efficiently utilized almost all the time. Actions of households and firms negate any effect the government may have. Government expenditures displace private expenditures, making fiscal policy ineffective except insofar as it diverts resources from private to public uses. Deficit financing has no effect, as increased private savings have an exactly offsetting effect. When government does affect the economy, it more often makes matters worse than better. The prescription: the government should stop mucking around in the economy. It should adopt rules, rather than use discretionary policy.

Real business-cycle theorists	There is no role for government in stabilizing the economy. Monetary policy has no effect, but does no harm.
Monetarists/New classical economists	Because of the sluggish adjustment of prices, in the short run monetary policy can have real effects. Government does more harm than good; it has been responsible (particularly through monetary policy) for major economic downturns.

INTERVENTIONIST THEORIES

Markets often respond slowly, so there may be extended periods of unemployment. Some government instruments are effective. While the government makes mistakes, on balance government policy is beneficial and is becoming increasingly so as we learn more about how the economy functions.

New Keynesians	Government should use discretionary policy to offset forces of economic shocks, rather than binding itself to fixed rules; changing economic circumstances require changes in economic policy.
Traditional business-cycle theorists	Government should design built-in stabilizers to make the economy more stable, reducing the endogenous forces that give rise to cycles.

EVALUATING ALTERNATIVE INSTRUMENTS

For new Keynesians and others favoring government intervention in the macroeconomy, the various noninterventionist schools have served an important function in addition to their contributions to macroeconomic analysis. They have taught that government intervention should not blithely be thought of as cost-free or necessarily effective. If undertaken at all, it should be undertaken with care. We now look at the different policy options the government has at its disposal.

THE POLICY INSTRUMENTS

If the government is to intervene in the economy, the question remains, how should it do so? The term "instrument" is used here to mean a way in which the government affects the economy. Fiscal policy instruments include the cutting (or raising) of taxes or the increasing (or decreasing) of government expenditures. A tax cut could be a lowering of the taxes faced by individuals, which might stimulate consumption, or a tax break for corporations, which may stimulate investment. It can be temporary or permanent. Each policy has effects that go beyond macroeconomics; for instance, lowering taxes on the poor more than on the rich may have the combined effect of increasing equality while at the same time stimulating consumption more than if taxes were lowered uniformly. A decrease in government expenditures could be for welfare or for an investment like road construction, to take two examples. In one case, the poor are adversely affected; in the other, future generations.

The government can also try to target particular sectors of the economy. For example, it can provide investment tax credits to stimulate investment in real estate, or it can provide export subsidies to stimulate exports. Parts Four and Five showed how each of these instruments works.

Monetary policy instruments include open market operations and changes in reserve requirements or discount rates. Monetary policies lowering interest rates, as we have seen, may stimulate investment by firms, exports, and household purchases of durables. Higher rates have the opposite effect and thus dampen the economy.

INSTRUMENTS OF GOVERNMENT POLICY

Fiscal instruments
    Changes in tax rates facing consumers and/or business firms
    Changes in levels of expenditures

Monetary instruments
    Open market operations
    Reserve requirements
    Discount rate

Unfortunately, the fiscal or monetary instruments do not match up neatly with the principal goals of macroeconomic policy: full employment, high growth, and stable prices. There is no "growth" instrument, "employment" instrument, or "inflation" instrument. Many instruments simultaneously affect all three goals. Nor does using one instrument preclude using others. Choosing the best set of policy instruments is thus an important job for policymakers. The sections that follow explore the major considerations for choosing among them.

EFFECTIVENESS IN ATTAINING OBJECTIVES

The single most important criterion in choosing an instrument is the likelihood that it will be successful in attaining the desired objectives. Consider, for instance, the situation where the country is in a recession and policymakers want to stimulate the economy. Experts often question whether monetary instruments will work. Chapter 34 explained why in deep recessions the Federal Reserve may be relatively ineffective in encouraging banks to make more loans to increase investment. The banks see few good loan prospects. And even if banks were willing to lend more, firms might not be willing to undertake the risks of additional investment without a dramatic change in interest rates.

There is also a debate about whether fiscal instruments like tax cuts will stimulate the economy. Individuals might simply decide to put away much of their increased income rather than spend it. This may be especially true if they are nervous about the future, as they often are when the economy goes into a recession. In such a situation, a tax cut aimed directly at the poor may be the most effective option. In a prolonged recession, the poor have used up their savings and spend whatever income they can get. Increased government expenditures financed by borrowing may also successfully stimulate the economy. Particularly when there is access to foreign borrowing, such expenditures are unlikely to crowd out much investment.

Those who subscribe to the policy ineffectiveness proposition, as we learned earlier, argue that particularly with rational expectations, individuals will undertake actions that offset the government's actions. The effect of an increase in the money supply will be offset by an increase in prices. An increase in deficit spending will be offset by an increase in private savings. While new Keynesians are aware that private actions do offset some government actions, they believe that other government policies do not bring offsetting actions; these policies are, accordingly, more likely to be effective. For instance, when the government makes it cheaper to invest by increasing the investment tax credit, it stimulates investment; for such policies, there is no offsetting private action.

1074 • DIFFERING APPROACHES TO MACROECONOMIC POLICY (CH. 39)

EFFECT ON THE COMPOSITION OF OUTPUT

One particularly important consideration in choosing among instruments is the effect the instrument will have on the composition of national output. Chapter 28 identified four components of aggregate demand: consumption, investment, net exports, and government expenditures. Government policymakers can stimulate aggregate demand in a recession by increasing any one (or more) of these, and they can dampen aggregate demand in an inflationary boom by contracting any one. The different instruments available to the government determine whether consumption, investment, net exports, or government expenditures are expanded or contracted; they therefore affect the extent to which other objectives, such as high growth, are achieved. Instruments that stimulate the economy by encouraging investment are especially likely to be conducive to growth.

One way to encourage investment is through monetary policy, though as we have seen, in an open economy the effects of loose monetary policy may be felt more through an increase in exports, as a result of a depreciation of the domestic currency. Loose monetary policy may also encourage the purchase of consumer durables, thus increasing the production of automobiles, refrigerators, and other major purchases.

Another policy for stimulating investment is a reduction in the taxation of businesses, particularly reductions such as investment tax credits. Not only do appropriately designed tax cuts stimulate investment by increasing the after-tax return to investing, they also provide firms with additional resources for investing.

Some policies may stimulate the economy but have a much more limited effect in encouraging investment. For example, the first-round effect of cuts in the individual income tax is to stimulate consumption; investment will only increase as a by-product of greater business optimism. Other policies may actually decrease investment. When a country has limited access to foreign borrowing, an increase in government expenditures, financed by government borrowing, may raise interest rates and thus crowd out investment. The net effect may be positive—the increase in government expenditures may well exceed the reduction in investment. Even so, such a policy results in a higher current output at the price of a lower future capital stock. With an increasingly open international capital market, this effect has become much less important, as the United States borrows abroad to finance its deficit.

The crowding out of investment is an indirect effect of government expenditures. The direct effect depends on how the money is spent. An increase in government expenditures to build roads or schools or otherwise improve the infrastructure may make future generations better off and stimulate economic growth. On the other hand, if government spends more on Social Security payments or higher welfare payments, then only current consumption is increased.

BREADTH OF IMPACTS

Some economic policies have a large effect on a few narrowly defined sectors of the economy, with the repercussions spreading out from these points of impact. For instance, tight monetary policy has particularly strong and direct effects on those who depend on banks for credit or whose customers depend on credit. Small businesses and the consumer durable industries thus feel the brunt of tight monetary policy.

In today's increasingly integrated international economy, tight monetary policy often has particularly large effects on export and import competing industries. For example, the United States competes to export farm products, and American automakers face stiff competition from imports. High interest rates lead to an influx of foreign capital, bidding up the value of the dollar and making it more difficult for American firms to export their products and for American automobile firms to compete against foreign imports. Assume the government wants to reduce total aggregate demand by 5 percent. If the government limits itself to policies that affect, say, only a quarter of the economy, aggregate demand in those sectors would have to be reduced by four times as much, or by 20 percent.

On the other hand, dampening the economy by increasing the individual income tax decreases demand for a broad spectrum of consumer goods. These broader impacts reduce the economic dislocations associated with policies with more narrowly focused impacts. Many economists believe that it is undesirable to have too high a reliance on monetary policy for stabilizing the economy, because the first-round impacts are fairly narrow.

FLEXIBILITY AND SPEED OF IMPLEMENTATION

Different instruments differ in the speed with which they can be implemented. In many industrialized economies, including the United States, monetary and fiscal policies are set in different parts of government. In the United States, the Fed sets monetary policy, while fiscal policy is set by Congress and the president. Coordination is therefore difficult to start with. Furthermore, there are lags in the government's ability to recognize a downturn in economic activity, design a program to combat it, implement the program, and then allow the program to have its effects. Each of these steps takes time. And by the time the effects of the policy have begun to be felt, economic conditions may have changed again.

These delays are more important for fiscal than for monetary policy. In the United States, changes in the federal income tax rates have to be legislated by Congress. Almost inevitably, questions about how the burden of taxes should be shared arise. Should everyone have his taxes reduced by an equal proportion, or by an equal dollar amount? Which is fairer? As a result, changes in individual income tax rates take time—six months would be speedy—and are a clumsy instrument for stabilizing the economy. There have been two such changes in recent decades: a permanent tax reduction under President Kennedy to stimulate the economy in 1963, and a temporary tax increase in 1968 under President Johnson to reduce aggregate demand, to offset partially the increased expenditures on the Vietnam War.

In other countries, tax adjustments are more frequently used as an instrument of stabilization. Each year, the British prime minister announces the tax rates for the following year. These rates usually go into effect immediately, though they technically need to be ratified by Parliament. The speed with which changes can be made makes taxes a much more effective policy instrument in the United Kingdom than in the United States.

One of the major advantages of monetary instruments over fiscal instruments in the United States is their greater flexibility. It is relatively easy for the Fed to change course, to decide this week to make credit more available and next week to make it less so. The Fed holds a weekly meeting to make these decisions; at this time, it takes the pulse of the economy and makes a judgment about the dose of medicine that is required. But fiscal instruments involve the U.S. political process, with its often seemingly endless haggling, its wide array of interests, and the large numbers involved in decision making, a process ill-suited for arriving at such judgments quickly.

The lags in fiscal policy go beyond decision making. After a decision is made, the policy must be implemented. If the government decides to spend more to build additional roads, engineers must draw up plans before the contracts can be let. After a tax reduction is enacted and takes effect, it may take consumers a while to respond fully. Responses to an investment tax credit are likely to be even slower, as firms must draw up new investment plans and obtain the required capital.

Once implemented, monetary policy suffers such lags as well. The banking system responds to the Fed's actions by making credit more or less available; this is usually a fairly short lag, of a few weeks. And then firms must respond to the actions of the banking system, increasing or decreasing investment; this often takes considerably longer.

CERTAINTY OF CONSEQUENCES

The effect of most government programs depends in part on how consumers and firms respond. Will consumers spend most of a tax reduction, believing that it is permanent, or will they squirrel away the extra funds? Will firms increase investment in response to a reduction in the interest rate, or will they wait, hoping for still further reductions? Because of these questions and because the responses depend on expectations of future government actions, there is inevitably considerable uncertainty about the effects of many policy changes.

Even so, the effects of some policy instruments are more predictable than others. In a recession, there is much uncertainty about the effectiveness of monetary policy. For example, it may be uncertain whether a reduction in reserve requirements will lead to a significant amount of increased lending and investment by firms.

There is also considerable uncertainty associated with the effects of changes in income tax rates. If a tax reduction is taken to be temporary, people will treat it as a "windfall"—a onetime increase in spendable income. Individuals tend to save a large fraction of windfall gains, as the theories of consumption described in Chapter 29 suggest. If, however, the change is taken to be permanent, people may increase their consumption substantially. Announcements by the government are not always believed, largely because the government finds it difficult to commit itself. The government might announce that a tax change is temporary, yet taxpayers believe that political forces will make it permanent. Or the government might announce that a tax reduction is permanent, and taxpayers, seeing future government deficits, expect the "permanent" change to be quickly repealed.

The uncertainties about the consequences of policy changes extend to questions of how markets perform. If the government borrows more to finance increased government expenditures, will private investment be crowded out? This depends on the flow of funds from abroad. If the supply curve of funds from abroad is very elastic, then increased government borrowing will have little effect on interest rates or the availability of credit.

Another uncertainty involves how well monetary and fiscal policies mesh. A crucial determinant of the extent to which government expenditures crowd out private investment is the response of the Fed. If the Fed believes that there are inflationary pressures, it may respond to increased government expenditures by tightening monetary policy, making credit less available. Then the increased government expenditures may have little *net* effect on aggregate demand; they only change the demand's composition, with a larger proportion of the nation's output going into the public sector and a smaller proportion into investment.

These uncertainties have two important implications for economic policy. First, at any given time, the uncertainties associated with some instrument are likely to be greater than the uncertainties with other instruments. As the economy seems to be plunging headlong into a recession, the government may want to reverse quickly the recessionary psychology. If the data indicate that many consumers are spending what they can get hold of and are saving little, then a tax reduction may have more certain effects than monetary policy and therefore be the instrument of choice. While the government can be fairly confident that consumers will spend a large part of the extra money in their pockets, it may be quite uncertain whether, given the bad business climate, banks will be willing to lend much more or firms will be willing to invest much more in response to a change in reserve requirements, a lower discount rate, or even lower interest rates resulting from open market operations.

For instance, in January 1992, with pessimism about the economy growing, the Fed reduced its discount rate by an unprecedented full 1 percentage point in order to signal to the market that it was committed to getting the economy out of the recession. The economy responded, but not as much as the Fed had hoped, partly because the weakened banks were not able to make credit that much more available, and consumers were accordingly pessimistic about whether even a large dose of monetary policy would do the trick; and partly because many people believed that the Fed would not maintain the low interest rates, so longer-term interest rates—which are relevant for most firm and household decisions—changed relatively slowly.

Second, in some cases, the uncertainties can be quickly resolved, and government actions can be modified accordingly. In other cases, it will take a long time to resolve the uncertainties. Consumers, for instance, are more likely to respond quickly to a tax rate change, particularly if they see an immediate change in their take-home pay. The government can see how workers are responding, and then determine whether or how much further action is required. On the other hand, it may take firms months or in some cases years to change their investment plans.

There have been periods, particularly in the 1960s, when macroeconomists hoped to understand policy instruments well enough to "fine tune" the economy; that is, to make sure that the economy was kept constantly at the lowest unemployment rate consistent with stable prices. The long delays associated with many government instruments combined with the uncertainty as to their consequences imply that it is extremely difficult for the government to do this. Still, when the economy is in a prolonged downturn, when unemployment rates have persisted at high rates as they did in Europe through the 1980s and in the United States in the Great Depression, there will be loud calls for some form of macroeconomic intervention.

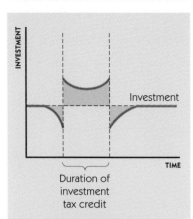

Figure 39.4 EFFECT OF TEMPORARY INVESTMENT TAX CREDIT OVER TIME

Temporary tax credits do not merely increase investment while they are in effect. They also decrease investment just before they go into effect, as firms reduce investment in anticipation of the tax credit and reduce investment just after they end. Firms modify investment timing to take advantage of the tax credit. The result may be that total investment is much the same over the longer period, but the pattern of investment is disrupted.

UNINTENDED SIDE EFFECTS

In choosing which instruments to use, the government wants to avoid unintended negative side effects. Temporary programs often have such side effects. For instance, in 1990, Congress enacted a luxury tax on boats costing over a certain amount. Most consumers thought the tax was temporary, and buying a boat was not such a necessity that it could not wait. Not surprisingly, boat sales dropped far more than a simple analysis based on the elasticity of demand would have predicted. Congress had aimed to increase revenue, but instead had only dampened the demand for boats.

Temporary tax measures may also have large effects outside the intended period. Consider the effect of a temporary investment tax credit. In effect, the credit reduces the costs of making investments during a certain period. The effects are illustrated in Figure 39.4. There is reduced investment right before the investment tax credit goes into effect and reduced investment right after it is removed, as investors try to shift their investment to the period in which it is being subsidized.

These effects may be undesirable for two reasons. First, the intent of the investment tax credit may be to stimulate investment, not to change the date at which investments are made. The temporary tax credit may have little effect on total investment. Second, the government may not want to reduce investment immediately after the removal of the tax credit or immediately before it goes into effect, for these decreases in demand may exacerbate recessionary pressures at those times.

CRITERIA FOR EVALUATING POLICY INSTRUMENTS

Effectiveness of instrument: Some policies may be more effective than others; in some cases, actions of the private sector may offset the effects of policy instruments.

Effect on composition of output: Among policies with similar effects on aggregate demand, some increase the relative size of the public sector, some increase current consumption, and some increase the future growth of the economy by stimulating investment.

Breadth of impact: Some policies, such as monetary policy, have narrow impacts; others, fiscal instruments like tax reductions, have more broadly based impacts.

Flexibility and speed of implementation: Some policies, such as monetary policy, are more flexible than others, and their impacts are felt more quickly.

Certainty of consequences: At any given time, the impact of some policies is more certain than that of others.

Presence of unintended side effects: Some policies have significant unintended (and often negative) side effects.

REVIEW AND PRACTICE

SUMMARY

1. Traditional business-cycle theorists believe economic fluctuations are caused by endogenous forces in the economy. Real business-cycle theorists believe fluctuations are the result of exogenous shocks to the economy, and the economy efficiently adapts to these shocks. Monetarists and new classical economists see government in general, and monetary policy in particular, as the source of the shocks. New Keynesians also believe that the shocks are exogenous but that the economy contains forces that amplify these shocks and make their effects persist.

2. Traditional business-cycle theory sees economic fluctuations as regular and predictable; the other theories see fluctuations as induced by randomly occurring shocks and thus largely unpredictable.

3. Noninterventionists, which include real business-cycle theorists, new classical economists, and monetarists, believe that the economy operates efficiently, at or near full employment, and that it responds quickly to external shocks. Government intervention is thus unnecessary.

4. Interventionists, which include new Keynesians, believe that periods of persistent unemployment are evidence that the economy sometimes does not adjust quickly and that at least in severe recessions, government policy can and should be used to stimulate the economy.

5. Real business-cycle theorists hold that monetary policy has no effect, but that does not matter, since the economy is generally near full employment. Monetarists and new classical economists believe the economy would be better off if the government stuck to simple rules, like expanding the money supply at a constant rate. New Keynesians believe that government can use both fiscal and monetary policy to effectively stabilize the economy.

6. In deciding which policy instrument to use, the government looks at several criteria: the effectiveness of the instrument, its effect on the composition of output, the breadth of its impact, the flexibility and speed of its implementation, the certainty of the consequences, and the possibility of unintended side effects.

KEY TERMS

multiplier-accelerator model   dynamic consistency

REVIEW QUESTIONS

1. What are the alternative explanations of the sources of the economy's fluctuations? What is the relationship between views about the nature of these fluctuations and views about the role of government?

2. What is the multiplier-accelerator model?

3. Describe the rules versus discretion debate.

4. Why do some economists believe that active government intervention in an attempt to stabilize the economy is either unnecessary or undesirable? What are the counter-arguments?

5. What are the relative advantages and disadvantages of the use of monetary versus fiscal instruments?

6. What is the problem of dynamic consistency? Give an example of dynamic inconsistency.

7. Provide some examples of how different policies or instruments affect different groups in society.

8. What are the principal criteria for evaluating alternative instruments?

PROBLEMS

1. Is fiscal or monetary policy more likely to affect consumption? investment? home buyers? exports? imports? Explain your answers.

2. If the tax code has been changing every year, would you expect consumer spending to decrease substantially when the government announces a "permanent" income tax increase? Explain. Why, under the same circumstances, might you expect consumer purchases of automobiles to decrease substantially when the government announces a "permanent" tax on the purchase of automobiles?

3. Use the concepts of income and substitution effects to explain the differences in effects of a temporary income tax and a temporary tax on consumer durables.

4. Assume that the government increases its spending by $10 billion, while the multiplier is 4 and the accelerator is 2. How much will the original increase in government spending increase national output? How much investment will result from that increase in output? How much will the increase in investment increase national output?

5. If the economy is in a boom, why might a multiplier-accelerator model predict that it will eventually slow down? If the economy is in a recession, why might the multiplier-accelerator model predict that it will eventually speed up?

6. What are some ways the government can use automatic stabilizers to help stabilize the economy?

7. If the economy is in a recession and the government wants to stimulate output in a way that will promote long-run growth, what instruments might the government favor to stimulate the economy?

8. If the economy is in a recession and the government is particularly concerned about how the rich have suffered during recent years, what instruments might the government favor to stimulate the economy?

9. Describe the effect on the composition of output of combining a tax cut with a tighter monetary policy.

CHAPTER 40

ALTERNATIVE ECONOMIC SYSTEMS

More than thirty years ago while giving a speech at the United Nations, Nikita Khrushchev pounded his shoe on the table and declared, "We will bury you!" Khrushchev, president of the Soviet Union, was referring to the rivalry between his country's communist economy and the mixed capitalist economies of Western Europe and the United States. Indeed, a number of reputable Western economists agreed with him then that it was only a matter of time before the Soviet Union caught up with and surpassed the United States.

Today most of the formerly communist countries are seeking to restructure their economies. Countries like Poland, Hungary, and Czechoslovakia look at their Western European neighbors, Germany, Italy, and the Scandinavian countries, and see higher standards of living. In a few momentous months in 1989, most of the Eastern European countries began to overhaul their systems into economies based on the market. In 1990, even Albania, the country seemingly most committed to communism, began to make market reforms. Events in the Soviet Union in 1991—including the attempted overthrow of President Gorbachev, the attainment of independence by the Baltic republics, and finally the breakup of the Union itself—set the stage for similar reforms there.

Nevertheless, the most populous country in the world, China, remains committed to some version of communism, though there is an ongoing debate in the country about how to most effectively improve its economy.

1. What were the economic conditions that gave rise to the socialist idea?

2. What were the central characteristics of Soviet-style socialism? How did it differ from the market system in the way it allocated resources?

3. Why did it fail?

4. What are some of the principal reforms of Soviet-style socialism that have been tried, and how have they fared?

5. What problems do the former socialist economies face in the process of transition to a market economy?

SOME TERMINOLOGY

A variety of terms are used to describe the alternative economic systems used in various parts of the world. Under **socialism**, the government owns and operates the basic means of production—the factories that make cars and steel, the mines, the railroads, the telephone system, and so on. Under **communism**, the government essentially owns all property—not only the factories, but also the houses and the land. In practice, no government has abolished all private property; people still own the clothes they wear, and if they are well enough off, they might even own cars and television sets.

The term "communism" is used to describe the economic system in the countries that came under the domination of the Soviet Union and China in the years after World War II, though there were in fact considerable variations in economic practices. In Poland, for instance, most land remained in the hands of the farmers who worked it. But by and large, these countries shared an economic system that involved not only state ownership of assets but also considerable central control of economic decisions, or **central planning**, and a political system that did not allow free elections, free speech, or the multitude of other rights found in democracies. Because of the important role played by central planning, these economies are sometimes referred to as planned economies or centrally planned economies. For simplicity, we will refer to the kind of economic system that evolved in the Soviet Union, Eastern Europe, and China as "Soviet-style socialist economies."

This chapter contrasts the Soviet-style economies with those of the United States and

Western Europe. Because of the important role played by private capital in the latter economies, they are commonly referred to as capitalist economies; further, since government plays a large role, they are often called mixed economies; and because of their heavy reliance on firms and households interacting in markets, they are also referred to as market economies. Again, there are considerable variations among these economies: for example, government plays a more important role in Sweden than it does in Switzerland. Yet they share much in common. The objective of this chapter is to enhance our understanding of the major differences between the market economies and the Soviet-style economies. Toward the end of the chapter, we will learn about the two major versions of socialism that differed from that of the Soviet Union: the worker cooperatives of the former Yugoslavia and the attempts by Hungary and China to incorporate some elements of a market into socialism.

Table 40.1 provides some data comparing living standards in the Soviet-style economies just before the revolutionary events of 1989–91 with those in the rest of the world.

Table 40.1 COMPARISON OF LIVING STANDARDS BETWEEN PLANNED AND MARKET ECONOMIES

	GNP per capita (1988 $)	Annual GNP growth rate (%) 1965–1988	Life expectancy at birth	Adult illiteracy (%)
Soviet-style economies:				
USSR	2,660	4.0	70	< 5
China	330	5.4	70	31
Hungary	2,460	5.1	71	< 5
Market economies:				
USA	19,840	1.6	76	< 5
India	340	1.8	58	57
Italy	13,330	3.0	77	< 5
Egypt	660	3.6	63	56
Sweden	19,300	1.8	77	< 5

THE ORIGINS OF SOCIALISM AND COMMUNISM

The eighteenth and nineteenth centuries produced the industrial revolution, and with it a dramatic change in the structures of the economies and societies it touched. The new technologies of the industrial revolution resulted in the development of the factory system and an increased movement of workers from rural to urban areas. In the fast-growing cities, workers often lived in squalid conditions. In order for families to eke out a living, children went alongside their parents to work in the factories, where they all worked long hours in unhealthy conditions. Periodically economies faced a recession or depression, and the workers were thrown out of their jobs and forced to beg, steal, or starve. Life for the unlanded peasants in the rural sectors was hardly more idyllic: in Ireland in the 1840s, for instance, a fifth of the population (half a million people) starved to death.

While the vast majority of people thus lived on the edge of survival, a few individuals had considerable wealth, often inherited. Between the very wealthy and the poor was a small but growing middle class, mainly commercial and professional. (By contrast, today in Europe and America, it is the middle class, consisting of professionals, businesspeople, and high-wage workers, that is dominant.)

Were these conditions inevitable? Could they be changed? If so, how? These questions were raised by numerous social thinkers from the late eighteenth century on. Many saw the culprit in the capitalist economic system. The most influential critic of the capitalist system was a German living in England, Karl Marx.

Marx, like many of the other critics, was concerned with both the efficiency and equity of the capitalist system, to use the terms that we would use today. He saw people working hard and long, but the fruits of their labor seemed to accrue largely to the owners of the firm. He spoke of the exploitation of the workers. Marx was concerned not just with the abject living standards of workers, but with the conditions in which they worked. While people spent most of their time sweating in workshops, the work was not a meaningful part of their lives; they were alienated from their work. The political process provided no relief, for Marx saw the government, consisting of individuals drawn from the upper and middle classes, as pursuing what he referred to as class interests, which were antagonistic to the interests of the workers and peasants.

Marx's prognosis for capitalism as an economic structure was bleak. He believed that wages would remain at a bare subsistence level; if they should happen to rise above this level, the population would increase fast enough that the greater supply of labor would drive wages back down. But capitalists—owners of firms, or those who supplied firms with the funds they needed—would not fare well either in the long run, in Marx's view. He saw capitalists as having an uncontrollable urge to accumulate capital, to save. They would run out of investment opportunities, and thus the return to capital would decline. Moreover, the goods produced in their factories would go unsold, and workers would be paid so little they would be able to do no more than survive. To put this last insight in modern terms, Marx saw a persistent deficiency in aggregate demand.

According to Marx, the only way out of this morass was a change in the economic system, a change that he thought was inevitable. Just as the force of history had led the economy to evolve from medieval feudalism to capitalism, he believed that the economy would evolve from capitalism to socialism and eventually to communism. Not only would there be no private property, the state would make all allocation decisions: "From each according to his ability," wrote Marx, "and to each according to his needs."[1] Clearly Marx's vision of socialism provided different answers than the market economy to the basic economic questions of what to produce and in what quantities, how to produce it, for whom it should be produced, and who makes the decisions. The state,

---

[1] *Critique of the Gotha Program* (1875).

not the market, would decide what, how, and for whom.[2]

Among those who found Marx's ideas particularly attractive was a Russian revolutionary, Vladimir Ilyich Lenin. In the early years of the twentieth century, Russia was among the most backward of the countries of Europe. Peasants lived in a close-to-feudal relationship with their landlords. The industrial revolution had hardly touched the country. The poor conditions became even worse during World War I, when millions of Russian soldiers were killed. As the war dragged on, the military became increasingly unhappy with the support it was receiving from the government. The country was ripe for a revolution, and toward the war's end in February 1917, the czar was overthrown. A democratic coalition of parties took over, but it was short-lived. In October 1917, the Bolsheviks—the party of Lenin, with Marxism as its official ideology—seized the government. The first "communist" government was established.

There is considerable debate over whether the Russian version of communism matched Marx's incompletely sketched vision. In fact, Marx's primary concern was not detailing a plan for an alternative economic system. Rather, he was more concerned with studying capitalism, both its origins and its future.

Translating Marx's ideology into a program for running a populous, poor, and largely undeveloped and rural country was no easy task. To a great extent, it was ironic that Russia, hardly touched by capitalism at the time of the revolution, became the first to try to implement Marx's ideas. Marx had predicted that countries would have to pass through the capitalist phase on the way to socialism, and he had therefore expected socialism to arise first in countries such as Britain or France.

Indeed, the economic system that we know today as communism is as much due to how Lenin and his successor, Joseph Stalin, adapted Marx's ideas to the situation they found in Russia as it is to Marx's original ideas. What Marx's reaction would be to what evolved there one can only guess, but a hint is provided by his comment on the ideas of the French Marxists: "As for me, I am not a Marxist."

THE DISILLUSIONMENT WITH MARKETS

It is difficult today to understand how viable an alternative communism seemed to be in the 1920s and 1930s. In the United States and other developed countries today, there is widespread confidence in markets and in the efficiency with which they allocate resources. To be sure, there are problems; there are market failures, periods of unemployment, and pockets of poverty. But we have seen in this book how markets by and large allocate resources efficiently. We have seen as well how selective government interventions can remedy the market failures and, if there is the political will, at least partially address the problem of the inequality of income generated by the market. Confidence in market-based economic systems is built on more than just economic theory: in market economies, living standards have soared well beyond the imagination of anyone living a century ago.

But this confidence has not always been present; neither is it universal now. When the United States went into the Great Depression in 1929, not to recover fully until

[2] In Marx's view, socialism itself was a transitional stage to an eventual time when the state would wither away. How production would be organized—how the basic decisions of what to produce, how to produce it, and for whom it should be produced would be made—in this eventual period was left unclear.

While there were many writers in the nineteenth century who advocated socialism, none was more influential than Karl Marx. His ideas not only influenced how socialism developed within the Soviet Union, they have given rise to a school of economics called the Marxist school. Like any major school, there is an evolution of ideas and disagreements among its members. Following are only a few of the major strands of thought.

One important idea concerns what determines, or should determine, prices. The answer given by the basic economic model is the law of supply and demand. Marx, by contrast, made use of what was called the labor theory of value, a set of ideas developed earlier by the British economist David Ricardo. The labor theory of value argued that the value of any good should be attributed to the workers who made it; a good that required more labor should be valued more highly, and vice versa. Marx considered the difference between what a good was sold for and the labor costs that went into making the good, the profits of the firm and the return to capital, as an exploitation of workers. By contrast, in market economies profits are viewed as providing firms with incentives, and capital is seen as a scarce factor—like any other scarce factor, such as land or labor—that will be efficiently allocated only when it fetches a return.

Another important strand in Marxist thought is that the economic system affects the nature of individuals and the evolution of technology. This book has taken the preferences of individuals as given. The demand curves for candy and CDs, for example, have been based on the trade-offs that people are willing to make. We have not asked why individuals like yogurt or cars or TVs. We have not asked why workers in many jobs will shirk if they are not provided incentives. Many Marxists believe

that under a different social system, people would behave differently. They would be less materialistic, more concerned about helping one another, more committed to their jobs. During wartime, we often see changes in attitudes and behavior. Whether human nature is sufficiently mutable that *some* social system might achieve these idealistic goals over long periods of time remains debatable; what is clear is that none of the Soviet-style economies, during their decades-long experiments, have succeeded.

A third strand of Marxist thought emphasizes the link between politics and economics. Marxists claim that the answer to the question of "for whom" is provided not just by the impersonal workings of the law of supply and demand in competitive markets, but by power—the economic power of monopolies and the political power of the wealthy. The wealthy use the government to gain for themselves what they cannot achieve in the marketplace. Marxists cite instances of the U.S. government spending hundreds of billions of dollars to fight a war to preserve business interests—as some allege was an important part of the motivation for the war in the Persian Gulf in 1990–91—while claiming it has insufficient money to finance the rebuilding of the ghettos of America's cities or to provide free college education to America's poor. The debate on the validity of these claims takes us beyond the boundaries of economics.

Marx stressed the importance of economic factors in determining the entire structure of society. Changes in technology bring about concomitant changes in economic relations. Such changes in the past had led the economy from feudalism to capitalism, and would lead from capitalism to socialism and on to communism. While Marx peered into the future with what from hindsight looks like a very cloudy crystal ball, he may have been correct in his emphasis on the importance of economic factors in determining the evolution of society. In an ironic twist of history, though, economic forces appear to have injured socialism more than capitalism. After all, it is the economic successes of the capitalist systems of the world's industrialized countries, combined with the economic failures of the Soviet-style socialist economies, that have led to the re-action against socialism in Eastern Europe and the Soviet Union, and to the ongoing changes in the political systems in those countries.

World War II, millions of Americans were thrown out of jobs. The capitalist economic system did not seem to be functioning well. Today, to the billions of people still living in abject poverty in India, elsewhere in Asia, and in Africa and South America, markets have failed to meet their rising aspirations. And even within the industrialized countries, there are many who have not partaken of the general prosperity; in their eyes, the market system has not worked.

It is not surprising, then, that many have sought an alternative economic system, which would be able at the same time to generate faster sustained economic growth and promote greater equality. Throughout the first half of this century, many saw socialism as the answer. They believed that if the government controlled the economy, not only would recessions be eliminated, so too would what they saw as the chaos of the marketplace, for instance the excess expansion of capacity in one industry accompanied by shortages in another industry.

HOW SOVIET-STYLE SOCIALIST ECONOMIES WORK

With its complete control over the economy, the government of a Soviet-style socialist economy has to provide all the answers to the basic economic questions—what is to be produced and in what quantities, how it is to be produced, for whom it is to be produced, and who makes the decisions. We saw in Chapter 2 the central role that private property, prices, and the profit incentive play in market economies. If these are to be abandoned, what is to replace them?

First, in Soviet-style economies, the coordination of economic activity was to be done by government ministries, through central planning. The government would make the decisions. Major decision making did not occur at the level of the plant, and at times not even in the ministry in charge of agriculture or mining or steel, but in a single ministry responsible for directing the economy. Five-year plans were drawn up, with well-defined targets—how much steel production was to be increased, how much food production, and so on. Individual plant managers were told not only what they were to produce, but how they were to produce it—what technologies to use, how much labor they would have, how much coal, and so forth.

Second, market incentive schemes were sometimes replaced by force. We saw in earlier chapters that some incentive schemes take the form of the carrot, some of the stick. The Soviet Union under Joseph Stalin preferred the stick: those who did not meet their targets were rewarded with a sojourn in Siberia.

Third, political controls and rewards also helped replace the lack of economic incentives. Key positions in the economy went to faithful members of the Communist party. In the early days of the revolution, these included many who really believed in socialism as an alternative, superior form of economic organization. Given their ideological commitment, economic incentives to work hard to meet the goals were relatively unimportant; and to the extent that incentives were important, they were provided by the potential for promotion. But as the years went by, membership in the party came to be seen as the vehicle for getting ahead. People joined the party not because they believed in anything it might have once stood for. Under Leonid Brezhnev, who was the first secretary of the Communist party (1964–1982), a term used to describe the actual head of the party, this cynical attitude spread; the party faithful not only received good jobs but enjoyed other benefits, including access to special stores at which goods not generally available could be acquired.

Another basic aspect of market economies, competition, was also shunned. Just as the Communist party had a monopoly in the political sphere, no competition with government enterprises was allowed, and the government enterprises did not compete with one another. The Soviet-style socialist governments failed to recognize the importance of competition in providing incentives and in deciding who was best suited to fulfill various roles in the economy. They did not, of course, eliminate all competition: there was still competition to be promoted to top positions and thus receive higher incomes and access to desirable goods. But success in this competition was not based on how efficiently you produced the goods that consumers wanted, or how innovative you were in devising new products. Rather, success was measured by how well you complied with the bureaucratic targets and requirements and how well you performed in the politics of the bureaucracy and party.

How well did central planning succeed in replacing markets? To answer that question, we need to take a closer look at each of the three principal markets.

THE LABOR MARKET

The United States is noted for its labor mobility. Young people try one job, then another, until they find a job for which they are well suited. As technology and market conditions change, firms are born and die, and jobs are born and die with them. When some skills, such as computer programming, are in short supply, programmers' wages are bid up. This scarce resource goes to where it is most needed, and the high wage attracts more people to computer programming. Job mobility is an important part of the capitalist economy's incentive structure. Those who perform well are rewarded with better jobs; those who perform badly will not be promoted and may even be fired.

Under Soviet-style socialism, there was little job mobility. A worker was assigned to a firm early in life and often stayed with it until retirement. If by bad luck you were assigned a job you did not like, you might have been stuck with it for life. Under Stalin, the Soviet government ordered thousands of people to take jobs in distant parts of the Soviet Union. Some workers from Moscow were assigned to the Baltic republics, others to the far eastern regions of the Union. With the government controlling the labor market, there was little choice; you could not decline the offer. Control of the labor market provided the government with enormous political control.

The system supplied some countervailing advantages, however. There was little evidence of unemployment, although there may have been high levels of "disguised" unemployment. In a capitalist economy, if a firm finds it no longer needs a worker, it lets the worker go. Competition forces it to do this. When markets work well, the worker laid off by one firm finds a job at another where she is needed. This continual reallocation of labor is essential for economic efficiency. In the Soviet-socialist economies, however, firms had little incentive to lay off workers, since they could run losses with impunity. There were no incentives to maximize profits, and strong incentives to avoid "causing trouble." Laying off workers would be viewed as causing trouble. For the system, the gains in job security were purchased at the price of a loss in economic efficiency, a trade-off depicted in Figure 40.1. Socialist economies choose a point such as A in the figure, with far more security and far less efficiency than the capitalist economies, which choose point B.

THE CAPITAL MARKET

Lenin, and Stalin after him, considered modernizing the economy the first task of the socialist system. If the country was to industrialize, it needed capital. Many developing countries, like the United States in the nineteenth century, have used foreign capital markets in the early stages of growth. This option was not available to the USSR, for two reasons. First, the new government faced an immediate hostile reaction from almost all the industrialized countries. Second, the new government refused to honor the debts incurred by the czarist government. Not surprisingly, then, it was cut off from credit and most trade. If capital was to be raised, it had to be raised internally.

There had been great inequality in czarist days, with a few individuals having much more wealth than others. But even after seizing what wealth it could, the new Communist government had insufficient capital to finance a development program. Furthermore, realizing its base of support was among the urban workers, the government was loath to tax them much to raise the funds. The only option was to raise funds from the peasants who lived in the rural sector, and who comprised the vast majority of the population at the time.

From the perspective of the peasants, all that had happened was that the exploitive landlords were replaced by an even more exploitive government. As the government attempted to tax them more, they produced less and less for the market. The resulting crisis persuaded Stalin that there was only one way out: to take control of the farms, to "collectivize" agriculture, in effect to organize agriculture more along the lines of a factory system. Rather than allowing a worker to run his own farm, the worker was made a state employee. The nationalization of the land accorded well with the general ideological commitment against private property. But in the process of the forced collectivization of agriculture, there were huge famines. Millions of people starved to death in Ukraine, a now-independent republic known as the country's "bread basket" for its fertile land, while output was being forcibly removed to feed people in the cities.

In private markets, investment funds go to where the marginal returns are highest. Interest rates are the "price" of capital; they measure its scarcity value. In the Soviet-style socialist economies, it was the government that decided where scarce investment funds went. But how did these governments decide where funds should go? How did they decide how much should go to each sector?

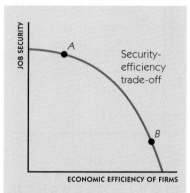

Figure 40.1 THE SECURITY-EFFICIENCY TRADE-OFF

Socialist countries have usually chosen a point like A, with far more security and far less efficiency, than the capitalist economies, which have chosen points more like B.

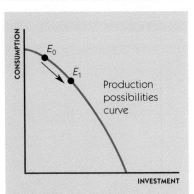

Figure 40.2 RAPID INDUSTRIALIZATION: MOVEMENTS ALONG THE PRODUCTION POSSIBILITIES CURVE

Soviet-style socialists believed that rapid growth of heavy industry was desirable, so they increased investment. But as the production possibilities curve shows, this can only be done at the expense of consumption. Central planners tried to move the economy toward a point such as E_1, with a high output of investment goods and a low output of consumption goods.

To a large extent, these decisions were based on a belief about the "correct" path of development. Stalin had two basic ideas. First, he recognized that resources that were not allocated to consumption could be given to investment. He was aware of the production possibilities curve, depicted in Figure 40.2, entailing a trade-off between consumption and investment. Thus, his first objective was to reduce consumption, and move the economy from a point such as E_0 to E_1. One of the aims of the collectivization of agriculture was to do just that, to squeeze the farmers as much as possible. But urban workers' wages were also kept low. By keeping wages low and the supply of consumer goods limited, the Soviet planners in effect "forced" the economy to have high savings.

The second idea was to focus investment on heavy industry. Stalin considered huge factories, such as steel mills, the central symbol of modern economies, which distinguished them from less developed, agrarian economies. He therefore invested primarily in heavy industry, providing little support for agriculture, consumer goods, or housing. The two ideas were in a sense intertwined: with low wages and low consumption, there was little need to invest in industries to provide consumption goods.

Thus, the central aspect of the Soviet-style socialist version of the capital market was low consumption, allowing the country as a whole to have a high savings rate, and heavy industrialization. The patterns initiated by the Soviet Union, including the collectivization of agriculture, were imitated by the other Communist governments.[3]

THE PRODUCT MARKET

In the USSR, government ministries decided what goods should be produced and how they should be produced. To a great extent, they also decided to whom goods were to be distributed. Many of the essentials of life, such as medical care and housing, were provided freely or at a modest price, though the individual had little choice about what she got. But not even the most enthusiastic government planner thought it was feasible for the government to decide how much each individual should receive of each good. Some discretion was left to the family. They could decide which foods or what clothing to purchase; to this extent, a market system was used to distribute goods. But even here, the government did not really rely on the price system. It set prices, but they were substantially below the market-clearing level, as illustrated in Figure 40.3, so there were shortages.

In Chapter 5, we learned what happens if prices are fixed at a level below market-clearing: there is excess demand. Shortages are pervasive. People have to wait in long lines to get the limited supply of goods. For durables like cars, shortages mean waiting for months, sometimes years, to get the goods, even if one has the cash. Shortages give enormous power to those who have discretion about who gets the goods in short supply. Thus, managers in the USSR were reputed to exchange "favors" with one another. For a manager to sell goods at a price higher than the official price would be a crime; but for the manager of a firm that manufactures television sets to allow the manager of a car plant to jump to the head of the line and get his TV, with the favor reciprocated, seemed not only acceptable but commonplace.

When prices are not set at their market-clearing level and are not responsive to changes in economic circumstances, it is clear that they will not serve the role in allocating resources that they do in market economies.

---

[3] With some minor exceptions. Poland never collectivized its agriculture.

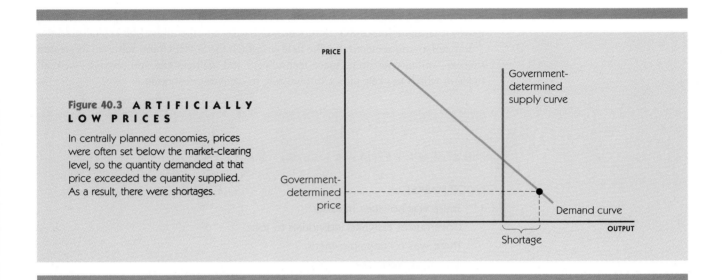

Figure 40.3 ARTIFICIALLY LOW PRICES

In centrally planned economies, prices were often set below the market-clearing level, so the quantity demanded at that price exceeded the quantity supplied. As a result, there were shortages.

While in market economies prices guide firms in making decisions about how their goods are to be produced—prices signal the relative scarcity of different inputs—in the socialist economy, prices could not perform that role. Ideology was important in two ways. First, government ministries associated the charging of interest with capitalism. They did not understand the important role that interest rates play in allocating one of society's scarce resources, capital. Second, as we have seen, they thought of heavy industrialization as the hallmark of a successful economy. Thus, Soviet-style economies tended to use very capital-intensive methods of production, and because of their failure to charge interest, they never realized how high the costs of these methods were.

By the same token, profits and losses do not serve the role in Soviet-style economies that they do in market economies. The quest for profits in market economies provides the incentive for entrepreneurs; equally important, losses are a signal for firms to close down. Returns to investment are the signals that determine how capital should be allocated. In socialist economies, with the state owning all firms and therefore all profits, profits provide little incentive; and losses are seldom used as a basis for shutting down establishments. If a firm makes a loss, the government meets the deficit. János Kornai, a Hungarian economist who teaches both in his native land and at Harvard, refers to this phenomenon as **soft budget constraints**, to contrast them with the harsh reality of budget constraints facing firms in a market economy. For the firm in a socialist system, there is no penalty for making losses and no incentive to conserve on resources.

In a way, it made sense for the Soviet government not to pay too much attention to profits, since the prices firms received for what they produced and the prices they paid for the inputs they used (including labor and capital) were not market-clearing prices; they did not represent the scarcity value of the resources used or of the goods produced. Thus, the profits were not a good measure of the benefits or costs of the firm's production. By the same token, since prices were not set at market-clearing levels, they did not reflect true scarcity, and hence returns to investment—measured in rubles—were not a sound guide for allocating investments. Prices and wages provided little guidance for whether firms should try to economize more on labor or capital or other inputs. There is an important lesson here: failure to use the market in one area (the product market) makes it virtually impossible to rely on the market in other areas (the capital market).

It is perhaps no accident that the fields in which the Soviet Union achieved its greatest success—military research, space technology, and mathematics and physics—were all fields in which markets play a limited role in capitalist economies.

THE THREE MARKETS, SOVIET STYLE

LABOR MARKET

    There was no labor mobility.

    Government assigned individuals to jobs.

    There was no unemployment.

    Incentives were low.

CAPITAL MARKET

    Government owned all capital.

    Government determined the savings rate.

      High savings, low consumption

    Government allocated all investment.

      Emphasis on heavy industry

PRODUCT MARKET

    Markets were used to distribute goods.

    Government kept prices below market-clearing levels.

      Pervasive shortages, long queues

      Prices failing to serve their allocative role

SOVIET-STYLE SOCIALISM AND INEQUALITY

The Soviet government, through its planning ministry, not only decided what was to be produced and how, it also provided the answer to the "for whom" question. In answering this question, three aspects of Soviet ideology played an important role. First, Soviet-style economies were committed to heavy industrialization and a de-emphasis on agriculture. Not surprisingly, then, a large part of the burden of the costs was borne by agriculture. Forced collectivization in agriculture kept agriculture wages low. In effect, there were high taxes on agriculture.

Second, the program of high savings and low consumption could be interpreted as putting an emphasis on the consumption of future generations at the expense of the consumption of the current generation.

Third, an attempt was made to reduce the inequality in society, or at least that is what leaders' rhetoric said. The government determined everyone's wages. It decided how much more a skilled worker got than an unskilled worker. Some goods it allocated directly, such as markets for housing and medical care. Whether or to what extent Soviet-style socialist systems were successful in reducing inequality remains debated. On the one hand, after confiscating all land and other property, there were no longer any very rich people. Also, free medicine and highly subsidized food and apartments provided what was referred to in Chapter 24 as a "safety net" for the poor.

But on the other hand, differences in life-style between the worst-off members of society and high party officials remained enormous. Among those who were not high party officials, whole families lived crowded together in one room. Though no one starved, long hours were spent in lines trying to obtain the barest necessities of life. By contrast, high party officials enjoyed vacations along the beaches of the Black Sea, could buy goods unavailable elsewhere at stores reserved for party members, and had chauffeur-driven cars and other powers and perquisites enjoyed by relatively few within the capitalist world. Among workers, there existed large wage differentials, commensurate with those observed in capitalist economies; though since so many things were provided cheaply by the state, the wage differentials translated into perhaps smaller differences in living standards.

Even the most vaunted achievements of socialism, the prevention of the abject extremes of poverty, have in recent years been thrown into doubt. In the period of 1960–61 in China, demographers now estimate that as many as 20 million Chinese starved to death. In the democracies, a free press would have presumably ensured that a calamity like this simply could not have occurred. Something would have been done. In China, it went almost unnoticed.

THE BASIC ECONOMIC QUESTIONS UNDER SOVIET-STYLE SOCIALISM

1. What is produced?

    Heavy industrial goods

    Other goods as the state sees fit

2. How are goods produced?

    With technologies and inputs decided upon by the state (often capital-intensive technologies)

3. For whom are they produced?

    For future generations (high forced savings rates)

    For present generations according to the wages set by government (high "taxes" on agriculture)

    For government officials, who get high rewards

4. Who makes the decisions?

    Central planning

THE FAILURE OF SOCIALISM

For several decades, Stalin's program appeared to enjoy a modicum of success. He was able to force net investment rates up to almost unprecedented levels of more than 23 percent of net national product in 1937. Many factories were built. The official statistics suggested that the high savings rates had spearheaded a path of rapid industrialization and growth. Though there is growing doubt about the reliability of the statistics, there is little doubt that what gains were made were accompanied by a high level of political repression. The USSR's economic progress was interrupted by World War II, in which 20 million Russians are believed to have died, and the economy was greatly disrupted.

The period after World War II saw the spread of Soviet-style socialism to Eastern Europe—Poland, Czechoslovakia, East Germany, Hungary, Romania, Bulgaria, Yugoslavia, and Albania—and, in 1949, to China.[4] In the case of the Eastern European countries, at least, the spread was hardly voluntary; it was the price they paid for being liberated from the Germans by Soviet troops at the end of the war. Before the war, some of the Eastern European countries had enjoyed reasonably high standards of living. Others, such as Albania, had been extremely poor and backward.

The ensuing decades witnessed several changes in attitudes toward the Soviet-style socialist experiment. At first, the "efficiency" virtues of the system were lauded. The planning mechanism replaced the perceived chaos of the marketplace. Investment could be directed in a rational way. Resources could be quickly mobilized. Moreover, the government could force the high levels of savings required for a successful development program. Textbooks as well as popular writings talked about a trade-off between growth and development on the one hand and freedom on the other. Strong central control was thought to be necessary for rapid growth. Moreover, it was thought that Soviet-style socialism could make possible a level of equality that the market economy had not been able to attain. Basic human services like health and education could be brought to the masses.

But economies like Czechoslovakia and Hungary, which had been prosperous before the war, fell behind other European countries; when this happened, concerns about the efficiency of the system began to be raised. Such systems could force their citizens to save more because they could repress consumption, but could they allocate resources efficiently? It became increasingly clear that the countries were not growing as fast as one would have thought. The higher savings rates did little more than offset the higher levels of inefficiency.

By the mid-1970s, inklings of an impending economic crisis became more and more apparent. While agricultural productivity in the United States and Western Europe had boomed, in the Soviet-style socialist countries it had stagnated. Nikita Khrushchev, who led Russia from the death of Stalin until he was replaced by Brezhnev in 1964, recognized the problems in agriculture and directed more of the country's investment there. But in 1973, the Soviet Union began buying massive amounts of wheat from the United

---

[4] Mongolia had adopted Soviet-style socialism much earlier, in 1924. Cuba adopted a variant much later under Castro, in 1959. North Korea and North Vietnam both adopted Soviet-style socialism as soon as their governments were established.

CLOSE-UP: ENVIRONMENTAL DAMAGE IN THE SOVIET UNION

One of the alleged advantages of centrally controlled economies was that unlike ruthless capitalists, socialist firms would take into account the costs and benefits to all members of society. In the area of environmental protection, that promise was not kept. In fact, in the words of one recent study, "When historians finally conduct an autopsy on the Soviet Union and Soviet Communism, they may reach the verdict of death by ecocide."

Market economies may often have difficulty dealing with pollution externalities. But in attempting to stimulate their economy, Soviet central planners often made pollution problems worse. For example, oil and energy prices were held deliberately low, as a form of assistance to manufacturers who used oil as an input. But lower prices encouraged wasteful use of energy, and when combined with a lack of antipollution measures, this produced a literally sickening air pollution. Today in the industrial center of what was called Industrial Magniogorsk, nine out of ten children become ill with pollution-related diseases like bronchitis, asthma, and cancer.

Highly intensive farming, in a situation where no one had a property right to the land and an incentive to protect it, led to massive pesticide use and soil erosion. Three-quarters of the surface water in what used to be the Soviet Union is now badly polluted, whether from industrial or agricultural sources.

Perhaps the most publicized result of all was the explosion at the Chernobyl nuclear power station in 1986, which exposed perhaps 20 million Soviet citizens to excessive levels of radiation. If that nuclear power plant had been forced to use high-priced safety equipment to avoid that externality, it might well have been shut down years earlier.

In many cities and republics, a protest against this environmental destruction formed part of the base of the popular movements that rebelled against the Soviet Union in the early 1990s. Rather than correcting the market failures that led to pollution, Soviet central planners had magnified them into ecological disasters.

Sources: "Rubbishing of a Superpower," *The Economist,* April 25, 1992, pp. 99–100; M. Feshbach and A. Friendly, *Ecocide in the USSR* (New York: Basic Books, 1992).

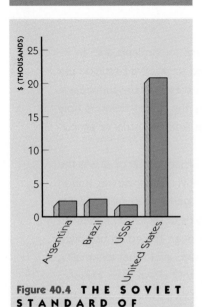

Figure 40.4 THE SOVIET STANDARD OF LIVING

Today, after decades of socialism, the average standard of living in the Soviet Union is close to that of Brazil, Argentina, and other less developed nations. *Sources: World Development Report* (1991), Table 1; World Bank, *World Tables* (1991).

States and other Western countries to feed its people. Meanwhile, the Eastern European countries' reputation for low-quality workmanship was underscored when a nuclear power plant at Chernobyl, in Ukraine, suffered a meltdown in 1986, releasing radiation across much of Europe.

As Mikhail Gorbachev, who came to power in 1985, attempted to introduce reforms to make the economy more efficient, the magnitude of the problems the country faced became clearer: it became evident that many of the statistics on industrial production had been more exaggerated than even many skeptics had thought. Indicators of well-being, such as infant mortality statistics, had similarly been spun out of thin air. Inadequate hospitals with substandard equipment had not only failed to keep pace with developments in the West, but may actually have become worse during recent decades.

The final verdict on the Soviet-style socialist experiment, in most economists' judgment, is that it has been a failure. Today, more than seventy years after the socialist experiment began in the Soviet Union, income per capita is a tenth of what it is in the United States. Far from having buried the United States, the Soviet Union finds its standard of living to be close to that of Brazil, Argentina, and other countries considered to be underdeveloped, as illustrated in Figure 40.4. The socialist experiment in the Soviet Union has had some remarkable achievements, like the Sputnik satellite, but a productive and growing economy is not among them.

REASONS FOR THE FAILURE

The continued success of the capitalist system and the failure of Soviet-style socialist economies can be attributed to incentives and markets, or the lack of them.

The socialists failed to recognize the importance of incentives. Workers, both in collective farms and in manufacturing firms, had no incentive to do more than was required. Managers similarly had no incentives. Firms could not keep any profits they made, and managerial pay in any case did not depend on the profitability of the enterprise. There was no competition, and the soft budget constraints—the fact that losses would be made up by the government—further attenuated managerial incentives.

Equally important, there was no incentive for innovation and growth. The increases in productivity of the labor force in capitalist economies over the past century, with the concomitant increases in wages, are in no small measure the result of the innovative efforts of entrepreneurs. These entrepreneurs almost surely did not succeed out of the desire to enhance the welfare of their workers; they were motivated by the lust for profits and the desire for returns to their savings. But as Adam Smith said, such motives provide a far surer guide to the enhancement of a nation's wealth than any other.

Socialists wanted to replace the market mechanism for allocating resources with central planning. But they encountered two further problems. First, the bureaucrats did not have the requisite information to know how to allocate resources efficiently. Managers of firms had no incentive to tell the central planners what the minimum inputs required to meet their production goals were. Rather, they had every incentive to claim they needed more than they really did. This made their job easier. And they had no incentive to exceed their goals; for if they did, the planners would raise their targets for the next year.

Second, planners could not perfectly monitor the various firms in the economy, to ensure that resources were used in the way intended. And firms had only limited incentives to comply with the planners' directives. They were not rewarded, and they knew they were only imperfectly monitored. Sometimes the managers could divert resources meant for the firm to their own private use. Their disdain for the planners was enhanced by the fact that the planners often put impossible demands on them, such as asking them to produce outputs without providing them the requisite inputs. To fulfill their quota, firms had to acquire the inputs from a "gray" market outside the planning system.

The socialists did not understand the importance of capital markets, interest rates, and profits. As this text has emphasized, capital is a scarce resource. It must be allocated efficiently. Prices provide the signals that make this possible. Because the Soviet-style socialist economies set prices by command rather than through markets, prices did not provide the necessary signals. Try as they might to use the planning mechanism to replace the market mechanism, socialist government planning boards simply did not have the requisite information to allocate investment efficiently.

Given the scarcity of capital, the Soviet strategy of heavy industrialization probably did not make much sense. It would have made more sense to focus attention on industries that require less capital.

The failure of worker incentives, the failure of planners to allocate resources efficiently, and the failure of firms to use resources efficiently largely accounted for the inefficiency of the system. But there were other factors as well. The drabness of life, the lack of opportunity afforded by the system, the long hours spent in lines trying to get rotten vegetables or a small portion of meat, all contributed to a social malaise, evidenced by a high incidence of alcoholism, which impaired worker productivity. The worker under Soviet-style socialism seemed truly alienated from his work.

CAUSES OF THE FAILURE OF SOVIET-STYLE SOCIALISM

1. Failure to provide adequate incentives to workers and managers
   A lack of competition, soft budget constraints, and a lack of incentives to stimulate innovation and growth were major factors.

2. Failure of planning mechanism to replace markets
   Planners lacked the requisite information to allocate resources efficiently.
   Planners lacked the ability to monitor firms and make sure resources were used in the ways intended.

REFORMS IN THE SOVIET-STYLE SOCIALIST ECONOMIES

As the failures of Soviet-style socialism became more evident, a variety of reforms were discussed. There were three possible tacks: try harder to make the socialist system work; give up on socialism and move to a market-based system; or find a third way, which would be neither capitalism nor socialism. For three decades, beginning with Khrushchev, the Soviet Union tried the first strategy. Workers were exhorted to work harder. Money poured into agriculture but seemed to disappear, leaving little traces of enhanced productivity. Antivodka campaigns were launched to increase worker productivity.

During 1990 and 1991, there was much debate over whether or not the first strategy should be abandoned. In October of 1990, Gorbachev announced that the Soviet Union would be converted to capitalism in five hundred days; but he soon dropped this program, whereupon the economists who had been advising him on the market strategy resigned and it appeared as if there would be another attempt to make socialism work. But then, following the attempted coup in August 1991 and the dissolution of the Soviet Union, directions were changed again: most of the newly created republics seemed committed to adopting some form of market system.

People who looked for a third solution sought ways of combining what they saw as the strengths of capitalism with those of socialism. While Hungary made some attempt to do this, perhaps the most successful experiment along these lines was performed in China, where the so-called responsibility system in agriculture essentially allowed farmers to sell most of what they produced in markets and to keep the proceeds. As a result, agricultural production skyrocketed during the late 1970s and early 1980s. The annual growth rate of grain production in the six years after the responsibility system was adopted (1978–1984) was 5 percent, compared with 3.5 percent in the thirteen years before the new system (1965–1978).

MARKET SOCIALISM

An important idea lying behind several of the reform movements was that of market socialism, which argued that an economy could combine the advantages of market mechanisms with public ownership of the means of production. Oskar Lange, who was a professor of economics at the University of Chicago before returning to Poland after World War II, eventually to become a vice-president of that country's communist government, was a leading advocate of this concept.

Under market socialism, prices would serve the same allocative role that they do in capitalist economies. Prices would be set so that demand equaled supply. Firms would act like competitive price takers. They would maximize their profits at the prices they faced. They would produce up to the point where price equaled marginal cost. They would hire labor up to the point where the value of the marginal product of labor was equal to the wage. Since the government owned all machines and buildings, it would have to take responsibility for all investment decisions. These decisions would be made according to a national plan, which defined the nation's priorities. The planning process would entail a close interaction between the government planners and the firms, with the firms informing the planners of what was required to meet various production goals.

In the 1930s, there was a great debate by the advocates of market socialism, including Oskar Lange, and a group of Austrian economists, including Ludwig von Mises and Nobel laureate Friedrich von Hayek. The Austrians did not believe that the government would have the information required to efficiently allocate investment. They thought that the task of allocating resources, or even setting market-clearing prices, was simply too complicated to be done by a government bureau. (As it turned out, they were largely correct.) And they did not believe that government-owned firms would act like private firms. In their view, market socialism was doomed to failure.

The advocates of market socialism emphasized the fact that there were, in modern terms, pervasive market failures. Capital and risk markets were imperfect. There were externalities. Competition was imperfect. The market gave rise to great inequality. And capitalist economies seemed prone to periodic chronic illnesses—to recessions and depressions.

PROBLEMS WITH MARKET SOCIALISM

Market socialism faces two key problems: obtaining the requisite information to set prices and providing managers with incentives.

First, in order to set prices at market-clearing levels, planners have to know, in effect, demand and supply curves; they have to know an enormous amount about what consumers want as well as firms' capabilities. They seldom have this information, partly, as has been noted, because firms have no incentive to tell planners what their capabilities are. Even with good information, it is extraordinarily difficult for a government bureaucracy to set prices at market-clearing levels. Lange hoped that with better computers the task could be done quickly, but as better and better computers have been developed, it has become increasingly clear that the problems of setting simultaneously the prices of the millions of goods produced in a modern market economy cannot be solved by a computer, however advanced.

Indeed, it has become clear that while prices play a central role in how the market economy functions, they are only part of the market's incentive systems. Customers care about the quality of the goods they purchase. For instance, for firms, having inputs delivered on time is essential. Consider the simple problem of producing nails in a socialist economy. Given a directive to produce so many nails, the nail factory produces short, stubby nails. When the directive is modified to include a specification for a longer nail, the factory responds by producing a nail with the cheapest steel it can get hold of; the result is that the nail splits when hit too hard. When told that the steel should not be too brittle, the firm finds a kind of steel that bends too easily to make it useful for many purposes.

In market economies, firms will not produce at the market price unless they know they can sell the goods. In a socialist economy, the producer simply delivers the goods to another government enterprise, whose problem it is to sell the good. When China set too high a price for fans, for example, the factories produced more fans than could be sold. Meanwhile, there were huge shortages of most other consumer goods.

While setting prices wrong for consumer goods causes inconvenience, setting prices wrong for producer goods causes further inefficiencies and dislocations. Shortages of inputs impair the entire production process. If a firm producing an intermediate good cannot get some input it needs, it will not be able to provide its product to the firms that need it. A shortage at one critical point can thus have reverberations through other parts of the economy.

A second problem with market socialism is that managers often lack incentives. When the enterprise makes a profit, they cannot keep the profit. And when the enterprise makes a loss, the government makes up the deficit. Market socialism therefore does not resolve the problem of soft budget constraints. Furthermore, competition, which lies at the heart of the market's incentive system, is absent, and this lack of competition is reflected in all aspects of behavior, including the incentive to produce goods that reflect what customers want.

Market socialists thought the central control of prices had one distinct advantage: the government could remedy some of the market failures that arise in capitalist economies. If a particular industry polluted the air, production of that industry's good would be limited and higher prices would be charged to reflect the externality. In principle, if there is an externality associated with burning coal, that it contributes to global warming, the socialist planner would let that be reflected in the price it announced for the use of coal.

But socialism, including market socialism, turned out far less willing to face up to these externalities than did capitalist economies. Each of the socialist countries has reported disastrous levels of air and water pollution: huge lakes that are being drained of life, smog rivaling anything seen in the West, rivers that have become chemical sewers. Evidently those in the economic ministries saw their responsibility as increasing production as fast as possible, regardless of the environmental cost; rather than raising the price of coal to discourage its use, they kept its price low as a means of encouraging production. Furthermore, the absence of democracy meant there was no forum in which those who had to suffer could register their protest.

Parts of the experiment with market socialism have been an unambiguous success, at least as compared with Soviet-style socialism. As was noted, the responsibility system of agriculture in China has resulted in huge increases in agricultural productivity. But other parts of the experiment are more debated. To some, market socialism lacks the best features of both capitalism and socialism: it lacks the market's incentive structure and traditional socialism's other mechanisms of economic control. Thus, within Hungary, which had gone the farthest along the road to market socialism before 1989, a consensus seems to have developed against market socialism.

WORKERS' COOPERATIVES IN YUGOSLAVIA

Yet another type of socialist experiment occurred in Yugoslavia. Marshal Tito, a communist who led the fight against the Nazis in Yugoslavia and became the country's leader after World War II, broke with Stalin in 1948. In the ensuing years, a new form of socialism evolved in which decentralization and decision making by firms played a much larger role. In effect, ownership of firms was turned over to the workers, who were responsible for choosing their own managers. In practice, the Communist party exercised considerable influence both in the choice of managers and in the decisions made.

The idea of worker-owned and -managed firms—cooperatives—has had a long history, with a variety of experiments performed throughout Europe and the United States. Even today in the United States, there are some enormously successful worker-owned firms—Amana, which makes refrigerators, Avis, the country's second largest car rental company, and W. W. Norton, the publisher of this book. Ulgar, a successful household appliances firm, began as a worker cooperative in Mondragón, Spain. Today, with thousands of workers located in many separate plants, it is still run as a cooperative.

Cooperatives have the advantage that because the worker is also a part owner, she has a greater commitment to the firm and more incentive to work hard. While this argument seems valid for cooperatives involving relatively few workers, it does not apply as well to large enterprises, and this proved to be a problem in Yugoslavia. Managers elected by a vote of the workers may be as remote as managers chosen by a board of directors. In cooperatives with thousands of workers, each worker gets back a negligible amount of any extra profits that result from anything he does. The most successful cooperatives thus are often the smaller ones.

In Yugoslavia, the cooperatives encountered another problem. What is the incentive to hire new workers? If new workers have the same rights as old workers, the profits of the enterprise must be divided more ways. Whether for this or another reason, Yugoslavia was plagued with high unemployment rates.

Investment posed still a third problem. When Yugoslavian workers left their cooperative, they received nothing. There was therefore little interest in investing, at least in the long term, or otherwise increasing the market value of the enterprise. Workers did not have an incentive to make investments that yielded returns beyond the date of their retirement. The investment problem was exacerbated by the employment problem: the reluctance to hire new workers resulted in an aging work force, and as the work force aged, incentives to invest were diminished. There was every incentive to pay high wages and to borrow to pay for any needed investment. Not surprisingly, the cooperatives' economic condition deteriorated steadily.[5]

Some of these problems are not *inherent* in cooperatives. For instance, in cooperatives in the United States and Europe, when a person retires or leaves the cooperative for any other reason, he takes his capital out. That is, he is viewed as a part owner of the enterprise; the share he owns depends on the rules of the cooperative, typically how long he has been with the cooperative and in what positions he has served. By the same token, when a worker joins a cooperative, she has in effect to buy a share. (The company may loan her the money, so her take-home pay may be reduced until she has contributed her capital share.) The better the cooperative does, the more valuable it is, the more she will be able to receive when she leaves. This provides an obvious incentive for the cooperative to make good investment decisions.

---

[5] This list of problems that Yugoslavia faced is not meant to be exhaustive. There were others: lack of competition among people who purchased farmers' produce, for instance, meant that farmers received lower prices for their goods, and this discouraged farmers' production.

THE TRANSITION TO MARKET ECONOMIES

Today many of the former socialist countries, including Hungary, Czechoslovakia, and Poland, are committed to transforming their economies into market economies. Others, such as Bulgaria, Romania, and Albania, want *some* market reforms, but how many and how fast remains uncertain. The following paragraphs describe some of the key problems facing those countries that are attempting to make the transition to a market economy. Studying these transition problems has enhanced economists' understanding of modern market economies.

The problems of transition faced by the Eastern European countries have been exacerbated by the economic chaos in the former Soviet Union. The Soviet Union was the main trading partner of the Eastern European countries. Thus, as they face the problem of making the transition to a market economy, they face the additional burden of finding new markets to replace sales to the Soviet Union, which have plummeted. To make matters worse, the kinds of goods they produced for the Soviet Union are not the kinds of high-quality goods consumers in Western Europe, Japan, and the United States want. Not only must they find new markets, they must reorient their production.

MACROECONOMIC PROBLEMS

The first hurdle Eastern European economies face in making a transition to markets is a period of disruption in which living standards, at least for some, fall below even the low level that they had been under socialism.

A central problem with socialism was that resources were inefficiently allocated. If the economy is to move from a point inside its production possibilities curve such as A in Figure 40.5 to a point on the curve, resources will have to be reallocated. Factories will have to be shut down. Workers will have to be let go. These disruptions will be reflected in high unemployment. Transitional unemployment is like frictional unemployment, the unemployment that occurs as workers move between jobs, just magnified many times over. Poland, the first country to attempt the transition, experienced unemployment rates variously estimated at between a quarter and a third. In Romania, miners, seeing their real wages cut by a third, rioted and succeeded in bringing down the market-oriented prime minister; the new prime minister, however, was an economist even more committed to market reforms.

Unemployment is particularly serious in Eastern European countries, because they do not have in place the same kinds of safety nets to protect people forced out of jobs as are found in Western Europe and the United States. This is not surprising, since under the previous regime unemployment was not a problem; firms retained workers even when they were no longer needed. They had no profit motive, no budget constraint. But now, in the transition, firms do face budget constraints. Moreover, capital markets are not yet working well, and new firms are not being created and old firms are not expanding production to absorb the workers who have been laid off.

Inflation receives considerable attention in Eastern European countries these days,

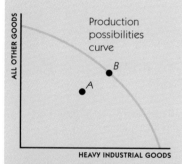

Figure 40.5

INEFFICIENCIES UNDER SOCIALISM

The Soviet-style socialist economies seemed to use their resources inefficiently, so that they operated substantially below the production possibilities curve, such as at point A. Moving the economy from A to a point like B, on the production possibilities curve, will entail substantial improvements in efficiency.

partly because it is felt by everyone, partly because typically wages do not keep pace with prices, so that living standards fall. But the fall in living standards is not really caused by the inflation; it is caused by the economic disruption of the transition process, which simultaneously reduces output, leads to inflation, and lowers living standards.

The reason that inflation always seems to arise in the transition is easy to see. The Soviet-style economies were run with prices below market-clearing levels; shortages were endemic. Hence, once prices were freed, an increase in prices was inevitable. One-time price increases, particularly of necessities like bread, which had been heavily subsidized (so much so that it was cheaper for farmers to buy bread to feed to their pigs than to buy grain), cause political problems: such price increases led to the downfall of the Polish government in 1989. But what also worries governments in most of these countries is the likelihood of the onset of inflation. Chapter 36 explained one reason for their worry: that inflationary expectations, once established, may perpetuate inflation.

Many of these countries, especially Russia and Poland, face another problem: the shortage of consumer goods has resulted in the accumulation of large holdings of money. This is referred to as the problem of **monetary overhang,** and it contributes to the inflationary pressures. The Soviet Union attempted to deal with this problem by calling in all notes of 50 rubles or more. (Before the economic crisis, the ruble was worth $2 at the official exchange rate; for the average Soviet citizen, 50 rubles was a substantial amount of money. By mid-1992, there were 200 rubles to the dollar, so 50 rubles amounted to a quarter.) Each individual was allowed to exchange a few old 50-ruble notes for new ones, but any excess was in effect confiscated by the government. This seemingly capricious action, while it did reduce the monetary overhang, increased the disaffection of the people toward their government.

Huge government deficits have also contributed to inflationary pressures. As the government's control over the economy weakens, its revenue sources also diminish. Under socialism, it could simply seize corporate profits; if it wanted to increase profits and thus its revenues, it could just increase the prices charged or reduce the wages paid. As the government abandoned its role in wage and price setting, it lost its ability to collect revenues in this way. But cutting back on expenditures seems no easier in Eastern Europe than elsewhere. Food subsidies are a major drain on the budget, but government threats to reduce them have met with stiff opposition. In the Soviet Union, the government deficit had reached 10 percent of GDP by 1990.

As the crisis in the Soviet economy unfolded in the late 1980s and early 1990s, inflation—and the threat of further inflation—and the unavailability of goods proved extremely disruptive to what remained of the old economic structure. Farmers, for instance, did not want to deliver food to the city in return for rubles that were constantly falling in value; and even if the rubles did not fall in value, people could not obtain goods with them. All the transition governments are committed to doing something about inflation. The range of instruments that a transition government has to control inflation, having abandoned direct price controls, are those discussed in Parts Four, Five, and earlier chapters in Six: cutting government expenditures, raising taxes, and restricting credit. But controlling the credit supply has proved both important and difficult in several of the countries in transition, such as Hungary. There are often several different lending institutions, with no central bank able to control the overall level of credit. Moreover, there is often considerable interfirm lending, so that firms that have access to credit extend it to others. Without any controls on the level of credit, it is easy to arrive at a situation in which there is excess demand for goods.

Poland did succeed in gaining control over credit, but with mixed effects on the economy: while aggregate demand was checked, the lack of credit impaired many firms' ability to produce. Firms need to have access to credit to purchase their inputs. Thus, the credit contraction not only decreased aggregate demand, it also decreased aggregate supply. Nonetheless, inflationary pressures were abated in Poland; other countries may not be so lucky.

PRIVATIZATION AND COMPETITION

Private property and competition are at the center of the market economy. *Allowing* competition is easy. The government can simply say that anyone who wants to set up a firm and has the necessary resources can do so. Generating and sustaining competition are more difficult.

One important way for Eastern European countries to promote competition is through trade liberalization—opening up the economy to competition from abroad. But while most economists believe that trade liberalization will enhance economic efficiency in the long run, some are concerned about those who lose out in the competition, including people who lose their jobs. They give a variant of the infant industry argument, which goes like this. Enterprises in the former socialist economies have been insulated from competition for decades. It is unfair to suddenly subject them to competition and make their survival depend on this market test. They need time to learn how to compete.

Another way to promote competition is to sell off different parts of existing state enterprises to private entrepreneurs. There are few problems in selling off small businesses—barbershops, retail stores, restaurants. The real difficulties come in selling large enterprises like automobile or cement factories. Selling them to foreigners raises a host of thorny problems. No country likes to see its factories owned by foreigners. And if a country sells the factories to buyers abroad at too low a price, it is as if the country is giving away its hard-earned savings to foreigners. In Eastern Europe, there is a further problem: people within these countries who have the most money include former party bosses. There is a bitter irony in seeing those who exploited the system under the Communist government for their own advantage retain their advantageous position, this time as capitalist bosses.

How the different countries will resolve these seeming dilemmas remains to be seen. Czechoslovakia, for one, first privatized stores, restricted purchases of the stores to citizens of the country (and prohibited their resale to foreigners for two years), and accepted the grim fact that many of the hated Communist bosses would now become capitalist bosses. Economic efficiency, in the minds of Czech reformers, was more important than revenge. The country distributed vouchers to all citizens, which the citizens used to bid for shares in the larger, privatized firms. Thus, in one stroke, Czechoslovakia hoped both to privatize and to establish a viable stock market. With the widely distributed ownership of firms, they planned to establish a people's capitalism. The next problem the Czechs face is one that was discussed in Chapter 21—with no shareholders having a large stake in a firm, managers will run the firm with little outside check on their behavior. There have been proposals to deal with this problem, such as the establishment of holding companies or investment banks, but no consensus has emerged.

By contrast, Hungary has taken the view that the advantages of foreign ownership—in particular, the advantage of foreigners' expertise—outweigh the disadvantages. Government officials point out that almost 40 percent of Belgian firms are foreign owned, with no adverse effects. They envisage a similar role for foreign ownership within their own economy.

While many of the countries have waited to figure out the best way of privatizing, they have broken up the large state enterprises into competing units, thus hoping to enjoy some of the benefits of competition. But in the absence of antitrust policies of the kind discussed in Chapter 17, there is a natural tendency for these separate enterprises to work together (as they put it) or to collude (perhaps a more apt description of what they are doing). The heads of the different companies had worked closely together in the years before the breakup, and it seems natural for them to work closely afterward.

The lack of competition has particularly harmful effects on agriculture. In Poland and what was formerly Yugoslavia, for instance, agriculture is now largely in private hands. The farmers used to have to sell their produce to state enterprises and buy their inputs (seeds, fertilizers, and tractors) from state enterprises. Now they find that they get equally low prices for their produce and pay equally high prices for their inputs; the prices are set not by the government but by the "new" noncompeting enterprises. If entry into the industries that supply inputs to farmers were easy, the high prices would attract competition that would drive prices down. But entry is not so easy. Most important, the uncertain economic environment makes foreigners less willing to make investments, and the small number of entrepreneurs within the country and their lack of access to capital impede entry. But even if foreigners are reluctant to invest, they are willing to trade, and the actual and potential competition from foreign firms may eventually provide a good substitute for the limited levels of domestic competition.

PRIVATIZATION OF LAND

In Hungary and Czechoslovakia, where memories are long and land is held in cooperatives and state farms, land privatization has proved controversial. One problem is how to treat old claims. The Communist government took away land without compensation. The original owners argue that if land is to become private, it should go to the person who owned it before the Communist regime. But in Hungary, there were **land reforms,** in which land was taken away from the large landowners and given to the peasants who actually worked the land, before the Communists took over. The Small Landowners party of Hungary wants the land returned to those who received it as part of the land reform. But others ask, why stop there? Why not undo the land reform itself, if private property is sacrosanct?

In Czechoslovakia, there are many farm cooperatives, which means in principle that farmers "voluntarily" contribute their land. If the cooperatives were dissolved, the land would return to its original owners. In both countries, four decades have left much changed: the original owners have died, most of the children have left the farms, others may have moved in. There is a general consensus among economists, but less so in the political sphere, that to sort out the old claims would be impossible. Let bygones be bygones.

SPEED OF TRANSITION

The former Soviet-style socialist economies face a difficult problem in deciding how fast to make the transition to capitalism. One approach is called "cold turkey": make the plunge, live through a short nightmarish period, and then enjoy a future prosperity.

The other approach calls for a more gradual transition and considers political as well as economic issues. For instance, will the pain caused by cold turkey be so great that support for the market will erode?

Poland tried the cold turkey approach, at least with respect to its macroeconomic adjustment. Inflation was brought under control, but at the expense of a drastic drop in output and employment and the defeat of the government that undertook the plan. And even after the macroadjustments are made, the microeconomic problems—for instance, making factories more efficient, reallocating labor and capital—remain. Most of the other countries have moved more cautiously.

The problem is that the success of market economies depends on a host of long-established institutions, not just on the abstract concept of markets. And all of these institutions have to be functioning reasonably well if the economy is to prosper. There must be credit institutions to sort out potential loan applicants, to monitor the loans, and to see that funds go where they are most productive and are used in the way promised. There must be a legal structure that ensures that contracts will be enforced, and that determines what happens when one party cannot fulfill its contract (bankruptcy). There must be an antitrust policy that ensures that firms compete against one another.

Beyond that, the more advanced developed countries have developed a set of safety nets to help certain segments of society, such as the unemployed. Since unemployment was not a problem in the socialist economies, these societies do not have such safety nets. There may be a huge human toll if the transition, with its attendant unemployment, proceeds before the safety nets are in place. Yet the budgetary problems facing all of these governments make it hard to institute such programs quickly.

Those who advocate a more gradual transition to market economies believe that the long-run success of these economies will be enhanced by thinking through each of the components, trying to design the best possible institutions, adapting to the particular situations in which they find themselves, and borrowing where appropriate from the United States, Western Europe, and Japan.

Whether slow or fast, the problems of the transition to a market economy are likely to be enormous. Yet Poland, Czechoslovakia, and Hungary, upon whom the Soviet-style socialist system was imposed by brute force, seem committed to making the transition. There are disagreements about how and how fast to get there, but not on the ultimate destination.

Within the republics of the former Soviet Union, where by now several generations have grown up under, been taught, and come to believe the Communist ideology, the debate about the destination—a reformed socialism, a humane capitalism, or a third system—goes on. There, a slow transition faces a major hurdle: for market reforms to work, market attitudes must be created. Those who make profits have to feel that they can keep them and that they will not be branded antisocial speculators. The government must be committed to enforcing contracts and must not interfere with wages and prices. Firms have to believe that budget constraints are firm, that they will not be bailed out if they make losses and threaten to close down. The great Harvard economist Joseph Schumpeter described the essence of capitalism as "creative destruction," a process of constant turmoil as old jobs and firms are eliminated and new, improved ones are created. There has to be general willingness to accept this creative destruction.

Today the republics of the former Soviet Union stand in limbo. The failure of the coup attempt in August 1991, followed by the banning of the Communist party, seemed to many a liberation from oppression much like the liberation of the countries of Eastern

Europe. Their citizens wanted to obtain all the fruits of this liberation: not only a democratic political system but also a market-oriented economic system. But old ideas die slowly. Both the political and economic systems are unsettled, and there is not a universal consensus on the desirability of all the features of capitalism. Without the commitment to a market economy, few entrepreneurs are coming forth, and the private economy is not getting off the ground. The planning apparatus, while it may have been inefficient, worked when accompanied by the strong system of political control. Today the planning apparatus seems to have largely broken down. As this book goes to press, there is economic chaos. Which way the country will turn remains unclear.

REVIEW AND PRACTICE

SUMMARY

1. Socialism grew out of the grave economic problems that characterized nineteenth-century industrial economies—severe recessions and depressions, unemployment, and bad working and living conditions.

2. Soviet-style socialism used central planning, under which government bureaucrats made all major decisions about what would be produced, how it would be produced, and for whom it would be produced. Competition was banned. Prices, set by the government, often did not reflect relative scarcities. Private property was restricted.

3. Socialism protected workers against layoffs. The trade-off was that this greater security created a lesser incentive for efficiency.

4. In Soviet-style economies, the government decided where investment funds went. The major Soviet aims in the capital market were a high savings rate (which meant low consumption) and heavy industrialization.

5. In socialist economies, firms had little incentive to make profits since profits went to the state, and little incentive to avoid losses since the government would meet any deficits. Firms thus faced "soft" budget constraints.

6. The Soviet-style socialist experiment is today considered a failure by most economists. The Soviet Union's standard of living is no higher than that of many underdeveloped countries.

7. Three possible reforms have been proposed for Soviet-style socialist economies: try harder to make socialism work; give up on socialism and move to a market-based system; find a third alternative between socialism and markets.

8. Among the problems faced by the countries of Eastern Europe and the former Soviet Union in their transition to a market economy are unemployment and inflation. These countries also do not have in place a safety net to protect those who are hurt in the transition process.

9. Privatizing state-controlled firms and land has proved difficult in practice. For instance, no one wants to sell factories to foreigners or former party bosses, and it is difficult to sort out old claims on land.

KEY TERMS

socialism

central planning

soft budget constraints

land reform

REVIEW QUESTIONS

1. What were some of the problems that motivated Karl Marx's criticism of capitalism?

2. What are some of the central characteristics of Soviet-style socialism?

3. How is the rate of national savings determined in a socialist economy, as opposed to a capitalist economy? How is the allocation of capital determined in a socialist economy, as opposed to a capitalist economy? Who determines what goods are produced in a socialist economy?

4. Why are budget constraints "soft" in socialist countries and "hard" in market economies?

5. What effect do the job-security policies of Soviet-style socialism have on the incentives of workers to put forward their strongest effort?

6. What is market socialism? What did its advocates claim? What are the main problems it faces?

7. What are worker cooperatives? What did its advocates claim for them? What were the problems of worker cooperatives in Yugoslavia?

8. What are the central problems facing countries trying to move from Soviet-style socialism to market economies? Why are inflationary pressures common in a socialist country that is moving toward a market economy? Why is rising unemployment common?

9. What benefits do socialist economies hope to gain from privatization? What are some of the problems facing privatization programs?

10. What are the advantages and disadvantages of the "cold turkey" approach for a socialist economy in transition?

PROBLEMS

1. Explain how the incentives of each of the following people are different in a socialist and a market economy:
    (a) the incentive of a manager to make wise decisions;
    (b) the incentive of workers to exert their best effort;
    (c) the incentive of a bank manager to screen prospective borrowers carefully.

2. Queues (lines) form when there is a shortage of goods. Use a supply and demand diagram to explain why socialist price controls tend to lead to queues.

3. Are the problems of soft budget constraints unique to socialist economies?

4. Why did the Soviet-style socialist economies have almost no safety nets of unemployment and welfare benefits?

5. In the Soviet-style socialist economies, there was a great scarcity of housing, and much of the housing was controlled by various firms. What consequences might this have for labor mobility?

6. If you were a top official in a country that practiced Soviet-style socialism, would you rather have a very high income or access to a special store where all items are guaranteed to be in stock? Why?

7. Imagine that you are sixty years old and you work for a worker cooperative in Yugoslavia. If you consider only your own self-interest, are you likely to support hiring more workers? Would you support long-term investments in capital?

CHAPTER 41

DEVELOPMENT

Three-quarters of the world's population live in what are often referred to as **less developed countries,** or **LDCs.** In the United States, one of the world's wealthier nations, the idea of "less developed" is often applied to rural areas, or to urban areas where the houses and businesses are dingy and run down. The problem of life in the LDCs is far more serious. It is not that houses are run down, but that a large percentage of the population may have no housing at all; not that people's diet is limited, but that they are starving to death; not that medical care is far off or costly, but that it may simply be unavailable. The contrast between life in some LDCs and life in the United States is significantly larger than the contrast between life in America today and two centuries ago.

The LDCs pose some of the most poignant problems in economics. There are no simple answers, no easy formulas that, if followed, will ensure successful solutions. Still, economists have learned a lot about the process of economic development during recent decades. This chapter discusses some of the more important theories that have been formulated as a result of this new knowledge.

KEY QUESTIONS

1. In what ways, besides their grinding poverty, do the developing countries differ from the United States, Japan, and the countries of Western Europe?

2. What are the impediments to the growth of developing countries?

3. What policies can these countries pursue to improve their standards of living? In particular, why have most of the success stories involved policies encouraging exports?

SOME BACKGROUND

Statistics cannot convey the full measure of what it means to live in a less developed country, but they can provide a start. In the United States, life expectancy at birth is about 76 years. In Peru, it is 62 years; in India, 58 years; in Nigeria and Bangladesh, 51 years. In the United States, 10 infants die for every 1,000 live births; in Brazil, 61; in Pakistan, 107; in Nepal, 126. The average American completes 12 years of schooling, while the average African gets only 5 years. India, with a population of nearly 815 million, has a GNP roughly one-twentieth that of the United States, which has a population of about 250 million. This means that per capita income in India is less than 2 percent of that in the United States. The industrial output of India is comparable to the output of the Netherlands, but the Netherlands has a population of less than 15 million, less than 2 percent of India's.

The statistics connect to one another in a vicious cycle. A lack of schools leads to widespread illiteracy; a lack of food brings malnutrition, starvation, and death; a lack of doctors and hospitals and clean water leads to more sickness and death. Life is hard in LDCs, and there is little hope that it will get better. In recent decades, many African countries, whose standards of living were already low enough, have had populations growing faster than national income, so that per capita income is falling; life is getting worse, not better.

The United Nations and the World Bank (a bank established by the major industrialized countries after World War II that provides loans to less-developed countries) group countries into three categories: low-income countries are those with a GNP per capita of $580 or less in 1989; high-income countries have a GNP per capita in excess of $6,000; and middle-income countries are those in between. The low-income countries

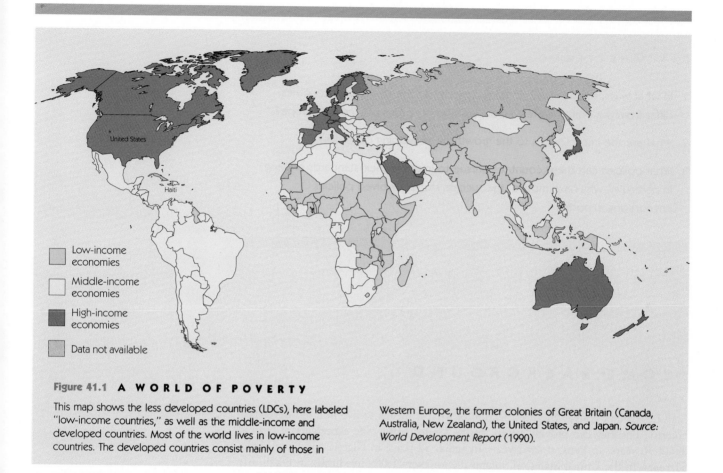

Figure 41.1 A WORLD OF POVERTY

This map shows the less developed countries (LDCs), here labeled "low-income countries," as well as the middle-income and developed countries. Most of the world lives in low-income countries. The developed countries consist mainly of those in Western Europe, the former colonies of Great Britain (Canada, Australia, New Zealand), the United States, and Japan. *Source: World Development Report* (1990).

Legend:
- Low-income economies
- Middle-income economies
- High-income economies
- Data not available

are the less developed countries, while the high-income countries are sometimes simply referred to as the **developed countries.** Because the basis of their higher level of income is their higher level of industrialization, they are also often referred to as the **industrialized countries.** Figure 41.1 is a map of the world showing the countries in their different categories. In the Western Hemisphere lie one of the richest countries, the United States, with a per capita income of $22,000 in 1990, and one of the poorest, Haiti, with a per capita income of $360, hardly 200 miles apart. Table 41.1 compares some of the relevant statistics for the United States and its neighbor to the south, Mexico.

The income gap among the more high-income countries, including the countries of Western Europe, the United States, Canada, Japan, Australia, and New Zealand, has narrowed considerably over the past hundred years, but the gap between the high-income countries and the low-income countries has not. Figure 41.2 shows per capita income in several different LDCs, ranging from $120 in Ethiopia to $370 in Pakistan. By way of comparison, note that the U.S. per capita income in 1990 was $22,000, 180

Table 41.1 **STANDARD OF LIVING MEASUREMENTS IN THE UNITED STATES AND MEXICO**

Category	U.S.	Mexico	U.S./Mexico
GNP per capita ($)	20,910	2,010	10.4
Life expectancy (years)	76	69	1.1
Agriculture as % of GNP	2	9	0.22
Energy consumption per capita (kilograms of oil equivalent)	7,794	1,288	6.05
Food as % of total household consumption	13	35	0.37
Medical care as % of total household consumption	14	5	2.8
Average annual inflation (GNP deflator): 1980–89[a]	3.9	72.8	0.05
Average annual growth of population (%): 1980–89	1	2.1	0.48
Infant mortality rate (per 1,000 live births)	10	40	0.25
Population per physician	470	1,242	0.38
Population in cities of 1 million or more as % of total population	36	32	1.13

Source: World Development Report (1991). Data are for the most recent year available, in most cases 1989.

[a]Like the GDP deflator discussed in Chapter 25, the GNP deflator is the measure of the price level used to adjust GNP for inflation.

and 60 times as large, respectively. However, there are signs that change is possible. Some countries have made notable progress in recent years.

First, several countries have moved from the circle of the LDCs to the ranks of the middle-income countries. These are sometimes referred to collectively as **newly industrialized countries,** or **NICs** for short. These success stories include the "gang of four": South Korea, Taiwan, Singapore, and Hong Kong. Just thirty years after the devastating Korean War, for instance, South Korea has moved from the category of backward country to that of major producer, not just of simple products such as textiles but of automobiles (the Hyundai) and computers (many of the IBM clones are made in South Korea), which require a reasonably high level of technological expertise. Even more impressive, Japan has moved from the ranks of middle-income countries to the position of one of the most prosperous countries in the world.

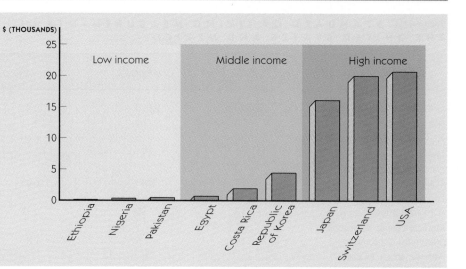

Figure 41.2

DIFFERENCES IN PER CAPITA INCOME

Some middle-income countries such as Egypt and Costa Rica have per capita incomes up to ten times that of the world's poorest nations and yet are up to ten times smaller than the per capita income of the world's wealthiest nations. *Sources:* Organization for Economic Cooperation and Development, *National Accounts* (1991); *WDR* (1991), Table 1. For high-income countries, the conversion uses purchasing power parity; for other countries, the conversion uses the exchange rate.

Second, there have been pockets of remarkable progress within the less developed countries. In the early 1960s, agricultural research centers around the world funded largely by the Rockefeller Foundation developed new kinds of seeds, which under the correct conditions increase the yields per acre enormously. The introduction and dissemination of these new seeds, accompanied by enormous improvements in agricultural practices—known as the **green revolution**—led to huge increases in output. India, for example, finally managed to produce enough food to feed its burgeoning population, and now sometimes can export wheat to other countries.

Third, even the grim statistics for life expectancy and infant mortality represent improvements for many countries. But these improvements have a darker side in some countries—a population explosion that is reminiscent of the Malthusian nightmare. Malthus, you will recall from Chapter 37, envisioned a world in which population growth outpaced increases in the food supply. In Kenya during the early 1980s, for instance, improved health conditions enabled the population to grow at the remarkable rate of 4.1 percent a year, implying a doubling of the population every eighteen years, while output increased only at the rate of 1.9 percent a year. Output increases do nothing to improve per capita income when the population grows at a faster rate.

The 1980s proved to be a particularly hard decade for some of the poorest countries, as Figure 41.3 shows. While sub-Saharan Africa[1] has basically stagnated for the past quarter century, during the 1980s per capita income actually fell at the rate of 2.4 percent per year. Latin America has grown an average of a little more than 2 percent a year in per capita income for a quarter century, but during the 1980s per capita income fell at the rate of .7 percent a year.

[1] A term that refers to all of Africa south of the Sahara except South Africa.

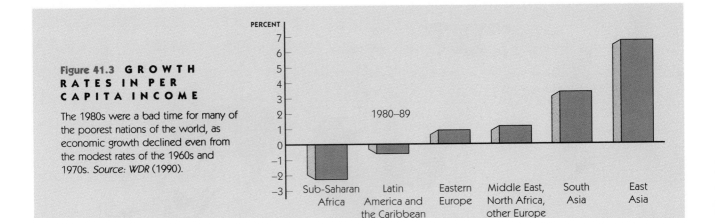

Figure 41.3 GROWTH RATES IN PER CAPITA INCOME

The 1980s were a bad time for many of the poorest nations of the world, as economic growth declined even from the modest rates of the 1960s and 1970s. Source: WDR (1990).

LIFE IN AN LDC

Just as there are large differences between the LDCs and the industrialized countries, so too are there large differences among the LDCs. The largest of them all, China, has a Communist government; the second largest, India, has an avowedly socialist government, but also functions as the world's largest democracy. Literacy standards and life spans in Costa Rica rank with those of the industrialized countries, while more than half of the adult population in sub-Saharan Africa is illiterate and the expected life span is roughly two-thirds that of the industrialized countries. Accordingly, one must be careful in generalizing about the less developed countries. Still, certain observations are true for *most* of these countries.

AGRICULTURE

Agriculture plays a much more important role in LDCs than in the more developed countries; we can see this in Figure 41.4. In wealthy countries like the United States and those of Western Europe, agriculture is generally 5 percent or less of the total gross domestic product. In poor countries, agriculture is often 40 percent or more of GNP.

Farms in less developed countries tend to be much smaller than in the United States—an acre or two on average compared with more than a hundred acres in the United States. The number of people working on each acre in LDCs is higher, but even so, output per worker is much, much lower. That is because these countries use less advanced farming techniques and less fertilizer. Developed countries use roughly twice as much

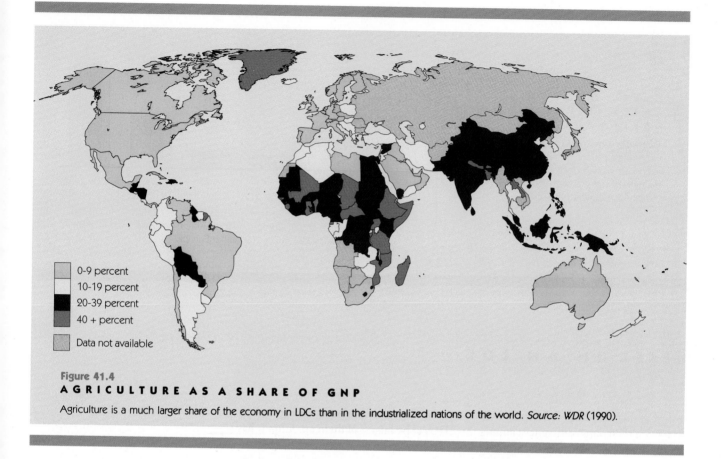

Figure 41.4

AGRICULTURE AS A SHARE OF GNP

Agriculture is a much larger share of the economy in LDCs than in the industrialized nations of the world. *Source: WDR* (1990).

Legend:
- 0-9 percent
- 10-19 percent
- 20-39 percent
- 40 + percent
- Data not available

fertilizer per acre of land than do less developed countries. They employ tractors, combines, and other equipment, while in LDCs a wealthy farmer may use oxen to plow his fields and a poor one may have nothing but a hand plow. The lack of productivity is not a result of lack of hard work; human and animal labor must substitute for a lack of fertilizer and machinery.

Some of the institutional arrangements in LDCs may also contribute to the lack of productivity. Much of the land in less developed countries is farmed under a share-cropping arrangement, in which the landlord takes a share of the output, usually between a third and a half. Sharecropping reduces the tenant farmers' incentives to work—if they work harder, they receive only one-half to two-thirds of the extra output, with the rest going to the landlord. In addition, since the workers do not own the land, they might not be as careful to maintain its quality, for instance by using the right kind and amount of fertilizer, by ensuring that drainage was proper, and so on. Absentee landlords do not, perhaps because they cannot, make their tenant farmers maintain the quality of the land in the same way that an owner-farmer would. Land that is not properly cared for can have its productivity decline significantly.

Sharecropping survives, in spite of its negative effects on productivity, because of the great inequality in wealth and land ownership prevalent in many LDCs. Given this inequality, sharecropping has certain advantages. Agriculture is extremely risky, especially in poor countries. When the weather is good, output is large; but if the weather is bad, output can drop dramatically. When the farmer grows crops intended to be sold in the world market, there is an additional source of uncertainty: the price received for crops may vary enormously. Poor farmers do not like bearing this risk. The landlords, who are often much wealthier than the workers, are in a better position to bear the risk. With sharecropping, landlord and workers can share the risk.

Land reforms may have an enormous effect in increasing output in LDCs. As we learned in Chapter 40, land reform is the redistribution of land ownership, usually by breaking it into smaller plots and giving the plots to those who work the land. With land reform, workers get all the return to their efforts, and thus they are motivated to work harder. When Taiwan introduced land reform in the 1950s, output per acre increased by 22 percent in only five years.

But to be successful, land reforms have to be carefully designed. In India, Peru, and the Philippines, the former tenants did not have the capital to run the farm or to buy fertilizer. They either did without, reducing productivity, or borrowed from the wealthy landlord. As tenants sank more into debt, many defaulted, and the land returned to the wealthy. In other cases, the land reforms, which limited the holdings of any single individual, were circumvented by placing the land in the names of different members of a single family.

THE DUAL ECONOMY: LIFE IN THE CITIES

Today in the more developed countries, 60 percent or more of the population live in urban centers, as Figure 41.5 shows. For the United States, the figure is 74 percent. In the LDCs, the figure is commonly around 30–40 percent. Though these urban areas represent a small fraction of the population, they are often responsible for a large fraction of national output. Thus, productivity in LDCs, measured in output per worker, is often considerably higher in urban areas. Cities may employ relatively modern manufacturing techniques, and the level of education, while still lower than in the developed economies, is typically far higher than in the rural sector. There is a marked contrast between the urban and rural sectors of the economy, a disparity known as the **dual economy**.

One aspect of these dual economies has been a particular source of concern—the high levels of urban unemployment. Wages in the urban sector are frequently far higher than in the rural sector, higher than can be accounted for by the differences in cost of living. The higher wages have an important and obvious consequence: workers migrate from the low-wage rural sector to the urban sector even if they are not sure of obtaining a job. Because of the lure of higher wages, they are willing to spend a considerable length of time looking for a job in the city. In some LDCs, unemployment has risen as high as 20 percent or more of the urban labor force. These unemployed are of concern not only because they represent underutilized human resources, but also because they may be a source of political unrest.

Visitors to LDCs do not see a pretty sight; they see rural poverty and urban squalor. While average incomes of those employed may be far higher in the urban sector, visitors cannot help but notice the homeless sleeping in the streets, the shantytowns with

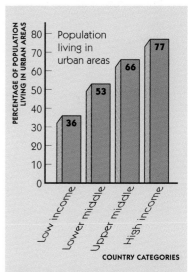

Figure 41.5 RATES OF URBANIZATION

The percentage of the population living in urban areas tends to be higher in developed countries than in LDCs. *Source: WDR* (1990).

cardboard houses and open sewers that house the recent migrants, the children begging in tattered clothes. It is hard not to want to do something. But to know what to do, we must understand the causes of the predicament in which these countries find themselves.

SOME IMPORTANT DIFFERENCES BETWEEN DEVELOPED AND LESS DEVELOPED COUNTRIES

	DEVELOPED COUNTRIES	LDCs
Per capita income	Over $6,000	Less than $580 per year
Production/Employment	Less than 10% of the work force is in agriculture	More than 70% of the work force is in agriculture
Urbanization	Less than 30% live in rural areas	More than 60% live in rural areas
Population growth rate	Less than 1.0%	Often more than 3.0%

EXPLANATIONS OF UNDERDEVELOPMENT

Chapter 35 related growth to increases in physical capital (machines, plants) and human capital (education), to the efficiency with which resources are used, and to technological progress. Similarly, the lack of development in LDCs is related to the lack of machines and equipment and an educated labor force, the failure to use resources efficiently, and the failure to take full advantage of technological progress.

But while there are some similarities between the problems of growth in developed countries and in LDCs, there are some important differences. The essential problem can be stated simply: the institutions and structure of less developed economies do not facilitate growth. For instance, not only is there a shortage of capital, but capital markets do not function well, so capital is often not allocated wisely. The following paragraphs examine this and other major impediments to development.

CAPITAL

The description of economic growth in Chapter 37 emphasized the importance of capital. The less developed countries have much less capital per capita. The low capital is not for want of trying: as Figure 41.6 shows, savings rates in most LDCs are higher than

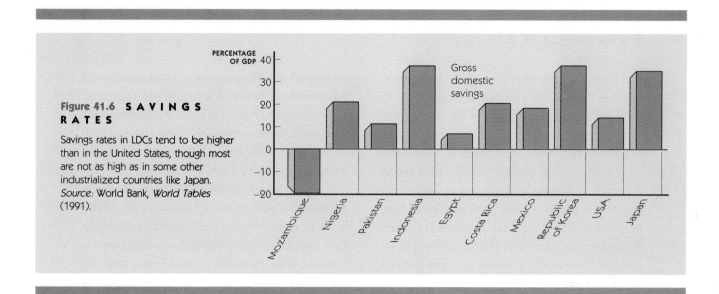

Figure 41.6 SAVINGS RATES

Savings rates in LDCs tend to be higher than in the United States, though most are not as high as in some other industrialized countries like Japan. *Source:* World Bank, *World Tables* (1991).

in the United States, though not so high as in Japan and Korea. Indonesia, which has been growing rapidly, is an exception. The accumulation of capital has been an important component of virtually all successful development programs. But incomes are so low that even a high savings rate does not permit a rapid increase in the capital stock.

Foreign Aid as a Remedy   Those who hold the view that the major problem in less developed economies is a shortage of capital have emphasized the importance of extending loans (or grants) to the LDCs. The United States and several other industrialized countries provide foreign aid to the LDCs to help build their roads and ports, to assist in the construction of new factories, and to help develop educational and health systems. Total aid in recent years from the developed to the less developed countries has exceeded $50 billion per year. The United States has been less charitable than the major European countries; aid as a percentage of national income is smaller, and more of it is linked to U.S. defense efforts. Pure economic aid from the United States now is less than $10 billion a year.

Today much of the aid from the more advanced countries to the LDCs is channeled through multilateral international agencies in which the donor countries work together. The most important of these agencies is the World Bank, which currently lends over $10 billion a year to the less developed countries. But loans from the World Bank or elsewhere eventually lead to an improvement in the standard of living only if they yield returns in excess of the interest the countries must pay. Many LDCs have faced financial crises as they have found it increasingly difficult to make the required interest payments, let alone the repayment of the principal.

Other Sources of Capital   Another source of capital is direct foreign investment, which has one major advantage over loans. The foreign companies making the investment risk their own capital; if the investment fails to yield a return, they, not the country,

CLOSE-UP: TRANSNATIONAL CORPORATIONS AS A SOURCE OF CAPITAL

Less developed countries have all the unskilled labor they need. What they lack is capital, both to build the physical tools needed for greater production and to increase the human capital of their population. But where is that capital to come from?

LDCs can, through savings, provide some capital themselves. Countries like Mexico, Brazil, and South Korea have shown a capacity to save more than 20 percent of GDP per year. By world standards, those countries are fairly well off. The poorest countries, like many in Africa or Asia, save only about 7 percent of GDP.

The other alternatives all involve investment capital coming in from abroad, whether it is through foreign aid, private bank loans, or direct foreign investment. The problem with depending on foreign aid is that there is not enough of it. For example, in one recent year the total foreign aid received by all less developed nations was perhaps 1 percent of their combined GDP, which helps, but is not much.

Another possibility is private financial capital, commonly in the form of bank loans. This method of sending capital to LDCs was tried with a vengeance in the 1970s. But after the experience of countries like Brazil, Argentina, and Mexico not being able to repay their loans on time in the 1980s, U.S. banks are not eager to plunge into a massive new round of lending.

The final possibility is direct foreign investment, more commonly known as investment by multinational or transnational corporations. This method has some obvious advantages. The transnational company has an interest in looking after its investment and managing it carefully, which means that the money is less likely to be spent inefficiently,

such as on a grandiose project. In addition, direct investment is not a loan; the country need not repay it. Finally, the company doing the investment will often send new technology to the LDC and train workers there. Regardless of whether the investment works out, the training helps.

The main disadvantage of direct investment is political. The governments of LDCs generally prefer loans or grants that they can spend as they wish over investment controlled by foreign business executives. LDCs have often passed laws that discouraged foreign companies from investing. But as the options for obtaining capital from other sources are dwindling, transnational corporations are looking better and better as an alternative. The current level of direct foreign investment in LDCs is only about $10 billion now. However, according to a recent United Nations report:

> There is a growing awareness—in countries at all levels of development . . . that many public goals can best be achieved in a decentralized fashion, through the operation of market forces. The revision by a large number of developing countries of their laws and regulations in the area of foreign direct investment is part and parcel of this broader process. There has been a marked decline in the incidence of nationalization and an increase in the arbitration of disputes between transnational corporations and host country Governments. To be sure, the straitened economic circumstances that many countries are facing has left them with no other option. But, generally, foreign investment and transnational corporations have come to be seen in a more favourable—and more technical and less political—light. . . .
>
> In an era of large international capital flows and rapid technological change, developing countries

will increasingly look to transnational corporations for economic stimulation. For their part, transnational corporations will frequently be in a position to provide significant long-term benefits to many developing countries. An important component in the next generation of development policies is that this mutuality of interest continues to grow.

Source: United Nations Center on Transnational Corporations, *Transnational Corporations in World Development* (New York: United Nations, 1988), pp. 10–11.

suffer the loss. And the fact that they bear this risk provides them with greater incentive to make sure the investment pays off. Foreign investment may also facilitate the transfer of modern technology and know-how. But in spite of these advantages, many countries have resisted foreign investment from fear that somehow it compromises their sovereignty or that the foreign companies will take advantage of them. In some cases, for instance when a foreign company is extracting the country's natural resources, there may be legitimate cause for concern; the country may be receiving less for the natural resources than they are really worth. Or the company may convince the country to provide trade protection, which amounts to a hidden subsidy to the firm paid by consumers within the country.

For foreign companies to be willing to invest, they must feel that the political environment is stable and conducive to business. When it is not, they can run up against a host of problems. In the past, LDCs have nationalized foreign-owned companies, paying them inadequate compensation for their investments; they have imposed taxes that effectively confiscate most of the profits; they have imposed foreign exchange restrictions that make it difficult for companies to obtain needed inputs; or they have imposed licensing requirements that make it difficult for foreign firms to operate. The governments of the United States and many European countries provide insurance for their companies investing in LDCs against the risk of nationalization, but there remain many other risks. Providing a politically stable environment has proved a difficult problem for many LDCs.

Importance of Capital   How much of the difference between developed and less developed countries can actually be attributed to lack of capital? If a shortage of capital in LDCs were the major difference between the developed and less developed countries, then the law of diminishing returns would predict that the return to capital in the industrialized countries would be much lower than the return in LDCs. The more capital a country has relative to the size of its population, the lower is the output per machine and the lower is the marginal return to capital. In other words, the shortage of capital should make the return to capital greater. This difference in returns would naturally result in a movement of capital from the more developed to the less developed countries, as business firms searched out profitable investment opportunities.

While the evidence does show some differences in the return to capital, they are too small to demonstrate that a capital shortage is the major problem faced by the LDCs. Moreover, if a capital shortage were the major problem, the LDCs would use what capital they have very intensively. But this does not seem to happen; for example, factories run extra daily shifts more often in developed countries than in LDCs.

Misallocation of Capital An important impediment to growth in many less developed countries is the lack of efficiency in how the scarce funds that are available are used. In Venezuela, which tried to invest its oil dollars as fast as they came in during the 1970s, output increased by 10 cents for every dollar invested in capital equipment. In contrast, in the United States and other developed countries, each extra dollar of investment results on average in an increase of output of between 30 and 50 cents— three to five times higher. In many LDCs, greater investment simply does not lead to much increased output.

There are a number of reasons for this. Some economists, such as Walter Rostow of the University of Texas, have argued that at any moment a country has only a limited absorptive capacity for more capital. It lacks the human capital, the experience, and technological know-how to pursue many projects simultaneously. The absorptive capacity is most limited in the poorest countries. When investments are pushed beyond the absorptive capacity, they yield very low returns.

As we will see below, in many LDCs governments have taken a strong role in allocating capital, partly because capital markets are underdeveloped. But by taking a strong role, the government may have hindered the development of capital markets. In many cases, governments have not proved particularly adept at allocating capital efficiently, and have invested in enterprises that do not reflect the economy's comparative advantage.

More generally, the lack of developed capital markets to facilitate the allocation of capital to its most productive uses and the lack of entrepreneurs who could find new projects well suited for the particular conditions of the LDCs have together contributed to the low returns obtained on capital in many LDCs.

POPULATION GROWTH AND LABOR SUPPLY

A second explanation for the predicament of the LDCs is that while their overall population is growing too rapidly, they have an inadequate supply of trained workers. There is a shortage of human capital. Figure 41.7A shows the growth rate of the population in the less developed regions of the world in comparison with that of high-income countries; panel B shows the levels of education. The populations in LDCs are growing more rapidly, but they have a much lower level of education.

In the developed countries, the Malthusian forecast has not been realized. Food production has increased more rapidly than he anticipated because of technological change, and population has grown less rapidly. Higher living standards and improved medicine have resulted in greater longevity, lower infant mortality, and a lower incidence of sterility. These factors might have contributed to the growth of the population, but at the same time, family planning has become widely accepted; as a result, population sizes have stabilized.

The LDCs have benefited from the improved medicine, but in most of these countries family planning has not yet taken hold to the extent necessary to offset its effects. Families are still large. One reason is lack of information. Another has to do with economic forces: in agricultural societies without social security programs, children provide both a source of labor and a source of support in old age. In developed countries, children have become more of an economic liability than an asset.

Whatever the reason, populations in LDCs are burgeoning. This presents several problems. First, the higher population growth rate leads to an increase in the fraction

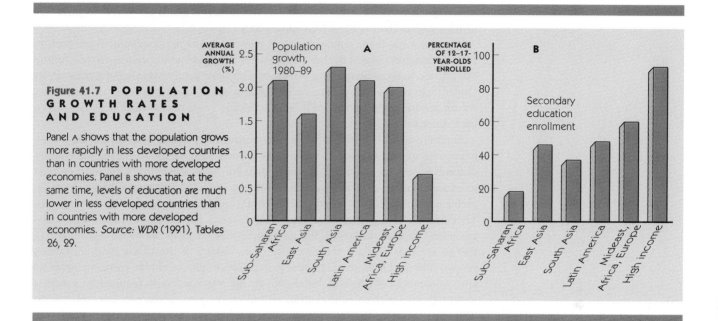

Figure 41.7 POPULATION GROWTH RATES AND EDUCATION

Panel A shows that the population grows more rapidly in less developed countries than in countries with more developed economies. Panel B shows that, at the same time, levels of education are much lower in less developed countries than in countries with more developed economies. *Source: WDR* (1991), Tables 26, 29.

of the population in childhood years who have to be supported by others. In sub-Saharan Africa, almost half the population is under fourteen years old, as seen in Figure 41.8, while in the typical developed country, one in four is under fourteen. When the ratio of dependents to working adults is high, per capita incomes and savings will be lower. Moreover, as these children grow up and enter the labor force, the stock of capital goods available for each worker will suffer. Just to provide the new entrants with the additional

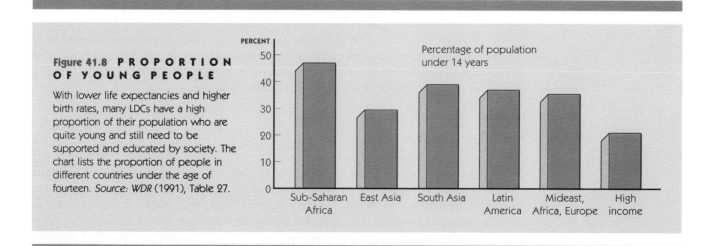

Figure 41.8 PROPORTION OF YOUNG PEOPLE

With lower life expectancies and higher birth rates, many LDCs have a high proportion of their population who are quite young and still need to be supported and educated by society. The chart lists the proportion of people in different countries under the age of fourteen. *Source: WDR* (1991), Table 27.

capital goods required to sustain a given level of capital goods per worker requires high savings, higher than many LDCs can manage.

In many ways, then, rapid population growth impairs the development prospects for LDCs. Therefore, one of the most effective forms of aid that the industrialized countries can provide to these countries is assistance with their family planning programs. In the United States, however, where such programs touch upon politically divisive issues, aid for family planning has itself become highly controversial. President Reagan cut back American support for these programs.

Another way to help the LDCs is to offer education to their citizens, in the form of fellowships to their students to study in the United States or another developed country, or funds to assist in the development of their educational systems. Care must be taken in educational aid as well, however. While the lack of skilled workers is an important problem in some LDCs, others, such as India and Kenya, have the opposite problem. They cannot seem to generate enough jobs that will use the skills of their high school graduates. In some instances, the problem is that the skills for which individuals are trained are not the skills the economy needs. Many of the LDCs have educational systems inherited from their colonial past. Students may be able to recite the list of the kings and queens of England, but do not get the vocational skills required for a modern industrialized society. Cultural attitudes and values may reinforce these problems; students may aspire to be a government bureaucrat rather than an engineer or an entrepreneur (though in many cases the high pay of government jobs combined with the security of employment provide a simple economic rationale for these aspirations).

LACK OF NATURAL RESOURCES AND TECHNOLOGY

Some of the poorest of the LDCs are poor simply by virtue of a lack of natural resources. The countries that border on the Sahara Desert, with little land that is suitable for farming and, so far, no mineral wealth, are the most dramatic examples. Natural resources are, of course, neither necessary nor sufficient for development. Switzerland is a country that has made up for its limited natural resources with capital—human and physical. And some African and Middle Eastern countries remain less developed, in spite of large incomes from natural resources, particularly oil.

Also, less developed countries often do not use well what limited resources they have. This is due partly to lack of technological know-how, really another manifestation of the lack of human capital. For instance, by training farmers to use better techniques, as well as providing them with better seeds, agricultural productivity may be greatly enhanced.

MARKET FAILURES

Another important respect in which LDCs and more developed countries differ is that market failures are much more pervasive within LDCs. And among the most important is the *absence* of markets. As we have seen throughout this book, markets serve an important function in helping ensure that resources are allocated efficiently. When markets are absent or do not work well, as is so often the case in LDCs, then resources are not efficiently allocated. Thus, not only do LDCs face a scarcity of capital and trained labor, what human and physical capital they have may not be put to its best use.

We get a picture of how underdeveloped capital markets are in LDCs by considering the ratio of net financial assets (bank accounts, stocks, etc.) to GNP. This is an indicator of the strength of the financial institutions. In most LDCs, this ratio is about one-third of the ratio in developed countries.

Labor markets also do not work well—they do not allow individuals to move easily from one employer to another or from one city to another. Ethnic divisions and language barriers divide many LDCs into small labor markets, with limited flows between them.

UNEMPLOYMENT

Among the most important aspects of market failure in LDCs is the pervasive unemployment. Unemployment, a major cause of the extremes of poverty, is concentrated in cities. In rural areas, the problem is underemployment; families may have more than enough labor to work their farms. This underemployment is best considered as disguised unemployment. In his classic 1954 study of the development process, Nobel laureate Arthur Lewis emphasized the importance of this ready supply of labor, which he called **surplus labor,** for the development process. The migration of surplus labor to the cities made industrialization possible with very little rise in wages, and this in turn enabled a flow of profits to be generated and capital to be accumulated. In the 1960s, a darker side of this rural to urban migration became apparent: urban centers faced unemployment rates of 15, 20, or 25 percent.

Because of the massive and conspicuous unemployment in many cities in LDCs, it is safe to assume that wages there are higher than they would be in a competitive equilibrium, in which wages are set at market-clearing levels. Because wages do not reflect the true scarcity value of labor, many LDCs have encouraged public enterprises to choose techniques that require more labor than more advanced techniques that are designed to save on the use of labor. Economists sometimes refer to the true social value or cost of a resource as its **shadow price.** For example, when there is unemployment, the shadow wage may be below the market wage. Thus, to encourage the use of more labor-intensive techniques, many LDCs have instructed their public enterprises to use shadow prices and wages rather than market prices and wages when choosing techniques of production.

LACK OF ENTREPRENEURSHIP

A critical problem in many LDCs is the lack of entrepreneurs. Entrepreneurs can be thought of as the individuals who have the ability and the incentive to recognize ways in which markets are not supplying needed products and to undertake new enterprises that will supply these products. Not only is there a lack of entrepreneurs, but what limited entrepreneurial talent that is available is often not well used, at least from a social perspective. For instance, entrepreneurs may spend their time dealing with the obstacles that government bureaucrats impose on private firms.

Economists do not know why there is a lack of entrepreneurs. Economic historians and psychologists have also tried to explain the lack, without any clear answers. In some cases, as in West Africa, there is considerable evidence of some forms of entrepreneurship, such as small-scale marketing, but this is seldom translated into larger-scale enterprises. Lack of capital and imperfectly functioning capital markets that prevent entrepreneurs from obtaining capital are obvious hindrances. The colonial experience, in which

Borrowing from abroad can make sound economic sense. For instance, much of the development of the American railroad network in the nineteenth century was financed by bonds issued in Europe. Over the past two decades, many firms and governments of less developed countries borrowed billions of dollars from banks in the United States and other developed countries, as the table here shows. But while the nineteenth-century U.S. railroad companies were able to repay investments, it became apparent in the 1980s that some of the countries that had borrowed heavily—particularly Brazil, Argentina, and Mexico—could not repay what they owed. The resulting crisis threatened the economic prospects of the LDCs and the financial viability of many American banks. How the problem arose and what should be done about it remain hotly debated questions.

The immediate cause of the problem was apparent. In the 1970s, real interest rates were low, and banks were flush with "petro dollars"—dollars that oil producers, particularly in the Middle East, had earned from selling their oil at the high prices that prevailed beginning in 1973—and wanted to invest or deposit abroad. Both borrowers and lenders were optimistic that the loans would create economic growth, and repayment would be an easy matter.

Then three things happened. First, nominal and real interest rates soared in the late 1970s, and since most of the loans had adjustable rates, the interest payments rose far beyond any level that the borrowers had imagined. Second, the world entered a recession in the early 1980s, and the worldwide slowdown in growth made it more difficult for the LDCs to pay back what they owed. Third, oil prices fell in the early 1980s. Some of the largest borrowers had been oil producers, like Mex-

ico and Indonesia, and they had intended to repay their loans by selling oil.

But bad luck is not the only culprit; the banks are also to blame for failing to take into account the risks associated with the loans they were making. They should have realized, for instance, that prices for goods like oil are volatile. They did not take into account the fact that when foreign borrowers refuse to pay, U.S. lenders cannot sue to recover some of their losses, as they can when the borrower is American. And they failed to learn the lesson of diversification: they put too many of their eggs in the same basket.

The banks also seem to have placed too much trust in the assurance of foreign governments that the loans would be invested productively. At least some of the funds were siphoned off from the investment projects for which they were intended and, it is claimed, used by wealthy Argentineans, Mexicans, and Brazilians to purchase real estate in the United States. Moreover, much of the money was invested in projects that were probably not economically viable from the start. By contrast, some better-managed countries like the Republic of Korea borrowed heavily but invested the money wisely and have been able to repay it.

Finally, some economists believe that deposit insurance is partly responsible: since depositors knew they would get their money back no matter how risky the loans made by their banks, they had no reason to monitor their banks and raise warning flags about the more risky loans to LDCs.

So far, massive defaults on loans have been avoided by debt rescheduling, which means that as a payment comes due, the banks lend the country more money, in effect postponing the date at which repayment is to occur. As a condition for this rescheduling, the lenders have insisted that the borrowers "put their houses in order," cutting back, for instance, on their huge budget deficits. But this strategy of squeezing the LDCs to pay does not seem likely to work; they simply do not have the money, and pressuring them can destabilize their economies and governments. An alternative strategy would be to help the countries grow, so they could afford to repay at least some of their debt. But growth may require additional capital, which foreign lenders are reluctant to provide. The only way out may be to forgive some of the debt and then count on the rest being repaid.

Debt forgiveness, which amounts to a gift to the debtor countries, has its own problems. If banks are forced to forgive the debts, they will suffer financially. Moreover, many worry about the incentives and fairness of forgiving debt. Will forgiveness encourage countries to borrow more in the future than they have the capacity to repay? Is Brazil more deserving of such a multibillion-dollar gift than many poorer countries in Latin America or Africa, just because it borrowed more?

Country	Public or publicly guaranteed external debt in 1989
Brazil	$84 billion
Mexico	$76 billion
India	$54 billion
Argentina	$51 billion
Indonesia	$41 billion
Egypt	$40 billion
China	$37 billion
Poland	$35 billion
Turkey	$35 billion
Nigeria	$32 billion
Venezuela	$25 billion
Algeria	$24 billion
Philippines	$23 billion
Morocco	$19 billion
Korea	$17 billion

Source: World Development Report (1991), Table 21.

foreigners dominated the nonagricultural sector, may be another. Even today in many LDCs, foreign firms predominate in the industrial sector. These firms may fail to train the indigenous population in entrepreneurship, and the indigenous population may think of entrepreneurship as foreign to their culture. Governments provide a variety of additional obstacles, including bureaucratic delays in obtaining permits, licenses, and foreign exchange; sometimes entrepreneurs are required to pay bribes to obtain them.

EXTERNALITIES

Another problem with markets in LDCs is externalities. Chapters 7 and 23 showed that when there are important externalities, markets will not work well. One of the problems facing many firms in the early stages of development is finding workers who work effectively within large organizations. In developed countries, employers are lucky in being able to draw upon a well-educated labor pool (educated largely in public schools) for skilled labor. In LDCs, more of the burden of training falls upon firms. Firms, in hiring and training workers with little previous experience, contribute to the pool of individuals with manufacturing skills. Once trained, a worker may move on to another company, which will benefit from the skills the worker acquired in the first firm. There is thus an externality. Firms collectively will not hire and train as many workers as society would like them to because they cannot capture this externality.

INEQUALITY

Visitors to many LDCs are struck by the extremes in inequality, such as homeless people sleeping in the streets along which the wealthy travel in Mercedes cars. Politicians in LDCs find it popular to attack the wealthy, suggesting that if only their wealth could be directed away from conspicuous consumption and toward productive uses, the country's development problems would be solved. Unfortunately, as much money as the wealthy may have, even if all their wealth were confiscated and invested, it would only make a small dent in the problems these countries face.

Programs of redistribution, if well designed, can still play a positive role in the development effort. Earlier we saw how sharecropping attenuated workers' incentives. Land reforms such as that of Taiwan can have a large effect on agricultural productivity. The use of excessively high income tax rates to redistribute wealth, however, can have a deleterious effect. They reduce the incentives for entrepreneurship, and within the urban sector they may reduce the funds available for reinvestment by successful enterprises. Many LDCs have imposed tax rates on upper-income groups in excess of 80 or even 90 percent. These rates, however, turn out to be more statements of ideology; the taxes are seldom effectively enforced.

The magnitude of the inequality colors all aspects of development policy. A policy is evaluated not only in terms of its effect on national output, but in terms of its impact on unemployment and, more generally, on what the policy will do to inequality. The grinding poverty in which so much of the population lives often makes it impossible to pursue policies that would maximize the rate of growth. Governments often feel themselves forced to spend much of their scarce revenues on food subsidies rather than on investments; and when governments have attempted to cut back on these food subsidies, as happened in the Dominican Republic or Morocco, there are riots.

Perhaps the way in which great inequality most impairs development is through its effects on the political process: inequality frequently gives rise to political instability, and political instability has strong adverse effects on the economic climate. In such an atmosphere, both domestic and foreign firms will feel reluctant to invest.

IMPEDIMENTS TO DEVELOPMENT

Capital
  Insufficient supply
  Absence of capital markets, leading to inefficient allocation
Population/Labor
  High population growth rates
  Insufficient number of trained individuals
Lack of natural resources and technology

Market failures

    Imperfect labor and capital markets

    Unemployment

    Lack of entrepreneurs

    Externalities, such as are associated with the development of a pool of educated
        workers

Inequality

    Direct effects, such as attenuation of incentives in sharecropping

    Indirect effects, like the possibility of political instability, which creates an unfa-
        vorable investment climate

SHOULD GOVERNMENT MAKE THE BASIC ECONOMIC DECISIONS?

How can less developed countries find their way to sustained economic growth? Economists break this question down into two issues. Who should make and carry out the decisions about resource allocation, government or markets? And, assuming the government does intervene in resource allocation, in which direction should it push (or pull) the economy? We now look at each of these issues in turn.

A QUESTIONABLE ROLE: PLANNING

A popular view among development economists in the 1960s was that governments in the LDCs should take a central role in planning the growth of the economy, to avoid market failures. A "Ministry of Planning" would draw up a detailed plan, perhaps for five years, specifying how much each sector of the economy would grow, how much investment would occur in each sector, where the output of each sector would go, and where each sector would receive its inputs. The Ministry of Planning would have enormous powers, among them allocating investment funds and the foreign exchange required to import raw materials from abroad.

The spread of the planning model was greatly influenced by the seeming success of the Soviet Union in the early stages of its industrialization program. In most LDCs that used the planning approach, such as India, the government did not have the all-pervasive role that it did in the Soviet Union, where not only did the government plan the investment, but government enterprises actually undertook the investment. In India and other LDCs, the government did undertake some of the investments itself, but it also gave powerful inducements to private firms to conform to the dictates of the government's plan—for example, by restricting access to needed foreign exchange only to approved investment projects or by making credit more readily available for approved investment projects.

In the last decade, there has been considerable disillusionment with planning. This disillusionment set in even before the failures of the Soviet-style system became widely evident. Planned economies like India have not done better than unplanned economies like Hong Kong and Taiwan—in fact, in most cases they have done worse. There are good reasons for this. The 1960s views on the need for planning ignored the extensive planning that goes on in all economies. For example, when U.S. Steel decided to build a steel mill on the southern shores of Lake Michigan in the early twentieth century, it made sure that there were sources of inputs and the transportation facilities to deliver these inputs—limestone from southern Indiana, coal and coke from Illinois, and iron ore from Minnesota. It also made sure that there was a source of demand. The issue is not whether planning is needed—it surely is—but whether the most effective place to do the planning is in a government centralized bureau or at the level of the firm. Today most economists are skeptical about the ability of a centralized bureau to do effective planning

One of the main arguments for centralized planning was its presumed greater ability to coordinate. But the experience of the past quarter century has shown that centralized planning offices generally do not do a good job at coordination. One reason is that they often do not have the requisite information. Another is that the details of investment projects—deciding what kind of plant to construct, how to construct it, making sure that it is constructed in an efficient way, and so on—are details firms can more easily deal with than government bureaucrats, and these details, more than anything else, determine the success of the projects.

WHEN GOVERNMENT BECOMES THE PROBLEM

Sometimes government has actually impeded the development process. It has done this both by allocating inefficiently those resources over which it has direct control and by interfering in the function of markets so that *they* could not efficiently allocate resources. Countries following the Soviet model attempted to imitate not only its reliance on planning, but also its pattern of development, with heavy emphasis on industries such as steel, whether such a pattern of industrialization was appropriate for those countries or not.

When Mao Tse-tung decided that China should grow more wheat, perhaps because he saw that wheat was the predominant grain consumed in the more developed countries, he directed that vast areas be converted from rice to wheat. This land was not suited for wheat growing, and agricultural productivity suffered. Moreover, the conversion to wheat fields depleted the land of its fertility, so that when it was eventually returned to growing rice, productivity was lower.

Of course, private firms make mistakes as well. There are flops, like the Edsel or the nicotine-free cigarette, mistakes that cost the companies making them hundreds of millions of dollars. But the firm (its owners) bears the costs of these mistakes, and when this is the case, these kinds of mistakes seem to get made less often. The firm has a strong incentive to avoid making them. A company that makes a mistake cannot finance itself for a long time. When the Ford Motor Company discovered that the Edsel was a mistake, it quickly discontinued production, cutting its losses; it knew, and acted upon, the basic lesson that such costs should be treated as bygones.

The government, by contrast, can support an unprofitable firm for many years. Also, the scale of the mistakes that governments sometimes make sets them apart from the mistakes of private firms. If a single farmer mistakenly decides to grow wheat rather than rice, the costs he faces are not comparable to the costs borne by China when Mao made his mistaken judgment.

Mao's mistake was an honest one; it was a mistake of judgment, not a consequence of his pursuit of private interests. But some of the problems facing the LDCs arise from governmental corruption, and here private interests conflict with public ones. Corruption is often associated with the large role that government plays in an LDC, particularly in restricting foreign trade. When the government imposes a high tariff or otherwise protects an industry, the protected firms can raise their prices and thereby increase their profits. If there are only one or two such firms, they will be tempted to share some of the resulting profits with the government official responsible for the protection. And the government official, knowing this, has a strong incentive to ask the private firms to share some of the profits.

In those countries where the government controls foreign exchange, manufacturers needing inputs from abroad can also find themselves at the whim of a foreign exchange official. The refusal to provide the foreign exchange required to purchase inputs can be disastrous for a manufacturer, and delays in granting the import permits can be costly. There is a clear incentive for corrupt behavior. By the same token, whenever there are government regulations that must be satisfied, government officials almost always have some discretion in implementing the regulations. They may not be able to prohibit the planned activity, such as a new plant or product, but they may be able to delay the approvals, and the delays can be costly. Again, the economic incentives to bribe a quick approval from the appropriate government officials are frequently overwhelming.

These problems arise in all countries: the building inspectors in New York have periodically been charged with accepting bribes to speed approvals, for instance. However, these problems are more likely to arise in countries such as LDCs, where government salaries are low relative to the size of the bribes being offered, where institutions like a free press that might closely monitor this kind of corruption do not exist, and where government regulations are more pervasive.

Between honest mistakes and corruption lies a third category: rent-seeking activities, first discussed in Chapter 17. If the government has the power to confer special benefits, people will seek those benefits for themselves. Firms will try to persuade government that they deserve protection from foreign competition, knowing that such protection will increase their profits. They may give outright bribes, or they may simply spend funds to help elect officials who are sympathetic to their views.

Critics of an activist role for government in development, such as Anne Krueger of Duke University, formerly vice-president of the World Bank, thus argue that while we might *imagine* a government's improving on the market, if we look more closely at how governments actually behave, and take into account the natural incentives for counterproductive behavior on the part of government bureaucrats as opposed to the incentives for efficiency on the part of private firms, we see that government activity can and often does impede development.

CLOSE-UP: ZAMBIA AND MALAWI

Zambia and Malawi are two African countries that sit side by side. Each won independence from Britain in 1963, and each has a population of about 7 million. Both countries are dreadfully poor. In 1989, GDP per capita in Zambia was only $390 per person; in Malawi, it was a mere $180. But although the two countries are similar in the extent of their poverty, the economy in Malawi has grown up to its present poverty level, while the economy in Zambia has shrunk down. In 1965, for example, per capita income in Malawi was only $117, but per capital income in Zambia was about $430.

How did this happen? Clearly, changes in per capita income involve two factors: economic growth and population growth. Population growth in Zambia was about .2 percent faster each year than in Malawi over those two decades, so the Zambian economy would have had to grow .2 percent faster a year just to keep its edge in per capita income. However, economic growth in Zambia was

actually much slower. The economy in Malawi grew at an annual rate of 5.5 percent a year from 1965 to 1980, but then slowed to a growth rate of 2.7 percent a year in the 1980s. The economy in Zambia, by comparison, grew at only 2.0 percent a year from 1965 to 1980, and only .8 percent a year in the 1980s.

These differences in economic growth are not accidental. Zambia's economic errors consisted of printing extra money to finance its budget deficits, thus fueling inflation; keeping farm prices low to benefit consumers, thus damaging its agricultural sector; going deeply into debt without investing the money in economically profitable ventures; and persistent incompetence and corruption, particularly in the important copper mining industry. Copper reserves are likely to be exhausted within a few years, and much of the population today is heavily infected with AIDS.

Malawi, on the other hand, has focused on build-

ing rural roads and railways and on subsidizing fertilizer so farmers could expand their production. The government has imposed some price and production controls, but has adjusted those controls to compensate for market realities. Although a war in neighboring Mozambique has been flooding Malawi with refugees, the short-term outlook for Malawi is not as bleak as that for Zambia.

Both countries remain desperately poor. The poor in Malawi complain that their relatively laissez-faire government has not done more to subsidize lower prices for food and medical care. The poor in Zambia have gotten steadily poorer over the last two decades, and they did not have much to start with. Clearly, the governments of such countries face heart-wrenching choices; just as clearly, those choices make a major difference to their people.

Sources: World Development Report (1991), various charts; *The Economist,* February 18–24, 1989, pp. 88–89.

A CLEAR ROLE: PROVIDING INFRASTRUCTURE

The debate about the role of government in developing countries is a long-standing one, but most economists agree that there are certain things government must do if there is to be a successful development program. Government must provide the necessary economic **infrastructure**—the roads, bridges, and ports—without which no economy can function well. In recent years, economists have extended the concept of infrastructure to include the legal system, specifically the set of property rights that can be enforced. If Harry has a painting to sell, Maria will be willing to buy it only if she can be sure that Harry actually owns the painting and that after she buys it she will really own it. If Amy lends Adam money, it is useful to have a legal system that will require Adam to repay the money; otherwise Amy will be less willing to lend.

If property rights are not well defined by the legal system, economic efficiency may suffer. If title to land is not clear, so that disputes can easily arise about who really owns a particular piece of real estate, the capital market will be impaired. Individuals will find it difficult to borrow using land as collateral; and "owners" of land will have an insufficient incentive to maintain it (making sure, for instance, that its fertility is not damaged), since they may not be able to bear the fruits of these efforts.

Although economists agree that government should establish and maintain the economic and legal infrastructure, they disagree about what form government intervention should take and how extensive it should be. Those who see the government as a major hindrance in development think that the best policy is to stop meddling: without government interference, markets could forward the development effort enormously. But others, noting widespread market failures, including important externalities, call for government direction, albeit in a more limited form than what the planning boards would provide. In Japan, for instance, the Ministry for International Trade and Industry (MITI) has played an active role in coordinating public and private sector activities in many industries. In South Korea and other successful Asian countries, governments have tried to tilt the economy in certain directions, as we will now see.

WHO SHOULD MAKE THE DECISIONS?

Questionable role for government: Planning
   Planning goes on in the private sector anyway
   Governments lack requisite information to do a good job at planning
Government misdirects resources
   From misguided theories
   Because of corruption
   Because of rent-seeking behavior
Clear role for government
   Providing economic infrastructure
   Providing legal infrastructure (property rights)

TILTING THE ECONOMY

If there is to be government intervention, the question is, what should the governments in LDCs try to encourage? There are several directions in which the government can attempt to tilt the economy. It can try to either encourage exports or encourage domestically produced goods in place of imports. Or it can try to promote either agriculture or industry. Both of these policy issues have been the subject of much discussion in recent years.

EXPORT-LED GROWTH

Most economists who see a role for government in LDCs in tilting the direction of the market believe the government should encourage the production and export of goods in which the country has a comparative advantage. This strategy is referred to as **export-led growth,** and is closely tied to the belief that there is a well-developed international market for goods. With exports, the demand for the goods produced by LDCs is not limited by the low incomes of their citizens.

   Advocates of export-led growth also believe that the high level of competition provided by the export market is an important stimulus to efficiency and modernization. The only way a firm can succeed in the face of keen international competition is to produce what consumers want, at the quality they want, and at the lowest possible costs. This keen competition forces specialization in areas where low-wage, less developed countries have a comparative advantage, such as labor-intensive products. It also forces firms to look for the best ways of producing. International firms often take a role in helping to enhance efficiency. For instance, the clothing store chain Benetton has developed production techniques that combine large production runs with rapid adaptability in style and color. In this way, the firm has been able to take advantage of low-wage LDCs by producing most of what it sells in these countries.

Another advantage of export-led growth is that there is a natural test of its success: can the country compete effectively with foreign producers?

While some economists believe that no government intervention is required for export-led growth—that firms on their own will find it profitable to export the goods in which the country has a comparative advantage—some of the most notable success stories entail active government encouragement. For example, as part of the successful development programs in both Japan and Korea, the government provided export subsidies and the credit necessary for the expansion of the export sectors. Japan's development efforts were spurred and coordinated by its powerful Ministry for International Trade and Industry. Within the space of less than two decades, it reversed its image from a producer of cheap, low-quality products to a manufacturer of quality high-tech products, including cameras, automobiles, and electronic equipment. Korea's success is no less notable, though since it started at a much lower level, it still has a long way to go to catch up to the more developed countries.

Critics of export-led growth cite three main problems with this approach. First, they worry that if countries simply play to their current comparative advantage, they will specialize in cheap, labor-intensive goods and in agricultural products like coffee, cocoa, and bananas, for which they have a comparative advantage based on climate. Their incomes may rise slightly, but they will not become developed.

Second, critics do not believe that it is as easy (or profitable) to export as those in favor of the export-led growth approach believe. The world market runs not just on price, but on trade patterns that have been established over long periods of time. The success of many products is based on reputations, which are not easy to establish. Developing export markets may be difficult even for products for which one might think there was a well-developed international market, like rice. Different countries come to rely on different sources of rice; there are variations in the quality of rice about which some consumers feel quite strongly. And a rice-growing country like Thailand, which is dependent on exports, puts itself at the mercy of others' foreign trade policies. Thus, when the U.S. government increased its protection of American rice farmers in 1986, Thailand saw an important part of its market disappear, and the price Thai farmers received fell by a third.

Third, critics are concerned that export-led growth has helped to perpetuate the dual structure of many LDCs, in which some parts of the economy are quite advanced but others remain at much lower stages of development. Export-led growth may create only isolated pockets of development, loosely connected with the rest of the economy. This may not pose a problem for small islands, like Hong Kong, Taiwan, and Singapore, but it does for the larger developing economies.

Supporters of export-led growth agree that there have been instances in which these concerns are valid. But they also point out that the most important such instances either are special cases—such as used to be the case in Malaysia, with its rubber plantation enclaves—or involve export industries that have developed as a result of government protection, with little relation to the rest of the country. When the exports are based on the country's comparative advantages, when they are labor intensive and have strong links with the rest of the economy, then the growth in the export industries will inevitably spill over to other sectors.

IMPORT SUBSTITUTION

A contrasting strategy, known as **import substitution,** stresses the development of a domestic market, by substituting domestically produced goods for goods that were previously imported. In this view, the hallmark of a developed country is modern industry. Rather than importing steel, automobiles, TV sets, computers, and other such products, a nation should produce them itself in order to develop the skills necessary for modernization. It should produce, in other words, all the goods that it had previously imported from the industrialized economies. This is the road to development that most of the larger LDCs, including India, China, and Brazil, undertook in the years after World War II. At times, each of these countries has taken import substitution to extremes, insisting, for example, on domestically produced computers even when they might not be able to perform the functions of imported computers.

India, like many other LDCs, has also placed a heavy emphasis on domestically owned businesses. At least 50 percent of each company must be owned by Indians. When Coca-Cola refused to disclose the secret of its closely guarded formula to its Indian-controlled subsidiary, the government shut down Coca-Cola. At times, it seemed as if "Indian-made cola for Indians" would become a rallying point for Indian nationalism, just as "Buy American" campaigns have been a rallying point for protectionism in America.

But the import substitution approach has disadvantages of its own. Trade barriers set up to protect domestic firms can end up protecting inefficient producers. The absence of foreign competition means that there is an insufficient spur to innovation and efficiency. The profits to which trade barriers frequently give rise provide a source of government corruption. And the trade barriers remain years after they are introduced.

In some cases, the value added of the protected industry is actually negative. Consider an Indian car producer. Many of the car parts have to be imported. The value added of the car manufacturer is not the total value of the car, but only the difference between the value of the car and the value of the imported components. Assume that because of sloppy manufacturing, a significant fraction of the imported parts are damaged. It might be cheaper for the country to import the entire car than import the components and assemble the car. Of course, with protection, the Indian car manufacturer may still be making profits. Consumers suffer, because they have to pay higher prices.

The problems are even worse when the protected industry is one like steel, whose product is used in other industries. An Indian car manufacturer might be profitable if it could only purchase steel at international prices. But if it is forced to pay inflated prices to buy Indian steel, it cannot compete with foreign producers. The government might try to offset this by subsidizing the car manufacturers. A subsidy or trade protection in one sector thus grows into a complex of subsidies and trade protection in other sectors.

While in general trade protection to stimulate import substitution seems to lead to massive inefficiencies, it has proved successful for a time in some countries such as Brazil, which enjoyed several decades of rapid growth before the debt crisis of the 1980s tainted that picture somewhat. Also, supporters of import substitution note that many of the most rapid bursts of growth of the current developed countries occurred in wartimes, when the economy was inwardly directed, not export oriented. These same supporters, looking at the experience of Japan, argue that at least for industrial goods, import substitution—the development of a domestic market—must precede exports. Before Japan was able successfully to sell cars abroad, it first had to develop a market for Japanese cars at home.

CHOOSING BETWEEN EXPORT-LED AND IMPORT SUBSTITUTION POLICIES

There is one respect in which those who advocate government intervention to stimulate export-led growth and those who advocate government intervention to stimulate import substitution agree: *current* comparative advantage is not the appropriate basis for the design of a development strategy. In the modern economy, a dynamic comparative advantage is what is important, one based not so much on current resource endowments as on acquired skills. Chapter 18 stressed the importance of learning by doing, of the improvement in skills and productivity that comes from the experience of production. Twenty years ago, Japan could not compete with the United States in the production of computer chips. Then the Japanese government subsidized the chip industry, and as the nation's firms gained experience, they became effective competitors, to the point where government subsidies were no longer needed. This is the infant industry argument for government assistance.

Today the question of export-led growth versus import substitution is viewed as one of balance. A competitive export sector is essential for a successful development program. A highly protected domestic import substitution sector can be an important barrier to development, but limited forms of government encouragement—for both exports and import substitution—may play an important positive role. And the more developed countries can provide effective assistance to LDCs by encouraging their firms to trade with these countries. At the very least, they should not construct trade barriers that keep products of LDCs out.

EXPORT-LED GROWTH VERSUS IMPORT SUBSTITUTION

General principles:
   Resources should be allocated on the basis of dynamic comparative advantage
      rather than current comparative advantage.
Export-led growth
   Strengths:
      The demand for goods is not limited by the income of the country.
      High levels of competition stimulate efficiency and modernization.
      The ability to compete with foreign producers provides a strong market test.

Problems:

May lead countries to specialize in cheap, labor-intensive goods and agriculture with little long-run growth potential.

It may not be easy to develop export markets.

May lead to an economy with a developed export sector and the rest of the economy remaining less developed.

Import substitution

Strength:

Helps country develop broad range of skills necessary for modernization.

Problems:

Trade barriers can discourage innovation and efficiency and encourage corruption.

It is often difficult to remove trade barriers once imposed.

When a protected industry makes goods used as inputs for firms in other sectors, this raises costs and lowers the competitiveness of these other sectors.

AGRICULTURE VERSUS INDUSTRY

A debate much like the one between export-led growth and import substitution concerns the role of agriculture versus industry in the development process. Many LDCs decided that growth must be based on the development of the industrialized sector. They therefore taxed the agriculture sector to provide the revenues required to support industrialization and to provide food subsidies to people living in the urban sector. This strategy has been criticized on the grounds of both efficiency and equity.

The comparative advantage of many LDCs lies in agriculture. While development may entail the growth of the urban sector, that growth in turn is based on a prosperous and productive rural sector. In the last decade, there has been a shift in development strategies to limit the taxes imposed on agriculture. The World Bank has focused much of its efforts on agriculture, aiding, for instance, the development of irrigation systems. China has returned control of much of the agricultural land to families, and has realized that the taxes it had been imposing on agriculture were so severe that production was badly discouraged. Placing the burden for raising resources for development on the rural sector through higher taxes is often viewed as inequitable, since those in the rural sector are poorer on average than those in the urban sector.

The agriculture-industry conflict has long played a role in America's history. The U.S. Constitution prohibited export taxes partly because the southern states were worried that the more populous and commercial North would impose taxes on their exports, which were agricultural. With prices for the goods exported by the South fixed in the international market, export taxes would have had the effect of reducing the prices received by farmers. The burden of export taxes would thus have lain on the backs of the agricultural South. Later the northern states discovered that exactly the same effect could be achieved by imposing tariffs on imported industrial goods. The prices of these goods, produced in the North, increased relative to the prices of agricultural goods, produced in the South. Those in the agricultural South bore the burden of the taxes, not through the prices they received for the cotton they sold, but through the prices they paid for the goods they bought. This conflict formed part of the background of the dissension between the two parts of the country that led to the Civil War.

THE PROSPECTS

The Bible says, "The poor ye always have with you" (Matthew 26:11). For centuries, people seemed engaged in a race between population and the economy's ability to support that population. The industrial and scientific revolutions of the past two centuries, and the enhanced means of production that resulted, have meant ever-rising living standards for most of those lucky enough to live in the developed countries of Europe and North America. And the past fifty years have extended the benefits to an increasing number of countries—to Japan in full measure, and to a lesser extent to a number of middle-income countries such as Singapore, South Korea, and Taiwan.

Elsewhere, there are pockets of success—the area around São Paulo in Brazil has the look and feel of prosperity. India, as noted above, has become self-sufficient with regard to food. Thailand has been having a boom. But their success is precarious; the debt crisis of the 1980s represented a major setback for many of these countries, including Mexico. Still, the outstanding lesson of recent decades is that success is possible: there is the real prospect that more and more of these countries, if they pursue wise policies and enjoy political stability, will be able to pull themselves out of the cycle of poverty in which they have lived for centuries.

But for the most unfortunate countries, such as sub-Saharan Africa, which lack human and physical resources and have burgeoning populations that consume much of whatever gains they are able to obtain, the prospects are less optimistic. And the lack of hope contributes to political instability, making economic progress all the more difficult.

AN AGENDA FOR DEVELOPMENT

How the developed countries can help
   Reduce trade barriers
   Increase foreign aid
   Facilitate foreign investment
Growth-oriented policies for LDCs
   Reduce rates of growth of the population
   Increase quantity and quality of education

> Provide a basic infrastructure (roads, ports, a legal system)
>
> Provide a favorable climate for investment, including foreign investment
>
> Facilitate the development of capital markets (financial intermediaries)
>
> Spend more of government revenues on investment rather than consumption, such as food subsidies
>
> Develop a competitive export sector

Policies that may inhibit growth

> Trade protection
>
> Regulations, licensing

REVIEW AND PRACTICE

SUMMARY

1. In less developed countries, or LDCs, life expectancies are usually shorter, infant mortality is higher, and people are less educated than in developed countries. Also, a larger fraction of the population lives in the rural sector, and population growth rates are higher.

2. In recent years, newly industrialized countries such as South Korea, Singapore, Hong Kong, and Taiwan have managed to improve their economic status dramatically. Other LDCs, like India, have expanded food production considerably. But the standard of living in some of the poorest LDCs, such as many African nations, has actually been declining, as population growth has outstripped economic growth.

3. Among the factors contributing to underdevelopment are a rapidly growing population, a lack of educated workers, market failures such as the absence of markets to efficiently allocate capital, a lack of entrepreneurs, and extremes of inequality.

4. Central planning has not been effective in LDCs. Governments lack the requisite information and often misdirect resources. On the other hand, governments have played an important role in providing an economic and legal infrastructure.

5. Some economists believe LDCs should tilt the economy by pursuing export-led economic growth. Others advocate a strategy of import substitution, where the goal is to develop skills and self-sufficiency by replacing imports. Both groups agree that resources should be allocated on the basis of dynamic comparative advantage.

6. Most LDCs have a comparative advantage in agriculture, but governments have often attempted to tilt the economy more toward industry. More recent development strategies have focused on improving productivity in the rural sector.

KEY TERMS

less developed countries
  (LDCs)
developed or
  industrialized
  countries

newly industrialized
  countries (NICs)
green revolution
dual economy
surplus labor

shadow price
infrastructure
export-led growth
import substitution

REVIEW QUESTIONS

1. List some of the important ways in which LDCs differ from more developed countries.

2. Why may a land reform increase agricultural output? What factors would hinder the success of a land reform?

3. What does it mean to say that less developed countries have a dual economy?

4. What are the most important factors inhibiting growth in the LDCs?

5. What can be done to help overcome the problem of capital shortage?

6. Why is capital often inefficiently allocated in LDCs?

7. How does rapid population growth make it more difficult to increase a country's standard of living?

8. What are the important instances of market failures in LDCs? In what ways are market failures more pervasive in LDCs than in developed countries? What are the consequences of market failures in LDCs?

9. Why has government planning failed?

10. Why have governments in LDCs put more emphasis on agriculture in recent years?

PROBLEMS

1. In the United States, the economy grew by 3.3 percent per year (in real terms) during the 1980s. In India, the economy grew by 5.3 percent during the 1980s. However, population growth in the United States was .8 percent annually, while population growth in India was 2.1 percent annually. Which country increased its standard of living faster for the average citizen? By how much?

2. Nominal GNP in Kenya was 9 billion shillings in 1967 and 135 billion shillings in 1987. The price level in Kenya (using 1980 as a base year) rose from 40 in 1967 to 200 in 1987. And the population of Kenya increased from 10 million to 22 million in those twenty years. What was the total percentage change in real GNP per capita in Kenya from 1967 to 1987?

3. True or false: "LDCs do not have much capital because their rates of saving are low. If they saved more or received more foreign aid, they could rapidly expand their economic growth." Discuss.

4. How might each of the following hinder entrepreneurs in LDCs?
   (a) a lack of functioning capital markets;
   (b) pervasive government control of the economy;
   (c) a lack of companies that offer business services;
   (d) a tradition of substantial foreign control of large enterprises.

5. What is the economist's case for having the government be responsible for providing infrastructure? (Hint: You may wish to review the concept of a public good from Chapter 7.)

6. If many LDCs simultaneously attempted to pursue export-led growth, what would be the effect in world markets on the quantities and prices of products mainly sold by LDCs, like minerals, agricultural goods, and textiles? What effect might these quantities and prices have on the success of such export-led growth policies?

7. Explain how the idea of import substitution conflicts in the short run with the idea of comparative advantage. Need the two ideas conflict in the long run? Why or why not?

8. Why does sharecropping reduce a farmer's incentive to work hard? Why is sharecropping nonetheless so prevalent in LDCs?

9. Why might a family in an LDC have an economic pressure toward having more children than a family in a developed country?

GLOSSARY

absolute advantage: a country has an absolute advantage over another country in the production of a good if it can produce that good more efficiently (with fewer inputs)

accelerator: the effect on GDP of the increase in investment that results from an increase in output. For instance, the greater output leads a firm to believe the demand for its products will rise in the future; the resulting increase in investment leads to growth in output and still further increases in investment, accelerating the expansion of the economy

acquired endowments: resources a country builds for itself, like a network of roads or an educated population

adaptive expectations: expectations based on the extrapolation of events in the recent past into the future

aggregate demand curve: a curve relating the total demand for the economy's goods and services at each price level, given the level of wages

aggregate supply curve: a curve relating the total supply of the economy's goods and services at each price level, given the level of wages

aggregate expenditures schedule: a curve that traces out the relationship between expenditures—the sum of consumption, investment, government expenditures, and net exports—and national income, at a fixed price level

antitrust laws: laws that discourage monopoly and restrictive practices and encourage greater competition

appreciation: a change in the exchange rate that enables a unit of currency to buy more units of foreign currencies

arbitrage: the process by which assets with comparable risk, liquidity, and tax treatment are priced to yield comparable expected returns

asset: any item that is long-lived, purchased for the service it renders over its life and for what one will receive when one sells it

assistance in kind: public assistance that provides particular goods and services, like food or medical care, rather than cash

asymmetric information: a situation in which the parties to a transaction have different information, as when the seller of a used car has more information about its quality than the buyer

autonomous consumption: that part of consumption that does not depend on income

average costs: the total costs divided by the total output

average productivity: the total quantity of output divided by the total quantity of input

average variable costs: the total variable costs divided by the total output

barriers to entry: factors that prevent firms from entering a market, such as government rules or patents

basic competitive model: the model of the economy that pulls together the assumptions of self-interested consumers, profit-maximizing firms, and perfectly competitive markets

bequest savings motive: people save so that they can leave an inheritance to their children

Bertrand competition: an oligopoly in which each firm believes that its rivals are committed to keeping their prices fixed and that customers can be lured away by offering lower prices

bilateral trade: trade between two parties

boom: a period of time when resources are being fully used and GDP is growing steadily

capital gain: the increase in the value of an asset between the time it is purchased and the time it is sold

capital goods: the machines and buildings firms invest in, with funds obtained in the capital market

capital market: the market in which savings are made available to those who need additional funds, such as firms that wish to invest, and in which ownership claims on different assets and their associated risks are exchanged

cartel: a group of producers with an agreement to collude in setting prices and output

categorical assistance: public assistance aimed at a particular category of people, like the elderly or the disabled

causation: the relationship that results when a change in one variable is not only correlated with but actually causes a change in another variable; the change in the second variable is a consequence of the change in the first variable, rather than both changes being a consequence of a change in a third variable

central bank: the bank that oversees and monitors the rest of the banking system and serves as the bankers' bank

central planning: the system in which central government bureaucrats (as opposed to private entrepreneurs or even local government bureaucrats) determine what will be produced and how it will be produced

centralization: organizational structure in which decision making is concentrated at the top

centrally planned economy: an economy in which most decisions about resource allocation are made by the central government

certificate of deposit (CD): an account in which money is deposited for a preset length of time, that yields a slightly higher return to compensate for the reduced liquidity

circular flow: the way in which funds move through the capital, labor, and product markets between households, firms, the government, and the foreign sector

classical economists: economists prevalent before the Great Depression who believed that the basic competitive model provided a good description of the economy and that if short periods of unemployment did occur, market forces would quickly restore the economy to full employment

classical unemployment: unemployment that occurs as a result of too-high real wages; it occurs in the supply-constrained equilibrium, so that rightward shifts in aggregate supply reduce the level of unemployment

closed economy: an economy that neither exports nor imports

Coase's theorem: the assertion that if property rights are properly defined, then people will be forced to pay for any negative externalities they impose on others, and market transactions will produce efficient outcomes

comparative advantage: a country has a comparative advantage over another country in one good as opposed to another good if its *relative* efficiency in the production of the first good is higher than the other country's

compensating wage differentials: differences in wages that can be traced to nonpecuniary attributes of a job, such as the degree of autonomy and risk

competitive equilibrium price: the price at which the quantity supplied and the quantity demanded are equal to each other

complement: two goods are complements if the demand for one (at a given price) decreases as the price of the other increases

consumer price index: a price index in which the basket of goods is defined by what a typical consumer purchases

consumer protection legislation: laws aimed at protecting consumers, for instance by assuring that consumers have more complete information about items they are considering buying

consumer surplus: the difference between what a person would be willing to pay and what he actually has to pay to buy a certain amount of a good

consumption function: the relationship between disposable income and consumption

contingency clauses: statements within a contract that make the level of payment or the work to be performed conditional upon various factors

corporate income tax: a tax based on the income, or profit, received by a corporation

corporation: a firm with limited liability, owned by shareholders, who elect a board of directors that chooses the top executives

correlation: the relationship that results when a change in one variable is consistently associated with a change in another variable

cost-push inflation: inflation whose initial cause is a rise in production costs

Cournot competition: an oligopoly in which each firm believes that its rivals are committed to a certain level of production and that rivals will reduce their prices as needed to sell that amount

credentials competition: the trend in which prospective workers acquire higher educational credentials, not so much because of anything they actually learn in the process but to convince potential employers to hire them by signaling that they will be more productive employees than those with weaker credentials

credit constraint effect: when prices fall, firms' revenues also fall, but the money they owe creditors remains unchanged; as a result, firms have fewer funds of their own to invest. Because of credit rationing, firms cannot make up the difference; accordingly, investment decreases

credit rationing: credit is rationed when no lender is willing to make a loan to a borrower or the amount lenders are willing to lend to borrowers is limited, even if the borrower is willing to pay more than other borrowers of comparable risk who are getting loans

cross subsidization: the practice of charging higher prices to one group of consumers in order to subsidize lower prices for another group

crowding out: a decrease in private investment resulting from an increase in government expenditures

debt: capital, such as bonds and bank loans, supplied to a firm by lenders; the firm promises to repay the amount borrowed plus interest

decentralization: organizational structure in which many individuals or subunits can make decisions

decision tree: a device for structured decision making that spells out the choices and possible consequences of alternative actions

deficit spending: the situation that exists when government expenditures are greater than revenues

deflation: a persistent decrease in the general level of prices

demand curve: the relationship between the quantity demanded of a good and the price, whether for an individual or for the market (all individuals) as a whole

demand deposits: deposits that can be drawn upon instantly, like checking accounts

demand-constrained equilibrium: the equilibrium that occurs when prices are stuck at a level above that at which aggregate demand equals aggregate supply; output is equal to aggregate demand

demand-pull inflation: inflation whose initial cause is aggregate demand exceeding aggregate supply at the current price level

demographic effects: effects that arise from changes in characteristics of the population such as age, birthrates, and location

depreciation: (a) the decrease in the value of an asset; in particular, the amount that capital goods decrease in value as they are used and become old; (b) a change in the exchange rate that enables a unit of one currency to buy fewer units of foreign currencies

deregulation: the lifting of government regulations to allow the market to function more freely

devaluation: a reduction in the rate of exchange between one currency and other currencies under a fixed exchange rate system

developed or **industrialized countries:** the wealthiest nations in the world, including Western Europe, the United States, Canada, Japan, Australia, and New Zealand

diminishing marginal utility: the principle that says that as an individual consumes more and more of a good, each successive unit increases her utility, or enjoyment, less and less

diminishing returns: the principle that says that as one input increases, with other inputs fixed, the resulting increase in output tends to be smaller and smaller

discount rate: the interest rate charged to banks when they wish to borrow from the central bank

discouraged workers: workers who would be willing to work but have given up looking for jobs, and thus are not officially counted as unemployed

dividends: that portion of corporate profits paid out to shareholders

downward rigidity of wages: the situation that exists when wages do not fall quickly in response to a shift in the demand or supply curve for labor, resulting in an excess supply of labor

dual economy: the separation in many LDCs between an impoverished rural sector and an urban sector that has higher wages and more advanced technology

duopoly: an industry with only two firms

durable goods: goods that provide a service over a number of years, such as cars, major appliances, and furniture

dynamic consistency: a policy is said to have dynamic consistency when government announces a course of action and then has the incentives to actually carry out that policy

economic rents: payments made to a factor of production that are in excess of what is required to elicit the supply of that factor

economies of scope: the situation that exists when it is less expensive to produce two products together than it would be to produce each one separately

efficiency wage: the wage at which total labor costs are minimized

efficiency wage theory: the theory that paying higher wages (up to a point) lowers total production costs, for instance by leading to a more productive labor force

efficient market theory: the theory that all available information is reflected in the current price of an asset

elasticity of labor supply: the percentage change in labor supplied resulting from a 1 percent change in wages

elasticity of supply: see **price elasticity of supply**

equilibrium price: see **competitive equilibrium price**

equity, shares, stock: terms that indicate part ownership of a firm; the firm sells these in order to raise money, or capital

equity capital: capital, such as shares (or stock), supplied to a firm by shareholders; the returns received by the shareholders are not guaranteed but depend on how well the firm does

excess demand: the situation in which the quantity demanded at a given price exceeds the quantity supplied

excess supply: the situation in which the quantity supplied at a given price exceeds the quantity demanded

exchange efficiency: the condition in which whatever the economy produces is distributed among people in such a way that there are no gains to further trade

exchange rate: the rate at which one currency (such as dollars) can be exchanged for another (such as marks, yen, or pounds)

excise tax: a tax on a particular good or service

expected return: the average return—a single number that combines the various possible returns per dollar invested with the chances that each of these returns will actually be paid

export-led growth: the strategy that government should encourage exports in which the country has a comparative advantage to stimulate growth

exports: goods produced domestically but sold abroad

externality: a phenomenon that arises when an individual or firm takes an action but does not bear all the costs (negative externality) or receive all the benefits (positive externality)

factor demand: the amount of an input demanded by a firm, given the price of the input and the quantity of output being produced; in a competitive market, an input will be demanded up to the point where the value of the marginal product of that input equals the price of the input

federal governmental structure: a system in which government activity takes place at several levels—national, state, county, city, and others

financial intermediaries: institutions that form the link between savers who have extra funds and borrowers who desire extra funds

firm wealth effect: lower prices or lower demand cause firms' profits and net worth to fall, and this makes them less willing to undertake the risks involved with investment

fiscal policies: policies that affect the level of government expenditures and taxes

fixed costs: the costs resulting from fixed inputs, sometimes called **overhead costs**

fixed exchange rate system: an exchange rate system in which the value of each currency is fixed in relationship to other currencies

fixed or **overhead inputs:** (a) inputs that do not change depending on the quantity of output; (b) fixed inputs also sometimes refer to inputs that are fixed in the short run—that is, they do not depend on *current* output—but may depend on output in the long run

flexible or **floating exchange rate system:** a system in which exchange rates are determined by market forces, the law of supply and demand, without government interference

flow statistics: measurements of a certain rate or quantity per period of time, such as GDP, which measures output per year

free-rider problem: the problem that occurs when someone thinks he may be able to enjoy something without paying for it, and so fails to contribute to the cost; free-rider problems arise in the provision of public goods

full-employment deficit: the budget deficit that would have prevailed if the economy were at full employment, thus with higher tax revenues and lower public assistance expenditures

full-employment or **potential output:** the level of output that would prevail if labor were fully employed (output may exceed that level if workers work more than the normal level of overtime)

gains from trade: the benefits that each side enjoys from a trade

GDP deflator: a weighted average of the prices of different goods and services, where the weights represent the importance of each of the goods and services in GDP

GDP per capita: the value of all goods and services produced in the economy divided by the population

general equilibrium analysis: a simultaneous analysis of all capital, product, and labor markets throughout the economy; it shows, for instance, the impact on all prices and quantities of immigration or a change in taxes

Gini coefficient: a measure of inequality (equal to twice the area between the 45-degree line and the Lorenz curve)

green revolution: the invention and dissemination of new seeds and agricultural practices that led to vast increases in agricultural output in less developed countries during the 1960s and 1970s

gross domestic product (GDP): the total money value of the goods and services produced by the residents of a nation during a specified period

gross national product (GNP): a measure of the incomes of residents of a country, including income they receive from abroad but subtracting similar payments made to those abroad

horizontal equity: the principle that says that those who are in identical or similar circumstances should pay identical or similar amounts in taxes

horizontal merger: a merger between two firms that produce the same goods

human capital: the stock of accumulated skills and experience that make workers more productive

imperfect competition: any market structure in which there is some competition but firms face downward-sloping demand curves

imperfect information: a situation in which market participants lack information (such as information about prices or characteristics of goods and services) important for their decision making

implicit contract: an unwritten understanding between two groups involved in an exchange, such as an understanding between employer and employees that employees will receive a stable wage throughout fluctuating economic conditions

import function: the relationship between imports and national income

import substitution: the strategy that focuses on the substitution of domestic goods for goods that were previously imported

imports: goods produced abroad but bought domestically

income effect: the reduced consumption of a good whose price has increased that is due to the reduction in a person's buying power, or "real" income; when a person's real income is lower, normally she will consume less of all goods, including the higher-priced good

income elasticity of demand: the percentage change in quantity demanded of a good as the result of a 1 percent change in income (the percentage change in quantity demanded divided by the percentage change in income)

incomplete markets: situations in which no market may exist for some good or for some risk, or in which some individuals cannot borrow for some purposes

increasing, constant, or **diminishing returns to scale:** when all inputs are increased by a certain proportion, output increases by a greater, equal, or smaller proportion, respectively; increasing returns to scale are also called **economies of scale**

indexing: the formal linking of any payment to a price index

individual income tax: a tax based on the income received by an individual or household

infant industry argument for protection: the argument that industries must be protected from foreign competition while they are young, until they have a chance to acquire the skills to enable them to compete on equal terms

inferior good: a good the consumption of which falls as income rises

infinite elasticity of demand: the situation that exists when any amount will be demanded at a particular price, but nothing will be demanded if the price increases even a small amount

infinite elasticity of supply: the situation that exists when any amount will be supplied at a particular price, but nothing will be supplied if the price declines even a small amount

inflation rate: the percentage increases in the general level of prices

inflation tax: the decrease in buying power (wealth) that inflation imposes on those who hold currency (and other assets, like bonds, the payments for which are fixed in terms of dollars)

inflationary spiral: a self-perpetuating system in which price increases lead to higher wages, which lead to further price increases

infrastructure: the roads, ports, bridges, and legal system that provide the necessary basis for a working economy

insider-outsider theory: the theory that firms are reluctant to pay new workers (outsiders) a lower wage than current workers (insiders), because current workers will fear being replaced by the new, low-wage workers and will not participate in cooperating with and training them

interest: the return a saver receives in addition to the original amount she deposited (loaned), and the amount a borrower must pay in addition to the original amount he borrowed

interest rate effect: the situation that exists when lower interest rates (resulting from an increase in the money supply or a fall in the price level) induce firms to invest more

investment: the purchase of an asset that will provide a return over a long period of time

investment schedule: the relationship between the level of investment and the (real) rate of interest

investment tax credit (ITC): a provision of the tax code in which the government reduces a company's tax bill by an amount equal to a percentage of its spending on investment

involuntary unemployment: the situation that occurs when the supply of those willing to work at the going market wage exceeds the demand for labor

Keynesian unemployment: unemployment that occurs as a result of insufficient aggregate demand; it arises in the demand-constrained equilibrium (where aggregate demand is less than aggregate supply), so that rightward shifts in aggregate demand reduce the level of unemployment

kinked demand curve: the demand curve perceived by an oligopolist who believes that rivals will match any price cuts but will not match price increases

labor force participation rate: the fraction of the working-age population that is employed or seeking employment

labor market: the market in which labor services are bought and sold

labor turnover rate: the rate at which workers leave jobs

land reform: the redistribution of land by the government to those who actually work the land

learning by doing: the increase in productivity that occurs as a firm gains experience from producing, and that results in a decrease in the firm's production costs

learning curve: the curve describing how costs of production decline as cumulative output increases over time

less developed countries (LDCs): the poorest nations of the world, including much of Africa, Latin America, and Asia

life-cycle hypothesis: the theory that individuals typically save when they are young and working and spend their savings as they age and retire

life-cycle savings motive: people save during their working lives so that they can consume more during retirement

limit pricing: the practice of charging a lower price than the level at which marginal revenue equals marginal cost, as a way of deterring entry by persuading potential competitors that their profits from entering are likely to be limited

liquidity: the ease with which an asset can be sold

Lorenz curve: a curve that shows the cumulative proportion of income that goes to each cumulative proportion of the population, starting with the lowest income group

Luddites: early nineteenth-century workmen who destroyed labor-saving machinery rather than see it take over their jobs

M1, M2, M3: measures of the money supply: M1 includes currency and checking accounts; M2 includes M1 plus savings deposits, CDs, and money market funds; M3 includes M2 plus large-denomination savings deposits and institutional money-market mutual funds

macroeconomics: the top-down view of the economy, focusing on aggregate characteristics

managerial slack: the lack of managerial efficiency (for instance, in cutting costs) that occurs when firms are insulated from competition

marginal cost: the additional cost corresponding to an additional unit of output produced

marginal costs and benefits: the extra costs and benefits that result from choosing a little bit more of one thing

marginal product: the amount output increases with the addition of one unit of an input

marginal propensity to consume: the amount by which consumption increases when disposable income increases by a dollar

marginal propensity to import: the amount by which imports increase when disposable income increases by a dollar

marginal propensity to save: the amount by which savings increase when disposable income increases by a dollar

marginal revenue: the extra revenue received by a firm for selling one additional unit of a good

marginal utility: the extra utility, or enjoyment, a person receives from the consumption of one additional unit of a good

market clearing: the situation that exists when supply equals demand, so there is neither excess supply nor excess demand

market economy: an economy that allocates resources primarily through the interaction of individuals (households) and private firms

market failure: the situation in which a market economy fails to attain economic efficiency

market failures approach: the argument that government may have an economic role to play when markets fail to produce efficient outcomes

market labor supply curve: the relationship between the wage paid and the amount of labor willingly supplied, found by adding up the labor supply curves of all the individuals in the economy

median voter: the voter such that half the population have preferences on one side of this voter (for instance, they want higher government expenditures and taxes), while the other half of the population have preferences on the other side of this voter (they want lower taxes and expenditures)

medium of exchange: any item that can be commonly exchanged for goods and services throughout the economy

menu costs: the costs to firms of changing their prices

merit goods and bads: goods that are determined by government to be good or bad for people, regardless of whether people desire them for themselves or not

microeconomics: the bottom-up view of the economy, focusing on individual households and firms

mixed economy: an economy that allocates resources through a mixture of public (governmental) and private decision making

model: a set of assumptions and data used by economists to study an aspect of the economy and make predictions about the future or about the consequences of various policy changes

Modigliani-Miller theorem: the theorem that says that under a simplified set of conditions, the manner in which a firm finances itself does not matter

monetarists: economists who emphasize the importance of money in the economy; they tend to believe that an appropriate monetary policy is all the economy needs from government, and market forces will otherwise solve any macroeconomic problems

monetary policies: policies that affect the supply of money and credit and the terms on which credit is available to borrowers

money: any item that serves as a medium of exchange, a store of value, and a unit of account

money multiplier: the amount by which a new deposit into the banking system (from the outside) is multiplied as it is loaned out, redeposited, reloaned, etc., by banks

monopolistic competition: the form of imperfect competition in which the market has sufficiently few firms that each one faces a downward-sloping demand curve, but enough that each can ignore the reactions of rivals to what it does

monopoly: a market consisting of only one firm

moral hazard: the principle that says that those who purchase insurance have a reduced incentive to avoid what they are insured against

multilateral trade: trade between more than two parties

multiplier: the factor by which a change in a component of aggregate demand, like investment or government spending, is multiplied to lead to a larger change in equilibrium national output

multiplier-accelerator model: a model that relates business cycles to the internal working of the economy, showing how changes in investment and output reinforce each other; the central ingredients of the model are the multiplier and the accelerator

mutual fund: a fund that gathers money from different investors and purchases a range of assets; each investor then owns a portion of the entire fund

nationalization: the process whereby a private industry is taken over by the government, whether by buying it or simply seizing it

natural endowments: a country's natural resources, such as good climate, fertile land, or minerals

natural monopoly: a monopoly that exists because average costs of production are declining beyond the level of output demanded in the market, thus making entry unprofitable and making it efficient for there to be a single firm

natural rate of unemployment: the rate of unemployment at which the rate of inflation is zero

net export function: a curve that gives the level of net exports at each level of income

net domestic product (NDP): GDP minus the value of the depreciation of the country's capital goods

new classical economists: economists who, beginning in the 1970s, built on the tradition of classical economists and believed that by and large, market forces, if left to themselves, would solve the problems of unemployment and recessions

new growth economists: economists who, beginning in the 1980s, sought to understand better the basic forces that led the economy to grow fast at one time and slower at another, or some countries to grow faster than others

new Keynesian economists: economists who, beginning in the 1980s, built on the tradition of Keynesian economists and focused attention on unemployment; they sought explanations for the failure of wages and prices to adjust to make labor markets and possibly other markets clear

newly industrialized countries (NICs): nations that have recently moved from being quite poor to being middle-income countries, including South Korea, Taiwan, Singapore, and Hong Kong

normal good: a good the consumption of which rises as income rises

normative economics: economics in which judgments about the desirability of various policies are made; the conclusions rest on value judgments as well as facts and theories

Okun's law: the observation that as the economy pulls out of a recession, output increases more than proportionately to increases in employment

oligopoly: the form of imperfect competition in which the market has several firms, sufficiently few that each one must take into account the reactions of rivals to what it does

open economy: an economy that is actively engaged in international trade

open market operations: central banks' purchase or sale of government bonds in the open market

opportunity cost: the cost of a resource, measured by the value of the next-best, alternative use of that resource

opportunity sets: a summary of the choices available to individuals, as defined by budget constraints and time constraints

Pareto-efficient allocations: resource allocations that cannot make any person better off without making someone else worse off

partial equilibrium analysis: an analysis that focuses on only one or a few markets at a time

partnership: a business owned by two or more individuals, who share the profits and are jointly liable for any losses

patent: a government decree giving an inventor the exclusive right to produce, use, or sell an invention

paternalism: the making of judgments by government about what is good for people to have, rather than letting people choose on their own

payroll tax: a tax based on payroll (wages) that is used to finance the Social Security and Medicare programs

perfect competition: a situation in which each firm is a price taker—it cannot influence the market price; at the market price, the firm can sell as much as it wishes, but if it raises its price, it loses all sales

perfectly mobile capital: capital that responds quickly to changes in returns in different countries

permanent income hypothesis: the theory that individuals base their current consumption levels on their permanent (long-run average) income

permanent-income savings motive: people save in good years to tide them over in bad years; they choose their pattern of saving and spending year by year to average, or smooth, their consumption over good years and bad

Phillips curve: the trade-off between unemployment and inflation such that a lower level of unemployment is associated with a higher level of inflation

piece-rate system: a compensation system in which workers are paid specifically for each item produced

planned and **unplanned inventories:** planned inventories are those firms choose to have on hand because they make business more efficient; unplanned inventories result when firms cannot sell what they produce

policy ineffectiveness proposition: the proposition that government policies are ineffective—policies aimed at stimulating aggregate demand at most change the price level

portfolio theories of monetary policy: theories that argue that monetary policy affects output through its effect on prices of various assets, in particular the prices of stocks

portfolio: an investor's entire collection of assets and liabilities

positive economics: economics that describes how the economy behaves and predicts how it might change—for instance, in response to some policy change

potential GDP: a measure of what the value of GDP would be if the economy's resources were fully employed

precautionary savings motive: people save so that they will be able to meet the costs of an unexpected illness, accident, or other emergency

predatory pricing: the practice of cutting prices below the marginal cost of production to drive out a new firm (or to deter future entry), at which point prices can be raised again

present discounted value: how much an amount of money to be received in the future is worth right now

price ceiling: a maximum price above which market prices are not legally allowed to rise

price discrimination: the practice of a firm charging different prices to different customers or in different markets

price dispersion: a situation that occurs when the same item is sold for different prices by different firms

price elasticity of demand: the percentage change in quantity demanded of a good as the result of a 1 percent change in price (the percentage change in quantity demanded divided by the percentage change in price)

price elasticity of supply: the percentage change in quantity supplied of a good as the result of a 1 percent change in price (the percentage change in quantity supplied divided by the percentage change in price)

price floor: a minimum price below which market prices are not legally allowed to fall

price index: a measure of the level of prices found by comparing the cost of a certain basket of goods in one year with the cost in a base year

principal: the original amount a saver deposits in a bank (lends) or a borrower borrows

principal-agent problem: any situation in which one party (the principal) needs to delegate actions to another party (the agent), and thus wishes to provide the agent with incentives to work hard and make decisions about risk that reflect the interests of the principal

principle of consumer sovereignty: the principle that holds that each individual is the best judge of what makes him better off

Prisoner's Dilemma: a situation in which the noncooperative pursuit of self-interest by two parties makes them both worse off

private marginal cost: the marginal cost of production borne by the producer of a good; when there is a negative externality, such as air pollution, private marginal cost is less than social marginal cost

privatization: the process whereby functions that were formerly undertaken by government are delegated instead to the private sector

producer price index: a price index that measures the average level of producers' prices

product differentiation: the fact that similar products (like breakfast cereals or soft drinks) are perceived to differ from one another and thus are imperfect substitutes

product liability: the obligation of a producer to compensate victims of a defective product that has injured them

product market: the market in which goods and services are bought and sold

product-mix efficiency: the condition in which the mix of goods produced by the economy reflects the preferences of consumers

production efficiency: the condition in which firms cannot produce more of some goods without producing less of other goods; the economy is on its production possibilities curve

production function: the relationship between the inputs used in production and the level of output

production possibilities curve: a curve that defines the opportunity set for a firm or an entire economy and gives the possible combinations of goods (outputs) that can be produced from a given level of inputs

productivity, or **GDP per hour worked:** how much an average worker produces per hour, calculated by dividing real GDP by hours worked in the economy

profits: total revenues minus total costs

progressive tax: a tax in which the rich pay a larger fraction of their income than the poor

property tax: a tax based on the value of property

proprietorship: a business owned by a single person, usually a small business

protectionism: the policy of protecting domestic industries from the competition of foreign-made goods

public good: a good, such as national defense, that costs little or nothing for an extra individual to enjoy, and the costs of preventing any individual from the enjoyment of which are high; public goods have the properties of nonrivalrous consumption and nonexcludability

pure profit or **monopoly rents:** the profit earned by a monopolist that results from its reducing output and increasing the price from the level at which price equals marginal cost

quantity theory of money: the theory that velocity is constant, so that changes in the money supply lead to proportionate changes in nominal income (which also equals the value of output)

random walk: a term used to describe the way the prices of stocks move; the next movement cannot be predicted on the basis of previous movements

rational expectations: the expectations of individuals that are formed by using all available information

rationing systems: ways of distributing goods that do not rely on prices, such as queues, lotteries, and coupons

real balance effect: as prices fall, the real value of people's money holdings increases, and they consume more

real business-cycle theorists: a school of economists who contend that the economy's fluctuations have nothing to do with monetary policy but are determined by real forces

real exchange rates: exchange rates adjusted for changes in the relative price levels in different countries

real GDP: the real value of all final goods and services produced in the economy, measured in dollars adjusted for inflation

real income: income measured by what it can actually buy, rather than by the amount of money

real interest rate: the real return to saving, equal to the nominal interest rate minus the rate of inflation

real product wage: the wage divided by the price of the good being produced

recession: two consecutive quarters of a year during which GDP falls

regressive tax: a tax in which the poor pay a larger fraction of their income than the rich

regulatory capture: a term used to describe a situation in which regulators serve the interests of the regulated rather than the interests of consumers

relative performance compensation: pay based on performance on the job relative to others who have similar responsibilities and authority

rent: see **economic rent**

rent seeking: the name given to behavior that seeks to obtain benefits from favorable government decisions, such as protection from foreign competition

reserve requirements: the minimum level of reserves that the central bank requires be kept on hand or deposited with the central bank

reserve: money kept on hand by a bank in the event that those who have made deposits wish to withdraw their money

revenue curve: the relationship between a firm's total output and its revenues

revenues: the amount a firm receives for selling its products, equal to the price received multiplied by the quantity sold

right-to-work laws: laws that prevent union membership from being a condition of employment

risk averse, risk loving, risk neutral: given equal expected returns and different risks, risk-averse people will choose assets with lower risk, risk-loving people will choose assets with higher risk, and risk-neutral individuals will not care about differences in risk

risk premium: the additional interest required by lenders as compensation for the risk that a borrower may default; more generally, the extra return required to compensate an investor for bearing risk

screening: the process of differentiating among job candidates, when there is incomplete information, to determine who will be the most productive

shadow price: the true social value of a resource

signaling: conveying information, for example a prospective worker's earning a college degree to persuade an employer that he has desirable characteristics that will enhance his productivity

slope: the amount by which the value along the vertical axis increases as the result of a change in one unit along the horizontal axis; the slope is calculated by dividing the change in the vertical axis (the "rise") by the change in the horizontal axis (the "run")

Smith's "invisible hand": the idea that if people act in their own self-interest, they will often also be acting in a broader social interest, as if they had been directed by an "invisible hand"

smoothing consumption: consuming similar amounts in the present and future, rather than letting year-to-year income dictate consumption

social marginal cost: the marginal cost of production, including the cost of any negative externality, such as air pollution, borne by individuals in the economy other than the producer

socialism: an economic system in which the means of production are controlled by the state

soft budget constraints: budget constraints facing a firm in which the government subsidizes any losses

static expectations: the belief of individuals that today's prices and wages are likely to continue into the future

sticky prices: prices that do not adjust or adjust only slowly toward a new equilibrium

sticky wages: wages that are slow to adjust in response to a change in labor market conditions

stock statistics: measurements of the quantity of a certain item at a certain point in time, such as capital stock, the total value of buildings and machines

store of value: something that can be accepted as payment in the present and exchanged for items of value in the future

substitute: two goods are substitutes if the demand for one increases when the price of the other increases

substitution effect: the reduced consumption of a good whose price has increased that is due to the changed trade-off, the fact that one has to give up more of other goods to get one more unit of the high-priced good; the substitution effect is associated with a change in the slope of the budget constraint

sunk cost: a cost that has been incurred and cannot be recovered

supply curve: the relationship between the quantity supplied of a good and the price, whether for a single firm or the market (all firms) as a whole

supply-constrained equilibrium: the equilibrium that occurs when prices are stuck at a level below that at which aggregate demand equals aggregate supply; in a supply-constrained equilibrium, output is equal to aggregate supply but less than aggregate demand

surplus labor: a great deal of unemployed or underemployed labor, readily available to potential employers

target savings motive: people save for a particular target, for example to make a down payment on a house or to pay college tuition

theory: a set of assumptions and the conclusions derived from those assumptions put forward as an explanation for some phenomena

thin markets: markets with relatively few buyers and sellers

total costs: the sum of all fixed costs and variable costs

trade deficit: the excess of imports over exports

trade secret: an innovation or knowledge of a production process that a firm does not disclose to others

transactions costs: the extra costs (beyond the price of the purchase) of conducting a transaction, whether those costs are money, time, or inconvenience

transactions demand for money: the demand for money arising from its use in buying goods and services

transfer programs: programs directly concerned with redistribution, such as AFDC and Medicaid, that move money from one group in society to another

Treasury bills (T-bills): bills the government sells in return for a promise to pay a certain amount in a short period, usually less than 180 days

unemployment rate: the fraction of the labor force (those unemployed *plus* those seeking jobs) who are seeking jobs but are unable to find them

union shops: unionized firms in which all workers are required to join the union as a condition of employment

unit of account: something that provides a way of measuring and comparing the relative values of different goods

utility: the level of enjoyment an individual attains from choosing a certain combination of goods

utility possibilities curve: a curve showing the maximum level of utility that one individual can attain, given the level of utility attained by others

variable costs: the costs resulting from variable inputs

variable inputs: inputs that rise and fall with the quantity of output

velocity: the speed with which money circulates in the economy, defined as the ratio of income to the money supply

vertical equity: the principle that says that people who are better off should pay more taxes

vertical merger: a merger between two firms, one of which is a supplier or distributor for the other

voluntary unemployment: a situation in which workers voluntarily drop out of the labor force when the wage level falls

voting paradox: the fact that under some circumstances there may be no determinate outcome with majority voting: choice A wins a majority over B, B wins over C, and C wins over A

wholesale price index: a price index that measures the average level of wholesale prices

work sharing: reducing all employees' hours by equal amounts rather than firing some workers

zero elasticity of demand: the situation that exists when the quantity demanded will not change, regardless of changes in price

zero elasticity of supply: the situation that exists when the quantity supplied will not change, regardless of changes in price

CREDITS

INDEX